I0006153

THE WORKS

OF

GEOFFREY CHAUCER

The Globe Edition

THE WORKS

OF

GEOFFREY CHAUCER

EDITED BY.

ALFRED W. POLLARD

H. FRANK HEATH   MARK H. LIDDELL

W. S. McCORMICK

London

MACMILLAN AND CO., Limited

NEW YORK: THE MACMILLAN COMPANY

1898

2425.8.3

C

V

TO

FREDERICK JAMES FURNIVALL, Ph.D.

FOUNDER AND DIRECTOR

OF THE CHAUCER AND EARLY ENGLISH TEXT SOCIETIES

THIS POPULAR EDITION OF THE POET

FOR WHOM HE HAS DONE SO MUCH

IS DEDICATED IN GRATITUDE

AND ESTEEM

PREFACE

EXACTLY a third of a century ago, in the year 1864, the publishers of this edition of Chaucer brought out their 'Globe' edition of Shakespeare, and it was their desire from the outset that it should be followed with as little delay as possible by a similar edition of the works of the greatest of his predecessors. The 'Globe' Shakespeare had been made possible by the previous publication of the splendid 'Cambridge' edition, in which everything that industry and scholarship could effect had been done to obtain a trustworthy text. It was naturally, therefore, to Cambridge that Mr. Alexander Macmillan turned for an edition of Chaucer, and in January 1864 he wrote to Henry Bradshaw, from whose *Memoir* by Mr. G. W. Prothero I am quoting,[1] to ask him 'to join Mr. Earle and Mr. Aldis Wright in editing a "Library" edition of Chaucer's works.' It is clear that this 'Library' edition was proposed mainly to settle the text for a 'Globe' edition, and it seems almost immediately to have been arranged that the Clarendon Press, with which Mr. Macmillan had intimate relations, should have the honour of publishing the 'Library' edition, and that the text should afterwards be used for the 'Globe.'[2] In March 1866 Mr. Macmillan could write to Bradshaw of his delight at hearing that 'the great Chaucer' was in 'so prosperous a condition,' and of his willingness to wait for the 'Globe' edition till after its completion; but a year or two later, Mr. Prothero tells us, it became apparent that the prospect of a large edition was becoming very uncertain, and the idea of the independent publication of a 'Globe' Chaucer was revived. 1870 brought a new scheme, Professor Earle retiring from the task and Bradshaw undertaking to edit

[1] *A Memoir of Henry Bradshaw*, Fellow of King's College, Cambridge, and University Librarian. By G. W. Prothero (London: Kegan Paul, Trench and Co., 1888), page 108.

[2] This seems the most probable explanation of the apparent discrepancy between Mr. Prothero's precise statement already quoted and his subsequent remark (p. 223) that 'the standard edition of Chaucer, to range with that of Shakespeare,' was undertaken in 1864 by Professor Earle, with Mr. Aldis Wright and Mr. Bradshaw as collaborators, for the Clarendon Press.

the 'Library' edition for the Clarendon Press, with Mr. Aldis Wright and Professor Skeat as his collaborators, and twenty-four years afterwards this idea bore fruit in the noble 'Oxford Chaucer' edited by Professor Skeat, to which it is a pleasure to the present editors to doff their caps.   But in the seventies Chaucer had still to stand waiting.   The 'Globe' edition, as Mr. Prothero remarks, fared no better than the 'Library' one.   'From time to time Mr. Macmillan and Dr. Furnivall stirred Bradshaw up, but to no purpose.   At length, in 1879, it was suggested that Bradshaw and Furnivall should do the edition together, and Bradshaw assented.   They got as far as discussing the title-page, on which Bradshaw wanted his partner's name to stand first ; some specimen pages were put in type" and there the matter ended.   In February 1886 Bradshaw died, having done for Chaucer what he had done for many other subjects— marked out the lines on which alone good work could be done, and communicated to others something of his own enthusiasm.   That so much of his learning should have died with him, is a calamity which Chaucer-students have to regret in common with philologists, bibliographers, and antiquaries of every kind.   In December 1887, with the lightheartedness of his inextinguishable youth, Dr. Furnivall invited the present writer to become his collaborator, and an agreement with the Messrs. Macmillan was duly signed by us both, embracing both a 'Library' and a 'Globe' edition.   But, as I have already written, 'the giant in the partnership had been used for a quarter of a century to doing, for nothing, all the hard work for other people,' and, like Bradshaw, 'could not spare from his pioneering the time necessary to enter into the fruit of his own Chaucer labours.   Thus the partner who was not a giant was left to go on pretty much by himself.'[1]   With the *Canterbury Tales* there was no great difficulty, for the seven manuscripts printed by the Chaucer Society made it possible to produce an adequate text without other help.   But for most of the rest of Chaucer's work it was essential for success to get into touch with the manuscripts themselves, and this was for me impossible.   Years previously Bradshaw had written, in excuse for his failure to produce a 'Globe' text, 'the fact is that the work would require an amount of *daylight leisure* which I can't give, and which no amount of money would enable me to buy,' and this humbler librarian was pulled up by the same difficulty Only the length of the King's Library separated me from all the Chaucer manuscripts of the British Museum, but though the consciousness that they were there was pleasing, they were as inaccessible for continuous study as those of Oxford or Cambridge.   Fortunately, I was able to find, with Dr. Furnivall's aid, first one, and then a second, and then a third helper, who could not only work at the treasures which a librarian may help to guard but must not study for his own ends, but who also possessed the scientific

---

[1] Preface to the 'Eversley' edition of Chaucer's *Canterbury Tales* (Macmillan, 1894).

training in the English language for which Oxford offered far fewer opportunities when I was an undergraduate than it does now. It is pleasant to me to know that two of my collaborators have completed this training at the feet of those distinguished foreign scholars, Ten Brink and Zupitza ; Dr. Heath and myself, like Chaucer, are Londoners ; Professor McCormick is a successor of the Scottish poets and students who in the fifteenth century did so much for Chaucer's honour ; and Professor Liddell is an American just called to the Chair of English Literature in the University of Texas. Thus in this popular edition of Chaucer, which, mainly through the steady persistence of the publishers, now sees the light a third of a century after its first proposal, the final workers may at least claim that they represent, however inadequately, all the different countries in which their favourite poet has been especially loved and studied.

In the division of labour which has thus been effected I have myself remained responsible for the *Canterbury Tales*, the *Legende of Good Women*, the Glossary, and the General Introduction ; Professor Liddell has taken the *Boece*, the *Treatise on the Astrolabe*, and the *Romaunt of the Rose;* Professor McCormick, *Troilus and Criseyde;* Dr. Heath, the *Hous of Fame*, *Parlement of Foules*, and all the shorter pieces. Each editor is responsible for his own work and for that only, and in some minor matters, as will be explained, we have each gone our own way. In the main essential, however, we have been from the first in entire agreement, for we all believe that in the present stage of our knowledge the most conservative treatment, consistent with the necessities of common sense and the known rules of Chaucerian usage, is also the best. We have endeavoured, therefore, as far as may be, to produce texts which shall offer an accurate reflection of that MS. or group of MSS. which critical investigation has shown to be the best, with only such emendation upon the evidence of other manuscripts as appeared absolutely necessary, and with the utmost parsimony of 'conjecture.' Our notes of variant readings have been greatly curtailed by consideration of space, but we have endeavoured to record most of those which have any literary or metrical importance, and I think I may say that in some cases, notably in the *Boece, Troilus*, and *Hous of Fame*, a real step forward has been taken towards a thoroughly critical text. As regards spelling, we are agreed in our dislike to any attempt at a uniform orthography determined by philological considerations. In the present state of our knowledge any such attempt must come perilously near that 'putting our own crotchets in place of the old scribes' habits' which Mr. Bradshaw once deprecated in editions of mediæval Latin, and which is as little to be desired as it is difficult to carry out. At the same time, every manuscript has its percentage of clerical errors or unusually repellent forms, and to reproduce these in a popular edition would be in the former case absurd, in the latter more or less undesirable. Thus, while we

have all adopted the modern usage of *u* and *v*, *i* and *j*, in other matters
each editor has used his own judgment as to the extent of alteration
necessary, and has explained what he has done in his introductory remarks.
With our common belief that the difficulties raised by variations of spelling
have been absurdly exaggerated, and our knowledge of how the balance of
advantage shifts with every change of manuscripts, we see no reason to
regret that while in some cases a few uncouth forms have been left in order
that it might be understood that the text is taken, with only specified
alterations, from a given manuscript, in other instances it has seemed advisable to do more to conciliate the eye of a modern reader.   Where such
alterations have been made, forms found in the Ellesmere MS. of the
Canterbury Tales have been adopted.

Our refusal to reduce the spelling of the manuscripts to a dead level of
philological correctness—were this attainable—has compelled us to use an
unobtrusive dot to indicate when the letter *e* is to be fully sounded.   This
is the less to be regretted as Chaucer's usage in this respect is not quite
so rigidly uniform as it is sometimes represented, and few readers will be
inclined to grumble at this help which we have endeavoured to offer as
modestly as possible.

As regards the order in which Chaucer's works are printed in this edition,
the *Canterbury Tales* have been placed first, a precedence which was
assigned them in all the old editions, and which is now further justified by
our knowledge that they include some of the poet's earliest work, as well
as much of his latest.   The other pieces are arranged, to the best of my
ability, in their chronological order, the Minor Poems being roughly grouped
together as Earlier and Later.

There is one last word which I should like to add.   The appearance of
this 'Globe' edition, so soon after the *Oxford Chaucer* and the *Student's
Chaucer*, which we owe to Professor Skeat, may perhaps seem superfluous,
and even intrusive.   Against such a criticism the fact that the publishers
have contemplated this edition since 1864, while the present writer began
it in 1887, these being personal matters, would be no good defence.   But
I think the case for the present book can be put on higher ground than
this.   I am so good a Chaucer-lover as to hope that in the near future the
student may have not merely two texts from which to choose, but half a
dozen.   So long as each editor does his work afresh, each new attempt
must add something to the common stock.   Where independent examination of the materials gathered by the Chaucer Society, or still unprinted,
has led to different results, the best text will in the end survive ; where the
results are the same, every fresh witness adds to the authority of the last.
In some cases the texts formed by my colleagues appear to me to take the
more adventurous course ; but, for myself, the results I have to show for
my own collations must set me quoting :—

For wel I wot, that ye han her-biforne
Of makynge ropen and lad awey the corne,
And I come after glenynge here and there,
And am ful glad if I may finde an ere
Of any goodly word that ye han left.

I hope that, more especially in the *Legende*, some three or four of such 'goodly words' may be found, but in editing both this poem and the *Canterbury Tales*, and even more in the tedious task of compiling a glossary, my admiration for the thoroughness and precision of my predecessor has been continually increased. But if some future editor can find new manuscripts or overlooked readings helpful to a better text, I am sure that Dr. Skeat will join me in congratulating him on his good luck.

ALFRED W. POLLARD.

CONTENTS

* The bracketed references in Roman numerals are to the pages of the Introduction which concern the poem.

INTRODUCTION

LIFE OF CHAUCER

(ALFRED W. POLLARD)

GEOFFREY CHAUCER was the son of John Chaucer, a citizen and vintner of London. His grandfather, Robert le Chaucer, the first member of the family of whom we hear, was in 1310 appointed one of the collectors in the Port of London of the new customs upon wine granted by the merchants of Aquitaine. At the time of his death Robert held a small property in Ipswich of the annual value of twenty shillings or thereabouts, *i.e.* some £15 of our present money. The ultimate remainder of other lands in Suffolk was settled on his son John (the poet's father), and apparently for the sake of this property the lad was kidnapped on 3rd December 1324, when he was between twelve and fourteen years of age, with the object of forcibly marrying him to a certain Joan de Westhale, who had also an interest in it. John's stepfather [1] took up his cause; his kidnappers were fined £250 (a crushing amount in those days), and from a subsequent plea to Parliament for the mitigation of this penalty we learn that in 1328 John Chaucer was still unmarried. On the 12th June 1338 a protection against being sued in his absence was granted to him with some forty-five others who were crossing the sea with the King, and ten years later he acted as deputy to the King's Butler in the port of Southampton. At the time of his death, in 1366, he owned a house in Thames Street, London, and was married to Agnes, niece of Hamo de Compton,[2] whom we first hear of as his wife in 1349, and who, soon after his death, married again another vintner, Bartholomew atte Chapel, in May 1367. Thus we know that the poet was born after 1328, that (if his father was only married once) his mother was this Agnes, niece of Hamo de Compton, and that he may have been born in the house in Thames Street, which he subsequently inherited and sold. In October 1386, when he was called upon to give evidence in the suit between Richard, Lord Scrope, and Sir Robert Grosvenor, his age was entered as 'forty years or more,' a statement the value of which is diminished, but not destroyed, by the proved carelessness of entries as to one or two other witnesses. We shall find that the date of about 1340, which this entry suggests as that of Chaucer's birth, fits in very fairly

---

[1] The biographical sections of this Introduction are mainly taken, with some revision and alteration, from my *Chaucer Primer* (Macmillan, 1895).
[2] John's mother Mary married three times; first one Heyroun, secondly Robert le Chaucer, and thirdly his kinsman or namesake, Richard Chaucer, who at one time was supposed to have been the poet's grandfather. John's kidnapper was Thomas Stace of Ipswich, who may have been a kinsman on his mother's side.

well with everything we know of his career, and until more precise evidence is forth-coming it may be accepted as approximately correct.

The first certain information we have about Chaucer himself is of his service in the household of Elizabeth de Burgh, Countess of Ulster, and wife of Lionel, third son of Edward III. The fragments of her Household Accounts, which contain the name Galfridus Chaucer, were found, appropriately enough, in the covers of a manu-script at the British Museum, containing Lydgate's *Storie of Thebes* and Hoccleve's *Regement of Princes*. The accounts show that in April 1357 the Countess was in London, and that an entire suit of clothes, consisting of a paltock, or short cloak, a pair of red and black breeches, and shoes, was then provided for Geoffrey Chaucer, at a cost of seven shillings (*i.e.* about five guineas present value), and another purchase of clothing for him was recorded the next month. In the following December, when the Countess was at her seat at Hatfield, in Yorkshire, there is an entry of two shillings and sixpence paid to Geoffrey Chaucer 'for necessaries at Christmas.' The entries of similar payments made to other members of the Countess of Ulster's house-hold are for much larger amounts, and we must therefore conclude that, on account either of his youth or of his not being of noble birth, Chaucer's position among her retainers was not a high one. It was probably, however, sufficiently good to enable him to be present at several great festivities at Court in which we know that the Countess took part, and it may have been during the visit which John of Gaunt paid to Hatfield towards the close of 1357 that the poet first attracted his notice.

In 1359, according to his evidence in the Scrope suit, Chaucer took part in the unlucky campaign in France, serving before the town of ' Retters ' (probably Réthel, not far from Rheims), until he was taken prisoner. His imprisonment did not last long, as on 1st March 1360 the King contributed £16 (£240 present value) to his ransom, a sum sufficiently large to show that both by his captors and his ransomers he was regarded as a person of some little importance. This may have arisen from his going to the war in the suite either of Prince Lionel or of the King himself. In any case, he must have been taken into the King's household about this time, as on 20th July 1367, in consideration of his past and future services, Edward III. granted him a pension, or annual salary, of twenty marks (£13 : 6 : 8) for life, under the title *dilectus valettus noster*. Chaucer was thus one of the yeomen of the King's chamber, and by Christmas 1368 had been promoted to be an esquire ' of less degree.'

On 12th September 1366 a Philippa Chaucer, one of the damoiselles of the Queen's chamber (*una domicellarum cameræ Reginæ*), was granted a pension of ten marks yearly for life. We know that this Philippa Chaucer in 1374, and occasionally in subsequent years, received part of her pension by the hands of Geoffrey Chaucer, her husband, and there seems to be no good reason to doubt that they were married as early as 1366. It is probable, though far from certain, that the damoiselle of the Queen's chamber may be identified with Philippa Roet, daughter of Sir Payne Roet of Hainault, and sister of Katherine Roet, who, after the death of her husband, Sir Hugh Swynford, became the third wife of John of Gaunt, in whose family she had been governess. Such a roundabout connection with John of Gaunt would help to explain the many marks of favour which he bestowed on both Chaucer and his wife ; but the evidence for it is at present rather slender. If we believe it, we must also hold it probable that Geoffrey and Philippa Chaucer were the parents of a Thomas Chaucer, a man of wealth and note in the next reign, who, towards the close of his life, exchanged the Chaucer arms for those of Roet ; also, perhaps, of the Elizabeth Chaucer for whose novitiate at the Abbey of Barking John of Gaunt paid a consider-able sum in 1381. But the only child of the poet about whom we have certain knowledge is the little Lewis, for whom he compiled a treatise on the Astrolabe, calculated for the year 1391, when the boy was ten years old.

In 1369, the year after his promotion to be an esquire, Chaucer took part in the war in France. We know this from the record of a loan of £10 advanced to him by a certain Henry de Wakefield, but the record tells us nothing else. In 1370 Chaucer was abroad on the King's service, and obtained letters of protection from creditors till Michaelmas, when he returned and received his pension on 8th October. He received his pension with his own hands in 1371 and 1372, but we know nothing of his doings until 12th November of the latter year, when he was joined in a commission with two citizens of Genoa to treat with the Duke, citizens, and merchants of that place for the choice of some port in England where Genoese merchants might settle and trade. For his expenses he was allowed an advance of a hundred marks, and a further sum of thirty-eight marks was paid after his return, which took place before 22nd November 1373, when he received his pension in person.

After his return from Genoa Chaucer's affairs prospered greatly. On St. George's Day 1374 the King, then at Windsor, granted him a pitcher of wine daily. He received money in lieu of this in 1377, and the next year it was commuted for a second pension of twenty marks. In May 1374 he leased from the Corporation of London the dwelling-house over the gate of Aldgate. In June he was appointed Comptroller of the Customs and Subsidy of Wools, Skins, and tanned Hides in the Port of London, with the obligation to keep the records of his office with his own hand, and to be continually present. On the 13th of the same month John of Gaunt granted a pension of £10 to Chaucer and his wife for good services rendered by them 'to the said Duke, his Consort, and his mother the Queen.'[1] In 1375 two wardships were granted Chaucer, one of which, that of Edward Staplegate of Kent, subsequently brought him in £104. In 1376 the King made him a grant of £71 : 4 : 6, the price of some wool forfeited at the Customs for non-payment of duty ; and just before Christmas he received ten marks as his wages, as one of the retinue of Sir John Burley, on some secret service. In 1377 he went to Flanders with Sir Thomas Percy on another secret mission, and later in the same year was engaged in France, probably with the King's ambassadors, who were then negotiating a peace.

Edward III.'s death on 21st June 1377 caused no interruption in Chaucer's prosperity. Early in the next year he probably took part in a second embassy to France, to negotiate a marriage between Richard II. (then twelve years old) and a daughter of the French king. In May 1378, again, we find him preparing to accompany Sir Edward Berkeley on a mission to Lombardy, there to treat on military matters with Bernabo Visconti, Lord of Milan, and with the English free-lance, Sir John Hawkwood. He obtained the usual letters of protection, and appointed two friends, Richard Forrester and the poet Gower, his agents during his absence. The arrears of his pension (£20), with an advance of two marks on the current quarter, were paid him, and on 28th May he received one hundred marks for his wages and expenses during his mission. Of the mission itself we know nothing, but we find Chaucer at home again on 3rd February 1379, when he drew his arrears of pension for the time he had been absent.

As far as we know, with this journey to Lombardy Chaucer's career as a diplomatist came to an end, and for the next five years or so we must picture him as attending to his duties as Comptroller of the Customs and Subsidies, receiving his

---

[1] A pension of the same amount had been previously granted by the Duke to Philippa Chaucer on 30th August 1372, and it is possible that the 1374 pension was only a re-grant of this made out in the joint names of husband and wife.

b

own and his wife's pensions at irregular intervals, and probably dunning the Treasury for £22 due to him for his last French mission, until in March 1381 it was finally paid.[1] On three successive New Year's Days (1380-82) his wife was presented with a silver gilt cup and cover by the Duke of Lancaster, and in May 1382 Chaucer himself was appointed to an additional Comptrollership, that of the Petty Customs of the Port of London, with leave to exercise his office by deputy. In February 1385 the same privilege was allowed him in regard to his old Comptrollership, after he had been granted a month's leave of absence at the end of the previous year. In October 1386 he sat in the Parliament at Westminster as one of the Knights of the Shire for Kent, and on the 15th of the same month gave evidence in favour of Lord Scrope in the suit between him and Sir Robert Grosvenor as to the right to a certain coat of arms, which he swore that he had constantly seen Henry le Scrope bearing in the campaign before ' Retters ' seven-and-twenty years previously. That campaign had ended for Chaucer himself in a short imprisonment, but since his ransom by Edward III. he had enjoyed, as far as we can tell, an uninterrupted career of prosperity, with a considerable income from his pension and official employments, and with his various diplomatic missions to increase his knowledge of the world.

To no small extent Chaucer's good fortune was due to the favour of his patron John of Gaunt, and now the latter had left England in the spring of 1386 to prosecute his claims to the throne of Castile. The Parliament in which Chaucer had sat had demanded a change in the royal advisers, and though the King at first resisted, the Duke of Gloucester was too strong for him. A Board of eleven was appointed to overlook the royal household and treasury, and Chaucer, who belonged to the King's party, lost both his Comptrollerships, his successors in them being nominated in December. Shortly before this he must have given up his house in Aldgate, for in October of this year it was let to another tenant, and we have no knowledge where the poet lived during the next thirteen years. Some time in the second half of 1387 it is probable that he lost his wife, for there is no record of any payment of her pension after midsummer in that year. By May 1388 he must have been in serious financial straits, for we find him assigning both his pensions (i.e. the original pension of twenty marks and the twenty marks allowed him instead of his pitcher of wine) to a certain John Scalby, who presumably gave him a lump sum in exchange for them. Exactly a year later (May 1389) the King dismissed Gloucester and the other Lords Appellant from his counsels, and declared his determination no longer to live under governance, and with the return of John of Gaunt to England Chaucer, no doubt, hoped for better times. A brief spell of prosperity came to him by his appointment on the 12th July 1389 to be Clerk of the King's Works at the Palace of Westminster, the Tower of London, and various royal manors, at a salary of two shillings a day, with power to employ a deputy. A year later he was ordered to procure workmen and materials for the repair of St. George's Chapel, Windsor, and was paid the costs of putting up scaffolds in Smithfield for the King and Queen to see

---

[1] These years, otherwise apparently uneventful, were broken by one unpleasant incident, for on 1st May 1380 a certain Cecilia de Chaumpaigne executed an absolute release to Chaucer from all liability *de meo raptu*. Quite recently, Mr. Reginald R. Sharpe has printed in the *Athenæum* for 14th August 1897 extracts from the Rolls of Pleas and Memoranda at the Guildhall, which show that on 26th June in the same year 1380 Cecilia Chaumpaigne executed a general release 'racione cuiuscunque cause a principio mundi,' to Richard Goodchild ' coteler ' and John Grove ' armurer,' and that on the same day Goodchild and Grove executed a similar release to Chaucer. On the 2nd of the next month Grove gave Cecilia Chaumpaigne a recognisance for £10 to be paid at Michaelmas, as was duly done. Mr. Sharpe suggests that the £10 may have been paid to the lady by Grove on Chaucer's account, but I do not agree as to this. Unfortunately the interpretation most favourable to the poet points to his having been accessory to some such attempt on Cecilia de Chaumpaigne as the Staces had practised against his own father.

the jousts in May. In the intervening March he had been named, with five others, as a commissioner for the repair of the roadways on the banks of the river between Greenwich and Woolwich, but by the summer of 1391 he had lost both his lucrative clerkships, though he received various payments in connection with them as late as 1393.

Even these short two years of renewed prosperity were marked by at least one unpleasant incident, for on 6th September 1390 Chaucer, by a strange misfortune, was robbed twice on the same day by members of the same gang of highwaymen—the first time at Westminster of £10, the second at Hatcham, near the 'foul oak,' of £9 : 3 : 8. The money was not his own, but the King's, and was forgiven him by writ on 6th January 1391. One of the gang turned 'approver' or informer against the rest ; but being challenged to a wager by battle and defeated, was himself hanged, a fate which seems eventually to have befallen most of his comrades.

After the loss of his clerkships Chaucer's means of subsistence, so far as we have certain knowledge of them,[1] were reduced to the proceeds of his commissionership of the roadway between Greenwich and Woolwich. From one of these places, probably in 1393, he wrote to his friend Scogan, as one 'at the stremé's hede Of grace, of alle honour and of worthynesse' (*i.e.* the Court at Windsor), a humorous poem which ended with the serious request 'myndé thy frend ther it may fructifye,' and it was possibly at Scogan's request that Richard II. came to Chaucer's relief with a grant of a new pension of £20 a year for life. During the next few years we find the poet frequently obtaining loans from the Treasury in advance of his pension, and on two occasions these loans are as small as 6s. 8d. (£5 modern value). In May 1398 he obtained from the King letters of protection against enemies suing him, and the protection was needed, for we know that just at this time he was being sued for a debt of a little over £14, nearly three-quarters of a year's pension. In October of this year Richard granted him a tun of wine yearly in answer to a petition which seems to have begged it somewhat pitifully 'for the sake of God and as a work of charity.' A few months later the King himself was deposed. To Chaucer, however, as a follower of John of Gaunt, the change was only that from a good friend to a better, for a poem entitled a *Compleynt to his Purs*, addressed to Henry IV., elicited in October 1399 a fresh pension of forty marks in addition to the £20 granted by Richard II. Thus assisted, Chaucer, on 24th December, took a lease of a tenement in the garden of St. Mary's Chapel, Westminster, for no less than fifty-three years. He drew an instalment of one pension on 21st February 1400, and £5 on account of another on 5th June, by the hands of a friend. On 25th October, just ten months after he had taken his long lease, he died, and was buried in St. Benet's Chapel, in Westminster Abbey, where his grave has since been surrounded by those of many later poets.

The fact that Chaucer was a servant of the Crown, and the care with which the public records of this period have been preserved, enable us to trace the poet's external or business life with a certainty and particularity in strong contrast with the little we know of the lives of most of the men of letters of the next two centuries. The additional information which we can glean from his poems is for the most part

[1] Between June 1390 and June 1391 a Geoffrey Chaucer was appointed Forester of North Petherton Park, in Somersetshire. The post was in the gift of the descendants of Chaucer's first patroness, the Countess of Ulster, but even with this to help us, it is hardly safe to assume the identity of the forester and the poet. The fact that in 1416-17 a Thomas Chaucer was appointed to the same post certainly does not carry us any farther, even if we believe that the Thomas who assumed the Roet arms was the poet's son. In the fourteenth century Chaucer or Le Chaucer (the shoemaker) was not an uncommon name.

vague and uncertain. The first of his works which we can date, the *Boke of the Duchesse* (an allegorical lament for the death of John of Gaunt's first wife, Blanche of Lancaster, who died in 1369), contains an allusion to an eight years' sickness which has caused much conjecture. Nature, he writes, will not suffer a man to live without sleep and in sorrow.

> And I ne may, no nyght ne morwe,
> Slepe ; and this melancolye
> And drede I havé for to dye,
> Defaute of slepe and hevynesse,
> Hath sleyn my spirit of quyknesse
> That I have lost al lustihede.
> Suche fantasyes been in myn hede
> So I noot what is best to do.
>   But men myghte axé me why so
> I may not slepe, and what me is ?
> But nathéless, who aské this
> Leseth his asking trewély.
> My selven can not tellé why
> The sothe ; but trewely, as I gesse,
> I holdé hit ben a siknesse
> That I have suffred this eight yere,
> And yet my booté is never the nere ;
> For ther is phisicien but oon
> That may me hele ; but that is doon.
> Passe we over until eft ;
> That wil not be, moot nede be left.

It is usual to join with this passage *The Compleynte unto Pite*, or, as it is otherwise called, *The Exclamacion of the Deth of Pite*, a fine but rather artificial poem, in which Chaucer tells us how, when he ran to beg pity to avenge him on cruelty, 'I fond hir deed and buried in an herte.' If, however, we are to search for autobiography in Chaucer's love-poems, *A Compleynte to his Lady* (pp. 334-336), which is even more artificial than the *Pite*, contains some far more explicit phrases as to a hopeless love, and its ill effects in melancholy and loss of sleep. Part of this poem is in *terza rima*, and for this and other reasons it seems impossible to assign it to so early a date as 1369. If we separate these two poems from the passage in the *Boke of the Duchesse*, we are left without any clue to the meaning of the allusion to the eight years' 'sickness' and the one 'physician' who could heal it. It is possible that the 'sickness,' which seems to have been mysterious to Chaucer himself ('myselven can not telle why'), may have been nothing more definite than the vague melancholy and unrest apt to beset young poets when they do not see their way clear, and in that case the physician may be the 'great physician,' God. It is possible also that the allusion is to a love unrequited, and perhaps unrequitable. It is idle to speculate. All we know is that any passion which Chaucer may have felt left but little trace on his verse, except possibly in the beauty and purity of the fine passage on the relations of lover and mistress in the *Boke of the Duchesse* itself. Save in this one piece Chaucer's contributions to English love-poetry may almost be called insignificant.

If we should be cautious in accepting any theory of an unrequited love upon too slender evidence, we should be no less careful to avoid the exaggeration which interprets the conventional satire which Chaucer in his later poems directs against women as a proof that the poet's relations with his wife Philippa were unhappy. If read as the work of any other fourteenth century writer would be read, there is nothing in Chaucer's poetry on which to rest such a theory, and it is even possible to contend that if we compare the poems written during his wife's lifetime with those generally assigned to the period after its close, we have some ground for believing that her death removed a moral influence which had previously made itself felt. On the other hand, we are tempted to conjecture that it was the influence of the ex-damoiselle of the bed-chamber which kept Chaucer so long occupied with the fashionable artificial poetry of the day, and that this may have been one of the causes of his abnormally late poetic development.

To pass to matters of more certainty, we find in the *Boke of the Duchesse* an illustration from the side of his poetry of Chaucer's relation with John of Gaunt, while in the two prologues to the *Legende of Good Women* we see him intending to present his book to the Queen, to whose patronage of him we have no external allusions. Lastly, we may note the well-known passages in the *Hous of Fame* (ii. 139-152) and *Legende of Good Women* (29-50), in which the poet alludes to his studious habits and love of flowers, and the remarks of the Host in the *Canterbury Tales* (B. 1884-1894) when he calls upon him for his story. These give us a picture of Chaucer as he imagined that other men would see him, and we have a notable additional help towards realising his appearance in the well-known portrait which his follower, Thomas Hoccleve, caused to be painted on one of the leaves of his own *Regement of Princes*, now Harleian MS. 4866 in the British Museum. Dr. Furnivall's description and comments on this portrait bring out its qualities so well that we cannot do better than quote them. 'The face,' he says, 'is wise and tender, full of a sweet and kindly sadness at first sight, but with much bonhomie in it on a further look, and with deep-set, far-looking grey eyes. Not the face of a very old man, a totterer, but of one with work in him yet, looking kindly, though seriously, out on the world before him. Unluckily the parted grey moustache and the vermilion above and below the lips render it difficult to catch the expression of the mouth ; but the lips seem parted, as if to speak. Two tufts of white beard are on the chin ; and a fringe of white hair shows from under the black hood. One feels one would like to go to such a man when one was in trouble, and hear his wise and tender speech.' Other portraits exist, but they are less carefully drawn. They serve, however, by their general resemblance to show us that the one which we owe to the piety of Hoccleve is no mere fancy sketch.

The foregoing account of Chaucer's career has been based entirely on authentic records, without any turning aside to notice the many fanciful statements about him, now known to be false. A full account of these will be found in the interesting chapter entitled 'the Chaucer Legend' in Professor T. R. Lounsbury's *Studies in Chaucer*,[1] to another chapter in which[2] students may be referred for an account of the books which we know, from his use of them in his works, that Chaucer must have read. That from our biographical sketch all mention of the poet's works has been so rigorously excluded is mainly due to the fact that, although the sequence of most of these is now well established, by evidence which I have epitomised in my *Chaucer Primer* (pp. 36-60), only in a few cases can we be absolutely sure of the year in which any given poem was begun or ended. In the case, indeed, of many of the poems we cannot even fix the date within five years, and it therefore

---

[1] Vol. i. pp. 129-224.
[2] Vol. ii. 169-426. A brief sketch of the same subject will be found in my *Chaucer Primer*, pp. 25-36. Professor Lounsbury seems to me a little unduly hard on Chaucer's inaccuracy as a scholar.

seemed impossible to introduce references to his poetry into an account of the poet's external life, of which most of the details we have are so singularly precise. The generalisation which has been accepted of recent years that Chaucer in the earliest stage of his career as a poet was subject only to the influences of French models, that he subsequently transferred his allegiance from Machault and Guillaume de Lorris to Dante, Petrarch, and Boccaccio, and finally became his own master and developed an 'English' style all his own,—such a generalisation as this may pass muster well enough, but when we attempt to define the years within which these stages were accomplished difficulties spring up on every side.

The date 1369 as that of the composition of the *Boke of the Duchesse* is, if not really a landmark, at least solid ground, but one of the few questions of sequence still undecided is as to on which side of the *Boke of the Duchesse* we should place the translation of the *Romaunt of the Rose*, the *A B C*, and the *Pite*.

Again, it is usual to date Chaucer's ' Italian period' from his Genoa mission of 1372-1373, but if we except a few lines in the invocation before the legend of St. Cecilia, which have the appearance of being translated from Dante (they may be a later addition or derived from a common original), we have no real proof that Chaucer was possessed of any Italian books until his Milan mission of 1378-1379, or indeed that he could read Italian until this date.[1]

Once more, though we have good reason for believing that the plan of the *Canterbury Tales* took shape about the years 1386-1388, we have no clue whatever to the number of years during which Chaucer continued writing them. The authenticity of the *Retraction* at the end of the *Tales* has been doubted, but with the distinct forecast of it given in the conclusion of the *Troilus*, the doubts seem themselves indefensible. It is possible that the unfinished treatise on the Astrolabe, compiled in 1391, practically marks the end of the *Tales*. It is possible, on the other hand, that the poet continued writing them almost to the last, though in this case, as he would hardly have abstained from publication during so many years, it is probable that we should have had a distinct group of manuscripts, containing only a portion of the extant series, put into circulation before the rest were written. But questions of this kind are never likely to be settled, and they are alluded to here chiefly to show how impossible it is to bring the two sides of Chaucer's life into as close connection as we could wish.

When we turn from the attempt to fix the precise date of the beginning or completion of any given poem to trace the development of Chaucer's genius our task becomes much easier. At first sight, indeed, it may seem that here we are merely arguing in a circle, deducing results from an arrangement especially contrived to produce them. But the sequence of Chaucer's poems, though in the early days of the Chaucer Society it was mapped out largely by this very test of development, has since been confirmed by a variety of other tests, and is strongly supported by every approximation to a precise date which we have attained. Thus Chaucer's gradual growth in poetic freedom and power is a real fact, and, as a fact, is worth studying. And at the outset we may note the strong probability that he started as a poet comparatively late in life. He himself went to school before the fashion of construing Latin into French and not into English had been abandoned, and it is probable that in the early years of his service at Court poetry in English would still

---

[1] The story of Griselda, which is generally and rightly regarded as written soon after the first Italian mission, was translated, not from the vernacular version of Boccaccio, but from the Latin of Petrarch. The sections, again, of the *Monk's Tale*, which are usually regarded as early, are taken from a Latin, not an Italian, work, the *De Casibus Virorum et Mulierum Illustrium* of Boccaccio.

have been rather looked down on, as a little vulgar or, at least, unfashionable. Certainly when Chaucer did begin to write, whether it was with his translation of the *Roman de la Rose*, or with the lost *Boke of the Leoun* (almost certainly a translation of Guillaume Machault's *Dit du Lion*),[1] or with the *A B C* translated from Guillaume de Deguilleville, or with the *Boke of the Duchesse*, in which, in addition to some (not very important) direct borrowings from Machault and the *Roman de la Rose*, the form of the whole poem is French,—whichever of these works we may choose to regard as the earliest, there can be no doubt that Chaucer was at starting wholly under the French influences which we may presume to have been predominant at Court, and which indeed were the only ones then open to him. From the three (or should we say the *two ?*) extant works we see that even in these days of his apprenticeship Chaucer's verse is full of music, but that he will condescend to very poor padding when he is translating and has to fill out his stanza. In the *Boke of the Duchesse* he is throughout conventional, even his often praised portrait of the knight's lady lacking the individuality which in later years he would have given it with far fewer touches and less piling up of pretty adjectives. Yet with all its conventions the *Boke of the Duchesse* has a certain charm in it, quite different from anything in Chaucer's later work. He writes as the timid lover, who dreams of women afar off; and it is noticeable how in the three next poems which we may attribute to him, the *Lyf of Seint Cecyle*, the story of Griselde and the story of the Emperor's daughter Constance (see below, Introduction to *Canterbury Tales*), he, in each case, takes as his heroines personified virtues whom he certainly never realised to himself as living women. All these poems, it should be noted again, are more or less didactic and religious, though the religious feeling in them is eminently artificial. All three in their present form (more especially the story of Constance, now the *Man of Lawes Tale*) show marks of revision at a later date. But the adoption of the decasyllabic seven-line stanza instead of the octosyllabic couplet, and the breaking away from French influences to a more straightforward method of narration, must have marked them from the beginning.

It was impossible for Chaucer to remain long content with these graceful and tender, but very unreal, personifications of religious zeal, patience, and constancy. Between 1369 and 1379 was, if not the busiest, certainly the most adventurous decade of his life, the period when he was moving about and seeing much of men and things, and also becoming acquainted with a new world of literature. The second and third of the three poems we have mentioned show that he had already learnt his art, was no longer a servile translator, unhappy how to fill out a verse when his original failed him. By this time he was ready to improve on the author he followed, introducing touches of his own, some of which show the first traces of his sly humour,

---

[1] This lost work is mentioned in the *Retraction*, already alluded to, found in many manuscripts of the *Canterbury Tales*. Other lost works are *Origenes upon the Maudeleyn*, i.e. a translation of the homily on St. Mary Magdalene, falsely attributed to Origen, and the *Wrecched Engendring of Mankynde*, a translation of Innocent III.'s treatise *De Miseria Conditionis humanæ*. Both these are mentioned in the Prologue to the *Legende of Good Women*, though the latter only in the earlier draft. This list (*Legende*, ll. 414-430), with that in the *Retraction*, and a passage in the Prologue to the *Man of Lawes Tale* (B, 57-89), mentions all Chaucer's more important works. Others are vouched for by Lydgate, or have been preserved in the writing of Chaucer's younger contemporary John Shirley (1366?-1456), or are ascribed to the poet in good manuscripts. A severely tabular statement of the evidence for the authenticity of each poem will be found in my *Chaucer Primer* (chapter iii.), where also I have epitomised (appendix, § 85) the evidence in which various poems at one time commonly attributed to Chaucer are now known not to be by him. For a fuller discussion of these supposititious pieces, see Lounsbury's *Studies in Chaucer* (vol. i.) and more especially Professor Skeat's valuable supplement to his six-volume edition of Chaucer, entitled *Chaucerian and other Pieces* (Clarendon Press, 1897).

and strengthening the web of his poetry with thoughts and reflections culled wherever he could find them.   His prose translation of Boethius and his study of Dante now came to help this reflective vein, and on the other hand he had made acquaintance with two of Boccaccio's masterpieces, not the *Decamerone*, which it is probable he never knew, but the *Teseide* and the *Filostrato*.   The story of Palamon and Arcite, which, after at least one recasting, has come down to us as the *Knightes Tale*, represents his work on the *Teseide*, and *Troilus and Criseyde* that on the *Filostrato*, and these two splendid poems, full of all the colour of mediæval chivalry and love and thought, relieved ever and anon with subtle touches of humour, are the striking achievements of his middle period.   In the *Parlement of Foules*, written in 1382, he returns, to please the Court, to the French models of his earlier days, only to show how far he had progressed since the *Boke of the Duchesse* of thirteen years earlier. In the *Hous of Fame* he is much less happy.   I think there can be no doubt that Dr. Heath is right in his conjecture (see his Introduction to the poem) that Books i. and ii. were separated from Book iii. by some interval, but the poem raises many difficulties, some of which we are not likely ever to solve.   Perhaps it is not amiss to remark here that Chaucer, though one of the world's great story-tellers, is not remarkable for inventiveness.   Probably all, or nearly all, of his plots are borrowed, and in the fourteenth century books from which he could borrow were not easily come at.   He had brought back the *Teseide* and *Filostrato* from one of his visits to Italy, and perhaps had strained his purse to do it; but when he had used them he was thrown back on the rather jejune material he could find in the books around him. At an earlier period he had probably been driven by some such straits to compile the dreary tragedies of misfortune which we know as the *Monkes Tale*.   In the first two Books of the *Hous of Fame* we find him narrating or alluding to almost all the tragedies of hapless love which he soon set himself to tell, till he wearied of them, in the *Legende of Good Women*.   The third Book of the *Fame* is in quite a different style, cast in Chaucer's happy discursive vein, and only failing for lack of a climax.   In the *Legende* it is the Prologue, in its two drafts, which gives him his opportunity.   Of the nine stories of loving women which he had patience to complete, only the first three (those of Cleopatra, Thisbe, and Dido) are in any way worthy of him.

The *Legende of Good Women* was perforce abandoned because of its deadly and inevitable monotony, and it was perhaps Chaucer's sense that this monotony must be avoided at all costs that caused him to conceive the plan of the *Canterbury Tales*, of which diversity, the exchange of stories between gentle and simple, bookmen and the bookless, the religious and the irreligious, is the very essence.   Once more the scheme was left unfinished, but in this case there is little to regret.   If indeed Chaucer had been in the mood, he might have described the adventures of the pilgrims at Canterbury, and the final supper at the Taberd on their return to Southwark, with all the richness of humour which marks the General Prologue or that of the Wife of Bath. But there is some gain in being left with the picture of the pilgrims as still journeying along the Kentish roads, and as for the *Tales*, they run the whole length of the gamut, and seem to leave no note wanting.   As is generally agreed, some of the tales of the gentle folk had probably been written at earlier dates, and had now only to be revised and fitted into their places, but his scheme gave Chaucer an excuse for displaying the same mastery in the broad humours of narration as he had shown in his *Troilus* and *Knightes Tale* in the fields of romance.   It is too true that several of these tales must be reckoned among those which, as the *Retraction* phrases it, 'sounen into sin,' but it is as unfair to take them too seriously as it would be to expose the essential immorality of most fairy-tales, and there can be no question as to the extraordinary skill with which the tales of the Miller, Reeve, and Summoner, no less than the gentler humours of that of the Nun's Priest, are set forth.

Along with their many masterpieces of humour and romance, the *Canterbury Tales* contain some poorer stories, the very feeble version of the death of Virginia, for instance, and the Manciple's tale of Phœbus and the Crow, and it is not easy to tell whether these represent earlier work foisted into the cycle, or whether we have here the fruits of Chaucer's failing powers. It needs some acquaintance with the workings of the mediæval mind to imagine how, at any period of his career, he could have cared to set forth the weariful prose discourses of Dame Prudence. The Parson's sermon, long as it is, is much more endurable, and though nobody is likely, except for professional reasons, to read it through, as I have done, at least six times, the task is not so repellent as might be imagined. The prose treatise on the Astrolabe, written for little Lewis Chaucer in 1391, though only a tenth of its length, is much more formidable. But in all his prose work Chaucer is merely as any other fourteenth century writer, without a touch of the grace and humour with which his poems are filled. As a poet he needs to-day no one to praise him. He has been praised already, wisely and well, by many clever writers. All that is now needed is that the praise shall no longer be taken contentedly on trust, but that his poems, which in their freshness and restfulness must in this century have more power of pleasure-giving than ever before, should be allowed to speak for themselves to ears no longer deaf.

THE CANTERBURY TALES

(ALFRED W. POLLARD)

The *Canterbury Tales* are given the place of honour in this edition partly out of deference to a time-honoured precedent, which might fairly claim some weight even against the chronological arrangement which commends itself to modern scholarship, but partly also because their assignment to any other position would be misleading. In addition to two long treatises in prose they contain some 18,000 lines of verse, and it is quite certain that not all of these 18,000 lines sprang from Chaucer's brain after he had conceived the plan which was to link together this wonderful medley. That one, at least, of the tales was written at an earlier period of his career we have clear evidence. In the Prologue to the *Legende of Good Women* we find the *Second Nun's Tale* already alluded to as the *Lyf of Seint Cecyle*, and in its introduction the narrator is made to speak as an 'unworthy sone of Eve' (l. 60) instead of as a woman, and to address those 'that reden that I write' (l. 78) instead of the listeners to a tale told along the highway to Canterbury. Again, with our suspicions thus aroused, we note Chaucer's distinct statement that he learnt the story of Grisilde at Padua of 'Fraunceys Petrak,' who died in 1374, and whom the English poet may have met on his Genoa mission of 1373, when Petrarch was living at Arqua, near Padua. Chaucer was not so well off for subjects for it to be probable that if he learnt this story from Petrarch in 1373 he would have left it unused for a dozen years or more, and there is a general agreement in the belief that he wrote his English version of Petrarch's Latin shortly after his return to England. In the *Monk's Tale*, again, the wearisome tragedies fall into two distinct groups, one of twelve stories of old time, derived from the Bible, Boccaccio's *De Casibus Virorum et Feminarum Illustrium* and *De Claris Mulieribus*, and the *Roman de la Rose ;* the other, of five modern instances, mostly very briefly treated, and one of them recording the death of Bernabo Visconti, Lord of Milan, which occurred as late as 1385. One of the modern stories, that of Ugolino of Pisa, is partly taken from Dante, and is strikingly better than all the rest. In the early stories, though the verse is good enough, the treatment is often careless and unsympathetic, and Chaucer was clearly not interested in them. It cannot be said dogmatically that they show early work, but it seems probable that at some time towards the close of the decade 1369-1379 (to which, it must be remembered, there is strikingly little of his poetry which can be positively assigned) Chaucer began a poem on the same plan as that afterwards adopted by his follower Lydgate in his *Falls of Princes*, and then abandoned it till the need came to suit the Monk with an unexpected but appropriate theme, when it was revised and enlarged. The *Man of Lawes Tale*, once more a curiously inappropriate one, is cast in the same seven-line stanza as the *Seint Cecyle* and the *Grisilde*, and from its subject, style, and tone appears to have been written towards the close of the same period. On the other hand, the *Prioress's Tale* of the little chorister, though it goes back in feeling to this earlier period, is clearly written after the conception of the plan of the *Canterbury Tales*, as is proved by the 'quod she' with which the narration is interrupted (B 1644), while its ripe and mature beauty fully agrees with this evidence.

Whether any of the other *Tales*—all of which, except the Sir Thopas parody, are written in heroic couplets—should be assigned to a date earlier than the immortal General Prologue, is a point much more difficult to determine. Outside the *Canterbury Tales* the only extant poem in which Chaucer used the heroic couplet is the *Legende of Good Women*, and as this certainly preceded the *Canterbury Tales* as a whole, there is a general inclination to regard this as Chaucer's first essay in the couplet, rather than to give any individual Tale precedence over it. On the other hand, there is an allusion in the already oft-quoted list of Chaucer's works in the *Legende* to a poem enshrining

> Al the love of Palamon and Arcyte
> Of Thebes, thogh the story is knowen lyte.

It is difficult to believe that the reference here is to the fragment of *Queen Anelida and Fals Arcyte* which has come down to us, as it ought to point to a poem which kept much more closely to the loves of the two knights as narrated in the *Teseide*. Our natural inclination would therefore be to identify this poem with the *Knightes Tale*, as we now have it, but the ingenuity of Chaucer's commentators has discovered that there are ten seven-line stanzas translated from the *Teseide* in *Anelida and Arcyte*, sixteen in the *Parlement of Foules*, and three in *Troilus and Criseyde*. Hence has arisen a theory that in addition to the *Anelida* and the *Knightes Tale* Chaucer composed a more literal translation of the *Teseide* in seven-line stanzas, subsequently withdrew it from circulation, and used some of his old material in later poems. Ingenious as this theory is, the supposition of the writing and suppression of a poem, necessarily of considerable length, is no light matter, and if Chaucer really wrote such a poem and subsequently used fragments of it in other works it is extraordinary that he should have called attention to a tale thus cruelly treated by an entirely gratuitous reference in the *Legende*. As for the fragments of the *Teseide* found in the three seven-line poems, there is a parallel instance, of the nearly simultaneous use of the same material in two different metres, in the story of Dido and Æneas, which we find first in the octosyllabic couplets of the *Hous of Fame*, and again in the decasyllabic couplets of the *Legende of Good Women*. On the whole, and with all deference to the great authority of the scholars who have held the opposite view, it seems best to regard the theory of a lost seven-line version of *Palamon and Arcyte* as a needless hypothesis. If this be so, the reference in the *Legend* must be almost certainly to the *Knightes Tale*, and this fine poem is thus brought back nearer to the period of the *Troilus*, with which it is so closely allied in style and temper.

If the *Knightes Tale* is thus brought back, other Tales, notably those of the Franklin (one of Chaucer's great successes) and the Squire, may perhaps come with it, and we need not hesitate, on the score of their metre, to relegate such poor work as the story of Appius and Virginia as told by the Doctor of Phisik, and the Manciple's tale of Apollo and the Crow, to a less happy period of Chaucer's career than that in which he was writing the Prologue and others of his finest works. Without wishing to press this point too far, it seems fair to point out that there is nothing unreasonable in supposing that when Chaucer conceived his immensely ambitious scheme of the *Canterbury Tales* he had a really considerable amount of material already at his disposal. It is sufficient, however, here to emphasise the fact that inclusion in the Canterbury series of itself tells us absolutely nothing as to the date at which any given poem was written, and that we must therefore place the *Tales* as a whole entirely outside the chronological sequence of the poet's other works.

As regards the date at which the idea took shape of a Canterbury Pilgrimage as a framework by which to connect a number of otherwise distinct stories, we have only two or three years from which to choose, and we must not attempt to pin it down too precisely to any one of them. We have various good reasons for believing that the six years which succeeded 1379 produced the *Boece, Troilus, Parlement of Foules, Hous of Fame* and *Legende of Good Women*, and it is therefore inconceivable that Chaucer should have planned the *Canterbury Tales* earlier than the end of 1385 or beginning of 1386. Again, no one who has read the talks by the way can doubt that the poet himself had travelled over the ground, while we know that until on 17th February 1385 he was permitted to appoint a deputy in his Comptrollership he was closely tied to his official work, a bondage of which he complains bitterly in the *Hous of Fame.* Chaucer's own pilgrimage, then, may have been made in 1385 or in any subsequent year, but hardly before this. On the other hand, the short poems written towards the close of his life show that the not very advanced age to which he attained pressed heavily on him, and it would be unreasonable to assign the plan of the *Tales* to his last decade. If, as is highly probable, the *Legende* was begun in 1385 and soon afterwards left unfinished in despair, everything points to the scheme of the *Canterbury Tales* as taking form during the next two or three years, 1386-1388. Nearer than this it is not easy to go with safety, for in drawing conclusions from the indications of date which we find in the talks by the road we must remember that Chaucer may have fitted them in either to the year in which he was writing, or back to the year in which he himself took his holiday. In the latter case the dates would be more likely to be real dates, while if we prefer to believe that they are taken from the year in which he was writing, we can hardly imagine that Chaucer was likely to trouble himself to consider too curiously whether this or that week would be a convenient one for some of his imaginary characters to make their pilgrimage. Thus, in drawing conclusions from the mention of 18th April in the talk which precedes the *Man of Law's Tale* (B 5), I do not think we can absolutely rule out of court the year 1386, on the ground that in that year 18th April fell in Holy Week, 'when the Parson and others would be much in request for the duties which the season imposed on them,'[1] or reject 1388 because 19th April then fell on a Sunday, and 'if Sunday travelling had been intended, something would have been said about the hearing of mass.'[1] With this caution, however, I am quite prepared to accept Professor Skeat's assurance that in 1387 'everything comes right,' since the pilgrims could assemble at the Tabard on Tuesday, 16th April, with four clear days before them, and the journey ending conveniently on a Saturday. Whether we should assign this year to that of Chaucer's own pilgrimage, or to that of his imaginary pilgrims, must remain undetermined. In any case we cannot be wrong in believing that in or about 1387 is the most probable date for the *Canterbury Tales* to have been begun. As to whence the idea of this particular framework for story-telling came to the poet, 'out of his own head' seems in every way the best answer. Certainly there is no shred of evidence to prove that he copied it from the very inferior scheme of Boccaccio's *Decamerone*.

The fame of Becket's shrine, the popularity of the pilgrimage to it, and the mediæval habit of turning a pilgrimage into a kind of religious holiday, are all matters of such common knowledge that they do not need illustrating here. Nor need we stop to prove the futility of the idea once current, that the pilgrims were in so great a hurry to bring their holiday to an end as to have accomplished the then well-nigh impossible feat of travelling fifty-six miles over heavy roads in a single day. In 1358 the queen-mother Isabella, on her own pilgrimage, left London 7th June, slept that night at Dartford, slept at Rochester on the 8th, and at Ospringe on the 9th, and reached Canterbury the next day. Two years later John of France slept at Dartford 1st July, dined there next day, slept at Rochester on the 2nd, dined at Sittingbourne and slept at Ospringe on the 3rd, and reached Canterbury 4th July. The records of other fourteenth century journeys confirm the presumption that Dartford, Rochester, and Ospringe (where some traces of the old Pilgrim's House still exists) were the regular sleeping-places on the road, and there can be no doubt that Chaucer intended his pilgrims to make the journey by these stages, and to take four days over it.

As to the exact route they followed some little uncertainty prevails, owing to the line of the modern road not coinciding everywhere with that of the old 'pilgrim's way,' but we have references to Deptford and Greenwich in the talk before the *Reeve's Tale* (A 3906, 3907), to Rochester in the Host's address to the Monk (B 3116), to Sittingbourne in the quarrel between the Friar and the Summoner (D 847), and to Boughton-under-Blee in the *Canon's Yeoman's Prologue* (G 556), and to the still mysterious Bobbe-up-and-doun, 'under the Blee,' in the *Manciple's* (H 2). Rochester could not possibly be reached after Sittingbourne, and guided by this fact Henry Bradshaw and Dr. Furnivall were able to correct a mistake in arrangement, found even in the best MSS., by which the five Tales of the Shipman, Prioress, Chaucer, the Monk, and the Nun's Priest (all linked together by the talks on the road) were placed immediately before that of the Second Nun, instead of between that of the Man of Law (with which the tales of the second day were begun) and that of the Wife of Bath, in which Sittingbourne is mentioned. By a less necessary alteration the position of the Tales of the Doctor and Pardoner, which in the best manuscripts come before the Shipman's group, were brought back along with it, but placed after instead of before. There are no references to place or time in these two tales, so that the alteration matters little either way, and we now have the twenty-four extant tales and fragments in a reasonable and probable order. Some of these tales (as has been mentioned in the case of the Shipman's group) are linked together by references, backwards or forwards, in the talks on the road ; in other cases there is no link of any kind between

---

[1] Skeat's *Chaucer*, vol. iii. p. 373.

one tale and the next, Chaucer having left the intermediate talk to be filled in when he had written more of the sixty (or a hundred and twenty!) stories which he at one time contemplated. In this and other editions, since the Chaucer Society issued its great Six-Text edition of the best manuscripts, each group of tales is now marked by a letter of the alphabet (A-I), the line-numeration being consecutive throughout the tales of the group.

The mention of the Six-Text edition, which has been the foundation of all subsequent Chaucer work, must lead to a brief statement as to the manuscripts followed, and the method of quoting them, in this text. The extant manuscripts of the *Tales* are very numerous, but there have here been used only the seven printed by the Chaucer Society, viz. the Ellesmere (E), Cambridge University MS. Gg 4. 27 (Cam.), the Hengwrt MS. 154 (Heng.), the Corpus Christi College, Oxford MS. (Corp.), the Petworth (Pet.), and the Lansdowne MS. 851 (Lansd.), being the Society's Six-Texts, and the very important Harleian MS. 7334 (H), which it subsequently printed. As regards the Harleian MS., there is an interesting footnote in Prothero's *Life of Henry Bradshaw* (p. 225) stating, on the authority of Mr. Aldis Wright, that one of Bradshaw's reasons for stopping short in his project of editing Chaucer ' was his inability to account for the wide divergences which distinguish the Harleian MS. of the *Canterbury Tales* from all the other manuscripts.' Thus the Harleian has much to answer for, and there can be no doubt, also, that its readings are often extraordinarily careless, and even absurd. On the other hand, it has a number of readings (cp. A 74, 257, 363, 415, 559, 727, 782, 791, 799, 803, *smyteth off myn heed* for *I wol yeve you myn heed* in l. 782 being a notable instance) as good or better than those found in any other manuscript, and many of them of a kind which it is very improbable that a copyist would have introduced in transcription. The most probable explanation seems to be that many of these readings represent Chaucer's own ' second thoughts,' introduced into a manuscript which passed through his hand after the *Tales* were already in circulation, and that the Harleian MS. is a careless copy of this manuscript.

At the extreme opposite pole to the Harleian stands the Ellesmere, a most carefully written MS., well spelt and observant of grammatical forms, with readings always straightforward and intelligible. Its discovery by the workers of the Chaucer Society was, perhaps, their greatest achievement.

Between the Ellesmere and the Harleian stand the other five manuscripts, of which the Cambridge and the Hengwrt are both very closely akin to the Ellesmere, while the Lansdowne, Corpus, and Petworth approach, more and more nearly, to the Harleian in their general characteristics, though they seldom agree with it in its most important variants. In all these five manuscripts the process of 'contamination,' *i.e.* the correction or completion of a manuscript of one group by one of another, has been at work, *e.g.* in the *Doctor's Tale* the Cambridge MS. deserts the Ellesmere and Hengwrt to join the Harleian and the other three in a number of readings, a few of which are possible, while many are absurd. But on the whole the relations of manuscript and manuscript are fairly constant. The text of the present edition is based on E, mere clerical errors avoided by the other MSS. being silently corrected, while variants of literary or metrical interest are recorded in the notes, or very sparingly introduced into the text. In recording variants E and H are regarded as mutually exclusive, so that if the reading in the note is assigned to H, that in the text is from E, and *vice versa*. To show further the amount of support accorded to any rejected reading of E or H, an index number is added to the letter. Thus a reading followed by the letter E denotes that the text follows the other six manuscripts, and the variation is supported by the Ellesmere only. E^2 shows that it is supported by the Ellesmere and one other, almost certainly the Cambridge ; E³ that it is supported by Ellesmere and two others, almost certainly Cambridge and Hengwrt. The numbers 4-6 show the additional support of one, two, or three of the inferior manuscripts, Corpus, Petworth, and Lansdowne. Similarly, a variant followed by the letter H denotes that the text has the support of the Ellesmere and other five manuscripts. H² indicates the agreement of one other manuscript, probably the Petworth, with H ; H³, H⁴ the support of one or two more, almost certainly Corpus and Lansdowne ; H⁵ that these are again reinforced, probably by Hengwrt ; H⁶ that even the Cambridge deserts the Ellesmere. I do not claim for this system of abridged collation that it is entirely satisfactory, but it gives a rough view of the authorities on either side at a glance, and makes it possible to record variants which otherwise would have to be omitted.

As regards spelling, the modern usage as regards *i* and *j*, *u* and *v*, has been followed throughout. I have also to confess that a personal dislike to the forms *hise*, *evere*, and *nevere* has led me to alter them throughout to *his*, *ever*, and *never*, though Professor McCormick has since convinced me that Chaucer probably pronounced the two latter words as *ev're* and *nev're*. A few accidental misspellings have been altered here and there ; otherwise the excellent spelling of the Ellesmere manuscript has been carefully followed.

For full information as to the sources from which Chaucer drew his stories, students interested in such questions will naturally refer to the *Originals and Analogues* printed by the Chaucer Society, or to the treatment of the subject by Professor Skeat in vol. iii. of the *Oxford Chaucer*, where all the information gleaned by the Chaucer Society, together with the results of the Editor's own researches, will be found set forth. In this edition, to save referring back, the briefest possible indication of the sources, where known, of each Tale has been prefixed to it by way of a preliminary note, and not much need here be added. As we have remarked before, inventiveness in the matter of plots was not a striking feature in Chaucer's equipment as a poet, but given the barest outline of a story he could develop it in his own inimitable manner, and his power in this respect seems to have steadily increased. Thus his indebtedness takes every form from the almost servile translation in the *Lyf of Seint Cecyle* to the re-telling in his own fashion of a tale like that of the *Canon's Yeoman* which he may have heard in the streets. For about one-third of the *Tales* no 'original' properly so called is known to exist, but from the far East or from France, Italy or Germany stories with similar plots have been unearthed which show that the idea was already in existence and only waited for Chaucer to develop it. This is the case with the tales of *The Miller*, *The Reeve*, *The Shipman*, *The Prioress*, *The Nun's Priest*, *The Pardoner*, *The Wife of Bath*, *The Friar*, *The Summoner and the Merchant*. The fable, or apologue or fabliau which can now be produced may be more or less close to the story as Chaucer tells it, but the literary setting is entirely his own, and in no case is there any need to suppose that he had a written original before him as he wrote. If he had once been told the story (as Tennyson, to take a modern instance, was told that of *Enoch Arden*) he would have obtained all the help he needed. In the case of the dull tale of the *Manciple* Chaucer doubtless followed the version of Ovid (*Metamorphoses* ii. 534-632), in that of the Doctor he professes to take Livy's account of the death of Virginia, but really borrowed from the *Roman de la Rose* (ll. 5613-5682). For the story of Dorigen, which he assigns to the *Franklin*, he distinctly mentions his obligation to a Breton 'lay' (F 709-715) and adduces as his authority for the length of Arviragus's absence the fact that 'the book seith thus' (l. 813). Unluckily no such 'lay' can now be found, though Mr. Clouston has discovered several Eastern analogues, from which not only Chaucer's story, but the similar one (with quite different incidents) told by Boccaccio (*Decam.* x. 5), must be sprung. The loss of the original in this case is regrettable, as it would have been curious to have noted how much of a story so well told was borrowed. Unfortunately there can be no doubt that the one blot in the telling, the unmercifully long recital of the martyrs of chastity drawn from S. Jerome 'contra Jovinianum,' is of Chaucer's own introduction. The original of *The Squire's Tale* has in the same way defied detection, though its sources are plainly Eastern. Even the attempt to prove direct indebtedness to the *Travels of Marco Polo* is something less than convincing. From the fact that the tale is unfinished it seems not un- reasonable to believe that Chaucer borrowed only the materials of this story and broke down for lack of a plot ready furnished to him. Of the poet's own *Tale of Sir Thopas*, so rudely interrupted by the Host, the 'original' is to be looked for in the numerous metrical romances which he here parodied so delightfully, and many of the passages which he selected to satirise have been duly pointed out by Dr. E. Kölbing (*Englische Studien*, xi.).

There remain seven tales derived wholly or in part from literary originals still extant. Chaucer's prose story of Prudence and Melibee is derived from Jean de Meung's adaptation of the *Liber Consolationis et Consilii* of Albertano of Brescia, a jurist who flourished in the first half of the thirteenth century. The *Parson's Tale* is similarly derived, but with alterations and additions, from the *Somme des Vices et des Vertus* of Frère Lourens, who died in 1279, a recent German theory that it was tampered with, after Chaucer's death, or with his consent, by some orthodox priest, being quite unnecessary. I cannot, however, agree with Professor Skeat that this Tale 'was once an independent Treatise, which people could either "herkne or rede," and was probably written before 1380, at much the same time as the *Tale of Melibeus*, which it somewhat resembles in style.' The words 'herkne or rede' occur, not in the Tale itself, but in *Envoy* or *Retraction*, and I see no reason to doubt that this was really the work of Chaucer's old age. When the *Melibee* was translated is nearly as difficult to imagine as why it was ever translated at all.

At the outset of this introduction to the *Canterbury · Tales* the sources of the Tales of the Second Nun (*Lyf of Seint Cecyle*), Clerk and Monk have already been indicated. The Man of Lawes story of Constance is derived from the Anglo-French chronicle of Nicholas Trivet, an English Dominican of the first half of the fourteenth century; the Knight's Tale from Boccaccio's *Teseide*, and in the *Eversley Edition* of the *Tales* I have already pointed out with some minuteness how the four Tales of the Nun, Clerk, Lawyer, and Knight illustrate the increasing freedom with which Chaucer handled his material as he felt his mastery in his art increase. In the Second Nun's Tale he is at first servile, but at last begins to condense from sheer weariness and even adds a touch here and there. In the Clerk's, with a better original, he translates with much greater ease, and shows some healthy symptoms of rebellion at the severity alike of Grisilde's trials and her patience. In the story of Constance he is no longer a translator but an adapter, introducing as poetic ornament moral reflections from the *De Contemptu Mundi*, astrological lore from a variety of authors, and, best of all, some very fine speeches and descriptions out of his own head. Lastly in the Knight's Tale we find him improving on the *Teseide* at every turn. It is he who allows Palamon to see Emily first and so have the better claim to her; it is to him we owe the fierce quarrel in prison, the vision of Mercury that sends Arcyte back to Athens, the overheard soliloquy in the wood, and the outburst of anger when Theseus discovers the prison-breakers. When he wrote this story of *Palamon and Arcyte* Chaucer had no longer anything to learn from others, and thenceforth he might take his plots where he could find them with as good a right as that of Shakespeare to such treasure trove.

MINOR POEMS

(H. Frank Heath)

A text of Chaucer's Minor Poems which shall be even fairly satisfactory is no easy achievement.   There is scarcely one of his shorter works which does not offer serious difficulties to the editor.   In some cases the poem is found in only one MS. (*e.g. To Rosemounde*) ; in some, though there may be two or three authorities, they are copied one from the other (*e.g. A Compleynt to his Lady*) ; in others, though there may be many MSS. extant, they show so much mutual contamination that it is impossible to construct a complete genealogy, and sometimes very difficult to assign some of these authorities to any one group (*e.g.* the *Parlement of Foules*).   In all cases the MSS. are much later in date than an editor would desire, and are far removed from the original or originals.   A critical study leads one to feel sure that Chaucer was often responsible for more than one draft of the same poem, and took little or no pains to maintain verbal identity.   There is also little doubt that he not infrequently made corrections in later copies of his works which may have fallen in his way.   Neither of these practices lightens the labours of a conscientious editor.   One example must suffice here.   There can be no reasonable doubt that the group of MSS. which read 'lyke' (l. 5), 'amonge us' (l. 10), 'man' (l. 17), and 'wed' (l. 28) in the Balade *Lak of Stedfastnesse* must be traced to a different original from the group to which MS. Harl. 7333 belongs, and which I have followed in this edition.

It is impossible within the limits of this volume to give all the apparatus necessary for a full critical edition, but the text here printed is the result of a careful collation and critical investigation of all the MSS. printed in the Chaucer Society's publications, and of the MSS. in the British Museum, in all cases where it was advisable or necessary to consult them.

As regards the spelling here adopted, in addition to abandoning the mediæval use of *u* for *v*, and *i* (or *I*) for *j*, and the casual use of capitals in the MSS., I have adopted the modern spelling of the pronouns *thou, you, your, our*, etc.   With these concessions to modern practice, the spelling of the text has been assimilated so far as possible to that of the Ellesmere MS.   I have been rather more consistent, perhaps, than the fifteenth century scribe of the Ellesmere, particularly where grammatical forms were in question (*e.g.* in the distinction of the preterite and past participle, *hadde, had ; broghte, broght*, etc.) ; but Chaucer must also have been more particular in these matters, and, be that as it may, the distinction certainly has the advantage of making the construction of the sentence and frequently the run of the verse clearer to the modern reader.

THE DETHE OF THE DUCHESSE

This poem was written soon after 1369, in which year John of Gaunt's first wife, Blaunche of Lancaster, died at the age of twenty-nine, her husband being then of the same age.   The poem is clearly the work of a young poet, for, though it strikes a true note of pathos at the close, it is unduly long in approaching the climax, and it has no touch of the characteristic humour and irony which so constantly relieve Chaucer's later work, even when the theme is a romantic one. Nor is the form marked by any originality. It is a dream-poem of the typical discursive order, for which the *Roman de la Rose* was responsible throughout European literature of the fourteenth and fifteenth centuries, with the usual furniture and scenery of twittering birds, the hunt, and the May morning. It has indeed been claimed altogether for France by Taine, who heartily despised English literature prior to Shakespeare as 'mere servile imitation.' But the *Dethe of the Duchesse*, though it has recollections in it of both the *Roman de la Rose* and the *Remède de Fortune*, is not a translation or imitation of either. The incident of 'Seys' with which it opens is taken from the *Metamorphoses* of Ovid, in which the story of Alcione's appearance to his faithful wife Ceyx is told, and Machault (possibly to Chaucer's knowledge) imitated the same passage in his *Dit de la Fontaine Amoureuse*, but beyond this the matter of the English poem is original.

Of the three MSS. Fairfax 16 is certainly the best, and closely related to it the Bodley MS. My own independent investigation of the MSS. gave the same result as those of Koch[1] and Max Lange,[2] and I therefore reproduce the following genealogy with the more confidence :—

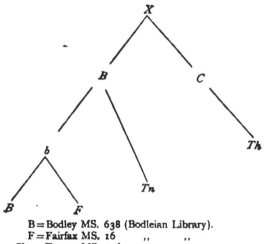

B = Bodley MS. 638 (Bodleian Library).
F = Fairfax MS. 16   ,,   ,,
Tn. = Tanner MS. 346   ,,   ,,
Th. = Thynne's Edition (1532).

The conservative treatment of the authorities in this edition will lead readers to the conclusion, I hope, that Chaucer allowed himself licences in the handling of the four-beat line at the beginning of his life which he refused afterwards in the *Hous of Fame*, and certainly would never have allowed in the five-beat line. In other words, they will, I trust, be willing to assume for Chaucer a development in technique similar to that of Shakespeare and some other poets. They will also, if they agree

[1] In *Anglia*, vol. iv. Auz. p. 95.
[2] In his *Untersuchungen über Chancer's Boke of the Duchesse*, Halle, 1883.

with the present editor, resist the temptation of setting down these 'freely' constructed lines either to the poet's bad ear or (when all the MS. authorities agree) to the copyist's careless hand, but will look for an explanation in the survival of that rhythmic but non-syllabic system of verse which still lived on in England down to Chaucer's day, though much corrupted from its original purity.   These native measures must have echoed in the young poet's ear when he first began to write in the foreign manner, and hence most of the so-called lame lines in the *Boke of the Duchesse.*

THE A B C

About the same time as the *Boke of the Duchesse*, perhaps a little later,[1] Chaucer wrote this poetical prayer to the Virgin.   It is based upon a similar *A B C* contained in Guillaume de Deguilleville's *Pèlerinage de la vie humaine*, a French Pilgrim's Progress of the fourteenth century.[2]   Chaucer simplified the measure by increasing the number of rhymes from two to three, and reducing the length of the stanzas from twelve to eight; but the result is little more than an exercise.   He would fain be a literal translator, but is forced by the exigences of the verse away from his model, only rising here and there, notably in the opening and the nineteenth strophes, above mechanical excellence.

There are thirteen MSS. and one printed edition (that of Speght 1602) available as authorities for this poem.   I agree with Koch in the following classification :—

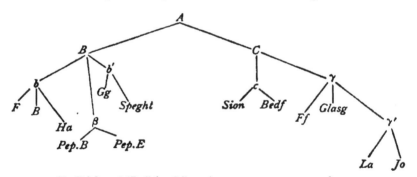

F = Fairfax 16 (Bodleian Library).
B = Bodley 638 (Oxford).
Ha. = Harleian 7578 (British Museum), incomplete.
Pep. B }
Pep. E } = Pepys 2006, Magdalene College, Cambridge (two copies), both incomplete.
Gg = Cambridge University Library, Gg 4. 27.
Sion = Sion College MS. (Shirley's).
Bedf. = Bedford MS. (Bedford Library).
Ff = MS. Ff 5. 30 in Cambridge University Library.
Glasg. = Glasgow, Hunterian Museum, Q 2. 25.
La. = Laud 740 (Bodleian Library).
John = St. John's College, Cambridge, G. 21.
Speght = Speght's Edition, 1602.

---

[1] Ten Brink places it as late as 1374.   [2] It was commenced in 1330.

The thirteenth MS. Harl. 2257 cannot with certainty be assigned its place in the above scheme. It has general similarity with group B, but it is of little or no value. The best group is C, which is used as the basis of the text.

THE COMPLEYNT UNTO PITE

This is a better poem than the preceding one, and the mark of sincerity and deep feeling is upon it, though the metaphor is carried too far here and there for clearness. It is usual to place this poem before 1369, and to make it Chaucer's first original work extant, but both the style and the verse lead me to agree with Ten Brink (whose critical edition of the poem should be a pattern for all editors) in assigning a later date than this somewhere in the two years subsequent to the writing of the *Dethe of the Duchesse*. Whatever the date, this poem is the earliest example of the famous Chaucer stanza, or 'rhyme royal,' as it was subsequently called. Professor Skeat has pointed out recollections of a phrase or two from the *Thebeis* (Book xi.), and Mr. Pollard suggests a parallel between the adversaries of Pity and the first part of the *Roman de la Rose*. But the poem, French in style as it is, is yet original, and is generally interpreted, together with a passage of similar feeling in the *Boke of the Duchesse* (l. 30 ff.), as referring to an incident of unrequited love in the poet's life.

There are nine extant MSS., eight of which (in agreement with Ten Brink and Koch) I would arrange in the following scheme :—

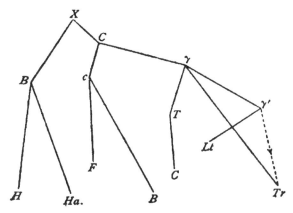

T = Tanner MS. 346 (Bodleian Library).
F = Fairfax MS. 16   ,,   ,,
B = Bodley MS. 638   ,,   ,,
Ha. = Harleian 7578 (British Museum).
H = Harleian 78   ,,   ,,
C = Cambridge University Library, Ff 1. 6.
Lt. = Longleat MS. 258 (Marquis of Bath).
Tr. = Trinity College, Cambridge, R 3. 19.

The dotted line is intended to show that there is evidence of contamination.

MS. Harleian 7578 clearly belongs to the same group as H, but is a much better authority, and more frequently agrees with the derivatives from C. In several cases it supports emendations made by Ten Brink without consulting it (*e.g.* ll. 15, 19, and 101). I am in some doubt whether H and Ha. should be traced from the same original as the other MSS., or whether we should not rather in this case as in others look on H and Ha. as derivatives from an earlier draft of the poem made by Chaucer himself. MS. Phillipps 9053 I have not yet collated. The best group of MSS. is that marked C in the diagram, and of these MS. F has been used as the basis for the text.

THE COMPLEYNT OF MARS

This poem falls well within the second period of Chaucer's work, and was probably written after the poet's second mission to Italy in 1378-79, while the *A B C* and the *Compleynt unto Pite* came in all probability soon after the date of the first mission in 1372-73. The story is founded on one told in the *Metamorphoses* iv. 170-189 of the love of Mars for Venus and its discovery by Apollo. With this story Chaucer combines the popular astronomy of the day in accordance with which the planet Mars is in conjunction with the planet Venus in the sign of Taurus. Taurus is one of the two astrological houses of Venus, and into this the Sun (Phœbus Apollo) enters on April 12th each year. On the basis of two notes made by Shirley in the Trinity College MS. this astrological mythical story is also an allegory written 'at the comandement of the renowned and excellent Prynce my lord the Duc John of Lancastre,' and 'made by (*i.e.* about) my lady of York, doughter to the kyng of Spaygne and my lord huntingdoon, some tyme Duc of Excestre.' The 'lady of York' was John of Gaunt's sister-in-law, through his second wife Constance of Castile. 'My lord huntingdon' was John Holande, half-brother to Richard II., who married Elizabeth, daughter of Blaunche, first Duchess of Lancaster. There are eight extant MSS. and one edition (that of Julian Notary 1499-1502) available as authorities. Of these the Fairfax, Tanner, and Longleat MSS., which belong to one group, are the best on the whole. The remaining authorities are difficult to arrange with certainty, but the following scheme expresses my view of their general interconnection. There is some room for doubt as to whether groups B and C should be traced to a single original rather than two drafts made by the poet at different times.

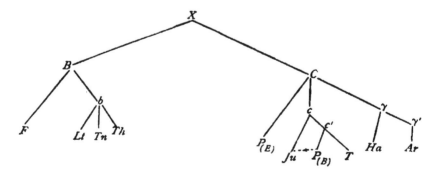

F = Fairfax MS. 16 (Bodleian Library).
Lt. = Longleat MS. 258 (Marquis of Bath).
Tn. = Tanner 346 (Bodleian Library).
P(E) = Pepys 2006 Hand E (Magdalene College, Cambridge).
P(B) = Pepys 2006 Hand B   ,,   ,,   ,,
    T = Trinity College, Cambridge, R 3. 20.
Ha. = Harleian 7333 (British Museum).
Ar. = Arch. Selden B 24 (Bodleian Library).
Ju. = Julian Notary's Edition, 1499-1502.
Th. = William Thynne's Edition, London 1532.

The dotted line is intended to show that there is evidence of contamination.

The MSS. belonging to group B are certainly better on the whole than any single MS. in group C, but were a satisfactory example of this latter tradition available it would undoubtedly be the one to form the basis of a text. In ll. 1, 3, 4, 11, and many others the right reading is clearly furnished by one or more of this group, which has possibly been neglected because it has been seen to include such MSS. as the Harleian 7333 and Arch. Selden. These two authorities are of little or no independent value, more particularly the latter, which gives a text that has been purposely edited, yet they sometimes support good readings in MSS. of the B group in opposition to other MSS. of their own group, and such testimony is valuable. Examples are— l. 20, *to dure* for *to endure*; l. 75, *is* for *was*; l. 120, *this* for *the*, and *smoking* for *smoketh* or *smoked*; l. 143, *Venus weping* for *weping Venus*, etc. Had P(E) been complete, it would have been the best basis for this text; as it is, some approach to a satisfactory result has, it is hoped, been obtained by a combination of P(E) as far as it goes (viz. to l. 84) and P(B), with aid here and there from Ju. and T, and the adoption where called for of readings from the B group, such as *e.g.* l. 66, where the C group read *that thilke*, l. 80, where they read *he fil* (= fell), and some others, among them ll. 20, 75, 120, and 143 referred to above.

A COMPLEYNT TO HIS LADY

This interesting *pot pourri* of verse-forms is found in only two MSS. and one edition, that of Stowe 1561. The two MSS. are Harleian 78 (by Shirley), and MS. Phillipps 9053 at Cheltenham, which last I have not been able to consult except indirectly through the critical notes in Professor Skeat's six-volume edition of Chaucer. He there says that Ph. is copied from Harleian 78, and this seems to be the case. All three authorities tack this fragment on to the *Compleynt unto Pite*, which is, how-ever, complete without it. The poem is clearly intended as a metrical experiment, or series of experiments, and should not be taken too seriously. The similarity of a phrase here and there to the *Anelida and Arcite*, and of the opening of the third section with the *Parlement of Foules* (ll. 90, 91), which are both serious poems, may just as well point to this work preceding them as following them in date. Some time shortly after 1373-74 seems, therefore, still to be most probable.

ANELIDA AND ARCYTE

This poem, like the preceding one, is chiefly interesting for the elaborate metrical experiments for which Chaucer made it the excuse. It opens with three stanzas from the *Teseide*, which Chaucer recast later into heroic couplets for his *Knightes Tale*. These are followed by four based partly on Statius, and these in turn by three more from the *Teseide*. It is possible that at least the first six stanzas and a half formed part of an earlier translation of the *Teseide*, now lost, and that the poet refers to this earlier work in the Prologue to the *Legende of Good Women* when he says 'he made . . . al the love of Palamon and Arcyte of Thebes, thogh the story is knowen lyte.' At l. 47 commences the story of 'quene Anelida and fals Arcite,' and this continues down to l. 210. What the source of this tale may be we do not know. At l. 211 begins the elaborate ' Compleynt of feire Anelida upon fals Arcite,' a more ambitious poem of the same kind as the *Compleynt to his Lady*. The fourteen stanzas of which it consists are arranged in a proem or introduction, two movements of six stanzas each, and a conclusion. With the exception of the last two stanzas in each of the movements of six, the stanzas are of nine decasyllabic lines rhyming *aab*, *aab*, *bab*. The fifth stanzas in the two movements or Strophes of six are divided into two parts, each of eight lines of octosyllabics, except the fourth and eighth which are decasyllabic. In the first part the rhymes run *aaab*, *aaab*, in the second the same rhymes are used in the reverse order *bbba*, *bbba*. The sixth stanza in each of the movements is of nine decasyllabics, rhymed as in the main body of the poem, but with the additional ornament of. an internal rhyme on the fourth and eighth syllable of each line.

At the conclusion of the Compleynt the story is resumed, but breaks off after a single stanza which is only found in five of the eleven MSS. Chaucer doubtless intended to reintroduce Theseus, with whom the poem opens, as the avenger of Anelida.

There are eleven MSS. and one edition (Caxton's) of this poem, which I agree with Koch in arranging as follows :—

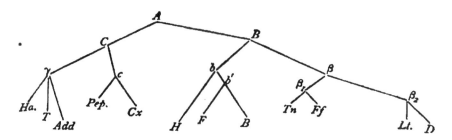

Ha. = Harleian 7333 (British Museum).
T = Trinity College, Cambridge, R 3. 20.
Add. = Shirley's Additional 16,165 (British Museum).
Pep. = Pepys 2006 (Magdalene College, Cambridge).
H = Harleian 372 (British Museum).
F = Fairfax 16 (Bodleian Library).
B = Bodley 638   ,,   ,,
Tn. = Tanner 346   ,,   ,,
Ff = MS. Ff 5. 30 (Cambridge University Library).
Lt. = Longleat MS. 258 (Marquis of Bath).
D = Digby 181 (Bodleian Library).
Cx. = Caxton's Edition, c. 1477-78.

The best group of MSS. is C, and this is the one used as the basis of the text.

THE PARLEMENT OF FOULES

This charming fancy is the only poem of any length written during the years that Chaucer was engaged upon his great masterpiece, the *Troilus and Cresseida*. As Dr. Koch has shown, the poet must have been commissioned in the summer of 1382 to celebrate the wooing and winning of Anne of Bohemia by Richard II. The marriage had taken place on January 14th of that year, after the successful mission of the English ambassadors to Bohemia in the previous January. Anne is represented in the poem by the formel (*i.e.* female) eagle and Richard by the royal eagle, while the two tercels (*i.e.* males), 'of lower kind,' who plead for her love, are the Prince of Bavaria and the Margrave of Misnia, to each of whom Anne had been in turn contracted.

The material supplied him was too slight in itself for a poem of sufficient length and dignity, so the poet elaborated and ornamented his theme by a summary of Cicero's *Somnium Scipionis*, a description of the Garden of Love taken from the *Teseide* of Boccaccio and a description of Nature and her birds based upon a passage in the *Planctus Naturæ* of Alain de l'Isle, though the Cistercian bishop had represented them in mediæval manner as embroidered on the garment of the Goddess, not, as Chaucer does, full of life and wit. His use of other men's work is seen to be much freer than it once was, and the poem is in all real senses an original one.

There are fourteen MSS. and one printed edition (Caxton's) which serve as authority for this poem, but some of them are so corrupt and show so much evidence of contamination that it is very difficult to discover their relation to the rest. These doubtful MSS. are printed below the remainder, which I agree with Koch in arranging as follows :—

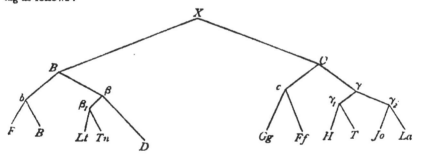

F = Fairfax 16 (Bodleian Library).
B = Bodley 638   ,,   ,,
Lt. = Longleat MS. 258 (Marquis of Bath).
Tn. = Tanner 346 (Bodleian Library).
D = Digby 181   ,,   ,,
Gg = Cambridge University MS. Gg 4. 27.
Ff = Cambridge University MS. Ff 1. 6.
H = Shirley's Harleian MS. 7333 (British Museum).
T = Trinity College, Cambridge, MS. R 3. 20.
Jo. = St. John's College, Oxford, MS. lvii.
La. = Laud MS. 416 (Bodleian Library).

Seld. = Archibald Selden B 24.
Hh = Cambridge University MS. Hh 4. 12.
  P = Pepys 2006 (Magdalene College, Cambridge).
Cx. = Caxton's Edition (1477-78).

The best group of MS. is C, and this is the one used as the basis of the text.

BOECE

(Mark H. Liddell)

The *Consolation of Philosophy* was one of the most popular books of the four-teenth century, and it is not to be wondered that Chaucer should have undertaken a translation of it.   How great an interest this classic had over him can be seen from the numerous quotations from it he makes all through his work.   His Latin scholar-ship, however, was by no means adequate to the task, a deficiency which he probably felt himself, for he makes very free use of an existing French version now commonly ascribed to Jehan de Meung.   He used also the paraphrase which was common in early texts of the *Consolation*, as well as the commentary ascribed by tradition to Thomas Aquinas, and printed in fifteenth century editions of Boethius.

Despite these props and stays, however, Chaucer makes blunders which cannot be charged to the incompetent scholarship of the time, but must be laid directly to his own insufficient knowledge of Latin idiom, a fault doubtless due to the fact that the *Boece* is one of the earliest of his longer works.

This edition contains a critical text made from all the known MSS. in which the translation has been preserved to us (including two newly-discovered ones). It follows MS. Ii i. 38 (C_1) Cambridge University Library, with such de-partures as are justified by critical examination of the other known MSS.   These are :—MS. Additional 16,165 (A_2) ; MS. Harleian 2421 (H) ; MS. Bodley 797 (B) ; MS. Hengwrt 393 (Hn), at Peniarth ; MS. Ii 3. 21 (C_2) of the Cambridge Univer-sity Library ; MS. Additional 10,340 (A_1) ; MS. Salisbury 13 (Sal.), in Salisbury Cathedral ; MS. Auct. 3. 5 (Com.), in the Bodleian Library.   Caxton's edition, made from a with frequent readings from Hn., is denoted by Cx. ; Jehan de Meung's French translation is quoted from MS. Fr. 1079 (Fr.) unless otherwise noted. The text is based upon the following arrangement of the MSS., each of which, except Sal., which is a copy of A_1, has been collated all through the work.

The orthography is that of C_1, except where the few northern forms peculiar to the MS. have been changed to Chaucer's spelling.   Several nonsensical sentences are set right for the first time by the critical method followed, but there still remain some passages which evidently got wrong in the original ; it is very fortunate for us that the French version makes almost all of these clear.

TROILUS AND CRISEYDE

(W. S. McCORMICK)

Troilus and Criseyde is based upon Boccaccio's *Il Filostrato*, from which nearly a third is translated or adapted. The characters of the hero and heroine are, however, considerably modified, and Pandarus, who is transformed from the cousin to the uncle of Cressida, is practically Chaucer's own creation. For the development of the story in Book v., Chaucer evidently consulted the *Roman de Troie* of Benoît de Sainte-More, possibly also the *Historia Troiana* of Guido delle Colonne; and for the incidents in Cassandra's exposition of Troilus' dream Chaucer is indebted to Ovid and Statius.

Chaucer's further borrowings are few. Petrarch's eighty-eighth sonnet forms Troilus' love-song in Book i. 400-420. There are three considerable passages from Boethius' *De Consolatione Philosophiæ*, which Chaucer was probably translating about the time of the composition of *Troilus*. The first (iii. 813-833) on 'fals felicité' is put into the mouth of Cressida; in the second (iii. 1744-1768) Boethius' celebration of divine love serves Troilus for another love-song; while the third (iv. 953-1085), Troilus' dreary moralising in the temple, is a fairly close rendering of Boethius' chapter on Free Will and Predestination. In Book v. two passages (ll. 1-14, and ll. 1807-1837) are taken from Boccaccio's *Teseide*, and the first three lines of the last stanza from Dante's *Paradiso*.

It is worth remarking that three of the above passages from *Boethius* and the *Teseide*, viz. iii. 1744-1768, iv. 953-1085, v. 1807-1827, are omitted in some MSS.

The relations of the MSS. of *Troilus and Criseyde* to each other are so complicated and variable, that a detailed statement is here impossible. In many cases portions of the same manuscript have been taken from different sources; and few manuscripts are without traces of contamination. They fall, however, for the most part, into three families (designated here *a*, *β*, and *γ*), which seem to represent three distinct editions or revisions; although in a number of passages, more especially in Book v., the *a* and *β* manuscripts frequently alter their relations to each other, and throughout the poem the variations among the *β* manuscripts are considerable. It appears probable, from a comparison of the readings of the three types with the originals from which Chaucer was translating, that in *a* type we have the first draft of the poem, copied in parts during its composition; that manuscripts of the *β* type give more than one partial revision by Chaucer of copies of his work before or after its completion; and that the *γ* type represents a later copy, either carelessly corrected by the author, or collated by some hand after Chaucer's death.

The following list of authorities may serve to indicate in a general way the relations of the MSS., or portions of MSS., to each type, at least for the first four Books.

MANUSCRIPTS

I. P—MS. Phillipps 8252.
    a throughout.

II. H₃—MS. Harl. 3943.
    a (close to P) till iv. 196; *β* (close to H₄) later.

III. H₄—MS. Harl. 2392.
    a (with *β* readings) till iii. 231 (?); *β* (with *a* readings) later.

IV. G—MS. Gg 4. 27, Cambridge (first and last leaves of all the Books cut out).
β till II. III. ; α later.

V. H₂—MS. Harl. 4912—(ends at IV. 686).
β till II. III. ; α later. Throughout close to G.

VI. J—MS. LI. St. John's College, Cambridge.
β (with α readings) till IV. 400 (?) ; α later.

VII. R—MS. Rawlinson Poet 163. Bodleian.
β throughout ; omits Prologues to Books II. III. and IV.

VIII. H₃—MS. Harl. 1239.
β till II. 1033 ; γ from II. 1034 till III. 231 ; later, collated from various sources, but keeping close to α through Book IV.

IX. S—MS. Arch. Selden B 24. Bodleian.
collated throughout from γ and β, and following many of the errors of γ till II. 516.

X. A—MS. Addit. 12,044, British Museum. (Ends at V. 1820.)
γ throughout (with occasional α or β reading).

XI. D—MS. v. ii. 13. Durham.
close to A.

XII. S₂—MS. Arch. Selden *supra* 56. Bodleian.
γ throughout (with occasional α or β reading).

XIII. Dg—MS. Digby 181. Bodleian. (Ends at III. 532.)
close to S₂.

XIV. Cp.—MS. 61 Corpus Christi College, Cambridge.
γ throughout.

XV. H₁—MS. Harl. 2280.
close to Cp.

XVI. Cl.—MS. Campsall.
close to Cp. and H₁.

[To these may be added two MS. fragments printed in *Odd Texts of Chaucer's Minor Poems* (Chaucer Society, 1880) ; and one MS. fragment of Book v. 1443-1498 in Cambridge University Library.]

EDITIONS

XVII. Cx.—Caxton's Edition (1484).
β throughout (with γ readings).

XVIII. Th.—Thynne's Edition (1532).
γ throughout (with Cx. and α readings, more especially in Books I. and II.)

[The Editions of Wynkyn de Worde (1517) and of Pynson (1526) are reprints of Caxton's text. In Sir Francis Kinaston's Latin Translation of the first two Books (1635), the English text is a reprint of Thynne's.]

MSS. J, Cp., H₁, and Cl. are the most accurate as to grammatical forms ; but none can be depended upon.

The present text is based upon J (MS. LI. St. John's College), and has been corrected throughout from readings of α and β types alone. But all the authorities have been examined, and all the important variations of γ type are given. In order to curtail the critical notes as much as possible, the mistakes occurring in J *alone* are corrected, and the spelling (including the insertion or deletion of final *e*) is normalised, in most cases, without special mention ; also, where possible, α, β, and γ have been employed to represent the MSS., or the majority of the MSS., belonging to these types respectively.

In printing the text for this edition, some assistance has been offered to the general reader by the indication of stressed syllables, by the use of the dotted *e* to denote a separate syllable in the middle of the line, and by marking elision in such words as *n'as*, *n'il*, *n'olde*, *n'ot*, *th'ilke*, *th'effect*, *m'asterte*, *this'* (for *this is*), etc. The modern use of *i* and *j*, and of *u* and *v*, has been adopted, as well as the modern spelling of *thou*, *you*, *our*, etc. In *her* (= *her*), and *hir* (= *their*), *o* (interjection), and *oo* (= *one*), *on* and *oon* (= *one*), *of* and *off*, *the*, *thee*, and *thé* (= *thrive*), the spelling has been differentiated to indicate the meaning ; and in French words ending in *é*, the accent has been retained. The final *e* of *evere*, *nevere*, *levere*, etc., has been retained, as Chaucer's pronunciation was evidently *ev're*, *nev're*, *lev're*, etc.

CHAUCER'S WORDS UNTO ADAM HIS OWNE SCRIVEYN

This keen *jeu d'esprit* is only found in one manuscript (Trin. Coll. Camb. MS. R 3. 20) and in Shirley's edition of 1561. There can be no doubt as to its authenticity. Its probable date is 1385. (H. F. H.)

THE HOUS OF FAME

(H. FRANK HEATH)

With the *Hous of Fame* we leave the period of the poet's finished work. From this time on his plans were far more ambitious, but they were doomed to remain unfinished. The *Hous of Fame*, the *Legende of Good Women*, and, greatest of all, the *Canterbury Tales*, were none of them completed. At the close of the *Troilus* Chaucer had uttered the hope that God would 'Sende (him) might to make in som comedie,' and most critics are agreed that the *Hous of Fame* was meant to be the fulfilment of this intention. There is some reason for thinking, I believe, that the *Hous of Fame* had been commenced some years before 1383, and then laid aside. When the *Troilus* was complete, this unfinished ' comedy ' came to Chaucer's mind, and hence the prayer. It is difficult, on any other assumption, to understand the use of the short couplet, an unsatisfactory measure at best, particularly for such a theme as the story of Æneas, which takes up the major part of the first book. Having finished the second book—in which the story advances rapidly enough, and with a light humorous touch throughout—the work was laid aside. When it was again taken in hand on the completion of the *Troilus* a new tone is noticeable, and a new invocation to Apollo, 'god of science and of light,' marks the fresh start. This is followed by an apology for the 'light and lewd' verse. It is not 'craft' but 'sentence' which is his aim, and throughout the humour is no longer playful but deeply ironical, for the poet has learnt to see his art and life in the light of common day. The close of the fragment describing the hall of Fame and the petitioners to the goddess is the purest piece of satire Chaucer ever wrote. But all this destroyed the original playful plan and rendered some striking close necessary. Failing this, no wonder the poet's golden eagle, having borne him up to the realm of Fame, finds it hard, as has been remarked, to get down again. No wonder 'the workmanship of the separate parts of the poem is much more masterly,' as the same critic adds, 'than the general plan.' The fragment we possess of the third book is longer than the first two put together. Chaucer had put new wine into an old bottle.[1] The care bestowed on the poem is evident from the number of sources from which the poet drew. The mediæval machinery of a dream with a description of the temple of Venus offers the opportunity for giving an outline of the story of the *Æneid*. Then follows the appearance of the eagle and the journey to the house of Fame, the description of which is taken from the *Metamorphoses* xii. 33-63. Professor Ten Brink was the first to point out that in general plan and in a number of individual passages the influence of the *Divina Commedia* can be traced. Both poems are visions, in both there is a heaven-sent guide who may but accompany the poet in parts of his journey; both are divided into three books. Very probably the importance of Vergil in Dante's poem suggested the story of the *Æneid*. Certainly the idea of the golden eagle is taken from him (*Purgat*. ix.). The apostrophe to 'Thought,' at the opening of the second book, was suggested by the *Inferno* (ii. 7-9), the invocation in the third book by that at the beginning of the *Paradiso* (i. 13-27). The philosophy, however, is not Dante's, but rather—as the poet himself suggests—that of Boethius (ii. 464 ff.); yet the poem as a whole is Chaucer's, and none but his.

The *Hous of Fame* was not likely to be popular, and there are unfortunately only three MSS. and two editions to serve as authorities. I arrange them as follows:—

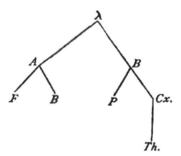

F = Fairfax 16 (Bodleian Library).
B = Bodley 638 ,, ,,
P = Pepys 2006 (Magdalene College, Cambridge), incomplete.
Cx. = Caxton's Edition (1477-78).
Th. = W. Thynne's Edition (1532).

The better group is B, and MS. P has been used as the basis of the text so far as it is available. From that point on Cx. and Th. were used with the aid of F and B. Th., it should be remarked, is not merely a reprint of Cx., for Thynne certainly had access to and made use of other authorities.

---

[1] Some support appears to be lent to this theory by the Fairfax MS., which commences the third book on f. 169, after a wide space, with a large illuminated capital, similar to that used at the opening of the poem; whilst the second book, which commences on f. 161, runs straight on after the close of the first without any space, and with a capital, which, though similar in design to that used for the other two books, is not quite so large.

THE LEGENDE OF GOOD WOMEN

(ALFRED W. POLLARD)

The Legende of Good Women, as Chaucer planned it, was intended to consist of a Prologue, the stories of nineteen women who have been true to love, and lastly, the legend of the crown of womanhood, Queen Alcestis, who gave up her own life to save her husband's. Such a series of poems had plainly been for some time in Chaucer's mind. The goodness of Alceste is the subject of two stanzas in the *Troilus*, and in the *Hous of Fame* (Bk. i. ll. 388-426), after telling the story of Dido out of Virgil's *Æneid*, he gives quite a list of other faithful women, to whom, doubtless, he meant to apply the phrase he uses of Dido, that if it were not too long to endite he would have liked to write her love in full. Chaucer was certainly oc-cupied with the *Hous of Fame* in 1383-1384, and the *Legende*—in which it is mentioned first in the poet's list of his own writings—must have immediately succeeded it. We know that on 17th February 1385 he obtained permission to exercise his Comptroller-ship by deputy, and it has been conjectured that the intention he expresses of sending this new poem to the Queen (ll. 496, 497), and the probability that she was meant to be identified with the good Alceste, are marks of gratitude for this particular favour, which may have been obtained through her intervention. Lydgate, in the Prologue to his *Fall of Princes*, even says that the *Legende* was written 'at the request of the quene,' but if so it would surely have been duly completed. Every-thing, however, points to 1385 as the year of its composition.

Of the nineteen (or twenty) legends planned, only nine were written. These celebrate (1) Cleopatra, who is represented (not quite in accordance, as Chaucer imagines, with 'storial sooth') as a martyr to her love for Antony ; (2) Thisbe, who refused to survive her lover Pyramus (see Bottom's play in the *Midsummer Night's Dream ;* (3) Dido ; (4) the two victims of Jason's treachery, Hypsipyle and Medea ; (5) Lucretia ; (6) Ariadne ; (7) Philomela, the victim of Tereus ; (8) Phyllis, who slew herself for love of Demophon ; (9) Hypermnestra, who accepted death at her father's hands rather than treacherously kill her husband. By the aid of some hints in the Prologue, and of a curious mention of these 'seintes legendes of Cupide' in the talk which precedes the Man of Law's story in the *Canterbury Tales*, it is possible to make a fair guess as to the names of the other ten women, in addition to Alcestis, whose praises Chaucer was too tired to sing. They belong to the same class of heroines as the nine he wrote of, and we need not trouble about them here. For the nine legends Chaucer had recourse chiefly to the *Metamorphoses* and *Heroides* of Ovid, but he used also two Latin works by Boccaccio, viz. his *De Claris Mulieribus* and *De Genealogia Deorum*, while the story of Dido is taken mainly from Virgil, and that of Hypsipyle and Medea from the *Historia Trojana* of Guido delle Colonne. The only other point that need be mentioned is that the Prologue (much the most interesting part of the poem) exists in two different versions. The one which appears to be the earlier has 545 lines, of which 90—including one long passage on love tales, and a reference to Chaucer's own library of 'sixty bookes olde and newe' all full of stories—do not reappear in the revised text. In this many lines are altered, the position of others transposed, and the 90 omitted lines replaced by 124 new ones, bringing the number in the second version to 579. Some of the alterations seem intended to make the poem more acceptable to the Queen, the rest are poetical improvements which may easily be studied in the parallel columns in which they are printed in this edition.

Nine MSS., besides Thynne's Edition (Th.), have been collated, as printed by the Chaucer Society, for the text of this poem, viz. Gg 4. 27, Cambridge (quoted as Gg); Fairfax (F); Tanner (Tan.); R 3. 19, Trinity College, Cambridge (Trin.); Arch. Seld. B 24, Bodleian Library (Arch. Seld.); Bodley MS. 638 (B); British Museum Additional MS. 9832 (Add.), and 12,524 (Add.$_2$); and Pepys MS. 2006 (Pepys).

Of these MSS. F and B must be derived immediately from the same original, and Tan., which shares most of their glaring faults, from the original of that. The text of Thynne's edition belongs to the same group, but Thynne must have collated it with other MSS., as he has supplied lines and words which F, B, and Tan. omit. In my notes F^2 stands for F and B; F^3 for F, B, and Tan.; F^4 for F, B, Tan., and Thynne.

The leading MS. in a second group is Trin., with which must be reckoned Add., which, however, stops at l. 1986. These two MSS. are almost as nearly identical as F and B, and contain a number of good readings. The other Museum fragment Add.$_2$, which only begins at l. 1640, belongs to the same group, as also does Arch. Seld. The latter, however, is a dangerous MS. to use, as its scribe, who may have worked from the same original used for Trin. and Add., has plainly introduced many emendations of his own to smooth away difficulties of sense or metre. I have occasionally denoted the agreement of Trin. and Add. by Trin.^{2}; of Trin. Add. and Arch. Seld. by Trin.^{3}; and of Trin. Add. Arch. Seld. and Add.$_2$ by Trin.^{4}

The Cambridge MS. Gg stands by itself, in virtue of its possession of the first draft of the Prologue. Its readings are throughout of great importance, but its spelling is bad, and it lacks ll. 1836-1907. The Pepys fragment, which stops at l. 1367, though it has the second draft of the Prologue, is linked to Gg by possessing ll. 960, 961, which the other MSS. omit; but it sometimes agrees with the Trin. group against Gg. Its independent readings (with the possible exception of *yiftes* in l. 1126) are of no value.

In making my text I am sorry now that I did not take the Trinity MS. as my starting-point, but I for a long time suspected it of being overmuch edited. Thus the completeness and comparatively good spelling of Fairfax gave it the preference, but in my final revision I have systematically substituted the readings of the Trinity group, or of Gg, for those of the Fairfax where there was any possibility of doubt. In the matter of spelling I have cleared away a good many of the double vowels (especially *oo*) which are the chief disfigurement of F, and have removed a few eccentricities, though with a very sparing hand.

LATER MINOR POEMS

(H. FRANK HEATH)

TO ROSEMOUNDE

To the *Troilus* period belongs this playful ballade, which, like the preceding poem, is only found in one MS. (Rawl. Poet. 163, leaf 114) in the Bodleian Library, where it was discovered some years since by Dr. Furnivall, and afterwards rediscovered and first published by Professor Skeat. The metaphor with which the third stanza opens, and the ironical humour of its combination with the story of Isolde, unmistakably declare the authorship.

THE FORMER AGE

This pleasant rhapsody upon the good old times is based upon Boethius' *De Consolatione Philosophiæ* (ii. met. v.), with echoes here and there from the *Roman de la Rose*. It is only found in two MSS., both in the University Library at Cambridge. Their press marks are Ii 3. 21 and Hh 4. 12. The former is the better of the two, and has been used as the basis of the text. This and the next four poems cannot be exactly dated. They were written after 1382, and probably before 1390.

FORTUNE

Balades de visage sans peinture, as this poem is called in the MSS., are a series of ballades, or rather a triple ballade, with a single envoy of seven, and possibly only six lines, in praise of the friend of the 'unpainted face,' who is faithful in adversity. It was possibly written after Chaucer's loss of office in 1386.

There are eight MSS. and one edition of this poem, which I arrange as follows :—

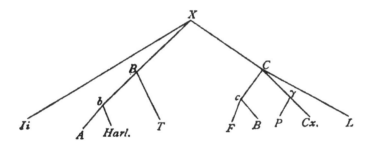

    Ii = Cambridge University Library MS. Ii 3. 21.
    A = Shirley's Ashmole MS. 59 (Bodleian Library).
Harl. = Harleian MS. 2251 (British Museum).
    T = Shirley's Trinity College, Cambridge, MS. R 3. 20 (sheet 7 lacking).
    F = Fairfax MS. 16 (Bodleian Library).
    B = Bodley 638 (Bodleian Library).
    P = Pepys 2006 (Magdalene College, Cambridge).
    L = Lansdowne MS. 699 (British Museum).
    Cx. = Caxton's Edition (1477-78).

Ii is decidedly the best authority, and this has been made the basis of the text.

TRUTH

This ballade and the next, called *Gentilesse*, show Chaucer in his gravest mood, and reveal the finely-tempered spirit which underlay his ironical and sometimes cynical humour. Both poems, like the *Lak of Stedfastnesse*, owe their suggestion, no doubt, to Boethius, but *Truth* (which is the finest) less so than the others, while they all strike an intensely personal note.

There are thirteen MSS. and one printed edition of *Truth*, which I arrange in the following way :—

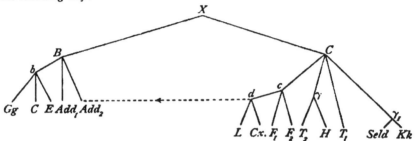

The dotted line is intended to show that there is evidence of contamination.

Gg = Cambridge University Library Gg 4. 27.
C = Cotton MS. Cleopatra D vii. (British Museum).
E = Ellesmere MS.
Add.[1] = Additional MS. 10,340 (British Museum).
Add.[2] = Additional MS. 22,139　　,,　　　,,
L = Lansdowne MS. 699　　　,,　　　,,
F₁ = Fairfax MS. 16 (Bodleian Library).
F₂ = Fairfax MS. 16 (Bodleian Library), second copy of the poem.
T₁ = Shirley's Trinity College, Cambridge, MS. R 3. 20.
T₂ = Shirley's Trinity College, Cambridge, MS. R 3. 20, second copy of the poem.
H = Shirley's Harleian MS. 7333 (British Museum).
Seld. = Arch. Selden B 24 (Bodleian Library).
Kk = Cambridge University Library Kk 1. 5.
Cx. = Caxton's Edition (1477-78).

Group B is the better of the two main groups into which the authorities fall, and of this group sub-group *b* is the better. I have used Gg as the basis of the text.

GENTILESSE

This fine ballade on the qualities that make a gentleman reminds one of the speech in which the Wife of Bath discourses upon 'gentillesse' (*Wife of Bath's Tale*, D 1109-1176). There are eight MSS. and one printed edition of this poem, which I arrange as follows :—

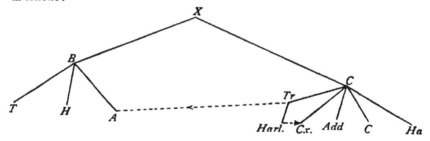

T = Shirley's Trinity College, Cambridge, MS. R 3. 20.
H = Shirley's Harleian MS. 7333 (British Museum).
A = Shirley's Ashmole MS. 59 (Oxford).
Tr. = Trinity College, Cambridge, MS. R 14. 51.
Harl. = Harleian MS. 2251 (British Museum).
Add. = Additional MS. 22,139 (British Museum).
C = Cotton MS. Cleopatra D vii. (British Museum).
Ha. = Harleian MS. 2257 (British Museum).
Cx. = Caxton's Edition (1477-78).

The dotted lines are intended to show that there is evidence of contamination.

Group C is the better of the two main groups, and has been used as the basis of the text.

LAK OF STEDFASTNESSE

This ballade, which is chiefly notable for its envoy to King Richard, Shirley and others have placed between 1393 and 1399. But it is difficult to account for Chaucer's sudden accession of reformatory zeal towards the man who could alone fill his quickly-emptying purse. The poet, if we except this poem, had none of Langland's spirit, and was always of the Court party. Mr. Pollard has suggested, and with great show of reason, that this address to the King and reference to the instability of the times probably dates from the time when the young Richard was taking the government into his own hands, and throwing over the tutelage of his guardian uncles with the support of all his people's hopes. This would place the composition in or about 1389, and when read with this in mind the whole poem gains an added force. There are eight MSS. and one printed edition of this poem, which I agree with Koch in arranging as follows :—

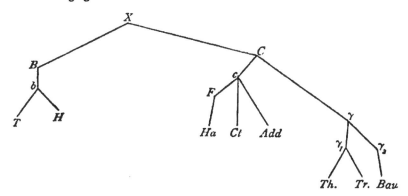

T = Shirley's Trinity College, Cambridge, MS. R 3. 20.
H = Shirley's Harleian MS. 7333 (British Museum).
F = Fairfax 16 (Bodleian Library).
Ha. = Harleian MS. 7578 (British Museum).
Ct. = Cotton MS. Cleopatra D vii. (British Museum).
Add. = Additional MS. 22,139 (British Museum).
Tr. = Trinity College, Cambridge, R 14. 51.

Ban. = Bannatyne MS. 1568 (Hunterian Museum, Glasgow).
Th. = Thynne's Edition (1532).

Group B is the better of the two main groups of authorities, and MS. H has been used as the basis of the text (cp. *supra*, p. xxxii).

THE COMPLEYNT OF VENUS

These three ballades, to which Shirley gave the above title, are translations, more or less free, from the famous Savoyard poet, Sir Otes de Granson,[1] made probably to please Isabella, Duchess of York, the doubtful heroine of the *Compleynt of Mars*. The envoy, which is the best part of the poem, is wholly original. The date is hard to assign, but it is probably somewhere near 1393. There are eight MSS. and one printed edition of this poem, which I arrange as follows :—

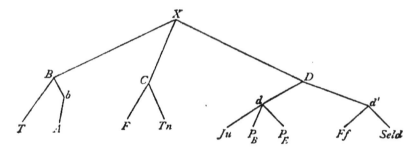

T = Shirley's Trinity College, Cambridge, R 3. 20.
A = Shirley's Ashmole 59 (Oxford).
F = Fairfax 16 (Bodleian Library).
Tn. = Tanner 346 ,, ,,
P(B) = Pepys 2006 Hand B (Magdalene College, Cambridge), ll. 65-72 are wanting.
P(E) = Pepys 2006 Hand E ,, ,, ,, contains only ll. 45-82.
Ff = Cambridge University Library MS. Ff 1. 6.
Seld. = Arch. Selden MS. B 24 (Bodleian Library).
Ju. = Julian Notary's Edition (1499-1502).

The best group of MSS. is B, and I have used this as the basis of the text.

ENVOY TO SCOGAN

About the same time as *The Compleynt of Venus*, Chaucer wrote this playful reproach to his friend Henry Scogan for having given up his lady at ' Michelmesse,' when he found her careless of his distress. But some year or two earlier, in 1391, the poet had lost his post as Clerk of the King's Works, and he makes this an opportunity of begging for his friend's influence on behalf of the needy road-com-

---

[1] For more concerning Granson, cp. Piaget, ' Oton de Granson and ses Poesies,' *Romania*, vol. xix. 1890.

missioner exiled in the 'solitarie wildernesse' of Greenwich. The prayer may have borne fruit in the pension granted him next year.

There are three MSS. (MS. Gg 4. 27, Univ. Libr. Camb. ; MS. Fairfax 16, Bodleian Libr. ; and MS. Pepys 2006, Magd. Coll. Camb.) and one edition (that of Thynne 1532) which serve as authorities for this poem. They all seem to belong to one group ; there is certainly no sufficient evidence for dividing them, though MS. Fairfax is, on the whole, the best, and has been used as the basis for this text.

ENVOY TO BUKTON

This bitter-sweet ballade, in stanzas of eight lines, touches marriage, and is quite characteristic of the poet. It was written in 1396, as we know by the reference to the English prisoners taken in the expedition against Friesland of that year. There is only one MS. (Fairfax 16) besides two early printed editions of this poem, that of Julian Notary (1499-1502), and that of Thynne (1532). The text is based upon the Fairfax MS.

COMPLEYNT TO HIS PURSE

This sadly humorous poem must be one of the last, if not quite the last, we have from the poet's pen. It was addressed to Henry of Bolingbroke, 'the Conqueror of Brutes Albioun,' and it won from him an additional pension of forty marks, which ensured Chaucer against penury in the closing months of his life. Professor Skeat thinks it probable that all the poem except the envoy was written at an earlier date, but without, it seems to me, sufficient ground. There are six MSS. and one early printed edition of this poem, which I arrange as follows :—

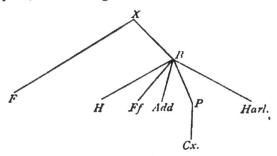

F = Fairfax 16 (Bodleian Library).
H = Shirley's Harleian MS. 7333 (British Museum).
Ff = Cambridge University Library MS. Ff 1. 6.
Add. = Additional MS. 22,139 (British Museum).
P = Pepys MS. 2006 (Magdalene College, Cambridge).
Harl. = Harleian MS. 2251 (British Museum).
Cx. = Caxton's Edition (1477-78).

The best MS. is the Fairfax, which has been used as the basis of the text.

PROVERBS

These two proverbs, if indeed they are Chaucer's, add nothing to his reputation. There are three MSS. of these trifles, two of which, the Fairfax and the Harleian 7578, ascribe the authorship to the poet. I arrange the authorities as follows :—

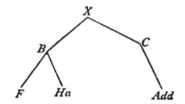

F = Fairfax 16 (Bodleian Library).
Ha. = Harleian MS. 7578 (British Museum).
Add. = Additional MS. 16,165 (British Museum).

B is the better of the two groups of MSS., and MS. F has been made the basis of the text.

DOUBTFUL MINOR POEMS

(H. Frank Heath)

MERCILES BEAUTE

This triple roundel immediately follows several of Chaucer's genuine poems in the only MS. (Pepys 2006) in which it is found. Its manner is quite that of the poet, and it seems to have been well known, for its first line is quoted in Lydgate's ' Ballade in commemoration of our Ladie,' St. 22.

The poems that follow have no direct evidence as to their authorship, but they are sufficiently in Chaucer's manner, though they do not show him at his best, if they are his. They are all of an erotic turn.

AGAINST WOMEN UNCONSTANT

The Ballade ' Against Women Unconstant ' is found in three MSS. (viz. Cotton Cleopatra D vii.; Harleian 7578 ; Fairfax 16), and in Stowe's edition of the works published in 1561. These authorities fall into two main groups, one of which consists of the Fairfax MS., the authority nearest to the original on the whole, and therefore made the basis of this text. The remaining authorities constitute the second group, within which the Cotton MS. and Stowe's edition form a subdivision traceable to a copy of the MS., of which Harleian 7578 was a copy.

The subheading of this poem is from the edition of 1561 which reads—' A Balade whiche Chaucer made agaynst women unconstant.'

COMPLEYNT DAMOURS

The *Compleynt Damours*, much the poorest of these doubtful poems, is also found in three MSS. (Fairfax 16; Bodley 638; and Harleian 7333). They fall into two groups, of which the Harleian MS. forms one, and the remaining MSS. the other. The common source of these two groups was almost certainly a MS. itself one or more removes from the original. None of the existing MSS. are good, but A on the whole forms the best basis for a text, and has been so used in this edition.

The reference to and quotation from the *Parlement of Foules* in the last stanza seems to be no evidence of its genuineness, whilst the subheading given in the Harleian MS. is cryptic and apparently nonsense.[1]

BALADE OF COMPLEYNT, ETC.

The *Balade of Compleynt* is found in only one MS. (Addit. 16,165, fol. 256b in the British Museum); and the same is true of the *Balade that Chaucier made* (Addit. MS. 34,360, f. 21b), which was first printed in the *Athenæum.*

TREATISE ON THE ASTROLABE

(MARK H. LIDDELL)

The *Astrolabe* gives us evidence of Chaucer's interest in exact science, as the *Boece* shows his leaning to philosophy. The *Astrolabe*, however, as a translation is far superior. Ripeness of scholarship, certainty of style, clearness of judgment; all these come out clearly in this later work.

For the evidence of the introduction and the dates given in the body of the tract point to a late period of Chaucer's life. There is little of that uncertainty which characterises the *Boece*, and no infelicities of idiom or mistakes in construing the Latin. It is interesting to note in this connection that the testimony of the Colophon in the St. John's (Cambridge) MS. to the effect that Chaucer wrote the tract for his son Lewis, then under the tutelage of (? Ralph) Strode at Merton College, is borne out by the fact that the problems are adapted to the latitude of Oxford, and that MS. Bodley 619, the best of those that have come down to us, bears evidence of having been written by an Astronomer of Merton College. Chaucer's plan was an ambitious one, and comprehended a complete treatise on the subject (cp. his *First Partie*). He either did not live to complete it or tired of his work and abandoned it. The sources of the tract are Messahala's treatise for most of the 'conclusions,' and John de Sacrobosco's *de Sphæra* for the definitions and descriptive astronomy. The few conclusions not traceable to Messahala may be accounted for by assuming an edition in which there were extra conclusions inserted like those in

---

[1] It runs as follows :—And next folowyng begynnith an amerowse compleynte made at Wyndesore in the laste May sofore Novembre.

group γ of Chaucer's own tract. The few definitions not directly traceable to Sacro-bosco are perhaps additions of Chaucer's own.

The technical character of the work has preserved it in a number of MSS. ; eighteen are now known. Many of them are very poor, but, fortunately for a critical text, the inferior ones all derive from the same source which is itself preserved to us in good MSS. The following have been used for the text :—MS. Bodley 619 (B_1), the basis of the text ; E. Museo 54 (M_1), in the Bodleian Library ; Dd 3. 53 of the Cambr. Univ. Library ; Rawl. D. 913 (R_1), in the Bodleian ; Dd 12. 51 (Dd_2), Cambr. Univ. Library ; Ashmole 391 (A_1) (fragmentary), Bodleian Library ; Ashmole 360 (A_2), Bodleian ; Bodley 68 (B_2) ; E. Museo 216 (M_2) (fragmentary), Bodleian ; Rawl. Misc. 3, Bodleian.

MS. Bodley 619 (which was evidently copied by an astronomer) has been made the basis of the text on account of the almost uniform excellence of its readings. The text is critical, based upon an arrangement of the MSS. as roughly shown in the following table :—

$$
O \longrightarrow \begin{cases} B_1 \\ \alpha \longrightarrow \begin{cases} M_1 \\ Dd_1 \end{cases} \\ \beta \longrightarrow \begin{cases} R_1 \\ (?)\ Dd_2 \\ \gamma \longrightarrow \end{cases} \begin{cases} (\textit{not classified.}) \\ A_2.\ Eg.\ M_2.\ Add. \\ B_2.\ R_2. \\ \text{Thynne's ed.} \\ \text{Brae's ed.} \end{cases} \Big\} (\text{Edd.}) \end{cases}
$$

γ shows a confusion in the arrangement of Pt. II., is late, and contains a number of spurious conclusions.

ROMAUNT OF THE ROSE

(MARK H. LIDDELL)

The chief interest that attaches to *The Romaunt of the Rose* is due to the possibility of its being wholly or in part the work of Chaucer. Its felicity as a translation, making anew, as it were, the French poém, the beauty and ease of its versification, the fact that Chaucer did translate Jehan de Meung's French poem, and that a large part of this version offers little to hang an objection to as far as Chaucerian grammar is concerned, have combined to enable it to resist most successfully all attempts to fix it among the spurious Chaucer pieces.

As the matter now stands it is generally agreed that Chaucer could not have written the part beginning somewhere about v. 1705 [1] and ending with v. 5810. The last part, extending from this point to the end and commonly called C by scholars, may possibly have been written by Chaucer, though it contains some rhymes that are, to say the least, unusual in Chaucer. The first part, known as A, though brief when compared to B and C, has been held by many to be of Chaucer's early work. It is not possible to decide this question yet. All that we can say at present is that A (vv. 1·1705) may be part of the translation Chaucer says he made ; that C is

---

[1] B is usually supposed to begin with v. 1706, but cp. the note to the verse.

also possibly Chaucer's, but this assumption is less likely than the former; that B (vv. 1706-5810) is probably the interpolation of a northern writer later than Chaucer who made an attempt to join the two parts of the poem A and C, and make a complete translation, but wearied of his task and dropped it at v. 5810. But it is just this part that Chaucer specifically refers to in *Leg.* 430, 431, where he speaks of ' misseying ' women. This horrible slander is contained in vv. 4252-4266 of the English version. His translation must, therefore, have extended at least to this point, so that our version, if it is Chaucer's, was originally more complete than it is now. But who-ever wrote it, the translation is well worthy to take a place beside Chaucer's best work ; and it is difficult to understand how this comes to be the only surviving work of a poet who was such a master of English verse and had such power of reproducing with added skilful touches of his own Jehan de Meung's *Roman de la Rose.*

The present edition offers a text based almost solely upon the Glasgow MS. By comparison with the French original, many unintelligible lines have for the first time been corrected so as to make good Middle-English sense. Many unintelligible words have been put back into their proper form by observing the recurrence of certain scribal errors in the Glasgow MS. *e.g. i* and *y* for *e, a* for *o, e* for *o, u* for *ou, w* for *v, b* for *l.* The notes give such variants as are of any importance, together with such citations of the French original as are necessary to understand the English version.

Throughout the poem *u* and *v, i* and *j* are used with their modern values, except that I is retained for modern J. The dotted *ė* is used to denote a separate syllable in the middle of the line.

THE CANTERBURY TALES

THE PROLOGUE

Here bygynneth the Book of the tales of Caunterbury

WHÁN that Apríllé with his shourés soote
The droghte of March hath percéd to the roote,
And bathéd every veyne in swich licóur
Of which vertú engendred is the flour ;
Whan Zephirus eek with his sweté breeth
Inspiréd hath in every holt and heeth
The tendré croppés, and the yongé sonne
Hath in the Ram his halfé cours y-ronne,
And smalé fowelés maken melodye,   9
That slepen al the nyght with open eye,—
So priketh hem Natúre in hir coráges,—
Thanne longen folk to goon on pilgrim-
          ages,
And palmeres for to seken straungé strondes,
To ferné halwés, kowthe in sondry londes ;
And specially, from every shirés ende
Of Engélond, to Caunturbury they wende,
The hooly blisful martir for to seke,
That hem hath holpen whan that they were seeke.

Bifil that in that seson on a day,
In Southwerk at the Tabard as I lay,   20
Redy to wenden on my pilgrymage
To Caunterbury with ful devout corage,

At nyght were come into that hostelrye
Wel nyne-and-twenty in a compaignye,
Of sondry folk, by áventure y-falle
In felaweshipe, and pilgrimes were they alle,
That toward Caunterbury wolden ryde.
The chambres and the stables weren wyde,
And wel we weren eséd atté beste.   29
And shortly, whan the sonné was to reste,
So hadde I spoken with hem everychon,
That I was of hir felaweshipe anon,
And madé forward erly for to ryse,
To take oure wey, ther as I yow devyse.
   But nathélees, whil I have tyme and space,
Er that I ferther in this talé pace,
Me thynketh it accordaunt to resoun
To tellé yow al the condicioun
Of ech of hem, so as it seméd me,
And whiche they weren and of what degree,   40
And eek in what array that they were inne ;
And at a Knyght than wol I first bigynne.

A KNYGHT ther was and that a worthy man,
That fro the tymé that he first bigan
To riden out, he lovéd chivalrie,
Trouthe and honóur, fredom and curteisie.
Ful worthy was he in his lordés werre,
And therto hadde he riden, no man ferre,
As wel in cristendom as in hethénesse,
And ever honoured for his worthynesse. 50

8. *the Ram*. The sun runs one half course in the sign of the Ram in March, and the second half course in April. The latter ends April 11th.
17. *martir, i.e.* Thomas à Becket.

23. *was* for *werre*, H⁶.

At Alisaundre he was whan it was wonne ;
Ful ofté tyme he hadde the bord bigonne
Aboven allé nacïons in Pruce.
In Lettow hadde he reyséd and in Ruce,—
No cristen man so ofte of his degree.
In Gernade at the seege eek hadde he be
Of Algezir, and riden in Belmarye.
At Lyeys was he, and at Satalye,
Whan they were wonne ; and in the
     Greté See
At many a noble armee hadde he be.   60
   At mortal batailles hadde he been fiftene,
And foughten for oure feith at Tramys-
     sene
In lystés thriés, and ay slayn his foo.
This ilké worthy knyght hadde been also
Somtymé with the lord of Palatye
Agayn another hethen in Turkye ;
And evermoore he hadde a sovereyn prys.
And though that he were worthy, he was
     wys,
And of his port as meeke as is a mayde.
He never yet no vileynye ne sayde,   70
In al his lyf, unto no maner wight.
He was a verray parfit, gentil knyght.
   But for to tellen yow of his array,
His hors weren goode, but he ne was nat
     gay ;
Of fustian he weréd a gypon
Ál bismótered with his habergeon,
For he was late y-come from his viage,
And wenté for to doon his pilgrymage.
   With hym ther was his sone, a yong
     SQUIÉR,
A lovyere and a lusty bacheler,   80

51. *Alisaundre*, Alexandria, taken by Pierre de Lusignan in 1356.
52. *the bord bigonne*, taken the head of the table.
53. *Pruce*, Prussia, *i.e.* in company with the Teutonic Knights.
54. *Lettow*, Lithuania.   *Ruce*, Russia.
56. *Gernade*, Granada.
57. *Algezir*, taken from the Moors in 1344.
57. *Belmarye*, perhaps Palmyra.
58. *Lyeys*, in Armenia, taken from the Turks 1307.
58. *Satalye*, Attalia, taken from Turks 1352.
59. *the Grete See*, the Mediterranean.
60. *armee*, an expedition, especially one by sea ; *aryve*, a disembarkation, H².
62. *Tramyssene*, in Africa.
65. *Palatye*, a Christian lordship in Anatolia.
74. *was* for *weren*, H², but *hors* may be plural, and refer to the knight's horses in general.

With lokkés crulle as they were leyd in
     presse.
Of twenty yeer of age he was, I gesse.
Of his statúre he was of evene lengthe,
And wonderly delyvere and greet of
     strengthe ;
And he hadde been somtyme in chyvachie,
In Flaundrés, in Artoys and Pycardie,
And born hym weel, as of so litel space,
In hope to stonden in his lady grace.   88
Embrouded was he, as it were a meede
Al ful of fresshé flourés whyte and reede ;
Syngynge he was, or floytynge, al the day ;
He was as fressh as is the monthe of May.
Short was his gowne, with slevés longe
     and wyde ;
Wel koude he sitte on hors and fairé ryde ;
He koudé songés make and wel endite,
Juste and eek daunce and weel purtreye
     and write.
So hoote he lovéde that by nyghtertale
He sleep namoore than dooth a nyghtyn-
     gale.
Curteis he was, lowely and servysáble,
And carf biforn his fader at the table.   100

   A YEMAN hadde he and servántz namo
At that tyme, for hym listé ridé soo ;
And he was clad in cote and hood of grene.
A sheef of pocok arwés, bright and kene,
Under his belt he bar ful thriftily—
Wel koude he dresse his takel yemanly ;
His arwés droupéd noght with fetherés
     lowe—
And in his hand he baar a myghty bowe.
A not-heed hadde he, with a broun viságe.
Of woodécraft wel koude he al the uságe.
Upon his arm he baar a gay bracér,   111
And by his syde a swerd and a bokeler,
And on that oother syde a gay daggere,
Harneiséd wel and sharpe as point of spere ;
A Cristophere on his brest of silver sheene ;
An horn he bar, the bawdryk was of grene.
A forster was he, soothly as I gesse.

   Ther was also a Nonne, a PRIORESSE,

86. *In Flaundres*, *i.e.* in minor expeditions against the French.
88. *lady grace* : ' lady ' is here a genitive.
115. *Cristophere*, a small figure of St. Christopher worn as a protection from evil.

That of hir smylyng was ful symple and
  coy ;
Hire gretteste ooth was but by seinté
  Loy,   120
And she was clepéd madame Eglentyne.
Ful weel she soong the servicé dyvyne,
Entunéd in hir nose ful semély,
And Frenssh she spak ful faire and fetisly
After the scole of Stratford-atté-Bowe,
For Frenssh of Parys was to hire un-
  knowe.
At meté wel y-taught was she with-alle,
She leet no morsel from hir lippés falle,
Ne wette hir fyngrés in hir saucé depe.
Wel koude she carie a morsel and wel
  kepe,   130
Thát no drope ne fille upon hire breste ;
In curteisie was set ful muchel hir leste.
Hire over-lippé wypéd she so clene,
That in hir coppe ther was no ferthyng
  sene
Of grecé, whan she dronken hadde hir
  draughte.
Ful semély after hir mete she raughte,
And sikerly she was of greet desport,
And ful plesáunt and amyable of port,
And peynéd hire to countrefeté cheere 139
Of Court, and been estatlich of manere,
And to ben holden digne of reverence.
But for to speken of hire conscïence,
She was so charitable and so pitous
She wolde wepe, if that she saugh a mous
Kaught in a trappe, if it were deed or
  bledde..
Of smalé houndés hadde she that she fedde
With rosted flessh, or milk and wastel
  breed ;
But sooré wepte she if oon of hem were
  deed,   148
Or if men smoot it with a yerdé smerte ;
And al was conscïence and tendré herte.

Ful semyly hir wympul pynchéd was ;
Hire nose tretys, hir eyen greye as glas,
Hir mouth ful smal and ther-to softe and
  reed,
But sikerly she hadde a fair forheed ;
It was almoost a spanné brood I trowe,
For, hardily, she was nat undergrowe.
Ful fetys was hir cloke, as I was war ;
Of smal coral aboute hire arm she bar
A peire of bedes, gauded al with grene,
And ther-on heng a brooch of gold ful
  sheene,   160
On which ther was first write a crownéd A,
And after *Amor vincit omnia.*
Another NONNÉ with hire haddé she
That was hire Chapéleyne, and PREESTÉS
  thre.

A MONK ther was, a fair for the
  maistrie,
An outridere, that lovéde venerie ;
A manly man, to been an abbot able.
Ful many a deyntee hors hadde he in stable,
And whan he rood men myghte his
  brydel heere   169
Gýnglen in a whistlynge wynd als cleere,
And eek as loude, as dooth the chapel belle,
Ther as this lord was kepere of the celle.
The reule of seint Maure or of seint Beneit,
By-cause that it was old and som-del
  streit,—
This ilké Monk leet oldé thyngés pace,
And heeld after the newé world the space.
He yaf nat of that text a pulléd hen
That seith that hunters beth nat hooly men,
Ne that a Monk whan he is recchélees
Is likned til a fissh that is waterlees ; 180
This is to seyn, a Monk out of his cloystre.
But thilké text heeld he nat worth an oystre ;
And I seyde his opinioun was good.

120. *seinté Loy.* St. Eligius refused to take an
oath which King Dagobert demanded of him, so
perhaps this means the Prioress did not swear at
all.

125. *After the scole of Stratford-atté-Bowe,*
i.e. Anglo-Norman French, still in use in convents
such as the Benedictine nunnery at Stratford-le-
Bow, where Chaucer probably means that his
Prioress was educated. The French spoken at
Court at this date would be French ' of Paris.'

. 127. *At mete,* etc., a reminiscence of a passage
in the *Roman de la Rose,* l. 13,612 *sqq.*

159. *gauded,* dyed, especially dyed green ; or
perhaps, having in green the gawdies, or large
beads which stood for the Lord's Prayer.

162. *Amor vincit omnia :* Love overcomes all
things.

173. *seint Maure,* a disciple of *seint Beneit*
or Benedict, established the Benedictine Order
in France.

177. *that text,* from the Decretal of Gratian,
' Sicut piscis sine aqua caret vita, ita sine
monasterio monachus.'

179. *recchelees,* reckless ; *cloysterles,* H only ;
neither reading is satisfactory.

3

What sholde he studie and make hym-
   selven wood,
Upon a book in cloystre alwey to poure,
Or swynken with his handès and labóure,
As Austyn bit? how shal the world be
   served?
Lat Austyn have his swynk to him reserved.
Therfore he was a prikasour aright;
Grehoundes he hadde, as swift as fowel
   in flight: 190
Of prikyng and of huntyng for the hare
Was al his lust, for no cost wolde he spare.
I seigh his sleves y-purfiled at the hond
With grys, and that the fyneste of a lond;
And for to festne his hood under his chyn
He hadde of gold y-wrogh t a ful curious pyn,
A love knotte in the gretter ende ther was.
His heed was balled that shoon as any glas,
And eek his face as he hadde been enoynt.
He was a lord ful fat and in good poynt;
Hise eyén stepe and rollynge in his heed,
That stemèd as a forneys of a leed; 202
His bootès souple, his hors in greet estaat.
Now certeinly he was a fair prelaat.
He was nat pale, as a forpynèd goost:
A fat swan loved he best of any roost;
His palfrey was as broun as is a berye.

A FRERE ther was, a wantowne and
   a merye,
A lymytour, a ful solempné man, 209
In allè the ordrès foure is noon that kan
So muchel of daliaunce and fair langage;
He haddè maad ful many a marïage
Of yongè wommen at his owene cost:
Unto his ordre he was a noble post,
Ful wel biloved and famulier was he
With frankeleyns over al in his contree;
And eek with worthy wommen of the toun,
For he hadde power of confessïoun,
As seyde hym-self, moorè than a curát,
For of his ordre he was licenciat. 220
Ful swetely herdè he confessioun,
And plesaunt was his absolucioun.

He was an esy man to yeve penaunce
Ther as he wiste to have a good pitaunce;
For unto a poure ordre for to yive
Is signè that a man is wel y-shryve;
For, if he yaf, he dorstè make avaunt
He wistè that a man was répentaunt:
For many a man so harde is of his berte
He may nat wepe al thogh hym soorè
   smerte,   230
Therfore in stede of wepynge and preyères
Men moote yeve silver to the pourè freres.
His typet was ay farsed full of knyves
And pynnès, for to yeven yongè wyves;
And certeinly he hadde a murye note;
Wel koude he synge and pleyen on a rote:
Of yeddynges he baar outrèly the pris;
His nekkè whit was as the flour-de-lys,
Ther-to he strong was as a champioun.
He knew the tavernes well in all the toun
And everich hostiler and tappestere 241
Bet than a lazar or a beggestere;
For unto swich a worthy man as he
Acordèd nat, as by his facultee,
To have with sikè lazars aqueyntaunce;
It is nat honeste, it may nat avaunce
Fór to deelen with no swiche poraille;
But al with riche and selleres of vitaille.
And over al, ther as profit sholde arise,
Curteis he was and lowely of servyse, 250
Ther nas no man nowher so vertuous.
He was the bestè beggere in his hous,*
For thogh a wydwe haddè noght a sho,
So plesaunt was his *In principio*,
Yet wolde he have a ferthyng er he wente:
His purchas was wel bettre than his rente.
And rage he koudè, as it were right a
   whelpe.

---

199. *hè*, E *it*.
210. *ordrès foure*, Dominicans, Carmelites,
Franciscans, and Augustinians.
212. *ful many a marïcge*, etc., *i.e.* he found
husbands for women he had himself seduced.
220. *licenciat*, *i.e.* he was licensed to hear con-
fessions without asking leave of the parson.

252. Hengwrt MS. here inserts two lines:
   'And yaf a certeyn ferme for the graunt,
    Noon of his bretheren cam ther in his haunt.'
i.e. paid rent for his privilege and was left undis-
turbed by his brethren. The couplet is probably
Chaucer's, but may have been deliberately
omitted by him, as it interrupts the sentence.
254. *In principio*, the first two words of St.
John's Gospel: the beginning of a Friar's
address.
256. *His purchas*, etc. He earnt more than
he received from fixed property: a proverbial
phrase pointed here by the fact that of fixed
property friars had none.
257. H reads 'and rage he couthe and
pleye[n] as a whelpe.'

4

In lové-dayes ther koude he muchel helpe,
For there he was nat lyk a cloysterer
With a thredbare cope, as is a poure scolér,
But he was lyk a maister, or a pope ; 261
Of double worstede was his semycope,
That rounded as a belle out of the presse.
Somwhat he lipséd for his wantownesse,
To make his Englissh sweet upon his tonge,
And in his harpyng, whan that he hadde
    songe,
His eyén twynkled in his heed aryght
As doon the sterrés in the frosty nyght.
This worthy lymytour was cleped Huberd.

A MARCHANT was ther with a forkéd
    berd, 270
In mottéleye, and hye on horse he sat ;
Upon his heed a Flaundryssh bevere hat;
His bootés claspéd faire and fetisly ;
His resons he spak ful solempnély,
Sownynge alway thencrees of his wynnyng.
He wolde the see were kept for any thing
Bitwixé Middelburgh and Orèwelle.
Wel koude he in eschaungé sheeldés selle.
This worthy man ful wel his wit bisette,
Ther wisté no wight that he was in dette,
So estatly was he of his governaunce 281
With his bargaynes and with his
    chevyssaunce.
For sothe he was a worthy man with-alle
But, sooth to seyn, I noot how men hym
    calle.

A CLERK ther was of Oxenford also
That unto logyk haddé longe y-go.
As leené was his hors as is a rake,
And he nas nat right fat, I undertake,
But lookéd holwe, and ther-to sobrely ;
Ful thredbare was his overeste courtepy ;
For he hadde geten hym yet no benefice,
Ne was so worldly for to have office ;
For hym was levere have at his beddes heed
Twénty bookés clad in blak or reed
Of Aristotle and his philosophie,
Than robés riche, or fithele, or gay sautrie :

But al be that he was a philosophre,
Yet haddé he but litel gold in cofre ;
But al that he myghte of his freendes hente
On bookés and his lernynge he it spente,
And bisily gan for the soulés preye 301
Of hem that yaf hym wher-with to scoleye.
Of studie took he moost cure and moost
    heede,
Noght o word spak he mooré than was
    neede,
And that was seyd in forme and reverence,
And short and quyk and ful of hy senténce.
Sownynge in moral vertu was his speche
And gladly wolde he lerne and gladly teche.

A SERGEANT OF THE LAWÊ, war and
    wys,
That often haddé been at the Parvys, 310
Ther was also, ful riche of excellence.
Discreet he was, and of greet reverence ;
He seméd swich, hise wordés weren so
    wise.
Justice he was ful often in Assise,
By patente and by pleyn commissioun :
For his science and for his heigh renoun.
Of fees and robés hadde he many oon ;
So greet a purchasour was nowher noon.
Al was fee symple to hym in effect,
His purchasyng myghté nat been infect.
Nowher so bisy a man as he ther nas, 321
And yet he seméd bisier than he was.
In termés hadde he caas and doomés alle
That from the tyme of kyng William
    were falle ;
Ther-to he coude endite and make a thyng,
Ther koudé no wight pynchen at his
    writyng ;
And every statut coude he pleyn by rote.
He rood but hoomly in a medlee cote,
Girt with a ceint of silk, with barrés smale ;
Of his array telle I no lenger tale. 330

A FRANKÈLEYN was in his compaignye.

---

777. *Middelburgh*, nearly opposite the Orwell
on the Dutch coast. Professor Hales notes that
between 1384 and 1388 the wool-staple was at
Middelburgh instead of at Calais.
278. *sheeldes*, French crowns or *écus*: he
could profit by the turn of exchange.

297. *philosophre*, an allusion to the philosophy
of the alchemists.
310. *Parvys*, church-porch, *i.e.* of St. Paul's,
where lawyers met for consultation.
319. *fee symple*. The meaning may be either
(literally) that the Sergeant could overcome all
restrictions on ownership, or (metaphorically)
that he could carry all before him.

Whit was his berd as is a dayésye,
Of his complexioun he was sangwyn.
Wel loved he by the morwe a sope in wyn;
To lyven in delit was ever his wone,
For he was Epicurus owené sone,
That heeld opinioun that pleyn delit
Was verraily felicitee parfit.
An housholdere, and that a greet, was he:
Seint Julian was he in his contree ;   340
His breed, his ale, was alweys after oon ;
A better envynéd man was nowher noon.
Withouté baké mete was never his hous,
Of fissh and flessh, and that so plenteuous
It snewéd in his hous of mete and drynke.
Of allé deyntees that men koudé thynke
After the sondry sesons of the yeer,
So chaungéd he his mete and his soper.
Ful many a fat partrich hadde he in muwe
And many a breem and many a luce in
    stuwe.   350
Wo was his cook but if his saucé were
Poynaunt and sharpe and redy al his geere.
His table dormant in his halle alway,
Stood redy covered al the longé day.
At sessiouns ther was he lord and sire ;
Ful ofté tymé he was knyght of the shire.
An anlaas, and a gipser al of silk,
Heeng at his girdel, whit as morné milk ;
A shirreve hadde he been, and a countour.
Was nowher such a worthy vavasour.   360

An HABERDASSHERE, and a CAR-
    PENTER,
A WEBBE, a DYERE, and a TAPYCER,—
And they were clothed alle in o lyveree
Of a solémpne and greet fraternitee ;
Ful fressh and newe hir geere apikéd was ;
Hir knyvés weré chapéd noght with bras,
But al with silver, wroght ful clene and
    weel,
Hire girdles and hir pouches everydeel.
Wel seméd ech of hem a fair burgeys
To sitten in a yeldehalle, on a deys.   370

Éverich for the wisdom that he kan
Was shaply for to been an alderman.
For catel haddé they ynogh and rente,
And eek hir wyvés wolde it wel assente ;
And ellés certeyn weré they to blame.
It is ful fair to been y-cleped *Madame*,
And goon to vigiliés al bifore,
And have a mantel roialliche y-bore.

A COOK they haddé with hem for the
    nones,   379
To boille the chiknés with the marybones,
And poudré-marchant tart and galyngale ;
Wel koude he knowe a draughte of
    Londoun ale ;
He koudé rooste and sethe and boille
    and frye,
Máken mortreux and wel bake a pye.
But greet harm was it, as it thoughté me,
That on his shyne a mormal haddé he.
For blankmanger, that made he with the
    beste.

A SHIPMAN was ther, wonynge fer by
    weste ;
For aught I woot he was of Dertémouthe.
He rood upon a rouncy as he kouthe,   390
In a gowne of faldyng to the knee.
A daggere hangynge on a laas hadde he
Aboute his nekke under his arm adoun.
The hooté somer hadde maad his hewe
    al broun ;
And certeinly he was a good felawe.
Ful many a draughte of wyn hadde he
    y-drawe
Fro Burdeuxward whil that the Chapman
    sleepe.
Of nycé conscïence took he no keepe.   398
If that he faught, and hadde the hyer hond ;
By water he sente hem hoom to every lond.
But of his craft to rekene wel his tydes,
His stremés and his daungers hym bisides,
His herberwe and his moone, his lode-
    menage,
Ther nas noon swich from Hullé to Cartage.
Hardy he was, and wys to undertake :
With many a tempest hadde his berd
    been shake ;

332. *heed* for *berd*, E.
340. St. Julian was famed for providing his votaries with good entertainment.
341. *after oon*, of one kind, *i.e.* the best.
363. *o*, one. H reads 'Weren with uss eeke clothed in oo lyvere.'
364. E⁶ add *a* before *greet*, with which reading we must scan : ' Of a só | lempne and | ,' etc.
400. *By water*, etc., *i.e.* he drowned his prisoners.

6

He knew wel alle the havenes, as they were,
From Gootlond to the Cape of Fynystere,
And every cryke in Britaigne and in Spayne.
His barge y-clepèd was the Maudélayne.

With us ther was a DOCTOUR OF
PHISIK ;   411
In all this world ne was ther noon hym lik,
To speke of phisik and of surgerye ;
For he was grounded in astronomye.
He keptè his pacïent a ful greet deel
In hourès, by his magyk natureel.
Wel koude he fortunen the ascendent
Of his ymáges for his pacïent.
He knew the cause of everich maladye,
Were it of hoot, or cold, or moyste, or drye,
And where they engendred and of what
        humour ;   421
He was a verray parfit praktisour.
The cause y-knowe and of his harm the
        roote,
Anon he yaf the sikè man his boote.
Ful redy hadde he his apothecaries
To sende him droggès and his letuaries,
For ech of hem made oother for to wynne,
Hir frendshipe nas nat newè to bigynne.
Wel knew he the oldè Esculapius
And Deÿscorides, and eek Rufus,   430
Olde Ypocras, Haly and Galyen,
Serapion, Razis and Avycen,
Averrois, Damascien and Constantyn,

Bernard and Gatésden and Gilbertyn.
Of his dieté mesurable was he,
For it was of no superfluitee,
But of greet norissyng and digestible.
His studie was but litel on the Bible.
In sangwyn and in pers he clad was al,
Lynèd with taffata and with sendal.   440
And yet he was but esy of dispence,
He keptè that he wan in pestilence.
For gold in phisik is a cordial,
Therfore he lovède gold in special.

A GOOD WIF was ther of bisidè BATHE,
But she was som-del deef, and that was
        scathe.
Of clooth-makyng she haddè swich an
        haunt
She passèd hem of Yprès and of Gaunt.
In al the parisshe wif ne was ther noon
That to the offrynge bifore hire sholdè
        goon ;   450
And if ther dide, certeyn so wrooth was
        she,
That she was out of allè charitee.
Hir coverchiefs ful fynè weren of ground,—
I dorstè swere they weyèden ten pound,—
That on a Sonday weren upon hir heed.
Hir hosen weren of fyn scarlet reed,
Ful streite y-teyd, and shoes ful moyste
        and newe ;
Boold was hir face, and fair, and reed of
        hewe.
She was a worthy womman al hir lyve,
Housbondes at chirchè dore she haddè
        fyve,   460
Withouten   oother   compaignye   in
        youthe,—

408. *Gootlond,* Jutland ; *Scotland,* H.
411. *With us ther was,* E⁶ ; *Ther was also,* H.
415. *a full greet deel,* E⁶ ; *wondurly wel,* H.
416. *In houres, i.e.* the astrological hours.
418. *ymages,* astrological figures, cp. *Hous of Fame,* iii. 175-180.
420. *hoot, or cold,* etc., the four elements of which the world was believed to be composed.
430. *Deyscorides,* Dioscorides, a physician of the 2nd century A.D., born in Cilicia.
430. *Rufus,* a physician of Ephesus, about the time of Trajan.
431. *Olde Ypocras,* Hippocrates, born in Cos about 460 B.C.
431. *Haly,* or Hali, an Arabian commentator on Galen in the 11th century : John Serapion and the famous Avicenna were his contemporaries.
431. *Galyen,* Galen, born at Pergamus 130 A.D.
432. *Razis,* or Rhazes, an Arabian physician of the 10th century.
433. *Averrois,* born at Cordova 1126.
433. *Damascien,* John Damascene, an Arab physician and theologian of the 9th century.
433. *Constantyn,* Constantinus Afer, born at Carthage in the 12th century.

434. *Bernard,* Bernardus Gordonius, a contemporary of Chaucer, Professor of Medicine at Montpellier.
434. *Gatesden,* John Gatesden, Fellow of Merton College, Oxford, and court physician in the first half of the 14th century. He wrote a medical treatise called *Rosa Anglica.*
434. *Gilbertyn,* Gilbertus Anglicus, one of the earliest English writers on medicine, fl. 1250.
442. *pestilence.* The great plague of the 14th century was in 1349, but lesser ones recurred every few years.
450. *to the offrynge.* Offerings in kind or money at mass and other services were presented by the people going up in order to the priest.
460. *at chirche dore.* The first part of the marriage service used to be read there.

But ther-of nedeth nat to speke as
    nowthe,—
And thriès hadde she been at Jerusálem;
She haddè passèd many a straungè strem;
At Rome she haddè been, and at Boloigne,
In Galice at Seint Jame, and at Coloigne,
She koudè muchel of wandrynge by the
    weye.
Gat-tothèd was she, soothly for to seye.
Upon an amblere esily she sat,   469
Y-wymplèd wel, and on hir heed an hat
As brood as is a bokeler or a targe;
A foot mantel aboute hir hipès large,
And on hire feet a paire of sporès sharpe.
In felaweshipe wel koude she laughe and
    carpe;
Of remedies of love she knew per chaunce,
For she koude of that art the oldè daunce.

A good man was ther of religioun,
And was a POURE PERSOUN OF A TOUN;
But riche he was of hooly thoght and werk;
He was also a lernèd man, a clerk,   480
That Cristès Gospel trewèly wolde preche:
His parisshens devoutly wolde he teche.
Benygne he was, and wonder diligent,
And in adversitee ful pacient;
And swich he was y-prevèd oftè sithes.
Ful looth were hym to cursen for his tithes,
But rather wolde he yeven, out of doute,
Unto his pourè parisshens aboute,
Of his offrýng and eek of his substaunce:
He koude in litel thyng have suffisaunce.
Wyd was his parisshe, and houses fer
    asonder,   491
But he ne laftè nat for reyn ne thonder,
In siknesse nor in meschief to visíte
The ferreste in his parisshe, mucheand lite,
Upon his feet, and in his hand a staf.
This noble ensample to his sheepe he yaf
That firste he wroghte and afterward he
    taughte.
Out of the gospel he tho wordès caughte,

465. *Boloigne*, Boulogne, where an image of
the Blessed Virgin was exhibited to pilgrims.
466. *In Galice at S. Jame, i.e.* at the shrine of
St. James of Compostella in Galicia in Spain.
466. *Coloigne*, to the shrine of the Three Kings
of the East at Cologne.
476. *koude the oldè daunce* ('Qu'el scet toute
la vielle dance,' *Rom. de la Rose*), knew the
ancient custom.

And this figure he added eek therto,
That if gold rustè what shal iren doo? 500
For if a preest be foul, on whom we truste,
No wonder is a lewèd man to ruste;
And shame it is, if a prest takè keepe,
A shiten shepherde and a clenè sheepe.
Wel oghte a preest ensample for to yive
By his clennesse how that his sheepe
    sholde lyve.
He settè nat his benefice to hyre
And leet his sheepe encombred in the myre,
And ran to Londoun, unto Seïnt Poules,
To seken hym a chaunterie for soules; 510
Or with a bretherhed to been withholde,
But dwelte at hoom and keptè wel his folde,
So that the wolf ne made it nat myscarie,—
He was a shepherde, and noght a
    mercenarie:
And though he hooly were and vertuous,
He was to synful man nat despitous,
Ne of his spechè daungerous ne digne,
But in his techyng déscreet and benygne,
To drawen folk to hevene by fairnesse,
By good ensample, this was his bisynesse:
But it were any persone obstinat,   521
What so he were, of heigh or lough estat,
Hym wolde he snybben sharply for the
    nonys.
A bettrè preest I trowe that nowher
    noon ys;
He waited after no pompe and reverence,
Ne maked him a spicèd conscience,
But Cristès loore, and his Apostles twelve,
He taughte, but first he folwed it hym
    selve.

With hym ther was a PLOWMAN, was
    his brother,
That hadde y-lad of dong ful many a
    fother,—   530
A trewè swynkere and a good was he,
Lyvynge in pees and parfit charitee.
God loved he best, with al his hoolè herte,
At allè tymès, thogh him gamed or smerte,
And thanne his neighèbore right as hym-
    selve.
He woldè thresshe, and therto dyke and
    delve,
For Cristès sake, for every pourè wight,
Withouten hire, if it lay in his myght.

His tithès paydé he ful faire and wel,
Bothe of his proprè swynk and his catel.
In a tabard he rood upon a mere.   541

Ther was also a REVE and a MILLERE,
A SOMNOUR and a PARDONER also,
A MAUNCIPLE and myself,—ther were
    namo.
The MILLERE was a stout carl for the
    nones,
Ful byg he was of brawn and eek of bones;
That provèd wel, for over-al, ther he cam,
At wrastlynge he wolde have awey the ram.
He was short-sholdred, brood, a thikkè
    knarre,
Ther nas no dore that he nolde heve of
    harre,   550
Or breke it at a rennyng with his heed.
His berd, as any sowe or fox, was reed,
And therto brood, as though it were a spade.
Upon the cope right of his nose he hade
A werte, and theron stood a toft of herys,
Reed as the brustles of a sowes erys;
His nosèthirlès blakè were and wyde;
A swerd and a bokeler bar he by his syde;
His mouth as wyde was as a greet forneys,
He was a janglere and a goliardeys,   560
And that was moost of synne and harlotriës.
Wel koude he stelen corn and tollen thriës,
And yet he hadde a thombe of gold, pardee.
A whit cote and a blew hood werèd he.
A baggèpipe wel koude he blowe and
    sowne,
And therwithal he broghte us out of towne.

A gentil MAUNCIPLE was ther of a
    temple,
Of which achátours myghtè take exemple
For to be wise in byynge of vitaille;
For, wheither that he payde or took by
    taille,   570
Algate he wayted so in his achaat
That he was ay biforn and in good staat.

Now is nat that of God a ful fair grace
That swich a lewèd mannès wit shal pace
The wisdom of an heepe of lerned men?
Of maistrès hadde he mo than thriës ten,
That weren of lawe expert and curious,
Of whiche ther weren a duszeyne in that
    hous
Worthy to been stywardes of rente and lond
Of any lord that is in Engèlond,   580
To maken hym lyvè by his proprè good
In honour dettèlees, but he were wood,
Or lyve as scarsly as hym list desire;
And able for to helpen al a shire
In any caas that myghtè falle or happe;
And yet this Manciple sette hir aller cappe.

The REVÈ was a sclendrè colerik man,
His berd was shave as ny as ever he kan;
His heer was by his erys round y-shorn,
His tope was dokèd lyk a preest biforn,
Ful longè were his leggès and ful lene,
Y-lyk a staf, ther was no calf y-sene.   592
Wel koude he kepe a gerner and a bynne,
Ther was noon auditour koude on him
    wynne.
Wel wiste he, by the droghte and by the
    reyn,
The yeldynge of his seed and of his greyn.
His lordès sheepe, his neet, his dayèrye,
His swyn, his hors, his stoor, and his
    pultrye,
Was hoolly in this revès governyng,
And by his covenant yaf the rekenyng   600
Syn that his lord was twenty yeer of age;
Ther koude no man brynge hym in
    arrerage.
There nas baillif, ne hierde, nor oother
    hyne,
That he ne knew his sleighte and his
    covyne;
They were adrad of hym as of the deeth.
His wonyng was ful faire upon an heeth,
With grenè trees y-shadwèd was his
    place.

---

548. *swey*, E³ *alwey*.
559. *wyde*, H; *greet*, E⁶.
562. *tollen thries*, take threefold his due.
563. *yet he hadde a thombe of gold.* Millers are said to test samples with their thumb. Hence the proverb 'An honest miller has a thumb of gold,' which suggests the meaning here to be 'yet he was honest,—for a miller.'
570. *by taille*, on trust, the debt being scored on a tally.

581. *by his proprè good*, on his own property.
586. *sette hir aller cappe*, set the caps of, *i.e.* befooled, them all.
594. *on*, E *of*.
595. *Wel wiste he*, etc., *i.e.* when he had to present his accounts he attributed the loss of the corn he had stolen to bad weather.
604. *he*, *i.e.* the Reeve, though H reads *they*.

9

He koudė bettrė than his lord purchace.
Ful riche he was a-storėd pryvely,
His lord wel koude he plesen subtilly 610
To yeve and lene hym of his owene good
And have a thank, and yet a gowne and
     hood.
In youthe he lernėd hadde a good myster,
He was a wel good wrighte, a carpenter.
This Revė sat upon a ful good stot,
That was al pomely grey, and hightė
     Scot ;
A long surcote of pers upon he hade,
And by his syde he baar a rusty blade.
Of Northfolk was this Reve of which I
     telle,
Biside a toun men clepen Baldėswelle.
Tukkėd he was as is a frere, aboute, 621
And ever he rood the hyndreste of oure
     route.

A SOMONOUR was ther with us in
     that place,
That hadde a fyr-reed cherubynnės face,
For sawcėfleem he was, with eyen narwe.
As hoot he was, and lecherous, as a sparwe,
With scalėd browės blake and pilėd berd,—
Of his visagė children were aferd.
Ther nas quyk-silver, lytarge, ne brym-
     stoon,
Boras, ceruce, ne oille of Tartre noon, 630
Ne oynėment that woldė clense and byte,
That hym myghte helpen of the whelkės
     white,
Nor of the knobbės sittynge on his chekes.
Wel loved he garleek, oynons, and eek
     lekes,
And for to drynken strong wyn, reed as
     blood ;
Thanne wolde he speke, and crie as he
     were wood.
And whan that he wel dronken hadde
     the wyn,
Than wòlde he speke no word but Latyn.
A fewė termės hadde he, two or thre,
That he had lernėd out of som decree,—
No wonder is, he herde it al the day, 641
And eek ye knowen wel how that a jay

624. *cherubynnes face.* The author of the *Philo-biblon* speaks of books brilliantly illuminated as 'cherubici libri.'

Kan clepen *Watte* as wel as kan the pope.
But whoso koude in oother thyng hym
     grope,
Thanne hadde he spent al his philosophie ;
Ay *Questio quid juris* wolde he crie.
He was a gentil harlot and a kynde ;
A bettre felawe sholdė men noght fynde.
He woldė suffre, for a quart of wyn,
A good felawe to have his concubyn 650
A twelf monthe, and excuse hym attė fulle ;
And privėly a fynch eek koude he pulle ;
And if he foond owher a good felawe,
He woldė techen him to have noon awe,
In swich caas, of the Ercėdekenes curs,
But-if a mannės soule were in his purs ;
For in his purs he sholde y-punysshed be :
' Purs is the Ercėdekenes helle,' seyde he.
But wel I woot he lyėd right in dede,
Of cursyng oghte ech gilty man him drede,
For curs wol slee,—right as assoillyng
     savith ; 661
And also war him of a *Significavit.*
In daunger hadde he at his owėne gise
The yongė girlės of the diocise,
And knew hir conseil, and was al hir reed.
A gerland hadde he set upon his heed,
As greet as it were for an alė-stake ;
A bokeleer hadde he maad him of a cake.

With hym ther rood a gentil PARDONER
Of Rouncivale, his freend and his compeer,
That streight was comen fro the court of
     Romė. 671
Ful loude he soong *Com hider, lovė, to me!*
This Somonour bar to hym a stif burdoun,
Was never trompe of half so greet a soun.
This Pardoner hadde heer as yelow as wex
But smothe it heeng as dooth a strike of
     flex ;

643. *Kan clepen Watte,* can call Walter.
646. *Questio quid juris,* the question is, what is the law?
652. *pulle a fynch,* as we should say 'pluck a pigeon,' plunder a fool.
662. *Significavit,* the opening word of a writ for imprisoning an excommunicated person.
664. *girles,* youths of both sexes.
670. *Of Rouncivale.* 'An Hospital *Beata Maria de Rouncyvalle in Charing, London* is mentioned in the *Monasticon* [Dugdale's], t. ii. p. 443, and there was a Runceval Hall in Oxford. So that perhaps it was the name of some confraternity.' —Tyrwhitt. The parent Roncevaux was in Navarre.

By ounces henge his lokkės that he hadde,
And therwith he his shuldres overspradde.
But thynne it lay by colpons oon and oon;
But hood, for jolitee, ne wered he noon,
For it was trussėd up in his walėt.   681
Hym thoughte he rood al of the newė jet;
Dischevelee, save his cappe, he rood al bare.
Swiche glarynge eyen hadde he as an hare,
A vernycle hadde he sowed upon his cappe;
His walet lay biforn hym in his lappe
Bret-ful of pardon, comen from Rome al
      hoot.
A voys he hadde as smal as hath a goot;
No berd hadde he, ne never sholdė have,
As smothe it was as it were latė shave;
I trowe he were a geldyng or a mare.   691
But of his craft, fro Berwyk unto Ware
Ne was ther swich another pardoner,
For in his male he hadde a pilwė-beer,
Which that, he seydė, was oure lady veyl;
He seydė he hadde a gobet of the seyl
That Seintė Peter hadde, whan that he wente
Upon the see, til Jhesu Crist hym hente.
He hadde a croys of latoun, ful of stones,
And in a glas he haddė piggės bones.   700
But with thise relikės, whan that he fond
A pourė person dwellynge upon lond,
Upon a day he gat hym moore moneye
Than that the person gat in monthės tweye;
And thus with feynėd flaterye and japes
He made the person and the peple his apes.
But, trewėly to tellen attė laste,
He was in chirche a noble ecclesiaste;
Wel koude he rede a lessoun or a storie,
But alderbest he song an Offertorie;   710
For wel he wistė, whan that song was
      songe,
He mostė preche, and wel affile his tonge
To wynnė silver, as he ful wel koude;
Therefore he song the murierly and loude.
  Now have I toold you shortly, in a
      clause,
The staat, tharray, the nombre, and eek
      the cause
Why that assembled was this compaignye
In Southwerk, at this gentil hostelrye,
That highte the Tabard, fastė by the Belle.
But now is tymė to yow for to telle   720
How that we baren us that ilkė nyght,
Whan we were in that hostelrie alyght;

And after wol I telle of our viage
And al the remenaunt of oure pilgrimage.
  But first, I pray yow of youre curteisye,
That ye narette it nat my vileynye,
Thogh that I pleynly speke in this mateere
To tellė yow hir wordės and hir cheere,
Ne thogh I speke hir wordės proprely;
For this ye knowen al-so wel as I,   730
Whoso shal telle a tale after a man,
He moote reherce, as ny as ever he
      kan,
Everich a word, if it be in his charge,
Al speke he never so rudėliche or large;
Or ellis he moot telle his tale untrewe,
Or feynė thyng, or fyndė wordės newe.
He may nat spare, althogh he were his
      brother;
He moot as wel seye o word as another.
Crist spak hymself ful brode in hooly writ,
And wel ye woot no vileynye is it.   740
Eek Plato seith, whoso that kan hym rede,
' The wordės moote be cosyn to the dede.'
  Also I prey yow to foryeve it me
Al have I nat set folk in hir degree
Heere in this tale, as that they sholdė
      stonde;
My wit is short, ye may wel understonde.
  Greet chierė made oure hoost us
      everichon,
And to the soper sette he us anon,
And servėd us with vitaille at the beste :
Strong was the wyn and wel to drynke
      us leste.   750
  A semely man OURE HOOSTĖ was
      with-alle
For to han been a marchal in an halle.
A largė man he was, with eyen stepe,
A fairer burgeys is ther noon in Chepe;
Boold of his speche, and wys and well
      y-taught
And of manhod hym lakkedė right naught.
Eek therto he was right a myrie man,
And after soper pleyen he bigan,
And spak of myrthe amongės othere
      thynges,
Whan that we haddė maad our rekenynges;

727. *pleynly speke*, E⁶; *speke al pleyn*, H.
741. *Eek Plato seith.* Chaucer takes his
quotation from Boethius, *De Consolatione*, bk.
iii. prose 12.
753. *is*, E² *was*.

11

And seydé thus : ' Now, lordynges, trewély,   761
Ye been to me right welcome, hertély ;
For by my trouthe, if that I shal nat lye,
I ne saugh this yeer so myrie a compaignye
At onés in this herberwe as is now ;
Fayn wolde I doon yow myrthé, wiste I how.
And of a myrthe I am right now bythoght,
To doon yow ese, and it shal costé noght.
    ' Ye goon to Canterbury—God yow speede,   769
The blisful martir quité yow youre meede !
And, wel I woot, as ye goon by the weye,
Ye shapen yow to talen and to pleye ;
For trewély confort ne myrthe is noon
To ridé by the weye doumb as a stoon ;
And therfore wol I maken yow disport,
As I seydé erst, and doon yow som confort.
And if you liketh alle, by oon assent,
Now for to stonden at my juggément,
And for to werken as I shal yow seye,
To-morwé, whan ye riden by the weye,
Now, by my fader soulé, that is deed,   781
But ye be myrie, smyteth of myn heed !
Hoold up youre hond, withouten mooré speche.'
    Oure conseil was nat longé for to seche ;
Us thoughte it was noght worth to make it wys,
And graunted hym withouten moore avys,
And bad him seye his verdit, as hym leste.
    ' Lordynges,' quod he, ' now herkneth for the beste ;
But taak it nought, I prey yow, in desdeyn ;
This is the poynt, to speken short and pleyn,   790
That ech of yow, to shorté with your weye,
In this viage shal tellé talés tweye,—
To Caunterburyward, I mean it so,
And homward he shal tellen othere two,—
Of aventúres that whilom han bifalle.

And which of yow that bereth hym beste of alle,
That is to seyn, that telleth in this caas
Talés of best senténce and moost solaas,
Shal have a soper at oure aller cost,   799
Heere in this placé, sittynge by this post,
Whan that we comeagayn fro Caunterbury.
And, for to maké yow the mooré mury,
I wol myselven gladly with yow ryde
Right at myn owene cost, and be youre gyde ;
And whoso wole my juggément withseye
Shal paye al that we spenden by the weye.
And if ye vouché-sauf that it be so
Tel me anon, withouten wordés mo,
And I wol erly shapé me therfore.'
    This thyng was graunted, and oure othés swore   810
With ful glad herte, and preyden hym also
That he would vouché-sauf for to do so,
And that he woldé been oure governour,
And of our talés juge and réportour,
And sette a soper at a certeyn pris,
And we wol reuléd been at his devys
In heigh and lough ; and thus, by oon assent,
We been acorded to his juggément.
And therupon the wyn was fet anon ;
We dronken, and to resté wente echon,
Withouten any lenger taryynge.   821
    Amorwé, whan that day gan for to sprynge,
Up roos oure Hoost and was oure aller cok,
And gadrede us togidre alle in a flok,
And forth we riden, a litel moore than paas,
Unto the wateryng of Seint Thomas ;
And there oure Hoost bigan his hors areste
And seydé, ' Lordynges, herkneth, if yow leste :
Ye woot youre foreward and I it yow recorde.
If even-song and morwé-song accorde,   830
Lat se now who shal telle the firsté tale.
As ever mote I drynké wyn or ale,
Whoso be rebel to my juggément
Shal paye for all that by the wey is spent !

782. For *smyteth of* (*i.e. off*), E6 read *I wol yeve yow.*
791. E5 read *oure* for *your*, but this makes the Host too precipitate.
793, 794. As the pilgrims progress we see clearly that they are only to tell *one* tale each on their way to Canterbury.

799. *oure aller*, of us all. *your aller*, H.
803. *gladly*, E6 *goodly.*
826. *the watering of St. Thomas*, a brook near the second milestone on the Canterbury Road, where pilgrims watered their horses.

Now draweth cut, er that we ferrer twynne.
He which that hath the shorteste shal
    bigynne.
Sire Knyght,' quod he, 'my mayster and
    my lord,
Now draweth cut, for that is myn accord.
Cometh neer,'quod he, 'my lady Prioresse,
And ye sire Clerk, lat be your shame-
    fastnesse,   840
Ne studieth noght; ley hond to, every man.'

Anon to drawen every wight bigan,
And, shortly for to tellen as it was,
Were it by áventúre, or sort, or cas,
The sothe is this, the cut fil to the knyght,
Of which ful blithe and glad was every
    wyght :

And telle he moste his tale, as was resoun,
By foreward and by composicioun,
As ye han herd ; what nedeth wordès
    mo?
And whan this goode man saugh that it
    was so,   850
As he that wys was and obedient
To kepe his foreward by his free assent,
He seydè, 'Syn I shal bigynne the game,
What, welcome be the cut, a Goddès
    name !
Now lat us ryde, and herkneth what I
    seye.'
And with that word we ryden forth oure
    weye ;
And he bigan with right a myrie cheere
His tale anon, and seyde in this manère.

[TALES OF THE FIRST DAY]

[GROUP A]

KNIGHT'S TALE

Heere bigynneth The Knyghtes Tale

WHILOM, as oldè stories tellen us,
Ther was a duc that hightè Thesëus; 860
Of Atthenes he was lord and governour,
And in his tymè swich a conquerour,
That gretter was ther noon under the sonne.
Ful many a richè cóntree hadde he wonne ;
That with his wysdom and his chivalrie
He conquered al the regne of Femenye,
That whilom was y-clepèd Scithia ;
And weddedè the queene Ypolita,
And broghte hire hoom with hym in his
    contrée
With muchel glorie and greet solempnytee,
And eek hir fairè suster Emelye.   871
And thus with victorie and with melodye
Lete I this noble duc to Atthenes ryde,
And al his hoost in armès hym bisyde.

Knight's Tale. A discussion of Chaucer's
adaptation of Boccaccio's *Teseide* in this tale
will be found in the Introduction.
866. *the regne of Femenye*, the kingdom of the
Amazons.
871. *fairè*, H⁶ *yonge*.

And certès, if it nere to long to heere,
I wolde han told yow fully the manere
How wonnen was the regne of Femenye
By Thesëus and by his chivalrye ;
And of the gretè bataille for the nones
Bitwixen Atthenès and Amazones ;   880
And how assegèd was Ypolita,
The fairè, hardy queene of Scithia,
And of the feste that was at hir weddýnge,
And of the tempest at hir hoom-comýnge ;
But al that thyng I moot as now forbere.
I have, God woot, a largè feeld to ere,
And waykè been the oxen in my plough.
The remenant of the tale is long ynough,
I wol nat letten eek noon of this route.
Lat every felawe telle his tale aboute, 890
And lat se now who shal the soper wynne ;
And ther I lefte I wol ageyn bigynne.

This duc, of whom I makè mencioun,
Whan he was come almost unto the
    toun,
In al his wele, and in his moostè pride,
He was war, as he castè his eye aside,
Where that ther kneled in the hyè weye
A compaignye of ladyes, tweye and tweye,

Ech after oother, clad in clothės blake ;
But swich a cry and swich a wo they make
That in this world nys creäture lyvynge
That herdė swich another waymentynge :
And of this cry they noldė nevere stenten,
Til they the reynės of his brydel henten.
   'What folk been ye, that at myn
      hom-comýnge
Perturben so my festė with criýnge ?'
Quod Theseüs. 'Have ye so greet envye
Of myn honoúr, that thus compleyne and
   crye ?
Or who hath yow mysboden or offended ?
And telleth me if it may been amended,
And why that ye been clothėd thus in
   blak ? '   911
   The eldeste lady of hem allė spak
Whan she haddė swownėd with a deedly
   cheere,
That it was routhė for to seen and heere,
And seydė, ' Lord, to whom fortune hath
   yeven
Victorie, and as a conqueror to lyven,
Nat greveth us youre glorie and youre
   honoúr,
But we biseken mercy and socoúr.
Have mercy on oure wo and oure distresse :
Som drope of pitee, thurgh thy gentillesse,
Upon us wrecchėd wommen lat thou falle :
For certės, lord, ther is noon of us alle
That she ne hath been a duchesse or a
   queene.
Now be we caytyves, as it is wel seene :
Thankėd be Fortune and hire falsė wheel,
That noon estat assureth to be weel.
And certės, lord, to abyden youre presence,
Heere in the temple of the goddesse
   Clemence
We han ben waitynge al this fourtė-
   nyght ;
Now help us, lord, sith it is in thy
   myght.   930
   'I wrecchė, which that wepe and
      waillė thus,
Was whilom wyf to kyng Cappanëus,
That starf at Thebės ; cursėd be that
   day !
And allė we that been in this array,
And maken al this lamentacioun,

931. *waille,* E³ *crie.*

We losten alle oure housbondes at that
   toun,
Whil that the seegė ther-aboutė lay,
And yet now the oldė Creon, weylaway !
That lord is now of Thebės, the citee,   940
Fulfild of ire and of iniquitee,
He, for despit and for his tirannye,
To do the dedė bodyes vileynye
Of alle oure lordės, whichė that been
   slawe,
Hath alle the bodyes on an heepe y-drawe,
And wol nat suffren hem, by noon assent,
Neither to been y-buryed nor y-brent,
But maketh houndės ete hem in despit.'
   And with that word, withouten moore
      respit,
They fillen gruf, and criden pitously,
' Have on us wrecched wommen som
      mercy,   950
And lat oure sorwė synken in thyn herte.'
   This gentil duc doun from his courser
      sterte
With hertė pitous, whan he herde hem
      speke.
Hym thoughtė that his hertė woldė breke
Whan he saugh hem, so pitous and so maat,
That whilom weren of so greet estaat ;
And in his armės he hem alle up hente,
And hem conforteth in ful good entente,
And swoor his ooth, as he was trewė
      knyght,   959
He woldė doon so ferforthly his myght
Upon the tiraunt Creon hem to wreke,
That all the peple of Grecė sholdė speke
How Creon was of Theseüs y-served
As he that haddė his deeth ful wel
   deserved.
And right anoon, withouten moore abood,
His baner he desplayeth and forth rood
To Thebėsward, and al his hoost biside.
No neer Atthénės wolde he go ne ride,
Ne take his esė fully half a day,   969
But onward on his wey that nyght he lay ;
And sente anon Ypolita the queene,
And Emelye, hir yongė suster sheene,
Unto the toun of Atthenės to dwelle,
And forth he rit ; ther is namoore to telle.
   The redė statue of Mars with spere
      and targe

949. *fillen gruf,* fell on their faces.

So shyneth in his whité baner large,
That alle the feeldés glyteren up and doun,
And by his baner born is his penoun
Of gold ful riche, in which ther was y-bete
The Mynotaur, which that he slough in
    Crete.   980
Thus rit this duc, thus rit this con-
    querour,
And in his hoost of chivalrie the flour,
Til that he cam to Thebés, and alighte
Faire in a feeld, ther as he thoughté fighte.
But, shortly for to speken of this thyng,
With Creon, which that was of Thebés
    kyng,
He faught, and slough hym manly as a
    knyght,
In pleyn bataille, and putte the folk to
    flyght,
And by assaut he wan the citee after,
And rente adoun bothe wall and sparre
    and rafter   990
And to the ladyes he restored agayn
The bonés of hir housbondes that weren
    slayn,
To doon obsequies as was tho the gyse.
But it were al to longe for to devyse
The greté clamour and the waymentynge
Thát the ladyes made at the brennynge
Óf the bodies, and the grete honóur
That Thesëus, the noble conquerour,
Dooth to the ladyes whan they from hym
    wente ;
But shortly for to telle is myn entente.
    Whan that this worthy duc, this
        Thesëus,   1001
Hath Creon slayn, and wonné Thebés thus,
Stille in that feeld he took al nyght his reste,
And dide with al the contree as hym leste.
    To ransake in the taas of bodyes dede,
Hem for to strepe of harneys and of wede,
The pilours diden bisynesse and cure
After the bataille and disconfiture.
And so bifel that in the taas they founde,
Thurgh-girt with many a grevous, blody
    wounde,   1010
Two yongé knyghtés, liggynge by and by,
Bothe in oon armés, wroght ful richély,

977. *the feeldes,* the heraldic fields or ground
of his banner.
993. *obsequies,* H *exequies.*

Of whiché two Arcita highte that oon,
Ánd that oother knyght highte Palamon.
Nat fully quyke, ne fully dede they were,
But by here cote-armures and by hir gere
The heraudes knewe hem best in special,
As they that weren of the blood roial
Of Thebés, and of sustren two y-born.
Out of the taas the pilours han hem torn
And han hem caried softe unto the tente
Of Theseus, and ful sooné he hem sente
To Atthenés, to dwellen in prisoun
Perpetuelly, he noldé no raunsoun.
And whan this worthy duc hath thus y-don,
He took his hoost and hoom he rood anon,
With laurer crownéd as a conqueróur ;
And ther he lyveth in joye and in honóur
Terme of his lyve ; what nedeth wordés mo?
And in a tour, in angwissh and in wo, 1030
This Palamon and his felawe Arcite
For evermoore ; ther may no gold hem
    quite.
This passeth yeer by yeer and day by day,
Till it fil onés, in a morwe of May,
That Emelye, that fairer was to sene
Than is the lylie upon his stalké grene,
And fressher than the May with flourés
    newe,—
For with the rosé colour stroof hire hewe,
I noot which was the fyner of hem two,—
Er it were day, as was hir wone to do,
She was arisen and al redy dight :   1041
For May wole have no slogardrie a nyght,
The sesoun priketh every gentil herte
And maketh hym out of his slepe to sterte,
And seith, 'Arys, and do thyn óbservaunce.'
This makéd Emelye have rémembráunce
To doon honóur to May, and for to ryse.
Y-clothéd was she fresshe, for to devyse ;
Hir yelow heer was broyded in a tresse
Bihynde hir bak, a yerdé long, I gesse ; 1050
And in the gardyn, at the sonne up-riste,
She walketh up and doun, and as hire liste
She gadereth flourés, party white and rede,
To make a subtil gerland for hire hede,
And as an aungel hevenysshly she soong.
    The greté tour, that was so thikke and
        stroong,
Which of the castel was the chief dongeóun
(Ther as the knyghtés weren in prisóun,
Of whiche I toldé yow and tellen shal),

Was evene joynant to the gardyn wal,
Ther as this Emelye hadde hir pleyynge.
Bright was the sonne, and cleer that
    morwenynge,
And Palamon, this woful prisoner,
As was his wone, bi leve of his gayler,
Was risen, and romèd in a chambre on
    heigh,   1065
In which he al the noble citee seigh,
And eek the gardyn, ful of braunches grene,
Ther as this fresshè Emelye the sheene
Was in hire walk and romèd up and doun.
This sorweful prisoner, this Palamoun,
Goth in the chambrè romynge to and fro,
And to hymself compleynynge of his wo ;
That he was born, ful ofte he seyde, 'allas !'
And so bifel, by áventure or cas,
That thurgh a wyndow, thikke of many
    a barre   1075
Of iren, greet and square as any sparre,
He cast his eyen upon Emelya,
And therwithal he bleynte and cridè, 'A !'
As though he stongen were unto the herte.
And with that cry Arcite anon up sterte,
And seydè, 'Cosyn myn, what eyleth thee,
That art so pale and deedly on to see ?
Why cridestow ? who hath thee doon
    offence ?
For Goddès love, taak al in pacience
Oure prisoun, for it may noon oother be ;
Fortune hath yeven us this adversitee.
Som wikke aspèct or disposicioun
Of Saturne, by sum constellacioun,
Hath yeven us this, although we hadde
    it sworn ;
So stood the hevene whan that we were
    born ;   1090
We moste endure : this is the short and
    playn.'
    This Palamon answerde, and seyde
    agayn,
'Cosyn, for sothe of this opinioun
Thow hast a veyn ymaginacioun ;
This prison causèd me nat for to crye,
But I was hurt right now thurghout myn eye
Into myn herte, that wol my banè be.
The fairnesse of that lady that I see
Yond in the gardyn romen to and fro,
Is cause of al my criyng and my wo.   1100
I noot wher she be womman or goddesse,

But Venus is it, soothly, as I gesse.'
And therwithal on kneës doun he fil,
And seydè : 'Venus, if it be thy wil
Yow in this gardyn thus to transfigure
Bifore me, sorweful, wrecchè creäture,
Out of this prisoun helpe that we may
    scapen.
And if so be my destynee be shapen,
By eternè word, to dyen in prisóun,
Of our lynage have som compassioun,   1110
That is so lowe y-broght by tirannye.'
    And with that word Arcitè gan espye
Wher as this lady romèd to and fro,
And with that sighte hir beautee hurte
    hym so,
That if that Palamon was wounded sore,
Arcite is hurt as moche as he, or moore ;
And with a sigh he seydè pitously :
'The fresshè beautee sleeth me sodeynly
Of hire that rometh in the yonder place,
And but I have hir mercy and hir grace,
That I may seen hire attè leestè weye,   1121
I nam but deed ; ther is namoore to seye.'
    This Palamon, whan he tho wordès
    herde,
Dispitously he lookèd, and answerde,
'Wheither seistow this in ernest or in pley ?'
    'Nay,' quod Arcite, 'in ernest, by my
    fey !
God helpe me so, me list ful yvele pleye.'
    This Palamon gan knytte his browès
    tweye,
'It nere,' quod he, 'to thee no greet
    honóur,
For to be fals, ne for to be traitóur   1130
To me, that am thy cosyn and thy brother
Y-sworn ful depe, and ech of us til oother,
That never, for to dyen in the peyne,
Til that deeth departè shal us tweyne,
Neither of us in love to hyndrè oother,
Ne in noon oother cas, my leevè brother,
But that thou sholdest trewely forthren me
In every cas, as I shal forthren thee.
This was thyn ooth, and myn also certeyn ;
I woot right wel thou darst it nat withseyn.
Thus artow of my conseil, out of doute :
And now thow woldest falsly been aboute
To love my lady, whom I love and serve,
And ever shal, til that myn hertè sterve.
Nay certès, false Arcite, thow shalt nat so ;

16

I loved hire first, and tolde thee my wo
As to my conseil, and my brother sworn
To forthre me, as I have toold biforn.
For which thou art y-bounden as a knyght
To helpen me, if it lay in thy myght ; 1150
Or elles artow fals, I dar wel seyn.'
  This Arcite ful proudly spak ageyn ;
Thow shalt,' quod he, ' be rather fals
      than I ;
And thou art fals, I telle thee, outrely,
For *par amour* I loved hire first er thow.
What wiltow seyn? thou wistest nat yet now
Wheither she be a womman or goddesse !
Thyn is affeccioun of hoolynesse,
And myn is love as to a creäture ;
For which I tolde thee myn aventure 1160
As to my cosyn and my brother sworn.
I pose that thow lovedest hire biforn,
Wostow nat wel the olde clerkes sawe,
That who shal yeve a lovere any lawe ;
Love is a gretter lawe, by my pan,
Than may be yeve of any erthely man ?
And therfore positif lawe and swich decree
Is broken al day for love, in ech degree.
A man moot nedes love, maugree his heed;
He may nat flee it, thogh he sholde be
      deed,   1170
Al be she mayde, or wydwe, or elles wyf ;
And eek it is nat likly, al thy lyf,
To stonden in hir grace ; namoore shal I ;
For wel thou woost thyselven, verraily,
That thou and I be dampned to prisoun
Perpetuelly ; us gayneth no raunsoun.
We stryven as dide the houndes for the
      boon,
They foughte al day, and yet hir part
      was noon ;
Ther cam a kyte, whil that they weren
      so wrothe,
And baar awey the boon bitwixe hem
      bothe ;   1180
And therfore, at the kynges court, my
      brother,   .

Ech man for hymself, ther is noon oother.
Love, if thee list, for I love and ay shal,
And soothly, leeve brother, this is al.
Heere in this prisoun moote we endure
And everich of us take his aventure.'
  Greet was the strif, and long, bitwix
      hem tweye,
If that I hadde leyser for to seye ;
But to theffect. It happed on a day,—
To telle it yow as shortly as I may,— 1190
A worthy duc, that highte Perotheus,
That felawe was unto duc Theseus,
Syn thilke day that they were children lite,
Was come to Atthenes, his felawe to visite,
And for to pleye, as he was wont to do ;
For in this world he loved no man so,
And he loved hym as tendrely agayn.
So wel they lovede, as olde bookes sayn,
That whan that oon was deed, soothly to
      telle,
His felawe wente and soughte hym doun
      in helle,—   1200
But of that storie list me nat to write.
Duc Perotheus loved wel Arcite,
And hadde hym knowe at Thebes, yeer
      by yere ;
And finally, at request and preyere
Of Perotheus, withouten any raunsoun,
Duc Theseus hym leet out of prisoun
Frely to goon wher that hym liste over-al,
In swich a gyse as I you tellen shal.
  This was the forward, pleynly for tendite,
Bitwixen Theseus and hym Arcite ; 1210
That if so were that Arcite were y-founde,
Ever in his lif, by day or nyght, oo stounde,
In any contree of this Theseus,
And he were caught, it was acorded thus,
That with a swerd he sholde lese his heed :
Ther nas noon oother remedie, ne reed,
But taketh his leve and homward he him
      spedde :
Lat hym be war, his nekke lith to wedde.
  How greet a sorwe suffreth now Arcite !

1147. For *conseil* Lansdowne MS. reads *cosin*,
cp. l. 1161.
1163. *olde clerkes sawe*. The proverb is found
in Boethius, *De Consolatione Philosophiae*, lib.
iii. met. 12, translated by Chaucer : ' But what
is he that may yeve a lawe to loveres ? Love is
a gretter law and a strengere to hymself than any
lawe that men may yeven.'

1193. Chaucer is out here in his mythology,
for Pirithous, King of Thessaly, was originally
the enemy of Theseus, and invaded Attica.
1200. Chaucer takes this from the *Roman de
la Rose*. According to the original legend
Theseus and Pirithous visited hell, when the
latter was minded to carry off its queen, Proserpina.
1212. *oo*, MSS. *or*.

C   17

The deeth he feeleth thurgh his hertė
   smyte ;   1220
He wepeth, wayleth, crieth pitously ;
To sleen hymself he waiteth privėly.
He seyde, 'Allas that day that I was born !
Now is my prisoun worsė than biforn ;
Now is me shape eternally to dwelle,
Nat in my purgatórie, but in helle.
Allas that ever knew I Perothëus !
For ellės hadde I dwelled with Thesëus,
Y-fetered in his prisoun evermo.
Thanne hadde I been in blisse, and nat
   in wo,   1230
Oonly the sighte of hire, whom that I
   serve,—
Though that I never hir gracė may
   deserve,—
Wolde han suffisėd right ynough for me.
O deerė cosyn Palamon,' quod he,
'Thyn is the victorie of this áventure !
Ful blisfully in prison maistow dure,—
In prisoun ? certės nay, but in paradys !
Wel hath Fortúne y-turnėd thee the dys,
That hast the sighte of hire and I
   thabsence.   1239
For possible is, syn thou hast hire presence,
And art a knyght, a worthy and an able,
That by som cas, syn Fortune is chaunge-
   able,
Thow maist to thy desir some tyme atteyne,
But I, that am exilėd and bareyne
Of allė grace, and in so greet dispeir,
That ther nys erthė, water, fir, ne eir,
Ne creätuure, that of hem makėd is,
That may me heele, or doon confort in
   this—
Wel oughte I sterve in wanhope and
   distresse ;   1249
Farwel, my lif, my lust and my gladnesse !
   'Allas, why pleynen folk so in commúne
Of purvieaunce of God, or of Fortúne,
That yeveth hem ful ofte in many a gyse
Wel bettre than they kan hem self devyse?
Som man desireth for to han richésse,
That cause is of his moerdre, or greet
   siknesse ;
And som man wolde out of his prisoun fayn,
That in his hous is of his meynee slayn.

Infinite harmės been in this mateere,   1259
We witen nat what thing we preyen heere.
We faren as he that dronke is as a mous.
A dronkė man woot wel he hath an hous,
But he noot which the rightė wey is thider,
And to a dronkė man the wey is slider ;
And certės in this world so faren we,—
We seken faste after felicitee,
But we goon wrong ful often, trewėly.
Thus may we seyėn alle, and namely I,
That wende and hadde a greet opinioun
That if I myghte escapen from prisoun,
Thanne hadde I been in joye and perfit
   heele,   1271
Ther now I am exilėd fro my wele.
Syn that I may nat seen you, Emelye,
I nam but deed, there nys no remedye.'
   Upon that oother sydė, Palamon,
Whan that he wiste Arcitė was agon,
Swich sorwe he maketh that the gretė tour
Resounėd of his youlyng and clamóur ;
The purė fettres on his shynės grete
Weren of his bittre, saltė teerės wete.   1280
'Allas !' quod he, 'Arcita, cosyn myn,
Of al oure strif, God woot, the fruyt is
   thyn ;
Thow walkest now in Thebės at thy large,
And of my wo thow yevest litel charge.
Thou mayst, syn thou hast wysdom and
   manhede,
Assemblen alle the folk of oure kynrede,
And make a werre so sharpe on this citee,
That by som áventure, or som tretee,
Thow mayst have hire to lady and to wyf,
For whom that I moste nedės lese my lyf.
For, as by wey of possibilitee,   1291
Sith thou art at thy large, of prisoun free,
And art a lord, greet is thyn ávauntage,
Moore than is myn that sterve here in a
   cage ;
For I moot wepe and waylė while I lyve,
With al the wo that prison may me yeve,
And eek with peyne that love me yeveth
   also,
That doubleth al my torment and my wo.'
Therwith the fyr of jalousie up-sterte
Withinne his brest, and hente him by the
   herte   1300
So woodly, that he lyk was to biholde

1226. *my*, om. H⁶.
1248. *heele*, H⁶ *helpe*.

1278. *Resouned*, H⁶ *resouneth*.

The boxtree, or the asshen, dede and
    colde.
Thanne seyde he, 'O crueel goddes
    that govérne
This world with byndyng of youre word
    eterne,
And writen in the table of atthamaunt
Youre parlément and youre eterné graunt,
What is mankyndé moore unto you holde
Than is the sheepe that rouketh in the
    folde ?   1308
For slayn is man, right as another beest,
And dwelleth eek in prison and arreest,
And hath siknesse and greet adversitee,
And ofté tymés giltélees, *pardee.*
   'What governance is in this prescience,
That giltélees tormenteth innocence ?
And yet encresseth this al my penaunce,
That man is bounden to his óbservaunce
For Goddés sake to letten of his wille,
Ther as a beest may al his lust fulfille ;
And whan a beest is deed he hath no peyne,
But after his deeth man moot wepe and
    pleyne,   1320
Though in this world he havé care and wo ;
Withouten douté it may stonden so.
The answere of this I leté to dyvynys,
But well I woot that in this world greet
    pyne ys.
Allas ! I se a serpent or a theef,
That many a trewé man hath doon
    mescheef,
Goon at his large, and where hym list
    may turne ;
But I moot been in prisoun thurgh Saturne,
And eek thurgh Juno, jalous and eek
    wood,
That hath destroyéd wel ny al the
    blood   1330
Of Thebés, with his wasté wallés wyde ;
And Venus sleeth me on that oother syde
For jalousie and fere of hym Arcite.'
   Now wol I stynte of Palamon a lite
And lete hym in his prisoun stillé dwelle,
And of Arcita forth I wol yow telle.

1320. *But after his deeth man*, etc., so E⁴,
throwing a stress, which accords well with the
sense, on *his ;* H⁸ more smoothly, *But man after
his deeth,* etc.
   1323. *I lete,* E⁶ *lete I,* spoiling the accents
throughout the line.

The sommer passeth, and the nyghtés
    longe
Encressen double wise the peynés stronge
Bothe of the lovere and the prisoner. 1339
I noot which hath the wofuller mester ;
For shortly for to seyn this Palamoun
Perpetuelly is dampnéd to prisoun,
In cheynés and in fettres to been deed,
And Arcite is exiled upon his heed
For ever-mo, as out of that contree,
Ne never-mo he shal his lady see.
   Yow loveres axe I now this questioun,
Who hath the worse, Arcite or Palamoun?
That oon may seen his lady day by day,
But in prison he moot dwelle alway ; 1350
That oother wher hym list may ride or go,
But seen his lady shal he never mo.
Now demeth as yow listé, ye that kan,
For I wol tellé forth as I bigan.

PART II

Whan that Arcite to Thebés comen was,
Ful ofte a day he swelte and seyde, 'Allas !'
For seen his lady shal he never mo.
And, shortly to concluden al his wo,
So muché sorwe hadde never creáture
That is, or shal, whil that the world may
    dure.   1360
His slepe, his mete, his drynke, is hym
    biraft,
That lene he wexe and drye as is a shaft ;
His eyen holwe, and grisly to biholde,
His hewé falow, and pale as asshen colde,
And solitarie he was and ever allone,
And waillynge al the nyght, makynge his
    mone :
And if he herdé song or instrument
Thanne wolde he wepe, he myghté nat
    be stent.
So feble eek were his spiritz and so lowe,
And chaungéd so that no man koudé
    knowe   1370
His speché nor his voys, though men it
    herde :
And in his geere for al the world he ferde,
Nat oonly like the loveris maladye

1337. *sommer,* E *sonne.*
1344. *upon his heed,* on pain of losing his head.
1362. *wexe,* E³ *wexeth.*

Of Hereos, but rather lyk manye,
Engendred of humóur maléncolik,
Biforn, in his owene cellè fantastik.
And, shortly, turnèd was al up-so-doun
Bothe habit and eek disposicioun
Of hym, this woful lovere daun Arcite.
  What sholde I al day of his wo endite?
Whan he endurèd hadde a yeer or two 1381
This crueel torment and this peyne and
   woo,
At Thebès, in his contree, as I seyde,
Upon a nyght, in sleepe as he hym leyde,
Hym thoughte how that the wyngèd god
   Mercúrie
Biforn hym stood and bad hym to be
   murie ;
His slepy yerde in hond he bar uprighte,
An hat he werede upon his heris brighte.
Arrayèd was this god, as he took keepe,
As he was whan that Argus took his sleepe,
And seyde hym thus, 'To Atthénès
   shaltou wende ;   1391
Ther is thee shapen of thy wo an ende.'
And with that word Arcitè wook and
   sterte,—
' Now trewély, hou soorè that me smerte,'
Quod he, 'to Atthénès right now wol I fare,
Ne for the drede of deeth shal I nat spare,
To se my lady that I love and serve ;
In hire presence I recchè nat to sterve.'
  And with that word he caughte a
   greet miróur   1399
And saugh that chaungèd was al his colóur
And saugh his visage al in another kynde ;
And right anon it ran hym in his mynde,
That sith his facè was so disfigúred
Of maladye the which he hadde endured,
He myghtè wel, if that he bar hym lowe,
Lyve in Atthénès evermore unknowe,
And seen his lady wel ny day by day.
And right anon he chaungèd his array
And cladde hym as a pourè laborer,

And al allone,—save oonly a squiér 1410
That knew his privétee and al his cas,
Which was disgised pourely as he was,—
To Atthénès is he goon the nextè way,
And to the court he wente upon a day,
And at the gate he profreth his servyse
To drugge and drawe, what so men wol
   devyse.
And, shortly of this matere for to seyn,
He fil in office with a chamberleyn
The which that dwellynge was with
   Emelye ;   1419
For he was wys and koude soone espye
Of every servaunt which that serveth here.
Wel koude he hewen wode and water bere,
For he was yong, and myghty for the nones,
And therto he was long and big of bones,
To doon that any wight kan hym devyse.
A yeer or two he was in this servyse,
Page of the chambre of Emelye the brighte,
And Philostrate he seydè that he highte.
But half so wel biloved a man as he 1429
Ne was ther never in court of his degree ;
He was so gentil of his condicioun
That thurghout al the court was his renoun.
They seyden that it were a charitee
That Theseus wolde enhauncen his degree,
And putten hym in worshipful servyse,
Ther as he myghte his vertu exercise.
And thus withinne a while his name is
   spronge,
Bothe of his dedès and his goodè tonge,
That Theséus hath takèn hym so neer,
That of his chambre he made hym a squiér,
And yaf him gold to mayntene his degree;
And eek men broghte hym out of his
   contree,
From yeer to yeer, ful pryvély, his rente ;
But honestly and slyly he it spente
That no man wondred how that he it hadde.
And thre yeer in this wise his lif he ladde
And bar hym so in pees, and eek in werre,
Ther was no man that Theséus hath derre.
And in this blissè lete I now Arcite
And speke I wole of Palamon a lite. 1450

  1374. *Hereos*, Eros, Love.
  1376. *Biforn, in his owene celle fantastik ; in* is from H only ; *owene* from E³ only. According to medieval theory Mania was begotten in the front cell of the head which was appropriated to the imagination.
  1387. *yerde*, Mercury's *caduceus.*
  1389. *he*, E *I.*
  1390. *Argus*, the hundred-eyed guardian of Io. Mercury lulled him with music and slew him.

  1424. *long*, EH³ ; Hengwrt⁴, *strong.*
  1428. *Philostrate :* in the *Teseide* Arcite takes the name of Pentheo. The name Philostrate was probably suggested to Chaucer by Boccaccio's poem *Filostrato*, the original of *Troilus and Cressida.*

In derknesse and horrible and strong
    prison
Thise seven yeer hath seten Palamon.
Forpynéd, what for wo and for distresse.
Who feeleth double soor and hevynesse
But Palamon? that love destreyneth so
That wood out of his wit he goth for wo;
And eek ther-to he is a prisoner
Perpetuelly, noght only for a yer.
    Who koudé ryme in Englyssh proprely
His martirdom? for sothe it am nat I;
Therfore I passe as lightly as I may. 1461
    It fel that in the seventhe yer, in May,
The thriddé nyght, as oldé bookés seyn,
That al this storie tellen mooré pleyn,
Were it by áventure or destynee,—
As whan a thyng is shapen it shal be,—
That soone after the mydnyght, Palamoun,
By helpyng of a freend brak his prisoun
And fleeth the citee, faste as he may go,
For he hade yeve his gayler drynké so,
Of a clarree, maad of a certeyn wyn, 1471
With nercotikes, and opie of Thebés fyn,
That al that nyght, thogh that men wolde
    him shake,
The gayler sleepe, he myghté nat awake;
    And thus he fleeth, as faste as ever
    he may.
The nyght was short and fasté by the day,
That nedés-cost he moot hymselven hyde,
And til a grové, fasté ther bisyde,
With dredeful foot, thanne stalketh Pala-
    moun.
For, shortly, this was his opinioun, 1480
That in that grove he wolde hym hyde al
    day,
And in the nyght thanne wolde he take
    his way
To Thebés-ward, his freendés for to preye
On Theséus to helpe him to werreye;
And, shortly, outher he woldé lese his lif,
Or wynnen Emelye unto his wyf.
This is theffect and his ententé pleyn.
    Now wol I turné to Arcite ageyn,
That litel wiste how ny that was his care,
Til that Fortúne had broght him in the
    snare.   1490

The bisy larké, messager of day,
Salueth in hir song the morwé gray;
And firy Phebus riseth up so brighte
That al the orient laugheth of the lighte,
And with his stremés dryeth in the greves
The silver dropés, hangynge on the leves.
And Arcita, that is in the court roiál
With Theséus, his squier principal,
Is risen, and looketh on the myrie day;
And for to doon his óbservaunce to May,
Remembrynge on the poynt of his desir,
He on a courser, stertyng as the fir,
Is riden into the feeldés hym to pleye,
Out of the court, were it a myle or tweye;
And to the grove of which that I yow tolde,
By áventure, his wey he gan to holde,
To maken hym a gerland of the greves,
Were it of wodébynde, or hawethorn leves,
And loude he song ageyn the sonné shene:
' Máy, with alle thy floures and thy grene,
Wélcome be thou, fairé, fresshé May, 1511
In hope that I som grené geté may.'
And from his courser with a lusty herte
Into a grove ful hastily he sterte,
And in a path he rometh up and doun,
Ther as by áventure this Palamoun
Was in a bussh, that no man myghte
    hym se,
For soore aferéd of his deeth was he.
No-thyng ne knew he that it was Arcite:
God woot he wolde have trowéd it ful lite;
But sooth is seyd, gon sithen many yeres,
That feeld hath eyen, and the wode hath
    eres.
It is ful fair a man to bere hym evene,
For al day meeteth men at unset stevene.
Ful litel woot Arcite of his felawe
That was so ny to herknen al his sawe,
For in the bussh he sitteth now ful stille.
    Whan that Arcite hadde roméd al his
    fille,
And songen al the roundel lustily,
Into a studie he fil al sodeynly,   1530
As doon thise loveres in hir queynté
    geres,—
Now in the cropé, now doun in the breres,

1454. *soor*, E⁵; H², *sorwe*.
1472. *Thebes*, in Egypt, not in Greece.
1472. *with*, E *of*.

1494. *That al the orient laugheth*: Dante, *Purg.* i. 20, ' faceva tutto rider l' oriente.' (Skeat.)
1522. *That feeld hath eyen*: 'Campus habet lumen et habet nemus auris acumen.'
1524. *unset stevene*, unappointed time.

Now up, now doun, as boket in a welle.
Right as the Friday, soothly for to telle,
Now it shyneth, now it reyneth faste,
Right so kan geery Venus overcaste
The hertès of hir folk ; right as hir day
Is gereful, right so chaungeth she array,—
Selde is the Friday al the wowke y-like.
   Whan that Arcite had songe, he gan
     to sike,   1540
And sette hym doun withouten any moore :
'Allas,' quod he, 'that day that I was
     bore !
How longè, Juno, thurgh thy crueltee,
Woltow werreyen Thebès the citee ?
Allas, y-broght is to confusioun
The   blood   roiál   of   Cadme   and
     Amphioun,—
Of Cadmus, which that was the firstè man
That Thebès bulte, or first the toun bigan,
And of the citee first was crounèd kyng.
Of his lynage am I, and his ofspryng   1550
By verray ligne, as of the stok roiál ;
And now I am so caytyf and so thral,
That he that is my mortal enemy,
I serve hym as his squier pourèly.
And yet dooth Juno me wel moorè shame,
For I dar noght biknowe myn owene name ;
But ther as I was wont to highte Arcite,
Now highte I Philostrate, noght worth a
     myte.
Allas, thou fellè Mars ! allas, Juno !   1559
Thus hath youre ire oure kynrede al fordo,
Save oonly me, and wrecched Palamoun,
That Theseüs martireth in prisoun.
And over al this, to sleen me outrely,
Love hath his firy dart so brennyngly
Y-stikèd thurgh my trewè, careful herte,
That shapen was my deeth erst than my
     sherte.
Ye sleen me with youre eyèn, Emelye !
Ye been the causè wherfore that I dye !
Of al the remenant of myn oother care
Ne sette I nat the montance of a tare,
So that I koude doon aught to youre
     plesaunce.'   1571
And with that word he fil doun in a traunce
A longè tyme, and afterward up-sterte.

This Palamoun, that thoughte that
     thurgh his herte
He felte a coold swerd sodeynlichè glyde,
For ire he quook, no lenger wolde he byde.
And whan that he had herd Arcitès tale,
As he were wood, with facè deed and pale,
He stirte hym up out of the buskès thikke,
And seide, 'Arcité, falsè traytour wikke !
Now artow hent, that lovest my lady so,
For whom that I have al this peyne and wo,
And art my blood, and to my conseil sworn,
As I ful ofte have seyd thee heer-biforn,
And hast byjapèd heere duc Theseüs,
And falsly chaungèd hast thy namè thus ;
I wol be deed, or ellès thou shalt dye ;
Thou shalt nat love my lady Emelye,
But I wol love hire oonly, and namo ;
For I am Palamon, thy mortal foo,   1590
And though that I no wepene have in
     this place,
But out of prison am astert by grace,
I dredè noght that outher thow shalt dye,
Or thow ne shalt nat loven Emelye.
Chees which thou wolt, for thou shalt
    •   nat asterte !'
   This Arcité, with ful despitous herte,
Whan he hym knew, and hadde his talè
     herd,
As fiers as leoun pullèd out his swerd,
And seydè thus, ' By God that sit above,
Nere it that thou art sik and wood for love,
And eek that thow no wepne hast in this
     place,   1601
Thou sholdest never out of this grovè pace,
That thou ne sholdest dyen of myn hond,
For I defye the seurete and the bond
Which that thou seist that I have maad
     to thee.
What, verray fool, thynk wel that love is fre !
And I wol love hire mawgree al thy myght.
But for as muche thou art a worthy knyght,
And wilnest to darreyne hire by bataille,
Have heer my trouthe, tomorwe I wol
     nat faile,   1610
Withoutè wityng of any oother wight,
That heere I wol be founden as a knyght,
And bryngen harneys right ynough for
     thee,—

1536. *kan*, H⁴ *gan*.
1566. *sherte*, shirt ; cp. *Legend of Good
Women*, l. 2626, and *Troilus*, 734.

1584. *seyd*, H⁶ *told*.
1595. *for*, E⁶ *or*.   1598. *his*, H³ *a*.

And chese the beste and leve the worste
    for me,—
And mete and drynké this nyght wol I
    brynge
Ynough for thee, and clothes for thy
    beddynge ;
And if so be that thou my lady wynne
And sle me in this wode ther I am inne,
Thou mayst wel have thy lady, as for me.'
    This Palamon answerde, ' I graunte it
    thee.'   1620
And thus they been departed til a-morwe,
Whan ech of hem had leyd his feith to
    borwe.

O Cupide, out of allé charitee !
O regne, that wolt no felawe have with
    thee !
Ful sooth is seyd that lové ne lordshipe
Wol noght, his thankés, have no felawe-
    shipe.
Wel fynden that Arcite and Palamoun !
    Arcite is riden anon unto the toun,
And on the morwe, er it were dayés light,
Ful privély two harneys hath he dight, 1630
Bothe suffisaunt and meté to darreyne
The bataille in the feeld betwix hem
    tweyne ;
And on his hors, allone as he was born,
He carieth al the harneys hym biforn :
And in the grove, at tyme and place y-set,
This Arcite and this Palamon ben met.
To chaungen gan the colour in hir face,
Right as the hunters, in the regne of
    Trace,
That stondeth at the gappé with a spere,
Whan hunted is the leoun or the bere,
And hereth hym come russhyng in the
    greves,   1641
And breketh both bowés and the leves,
And thynketh, ' Heere cometh my
    mortal enemy,
With-outé faile he moot be deed or I ;
For outher I moot sleen hym at the gappe,
Or he moot sleen me, if that me
    myshappe ' :
So ferden they in chaungyng of hir hewe,
As fer as everich of hem oother knewe.
    Ther nas no ' Good day,' ne no saluyng,

1637. *To,* H¹ *tho.*

But streight, withouten word or re-
    hersyng,   1650
Everich of hem heelpe for to armen oother,
As frendly as he were his owene brother ;
And after that, with sharpé sperés stronge,
They foynen ech at oother wonder longe.
Thou myghtest wené that this Palamoun,
In his fightyng were a wood leoun,
And as a crueel tigre was Arcite :
As wildé borés gonné they to smyte,
That frothen whit as foom for iré wood,—
Up to the ancle foghte they in hir blood.
    And in this wise I lete hem fightyng
    dwelle,   1661
And forth I wole of Thesëus yow telle.

    The Destinee, ministré general,
That executeth in the world over al,
The purveiaunce that God hath seyn biforn,
So strong it is that, though the world had
    sworn
The contrarie of a thyng by ye or nay,
Yet somtyme it shal fallen on a day
That falleth nat eft withinne a thousand
    yeere.
For certeinly oure appetités heere,   1670
Be it of werre, or pees, or hate, or love,
Al is this reuléd by the sighte above.
    This mene I now by myghty Thesëus,
That for to hunten is so desirús,
And namely at the greté hert in May,
That in his bed ther daweth hym no day
That he nys clad, and redy for to ryde
With hunte and horne, and houndés hym
    bisyde.
For in his huntyng hath he swich delit,
That it is al his joye and appetit   1680
To been hymself the greté hertés bane,
For after Mars he serveth now Dyane.
    Cleer was the day, as I have toold er
    this,
And Thesëus, with allé joye and blis,
With his Ypolita, the fairé queene,
And Emelyë, clothéd al in grene,
On huntyng be they riden roially ;
And to the grove, that stood ful fasté by,
In which ther was an hert, as men hym
    tolde,
Duc Thesëus the streighté way hath
    holde ;   1690

And to the launde he rideth hym ful
   right,—
For thider was the hert wont have his
   flight,—
And over a brook, and so forth in his weye.
This duc wol han a cours at hym, or tweye,
With houndès, swiche as that hym list
   commaunde.
   And whan this duc was come unto the
     launde
Under the sonne he looketh, and anon,
He was war of Arcite and Palamon,
That foughten breme, as it were borès
   two.   1699
The brightè swerdès wenten to and fro
So hidously, that with the leestè strook
It semèd as it woldè fille an ook ;
But what they werè no thyng he ne woot.
This duc his courser with his sporès smoot,
And at a stert he was bitwix hem two,
And pullèd out a swerd, and cridè, 'Hoo!
Namoore, up peyne of lesynge of youre
   heed !
By myghty Mars, he shal anon be deed
That smyteth any strook, that I may seen.
But telleth me what mystiers men ye been,
That been so hardy for to fighten heere 1711
Withouten juge, or oother officere,
As it were in a lystès roially ? '
   This Palamon answerdè hastily
And seydè, 'Sire, what nedeth wordès mo?
We have the deeth disservèd bothè two.
Two woful wrecches been we, two caytyves,
That been encombred of oure owene lyves,
And as thou art a rightful lord and juge,
Ne yeve us neither mercy ne refuge, 1720
But sle me first, for seintè charitee,
But sle my felawe eek as wel as me ;
Or sle hym first, for though thow
     knowest it lite,
This is thy mortal foo, this is Arcite,
That fro thy lond is banysshed on his heed,
For which he hath deservèd to be deed ;
For this is he that cam unto thy gate
And seydè that he hightè Philostrate ;
Thus hath he japèd thee ful many a yer,
And thou hast makèd hym thy chief
     squiér ;   1730
And this is he that loveth Emelye ;
For sith the day is come that I shal dye,

I makè pleynly my confessioun
That I am thilkè woful Palamoun,
That hath thy prisoun broken wikkedly.
I am thy mortal foo, and it am I
That loveth so hoote Emelye the brighte
That I wol dyè present in hir sighte.
Therfore I axè deeth and my juwise ;
But sle my felawe in the samè wise, 1740
For bothe han we deservèd to be slayn.'
   This worthy duc answerde anon agayn,
And seyde, ' This is a short conclusioun :
Youre owene mouth, by youre confessioun,
Hath dampnèd yow, and I wol it recorde,
It nedeth noght to pyne yow with the
     corde,
Ye shal be deed, by myghty Mars the
     rede ! '
   The queene anon, for verray womman-
     hede,
Gan for to wepe, and so dide Emelye,
And alle the ladyes in the compaignye.
Greet pitee was it, as it thoughte hem alle,
That ever swich a chauncè sholde falle,
For gentil men they were, of greet estaat,
And no thyng but for love was this
     debaat,—
And saugh hir blody woundès, wyde and
     soore,
And allè crieden, bothè lasse and moore,
' Have mercy, lord, upon us wommen alle ! '
And on hir barè knees adoun they falle,
And wolde have kist his feet ther as he
     stood,
Til at the laste aslakèd was his mood, 1760
For pitee renneth soone in gentil herte,
And though he first for irè quook and sterte,
He hath considered shortly, in a clause,
The trespas of hem bothe, and eek the
     cause,
And although that his ire hir gilt accused,
Yet in his resoun he hem bothe excused,
And thus he thoghtè wel, that every man
Wol helpe hymself in love, if that he kan,
And eek delivere hymself out of prisoun ;
And eek his hertè hadde compassioun 1770
Of wommen, for they wepen ever in oon ;

1746. *to pyne yow with the corde*, put you to
torture, *i.e.* to extract a confession.
   1761. *For pitee*, etc. This beautiful line occurs
four times in Chaucer.

And in his gentil herte he thoughte anon,
And softe unto hym-self he seyde, ' Fy
Upon a lord that wol have no mercy,
But been a leoun, bothe in word and dede,
To hem that been in répentaunce and
    drede,
As wel as to a proud despitous man
That wol maynteyné that he first bigan ;
That lord hath litel of discrecioun,
That in swich cas kan no divisioun,   1780
But weyeth pride and humblesse after oon.'
And shortly, whan his ire is thus agoon,
He gan to looken up with eyèn lighte,
And spak thise samé wordés, al on highte.
  ' The god of love, a *benedicite*,
How myghty and how greet a lord is he !
Ageyns his myght ther gayneth none
    obstácles,
He may be cleped a god for his myrácles,
For he kan maken, at his owene gyse,
Of everich herte as that hym list divyse.
  ' Lo heere this Arcite, and this
    Palamoun,   1791
That quitly weren out of my prisoun,
And myghte han lyved in Thebès roially,
And witen I am hir mortal enemy,
And that hir deth lith in my myght also,
And yet hath love, maugree hir eyèn two,
Y-broght hem hyder, bothé for to dye.
Now looketh, is nat that an heigh folye ?
  ' Whó may been a fole, but if he love ?
Bihoold, for Goddès sake that sit above,
Se how they blede ! be they noght wel
    arrayed ?   1801
Thus hath hir lord, the god of love, y-payed
Hir wages and hir fees for hir servyse :
And yet they wenen for to been ful wyse
That serven love, for aught that may bifalle.
But this is yet the besté game of alle,
That she, for whom they han this jolitee,
Kan hem ther-fore as muché thank as me.
She woot namoore of al this hooté fare,
By God, than woot a cokkow or an hare.
But all moot ben assayèd, hoot and coold ;
A man moot ben a fool, or yong or oold,—
I woot it by myself ful yore agon,

For in my tyme a servant was I oon.
And therfore, syn I knowe of lovès peyne,
And woot how soore it kan a man distreyne,
As he that hath ben caught ofte in his laas,
I yow foryeve al hoolly this trespaas,
At réqueste of the queene, that kneleth
    heere,
And eek of Emelye, my suster deere.   1820
And ye shul bothe anon unto me swere,
That never mo ye shal my contree dere,
Ne maké werre upon me, nyght ne day,
But been my freendés in al that ye may.
I yow foryeve this trespas every deel.'
And they him sworen his axyng, faire
    and weel,
And hym of lordshipe and of mercy preyde,
And he hem graunteth grace, and thus he
    seyde :—
  ' To speke of roial lynage and richesse,
Though that she were a queene or a
    princesse,   1830
Ech of you bothe is worthy, doutèlees,
To wedden whan tyme is, but nathèlees,—
I speke as for my suster Emelye,
For whom ye have this strif and jalousye,—
Ye woot your self she may nat wedden two
At onès, though ye fighten evermo.
That oon of you, al be hym looth or lief,
He moot go pipen in an yvy leef :
This is to seyn, she may nought havé
    bothe,   1839
Al be ye never so jalouse ne so wrothe ;
And for-thy, I yow putte in this degree,
That ech of yow shal have his destynee
As hym is shape, and herkneth in what
    wyse ;
Lo, heere your ende of that I shal devyse.
  ' My wyl is this, for plat conclusioun
Withouten any repplicacioun,—
If that you liketh, take it for the beste,—
That everich of you shal goon where
    hym leste
Frely, withouten raunson or daunger ;
And this day fifty wykès, fer ne ner,   1850
Everich of you shal brynge an hundred
    knyghtes   ·

1799. *Who may*, etc., *i.e.* your lover is your only perfect fool. The reading of H, '*who may be a fole if that he love*,' necessitates the insertion of *not* after *may*.

1838. *go*, om. E. The phrase, equivalent to our *go whistle*, is used by Wyclif.
1850. *fer ne ner*, no later or sooner ; *fifty wykes* are of course used here for a year, Boccaccio's *un anno intero*.

25

Arméd for lystés up at allé rightes,
Al redy to darreyne hire by bataille ;
And this bihote I yow with-outen faille
Upon my trouthe and as I am a knyght,
That wheither of yow bothé that hath
    myght,
This is to seyn, that wheither he or thow
May with his hundred, as I spak of now,
Sleen his contrarie, or out of lystés dryve,
Him shal I yeve Emelya to wyve,   1860
To whom that Fortune yeveth so fair a
    grace.
The lystés shal I maken in this place,
And God so wisly on my soulé rewe
As I shal evene jugé been, and trewe.
Ye shul noon oother endé with me maken
That oon of yow ne shal be deed or taken ;
And if yow thynketh this is weel y-sayd,
Seyeth youre avys and holdeth you apayd.
This is youre ende and youre conclusioun.'
   Who looketh lightly now but Pala-
    moun ?   1870
Who spryngeth up for joyé but Arcite ?
Who kouthé tellé, or who kouthe endite,
The joyé that is makéd in the place
Whan Thesëus hath doon so fair a grace ?
But doun on knees wente every maner
   • wight
And thonken hym with al hir herte and
    myght ;
And namély the Thebans often sithe.
And thus with good hope and with herté
    blithe
They taken hir leve, and homward gonne
    they ride   1879
To Thebés, with his oldé wallés wyde.

PART III

I trowe men woldé deme it necligence
If I forgete to tellen the dispence
Of Thesëus, that gooth so bisily
To maken up the lystés roially,
That swich a noble theatre as it was
I dar wel seyn that in this world there nas.
The circuit a mylé was aboute,
Walléd of stoon and dychéd al withoute.
Round was the shape, in manere of
    compaas,   1889
Ful of degrees, the heighte of sixty pas,

That whan a man was set on o degree,
He letté nat his felawe for to see.
   Estward ther stood a gate of marbul whit,
Westward right swich another in the
    opposit.
And, shortly to concluden, swich a place
Was noon in erthe, as in so litel space ;
For in the lond ther was no crafty man
That geométrie or ars-metrik kan,
Ne portreitour, ne kervere of ymáges,
That Thesëus ne yaf him mete and wages,
The theatre for to maken and devyse.   1901
And, for to doon his ryte and sacrifise,
He estward hath, upon the gate above,
In worshipe of Venús, goddesse of love,
Doon make an auter and an oratórie ;
And westward, in the mynde and in
    memórie
Of Mars, he makéd hath right swich
    another,
That costé largély of gold a fother.
And northward, in a touret on the wal,
Of alabastre whit and reed coral,   1910
An oratorie riché for to see,
In worshipe of Dyane of chastitee,
Hath Thesëus doon wroght in noble wyse.
   But yet hadde I forgeten to devyse
The noble kervyng and the portreitures,
The shape, the contenaunce, and the
    figures
That weren in thise oratories thre.
   First, in the temple of Venus maystow
    se,   1918
Wroght on the wal, ful pitous to biholde,
The broken slepés, and the sikés colde,
The sacred teeris, and the waymentynge,
The firy strokés, and the desirynge,
That lovés servauntz in this lyf enduren ;
The othés that her covenantz assuren ;
Plesaunce and Hope, Desir, Foolhardy-
    nesse,
Beautee and Youthé, Bauderie, Richesse,
Charmés and Force, Lesyngés, Flaterye,
Despensé, Bisynesse and Jalousye,
That wered of yelewe gooldés a gerland

1900. *kim*, om. E³ ; H, *hem.*
1906. *And westward,* etc., text from H ; *and
on the westward in memorie,* E⁵ ; *and on the
westward side in memorie,* Petworth.
1921. *sacred,* Cambridge MS. *secret,* an at-
tractive reading.

Ánd a cokkow sitynge on hir hand ;   1930
Féstes, instrumentz, caróles, daunces,
Lust and array, and alle the circum-
  staunces
Of love, whiche that I reken, and rekne
  shal,
By ordre weren peynted on the wal,
And mo than I kan make of mencioun ;
For soothly al the mount of Citheroun,
Ther Venus hath hir principal dwellynge,
Was shewéd on the wal in portreyynge,
With al the gardyn and the lustynesse.
Nat was forgeten the porter Ydelnesse,
Ne Narcisus the faire of yore agon,   1941
Ne yet the folye of kyng Salamon,
Ne yet the greté strengthe of Ercules,
Thenchauntementz of Medea and Circes,
Ne of Turnus, with the hardy fiers corage,
The riché Cresus, kaytyf in servage.
Thus may ye seen that Wysdom ne
  Richésse,
Beautee ne Sleighté, Strengthé, Hardy-
  nesse,
Ne may with Venus holdé champartie,
For as hir list the world than may she
  gye.   1950
Lo, alle thise folk so caught were in hir las
Til they for wo ful ofté seyde, 'Allas !'
Suffiseth heere ensamplés oon or two,
And though I koudé rekene a thousand mo.
  The statue of Venus, glorious for to se,
Was naked, fletynge in the largé see,
And fro the navele doun al covered was
With wawés grene, and brighte as any
  glas.
A citole in hir right hand haddé she,
And on hir heed, ful semely for to se,   1960
A rosé gerland, fressh and wel smellynge,
Above hir heed hir dowvés flikerynge.
Biforn hire stood hir soné Cupido,
Upon his shuldrés wyngés hadde he two,
And blind he was, as it is often seene;
A bowe he bar and arwés brighte and kene.

Why sholde I noght as wel eek telle
  yow al
The portreiture that was upon the wal
Withinne the temple of myghty Mars the
  rede ?
Al peynted was the wal, in lengthe and
  brede,   1970
Lyk to the estrés of the grisly place
That highte the greté temple of Mars in
  Trace,
In thilké coldé, frosty regioun
Ther as Mars hath his sovereyn mansioun.
  First, on the wal was peynted a forest,
In which ther dwelleth neither man nor
  best,
With knotty, knarry, bareyne treés olde
Of stubbés sharpe and hidouse to biholde,
In which ther ran a rumbel and a swough,
As though a storm sholde bresten every
  bough ;   1980
And dounward from an hille, under a
  bente,
Ther stood the temple of Mars army-
  potente,
Wroght al of burnéd steel, of which the
  entree
Was long and streit, and gastly for to see ;
And ther out came a rage, and such a veze
That it made all the gatés for to rese.
The northren lyght in at the dorés
  shoon,—
For wyndowe on the wal ne was ther noon
Thurgh which men myghten any light
  discerne,—
The dores were al of adamant eterne,   1990
Y-clenchéd overthwart and endélong
With iren tough, and for to make it strong,
Every pylér, the temple to sustene,
Was tonné greet, of iren bright and shene.
  Ther saugh I first the derke ymaginyng
Of felonye, and al the compassyng ;
The crueel ire, reed as any gleede ;
The pyképurs, and eke the palé drede ;

1933. *reken*, Cambridge MS. ; E, *rekned have* ; H⁵, *rekned*.
1936. *Citherroun*. Chaucer seems to confuse the island of *Cythera*, the home of Venus, with *Mt. Citheron*, on the borders of Attica, sacred to Bacchus and the Muses.
1940. *the porter Ydelnesse*, cp. *Romaunt of the Rose*, ll. 531-593.
1951. *las*, snare ; H, *trace*.

1972 *greté temple of Mars in Trace*, i.e. the temple under Mt. Hæmus, described by Statius in the seventh book of the *Thebaid*, lines 40-63. Statius here served as a model to Boccaccio.
1979. *rumbel*, H *rwymbel*, moaning (of wind).
1986. *gates*, E³ *gate*.
1990. *dores were*, E³ *dore was*.
1998. *pykepurs*. The pickpurse is not mentioned in Boccaccio. Wright explains it to refer to the

The smylere, with the knyfe under the
   cloke ;
The shepné, brennynge with the blakè
   smoke ;   2000
The tresoun of the mordrynge in the
   bedde ;
The open werre, with woundès al bi-
   bledde ;
Contek, with blody knyf, and sharpe
   manace ;
Al ful of chirkyng was that sory place.
The sleere of hymself yet saugh I ther,
His hertè blood hath bathèd al his heer ;
The nayl y-dryven in the shode a-nyght ;
The coldè deeth, with mouth gapyng up-
   right.
Amyddès of the temple sat Meschaunce,
With disconfort and sory contenaunce.
Yet saugh I Woodnesse, laughynge in
   his rage,   2011
Armèd compleint, out - hees, and fiers
   outrage,
The careyne, in the busk, with throte
   y-corve,
A thousand slayn and nat of qualm y-
   storve ;
The tiraunt, with the pray by force y-raft ;
The toun destroyéd, ther was nothyng laft.
Yet saugh I brent the shippes hoppe-
   stères ;
The huntè strangled with the wildè beres ;
The sowè freten the child right in the
   cradel ;   2019
The cook y-scalded, for al his longè ladel.
  Noght was forgeten by the infortune
   of Marte,
The cartere over-ryden with his carte ;
Under the wheel ful lowe he lay adoun.

riflers of the dead after a battle. But in Wright's
own quotation from the *Compost of Ptolomeus* it
is said, ' Under Mars is borne *theves* and *robbers*
that kepe hye wayes.'
2009. *Meschaunce.* Statius 'virtus tristissima.'
2012. *Armed compleint.* Statius has 'Mors
armata.'
2014. *and nat,* E *and nat oon,* a good reading
if we omit *and.*
2017. *the shippes hoppesteres,* the dancing
ships. Chaucer is translating *Teseide,* vii. 37,
'Vedevi ancor le navi bellatrici,' and probably
read the last word ' ballatrici ' in error.
2018. *huntè,* hunter. H ends the line 'with
wilde bores corage' to rhyme with 'rage' in
2011, omitting all between.

Ther were also of Martes divisioun,
The barbour and the bocher, and the smyth
That forgeth sharpè swerdès on his styth ;
And al above, depeynted in a tour,
Saugh I Conquést sittynge in greet honour
With the sharpè swerd over his heed
Hángynge by a soutil twynès threed. 2030
  Depeynted was the slaughtre of Julius,
Of grete Nero, and of Antonius, —
Al be that thilkè tyme they were unborn,
Yet was hir deth depeynted ther-biforn
By manasynge of Mars, right by figure,
So it was shewèd in that portreiture
As is depeynted in the sterres above
Who shal be slayn or ellès deed for love ;
Suffiseth oon ensample in stories olde, 2039
I may nat rekene hem allè though I wolde.
  The statue of Mars upon a cartè stood,
Armèd, and lookèd grym as he were wood,
And over his heed ther shynen two figures
Of sterrès that been clepéd in scriptures,
That oon Puella, that oother Rubëus.
This god of armès was arrayèd thus :
A wolf ther stood biforn hym at his feet
With eyen rede, and of a man he eet.
With soutil pencel depeynted was this
  storie   2049
In rédoutynge of Mars and of his glorie.
  Now to the temple of Dyane the chaste,
As shortly as I kan, I wol me haste
To tellè yow al the descripsioun.
Depeynted been the wallès up and doun
Of huntyng and of shamefast chastitee.
Ther saugh I how woful Calistopee,
Whan that Diane agrevèd was with here,
Was turnèd from a womman to a bere,
And after was she maad the loodè-sterre ;
Thus was it peynted, I kan sey yow no
  ferre.   2060
Hir sone is eek a sterre, as men may see.

2025. *barbour, i.e.* barber - surgeon. In
Wright's extract from the *Compost of Ptolomeus* it is said, 'These men of Mars . . . wyll
be gladly Smythes or workers of iron . . . good
to be a barboure and a blode letter and to drawe
tethe.'
2037. *sterres,* E⁶ *sertres* or *certres.*
2045. *Puella.* 'Signifieth Mars retrograde
and Rubeus, Mars direct' (Speght).
2049. *depeynted was,* E⁶ *was depeynted.*
2056. *Calistopee, i.e.* the Arcadian nymph
Callisto.
2061. *eek a sterre,* the constellation Boötes.

Ther saugh I Dane, y-turned til a tree,—
I menè nat the goddessè Diane,
But Penneus doughter which that hightè
    Dane.
Ther saugh I Attheon an hert y-maked,
For vengeance that he saugh Diane al
    naked ;
I saugh how that his houndès have hym
    caught
And freeten hym, for that they knewe
    hym naught.
    Yet peynted was a litel forther moor
How Atthalante hunted the wildè boor,
And Meleagre, and many another mo,
For which Dyanè wroghte hym care and
    wo.
Ther saugh I many another wonder storie,
The whiche me list nat drawen to memórie.
    This goddesse on an hert ful hyè seet,
With smalè houndès al aboute hir feet,
And undernethe hir feet she hadde a
    moone,
Wexynge it was, and sholdè wanye soone.
In gaudè grene hir statue clothèd was,
With bowe in honde and arwès in a cas ;
Hir eyen castè she ful lowe adoun   2081
Ther Pluto hath his derkè regioun.
    A womman travaillynge was hire biforn,
But, for hir child so longe was unborn,
Ful pitously Lucyna gan she calle
And seydè, 'Helpe, for thou mayst best
    of alle.'
Wel koude he peynten lifly, that it wroghte ;
With many a floryn he the hewès boghte.
    Now been the lystès maad, and Theseüs,
That at his gretè cost arrayèd thus   2090
The templès, and the theatre every deel,
Whan it was doon hym lykèd wonder weel ;
But stynte I wole of Theseüs a lite,
And speke of Palamon and of Arcite.
    The day approcheth of hir retournynge,
That everich sholde an hundred knyghtès
    brynge,
The bataille to dareyne, as I yow tolde,

2062. *Dane*, i.e. Daphne.
2065. *Attheon*, Actæon.
2070. *Atthalante*, Atalanta.
2072. *kym*, H *hem*.
2085. *Lucyna*, the name of Diana as helper of
women in labour.
2089. *the*, H⁶ *thise*.

And til Atthenes, hir covenantz for to
    holde,
Hath everich of hem broght an hundred
    knyghtes   2099
Wel armèd for the werre at allè rightes ;
And sikerly ther trowèd many a man
That never, sithen that the world bigan,
As for to speke of knyghthod of hir hond,
As fer as God hath makèd see or lond,
Nas, of so fewe, so noble a compaignye ;
For every wight that lovède chivalrye
And wolde, his thankès, han a passant
    name,
Hath preyèd that he myghte been of that
    game ;
And wel was hym that ther-to chosen was ;
For if ther fille tomorwè swich a caas,   2110
Ye knowen wel that every lusty knyght
That loveth paramours, and hath his
    myght,
Were it in Engèlond or ellès-where,
They wolde, hir thankès, wilnen to be
    there.
To fightè for a lady,—*benedicitee !*
It were a lusty sightè for to see.
And right so ferden they with Palamon.
With hym ther wenten knyghtès many
    oon ;
Som wol ben armèd in an haubergeoun,
In a bristplate and in a light gypoun ;
And somme woln have a pairè platès
    large ;   2121
And somme woln have a Pruce sheeld or
    a targe ;
Somme woln ben armèd on hir leggès weel,
And have an ax, and somme a mace of
    steel ;
Ther is no newè gyse that it nas old.
Armèd were they, as I have yow told,
Everych after his opinion.
    Ther maistow seen comynge with
    Palamon
Lygurge hymself, the gretè kyng of Trace ;
Blak was his berd, and manly was his
    face ;   2130
The cercles of his eyen in his heed,
They glowèden bitwyxen yelow and reed ;
And lik a grifphon lookèd he aboute,

2129. *Lygurge*, Lycurgus. In the *Teseide* he
fights on Arcite's side.

With kempë heeris on his browës stoute;
His lymës grete, his brawnës harde and stronge,
His shuldrës brode, his armës rounde and longe,
And, as the gysë was in his contree,
Ful hye upon a chaar of gold stood he,
With fourë whitë bolës in the trays.
In stede of cote-armure, over his harnays   2140
With naylës yelewe, and brighte as any gold,
He hadde a berës skyn, col-blak, for-old.
His longë heer was kembd bihynde his bak ;
As any ravenes fethere it shoon for-blak ;
A wrethe of gold, arm-greet, of hugë wighte,
Upon his heed, set ful of stonës brighte,
Of fynë rubyes and of dyamauntz ;
Aboute his chaar ther wenten white alauntz,
Twenty and mo, as grete as any steer,
To hunten at the leoun or the deer ;   2150
And folwëd hym with mosel faste y-bounde,
Colered of gold and tourettes fylëd rounde.
An hundred lordës hadde he in his route,
Armëd ful wel, with hertës stierne and stoute.

With Arcita, in stories as men fynde,
The grete Emetrëus, the kyng of Inde,
Upon a steedë bay, trappëd in steel,
Covered in clooth of gold, dyapred weel,
Cam ridynge, lyk the god of armës, Mars.
His cote armurë was of clooth of Tars
Couchëd with perlës, white and rounde and grete ;   2161
His sadel was of brend gold, newe y-bete;
A mantelet upon his shulder hangynge,
Brat-ful of rubyes rede, as fyr sparklynge ;
His crispë heer, lyk ryngës was y-ronne,
And that was yelow, and glytered as the sonne.
His nose was heigh, his eyen bright citryn ;
His lippës rounde, his colour was sangwyn ;

A fewë frakenes in his face y-spreynd,
Bitwixen yelow and somdel blak y-meynd,
And as a leoun he his lookyng caste.   2171
Of fyve and twenty yeer his age I caste ;
His berd was wel bigonnë for to sprynge;
His voys was as a trompë thondrynge ;
Upon his heed he wered, of laurer grene,
A gerland, fressh and lusty for to sene.
Upon his hand he bar, for his deduyt,
An egle tame, as any lilye whyt.
An hundred lordës hadde he with hym there,
Al armëd, save hir heddes, in al hir gere,
Ful richëly in allë maner thynges ;   2181
For trusteth wel that dukës, erlës, kynges,
Were gadered in this noble compaignye,
For love and for encrees of chivalrye.
Aboute this kyng ther ran on every part
Ful many a tame leoun and leopard.
And in this wise these lordës, alle and some,
Been on the Sonday to the citee come
Aboutë pryme, and in the toun alight.

   This Thesëus, this duc, this worthy knyght,   2190
Whan he had broght hem into his citee
And innëd hem, everich in his degree,
He festeth hem, and dooth so greet labóur
To esen hem, and doon hem al honóur,
That yet men weneth that no mannës wit
Of noon estaat ne koude amenden it.

   The mynstralcye, the service at the feeste,
The gretë yiftes to the meeste and leeste,
The riche array of Thesëus paleys,
Ne who sat first, ne last, upon the deys,
What ladyes fairest been, or best daunsynge,   2201
Or which of hem kan dauncen best and synge,
Ne who moost felyngly speketh of love ;
What haukës sitten on the perche above,
What houndës liggen in the floor adoun,—
Of al this make I now no mencioun,
But al theffect, that thynketh me the beste ;

2160. *clooth of Tars, i.e.* Tartary, Chinese stuffs which passed through Tartary on their way to Europe.

2177. *deduyt*, delight ; H², *delite*.
2188. *the Sonday, i.e.* the 'this day fifty wykes' from the Saturday May 5th in which Palamon and Arcite first fought (see l. 1850).
2207. *al*, H *of*, perhaps rightly.

Now cometh the point, and herkneth if
    yow leste.
The Sonday nyght, er day bigan to
    sprynge,   2209
Whan Palamon the larkė herdė synge,
Al though it nere nat day by hourės two,
Yet song the larke, and Palamon also.
With hooly herte and with an heigh corage,
He roos to wenden on his pilgrymage
Unto the blisful Citherea benigne,—
I menė Venus, honurable and digne,—
And in hir houre he walketh forth a paas
Unto the lystės, ther hire temple was,
And doun he kneleth with ful humble cheer
And hertė soor, and seyde in this
    manere :—   2220
   ' Faireste of faire, o lady myn, Venus,
Doughter to Jove, and spouse of Vulcanus,
Thow gladere of the mount of Citheron,
For thilkė love thow haddest to Adoon,
Have pitee of my bittrė teeris smerte,
And taak myn humble preyere at thyn
    herte.
Allas ! I ne havė no langage to telle
Theffectės ne the tormentz of myn helle ;
Myn hertė may myne harmės nat biwreye ;
I am so cónfus that I kan noght seye.   2230
But mercy, lady bright, that knowest weele
My thought, and seest what harmės that
    I feele,
Considere al this and rewe upon my soore
As wisly as I shal for evermoore,
Emforth my myght, thy trewė servant be,
And holden werre alwey with chastitee ;
That make I myn avow, so ye me helpe.
I kepė noght of armės for to yelpe.
Ne I ne axe nat tomorwe to have victórie,
Ne rénoun in this cas, ne veynė glorie   2240
Of pris of armės, blowen up and doun,
But I wolde have fully possessioun
Of Emelye, and dye in thy servyse.

2217. *in hir houre.* The first hour of each day
belonged to that one of the seven deities, Saturn,
Jupiter, Mars, Sol, Venus, Mercury, Luna, to
whom the day was dedicated ; the second to the
next on the list, the third to the next, and so on.
Sunday being dedicated to Sol, Venus would
preside over the second, ninth, sixteenth and
twenty-third hours, the last of which would begin
two hours before day-break on Monday.
2219. *with ful,* H⁶ *and with.*
2220. *and seyde in this manere,* H⁶ *he seide as
ye shal here.*

Fynd thow the manere how, and in what
    wyse ;
I recchė nat, but it may bettre be,
To have victorie of hem, or they of me,
So that I have my lady in myne armes,
For though so be that Mars is god of
    armes,
Youre vertu is so greet in hevene above
That, if yow list, I shal wel have my love.
Thy temple wol I worshipe evermo,   2251
And on thyn auter, wher I ride or go,
I wol doon sacrifice and firės beete ;
And if ye wol nat so, my lady sweete,
Thanne preye I thee, tomorwe with a spere
That Arcita me thurgh the hertė bere ;
Thanne rekke I noght, whan I have lost
    my lyf,
Though that Arcita wynne hire to his wyf :
This is theffect and ende of my preyėre,—
Yif me my love, thow blisful lady deere.'
   Whan the orison was doon of Palamon,
His sacrifice he dide, and that anon,
Ful pitously with allė circumstaunces,
Al telle I noght as now his observaunces ;
But attė laste the statue of Venus shook
And made a signė, wher-by that he took
That his preyėre accepted was that day ;
For thogh the signė shewėd a delay,
Yet wiste he wel that graunted was his
    boone,
And with glad herte he wente hym hoom
    ful soone.   2270
   The thridde houre in - equál that
    Palamon
Bigan to Venus temple for to gon,
Up roos the sonne and up roos Emelye,
And to the temple of Dyane gan she hye.
Hir maydens, that she thider with hire
    ladde,
Ful redily with hem the fyr they hadde,
Thencens, the clothės, and the remenant al
That to the sacrificė longen shal,
The hornės fulle of meeth, as was the
    gyse,—   2279

2271. *The thridde houre in-equal,* three hours
after 'two hours before sunrise,' *i.e.* the first
hour on Monday, that dedicated to Luna or
Diana : *in-equal* shows that the reckoning is by
planetary hours, which vary with the length of
the day.
2274. *she,* om. E⁵.

Ther lakkėd noght to doon hir sacrifise.
Smokynge the temple, ful of clothės
faire,
This Emelye, with hertė debonaire,
Hir body wessh with water of a welle ;
But how she dide hir ryte I dar nat telle,
But it be any thing in general ;
And yet it were a game to heeren al ;
To hym that meneth wel it were no charge,
But it is good a man been at his large.
Hir brightė heer was kempd, un-
tressėd al,
A coroune of a grene ook cerial   2290
Upon hir heed was set, ful faire and meete;
Two fyrės on the auter gan she beete,
And dide hir thyngės, as men may biholde
In Stace of Thebės, and thise bookės olde.
Whan kyndled was the fyr, with pitous
cheere,
Unto Dyane she spak as ye may heere :—
'O chastė goddesse of the wodės grene,
To whom bothe hevene and erthe and
see is sene,
Queene of the regne of Pluto, derk and
lowe,
Goddesse of maydens, that myn herte hast
knowe   2300
Ful many a yeer, and woost what I desire,
As keepe me fro thy vengeaunce and
thyn ire,
That Attheon aboughtė cruelly ;
Chastė goddessė, wel wostow that I
Desire to ben a mayden al my lyf,
Ne never wol I be no love, ne wyf.
I am, thow woost, yet of thy compaignye,
A mayde, and love huntynge and venerye,
And for to walken in the wodės wilde,
And noght to ben a wyf and be with childe ;
Noght wol I knowe the compaignye of man.
Now helpe me, lady, sith ye may and kan,
For tho thre formes that thou hast in thee.
And Palamon, that hath swich love to me,
And eek Arcite, that loveth me so soore,

2290. *grene ook cerial*, Boccaccio's ' quercia
cereale,' the holm oak.
2294. *In Stace of Thebes, i.e.* the *Thebais* of
Statius, where, however, no description of these
observances occurs.
2303. *Attheon*, Actæon.
2313. *tho thre formes.* Diana, a ' diva
triformis,' was known as Luna in heaven, Diana
or Lucina on earth, and Proserpina in hell.

This grace I preyė thee withoutė moore ;
As sendė love and pees bitwixe hem two,
And fro me turne awey hir hertės so
That al hire hootė love and hir desir,
And al hir bisy torment and hir fir,   2320
Be queynt, or turnėd in another place.
And if so be thou wolt do me no grace,
Or if my destynee be shapen so
That I shal nedės have oon of hem two,
As sende me hym that moost desireth me.
Bihoold, goddesse of clenė chastitee,
The bittrė teeres that on my chekės falle.
Syn thou art mayde, and kepere of us alle,
My maydenhede thou kepe and wel
conserve   2329
And whil I lyve a mayde I wol thee serve.'
The firės brenne upon the auter cleere
Whil Emelye was thus in hir preyėre,
But sodeynly she saugh a sightė queynte,
For right anon oon of the fyrės queynte,
And quyked agayn, and after that, anon
That oother fyr was queynt and al agon,
And as it queynte it made a whistėlynge,
As doon thise wetė brondes in hir
brennynge ;
And at the brondės ende out-ran anon
As it were blody dropės, many oon ;   2340
For which so soore agast was Emelye
That she was wel ny mad, and gan to crye,
For she ne wistė what it signyfied,
But oonly for the feere thus hath she cried,
And weep that it was pitee for to heere;
And ther-with-al Dyanė gan appeere,
With bowe in honde, right as an hunteresse,
And seydė, ' Doghter, stynt thyn hevy-
nesse.
Among the goddės hye it is affermed,   2349
And by eternė word writen and confermed,
Thou shalt ben wedded unto oon of tho
That han for thee so muchel care and wo,
But unto which of hem I may nat telle.
Farwel, for I ne may no lenger dwelle.
The firės whiche that on myn auter brenne
Shulle thee declaren, er that thou go
henne,
Thyn áventure of love, as in this cas.'
And with that word the arwės in the caas
Of the goddessė clateren faste and rynge,

2338. *brondes*, brands ; H, *as doth a wete brond
in his brennyng.*

And forth she wente and made a
    vanysshynge,   2360
For which this Emelye astonéd was,
And seydé, ' What amounteth this, allas !
I putté me in thy proteccioun,
Dyane, and in thy disposicioun.'
And hoom she goth anon the nexté weye.
This is theffect, ther is namoore to seye.
    The nexté houre of Mars folwynge this,
Arcite unto the temple walkéd is
Of fiersé Mars, to doon his sacrifise   2369
With alle the rytés of his payen wyse.
With pitous herte and heigh devocioun
Right thus to Mars he seyde his
    orisoun :—
    ' O strongé god, that in the regnés colde
Of Trace honóured art and lord y-holde,
And hast in every regne and every lond
Of armés al the brydel in thyn hond,
And hem fortúnest as thee lyst devyse,
Accepte of me my pitous sacrifise.
If so be that my youthé may deserve,
And that my myght be worthy for to serve
Thy godhede, that I may been oon of
    thyne,   2381
Thanne preye I thee to rewe upon my pyne.
For thilké peyne, and thilké hooté fir,
In which thou whilom brendest for desir,
Whan that thou usedeste the béautee
Of fairé, yongé, fresshé Venus free,
And haddest hire in armés at thy wille,
Al-though thee onés on a tyme mysfille,
Whan Vulcanus hadde caught thee in
    his las,   2389
And foond thee liggynge by his wyf, allas !
For thilké sorwé that was in thyn herte,
Have routhe as wel upon my peynés smerte.
I am yong and unkonnynge, as thow woost,
And, as I trowe, with love offended moost
That ever was any lyvés creature ;
For she that dooth me al this wo endure
Ne reccheth never wher I synke or fleete.
And wel I woot, er she me mercy heete,
I moot with strengthé wynne hire in the
    place ;   2399
And wel I woot withouten helpe or grace
Of thee, ne may my strengthé noght availle.

2367. *The nexte houre of Mars*, the fourth
hour of the day.
2369. *Of fierse Mars*, H *To fyry Mars.*

Thanne helpe me, lord, tomorwe in my
    bataille,
For thilké fyr that whilom brenté thee,
As well as thilké fyr now brenneth me,
And do that I tomorwe have victorie.
Myn be the travaille, and thyn be the
    glorie !
Thy sovereyn temple wol I moost
    honouren
Of any place, and alwey moost labouren
In thy plesaunce, and in thy craftés
    stronge ;   2409
And in thy temple I wol my baner honge,
And alle the armés of my compaignye,
And ever mo, un-to that day I dye,
Eterné fir I wol biforn thee fynde :
And eek to this avow I wol me bynde.
My beerd, myn heer, that hongeth long
    adoun,
That never yet ne felte offensioun
Of rasour nor of shere, I wol thee yive,
And ben thy trewé servant whil I lyve.
Now, lord, have routhe upon my sorwés
    soore,   2419
Yif me the victorie, I aske thee namoore !'
    The preyére stynt of Arcita the stronge,
The ryngés on the temple dore that honge,
And eek the dorés, clatereden ful faste,
Of which Arcita som-what hym agaste.
The fyrés brenden upon the auter brighte,
That it gan al the temple for to lighte ;
And sweeté smel the ground anon up yaf,
And Arcita anon his hand up-haf,
And moore encens into the fyr he caste,
With othere rytés mo, and atté last   2430
The statue of Mars bigan his hauberk
    rynge ;
And with that soun he herde a mur-
    murynge
Ful lowe and dym, and seydé thus :
    ' Victorie !'
For which he yaf to Mars honour and
    glorie.
And thus with joye and hopé wel to fare,
Arcite anon unto his inne is fare,
As fayn as fowel is of the brighté sonne.
    And right anon swich strif ther is
    bigonne
For thilké grauntyng in the hevene above,
Bitwixé Venus, the goddesse of love,   2440

D   33

And Mars, the stiernė god armypotente,
That Juppiter was bisy it to stente ;
Til that the palė Saturnus the colde,
That knew so manye of aventures olde,
Foond in his olde experience an art
That he ful soone hath plesėd every part.
As sooth is seyd, elde hath greet ávantáge ;
In elde is bothė wysdom and uságe ;
Men may the olde at-renne and noght
    at-rede.   2449
Saturne anon, to stynten strif and drede,
Al be it that it is agayn his kynde,
Of al this strif he gan remédie fynde.
    ' My deerė doghter Venus,' quod
        Saturne,
' My cours, that hath so wydė for to turne,
Hath moorė power than woot any man ;
Myn is the drenchyng in the see so wan,
Myn is the prison in the derkė cote,
Myn is the stranglyng and hangyng by
    the throte,
The murmure and the cherlės rėbellyng,
The groynynge and thc pryvee empoy-
    sonyng ;   2460
I do vengeance and pleyn correccioun
Whil I dwelle in signe of the leoun ;
Myn is the ruyne of the hyė halles,
The fallynge of the toures and of the
    walles,
Upon the mynour or the carpenter,—
I slow Sampsoun, in shakynge the piler,—
And mynė be the maladýės colde,
The derkė tresons and the castės olde ;
My lookyng is the fader of pestilence ;
Now weepe namoore, I shal doon dili-
    gence   2470
That Palamon, that is thyn owene knyght,
Shal have his lady, as thou hast him hight.
Though Mars shal helpe his knyght, yet
    nathėlees,

Bitwixė yow ther moot be som tyme pees,
Al be ye noght of o compleccioun,
That causeth al day swich divisioun.
I am thyn aiel, redy at thy wille ;
Weepe now namoore, I wol thy lust
    fulfille.'
    Now wol I stynten of the goddes above,
Of Mars, and of Venús, goddesse of love,
And tellė yow, as pleynly as I kan,   2481
The grete effect for which that I bygan.

PART IV

    Greet was the feeste in Atthenės that
        day,
And eek the lusty seson of that May
Made every wight to been in such
    plesaunce,
That al that Monday justen they and
    daunce,
And spenten it in Venus heigh servyse ;
But, by the cause that they sholdė ryse
Éerly, for to seen the gretė fight,
Unto hir restė wenten they at nyght.   2490
And on the morwė, whan that day gan
    sprynge,
Of hors and harneys noyse and claterynge
Ther was in hostelryës al aboute,
And to the paleys rood ther many a route
Of lordės, upon steedės and palfreys.
Ther maystow seen divisynge of harneys
So unkouth and so riche, and wroght so
    weel
Of goldsmythrye, of browdynge, and of
    steel,
The sheeldės brighte, testerės, and
    trappúres ;
Gold-hewen helmės, hauberkes, cote
    armúres ;   2500
Lordės in paramentz on hir courseres ;
Knyghtės of retenue, and eek squieres,
Nailynge the speres, and helmės bokėlynge,
Giggynge of sheeldės, with layneres
    lacynge ;
There, as nede is, they weren no thyng
    ydel.
The fomy steedės on the golden brydel
Gnawynge, and faste the armurers also,

2445. *an*, E² *and*.
2449. The line is a proverb.
2454. *My cours*. The reference is to the supposed malign influence of the planet Saturn :
for its 'width' Wright quotes the *Compost of
Ptolomeus*, which gives Saturn an orbit of more
than thirty years.
2459. *cherles rebellyng*. Possibly Chaucer had
in his mind 'he Jacke Strawe and his meynee';
cp. Group B₁ l. 4584.
2462. *in signe of the leoun*. Prof. Skeat notes
that the first ten degrees of the sign *Leo* are
called the 'face of Saturn.'

2500. *Gold-hewen*, H *Gold-beten*.

34

With fyle and hamer, prikynge to and fro;
Yemen on foote, and communes many oon
With shorté stavés, thikke as they may
    goon;   2510
Pýpés, trompés, nakers, clariounes,
That in the bataille blowen blody sounes;
The paleys ful of peplés up and doun,—
Heere thre, ther ten, holdynge hir
    questioun,
Dyvynynge of thise Thebane knyghtés two.
Somme seyden thus, somme seyde it shal
    be so,
Somme helden with hym with the blaké
    berd,
Somme with the balled, somme with the
    thikké herd,
Some seyde he lookéd grymme and he
    wolde fighte,
He hath a sparth of twenty pound of
    wighte,—   2520
Thus was the hallé ful of divynynge
Longe after that the sonné gan to sprynge.
    The greté Theseus, that of his sleepe
    awaked
With mynstralcie and noysé that was
    maked,
Heeld yet the chambre of his paleys riche,
Til that the Thebane knyghtés, bothe y-
    liche
Honured, were into the paleys fet.
Duc Theséus was at a wyndow set,
Arrayed right as he were a god in trone.
The peple preesseth thiderward ful soone
Hym for to seen, and doon heigh
    reverence,   2531
And eek to herkne his heste and his
    sentence.
    An heraud on a scaffold made an 'Ho!'
Til al the noyse of peple was y-do;
And whan he saugh the peple of noyse
    al stille
Tho shewéd he the myghty dukés wille.
    ' The lord hath of his heih discrecioun
Considered that it were destruccioun
To gentil blood to fighten in the gyse 2539
Of mortal bataille now in this emprise;
Wherfore, to shapen that they shal nat dye,
He wolde his firsté purpos modifye.
    ' No man ther-fore, up peyne of los of
    lyf,

No maner shot, ne polax, ne shorte knyf,
Into the lystés sende, ne thider brynge;
Ne short swerd, for to stoke with poynt
    bitýnge,
No man ne drawe, ne beré by his syde.
Ne no man shal unto his felawe ryde
But o cours with a sharpe y-groundé spere;
Foyne, if hym list, on foote, hym self to
    were.   2550
And he that is at meschief shal be take,
And noght slayn, but be broght unto the
    stake
Thát shal ben ordeyned on either syde;
But thider he shal by force, and there
    abyde.
    ' And if so falle the chiëftayn be take
On outher syde, or ellés sleen his make,
No lenger shal the turneiyngé laste.
God spedé you! gooth forth, and ley on
    faste!
With long swerd and with maces fighteth
    youre fille.
Gooth now youre wey, this is the lordés
    will.'   2560
    The voys of peple touchédé the hevene,
So loudé cridé they, with murie stevene,
' God savé swich a lord, that is so good,
He wilneth no destruccion of blood!'
    Up goon the trompés and the melodye
And to the lystës rit the compaignye
By ordinance, thurgh-out the citee large,
Hangéd with clooth of gold, and nat
    with sarge.
Ful lik a lord this noble duc gan ryde,
Thise two Thebánes upon either side; 2570
And after rood the queene and Emelye,
And after that another compaignye
Of oon and oother, after hir degre;
And thus they passen thurgh-out the citee,
And to the lystés comé they by tyme.
It nas not of the day yet fully pryme
Whan set was Theséus ful riche and hye,
Ypolita the queene and Emelye,
And othere ladys in degrees aboute.
Unto the seettés preesseth al the route,
And westward, thurgh the gatés under
    Marte,   2581
Arcite, and eek the hondred of his parte,
With baner reed is entred right anon.

2555. *chieftayn, cheventein* H².

35

And in that selvè moment Palamon
Is under Venus, estward in the place,
With baner whyt, and hardy chiere and
   face.
In al the world to seken up and doun
So evene, withouten variacioun,
Ther nerè swichè compaignýes tweye ;
For ther was noon so wys that koudè seye
That any hadde of oother avauntage 2591
Of worthynesse, ne of estaat, ne age,
So evene were they chosen, for to gesse ;
And in two rengès fairè they hem dresse.
   Whan that hir namès rad were
     everichon,
That in hir nombrè gylè were ther noon,
Tho were the gatès shet, and cried was
   loude,
'Do now youre devoir, yongè knyghtès
   proude !'
   The heraudes lefte hir prikyng up and
     doun ;   2599
Now ryngen trompès loude and clarioun ;
Ther is namoore to seyn, but west and est
In goon the speres ful sadly in arrest ;
In gooth the sharpè spore into the syde.
Ther seen men who kan juste and who
   kan ryde ;
Ther shyveren shaftès upon sheeldès
   thikke ;
He feeleth thurgh the hertè-spoon the
   prikke.
Up spryngen sperès twenty foot on highte ;
Out gooth the swerdès as the silver
   brighte ;
The helmès they to-hewen and to-shrede,
Out brest the blood with stiernè stremès
   rede ;   2610
With myghty maces the bonès they to-
   breste.
He, thurgh the thikkeste of the throng
   gan threste,
Ther, stomblen steedès stronge, and doun
   gooth al ;
He, rolleth under foot as dooth a bal ;
He, foyneth on his feet with his tronchoun,
And he hym hurtleth with his hors adoun ;
He, thurgh the body is hurt and sithen
   y-take,
Maugree his heed, and broght unto the
   stake,

As forward was, right ther he moste abyde.
Another lad is on that oother syde.   2620
And som tyme dooth hem Thesèus to
   reste,
Hem to refresshe and drynken, if hem leste.
Ful ofte a-day han thise Thebánes two,
Togydre y-met and wroght his felawe wo ;
Unhorsèd hath ech oother of hem tweye.
Ther nas no tygre in the vale of Galgo-
   pheye,
Whan that hir whelpe is stole whan it is
   lite,
So crueel on the hunte, as is Arcite
For jelous herte upon this Palamoun ;
Ne in Belmarye ther nys so fel leoun, 2630
That hunted is, or for his hunger wood,
Ne of his praye desireth so the blood,
As Palamoun, to sleen his foo Arcite.
The jelous strokès on hir helmes byte ;
Out renneth blood on bothe hir sydès rede.
   Som tyme an ende ther is of every dede,
For, er the sonne unto the restè wente,
The strongè kyng Emetrèus gan hente
This Palamon, as he faught with Arcite,
And made his swerd depe in his flessh to
   byte,   2640
And by the force of twenty is he take
Unyolden, and y-drawe unto the stake.
And in the rescus of this Palamoun
The strongè kyng Lygurge is born adoun,
And kyng Emetrèus, for al his strengthe,
Is born out of his sadel a swerdès lengthe :
So hitte him Palamoun, er he were take ;
But al for noght ; he was broght to the
   stake.
His hardy hertè myghte hym helpè naught :
He moste abydè, whan that he was caught,
By force, and eek by composicioun.   2651
   Who sorweth now but woful Palamoun,
That moot namoorè goon agayn to fighte ?
And whan that Theseus haddè seyn this
   sighte
Unto the folk that foghten thus echon
He crydè, 'Hoo ! namoore, for it is doon !
I wol be trewè juge, and no partie ;
Arcite of Thebès shall have Emelie

2626. *Galgopheye*. Prof. Skeat identifies this
with the valley of Gargaphie (in Bœotia), where
Actæon was torn in pieces. Tyrwhitt suggests a
town called Galapha in Mauritania Tingitana.
2630. *Belmarye*, perhaps Palmyra.

That by his fortune hath hire faire y-
   wonne.'
   Anon ther is a noyse of peple bigonne,
For joye of this, so loude and heighe
   with-alle,   2661
It semèd that the lystès sholde falle.
   What kan now faire Venus doon above?
What seith she now, what dooth this
   queene of love,
But wepeth so, for wantynge of hir wille,
Til that hir teerès in the lystès fille?
She seyde, 'I am ashamèd doutèlees.'
Saturnus seydè, 'Doghter, hoold thy pees,
Mars hath his wille, his knyght hath al
   his boone,
And, by myn heed, thow shalt been esèd
   soone.'   2670
   The trompès, with the loudè myn-
   stralcie,
The heraudes, that ful loudè yolle and crie,
Been in hire wele, for joye of daun Arcite.
But herkneth me, and stynteth now a lite,
Which a myrácle ther bifel anon.
   This fierse Arcite hath of his helm y-don,
And on a courser, for to shewe his face,
He priketh endèlong the largè place,
Lokynge upward up-on this Emelye,   2679
And she agayn hym caste a freendlich eye
(For wommen, as to speken in comune,
Thei folwen all the favour of Fortune),
And was al his, in chiere, as in his herte.
   Out of the ground a fyr infernal sterte,
From Pluto sent, at réqueste of Saturne,
For which his hors for ferè gan to turne,
And leep aside, and foundred as he leep,
And er that Arcitè may taken keep,
He pighte hym on the pomel of his heed,
That in the place he lay as he were deed,
His brest to-brosten with his sadel-bowe.
As blak he lay as any cole or crowe,

2683. *And was al his, in chiere, as in his
herte.* This is Dr. Furnivall's emendation, no
MS. containing the first *in*—'she was all his in
her looks, as the queen of his heart'; H reads
and for *as*; Hengwrt, *And she was al his
cheers*, etc., *i.e.* 'all his delight, as regarded his
heart,' but this is not the use of *cheers* here
wanted.
2684. *fyr, E³ furie.* In Boccaccio (*Tes.* ix. 4)
it is a fury raised by Venus.
2691. *sadel-bowe.* The 'bow' was a curved
piece of wood fixed before and behind the saddle
to hold the rider in his seat.

So was the blood y-ronnen in his face.
Anon he was y-born out of the place,
With hertè soor, to Thesëus paleys.
Tho was he korven out of his harneys,
And in a bed y-brought ful faire and blyve;
For he was yet in memorie and alyve,
And alwey criynge after Emelye.   2699
   Duc Thesëus with al his compaignye
Is comen hoom to Atthenes his citee,
With allè blisse and greet solempnitee;
Al be it that this áventure was falle,
He noldè noght disconforten hem alle,—
Men seyden eek that Arcite shal nat dye,
He shal been heelèd of his maladye.
   And of another thyng they weren as
   fayn,
That of hem allè was ther noon y-slayn;
Al were they soore y-hurt, and namely oon,
That with a spere was thirlèd his brest
   boon.   2710
To otherè woundes and to broken armes,
Somme hadden salvès and somme hadden
   charmes,
Fermaciës of herbès, and eek save
They dronken, for they wolde hir lymès
   have.
For which this noble duc, as he wel kan,
Conforteth and honóureth every man,
And madè revel al the longè nyght
Unto the straungè lordès, as was right;
Ne ther was holden no disconfitynge
But as a justès, or a tourneiynge;   2720
For soothly ther was no disconfiture,
For fallyng nys nat but an áventure,
Ne to be lad by force unto the stake
Unyolden, and with twenty knyghtès take,
Ó persone allone, withouten mo,
And haryed forth by armè, foot and too,
And eke his steedè dryven forth with
   staves,
With footmen, bothè yemen and eek
   knaves,—
It nas aretted hym no vileynye;
Ther may no man clepen it cowardye.   2730
   For which anon duc Thesëus leet crye,
To stynten allè rancour and envye,
The gree as wel of o syde as of oother,
And eyther syde y-lìk as ootheres brother;
And yaf hem yiftès after hir degree,
And fully heeld a feestè dayès three,

And convoyèd the kyngès worthily
Out of his toun, a journee largèly,
And hoom wente every man the rightè
　　way ;
Ther was namoore, but ' Fare wel!'
　　' Have good day ! '　　　　2740
Of this bataille I wol namoore endite,
But speke of Palamoun and of Arcyte.
　　Swelleth the brest of Arcite, and the
　　　　soore
Encreesseth at his hertè moore and moore.
The clothered blood, for any lechécraft,
Corrupteth, and is in his bouk y-laft,
That neither veynè-blood ne ventusynge,
Ne drynke of herbès may ben his
　　helpynge ;
The vertu èxpulsif, or animal,
Fro thilkè vertu clepéd natural,　　2750
Ne may the venym voyden ne expelle.
The pipès of his longès gonne to swelle,
And every lacerte in his brest adoun
Is shent with venym and corrupcioun.
Hym gayneth neither, for to gete his lif,
Vomyt upward, ne dounward laxatif ;
Al is to-brosten thilkè regioun ;
Nature hath now no dominacioun ;
And certeinly, ther Nature wol nat wirche,
Farewel, phisik ! go ber the man to chirche!
This al and som, that Arcita moot dye,
For which he sendeth after Emelye,
And Palamon, that was his cosyn deere.
Thanne seyde he thus as ye shal after
　　heere :
　　' Naught may the woful spirit in myn
　　herte
Declare o point of alle my sorwès smerte
To yow, my lady, that I lovè moost,
But I biquethe the servyce of my goost
To yow aboven every creäture,　　2769
Syn that my lyf ne may no lenger dure.
Allas the wo ! allas, the peynès stronge,
That I for yow have suffred, and so longe !
Allas, the deeth ! allas, myn Emelye !
Allas, departynge of our compaignye !
Allas, myn hertès queene ! allas, my wyf !
Myn hertès lady, endere of my lyf !
What is this world ? what asketh men to
　　have ?
Now with his love, now in his coldè grave

Allone, withouten any compaignye.　2779
Farewel, my swetè foo, myn Emelye !
And softè taak me in youre armès tweye
For love of God, and herkneth what I seye.
　' I have heer with my cosyn Palamon
Had strif and rancour, many a day agon,
For love of yow, and for my jalousye,
And Juppiter so wys my soulè gye
To speken of a servaunt proprely,
With allè circumstances trewèly,—
That is to seyn, trouthe, honour, and
　　knyghthede,
Wysdom, humblesse, estaat and heigh
　　kynrede,　　　　　　　　　　2790
Fredom, and al that longeth to that art,—
So Juppiter have of my soulè part,
As in this world right now ne knowe I non
So worthy to ben loved as Palamon,
That serveth yow and wol doon al his lyf.
And if that ever ye shul ben a wyf,
Forget nat Palamon, the gentil man,'—
And with that word his spechè faillè gan,
For from his feet up to his brest was come
The coold of deeth, that hadde him over·
　　come ;　　　　　　　　　　2800
And yet moore-over, in his armès two,
The vital strengthe is lost and al ago.
Oonly the intellect, withouten moore
That dwellèd in his hertè syk and soore,
Gan faillen when the hertè feltè deeth,
Duskèd his eyen two and faillèd breeth.
But on his lady yet caste he his eye ;
His lastè word was, ' Mercy, Emelye ! '
His spirit chaungèd hous, and wentè ther,
As I cam never, I kan nat tellen wher.
Therfore I stynte, I nam no divinistre ;
Of soulès fynde I nat in this registre,
Ne me ne list thilke opinions to telle,
Of hem, though that they writen wher
　　they dwelle.
Arcite is coold, ther Mars his soulè gye ;
Now wol I speken forth of Emelye.
　　Shrighte Emelye, and howleth Palamon,
And Thesëus his suster took anon
Swownynge, and baar hire fro the corps
　　away.
What helpeth it to tarien forth the day,

2799. *feet*, EH³ *herte* ; Petworth, *for from his
fete unto the herte.*
2801. *in*, E⁶ *for in.*

2770. *ne*, supplied by Tyrwhitt.

To tellen how she weepe, bothe eve and
   morwe ?   2821
For in swich cas wommen have swiche
   sorwe,
Whan that hir housbonds ben from hem
   ago,
That, for the mooré part, they sorwen so,
Or ellis fallen in swich maladye,
That, at the lasté, certeinly they dye.
   Infinite been the sorwés and the teeres
Of oldé folk, and folk of tendré yeeres,
In all the toun for deeth of this Theban ;
For hym ther wepeth bothé child and
   man ;   2830
So greet a wepyng was ther noon, certayn,
Whan Ector was y-broght al fressh y-slayn
To Troye. Allas ! the pitee that was ther,
Cracchynge of chekés, rentynge eek of
   heer.
   ' Why woldestow be deed ? ' thise
   wommen crye,
' And haddest gold ynough, and Emelye.'
   Nó man myghté gladen Theseus,
Savynge his oldé fader Egeus,
That knew this worldés transmutacioun,
As he hadde seyn it chaungen, up and
   doun,   2840
Joye after wo, and wo after gladnesse,
And shewéd hem ensamples and liknesse.
   ' Right as ther dyéd never man,' quod
   he,
' That he ne lyvede in erthe in som degree,
Right so ther lyvéde never man,' he seyde,
' In all this world, that som tym he ne
   deyde ;
This world nys but a thurghfare ful of wo,
And we been pilgrymes, passynge to and
   fro ;
Deeth is an ende of every worldly soore';
And over al this yet seyde he muchel
   moore   2850
To this effect, ful wisely to enhorte
The peple that they sholde hem reconforte.
   Duc Thesëus, with all his bisy cure,
Cast busily wher that the sepulture
Of goode Arcite may best y-makéd be,

2840. *chaungen*, from Hengwrt ; H *torne* ; E[5]
om.
2849. *worldly*, E *worldés*.
2854. *busily*, E[6] *now*.

And eek moost honurable in his degree ;
And at the laste he took conclusioun
That ther as first Arcite and Palamoun
Hadden for love the bataille hem bitwene,
That in that selvé grové, swoote and
   grene,   2860
Ther as he hadde his amorouse desires,
His compleynte, and for love his hooté
   fires,
He woldé make a fyr in which the office
Fúneral he myghte al accomplice ;
And leet comande anon to hakke and
   hewe
The okés olde, and leye hem on a rewe,
In colpons, wel arrayéd for to brenne.
His officers with swifté feet they renne,
And ryden anon at his comandément.
And after this Thesëus hath y-sent   2870
After a beere, and it al over spradde
With clooth of gold, the richeste that he
   hadde ;
And of the same suyte he clad Arcite.
Upon his hondés hadde he glovés white,
Eek on his heed a coroune of laurer grene,
And in his hond a swerd ful bright and
   kene.
He leyde hym, bare the visage, on the
   beere.
Ther-with he weep that pitee was to heere ;
And, for the peple sholdé seen hym alle,
Whan it was day he broghte hym to the
   halle,   2880
That roreth of the criyng and the soun.
   Tho cam this woful Theban Palamoun,
With flotery berd and ruggy asshy heeres,
In clothés blake, y-droppéd al with teeres ;
And passynge othere of wepynge, Emelye,
The rewefulleste of al the compaignye.
In as muche as the servyce sholdé be
The mooré noble and riche in his degree,
Duc Thesëus leet forth thre steedés
   brynge,
That trappéd were in steele al gliterynge
And covered with the armes of daun
   Arcite.   2891
Upon thise steedes, that weren grete and
   white,
Ther sitten folk, of whiche oon baar his
   sheeld,
Another his spere up in his hondés heeld,

The thridde baar with hym his bowe
    Turkeys   2895
(Of brend gold was the caas, and eek the
    harneys) ;
And riden forth a paas with sorweful
    cheere,
Toward the grove, as ye shul after heere.
The nobleste of the Grekes that ther were
Upon hir shuldres caryeden the beere,
With slake paas, and eyen rede and wete,
Thurgh-out the citee, by the maister strete,
That sprad was al with blak, and wonder
    hye
Right of the same is al the strete y-wrye.
    Upon the right hond wente olde Egeus,
And on that oother syde duc Theseus,
With vessels in hir hand of gold ful fyn
Al ful of hony, milk, and blood, and wyn :
Eek Palamon, with ful greet compaignye,
And after that cam woful Emelye,   2910
With fyr in honde, as was that tyme the
    gyse
To do the office of funeral servyse.
    Heigh labour, and ful greet apparail-
    lynge,
Was at the service and the fyr makynge,
That with his grene tope the heven
    raughte,
And twenty fadme of brede the armes
    straughte ;
This is to seyn, the bowes weren so brode.
Of stree first ther was leyd ful many a lode ;
But how the fyr was maked up on highte,
And eek the names that the trees highte,—
As ook, firre, birch, aspe, alder, holm,
    popeler,   2921
Wylugh, elm, plane, assh, box, chasteyn,
    lynde, laurer,
Mapul, thorn, bech, hasel, ew,
    whippeltre,—
How they weren feld shal nat be toold
    for me ;
Ne how the goddes ronnen up and doun,
Disherited of hire habitacioun,
In whiche they woneden in reste and pees,
Nymphes, fawnes, and amadriades ;
Ne how the beestes and the briddes alle
Fledden for fere, whan the wode was falle ;
Ne how the ground agast was of the light,

That was nat wont to seen the sonne
    bright ;
Ne how the fyr was couched first with
    stree,
And thanne with drye stokkes, cloven a
    thre,
And thanne with grene wode and spicerye,
And thanne with clooth of gold, and
    with perrye,
And gerlandes, hangynge with ful many
    a flour,
The mirre, thencens, with al so greet
    odour ;
Ne how Arcite lay among al this,
Ne what richesse aboute his body is,   2940
Ne how that Emelye, as was the gyse,
Putte in the fyr of funeral servyse,
Ne how she swowned whan men made
    the fyr,
Ne what she spak, ne what was hir desyr,
Ne what jeweles men in the fyr tho caste
Whan that the fyr was greet and brente
    faste ;
Ne how somme caste hir sheeld, and
    somme hir spere,
And of hire vestimentz, whiche that they
    were,
And coppes full of wyn, and milk, and
    blood,
Into the fyr, that brente as it were
    wood ;   2950
Ne how the Grekes, with an huge route,
Thries riden al the place aboute
Upon the left hand, with a loud shoutynge,
And thries with hir speres claterynge,
And thries how the ladyes gonne crye,
And how that lad was homward Emelye ;
Ne how Arcite is brent to asshen colde,
Ne how that lychewake was y-holde
Al thilke nyght ; ne how the Grekes pleye
The wake-pleyes ; ne kepe I nat to seye
Who wrastleth best naked, with oille
    enoynt,   2961
Ne who that baar hym best in no disjoynt.
I wol nat tellen eek how that they goon
Hoom til Atthenes, whan the pleye is
    doon ;
But shortly to the point thanne wol I
    wende,
And maken of my longe tale an ende.

By processe and by lengthe of certeyn
    yeres,
Al styntyd is the moornynge and the teres
Of Grekės, by oon general assent.   2969
Thanne semėd me ther was a parlėment
At Atthenes, upon certein poyntz and caas ;
Among the whichė poyntz y-spoken was,
To have with certein contrees alliaunce,
And have fully of Thebans obeissaunce.
For which this noble Thesëus anon
Leet senden after gentil Palamon,
Unwist of hym what was the cause and
    why ;
But in his blakė clothės sorwefully
He cam at his comandėment in hye.
Tho sentė Thesëus for Emelye.   2980
Whan they were set, and hust was al
    the place,
And Thesëus abiden hadde a space
Er any word cam fram his wisė brest,
His eyen sette he ther as was his lest,
And with a sad visage he sikėd stille,
And after that right thus he seyde his wille :
'The Firstė Moevere of the cause above,
Whan he first made the fairė cheyne of love,
Greet was theffect and heigh was his
    entente ;
Wel wiste he why and what therof he
    mente,   2990
For with that fairė cheyne of love he bond
The fyr, the eyr, the water and the lond,
In certeyn boundės that they may nat flee.
That same Prince, and that same
    Moevere,' quod he,
'Hath stablissed in this wrecchėd world
    adoun
Certeynė dayės and duracioun
To al that is engendrid in this place,
Over the whichė day they may nat pace,—
Al mowe they yet tho dayės wel abregge,
Ther nedeth noon auctoritee allegge   3000
For it is preevėd by experience,
But that me list declaren my sentence.
Thanne may men by this ordrė wel
    discerne

That thilkė Moevere stable is and eterne.
Wel may men knowė, but it be a fool,
That every part dirryveth from his hool ;
For nature hath nat taken his bigynnyng
Of no partie, ne cantel, of a thyng,
But of a thyng that parfit is and stable,
Descendynge so, til it be corrumpable.
And therfore of his wisė purveiaunce   3011
He hath so wel biset his ordinaunce,
That speces of thyngės and progressiouns
Shullen enduren by successiouns,
And nat eterne, withouten any lye ;
This maystow understonde, and seen at
    eye.
'Loo the ook, that hath so long a
    norisshynge
From tymė that it first bigynneth sprynge,
And hath so long a lif as we may see,
Yet at the lastė wasted is the tree.   3020
'Considereth eek how that the hardė
    stoon
Under oure feet, on which we trede and
    goon,
Yit wasteth it, as it lyth by the weye ;
The brodė ryver somtyme wexeth dreye ;
The gretė tounės se we wane and wende ;
Thanne may ye se that al this thyng hath
    ende.
'Of man and womman seen we wel
    also,
That nedeth in oon of thisė termės two,
This is to seyn, in youthe or ellės age,
He moot be deed, the kyng as shal a
    page ;   3030
Som in his bed, som in the depė see,
Som in the largė feeld, as men may se ;
Ther helpeth noght, al goth that ilkė
    weye :
Thanne may I seyn that al this thyng
    moot deye.
'What maketh this but Juppiter, the
    kyng,
The which is prince, and cause of allė
    thyng,
Convertynge al unto his proprė welle,
From which it is dirryvėd, sooth to telle?

2987-3016. *The Firste Moevere*, etc. Theseus
takes the arguments of this speech from
Boethius, *De Consolatione*, bk. ii. met. 8 ; bk.
iv. pr. 6 ; bk. iii. pr. 10.
2994. *and that same Moevere*, Heng.[2] om.
that ; Hl. *and moevere eek*.

3015. H *And nat eterne be, withoute lye.*
3025. *tounes*, E *toures.*
3034. *that*, om. E[2].
3036. *The which*, E[6] *that.*

And here-agayns no creäture on lyve,
Of no degree, availleth for to stryve. 3040
'Thanne is it wysdom, as it thynketh me,
To maken vertu of necessitee,
And take it weel that we may not eschue,
And namély that to us alle is due.
And whoso gruccheth ought, he dooth
    folye,
And rebel is to hym that al may gye ;
And certeinly a man hath moost honour,
To dyen in his excellence and flour,
Whan he is siker of his goodé name ;
Thanne hath he doon his freend, ne hym,
    no shame, 3050
And gladder oghte his freend been of his
    deeth,
Whan with honour up-yolden is his breeth,
Than whan his name apalléd is for age,
For al forgeten is his vassellage.
Thanne is it best, as for a worthy fame,
To dyen whan that he is best of name.
'The contrarie of al this is wilfulnesse.
Why grucchen we, why have we hevynesse,
That goode Arcite, of chivalrié flour,
Departed is, with duetee and honour, 3060
Out of this foulé prisoun of this lyf?
Why grucchen heere his cosyn and his wyf
Of his welfare that loved hem so weel ?
Kan he hem thank ?—Nay, God woot,
    never a deel—
That bothe his soule and eek hem-self
    offende,
And yet they mowe hir lustés nat amende.
'What may I conclude of this longé
    serye,
But after wo, I rede us to be merye,
And thanken Juppiter of al his grace ?
And er that we departen from this place
I redé that we make of sorwés two 3071
O parfit joyé, lastynge evermo.
And looketh now, wher moost sorwe is
    her-inne,
Ther wol we first amenden and bigynne.
'Suster,' quod he, 'this is my fulle
    assent,
With all thavys heere of my parlèment,
That gentil Palamon, thyn owene knyght,
That serveth yow with willé, herte, and
    myght,

3077. *thyn*, H⁶ *your*.

And ever hath doon, syn that ye first
    hym knewe,
That ye shul of your grace upon hym
    rewe, 3080
And taken hym for housbonde and for
    lord ;
Lene me youre hond, for this is oure
    accord.
Lat se now of youre wommanly pitee ;
He is a kyngès brother sone, *pardee*,
And though he were a pouré bacheler,
Syn he hath servéd yow so many a yeer
And had for yow so greet adversitee,
It mosté been considered, leeveth me,
For gentil mercy oghte to passen right.'
    Thanne seyde he thus to Palamon ful
    right : 3090
'I trowe ther nedeth litel sermonyng
To maké yow assenté to this thyng ;
Com neer, and taak youre lady by the
    hond.'
Bitwixen hem was maad anon the bond
That highté matrimoigne, or mariage,
By al the conseil and the baronage ;
And thus with allé blisse and melodye
Hath Palamon y-wedded Emelye,
And God, that al this wydé world hath
    wroght,
Sende hym his love that it hath deere
    aboght, 3100
For now is Palamon in allé wele,
Lyvynge in blisse, in richesse, and in
    heele ;
And Emelye hym loveth so tendrely,
And he hire serveth al-so gentilly,
That never was ther no word hem bitwene
Of jalousie, or any oother tene.
    Thus endeth Palamon and Emelye ;
And God save al this fairé compaignye.
               Amen.

*Heere folwen the wordes bitwene the
    Hoost and the Millere*

Whan that the Knyght had thus his
    tale y-toold,
In al the routé ne was ther yong ne
    oold 3110

3106. *or any*, H *ne of non*.

'hat he ne seyde it was a noble storie,
,nd worthy for to drawen to memorie ;
,nd namely the gentils everichon.
  Oure Hooste lough and swoor, 'So
    moot I gon,
'his gooth aright; unbokeled is the male ;
,at se now who shal telle another tale ;
'or trewely the game is wel bigonne.
'ow telleth on, sire Monk, if that ye
    konne
umwhat to quite with the Knyghtes tale.'
  The Millere, that for-dronken was al
    pale,   3120
o that unnethe upon his hors he sat,
Ie nolde avalen neither hood ne hat,
;e abyde no man for his curteisie,
;ut in Pilates voys he gan to crie,
,nd swoor by armes, and by blood and
    bones,
I kan a noble tale for the nones,
Vith which I wol now quite the
    Knyghtes tale.'
  Oure Hooste saugh that he was dronke
    of ale,
,nd seyde, 'Abyd, Robyn, my leeve
    brother,   3129
om bettre man shal telle us first another ;
byde, and lat us werken thriftily.'
  ' By Goddes soule,' quod he, ' that wol
    nat I,
or I wol speke, or elles go my wey.'
  Oure Hoost answerde, ' Tel on a
    devele wey !
hou art a fool, thy wit is overcome.'
  ' Now herkneth,' quod the Millere,
    ' alle and some ;
at first I make a protestacioun
hat I am dronke, I knowe it by my
    soun ;
nd, therfore, if that I mysspeke or seye,
;yte it the ale of Southwerk, I you
    preye ;   3140
or I wol telle a legende and a lyf,

Bothe of a carpenter and of his wyf,
How that a clerk hath set the wrightes
    cappe.'
  The Reve answerde and seyde, ' Stynt
    thy clappe !
Lat be thy lewed, dronken harlotrye ;
It is a synne, and eek a greet folye
To apeyren any man, or hym defame,
And eek to bryngen wyves in swich fame ;
Thou mayst ynogh of othere thynges seyn.'
  This dronke Millere spak ful soone
    ageyn   3150
And seyde, ' Leve brother Osewold,
Who hath no wyf he is no cokewold,
But I sey nat therfore that thou art oon,
Ther been ful goode wyves many oon,
And ever a thousand goode ayeyns oon
    badde ;
That knowestow wel thyself, but if thou
    madde.
Why artow angry with my tale now ?
I have a wyf *pardee*, as wel as thow,
'Yet nolde I, for the oxen in my plogh,
Taken upon me moore than ynogh ;   3160
Though that thou deme thiself that thou
    be oon,
I wol bileve wel that I am noon.
An housbonde shal nat been inquisityf
Of Goddes pryvetee, nor of his wyf ;
So he may fynde Goddes foysoun there,
Of the remenant nedeth nat enquere.'

  What sholde I moore seyn, but this
    Millere
He nolde his wordes for no man forbere,
But told his cherles tale in his manere.
Mathynketh that I shal reherce it heere ;
And therfore every gentil wight I preye,
For Goddes love, demeth nat that I seye
Of yvel entente, but for I moot reherce
Hir tales alle, be they bettre or werse,
Or elles falsen som of my mateere :   3175
And therfore, who-so list it nat y-heere,

3112. *for to drawen to,* H *to be drawen in.*
3114. *lough,* H *tho lough.*
3115. *aright,* H *right wel.*
3117. *on,* H⁶ *ye.*
3124. *in Pilates voys.* the ranting tone assigned
Pilate in the Miracle Plays.
3128. *saugh that he was dronke,* H *saugh wel
nv dronke he was.*
3138. *it,* H *wel.*

3148. *swich fame,* H *yllname.*
3161. *Though,* etc. This reading of H (partly
supported by Camb.) is much better than the
' *As demen of myself that I were oon* ' of E⁵.
3167. *moore seyn but this,* H *seye but that this
proud.*
3173. *for,* E² *that.*
3174. *Hir tales alle, be they,* etc., H *Here
wordes alle, al be they,* etc.

Turne over the leef and chese another tale;
For he shal fynde ynowe, bothe grete
    and smale,
Of storial thyng that toucheth gentillesse,
And eek moralitee, and hoolynesse,— 3180
Blameth nat me if that ye chese amys.
The Millere is a cherl, ye knowe wel this,
So was the Reve, and othere manye mo,
And harlotrie they tolden bothe two.
Avyseth yow, putteth me out of blame ;
And eek men shal nat maken ernest of
    game.

MILLER'S TALE

Heere bigynneth The Millere his Tale

Whilom ther was dwellynge at Oxenford
A riche gnof, that gestes heeld to bord,
And of his craft he was a carpenter.
With hym ther was dwellynge a poure
    scoler,   3190
Hadde lerned art, but al his fantasye
Was turned for to lern astrologye,
And koude a certeyn of conclusiouns,
To demen by interrogaciouns,
If that men asked hym in certein houres
Whan that men sholde have droghte or
    elles shoures,
Or if men asked hym what sholde bifalle
Of every thyng, I may nat rekene hem
    alle.
This clerk was cleped hende Nicholas.
Of deerne love he koude, and of solas,
And ther-to he was sleigh and ful privee,
And lyk a mayden meke for to see.   3202
A chambre hadde he in that hostelrye
Allone, withouten any compaignye,
Ful fetisly y-dight, with herbes swoote,
And he hymself as sweete as is the roote
Of lycorys, or any cetewale.
His Almageste, and bookes grete and
    smale,

His astrelabie, longynge for his art,
His augrym stones, layen faire apart, 3210
On shelves couched at his beddes heed,
His presse y-covered with a faldyng reed,
And all above ther lay a gay sautrie,
On which he made a-nyghtes melodie
So swetely, that al the chambre rong,
And *Angelus ad Virginem*, he song ;
And after that he song the 'kynges
    noote ' ;
Ful often blessed was his myrie throte,
And thus this sweete clerk his tyme
    spente   3219
After his freendes fyndyng and his rente.
    This carpenter hadde wedded newe a
        wyf,
Which that he lovede moore than his lyf ;
Of eighteteene yeer she was of age.
Jalous he was, and heeld hire narwe in
    cage,
For she was yong and wylde, and he was
    old,
And demed hymself been lik a cokewold.
He knew nat Catoun, for his wit was
    rude,—
That bad man sholde wedde his
    simylitude.
Men sholde wedden after hire estaat, 3229
For youthe and elde is often at debaat ;
But sith that he was fallen in the snare,
He moste endure, as oother folk, his care.
    Fair was this yonge wyf, and therwithal.
As any wezele, hir body gent and smal.
A ceynt she werede, y-barred al of silk ;
A barmclooth eek, as whit as morne milk,
Upon hir lendes, ful of many a goore ;
Whit was hir smok, and broyden al bifoore,
And eek bihynde, on hir coler aboute,
Of colblak silk withinne and eek withoute.

The Millere his Tale. No original or analogue
has been discovered for this story, and there is
no reason to doubt that it is of Chaucer's own
invention.

3208. *Almageste*, the chief work of the astron-
omer Ptolemy, called by the Greeks Μεγάλη
Σύνταξις τῆς Ἀστρονομίας, a name which the
Arabs by substituting a superlative turned into
Al-megiste, or *Almagest*.

3216. *Angelus ad Virginem*. The music of a
13th-century chant to these words is extant at
the British Museum. Of the 'kynges noote '
nothing appears to be known.

3227. *He knew nat Catoun*. The maxim here
alluded to is not properly one of Cato's ; but I
find it in a kind of Supplement to the Moral
Distichs, entitled *Facetus* int. Auctores octo
morales, Lugd. 1538, cap. iii.
    ' Duc tibi prole parem sponsam moresque venustam.
    Si cum pace velis vitam deducere justam '
(Tyrwhitt). The sentiment is as old as the
Seven Sages.
3231. *fallen in*, H *brought into.*
3232. *folk*, H *doon.*

44

The tapés of hir whité voluper   3241
Were of the samé suyte of hir coler ;
Hir filet brood, of silk and set ful hye ;
And sikerly she hadde a likerous eye.
Ful smale y-pulléd were hire browés two,
And tho were bent, and blake as any sloo.
She was ful mooré blisful on to see
Than is the newé pereionetté tree,
And softer than the wolle is of a wether ;
And by hir girdel heeng a purs of lether,
Tasseled with grene and perléd with
    latoun.   3251
In al this world, to seken up and doun,
There nas no man so wys that koudé
    thenche
So gay a popelote, or swich a wenche.
Ful brighter was the shynyng of hir hewe
Than in the Tour the noble y-forgéd newe.
But of hir song it was as loude and yerne
As any swalwé chitteryng on a berne.
Therto she koudé skippe and maké game,
As any kyde, or calf, folwynge his dame.
Hir mouth was sweete as bragot or the
    meeth,   3261
Or hoord of apples leyd in hey or heeth.
Wynsynge she was, as is a joly colt ;
Long as a mast and uprighte as a bolt.
A brooch sche baar upon hir love coler,
As brood as is the boos of a bokeler ;
Hir shoes were lacéd on hir leggés hye ;
She was a prymerole, a piggesnye
For any lord, to leggen in his bedde,
Or yet for any good yeman to wedde.   3270
    Now, sire, and eft, sire, so bifel the cas,
That on a day this hendé Nicholas,
Fil with this yongé wyf to rage and pleye,
Whil that hir housbonde was at Oséneye,
As clerkés ben ful subtile and ful queynte ;
And privély he caughte hire by the queynte,
And seyde, ' Y-wis, but if ich have my
    wille,
For deerné love of thee, lemman, I
    spille ' ;
And heeld hire hardé by the haunché
    bones,

And seydé, ' Lemman, love me al atones,
Or I wol dyen, also God me save ! '   3281
    And she sproong, as a colt doth in the
    trave,
And with hir heed sche wryéd faste awey,
And seyde, ' I wol nat kisse thee, by
    my fey !
Why, lat be ! ' quod she, ' lat be,
    Nicholas !
Or I wol crie, "out, Harrow,"and "Allas !"
Do wey youre handés, for your curteisye !'
This Nicholas gan mercy for to crye,
And spak so faire, and profréd hym so
    faste,
That she hir love hym graunted atté laste,
And swoor hir ooth, by Seint Thomas of
    Kent,   3291
That she wol been at his comandément
Whan that she may hir leyser wel espie.
' Myn housbonde is so ful of jalousie,
That but ye wayté wel and been privee,
I woot right wel I nam but deed,' quod
    she ;
' Ye mosté been ful deerne, as in this cas.'
    ' Nay, ther-of care thee noght,' quod
    Nicholas.
' A clerk hadde litherly biset his whyle
But if he koude a carpenter bigyle.'   3300
And thus they been accorded and y-sworn
To wayte a tyme, as I have told biforn.
    Whan Nicholas had doon thus everideel,
And thakkéd hire aboute the lendés weel,
He kist hire sweete, and taketh his sawtrie,
And pleyeth faste, and maketh melodie.
    Thanne fil it thus, that to the paryssh
    chirche,
Christés owené werkés for to wirche,
This goodé wyf went on an haliday ;   3309
Hir forheed shoon as bright as any day,
So was it wasshen whan she leet hir werk.
    Now was ther of that chirche a parissh
    clerk,
The which that was y-clepéd Absolon ;
Crul was his heer and as the gold it
    shoon,
And strouted as a fanné, large and brode,

3256. *Tour*, *i.e.* the Tower of London, where
the Mint was.
3256. *the noble*, a gold coin (6s. 8d.), first
minted by Edward III.
3258. *chitteryng*, E⁴ *sittynge*.
3274. *Oséneye*, Osney, a village near Oxford.

3282. H *and she sprang out as doth a colt in
trave.*
3283. *Nicholas*, H *thou Nicholas.*
3289. *hym*, E *hire.*

Ful streight and evene lay his joly shode.
His rode was reed, his eyen greye as
    goos ;
With Powlës wyndow corven on his shoos,
In hoses rede he wentë fetisly.
Y-clad he was ful smal and proprëly,   3320
Al in a kirtel of a lyght waget,
Ful faire and thikkë been the poyntës set ;
And therupon he hadde a gay surplys,
As whit as is the blosme upon the rys.
A myrie child he was, so God me save,
Wel koude he laten blood and clippe
    and shave,
And maken a chartre of lond or acquit-
    aunce.
In twenty manere koude he trippe and
    daunce
(After the scole of Oxenfordë tho),
And with his leggës casten to and fro,   3330
And pleyen songës on a small rubible ;
Therto he song somtyme a loud quynyble,
And as wel koude he pleye on his giterne.
In al the toun nas brewhous ne taverne
That he ne visited with his solas,
Ther any gaylard tappesterë was.
But, sooth to seyn, he was somdel
    squaymous
Of fartyng, and of spechë daungerous.
    This Absolon, that jolif was and gay,
Gooth with a sencer on the haliday,   3340
Sensynge the wyvës of the parisshe faste,
And many a lovely look on hem he caste,
And namely on this carpenteris wyf.
To loke on hire hym thoughte a myrie lyf,
She was so propre, and sweete, and
    likerous.
I dar wel seyn if she hadde been a mous,
And he a cat, he wold hire hente anon.
    This parissh clerk, this joly Absolon,
Hath in his hertë swich a love longynge,
That of no wyf ne took he noon offrynge ;
For curteisie, he seyde, he woldë noon.
    The moone, whan it was nyght, ful
    brightë shoon,   3352

And Absolon his gyterne hath y-take,
For paramours he thoghtë for to wake ;
And forth he gooth, jolif and amorous,
Til he cam to the carpenterës hous,
A litel after cokkës hadde y-crowe,
And dressëd hym up by a shotwyndowe,
That was upon the carpenteris wal.
He syngeth in his voys gentil and smal :
' *Now, deerë lady, if thy willë be,*   3361
I prayë yow that ye wole thynke on me, '
Ful wel acordaunt to his gyternynge.
    This carpenter awook, and herdë synge,
And spak unto his wyf, and seyde anon,
' What, Alison, herestow nat Absolon,
That chaunteth thus under oure bourës
    wal ? '
And she answerde hir housbonde ther-
    withal,
' Yis, God woot, John, I heere it every del.'
    This passeth forth ; what wol ye bet
    than weel ?   3370
Fro day to day this joly Absolon
So woweth hire that hym is wo bigon ;
He waketh al the nyght and al the day,
He kembeth his lokkës brode, and
    made hym gay,
He woweth hire by meenës and brocage,
And swoor he woldë been hir owene page ;
He syngeth, brokkynge as a nyghtyngale ;
He sente hire pyment, meeth, and spicëd
    ale,
And wafres, pipyng hoot out of the gleede ;
And, for she was of toune, he profreth
    meede ;   3380
For som folk wol ben wonnen for richesse,
And somme for strokes, and somme for
    gentillesse.
    Somtyme to shewe his lightnesse and
    maistrye
He pleyeth Heródës, on a scaffold hye,
But what availleth hym, as in this cas ?
She loveth so this hendë Nicholas,

3318. *Powles wyndow.* The reference is to the open-work tracery, like that of the great Rose window at Old St. Paul's, in the fashionable shoes of the time.   H² *wyndowes.*
3321. *lyght,* H *fyn.*
3322. H *Schapen with goores in the newe get.*
3352. *whan it was nyght, ful,* H *at night ful clers and.*

3354. *thoghte for to wake,* H *seyde he wolde awake.*
3362. *thynke,* H *rewe.*
3374. *He kembeth,* H *To kembe,* an amusing but unlikely variant.
3377. *brokkynge,* warbling ? ; H *crowyng.*
3384. *He pleyeth Herodes,* etc. The Miracle Plays were at first chiefly acted by clerks ; the stage or ' scaffold ' often had three compartments to represent Heaven, Earth, and Hell.

That Absolon may blowe the bukkès horn,
He ne haddè for his labour but a scorn,
And thus she maketh Absolon hire ape
And al his ernest turneth til a jape.   3390
Ful sooth is this proverbe, it is no lye,
Men seyn right thus, ' Alwey the nyè slye
Maketh the ferrè leevè to be looth ' ;
For though that Absolon be wood or wrooth,
By-causè that he fer was from hire sighte,
This nyè Nicholas stood in his lighte.
    Now bere thee wel, thou hendè Nicholas,
For Absolon may waille and synge, allas !
And so bifel it on a Saterday
This carpenter was goon til Osènay,   3400
And hendè Nicholas and Alisoun
Acorded been to this conclusioun,
That Nicholas shal shapen hym a wyle
This sely, jalous housbonde to bigyle ;
And, if so be the gamè wente aright,
She sholdè slepen in his arm al nyght,
For this was his desir and hire also.
And right anon, withouten wordès mo,
This Nicholas no lenger woldè tarie,
But dooth ful softe unto his chambrè carie   3410
Bothe mete and drynkè for a day or tweye ;
And to hire housbonde bad hire for to seye,
If that he axèd after Nicholas,
She sholdè seye she nystè where he was,
Of al that day she saugh hym nat with eye ;
She trowèd that he was in maladye,
For for no cry hir maydè koude hym calle,
He nolde answere for nought that myghtè falle.
    This passeth forth al thilkè Saterday
That Nicholas stille in his chambrè lay,
And eet and sleepe, or didè what hym leste,   3421
Til Sonday, that the sonnè gooth to reste.
    This sely carpenter hath greet merveyle

Of Nicholas, or what thyng myghte hym eyle,
And seyde, ' I am adrad, by Seint Thomas
It stondeth nat aright with Nicholas.
God shildè that he deydè sodeynly ;
This world is now ful tikel, sikerly ;
I saugh to day a cors y-born to chirche,
That now on Monday last I saugh hym wirche.   3430
' Go up,' quod he unto his knave anoon,
'Clepe at his dore, or knokkè with a stoon ;
Looke how it is, and tel me boldèly.'
    This knavè gooth him up ful sturdily
And at the chambrè dorè, whil he stood,
He cride and knokkèd as that he were wood,—
' What ! how ! what do ye, maister Nicholay ?
How may ye slepen al the longè day ? '
    But al for noght, he herdè nat a word.
An hole he foond, ful lowe upon a bord,
Ther as the cat was wont in for to crepe,
And at that hole he lookèd in ful depe,
And at the laste he hadde of hym a sighte.
This Nicholas sat gapyng ever uprighte,
As he had kikèd on the newè moone.
Adoun he gooth and tolde his maister soone
In what array he saugh this ilkè man.
    This carpenter to blessen hym bigan,
And seydè, ' Help us, Seintè Frydeswyde !
A man woot litel what hym shal bityde ;
This man is fallè, with his astromye,   3451
In som woodnesse, or in some agonye.
I thoghte ay wel how that it sholdè be,
Men sholde nat knowe of Goddès pryvetee.
Ye, blessèd be alwey a lewèd man,
That noght but oonly his bilevè kan.
So ferde another clerk with astromye ;
He walkèd in the feeldès, for to prye
Upon the sterrès, what ther sholde bifalle,
Til he was in a marlè pit y-falle ;   3460
He saugh nat that. But yet by Seint Thomas,
Me reweth soore of hendè Nicholas !

3387. *blowe the bukkes horn*, a phrase meaning have his trouble for nothing.'
3405. *be the*, H *were this*.
3416. *that he was in*, H *he were falle in som*.
3417. *For for no cry hir maydè*, H *For no cry 'hat hir maydè*, to be taken with next line.

3449. *Seinte Frydeswyde*, still the patron saint of one of the Oxford parishes.
3451. *astromye*, a corruption of 'astronomye'; the latter word is the reading of H4, but both here and in 3457 it spoils the metre.
3457. *another clerk*, Thales.

He shal be ratėd of his studiyng,
If that I may, by Jhesus, hevene kyng !
　'Get me a staf, that I may underspore,
Whil that thou, Robyn, hevest of the dore :
He shal out of his studiyng, as I gesse.'
And to the chambrė dore he gan hym
　　dresse ;
His knavė was a strong carl, for the
　　noones,
And by the haspe he haaf it of atones,
Into the floor the dorė fil anon.　　3471
This Nicholas sat ay as stille as stoon,
And ever gapėd upward into the eir.
This carpenter wende he were in despeir,
And hente hym by the sholdrės myghtily
And shook hym harde and cridė spitously,
'What, Nicholay ! what how ! what,
　　looke adoun !
Awake ! and thenk on Cristės passioun !
I crouchė thee from elvės and fro wightes.'
Therwith the nyghtspel seyde he anon-
　　rightes,　　3480
On fourė halvės of the hous aboute,
And on the thresshfold of the dore
　　withoute :

'Jhesu Crist and Seint Benedight,
Blesse this hous from every wikked wight
For nyghtės verye the whitė Pater noster.
Where wentestow, Seint Petres soster ?'

And attė laste this hendė Nicholas
Gan for to sikė soore, and seyde, 'Allas !
Shal al this world be lost eftsoonės now ?'
　This carpenter answerdė, 'What
　　seystow ?　　3490
What, thynk on God, as we doon, men
　　that swynke.'
　This Nicholas answerdė, 'Fecche me
　　drynke ;

3477. *what* (3rd), H *man ;* Heng.⁵ om.
3483. *Jhesu,* H *Lord Jhesu.*
3485. *For nyghtes,* etc. Tyrwhitt reads : *Fro*
the nyghtes mare the wite pater-noster (may
pater-noster defend thee from night-mare); Morris:
Fro nyghtes mare werye the with pater-noster
(guard thyself with pater-noster). But a charm
of the 16th century quoted by Mr. Gilman runs :
　'White Pater Noster, St. Peter's brother,
　What hast thou in one hand ? White-Book Leaves.
　What hast i' th' other ? Heaven Gate keys.
　Open Heaven Gates and steike Hell Gates,
　And let every crysom child creep to its own mother :
　White Pater Noster. Amen.'
If this be genuine the *white* must stand.

And after wol I speke, in pryvėtee,
Of certeyn thyng that toucheth me and
　　thee ;
I wol telle it noon oother man, certeyn.'
　This carpenter goth doun and comth
　　ageyn,
And broghte of myghty ale a largė quart,
And whan that ech of hem had dronke
　　his part,
This Nicholas his dorė fastė shette　　3499
And doun the carpenter by hym he sette.
　He seydė, 'John, myn hoostė, lief
　　and deere,
Thou shalt upon thy trouthė swere me
　　heere
That to no wight thou shalt this conseil
　　wreye,
For it is Cristės conseil that I seye ;
And if thou tellė man thou art forlore,
For this vengauncė thou shalt han therfore,
That if thou wreyė me thou shalt be wood.'
　'Nay, Crist forbede it, for his hooly
　　blood,'　　3508
Quod tho this sely man, 'I nam no labbe,
Ne, though I seye, I am nat lief to gabbe ;
Sey what thou wolt, I shal it never telle
To child ne wyf, by hym that harwėd
　　helle !'
　'Now, John,' quod Nicholas, 'I
　　wol nat lye,
I have y-founde in myn astrologye,
As I have lookėd in the moonė bright,
That now a Monday next, at quarter nyght,
Shal fallė a reyn, and that so wilde and
　　wood,
That half so greet was never Noees flood.
This world,' he seyde, 'in lassė than an hour
Shal al be dreynt, so hidous is the shour ;
Thus schal mankyndė drenche and lese
　　hir lyf.'　　3521
　This carpenter answerde, 'Allas, my
　　wyf !
And shal she drenche ? Allas, myn
　　Alisoun !'
For sorwe of this he fil almoost adoun,
And seyde, 'Is ther no remedie in this cas ?'

3499. *faste shette,* etc. ; H *gan to schitte, And*
dede this carpenter doun by him sitte.
3510. *Ne, though I seye,* H *though I it seye.*
3520. *Shal al be dreynt,* H *Shal ben i-dreynt.*

48

'Why, yis, for Gode,' quod hendè Nicholas,
'If thou wolt werken aftir loore and reed ;
Thou mayst nat werken after thyn owene heed,
For thus seith Salomoun, that was ful trewe,
"Werk al by conseil and thou shalt nat rewe " ;   3530
And if thou werken wolt by good conseil,
I undertake, withouten mast and seyl,
Yet shal I saven hire and thee and me.
Hastow nat herd how savèd was Noè,
Whan that oure Lord hadde warnèd hym biforn
That al the world with water sholde be lorn ?'
'Yis,' quod this carpenter, 'ful yoore ago.'
'Hastou nat herd,'quod Nicholas, 'also,
The sorwe of Noè with his felaweshipe
Er that he myghtè brynge his wyf to shipe ?
Hym hadde be levere, I dar wel undertake,
At thilkè tyme, than alle his wetheres blake,   3542
That she hadde had a shipe hir-self allone.
And therfore, woostou what is best to doone ?
This asketh haste, and of an hastif thyng
Men may nat preche or maken tariyng.
'Anon go gete us faste into this in
A knedyng trogh, or ellis a kymèlyn,
For ech of us, but loke that they be large,
In whiche we mowè swymme as in a barge,
And han ther-inne vitaillè suffisant   3551
But for a day,—fy on the remenant,—
The water shal aslake and goon away
Aboutè pryme upon the nextè day.
But Robyn may nat wite of this, thy knave,
Ne eek thy maydè Gille I may nat save ;
Axè nat why, for though thou askè me,
I wol nat tellen Goddès pryvètee ;
Suffiseth thee, but if thy wittès madde,
To han as greet a grace as Noè hadde.
Thy wyf shal I wel saven, out of doute.

3540. *Er that he myghte brynge*, H *that he had or he gat.* In the Miracle Plays Noah's wife refused to be saved without her gossips, and when dragged in broke her husband's head.
3550. *In whiche we mowe swymme*, H *In which that we may row.*

Go now thy wey and speed thee heer aboute.   3562
'But whan thou hast for hire and thee and me
Y-geten us thise knedyng-tubbès thre,
Thanne shaltow hange hem in the roof ful hye,
That no man of oure purveiauncè spye,
And whan thou thus hast doon as I have seyd,
And hast oure vitaille faire in hem y-leyd,
And eek an ax to smyte the corde atwo,
Whan that the water comth, that we may go ;   3570
And broke an hole, an heigh upon the gable,
Unto the gardynward, over the stable,
That we may frely passen forth oure way,
Whan that the gretè shour is goon away ;
Thanne schalt thou swymme as myrie, I undertake,
As dooth the whitè doke after hire drake ;
Thanne wol I clepe "how Alisoun, how John,
Be myrie, for the flood wol passe anon,"
And thou wolt seyn, "Hayl, maister Nicholay !   3579
Good morwe, I se thee wel for it is day !"'
And thanne shul we be lordès al oure lyf
Of al the world, as Noë and his wyf.
'But of o thing I warnè thee ful right,
Be well avysèd on that ilkè nyght
That we ben entred into shippès bord,
That noon of us ne spekè nat a word,
Ne clepe, ne crie, but been in his preyère,
For it is Goddès owene heestè deere.
Thy wyf and thou moote hangè fer atwynne,
For that bitwixè yow shal be no synne,
Na moore in lookyng than ther shal in deede ;   3591
This ordinance is seyd ; so God thee speede ;
Tomorwe at nyght, whan folk ben alle aslepe,
Into our knedyng-tubbès wol we crepe,
And sitten there, abidyng Goddès grace.
Go now thy wey, I have no lenger space

3578. *wol passe*, H *passeth.*
3593. *folk ben alle*, H *men ben.*

E   49

To make of this no lenger sermonyng,—
Men seyn thus, "Sende the wise and sey
   nothyng";
Thou art so wys it needeth nat thee teche,
Go save oure lyf, and that I the biseche.'
  This sely carpenter goth forth his wey;
Ful ofte he seith 'Allas,' and 'Weylawey,'
And to his wyf he tolde his pryveetee,
And she was war, and knew it bet than he,
What al this queyntë cast was for to seye;
But nathélees she ferde as she wolde deye,
And seyde, 'Allas! go forth thy wey anon,
Help us to scape or we been lost echon!
I am thy trewé, verray, wedded wyf,
Go, deerë spouse, and help to save oure
   lyf!'   3610
  Lo which a greet thyng is affeccioun!
Men may dyen of ymaginacioun,
So depé may impressioun be take.
This sely carpenter bigynneth quake;
Hym thynketh verraily that he may see
Noëes flood, come walwynge as the see,
To drenchen Alisoun, his hony deere.
He wepeth, weyleth, maketh sory cheere;
He siketh, with ful many a sory swogh;
He gooth and geteth hym a knedyng trogh,
And after that a tubbe and a kymelyn,
And pryvély he sente hem to his in,
And heng hem in the roof in pryvétee.
His owene hande he made laddrés thre,
To clymben by the rongés and the stalkes,
Into the tubbés, hangynge in the balkes;
And hem vitailleth, bothé trogh and tubbe,
With breed and chese and good ale in a
   jubbe,
Suffisynge right ynogh as for a day;
But er that he hadde maad al this array,
He sente his knave, and eek his wenche
   also,   3631
Upon his nede to London for to go;
And on the Monday, whan it drow to
   nyght,
He shette his dore withouté candel lyght,
And dresseth al this thyng as it shal be;
And shortly, up they clomben allé thre;
They sitten stillë, wel a furlong way.
  'Now, *Pater noster,* clom,' seydé
   Nicholay;

And 'Clom,' quod John, and 'Clom,'
   seyde Alisoun.
This carpenter seyde his devocioun,   3640
And stille he sit and biddeth his preyere,
Ay waitynge on the reyn, if he it heere.
  The dedé sleepe, for verray bisynesse,
Fil on this carpenter, right as I·gesse
Aboutë corfew-tyme, or litel more;
For travaille of his goost he groneth soore,
And eft he routeth, for his heed myslay.
Doun of the laddré stalketh Nicholay,
And Alisoun ful softe adoun she speddé;
Withouten wordés mo they goon to beddé.
Ther as the carpenter is wont to lye,   3651
Ther was the revel and the melodye.
And thus lith Alison and Nicholas,
In bisynesse of myrthe and of solas,
Til that the belle of laudés gan to rynge,
And freré in the chauncel gonné synge.
  This parissh clerk, this amorous Ab-
   solon,
That is for love alwey so wo-bigon,
Upon the Monday was at Oséneye
With compaignye, hym to disporte and
   pleye,   3660
And axéd upon cas a cloisterer
Ful prively after John the carpenter.
And he drough hym a-part out of the
   chirche,
And seyde, 'I noot, I saugh hym heere
   nat wirche
Syn Saterday; I trow that he be went
For tymber ther our abbot hath hym sent;
For he is wont for tymber for to go,
And dwellen at the grange a day or two;
Or ellés he is at his hous, certeyn;   3669
Where that he be I kan nat soothly seyn.'
  This Absolon ful joly was and light,
And thoghté, 'Now is tymé wake al nyght,
For sikirly I saugh him nat stirynge
Aboute his dore, syn day bigan to sprynge.
So moot I thryve I shal, at cokkés crowe,
Ful pryvély go knokke at his wyndowe,
That stant ful lowe upon his bourés wal.
To Alison now wol I tellen al
My love-longynge; for yet I shal nat
   mysse   3679
That at the lesté wey I shal hire kisse.

3612. *Men may dyen* (slur *may*), H *A man*
may dye.

3643. *verray,* E³ *wery.*
3658. *alwey so,* H *so hard and.*

50

om maner confort shal I have, parfay.
 Iy mouth hath icchèd al this longè day,
That is a signe of kissyng atté leste.
Al nyght me mette eek I was at a feeste;
Therfore I wol goon slepe an houre or
    tweye,
And al the nyght thanne wol I wake
    and pleye.'
   Whan that the firstè cok hath crowe
    anon
Up rist this joly lovere Absolon,
And hym arraieth gay, at poynt devys ;
But first he cheweth greyn and lycorys,
To smellen sweete, er he hadde kembd
    his heer.   3691
Under his tonge a trewè-love he beer,
For ther-by wende he to ben gracious.
He rometh to the carpenterès hous,
And stille he stant under the shot-wyn-
    dowe,—
Into his brist it raughte, it was so lowe,—
And softe he knokketh with a semysoun :
What do ye, hony-comb, sweete Alisoun,
My fairè bryd, my sweetè cynamome ?
Awaketh, lemman myn, and speketh to me.
Wel litel thynken ye upon my wo   3701
That for youre love I swetè ther I go.
No wonder is, thogh that I swelte and
    swete,
I moorne as dooth a lamb after the tete ;
I-wis, lemman, I have swich love-long-
    ynge,
That lik a turtel trewe is my moornynge ;
I may nat ete na moorè than a mayde.'
   'Go fro the wyndow, jakkè-fool,' she
    sayde,
As help me God, it wol nat be, "com
    ba me " ;   3709
I love another, and elles I were to blame,
Wel bet than thee, by Jhesu, Absolon.
Go forth thy wey, or I wol caste a ston,
And lat me slepe, a twenty devel wey ! '
   ' Allas,' quod Absolon, 'and weylawey,
That trewè love was ever so yvel biset !
Thanne kyssè me, syn it may be no bet,
For Jhesus love, and for the love of me.'
   'Wiltow thanne go thy wey ?' therwith
    quod she.

3697. *knokketh*, H⁴ *cowhith, cougheth, coughed.*
3702. *swete*, H *swelte*, faint.

   'Ye certès, lemman,' quod this Absolon.
   'Thanne make thee redy,' quod she,
    ' I come anon,'   3720
And unto Nicholas she seydè stille,
' Now hust and thou shalt laughen al
    thy fille.'
   This Absolon doun sette hym on his
    knees,
And seydè, ' I am lord at alle degrees,
For after this I hope ther cometh moore.
Lemman, thy grace, and sweetè bryd,
    thyn oore.'
   The wyndow she undoth, and that in
    haste,
' Have do,' quod she, 'com of, and speed
    the faste,
Lest that oure neighèborès thee espie.'
   This Absolon gan wype his mouth ful
    drie :   3730
Dirk was the nyght as pich, or as the cole,
And at the wyndow out she pitte hir hole,
And Absolon hym fil no bet ne wers,
But with his mouth he kiste hir naked ers,
Ful savourly, er he was war of this.
Abak he stirte, and thoughte it was amys,
For wel he wiste a womman hath no berd.
He felte a thyng al rough and long y-herd,
And seydè, ' Fy, allas, what have I do?'
' Tehee ! ' quod she, and clapte the
    wyndow to,   3740
And Absolon gooth forth a sory pas.
' A berd, a berd ! ' quod hendè Nicholas,
' By Goddès corps, this game goth faire
    and weel.'
   This sely Absolon herde every deel,
And on his lippe he gan for anger byte,
And to hymself he seydè, ' I shal thee
    quyte.'
   Who rubbeth now, who froteth now
    his lippes
With dust, with sond, with straw, with
    clooth, with chippes,
But Absolon?—that seith ful ofte, 'Allas !
My soule bitake I unto Sathanas,   3750
But me were levere than al this toun,'
    quod he,
' Of this despit awroken for to be.
Allas,' quod he, 'allas, I ne hadde
    y-bleynt.'
His hootè love was coold and al y-queynt ;

For fro that tyme that he hadde kiste
   her ers,
Of paramours he setté nat a kers ;
For he was heeléd of his maladie.
Full ofté paramours he gan deffie,
And weepe as dooth a child that is y-bete.
A softé paas he wente over the strete   3760
Until a smyth men clepéd daun Gerveys,
That in his forgé smythéd plough
   harneys,—
He sharpeth shaar and kultour bisily.
This Absolon knokketh al esily,
And seyde, 'Undo, Gerveys, and that
   anon.'
   'What, who artow ?'   'It am I, Ab-
   solon.'
'What, Absolon! For Cristés sweeté tree,
Why risé ye so rathe ? ey *benedicitee !*
What eyleth yow? Som gay gerl, God
   it woot,
Hath brought yow thus upon the
   viritoot ;   3770
By seinté Note, ye woot wel what I mene.'
   This Absolon ne roghté nat a bene
Of al his pley ; no word agayn he yaf ;
He haddé mooré tow on his distaf
Than Gerveys knew, and seydé, 'Freend
   so deere,
That hooté kultour in the chymenee heere,
As lene it me, I have therwith to doone,
And I wol brynge it thee agayn ful soone.'
   Gerveys answerdé, 'Certés, were it
   gold,
Or in a poké nobles alle untold,   3780
Thou sholdest have, as I am trewé smyth ;
Ey, Cristés foo, what wol ye do ther-
   with ?'
'Ther-of,' quod Absolon, 'be as be may,
I shall wel telle it thee to-morwé day,'
And caughte the kultour by the coldé stele.
Ful softe out at the dore he gan to stele,
And wente unto the carpenteris wal.
He cogheth first, and knokketh therwithal
Upon the wyndowe, right as he dide er.
   This Alison answerdé, 'Who is ther,
That knokketh so ? I warante it a theef.'

3770. *viritoot*, meaning doubtful—H *very trot*,
Camb. *merytot.*
3771. *Note*, St. Neot.
3781. *Thou sholdest have*, H *Ye skul hem
have.*

'Why nay,' quod he, 'God woot, my
   sweeté leef,
I am thyn Absolon, my deerélyng.
Of gold,' quod he, 'I have thee broght
   a ryng ;
My mooder yaf it me, so God me save :
Ful fyn it is, and therto wel y-grave ;
This wol I yevé thee, if thou me kisse.'
   This Nicholas was risen for to pisse,
And thoughte he wolde amenden al the
   jape,   3799
He sholdé kisse his ers, er that he scape ;
And up the wyndowe dide he hastily,
And out his ers he putteth pryvély,
Over the buttok to the haunché bon.
And ther-with spak this clerk, this
   Absolon ;
'Spek, sweeté bryd, I noot nat where
   thou art.'
This Nicholas anon leet fle a fart,
As greet as it had been a thonder dent,
That with the strook he was almoost
   y-blent ;
And he was redy with his iren hoot,
And Nicholas amydde the ers he smoot.
   Of gooth the skyn, an handé brede
   aboute,   3811
The hooté kultour brende so his toute ;
And for the smert he wendé for to dye.
As he were wood for wo he gan to crye,
'Help, water, water, help, for Goddés
   herte !'
   This carpenter out of his slomber stertc,
And herde oon crien 'water,' as he were
   wood,
And thoughte, 'Allas, now comth Nowelis
   flood !'
He sit hym up withouten wordés mo,
And with his ax he smoot the corde at wo,
And doun gooth al ; he foond neither to
   selle,   3821
Ne breed ne ale, til he cam to the celle
Upon the floor and ther aswowne he lay.
   Up stirte hire Alison and Nicholay,
And criden, 'Out and harrow !' in the
   strete.
The neighéborés, bothé smale and grete,
In ronnen for to gauren on this man,
That yet aswowné lay, bothe pale and wan,
For with the fal he brosten hadde his arm.

But stonde he moste unto his owene harm,
For whan he spak he was anon bore doun
With hendė Nicholas and Alisoun.   3832
They tolden every man that he was wood,
He was agast so of Nowelis flood
Thurgh fantasie, that of his vanytee
He haddė y-boght hym knedyng-tubbės thre,
And haddė hem hangėd in the rove above;
And that he preydė hem, for Goddės love,
To sitten in the roof, *par compaigyne.*

The folk gan laughen at his fantasye;
Into the roof they kiken and they gape,
And turnėd al his harm unto a jape; 3842
For, what-so that this carpenter answerde,
It was for noght, no man his reson herde;
With othės grete he was so sworn adoun,
That he was holdė wood in al the toun;
For every clerk anonright heeld with oother;
They seyde, 'The man was wood, my leevė broother';
And every wight gan laughen of this stryf.
Thus swyvėd was this carpenteris wyf,
For al his kepyng and his jalousye; 3851
And Absolon hath kist hir nether eye,
And Nicholas is scalded in the towte:
This tale is doon, and God save al the rowte.

REEVE'S TALE

The prologe of the Reves Tale

Whan folk haddė laughen at this nycė cas
Of Absolon and hendė Nicholas,
Diversė folk diversėly they seyde,
But for the moorė part they loughe and pleyde;
Je at this tale I saugh no man hym greve,
But it were oonly Osėwold the Reve. 3860
Y-cause he was of carpenteris craft
A litel ire is in his herte y-laft.
He gan to grucche and blamėd it a lite.
'So theek,' quod he, 'ful wel koude I the quite,
With bleryng of a proud millėrės eye,—

If that me listė speke of ribaudye,—
But ik am oold, me list not pley for age,
Gras tyme is doon, my fodder is now forage;
This whitė tope writeth myne oldė yeris;
Myn herte is also mowlėd as myne heris,
But if I fare as dooth an openers; 3871
That ilkė fruyt is ever lenger the wers
Til it be roten in mullok, or in stree.
'We oldė men, I drede, so farė we;
Til we be roten kan we nat be rype.
We hoppen ay whil that the world wol pype,
For in oure wyl ther stiketh ever a nayl,
To have an hoor heed and a grenė tayl,
As hath a leek; for, thogh oure myght be goon,
Oure wyl desireth folie ever in oon; 3880
For whan we may nat doon, than wol we speke,
Yet in oure asshen olde is fyr y-reke.
Foure gleedės han we, whiche I shal devyse,
Avauntyng, liyng, anger, coveitise.
Thise fourė sparkles longen unto eelde.
Oure oldė lemės mowe wel been unweelde,
But wyl ne shal nat faillen, that is sooth;
And yet ik have alwey a coltės tooth,
As many a yeer as it is passėd henne
Syn that my tappe of lif bigan to renne;
For sikerly, whan I was bore, anon 3891
Deeth drough the tappe of lyf and leet it gon,
And ever sithe hath so the tappe y-ronne,
Til that almoost al empty is the tonne.
The streem of lyf now droppeth on the chymbe;
The sely tongė may wel rynge and chymbe
Of wrecchednesse that passėd is ful yoore;
With oldė folk, save dotage, is namoore.'
Whan that oure Hoost haddė herd this sermonyng,
He gan to speke as lordly as a kyng. 3900
He seidė: 'What amounteth al this wit?
What, shul we speke alday of hooly writ?
The devel made a Revė for to preche,
Or of a soutere shipman or a leche.

3858. *moore,* H *moste.*

3871. *But if,* H *But yit.*
3887. *faillen,* H *fayle us.*
3904. *soutere,* 'a cobbler may as well turn

Sey forth thy tale, and tarie nat the tyme,—
Lo, Depèford, and it is half wey pryme.
Lo, Grenèwych, ther many a shrewe is
    inne,
It were al tyme thy talè to bigynne.'
    ' Now, sirès,' quod this Osèwold the
        Reve,   3909
' I pray yow allè that ye nat yow greve,
Thogh I answére and somdeel sette his
    howve,
For leveful is, with forcè force of showvve;
This dronkè Millere hath y-toold us heer
How that bigylèd was a carpenteer,
Peráventure in scorn for I am oon ;
And, by youre leve, I shal him quite anoon.
Right in his cherlès termés wol I speke ;
I pray to God his nekkè motè breke.
He kan wel in myn eyè seen a stalke,
But in his owene he kan nat seen a balke.'

Heere bigynneth The Reves Tale

    At Trumpyngtoun, nat fer fro Cantè-
        brigge,   3921
Ther gooth a brook, and over that a brigge,
Upon the whichè brook ther stant a melle ;
And this is verray sooth that I yow tell.
A millere was ther dwellynge many a day,
As eny pecok he was proud and gay.
Pipen he koude and fisshe, and nettès beete,
And turnè coppès, and wel wrastle and
    sheete ;
And by his belt he baar a long panade,
And of a swerd ful trenchant was the
    blade.   3930

sailor or physician as a reeve take to preaching.'
' Ex sutore nauclerus,' 'ex sutore medicus,' were
proverbial expressions.
    3906. *Depeford,* Deptford.
    3906. *half wey pryme,* 7.30 A.M. ; H, *passed
pryme* ; Petworth, *almost prime.*
    3910. *that ye nat yow greve,* H *that noon of
you him greve.*
    3911. *howve,* cap ; for the phrase cp. line 586.
    3912. *of, i.e.* off ; H² *to.*
    The Reves Tale: probably taken by Chaucer
from the French fabliau, *De Gombert et des Deux
Clers,* by Jean de Boves, with hints also from
another fabliau now in the library at Berne, in
which the clerks lodge with a thieving miller and
not with a ' vilein,' as in *Gombert.* Cp. also
Boccaccio, *Decameron,* D. ix. N. 6. All the
local colour is of course supplied by Chaucer
himself, who sets off the Cambridge clerks and
their miller against the Oxford clerk and the
carpenter.

A joly poppere baar he in his pouche,
Ther was no man, for peril, dorste hym
    touche ;
A Sheffeld thwitel baar he in his hose.
Round was his face, and camuse was his
    nose ;
As pilèd as an apè was his skulle ;
He was a market-betere attè fulle ;
Ther dorstè no wight hand upon hym
    legge,
That he ne swoor he sholde anon abegge.
    A theef he was, for sothe, of corn and
        mele,
And that a sly and usaunt for to stele. 3940
His name was hootè, deynous, Symèkyn.
A wyf he hadde, y-comen of noble kyn,—
The person of the toun hir fader was,—
With hire he yaf ful many a panne of bras
For that Symkyn sholde in his blood allye.
She was y-fostred in a nonnerye,
For Symkyn woldè no wyf, as he sayde,
But she were wel y-norissed and a maydè,
To saven his estaat of yomanrye.   3949
And she was proud and peert as is a pye.
A ful fair sighte was it upon hem two
On haly dayes ; biforn hire wolde he go
With his typet y-bounde about his heed ;
And she cam after in a gyte of reed ;
And Symkyn haddè hosen of the same.
Ther dorstè no wight clepen hire but
    ' Dame ' ;
Was noon so hardy that wente by the weye
That with hire dorstè rage, or onès pleye,
But if he wolde be slayn of Symèkyn,
With panade, or with knyf, or boidèkyn ;
For jalous folk ben perilous evermo ;   3961
Algate they wolde hire wyvès wenden so.
And eek, for she was somdel smoterlich,
She was as digne as water in a dich,
As ful of hoker, and of bisèmare.
Hir thoughtè that a lady sholde hire spare,
What for hire kynrede and hir nortelrie,
That she hadde lernèd in the nonnerie.

    3949. *of,* H *and.*
    3953. *y-bounde,* E² *bounde, bounden* ; Heng.³
wounden.
    3956. *clepen hire but ' Dame,'* H *clepe hir
but ' Madame' ;* cp. line 376.
    3957. *that wente,* H *walkyng.*
    3958. *ones,* H *elles.*
    3966. *a lady sholde hire spare,* H *ladyes
oughten hir to spare, i.e.* be considerate to.

A doghter hadde they bitwixe hem two,
Of twenty yeer, withouten any mo,   3970
Savynge a child that was of half yeer age ;
In cradel it lay, and was a propre page.
This wenche thikke and wel y-growen was,
With kamuse nose, and eyen greye as glas ;
Buttokes brode, and brestes rounde and
     hye,
But right fair was hire heer, I wol nat lye.
   This person of the toun, for she was feir,
In purpos was to maken hire his heir,
Both of his catel and his mesuage,   3979
And straunge he made it of hir mariage.
His purpos was for to bistowe hire hye
Into som worthy blood of auncetrye ;
For hooly chirches good moot been
     despended
On hooly chirches blood that is descended ;
Therfore he wolde his hooly blood honoure,
Though that he hooly chirche sholde
     devoure.
   Gret- sokene hath this millere, out of
     doute,
With whete and malt of al the land aboute ;
And nameliche, ther was a greet collegge,
Men clepen the Soler Halle at Cante-
     bregge ;   3990
Ther was hir whete and eek hir malt
     y-grounde.
And on a day it happed in a stounde,
Sik lay the maunciple on a maladye—
Men wenden wisly that he sholde dye,—
For which this millere stal bothe mele
     and corn
An hundred tyme moore than biforn :
For ther-biforn he stal but curteisly,
But now he was a theef outrageously ;
For which the wardeyn chidde and made
     fare ;   3999
But ther-of sette the millere nat a tare ;
He craketh boost, and swoor it was nat so.
   Thanne were ther yonge, poure clerkes
     two,
That dwelten in this halle of which I seye ;

Testif they were, and lusty for to pleye ;
And, oonly for hire myrthe and revelrye,
Upon the wardeyn bisily they crye,
To yeve hem leve, but a litel stounde,
To goon to mille and seen hir corn
     y-grounde,
And hardily they dorste leye hir nekke,
The millere shold nat stele hem half a
     pekke   4010
Of corn, by sleighte, ne by force hem reve.
And at the laste the wardeyn yaf hem leve.
John highte that oon, and Aleyn highte
     that oother ;
Of o toun were they born, that highte
     Strother,
Fer in the North, I kan nat telle where.
   This Aleyn maketh redy al his gere,
And on an hors the sak he caste anon.
Forth goth Aleyn the clerk, and also John,
With good swerd and with bokeler by
     hir side.   4019
John knew the wey, hem nedede no gyde ;
And at the mille the sak adoun he layth.
Aleyn spak first, ' Al hayl, Symond,
     y-fayth !
How fares thy faire doghter, and thy wyf ? '
   ' Aleyn, welcome,' quod Symkyn, ' by
     my lyf !
And John also, how now ? what do ye
     heer ? '
   ' Symond,' quod John, ' by God, nede
     has na peer,
Hym boes serve hym-self that has na
     swayn,
Or elles he is a fool, as clerkes sayn.   4028
Oure manciple, I hope he will be deed,
Swa werkes ay the wanges in his heed ;
And forthy is I come, and eek Alayn,
To grynde oure corn and carie it ham
     agayn.
I pray yow spede us heythen that ye may.'
   ' It shal be doon,' quod Symkyn, ' by
     my fay !
What wol ye doon, whil that it is in hande ? '
   ' By God, right by the hopur wil I stande,'
Quod John, ' and se how that the corn
     gas in.

3980. *he*, om. H.
3985. *hooly*, H *joly*.
3990. *Soler Halle*, the hall with the solers, or
un-chambers, *i.e.* rooms with bay-windows,
probably King's Hall, one of the predecessors
f Trinity College.
3996. *An hundred tyme*, H *a thousend part.*
3998. *was*, H *is.*

4026. *na peer*. The two clerks speak throughout in northern dialect.
4027. *Hym boes*, behoves him ; H, *falles* ;
Camb. *muste* ; rest *bihoves, byhoveth.*

Yet saugh I never, by my fader kyn,
How that the hopur waggès til and fra.'
  Aleynanswérdè, 'John, and wiltowswa?
Thanne wil I be bynethè, by my croun !
And se how that the melè fallès doun
Into the trough,—that sal be my disport ;
For John, y-faith, I may been of youre
    sort,
I is as ille a millere as are ye.'
  This millere smylèd of hir nycètee,
And thoghte, 'Al this nys doon but for
    a wyle ;
They wenè that no man may hem bigile ;
But by my thrift yet shal I blere hir eye,
For al the sleighte in hir philosophye. 4050
The moorè queyntè crekès that they
    make,
The moorè wol I stelè whan I take.
In stide of flour yet wol I yeve hem bren;
The gretteste clerkès been noght wisest
    men,
As whilom to the wolf thus spak the mare;
Of al hir art ne counte I noght a tare.'
  Out at the dore he gooth ful pryvèly,
Whan that he saugh his tymè softèly.
He looketh up and doun til he hath founde
The clerkès hors, ther as it stood y-bounde
Bihynde the mille, under a levèsel,   4061
And to the hors he gooth hym faire and
    wel ;
He strepeth of the brydel right anon,
And whan the hors was laus, he gynneth gon
Toward the fen, ther wildè marès renne,—
Forth with ' Wehee !' thurgh thikkè and
    thurgh thenne.
  This millere gooth agayn, no word he
    seyde,
But dooth his note and with the clerkès
    pleyde,

Til that hir corn was faire and weel
    y-grounde ;
And whan the mele is sakkèd and
    y-bounde,   4070
This John goth out, and fynt his hors away,
And gan to crie, ' Harrow !' and, ' Weyl-
    away !
Oure hors is lorn ; Alayn, for Goddès banes
Stepe on thy feet ; com out, man, al atanes !
Allas, our wardeyn has his palfrey lorn !'
This Aleyn al forgat, bothe mele and corn ;
Al was out of his mynde his housbondrie.
'What, whilk way is he geen ?' he gan
    to crie.
  The wyf cam lepynge inward with a ren ;
She seyde, 'Allas, youre hors goth to
    the fen   4080
With wildè mares, as faste as he may go ;
Unthank come on his hand that boond
    hym so,
And he that bettrè sholde han knyt the
    reyne !'   .
  ' Allas,' quod John, ' Aleyn, for Cristès
    peyne,
Lay doun thy swerd, and I wil myn alswa.
I is ful wight, God waat, as is a raa ;
By Goddès hertè ! he sal nat scape us
    bathe.
Why nadstow pit the capul in the lathe ?
Il-hayl, by God, Aleyn, thou is a fonne.'
  Thise sely clerkès han ful faste y-ronne
Toward the fen, bothe Aleyn and eek
    John ;   4091
And whan the millere saugh that they
    were gon,
He half a busshel of hir flour hath take,
And bad his wyf go knede it in a cake.
He seyde, 'I trowe the clerkès were aferd ;
Yet kan a millere make a clerkès berd,
For al his art ; now lat hem goon hir weye !
Lo wher they goon ; ye, lat the children
    pleye ;
They gete hym nat so lightly, by my
    croun !'
  Thise sely clerkes rennen up and doun
With ' Keepe ! keepe ! stand ! stand !
    Jossa warderere !   4101

4046. *smyled of*, H *smyleth for*.
4051. *crekes*, H *knakkes*.
4053. *flour*, H *mele*.
4055. *As whilom*, etc. 'The story alluded to is told of a Mule in *Cent. Nov. Ant.* No. 91. The Mule pretends that his name is written upon the bottom of his hind-foot. The Wolf attempting to read it, the Mule gives him a kick on the forehead and kills him. Upon which the Fox, who was present, observes : *Ogni huomo, che sa lettera, non è savio*' (Tyrwhitt). A variant of the story occurs in *Reynard the Fox*.
4064. *gynneth*, H *gan to*.
4066. *and*, H *and eek*.

4090. *han ful faste y-ronne*, H *speeden hem anoon*.
4095. *were*, H *ben*.

Ga wyghtly thou, and I shal kepe him
    heere.'
But shortly, til that it was verray nyght,
They koudè nat, though they dide al hir
    myght,
Hir capul cacche, he ran alwey so faste,
Til in a dych they caughte hym attè laste.
    Wery and weet, as beest is in the reyn,
Comth sely John, and with him comth
    Aleyn.
'Allas!' quod John, 'the day that I was
    born!   4109
Now are we dryve til hethyng and til scorn;
Oure corn is stoln, men wil us foolès calle,
Bathè the wardeyn and oure felawes alle,
And namèly the millere, weylaway!'
    Thus pleyneth John, as he gooth by
    the way
Toward the mille, and Bayard in his hond.
The millere sittynge by the fyr he fond,—
For it was nyght and forther myghte they
    noght,—
But for the love of God they hym bisoght
Of herberwe and of ese, as for hir peny.
    The millere seyde agayn, "If ther be
    eny,   4120
Swich as it is, yet shal ye have youre part;
Myn hous is streit, but ye han lernèd art,
Ye konne by argumentès make a place
A mylè brood of twenty foot of space.
Lat se now if this placè may suffise,
Or make it rowm with speche, as is youre
    gise.'
    'Now, Symond,' seydè John, 'by Seint
    Cutberd,
Ay is thou myrie, and this is faire answérd.
I have herd seyd, "Man sal taa of twa
    thynges,
Slyk as he fyndes, or taa slyk as he
    brynges";   4130
But specially I pray thee, hoostè deere,
Get us som mete and drynke, and make
    us cheere,
And we wil payen trewely attè fulle;
With empty hand men may none haukès
    tulle;
Loo, heere our silver, redy for to spende.'
    This millere into toun his doghter sende

For ale and breed, and rosted hem a goos,
And boond hire hors, it sholdè nat goon
    loos,
And in his owene chambre hem made a
    bed,   4139
With sheetès and with chalons faire y-spred,
Noght from his owene bed ten foot or
    twelve.
His doghter hadde a bed al by hir-selve,
Right in the samè chambre by and by;
It myghtè be no bet, and causè why?
Ther was no roumer herberwe in the place.
They soupen, and they speke hem to solace,
And drynken ever strong ale attè beste.
Aboutè mydnyght wentè they to reste.
    Wel hath this millere vernysshèd his
    heed: 4149
Ful pale he was for-dronken, and nat reed.
He yexeth, and he speketh thurgh the nose,
As he were on the quakke or on the pose.
To bedde he goth, and with hym goth
    his wyf,
As any jay she light was and jolyf;
So was hir joly whistle wel y-wet;
The cradel at hir beddès feet is set,
To rokken, and to yeve the child to sowke:
And whan that dronken al was in the
    crowke,   4158
To beddè went the doghter right anon;
To beddè wente Aleyn, and also John;
Ther nas na moore; hem neededè no dwale.
This millere hath so wisely bibbèd ale
That as an hors he snorteth in his sleepe;
Ne of his tayl bihynde he took no keepe;
His wyf bar him a burdon, a ful strong,
Men myghte hir rowtyng heerè two furlong;
The wenchè rowteth eek, *par compaignye*.
    Aleyn the clerk, that herd this melodye,
He pokèd John, and seydè, 'Slepestow?
Herdistow ever slyk a sang er now?   4170
Lo, whilk a compline is y-mel hem alle!
A wildè fyr upon thair bodyes falle!
Wha herkned ever slyk a ferly thyng?
Ye, they sal have the flour of il endyng!
This langè nyght ther tydès me na reste,
But yet, nafors; al sal be for the beste,
For, John,' seydè he, 'als ever moot
    I thryve,

4102. *wyghtly*, E⁶ *whistle*.
4105. *he ran alwey*, H *it ran away*.

4138. *it sholde nat goon*, H⁶ *he schold no more go*.

If that I may, yon wenché wil I swyve.
Som esément has lawe y-shapen us ;   4179
For, John, ther is a lawé that says thus,
That gif a man in a point be y-greved,
That in another he sal be releved.
Oure corn is stoln, sothly it is na nay,
And we han had an il fit al this day ;
And syn I sal have neen amendément
Agayn my los, I wil have esément.
By Goddes sale ! it sal neen other bee.'
  This John answerde, 'Alayn, avysé thee ;
The millere is a perilous man,' he seyde,
'And gif that he out of his sleepe abreyde,
He mighté doon us bathe a vileynye.'   4191
  Aleyn answerde, 'I count hym nat a flye.'
And up he rist, and by the wenche he
    crepte.
This wenché lay uprighte, and fasté slepte
Til he so ny was, er she myghte espie,
That it had been to laté for to crie ;
And, shortly for to seyn, they were at on.
Now pley, Aleyn, for I wol speke of John.
  This John lith stille a furlong wey or two,
And to hymself he maketh routhe and wo ;
'Allas !' quod he, 'this is a wikked jape ;
Now may I seyn that I is but an ape ;
Yet has my felawe somwhat for his harm,—
He has the milleris doghter in his arm,
He auntred hym, and has his nedés sped,
And I lye as a draf sak in my bed ;
And when this jape is tald another day,
I sal been halde a daf, a cokénay.
I wil arise and auntre it, by my fayth ;
" Unhardy is unseely," thus men sayth.'
And up he roos and softély he wente   4211
Unto the cradel, and in his hand it hente,
And baar it softe unto his beddés feet.
  Soone after this the wyf hir rowtyng leet,
And gan awake and wente hire out to pisse,
And cam agayn, and gan hir cradel mysse,
And groped heer and ther, but she foond
    noon.
'Allas !' quod she, 'I hadde almoost
    mysgoon ;
I hadde almoost goon to the clerkés bed.
Ey, *benedicite !* thanne hadde I foule
    y-sped.'   4220

4183. *sothly,* E² *shortly.*
4199. *wey,* H *while.*
4200. *he maketh routhe and wo,* H *compleyned
of his wo.*

And forth she gooth til she the cradel fond :
She gropeth alwey forther with hir hond,
And foond the bed and thoghté noght
    but good,
By-causé that the cradel by it stood,
And nysté wher she was, for it was derk,
But faire and wel she creepe into the clerk ;
And lith ful stille and wolde han caught
    a sleepe.
Withinne a while this John the clerk up
    leepe,   4228
And on this goodé wyf he leith on soore ;
So myrie a fit ne hadde she nat ful yoore ;
He priketh harde and soore as he were mad.
This joly lyf han thise two clerkés lad,
Til that the thriddé cok bigan to synge.
  Aleyn wax wery in the dawénynge,
For he had swonken al the longé nyght ;
And seydé, 'Fare weel, Malyne, sweeté
    wight.
The day is come, I may no lenger byde ;
But evermo, wher so I go or ryde,
I is thyn awen clerk, swa have I seel.'
  'Now, deeré lemman,' quod she, 'go,
    fareweel !   4240
But, er thow go, o thyng I wol thee telle ;
Whan that thou wendest homward by the
    melle,
Right at the entree of the dore bihynde,
Thou shalt a cake of half a busshel fynde,
That was y-maked of thyn owene mele,
Which that I heelpe my fader for to stele ;
And, goodé lemman, God thee save and
    kepe !'
And with that word almoost she gan to
    wepe.
  Aleyn up rist and thoughte, 'Er that
    it dawe,
I wol go crepen in by my felawe' ;   4250
And fond the cradel with his hand anon.
'By God !' thoughte he, 'al wrang I
    have mysgon ;
Myn heed is toty of my swynk to nyght,
That maketh me that I go nat aright ;
I woot wel by the cradel I have mysgo ;
Heere lith the millere and his wyf also.'
And forth he goth, a twenty devel way,
Unto the bed ther as the millere lay.

4225. *And nysté,* H *Nat knowyng.*
4231. *soore,* H⁵ *deepe.*

He wende have cropen by his felawe John,
And by the millere in he crepe anon,   4260
And caughte hym by the nekke, and softe
    he spak ;
He seyde, ' Thou John, thou swynės-
    heed, awak,
For Cristès saule, and heer a noble game ;
For by that lord that callèd is seint Jame,
As I have thriės in this shortė nyght
Swyvèd the milleres doghter bolt upright,
Whil thow hast as a coward been agast.'
    ' Ye, falsèharlot,' quod the millere, 'hast ?
A ! falsè traitour ! falsè clerk ! ' quod he,
' Thow shalt be deed, by Goddės dignitee !
Who dorstė be so boold to disparage   4271
My doghter, that is come of swich lynage ?'
And by the throtė-bolle he caughtė Alayn ;
And he hente hym despitously agayn,
And on the nose he smoot hym with his
    fest.
Doun ran the blody streem upon his brest,
And in the floor, with nose and mouth
    to-broke,
They walwe as doon two piggės in a poke ;
And up they goon and doun agayn anon,
Til that the millere spornėd at a stoon,
And doun he fil bakward upon his wyf,
That wistė no thyng of this nycė stryf ;
For she was falle aslepe a litė wight
With John the clerk, that wakėd hadde
    al nyght ;
And with the fal out of hir sleepe she
    breyde.
' Help, hooly croys of Bromėholm,' she
    seyde,
' *In manus tuas*, Lord, to thee I calle !
Awak, Symond ! the feend is on us falle !
Myn herte is broken ! help ! I nam but
    deed !
Ther lyth oon upon my wombe and on
    myn heed.   4290
Helpe, Symkyn, for the falsè clerkės fighte!'
    This John stirte up, as soone as ever
    he myghte,
And graspeth by the wallės to and fro

4264. *called*, H *cleped.*
4272. *swich*, H *hik.*
4279. *agayn*, H *they goon.*
4280. *sporned*, H *stumbled.*
4286. *Bromeholm*, a Norfolk priory.
4288. *is on us falle*, H *is in thi halle.*

To fynde a staf, and she stirte up also,
And knewe the estrės bet than dide this
    John,
And by the wal a staf she foond anon,
And saugh a litel shymeryng of a light,
For at an hole in shoon the moonė bright ;
And by that lightshesaugh hem bothė two,
But sikerly she nystė who was who ;   4300
But as she saugh a whit thyng in hir eye ;
And whan she gan the whitė thyng espye,
She wende the clerk hadde wered a
    volupeer,
And with the staf she drough ay neer
    and neer
And wende han hit this Aleyn at the fulle ;
And smoot the millere on the pylėd skulle,
And doun he gooth, and cride, ' Harrow !
    I dye ! '
Thise clerkės beete hym weel and lete
    hym lye,
And greythen hem, and tooke hir hors anon,
And eek hire mele, and on hir wey they
    gon,   4310
And at the millė yet they tooke hir cake
Of half a busshel flour ful wel y-bake.
    Thus is the proude millerė wel y-bete,
And hath y-lost the gryndynge of the whete,
And payėd for the soper everideel
Of Aleyn and of John, that bette hym weel ;
His wyf is swyvėd, and his doghter als.
Lo ! swich it is a millere to be fals ;
And therfore this proverbe is seyd ful sooth,
' Hym thar nat wenė wel that yvele dooth,'
A gylour shal hymself bigylėd be,—   4321
And God, that sitteth heighe in Trinitee,
Save al this compaignyė, grete and smale.
Thus have I quyt the Millere in my tale.

COOK'S TALE

The prologe of the Cokes Tale

The Cook of Londoun, whil the Revė
    spak,

4296. *a staf she foond*, H *sche took a staf.*
4297. *shymeryng*, H *glymeryng.*
4304. *ay*, H *hir.*
4309. *greythen*, equip ; H *greyth hem wel.*
4310. *on hir wey*, H *hoom anon.*
4311. *at the millė yet*, H *at the millen dore.*
4322. *Trinitee*, H *Magestee.*

For joye him thoughte he clawed him on
    the bak ;
'Ha, ha!' quod he, 'for Cristès passioun
This millere hadde a sharpe conclusioun
Upon his argument of herbergage ;
Wel seydè Salomon, in his langage,   4330
"Ne brynge nat every man into thyn hous,"
For herberwynge by nyghte is perilous.
Wel oghte a man avysèd for to be
Whom that he broghte into his pryvètee.
I pray to God, so yeve me sorwe and care,
If ever, sitthe I hightè Hogge of Ware,
Herde I a millere bettre y-set a werk ;
He hadde a jape of malice in the derk.
But God forbedè that we styntè heere,
And therfore if ye vouchè-sauf to heere
A tale of me, that am a pourè man,   4341
I wol yow telle, as wel as ever I kan,
A litel jape that fil in oure citee.'
    Oure Hoost answèrde and seide, 'I
    graunte it thee ;
Now telle on, Roger, looke that it be good ;
For many a pastee hastow laten blood,
And many a jakke of Dovere hastow soold,
That hath been twiès hoot and twiès coold ;
Of many a pilgrym hastow Cristès curs,
For of thy percely yet they fare the
    wors,   4350
That they han eten with thy stubbel goos;
For in thy shoppe is many a flyè loos.
Now telle on, gentil Roger by thy name.
But yet I pray thee be nat wroth for game,
A man may seye ful sooth in game and
    pley.'
    'Thou seist ful sooth,' quod Roger,
    'by my fey !
But "sooth pley quaad pley," as the
    Flemyng seith ;
And therfore, Herry Bailly, by thy feith,
Be thou nat wrooth, er we departen heer
Though that my tale be of an hostileer :
But nathèlees I wol nat telle it yit ; 4361
But er we parte, y-wis, thou shalt be quit.'
And therwithal he lough and madè cheere,
And seyde his tale, as ye shul after heere.

4335. *so geve me sorwe*, H *so gyf my body.*
4347. *a jakke of Dovere*, said to be 'a sea-
fish,' but more probably a pudding.
4357. *sooth pley quaad pley*, true jest, bad
jest. Cp. 'soth bourd is no bourd.'

Heere bigynneth The Cookes Tale

A prentys whilom dwelled in oure citee,
And of a craft of vitailliers was hee.
Gaillard he was as goldfynch in the shawe ;
Broun as a berye, a propre short felawe,
With lokkès blake, y-kempd ful fetisly.
Dauncen he koude so wel and jolily,   4370
That he was clepèd Perkyn Revelour.
He was as ful of love and paramour
As is the hyvè ful of hony sweete.
Wel was the wenchè with hym myghtè
    meete ;
At every bridale wolde he synge and hoppe,
He lovèd bet the taverne than the shoppe.
For whan ther any ridyng was in Chepe,
Out of the shoppè thider wolde he lepe ;
Til that he haddè al the sightè y-seyn,
And dauncèd wel, he wolde nat come
    ageyn ;   4380
And gadered hym a meynee of his sort,
To hoppe and synge and maken swich
    disport ;
And ther they setten stevene for to
    meete,
To pleyen at the dys in swich a streete ;
For in the toun ne was ther no prentys
That fairer koudè caste a paire of dys
Than Perkyn koude, and therto he was
    free
Of his dispense, in place of pryvètee.
That fond his maister wel in his chaffare,
For often tyme he foond his box ful bare :
For sikerly a prentys revelour,   4391
That haunteth dys, riot, or paramour,
His maister shal it in his shoppe abye,
Al have he no part of the mynstralcye ;
For thefte and riot they been convertible,
Al konne he pleye on gyterne or ribible.
Revel and trouthe, as in a lowe degree,
They been ful wrothe al day, as men
    may see.
    This joly prentys with his maister bood,
Til he were ny out of his prentishood ;
Al were he snybbèd bothe erly and late,
And somtyme lad with revel to Newègate :
But attè laste his maister hym bithoghte,

4370. *jolily*, H *pratety.*
4373. *hyve ful*, H *hony-combe.*
4391. *sikerly a*, H *such a joly.*
4392. *riot*, H *revel.*

Upon a day, whan he his papir soghte,
Of a proverbe that seith this samé word,
'Wel bet is roten appul out of hoord,
Than that it rotie al the reménaunt.'
So fareth it by a riotous servaunt,
It is wel lassé harm to lete hym pace
Than he shende alle the servauntz in the
    place.   4410
Therfore his maister yaf hym acquitance,
And bad hym go with sorwe and with
    meschance ;
And thus this joly prentys hadde his leve.
Now lat him riote al the nyght or leve.
And for ther is no theef withoute a
    lowke,
That helpeth hym to wasten and to sowke,

Of that he brybé kan or borwe may,
Anon he sente his bed and his array
Unto a compier of his owene sort,   4419
That lovéde dys, and revel and disport,
And hadde a wyf that heeld for contenance
A shoppe, and swyvéd for hir suste-
    nance . . .

Of this Cokes Tale maked Chaucer
na more

4422. *Of this Cokes tale*, etc., from Hengwrt
MS. In many MSS. here follows the Tale of
Gamelyn, which Chaucer probably meant to re-
write and assign to the Yeoman; but the tale, as
it stands, is none of Chaucer's, and is therefore
not printed here. The rest of the tales supposed
to be told on the first day of the Pilgrimage are
lacking, and, almost certainly, were never written.

TALES OF THE SECOND DAY

GROUP B

The wordes of the Hoost to the
compaignye

OURE Hosté saugh wel that the
    brighté sonne
The ark of his artificial day hath ronne
The ferthé part, and half an houre and
    moore,
And though he were nat depe experte in
    loore,
He wiste it was the eightétethé day
Of Aprill, that is messager to May ;
And saugh wel that the shadwe of every
    tree
Was, as in lengthe, the samé quantitee
That was the body erect that causéd it ;
And therfore by the shadwe he took his
    wit   10
That Phebus, which that shoon so clere
    and brighte,

Degrees was fyve and fourty clombe on
    highte ;
And for that day, as in that latitude,
It was ten of the clokke, he gan conclude ;
And sodeynly he plighte his hors aboute.
   'Lordynges,' quod he, 'I warne yow,
    al this route,
The fourthé party of this day is gon.
Now for the love of God and of Seint John,
Leseth no tyme, as ferforth as ye may.
Lordynges, the tymé wasteth nyght and
    day   20
And steleth from us,—what pryvély
    slepýnge,
And what thurgh necligence in oure
    wakýnge,—
As dooth the streem that turneth never
    agayn,
Descendynge fro the montaigne into playn.
   'Wel kan Senec, and many a philo-
    sophre,
Biwaillen tymé moore than gold in cofre ;
For "losse of catel may recovered be,

2. *his artificial day*, *i.e.* between sunrise and
sunset as opposed to the day of 24 hours.
3. *The ferthe part*, etc. On April 18th (April
26th of the reformed calendar) the sun would have
accomplished the fourth part of his day's journey
at 9.20 A.M., leaving 40 minutes, or 'half-an-hour
and more,' to 10 o'clock.
4. *experte*, om. H ; *y-stert*, E².
11. *clere*, H *fair*.

12. *Degrees*, etc. The sun attained this altitude
exactly at 9.58.
20. *the tyme*, etc. Imitated from the *Roman
de la Rose*, cp. the English translation, ll. 369
sqq.

But losse of tymė shendeth us," quod he ;
It wol nat come agayn, withouten drede,
Namoorė than wole Malkynes mayden-
    hede,   30
Whan she hath lost it in hir wantow-
    nesse ;
Lat us nat mowlen thus in ydelnesse.
  ' Sire Man of Lawe,' quod he, ' so have
    ye blis,
Telle us a tale anon, as forward is ;
Ye been submytted thurgh youre free
    assent
To stonden in this cas at my juggėment.
Acquiteth yow and holdeth youre biheeste,
Thanne have ye doon youre devoir attė
    leeste.'
  ' Hostė,' quod he, ' *depardieux* ich
    assente ;
To brekė forward is nat myn entente. 40
Biheste is dette, and I wole holdė fayn
Al my biheste, I kan no bettrė sayn ;
For swich lawe as man yeveth another
    wight
He sholde hym-selven usen it by right ;
Thus wole oure text ; but nathéless certeyn
I kan right now no thrifty talė seyn,
But Chaucer, thogh he kan but lewedly,
On metres and on rymyng craftily,
Hath seyd hem, in swich Englissh as he
    kan,
Of oldė tyme, as knoweth many a man. 50
And if he have noght seyd hem, levė
    brother,
In o book, he hath seyd hem in another.
For he hath toold of loveris up and doun
Mo than Ovidė made of mencioun
In his Epistellės, that been ful olde.
What sholde I tellen hem, syn they ben
    tolde ?
  ' In youthe he made of Ceys and
    Alcione,
And sithen hath he spoken of everichone
Thise noble wyvės and thise loveris eke.
Who so that wole his largė volume seke,

Clepėd the Seintės Legende of Cupide,
Ther may he seen the largė woundės wyde
Of Lucresse and of Babilan Tesbee ;
The swerd of Dido for the false Enee ;
The tree of Phillis for hire Demophon ;
The pleinte of Dianire and of Hermyon ;
Of Adriane and of Isiphilee ;
The bareyne ylė stondynge in the see ;
The dreyntė Leandrė for his Erro ;
The teeris of Eleyne ; and eek the wo 70
Of Brixseyde, and of the, Ladómya !
The crueltee of the, queene Mėdea !
Thy litel children hangynge by the hals,
For thy Jasón, that was in love so fals !
O Ypermystra, Penolopee, Alceste,
Youre wifhede he comendeth with the
    beste !
  ' But certeinly no word ne writeth he
Of thilkė wikke ensample of Canacee,
That loved hir owenė brother synfully ;
(Of swichė cursėd stories I sey fy !)   80
Or ellis of Tyro Appollonius,
How that the cursėd kyng Antiochus
Birafte his doghter of hir maydenhede,
That is so horríble a talė for to rede,
Whan he hir threw upon the pavėment ;
And therfore he, of ful avysėment,
Nolde nevere write in none of his sermons
Of swiche unkynde abhomynacions,
Ne I wol noon reherce, if that I may.
  ' But of my tale how shall I doon this
    day ?   90
Me werė looth be likned, doutėlees,

61. *the Seintes Legende of Cupide* (H
Legendes), the *Legend of Good Women*, *i.e.* of
Cupid's Saints. In the list which follows, the
Man of Law omits the names of Cleopatra and
Philomela, of whom Chaucer wrote, while of
Deianira, Hermione, Hero, Helen, Briseis,
Laodameia, Penelope and Alcestis no legends
remain.
63. *Babilan Tesbee*, Thisbe of Babylon.
67. *Adriane*, Ariadne.
67. *Isiphilee*, Hypsipyle.
68. *The bareyne ylė*, Naxos.
74. *thy*, H *thilke*.
74. *in*, H *of.*
78. *Canacee.* ' This and the story of Apollonius of Tyre are told in Gower's *Confessio
Amantis*, whence it has been supposed that
Chaucer intended here to blame that writer—a
notion for which there appears to be no good
foundation ' (Wright).
80. *Of swiche*, H *On whiche.*
84. *for to*, H *as man may.*

57. *of Ceys and Alcione*, the story of Ceyx and
Alcyone, from Ovid, *Metam.* bk. xi. It forms
the subject of ll. 62-220 of Chaucer's *Book of the
Duchesse*, which may have been originally an
independent poem. The *Book of the Duchesse*
was written in 1368, when Chaucer was nearly
thirty.

To Muses that men clepe Pierides,—
Methamorphosios woot what I mene,—
But nathélees, I recché noght a bene,
Though I come after hym with hawébake;
I speke in prose, and lat him rymés make.'
And with that word, he with a sobré cheere
Bigan his tale, as ye shal after heere.

MAN OF LAW'S TALE

The Prologe of the Manne of Lawes Tale

O hateful harm ! condicion of poverte !
With thurst, with coold, with hunger so
    confoundid !   100
To asken help thee shameth in thyn herte;
If thou noon aske so soore artow y-woundid,
That verray nede unwrappeth al thy
    wounde hid !
Maugree thyn heed, thou most for indigence
Or stele, or begge, or borwé thy despence !

Thow blamest Crist, and seist ful bitterly,
He mysdeparteth richesse temporal ;
Thy neighébore thou wytest synfully,
And seist thou hast to lite and he hath al.
'*Parfay*,' seistow, 'somtyme he rekene
    shal,   110
Whan that his tayl shal brennen in the
    gleede,
For he noght helpeth needfulle in hir neede.'

Herké what is the sentence of the wise:
'Bet is to dyen than have indigence';
Thy selvé neighébor wol thee despise,
If thou be poure, farwel thy reverence !
Yet of the wisé man take this sentence :
'Allé the dayes of pouré men been wikke';
Be war therfore, er thou come to that
    prikke !   119

If thou be poure thy brother hateth thee,
And alle thy freendés fleen from thee, allas !

O riché marchauntz, ful of wele been yee,
O noble, o prudent folk, as in this cas !
Youre baggés been nat fild with *ambés as*,
But with *sys cynk*, that renneth for youre
    chaunce ;
At Cristémasse wel myrie may ye daunce !

Ye seken lond and see for yowre
    wynnynges ;
As wisé folk ye knowen all thestaat
Of regnés ; ye been fadrés of tidynges
And talés, bothe of pees and of debaat. 130
I were right now of talés desolaat,
Nere that a marchant—goon is many a
    yeere—
Me taughte a talé, which that ye shal heere.

*Heere begynneth The Man of Lawe his
Tale*

PART I

In Surrye whilom dwelte a compaignye
Of chapmen riche, and therto sadde and
    trewe,
That wydé-where senten hir spicerye,
Clothés of gold, and satyns riche of hewe.
Hir chaffare was so thrifty and so newe
That every wight hath deyntee to chaffare
With hem, and eek to sellen hem hire ware.

Now fil it that the maistrés of that sort 141
Han shapen hem to Romé for to wende,
Were it for chapmanhode, or for disport,
Noon oother message wolde they thider
    sende,
But comen hem-self to Rome, this is the
    ende ;
And in swich place as thoughte hem
    ávantage
For hire entente, they take hir herbergage.

Sojourned han thise marchantz in that
    town
A certein tyme, as fil to hire plesance ;

---

92. *Pierides*, 'the daughters of Pierus, that contended with the Muses, and were changed into Pies, Ovid, *Metam.* v.' (Tyrwhitt).

99. ll. 99-103, 1c6-8, 112, 113-5, 118, 120-1, are imitated from the sixteenth chapter of Pope Innocent III.'s *De Contemptu Mundi*. The two Biblical quotations are from Ecclus. xl. 29 and Prov. xiv. 20.

Heere begynneth, etc. The tale which follows is taken in the main from the Anglo-French Chronicle of Nicholas Trivet, an English Dominican who died some time after 1334. The translation is nowhere very close, and 'of the 1029 lines of which the tale consists, about 350 are Chaucer's additions' (Brock).

And so bifel that thexcellent renoun   150
Of the Emperoures doghter, dame
    Custance,
Reported was, with every circumstance,
Unto thise Surryen marchantz in swich
    wyse,
Fro day to day, as I shal yow devyse.

    This was the commune voys of every
      man :
' Oure Emperour of Rome, God hym see !
A doghter hath that, syn the world bigan,
To rekene as wel hir goodness as beautee,
Nas never swich another as is shee.
I prey to God, in honour hire susteene,
And wolde she were of all Europe the
    queene !   161

In hire is heigh beautee, withoute pride,
Yowthe, withoute grenehede or folye ;
To alle hire werkes vertu is hir gyde ;
Humblesse hath slayn in hire al tirannye ;
She is miróur of alle curteisye,
Hir herte is verray chambre of hoolynesse,
Hir hand ministre of fredam for almesse.'

And al this voys was sooth, as God is
    trewe ;
But now to purpos lat us turne agayn. 170
Thise marchantz han doon fraught hir
    shippes newe,
And whan they han this blisful mayden
    sayn,
Hoom to Surryë been they went ful fayn,
And doon hir nedes as they han doon yoore,
And lyven in wele ; I kan sey yow namoore.

    Now fil it that thise marchantz stode
      in grace
Of hym that was the sowdan of Surrye ;
For whan they cam from any strange place
He wolde of his benigne curteisye
Make hem good chiere and bisily espye 180
Tidynges of sondry regnes, for to leere
The wondres that they myghte seen or
    heere.

Amonges othere thynges specially,
Thise marchantz han hym toold of dame
    Custance

168. *for*, H *and*.

So greet noblesse in ernest, ceriously,
That this sowdan hath caught so greet
    plesance
To han hir figure in his remembrance,
That all his lust, and al his bisy cure,
Was for to love hire while his lyf may dure.

Paráventure in thilke large book,   190
Which that men clipe the hevene, y·
    writen was
With sterres, whan that he his birthe took,
That he for love sholde han his deeth, allas !
For in the sterres, clerer than is glas,
Is written, God woot, whoso koude it rede,
The deeth of every man, withouten drede.

In sterres many a wynter ther biforn
Was writen the deeth of Ector, Achilles,
Of Pompei, Julius, er they were born,
The strif of Thebes, and of Ercules,   200
Of Sampson, Turnus, and of Socrates
The deeth ; but mennes wittes ben so dulle
That no wight kan wel rede it atte fulle.

    This sowdan for his privee conseil sente,
And, shortly of this matiere for to pace,
He hath to hem declared his entente,
And seyde hem, certein, but he myghte
    have grace
To han Custance withinne a litel space,
He nas but deed, and charged hem in hye
To shapen for his lyf som remedye.   210

    Diverse men diverse thynges seyden,
They argumenten, casten up and doun ;
Many a subtil resoun forth they leyden ;
They speken of magyk and abusioun ;
But finally, as in conclusioun,
They kan nat seen in that noon avantage,
Ne in noon oother wey, save mariage.

185. *ceriously*, glossed *ceriose* in E², which may be meant either for *serie* (seriously) or *seriatim* (in order) ; Camb. *certeynly*, Lansd. *curiously*, H *so rially* (? for *serially*).
190. *Paraventure*. This and the next five stanzas are Chaucer's own, and probably later work. In ll. 197-201 he is imitating some lines from the *Megacosmus* of Bernardus Sylvestris beginning—

    ' Praejacet in stellis series, quam longior aetas
      Explicet et spatiis temporis ordo suis.'

201. *Turnus*, the opponent of Æneas.

Thanne sawe they ther-inne swich
 difficultee,
By wey of reson, for to speke al playn,
By-cause that ther was swich diversitee 220
Bitwene hir bothe lawes, that they sayn,
They trowe that ' no cristene prince wolde
 fayn
Wedden his child under oure lawe sweete,
That us was taught by Mahoun, oure
 prophete.'

And he answerde, ' Rather than I lese
Custance, I wol be cristned, doutelees ;
I moot been hires, I may noon oother chese.
I prey yow hoold youre argumentz in pees ;
Saveth my lyf, and beth noght recchelees
To geten hire that hath my lyf in cure ; 230
For in this wo I may nat longe endure."

What nedeth gretter dilatacioun ?
I seye, by tretys and embassadrie,
And by the popes mediacioun,
And al the chirche, and al the chivalrie,
That in destruccioun of maumettrie,
And in encrees of Cristes lawe deere,
They been acorded, so as ye shal heere :

How that the sowdan and his baronage,
And alle his liges, sholde y-cristned be,
And he shal han Custance in mariage, 241
And certein gold, I noot what quantitee ;
And heer-to founden sufficient suretee.
This same accord was sworn on eyther syde.
Now, faire Custance, almyghty God thee
 gyde !

Now wolde som men waiten, as I gesse,
That I sholde tellen al the purveiance
That themperoure, of his grete noblesse,
Hath shapen for his doghter, dame
 Custance.
Wel may men knowen that so greet
 ordinance 250
May no man tellen in a litel clause,
As was arrayed for so heigh a cause.

Bisshopes been shapen with hire for to
 wende,
Lordes, ladies, knyghtes of renoun,

And oother folk ynogh, this is the ende ;
And notified is thurgh-out the toun
That every wight, with greet devocioun,
Sholde preyen Crist, that he this mariage
Receyve in gree and spede this viage.

The day is comen of hir departynge—
I seye, the woful day fatal is come, 261
That ther may be no lenger tariynge,
But forthward they hem dressen alle and
 some.
Custance, that was with sorwe al overcome,
Ful pale arist, and dresseth hire to wende,
For wel she seeth ther is noon oother ende.

Allas ! what wonder is it thogh she wepte,
That shal be sent to strange nacioun,
Fro freendes that so tendrely hire kepte,
And to be bounde under subjeccioun 270
Of oon she knoweth nat his condicioun ?
Housbondes been alle goode, and han
 ben yoore ;
That knowen wyves, I dar say yow na
 moore.

' Fader,' she seyde, ' thy wrecched
 child, Custance,
Thy yonge doghter, fostred up so softe,
And ye, my mooder, my soverayn plesance,
Over alle thyng, out-taken Crist on lofte,
Custance, youre child, hire recomandeth
 ofte
Unto your grace ; for I shal to Surrye,
Ne shal I never seen yow moore with eye.

Allas ! unto the Barbre nacioun 281
I mooste anoon, syn that it is youre wille ;
But Crist, that starf for our savacioun,
So yeve me grace his heestes to fulfille ;
I, wrecche womman, no fors though I spille !
Wommen are born to thraldom and
 penance
And to been under mannes governance.'

I trowe at Troye, when Pirrus brak
 the wal
Or Ilion brende, at Thebes the citee,

230. *To geten*, H *Goth, geteth.*
231. *nat longe*, H *no lenger.*
254. *Lordes*, Camb. *Lordyngis.*

282. *anoon*, E *goon.*
283. *savacioun*, H^b *redempcioun.*
289. *Ilion*, the citadel of Troy.

F   65

Nat Rome, for the harm thurgh Hanybal,
That Romayns hath venquysshed tymes
  thre, 291
Nas herd swich tendre wepyng for pitee,
As in the chambre was for hire partynge;
But forth she moot, wher so she wepe or
  synge.

O firste moevyng, crueel firmament,
With thy diurnal sweigh that crowdest ay,
And hurlest al from Est til Occident,
That naturelly wolde holde another way;
Thy crowdyng set the hevene in swich array
At the bigynnyng of this fiers viage, 300
That crueel Mars hath slayn this mariage!

Infortunat ascendent tortuous,
Of which the lord is helplees, falle, allas,
Out of his angle into the derkeste hous.
O Mars, O atazir, as in this cas!
O fieble Moone, unhappy been thy pas!
Thou knyttest thee ther thou art nat
  receyved;
Ther thou were weel, fro thennes artow
  weyved.

Imprudent emperour of Rome, allas! 309
Was ther no philosophre in al thy toun?
Is no tyme bet than oother in swich cas?
Of viage is ther noon eleccioun,
Namely to folk of heigh condicioun,
Noght whan a roote is of a burthe y-knowe?
Allas! we been to lewed or to slowe!

  To ship is brought this woful, faire
    mayde,
Solempnely, with every circumstance.

293. *partynge*, E⁶ *departynge*.
295. *O firste moevyng*, etc. The *Primum Mobile* is the outermost of the nine spheres, and revolves daily from east to west, carrying the inner spheres with it.
304. *Out of his angle*. The angles were the highest parts of the sphere, and Mars had fallen from his angle to the lowest house in the sphere.
305. *atasir*, planetary influence.
312. *Of viage is ther noon eleccioun*. Only rich people could pay for the calculation of their horoscope from its 'root'; but, when the horoscope was made, the choice of a time for any business became easy, because it was known which planets would be favourable to the undertaker.
316. *brought*, E *come*.

'Now Jhesu Crist be with yow alle,'
  she sayde.
Ther nys namoore, but 'Farewel, faire
  Custance!' 319
She peyneth hire to make good contenance;
And forth I lete hire saille in this manere,
And turne I wole agayn to my matere.

  The mooder of the sowdan, welle of
    vices,
Espied hath hir sones pleyn entente,
How he wol lete his olde sacrifices;
And right anon she for hir conseil sente;
And they been come, to knowe what she
  mente;
And whan assembled was this folk in-feere,
She sette hire doun and seyde as ye shal
  heere.

  'Lordes,' she seyde, 'ye knowen
    everichon, 330
How that my sone in point is for to lete
The hooly lawes of oure Alkaron,
Yeven by Goddes message Makomete;
But oon avow to grete God I heete,
The lyf shal rather out of my body sterte,
Than Makometes lawe out of myn herte!

  What sholde us tyden of this newe lawe,
But thraldom to our bodies and penance,
And afterward in helle to be drawe,
For we reneyed Mahoun oure creance?
But, lordes, wol ye maken assurance 341
As I shal seyn, assentynge to my loore,
And I shal make us sauf for everemoore.'

  They sworen, and assenten every man
To lyve with hire, and dye, and by hire
  stonde,
And everich, in the beste wise he kan,
To strengthen hire shal alle his frendes
  fonde.
And she hath this emprise y-take on honde
Which ye shal heren that I shal devyse;
And to hem alle she spak right in this
  wyse:

323. *welle*, H *full*.
330. *she seyde*, H⁶ *quod sche*. The speeches are Chaucer's.
336. *Than*, H⁴ *Or*.

'We shul first feyne us cristendom to
take,   351
(Coold water shal nat greve us but a lite),
And I shal swiche a feeste and revel make,
That as I trowe I shal the sowdan quite;
For thogh his wyf be cristnéd never so
white
She shal have nede to wasshe awey the rede,
Thogh she a font-ful water with hire lede!'

O sowdanesse, roote of iniquitee!
Virago thou, Semyrame the secounde,
O serpent, under femynynytee,   360
Lik to the serpent depe in helle y-bounde!
O feynéd womman, al that may confounde
Vertu and innocence thurgh thy malice
Is bred in thee, as nest of every vice!

O Sathan, envious syn thilké day
That thou wert chacéd from oure heritage,
Wel knowestow to wommen the oldé way!
Thou madest Eva brynge us in servage,
Thou wolt fordoon this cristen mariage.
Thyn instrument so, weylawey the while!
Makestow of wommen whan thou wolt
bigile.   371

This sowdanesse, whom I thus blame
and warye,
Leet privély hire conseil goon hire way.
What sholde I in this talé lenger tarye?
She rydeth to the sowdan on a day,
And seyde hym that she wolde reneye
hir lay,
And cristendom of preestés handés fonge,
Repentynge hire she hethen was so longe;

Bisechynge hym to doon hire that honóur,
That she moste han the cristen folk to
feeste,—   380
'To plesen hem, I wol do my labóur.'
The sowdan seith, 'I wol doon at youre
heeste';
And knelynge, thanketh hire of that
requeste;
So glad he was he nysté what to seye.
She kiste hir sone, and hoome she gooth
hir weye.

358. *sowdanesse*, Sultaness. The apostrophe
is Chaucer's.
360. *under femynynytee*, in woman's form.

PART II

Arryvéd been this cristen folk to londe
In Surrye, with a greet solempné route;
And hastily this sowdan sente his sonde,
First to his mooder, and all the regne
aboute,
And seyde his wyf was comen, oute of
doute,   390
And preyde hire for to ryde agayn the
queene,
The honour of his regné to susteene.

Greet was the prees, and riché was tharray
Of Surryens and Romayns met yfeere.
The mooder of the sowdan, riche and gay,
Recyveth hire with al-so glad a cheere
As any mooder myghte hir doghter deere,
And to the nexté citee ther bisyde,
A softé paas solempnély they ryde.   399

Noght trowe I the triúmphe of Julius,—
Of which that Lucan maketh swich a
boost,—
Was roialler ne mooré curius,
Than was thassemblee of this blisful hoost;
But this scorpioun, this wikked goost,
The sowdanesse, for all hire flaterynge,
Caste under this ful mortally to stynge.

The sowdan comth hymself soone after this
So roially that wonder is to telle,
And welcometh hire with allé joye and blis;
And thus in murthe and joye I lete hem
dwelle;   410
The fruyt of this matiere is that I telle.
Whan tymé cam, men thoughte it for the
beste
That revel stynte and men goon to hir reste.

The tymé cam this oldé sowdanesse
Ordeynéd hath this feeste of which I tolde,
And to the feesté cristen folk hem dresse
In general, ye, bothé yonge and olde.
Heere may men feeste and roialtee biholde,
And deyntees mo than I kan yow devyse,
But all to deere they boghte it, er they ryse.

400. *the triumphe of Julius*. The stanza is
Chaucer's addition.

67

O sodeyn wo! that ever art súccessóur
To worldly blisse! Spreynd is with
　bitternesse
The ende of the joye of oure worldly
　labóur !
Wo occupieth the fyn of oure gladnesse.
Herké this conseil, for thy sikernesse,
Upon thy gladé day have in thy mynde
'The unwar wo, or harm, that comth
　bihynde.

For schortly for to tellen, at o word,
The sowdan and the cristen everichone 429
Been al to-hewe, and stikéd at the bord,
But it were oonly dame Custance allone.
This oldé sowdanessé, curséd krone !
Hath with hir freendés doon this curséd
　dede,
For she hir-self wolde all the contree lede.

Nether was Surryén noon, that was con-
　verted,
That of the conseil of the sowdan woot,
That he nas al to-hewe er he asterted,
And Custance han they take anon, foot-
　hoot,
And in a ship all steerélees, God woot,
They han hir set and biddeth hire lerné
　saille　　　　　　　　　　　　 440
Out of Surrye, agaynward to Ytaille.

A certein tresor that she thider ladde,
And, sooth to seyn, vitaillé greet plentee,
They han hire yeven, and clothés eek she
　hadde,
And forth she sailleth in the salté see !
O my Custance, ful of benignytee,
O emperourés yongé doghter deere,
He that is lord of fortune be thy steere !

She blesseth hire, and with ful pitous
　voys,　　　　　　　　　　　　 449
Unto the croys of Crist thus seydé she :
' O cleere, O weleful auter, hooly croys,

Reed of the Lambés blood, ful of pitee,
That wesshe the world fro the olde
　iniquitee,
Me fro the feend and fro his clawés kepe,
That day that I shal drenchen in the depe !

Victorious tree, proteccïoun of trewe,
That oonly worthy weré for to bere
The Kyng of Hevene with his woundés
　newe,
The whité Lamb that hurt was with the
　spere ;　　　　　　　　　　　　 459
Flemere of feendés out of hym and here,
On which thy lymés feithfully extenden,
Me helpe, and yif me myght my lyf
　tamenden.'

Yerés and dayés fleteth this creäture
Thurghout the see of Grece unto the strayte
Of Marrok, as it was hire áventure.
On many a sory meel now may she
　bayte ;
After hir deeth ful often may she wayte,
Er that the wildé wawés wol hire dryve
Unto the placé ther she shal arryve.

Men myghten asken why she was nat
　slayn ?　　　　　　　　　　　　 470
Eek at the feeste who myghte hir body save ?
And I answere to that demande agayn,
Who savéd Danyel in the horríble cave,
Ther every wight save he, maister and
　knave,
Was with the leoun frete, er he asterte ?
No wight but God, that he bar in his herte.

God liste to shewe his wonderful myrácle
In hire, for we sholde seen his myghty
　werkis.
Crist, which that is to every harm triácle,
By certeine meenés ofte, as knowen clerkis,
Dooth thyng for certein endé that ful derk is
To mannés wit, that for oure ignorance
Ne konne noght knowe his prudent
　purveiance.

Now sith she was nat at the feeste y-slawe,
Who kepte hire fro the drenchyng in the
　see ?

421. *O sodeyn wo !* The stanza is Chaucer's
addition, taken from the *De Contemptu Mundi*,
i. 23.
427. *or harm that comth,* H *that cometh ay.*
428. *schortly,* E *soothly.*
442. *thider,* E *with hire.*
449-62. Chaucer's addition.

459. *the spere,* H⁶ *a spere.*
470-504. Chaucer's addition.

Who keptė Jonas in the fisshės mawe,
Til he was spouted up at Nynyvee?
Wel may men knowe it was no wight
     but He
That keptė peple Ebrayk from hir
     drenchynge,   489
With dryė feet thurgh-out the see passynge.

Who bad the fourė spirites of tempest,
That power han tanoyen lond and see,
'Bothe north and south, and also west
     and est,
Anoyeth neither see, ne land, ne tree'?
Soothly the comandour of that was He
That fro the tempest ay this womman kepte
As wel when she awok as whan she slepte.

Where myghte this womman mete and
     drynkė have,
Thre yeer and moore? how lasteth hire
     vitaille?
Who feddethe Egypcien Marie in the cave,
Or in desert?   No wight but Crist, *sanz*
     faille.   501
Fyve thousand folk it was as greet mervaille
With lovės fyve, and fisshės two, to feede.
God sente his foyson at hir gretė neede.

She dryveth forth into oure occian,
Thurgh-out oure wildė see, til attė laste
Under an hoold, that nempnen I ne kan,
Fer in Northumberlond the wawe hire
     caste,
And in the sond hir ship stikėd so faste
That thennės wolde it noght of al a tyde.
The wyl of Crist was that she sholde abyde.

The constable of the castel doun is fare
To seen this wrak, and al the ship he
     soghte,
And foond this wery womman, ful of care;
He foond also the tresor that she broghte.
In hir langagė mercy she bisoghte,
The lyf out of hire body for to twynne,
Hire to delivere of wo that she was inne.

493. See Rev. vii. 2, 3.
497. *awok*, E³ *wook*, throwing stress on *As*.
500. *the Egypcien Marie*, St. Mary of Egypt,
who lived forty-seven years in the desert as a
penitent.

A maner Latyn corrupt was hir speche,
But algates ther-by was she understonde.
The constable, whan hym lyst no lenger
     seche,   521
This woful womman broghte he to the
     londe;
She kneleth doun and thanketh Goddės
     sonde;
But what she was she woldė no man seye,
For foul ne fair, thogh that she sholdė
     deye.

She seyde she was so mazėd in the see
That she forgat hir myndė, by hir trouthe.
The constable hath of hire so greet pitee,
And eke his wyf, that they wepen for routhe.
She was so diligent, withouten slouthe,
To serve and plese everich in that place,
That alle hir loven that looken in hir face.

This constable and dame Hermengyld,
     his wyf,   533
Were payens, and that contree everywhere;
But Hermengyld loved hire right as hir lyf,
And Custance hath so longe sojournėd
     there,
In orisons, with many a bitter teere,
Til Jhesu hath converted, thurgh his grace,
Dame Hermengyld, constablesse of that
     place.

In al that lond no cristen dorstė route,   540
Allė cristen folk been fled fro that contree,
Thurgh payens, that conquereden al aboute
The plagės of the North, by land and see.
To Walys fledde the cristyanytee
Of oldė Britons dwellynge in this ile;
Ther was hir refut for the meenė while.

But yet nere cristene Britons so exiled
That ther nere somme, that in hir privėtee
Honóurėd Crist, and hethen folk bigiled;
And ny the castel swiche ther dwelten
     three.   550
That oon of hem was blynd and myghte
     nat see,
But it were with thilke eyen of his mynde,
With whiche men seën whan that they
     ben blynde.

536. *sojourned*, H *herberwed*.

69

Bright was the sonne, as in that someres day,
For which the constable and his wyf also,
And Custance, han y-take the righté way
Toward the see, a furlong wey or two,
To pleyen and to romen to and fro ;   558
And in hir walk this blyndé man they mette,
Crokéd and oold, with eyen faste y-shete.

'In name of Crist,' cridé this olde Britoun,
'Dame Hermengyld, yif me my sighte
    agayn !'
This lady weex affrayéd of the soun,
Lest that hir housbonde, shortly for to sayn,
Wolde hire for Jhesu Cristés love han
    slayn ;
Til Custance made hire boold, and bad
    hire wirche
The wyl of Crist, as doghter of his chirche.

The constable weex abasshéd of that sight,
And seydé, 'What amounteth all this fare !'
Custance answérde, 'Sire, it is Cristés
    myght   570
That helpeth folk out of the feendés snare' :
And so ferforth she gan oure lay declare,
That she the constable, er that it were eve,
Converteth, and on Crist maketh hym
    bileve.

This constable was no-thyng lord of this
    place
Of which I speké, ther he Custance fond,
But kepte it strongly, many wyntrés space,
Under Alla, kyng of al Northhumbrelond,
That was ful wys and worthy of his hond,
Agayn the Scottés, as men may wel heere ;
But turne I wole agayn to my mateere.

Sathan, that ever us waiteth to bigile,
Saugh of Custance al hire perfeccioun,
And caste anon how he myghte quite hir
    while,
And made a yong knyght, that dwelte
    in that toun,
Love hire so hoote, of foul affeccioun,
That verraily hym thoughte he sholdé spille
But he of hire myghte onés have his wille.

He woweth hire, but it availleth noght,
She woldé do no synné, by no weye ;   590
And for despit he compassed in his thoght
To maken hire on shameful deeth to deye.
He wayteth whan the constable was aweye,
And pryvély upon a nyght he crepte
In Hermengyldés chambre, whil she slepte.

Wery, for-wakéd in hire orisouns,
Slepeth Custance, and Hermengyld also.
This knyght, thurgh Sathanas tempta-
    ciouns,
All softély is to the bed y-go,
And kitte the throte of Hermengyld atwo,
And leyde the blody knyf by dame
    Custance,   601
And wente his wey, ther God yeve hym
    meschance !

Soone after cometh this constable hoom
    agayn,
And eek Alla, that kyng was of that lond,
And saugh his wyf despitously y-slayn,
For which ful ofte he weepe and wroong
    his hond,
And in the bed the blody knyf he fond
By dame Custance ; allas ! what myghte
    she seye ?
For verray wo, hir wit was al aweye.

To kyng Alla was toold al this meschance
And eek the tyme, and where, and in
    what wise   611
That in a ship was founden this Custance,
As heer-biforn that ye han herd devyse.
The kyngés herte of pitee gan agryse,
Whan he saugh so benigne a creäture
Falle in disese, and in mysáventure :

For as the lomb toward his deeth is broght,
So stant this innocent bifore the kyng.
This falsé knyght, that hath this tresoun
    wroght,
Berth hire on hond that she hath doon
    thys thyng ;   620
But nathélees, thér was greet moornyng

567. *his*, H *holy*.
578. *Alla*, reigned A.D. 560-588.

610-666. These eight stanzas are Chaucer's
addition. In Trivet the king does not arrive till
after the miracle.
612. *this*, E *dame*.

Among the peple, and seyn they kan nat
   gesse
That she had doon so greet a wikkednesse:

For they han seyn hire ever so vertuous,
And lovynge Hermengyld right as hir lyf.
Of this baar witnesse everich in that hous,
Save he that Hermengyld slow with his
   knyf.
This gentil kyng hath caught a greet motyf
Of this witnesse, and thoghte he wolde
   enquere
Depper in this, a trouthe for to lere. 630

Allas ! Custance, thou hast no cham-
   pioun,
Ne fighte kanstow noght, so weylaway !
But he that starf for our redempcioun,
And boond Sathan,—and yet lith ther
   he lay,—
So be thy stronge champion this day ;
For, but if Crist open myracle kithe,
Withouten gilt thou shalt be slayn as
   swithe.

She sette hire doun on knees and thus she
   sayde
' Immortal God, that savedest Susanne
Fro false blame, and thou, merciful mayde,
Mary I meene, doghter to Seïnt Anne, 641
Bifore whos child angeles synge Osanne,
If I be giltlees of this felonye
My socour be, for ellis shal I dye !'

Have ye nat seyn som tyme a pale face
Among a prees, of hym that hath be lad
Toward his deeth, wher-as hym gat no
   grace ?
And swich a colour in his face hath had,
Men myghte knowe his face that was bistad,
Amonges alle the faces in that route ; 650
So stant Custance, and looketh hire aboute.

O queenes, lyvynge in prosperitee !
Duchesses, and ye ladyes everichone !
Haveth som routhe on hire adversitee.
An emperoures doghter stant allone ;
She hath no wight to whom to make hir
   mone !

O blood roial, that stondest in this drede,
Fer been thy freendes at thy grete nede !

This Alla, kyng, hath swich compas-
   sioun,
As gentil herte is fulfild of pitee,   660
That from his eyen ran the water doun.
' Now hastily do fecche a book,' quod he,
' And if this knyght wol sweren how
   that she
This womman slow, yet wol we us avyse
Whom that we wole that shal been our
   justise.'

A Briton book written with Evaungiles
Was fet, and on this book he swoor anoon
She gilty was, and in the meene whiles
An hand hym smoot upon the nekke boon,
That doun he fil atones as a stoon ; 670
And bothe his eyen broste out of his face
In sighte of every body in that place !

A voys was herd in general audience
And seyde, ' Thou hast desclaundred,
   giltelees,
The doghter of hooly chirche in heigh
   presence ;
Thus hastou doun, and yet holde I my
   pees !'
Of this mervaille agast was al the prees ;
As mazed folk they stoden everichone,
For drede of wreche, save Custance allone.

Greet was the drede, and eek the
   repentance,   680
Of hem that hadden wronge suspecioun
Upon this sely, innocent Custance ;
And for this miracle, in conclusioun,
And by Custances mediacioun,
The kyng, and many another in that place,
Converted was,—thanked be Cristes grace !

This false knyght was slayn for his
   untrouthe
By juggement of Alla, hastifly ;
And yet Custance hadde of his deeth
   greet routhe ;
And after this Jhesus, of his mercy, 690
Made Alla wedden, ful solempnely,

This hooly mayden, that is so bright and
    sheene ;
And thus hath Crist y-maad Custance a
    queene.

But who was woful—if I shal nat lye—
Of this weddyng but Donegild and na mo,
The kyngės mooder, ful of tirannye ?
Hir thoughte hir cursėd hertė brast atwo,—
She woldė noght hir sonė had do so.
Hir thoughte a despit that he sholdė take
So strange a creäture unto his make.   700

Me list nat of the chaf, ne of the stree,
Maken so long a tale as of the corn.
What sholde I tellen of the roialtee
At mariage, or which cours goth biforn,
Who bloweth in the trumpe, or in an horn?
The fruyt of every tale is for to seye,
They ete, and drynke, and daunce, and
    synge and pleye.

They goon to bedde, as it was skile and
    right,
For thogh that wyvės be ful hooly thynges,
They mostė take in pacïence at nyght   710
Swiche manere necessaries as been
    plesynges
To folk that han y-wedded hem with rynges,
And leye a lite hir hoolynesse aside,
As for the tyme,—it may no bet bitide.

On hire he gat a knavė childe anon,
And to a bisshop, and his constable eke,
He took his wyf to kepe, whan he is gon
To Scotlondward, his foomen for to seke.
Now faire Custance, that is so humble
    and meke,
So longe is goon with childė, til that stille
She halt hire chambre, abidyng Cristės
    wille.   721

The tyme is come a knavė child she beer,—
Mauricius at the fontstoon they hym calle.
This constable dooth forth come a
    messageer,
And wroot unto his kyng, that cleped
    was Alle,
How that this blisful tidyng is bifalle,

713. H and halvendel hir holynesse ley aside.

And othere tidynges spedeful for to seye.
He taketh the lettre and forth he gooth
    his weye.   728

This messager, to doon his ávantage,
Unto the kyngės mooder rideth swithe,
And salueth hire ful faire in his langage :
'Madame,' quod he, 'ye may be glad
    and blithe,
And thanketh God an hundred thousand
    sithe,
My lady queene hath child withouten doute,
To joye and blisse of al this regne aboute.

Lo, heere the lettrės selėd of this thyng,
That I moot bere with al the haste I may.
If ye wol aught unto youre sone the kyng,
I am youre servant bothė nyght and day.'
Donegild answerde, 'As now, at this
    tyme, nay ;   740
But heere al nyght I wol thou take thy reste.
To-morwė wol I seye thee what me leste.'

This messager drank sadly ale and wyn,
And stolen were his lettrės pryvėly,
Out of his box whil he sleep as a swyn,
And countrefeted was ful subtilly
Another lettrė, wroght ful synfully,
Unto the kyng direct, of this mateere,
Fro his constable, as ye shal after heere.

The lettrė spak, the queene delivered was
Of so horrıble a feendly creäture,   751
That in the castel noon so hardy was
That any whilė dorstė ther endure.
The mooder was an elf, by áventure,
Y-comen by charmės, or by sorcerie,
And every wight hateth hir compaignye.

Wo was this kyng whan he this lettre
    had sayn,
But to no wight he tolde his sorwės soore,
But of his owene hand he wroot agayn :
'Welcome the sonde of Crist for ever-
    moore,   7(·)
To me that am now lernėd in his loore !

727. tidynges, H thynges.
746. countrefeted was ful, H countrefeet they
were.
747. Another lettre, wroght, H Another sche
him wrote.

Lord, welcome be thy lust and thy
　　plesaunce :
My lust I putte al in thyn ordinaunce.

Kepeth this child, al be it foul or feir,
And eek my wyf unto myn hoom-comýnge ;
Crist whan hym list may sendé me an heir
Moore ágreáble than this to my likýnge.'
This lettre he seleth, pryvély wepynge,
Which to the messager was také soone,
And forth he gooth ; ther is na moore to
　　doone.　　　　　770

O messager, fulfild of dronkenesse !
Strong is thy breeth, thy lymés faltren ay,
And thou biwreyest allé secreenesse.
Thy mynde is lorn, thou janglest as a jay;
Thy face is turnéd in a newe array !
Ther dronkenesse regneth in any route,
Ther is no conseil hyd, withouten doute.

O Donégild ! I ne have noon Englissh
　　digne
Unto thy malice and thy tirannye,
And therfore to the feend I thee resigne,
Lat hym enditen of thy traitorie !　　781
Fy, mannysh, fy,—O nay, by God, I lye,—
Fy, feendlych spirit, for I dar wel telle,
Thogh thou heere walke, thy spirit is in
　　helle.

This messager comth fro the kyng agayn,
And at the kyngés moodrés court he lighte ;
And she was of this messager ful fayn,
And pleséd hym, in al that ever she myghte.
He drank, and wel his girdel underpighte ;
He slepeth, and he snoreth in his gyse　790
All nyghté, til the sonné gan aryse.

Eft were his lettrés stolen everychon,
And countrefeted lettrés in this wyse :
' The king comandeth his constable anon,
Up peyne of hangyng, and on heigh juyse,
That he ne sholdé suffren, in no wyse,
Custance in-with his reawmé for tabyde
Thre dayés and o quarter of a tyde ;

But in the samé ship as he hire fond,
Hire, and hir yongé sone, and al hir geere
He sholdé putte, and croude hire fro the
　　lond,　　　　　801
And chargen hire she never eft coome
　　theere ! '
O my Custance, wel may thy goost have
　　feere,
And slepynge in thy dreem been in pen-
　　ance,
Whan Donégild cast al this ordinance.

This messager on morwé, whan he wook,
Unto the castel halt the nexté way,
And to the constable he the lettré took ;
And whan that he this pitous lettré say,
Ful ofte he seyde, ' Allas ! and weylaway ! '
' Lord Crist,' quod he, ' how may this
　　world endure ?　　　　811
So ful of synne is many a creäture !

' O myghty God, if that it be thy wille,
Sith thou art rightful juge, how may it be
That thou wolt suffren innocentz to spille,
And wikked folk regne in prosperitee ?
O goode Custance ! Allas, so wo is me,
That I moot be thy tormentour, or deye
On shamés deeth ; ther is noon oother
　　weye.'

Wepen bothe yonge and olde in al
　　that place,　　　　820
Whan that the kyng this cursed lettré
　　sente,
And Custance, with a deedly palé face,
The ferthé day toward the ship she wente ;
But nathélees she taketh in good entente
The wyl of Crist, and knelynge on the
　　stronde,
She seydé, ' Lord, ay welcome be thy sonde ;

He that me kepté fro the falsé blame,
While I was on the lond amongés yow,
He kan me kepe from harm, and eek fro
　　shame,
In salté see, al-thogh I se noght how.　830
As strong as ever he was he is yet now.
In hym triste I, and in his mooder deere,—
That is to me my seyl, and eek my
　　steere.'

771-784. The next two stanzas are Chaucer's
addition from the *De Contemptu Mundi*, ii. 19.
798. *Thre dayes and o quarter of a tyde*,
' deynz quatre iours' (Trivet); as soon as the
tide began to rise on the fourth day.

Hir litel child lay wepyng in hir arm,
And knelynge, pitously to hym she seyde,
'Pees, litel sone, I wol do thee noon harm !'
With that hir coverchief of hir heed she
　　breyde,
And over his litel eyen she it leyde,
And in hir arm she lulleth it ful faste,
And into hevene hire eyen up she caste.

'Mooder,' quod she, 'and maydé,
　　bright Marie,　　　　841
Sooth is that thurgh wommanès eggèment
Mankynde was lorn, and damnèd ay to dye,
For which thy child was on a croys y-
　　rent,—
Thy blisful eyen sawe al his torment,—
Thanne is ther no comparison bitwene
Thy wo and any wo man may sustene.

Thow sawe thy child y-slayn bifore thyne
　　eyen,
And yet now lyveth my litel child, *parfay!*
Now, lady bright, to whom alle woful
　　cryen,—　　　　850
Thow glorie of wommanhede, thow fairé
　　May,
Thow haven of refut, brightè sterre of
　　day,—
Rewe on my child, that of thy gentillesse
Ruest on every reweful in distresse.

'O litel child, allas ! what is thy gilt,
That never wroghtest synne as yet, *pardee?*
Why wil thyn hardé fader han thee spilt ?
O mercy, deeré constable,' quod she,
'As lat my litel child dwelle heer with thee ;
And if thou darst nat saven hym for blame,
Yet kys hym onès in his fadrès name !' 861

Ther-with she lookèd bakward to the londe,
And seydé, 'Farewel, housbonde routhé-
　　lees ! '
And up she rist, and walketh doun the
　　stronde
Toward the ship,—hir folweth al the
　　prees,—
And ever she preyeth hire child to hold
.　　his pees ;
And taketh hir leve, and with an hooly
　　entente,
She blissèd hire and into ship she wente.

Vitaillèd was the ship, it is no drede,
Habundantly for hire ful longè space ; 870
And othere necessaries that sholdé nede
She hadde ynogh, heryéd be Goddès grace !
For wynd and weder, almyghty God
　　purchace !
And brynge hire hoom, I kan no bettré seye ;
But in the see she dryveth forth hir weye.

PART III

Alla the kyng comth hoom soone after
　　this
Unto his castel of the which I tolde,
And asketh where his wyf and his child is?
The constable gan aboute his hertè colde,
And pleynly al the manere he hym tolde,
As ye han herd,—I kan telle it no bettre,—
And sheweth the kyng his seelé and his
　　lettre ;

And seydé, 'Lord, as ye comanded me,
Up peyne of deeth, so have I doon certein.'
This messager tormented was til he
Mostè biknowe, and tellen, plat and pleyn,
Fro nyght to nyght in what place he had
　　leyn ;
And thus by wit and sobtil enquerynge
Ymagined was by whom this harm gan
　　sprynge.

The hand was knowé that the lettre
　　wroot,　　　　890
And all the venym of this cursèd dede ;
But in what wisé certeinly I noot.
Theffect is this, that Alla, out of drede,
His mooder slow,—that may men pleynly
　　rede,—
For that she traitoure was to hire ligeance.
Thus endeth oldé Donegild with mes-
　　chance.

The sorwè that this Alla nyght and day
Maketh for his wyf, and for his child also,
Ther is no tongé that it tellé may ;
But now wol I unto Custancé go, 900
That fleteth in the see, in peyne and wo,

870. *ful longè space,* five years according to
Trivet.
873. *weder,* H *water.*

Fyve yeer and moore, as likèd Cristes
    sonde,
Er that hir ship approched unto the londe.

Under an hethen castel attè laste—
Of which the name in my text noght I
    fynde,—
Custance, and eek hir child, the see up
    caste.
Almyghty God, that saveth al mankynde,
Have on Custance and on hir child som
    mynde,
That fallen is in hethen hand eft-soon,
In point to spille, as I shal telle yow soone.

Doun fro the castel comth ther many
    a wight,   911
To gauren on this ship, and on Custance;
But, shortly, from the castel on a nyght,
The lordès styward,—God yeve him mes-
    chance !—
A theef, that hadde reneyèd oure creance,
Came into the ship allone, and seyde he
    sholde
Hir lemman be, wher-so she wolde or
    noldc.

Wo was this wrecched womman tho
    bigon ;
Hir childè cride, and she cride pitously ;
But blisful Marie heelp hire right anon,
For with hir struglyng wel and myghtily,
The theef fil over bord al sodeynly,
And in the see he dreyntè for vengeance;
And thus hath Crist unwemmèd kept
    Custance !

O foulè lust of luxurie, lo, thyn ende !
Nat only that thou feyntest mannès mynde,
But verraily thou wolt his body shende.
Thende of thy werk, or of thy lustes blynde,
Is cómpleynyng. How many oon may
    men fynde
That noght for werk somtyme, but for
    thentente   930
To doon this synne, been outher slayn or
    shente !

How may this waykè womman han this
    strengthe
Hire to defende agayn this renegat ?
O Golias, unmeasurable of lengthe,
How myghtè David makè thee so maat ?
So yong and of armure so desolaat,
How dorste he looke upon thy dredful face?
Wel may men seen it nas but Goddès grace.

Who yaf Judith coráge or hardynesse
To sleen hym Olofernes in his tente,   940
And to deliveren out of wrecchednesse
The peple of God ? I seye, for this
    entente,
That right as God spirit of vigour sente
To hem, and savèd hem out of meschance,
So sente he myght and vigour to Custance.

Forth gooth hir ship thurgh-out the
    narwè mouth
Of Jubaltare and Septè, dryvynge alway,
Som-tymè West and som-tyme North
    and South,
And som-tyme Est, ful many a wery day,
Til Cristès mooder—blessed be she ay !—
Hath shapen, thurgh hir endèlees good-
    nesse,   951
To make an ende of al hir hevynesse.

Now lat us stynte of Custance but a
    throwe,
And speke we of the Romayn emperour,
That out of Surrye hath by lettres knowe
The slaughtre of cristen folk, and dis-
    honóur
Doon to his doghter by a fals traytour,—
I mene the cursèd wikked sowdanesse,
That at the feeste leet sleen both moore
    and lesse ;

For which this emperour hath sent anon
His senatour with roial ordinance,   961
And othere lordès, God woot many oon,
On Surryens to taken heigh vengeance.
They brennen, sleen, and brynge hem to
    meschance

925-945. The next three stanzas are Chaucer's
addition, again suggested by the *De Contemptu
Mundi*, ii. 21.

947. *Jubaltare*, Gibraltar.
947. *Septe*, on the opposite coast. Trivet had
made the 'hethen castel' (904) in Spain.
961. *senatour*. His name was Arsemius.

Ful many a day, but, shortly, this is thende,
Homward to Rome they shapen hem to
    wende.

This senatour repaireth with victorie
To Romé-ward, saillynge ful roially,
And mette the ship dryvynge, as seith
    the storie,
In which Custancé sit ful pitously.   970
No-thyng ne knew he what she was, ne why
She was in swich array ; ne she nyl seye
Of hire estaat, althogh she sholdé deye.

He bryngeth hire to Rome, and to his wyf
He yaf hire, and hir yongé sone also ;
And with the senatour she ladde hir lyf.
Thus kan oure lady bryngen out of wo
Woful Custance and many another mo ;
And longé tymé dwelled she in that place,
In hooly werkés ever, as was hir grace.

The senatourés wyf hir aunté was,   981
But for all that she knew hire never the
    moore.
I wol no lenger tarien in this cas,
But to kyng Alla, which I spake of yoore,
That wepeth for his wyf and siketh soore,
I wol retourne, and lete I wol Custance
Under the senatourés governance.

Kyng Alla, which that hadde his
    mooder slayn,
Upon a day fil in swich répentance,   989
That, if I shortly tellen shal and playn,
To Rome he comth to receyven his
    penance,
And putte hym in the popés ordinance,
In heigh and logh ; and Jhesu Crist bisoghte
For yeve his wikked werkés that he wroghte.

The fame anon thurghout the toun is
    born,
How Alla kyng shal comen on pilgrymage,
By herbergeours that wenten hym biforn ;
For which the senatour, as was usage,
Rood hym agayns, and many of his lynage,

As wel to shewen his beighe magnificence,
As to doon any kyng a reverence.   1001

Greet cheeré dooth this noble senatour
To kyng Alla, and he to hym also ;
Everich of hem dooth oother greet honour ;
And so bifel that in a day or two
This senatour is to kyng Alla go
To feste, and, shortly, if I shal nat lye,
Custancés sone wente in his compaignye.

Som men wolde seyn at réqueste of
    Custance
This senatour hath lad this child to
    feeste,—   1010
I may nat tellen every circumstance ;
Be as be may, ther was he at the leeste ;
But sooth is this, that at his moodrés heeste
Biforn Alla, durynge the metés space,
The child stood, lookynge in the kyngés
    face.

This Alla kyng hath of this child greet
    wonder,
And to the senatour he seyde anon,
' Whos is that fairé child, that stondeth
    yonder ? '
' I noot,' quod he, ' by God and by
    Seint John !   1019
A mooder he hath, but fader hath he noon,
That I of woot '; but shortly, in a stounde
He tolde Alla how that this child was
    founde ;

' But God woot,' quod this senatour also,
' So vertuous a lyvere in my lyf
Ne saugh I never as she, ne herde of mo,
Of worldly wommen, maydé, ne of wyf ;
I dar wel seyn hir haddé levere a knyf
Thurgh out hir brest, than ben a womman
    wikke ;
There is no man koude brynge hire to
    that prikke.'   1029

Now was this child as lyke unto Custance
As possible is a creäture to be.

981. *hir aunte*, really her cousin. According to Trivet, Arsemius married Helen, daughter
of Sallustius, Constance's uncle.
995. *thurghout the toun*, H⁶ *thurgh Rome
toun*.

1009. *Som men wolde seyn, i.e.* Trivet.
1010. *this child.* With the usual medieval
prodigality of time Trivet makes Maurice now
seventeen.
1014. *Biforn Alla*, H *Biforn hem alle.*

This Alla hath the face in remembrance
Of dame Custance, and theron mused he,
If that the childes mooder were aught she
That is his wyf, and pryvely he sighte,
And spedde hym fro the table that he
    myghte.

'*Parfay!*' thoghte he, 'fantome is in
    myn heed!
I oghte deme, of skilful juggement,
That in the salte see my wyf is deed';
And afterward he made his argument, 1040
'What woot I, if that Crist have hyder
    y-sent
My wyf by see, as wel as he hire sente
To my contree fro thennes that she wente?'

And after noon, hoom with the senatour
Goth Alla, for to seen this wonder chaunce.
This senatour dooth Alla greet honour,
And hastifly he sente after Custaunce;
But trusteth weel hire liste nat to daunce,
Whan that she wiste wherfore was that
    sonde;   1049
Unnethe upon hir feet she myghte stonde.

    Whan Alla saugh his wyf, faire he hire
    grette,
And weep, that it was routhe for to see;
For at the firste look he on hire sette,
He knew wel verraily that it was she,
And she for sorwe as doumb stant as a tree;
So was hir herte shet in hir distresse
When she remembred his unkyndenesse.

Twyes she swowned in his owene sighte.
He weep, and hym excuseth pitously:
'Now God,' quod he, 'and alle his
    halwes brighte,   1060
So wisly on my soul as have mercy,
That of youre harm as giltelees am I,
As is Maurice my sone, so lyk your face;
Elles the feend me fecche out of this place!'

    Long was the sobbyng and the bitter
    peyne,
Er that hir woful hertes myghte cesse;

Greet was the pitee for to heere hem pleyne,
Thurgh whiche pleintes gan hir wo en-
    cresse.
I pray yow all my labour to relesse,
I may nat tell hir wo until to-morwe, 1070
I am so wery for to speke of sorwe.

But finally, whan that the sothe is wist,
That Alla giltelees was of hir wo,
I trowe an hundred tymes been they kist;
And swich a blisse is ther bitwix hem two,
That, save the joye that lasteth evermo,
Ther is noon lyk that any creäture
Hath seyn, or shal, whil that the world
    may dure.

Tho preyde she hir housbonde, mekely,
In relief of hir longe pitous pyne,   1080
That he wolde preye hir fader specially,
That of his magestee he wolde enclyne
To vouche-sauf som day with hym to dyne.
She preyde hym eek he wolde, by no weye,
Unto hir fader no word of hire seye.

    Som men wold seyn how that the child
    Maurice
Dooth this message unto the emperour,
But, as I gesse, Alla was nat so nyce
To hym, that was of so sovereyn honour
As he that is of cristen folk the flour,   1090
Sente any child; but it is bet to deeme
He wente hymself, and so it may well
    seeme.

This emperour hath graunted gentilly
To come to dyner, as he hym bisoughte,
And wel rede I, he looked bisily
Upon this child, and on his doghter thoghte.
Alla goth to his in, and as him oghte,
Arrayed for this feste in every wise,
As ferforth as his konnyng may suffise.

    The morwe cam, and Alla gan hym
    dresse,   1100
And eek his wyf, this emperour to meete;
And forth they ryde in joye and in
    gladnesse;
And whan she saugh hir fader in the strete,
She lighte doun and falleth hym to feete;

1037. The stanza is Chaucer's addition.
1038. *skilful*, H *rightful*.
1051-1078. Chaucer's addition.

1086. *Som men*, *i.e.* Trivet.

77

'Fader,' quod she, 'youre yongė child,
   Custance,
Is now ful clene out of youre rémembrance.

I am youre doghter Custancė,' quod she,
'That whilom ye han sent unto Surrye.
It am I, fader, that in the saltė see   1109
Was put allone, and dampnėd for to dye.
Now, goodė fader, mercy, I yow crye !
Sende me namoore unto noon hethėnesse,
But thonketh my lord heere of his kyndė-
   nesse.'

Who kan the pitous joyė tellen al
Bitwixe hem thre, syn they been thus
   y-mette ?
But of my talė make an ende I shal,—
The day goth faste, I wol no lenger lette.
This gladė folk to dyner they hem sette.
In joye and blisse at mete I lete hem dwelle,
A thousand foold wel moore than I kan
   telle.   1120

This child Maurice was sithen emperour
Maad by the pope and lyvėd cristenly.
To Cristės chirchė he dide greet honour ;
But I lete all his storie passen by ;
Of Custance is my talė specially.
In the oldė Romane Geestės may men
   fyndė
Mauricės lyf, I bere it noght in mynde.

This kyng Alla, whan he his tymė say,
With his Custance, his hooly wyf so sweete,
To Engelond been they come the rightė
   way,   1130
Wher as they lyve in joye and in quiete ;
But litel while it lasteth, I yow heete.
Joye of this world for tyme wol nat abyde,
Fro day to nyght it changeth as the tyde.

Who lyved ever in swich delit o day
That hym ne moevėd outher conscience,
Or ire, or talent, or som kynnes affray,

Envye, or pride, or passion, or offence ?
I ne seye but for this endė this sentence,
That litel while in joye, or in plesance,   1140
Lasteth the blisse of Alla with Custance ;

For Deeth, that taketh of heigh and logh
   his rente,
Whan passed was a year, evene as I gesse,
Out of this world this kyng Alla he hente.
For whom Custance hath ful greet hevy-
   nesse.
Now lat us prayen God his soulė blesse !
And dame Custancė, finally to seye,
Toward the toun of Romė goth hir weye.

To Rome is come this hooly creäture,
And fyndeth hire freendės ther bothe
   hoole and sounde.   1150
Now is she scapėd al hire áventure,
And whan that she hir fader hath y-foundė,
Doun on hir kneės falleth she to groundė :
Wepynge for tendrenesse in hertė blithe,
She heryeth God an hundred thousand
   sithe.

In vertu and in hooly almus-dede
They lyven alle, and nevere asonder wende.
Til deeth departed hem this lyf they lede,
And fareth now weel, my tale is at an ende.
Now Jhesu Crist, that of his myght may
   sende   1160
Joye after wo, governe us in his grace,
And kepe us allė that been in this place.
   Amen.

[*Words of the Host, the Parson, and the
Shipman*]

Oure Hoste upon his stiropes stode anon,
And seydė, 'Good men, herkeneth,
   everichon !
This was a thrifty talė for the nones !
Sir Parish Prest,' quod he, 'for Goddės
   bones,

1122. *Maad by the pope.* Trivet says by his grandfather 'par l'assent del pape Pelagie e de tout le senat de Rome.'
1126. *the oldė Romane Geestes, i.e.* the *Gesta Romanorum ;* H om. *the.*
1135. From *De Contemptu Mundi,* i. 22.
1137. *kynnes,* H *maner.*

1149. *hooly,* H *nobil.*
1163-1190. The text is taken from MS. Arch. Seld. B. 14, the only MS. which preserves the reading *Shipman* in line 1179.
1165. *a thrifty tale,* an allusion to the same phrase in B. 46, showing that the reference is to the Man of Law's Tale.

Tell us a tale, as was thy forward yore ;
I se wel that ye lernèd men in lore
Can mochè good, by Goddès dignitee ! '
    The Persone him answérde, '*Benedicite!*
What eyleth the man so sinfully to
    swere ? '   1171
    Our Hoste answérde, 'O Jankyn, be
    ye there ?
I smelle a Loller in the wind,' quod he.
'Nowe, good men,' quod our Hostè,
    'herkneth me,
Abydeth, for Goddès dignè passioun,
For we shul han a predicacioun ;
This Loller here wol prechen us somwhat.'
    'Nay, by my fader soule ! that shal
    he nat ! '
Seydè the Shipman ; 'here shal he nat
    preche ;   1179
He shal no gospel glosen here, ne teche.
We leven alle in the grete God,' quod he,
' He woldè sowen som difficulte,
Or sprengen cokkel in our clenè corn ;
And therfore, Hoste, I warnè the biforn,
My joly body shal a talè telle,
And I shal clynken yow so mery a belle
That I shal wakyn al this companye ;
But it shal nat ben of philosophye,
Ne of phisyk, ne termès queint of lawe ;
There is but litel Latin in my mawe.' 1190

SHIPMAN'S TALE

Heere bigynneth The Shipmannes Tale

    A marchant whilom dwelled at Seint
    Denys,
That richè was, for which men heldè
    hym wys ;
A wyf he haddè of excellent beautee,

1173. *a Loller*, a Lollard. That Chaucer
allowèd this name to be given to his good parson
does not prove that he sympathised with Wyclif's
doctrines. Any priest who lived a strict life just
then might incur the charge of Lollardy.
    1174. *Nowe*, from H ; rest *Howe*.
    1178. *my fader*, Arch. Seld. *godis*.
    1179. *Shipman*, Heng.[5] *Squier*, H *Sompnour*.
    1183. *cokkel*, an allusion to the derivation of
Lollard from *lolium*.
    1186-1190. *The Shipmannes Tale*. In Heng.[6]
here follows the Squire's Tale. No original of
the Shipman's Tale has yet been found.

And compaignable and revelous was she,
Which is a thyng that causeth more
    dispence
Than worth is al the chiere and reverence
That men hem doon at festès and at
    daunces.   1197
Swiche salutaciouns and contenaunces
Passen as dooth a shadwe upon the wal ;
But wo is hym that payen moot for al !
'The sely housbonde algate he moste paye ;
He moot us clothe and he moot us arraye,
Al for his owene worship richély,
In which array we dauncè jolily.
And if that he noght may, par áventure,
Or ellis list no swich dispence endure,
But thynketh it is wasted and y-lost,
Thanne moot another payen for oure cost,
Or lene us gold, and that is perilous.'
    This noblè marchaunt heeld a worthy
    hous,   1210
For which he haddè alday so greet repair
For his largesse, and for his wyf was fair,
That wonder is ; but herkneth to my tale.
    Amongès alle his gestès, grete and
    smale,
Ther was a monk, a fair man and a
    boold,—
I trowe of thritty wynter he was oold,—
That ever in oon was comynge to that
    place.
This yongè monk, that was so fair of face,
Aqueynted was so with the goodè man
Sith that hir firstè knowelichè bigan, 1220
That in his hous as famulier was he
As it is póssible any freend to be.
And for as muchel as this goodè man
And eek this monk, of which that I bigan,
Were bothè two y-born in o village,
The monk hym claymeth as for cosynage ;
And he agayn he seith nat onès nay,
But was as glad therof as fowel of day ;
For to his herte it was a greet plesaunce.
Thus been they knyt with eterne alliaunce,
And ech of hem gan oother for tassure 1231
Of bretherhede whil that hir lyf may dure.

1202. *and he moot us*, H *in ful good*.
1206. *list no*, H *will not*.
1210. *worthy*, H[5] *noble*.
1217. *comynge*, H[6] *drawyng*.
1222. *is*, om. E ; H reads *as it possible is a
friend to be*.

79

Free was Daun John, and namely of
    dispence,
As in that hous, and ful of diligence
To doon plesaunce, and also greet costage:
He noght forgat to yeve the leeste page
In al the hous; but after hir degree
He yaf the lord and sitthe al his meynee,
Whan that he cam, som manere honest
    thyng,
For which they were as glad of his comyng
As fowel is fayn whan that the sonne
    upriseth ;   1241
Na moore of this as now, for it suffiseth.

    But so bifel this marchant on a day
Shoop hym to make redy his array
Toward the toun of Brugges for to fare,
To byen there a porcioun of ware ;
For which he hath to Parys sent anon
A messager, and preyed hath Daun John
That he sholde come to Seint Denys, to
    pleye   1249
With hym and with his wyf a day or tweye,
Er he to Brugges wente, in alle wise.

    This noble monk, of which I yow devyse,
Hath of his abbot, as hym list, licence,—
By-cause he was a man of heigh prudence,
And eek an officer,—out for to ryde,
To seen hir graunges and hire bernes wyde,
And unto Seint Denys he comth anon.
Who was so welcome as my lord Daun
    John,
Oure deere cosyn, ful of curteisye ?
With hym broghte he a jubbe of malvesye
And eek another, ful of fyn vernage, 1261
And volatyl, as ay was his usage.
And thus I lete hem ete and drynke and
    pleye,
This marchant and this monk, a day or
    tweye.

    The thridde day this marchant up
    ariseth,
And on his nedes sadly hym avyseth,
And up into his countour-hous gooth he,
To rekene with hymself, as wel may be,
Of thilke yeer, how that it with hym stood,
And how that he despended hadde his
    good,   1270
And if that he encressed were or noon.
His bookes and his bagges, many oon,
He leith biforn hym on his countyng-bord.

Ful riche was his tresor and his hord,
For which ful faste his countour dore he
    shette ;
And eek he nolde that no man sholde
    hym lette
Of his accountes, for the meene tyme ;
And thus he sit til it was passed pryme.

    Daun John was rysen in the morwe also
And in the gardyn walketh to and fro, 1280
And hath his thynges seyd ful curteisly.
This goode wyf cam walkynge pryvely
Into the gardyn, there he walketh softe,
And hym saleweth, as she hath doon ofte.
A mayde child cam in hire compaignye,
Which as hir list she may governe and gye,
For yet under the yerde was the mayde.
'O deere cosyn myn, Daun John,' she
    sayde,
'What eyleth yow, so rathe for to ryse ? '
    'Nece,' quod he, 'it oghte ynough suffise
Fyve houres for to slepe upon a nyght, 1291
But it were for an old appalled wight,
As been thise wedded men that lye and
    dare,
As, in a fourme, sit a wery hare
Were al forstraught with houndes grete
    and smale ;
But, deere nece, why be ye so pale ?
I trowe certes that oure goode man
Hath yow laboured sith the nyght bigan,
That yow were nede to resten hastily ' ;
And with that word he lough ful murily
And of his owene thought he wax al reed.

    This faire wyf gan for to shake hir heed,
And seyde thus : 'Ye, God woot al,'
    quod she,
'Nay, cosyn myn, it stant nat so with me,
For by that God that yaf me soule and lyf,
In al the reawme of France is ther no wyf
That lasse lust hath to that sory pleye ;
For I may synge allas and weylawey
That I was born ; but to no wight,'
    quod she,
'Dar I nat telle how that it stant with me ;
Wherfore I thynke out of this lande to
    wende,   1311
Or elles of myself to make an ende,
So ful am I of drede and eek of care.'

    This monk bigan upon this wyf to stare,
And seyde, ' Allas, my nece, God forbede

That ye, for any sorwe or any drede,
Fordo youreself; but tel me of youre grief;
Paráventure I may in youre meschief   1318
Conseille or helpe; and therfore telleth me
All youre anoy, for it shal been secree ;
For on my porthors here I make an ooth
That never in my lyf, for lief ne looth,
Ne shal I of no conseil yow biwreye.'
   ' The same agayn to yow,' quod she,
     ' I seye,
By God and by this porthors I yow swere,
Though men me wolde al into pieces tere,
Ne shal I never, for to goon to helle,
Biwreye a word of thyng that ye me telle,
Nat for no cosynage ne alliance,
But verraily for love and affiance.'   1330
Thus been they sworn, and heer-upon
    they kiste,
And ech of hem tolde oother what hem
    liste.
   ' Cosyn,' quod she, ' if that I hadde
     a space,   .
As I have noon, and namely in this place,
Thanne wolde I telle a legende of my lyf,
What I have suffred sith I was a wyf
Vïth myn housbonde, al be he of youre
    kyn.'
   ' Nay,' quod this monk, ' by God,
     and Seint Martyn !
He is na mooré cosyn unto me   1339
Than is this lief that hangeth on the tree.
I clepe hym so, by Seint Denys of Fraunce !
To have the mooré cause of áqueyntaunce
Of yow, which I have lovéd specially,
Aboven allé wommen sikerly ;
This swere I yow on my professioun.
Telleth youre grief, lest that he come adoun,
And hasteth yow, and gooth youre wey
    anon.'
   ' My deeré love,' quod she, ' O my
     Daun John,
Ful lief were me this conseil for to hyde,
But out it moot, I may namoore abyde ! 1350
Myn housbonde is to me the worsté man
That ever was sith that the world bigan,
But sith I am a wyf, it sit nat me

To tellen no wight of oure privetee,
Neither a-bedde ne in noon oother place—
God shilde I sholde it tellen for his grace !
A wyf ne shal nat seyn of hir housbonde
But al honóur, as I kan understonde,
Save unto yow, thus muche I tellen shal;
As helpe me God, he is noght worth at al
In no degree the value of a flye ;   1361
But yet me greveth moost his nygardye.
And wel ye woot that wommen naturelly
Desiren thyngés sixe, as wel as I :
They woldé that hir housbondes sholdé be
Hardy and wise, and riche, and therto free,
And buxom unto his wyf, and fressh
    abedde;
But by that ilké Lord that for us bledde,
For his honóur myself for to arraye,
A Sonday next, I mosté nedés paye   1370
An hundred frankes, or ellis I am lorn ;
Yet were me levere that I were unborn
Than me were doon a sclaundre or
    vileynye ;
And if myn housbonde eek it myghte espye
I nere but lost, and therfore I yow preye,
Lene me this somme, or ellis moot I deye.
Daun John, I seye, lene me thise
    hundred frankes ;
Pardee, I wol nat faillé yow my thankes,
If that yow list to doon that I yow praye,
For at a certeyn day I wol yow paye,   1380
And doon to yow what plesance and service
That I may doon, right as yow list devise,
And but I do, God take on me vengeance
As foul as ever hadde Genyloun of France !'
   This gentil monk answerde in this
    manere :
' Now trewély, myn owene lady deere,
I have,' quod he, ' on yow so greet a routhe,
That I yow swere, and plighté yow my
    trouthe,
That whan youre housbonde is to
    Flaundrés fare
I wol delyvere yow out of this care ;   1390
For I wol bryngé yow an hundred frankes';

1317. *tel,* H⁶ *telleth.*
1331. *they kiste,* H⁴ *i-kiste, kist.*
1337. *al be he of youre kyn,* H *though he be your cosyn.*

1368. H reads : *But by that lord that for us alle bledde.*
1370. H reads : *A sonday next comyng yit moste I praye.*
1384. *Genyloun,* the betrayer of Roland.
1387. H reads : *I have on yow so greet pité and routhe.*

And with that word he caughte hire by
the flankes
And hire embraceth harde and kiste hire
ofte.
'Gooth now youre wey,' quod he, 'all
stille and softe,
And lat us dyne as soone as that ye may,
For by my chilyndre it is pryme of day.
Gooth now, and beeth as trewe as I shal
be.'
'Now ellès God forbedè, sire,' quod
she ;
And forth she gooth as jolif as a pye,
And bad the cookès that they sholde
hem hye,   1400
So that men myghtè dyne and that anon.
Up to hir housbonde is this wyf y-gon,
And knokketh at his countour boldèly.
'Qy la ?' quod he.   'Peter ! it am I,'
Quod she ; 'what, sire, how longè wol
ye faste ?
How longè tymè wol ye rekene and caste
Youre sommès, and youre bookès, and
youre thynges ?
The devel have part on alle swiche
rekenynges !
Ye have ynough, pardee, of Goddès sonde ;
Com doun to-day, and lat youre baggès
stonde.   1410
Ne be ye nat ashamèd that Daun John
Shal fasting al this day alengè goon ?
What ! lat us heere a messe, and go we
dyne !'
'Wyf,' quod this man, 'litel kanstow
devyne
The curious bisynessè that we have ;
For of us chapmen,—al-so God me save,
And by that lord that clepid is Seint Yve,—
Scarsly amongès twelvè two shuln thryve,
Continuelly lastynge unto oure age.   1419
We may wel makè chiere and good visage,
And dryvè forth the world as it may be,
And kepen oure estaat in pryvètee
Til we be deed ; or ellès that we pleye
A pilgrymage, or goon out of the weye ;
And therfore have I greet necessitee

Upon this queyntè world tavysè me,
For, evermoorè we moote stonde in drede
Of hap and fortune in oure chapmanhede.
'To Flaundrès wol I go to-morwe at
day,   1429
And come agayn as soone as ever I may ;
For which, my deerè wyf, I thee biseke
As be to every wight buxom and meke,
And for to kepe oure good be curious,
And honestly governè wel oure hous.
Thou hast ynough in every maner wise,
That to a thrifty housbold may suffise ;
Thee lakketh noon array ne no vitaille,
Of silver in thy purs shaltow nat faille.'
And with that word his countour dore he
shette,
And doun he gooth, no lenger wolde he
lette ;   1440
But hastily a messè was ther seyd,
And spedily the tables were y-leyd,
And to the dyner fastè they hem spedde,
And richèly this monk the chapman fedde.
   At after dyner Daun John sobrèly
This chapman took apart and privèly
He seyde hym thus : 'Cosyn, it standeth
so
That, wel I se, to Bruggès wol ye go.
God and Seint Austyn spedè yow and gyde !
I prey yow, cosyn, wisely that ye ryde ;
Governeth yow also of youre diete   1451
Atemprèly, and namely in this hete.
Bitwix us two nedeth no strangè fare ;
Fare wel, cosyn, God shildè yow fro care !
And if that any thyng, by day or nyght,
If it lye in my power and my myght,
That ye me wol comande in any wyse,
It shal be doon, right as ye wol devyse.
   'O thyng, er that ye goon, if it may be,
I woldè prey yow for to lenè me   1460
An hundred frankès for a wyke or tweye,
For certein beestès that I mostè beye,
To stoorè with a placè that is oures,—
God helpe me so, I wolde it werè youres !
I shal nat faillè surely of my day,
Nat for a thousand frankes a milè way !
But lat this thyng be secree, I yow preye,
For yet to-nyght thise beestès moot I beye ;
And fare now wel, myn owene cosyn deere,

1417. *Seint Yve*, Saint Ivo.
1418. *two*, E³ *ten*, Corp.³ *tweye*.
1423, 24. *we pleye A pilgrymage*, as a pretext
for keeping out of the way of creditors.

1438. *shaltow*, H⁴ *thou mayst*.
1445. *At*, H⁴ *And*.

82

Graunt mercy of youre cost and of youre
    cheere ! '   1470
This noble marchant gentilly anon
Answerde and seyde, ' O cosyn myn,
    Daun John,
Now sikerly this is a smal requeste,
My gold is youres whan that it yow leste,
And nat oonly my gold, but my chaffare;
Take what yow list, God shildè that ye
    spare !
' But o thyng is, ye knowe it wel ynogh,
Of chapmen, that hir moneie is hir plogh;
We may creauncè whil we have a name,
But goldlees for to be, it is no game ;   1480
Paye it agayn whan it lith in youre ese ;
After my myght ful fayn wolde I yow plese.'
    Thise hundred frankes he fette hym
    forth anon
And privèly he took hem to Daun John ;
No wight in all this world wiste of this
    loone,
Savynge this marchant and Daun John
    allone.
They drynke, and speke, and rome a
    while and pleye,
Til that Daun John rideth to his abbeye.
    The morwè cam and forth this mar-
    chant rideth
To Flaundrès-ward,—his prentys wel
    hym gydeth,—   1490
Til he cam into Bruggès murily.
Now gooth this marchant, faste and bisily
Aboute his nede, and byeth and creaun-
    ceth ;
He neither pleyeth at the dees, ne daun-
    ceth,
But as a marchant, shortly for to telle,
He lad his lyf, and there I lete him dwelle.
    The Sonday next this marchant was
    agon,
To Seint Denys y-comen is Daun John,
With crowne and berde all fressh and
    newe y-shave.   1499
In al the hous ther nas so litel a knave,
Ne no wight ellès, that he nas ful fayn
For that my lord Daun John was come
    agayn ;
And shortly, to the point right for to gon,
This fairè wyf accorded with Daun John

1483. *hym*, om. H⁶.

That for thise hundred frankes he sholde
    a nyght
Háve hire in his armès bolt upright ;
And this acord parfournèd was in dede.
In myrthe al nyght a bisy lyf they lede
Til it was day, that Daun John wente
    his way,
And bad the meynee, Fare wel, have
    good day !   1510
For noon of hem, ne no wight in the toun,
Hath of Daun John right no suspecioun ;
And forth he rydeth hoom to his abbeye,
Or where hym list; namoore of hym I
    seye.
    This marchant, whan that ended was
    the faire,
To Seint Denys he gan for to repaire,
And with his wyf he maketh feeste and
    cheere,
And telleth hire that chaffare is so deere
That nedès moste he make a chevyssaunce,
For he was bounden in a reconyssaunce,
To payè twenty thousand sheeld anon ;
For which this marchant is to Parys gon,
To borwe of certeine freendès that he
    hadde
A certeyn frankes ; and somme with him
    he ladde.
And whan that he was come into the toun,
For greet chiertee, and greet affeccioun,
Unto Daun John he gooth hym first, to
    pleye,—
Nat for to axe or borwe of hym moneye,—
But for to wite and seen of his welfare,
And for to tellen hym of his chaffare,   1530
As freendès doon whan they been met
    y-feere.
Daun John hym maketh feeste and muryè
    cheere,
And he hym tolde agayn, ful specially,
How he hadde wel y-boght and gra-
    ciously,—
Thankèd be God !—al hool his mar-
    chandise,
Save that he moste, in allè maner wise,
Maken a chevyssaunce as for his beste,
And thanne he sholdè been in joye and
    reste.

1528. H reads: *Nought for to borwe of hym
no kyn monay*, so Corp.⁸ omitting *kyn*.

Daun John answérdė, 'Certės I am
   fayn,   1539
That ye in heele ar comen hom agayn,
And if that I were riche, as have I blisse,
Of twenty thousand sheeld shold ye nat
   mysse,
For ye so kyndély this oother day
Lentė me gold ; and as I kan and may
I thankė yow, by God and by Seint Jame !
But nathélees I took unto oure dame,
Youre wyf, at hom, the samė gold ageyn
Upon youre bench ; she woot it wel certeyn,
By certeyn tokenes that I kan yow telle.
Now by youre leve I may no lenger
   dwelle ;   1550
Oure abbot wole out of this toun anon,
And in his compaignÿė moot I goon.
Grete wel oure dame, myn owene necė
   sweete,
And fare wel, deerė cosyn, til we meete !'
   This marchant, which that was ful war
   and wys,
Creancėd hath and payd eek in Parys
To certeyn Lumbardes, redy in hir hond,
The somme of gold, and hadde of hem
   his bond ;
And hoom he gooth, murie as a papejay,
For wel he knew he stood in swich array
That nedės moste he wynne in that viage
A thousand frankes aboven al his costage.
   His wyf ful redy mette hym attė gate,
As she was wont of oold usage algate,
And al that nyght in myrthė they bisette ;
For he was riche and cleerly out of dette.
Whan it was day this marchant gan
   embrace
His wyf al newe, and kiste hire on hir face,
And up he gooth and maketh it ful tough.
   'Namoore,' quod she, 'by God, ye
   have ynough !'   1570
And wantownely agayn with hym she
   pleyde ;
Til attė lastė thus this marchant seyde :
'By God,' quod he, 'I am a litel wrooth
With yow, my wyf, although it be me
   looth ;
And woot ye why ? By God, as that I
   gesse

1549: *yow*, H⁴ *hir*.
1557. *Lumbardes*, Lombard money-dealers.

That ye han maad a manere straungénesse
Bitwixen me and my cosyn daun John,—
Ye sholde han warnėd me, er I had gon,
That he yow hadde an hundred frankės
   payed,
By redy tokene,—and heeld hym yvele
   apayed   1580
For that I to hym spak of chevyssaunce,—
Me semėd so, as by his contenaunce—
But nathélees, by God, oure hevene kyng,
I thoughtė nat to axen hym no thyng.
I prey thee, wyf, as do namoorė so ;
Telle me alwey, er that I fro thee go,
If any dettour hath in myn absence
Y-payėd thee, lest thurgh thy necligence
I myghte hym axe a thing that he hath
   payed.'
   This wyf was nat aferėd nor affrayed,
But boldėly she seyde, and that anon,   1591
'Marie, I deffie the falsė monk, Daun
   John !
I kepe nat of his tokenes never a deel !
He took me certeyn gold, that woot I weel.
What, yvel thedam on his monkės snowte !
For, God it woot, I wende withouten doute
That he hadde yeve it me bycause of yow,
To doon therwith myn honour and my
   prow,
For cosynage, and eek for beelė cheere,
That he hath had ful oftė tymės heere.
But sith I se I stonde in this disjoynt,   1601
I wol answére yow shortly to the poynt.
Ye han mo slakkere dettours than am I,
For I wol paye yow wel and redily
Fro day to day, and if so be I faille,
I am youre wyf, score it upon my taille,
And I shal paye as soone as ever I may ;
For by my trouthe, I have on myn array,
And nat on wast, bistowėd every deel ;
And for I have bistowėd it so weel   1610
For youre honóur, for Goddės sake, I seye,
As be nat wrooth, but lat us laughe and
   pleye.
Ye shal my joly body have to wedde ;
By God ! I wol nat paye yow but abedde.
Foryive it me, myn owene spousė deere,
Turne hiderward, and maketh bettrė
   checre !'
   This marchant saugh ther was no
   remedie,

And for to chide it nere but greet folie,
Sith that the thyng may nat amended be.
'Now, wyf,' he seyde, 'and I foryeve
        it thee,   1620
But by thy lyf ne be namoore so large ;
Keepe bet oure good, this yeve I thee in
        charge.'
Thus endeth now my tale, and God us
        sende
Talynge ynough unto oure lyves ende.
        Amen.

*Bihoold the murie wordes of the Hoost to
the Shipman, and to the lady Prioresse*

    'Wel seyd ! by *corpus dominus,'*
        quod our Hoost ;
' Now longe moote thou saille by the cost,
Sire gentil maister, gentil maryneer !
God yeve this monk a thousand last
        quade yeer !
A ha, felawes, beth ware of swiche a jape !
The monk putte in the mannes hood an
        ape,   1630
And in his wyves eek, by Seint Austyn !
Draweth no monkes moore unto youre in.
    ' But now passe over, and lat us seke
        aboute,
Who shal now telle first of al this route
Another tale'; and with that word he sayde,
As curteisly as it had ben a mayde,
' My lady Prioresse, by youre leve,
So that I wiste I sholde yow nat greve,
I wolde demen that ye tellen sholde
A tale next, if so were that ye wolde. 1640
Now wol ye vouchesauf, my lady deere ?'
    ' Gladly,' quod she, and seyde as ye
        shal heere.

PRIORESS'S TALE

The Prologe of the Prioresses Tale

' O Lord, oure Lord, thy name how
        merveillous

1618. *nere but greet,* H⁶ om. *greet,* H *nas* for
nere.
1622. *oure,* H⁸ *my,* Heng. *thy.*
1643. *O Lord, oure Lord,* etc., the beginning
of Ps. viii.

Is in this large world y-sprad,' quod she ;
' For noght oonly thy laude precious
Parfourned is by men of dignitee,
But by the mouth of children thy bountee
Parfourned is ; for on the brest soukynge
Somtyme shewen they thyn heriynge.

Wherfore, in laude as I best kan or may,
Of thee, and of the white lylye flour, 1651
Which that the bar and is a mayde alway,
To telle a storie I wol do my labour ;
Nat that I may encreessen hir honour,
For she hirself is honour and the roote
Of bountee, next hir sone, and soules
        boote.

O mooder mayde ! O mayde mooder fre !
O bussh unbrent, brennynge in Moyses
        sighte !
That ravysedest doun fro the Deitee,
Thurgh thyn humblesse, the Goost that in
        thalighte ;   1660
Of whos vertu, whan He thyn herte lighte,
Conceyved was the Fadres sapience,
Helpe me to telle it in thy reverence !

Lady, thy bountee, thy magnificence,
Thy vertu, and thy grete humylitee,
Ther may no tonge expresse in no science ;
For somtyme, lady, er men praye to thee,
Thou goost biforn of thy benygnytee,
And getest us the lyght, thurgh thy preyere,
To gyden us unto thy Sone so deere. 1670

My konnyng is so wayk, O blisful queene,
For to declare thy grete worthynesse,
That I ne may the weighte nat susteene ;
But as a child of twelf monthe oold or lesse,
That kan unnethes any word expresse,
Right so fare I, and therfore I yow preye,
Gydeth my song that I shal of yow seye.'

Heere bigynneth The Prioresses Tale

    Ther was in Asye, in a greet citee,
Amonges cristene folk, a Jewerye,

1667-1669. Imitated from Dante, *Paradiso*
xxxiii. 16-18, a passage from which, or from some
Latin original, Chaucer had already borrowed in
the proem to the ' Tale of St. Cecilia,' assigned
in the *Canterbury Tales* to the second Nun.
    The Prioresses Tale. A poem of a Paris beggar-

85

Sustenèd by a lord of that contree,   1680
For foule usure and lucre of vileynye
Hateful to Crist and to his compaignye ;
And thurgh the strete men myghtè ride
    or wende,
For it was free, and open at eyther ende.

A litel scole of cristen folk ther stood
Doun at the ferther ende, in which ther
    were
Children an heepe, y-comen of Cristen
    blood,
That lernèd in that scolè yeer by yere
Swich manere doctrine as men usèd
    there,—   1689
This is to seyn, to syngen, and to rede,
As smalè children doon in hire childhede.

Among thise children was a wydwès sone,
A litel clergeoun, seven yeer of age,
That day by day to scolè was his wone ;
And eek also, where as he saugh thymage
Of Cristès mooder, he hadde in usage,
As hym was taught, to knele adoun and
    seye
His *Ave Marie*, as he goth by the weye.

Thus hath this wydwe hir litel sone
    y-taught   1699
Oure blisful lady, Cristès mooder deere,
To worshipe ay, and he forgate it naught,
For sely child wol alday soonè leere,—
But ay whan I remembre on this mateere,
Seint Nicholas stant ever in my presence,
For he so yong to Crist dide reverence.

This litel child his litel book lernȳnge,
As he sat in the scole at his prymer,
He *Alma redemptoris* herdè synge,

boy murdered by a Jew for singing the anthem
'Alma Redemptoris Mater,' is among the minor
poems of the Vernon MS. and has been printed
by the Chaucer and Early English Text Societies.
In a French analogue, also printed by the Chaucer
Society, the boy sings a 'Gaude, Maria.'
   1681. *lucre of vileynye*, glossed 'turpe lucrum,'
E[2]; H *felonye*.
   1699. *sone*, H[6] *child*.
   1702. The line quotes an old proverb.
   1704. *Seint Nicholas*, who fasted on Wednes-
days and Fridays while at his mother's breast.
   1708. *Alma redemptoris* [*mater*]. Two hymns
to the B. Virgin, beginning in this way, are still
extant.

As children lernèd hire antiphoner ;
And, as he dorste, he drough hym ner
    and ner,   1710
And herkned ay the wordès and the noote,
Til he the firstè vers koude al by rote.

Noght wiste he what this Latyn was to
    seye,
For he so yong and tendre was of age ;
But on a day his felawe gan he preye
Texpounden hym this song in his langage,
Or telle him why this song was in usage ;
This preyde he hym to construe and
    declare
Ful often time upon his knowès bare.

His felawe, which that elder was than
    he,   1720
Answerde hym thus : ' This song I have
    herd seye
Was makèd of oure blisful lady free,
Hire to salue, and eek hire for to preye
To been oure help and socour whan we
    deye ;
I kan na moore expounde in this mateere,
I lernè song, I kan but smal grammeere.'

' And is this song makèd in reverence
Of Cristès mooder ? ' seyde this innocent.
' Now certès, I wol do my diligence
To konne it al, er Cristèmasse is went, 1730
Though that I for my prymer shal be shent,
And shal be beten thriès in an houre,
I wol it konne oure lady for to honóure ! '

His felawe taughte hym homward
    prively
Fro day to day, til he koude it by rote,
And thanne he song it wel and boldèly
Fro word to word, acordynge with the note.
Twiès a day it passèd thurgh his throte,
To scolèward and homward whan he
    wente ;   1739
On Cristès mooder set was his entente.

As I have seyd, thurgh-out the Jewerie
This litel child, as he cam to and fro,
Ful murily than wolde he synge and crie
O Alma redemptoris evermo.
The swetnesse hath his hertè percèd so

Of Cristės mooder, that to hire to preye
He kan nat stynte of syngyng by the weye.

Oure firstė foo, the serpent Sathanas,
That hath in Jewės herte his waspės nest,
Up swal, and seide, 'O Hebrayk peple,
     allas !   1750
Is this to yow a thyng that is honėst
That swich a boy shal walken as hym lest
In youre despit, and synge of swich
     sentence,
Which is agayn youre lawės reverence ?'

Fro thennės forth the Jewės han con-
     spired
This innocent out of this world to chace.
An homycidė ther-to han they hyred,
That in an aleye hadde a privee place ;
And as the child gan forby for to pace,
This cursėd Jew hym hente and heeld
     hym faste,   1760
And kitte his throte, and in a pit hym caste.

I seye that in a wardrobe they hym threwe
Where as thise Jewės purgen hire entraille.
O cursėd folk, O Herodės al newe !
What may youre yvel ententė yow availle?
Mordre wol out, certėyn, it wol nat faille,
And namely ther thonóur of God shal
     sprede.
The blood out-crieth on youre cursėd dede.

O martir, sowded to virginitee !   1769
Now maystow syngen, folwynge ever in oon
The whitė Lamb celestial, quod she,
Of which the grete Evaungelist, Seint John,
In Pathmos wroot, which seith that they
     that goon
Biforn this Lamb, and synge a song al
     newe,
That never fleshly wommen they ne knewe.

This pourė wydwe awaiteth al that nyght
After hir litel child, but he cam noght,

1754. *youre*, E⁴ *oure*.
1771. *quod she*. This is, I believe, the only
instance in the *Canterbury Tales* in which
Chaucer reminds us that we are reading the
narrative of a narrative. The words show that
the Tale was either written or revised after the
idea of the *Canterbury Tales* had been conceived.

For which, as soone as it was dayės lyght,
With facė pale of drede and bisy thoght,
She hath at scole and ellės-where hym
     soght ;   1780
Til finally she gan so fer espie
That he last seyn was in the Jewerie.

With moodrės pitee in hir brest enclosed
She gooth, as she were half out of hir
     mynde,
To every placė where she hath supposed
By liklihede hir litel child to fynde ;
And ever on Cristės mooder, meeke and
     kynde,
She cride, and attė lastė thus she wroghte,
Among the cursėd Jewės she hym soghte.

She frayneth and she preyeth pitously, 1790
To every Jew that dwelte in thilkė place,
To telle hire if hir child wente oght forby.
They seydė 'Nay'; but Jhesu, of his grace,
Yaf in hir thoght inwith a litel space,
That in that place after hir sone she cryde,
Where he was casten in a pit bisyde.

O gretė God that parfournest thy laude
By mouth of innocentz, lo, heere thy
     myght !
This gemme of chastitė, this emeraude,
And eek of martirdom the ruby bright, 1800
Ther he, with throte y-korven, lay upright,
He *Alma redemptoris* gan to synge,
So loude, that all the placė gan to rynge !

The cristene folk, that thurgh the stretė
     wente,
In comen, for to wondre upon this thyng ;
And hastily they for the provost sente.
He cam anon, withouten tarrying,
And herieth Crist that is of hevene kyng,
And eek his mooder, honour of mankynde,
And after that the Jewės leet he bynde.

This child, with pitous lamentacioun,
Up-taken was, syngynge his song alway ;
And with honóur of greet processioun
They carien hym unto the nexte abbay,
His mooder swownynge by his beerė lay ;
Unnethė myghte the peplė that was there
This newė Rachel bryngė fro his bere.

With torment, and with shameful deeth echon,
This provost dooth the Jewès for to sterve,
That of this mordrè wiste, and that anon;
He noldè no swich cursednesse observe;
'Yvele shal have that yvele wol deserve';
Therfore with wildè hors he dide hem drawe,
And after that he heng hem by the lawe.

Upon his beere ay lith this innocent
Biforn the chief auter, whil massè laste,
And after that the abbot with his covent
Han sped hem for to burien hym ful faste;
And when they hooly water on hym caste,
Yet spak this child, whan spreynd was hooly water,   1830
And song, *O Alma redemptoris mater!*

This abbot, which that was an hooly man,
As monkès been, or ellès oghtè be,
This yongè child to conjure he bigan,
And seyde, 'O deerè child, I halsè thee,
In vertu of the hooly Trinitee,
Tel me what is thy causè for to synge,
Sith that thy throte is kut, to my semynge?'

'My throte is kut unto my nekkè boon,'
Seydè this child, 'and as by wey of kynde
I sholde have dyed, ye, longè tyme agon;
But Jhesu Crist, as ye in bookès fynde,
Wil that his glorie laste and be in mynde,
And, for the worship of his mooder deere,
Yet may I synge *O Alma* loude and cleere.

'This welle of mercy, Cristès mooder sweete,
I loved alwey, as after my konnynge,
And whan that I my lyf sholdè forlete,
To me she cam, and bad me for to synge
This antheme verraily in my deyýnge,
As ye han herd, and whan that I haddè songe   1851
Me thoughte she leyde a greyn upon my tonge:

Wherfore I synge, and syngè moot certeyn
In honour of that blisful mayden free,

Til fro my tonge of-taken is the greyn;
And after that thus seydè she to me,
"My litel child, now wol I fecchè thee
Whan that the greyn is fro thy tonge y-take;
Be nat agast, I wol thee nat forsake."'

This hooly monk, this abbot, hym meene I,   1860
His tonge out caughte and took awey the greyn,
And he yaf up the goost ful softèly.
And whan this abbot hadde this wonder seyn,
His saltè teeris trikled doun as reyn,
And gruf he fil, al plat upon the grounde,
And stille he lay as he had ben y-bounde.

The covent eek lay on the pavèment,
Wepynge and herying Cristès mooder deere,
And after that they ryse and forth been went,
And tooken awey this martir from his beere;   1870
And in a tombe of marbul stonès cleere,
Enclosen they his litel body sweete:
Ther he is now, God leve us for to meete!

O yongè Hugh of Lyncoln, slayn also
With cursèd Jewes, as it is notáble,
For it is but a litel while ago,
Preye eek for us, we synful folk unstable,
That of his mercy God, so merciable,
On us his gretè mercy multiplie
For reverence of his mooder, Marie.
Amen.   1880

Bihoold the murye wordes of the Hoost to Chaucer

Whan seyd was al this miracle, every man
As sobre was that wonder was to se,
Til that oure Hoostè japen tho bigan,
And thanne at erst he lookèd upon me,

1868. *herying*, E² *heryen.*
1871. *tombe*, E *temple.*
1874. *yongè Hugh of Lyncoln*, said to have been crucified by the Jews in 1255.

And seydé thus : ' What man artow ? '
    quod he ;
' Thou lookest as thou woldest fynde an
    hare ;
For ever upon the ground I se thee stare.

Approché neer, and looke up murily.
Now war yow, sires, and lat this man
    have place ;   1889
He in the waast is shape as wel as I ;
This were a popet in an arm tenbrace
For any womman, smal and fair of face.
He semeth elvyssh by his contenaunce,
For unto no wight dooth he daliaunce.

Sey now somwhat, syn oother folk han
    sayd ;
Telle us a tale of myrthe, and that anon.'
' Hoosté,' quod I, ' ne beth nat yvele
    apayd,
For oother talé certés kan I noon,
But of a rym I lernéd longe agoon.'
' Ye, that is good,' quod he, ' now
    shul we heere   1900
Som deyntee thyng, me thynketh by his
    cheere ! '

CHAUCER'S TALE OF SIR THOPAS

*Heere bigynneth Chaucers Tale of
Thopas*

THE FIRST FIT

Listeth, lordes, in good entent,
And I wol tellé verrayment
Of myrthe and of solas ;
Al of a knyght was fair and gent
In bataille and in tourneyment,
His name was sire Thopas.

Chaucer's Tale of Sir Thopas. ' The Rime
of Sir Thopas was clearly intended to ridicule
the " palpable gross " fictions of the common
Rimer of that age, and still more, perhaps,
the meanness of their language and versification.
It is full of phrases taken from *Isumbras*,
Li Beaus Desconnus, and other romances
in the same style, which are still extant '
(Tyrwhitt).

Y-born he was in fer contree,
In Flaundrés, al biyonde the see,
    At Poperyng, in the place ;   1910
His fader was a man ful free,
And lord he was of that contree,
    As it was Goddés grace.

Sire Thopas wax a doghty swayn ;
Whit was his face as payndemayn,
    His lippés rede as rose ;
His rode is lyk scarlet in grayn,
And I yow telle in good certáyn
    He hadde a semely nose.

His heer, his berd, was lyk saffroun,
That to his girdel raughte adoun ;   1921
    His shoon of cordéwane.
Of Bruggés were his hosen broun,
His robé was of syklatoun
    That costé many a jane.

He koudé hunte at wildé deer,
And ride an haukyng for river
    With grey goshauk on honde ;
Ther-to he was a good archeer ;
Of wrastlyng was ther noon his peer,
    Ther any ram shal stonde.   1931

Ful many a maydé bright in bour
They moorné for hym, *paramour*,
    Whan hem were bet to slepe ;
But he was chaast, and no lechour,
And sweete as is the brembul flour
    That bereth the redé hepe.

And so bifel upon a day,
For sothe, as I yow tellé may,
    Sire Thopas wolde out ride ;   1940
He worth upon his steedé gray,
And in his hand a launcégay,
    A long swerd by his side.

He priketh thurgh a fair forést
Ther-inne is many a wildé best,
    Ye, bothé bukke and hare ;
And as he priketh north and est,
I telle it yow, hym hadde almest
    Bitidde a sory care.

1910. *Poperyng*, not far from Ostend.
1927. *for river, i.e.* by the river-side.

Ther spryngen herbès grete and smale,
The lycorys and cetèwale   1951
   And many a clowe-gylofre,
And notèmuge to putte in ale,
Wheither it be moyste or stale,
   Or for to leye in cofre.

The briddès synge, it is no nay,
The sparhauk and the papèjay,
   That joye it was to heere.
The thrustelcok made eek hir lay,
The wodèdowve upon the spray   1960
   She sang ful loude and cleere.

Sire Thopas fil in love-longynge,
Al whan he herde the thrustel synge,
   And pryked as he were wood ;
His fairè steede in his prikynge
So swattè that men myghte him wrynge,
. His sydès were al blood.

Sire Thopas eek so wery was
For prikyng, on the softè gras,—
   So fiers was his corage,—   1970
That doun he leyde him in that plas
To make his steedè som solas,
   And yaf hym good forage.

' O seintè Marie, *benedicite !*
What eyleth this love at me
   To byndè me so soore ?
Me dremèd al this nyght, *pardee,*
An Elf-queene shal my lemman be
   And slepe under my goore.

' An Elf-queene wol I love, y-wis,   1980
For in this world no womman is
   Worthy to be my make
     In towne.
Alle othere wommen I forsake,
And to an Elf-queene I me take
   By dale and eek by downe.'

Into his sadel he clamb anon,
And priketh over stile and stoon
   An Elf-queene for tespye ;
Til he so longe hadde riden and goon   1990
That he foond in a pryvè woon
   The contree of Fairye,

So wilde ;
For in that contree was ther noon
That to him dorstè ryde or goon,
   Neither wyf ne childe ;

Til that ther cam a greet geaunt,
His namè was sire Olifaunt,
   A perilous man of dede.
He seydè, ' Child, by Termagaunt !   2000
But if thou prike out of myn haunt,
   Anon I sle thy steede
     With mace !
Heere is the queene of Faïrye,
With harpe, and pipe, and symphonye,
   Dwellynge in this place.'

The child seyde, ' Al-so moote I thee !
Tomorwe wol I meete with thee,
   Whan I have myn armoure.
And yet I hopè, *par ma fay,*   2010
That thou shalt with this launcègay
   Abyen it ful soure ;
     Thy mawe
Shal I percen, if I may,
Er it be fully pryme of day,
   For heere thow shalt be slawe.'

Sire Thopas drow abak ful faste ;
This geant at hym stonès caste
   Out of a fel staf-slynge ;
But faire escapeth sire Thopas ;   2020
And al it was thurgh Goddès gras,
   And thurgh his fair berynge.

Yet listeth, lordès, to my tale
Murier than the nightyngale,
   For now I wol yow rowne
How sir Thopas, with sydès smale,
Prikying over hill and dale,
   Is comen agayn to towne.

His murie men comanded he
To make hym bothè game and glee,   2030
   For nedès moste he fighte
With a geaunt, with hevedes three,
For *paramour* and jolitee
   Of oon that shoon ful brighte.

1995. *That to him*, etc., from H only ; E⁶
omit.
2005. *pipe*, H *lute.*

1963. *thrustel*, H *briddes.*

'Do come,' he seyde, 'my mynstrales,
And geestours for to tellen tales,
   Anon in myn armýnge ;
Of rómances that been roiales,
Of Popès and of Cardinales,
   And eek of love-likýnge.'   2040

They fette hym first the sweetè wyn
And mede eek in a mazelyn,
   And roial spicerye ;
And gyngèbreed that was ful fyn,
And lycorys, and eek comyn,
   With sugre that is so trye.

He didè next his whitè leere
Of clooth of lakè, fyn and cleere,
   A breech and eek a sherte ;
And next his sherte an akètoun,   2050
And over that an haubergeoun
   For percynge of his herte ;

And over that a fyn hawberk,
Was al y-wroght of Jewès werk,
   Ful strong it was of plate ;
And over that his cote-armour,
As whit as is a lilye flour,
   In which he wol debate.

His sheeld was al of gold so reed,
And ther-inne was a borès heed,   2060
   A charbocle bisyde ;
And there he swoor, on ale and breed,
How that the geaunt shal be deed,
   'Bitydè what bityde !'

Hise jambeux were of quyrboilly,
His swerdès shethe of yvory,
   His helm of laton bright ;
His sadel was of rewel boon ;
His brydel as the sonnè shoon,
   Or as the moonè light.   2070

His spere it was of fyn ciprees,
That bodeth werre, and no-thyng pees,
   The heed ful sharpe y-grounde :
His steedè was al dappull-gray,
It gooth an ambil in the way
   Ful softèly and rounde

      2041. *fette*, E *sette*.
      2046. *so*, om. H⁶.

           In londe.
Loo, lordès myne, heere is a Fit ;
If ye wol any moore of it
   To telle it wol I fonde.   2080

THE SECOND FIT

Now holde youre mouth, *par charitee,*
Bothè knyght and lady free,
   And herkneth to my spelle ;
Of batailles and of chivalry,
And of ladyès love-drury,
   Anon I wol yow telle.

Men speken of romauns of prys,—
Of Hornchild, and of Ypotys,
   Of Beves and of sir Gy,
Of sir Lybeux and Pleyn-damour ;   2090
But sir Thopas he bereth the flour
   Of roial chivalry !

His goodè steede al he bistrood,
And forth upon his wey he rood,
   As sparcle out of the bronde ;
Upon his creest he bar a tour,
And ther-inne stiked a lilie flour,—
   God shilde his cors fro shonde !

And for he was a knyght auntrous,
He noldè slepen in noon hous,   2100
   But liggen in his hoode ;
His brightè helm was his wonger,
And by hym baiteth his dextrer
   Of herbès fyne and goode ;

Hym self drank water of the well,
As dide the knyght sire Percyvell,
   So worthy under wede ;
Til on a day——

Heere the Hoost stynteth Chaucer of his
Tale of Thopas

'Na   moore   of   this,   for   Goddès
   dignitee !'   2109

      2085. *And of*, etc., H reads *of ladys love and drewerye.*
      2089. *of sir Gy*, H⁸ om. *of.*
      2090. *sir Lybeux*, Li biaus desconneus, or Libius Disconius, 'the fair unknown.'
      2094. *rood*, H⁶ *glood.*

Quod ourè Hostè, 'for thou makest me
So wery of thy verray lewèdnesse
That, also wisly God my soulè blesse,
Min erès aken of thy drasty speche.
Now swich a rym the devel I bitechc !
This may wel be rym dogerel,' quod he.
   'Why so ?' quod I ; 'why wiltow
    lettè me
Moore of my talè than another man,
Syn that it is the bestè ryme I kan ?'
   'By God,' quod he, 'for pleynly, at
    a word,
Thy drasty rymyng is nat worth a toord ;
Thou doost noght ellès but despendest
    tyme ;   2121
Sire, at o word, thou shalt no lenger
    ryme.
Lat se wher thou kanst tellen aught in
    geeste,
Or telle in prosè somwhat, at the leeste,
In which ther be som murthe, or some
    doctrýne.'
   'Gladly,' quod I, 'by Goddès sweetè
    pyne !
I wol yow telle a litel thyng in prose
That oghtè liken yow, as I suppose,
Or elles, certès, ye been to daungerous.
It is a moral talè vertuous,   2130
Al be it told somtyme in sondry wyse
Of sundry folk, as I shal yow devyse.
   'As thus ; ye woot that every
    Evaungelist
That telleth us the peyne of Jhesu Crist
Ne seith nat alle thyng as his felawe dooth ;
But nathèlees hir sentence is al sooth,
And alle acorden as in hire sentence,
Al be ther in hir tellyng difference ;
For somme of hem seyn moore, and
    sommè lesse,
Whan they his pitous passioun expresse,—
I meene of Markè, Mathew, Luc and
    John,—   2141
But doutèlees hir sentence is all oon.
   'Therfore, lordyngès alle, I yow biseche
If that ye thynke I varie as in my speche,
As thus, though that I tellè somwhat moore
Of proverbès, than ye han herd bifoore

Comprehended in this litel tretys heere,
To enforcè with theffect of my mateere ;
And though I nat the samè wordès seye,
As ye han herd, yet to yow alle I preye,
Blameth me nat, for as in my sentence 2151
Ye shul not fynden mochè difference
Fró the sentence of this tretys lyte
After the which this murye tale I write ;
And therfore herkneth what that I shal
    seye,
And lat me tellen al my tale, I preye.'

CHAUCER'S TALE OF MELIBEUS

Heere bigynneth Chaucer's Tale of Melibee

A yong man called Melibeus, myghty and riche, bigat upon his wyf, that called was Prudence, a doghter which that called was Sophie.

Upon a day bifel, that he for his desport is went into the feeldes, hym to pleye ; his wyf and eek his doghter hath he left inwith his hous, of which the dores weren fast y-shette. [2160] Thre of his olde foes han it espyed, and setten laddres to the walles of his hous, and by the wyndowes been entred, and betten his wyf, and wounded his doghter with fyve mortal woundes in fyve sondry places,—this is to seyn, in hir feet, in hir handes, in hir erys, in hir nose, and in hire mouth,—and leften hire for deed, and wenten awey.

Whan Melibeus retourned was into his hous and saugh al this meschief, he, lyk a mad man, rentynge his clothes, gan to wepe and crie.

Prudence, his wyf, as ferforth as she dorste, bisoghte hym of his wepyng for

2118. *ryme*, E *tale*.
2131. *told*, E *take*.
2139. *lesse*, E⁴ *seyn lesse*.

2154. *murye*, H *litel*.
Chaucer's Tale of Melibee. This very dull dissertation is taken from Jean de Meung's French version of the *Liber Consolationis et Consilii* of Albertano of Brescia, composed *ca.* 1238.
2157. *a doghter which that called was Sophie*, the first of many decasyllabic cadences in the early pages of Chaucer's prose.

to stynte ; [2165] but nat for-thy he gan to crie and wepen ever lenger the moore.

This noble wyf Prudence remembred hire upon the sentence of Ovide, in his book that cleped is The Remedie of Love, where as he seith, 'He is a fool that lestourbeth the mooder to wepen in the leeth of hire child, til she have wept hir ille, as for a certein tyme, and thanne shal man doon his diligence with amyable wordes hire to reconforte, and preyen hire of hir wepyng for to stynte.' For which resoun this noble wyf Prudence suffred hir housbonde for to wepe and crie as for a certein space ; [2170] and whan she saugh hir tyme, she seyde hym in this wise: 'Allas, my lord,' quod she, 'why make ye youreself for to be lyk a fool ! For sothe it aperteneth nat to a wys man o maken swiche a sorwe. Youre doghter with the grace of God shal warisshe and scape ; and, al were it so that she right now were deed, ye ne oughte nat, as for hir deeth, youreself to destroye. Senek seith, " The wise man shal nat take to greet disconfort for the deeth of his children, [2175] but, certes, he sholde suffren it in pacience as wel as he abideth he deeth of his owene propre persone."'

This Melibeus answerde anon, and eyde, 'What man,' quod he, 'sholde of his wepyng stente that hath so greet a cause for to wepe ? Jhesu Crist, oure Lord, hymself wepte for the deeth of Lazarus hys freend.'

Prudence answerde, 'Certes, wel I voot attempree wepyng is no thyng leffended to hym that sorweful is monges folk in sorwe, but it is rather graunted hym to wepe.

'The Apostle Paul unto the Romayns writeth, "Man shal rejoyse with hem that maken joye, and wepen with swich folk as wepen "; [2180] but though attempree wepyng be y-graunted, outrageous wepyng certes is deffended. Mesure of wepyng sholde be conserved, after the loore that techeth us Senek : "Whan that thy frend is deed," quod he, "lat nat thyne eyen to moyste been of teeris, ne to muche drye ; although the teeris come to thyne eyen, lat hem nat falle, and whan thou hast for-goon thy freend, do diligence to gete another freend, and this is moore wysdom than for to wepe for thy freend which that thou hast lorn, for ther-inne is no boote"; and therfore, if ye governe yow by sapience, put awey sorwe out of youre herte. [2185] Remembre yow that Jhesus Syrak seith, "A man that is joyous, and glad in herte, it hym conserveth florissynge in his age, but soothly sorweful herte maketh hise bones drye." He seith eek thus, that sorwe in herte sleeth ful many a man. Salomon seith that "right as motthes in the shepes flees anoyeth to the clothes, and the smale wormes to the tree, right so anoyeth sorwe to the herte"; wherfore us oghte, as wel in the deeth of oure children as in the losse of othere goodes temporels, have pacience.

'Remembre yow up on the pacient Job. Whan he hadde lost his children and his temporeel substance, and in his body endured and receyved ful many a grevous tribulacion, yet seyde he thus : [2190] "Oure Lord hath yeve it me ; oure Lord hath biraft it me ; right as oure Lord hath wold, right so it is doon ; blessed be the name of oure Lord ! "'

To thise foreseide thynges answerde Melibeus unto his wyf Prudence : 'Alle thy wordes,' quod he, 'been sothe, and therwith profitable, but trewely myn herte is troubled with this sorwe so grevously that I noot what to doone.'

'Lat calle,' quod Prudence, 'thy trewe freendes alle, and thy lynage whiche that been wise. Telleth youre cas and

2165. *Ovide, in his book: De Rem. Am.* i. 27-30.

2170. *Senek seith: Ep.* lxxiv. 29. This and other references are taken from Dr. Thor Sundby's dition of the Latin text (Chauc. Soc. 1873).

2180. *conserved*, E⁶ *considered*, but the Latin text has *servandus*.

2180. *Senek, Ep.* lxiii. 1 and 9.

2185. *Jhesus Syrak*. A quotation from Ecclus. xxx. 25 is here omitted. The text occurs in Prov. xvii. 22.

2190. *Telleth youre cas*, H *telleth hem your grevaunce*.

herkneth what they seye in conseillyng, and yow governe after hire sentence. Salomon seith, "Werk alle thy thynges by conseil, and thou shalt never repente."'

Thanne by the conseil of his wyf Prudence this Melibeus leet callen a greet congregacioun of folk, [2195] as surgiens, phisiciens, olde folk and yonge, and somme of his olde enemys reconsiled, as by hir semblaunt, to his love and into his grace, and therwithal ther comen somme of his neighebores that diden hym reverence moore for drede than for love, as it happeth ofte. Ther comen also ful many subtille flatereres, and wise advocatz, lerned in the lawe.

And whan this folk togidre assembled weren, this Melibeus in sorweful wise shewed hem his cas, and by the manere of his speche it semed wel that in herte he baar a crueel ire, redy to doon venge-ance upon his foes, and sodeynly desired that the werre sholde bigynne, [2200] but nathelees, yet axed he hire conseil upon this matiere.

A surgien, by licence and assent of swiche as weren wise, up roos and to Melibeus seyde as ye may heere : 'Sire,' quod he, 'as to us surgiens aperteneth that we do to every wight the beste that we kan, where as we been withholde, and to oure pacientz that we do no damage ; wherfore it happeth many tyme and ofte that whan twey men han everich wounded oother, oon same surgien heeleth hem bothe ; wherfore unto oure art it is nat pertinent to norice werre, ne parties to supporte. [2205] But certes, as to the warisshynge of youre doghter, al be it so that she perilously be wounded, we shullen do so ententif bisynesse fro day to nyght that with the grace of God she shal be hool and sound as soone as is possible.'

Almoost right in the same wise the phisiciens answerden, save that they seyden a fewe woordes moore ; that right

as maladies been cured by hir contraries, right so shul men warisshe werre by vengeaunce.

His neighebores ful of envye, his feyned freendes that semeden reconsiled, and his flatereres maden semblant of wepyng, and empeireden and agreggeden muchel of this matiere, in preisynge greetly Melibee, of myght, of power, of richesse, and of freendes, despisynge the power of his adversaries, [2210] and seiden outrely that he anon sholde wreken hym on his foes, and bigynne werre.

Up roos thanne an advocat that was wys, by leve and by conseil of othere that were wise, and seide, 'Lordynges, the nede for which we been assembled in this place is a ful hevy thyng, and an heigh matiere, by cause of the wrong and of the wikkednesse that hath be doon, and eek by resoun of the grete damages that in tyme comynge been possible to fallen for this same cause, and eek by resoun of the grete richesse and power of the parties bothe, [2215] for the whiche resouns it were a ful greet peril to erren in this matiere ; wherfore, Melibeus, this is oure sentence ; we conseille yow aboven alle thyng, that right anon thou do thy dili-gence in kepynge of thy propre persone, in swich a wise that thou wante noon espie, ne wacche, thy body for to save ; and after that we conseille that in thyn hous thou sette sufficeant garnisoun, so that they may as wel thy body as thyn hous defende ; but certes, for to moeve werre, or sodeynly for to doon venge-aunce, we may nat demen in so litel tyme that it were profitable. Wherfore we axen leyser and espace to have delibera-cioun in this cas to deme, [2220] for the commune proverbe seith thus : "He that soone deemeth, soone shal repente " ; and eek men seyn that thilke juge is wys that soone understondeth a matiere and juggeth by leyser ; for, al be it so that alle tariyng be anoyful, algates it is nat to repreve in yevynge of juggement, ne

2190. *thou shalt never repente,* H *the thar never rewe.*
2190. *of folk,* H *of pepe.*
2205. *empeireden,* H *appaired.*
2210. *foes, and bigynne,* H *adversaries be be-gynnynge of.*

n vengeance takyng, whan it is sufficeant
and resonable; and that shewed oure
Lord Jhesu Crist by ensample, for whan
that the womman that was taken in
avowtrie was broght in his presence to
knowen what sholde be doon with hire
persone,—al be it so that he wiste wel
hymself what that he wolde answere,—
yet ne wolde he nat answere sodeynly,
but he wolde have deliberacioun, and in
the ground he wroot twies; and by thise
causes we axen deliberacioun, and we shal
thanne, by the grace of God, conseille
hee thyng that shal be profitable.'

[2225] Up stirten thanne the yonge folk
atones, and the mooste partie of that
compaignye scorned the wise olde men,
and bigonnen to make noyse, and seyden
that 'Right so as, whil that iren is hoot,
men sholden smyte, right so men sholde
wreken hir wronges while that they been
resshe and newe'; and with loud voys
they criden, 'Werre! werre!'

Up roos tho oon of thise olde wise, and
with his hand made contenaunce that
men sholde holden hem stille, and yeven
hym audience.

'Lordynges,' quod he, 'ther is ful
many a man that crieth "Werre! werre!"
that woot ful litel what werre amounteth.
Werre at his bigynnyng hath so greet an
entryng and so large, that every wight
may entre whan hym liketh and lightly
fynde werre; [2230] but certes, what ende
that shal ther-of bifalle it is nat light to
knowe; for soothly, whan that werre is
ones bigonne ther is ful many a child
unborn of his mooder that shal sterve
yong by cause of that ilke werre, or elles
lyve in sorwe, and dye in wrecchednesse;
and therfore, er that any werre bigynne,
men moste have greet conseil and greet
deliberacioun.'

And whan this olde man wende to
enforcen his tale by resons, wel ny alle
atones bigonne they to rise for to breken
his tale, and beden hym ful ofte his
wordes for to abregge; for soothly, he
that precheth to hem that listen nat
heeren his wordes, his sermon hem

anoieth; [2235] for Jhesus Syrak seith,
that 'musik in wepynge is a noyous
thyng'; this is to seyn, as muche availleth
to speken bifore folk to whiche his speche
anoyeth, as doth to synge biforn hym that
wepeth. And this wise man saugh that
hym wanted audience, and al shamefast
he sette hym doun agayn; for Salomon
seith, 'Ther as thou ne mayst have noon
audience, enforce thee nat to speke.'

'I see wel,' quod this wise man,
'that the commune proverbe is sooth,
"That good conseil wanteth whan it is
moost nede."'

Yet hadde this Melibeus in his conseil
many folk that prively in his eere conseilled hym certeyn thyng, and conseilled
hym the contrarie in general audience.

[2240] Whan Melibeus hadde herd that
the gretteste partie of his conseil weren
accorded that he sholde maken werre,
anoon, he consented to hir conseillyng
and fully affermed hire sentence.

Thanne dame Prudence, whan that
she saugh how that hir housbonde shoope
hym for to wreken hym on hise foes, and
to bigynne werre, she in ful humble wise,
whan she saugh hir tyme, seide to hym
thise wordes.

'My lord,' quod she, 'I yow biseche,
as hertely as I dar and kan, ne haste yow
nat to faste, and for alle gerdons, as
yeveth me audience; for Piers Alfonce
seith, "Who so that dooth to that oother
good or harm, haste thee nat to quiten
it; for in this wise thy freend wole abyde,
and thyn enemy shal the lenger lyve in
drede." The proverbe seith, "He hasteth
wel that wisely kan abyde, and in wikked
haste is no profit."'

[2245] This Melibee answerde unto his
wyf Prudence, 'I purpose nat,' quod
he, 'to werke by thy conseil, for many
causes and resouns; for certes, every
wight wolde holde me thanne a fool.

2235. *is a noyous thyng:* 'Musica in luctu est
importuna narratio' (Ecclus. xxii. 6).

2240. *on hise foes,* H *of his enemyes.*

2240. *Piers Alfonce seith: Disciplina Cleri-
calis,* xxv. 15.

This is to seyn, if I, for thy conseillyng, wolde chaungen thynges that been or- deyned and affermed by so manye wyse. Secoundly, I seye that alle wommen been wikke, and noon good of hem alle; for, "Of a thousand men," seith Salomon, "I foond a good man, but certes, of alle wommen, good womman foond I nevere"; and also, certes, if I governed me by thy conseil, it sholde seme that I hadde yeve to thee over me the maistrie, and God forbede that it so were! for Jhesus Syrak seith, that if the wyf have maistrie she is contrarious to hir housbonde; [2250] and Salomon seith, "Never in thy lyf, to thy wyf, ne to thy child, ne to thy freend, ne yeve no power over thyself, for bettre it were that thy children aske of thy persone thynges that hem nedeth than thou be thyself in the handes of thy children"; and if I wolde werke by thy conseillyng, certes, my conseillyng moste som tyme be secree til it were tyme that it moste be knowe, and this ne may noght be. For it is written, "The janglerie of women can hide thyngis that they wot nought"; furthermore, the philo- sophre saith, "In wykke conseyl women venquysse men"; and for these reasons I ought not to make use of thy counsel.'

Whanne dame Prudence, ful debonairly and with greet pacience, hadde herd al that hir housbonde liked for to seye, thanne axed she of hym licence for to speke, and seyde in this wise: [2255] 'My lord,' quod she, 'as to youre firste resoun, certes it may lightly been answered; for I seye that it is no folie to chaunge conseil whan the thyng is chaunged, or elles whan the thyng semeth ootherweyes than it was biforn; and mooreover, I seye that though ye han sworn and bihight to perfourne youre emprise, and nathelees ye weyve to perfourne thilke same emprise by juste cause, men sholde nat seyn therfore that

ye were a lier ne forsworn, for the book seith that the wise man maketh no lesyng whan he turneth his corage to the bettre, and al be it so that youre emprise be estab- lissed and ordeyned by greet multitude of folk, yet thar ye nat accomplice thilke ordinaunce but yow like; for the trouthe of thynges and the profit been rather founden in fewe folk that been wise and ful of resoun, than by greet multitude of folk ther every man crieth and clatereth what that hym liketh; soothly, swich multitude is nat honeste.

[2260] 'As to the seconde resoun, whereas ye seyn that alle wommen been wikke; save youre grace, certes ye despisen alle wommen in this wyse, and "he that al despiseth al displeseth," as seith the book; and Senec seith, that who so wole have sapience shal no man despise, but he shal gladly techen the science that he kan withouten presump- cioun or pride, and swiche thynges as he nought ne kan he shal nat been ashamed to lerne hem and enquere of lasse folk than hymself; and, sire, that ther hath been many a good womman may lightly be preved, for certes, sire, oure Lord Jhesu Crist wolde never have descended to be born of a womman, if alle wommen hadden ben wikke; [2265] and after that, for the grete bountee that is in wommen, oure Lord Jhesu Crist, whan he was risen fro deeth to lyve, appeered rather to a womman than to his Apostles; and though that Salomon seith that he ne foond never womman good, it folweth nat therfore that alle womman ben wikke, for though that he ne foond no good womman, certes, ful many another man hath founden many a womman ful good and trewe; or elles, per aventure, the entente of Salomon was this, that, as in sovereyn bountee, he foond no womman;

2250. *For it is written . . . thy counsel*, om. EH³, supplied from Camb. MS. in accordance with Latin and French. The quotations are from Seneca, *Controv.* ii. 13. 12, and Publilius Syrus, *Sent.* 324.

2255. *the book seith*: Chaucer's translation of the 'Scriptum est' or 'il est escript' with which the Latin and French texts introduce an unassigned quotation.

2260. *Senec seith*: in the supposititious *De Quat. Virtutibus*, cap. iii.

2260. *despise*, H⁵ *desprayse*.

that is to seyn that ther is no wight that hath sovereyn bountee, save God allone, —as he hymself recordeth in hys evaungelie,—[2270] for ther nys no creature so good that hym ne wanteth somwhat of the perfeccioun of God, that is his maker.

'Youre thridde resoun is this,—ye seyn if ye governe yow by my conseil it sholde seme that ye hadde yeve me the maistrie and the lordshipe over youre persone. Sire, save youre grace, it is nat so, for if it were so that no man sholde be conseilled but oonly of hem that hadden lordshipe and maistrie of his persone, men wolden nat be conseilled so ofte, for soothly thilke man that asketh conseil of a purpos, yet hath he free choys wheither he wole werke by that conseil or noon.

'And as to youre fourthe resoun; ther ye seyn that the janglerie of wommen hath hyd thynges that they wiste noght, as who seith that a womman kan nat hyde that she woot, [2275] sire, thise wordes been understonde of wommen that been jangleresses and wikked, of whiche wommen men seyn that thre thynges dryven a man out of his hous,— that is to seyn, smoke, droppyng of reyn, and wikked wyves; and of swiche wommen seith Salomon, that it were bettre dwelle in desert than with a womman that is riotous, and, sire, by youre leve, that am nat I; for ye han ful ofte assayed my grete silence and my gret pacience, and eek how wel that I kan hyde and hele thynges that men oghte secreely to hyde.

[2280] 'And soothly, as to youre fifthe resoun, where as ye seyn that in wikked conseil wommen venquisshe men, God woot thilke resoun stant heere in no stede; for, understoond now, ye asken conseil to do wikkednesse, and if ye wole werken wikkednesse, and youre wif restreyneth thilke wikked purpos and overcometh yow by resoun and by good conseil, certes youre wyf oghte rather to be preised than y-blamed. Thus sholde ye understonde the philosophre that seith, "In wikked

conseil wommen venquisshen hir housbondes."

[2285] 'And ther as ye blamen alle wommen and hir resouns, I shal shewe yow by manye ensamples, that many a womman hath ben ful good, and yet been, and hir conseils ful hoolsome and profitable. Eek som men han seyd that the conseillynge of wommen is outher to deere, or elles to litel of pris ; but, al be it so that ful many a womman is badde and hir conseil vile and noght worth, yet han men founde ful many a good womman, and ful discrete and wise in conseillynge.

'Loo, Jacob, by good conseil of his mooder Rebekka, wan the benysoun of Yssak his fader, and the lordshipe over alle his bretheren : Judith, by hire good conseil, delivered the citee of Bethulie, in which she dwelled, out of the handes of Olofernus, that hadde it biseged and wolde have al destroyed it: [2290] Abygail delivered Nabal hir housbonde fro David the kyng that wolde have slayn hym, and apaysed the ire of the kyng by hir wit and by hir good conseillyng : Hester enhaunced greetly by hir good conseil the peple of God in the regne of Assuerus the kyng : and the same bountee in good conseillyng of many a good womman may men telle, and moore over, whan oure Lord hadde creat Adam oure forme fader, he seyde in this wise : "It is nat good to been a man alloone ; make we to hym an helpe semblable to hym self."

[2295] 'Heere may ye se that if that wommen were nat goode and hir conseils goode and profitable, oure Lord God of hevene wolde never han wroght hem, ne called hem "help" of man, but rather confusioun of man. And ther seyde oones a clerk in two vers, "What is bettre than Gold? Jaspre. What is bettre than Jaspre? Wisdom. And what is better than Wisdom? Wom-

---

2285. *ensamples*, H *resons and ensamples*.
2285. *benysoun*, H *blessyng*.
2295. *in two vers :*
'Quid melius auro? Jaspis. Quid Jaspide? Sensus. Quid sensu? Mulier. Quid Muliere? Nihil.'

man. And what is bettre than a good Womman? No thyng." And, sire, by manye of othre resouns may ye seen that manye wommen been goode, and hir conseils goode and profitable, [2300] and therfore, sire, if ye wol triste to my conseil, I shal restoore yow youre doghter hool and sound, and eek I wol do to yow so muche that ye shul have honour in this cause.'

Whan Melibee hadde herd the wordes of his wyf Prudence, he seyde thus : ' I see wel that the word of Salomon is sooth. He seith that wordes that been spoken discreetly, by ordinaunce, been honycombes, for they yeven swetnesse to the soule and hoolsomnesse to the body ; and, wyf, by-cause of thy sweete wordes, and eek for I have assayed and preved thy grete sapience and thy grete trouthe, I wol governe me by thy conseil in alle thyng.'

[2305] ' Now, sire,' quod dame Prudence, ' and syn ye vouchesauf to been governed by my conseil, I wol enforme yow how ye shul governe youreself in chesynge of youre conseillours. Ye shul first in alle youre werkes mekely biseken to the heighe God that he wol be youre conseillour, and shapeth yow to swich entente that he yeve yow conseil and confort, as taughte Thobie his sone : " At alle tymes thou shalt blesse God and praye hym to dresse thy weyes, and looke that alle thy conseils been in hym for everemoore." Seint Jame eek seith, " If any of yow have nede of sapience, axe it of God." [2310] And afterward, thanne shul ye taken conseil of youre self and examyne wel youre thoghtes of swich thyng as yow thynketh that is best for youre profit, and thanne shul ye dryve fro youre herte thre thynges that been contrariouse to good conseil,—that is to seyn, ire, coveitise, and hastifnesse.

' First, he that axeth conseil of hymself, certes he moste been withouten ire, for manye causes. The firste is this : he that hath greet ire and wratthe in hym self, he weneth alwey that he may do thyng that he may nat do. [2315] And secoundely, he that is irous and wrooth, he ne may nat wel deme, and he that may nat wel deme, may nat wel conseille. The thridde is this, that he that is irous and wrooth, as seith Senec, ne may nat speke but blameful thynges, and with his vicïouse wordes he stireth oother folk to angre and to ire. And eek, sire, ye moste dryve coveitise out of youre herte, [2320] for the Apostle seith that coveitise is roote of alle harmes ; and trust wel that a coveitous man ne kan noght deme, ne thynke, but oonly to fulfille the ende of his coveitise, and certes, that ne may never been accompliced, for ever the moore habundaunce that he hath of richesse the moore he desireth. And, sire, ye moste also dryve out of youre herte hastifnesse, for certes, ye ne may nat deeme for the beste a sodeyn thought that falleth in youre herte, but ye moste avyse yow on it ful ofte, [2325] for as ye herde biforn, the commune proverbe is this, that "he that soone deemeth, soone repenteth." Sire, ye ne be nat alwey in lyke disposicioun, for certes som thyng that somtyme semeth to yow that it is good for to do, another tyme it semeth to yow the contrarie.

' Whan ye han taken conseil of youre self and han deemed by good deliberacion swich thyng as you semeth best, thanne rede I yow that ye kepe it secree. [2330] Biwrey nat youre conseil to no persone, but if so be that ye wenen sikerly that thurgh youre biwreyyng youre condicioun shal be to yow the moore profitable ; for Jhesus Syrak seith, " Neither to thy foo, ne to thy frend, discovere nat thy secree, ne thy folie, for they wol yeve yow audience and lookynge and supportacioun in thy presence, and scorne thee in thyn absence." Another clerk seith, that scarsly shaltou fynden any persone that may kepe conseil sikerly.

2315. *as seith Senec,* rather Publil. Syrus, Sent. 281.
     2315. *but blameful,* E *but he blame.*
     2325. *as you semeth,* E *as you list.*
     2330. *Another clerk :* pseudo - Seneca, *De Moribus,* Sent. 16.

'The book seith, "Whil that thou kepest thy conseil in thyn herte, thou kepest it in thy prisoun, [2335] and whan thou biwreyest thy conseil to any wight he holdeth thee in his snare"; and therfore yow is bettre to hyde youre conseil in youre herte than praye him to whom ye han biwreyed youre conseil that he wole kepen it cloos and stille; for Seneca seith, "If so be that thou ne mayst nat thyn owene conseil hyde, how darstou prayen any oother wight thy conseil sikerly to kepe?"

'But nathelees, if thou wene sikerly that the biwreiyng of thy conseil to a persone wol make thy condicioun to stonden in the bettre plyt, thanne shaltou tellen hym thy conseil in this wise: first, thou shalt make no semblant wheither thee were levere pees or werre, or this or that, ne shewe hym nat thy wille and thyn entente,—[2340] for trust wel, that comunly thise conseillours been flatereres, namely the conseillours of grete lordes, for they enforcen hem alwey rather to speken plesante wordes, enclynynge to the lordes lust, than wordes that been trewe or profitable; and therfore men seyn, that the riche man hath seeld good conseil, but if he have it of hym self.

'And after that thou shalt considere thy freendes and thyne enemys; [2345] and as touchynge thy freendes thou shalt considere whiche of hem been moost feithful and moost wise, and oldest, and most approved in conseillyng, and of hem shalt thou aske thy conseil as the caas requireth.

'I seye that first ye shul clepe to youre conseil youre freendes that been trewe, for Salomon seith that "Right as the herte of a man deliteth in savour that is soote, right so the conseil of trewe freendes yeveth swetenesse to the soule"; he seith also, "Ther may no thyng be likned to the trewe freend, [2350] for certes

gold ne silver beth nat so muche worth as the goode wyl of a trewe freend"; and eck, he seith that "A trewe freend is a strong deffense; whoso that it fyndeth, certes, he fyndeth a greet tresour."

'Thanne shul ye eek considere if that youre trewe freendes been discrete and wise, for the book seith, "Axe alwey thy conseil of hem that been wise"; and by this same resoun shul ye clepen to youre conseil of youre freendes that been of age, swiche as han seyn and been expert in manye thynges, and been approved in conseillynges; for the book seith that in the olde men is the sapience, and in longe tyme the prudence; [2355] and Tullius seith, that grete thynges ne been nat ay accompliced by strengthe, ne by delivernesse of body, but by good conseil, by auctoritee of persones, and by science; the whiche thre thynges ne been nat fieble by age, but certes they enforcen and encreescen day by day. And thanne shul ye kepe this for a general reule; first, shul ye clepen to youre conseil a fewe of youre freendes that been especiale; for Salomon seith, "Manye freendes have thou, but among a thousand, chese thee oon to be thy conseillour," for, al be it so that thou first ne telle thy conseil but to a fewe, thou mayst afterward telle it to mo folk if it be nede. But looke alwey that thy conseillours have thilke thre condiciouns that I have seyd bifore, that is to seyn, that they be trewe, wise, and of oold experience. [2360] And werke nat alwey in every nede by oon counseillour allone, for somtyme bihooveth it to been conseilled by manye, for Salomon seith, "Salvacioun of thynges is where as ther been manye conseillours."

'Now, sith I have toold yow of which folk ye sholde been counseilled, now wol I teche yow which conseil ye oghte to eschewe. First, ye shul eschue the conseillyng of fooles, for Salomon seith, "Taak no conseil of a fool, for he ne kan noght conseille but after his owene lust

2330. *The book seith:* Petrus Alfonsi, *Discip. Cler.* iv. 3.
2335. *Seneca seith:* pseudo-Seneca, *De Moribus,* Sent. 16.

2355. *Tullius:* Cicero, *De Senect.* vi. 17.

and his affeccioun." The book seith that the propretee of a fool is this, "He troweth lightly harm of every wight, and lightly troweth alle bountee in hym self." [2365] Thou shalt eek eschue the conseillyng of flatereres, swiche as enforcen hem rather to preise youre persone by flaterye, than for to telle yow the soothfastnesse of thynges.

'Wherfore Tullius seith, "Amonges alle the pestilences that been in freendshipe the gretteste is flaterie"; and therfore is it moore nede that thou eschue and drede flatereres than any oother peple. The book seith, "Thou shalt rather drede and flee fro the sweete wordes of flaterynge preiseres than fro the egre wordes of thy freend that seith thee thy sothes." Salomon seith that "The wordes of a flaterere is a snare to cacche with innocentz." He seith also that "He that speketh to his freend wordes of swetnesse and of plesaunce, setteth a net biforn his feet to cacche hym"; [2370] and therfore, seith Tullius, "Enclyne nat thyne eres to flatereres, ne taaketh no conseil of the wordes of flaterye"; and Caton seith, "Avyse thee wel, and eschue the wordes of swetnesse and of plesaunce."

'And eek thou shalt eschue the conseillyng of thyne olde enemys that been reconsiled. The book seith that no wight retourneth saufly into the grace of his olde enemy; and Isope seith, "Ne trust nat to hem to whiche thou hast had som tyme werre or enemytee, ne telle hem nat thy conseil"; [2375] and Seneca

2360. *The book seith*: Cicero, *Tusc. D.* iii. 30. 37.
2365. *Tullius seith*: *De Amicitia*, xxv. 91.
2365. *The book seith*: pseudo-Seneca, *De Quat. Virt.* cap. iii. : 'Non acerba verba, sed blanda, timebis.'
2370. *Tullius*: *De Offic.* i. 26. 91.
2370. *Caton*: Dionysius Cato, *De Morib.* iii. 5.
2370. *The book seith*: Publil. Syrus, Sent. 91.
2370. *Isope seith*. In the Latin text the lines are quoted as :

'Ne confidatis secreta nec hijs detegatis
Cum quibus egistis pugnæ discrimina tristis.'

2375. *Seneca:* rather Publil. Syrus, Sent. 389 : 'Numquam ubi diu fuit ignis deficit vapor.'

telleth the cause why : "It may nat be," seith he, "that where greet fyr hath longe tyme endured, that ther ne dwelleth som vapour of warmnesse"; and therfore seith Salomon, "In thyn olde foo trust never"; for sikerly though thyn enemy be reconsiled and maketh thee chiere of humylitee, and lowteth to thee with his heed, ne trust hym never; for certes he maketh thilke feyned humilitee moore for his profit than for any love of thy person, by-cause that he deemeth to have victorie over thy persone by swich feyned contenance, the which victorie he myghte nat wynne by strif or werre. And Peter Alfonce seith, "Make no felawshipe with thyne olde enemys, for if thou do hem bountee they wol perverten it into wikkednesse."

[2380] 'And eek thou most eschue the conseillyng of hem that been thy servantz and beren thee greet reverence, for peraventure they doon it moore for drede than for love. And therfore seith a philosophre in this wise : "Ther is no wight parfitly trewe to hym that he to soore dredeth"; and Tullius seith, "Ther nys no myght so greet of any emperour that longe may endure, but if he have moore love of the peple than drede."

'Thou shalt also eschue the conseiling of folk that been dronkelewe, for they ne kan no conseil hyde; for Salomon seith, "Ther is no privetee ther as regneth dronkenesse." [2385] Ye shul also han in suspect the conseillyng of swich folk as conseille yow a thyng prively and conseille yow the contrarie openly ; for Cassidorie seith that "It is a manere sleighte to hyndre, whan he sheweth to doon a thyng openly and werketh prively the contrarie."

'Thou shalt also have in suspect the conseillyng of wikked folk, for the book seith, "The conseillyng of wikked folk is alwey ful of fraude"; and David seith,

2375. *Peter Alfonce*: *Disc. Cler.* iv. 4.
2380. *doon*, H[6] say.
2380. *Tullius seith*: *De Off.* ii. 7. 25.
2385. *Cassidorie*: *Variar. Ep.* Lib. x. Ep. 18.
2385. *have in suspect*, H *eschiewe*.

" Blisful is that man that hath nat folwed the conseilyng of shrewes." Thou shalt also eschue the conseillyng of yong folk, for hir conseil is nat rype.

[2390] ' Now, sire, sith I have shewed yow of which folk ye shul take youre conseil, and of which folk ye shul folwe the conseil, now wol I teche yow how ye shal examyne youre conseil, after the doctrine of Tullius.

' In the examynynge thanne of youre conseillour ye shul considere manye thynges. Alderfirst thou shalt considere, that in thilke thyng that thou purposest and upon what thyng thou wolt have conseil, that verray trouthe be seyd and conserved ; this is to seyn, telle trewely thy tale ; for he that seith fals may nat wel be conseilled in that cas of which he lieth.

[2395] ' And after this thou shalt considere the thynges that acorden to that thou purposest for to do by thy conseillours, if resoun accorde therto, and eek if thy myght may atteine therto ; and if the moore part and the bettre part of thy conseillours acorde therto or noon. Thanne shaltou considere what thyng shal folwe after hir conseillyng, as hate, pees, werre, grace, profit, or damage, and manye othere thynges. Thanne, of alle thise thynges, thou shalt chese the beste, and weyve alle othere thynges. Thanne shaltow considere of what roote is engendred the matiere of thy conseil, and what fruyt it may conceive and engendre. [2400] Thou shalt eek considere alle thise causes fro whennes they been sprongen.

' And whan ye han examyned youre conseil as I have seyd, and which partie is the bettre and moore profitable, and hast approved it by manye wise folk, and olde, thanne shaltou considere if thou mayst parfourne it and maken of it a good ende ; for certes, resoun wol nat that any man sholde bigynne a thyng, but if he myghte parfourne it as hym oghte, ne no

wight sholde take upon hym so hevy a charge that he myghte nat bere it ; [2405] for the proverbe seith, " He that to muche embraceth, distreyneth litel" ; and Catoun seith, " Assay to do swich thyng as thou hast power to doon, lest that the charge oppresse thee so soore that thee bihoveth to weyve thyng that thou hast bigonne." And, if so be that thou be in doute wheither thou mayst parfourne a thing or noon, chese rather to suffre than bigynne. And Piers Alphonce seith, " If thou hast myght to doon a thyng of which thou most repente thee, it is bettre ' nay ' than ' ye'" ; this is to seyn, that thee is bettre holde thy tonge stille than for to speke. [2410] Thanne may ye understonde by strenger resons that if thou hast power to parfourne a werk of which thou shalt repente, thanne is it bettre that thou suffre than bigynne. Wel seyn they that defenden every wight to assaye any thyng of which he is in doute wheither he may parfourne it or noon. And after, whan ye han examyned youre conseil, as I have seyd biforn, and knowen wel that ye may parfourne youre emprise, conferme it thanne sadly til it be at an ende.

' Now is it resoun and tyme that I shewe yow whanne and wherfore that ye may chaunge youre conseill withouten youre repreve. Soothly a man may chaungen his purpos and his conseil if the cause cesseth, or whan a newe caas bitydeth ; [2415] for the lawe seith that upon thynges that newely bityden bihoveth newe conseil ; and Senec seith, " If thy conseil is comen to the eeris of thyn enemy, chaunge thy conseil." Thou mayst also chaunge thy conseil if so be that thou mayst fynde that by errour, or by oother

---

2395. *conceive*, E *conserve*.
2400. *as hym oghte*, H *and make therof a good ende*.

2405. *the proverbe* 'qui nimis capit, parum stringit.'
2405. *Catoun, De Mor.* iii. 15 :
' Quod potes id tempta, operis ne pondere pressus Succumbat labor, et frustra temptata relinquas.'
2405. *Piers Alphonce, Disc. Cler.* vi. 12. The Latin ' si dicere metuas unde poeniteas semper est melius *non* quam *sic*' is much clearer than the English.
2410. *conseil*, E⁶ *conseillors*.
2415. *oother cause*, H *other processe*.

cause, harm or damage may bityde. Also if thy conseil be dishonest, or ellis cometh of dishoneste cause, chaunge thy conseil, for the lawes seyn that alle bihestes that been dishoneste been of no value, [2420] and eek if so be that it be inpossible or may nat goodly be parfourned or kept.

'And take this for a general reule, that every conseil that is affermed so strongly that it may nat be chaunged for no condicioun that may bityde, I seye that thilke conseil is wikked.'

This Melibeus, whanne he hadde herd the doctrine of his wyf, dame Prudence, answerde in this wyse : ' Dame,' quod he, ' as yet into this tyme ye han wel and covenablely taught me as in general how I shal governe me in the chesynge and in the withholdynge of my conseillours, but now wolde I fayn that ye wolde condescende in especial, [2425] and telle me how liketh yow, or what semeth yow by oure conseillours that we han chosen in oure present nede.'

' My lord,' quod she, ' I biseke yow in al humblesse that ye wol nat wilfully replie agayn my resouns, ne distempre youre herte, thogh I speke thyng that yow displese ; for God woot that as in myn entente I speke it for youre beste, for youre honour, and for youre profite eke ; and soothly I hope that youre benyngnytee wol taken it in pacience. Trusteth me wel,' quod she, ' that youre conseil as in this caas ne sholde nat, as to speke properly, be called a conseillyng, but a mocioun or a moevyng of folye, [2430] in which conseil ye han erred in many a sondry wise.

' First and forward ye han erred in thassemblynge of youre conseillours ; for ye sholde first have cleped a fewe folk to youre conseil, and after ye myghte han shewed it to mo folk, if it hadde been nede ; but certes, ye han sodeynly cleped to youre conseil a greet multitude of peple ful chargeant and ful anoyous for to heere. Also, ye han erred, for there

as ye sholden oonly have cleped to youre conseil youre trewe frendes olde and wise, [2435] ye han y-cleped straunge folk, and yong folk, false flatereres and enemys reconsiled, and folk that doon yow reverence withouten love. And eek also ye have erred for ye han broght with yow to youre conseil ire, coveitise, and hastifnesse ; the whiche thre thinges been contrariouse to every conseil honeste and profitable, the whiche thre ye han nat anientissed or destroyed hem, neither in youre self ne in youre conseillours, as yow oghte. Ye han erred also, for ye han shewed to youre conseillours youre talent and youre affeccioun to make werre anon, and for to do vengeance. [2440] They han espied by youre wordes to what thyng ye been enclyned, and therfore han they rather conseilled yow to youre talent than to youre profit.

' Ye han erred also, for it semeth that it suffiseth to han been conseilled by thise conseillours oonly, and with litel avys, where-as in so greet and so heigh a nede it hadde been necessarie mo conseillours and moore deliberacioun to parfourne youre emprise.

' Ye han erred also, for ye han nat examyned youre conseil in the forseyde manere, ne in due manere as the caas requireth. [2445] Ye han erred also, for ye han nat maked no divisioun bitwixe youre conseillours, this is to seyn, bitwixen youre trewe freendes and youre feyned conseillours ; ne ye han nat knowe the wil of youre trewe freendes, olde and wise ; but ye han cast alle hire wordes in an hochepot, and enclyned youre herte to the moore partie and to the gretter nombre, and there been ye condescended. And, sith ye woot wel that men shal alwey fynde a gretter nombre of fooles than of wise men, and therfore the conseils that been at congregaciouns and multitudes of folk, there as men take moore reward to the nombre than to the sapience of persones, [2450] ye se wel that in swiche conseillynges fooles han the maistrie.'

2415. *Also if*, etc., H .*lso thou change thy conseil if that it be dishoneste.*
2430. *thassemblynge*, H *the gaderyng*.

Melibeus answerde agayn, and seyde, 'I graunte wel that I have erred, but there as thou hast toold me heerbiforn that he nys nat to blame that chaungeth his conseillours in certein caas, and for certeine juste causes, I am al redy to chaunge my conseillours right as thow wolt devyse. The proverbe seith, that for to do synne is mannyssh, but certes, for to persevere longe in synne is werk of the devel.'

[2455] To this sentence answereth anon dame Prudence and seyde, 'Examineth,' quod she, 'youre conseil and lat us see the whiche of hem han spoken most resonablely, and taught yow best conseil ; and for as muche as that the examynacioun is necessarie, lat us bigynne at the surgiens and at the phisiciens that first speeken in this matiere. I sey yow that the surgiens and phisiciens han seyd yow in youre conseil discreetly as hem oughte, and in hir speche seyd ful wisely that to the office of hem aperteneth, to doon to every wight honour and profit, and no wight for to anoye, [2460] and in hir craft to doon greet diligence unto the cure of hem whiche that they han in hir gouvernaunce. And, sire, right as they han answered wisely and discreetly, right so rede I that they been heighly and sovereynly gerdoned for hir noble speche, and eek, for they sholde do the moore ententif bisynesse in the curacioun of youre doghter deere ; for, al be it so that they been youre freendes, therfore shal ye nat suffren that they serve yow for noght, [2465] but ye oghte the rather gerdone hem and shewe hem youre largesse.

'And as touchynge the proposicioun which that the phisiciens encreesceden in this caas ; this is to seyn, that in maladies that oon contrarie is warisshed by another contrarie ; I wolde fayn knowe how ye

understonde this text, and what is youre sentence.'

'Certes,' quod Melibeus, 'I understonde it in this wise : [2470] that right as they han doon me a contrarie, right so sholde I doon hem another ; for right as they han venged hem on me and doon me wrong, right so shal I venge me upon hem, and doon hem wrong, and thanne have I cured oon contrarie by another.'

'Lo, lo,' quod dame Prudence, 'how lightly is every man enclined to his owene desir and to his owene plesaunce ! Certes,' quod she, 'the wordes of the phisiciens ne sholde nat han been understonden in thys wise, [2475] for certes, wikkednesse is nat contrarie to wikkednesse, ne vengeance to vengeaunce, ne wrong to wrong, but they been semblable ; and therfore, o vengeaunce is nat warisshed by another vengeaunce, ne o wroong by another wroong, but everich of hem encreesceth and aggreggeth oother.

'But certes, the wordes of the phisiciens sholde been understonden in this wise ; for good and wikkednesse been two contraries, and pees and werre, vengeaunce and suffraunce, discord and accord, and manye othere thynges ; [2480] but certes, wikkednesse shal be warisshed by goodnesse, discord by accord, werre by pees, and so forth of othere thynges ; and heer-to accordeth Seint Paul the Apostle in manye places.

'He seith, "Ne yeldeth nat harm for harm, ne wikked speche for wikked speche ; but do wel to hym that dooth thee harm, and blesse hym that seith to thee harm." And in manye othere places he amonesteth pees and accord.

[2485] 'But now wol I speke to yow of the conseil which that was yeven to yow by the men of lawe, and the wise folk, that seyden alle by oon accord, as ye han herd bifore, that over alle thynges ye sholde doon youre diligence to kepen youre persone and to warnestoore youre hous ; and seyden also, that in this caas yow oghten for to werken ful avysely

2450. *The proverbe seith*, S. Chrysost. *Adhortatio ad Theod. lapsum*, i. 14 : 'Humanum enim est peccare, diabolicum vero perseverare.'
2455. *aperteneth*, H³ *appendith*.
2465. *encreesceden*, enlarged ou ; H *han shewed you*.
2465. *how ye understonde this text*, H *thilke text and how thay understonde it*.
2465. *sentence*, H *entente*.

and with greet deliberacioun. And, sire, as to the firste point that toucheth to the kepyng of youre persone, [2490] ye shul understonde that he that hath werre shal evermoore mekely and devoutly preyen, biforn alle thynges, that Jhesus Crist of his grete mercy wol han hym in his proteccioun and been his sovereyn helpyng at his nede ; for certes, in this world ther is no wight that may be conseilled ne kept sufficeantly withouten the kepyng of oure Lord Jhesu Crist.

' To this sentence accordeth the prophete David, that seith, " If God ne kepe the citee, in ydel waketh he that it kepeth." [2495] Now, sire, thanne shul ye committe the kepyng of youre persone to youre trewe freendes that been approved and knowe, and of hem shul ye axen helpe, youre persone for to kepe, for Catoun seith, " If thou hast nede of help, axe it of thy freendes, for ther nys noon so good a phisicien as thy trewe freend."

' And after this, thanne shul ye kepe yow fro alle straunge folk, and fro lyeres, and have alwey in suspect hire compaignye, for Piers Alfonce seith, " Ne taak no compaignye by the weye of straunge men, but if so be that thou have knowe hym of a lenger tyme. [2500] And if so be, that he be falle into thy compaignye, paraventure, withouten thyn assent, enquere thanne, as subtilly as thou mayst, of his conversacioun, and of his lyf bifore, and feyne thy wey,—seye that thou goost thider as thou wolt nat go,— and if he bereth a spere, hoold thee on the right syde, and if he bere a swerd, hoold thee on his lift syde." And after this thanne shul ye kepe yow wisely from all swich manere peple as I have seyd bifore, and hem and hir conseil eschewe.

' And after this, thanne shul ye kepe yow in swich manere [2505] that for any presumpcioun of youre strengthe, that ye ne dispise nat ne acounte nat the myght

of youre adversarie so litel that ye lete the kepyng of youre persone for youre presumpcioun; for every wys man dredeth his enemy, and Salomon seith, "Weleful is he that of alle hath drede, for certes, he that thurgh the hardynesse of his herte and thurgh the hardynesse of hymself hath to greet presumpcioun, hym shal yvel bityde." Thanne shul ye evermoore countrewayte embusshementz and alle espiaille. [2510] For Senec seith, that the wise man that dredeth harmes escheweth harmes, ne he ne falleth into perils that perils escheweth. And, al be it so that it seme that thou art in siker place, yet shaltow alwey do thy diligence in kepynge of thy persone ; this is to seyn, ne be nat necligent to kepe thy persone, nat oonly fro thy gretteste enemys, but fro thy leeste enemy. Senek seith, "A man that is wel avysed, he dredeth his leste enemye." [2515] Ovyde seith that the litel wesele wol slee the grete bole and the wilde hert. And the book seith, "A litel thorn may prikke a greet kyng ful soore, and an hound wol holde the wilde boor."

' But nathelees, I sey nat thou shalt be coward, that thou doute ther wher as is no drede. The book seith that somme folk han greet lust to deceyve, but yet they dreden hem to be deceyved. Yet shaltou drede to been empoisoned, and kepe yow from the compaignye of scorneres, [2520] for the book seith, "With scorneres make no compaignye, but flee hire wordes as venym."

' Now as to the seconde point ; where as youre wise conseillours conseilled yow to warnestoore youre hous with gret diligence, I wolde fayn knowe how that ye understonde thilke wordes, and what is youre sentence.'

Melibeus answerde and seyde, 'Certes, I understande it in this wise : That I

2495. *Catoun, De Moribus*, iv. 13 :
' Auxilium a notis petito, si forte laboras.
Ne- quisquam melior medicus quam fidus amicus.'
2495. *Piers Alfonce, Disc. Cler.* xviii. 10.

2510. *Senec seith*, Publilius Syrus, Sent. 542.
2510. *that dredeth*, E *he dredeth*.
2510. *Senek seith*, Publilius Syrus, Sentent.
255 : om. E.
2515. *Ovyde, De Rem. Am.* ii. 25, 26.
2520. *conseilled*, H *warnede*.

shal warnestoore myn hous with toures, swiche as han castelles, and othere manere edifices, and armure and artelries, by whiche thynges I may my persone and myn hous so kepen and deffenden, that myne enemys shul been in drede myn hous for to approche.'

[2525] To this sentence answerde anon Prudence. 'Warnestooryng,' quod she, 'of heighe toures and of grete edifices appertyneth somtyme to pryde and eek men make heihe toures with grete costages and with greet travaille, and whan that they been accompliced yet be they nat worth a stree, but if they be defended by trewe freendes that been olde and wise. And understoond wel that the gretteste and strongeste garnyson that a riche man may have, as wel to kepen his persone as his goodes, is that he be biloved amonges hys subgetz and with his neighebores; for thus seith Tullius, that ther is a manere garnysoun that no man may venquysse ne disconfite, and that is [2530] a lord to be biloved of his citezeins and of his peple.

'Now, sire, as to the thridde point, where as youre olde and wise conseillours seyden that yow ne oghte nat sodeynly ne hastily proceden in this nede, but that yow oghte purveyen and apparaillen yow in this caas with greet diligence and greet deliberacioun, trewely, I trowe that they seyden right wisely and right sooth, for Tullius scith, "In every nede er thou bigynne it, apparaille thee with greet diligence." [2535] Thanne seye I that in vengeance takyng, in werre, in bataille, and in warnestooryng, er thow bigynne, I rede that thou apparaille thee therto and do it with greet deliberacioun, for Tullius seith, "The longe apparaillyng biforn the bataille maketh short victorie,"

and Cassidorus seith, "The garnyson is stronger whan it is longe tyme avysed."

'But now lat us speken of the conseil that was accorded by youre neighebores, swiche as doon yow reverence withouten love, [2540] youre olde enemys reconsiled, youre flatereres, that conseilled yow certeyne thynges prively, and openly conseilleden yow the contrarie, the yonge folk also, that conseilleden yow to venge yow, and make werre anon. And certes, sire, as I have seyd biforn, ye han greetly erred to han cleped swich manere folk to youre conseil, which conseillours been ynogh repreved by the resouns aforeseyd.

[2545] 'But nathelees, lat us now descende to the special. Ye shuln first procede after the doctrine of Tullius. Certes, the trouthe of this matiere, or of this conseil, nedeth nat diligently enquere, for it is wel wist whiche they been that han doon to yow this trespas and vileynye, and how manye trespassours and in what manere they han to yow doon al this wrong and all this vileynye. And after this thanne shul ye examyne the seconde condicioun which that the same Tullius addeth in this matiere; [2550] for Tullius put a thyng which that he clepeth consentynge, this is to seyn, who been they, and how manye and whiche been they, that consenten to thy conseil, in thy wilfulnesse to doon hastif vengeance. And lat us considere also who been they, and how manye been they, and whiche been they, that consenteden to youre adversaries. And certes, as to the firste poynt, it is wel knowen whiche folk been they that consenteden to youre hastif wilfulnesse; for trewely, alle tho that conseilleden yow to maken sodeyn werre ne been nat youre freendes.

[2555] 'Lat us now considere whiche been they that ye holde so greetly youre freendes as to youre persone; for al be it so that ye be myghty and riche, certes, ye ne been nat but allone; for certes, ye ne han no child but a doghter, ne ye ne

---

2520. *kepen,* H *kepen and edifien.*
2525. *appertyneth . . . toures,* text from Corpus; EH⁵ om.
2525. *and strongeste,* H *strength or.*
2525. *Tullius,* rather Seneca, *De Clementia,* i. 19. 5: 'Unum est inexpugnabile munimentum, amor civium.'
2530. *Tullius, De Offic.* i. 21. 73.

2535. *Cassidorus, Variarum,* Lib. i. Ep. 17.
2545. *Tullius,* cp. *De Offic.* ii. 5. 18.

han bretheren, ne cosyns germayns, ne noon oother neigh kynrede, wherfore that youre enemys for drede sholde stinte to plede with yow, or to destroye youre persone. [2560] Ye knowen also that youre richesses mooten been dispended in diverse parties, and whan that every wight hath his part, they ne wollen taken but litel reward to venge thy deeth ; but thyne enemys been thre, and they han manie children, bretheren, cosyns, and oother ny kynrede, and though so were that thou haddest slayn of hem two or thre, yet dwellen ther ynowe to wreken hir deeth, and to sle thy persone. And though so be that youre kynrede be moore siker and stedefast than the kyn of youre adversarie, [2565] yet nathelees, youre kynrede nys but a fer kynrede, they been but litel syb to yow, and the kyn of youre enemys been ny syb to hem, and certes, as in that, hir condicioun is bet than youres.

'Thanne lat us considere also of the conseillyng of hem that conseilleden yow to taken sodeyn vengeaunce, wheither it accorde to resoun. And certes, ye knowe wel, nay ; for as by right and resoun, ther may no man taken vengeance on no wight but the juge that hath the jurisdiccioun of it, [2570] whan it is graunted hym to take thilke vengeance hastily or attemprely as the lawe requireth. And yet mooreover of thilke word that Tullius clepeth "consentynge," thou shalt considere if thy myght and thy power may consenten and suffise to thy wilfulnesse, and to thy conseillours. And certes, thou mayst wel seyn that nay ; for sikerly, as for to speke proprely, we may do no thyng, but oonly swich thyng as we may doon rightfully, [2575] and certes, rightfully ne mowe ye take no vengeance, as of youre propre auctoritee.

'Thanne mowe ye seen that youre power ne consenteth nat, ne accordeth nat, with youre wilfulnesse.

'Lat us now examyne the thridde point, that Tullius clepeth "consequent."

2560. *dispended*, H *departed*, Pet. *dalt*.

Thou shalt understonde that the vengeance that thou purposest for to take is the consequent, and therof folweth another vengeaunce, peril and werre, and othere damages with-oute nombre, of whiche we be nat war, as at this tyme. [2580] And as touchynge the fourthe point, that Tullius clepeth "engendrynge," thou shalt considere that this wrong which that is doon to thee is engendred of the hate of thyne enemys, and of the vengeance takynge upon that wolde engendre another vengeance, and muchel sorwe and wastynge of richesses, as I seyde.

'Now, sire, as to the point that Tullius clepeth "causes," which that is the laste point. Thou shalt understonde that the wrong that thou hast receyved hath certeine causes, [2585] whiche that clerkes clepen *Oriens* and *Efficiens*, and *Causa longinqua* and *Causa propinqua*, this is to seyn, the fer cause and the ny cause. The fer cause is Almyghty God, that is cause of alle thynges ; the neer cause is thy thre enemys. The cause accidental was hate, the cause material been the fyve woundes of thy doghter. [2590] The cause formal is the manere of hir werkynge that broghten laddres and cloumben in at thy wyndowes ; the cause final was for to sle thy doghter. It letted nat in as muche as in hem was.

'But for to speken of the fer cause, as to what ende they shul come, or what shal finally bityde of hem in this caas, ne kan I nat deme but by conjectynge and by supposynge. For we shul suppose that they shul come to a wikked ende by-cause that the book of decrees seith, "Seelden, or with greet peyne, been causes broght to good ende whanne they been baddely bigonne."

[2595] 'Now, sire, if men wolde axe me why that God suffred men to do yow this vileynye, certes, I kan nat wel answere, as for no soothfastnesse. For thapostle seith that the sciences and the

2590. *the book of decrees*: Decret. Gratiani, P. ii. Causa i. Qu. i. C. 25.
2595. *this vileynye*, H² *this wrong and vileynye*.

juggementz of oure Lord God Almyghty been ful depe,—ther may no man comprehende ne serchen hem suffisantly. Nathelees, by certeyne presumpciouns and conjectynges, I holde and bileeve, that God, which that is ful of justice and of rightwisnesse, hath suffred this bityde by juste cause, resonable.

[2600] 'Thy name is Melibee, this is to seyn, "a man that drynketh hony." Thou hast y-dronke so muchel hony of sweete temporeel richesses, and delices and honours of this world, that thou art dronken, and hast forgeten Jhesu Crist, thy creatour; thou ne hast nat doon to hym swich honour and reverence as thee oughte, ne thou ne hast nat wel ytaken kepe to the wordes of Ovide, that seith, [2605] "Under the hony of the goodes of the body is hyd the venym that sleeth the soule"; and Salomon seith, "If thou hast founden hony, ete of it that suffiseth, for if thou ete of it out of mesure, thou shalt spewe, and be nedy and poure"; and peraventure, Crist hath thee in despit, and hath turned awey fro thee his face and his ceris of misericorde, and also he hath suffred that thou hast been punysshed in the manere that thow hast y-trespassed. [2610] Thou hast doon synne agayn oure Lord Crist, for certes, the thre enemys of mankynde,—that is to seyn, the flessh, the feend and the world,—thou hast suffred hem entre into thyn herte wilfully by the wyndowes of thy body, and hast nat defended thy self suffisantly agayns hire assautes, and hire temptacious, so that they han wounded thy soule in five places; this is to seyn, the deedly synnes that been entred into thyn herte by thy five wittes. [2615] And in the same manere oure Lord Crist hath wold and suffred that thy thre enemys been entred into thyn hous by the wyndowes, and han y-wounded thy doghter in the foreseyde manere.'

'Certes,' quod Melibee, 'I se wel that ye enforce yow muchel by wordes to overcome me in swich manere that I

2600. Ovide, Amor. i. viii. 104.

shal nat venge me of myne enemys, shewynge me the perils and the yveles that myghten falle of this vengeance; but whoso wolde considere in alle vengeances the perils and yveles that myghte sewe of vengeance takynge, [2620] a man wolde never take vengeance; and that were harm, for by the vengeance takynge been the wikked men dissevered fro the goode men, and they that han wyl to do wikkednesse restreyne hir wikked purpos whan they seen the punyssynge and chastisynge of the trespassours.'

[And to this answered dame Prudence, 'Certes,' said she, 'I grant you that from vengeance come many evils and many benefits, and yet vengeance belongeth not to everyone but only to the judges, and to those who have jurisdiction over evildoers.]

[2625] 'And yet seye I moore, that right as a singuler persone synneth in takynge vengeance of another man, right so synneth the juge if he do no vengeance of hem that it han disserved; for Senec seith thus: That maister, he seith, is good that proveth shrewes. And, as Cassidore seith, "A man dredeth to do outrages whan he woot and knoweth that it displeseth to the juges and sovereyns." Another seith, "The juge that dredeth to do right maketh men shrewes," [2630] and Seint Paule the Apostle seith in his Epistle, whan he writeth unto the Romayns, that "The juges beren nat the spere withouten cause, but they beren it to punysse the shrewes and mysdoeres, and to defende the goode men." If ye wol thanne take vengeance of youre enemys, ye shul retourne, or have youre recours to the juge that hath the jurisdiccion upon hem, and he shal punysse hem as the lawe axeth and requireth.'

2615. sewe, H folwe.
2620. dissevered, H destruyed and dissevered.
2620. to do wikkednesse, H om. do.
2620. And to this answered, etc. The words in brackets are inserted from the French; they are not given in any of the seven MSS.
2625. Cassidore, Variar. i. 4.
2625. Another seith, Publil. Syrus, Sentent. 528.

'A!' quod Melibee, 'this vengeance liketh me no thyng. [2635] I bithenke me now, and take heede how Fortune hath norissed me fro my childhede, and hath holpen me to passe many a stroong paas. Now wol I assayen hire, trowynge with Goddes helpe that she shal helpe me my shame for to venge.'

'Certes,' quod Prudence, 'if ye wol werke by my conseil ye shul nat asseye Fortune by no wey, ne ye shul nat lene or bowe unto hire after the word of Senec, for thynges that been folily doon and that been in hope of Fortune shullen never come to goode ende. [2640] And, as the same Senec seith, "The moore cleer and the moore shynyng that Fortune is, the moore brotil and the sonner broken she is; trusteth nat in hire, for she nys nat stidefaste, ne stable, for whan thow trowest to be moost seur and siker of hire helpe, she wol faille thee and deceyve thee." And where as ye seyn that Fortune hath norissed yow fro youre childhede, I seye, that in so muchel shul ye the lasse truste in hire and in hir wit; [2645] for Senec seith, "What man that is norissed by Fortune she maketh hym a greet fool." Now thanne, syn ye desire and axe vengeance, and the vengeance that is doon after the lawe and bifore the juge ne liketh yow nat, and the vengeance that is doon in hope of Fortune is perilous and uncertein, thanne have ye noon oother remedie, but for to have youre recours unto the sovereyn juge that vengeth alle vileynyes and wronges, and he shal venge yow after that hym-self witnesseth, where as he seith, [2650] "Leveth the vengeance to me, and I shal do it."'

Melibee answerde, 'If I ne venge me nat of the vileynye that men han doon to me, I sompne or warne hem that han doon to me that vileynye, and alle othere, to do me another vileynye. For it is writen, "If thou take no vengeance of an·oold vileynye, thou sompnest thyne adversaries to do thee a newe vileynye." And also for my suffrance men wolden do to me so muchel vileynye that I myghte neither bere it ne susteene, [2655] and so sholde I been put and holden over lowe. For men seyn, "In muchel suffrynge shul manye thynges falle unto thee whiche thou shalt nat mowe suffre."'

'Certes,' quod Prudence, 'I graunte yow that over muchel suffraunce nys nat good, but yet ne folweth it nat ther-of that every persone to whom men doon vileynye take of it vengeance; for that aperteneth and longeth al oonly to the juges, for they shul venge the vileynyes and injuries; [2660] and therfore tho two auctoritees that ye han seyd above been oonly understonden in the juges, for whan they suffren over muchel wronges and the vileynyes to be doon withouten punysshynge, they sompne nat a man al oonly for to do newe wronges, but they comanden it. Also a wys man seith that the juge that correcteth nat the synnere comandeth and biddeth hym do synne; and the juges and sovereyns myghten in hir land so muchel suffre of the shrewes and mysdoeres, [2665] that they sholden, by swich suffrance, by proces of tyme wexen of swich power and myght that they sholden putte out the juges and the sovereyns from hir places, and atte laste maken hem lesen hire lordshipes.

'But lat us now putte that ye have leve to venge yow. I seye ye been nat of myght and power as now to venge yow; for if ye wole maken comparisoun unto the myght of youre adversaries, ye shul fynde in manye thynges that I have shewed yow er this that hire condicioun is bettre than youres; [2670] and therfore seye I that it is good as now that ye suffre and be pacient.

'Forthermoore, ye knowen wel that

2635. *stroong paas*, H *strayt passage*.
2635. *Senec*, Publil. Syrus, Sent. 320.
2640. *broken she is*, H² *breketh sche*: for the quotation see Publil. Syrus, Sentent. 189: 'Fortuna vitrea est et, cum splendet, frangitur.'
2645. *Senec*, Publil. Syrus, Sentent. 173.

2660. *a wys man*, Cæc. Balbus, *De Nugis Phil.*: 'Qui non corripit peccantem peccare imperat.'

after the comune sawe, it is a woodnesse a man to stryve with a strenger, or a moore myghty man than he is hymself; and for to stryve with a man of evene strengthe, that is to seyn, with as stronge a man as he, it is peril; and for to stryve with a weyker man, it is folie; and therfore sholde a man flee stryvynge as muchel as he myghte; [2675] for Salomon seith, "It is a greet worshipe to a man to kepen hym fro noyse and stryf." And if it so bifalle or happe that a man of gretter myght and strengthe than thou art do thee grevaunce, studie and bisye thee rather to stille the same grevaunce, than for to venge thee; for Senec seith, that "He putteth hym in greet peril that stryveth with a gretter man than he is hymself"; and Catoun seith, "If a man of hyer estaat or degree, or moore myghty than thou, do thee anoy or grevaunce, suffre hym, [2680] for he that oones hath greved thee, another tyme may releeve thee and helpe."

' Yet sette I caas ye have bothe myght and licence for to venge yow, I seye that ther be ful manye thynges that shul restreyne yow of vengeance-takynge, and make yow for to enclyne to suffre and for to han pacience in the thynges that han been doon to yow. First and fore-ward, if ye wole considere the defautes that been in youre owene persone, [2685] for whiche defautes God hath suffred yow have this tribulacioun, as I have seyd yow heer biforn; for the poete seith, that we oghte paciently taken the tribulacions that comen to us whan we thynken and consideren that we han disserved to have hem; and Seint Gregorie seith, that whan a man considereth wel the nombre of his defautes and of his synnes, the peynes and the tribulaciouns that he suff-reth semen the lesse unto hym; and in as muche as hym thynketh his synnes moore hevy and grevous, [2690] in so

muche semeth his peyne the lighter, and the esier unto hym.

' Also ye owen to enclyne and bowe youre herte to take the pacience of oure Lord Jhesu Crist, as seith Seint Peter in his Epistles: "Jhesu Crist," he seith, "hath suffred for us and yeven ensample to every man to folwe and sewe hym; for he dide never synne, ne never cam ther a vileynous word out of his mouth; whan men cursed hym he cursed hem noght, and whan men betten hym he manaced hem noght." [2695] Also the grete pacience which the seintes that been in paradys han had in tribulaciouns that they han y-suffred withouten hir desert or gilt oghte muchel stiren yow to pacience. Forthermoore, ye sholde en-force yow to have pacience, considerynge that the tribulaciouns of this world but litel while endure, and soone passed been and goone, and the joye that a man seketh to have by pacience in tribulaciouns is perdurable, after that, the Apostle seith in his Epistle, [2700] "The joye of God," he seith, "is perdurable," that is to seyn, everelastynge.

' Also trowe and bileveth stedefastly that he nys nat wel y-norissed, ne wel y-taught, that kan nat have pacience, or wol nat receyve pacience; for Salomon seith that the doctrine and the wit of a man is knowen by pacience. And in another place he seith that he that is pacient governeth hym by greet prudence. And the same Salomon seith, "The angry and wrathful man maketh noyses, and the pacient man atempreth hem and stilleth." [2705] He seith also, "It is moore worth to be pacient, than for to be right strong," and he that may have the lordshipe of his owene herte is moore to preyse than he that by his force or strengthe taketh grete citees; and ther-fore seith Seint Jame in his Epistle, that pacience is a greet vertu of perfeccioun.'

'Certes,' quod Melibee, 'I graunte yow, dame Prudence, that pacience is a greet vertu of perfeccioun, but every man may nat have the perfeccioun that ye

2670. *the common saw*, from Seneca, *De Ira*, ii. 34. I.
2675. *Senec*, Publilius Syrus, Sent. 483.
2675. *Catoun, De Moribus*, iv. 39.
2680. *greved thee*, H *don the a grievaunce*.

seken, [2710] ne I nam nat of the nombre of right parfite men, for myn herte may never been in pees unto the tyme it be venged ; and al be it so that it was greet peril to myne enemys to do me a vileynye in takynge vengeance upon me, yet tooken they noon heede of the peril, but fulfilleden hir wikked wyl, and hir corage ; and therfore, me thynketh, men oghten nat repreve me, though I putte me in a litel peril for to venge me, [2715] and though I do a greet excesse, that is to seyn, that I venge oon outrage by another.'

'A !' quod dame Prudence, 'ye seyn youre wyl and as yow liketh, but in no caas of the world a man sholde nat doon outrage, ne excesse, for to vengen hym ; for Cassidore seith that as yvele dooth he that vengeth hym by outrage as he that dooth the outrage ; and therfore, ye shul venge yow after the ordre of right, that is to seyn, by the lawe, and noght by excesse ne by outrage. [2720] And also, if ye wol venge yow of the outrage of youre adversaries in oother manere than right comandeth, ye synnen; and therfore seith Senec, that a man shal never vengen shrewednesse by shrewednesse. And if ye seye that right axeth a man to defenden violence by violence, and fightyng by fightyng, certes ye seye sooth, whan the defense is doon anon withouten intervalle or withouten tariyng or delay, for to deffenden hym and nat for to vengen hym. [2725] And it bihoveth that a man putte swich attemperance in his deffense that men have no cause ne matiere to repreven hym that deffendeth hym of excesse and outrage, for ellis were it agayn resoun. *Pardee* ye knowen wel that ye maken no deffense as now for to deffende yow, but for to venge yow; and so sheweth it that ye han no wyl to do youre dede attemprely, and therfore me thynketh that pacience is good, for Salomon seith that he that is nat pacient shal have greet harm.'

[2730] 'Certes,' quod Melibee, 'I graunte yow that whan a man is inpacient and wrooth, of that that toucheth hym noght and that aperteneth nat unto hym, though it harme hym, it is no wonder ; for the lawe seith that he is coupable that entremetteth or medleth with swych thyng as aperteneth nat unto hym. And Salomon seith, that he that entremetteth hym of the noyse or strif of another man is lyk to hym that taketh an hound by the eris ; for right as he that taketh a straunge hound by the eris is outherwhile biten with the hound, right in the same wise is it resoun that he have harm that by his inpacience medleth hym of the noyse of another man whereas it aperteneth nat unto hym. [2735] But ye knowen wel that this dede, that is to seyn, my grief and my disese, toucheth me right ny, and therfore, though I be wrooth and inpacient, it is no merveille ; and, savynge youre grace, I kan nat seen that it myghte greetly harme me though I tooke vengeaunce, for I am richer and moore myghty than myne enemys been. And wel knowen ye that by moneye and by havynge grete possessions been alle the thynges of this world governed ; [2740] and Salomon seith, that alle thynges obeyen to moneye.'

Whan Prudence hadde herd hir housbonde avanten hym of his richesse and of his moneye, dispreisynge the power of his adversaries, she spak, and seyde in this wise : 'Certes, deere sire, I graunte yow that ye been riche and myghty, and that the richesses been goode to hem that han wel y-geten hem and wel konne usen hem ; for, right as the body of a man may nat lyven withoute the soule, namoore may it lyve withouten temporeel goodes ; [2745] and for richesses may a man gete hym grete freendes. And therfore seith Pamphilles, "If a netherdes doghter," seith he, "be riche, she may chesen of a thousand men which she wol take to her

2715. *Cassidore, Variar.* i. 20.
2720. *Senec,* the pseudo-Seneca, *De Moribus,* 139.
2725. *sheweth,* H *semeth,* Camb.⁵ *seweth.*

2745. *Pamphilles,* Pamphilus, *De Amore :*
'Dummodo sit dives cujusdam nata bubulci
Eligit e mille quemlibet ipsa virum.'

110

housebonde," for of a thousand men oon wol nat forsaken hire ne refusen hire. And this Pamphilles seith also, "If thow be right happy, that is to seyn, if thou be right riche, thou shalt fynde a greet nombre of felawes and freendes; and if thy fortune change that thou wexe poure, farewel freendshipe and felaweshipe, [2750] for thou shalt be al alloone with-outen any compaignye, but if it be the compaignye of poure folk." And yet seith this Pamphilles moreover, that they that been thralle and bonde of lynage shullen been maad worthy and noble by the richesses. And right so as by richesses ther comen manye goodes, right so by poverte come ther manye harmes and yveles; for greet poverte constreyneth a man to do manye yveles, and therfore clepeth Cassidore poverte the mooder of ruyne,—[2755] that is to seyn, the mooder of overthrowynge or fallynge doun. And therfore seith Piers Alfonce, "Oon of the gretteste adversitees of this world is whan a free man, by kynde or by burthe, is constreyned by poverte to eten the almesse of his enemy"; and the same seith Innocent in oon of his bookes; he seith that sorweful and myshappy is the condicioun of a poure beggere, for if he axe nat his mete he dyeth for hunger, [2760] and if he axe, he dyeth for shame; and algates necessitee constreyneth hym to axe. And therfore seith Salomon that bet it is to dye than for to have swich poverte. And as the same Salomon seith, "Bettre it is to dye of bitter deeth than for to lyven in swich wise." By thise resons that I have seid unto yow, and by manye othere resons that I koude seye, I graunte yow that richesses been goode to hem that geten hem wel and to hem that wel usen tho richesses. [2765] And therfore wol I shewe yow how ye

2750. *Cassidore*, *Variar*. ix. 13: 'mater criminum necessitas.
2755. *Piers Alfonce*, *Discip. Cler.* iv. 5.
2755. *Innocent* [III.], *De Contemptu Mundi*, i. 14; the passage versified by Chaucer in the Prologue to the Man of Law's Tale.
2765. *wol I shewe you*, etc. The substance of the next seventy paragraphs is not given by

shul have yow, and how ye shul bere yow in gaderynge of richesses, and in what manere ye shul usen hem.
'First, ye shul geten hem withouten greet desir, by good leyser, sokyngly, and nat over hastily; for a man that is to desirynge to gete richesses abaundoneth hym first to thefte, and to alle other yveles; and therfore seith Salomon, "He that hasteth hym to bisily to wexe riche shal be noon innocent." He seith also, that the richesse that hastily cometh to a man soone and lightly gooth and passeth fro a man; [2770] but that richesse that cometh litel and litel wexeth alwey and multiplieth. And, sire, ye shul geten richesses by youre wit and by youre travaille unto youre profit, and that with-outen wrong or harm-doynge to any oother persone; for the lawe seith that ther maketh no man himselven riche if he do harm to another wight: this is to seyn, that nature deffendeth and forbedeth by right that no man make hymself riche unto the harm of another persone. [2775] And Tullius seith that no sorwe, ne no drede of deeth, ne no thyng that may falle unto a man, is so muchel agayns nature as a man to encressen his owene profit to the harm of another man. And though the grete men and the myghty men geten richesses moore lightly than thou, yet shaltou nat been ydel ne slow to do thy profit; for thou shalt in alle wise flee ydelnesse; for Salomon seith that ydelnesse techeth a man to do manye yveles. [2780] And the same Salomon seith that he that travailleth and bisieth hym to tilien his land shal eten breed, but he that is ydel and casteth hym to no bisynesse ne occupacioun shal falle into poverte, and dye for hunger. And he that is ydel and slow kan never fynde covenable tyme for to doon his profit; for ther is a versifiour seith that the ydel man excuseth hym in wynter by cause of

Albertanus Brixiensis in his *Liber Consolationis*, but he refers to a section of his own work *De Amore Dei et Proximi*, whence the French translator, whom Chaucer follows, doubtless took them.

the grete coold, and in somer by enche-soun of the heete. For thise causes seith Caton, "Waketh and enclyneth nat yow over muchel for to slepe, for over muchel reste norisseth and causeth manye vices." [2785] And therfore seith Seint Jerome, "Dooth somme goode deedes, that the devel, which is oure enemy, ne fynde yow nat unocupied. For the devel ne taketh nat lightly unto his werkynge swiche as he fyndeth occupied in goode werkes."

'Thanne thus in getynge richesses ye mosten flee ydelnesse; and afterward ye shul use the richesses whiche ye have geten by youre wit and by youre travaille, in swich a manere that men holde nat yow to scars, ne to sparynge, ne to fool large, —that is to seyn, over large a spendere; [2790] for right as men blamen an avaricious man by cause of his scarsetee and chyngerie, in the same wise is he to blame that spendeth over largely. And therfore seith Caton, "Use," he seith, "thy richesses that thou hast geten in swich a manere that men have no matiere ne cause to calle thee neither wrecche ne chynche; for it is a greet shame to a man to have a povere herte and a riche purs." [2795] He seith also, "The goodes that thou hast y-geten, use hem by mesure, that is to seyn, spende hem mesurably; for they that folily wasten and despenden the goodes that they han, whan they han namoore propre of hir owene, they shapen hem to take the goodes of another man."

'I seye thanne that ye shul fleen avarice, usynge youre richesses in swich manere that men seye nat that youre richesses been y-buryed, [2800] but that ye have hem in youre myght and in youre weeldynge; for a wys man repreveth the avaricious man and seith thus in two vers: "Wherto and why burieth a man his goodes by his grete avarice, and knoweth wel that nedes moste he dye, for deeth is the ende of every man, as in this present lyf; and for what cause or enchesoun joyneth he hym or knytteth he hym so faste unto his goodes [2805] that alle his wittes mowen nat disseveren hym or

departen hym from his goodes; and knoweth wel, or oghte knowe, that whan he is deed he shal no thyng bere with hym out of this world?" And therfore seith Seint Augustyn, that the avaricious man is likned unto helle, that the moore it swelweth the moore desir it hath to swelwe and devoure. And as wel as ye wolde eschewe to be called an avaricious man or chynche, [2810] as wel sholde ye kepe yow and governe yow in swich a wise that men calle yow nat fool-large. Therfore seith Tullius, "The goodes," he seith, "of thyn hous ne sholde nat been hyd, ne kept so cloos but that they myghte been opened by pitee and debonairetee,"— that is to seyn, to yeven part to hem that han greet nede,—"ne thy goodes shullen nat been so opene to been every mannes goodes."

'Afterward, in getynge of youre richesses and in usynge hem, ye shul alwey have thre thynges in youre herte, [2815] that is to seyn, oure Lord God, conscience, and good name. First, ye shul have God in youre herte, and for no richesse ye shullen do no thyng which may in any manere displese God, that is youre creatour and makere; for after the word of Salomon, "It is bettre to have a litel good with the love of God, than to have muchel good and tresour and lese the love of his Lord God." [2820] And the prophete seith that bettre it is to been a good man and have litel good and tresour, than to been holden a shrewe, and have grete richesses. And yet seye I ferthermoore, that ye sholde alwey doon youre bisynesse to gete yow richesses, so that ye gete hem with good conscience; and thapostle seith that ther nys thyng in this world of which we sholden have so greet joye as whan oure conscience bereth us good witnesse; [2825] and the wise man seith, "The substance of a man is ful good whan synne is nat in mannes con-science."

'Afterward, in getynge of youre richesses and in usynge of hem, yow moste have greet bisynesse and greet diligence that youre goode name be alwey kept and conserved, for Salomon seith that bettre it is and moore it availleth a man to have a good name than for to have grete richesses. And therfore he seith in another place, "Do greet diligence," seith Salomon, "in kepyng of thy freend and of thy goode name, [2830] for it shal lenger abide with thee than any tresour, be it never so precious." And certes, he sholde nat be called a gentil man that after God and good conscience, alle thynges left, ne dooth his diligence and bisynesse to kepen his good name. And Cassidore seith that it is signe of gentil herte whan a man loveth and desireth to han a good name. And therfore seith Seint Augustyn, that ther been two thynges that arn necessarie and nedefulle, and that is, good conscience and good loos; [2835] that is to seyn, good conscience to thyn owene persone inward, and good loos for thy neighebore outward. And he that trusteth hym so muchel in his goode conscience that he displeseth and setteth at noght his goode name or loos, and rekketh noght though he kepe nat his goode name, nys but a crueel cherl.

'Sire, now have I shewed yow how ye shul do in getynge richesses, and how ye shullen usen hem, and I se wel that for the trust that ye han in youre richesses ye wole moeve werre and bataille. [2840] I conseille yow that ye bigynne no werre in trust of youre richesses, for they ne suffisen noght werres to mayntene. And therfore seith a philosophre, "That man that desireth and wole algates han werre shal never have suffisaunce, for the richer that he is, the gretter despenses moste he make if he wole have worshipe and victorie." And Salomon seith that the gretter richesses that a man hath, the mo despendours he hath. And, deere sire, al be it so that for youre richesses ye mowe have muchel folk, [2845] yet bihoveth it nat, ne it is nat good to bigynne werre where as ye mowe in oother manere have pees unto youre worshipe and profit. For

the victories of batailles that been in this world lyen nat in greet nombre or multitude of the peple, ne in the vertu of man, but it lith in the wyl and in the hand of oure Lord God Almyghty.

'And therfore Judas Machabeus, which was Goddes knyght, whan he sholde fighte agayn his adversarie that hadde a greet nombre and a gretter multitude of folk and strenger than was this peple of Machabee, [2850] yet he reconforted his litel compaignye, and seyde right in this wise : "Als lightly," quod he, "may oure Lord God Almyghty yeve victorie to a fewe folk as to many folk, for the victorie of a bataile comth nat by the grete nombre of peple, but it come from oure Lord God of hevene."

'And, deere sire, for as muchel as ther is no man certein if he be worthy that God yeve hym victorie [no more than he is sure whether he is worthy of the love of God] or naught, after that Salomon seith, [2855] therfore every man sholde greetly drede werres to bigynne. And by cause that in batailles fallen manye perils, and happeth outher while that as soone is the grete man slayn as the litel man ; and as it is writen in the seconde book of Kynges, "The dedes of batailles been aventurouse and no thyng certeyne, for as lightly is oon hurt with a spere as another"; [2860] and for ther is gret peril in werre, therfore sholde a man flee and eschue werre, in as muchel as a man may goodly, for Salomon seith, "He that loveth peril shal falle in peril." '

After that dame Prudence hadde spoken in this manere, Melibee answerde and seyde, 'I see wel, dame Prudence, that by youre faire wordes, and by youre resouns that ye han shewed me, that the werre liketh yow no thyng ; but I have nat yet herd youre conseil, how I shal do in this nede.'

2845. *greet nombre*, H⁶ *gretter* for *greet*.
2850. *compaignye*, H *poeple*.
2850. [*no more*, etc.] The words bracketed are supplied from the French.
2855. *manye perils*, H *many mervayles and periles*.

[2865] 'Certes,' quod she, 'I con-seille yow that ye accorde with youre adversaries and that ye have pees with hem; for Seint Jame seith, in his Epistles, that by concord and pees the smale richesses wexen grete, and by debaat and discord the grete richesses fallen doun; and ye knowen wel that oon of the gretteste and moost sovereyn thyng that is in this world is unytee and pees. And therfore seyde oure Lord Jhesu Crist to his Apostles in this wise, [2870] "Wel happy and blessed been they that loven and purchacen pees, for they been called children of God." '

A!' quod Melibee, 'now se I wel that ye loven nat myn honour ne my worshipe. Ye knowen wel that myne adversaries han bigonnen this debaat and bryge by hire outrage, and ye se wel that they ne requeren ne preyen me nat of pees, ne they asken nat to be recon-siled. Wol ye thanne that I go and meke me and obeye me to hem and crie hem mercy? [2875] For sothe that were nat my worshipe; for right as men seyn that over greet hoomlynesse engendreth dispreisynge, so fareth it by to greet humylitee or mekenesse.'

Thanne bigan dame Prudence to maken semblant of wratthe, and seyde, 'Certes, sire, sauf youre grace, I love youre honour and youre profit as I do myn owene, and ever have doon; ne ye, ne noon oother, syen never the con-traire! [2880] And yit if I hadde seyd that ye sholde han purchaced the pees and the reconsiliacioun, I ne hadde nat muchel mystaken me, ne seyd amys; for the wise man seith, "the dissensioun bigynneth by another man and the recon-silyng bygynneth by thy self"; and the prophete seith, "Flee shrewednesse and do goodnesse, seke pees and folwe it, as muchel as in thee is." Yet seye I nat that ye shul rather pursue to youre ad-versaries for pees than they shuln to yow; [2885] for I knowe wel that ye been so

2880. *shrewednesse*, II *schame and schrewed-nesse*.

hard-herted that ye wol do no thyng for me; and Salomon seith, "He that hath over hard an herte atte laste he shal mys-happe and mystyde." '

Whanne Melibee hadde herd dame Prudence maken semblant of wratthe, he seyde in this wise: 'Dame, I prey yow that ye be nat displesed of thynges that I seye, for ye knowe wel that I am angry and wrooth, and that is no wonder, [2890] and they that been wrothe witen nat wel what they don, ne what they seyn; therfore the prophete seith that troubled eyen han no cleer sighte. But seyeth and conseileth me as yow liketh, for I am redy to do right as ye wol desire, and if ye repreve me of my folye I am the moore holden to love yow and preyse yow; for Salomon seith that he that repreveth hym that dooth folye [2895] he shal fynde gretter grace than he that deceyveth hym by sweete wordes.'

Thanne seide dame Prudence, 'I make no semblant of wratthe ne anger but for youre grete profit; for Salomon seith, "He is moore worth that repreveth or chideth a fool for his folye, shewynge hym semblant of wratthe, than he that supporteth hym and preyseth hym in his mysdoynge, and laugheth at his folye." And this same Salomon seith afterward that by the sorweful visage of a man, that is to seyn, by the sory and hevy conten-aunce of a man, [2900] the fool correcteth and amendeth hymself.'

Thanne seyde Melibee, 'I shal nat konne answere to so manye faire resouns as ye putten to me and shewen; seyeth shortly youre wyl and youre conseil, and I am al redy to fulfille and parfourne it.'

Thanne dame Prudence discovered al hir wyl to hym, and seyde, 'I conseille yow,' quod she, 'aboven alle thynges, that ye make pees bitwene God and yow, [2905] and beth reconsiled unto hym and to his grace; for as I have seyd yow heer biforn, God hath suffred yow to have this tribulacioun and disese for youre synnes, and if ye do as I sey yow, God

2900. *hir wyl*, H *hire counsail and hire wills*.

wol sende youre adversaries unto yow and maken hem fallen at youre feet redy to do youre wyl and youre comandementz; for Salomon seith, "Whan the condicioun of man is plesaunt and likynge to God, [2910] he chaungeth the hertes of the mannes adversaries and constreyneth hem to biseken hym of pees and of grace." And I prey yow, lat me speke with youre adversaries in privee place; for they shul nat knowe that it be of youre wyl or youre assent; and thanne, whan I knowe hir wil and hire entente, I may conseille yow the moore seurely.'

'Dame,' quod Melibee, 'dooth youre wil and youre likynge, [2915] for I putte me hoolly in youre disposicioun and ordinaunce.'

Thanne dame Prudence, whan she saugh the goode wyl of hir housbonde, delibered and took avys in hirself, thinkinge how she myghte brynge this nede unto a good conclusioun and to a good ende. And whan she saugh hir tyme she sente for thise adversaries to come unto hire into a pryvee place, and shewed wisely unto hem the grete goodes that comen of pees, [2920] and the grete harmes and perils that been in werre; and seyde to hem in a goodly manere how that hem oughten have greet repentaunce of the injurie and wrong that they hadden doon to Melibee, hir lord, and to hire, and to hire doghter.

And whan they herden the goodliche wordes of dame Prudence, they weren so surprised and ravysshed, and hadden so greet joye of hire, that wonder was to telle. [2925] 'A! lady,' quod they, 'ye han shewed unto us the blessynge of swetnesse after the sawe of David the prophete; for the reconsilynge which we been nat worthy to have in no manere, but we oghte requeren it with greet contricioun and humylitee, ye, of youre grete goodnesse, have presented unto us. Now se we wel that the science and the konnynge of Salomon is ful trewe, [2930] for he seith that sweete wordes multiplien and encreesen freendes, and

maken shrewes to be debonaire and meeke.

'Certes,' quod they, 'we putten oure dede and al oure matere and cause al hoolly in youre goode wyl, and been redy to obeye to the speche and comandement of my lord Melibee. And therfore, deere and benygne lady, we preien yow and biseke yow as mekely as we konne and mowen, that it lyke unto youre grete goodnesse to fulfillen in dede youre goodliche wordes, [2935] for we consideren and knowelichen that we han offended and greved my lord Melibee out of mesure, so ferforth that we be nat of power to maken his amendes; and therfore we oblige and bynden us and oure freendes to doon al his wyl and his comandementz. But peraventure he hath swich hevynesse and swich wratthe to usward by cause of oure offense, that he wole enjoyne us swich a peyne as we mowe nat bere ne susteene, [2940] and therfore, noble lady, we biseke to youre wommanly pitee to taken swich avysement in this nede that we, ne oure freendes, be nat desherited, ne destroyed, thurgh oure folye.'

'Certes,' quod Prudence, 'it is an hard thyng and right perilous that a man putte hym al outrely in the arbitracioun and juggement, and in the myght and power of his enemys, for Salomon seith, "Leeveth me, and yeveth credence to that I shal seyn; I seye," quod he, "ye peple, folk and governours of hooly chirche, [2945] to thy sone, to thy wyf, to thy freend, ne to thy broother, ne yeve thou never myght ne maistrie of thy body whil thou lyvest."

'Now sithen he deffendeth that man shal nat yeven to his broother, ne to his freend, the myght of his body, by strenger resoun he deffendeth and forbedeth a man to yeven hymself to his enemy. And nathelees I conseille you that ye mystruste nat my lord; [2950] for I woot wel and knowe verraily that he is debonaire and meeke, large, curteys, and no thyng desirous, ne coveitous of good ne richesse;

for ther nys nothyng in this world that he desireth, save oonly worshipe and honour. Forthermoore I knowe wel and am right seur that he shal no thyng doon in this nede withouten my conseil, and I shal so werken in this cause that, by grace of oure Lord God, ye shul been reconsiled unto us.'

[2955] Thanne seyden they with o voys, 'Worshipful lady, we putten us and oure goodes al fully in youre wil and disposicioun, and been redy to comen what day that it like unto youre noblesse to lymyte us or assigne us, for to maken oure obligacioun and boond as strong as it liketh unto youre goodnesse, that we mowe fulfille the wille of yow and of my lord Melibee.'

Whan dame Prudence hadde herd the answeres of thise men, she bad hem goon agayn prively, [2960] and she retourned to hir lord Melibee, and tolde hym how she foond his adversaries ful repentant, knowelechynge ful lowely hir synnes and trespas, and how they were redy to suffren all peyne, requirynge and preiynge hym of mercy and pitee.

Thanne seyde Melibee, 'He is wel worthy to have pardoun and foryifnesse of his synne that excuseth nat his synne, but knowlecheth it and repenteth hym, axinge indulgence. [2965] For Senec seith, "Ther is the remissioun and foryifnesse, where as confessioun is"; for confessioun is neighebore to innocence. And he saith in another place that he that hath shame of his synne, and knowlecheth it, is worthi remyssioun. And therfore I assente and conforme me to have pees; but it is good that we do it nat with-outen the assent and wyl of oure freendes.'

Thanne was Prudence right glad and joyeful, and seyde, [2970] 'Certes, sire,' quod she, 'ye han wel and goodly

2965. *Senec*, the pseudo-Seneca, *De Moribus*, 94.
2965. *And he saith . . . remyssioun*, text from Petworth and Lansdowne (the latter reading *mercy* for *remyssioun*); other MSS. omit wholly or in part.

answered, for right as by the conseil, assent and helpe of youre freendes, ye han been stired to venge yow and maken werre, right so withouten hire conseil shul ye nat accorden yow, ne have pees with youre adversaries; for the lawe seith, "Ther nys no thyng so good by wey of kynde as a thyng to been unbounde by hym that it was y-bounde."'

And thanne dame Prudence, withouten delay or tariynge, sente anon hire messages for hire kyn and for hire olde freendes, whiche that were trewe and wyse, [2975] and tolde hem by ordre, in the presence of Melibee, al this mateere as it is aboven expressed and declared, and preyden that they wolde yeven hire avys and conseil, what best were to doon in this nede. And whan Melibees freendes hadde taken hire avys and deliberacioun of the forseide mateere, and hadden examyned it by greet bisynesse and greet diligence, they yave ful conseil for to have pees and reste, [2980] and that Melibee sholde receyve with good herte hise adversaries to foryifnesse and mercy.

And whan dame Prudence hadde herd the assent of hir lord Melibee, and the conseil of his freendes accorde with hire wille and hire entencioun, she was wonderly glad in hire herte and seyde, 'Ther is an old proverbe,' quod she, 'seith that the goodnesse that thou mayst do this day, do it, [2985] and abide nat, ne delaye it nat til to morwe. And therfore I conseille that ye sende youre messages, swiche as been discrete and wise, unto youre adversaries, tellynge hem on youre bihalve, that if they wole trete of pees and of accord, [2990] that they shape hem, withouten delay or tariyng, to comen unto us.' Which thyng parfourned was in dede; and whanne thise trespassours and repentynge folk of hire folies,—that is to seyn, the adversaries of Melibee,— hadden herd what thise messagers seyden unto hem, they weren right glad and joyeful, and answereden ful mekely and benignely, yeldynge graces and thankynges to hir lord Melibee and to al his compaignye, [2995] and shopen hem withouten delay to go with the messagers, and obeye to the comandement óf hir lord Melibee.

And right anon they tooken hire wey to the court of Melibee, and tooken with hem somme of hire trewe freendes to maken feith for hem and for to been hire borwes. And whan they were comen to the presence of Melibee, he seyde hem thise wordes : 'It standeth thus,' quod Melibee, 'and sooth it is, that ye, [3000] causeless and withouten skile and resoun, han doon grete injuries and wronges to me and to my wyf Prudence, and to my doghter also ; for ye han entred in to myn hous by violence, and have doon swich outrage that alle men knowen wel that ye have disserved the deeth, and therfore wol I knowe and wite of yow [3005] wheither ye wol putte the punyssement and the chastisynge and the vengeance of this outrage in the wyl of me and of my wyf Prudence, or ye wol nat ?'

Thanne the wiseste of hem thre answerde for hem alle, and seyde, 'Sire,' quod he, 'we knowen wel that we been unworthy to comen unto the court of so greet a lord, and so worthy as ye been, for we han so greetly mystaken us, and han offended and agilt in swich a wise agayn youre heigh lordshipe that trewely we han disserved the deeth ; [3010] but yet for the grete goodnesse and debonairetee that al the world witnesseth in youre persone, we submytten us to the excellence and benignitee of youre gracious lordshipe, and been redy to obeie to alle youre comandementz, bisekynge yow that of youre merciable pitee ye wol considere oure grete repentaunce and lough submyssioun, and graunten us foryevenesse of oure outrageous trespas and offense ; [3015] for wel we knowe that youre liberal grace and mercy strecchen hem ferther into goodnesse than doon oure outrageouse giltes and trespas into wikkednesse ; al be it that cursedly and dampnablely we han agilt agayn youre heigh lordshipe.'

Thanne Melibee took hem up fro the ground ful benignely, and receyved hire obligaciouns and hir boondes by hire othes upon hire plegges and borwes, and assigned hem a certeyn day to retourne unto his court, [3020] for to accepte and receyve the sentence and juggement that Melibee wolde comande to be doon on hem by the causes aforeseyd ; whiche thynges ordeyned, every man retourned to his hous.

And whan that dame Prudence saugh hir tyme, she freyned and axed hir lord Melibee what vengeance he thoughte to taken of his adversaries.

To which Melibee answerde and seyde, 'Certes,' quod he, 'I thynke and purpose me fully [3025] to desherite hem of al that ever they han, and for to putte hem in exil for ever.'

'Certes,' quod dame Prudence, 'this were a crueel sentence and muchel agayn resoun ; for ye been riche ynough and han no nede of oother mennes good, and ye myghte lightly in this wise gete yow a coveitous name, which is a vicious thyng and oghte been eschued of every good man ; [3030] for after the sawe of the word of the Apostle, "Coveitise is roote of alle harmes." And therfore it were bettre for yow to lese so muchel good of youre owene than for to taken of hir good in this manere ; for bettre it is to lesen with worshipe, than it is to wynne with vileynye and shame ; and everi man oghte to doon his diligence and his bisynesse to geten hym a good name. And yet shal he nat oonly bisie hym in kepynge of his good name, [3035] but he shal also enforcen hym alwey to do som thyng by which he may renovelle his good name ; for it is writen " that the olde good loos and good name of a man is soone goon and passed whan it is nat newed ne renovelled."

'And as touchynge that ye seyn ye wole exile youre adversaries, that thynketh me muchel agayn resoun, and out of mesure, considered the power that they han yeve yow upon hemself. [3040] And it is writen that he is worthy to lesen his privilege that mysuseth the myght and the power that is yeven hym. And I sette cas, ye myghte enjoyne hem that peyne by right and by lawe, which I trowe ye mowe nat do; I seye ye mighte nat putten it to execucioun per-aventure, and thanne were it likly to retourne to the werre as it was biforn; [3045] and therfore if ye wole that men do yow obeisance, ye moste deemen moore curteisly, this is to seyn, ye moste yeven moore esy sentences and jugge-mentz. For it is writen that he that moost curteisly comandeth, to hym men moost obeyen. And therfore I prey yow that in this necessitee and in this nede ye caste yow to overcome youre herte. For Senec seith that he that overcometh his herte overcometh twies; [3050] and Tullius seith, "Ther is no thyng so comendable in a greet lord as whan he is debonaire and meeke, and appeseth lightly." And I prey yow that ye wole forbere now to do vengeance in swich a manere, that youre goode name may be kept and conserved, and that men mowe have cause and mateere to preyse yow of pitee and of mercy, [3055] and that ye have no cause to repente yow of thyng that ye doon; for Senec seith, "He overcometh in an yvel manere that repenteth hym of his victorie." Wher-fore, I pray yow, lat mercy been in youre mynde and in youre herte, to theffect and entente that God Almyghty have mercy on yow in his laste juggement; for Seint Jame seith in his Epistle, "Juggement withouten mercy shal be doon to hym that hath no mercy of another wight!"'

[3060] Whanne Melibee hadde herd the grete skiles and resouns of dame Prudence, and hire wise informaciouns and techynges, his herte gan enclyne to the wil of his wyf, consideryge hir trewe entente, and conformed hym anon and assented fully to werken after hir conseil; and thonked God, of whom procedeth al vertu and alle goodnesse, that hym sente a wyf of so greet discrecioun.

And whan the day cam that his adversaries sholde appieren in his pre-sence, [3065] he spak unto hem ful goodly, and seyde in this wyse: 'Al be it so that of youre pride and presumpcioun and folie, and of youre necligence and unkonnynge, ye have mysborn yow and trespassed unto me; yet, for as muche as I see and biholde youre grete humylitee, [3070] and that ye been sory and re-pentant of youre giltes, it constreyneth me to doon yow grace and mercy. Therfore I receyve yow to my grace and foryeve yow outrely alle the offenses, injuries and wronges that ye have doon agayn me and myne; to this effect and to this ende, that God of his endelees mercy wole at the tyme of oure diynge foryeven us oure giltes that we han trespassed to hym in this wrecched world; [3075] for doutelees if we be sory and repentant of the synnes and giltes whiche we han trespassed in the sighte of oure Lord God, he is so free and so merciable that he wole foryeven us oure giltes, and bryngen us to his blisse that never hath ende.' *Amen.*

The murye wordes of the Hoost to the Monk

Whan ended was my tale of Melibee, And of Prudence and hire benignytee, Oure Hostè seyde, 'As I am feithful man, And by that precious corpus Madrian, I haddè levere than a barel ale   3083 That goodè lief my wyf haddeherd this tale! For she nys no thyng of swich pacience As was this Melibeus wyf Prudence. By Goddès bonès! whan I bete my knaves, She bryngeth me forth the gretè clobbèd staves And crieth, "Slee the doggès everichoon,

---

3045. *Senec seith*, Publil. Syrus, Sent. 64: 'Bis vincit qui se in victoria vincit.'
3050. *Tullius, De Offic.* i. 25. 88.
3055. *Senec seith*, Publil. Syrus, Sent. 366.
3055. *mercy*, H *mercy and pite.*

3060. *conseil*, H *reed and counseil.*
3082. *corpus Madrian*, the body of S. Mathurin, which would not accept burial except in France, and then worked miracles.

And brek hem, bothè bak and every
    boon !"   3090
' And if that any neighèbore of myne
Wol nat in chirchè to my wyf enclyne,
Or be so hardy to hire to trespace,
Whan she comth home she rampeth in
    my face,
And crieth, " Falsè coward ! wrek thy wyf !
By corpus bonès ! I wol have thy knyf,
And thou shalt have my distaf and go
    spynne !"
Fro day to nyght, right thus she wol
    bigynne,—   3098
"Allas!" she seith, "that ever I was shape
To wedden a milksope or a coward ape,
That wol been overlad with every wight !
Thou darst nat stonden by thy wyvès
    right !"
' This is my lif, but if that I wol fighte ;
And out at dore anon I moot me dighte,
Or elles I am but lost, but if that I
Be lik a wildè leoun, fool-hardy.
I woot wel she wol do me slee som day
Som neighèbore, and thannè go my way ;
For I am perilous with knyf in honde ;
Al be it that I dar hire nat withstonde,
For she is byg in armès, by my feith,   3111
That shal he fynde that hire mysdooth
    or seith.
But lat us passe awey fro this mateere.
    ' My lord the Monk,' quod he, ' be
    myrie of cheere,
For ye shul tellè a talè trewèly.
Ló ! Rouchéstre stant heer fastè by !
Ryde forth, myn owenè lord, brek nat
    oure game,
But by my trouthe I knowè nat youre
    name,—   3118
Wher shal I callè you my lord daun John,
Or daun Thomás, or ellès daun Albón ?
Of what hous be ye, by youre fader kyn ?
I vowe to God, thou hast a ful fair skyn !
It is a gentil pasture ther thow goost ;
Thou art nat lyk a penant, or a goost.
Upon my feith, thou art som officer,
Som worthy sexteyn, or som celerer,
For by my fader soule, as to my doom
Thou art a maister, whan thou art at hoom ;
No pourè cloysterer, ne no novys,

3125. *som*, H *an.*

Bút a governour, wily and wys,   3130
And therwithal of brawnès and of bones,
A wel-farynge personè, for the nones.
I pray to God, yeve hym confusioun
That first thee broghte unto religioun.
Thou woldest han been a tredéfowel aright ;
Haddestow as greet a leeve as thou hast
    myght
To parfourne al thy lust in engendrure,
Thou haddest bigeten ful many a creäture.
Allas ! why werestow so wyd a cope ?   3139
God yeve me sorwe ! but and I were a pope,
Nat oonly thou, but every myghty man,
Though he were shorn ful hye upon his pan,
Sholde have a wyf,—for al the world is
    lorn ;
Religioun hath take up al the corn
Of tredyng, and we borel men been
    shrympes ;
Of fieble trees ther comen wrecched ympes.
This maketh that oure heirès beth so
    sklendre
And feble that they may nat wel engendre ;
This maketh that oure wyvès wole assaye
Religious folk, for ye mowe bettre paye
Of Venus paièmentz than mowè we.   3151
God woot, no Lusshèburghes payen ye !
But be nat wrooth, my lord, for that I
    pleye.
Ful ofte in game a soothe I have herd seye !'
    This worthy Monk took al in pacience
And seyde, ' I wol doon al my diligence,
As fer as sowneth into honestee,
To tellè yow a tale, or two, or three ;
And if yow list to herkne hyderward,
I wol yow seyn the lyf of Seint Edward,
Or ellis, first, tragédies wol I telle,   3161
Of whiche I have an hundred in my celle.
    ' Tragédie is to seyn a certeyn storie,
As oldè bookès maken us memórie,
Of hym that stood in greet prosperitee,
And is y-fallen out of heigh degree
Into myserie, and endeth wrecchedly ;
And they ben versifiéd communely
Of six feet, which men clepen exametron.
In prose eek been endited many oon,   3170

3137. *lust*, H *wil.*
3138. *ful*, om. H5.
3152. *Lussheburghes*, base coins imported
from Luxemburg.

And eek in meetre in many a sondry wyse;
Lo, this declaryng oghte ynogh suffise.
Now herkneth, if yow liketh for to heere;
But first, I yow biseeke in this mateere,
Though I by ordre tellé nat thise thynges
Be it of popés, emperours, or kynges,
After hir agés as men writen fynde,
But tellen hem, som bifore and som
    bihynde,
As it now comth unto my remembraunce,
Have me excusèd of myn ignoraunce.' ₃₁₈₀

MONK'S TALE

*Heere bigynneth The Monkes Tale, de
Casibus Virorum Illustrium*

I wol biwaille, in manere of tragédie,
The harm of hem that stoode in heigh
    degree,
And fillen so that ther nas no remédie
To brynge hem out of hir adversitee;
For certein, whan that Fortune list to flee,
Ther may no man the cours of hire with-
    holde.
Lat no man truste on blynd prosperitee;
Be war by thise ensamplés trewe and olde.

At LUCIFER,—though he an angel were,
And nat a man,—at hym wol I bigynne,
For though Fortuné may noon angel dere,
From heigh degree yet fel he for his synne
Doun into hellé, where he yet is inne.
O Lucifer! brightest of angels alle,
Now artow Sathanas, that mayst nat
    twynne
Out of miserie in which that thou art falle.

Lo ADAM, in the feeld of Damyssene,
With Goddés owné fynger wroght was he,
And nat bigeten of mannés sperme unclene,
And welte all paradys savynge o tree. ₃₂₀₀

De Casibus Virorum Illustrium. The title
indicates Chaucer's obligations to Boccaccio's *De
Cas. Vir. et Feminarum Illust.*, from which
and the same author's *De Claris Mulieribus*,
Boethius, *De Consolatione*, the *Roman de la
Rose*, and the Bible the monk takes his 'old ensamples.'
3189. *Lucifer*, Chaucer's addition; Boccaccio
begins with Adam.
3197. *Damyssene*, Damascus; Boccaccio's
'Ager, qui postea Damascenus.'

Hadde never worldly man so heigh degree
As Adam, til he for mysgovernaunce
Was dryven out of hys hye prosperitee
To labour, and to helle, and to mes-
    chaunce.

Lo SAMPSON, which that was annunciat
By angel, longe er his nativitee,
And was to God Almyghty consecrat,
And stood in noblesse whil he myghtè see.
Was never swich another as was hee,
To speke of strengthe, and therwith
    hardynesse;   ₃₂₁₀
But to his wyvés toolde he his secree,
Thurgh whiche he slow hymself for
    wrecchednesse.

Sampson, this noble almyghty champioun,
Withouten wepene save his handés tweye,
He slow and al to-rentè the leoun,
Toward his weddyng walkynge by the
    weye.
His falsé wyf koude hym so plese and
    preye
Til she his conseil knew; and she, un-
    trewe,
Unto his foos his conseil gan biwreye,
And hym forsook, and took another newe.

Thre hundred foxes took Sampson for ire,
And alle hir taylés he togydrè bond,
And sette the foxes taylés alle on fire,
For he on every tayl had knyt a brond;
And they brende alle the cornés in that
    lond,
And alle hire olyveres, and vynés eke.
A thousand men he slow eek with his
    hond,
And hadde no wepene but an asses cheke.

Whan they were slayn so thursted hym
    that he   ₃₂₂₉
Was wel ny lorn, for which he gan to preye
That God wolde on his peyne han som
    pitee,
And sende hym drynke, or ellés moste
    he deye
And of this asses cheké, that was dreye,

3205. *annunciat*, from Boccaccio 'Prænunci-
ante per angelum Deo,' but Chaucer takes his
points mainly from the Bible.

Out of a wang-tooth sprang anon a welle,
Of which he drank ynow, shortly to seyė;
Thus heelpe hym God, as *Judicum* can
    telle.

By verray force at Gazan, on a nyght,
Maugree Philistiens of that citee,
The gatės of the toun he hath up-plyght,
And on his bak y-caryed hem hath hee 3240
Hye on an hillė, that men myghte hem see.
O noble, almyghty Sampson, lief and deere,
Had thou nat toold to wommen thy secree,
In all this world ne haddė been thy peere !

This Sampson never ciser drank, ne wyn,
Ne on his heed cam rasour noon, ne sheere,
By precept of the messager dïvyn ;
For alle his strengthės in his heerės were ;
And fully twenty wynter, yeer by yeere,
He haddė of Israel the governaunce ; 3250
But soonė shal he wepė many a teere,
For wommen shal hym bryngen to mes-
    chaunce.

Unto his lemman Dalida he tolde
That in his heeris al his strengthė lay,
And falsly to his foomen she hym solde ;
And slepynge in hir barm upon a day
She made to clippe or shere his heres away,
And made his foomen al his craft espyen ;
And whan that they hym foond in this array,
They bounde hym faste and putten out
    his eyen.   3260

But er his heer were clippėd or y-shave,
Ther was no boond with which men
    myghte him bynde ;
But now is he in prison in a cave,
Where-as they made hym at the queernė
    grynde.
O noble Sampson, strongest of mankynde,
O whilom juge, in glorie and in richésse !
Now maystow wepen with thyne eyen
    blynde,
Sith thou fro wele art falle in wrecched-
    nesse.

Thende of this caytyf was as I shal seye ;
His foomen made a feeste upon a day,
And made hym as a fool biforn hem pleye ;

3236. *Judicum*, Book of Judges.

And this was in a temple of greet array ;
But attė laste he made a foul affray ;
For he the pilers shook and made hem
    falle,
And doun fil temple and al, and ther it lay ;
And slow hymself, and eek his foomen alle :

This is to seyn, the prynces everichoon ;
And eek thre thousand bodyes were ther
    slayn
With fallynge of the gretė temple of stoon.
Of Sampson now wol I namoorė sayn ; 3280
Beth war by this ensample oold and playn
That no men telle hir conseil til hir wyves
Of swich thyng as they wolde han secree
    fayn,
If that it touche hir lymės or hir lyvės.

Of HERCULES, the sovereyn conquer-
    our,
Syngen his werkės laude and heigh renoun ;
For in his tyme of strengthe he was the flour.
He slow, and rafte the skyn of the leoun ;
He of Centauros leyde the boost adoun ;
He Arpies slow, the crueel bryddės felle ;
He golden apples rafte of the dragoun ;
He drow out Cerberus, the hound of helle ;

He slow the crueel tyrant Busirus,
And made his hors to frete hym, flessh
    and boon ;
He slow the firy serpent venymus ;   3295
Of Acheloys two hornės he brak oon ;
And he slow Cacus in a cave of stoon ;
He slow the geant Anthëus the stronge ;
He slow the grisly boor, and that anon ;
And bar the hevene on his nekkė longe.

Was never wight sith that this world bigan,
That slow so manye monstrės as dide he ;
Thurghout this wydė world his namė ran,

3274. *the*, H⁶ *two*.
3285. *Hercules*. In this and the next stanza
Chaucer follows closely Boethius, *De Consolatione*, Bk. v. Met. 7, keeping some of the phrases
of his own translation.
3293. *Busirus*, Busiris, King of Egypt, who
offered strangers in sacrifice.
3296. *Acheloys*. The river-god turned himself
into a bull to fight Hercules the better.
3296. *brak*, H *raft*.
3297. *Cacus*, who stole the cattle of Hercules.
3298. *Anthëus*, Antæus.

What for his strengthe and for his heigh
    bountee,
And every reawmé wente he for to see.
He was so stroong that no man myghte
    hym lette ;
At bothe the worldés endés, seith Tro-
    phee,
In stide of boundés he a pileer sette.

A lemman hadde this noble champioun,
That highté Dianira, fressh as May ; 3310
And as thise clerkés maken mentioun,
She hath hym sent a sherté, fressh and gay.
Allas, this sherte—allas, and weylaway !—
Envenymed was so subtilly withalle,
That er that he had wered it half a day,
It made his flessh al from his bonés falle ;

But nathélees somme clerkés hire excusen
By oon that highté Nessus, that it maked.
Be as be may, I wol hire noght accusen ;
But on his bak this sherte he wered al
    naked, 3320
Til that his flessh was for the venym
    blaked ;
And whan he saugh noon oother remedye,
In hooté coles he hath hymselven raked ;
For with no venym deignéd hym to dye.

Thus starf this worthy, myghty Hercules.
Lo ! who may truste on Fortune any
    throwe ?
For hym that folweth al this world of
    prees,
Er he be war, is ofte y-leyd ful lowe.
Ful wys is he that kan hymselven knowe !
Beth war, for whan that Fortune list to
    glose, 3330
Thanne wayteth she hir man to over-
    throwe
By swich a wey as he wolde leest suppose.

The myghty trone, the precious tresor,
The glorious ceptre, and roial magestee
That hadde the kyng NABUGODONOSOR,

With tonge unnethé may discryvéd bee.
He twyés wan Jerusalem the citee ;
The vessel of the temple he with hym
    ladde.
At Babiloigné was his sovereyn see, 3339
In which his glorie and his delit he hadde.

The faireste children of the blood roial
Of Israel he leet do gelde anoon,
And makéd ech of hem to been his thral.
Amongés othere Daniel was oon,
That was the wiseste child of everychon,
For he the dremés of the kyng expowned,
Where-as in Chaldeye clerk ne was ther
    noon,
That wisté to what fyn his dremés sowned.

This proudé kyng leet maken a statue of
    gold, 3349
Sixty cubités long and sevene in brede,
To which ymagé bothé yonge and oold
Comanded he to loute, and have in drede,
Or in a fourneys, ful of flambés rede,
He shal be brent, that woldé noght obeye ;
But never wolde assenté to that dede
Daniel, ne his yongé felawes tweye.

This kyng of kyngés proud was and elaat ;
He wende that God that sit in magestee
Ne myghte hym nat bireve of his estaat ;
But sodeynly he loste his dignytee 3360
And lyk a beest hym seméd for to bee ;
And eet hey as an oxe, and lay theroute
In reyn ; with wildé beestés walkéd hee
Til certein tymé was y-come aboute ;

And lik an eglés fetheres wex his heres ;
His naylés lik a briddés clawés were ;
Til God relesséd hym a certeyn yeres,
And yaf hym wit, and thanne with many
    a teere
He thankéd God, and ever his lyf in feere
Was he to doon amys, or moore trespace ;
And, til that tyme he leyd was on his
    beere, 3371
He knew that God was ful of myght and
    grace.

3307. *Trophee.* E and Heng., wiser than any
modern commentator, append the note ' Ille
vates Chaldeorum Tropheus' !
3318. *Nessus*, the Centaur whom Hercules
slew.

3365. *wer*, emend. Skeat for *war* (E) and
were (H³) etc. of MSS.

His soné, which that highté BALTHA-
    SAR,
That heeld the regne after his fader day,
He by his fader koudé noght be war;
For proud he was of herte and of array,
And eek an ydolastré he was ay.
His hye estaat assuréd hym in pryde ;
But Fortune caste hym doun and ther
    he lay,
And sodeynly his regné gan divide.   3380

A feeste he made unto his lordés alle,
Upon a tyme, and bad hem blithé bee ;
And thanne his officerés gan he calle,—
'Gooth, bryngeth forth the vessellés,'
    quod he,
' Whiche that my fader in his prosperitee
Out of the temple of Jerusalem birafte,
And to our hyé goddés thanké we
Of honour that oure eldrés with us lafte.'

Hys wyf, his lordés, and his concubynes
Ay dronken, whil hire appetités laste, 3390
Out of thise noble vessels sondry wynes ;
And on a wal this kyng his eyen caste,
And saugh an hand, armlees, that wroot
    ful fast ;
For feere of which he quook, and sikéd
    soore.
This hand, that Balthasar so soore agaste,
Wroot *Mane, techel, phares,* and na moore.

In al that land magicien was noon
That koude expoundé what this lettré
    mente ;
But Daniel expownéd it anon,   3399
And seydé, ' King, God to thy fader sente
Glorie and honour, regné, tresour, rente,
And he was proud, and no-thyng God
    ne dradde,
And therfore God greet wreche upon
    hym sente,
And hym birafte the regné that he hadde ;

' He was out-cast of mannés compaignye ;
With asses was his habitacioun,
And eet hey as a beest in weet and drye,
Til that he knew, by grace and by resoun,

That God of hevene hath domynacioun
Over every regne and every creäture ; 3410
And thanne hadde God of hym com-
    passioun,
And hym restored his regne and his figúre.

' Eek thou that art his sone art proud also,
And knowest alle thise thyngés verraily,
And art rebel to God and art his foo ;
Thou drank eek of his vessels boldély ;
Thy wyf eek, and thy wenches, synfully
Dronke of the samé vessels sondry wynys,
And heryest false goddés cursedly ;
Therfore to thee y-shapen ful greet pyne ys.

' This hand was sent from God, that on
    the wal   3421
Wroot, " *Mane, techel, phares,*" trusté
    me,—
Thy regne is doon, thou weyest noght at al,
Dyvyded is thy regne, and it shal be
To Medés and to Persés yeve,' quod he.
And thilké samé nyght this kyng was
    slawe,
And Darius occupieth his degree,
Thogh he therto hadde neither right ne
    lawe.

Lordynges, ensample heer-by may ye
    take,   3429
How that in lordshipe is no sikernesse ;
For whan Fortúné wole a man forsake,
She bereth awey his regne and his richesse,
And eek his freendés, bothé moore and
    lesse ;
For what man that hath freendés thurgh
    Fortúne
Mishape wol maken hem enemys, as I
    gesse ;
This proverbe is ful sooth and ful com-
    múne.

CENOBIA, of Palymerie queene,—
As writen Persiens of hir noblesse,—
So worthy was in armés, and so keene,
That no wight passéd hire in hardynesse,
Ne in lynage, ne in oother gentillesse.

3384. *vesselles.* Only *Corpus* and *Lansdowne* make this a trisyllable here.

3437. *Cenobia.* The account of Zenobia follows closely, omitting details of battles, Boccaccio's *De Claris Mulieribus*, cap. 98.

Of kyngès blood of Perce is she descended;
I seyè nat that she hadde moost fairnesse,
But of hire shape she myghte nat been
    amended.

From hire childhede I fyndè that she fledde
Office of wommen, and to wode she went,
And many a wildè hertès blood she shedde
With arwès brodè that she to hem sente ;
She was so swift that she anon hem hente,
And whan that she was elder she wolde
    kille   3450
Leouns, leopardes, and berès al to-rente,
And in hir armès weelde hem at hir wille.

She dorstè wildè beestès dennès seke,
And rennen in the montaignes al the nyght,
And slepen under the bussh ; and she
    koude eke
Wrastlen, by verray force and verray myght,
With any yong man, were he never so
    wight.
Ther myghtè no thyng in hir armès stonde.
She kepte hir maydenhod from every
    wight ;   3459
To no man deignèd hire for to be bonde ;

But attè laste hir freendès han hire maried
To Onèdake, a prynce of that contree ;
Al were it so that she hem longè taried.
And ye shul understondè how that he
Hadde swichè fantasies as haddè she ;
But nathèlees, whan they were knyt in feere,
They lyved in joye and in felicitee,
For ech of hem haddè oother lief and deere,

Save o thyng, that she wolde never assente
By no wey that he sholdè by hire lye   3470
But onès, for it was hir pleyn entente
To have a child the world to multiplye ;
And also soone as that she myghtè espye
That she was nat with childè with that
    dede,
Thanne wolde she suffre hym doon his
    fantasye
Eft soone, and nat but oonès, out of drede ;

And if she were with childe at thilkè cast,

Na moorè sholde he pleyen thilkè game,
Til fully fourty dayès weren past ;
Thanne wolde she onès suffre hym do
    the same.   3480
Al were this Onèdakè wilde or tame
He gat na moore of hire, for thus she seyde,
It was to wyvès lecherie and shame,
In oother caas, if that men with hem pleyde.

Two sonès by this Onèdake hadde she,
The whiche she kepte in vertu and lettrure;
But now unto our talè turnè we.
I seye so worshipful a creature,
And wys ther-with, and largè with mesure,
So penyble in the werre, and curteis eke,
Ne moorè labour myghte in werre endure,
Was noon, though al this world men
    sholdè seke.

Hir riche array ne myghtè nat be told,
As wel in vessel as in hire clothyng.
She was al clad in perree and in gold,
And eek she laftè noght, for noon huntyng,
To have of sondry tongès ful knowyng,
Whan that she leyser hadde ; and for to
    entende
To lernè bookès was al hire likyng,   3499
How she in vertu myghtè hir lyf dispende.

    And, shortly of this storie for to trete,
So doghty was hir housbonde and eek she,
That they conquérèd manye regnès grete
In the Orient, with many a faire citee
Apertenaunt unto the magestee
Of Romè, and with strong hond held
    hem faste,
Ne never myghte hir foomen doon hem flee,
Ay, whil that Onèdakès dayès laste.

Hir batailles, whoso list hem for to rede,—
Agayn Sapor the kyng and othere mo,   3510
And how that al this proces fil in dede,
Why she conquered, and what title had
    therto,
And after of hir meschief and hire wo,
How that she was bisegèd and y-take,—

3477-80. Chaucer here misunderstands his original.

3487. *tale,* H *purpos.*
3492. H *It as nowher noon, in al this world to seeke.*
3501. *storie,* E *proces.*

Lat hym unto my maister Petrak go,
That writ ynough of this, I undertake.

   Whan Onėdake was deed she myghtily
The regnės heeld, and with hire proprė hond
Agayn hir foos she faught so cruelly
That ther nas kyng, ne prynce, in al that
    lond   3520
That he nas glad if he that gracė fond,
That she ne wolde upon his lond werreyc.
With hire they maden alliance by bond
To been in pees, and lete hire ride and
    pleye.

   The emperour of Romė, Claudius,
Ne hym bifore, the Romayn Galien,
Ne dorstė never been so corageous
Ne noon Ermyn, ne noon Egipcien,
Ne Surrien, ne noon Arabyen,
Withinne the feelde that dorstė with hire
    fighte   3530
Lest that she wolde hem with hir handės
    slen,
Or with hir meignee putten hem to flighte.

   In kyngės habit wente hir sonės two,
As heirės of hir fadrės regnės alle,
And Hermanno and Thymalao
Hir namės were, as Persiens hem calle ;
But ay Fortune hath in hire hony galle :
This myghty queenė may no while endure.
Fortune out of hir regnė made hire falle
To wrecchednesse and to mysáventure.

   Aurelian, whan that the governaunce
Of Romė cam into his handės tweye,
He shoope upon this queene to doon
    vengeaunce ;
And with his legions he took his weye
Toward Cenobie, and, shortly for to seye,
He made hire flee and attė last hire hente,
And fettred hire, and eek hire children
    tweye,
And wan the land, and hoom to Rome
    he wente.

   Amongės othere thyngės that he wan
Hir chaar, that was with gold wroght and
    perree,   3550
This gretė Romayn, this Aurelian,
Hath with hym lad, for that men sholde
    it see.
Biforen his triúmphė walketh shee
With gilté cheynės on hire nekke hangynge.
Corónėd was she after hir degree,
And ful of perree chargėd hire clothynge.

   Allas, Fortune ! she that whilom was
Dredeful to kyngės and to emperoures,
Now gaureth al the peple on hire, allas !
And she that helmėd was in starkė
    stoures,   3560
And wan by forcė townės stronge, and
    toures,
Shal on hir heed now were a vitremyte ;
And she that bar the ceptre ful of floures
Shal bere a distaf, hire costės for to quyte.

   O noble, o worthy PETRO, gloric of
    Spayne,
Whom Fortune heeld so hye in magestee,
Wel oghten men thy pitous deeth com-
    playne !
Out of thy land thy brother made thee flee,
And after, at a scege, by subtiltee,   3569
Thou were bitraysed and lad unto his tente,
Where-as he with his owene hand slow
    thee,
Succedynge in thy regne and in thy rente.

   The feeld of snow with thegle of blak
    therinne
Caught with the lymerod coloured as the
    gleede,
He brew this cursednesse and al this synne.

3565. *Petro,* Pedro the Cruel, killed by his brother Henry in 1369. In E, Heng. and Camb. this and the three other modern instances come at the end after *Crœsus,* but wrongly as the Host's talk shows.
3568. H⁴ read *Thy bastard brother made the to fle.*
3572. *regne,* H *lond.*
3573. Du Guesclin's arms were a black eagle on a silver shield, with a bend gules (the lymerod, or lime twig, coloured like a red coal). Wickednest is Sir Oliver de Mauny (mal-ni) of Brittany. The two trapped Pedro to the fatal meeting. The epithet Genylon refers to the Breton traitor who betrayed Roland.

3515. *Petrak, i.e.* Boccaccio, who, however, is never mentioned by Chaucer, for what reason is not clear.
3519. *so cruelly,* H *ful trewely,* Corp.³ *trewely.*
3520. *Ermyn,* Armenian.

The 'wikked-nest' was werker of this nede,
Noght Charlés-Olyvver, that took ay heede
Of trouthe and honour, but of Armorike
Genylon-Olyver, corrupt for meede,   3579
Broghté this worthy kyng in swiche a brike.

O worthy PETRO, kyng of Cipre also,
That Alisandre wan by heigh maistrie,
Ful many a hethen wroghtéstow ful wo,
Of which thyne owené ligés hadde envie,
And for no thyng but for thy chivalrie
They in thy bed han slayn thee by the
    morwe.
Thus kan Fortúne hir wheel governe and
    gye,
And out of joyé bryngé men to sorwe.

Of Melan, greté BARNABO VISCOUNTE,
God of delit, and scourge of Lumbardye,
Why sholde I nat thyn infortune acounte,
Sith in estaat thow cloumbé were so hye ?
Thy brother sone, that was thy double
    allye,
For he thy nevew was, and sone-in-lawe,
Withinne his prisoun madé thee to dye,—
But why, ne how, noot I that thou were
    slawe.

Of the erl HUGELYN OF PYZÉ the
    langour
Ther may no tongé tellé for pitee ;
But litel out of Pizé stant a tour,   3599
In whiché tour in prisoun put was he,
And with hym been his litel children thre ;
The eldeste scarsly fyf yeer was of age.
Allas, Fortúne ! it was greet crueltee
Swiche briddés for to putte in swiche a
    cage !

Dampnéd was he to dyen in that prisoun,
For Roger, which that bisshope was of Pize,

Hadde on hym maad a fals suggestioun
Thurgh which the peplé gan upon hym rise
And putten hym to prisoun, in swich wise
As ye han herd, and mete and drynke he
    hadde   3610
So smal, that wel unnethe it may suffise,
And therwithal it was ful poure and badde.

And on a day bifil that in that hour
Whan that his meté wont was to be broght,
The gayler shette the dorés of the tour.
He herde it wel, but he ne spak right
    noght,
And in his herte anon ther fil a thoght
That they for hunger woldé doon hym
    dyen.
'Allas !' quod he, 'allas, that I was
    wroght !'   3619
Therwith the teeris fillen from his eyen.

His yongé sone, that thre yeer was of age,
Unto hym seyde, 'Fader, why do ye wepe ?
Whanne wol the gayler bryngen oure
    potage ;
Is ther no morsel breed that ye do kepe ?
I am so hungry that I may nat slepe ;
Now woldé God that I myghte slepen
    evere !
Thanne sholde nat hunger in my wombé
    crepe ;
Ther is no thyng, but breed, that me were
    levere.'

Thus day by day this child bigan to crye,
Til in his fadrés barm adoun it lay,   3630
And seydé, ' Farewel, fader, I moot dye !'
And kiste his fader, and dyde the same
    day ;
And whan the woful fader deed it say,
For wo his armés two he gan to byte,
And seyde, 'Allas, Fortúne ! and weyl-
    away !
Thy falsé wheel my wo al may I wyte !'

His children wende that it for hunger was
That he his armés gnow, and nat for wo,
And seydé, ' Fader, do nat so, allas !
But rather ete the flessh upon us two ;
Oure flessh thou yaf us, take oure flessh
    us fro,   3641

3581. *Petro, kyng of Cipre*, Pierre de Lusignan, assassinated 1369.
3582. *Alisandre wan*, in 1365.
3589. *Barnabo*, Barnabo Visconti, deposed by his nephew, died in prison 1385.
3597. *Hugelyn of Pyze*, Ugolino of Pisa, starved to death in 1289. See Dante, *Inferno*, xxxiii., from which Chaucer has borrowed.
3601. *thre*, Dante says four.
3602. *scarsly fyf yeer*, a touch added by Chaucer.
3606. *Roger*, Ruggieri degli Ubaldini.

And ete ynogh,'—right thus they to
    hym seyde,
And after that, withinne a day or two,
They leyde hem in his lappe adoun and
    deyde.

Hymself, despeirèd, eek for hunger starf;
Thus ended is this myghty erl of Pize;
From heigh estaat Fortune awey hym carf.
Of this tragédie it oghte ynough suffise.
Whoso wol here it in a lenger wise,
Redeth the gretè poete of Ytaille   3650
That hightè Dant, for he kan al devyse
Fro point to point,—nat o word wol he
    faille.

Although that NERO were as vicious
As any feend that lith in helle adoun,
Yet he, as telleth us Swetonius,
This wydè world hadde in subjeccioun
Bothe est and west, north and septem-
    trioun;
Of rubies, saphires, and of peerlès white,
Were alle hise clothès brouded up and
    doon;
For he in gemmès greetly gan delite.   3660

Moore delicaat, moore pompous of array,
Moore proud, was never emperour than he;
That ilkè clooth that he hadde wered o day,
After that tyme he nolde it never see.
Nettès of gold threed hadde he greet plentee
To fisshe in Tybrè, whan hym listè pleye.
His lustès were al lawe in his decree,
For Fortune, as his freend, hym wolde
    obeye.

He Romè brende for his delicasie;
The senatours he slow upon a day,   3670
To heerè how men woldè wepe and crie;
And slow his brother, and by his suster lay.
His mooder made he in pitous array,
For he hire wombè slittè, to biholde
Where he conceyvèd was; so weilaway!
That he so litel of his mooder tolde.

No teere out of his eyen for that sighte
Ne cam, but seyde, 'A fair womman
    was she!'
Greet wonder is how that he koude or
    myghte
Be domèsman of hire dede beautee;   3680
The wyn to bryngen hym comanded he,
And drank anon,—noon oother wo he
    made.
Whan myght is joynèd unto crueltee,
Allas, to depè wol the venym wade!

In yowthe a maister hadde this emper-
    our,
To teche hym letterure and curteisye,—
For of moralitee he was the flour,
As in his tymè, but if bookès lye;
And whil this maister hadde of hym
    maistrye,   3689
He makèd hym so konnyng and so sowple,
That longè tyme it was er tirannye,
Or any vicè, dorste on hym uncowple.

This Seneca, of which that I devyse,
By-cause that Nero hadde of hym swich
    drede,
For he fro vices wolde hym ay chastise
Discreetly, as by word, and nat by dede;
'Sire,' wolde he seyn, 'an emperour
    moot nede
Be vertuous and hatè tirannye';
For which he in a bath made hym to blede
On bothe his armès, til he mostè dye.   3700

This Nero hadde eek of acustumaunce
In youthe agayns his maister for to ryse,
Which afterward hym thoughte a greet
    grevaunce;
Therfore he made hym dyen in this wise;
But nathèlees this Seneca the wise
Chees in a bath to dye in this manere
Rather than han another tormentise;
And thus hath Nero slayn his maister deere.

Now fil it so that Fortune liste no lenger
The hyè pryde of Nero to cherice,   3710
For though he werè strong, yet was she
    strenger;

3654. *in helle*, H⁶ *ful lowe.*
3655. *Swetonius.* Chaucer is more indebted
to the *Roman de la Rose* and to Boethius, *De
Cons.* lib. 2, met. 6.
3657. *north*, Chaucer's slip for *south*; Corp.³
om.

3680. Taken verbatim from Chaucer's version
of Boethius.

She thoughtė thus : 'By God, I am to nyce,
To sette a man that is fulfild of vice
In heigh degree, and emperour hym calle.
By God ! out of his sete I wol hym trice ;
Whan he leest weneth sonest shal he falle!'

The peplė roos upon hym on a nyght
For his defaute, and whan he it espied,
Out of his dores anon he hath hym dight
Allone, and, ther he wende han ben allied,
He knokkėd faste, and ay the moore he
cried   3721
The fastere shettė they the dorės alle ;
Tho wiste he weel he hadde hymself
mysgyed,
And wente his wey, no lenger dorste he
calle.

The peplė cride and rombled up and doun,
That with his erys herde he how they seyde,
' Where is this falsė tiraunt, this Neroun?'
For fere almoost out of his wit he breyde,
And to his goddės pitously he preyde
For socour, but it myghtė nat bityde.
For drede of this, hym thoughtė that he
deyde,   3731
And ran into a garden hym to hyde ;

And in this gardyn foond he cherlės tweye
That seten by a fyr, greet and reed ;
And to thise cherlės two he gan to preye
To sleen hym, and to girden of his heed,
That to his body, whan that he were deed,
Were no despit y-doon for his defame.
Hymself he slow, he koude no bettre reed,
Of which Fortúnė lough, and hadde a
game.   3740

Was never capitayn under a kyng
That regnės mo putte in subjeccioun,
Ne strenger was in feeld of allė thyng,
As in his tyme, ne gretter of renoun,
Ne moore pompous in heigh presumpcioun,
Than OLOFERNE, which that Fortune ay
kiste
So likerously, and ladde hym up and doun,
Till that his heed was of, er that he wiste.

Nat oonly that this world haddehym in awe
For lesynge of richesse or libértee,   3750
But he made every man reneyen his lawe.
' Nabugodonosor was god,' seyde hee,
' Noon oother god[ne] sholde adourėd bee.'
Agayns his heestė no wight dorst trespace
Save in Bethulia, a strong citee
Where Eliachim a preest was of that place.

But taak kepe of the deeth of Oloferne :
Amydde his hoost he dronkė lay a nyght,
Withinne his tentė, large as is a berne,
And yet, for al his pompe and al his myght,
Judith, a womman, as he lay upright 3761
Slepynge, his heed of smoot, and from
his tente
Ful pryvėly she stal from every wight,
And with his heed unto hir toun she wente.

What nedeth it of kyng ANTHIOCHUS
To telle his hyė roial magestee,
His hyė pride, his werkės venymus ?
For swich another was ther noon as he.
Redė which that he was in Machabee,
And rede the proudė wordės that he seyde,
And why he fil fro heigh prosperitee,
And in an hill how wreechedly he deyde.

Fortune hym haddė enhauncėd so in pride
That verraily he wende he myghte attayne
Unto the sterrės upon every syde ;
And in balancė weyen ech montayne ;
And alle the floodės of the see restraynė ;
And Goddės peplė hadde he moost in hate ;
Hem wolde he sleen in torment and in
payne,
Wenynge that God ne myghte his pride
abate.   3780

And for that Nichanore and Thymothee,
Of Jewės weren venquysshed myghtily,
Unto the Jewės swich an hate hadde he
That he bad greithen his chaar ful hastily,
And swoor, and seydė ful despitously
Unto Jerusalem he wolde eftsoone,
To wreke his ire on it ful cruelly ;
But of his purpos he was let ful soone.

3723. E and Heng. have the same line as in
3731 in place of this.
3746. *Olofernė*, Holofernes.

3749. *hym in*, H4 *of him.*
3752. *Nabugodonosor*, Nebuchadnezzar.
3752. *god*, H4 *lord.*
3753. *adourėd*, H4 *honoured.*
3769, 70. *Rede*, H4 *Redeth.*
3769. *Machabee*, Bk. ii. chap. 9.

God for his manace hym so soorè smoot
With invisíble wounde, ay incuráble, 3790
That in his guttès carf it so and boot,
Thát his peynès weren importable ;
And certeinly the wreche was resonable,
For many a mannès guttes dide he peyne ;
But from his purpos cursèd and dampnable
For all his smert he wolde hym nat
    restreyne ;

But bad anon apparaillen his hoost,—
And, sodeynly, er he was of it war,
God daunted al his pride and all his boost ;
For he so soorè fil out of his char,   3800
That it his lemès and his skyn to-tar,
So that he neyther myghtè go ne ryde,
But in a chayer men aboute hym bar
Ál for-brusèd, bothè bak and sydc.

The wreche of God hym smoot so cruelly,
That thurgh his body wikked wormès
    crepte,
And therwithal he stank so horriblely
That noon of al his meynee that hym kepte,
Wheither so he awook or ellis slepte, 3809
Ne myghtè noght for stynk of hym endure,
In this meschief he wayled and eek wepte,
And knew God lord of every creäture.

To all his hoost and to hym self also
Ful wlatsom was the stynk of his careyne ;
No man ne myghtè hym berè to ne fro ;
And in this stynk and this horríble peyne,
He starf ful wrecchedly in a monteyne.
Thus hath this robbour and this homycide,
That many a man madè to wepe and
    pleyne,   3819
Swich gerdoun as bilongeth unto pryde.

    The storie of ALISAUNDRE is so com-
      mune,
That every wight that hath discrecioun
Hath herd somwhat or al of his fortune.
This wydè world, as in conclusioun,
He wan by strengthe, or for his hye renoun
They weren glad for pees unto hym sende.
The pride of man and beest he leyde
    adoun,
Wher so he cam, unto the worldès ende.

Comparisoun myghte never yet been
    maked
Bitwixe hym and another conquerour ;
For al this world for drede of hym hath
    quaked.   3831
He was of knighthod and of fredom flour ;
Fortune hym made the heir of hire honour ;
Save wyn and wommen no thyng mighte
    aswage
His hye entente in armès and labour,
So was he ful of leonyn corage.

What preys were it to hym though I yow
    tolde
Of Dárius, and añ hundred thousand mo,
Of kyngès, princes, erlès, dukès bolde,
Whiche he conquered and broghte hem
    into wo ?   3840
I seye, as fer as man may ryde or go,
The world was his,—what sholde I moore
    devyse ?
For though I writ or tolde yow evermo
Of his knyghthode, it myghtè nat suffise.

Twelf yeer he regnèd, as seith Machabee.
Philippès sone of Macidoyne he was,
That first was kyng in Grecè the contree.
    O worthy, gentil Alisandre, allas !
That ever sholdè fallen swich a cas !
Empoysoned of thyn owenè folk thou
    weere ;   3850
Thy *sys* Fortune hath turned into *aas*,
And yet for thee ne weep she never a
    teere !

Who shal me yeven teeris to compleyne
The deeth of gentillesse and of franchise,
That al the world weelded in his demeyne ?
And yet hym thoughte it myghtè nat
    suffise,
So ful was his coráge of heigh emprise.
Allas ! who shal me helpè to endite
Falsè Fortúne, and poyson to despise,
The whichè two of al this wo I wyte ?

    By wisedom, manhede, and by greet
      labour   3861
From humble bed to roial magestee
Up roos he, JULIUS the conquerour,

3862. *humble bed*, Corp.³ *humblehede.*

That wan al thoccident, by land and see,
By strengthe of hand, or elles by tretee,
And unto Romè made hem tributarie ;
And sitthe of Rome the emperour was he
Til that Fortunè weex his adversarie.

O myghty Cesar ! that in Thessalie
Agayn Pompëus, fader thyn in lawe, 3870
That of the orient hadde all the chivalrie
As fer as that the day bigynneth dawe,
Thou thurgh thy knyghthod hast hem
    take and slawe,
Save fewè folk that with Pompëus fledde,
Thurgh which thou puttest al thorient in
    awe,—
Thankè Fortúnè, that so wel thee spedde !

But now a litel while I wol biwaille
This Pompëus, this noble governour
Of Romè, which that fleigh at this
    bataille.   3879
I seye, oon of his men, a fals traitour,
His heed of smoot, to wynnen hym favour
Of Julius, and hym the heed he broghte.
Allas, Pompeye, of thorient conquerour,
That Fortune unto swich a fyn thee
    broghte !

To Rome agayn repaireth Julius
With his triúmphè, lauriat ful hye ;
But on a tyme Brutus and Cassius,
That ever hadde of his hye estaat envye,
Ful privèly had maad conspiracye
Agayns this Julius in subtil wise,   3890
And caste the place in which he sholdè dye
With boydèkyns, as I shal yow devyse.

This Julius to the Capitolie wente
Upon a day, as he was wont to goon,
And in the Capitolie anon hym hente
This falsè Brutus, and his otherè foon,
And stikèd hym with boydèkyns anoon
With many a wounde, and thus they lete
    hym lye ;
But never gronte he at no strook but oon,
Or elles at two, but if his storie lye.   3900

So manly was this Julius of herte,
And so wel lovede estaatly honestee,

That though his deedly woundès soorè
    smerte,
His mantel over his hypès casteth he
For no man sholdè seen his privetee ;
And as he lay of diyng in a traunce,
And wistè verraily that deed was hee,
Of honestee yet hadde he remembrraunce.

Lucan, to thee this storie I recomende,
And to Swetoun, and to Valerius also,
That of this storie writen ord and ende,
How that to thise grete conqueróurès two
Fortúnè was first freend and sitthè foo.
No man ne truste upon hire favour longe,
But have hire in awayt for ever-moo ;
Witnesse on alle thise conqueróurès
    strongc.

This richè CRESUS, whilom kyng of
    Lyde,
Of whichè Cresus Cirus soore hym dradde,
Yet was he caught amyddès al his pryde
And to be brent men to the fyr hym ladde ;
But swich a reyn doun fro the welkne
    shadde,   3921
That slow the fyr and made hym to escape ;
But to be war, no gracè yet he hadde,
Til Fortune on the galwès made hym gape.

Whanne he escapèd was he kan nat stente
For to bigynne a newè werre agayn.
He wendè wel, for that Fortune hym sente
Swich hape that he escapèd thurgh the rayn,
That of his foos he myghtè nat be slayn ;
And eek a swevene upon a nyght he mette,
Of which he was so proud, and eek so fayn,
That in vengeance he al his hertè sette.

Upon a tree he was, as that hym thoughte,
Ther Juppiter hym wesshe, bothe bak
    and syde,
And Phebus eek a fair towaille hym
    broughte
To dryen hym with, and therfore wex
    his pryde ;

3910. *Valerius, i.e.* Valerius Maximus.
3911. *ord,* beginning ; Dr. Hickes' correction
for the *word* of the MSS.
3920. *And to be brent,* etc., cp. Boethius, *De
Consolatione,* Bk. ii. prose 2 ; H reads : *And to
the fuyr to brenne him men him ladde.*
3921. *welkne,* H *h-ven.*

3866. *tributarie,* H *contributarie.*

130

And to his doghter, that stood hym bisyde,
Which that he knew in heigh science
    habounde,
He bad hire telle hym what it signyfyde,
And she his dreem bigan right thus ex-
    pounde :   3940

'The tree,' quod she, 'the galwès is to
    meene ;
And Juppiter bitokneth snow and reyn,
And Phebus with his towaillè so clene,
Tho been the sonnè-bemès for to seyn ;
Thou shalt anhangèd be, fader, certeyn,—
Reyn shal thee wasshe and sonnè shal
    thee drye';
Thus warnèd she hym ful plat and ful
    pleyn,
His doghter which that called was Phanye.

An-hanged was Cresus, the proudè kyng ;
His roial tronè myghte hym nat availle.
    Tragédie is noon oother maner thyng ;
Ne kan in syngyng criè ne biwaille
But for that Fortune alwey wole assaille
With unwar strook the regnès that been
    proude ;
For whan men trusteth hire, thanne wol
    she faille,
And coverè hire brighte facè with a
    clowde—

*The Knight and the Host complain of
this Tale*

'Hoo !' quod the Knyght, 'good sire,
    namoore of this !
That ye han seyd is right ynough, y-wis,
And muchel moore ; for litel hevynesse
Is right ynough to muchè folk, I gesse.
I seye for me it is a greet disese,   3961
Where as men han been in greet welthe
    and ese,
To heeren of hire sodeyn fal, allas !
And the contrarie is joye and greet solas,
As whan a man hath ben in pourè estaat,
And clymbeth up, and wexeth fortunat,
And there abideth in prosperitee ;

Swich thyng is gladsom, as it thynketh
    me,
And of swich thyng were goodly for to
    telle.'
    'Ye,' quod oure Hoost, 'by Seintè
      Poulès belle !   3970
Ye seye right sooth ; this Monk he
    clappeth lowde ;
He spak how "Fortune covered with a
    clowde"
I noot never what, and als of a "tragédie"
Right now ye herde, and, *pardee*, no
    remédie
It is for to biwaillè, ne compleyne
That that is doon ; and als, it is a peyne,
As ye han seyd, to heere of hevynesse.
Sire Monk, namoore of this, so God yow
    blesse !
Youre tale anoyeth all this compaignye ;
Swich talkyng is nat worth a boterflye,
For therinne is ther no desport ne game.
Wherfore, sire Monk, or daun Piers by
    youre name,
I pray yow hertely, telle us somwhat elles,
For sikerly nere clynkyng of youre belles,
That on youre bridel hange on every
    syde,
By hevene kyng, that for us allè dyde !
I sholde er this han fallen doun for sleepe,
Althogh the slough had never been so
    deepe ;
Thanne hadde youre tale al be toold in
    veyn,   3989
For certeinly, as that thise clerkès seyn,
Where as a man may have noon audience,
Noght helpeth it to tellen his sentence ;
And wel I woot the substance is in
    me,
If any thyng shal wel reported be.
Sir, sey somwhat of huntyng, I yow preye.'
    'Nay !' quod this Monk, 'I have no
    lust to pleye ;
Now lat another telle, as I have toold.'
    Thanne spak oure Hoost with rudè
    speche and boold,
And seydè unto the Nonnès Preest anon,
'Com neer, thou preest, com hyder,
    thou sir John.   4000

3944. *sonnè-bemes*, H⁶ *sonne-stremes.*
3954. *With unwar strook.* The phrase is from
Boethius.

3972. *covered*, H *was clipped.*
3984. *clynkyng*, H *gingling.*

Telle us swich thyng as may oure hertės
    glade ;
Be blithė, though thou ryde upon a jade.
What thogh thyn hors be bothė foule
    and lene ?
If he wol serve thee, rekkė nat a bene ;
Looke that thyn herte be murie evermo.'
    ' Yis, sir,' quod he, ' yis, Hoost, so
      moot I go,
But I be myrie, y-wis I wol be blamed.'
And right anon his tale he hath attamed,
And thus he seyde unto us everichon,
This sweetė preest, this goodly man, sir
    John.   4010

NUN'S PRIEST'S TALE

*Heere bigynneth The Nonnes Preestes
Tale of the Cok and Hen,—Chauntecleer and Pertelote*

A poure wydwė, somdel stape in age,
Was whilom dwellyng in a narwe cotage
Beside a grevė, stondynge in a dale.
This wydwe, of which I tellė yow my
    tale,
Syn thilkė day that she was last a wyf,
In paci'ence ladde a ful symple lyf,
For litel was hir catel and hir rente.
By housbondrie of swich as God hire sente
She foond hirself, and eek hire doghtren
    two.   4019
Thre largė sowės hadde she, and namo ;
Three keen and eek a sheep that hightė
    Malle.
Ful sooty was hir bour, and eek hire halle,
In which she eet ful many a sklendre meel ;
Of poynaunt sauce hir neded never a deel.
No deyntee morsel passėd thurgh hir
    throte,
Hir diete was accordant to hir cote ;
Repleccioun ne made hire never sik,
Attempree diete was al hir phisik,
And exercise, and hertės suffisaunce.
The goutė lette hire no-thyng for to
    daunce,   4030
Napoplexïe shentė nat hir heed ;

The Nonnes Preestes Tale. A fable of Marie
de France, *Dou Coc et dou Werpil*, contains in
38 lines the germ of this tale.

No wyn ne drank she, neither whit ne
    reed ;
Hir bord was servėd moost with whit
    and blak,—
Milk and broun breed,— in which she
    foond no lak ;
Seynd bacoun and somtyme an ey or tweye,
For she was, as it were, a maner deye.
A yeerd she hadde, enclosėd al aboute
With stikkės, and a dryė dych withoute,
In which she hadde a cok, heet Chaun-
    tėcleer.   4039
In al the land of crowyng nas his peer.
His voys was murier than the murie orgon
On messė dayes that in the chirchė gon ;
Wel sikerer was his crowyng in his logge
Than is a clokke, or an abbey orlogge.
By nature knew he eche ascencioun
Of the equynoxial in thilkė toun ;
For whan degreės fiftene weren ascended,
Thanne crew he that it myghte nat been
    amended.
His coomb was redder than the fyn coral,
And batailled as it were a castel wal ; 4050
His byle was blak, and as the jeet it shoon ;
Lyk asure were his leggės and his toon ;
His naylės whiter than the lylye flour,
And lyk the burnėd gold was his colour.
    This gentil cok hadde in his gover-
      naunce
Sevene hennės for to doon al his plesaunce,
Whiche were his sustrės and his para-
    mours,
And wonder lyk to hym, as of colours ;
Of whiche the faireste hewėd on hir throte
Was clepėd faire damoysele Pertėlote. 4060
Curteys she was, discreet and debonaire,
And compaignable, and bar hyrself so
    faire
Syn thilkė day that she was seven nyght
    oold,
That trewėly she hath the herte in hoold
Of Chauntėcleer, loken in every lith ;
He loved hire so that wel was hym ther-
    with ;
But swiche a joye was it to here hem
    synge,
Whan that the brightė sonne bigan to
    sprynge,

4045. *knew he,* E² *he crew ; rest he knew.*

In sweete accord, 'My lief is faren in
    londe';   4069
For thilkė tyme, as I have understonde,
Beestės and briddės koudė speke and
    synge.
And so bifel, that in the dawėnynge,
As Chauntėcleer among his wyvės alle
Sat on his perchė, that was in the halle,
And next hym sat this fairė Pertelote,
This Chauntėcleer gan gronen in his throte,
As man that in his dreem is drecchėd
    soore.
And whan that Pertelote thus herde hym
    roore,
She was agast, and seyde, 'O hertė deere !
What eyleth yow, to grone in this manére?
Ye been a verray sleper ; fy, for shame !'
    And he answerde and seydė thus :
    ' Madame,
I pray yow that ye take it nat agrief ;
By God, me mette I was in swich meschief
Right now, that yet myn herte is soore
    afright.
Now God,' quod he, 'my swevene recche
    aright,
And kepe my body out of foul prisoun !
Me mette how that I romėd up and doun
Withinne our yeerd, wheer as I saugh a
    beest
Was lyk an hound, and wolde han maad
    areest   4090
Upon my body, and han had me deed.
His colour was bitwixė yelow and reed,
And tippėd was his tayl, and bothe his
    eeris,
With blak, unlyk the remenant of his
    heeris ;
His snowtė smal, with glowynge eyen
    tweye.
Yet of his look for feere almoost I deye ;
This causėd me my gronyng doutėlees.'
    ' Avoy !' quod she, ' fy on yow, hertė-
    lees !
Allas !' quod she, 'for by that God above !
Now han ye lost myn herte and al my love.
I kan nat love a coward, by my feith !
For certės, what so any womman seith,
We alle desiren, if it myghtė bee,

To han housbóndės hardy, wise, and free,
And secree, and no nygard, ne no fool,
Ne hym that is agast of every tool,
Nė noon avauntour, by that God above !
How dorste ye seyn, for shame, unto
    youre love
That any thyng myghte makė yow aferd ?
Have ye no mannės herte, and han a berd ?
    ' Allas ! and konne ye been agast of
    swevenys ?   4111
No thyng, God woot, but vanitee in
    swevene is.
Swevenes engendren of replecciouns,
And ofte of fume, and of complecciouns,
Whan humours been to habundant in a
    wight.
    ' Certės this dreem, which ye han
    met to-nyght,
Cometh of the greet superfluytee
Of yourė redė colera, *pardee,*
Which causeth folk to dreden in hir dremes
Of arwės, and of fyre with redė lemes, 4120
Of redė beestės, that they wol hem byte,
Of contekes and of whelpės, greet and lyte ;
Right as the humour of malencolie
Causeth ful many a man in sleepe to crie,
For feere of blakė beres, or bolės blake,
Or ellės blakė develes wole hem take.
Of othere humours koude I telle also
That werken many a man in sleepe ful wo ;
But I wol passe as lightly as I kan.
Lo, Catoun, which that was so wys a man,
Seyde he nat thus, "Ne do no fors of
    dremes " ?
    ' Now, sire,' quod she, ' whan we flee
    fro the bemes,
For Goddės love, as taak som laxatyf.
Up peril of my soule, and of my lyf,
I conseille yow the beste, I wol nat lye,
That bothe of colere and of malencolye
Ye purgė yow, and, for ye shal nat tarie,
Though in this toun is noon apothecarie,
I shal myself to herbės techen yow
That shul been for youre hele, and for
    youre prow ;   4140
And in oure yeerd tho herbės shal I fynde,
The whiche han of hire propretee by kynde

4089. *a beest.* The description is exactly that
of a ' col-fox ' (l. 4405).

4120. *lemes,* gleams ; H *beemes.*
4121. *redė,* E *greet.*
4130. *Catoun, Dist.* ii. 32 : ' somnia ne cures.'

133

To purgé yow, bynethe and eek above.
Forget nat this, for Goddés owené love !
Ye been ful coleryk of compleccioun.
Waré the sonne in his ascencioun
Ne fynde yow nat repleet of humours
    hoote ;
And if it do, I dar wel leye a grote
That ye shul have a fevere terciane,
Or an agu, that may be youré bane.   4150
A day or two ye shul have digestyves
Of wormés, er ye take youre laxatyves
Of lawriol, centaure and fumetere,
Or elles of ellébor that groweth there,
Of katapuce or of gaitrys beryis,
Of herbe yve, growyng in oure yeerd,
    ther mery is ;
Pekke hem up right as they growe and
    ete hem yn ;
Be myrie, housbonde, for youre fader kyn !
Dredeth no dreem ; I kan sey yow
    namoore.'
  'Madame,' quod he, '*graunt mercy* of
    youre loore,   4160
But nathélees, as touchyng daun Catoun,
That hath of wysdom swich a greet renoun,
Though that he bad no dremés for to
    drede,
By God, men may in oldé bookés rede
Of many a man, moore of auctorite
Than ever Caton was, so moot I thee !
That al the revers seyn of his sentence,
And han wel founden by experience
That dremés been significaciouns
As wel of joye as tribulaciouns,   4170
That folk enduren in this lif present.
Ther nedeth make of this noon argument,
The verray preevé sheweth it in dede.
  'Oon of the gretteste auctours that
    men rede
Seith thus, that whilom two felawés wente
On pilgrimage, in a ful good entente,
And happéd so they coomen in a toun,
Wher as ther was swich congregacioun
Of peple, and eek so streit of herbergage,
That they ne founde as muche as o cotage
In which they bothé myghté loggéd bee ;
Wherfore they mosten of necessitee,

4174. *auctours.* Cicero, *De Divin.* i. 27, relates
both this and the next story.
  4181. H reads : *In which that thay might both
i-loggéd be.*

As for that nyght, departen compaignye ;
And ech of hem gooth to his hostelrye,
And took his loggyng as it woldé falle.
That oon of hem was loggéd in a stalle,
Fer in a yeerd, with oxen of the plough ;
That oother man was loggéd wel ynough,
As was his áventure, or his fortúne,   4189
That us governeth alle as in commune.
  'And so bifel that longe er it were day,
This man mette in his bed, ther as he lay,
How that his felawe gan upon hym calle,
And seyde, "Allas ! for in an oxes stalle
This nyght I shal be mordred ther I lye ;
Now helpe me, deeré brother, or I dye ;
In allé hasté com to me !" he seyde.
  'This man out of his sleepe for feere
    abrayde ;
But whan that he was wakened of his
    sleepe,   4199
He turnéd hym and took of this no keepe ;
Hym thoughte his dreem nas but a vanitee.
Thus twiés in his slepyng dremed hee,
And atté thriddé tyme yet his felawe
Cam, as hym thoughte, and seide, "I am
    now slawe !
Bihoold my bloody woundés, depe and
    wyde ;
Arys up erly in the morwé tyde,
And at the west gate of the toun," quod he,
"A carté ful of donge ther shaltow se,
In which my body is hid ful privély ;
Do thilké carte arresten boldély ;   4210
My gold causéd my mordré, sooth to sayn."
And tolde hym every point how he was
    slayn,
With a ful pitous facé, pale of hewe ;
And trusté wel, his dreem he foond ful
    trewe ;
For on the morwe, as soone as it was day,
To his felawés in he took the way,
And whan that he cam to this oxes stalle,
After his felawe he bigan to calle.
  'The hostiler answerdé hym anon   4219
And seydé, "Sire, your felawe is agon ;
As soone as day he wente out of the toun."
  'This man gan fallen in suspecioun,—
Remembrynge on his dremés, that he
    mette,—
And forth he gooth, no lenger wolde he
    lette,

Unto the west gate of the toun, and fond
A dong carte, as it were to dongé lond,
That was arrayéd in that samé wise
As ye han herd the dedé man devyse ;
And with an hardy herte he gan to crye
Vengeance and justice of this felonye. 4230
" My felawe mordred is this samé nyght,
And in this carte he lith gapyng upright.
I crye out on the ministres," quod he,
" That sholden kepe and reulen this citee ;
Harrow ! allas ! heere lith my felawe
    slayn ! "
What sholde I moore unto this talé sayn ?
The peple out sterte and caste the cart to
    grounde,
And in the myddel of the dong they
    founde
The dedé man, that mordred was al newe.
   ' O blisful God, that art so just and
    trewe !   4240
Lo, how that thou biwreyest mordre alway !
Mordré wol out, that se we day by day ;
Mordre is so wlatsom, and abhomynable
To God, that is so just and resonable,
That he ne wol nat suffre it heléd be,
Though it abyde a yeer, or two, or thre ;
Mordré wol out, this my conclusioun.
And right anon, ministres of that toun
Han hent the carter, and so soore hym
    pyned,   4249
And eek the hostiler so soore engyned,
That they biknewe hire wikkednesse anon,
And were an-hanged by the nekké bon.
   ' Heere may men seen that dremés
    been to drede ;
And certés, in the samé book I rede,
Right in the nexté chapitre after this,—
I gabbé nat, so have I joye or blis,—
Two men that wolde han passéd over
    see,
For certeyn cause, into a fer contree,
If that the wynd ne haddé been contrarie,
That made hem in a citee for to tarie   4260
That stood ful myrie upon an haven syde ;
But on a day, agayn the even-tyde,
The wynd gan chaunge, and blew right
    as hem leste.
Jolif and glad they wente unto hir reste,
And casten hem ful erly for to saille.

' But to that o man fil a greet mer-
    vaille ;
That oon of hem in slepyng as he lay,
Hym mette a wonder dreem, agayn the
    day :
Him thoughte a man stood by his beddés
    syde   4269
And hym comanded that he sholde abyde,
And seyde hym thus : " If thou tomorwé
    wende,
Thou shalt be dreynt, my tale is at an
    ende."
   ' He wook, and tolde his felawe what
    he mette,
And preydé hym his viage for to lette ;
As for that day, he preydé hym to byde.
His felawe, that lay by his beddés syde,
Gan for to laughe, and scornéd him ful
    faste ;
" No dreem," quod he, " may so myn
    herte agaste,
That I wol letté for to do my thynges ;
I setté not a straw by thy dremynges, 4280
For swevenes been but vanytees and
    japes ;
Men dreme al day of owlés or of apes,
And eke of many a mazé therwithal ;
Men dreme of thyng that never was ne
    shal ;
But sith I see that thou wolt heere abyde,
And thus forslewthen wilfully thy tyde,
God woot it reweth me, and have good
    day ! "
And thus he took his leve, and wente his
    way ;
But er that he hadde half his cours
    y-seyled,
Noot I nat why, ne what myschaunce it
    eyled,   4290
But casuelly the shippés botmé rente,
And shipe and man under the water
    wente
In sighte of othere shippés it bisyde,
That with hem seyléd at the samé tyde !
And therfore, fairé Pertélote so deere,
By swiche ensamplés olde yet maistow
    leere,
That no man sholdé been to recchelees
Of dremés, for I seye thee doutélees,

That many a dreem ful soore is for to
    drede.   4299
  ' Lo, in the lyf of Seint Kenelm I rede,
That was Kenulphus sone, the noble kyng
Of Mercenrike, how Kenelm mette a
    thyng.
A lite er he was mordred, on a day
His mordre in his avysioun he say.
His norice hym expownèd every deel
His swevene, and bad hym for to kepe
    hym weel
For traisoun; but he nas but seven yeer
    oold,
And therfore litel talè hath he toold
Of any dreem, so hooly was his herte.
By God, I haddè levere than my sherte
That ye hadde rad his legende as have I.
Dame Pertèlote, I sey yow trewèly,
Macrobeus, that writ the avisioun
In Affrike of the worthy Cipioun,
Affermeth dremes, and seïth that they
    been
Warnynge of thyngès that men after seen;
And forther-moore, I pray yow looketh wel
In the Oldè Testament of Daniel,
If he heeld dremès any vanitee.
  ' Reed eek of Joseph, and ther shul
    ye see   4320
Wher dremès be somtyme,—I sey nat
    alle,—
Warnynge of thyngès that shul after falle.
Looke of Egipte the kyng, daun Pharao,
His baker and his butiller also,
Wher they ne feltè noon effect in dremes.
Whoso wol seken actes of sondry remes
May rede of dremès many a wonder thyng.
  ' Lo, Cresus, which that was of Lydè
    kyng,
Mette he nat that he sat upon a tree,
Which signified he sholde anhanged bee?
  ' Lo heere Andromacha, Ectorès wyf,
That day that Ector sholdè lese his lyf,
She dremèd on the samè nyght biforn,
How that the lyf of Ector sholde be lorne,
If thilkè day he wente into bataille;
She warnèd hym, but it myghte nat
    availle;
He wentè forth to fightè nathèles,

And he was slayn anon of Achilles;
But thilkè tale is al to longe to telle,
And eek it is ny day, I may nat dwelle;
Shortly I seye, as for conclusioun,   4341
That I shal han of this avisioun
Adversitee; and I seye forthermoor,
That I ne telle of laxatyves no stoor,
For they been venymès, I woot it weel;
I hem diffye, I love hem never a deel!
  ' Now let us speke of myrthe, and
    stynte al this;
Madamè Pertèlote, so have I blis,
Of o thyng God hath sent me largè grace;
For whan I se the beautee of yourè face,
Ye been so scarlet reed aboute youre
    eyen,   4351
It maketh al my dredè for to dyen,
For, al-so siker as *In principio*,
Mulier est hominis confusio,—
Madame, the sentence of this Latyn is,
" Womman is mannès joye, and al his
    blis ";
For whan I feele a-nyght your softè syde,
Al be it that I may nat on yow ryde,
For that oure perche is maad so narwe,
    allas !
I am so ful of joye and of solas,   4360
That I diffyè bothè swevene and dreem ':
And with that word he fly doun fro the
    beem,
For it was day, and eke his hennès alle;
And with a chuk he gan hem for to calle,
For he hadde foundè a corn, lay in the
    yerd.
Rèal he was, he was namoore aferd,
He fethered Pertèlotè twenty tyme,
And trad as oftè, er that it was pryme.
He looketh as it were a grym leoun,
And on his toos he rometh up and doun;
Hym deignèd nat to sette his foot to
    grounde.   4371
He chukketh whan he hath a corn
    y-founde,
And to hym rennen thanne his wyvès
    alle.
Thus roial, as a prince is in an halle,
Leve I this Chauntècleer in his pasture,
And after wol I telle his àventure.

4300. *Kenelm*, murdered by his tutor at the
desire of a wicked sister.

4353. The real meaning of the Latin is : In the
beginning, woman is man's destruction.

Whan that the monthe in which the
world bigan,
That highté March, whan God first
maké man,
Was compleet, and [y-] passéd were also,
Syn March bigan, thritty dayés and two,
Bifel that Chauntécleer in al his pryde,
His sevene wyvés walkynge by his syde,
Caste up his eyen to the brighté sonne
That in the signe of Taurus hadde y-ronne
Twenty degrees and oon, and som-what
moore,
And knew by kynde, and by noon oother
loore, ·
That it was pryme, and crew with blisful
stevene.
'The sonne,' he seyde, 'is clomben up
on hevene
Fourty degrees and oon, and moore y-wis.
Madamé Pertélote, my worldés blis, 4390
Herkneth thise blisful briddés how they
synge,
And se the fresshé flourés how they
sprynge;
Ful is myn herte of revel and solas!'
But sodeynly hym fil a sorweful cas;
For ever the latter ende of joy is wo.
God woot that worldly joye is soone
ago,
And if a rethor koudé faire endite,
He in a cronycle saufly myghte it write,
As for a sovereyn notabilitee. 4399
Now every wys man, lat him herkné me;
This storie is al so trewe, I undertake,
As is the book of Launcelot de Lake,
That wommen holde in ful greet reverence.
Now wol I torne agayn to my sentence.

A colfox, ful of sly iniquitee,
That in the grove hadde wonnéd yerés
three,
By heigh ymaginacioun forn-cast,
The samé nyght thurgh-out the heggés
brast
Into the yerd, ther Chauntécleer the faire
Was wont, and eek his wyvés, to repaire;
And in a bed of wortés stille he lay, 4411

Til it was passéd undren of the day,
Waitynge his tyme on Chauntécleer to
falle;
As gladly doon thise homycidés alle
That in await liggen to mordré men.
O falsé mordrour lurkynge in thy den!
O newé Scariot, newé Genyloun!
Falsé dissymulour, O Greek Synoun,
That broghtest Troye al outrély to sorwe!
O Chauntécleer, acurséd be that morwe,
That thou into that yerd flaugh fro the
bemes! 4421
Thou were ful wel y-warnéd by thy dremés
That thilké day was perilous to thee;
But what that God forwoot moot nedés
bee,
After the opinioun of certein clerkis.
Witnesse on hym that any parfit clerk is,
That in scole is greet altercacioun
In this mateere, and greet disputisoun,
And hath been of an hundred thousand
men;
But I ne kan nat bulte it to the bren, 4430
As kan the hooly doctour Augustyn,
Or Boece, or the bisshope Bradwardyn,
Wheither that Goddés worthy forwityng
Streyneth me nedély to doon a thyng,—
Nedély clepe I symple necessitee,—
Or ellés if free choys be graunted me
To do that samé thyng, or do it noght,
Though God forwoot it er that it was
wroght;
Or if his wityng streyneth never a deel,
But by necessitee condicioneel. 4440
I wil nat han to do of swich mateere,
My tale is of a cok, as ye may heere,
That took his conseil of his wyf with sorwe,
To walken in the yerd upon that morwe
That he hadde met that dreem that I
yow tolde.
Wommennés conseils been ful ofté colde;
Wommannés conseil broghte us first to wo
And made Adam fro Paradys to go,
Ther as he was ful myrie and wel at
ese; 4449
But for I noot to whom it myght displese,

4389. *Fourty*, H *Twenty*; but perhaps Chaucer
is laughing at the cock.
4399. E and Heng. assign the saying to Petrus
Comestor.

4417. *Genyloun*, the betrayer of Roland.
4432. *Boece*, Boethius.
4432. *Bradwardyn*, author of the 'De Causa
Dei contra Pelagium,' d. 1349.

If I conseil of wommen woldė blame,
Passe over, for I seyde it in my game.
Rede auctours where they trete of swich
　　mateere,
And what they seyn of wommen ye may
　　heere ;
Thise been the cokkės wordės, and nat
　　myne,
I kan noon harm of no womman divyne !
　　Faire in the soond, to bathe hire myrily,
Lith Pertėlote, and alle hire sustres by,
Agayn the sonne, and Chauntėcleer so free
Soong murier than the mermayde in the
　　see ;　　　　　　　・　　　　4460
For *Phisiologus* seith sikerly,
How that they syngen wel and myrily.
　　And so bifel that as he cast his eye
Among the wortės, on a boterflye,
He was war of this fox that lay ful lowe.
No-thyng ne liste hym thannė for to
　　crowe,
But cride anon, ' Cok, cok ! ' and up he
　　sterte,
As man that was affrayėd in his herte, —
For natureelly a beest desireth flee
Fro his contrárie, if he may it see,　　4470
Though he never erst hadde seyn it with
　　his eye.
　　This Chauntėcleer, whan he gan hym
　　espye,
He wolde han fled, but that the fox anon
Seyde, ' Gentil sire, allas ! wher wol ye
　　gon ?
Be ye affrayed of me that am youre
　　freend ?
Now, certės, I were worsė than a feend,
If I to yow wolde harm or vileynye.
I am nat come your conseil for tespye,
But trewėly the cause of my comynge
Was oonly for to herkne how that ye
　　synge ;　　　　　　　　　　　4480
For trewėly, ye have as myrie a stevene
As any aungel hath that is in hevene.
Therwith ye han in musyk moore feelynge
Than hadde Boece, or any that kan synge.
My lord youre fader, — God his soulė
　　blesse !

4461. *Phisiologus, i.e.* the *Physiologus de
naturis xii. animalium*, written by a certain
Theobaldus.
4484. *Boece.* Boethius wrote a treatise on music.

And eek youre mooder, of hire gentillesse,
Han in myn hous y-been to my greet
　　ese,
And certės, sire, ful fayn wolde I yow
　　plese.
But for men speke of syngyng, I wol
　　seye, —
So moote I broukė wel myne eyen
　　tweye, —　　　　　　　　　　4490
Save yow, I herdė never man so synge
As dide youre fader in the morwenynge.
Certės, it was of herte, al that he song ;
And for to make his voys the moorė strong,
He wolde so peyne hym that with bothe
　　his eyen
He mostėwynke, so loude he woldė cryen ;
And stonden on his tiptoon therwithal,
And strecchė forth his nekkė, long and
　　smal ;
And eek he was of swich discrecioun
That ther nas no man in no regioun　　4500
That hym in song or wisedom myghtė
　　passe.
I have wel rad, in " Daun Burnel the
' 　　Asse,"
Among his vers, how that ther was a cok,
For that a preestės sone yaf hym a knok
Upon his leg, whil he was yong and nyce,
He made hym for to lese his benefice ;
But certeyn, ther nys no comparisoun
Bitwixe the wisedom and discrecioun
Of yourė fader and of his subtiltee.
Now syngeth, sire, for seintė charitee ;　4510
Lat se, konne ye youre fader countrefete.'
　　This Chauntėcleer his wyngės gan to
　　bete,
As man that koude his traysoun nat espie,
So was he ravysshed with his flaterie.
　　Allas, ye lordės, many a fals flatour
Is in youre courtes, and many a losengeour,
That plesen yow wel moorė, by my feith,
Than he that soothfastnesse unto yow
　　seith, —
Redeth Ecclesiaste of flaterye, —
Beth war, ye lordės, of hir trecherye.　4520
　　This Chauntėcleer stood bye upon his
　　toos

4502. *Daun Burnel the Asse*, in the *Speculum
Stultorum* of Nigel Wireker.
4515. *ye lordės*, H *lordynges*.
4516. *courtes*, H *hous*.

Strecchynge his nekke, and heeld his eyen
   cloos,
And gan to crowe loude for the nones,
And daun Russell, the fox, stirte up atones,
And by the gargat hente Chauntecleer,
And on his bak toward the wode hym
   beer ;
For yet ne was ther no man that hym
   sewed.
  O destinee, that mayst nat been
   eschewed !
Allas, that Chauntecleer fleigh fro the
   bemes !   4529
Allas, his wyf ne roghte nat of dremes !
And on a Friday fil al this meschaunce.
O Venus, that art goddesse of plesaunce,
Syn that thy servant was this Chaunte-
   cleer,
And in thy servyce dide al his poweer,
Moore for delit than world to multiplye,
Why woltestow suffre hym on thy day to
   dye ?
O Gaufred, deere maister soverayn,
That, whan thy worthy kyng Richard
   was slayn
With shot, compleynedest his deeth so
   soore !
Why ne hadde I now thy sentence, and
   thy loore,   4540
The Friday for to chide, as diden ye ?—
For on a Friday, soothly, slayn was he.
Thanne wolde I shewe yow how that I
   koude pleyne
For Chauntecleres drede, and for his
   peyne.
  Certes, swich cry, ne lamentacioun,
Was never of ladyes maad whan Ylioun
Was wonne, and Pirrus with his streite
   swerd,
Whan he hadde hent kyng Priam by the
   berd,
And slayn hym,—as seith us *Eneydos*,— 4550
As maden alle the hennes in the clos,
Whan they had seyn of Chauntecleer the
   sighte.
But sovereynly dame Pertelote shrighte,
Ful louder than dide Hasdrubales wyf,

4537. *Gaufred*, Geoffrey of Vinesauf; author
a treatise on the art of poetry, in which, to
ow how such poems should be written, he be-
wailed the death of Richard.

Whan that hir housbonde hadde lost his lyf,
And that the Romayns hadde brend
   Cartage,—
She was so ful of torment and of rage,
That wilfully into the fyr she sterte,
And brende hirselven with a stedefast
   herte.
  O woful hennes, right so criden ye,
As, whan that Nero brende the citee 4560
Of Rome, cryden senatoures wyves,
For that hir husbondes losten alle hir
   lyves
Withouten gilt,—this Nero hath hem slayn.
Now wol I torne to my tale agayn.
  This sely wydwe, and eek hir doghtres
   two,
Herden thise hennes crie and maken wo,
And out at dores stirten they anon,
And syen the fox toward the grove gon,
And bar upon his bak the cok away,
And cryden, ' Out ! harrow ! and weyl-
   away !   4570
Ha ! ha ! the fox !' and after hym they
   ran,
And eek with staves many another man ;
Ran Colle, oure dogge, and Talbot, and
   Gerland
And Malkyn, with a dystaf in hir hand ;
Ran cow and calf, and eek the verray
   hogges,
So were they fered for berkynge of the
   dogges,
And shoutyng of the men and wommen
   eek ;
They ronne so hem thoughte hir herte
   breek.
They yolleden, as feendes doon in helle ;
The dokes cryden, as men wolde hem
   quelle ;   4580
The gees, for feere, flowen over the trees ;
Out of the hyve cam the swarm of bees ;
So hydous was the noys, *a benedicitee !*
Certes, he Jakke Straw, and his meynee,
Ne made never shoutes half so shrille,
Whan that they wolden any Flemyng
   kille,
As thilke day was maad upon the fox.
Of bras they broghten bemes, and of box,

4586. *Flemyng*, to whose competition the
English craftsmen objected.

Of horn, of boon, in whiche they blewe
   and powped,
And therwithal they skrikėd and they
   howped ;   4590
It semėd as that hevene sholdė falle.
   Now, goodė men, I pray yow herkneth
   alle ;
Lo, how Fortunė turneth sodeynly
The hope and prydė eek of hir enemy !
This cok, that lay upon the foxes bak,
In al his drede unto the fox he spak,
And seyde, ' Sire, if that I were as ye,
Yet wolde I seyn, as wys God helpė me,
" Turneth agayn, ye proudė cherlės alle !
A verray pestilence upon yow falle ; 4600
Now am I come unto the wodės syde,
Maugree youre heed, the cok shal heere
   abyde ;
I wol hym ete in feith, and that anon ! " '
   The fox answerde, ' In feith it shal
   be don ';
And as he spak that word, al sodeynly
This cok brak from his mouth delyverly,
And heighe upon a tree he fleigh anon ;
And whan the fox saugh that he was
   y-gon,—
   ' Allas !' quod he, ' O Chauntėcleer,
   allas !
I have to yow,' quod he, ' y-doon trespas,
In as muchę as I makėd yow aferd, 4611
Whan I yow hente and broght out of the
   yerd ;
But, sire, I dide it of no wikke entente.
Com doun, and I shal telle yow what I
   mente ;
I shal seye sooth to yow, God help me so !'
   ' Nay thanne,' quod he, ' I shrewe
   us bothė two,
And first I shrewe myself, bothe blood
   and bones,
If thou bigyle me any ofter than ones.
Thou shalt na moorė, thurgh thy flaterye,
Do me to synge, and wynkė with myn
   eye,   4620
For he that wynketh, whan he sholdė see,
Al wilfully, God lat him never thee !'

' Nay,' quod the fox, ' but God yeve
   hym meschaunce,
That is so undiscreet of governaunce
That jangleth whan he sholdė holde his
   pees.'
   Lo, swich it is for to be recchėlees,
And necligent, and truste on flaterye.
But ye that holden this tale a folye,—
As of a fox, or of a cok and hen,—
Táketh the moralitė, good men ; 4630
For Seint Paul seith that al that writen is,
To oure doctrine it is y-write y-wis ;
Taketh the fruyt and lat the chaf be stille.
Now, goodė God, if that it be thy wille,
As seith my lord, so make us alle goodė
   men,
And brynge us to his heighė blisse !
   Amen.

Words of the Host to the Nun's Priest

' Sire Nonnės Preest,' oure Hoostė
   seide anoon,
' I-blessėd be thy breche and every stoon !
This was a murie tale of Chaunticleer ;
But, by my trouthe, if thou were seculer,
Thou woldest ben a tredėfoul aright ; 4641
For if thou have coráge, as thou hast
   might,
The werė nede of hennės, as I wene,
Ye, mo than sevene tymės seventene !
Se, which braunės hath this gentil preest,
So gret a nekke, and swich a largė breest !
He loketh as a sparhawke with his eyen :
Him nedeth nat his colour for to dyen
With brasile, ne with greyn of Portyngale.
Now, sire, faire fallė yow for yourė tale.'
And after that, he with ful merie chere
Seide unto another as ye shullen heere.

   .   .   .   .

4637. *Sire Nonnes Preest.* Only three MSS.,
one at Camb. and two at the Brit. Mus., contain
this end-link. Its authenticity is not above
suspicion ; l. 4641 repeats B. 3135, and ' seide
unto *another*' could hardly have been written by
Chaucer.

[TALES OF THE THIRD DAY]

[GROUP C]

DOCTOR'S TALE

Heere folweth The Phisiciens Tale

THER was, as telleth Titus Livius,
A knyght that callèd was Virginius,
Fulfild of honour and of worthynesse,
And strong of freendès and of greet
  richesse.
  This knyght a doghter haddè by his
  wyf,—
No children haddè he mo in al his lyf.
Fair was this mayde in excellent beautee
Aboven every wight that man may see ;
For Nature hath with sovereyn diligence
Y-formèd hire in so greet excellence, 10
As though she woldè seyn, 'Lo, I, Natúre,
Thus kan I forme, and peynte a creäture,
Whan that me list,—who kan me countre-
  fete ?
Pigmalion ? Noght, though he ay forge
  and bete,
Or grave, or peyntè ; for I dar wel seyn
Apellès, Zanzis, sholdè werche in veyn,
Outher to grave, or peynte, or forge, or
  bete,
If they presumèd me to countrefete.
For He that is the Formere principal
Hath makèd me his vicaire-general 20
To forme and peynten erthely creäturis
Right as me list, and ech thyng in my
  cure is
Under the moonè that may wane and
  waxe ;
And for my werk right no thyng wol I axe ;

GROUP C. These two tales follow the Franklin's in E.   Dr. Furnivall is responsible for their present placing, which is not a matter of certainty.
  Doctor's Tale, taken, as to its incidents, as Prof. Lounsbury shows, including the reference to Livy, from the *Roman de la Rose*, ll. 6324-94. In this tale H⁶ differ greatly from E and Heng. ; though only a few of the variants can be here recorded.
6. *No children*, H⁵ *and never ne* (H only, *ne*).
16. *Zanzis*, Zeuxi·.
24. *werk right*, H⁵ *werke*.

My lord and I been ful of oon accord.
I made hire to the worshipe of my lord ;
So do I alle myne othere creätures,
What colour that they han, or what
  figures.'
Thus semeth me that Nature woldè seye.
  This mayde of agè twelve yeer was
  and tweye 30
In which that Nature haddè swich delit ;
For, right as she kan peynte a lilie whit,
And reed a rosé, right with swich peynture
She peynted hath this noble creäture,
Er she were born, upon hir lymès fre,
Where as by right swiche colours sholdè
  be ;
And Phebus dyèd hath hire tresses grete
Lyk to the stremès of his burnèd heete ;
And if that excellent was hire beautee,
A thousand-foold moore vertuous was she.
In hire ne lakkèd no condicioun 41
That is to preyse, as by discrecioun.
As wel in goost as body chast was she,
For which she flourèd in virginitee
With alle humylitee and abstinence,
With alle attemperaunce and pacience,
With mesure eek of beryng and array.
Discreet she was in answeryng alway,
Though she were wise as Pallas, dar I
  seyn ;
Hir facound eek, ful wommanly and
  pleyn ; 50
No countrefeted termès hadde she
To semè wys ; but after hir degree
She spak, and alle hire wordès, moore
  and lesse,
Sownynge in vertu and in gentillesse ;
Shamefast she was, in maydens shame-
  fastnesse,
Constant in herte, and ever in bisynesse
To dryve hire out of ydel slogardye.
Bacus hadde of hire mouth right no
  maistrie,

25. *ful of oon*, H⁵ *fully at.*

For wyn and youthė dooth Venus
     encresse,   59
As man in fyr wol casten oille or greesse.
And of hir owene vertu unconstreyned
She hath ful oftė tymė syk hire feyned,
For that she woldė fleen the compaignye
Where likly was to treten of folye,—
As is at feestės, revels, and at dauncces,
That been occasions of daliaunces.
Swich thyngės maken children for to be
To soonė rype and boold, as men may se,
Which is ful perilous, and hath been yoore,
For al to soonė may she lernė loore   70
Of booldnesse, whan she woxen is a wyf.

    And ye maistresses, in youre oldė lyf,
That lordės doghtrės han in governaunce,
Ne taketh of my wordes no displesaunce;
Thenketh that ye been set in governynges
Of lordės doghtrės, oonly for two thynges:
Outher for ye han kept youre honestee,
Or ellės ye han falle in freletee,
And knowen wel ynough the oldė daunce,
And han forsaken fully swich meschaunce
For evermo : therfore for Cristės sake   81
To teche hem vertu looke that ye ne
     slake.

    A theef of venysoun, that hath forlaft
His likerousnesse and al his oldė craft,
Kan kepe a forest best of any man ;
Now kepeth wel, for if ye wolde ye kan ;
Looke wel that ye unto no vice assente,
Lest ye be dampnėd for youre wikke
     entente ;
For who so dooth a traitour is certeyn ;
And taketh kepe of that that I shal seyn ;
Of allė tresons sovereyn pestilence   91
Is whan a wight bitrayseth innocence.

    Ye fadrės and ye moodrės eek, also,
Though ye han children, be it oon or mo,
Youre is the charge of al hir surveiaunce,
Whil that they been under youre gover-
     naunce ;
Beth war, if by ensample of youre lyvynge,
Or by youre necligence in chastisynge,
That they ne perisse ; for I dar wel seye,
If that they doon, ye shul it deere abeye.

Under a shepherde softe and necligent
The wolf hath many a sheepe and lamb
     to-rent.
Suffiseth oon ensample now as heere,
For I moot turne agayne to my matere.

    This mayde, of which I wol this tale
     expresse,
So kepte hir self hir neded no maistresse ;
For in hir lyvyng maydens myghten rede,
As in a book, every good word or dede
That longeth to a mayden vertuous,
She was so prudent and so bounteuous ;
For which the fame out sprong on every
     syde,   111
Bothe of hir beautee and hir bountee wyde,
That thurgh that land they preisėd hire,
     echone
That lovėd vertu, save Envye allone,
That sory is of oother mennės wele,
And glad is of his sorwe and his unheele ;
The doctour maketh this descripcioun.

    This mayde upon a day wente in the
     toun
Toward a temple, with hire mooder deere,
As is of yongė maydens the manere.   120
Now was ther thanne a justice in that toun,
That governour was of that regioun,
And so bifel this juge his eyen caste
Upon this mayde, avysynge hym ful faste,
As she cam forby, ther as this juge stood.
Anon his hertė chaungėd and his mood,
So was he caught with beautee of this
     mayde,
And to hymself ful pryvėly he sayde,
'This maydė shal be myn, for any man !'
    Anon the feend into his hertė ran,   130
And taughte hym sodeynly that he by
     slyghte
The mayden to his purpos wynnė myghte ;
For certės, by no force, ne by no meede,
Hym thoughte, he was nat able for to
     speede ;
For she was strong of freendės, and eek she
Confermėd was in swich soverayn
     bountee,
That wel he wiste he myghte hire never
     wynne

74. *wordės*, H⁴ *word*.
82. H⁵ read *Kepeth wel tho that ye undertake*.
84. *oldė*, H⁵ *theves*.
86. *if ye wolde*, H⁵ *and ye wil*.
94. *mo*, E² *two*.

105. *wol*, H⁵ *telle*.
117. *The doctour*, glossed 'Augustinus' in E².
125. *as this*, H⁵ *the*.

As for to maken hire with hir body synne;
For which by greet deliberacioun
He sente after a cherl, was in the toun, 140
Which that he knew for-subtil and for-
    boold.
This juge unto this cherl his tale hath
    toold
In secree wise, and made hym to ensure
He sholdė telle it to no creäture,
And if he dide he sholdė lese his heed.
Whan that assented was this cursėd reed
Glad was this juge, and makėd him
    greet cheere,
And yaf hym yiftės, preciouse and deere.
    Whan shapen was al hire conspiracie,
Fro point to point, how that his lecherie
Parfournėd sholdė been ful subtilly, 151
As ye shul heere it after openly,
Hoom gooth the cherl, that hightė
    Claudius.
This falsė jugė that hightė Apius,—
So was his namė, for this is no fable,
But knowen for historial thyng notable;
The sentence of it sooth is, out of doute,—
This falsė jugė gooth now faste aboute
To hasten his delit al that he may;
And so bifel soone after, on a day, 160
This falsė juge, as telleth us the storie,
As he was wont, sat in his consistórie:
And yaf his doomės upon sondry cas,
This falsė cherl cam forth, a ful greet pas,
And seydė, 'Lord, if that it be youre wille,
As dooth me right upon this pitous bille,
In which I pleyne upon Virginius;
And if that he wol seyn it is nat thus,
I wol it preeve, and fyndė good witnesse
That sooth is that my billė wol expresse.'
    The juge answerde, 'Of this in his
    absence
I may nat yeve diffynytyve sentence;
Lat do hym calle, and I wol gladly heere;
Thou shalt have al right and no wrong
    heere.'
    Virginius cam to wite the juges wille,
And right anon was rad this cursėd bille;
The sentence of it was as ye shul heere:—
    To yow, my lord, sire Apius so deere,

Sheweth youre pourė servant Claudius,
How that a knyght, callėd Virginius, 180
Agayns the lawe, agayn al equitee,
Holdeth, expres agayn the wyl of me,
My servant, which that is my thral by right,
Which fro myn hous was stole upon a
    nyght,
Whil that she was ful yong; this wol I preeve
By witnesse, lord, so that it nat yow greeve.
She nys his doghter, nat, what so he seye;
Wherfore to yow, my lord, the juge, I preye,
Yeld me my thral, if that it be youre wille.
Lo, this was al the sentence of his bille.
    Virginius gan upon the cherl biholde,
But hastily, er he his talė tolde,
And wolde have preevėd it, as sholde a
    knyght,
And eek by witnessyng of many a wight,
That it was fals that seyde his adver-
    sarie,—
This cursėd jugė woldė no thyng tarie,
Ne heere a word moore of Virginius,
But yaf his juggėment, and seydė thus:—
    'I deeme anon this cherl his servant
    have; 199
Thou shalt na lenger in thyn hous hir save.
Go, bryng hire forth, and put hire in
    oure warde.
The cherl shal have his thral; this I
    awarde.'
    And whan this worthy knyght,
    Virginius,
Thurgh sentence of this justice Apius,
Mostė by force his deerė doghter yeven
Unto the juge, in lecherie to lyven,
He gooth hym hoom and sette him in his
    halle,
And leet anon his deerė doghter calle,
And with a facė deed as asshen colde,
Upon hir humble face he gan biholde, 210
With fadrės pitee stikynge thurgh his herte,
Al wolde he from his purpos nat converte.
    'Doghter,' quod he, 'Virginia by thy
    name,
Ther been two weyės, outher deeth or
    shame,
That thou most suffre; allas! that I was
    bore!
For never thou deservedest wherfore
To dyen with a swerd, or with a knyf.

138. *makėn*, H⁶ *make.*
140. *cherl*, here and passim H⁵ read *clerk*; the
Roman de la Rose has *serjant.*

O deerè doghter, endere of my lyf,
Which I have fostred up with swich
   plesaunce
That thou were never out of my remem-
   braunce ;   220
O doghter, which that art my lastè wo,
And in my lyf my lastè joye also ;
O gemme of chastitee ! in pacience
Take thou thy deeth, for this is my
   sentence.
For love, and nat for hate, thou most be
   deed :
My pitous hand moot smyten of thyn
   heed !
Allas ! that ever Apius the say !
Thus hath he falsly juggèd the to day ' ;
And tolde hire al the cas, as ye bifore
Han herd, nat nedeth for to telle it moore.
    ' O mercy, deerè fader ! ' quod this
   mayde,   231
And with that word she both hir armès
   layde
About his nekke, as she was wont to do ;
The teeris bruste out of hir eyen two,
And seydè, ' Goodè fader, shal I dye ?
Is ther no grace, is ther no remedye ? '
    ' No, certès, deerè doghter myn,' quod
   he.
    ' Thanne yif me leyser, fader myn,'
   quod she,
' My deeth for to compleyne a litel space,
For *pardee* Jeptè yaf his doghter grace 240
For to compleyne, er he hir slow, allas !
And God it woot, no thyng was hir trespas,
But for she ran hir fader first to see,
To welcome hym with greet solempnitee.'
And with that word she fil aswowne anon,
And after, whan hir swowning is agon,
She riseth up, and to hir fader sayde,
' Blissed be God, that I shal dye a mayde ;
Yif me my deeth, er that I have a shame ;
Dooth with youre child youre wyl, a
   Goddès name ! '   250
    And with that word she preyèd hym
   ful ofte
That with his swerd he woldè smytè
   softe ;
And with that word aswownè doun she fil.
Hir fader, with ful sorweful herte and wil,

238. *leyser*, H⁵ *leve.*

Hir heed of smoot, and by the tope it
   hente,
And to the juge he gan it to presente,
As he sat yet in doom in consistórie ;
And whan the juge it saugh, as seith the
   storie,
He bad to take hym and anhange hym
   faste ;   259
But right anon a thousand peple in thraste,
To save the knyght, for routhe and for
   pitee ;
For knowen was the false iniquitee.
The peple anon hath suspect of this thyng,
By manere of the cherlès chalangyng,
That it was by the assent of Apius ;
They wisten wel that he was lecherus ;
For which unto this Apius they gon,
And caste hym in a prisoun right anon,
Wher as he slow hymself ; and Claudius,
That servant was unto this Apius,   270
Was demèd for to hange upon a tree ;
But that Virginius, of his pitee,
So preydè for hym that he was exiled,
And ellès, certès, he had been bigyled.
The remenant were anhangèd, moore and
   lesse,
That were consentant of this cursednesse.
    Heere men may seen how synne hath
   his merite.
Beth war, for no man woot whom God
   wol smyte,
In no degree ; ne in which manere wyse
The worm of consciencè may agryse 280
Of wikked lyf, though it so pryvee be
That no man woot ther-of but God and
   he ;
For be he lewèd man, or ellis lered,
He noot how soone that he shal been
   afered ;
Therfore, I redè yow, this conseil take,
Forsaketh synne, er synnè yow forsake.

*The wordes of the Hoost to the Phisicien
and the Pardoner*

    Oure Hoostè gan to swere as he were
   wood ;

275. *The remenant*, the witnesses promised
in l. 186.
278. *whom*, H⁵ *how.*
283. H⁵ read *Wher (whether) that he be lewed
man or lered.*

'Harrow !' quod he, 'by naylės, and
    by blood !
This was a fals cherl and a fals justise !
As shameful deeth as hertė may devyse
Come to thise jugės, and hire advocatz !
Algate this sely mayde is slayn, allas !
Allas ! to deerė boughtė she beautee !
Wherfore I seye al day, as men may see,
That yiftės of Fortúne and of Natúre
Been cause of deeth to many a creäture.
Hire beautee was hire deth, I dar wel
    sayn ;
Allas ! so pitously as she was slayn !
Of bothė yiftės that I speke of now
Men han ful oftė moorė harm than prow.
   'But trewėly, myn owene maister
    deere,   301
This is a pitous talė for to heere ;
But nathėlees, passe over, is no fors ;
I pray to God so save thy gentil cors,
And eek thyne urynals, and thy jurdones,
Thyn Ypocras, and eek thy Galiones,
And every boyste ful of thy letuarie ;
God blesse hem, and oure lady Seintė
    Marie !
So moot I theen, thou art a proprė man,
And lyk a prelat, by Seint Ronyan !   310
Seyde I nat wel, I kan nat speke in terme ?
But wel I woot thou doost myn herte to
    erme
That I almoost have caught a cardynacle.
By *corpus* bones ! but I have triacle,
Or elles a draughte of moyste and corny
    ale,
Or but I heere anon a myrie tale,
Myn herte is lost, for pitee of this mayde.
Thou *beel amy*, thou Pardoner,' he sayde,
'Telle us som myrthe, or japės, right
    anon !'
   'It shal be doon,' quod he, 'by
    Seint Ronyon !   320
'But first,' quod he, 'heere at this alė
    stake

289. *fals cherl and;* H⁴ *cursed they.*
290. *shameful,* H² *schendful.*
291, 292. H³ have the more vigorous couplet :

    So falle upon his body and his boones,
    The devel I bykenne him, al at oones.

317. *lost,* H *brost.*
319. H reads *Tel us a tale for thou canst
many oon,* ending next line *and that anoon.*

I wol bothe drynke and eten of a cake.'
   And right anon the gentils gonne to
    crye,
'Nay ! lat hym telle us of no ribaudye ;
Telle us som moral thyng, that we may
    leere
Som wit, and thannė wol we gladly heere.'
   'I grauntė, y-wis,' quod he, 'but I
    moot thynke
Upon som honeste thyng, while that I
    drynke.'

*Heere folweth The Preamble of the
    Pardoners Tale*

   'Lordynges,' quod he, 'in chirchės
    whan I preche,
I peynė me to han an hauteyn speche,
And rynge it out as round as gooth a
    belle,   331
For I kan al by rotė that I telle.
My theme is alwey oon, and ever was,—
Radix malorum est Cupiditas.
   'First, I pronouncė whennės that I
    come,
And thanne my bullės shewe I, alle and
    some ;
Oure ligė lordės seel on my patente,
That shewe I first, my bodý to warente,
That no man be so boold, ne preest, ne
    clerk,
Me to destourbe of Cristės hooly werk ;
And, after that, thanne telle I forth my
    tales,   341
Bullės of popės and of cardynales,
Of patriarkes and bishoppės I shewe,
And in Latyn I speke a wordės fewe
To saffron with my predicacioun,
And for to stire hem to devocioun ;
Thanne shewe I forth my longė cristal
    stones
Y-crammėd ful of cloutės and of bones,—
Relikes been they, as wenen they echoon ;
Thanne have I in latoun a sholder boon

326, 327. H reads *Gladly, quod he, and sayde
as ye schal heere, But in the cuppe wil I me be-
thinke.*
328. *thyng,* H *tale.*
329. *chirches,* H³ *chirche.*
331. *as round as gooth,* H *as lowd as doth.*
345. *saffron,* H⁴ *savore.*

L   145

Which that was of an hooly Jewès sheepe.
  ' "Goode men," I seye, " taak of my
     wordès keepe,—
If that this boon be wasshe in any welle,
If cow, or calf, or sheepe, or oxè swelle
That any worm hath ete, or worm
     y-stonge,
Taak water of that welle and wassh his
     tonge,
And it is hool anon ; and forthermoor
Of pokkès, and of scabbe, and every soor,
Shal every sheepe be hool that of this
     welle
Drynketh a draughte.   Taak kepe eek
     what I telle.   360
If that the goode-man that the beestès
     oweth
Wol every wyke, er that the cok hym
     croweth,
Fastyngè, drinken of this welle a draughte,
As thilkè hooly Jew oure eldrès taughte,
His beestès and his stoor shal multiplie.
And, sires, also it heeleth jalousie,
For though a man be falle in jalous rage,
Lat maken with this water his potage,
And never shal he moore his wyf
     mystriste,
Though he the the soothe of hir defautè
     wiste,—   370
Al had she taken preestes two or thre.
Heere is a miteyn eek, that ye may se ;
He that his hand wol putte in this mitayn,
He shal have multipliyng of his grayn,
Whan he hath sowèn, be it whete or otes,
So that he offrè pens, or ellès grotes.
  ' "Goode men and wommen, o thyng
     warne I yow,
If any wight be in this chirchè now
That hath doon synnè horrible, that he
Dar nat for shame of it y-shryven be,   380
Or any womman, be she yong or old,
That hath y-maad hir housbonde cokè-
     wold,
Swich folk shal have no power ne no
     grace
To offren to my relikes in this place ;
And whoso fyndeth hym out of swich blame
They wol come up and offre on Goddès
     name,

     385. *blame,* E *fame.*

And I assoille hem by the auctoritee
Which that by bulle y-graunted was to
     me."
  ' By this gaude have I wonnè, yeer
     by yeer,
An hundred mark sith I was Pardoner.
I stondè lyk a clerk in my pulpet,   391
And whan the lewèd peple is doun y-set,
I prechè so as ye han herd bifoore,
And telle an hundred falsè japès moore ;
Thanne peyne I me to strecchè forth the
     nekke,
And est and west upon the peple I bekke,
As dooth a dowvè, sittynge on a berne ;
Myne handès and my tongè goon so yerne,
That it is joye to se my bisynesse.
Of avarice and of swich cursednesse   400
Is al my prechyng, for to make hem free
To yeven hir pens, and namely unto me ;
For myn entente is nat but for to wynne,
And no thyng for correccioun of synne.
I rekkè never whan that they been beryed,
Though that hir soulès goon a-blakè-
     beryed ;
For certès many a predicacioun
Comth oftè tyme of yvel entencioun ;
Som for plesaunce of folk and flaterye,
To been avauncèd by ypocrisye ;   410
And som for veynè glorie, and som for
     hate,
For whan I dar noon oother weyes debate,
Thanne wol I stynge hym with my tongè
     smerte
In prechyng, so that he shal nat asterte
To been defamèd falsly, if that he
Hath trespased to my bretheren or to me ;
For though I tellè noght his proprè name,
Men shal wel knowè that it is the same,
By signès, and by othere circumstances.
Thus quyte I folk that doon us dis-
     plesances ;   420
Thus spitte I out my venym under hewe
Of hoolynesse, to semen hooly and trewe.
  ' But, shortly, myn entente I wol
     devyse,—
I preche of no thyng but for coveityse ;
Therfore my theme is yet and ever was,
Radix malorum est Cupiditas.
Thus kan I preche agayn that samè vice
Which that I use, and that is avarice ;

But though myself be gilty in that synne
Yet kan I maken oother folk to twynne
From avarice, and soore to repente ;   431
But that is nat my principal entente ;
I preche no thyng but for coveitise.
Of this mateere it oghte ynogh suffise.
   ' Thanne telle I hem ensamples many oon
Of olde stories longe tyme agoon,—
For lewed peple loven tales olde,—
Swiche thynges kan they wel reporte and holde.
What ! trowe ye, the whiles I may preche,
And wynne gold and silver for I teche,
That I wol lyve in poverte wilfully ?   441
Nay, nay, I thoghte it never, trewely,
For I wol preche and begge in sondry landes ;
I wol nat do no labour with myne handes,
Ne make baskettes and lyve therby,
By cause I wol nat beggen ydelly.
I wol noon of the Apostles countrefete,
I wol have moneie, wolle, chese and whete,
Al were it yeven of the povereste page,
Or of the povereste wydwe in a village,
Al sholde hir children sterve for famyne.
Nay, I wol drynke licour of the vyne,
And have a joly wenche in every toun ;
But herkneth, lordynges, in conclusioun.
   ' Youre likyng is that I shal telle a tale.
Now have I dronke a draughte of corny ale,
By God, I hope I shal yow telle a thyng
That shal by resoun been at youre likyng ;
For though myself be a ful vicious man,
A moral tale yet I yow telle kan,   460
Which I am wont to preche, for to wynne.
Now hoold youre pees, my tale I wol bigynne.'

PARDONER'S TALE

Heere bigynneth The Pardoners Tale

In Flaundres whilom was a compaignye
Of yonge folk, that haunteden folye,

As riot, hasard, stywes and tavernes,
Where-as with harpes, lutes and gyternes,
They daunce and pleyen at dees, bothe day and nyght,
And eten also, and drynken over hir myght,
Thurgh which they doon the devel sacrifise
Withinne that develes temple, in cursed wise,   470
By superfluytee abhomynable.
Hir othes been so grete and so dampnable
That it is grisly for to heere hem swere ;
Oure blissed Lordes body they to-tere ;
Hem thoughte that Jewes rente hym noght ynough,
And ech of hem at otheres synne lough ;
And right anon thanne comen tombesteres
Fetys and smale, and yonge frutesteres,
Syngeres with harpes, baudes, wafereres,
Whiche been the verray develes officeres,
To kyndle and blowe the fyr of lecherye,
That is annexed unto glotonye.
The Hooly Writ take I to my witnesse
That luxurie is in wyn and dronkenesse.
   ' Lo, how that dronken Looth, unkyndely,
Lay by his doghtres two unwityngly ;
So dronke he was he nyste what he wroghte.
Herodes, (who so wel the stories soghte,)
Whan he of wyn was repleet at his feeste,
Right at his owene table, he yaf his heeste
To sleen the Baptist John, ful giltelees.
   Seneca seith a good word, doutelees ;
He seith he kan no difference fynde
Bitwix a man that is out of his mynde
And a man which that is dronkelewe,
But that woodnesse, fallen in a shrewe,
Persevereth lenger than dooth dronkenesse.
O glotonye, ful of cursednesse ;
O cause first of oure confusioun ;
O original of oure dampnacioun ;   500
Til Crist hadde boght us with his blood agayn !
Lo, how deere, shortly for to sayn,

Pardoners Tale. The earliest form of this tale is a Buddhist Birth-Story in the *Vedabbha Jataka;* analogues exist in Persian, Arabic, etc., and in the *Cento Novelle Antiche,* but Chaucer's particular original is unknown.

474. *Oure blissed Lordes body,* etc. The phrase occurs also in the Parson's Tale.
492. *Seneca,* E[6] *Senec;* Corp.[2] reading *ech good wordes* for *a good word.* Tyrwhitt traces the reference to *Ep.* 83.

Aboght was thilkė cursėd vileynye ;
Corrupt was al this world for glotonye !
Adam oure fader, and his wyf also,
Fro Paradys, to labour and to wo
Were dryven for that vice, it is no
    drede,—
For whil that Adam fasted, as I rede,
He was in Paradys, and whan that he
Eet of the fruyt deffended, on the tree, 510
Anon he was out cast to wo and peyne.
O glotonye, on thee wel oghte us pleyne !
    O, wiste a man how manye maladyes
Folwen of excesse and of glotonyes,
He woldė been the moorė mesurable
Of his dietė, sittynge at his table !
Allas ! the shortė throte, the tendrė mouth,
Maketh that est and west, and north and
    south,
In erthe, in eir, in water, man to-swynke
To gete a glotoun deyntee mete and
    drynke !   520
Of this matiere, O Paul, wel kanstow
    trete !
' Mete unto wombe, and wombe eek
    unto mete,
Shal God destroyen bothe,' as Paulus seith.
Allas ! a foul thyng is it, by my feith,
To seye this word, and fouler is the dede
Whan man so drynketh of the white and
    rede,
That of his throte he maketh his pryvee,
Thurgh thilkė cursėd superfluitee.
    The Apostel wepyng seith ful pitously,
' Ther walken manye of whiche yow
    toold have I,   530
I seye it now wepyng with pitous voys,
That they been enemys of Cristės croys,
Of whiche the ende is deeth, wombe is
    hir god.'
O wombe ! O bely ! O stynkyng is thi
    cod !
Fulfilled of donge and of corrupcioun !
At either ende of thee foul is the soun ;
How greet labóur and cost is thee to
    fynde !
Thise cookės, how they stampe, and
    streyne, and grynde,

And turnen substaunce into accident,
To fulfillen al thy likerous talent !   540
Out of the hardė bonės knokkė they
The mary, for they castė noght awey
That may go thurgh the golet softe and
    swoote.
Of spicerie, of leef, and bark, and roote,
Shal been his sauce y-makėd by delit,
To make hym yet a newer appetit ;
But certės he that haunteth swiche delices
Is deed, whil that he lyveth in tho vices.
    A lecherous thyng is wyn, and dronke-
    nesse
Is ful of stryvyng and of wrecchednesse.
O dronkė man ! disfigured is thy face, 551
Sour is thy breeth, foul artow to embrace,
And thurgh thy dronkė nose semeth the
    soun,
As though thou seydest ay, ' Sampsoun !
    Sampsoun ! '
And yet, God woot, Sampsoun drank
    never no wyn.
Thou fallest as it were a stykėd swyn,
Thy tonge is lost and al thyn honeste cure ;
For dronkenesse is verray sepulture
Of mannės wit and his discrecioun ;
In whom that drynke hath dominacioun,
He kan no conseil kepe, it is no drede. 561
Now kepe yow fro the white ahd fro the
    rede,
And namely fro the whitė wyn of Lepe,
That is to selle in Fysshstrete, or in Chepe.
This wyn of Spaignė crepeth subtilly
In othere wynės growynge fastė by,
Of which ther ryseth swich fumositee,
That whan a man hath dronken draughtės
    thre,
And weneth that he be at hoom in Chepe,
He is in Spaigne right at the toune of
    Lepe,—   570
Nat at the Rochele, neat Burdeux-toun,—
And thannė wol he seye, ' Sampsoun,
    Sampsoun ! '
    But herkneth, lordyngs, o word, I yow
    preye,

539. *turnen substaunce into accident*, alter the whole character of. Chaucer is imitating the chapter De Gula in the *De Contemptu Mundi* of Innocent III.
563. *Lepe*, near Cadiz.
564. *Fysshstrete*, H *Fleetstreet*.

508. *as I rede*, glossed : Ieronimus contra Iouianum (Bk. ii. cap. 15).
534. *is thi*, om. E⁶.

148

That alle the sovereyn actès, dar I seye,
Of victories in the Oldè Testament,
Thurgh verray God that is omnipotent,
Were doon in abstinence and in preyere;
Looketh the Bible and ther ye may it
    leere.
Looke, Attilla, the gretè conquerour,
Deyde in his sleepe, with shame and
    dishonour,   580
Bledynge ay at his nose in dronkenesse.
A capitayn sholde lyve in sobrenesse;
And over al this avyseth yow right wel
What was comaunded unto Lamuel,—
Nat Samuel, but Lamuel seye I;
Redeth the Bible, and fynde it expresly
Of wyn-yevyng to hem that han justise.
Namoore of this, for it may wel suffise.

    And now that I have spoken of glo-
    tonye,
Now wol I yow deffenden hasardrye. 590
Hasard is verray mooder of lesynges,
And of deceite, and cursèd forswerynges,
Blaspheme of Crist, manslaughtre, and
    wast also
Of catel, and of tyme, and forthermo
It is repreeve and contrarie of honour
For to ben holde a commune hasardour
And ever the hyer he is of estaat,
The moorè is he holden desolaat.
If that a pryncè useth hasardrye
In allè governaunce and policye,   600
He is, as by commune opinioun,
Y-holde the lasse in reputacioun.

    Stilbon, that was a wys embassadour,
Was sent to Corynthe in ful greet honour
Fro Lacidomye to maken hire alliaunce;
And whan he cam, hym happedè *par
chaunce*
That alle the gretteste that were of that
    lond
Pléyynge attè hasard he hem fond;
For which, as soonè as it myghtè be,
He stal hym hoom agayn to his contree,
And seydè, 'Ther wol I nat lese my
    name,   611

Ne I wol nat take on me so greet defame,
Yow for to allie unto none hasardours;
Sendeth otherè wise embassadours,
For, by my trouthè, me were levere dye,
Than I yow sholde to hasardours allye;
For ye that been so glorious in honours,
Shul nat allyèn yow with hasardours,
As by my wyl, ne as by my tretee!'
This wisè philosophrè thus seyde hee. 620

    Looke eek that to the kyng Demetrius,
The kyng of Parthès, as the book seith us,
Sente him a paire of dees of gold, in scorn,
For he hadde usèd hasard ther-biforn;
For which he heeld his glorie or his
    renoun
At no value or reputacioun.
Lordès may fynden oother maner pley
Honeste ynough to dryve the day awey.

    Now wol I speke of othès false and
    grete
A word or two, as oldè bookès trete. 630
Gret sweryng is a thyng abhomináble,
And fals sweryng is yet moore reprevàble.
The heighè God forbad sweryng at al,—
Witnesse on Mathew, but in special
Of sweryng seith the hooly Jeremye,
'Thou shalt seye sooth thyne othès, and
    nat lye
And swere in doom, and eek in rightwis-
    nesse';
But ydel sweryng is a cursednesse.
Bihoold and se, that in the firstè table
Of heighè Goddès heestès, honurable, 640
How that the seconde heeste of hym is
    this:
'Take nat my name in ydel, or amys';
Lo, rather he forbedeth swich sweryng
Than homycide, or many a cursèd thyng;
I seye that as by ordrè thus it stondeth.
This knowen, that his heestès under-
    stondeth,
How that the seconde heeste of God is
    that;
And forther over, I wol thee telle, al plat,
That vengeance shal nat parten from his
    hous

584. *Lamuel*, the mysterious king of Prov.
xxxi. I.
603. *Stilbon*. The story is told in the *Polycraticus* (Bk. i. cap. v.) of John of Salisbury;
the ambassador's name there being given as
Chilon.

621. *Demetrius*. This story also is from the
Polycraticus.
641. *the seconde heeste*. By the Roman
Church the first and second commandments are
regarded as one, and the tenth divided into two.

That of his othes is to outrageous,— 650
'By Goddès precious herte,' and 'By
   his nayles,'
And 'By the blood of Crist that is in
   Hayles,'
'Sevene is my chaunce, and thyn is cynk
   and treye,
By Goddès armès, if thou falsly pleye,
This daggere shal thurghout thyn hertè
   go !'   •
This fruyt cometh of the bicchèd bonès
   two,
Forsweryng, irè, falsnesse, homycide.
Now for the love of Crist that for us dyde,
Leveth youre othès, bothè grete and
   smale.
But, sires, now wol I tellè forth my tale.
   Thise riotourès thre, of whiche I telle,
Longe erst er primè rong of any belle,
Were set hem in a taverne for to drynke ;
And as they sat they herde a bellè clynke
Biforn a cors, was caried to his grave.
That oon of hem gan callen to his knave :
'Go bet,' quod he, 'and axè redily
What cors is this that passeth heer forby,
And looke that thou reporte his namè
   weel.'
   'Sire,' quod this boy, 'it nedeth
   never a deel,   670
It was me toold er ye cam heere two
   houres ;
He was, *pardee*, an old felawe of youres,
And sodeynly he was y-slayn to-nyght,
For-dronke, as he sat on his bench upright ;
Ther cam a privee theef, men clepeth
   Deeth,
That in this contree al the peplè sleeth,
And with his spere he smoot his herte
   atwo,
And wente his wey withouten wordès mo.
He hath a thousand slayn this pestilence,
And, maister, er ye come in his presence,
Me thynketh that it werè necessarie   681
For to be war of swich an adversarie ;
Beth redy for to meete hym evermoore ;
Thus taughtè me my dame ; I sey na-
   moore.'
   'By Seinte Mariè !' seyde this taverner,

652. *Hayles*, Hailes Abbey in Gloucestershire.
659. *Leveth*, E² *Lete.*

'The child seith sooth, for he hath
   slayn this yeer
Henne over a mile, withinne a greet
   village,
Bothe man and womman, child, and
   hyne, and page ;
I trowe his habitacioun be there ;
To been avysèd greet wysdom it were, 690
Er that he dide a man a dishonour.'
   'Ye, Goddès armès !" quod this riotour,
'Is it swich peril with hym for to meete ?
I shal hym seke by wey, and eek by strete ;
I make avow to Goddès dignè bones !
Herkneth, felawès, we thre been al ones,
Lat ech of us holde up his hand til oother,
And ech of us bicomen otheres brother,
And we wol sleen this falsè traytour,
   Deeth ;   699
He shal be slayn, he that so manye sleeth,
By Goddès dignitee, er it be nyght !'
   Togidres han thise thre hir trouthès
   plight
To lyve and dyen ech of hem for oother,
As though he were his owene y-borè
   brother ;
And up they stirte, al dronken, in this
   rage ;
And forth they goon towardès that village
Of which the taverner hadde spoke biforn;
And many a grisly ooth thanne han they
   sworn ;
And Cristès blessed body they to-rente,—
Deeth shal be deed, if that they may
   hym hente.   710
   Whan they han goon nat fully half a
   mile,
Right as they wolde han troden over a
   stile,
An oold man and a pourè with hem mette ;
This oldè man ful mekèly hem grette,
And seydè thus : 'Now, lordès, God
   yow see !'
   The proudeste of thise riotourès three
Answerde agayn, 'What, carl with sory
   grace,
Why artow al for-wrappèd, save thy face ?
Why lyvèstow so longe in so greet age ?'
   This oldè man gan looke in his visage,
And seydè thus : 'For I ne kan nat fynde

704. *y-bore*, H³ *sworne.*

A man, though that I walkèd into Ynde,
Neither in citee, ne in no village,
That woldè chaunge his youthè for myn
    age ;
And therfore moot I han myn agè stille,
As longè tyme as it is Goddès wille.
Ne Deeth, allas ! ne wol nat han my lyf ;
Thus walke I, lyk a restèlees kaityf,
And on the ground, which is my moodrès
    gate,
I knokkè with my staf, erly and late,   730
And seyè, "Lèevè mooder, leet me in !
Lo, how I vanysshe, flessh and blood
    and skyn ;
Allas ! whan shul my bonès been at reste ?
Mooder, with yow wolde I chaungè my
    cheste
That in my chambrè longè tyme hath be,
Ye, for an heyrè-clowt to wrappè me ! "
But yet to me she wol nat do that grace,
For which ful pale and welkèd is my face.
' But, sires, to yow it is no curteisye
To speken to an old man vileynye,   740
But he trespasse in word, or elles in dede.
In Hooly Writ ye may your self wel rede,
Agayns an oold man, hoor upon his heed,
Ye sholde arise ; wherfore I yeve yow reed,
Ne dooth unto an oold man noon harm
    now,
Namoorè than ye wolde men did to yow
In agè, if that ye so longe abyde.
And God be with yow, where ye go or
    ryde ;
I moote go thider as I have to go.'
    ' Nay, oldè cherl, by God, thou shalt
    nat so ! '   750
Seydè this oother hasardour anon ;
' Thou partest nat so lightly, by Seint
    John !
Thou spak right now of thilkè traytour,
    Deeth,
That in this contree alle oure freendès
    sleeth ;
Have heer my trouthe, as thou art his
    espye,
Telle where he is, or thou shalt it abye,
By God and by the hooly sacrement !

For soothly, thou art oon of his assent
To sleen us yongè folk, thou falsè theef ! '
    ' Now, sires,' quod he, ' if that ye
    be so leef   760
To fyndè Deeth, turne up this croked wey,
For in that grove I laftè hym, by my fey,
Under a tree, and there he wole abyde ;
Noght for youre boost he wole him no
    thyng hyde.
Se ye that ook ? Right there ye shal
    hym fynde.
God savè yow that boghte agayn man-
    kynde,
And yow amende ! ' thus seyde this oldè
    man ;
And everich of thise riotourès ran
Til he cam to that tree, and ther they
    foundè,   769
Of floryns fyne, of gold y-coynèd rounde,
Wel ny a seven busshels, as hem thoughte.
No lenger thannè after Deeth they
    soughte,
But ech of hem so glad was of that sighte,
For that the floryns been so faire and
    brighte,
That doun they sette hem by this precious
    hoord.
The worste of hem he spak the firstè word.
    ' Bretheren,' quod he, ' taak kepè
    what I seye ;
My wit is greet, though that I bourde
    and pleye.
This tresor hath Fortúne unto us yeven
In myrthe and joliftee oure lyf to lyven,
And lightly as it comth so wol we spende.
Ey, Goddès precious dignitee ! who wende
To-day, that we sholde han so fair a
    grace ?
But myghte this gold be caried fro this
    place
Hoom to myn hous, or ellès unto
    youres,—
For wel ye woot that al this gold is
    oures,—
Thanne werè we in heigh felicitee.
But trewèly, by daye it may nat bee ;
Men woldè seyn that we were thevès
    stronge,   789
And for oure owenè tresor doon us honge.

732. *vanysshe*, H² *wane*.
756. *or thou shalt it abye*, H² *or elles thou shalt dye*.

771. *seven*, E³ *eighte*.

151

This tresor moste y-caried be by nyghte
As wisely and as slyly as it myghte.
Wherfore, I rede that cut among us alle
Be drawe, and lat se wher the cut wol
        falle ;
And he that hath the cut with hertè blithe
Shal rennè to the towne, and that ful
        swithe,
And brynge us breed and wyn ful privèly,
And two of us shul kepen subtilly
This tresor wel ; and if he wol nat tarie,
Whan it is nyght we wol this tresor carie,
By oon assent, where as us thynketh best.'
That oon of hem the cut broghte in his
        fest,
And bad hem drawe and looke where it
        wol falle ;
And it fil on the yongeste of hem alle,
And forth toward the toun he wente anon ;
And al so soonè as that he was gon,
That oon of hem spak thus unto that
        oother :
'Thow knowest wel thou art my swornè
        brother ;
Thy profit wol I tellè thee anon ;   809
Thou woost wel that oure felawe is agon,
And heere is gold, and that ful greet
        plentee,
That shal departèd been among us thre ;
But nathèlees, if I kan shape it so
That it departed were among us two,
Hadde I nat doon a freendès torn to thee ?'
        That oother answerde, 'I noot how
        that may be ;
He woot how that the gold is with us
        tweye ;
What shal we doon, what shal we to hym
        seye ?'
        'Shal it be conseil ?' seyde the firstè
        shrewe,   819
'And I shal tellen thee in wordès fewe
What we shal doon, and bryngen it wel
        aboute.'
        'I grauntè,' quod that oother, 'out
        of doute,
That by my trouthe I shal thee nat
        biwreye.'
        'Now,' quod the firste, 'thou woost
        wel we be tweye,
And two of us shul strenger be than oon.

Looke whan that he is set, and right
        anoon
Arys, as though thou woldest with hym
        pleye,
And I shal ryve hym thurgh the sydès
        tweye,
Whil that thou strogelest with hym as in
        game,
And with thy daggere looke thou do the
        same ;   830
And thanne shal al this gold departed be,
My deerè freend, bitwixen me and thee.
Thanne may we bothe oure lustès all
        fulfille,
And pleye at dees right at oure owene
        wille.'
And thus acorded been thise shrewès
        tweye,
To sleen the thridde, as ye han herd me
        seye.
        This yongeste, which that wente unto
        the toun,
Ful ofte in herte he rolleth up and doun
The beautee of thise floryns newe and
        brighte ;
'O Lord,' quod he, 'if so were that I
        myghte   840
Have al this tresor to my self allone,
Ther is no man that lyveth under the
        trone
Of God, that sholdè lyve so murye as I !'
And attè laste the feend, oure enemy,
Putte in his thought that he sholde poyson
        beye,
With which he myghtè sleen his felawes
        tweye ;
For-why the feend foond hym in swich
        lyvynge,
That he hadde levè hym to sorwè brynge,
For this was outrèly his fulle entente
To sleen hem bothe and never to repente.
And forth he gooth, no lenger wolde he
        tarie,   851
Into the toun, unto a pothecarie,
And preydè hym that he hym woldè selle
Som poysoun, that he myghte his rattès
        quelle ;
And eek ther was a polcat in his hawe,
That, as he seyde, his capouns hadde
        y-slawe,

And fayn he woldè wreke hym, if he
    myghte,
On vermyn, that destroyèd hym by
    nyghte.
    The pothecarie answerde, 'And thou
       shalt have
A thyng that, al so God my soulè save!
In al this world ther nis no creäture, 861
That eten or dronken hath of this con-
    fiture,
Noght but the montance of a corn of
    whete,
That he ne shal his lif anon forlete;
Ye, sterve he shal, and that in lassè while
Than thou wolt goon a-paas nat but a mile;
This poysoun is so strong and violent.'
    This cursèd man hath in his hond y-
    hent
This poysoun in a box, and sith he ran
Into the nextè strete unto a man,   870
And borwèd hym largè botellès thre,
And in the two his poyson pourèd he;
The thridde he kepte clene for his owenè
    drynke;
For al the nyght he shoope hym for to
    swynke
In cariynge of the gold out of that place.
And whan this riotour with sory grace
Hadde filled with wyn his gretè botels thre,
To his felawes agayn repaireth he.
    What nedeth it to sermone of it moore?
For right as they hadde cast his deeth
    bifoore,   880
Right so they han hym slayn, and that
    anon,
And whan that this was doon thus spak
    that oon:
'Now lat us sitte and drynke, and make
    us merie,
And afterward we wol his body berie';
And with that word it happèd hym,
    par cas,
To take the botel ther the poysoun was,
And drank and yaf his felawe drynke also,
For which anon they storven bothè two.
    But certès, I suppose that Avycen
Wroot never in no Canon, ne in no fen,
Mo wonder signès of empoisonyng   891

890. *fen*, the Arabic name of the sections of
Avicenna's Canon.

Than hadde thise wrecches two, er hir
    endyng.
Thus ended been thise homycidès two,
And eek the false empoysonere also.
    O cursèd synne of allè cursednesse!
O traytorous homycide! O wikkednesse!
O glotonye, luxurie, and hasardrye!
Thou blasphemour of Crist with vileynye,
And othès grete, of usage and of pride!
Allas! mankyndè, how may it bitide 900
That to thy Creätour which that thee
    wroghte,
And with his precious hertè-blood thee
    boghte,
Thou art so fals and so unkynde, allas!

    Now, goode men, God foryeve yow
    youre trespas,
And ware yow fro the synne of avarice.
Myn hooly pardoun may yow alle warice,
So that ye offre nobles, or sterlynges,
Or ellès silver broches, spoonès, rynges.
Boweth youre heed under this hooly bulle!
Cometh up, ye wyvès, offreth of youre
    wolle!   910
Youre names I entre heer in my rolle anon;
Into the blisse of hevene shul ye gon;
I yow assoillè by myn heigh power,—
Yow that wol offre,—as clene and eek as
    cleer
As ye were born; and lo, sires, thus I
    preche,
And Jhesu Crist, that is oure soulès leche,
So grauntè yow his pardoun to receyve;
For that is best; I wol yow nat deceyve.

    'But, sires, o word forgat I in my tale;
I have relikes and pardoun in my male
As faire as any man in Engelond,   921
Whiche were me yeven by the popès hond.
If any of yow wole of devocioun
Offren, and han myn absolucioun,
Com forth anon, and kneleth heere adoun,
And mekèly receyveth my pardoun;
Or ellès taketh pardoun as ye wende,
Al newe and fressh at every milès ende,—
So that ye offren, alwey newe and newe,
Nobles or pens, whiche that be goode
    and trewe.   930
It is an honour to everich that is heer

That ye mowe have a suffisant Pardoneer
Tassoillé yow in contree as ye ryde,
For áventúres whiche that may bityde.
Paráventure ther may 'fallen oon or two
Doun of his hors and breke his nekke atwo;
Looke which a seuretee is it to yow alle,
That I am in youre felaweshipe y-falle,
That may assoillé yow, bothe moore and lasse,
Whan that the soule shal fro the body passe. 940
I redé that oure Hoost heere shal bigynne,
For he is moost envoluped in synne !
Com forth, sire Hoost, and offré first anon,
And thou shalt kisse my relikes everychon,—
Ye, for a grote ! Unbokele anon thy purs.'
  'Nay, nay,' quod he, 'thanne have I Cristés curs !
Lat be,' quod he, 'it shal nat be, so theech !
Thou woldest make me kisse thyn oldé breech,
And swere it were a relyk of a seint,
Though it were with thy fundément depeint ; 950
But, by the croys which that Seint Eleyne fond,

935. *fallen*, H⁸ *falle.*   951. *Eleyne*, Helena.

I wolde I hadde thy coillons in myn hond
Instide of relikes, or of seintuarie.
Lat kutte hem of, I wol thee helpe hem carie,
They shul be shryned in an hogges toord.'
  This Pardoner answerdé nat a word ;
So wrooth he was no word ne wolde he seye.
  'Now,' quod oure Hoost, 'I wol no lenger pleye
With thee, ne with noon oother angry man.'
But right anon the worthy Knyght bigan,— 960
Whan that he saugh that al the peple lough,—
  'Namoore of this, for it is right ynough !
Sire Pardoner, be glad and myrie of cheere ;
And ye, sir Hoost, that been to me so deere,
I prey yow that ye kisse the Pardoner ;
And Pardoner, I prey thee drawe thee neer,
And as we diden, lat us laughe and pleye.'
Anon they kiste and ryden forth hir weye.

·   ·   ·   ·

GROUP D

The Prologue of the Wyves Tale of Bathe

  'EXPERIENCE, though noon auctoritee
Were in this world, were right ynogh to me
To speke of wo that is in mariage ;
For, lordynges, sith I twelf yeer was of age,—
Y-thonked be God, that is eterne on lyve !
Housbondes at chirché dore I have had fyve ;
For I so ofté have y-wedded bee ;

And alle were worthy men in hir degree.
But me was toold certeyn, nat longe agoon is,
That sith that Crist ne wente never but onis 10
To weddyng, in the Cane of Galilee,
Bý the same ensample taughte he me
That I ne sholdé wedded be but ones.
Herkne, eek, which a sharpe word for the nones,
Beside a wellé Jhesus, God and man,

GROUP D. In the Ellesmere MS. this group follows the Man of Law's Tale, but the mention of Sittingbourne (l. 847) shows that it must come after the Monk's Tale with its reference to Rochester.
  6. *at chirche dore*, where the first part of the service used to be read.

13. Against this line E has the note, 'Qui enim semel ivit ad nupcias docuit semel esse nubendum,' a quotation from St. Jerome, *Adversus Jovinianum*, a treatise in favour of chastity, some of the arguments in which the Wife of Bath from here to line 128 takes up and inverts or combats.

Spak in repreeve of the Samaritan :
" Thou hast y-had fyve housbondès," quod
   he,
" And that ilk man the which that hath
   now thee
Is noght thyn housbonde " ; thus seyde
   he certeyn.
What that he mente therby, I kan nat
   seyn ;   20
But that I axè, why the fifthè man
Was noon housbonde to the Samaritan ?
How manye myghte she have in mariage ?
Yet herde I never tellen, in myn age,
Upon this nombrè diffinicioun.
Men may devyne, and glosen up and doun,
But wel I woot, expres, withoutè lye,
God bad us for to wexe and multiplye ;
That gentil text kan I wel understonde.
Eek, wel I woot, he seydè myn housbonde
Sholde letè fader and mooder, and takè
   me ;   31
But of no nombrè mencioun made he,
Of bigamye, or of octogamye ;
Why sholdè men speke of it vileynye.
  ' Lo, heere the wisè kyng daun
   Salomon ;
I trowe he haddè wyves mo than oon ;
As, woldè God, it leveful were to me
To be refresshèd half so ofte as he !
Which yifte of God hadde he for alle his
   wyvys !
No man hath swich that in this world
   alyve is.   40
God woot, this noble kyng, as to my wit,
The firstè nyght had many a myrie fit
With ech of hem, so wel was hym on lyve.
  ' Y-blessed be God, that I have wedded
   fyve !
Welcome the sixtè, whan that ever he shal,
For sothe I wol nat kepe me chaast in al.
Whan myn housbonde is fro the world
   y-gon,
Som cristen man shal weddè me anon ;
For thanne, thapostle seith, I am free
To wedde, a Goddes half, where it liketh
   me.   50
He seith to be wedded is no synne ;
" Bèt is to be wedded than to brynne."

50. *a Goddes half*, on God's part, *i.e.* with His
consent.

What rekketh me thogh folk seye vileynye
Of shrewèd Lameth, and his bigamye ?
I woot wel Abraham was an hooly man,
And Jacob eek, as ferforth as I kan,
And ech of hem haddè wyvès mo than two,
And many another holy man also.
Whanne saugh ye ever in any manere age
That hyè God defended mariage   60
By expres word ? I pray you telleth me ;
Or where comanded he virginitee ?
I woot as wel as ye, it is no drede,
Thapostel whan he speketh of mayden-
   hede,
He seyde that precept ther-of hadde he
   noon.
Men may conseille a womman to been
   oon,
But conseillyng is nat comandèment.
He putte it in oure owene juggèment ;
For haddè God comanded maydenhede
Thanne hadde he dampnèd weddyng with
   the dede ;   70
And certein, if ther were no seed y-sowe,
Virginitee, wher-of thanne sholde it growe ?
Poul dorste nat comanden, attè leeste,
A thyng of which his maister yaf noon
   heeste.
The dart is set up of virginitee,
Cacche who so may, who renneth best
   lat see !
  ' But this word is nat taken of every
   wight,
But ther as God lust yive it of his myght.
I woot wel that the Apostel was a mayde,
But nathèlees, thogh that he wroot and
   sayde   80
He wolde that every wight were swich
   as he,
Al nys but conseil to virginitee ;
And for to been a wyf he yaf me leve
Of índulgence, so it is no repreve
To weddè me, if that my makè dye,
Withouten excepcioun of bigamye,
Al were it good no womman for to
   touche, —
He mente as in his bed or in his couche ;
For peril is bothe fyr and tow tassemble ;
Ye knowe what this ensample may
   resemble.   90
This is al and som, he heldè virginitee

Moore profiteth than weddyng in freletee ;
Freeltee clepe I, but if that he and she
Wolde leden al hir lyf in chastitee.
  ' I graunte it wel I havé noon envie
Thogh maydenhede preferré bigamye :
Hem liketh to be clené, body and goost.
Of myn estaat I nyl nat make no boost,
For wel ye knowe a lord in his houshold
He nath nat every vessel al of gold ;   100
Somme been of tree, and doon hir
     lord servyse.
God clepeth folk to hym in sondry wyse,
And everich hath of God a propre yifte,
Som this, som that, as hym liketh to
     shifte.
  ' Virginitee is greet perfeccioun,
And continence eek, with devocioun ;
But Crist, that of perfeccioun is welle,
Bád nat every wight sholdé go selle
All that he hadde and yive it to the poore,
And in swich wisé folwe hym and his foore.
He spak to hem that wolde lyve parfitly,
And, lordynges, by youre leve, that am
     nat I.
I wol bistowe the flour of al myn age
In the actés and in fruyt of mariage.
  ' Telle me also, to what conclusioun
Were membres maad of generacioun,
And for what profit was a wight
     y-wroght ?
Trusteth right wel, they were nat maad
     for noght.
Glose who so wole, and seye bothe up
     and doun,
That they were makyd for purgacioun   120
Of uryne, and oure bothé thyngés smale
Were eek to knowe a femele from a male,
And for noon oother causé,—sey ye no ?
The experience woot wel it is noght so ;
So that the clerkés be nat with me wrothe,
I sey this, that they beth maked for bothe ;
This is to seye, for office, and for ese
Of engendrure, ther we nat God displese.
Why sholde men ellés in hir bookés sette
That man shal yeldé to his wyf hire dette ?
Now wher-with sholde he make his
     paiément,   131
If he ne used his sely instrument ?
Thanne were they maad upon a creäture,

To purge uryne and eek for engendrure.
  ' But I seye noght that every wight is
     holde,
That hath swich harneys as I to yow tolde,
To goon and usen hem in engendrure,—
Thanne shuld men take of chastitee no
     cure.
Crist was a mayde and shapen as a man,
And many a seint sith that the world
     bigan,   140
Yet lyved they ever in parfit chastitee.
I nyl nat envye no virginitee ;
Lat hem be breed of puréd wheté seed,
And lat us wyvés hoten barly breed,
And yet with barly breed Mark tellé kan
Oure Lord Jhesu refresshéd many a man.
  ' In swich estaat as God hath clepéd us,
I wol persévere, I nam nat precius ;
In wyfhode I wol use myn instrument
As frely as my Makere hath it sent.   150
If I be daungerous, God yeve me sorwe ;
Myn housbonde shal it have bothe eve
     and morwe,
Whan that hym list com forth and paye
     his dette.
An housbonde I wol have, I nyl nat lette,
Which shal be bothe my dettour and my
     thral,
And have his tribulacioun withal
Upon his flessh, whil that I am his wyf.
I have the power, durynge al my lyf,
Upon his propré body, and noght he.
Right thus the Apostel tolde it unto me, 160
And bad oure housbondes for to love us
     weel ;
Al this sentence me liketh every deel.'
  Up stirte the Pardoner, and that anon ;
' Now, dame,' quod he, ' by God and
     by Seint John !
Ye been a noble prechour in this cas.
I was aboute to wedde a wyf, allas !
What, sholde I bye it on my flessh so
     deere ?
Yet hadde I levere wedde no wyf to-yeere !'
  ' Abyde,' quod she, ' my tale is nat
     bigonne.   169
Nay, thou shalt drynken of another tonne
Er that I go, shal savoure wors than ale ;
And whan that I have toold thee forth
     my tale

92. *profiteth*, H⁵ *parfit*.

Of tribulacioun in mariage,
Of which I am expert in al myn age,—
This to seyn, my self have been the whippe,—
Than maystow chesé wheither thou wolte sippe
Of thilké tonné that I shal abroche.
Be war of it, er thou to ny approche,
For I shal tell ensamples mo than ten,
"Whoso that nyl be war by othere men, 180
By hym shul othere men corrected be";
The samé wordes writeth Ptholomee;
Rede in his Almageste and take it there.'
'Dame, I wolde praye yow, if youre wyl it were,'
Seydé this Pardoner, 'as ye bigan
Telle forth youre talé; spareth for no man,
And teche us yongé men of youre praktike.'
'Gládly, sirès, sith it may yow like;
But yet I praye to al this compaignye,
If that I speke after my fantasye, 190
As taketh not agrief of that I seye,
For myn entente is nought but for to pleye.
'Now, sire, now wol I tellé forth my tale.
As ever moote I drynken wyn or ale,
I shal seye sooth, of housbondes that I hadde,
As thre of hem were goode, and two were badde.
The thre were goodé men and riche, and olde;
Unnethé myghté they the statut holde
In which that they were bounden unto me;
Ye woot wel what I meene of this, *pardee!*
As help me God, I laughé whan I thynke
How pitously a-nyght I made hem swynke!
And, by my fey, I tolde of it no stoor;
They had me yiven hir lond and hir tresoor,
Me neded nat do lenger diligence
To wynne hir love, or doon hem reverence;
They lovéd me so wel, by God above,

That I ne tolde no deyntee of hir love!
A wys womman wol sette hire, ever in oon, 209
To gete hire lové ther as she hath noon;
But sith I hadde hem hoolly in myn hond,
And sith they hadde me yeven all hir lond,
What sholde I taken heede hem for to plese,
But it were for my profit and myn ese?
I sette hem so a werké, by my fey,
That many a nyght they songen "weil-awey!"
The bacoun was nat fet for hem, I trowe,
That som men han in Essexe at Dunmowe. 218
I governed hem so wel after my lawe,
That ech of hem ful blisful was and fawe
To brynge me gayé thynges fro the fayre;
They were ful glad whan I spak to hem faire,
For, God it woot, I chidde hem spitously.
'Now herkneth how I baar me properly,
Ye wisé wyvés that kan understonde.
'Thus shul ye speke, and beren hem on honde;
For half so boldély kan ther no man
Swerè and lyé as a womman kan.
I sey nat this by wyvés that been wyse,
But if it be whan they hem mysavyse. 230
I-wis a wyf, if that she kan hir good,
Shal beré hym on hond the cow is wood,
And také witnesse of hir owene mayde
Of hir assent; but herkneth how I sayde.
'Sire, oldé kaynard, is this thyn array?
Why is my neighéborès wyf so gay?
She is honóuréd over al ther she gooth;
I sitte at hoom, I have no thrifty clooth.
What dostow at my neighéborès hous?
Is she so fair? artow so amorous? 240
What rowne ye with oure mayde? *Benedicite!*

---

209. *sette,* H⁵ *bisy.*
218. *Dunmowe.* The Dunmow flitch is still given as a prize to a husband and wife who have never quarrelled.
232. *cow,* chough or jackdaw, the reference being to a tale like the Manciple's.
235. From here to l. 315 Chaucer takes his text from a fragment of Theophrastus, *De Nuptiis,* preserved in §§ 313, 314 of St. Jerome's treatise against Jovinian.

182. *Ptholomee.* No one has yet verified the references to the Almagest here and in l. 324.
188. *sires,* H⁵ *quod sche.*
204. *lond,* E *gold.*

Sire, oldé lecchour, lat thy japès be !
And if I have a gossib or a freend,
Withouten gilt thou chidest as a feend,
If that I walke or pleye unto his hous.
Thou comest hoom as dronken as a mous
And prechest on thy bench with yvel
    preef :
Thou seist to me it is a greet meschief
To wedde a pouré womman for costage ;
And if she be riche and of heigh parage, 250
Thanne seïstow it is a tormentrie
To suffre hire pride and hire malencolie ;
And if that she be faire, thou verray
    knave,
Thou seyst that every holour wol hire
    have ;
She may no while in chastitee abyde
That is assailléd upon eché syde.
   ' Thou seyst som folk desire us for
    richesse,
Somme for oure shapé, somme for oure
    fairnesse,
And som for she kan either synge or
    daunce,
And som for gentillesse, and daliaunce,
Som for hir handés, and hir armés
    smale,—   261
Thus goth al to the devel by thy tale !
Thou seyst men may nat kepe a castel wal,
It may so longe assailled been over al.
   ' And if that she be foul, thou seist
    that she
Coveiteth every man that she may se,
For as a spaynel she wol on hym lepe,
Til that she fyndé som man hire to chepe ;
Ne noon so grey a goos gooth in the lake,
As, seïstow, wol been withouté make ; 270
And seyst it is an hard thyng for to welde
A thyng that no man wole, his thankés,
    helde.
Thus seistow, lorel, whan thow goost to
    bedde,
And that no wys man nedeth for to wedde,
Ne no man that entendeth unto hevene.
With wildé thonder dynt and firy levene
Mooté thy welkéd nekké be to-broke !
   ' Thow seyst that droppyng houses,
    and eek smoke,
And chidyng wyvés, maken men to flee
Out of hir owene hous, a ! *benedicitee !* 280

What eyleth swich an old man for to
    chide ?
   ' Thow seyst we wyvés wol oure vices
    hide
Til we be fast, and thanne we wol hem
    shewe,—
Wel may that be a proverbe of a shrewe.
   ' Thou seist that oxen, asses, hors, and
    houndes,
They been assayéd at diversé stoundes ;
Basyns, lavourés, er that men hem bye,
Spoonés and stooles, and al swich hous-
    bondrye,
And so been pottés, clothés, and array ;
But folk of wyvés maken noon assay 290
Til they be wedded,—oldé dotard shrewe !
Thanne, seïstow, we wol oure vices shewe.
   ' Thou seist also that it displeseth me
But if that thou wolt preysé my beautee,
And but thou poure alwey upon my face,
And clepe me "fairé dame" in every
    place ;
And but thou make a feeste on thilké day
That I was born, and make me fressh
    and gay ;
And but thow do to my norice honour,
And to my chamberere withinne my
    bour,   300
And to my fadrés folk and his allyes,—
Thus seistow, oldé barelful of lyes !
   ' And yet of oure apprentice Janékyn,
For his crispe heer, shynynge as gold so
    fyn,
And for he squiereth me bothe up and
    doun,
Yet hastow caught a fals suspecioun,—
I wol hym noght, thogh thou were deed
    to-morwe !
   ' But tel me this, why hydestow with
    sorwe
The keyés of thy cheste, awey fro me ?
It is my good, as wel as thyn, *pardee !*
What ! wenestow make an ydiot of oure
    dame ?   311
Now, by that lord that calléd is Seint
    Jame,
Thou shalt nat bothé, thogh thou weré
    wood,
Be maister of my body, and of my
    good ;

That oon thou shalt forgo, maugree thyne
    eyen !
What nedeth thee of me to enquere or
    spyen ?
I trowe thou woldest loke me in thy
    chiste ;
Thou sholdest seyé, "Wyf, go wher thee
    liste ;
Taak youre disport, I wol nat leve no
    talys ;
I knowe yow for a trewé wyf, dame Alys."
We love no man that taketh kepe, or
    charge,   321
Wher that we goon ; we wol ben at our
    large.
'Of allé men y-blessed moot he be,
The wise astrologien, Daun Ptholome,
That seith this proverbe in his Almageste,
"Of allé men his wysdom is the hyeste
That rekketh never who hath the world
    in honde."
By this proverbé thou shalt understonde,
Have thou ynogh, what thar thee recche
    or care
How myrily that othere folkés fare ? 330
For certeyn, oldé dotard, by youre leve,
Ye shul have queynté right ynogh at eve.
He is to greet a nygard that wolde werne
A man to lighte his candle at his lanterne.
He shal have never the lassé light, *pardee !*
Have thou ynogh, thee thar nat pleyné
    thee.
    'Thou seyst also, that if we make us
        gay
With clothyng, and with precïous array,
That it is peril of oure chastitee ;
And yet with sorwe thou most enforcé
    thee,   340
And seye thise wordés in the Apostles
    name :
"In habit maad with chastitee and shame,
Ye wommen shul apparaille yow," quod
    he,
    "And noght in tressed heer, and gay
        perree,
As perlés, ne with gold, ne clothés riche."
After thy text, ne after thy rubriche,
I wol nat wirche as muchel as a gnat.
Thou seydest this, that I was lyk a cat ;
For whoso woldé senge a cattés skyn,

Thanne wolde the cat wel dwellen in his
    in ;   350
And if the cattés skyn be slyk and gay,
She wol nat dwelle in housé half a day ;
But forth she wole, er any day be dawed,
To shewe hir skyn, and goon a-cater-
    wawed ;
This is to seye, if I be gay, sire shrewe,
I wol renne out my borel for to shewe.
    'Sire, oldé fool, what eyleth thee to
        spyen ?
Thogh thou preye Argus with his
    hundred eyen
To be my wardécors, as he kan best,
In feith, he shal nat kepe me but me
    lest ;   360
Yet koude I make his berd, so moot I
    thee !
    'Thou seydest eek, that ther been
        thyngés thre
The whiché thyngés troublen al this erthe,
And that no wight ne may endure the
    ferthe.
O leeve sire shrewé, Jhesu shorte thy lyf !
Yet prechestow and seyst an hateful wyf
Y-rekened is for oon of thise meschances.
Been ther none othere of thy resemblances
That ye may likne youre parables unto,
But if a sely wyf be oon of tho ?   370
    'Thou likénest wommenés love to
        helle,
To bareyne lond, ther water may nat
    dwelle ;
Thou liknest it also to wildé fyr,
The moore it brenneth the moore it hath
    desir
To consumen every thyng that brent wole
    be ;
Thou seyst, right as wormés shende a tree,
Right so a wyf destroyeth hire housbond
This knowé they that been to wyvés
    bonde.'
    Lordynges, right thus as ye have
        understonde
Baar I stifly myne olde housbondes on
    honde,   380
That thus they seyden in hir dronkenesse ;
And al was fals, but that I took witnesse

357. *eyleth*, H⁶ *helpith.*
361. *make his berd*, cheat him.

159

On Janėkyn, and on my nece also.
O Lord, the peyne I dide hem and the wo!
Ful giltėlees, by Goddės sweetė pyne!
For as an hors I koudė byte and whyne;
I koudė pleyne, thogh I were in the gilt,
Or ellės often tyme hadde I been spilt.
'Who so first cometh to the mille first
grynt';
I pleynėd first, so was oure werre y-stynt;
They were ful glad to excusen hem ful
blyve   391
Of thyng of which they never agilte hir
lyve.
Of wenches wolde I beren hem on
honde,
Whan that for syk unnethės myghte thay
stonde;
Yet tikled it his hertė, for that he
Wende that I hadde of hym so greet
chiertee!
I swoor that al my walkynge out by
nyghte
Was for tespyė wenches that he dighte.
Under that colour hadde I many a myrthe,
For al swich witte is yeven us in oure
byrthe,—   400
Deceitė, wepyng, spynnyng, God hath
yive
To wommen kyndėly whil they may lyve;
And thus of o thyng I avauntė me,
Atte ende I hadde the bettre in ech de-
gree,—
By sleighte, or force, or by som maner
thyng,
As by continueel murmure or grucchyng.
Namely abeddė hadden they meschaunce;
Ther wolde I chide and do hem no
plesaunce;
I wolde no lenger in the bed abyde,
If that I felte his arm over my syde,   410
Til he had maad his raunsoun unto me;
Thanne wolde I suffre hym do his
nycetee;
And therfore every man this tale I telle,—
Wynne who so may, for al is for to selle;
With empty hand men may none haukės
lure.
For wynnyng wolde I al his lust endure

380. From H; Heng.⁴ *Whoso that first to mylle comth first grynt.*

And makė me a feynėd appetit,
And yet in bacoun hadde I never delit;
That madė me that ever I wolde hem
chide;
For thogh the pope hadde seten hem
biside   420
I wolde nat spare hem at hir owene bord,
For, by my trouthe, I quitte hem word
for word.
As helpe me verray God omnipotent,
Though I right now sholde make my
testament,
I ne owe hem nat a word that it nys quit.
I broghte it so aboutė by my wit
That they moste yeve it up as for the
beste,
Or ellės hadde we never been in reste;
For thogh he lookėd as a wood leoun,
Yet sholde he faille of his conclusioun,
Thanne wolde I seyė, 'Goodė lief,
taak keepe,—   431
How mekely looketh Wilkyn, ourė
sheepe!
Com neer, my spousė, lat me ba thy
cheke;
Ye sholdė been al pacient and meke,
And han a sweetė, spicėd conscїence,
Sith ye so preche of Jobės pacїence.
Suffreth alwey, syn ye so wel kan preche,
And, but ye do, certein we shal yow
teche
That it is fair to have a wyf in pees.
Oon of us two moste bowen, doutėlees,
And sith a man is moorė resonable   441
Than womman is, ye mostė been suffrable.
What eyleth yow to grucchė thus and
grone?
Is it for ye woldė have my queynte allone?
Wy, taak it al! lo, have it every deel!
Peter! I shrewe yow, but ye love it
weel;
For if I woldė selle my belė chose
I koudė walke as fressh as is a rose;
But I wol kepe it for youre owene tooth.
Ye be to blame, by God! I sey yow sooth.'
Swiche manere wordės haddė we on
honde.   451
Now wol I speken of my fourthe
housbonde.
My fourthė housbonde was a revelour;

This is to seyn, he hadde a paramour;
And I was yong and ful of ragerye,
Stibourne and strong and joly as a pye.
Wel koude I daunce to an harpe smale,
And synge, y-wis, as any nyghtyngale,
Whan I had dronke a draughte of sweete
    wyn.
  Metellius, the foule cherl, the swyn! 460
That with a staf birafte his wyf hire lyf,
For she drank wyn; thogh I hadde been
    his wyf
He sholde nat han daunted me fro drynke!
And after wyn on Venus moste I thynke,
For al so siker as cold engendreth hayl,
A likerous mouth moste han a likerous tayl.
In wommen vinolent is no defence,—
This knowen lecchours by experience.
  But, Lord Crist! whan that it remem-
    breth me
Upon my yowthe, and on my jolitee, 470
It tikleth me aboute myn herte roote!
Unto this day it dooth myn herte boote
That I have had my world, as in my tyme.
But Age, allas! that al wole envenyme,
Hath me biraft my beautee and my pith,—
Lat go, fare wel, the devel go therwith!
The flour is goon, ther is namoore to telle,
The bren, as I best kan, now moste I selle;
But yet to be right myrie wol I fonde.
  Now wol I tellen of my fourthe housbonde.
  I seye I hadde in herte greet despit 481
That he of any oother had delit;
But he was quit, by God, and by Seint
    Joce!
I made hym of the same wode a croce.
Nat of my body in no foul manere,
But certeinly I made folk swich cheere,
That in his owene grece I made hym frye
For angre, and for verray jalousye.
By God, in erthe I was his purgatorie,
For which I hope his soule be in glorie! 490
For God it woot, he sat ful ofte and song
Whan that his shoo ful bitterly hym wrong.
Ther was no wight save God and he that
    wiste
In many wise how soore I hym twiste.

He deyde whan I cam fro Jerusalem,
And lith y-grave under the roode beem,
Al is his tombe noght so curyus
As was the sepulcre of hym Daryus,
Which that Appelles wroghte subtilly;
It nys but wast to burye hym preciously. 500
Lat hym fare wel, God yeve his soule reste,
He is now in his grave and in his cheste!
  Now of my fifthe housbonde wol I telle.
God lete his soule never come in helle!
And yet was he to me the mooste shrewe;
That feele I on my ribbes al by rewe,
And ever shal, unto myn endyng day;
But in oure bed he was so fressh and gay;
And therwithal so wel koude he me glose,
Whan that he wolde han my bele chose,
That thogh he hadde me bet on every bon,
He koude wynne agayn my love anon.
I trowe I loved hym beste for that he
Was of his love daungerous to me.
We wommen han, if that I shal nat lye,
In this matere a queynte fantasye;
Wayte! what thyng we may nat lightly
    have
Ther-after wol we crie al day and crave.
Forbede us thyng, and that desiren we;
Preesse on us faste and thanne wol we fle.
With daunger oute we al oure chaffare; 521
Greet prees at market maketh deere ware,
And to greet cheepe is holde at litel prys;
This knoweth every womman that is wys.
  My fifthe housbonde, God his soule
    blesse!
Which that I took for love, and no
    richesse,
He somtyme was a clerk of Oxenford,
And hadde left scole and wente at hom
    to bord
With my gossib, dwellynge in oure toun;
God have hir soule, hir name was Alisoun.
She knew myn herte, and eek my privetee,
Bet than oure parisshe preest, as moot
    I thee.
To hire biwreyed I my conseil al,
For hadde myn housbonde pissed on a
    wal,

460. *Metellius.* The story is from Valerius
Maximus, Bk. vi. ch. 3.
483. *Seint Joce.* Saint Judocus, a Breton
hermit of the 7th century.

498. *Daryus.* The tomb which Appelles wrought
for Darius by Alexander's order is described in
the 6th book of the *Alexandreis* of Gualtier de
Lille.

Or doon a thyng that sholde han cost his
    lyf,
To hire, and to another worthy wyf,
And to my nece, which that I lovèd weel,
I wolde han toold his conseil every deel ;
And so I dide ful often, God it woot,
That made his face ful often reed and hoot
For verray shame, and blamed hymself,
    for he   541
Had toold to me so greet a pryvètee.
    And so bifel that onès in a Lente,
So often tymes I to my gossyb wente,—
For ever yet I lovèd to be gay,
And for to walke in March, Averill and
    May,
Fro hous to hous to heerè sondry talys,—
That Jankyn clerk, and my gossyb dame
    Alys
And I myself into the feeldès wente.
Myn housbonde was at London al that
    Lente ;   550
I hadde the bettre leyser for to pleye,
And for to se, and eek for to be seye
Of lusty folk.   What wiste I wher my
    grace
Was shapen for to be, or in what place ?
Therfore I made my visitaciouns
To vigilies and to processiouns,
To prechyng eek, and to thise pilgrimages,
To pleyes of myracles, and to mariages,
And wered upon my gayè scarlet gytes.
Thise wormes, ne thise motthes, ne thise
    mytes,   560
Upon my peril frete hem never a deel.
And wostow why ?   For they were usèd
    weel.
    Now wol I tellen forth what happèd me.
I seye that in the feeldès walked we,
Till trewèly we hadde swich daliance,
This clerk and I, that of my purveiance
I spak to hym, and seyde hym how that he,
If I were wydwè, sholdè weddè me ;
For certeinly,—I sey for no bobance,—
Yet was I never withouten purveiance
Of mariage, nof othere thyngès eek.   571
I holde a mouses herte nat worth a leek
That hath but oon hole for to sterte to,
And if that faillè, thanne is al y-do.
    I bar hym on honde he hadde enchanted
    me,—

My damè taughtè me that soutiltee,—
And eek I seyde, I mette of hym al nyght,
He wolde han slayn me as I lay up right,
And al my bed was ful of verray blood ;
But yet I hope that he shal do me good,   580
For blood bitokeneth gold, as me was
    taught ;
And al was fals, I dremed of it right
    naught,
But I folwed ay my damès loore,
As wel of this as of othere thyngès moore.
    But now, sire,—lat me se,—what I
    shal seyn ?
A ha ! by God, I have my tale ageyn.
    Whan that my fourthè housbonde was
    on beere
I weepte algate and madè sory cheere,
As wyvès mooten, for it is usage,
And with my coverchief covered my
    visage ;   591
But, for that I was purveyed of a make,
I wepte but smal, and that I undertake !
    To chirche was myn housbonde born
    a-morwe
With neighèbores, that for hym maden
    sorwe,
And Jankyn, ourè clerk, was oon of tho.
As help me God, whan that I saugh hym go
After the beere, me thoughte he hadde a
    paire
Of leggès and of feet so clene and faire,
That al myn herte I yaf unto his hoold.
He was, I trowe, a twenty wynter oold,   600
And I was fourty, if I shal seye sooth ;
But yet I hadde alwey a coltès tooth.
Gat-tothed I was, and that bicam me weel,
I hadde the prente of seintè Venus seel.
As help me God, I was a lusty oon,
And faire and riche, and yong, and wel
    bigon,
And trewely, as myne housbondes toldè me,
I hadde the beste quonyam myghtè be ;
For certès, I am al Venerien   609
In feelynge, and myn herte is Marcien ;
Venus me yaf my lust, my likerousnesse,
And Mars yaf me my sturdy hardynesse.
Myn áscendent was Taur and Mars
    therinne ;
Allas, allas ! that ever love was synne !
I folwed ay myn inclinacioun

By vertu of my constellacioun,
That madé me I koudé noght withdrawe
My chambre of Venus from a good felawe.
Yet have I Martés mark upon my face,
And also in another, privee, place,   620
For God so wys be my savacioun,
I ne loved never by no discrecioun,
But ever folwedé myn appetit,—
Al were he short, or long, or blak, or whit;
I took no kepe, so that he likéd me,
How poore he was, ne eek of what degree.
  What sholde I seye, but at the monthés
    ende
This joly clerk, Jankyn, that was so hende,
Hath wedded me with greet solempnytee,
And to hym yaf I all the lond and fee,
That ever was me yeven ther-bifoore; 631
But afterward repented me ful soore.
He noldé suffre nothyng of my list ;
By God, he smoot me onés, on the lyst,
For that I rente out of his book a leef,
That of the strook myn eré wex al deef.
Stibourne I was as is a leonesse,
And of my tonge a verray jangleresse ;
And walke I wolde, as I had doon biforn,
From hous to hous, although he had it
    sworn ;   640
For which he often tymés woldé preche,
And me of oldé Romayn geestés teche ;
How he, Symplicius Gallus, lefte his wyf,
And hire forsok for terme of al his lyf,
Noght but for open-heedid he hir say
Lokynge out at his dore upon a day.
  Another Romayn tolde he me by name,
That, for his wyf was at a somerés game
Withouten his wityng, he forsook hire eke ;
And thanne wolde he upon his Bible seke
That ilké proverbe of Ecclesiaste, 651
Where he comandeth, and forbedeth faste,
Man shal nat suffre his wyf go roule
    aboute.
Thanne wolde he seye right thus, with-
    outen doute :
Whoso that buyldeth his hous al of salwes,
And priketh his blyndé hors over the falwes,
And suffreth his wyf to go seken halwes,
Is worthy to been hanged on the galwes ;

642. *geestes.* These stories of Sulpicius Gallus
and Sempronius Sophus are taken from Valerius
Maximus (Bk. vi. ch. 3).

But al for noght, I setté noght an hawe
Of his proverbés, nof his oldé sawe ; 660
Ne I wolde nat of hym corrected be.
I hate hym that my vices telleth me,
And so doo mo, God woot, of us than I.
This made hym with me wood al outrely ;
I noldé noght forbere hym in no cas.
  Now wol I seye yow sooth, by Seint
    Thomas !
Why that I rente out of his book a leef,
For which he smoot me so that I was
    deef.
He hadde a book that gladly, nyght
    and day,
For his desport he woldé rede alway. 670
He clepéd it ' Valerie ' and ' Theofraste,'
At whiché book he lough alwey ful faste ;
And eek ther was som-tyme a clerk at
    Rome,
A cardinal, that highté Seint Jerome,
That made a book agayn Jovinian,
In whiché book eek ther was Tertulan,
Crisippus, Trotula, and Helowys,
That was abbessé nat fer fro Parys ;
And eek the Parables of Salomon,
Ovídés Art, and bookés many on ; 680
And allé thise were bounden in o volume ;
And every nyght and day was his custume,
Whan he hadde leyser and vacacioun
From oother worldly occupacioun,
To reden on this book of wikked wyves.
He knew of hem mo legendés and lyves
Than been of goodé wyvés in the Bible ;
For, trusteth wel, it is an impossible
That any clerk wol speké good of wyves,—
But if it be of hooly Seintés lyves,— 690
Ne of noon oother womman never the mo.
Who peyntedé the leoun? Tel me who.
By God ! if wommen haddé writen stories,
As clerkés han withinne hire oratories,
They wolde han writen of men moore
    wikkednesse
Than all the mark of Adam may redresse.
The children of Mercúrie and Venus

671. *Valerie,* i.e. Walter Map's *Epistola*
Valerii ad Rufinum de non ducenda uxore
  671. *Theofraste.* See note to l. 235.
  676. *Tertulan,* perhaps Tertullian's treatise *De*
Exhortatione Castitatis.
  677. *Crisippus, Trotula,* not identified yet
with any probability.

Been in hir wirkyng ful contrarius ;
Mercúrie loveth wysdam and science,
And Venus loveth ryot and dispence ; 700
And for hire diverse disposicioun
Each falleth in otheres exaltacioun ;
And thus, God woot, Mercurie is desolat
In Pisces, wher Venus is exaltat ;
And Venus falleth ther Mercurie is reysed ;
Therefore no womman of no clerk is
    preysed.
The clerk whan he is oold, and may
    noght do
Of Venus werkès worth his oldè sho,
Thanne sit he doun and writ in his dotage
That wommen kan nat kepe hir mariage.
    But now to purpos why I toldè thee 711
That I was beten for a book, *pardee.*
Upon a nyght Jankyn, that was oure sire,
Redde on his book, as he sat by the fire,
Of Eva first, that for hir wikkednesse
Was al mankyndè broght to wrecched-
    nesse ;
For which that Jesus Crist hymself was
    slayn,
That boghte us with his hertè blood agayn.
Lo, heere expres of womman may ye fynde,
That womman was the los of al mankynde.
    Tho redde he me how Sampson loste
    his heres ;   721
Slepynge, his lemman kitte ·it with hir
    sheres ;
Thurgh which tresoun loste he bothe his
    eyen.
    Tho redde he me, if that I shal nat lyen,
Of Hercules and of his Dianyre,
That causèd hym to sette hymself afyre.
    No thyng forgat he the penaunce and wo
That Socrates hadde with his wyvès two ;
How Xantippa caste pisse upon his heed.
This sely man sat stille as he were deed ;
He wiped his heed, namoorè dorste he
    seyn   731
But, ' Er that thonder styntè comth a
    reyn ! '
    Of Phasifpha, that was the queene of
    Crete,

708. *worth*, etc., H *is not worth a scho.*
717-20. Omitted in H⁶.
727. *penaunce*, from Pet.³   E² *sorwe*, H²
care.
733. *Phasifpha*, Pasiphaè.

For shrewednesse hym thoughte the talè
    swete.
Fy ! speke namoore ; it is a grisly thyng,
Of hire horríble lust and hir likyng !
    Of Clitermystra, for hire lecherye
That falsly made hire housbonde for to
    dye ;
He redde it with ful good devociouñ.
    He tolde me eek for what occasioun 740
Amphiorax at Thebès loste his lyf ;
Myn housbonde hadde a legende of his
    wyf,
Eriphilem, that for an ouche of gold
Hath privély unto the Grekès told
Wher that hir housbonde hidde hym in
    a place,
For which he hadde at Thebès sory grace.
    Of Lyma tolde he me, and of Lucye ;
They bothè made hir housbondes for to
    dye,—
That oon for love, that oother was for hate.
Lyma hir housbonde, upon an even late,
Empoysoned hath, for that she was his
    fo ;
Lucia likerous loved hire housbonde so,
That, for he sholde alwey upon hire
    thynke,
She yaf hym swich a manere lovè-drynke
That he was deed, er it were by the
    morwe ;
And thus algatès housbondès han sorwe.
    Thanne tolde he me how oon Latumyus
Compleyned, unto his felawe Arrius,
That in his gardyn growèd swich a tree,
On which, he seyde, how that his wyvès
    thre   760
Hangèd hemself for hertè despitus.
    ' O leevè brother,' quod this Arrius,
' Yif me a plante of thilkè blissèd tree,
And in my gardyn planted it shal be ! '
    Of latter date of wyvès hath he red,
That somme han slayn hir housbondes in
    hir bed,
And lete hir lecchour dighte hire al the
    nyght,

743. *Eriphilem*, who betrayed Amphiaraus to
gain the necklace of Harmonia.
747. *Lyma*, an error for ' Livia, who poisoned
Drusus ; this instance and the next are taken
from Map.
757. *Latumyus*. Map calls him Pacuvius.

Whil that the corps lay in the floor
    upright ;
And somme han dryven naylès in hir brayn
Whil that they slepte, and thus they han
    hem slayn.   770
Somme han hem yeven poysoun in hire
    drynke ;
He spak moore harm than hertè may
    bithynke ;
And therwithal he knew of mo proverbes,
Than in this world ther growen gras or
    herbes.
' Bet is,' quod he, ' thyn habitacioun
Be with a leoun or a foul dragoun,
Than with a womman usynge for to
    chyde.'
' Bet is,' quod he, ' hye in the roof abyde,
Than with an angry wyf doun in the hous.'
They been so wikked and contrarious, 780
They haten that hir housbondes loven ay.
He seyde a womman cast hir shame away
Whan she cast of hir smok ; and forther
    mo,
A fair womman, but she be chaast also,
Is lyk a gold ryng in a sowès nose.
Who woldè wenè, or who wolde suppose,
The wo that in myn hertè was, and pyne ?
  And whan I saugh he woldè never fyne
To reden on this cursèd book al nyght,
Al sodeynly thre levès have I plyght 790
Out of his book, right as he radde, and eke
I with my fest so took hym on the cheke,
That in oure fyr he fil bakward adoun ;
And he up stirte as dooth a wood leoun,
And with his fest he smoot me on the
    heed,
That in the floor I lay as I were deed ;
And whan he saugh how stillè that I lay,
He was agast and wolde han fled his way,
Til attè laste out of my swogh I breyde.
' O hastow slayn me, falsè theef ? ' I seyde ;
' And for my land thus hastow mordred
    me ?   801
Er I be deed, yet wol I kissè thee.'
    And neer he cam, and knelèd faire
    adoun,
And seydè, ' Deerè suster Alisoun !
As help me God, I shal thee never smyte.
That I have doon it is thyself to wyte ;
Foryeve it me, and that I thee biseke ' ;

And yet, eft-soones, I hitte hym on the
    cheke,
And seyde, ' Theef ! thus muchel am I
    wreke.   809
Now wol I dye, I may no lenger speke.'
But attè laste, with muchel care and wo,
We fille acorded by us selven two.
He yaf me al the bridel in myn hond,
To han the governance of hous and lond,
And of his tonge, and of his hond also,
And made hym brenne his book anon
    right tho ;
And whan that I hadde geten unto me
By maistrie al the sovèraynètee,—
And that he seyde, ' Myn owene trewè wyf,
Do as thee lust to terme of al thy lyf ; 820
Keepe thyn honour, and keepe eek myn
    estaat,'—
After that day we hadden never debaat.
God helpe me so, I was to hym as kynde
As any wyf from Denmark unto Ynde,
And also trewe, and so was he to me.
I prey to God, that sit in magestee,
So blesse his soulè for his mercy deere.
Now wol I seye my tale, if ye wol heere.

*Biholde the wordes bitwene the Somonour
    and the Frere*

  The Frere lough whan he hadde herd
    al this ;
' Now, dame,' quod he, ' so have I joye
    or blis,   .   830
This is a long preamble of a tale.'
And whan the Somonour herde the Frere
    gale,
  ' Lo,' quod the Somonour, ' Goddès
    armès two !
A frere wol entremette him ever-mo.
Lo, goodè men, a flye, and eek a frere,
Wol falle in every dysshè and mateere.
What spekestow of '' preambulacioun '' ?
What ? amble, or trotte, or pees, or go
    sit doun !
Thou lettest oure disport in this manere.'
  ' Ye, woltow so, sire Somonour ? ' quod
    the Frere ;   840
' Now, by my feith ! I shal, er that I go,

836. *and*, Corp.³ *and eek*, a clumsy device to
help out the line.

165

Telle of a somonour swich a tale or two
That alle the folk shal laughen in this
    place.'
    'Now ellès, Frerè, I bishrewe thy face,'
Quod this Somonour, 'and I bishrewé me
But if I tellé talès, two or thre,
Of frerès, er I come to Sidyngborne,
That I shal make thyn hertè for to morne,
For wel I woot thy pacïence is gon.'
    Oure Hoostè cridè, ' Pees ! and that
        anon ' ;   850
And seydè, ' Lat the womman telle hire
    tale ;
Ye fare as folk that dronken ben of ale.
Do, dame, telle forth youre tale, and
    that is best.'
    ' Al redy, sire,' quod she, ' right as
        yow lest ;
If I have licence of this worthy Frere.'
    ' Yis, dame,' quod he, ' tel forth, and
        I wol heere.'

WIFE OF BATH'S TALE

In tholdè dayès of the Kyng Arthour,
Of which that Britons speken greet
    honour,
All was this land fulfild of faïrye.   859
The elf queene with hir joly compaignye
Dauncèd ful ofte in many a grenè mede.
This was the olde. opinion as I rede,—
I speke of manye hundred yeres ago,—
But now kan no man se none elvès mo,
For now the gretè charitee and prayeres
Of lymytours, and othere hooly freres,
That serchen every lond and every streem,
As thikke as motès in the sonnè beem,—
Bléssynge hallès, chambres, kichenes,
    boures,
Citees, burghes, castels, hyè toures,   870
Thrópès, bernès, shipnes, daÿeryes,—
This maketh that ther been no faïryes ;
For ther as wont to walken was an elf,
Ther walketh now the lymytour hymself,

In undermelès and in morwenynges,
And seyth his matyns and his hooly
    thynges
As he gooth in his lymytacioun.
Wommen may go now saufly up and doun ;
In every bussh or under every tree,
Ther is noon oother incubus but he,   880
And he ne wol doon hem non dishonour.
    And so bifel it that this kynge, Arthour,
Hadde in his hous a lusty bacheler
That on a day cam ridynge fro ryver,
And happèd that, allone as she was born,
He saugh a maydè walkynge hym biforn,
Of whichè mayde, anon, maugree hir heed,
By verray force birafte hire maydenhed ;
For which oppressioun was swich clamour,
And swich pursute unto the kyng Arthour,
That dampnèd was this knyght for to be
    deed   891
By cours of lawe, and sholde han lost his
    heed,—
Paráventure swich was the statut tho,—
But that the queene and othere ladyes mo,
So longè preyèden the kyng of grace,
Til he his lyf hym grauntèd in the place,
And yaf hym to the queene al at hir wille
To chesè wheither she wolde hym save
    or spille.
    The queene thanketh the kyng with al
        hir myght,   899
And after this thus spak she to the knyght,
Whan that she saugh hir tyme upon a day :
' Thou standest yet,' quod she, ' in swich
    array,
That of thy lyf yet hastow no suretee.
I grante thee lyf, if thou kanst tellen me
What thyng is it that wommen moost
    desiren,—
Be war, and keepe thy nekkè-boon from
    iren,—
And if thou kanst nat tellen it anon,
Yet shal I yeve thee levè for to gon
A twelf-month and a day, to seche and
    leere
An answere suffisant in this mateere ;   910
And suretee wol I han, er that thou pace,
Thy body for to yelden in this place.'

847. *Sidyngborne*, Sittingbourne.
Wife of Bath's Tale. No original of this tale
is known. Tyrwhitt compares it to the story of
Florent in Gower's *Confessio Amantis*, Bk. i.
867. *serchen*, H *sechen*.

878. *now*, om. EH⁴.
881. *non*, the reading of Camb. MS. only ;
E H⁶ *but*, which is pointless.

Wo was this knyght, and sorwefully he
    siketh ;
But what? he may nat do al as hym liketh,
And at the laste he chees hym for to
    wende,
And come agayn right at the yerés ende,
With swich answere as God wolde hym
    purveye,
And taketh his leve, and wendeth forth
    his weye.
He seketh every hous and every place
Where as he hopeth for to fyndé grace 920
To lerné what thyng wommen loven
    moost ;
But he ne koude arryven in no coost
Wher as he myghté fynde in this mateere
Two creäturés áccordynge in feere.
    Somme seydé wommen loven best
        richesse,
Somme seyde honóur, somme seydé joly-
    nesse,
Somme riche array, somme seyden lust
    abedde,
And ofté tymé to be wydwe and wédde.
Somme seydé that oure hertés been moost
    esed 929
Whan that we been y-flatered and y-plesed.
    He gooth ful ny the sothe, I wol nat
    lye,—
A man shal wynne us best with flaterye ;
And with attendance and with bisynesse,
Been we y-lyméd, bothé moore and lesse.
    And sommé seyen that we loven best
For to be free, and do right as us lest,
And that no man repreve us of oure vice,
But seye that we be wise and no-thyng
    nyce ;
For trewély ther is noon of us alle,
If any wight wol clawe us on the galle, 940
That we nyl kiké, for he seith us sooth.
Assay, and he shal fynde it that so dooth,
For, be we never so vicious with-inne,
We wol been holden wise and clene of
    synne.
    And sommé seyn that greet delit han we
For to been holden stable and eke secree,
And in o purpos stedefastly to dwelle,
And nat biwreyé thyng that men us telle ;
But that tale is nat worth a raké-stele.
Pardee, we wommen konné no thyng hele ;

Witnesse on Myda, — wol ye heere the
    tale ?   *   951
Ovyde, amongés othere thyngés smale,
Seyde Myda hadde under his longé heres,
Growynge upon his heed, two asses eres,
The whiché vice he hydde as he best
    myghte,
Ful subtilly, from every mannés sighte,
That save his wyf ther wiste of it namo.
He loved hire moost, and trusted hire also ;
He preydé hire that to no creäture
She sholdé tellen of his disfigure. 960
    She swoor him nay, for al this world
    to wynne,
She noldé do that vileynye or synne,
To make hir housbonde han so foul a
    name.
She nolde nat telle it for hir owene shame ;
But nathélees hir thoughté that she dyde,
That she so longé sholde a conseil hyde ;
Hir thoughte it swal so soore aboute hir
    herte,
That nedély som word hire moste asterte ;
And sith she dorsté telle it to no man,
Doun to a mareys fasté by she ran. 970
Til she came there her herté was a-fyre,
And as a bitore bombleth in the myre
She leyde hir mouth unto the water doun :
' Biwreye me nat, thou water, with thy
    soun,'
Quod she, ' to thee I telle it and namo,—
Myn housbonde hath longe asses erys two.
Now is myn herte all hool, now is it oute,
I myghte no lenger kepe it, out of doute.'
Heere may ye se, thogh we a tyme abyde,
Yet, out it moot, we kan no conseil hyde.
The remenant of the tale if ye wol heere,
Redeth Ovyde, and ther ye may it leere.
    This knyght, of which my tale is
    specially,
Whan that he saugh he myghte nat come
    therby,
That is to seye, what wommen lové moost,
Withinne his brest ful sorweful was the
    goost.
But hoom he gooth, he myghté nat
    sojourne,
The day was come that homward moste
    he tourne,

    951. *Myda*, Midas.

167

And in his wey it happéd hym to ryde
In al this care, under a forest syde,   990
Wher as he saugh upon a dauncé go
Of ladyes foure and twenty, and yet mo ;
Toward the whiché daunce he drow ful
    yerne,
In hopé that som wysdom sholde he lerne ;
But certeinly, er he came fully there,
Vanysshéd was this daunce, he nysté
    where.
No creäturé saugh he that bar lyf,
Save on the grene he saugh sittynge a wyf ;
A fouler wight ther may no man devyse.
Agayn the knyght this oldé wyf gan ryse,
And seyde, ' Sire knyght, heer-forth ne
    lith no wey ;   1001
Tel me what that ye seken, by youre fey !
Paráventure it may the bettre be ;
Thise oldé folk kan muchel thyng,' quod
    she.
    ' My leevé mooder,' quod this knyght,
      ' certeyn
I nam but deed but if that I kan seyn
What thyng it is that wommen moost
    desire :
Koude ye me wisse I wolde wel quite
    youre hire.'
    ' Plight me thy trouthe, heere in myn
    hand,' quod she,
' The nexté thyng that I requeré thee 1010
Thou shalt it do, if it lye in thy myght,
And I wol telle it yow, er it be nyght.'
    ' Have heer my trouthé,' quod the
    knyght, ' I graunte !'
    Thanné quod she, ' I dar me wel
    avaunte
Thy lyf is sauf, for I wol stonde therby ;
Upon my lyf, the queene wol seye as I.
Lat se, which is the proudeste of hem alle
That wereth on a coverchief or a calle,
That dar seye "nay" of that I shal thee
    teche.   1019
Lat us go forth withouten lenger speche.'
Tho rownéd she a pistel in his ere,
And bad hym to be glad and have no fere.
    Whan they be comen to the court, this
    knyght
Seyde he had holde his day as he hadde
    hight,
And redy was his answere, as he sayde.

Ful many a noble wyf, and many a mayde,
And many a wydwé, for that they had
    been wise,
The queene hirself sittynge as a justise,
Assembled been, his answere for to heere ;
And afterward this knyght was bode
    appere.   1030
To every wight comanded was silence,
And that the knyght sholde telle in
    audience
What thyng that worldly wommen loven
    best.
This knyght ne stood nat stille as doth
    a best,
But to his questioun anon answerde,
With manly voys, that al the court it herde.
    ' My ligé lady, generally,' quod he,
' Wommen desiren have sovereynetee,
As wel over hir housbond, as hir love,
And for to been in maistrie hym above.
This is youre mooste desir, thogh ye me
    kille.   1041
Dooth as yow list, I am heer at youre
    wille.'
    In al the court ne was ther wyf, ne
    mayde,
Ne wydwé, that contraried that he sayde,
But seyden he was worthy han his lyf ;
And with that word up stirte the oldé wyf,
Which that the knyght saugh sittynge on
    the grene ;
' Mercy !' quod she, ' my sovereyn lady
    queene !
Er that youre court departé, do me right ;
I taughté this answere unto the knyght,
For which he plighté me his trouthé there,
The firsté thyng I woldé hym requere,
He wolde it do, if it lay in his myght.
Bifore the court thanne, preye I thee, sir
    knyght,'
Quod she, ' that thou me take unto thy
    wyf,
For wel thou woost that I have kept thy lyf.
If I sey fals, sey "nay," upon thy fey !'
    This knyght answerde, ' Allas, and
    weylawey !
I woot right wel that swich was my biheste.
For Goddés love, as chees a newe
    requeste !   1060
Taak al my good, and lat my body go.'

'Nay, thanne,' quod she, 'I shrewe us
   bothé two !
For thogh that I be foul, and oold, and
   poore,
I nolde, for al the metal, ne for oore
That under erthe is grave, or lith above,
But if thy wyf I were, and eek thy love !'
   'My "love"!' quod he, 'nay, my
   dampnacioun !
Allas ! that any of my nacioun
Sholde ever so foulé disparáged be !'
But al for noght, the ende is this, that he
Constreynéd was, he nedés moste hire
   wedde,   1071
And taketh his oldé wyf, and gooth to
   bedde.
   Now wolden som men seye, pará-
   venture,
That for my necligence I do no cure
To tellen yow the joye and al tharray,
That at the feesté was that ilké day ;
To which thyng shortly answeren I shal ;
I seye, ther nas no joye ne feeste at al.
Ther nas but hevynesse, and muché sorwe,
For privély he wedded hire on a morwe,
And al day after hidde hym as an owle,
So wo was hym, his wyf lookéd so foule.
   Greet was the wo the knyght hadde in
   his thoght,
Whan he was with his wyf abedde y-broght,
He walweth, and he turneth to and fro ;
His oldé wyf lay smylynge evermo,
And   seyde,   'O   deeré   housbonde,
   benedicitee !
Fareth every knyght thus with his wyf,
   as ye ?
Is this the law of kyng Arthúrés hous ?
Is every knyght of his so dangerous ? 1090
I am youre owene love, and youré wyf ;
I am she which that savéd hath youre lyf,
And certes, yet dide I yow never unright,
Why fare ye thus with me, this firsté
   nyght ?
Ye faren lyk a man had lost his wit ;
What is my gilt ? For Goddés love tel it,
And it shal been amended, if I may.'
   'Amended !' quod this knyght, 'allas !
   nay, nay !
It wol nat been amended never mo,
Thou art so loothly, and so oold also, 1100

And ther-to comen of so lough a kynde,
That litel wonder is thogh I walwe and
   wynde.
So, woldé God ! myn herté woldé breste !'
   'Is this,' quod she, 'the cause of youre
   unreste ?'
   'Ye, certeinly,' quod he, 'no wonder is.'
   'Now, sire,' quod she, 'I koude
   amende al this,
If that me liste, er it were dayés thre ;
So wel ye myghté bere yow unto me.'
   'But for ye speken of swich gentillesse
As is descended out of old richesse, 1110
That therfore sholden ye be gentil men,
Swich arrogance is nat worth an hen.
Looke, who that is moost vertuous alway,
Pryvee and apert, and moost entendeth ay
To do the gentil dedés that he kan,
Taak hym for the grettest gentil man.
Crist wole we clayme of hym oure gentil-
   lesse,
Nat of oure eldrés for hire old richesse ;
For, thogh they yeve us al hir heritage,—
For which we clayme to been of heigh
   parage,—   1120
Yet may they nat biquethé for no thyng,
To noon of us, hir vertuous lyvyng,
That made hem gentil men y-called be,
And bad us folwen hem in swich degree.
   'Wel kan the wisé poete of Florence,
That highté Dant, speken in this sen-
   tence,—
Lo, in swich maner rym is Dantes tale,—
   'Ful selde up riseth by his branches
   smale
Prowesse of man, for God of his goodnesse
Wole   that   of   hym   we   clayme   oure
   gentillesse ;   1130
For oure eldrés may we no-thyng
   clayme,
But temporel thyng that man may hurte
   and mayme.'
   'Eek every wight woot this as wel as I,
If gentillesse were planted natureelly,
Unto a certeyn lynage doun the lyne,
Pryvee nor apert, thanne wolde they
   never fyne

1126. *Dant, Purgatorio,* vii. 121-3 : 'Rade
volte risurge per li rami L' umana probitate,' etc.
1131. *eldrés may we,* H *auncestres we.*

169

To doon of gentillesse the faire office ;
They myghte do no vileynye or vice.
　‹ Taak fyr and ber it in the darkeste
　　hous,　　　　　　　　　　　　　1139
Bitwix this and the mount of Kaukasous,
And lat men shette the dores and go
　　thenne,
Yet wole the fyr as faire lye and brenne
As twenty thousand men myghte it
　　biholde ;
His office natureel ay wol it holde,
Up peril of my lyf, til that it dye.
　‹ Heere may ye se wel how that
　　genterye
Is nat annexed to possessioun,
Sith folk ne doon hir operacioun
Alwey, as dooth the fyr, lo, in his kynde ;
For, God it woot, men may wel often fynde
A lordes sone do shame and vileynye ;
And he that wole han pris of his gentrye,
For he was boren of a gentil hous,
And hadde his eldres noble and vertuous,
And nyl hymselven do no gentil dedis,
Ne folwen his gentil auncestre that deed is,
He nys nat gentil, be he duc or erl ;
For vileyns synful dedes make a cherl ;
For gentillesse nys but renomee
Of thyne auncestres, for hire heigh
　　bountee,　　　　　　　　　　　1160
Which is a strange thyng to thy persone.
Thy gentillesse cometh fro God allone ;
Thanne comth oure verray gentillesse of
　　grace,
It was no thyng biquethe us with oure
　　place.
　‹ Thenketh how noble, as seith
　　Valerius,
Was thilke Tullius Hostillius,
That out of poverte roos to heigh noblesse.
Redeth Senek, and redeth eek Boece,
Ther shul ye seen expresse, that no drede
　　is,　　　　　　　　　　　　　1169
That he is gentil that dooth gentil dedis ;
And therfore, leeve housbonde, I thus
　　conclude ;
Al were it that myne auncestres weren
　　rude,

Yet may the hye God, and so hope I,
Grante me grace to lyven vertuously ;
Thanne am I gentil, whan that I bigynne
To lyven vertuously and weyve synne.
　‹ And ther as ye of poverte me repreeve
The hye God, on whom that we bileeve,
In wilful poverte chees to lyve his lyf,
And certes, every man, mayden, or wyf,
May understonde that Jhesus, hevene
　　kyng,　　　　　　　　　　　1181
Ne wolde nat chese a vicious lyvyng.
Glad poverte is an honeste thyng, certeyn ;
This wole Senec and othere clerkes seyn ;
Whoso that halt hym payd of his poverte,
I holde hym riche, al hadde he nat a
　　sherte ;
He that coveiteth is a povere wight,
For he wolde han that is nat in his
　　myght ;
But he that noght hath, ne coveiteth have,
Is riche, although ye holde hym but a
　　knave.　　　　　　　　　　　1190
　‹ Verray poverte, it syngeth proprely ;
Juvenal seith of poverte, myrily,
" The poure man, whan he goth by the
　　weye,
Bifore the theves he may synge and pleye."
Poverte is hateful good, and as I gesse
A ful greet bryngere-out of bisynesse,
A greet amendere eek of sapience,
To hym that taketh it in pacience,
Poverte is this, although it seme alenge,
Possessioun that no wight wol chalenge.
Poverte ful ofte, whan a man is lowe,
Maketh his God, and eek hymself, to
　　knowe.
Poverte a spectacle is, as thynketh me,
Thurgh which he may his verray freendes
　　see ;
And therfore, sire, syn that I noght yow
　　greve,
Of my poverte namoore ye me repreve.
　‹ Now, sire, of elde ye repreve me ;
And certes, sire, thogh noon auctoritee
Were in no book, ye gentils of honour

1159. *renomee*, renown ; cp. Boethius, Bk. iii.
Prose 6.
1165. *Valerius*, see Valerius Maximus, Bk.
iii. ch. 4.

1192. *Juvenal, Sat.* x. 22.
1195. *hateful* (Corp.³ *hatel*, hostile). E quotes
in the margin the answer to the question ‘ Quid
est paupertas (Odibile bonum, sanitatis mater,
etc.)’ from the Dialogue of Adrian and Secundus,
found in Vincent de Beauvais.

Seyn that men sholde an oold wight doon
   favóur,   1210
And clepe hym fader, for youre gentil-
   lesse,
And auctours shal I fynden, as I gesse.
   ' Now, ther ye seye that I am foul and
      old,
Than drede you noght to been a cokewold;
For filthe and eelde, al so moot I thee !
Been grete wardeyns upon chastitee :
But nathelees, syn I knowe youre delit,
I shal fulfille youre worldly appetit.
   ' Chese now,' quod she, ' oon of thise
      thynges tweye :   1219
To han me foul and old til that I deye,
And be to yow a trewe, humble wyf,
And never yow displese in al my lyf ;
Or elles ye wol han me yong and fair,
And take youre áventure of the repair
That shal be to youre hous by cause of me,
Or in som oother place may wel be ;
Now chese yourselven, wheither that yow
      liketh.'
   This knyght avyseth hym and sore
      siketh ;
But atté laste he seyde in this manere :
' My lady and my love, and wyf so deere,
I put me in youre wise governance ; 1231
Cheseth youre self which may be moost
   plesance,
And moost honóur to yow and me also ;
I do no fors the wheither of the two,
For as yow liketh it suffiseth me.'
   ' Thanne have I gete of yow maistrie,'
      quod she,
' Syn I may chese, and governe as me
      lest ? '
   ' Ye, certes, wyf,' quod he, ' I holde
      it best.'
   ' Kys me,' quod she, ' we be no lenger
      wrothe,
For, by my trouthe, I wol be to yow
      bothe,—   1240
This is to seyn, ye, bothe fair and good.
I prey to God that I moote sterven wood,
But I to yow be al so good and trewe,
As ever was wyf syn that the world was
   newe ;
And but I be to-morn as fair to seene
As any lady, emperice, or queene,

That is bitwixe the est and eek the west ;
Dooth with my lyf and deth right as yow
   lest.
Cast up the curtyn,—looke, how that it is.'
   And whan the knyght saugh verraily
      al this,   1250
That she so fair was, and so yong ther-to,
For joye he hente hire in his armes two,
His herte bathed in a bath of blisse ;
A thousand tyme arewe he gan hire kisse,
And she obeyed hym in every thyng
That myghte doon hym plesance or likyng.
   And thus they lyve unto hir lyves ende
In parfit joye ; and Jhesu Crist us sende
Housbondes meeke, yonge, fressh a-bedde,
And grace toverbyde hem that we wedde,
And eek, I praye Jhesu to shorte hir lyves
That nat wol be governed by hir wyves ;
And olde and angry nygardes of dispence,
God sende hem soone verray pestilence !

The prologe of the Freres Tale

   This worthy Lymytour, this noble Frere,
He made alway a maner louryng chiere
Upon the Somonour, but for honestee
No vileyns word as yet to hym spak he ;
But atté laste he seyde unto the Wyf,
' Dame,' quod he, ' God yeve yow right
      good lyf !   1270
Ye han heer touched, al so moot I thee !
In scole-matere greet difficultee.
Ye han seyd muche thyng right wel, I
      seye ;
But, dame, heere as we ryde by the weye
Us nedeth nat to speken but of game,
And lete auctoritees, on Goddes name,
To prechyng, and to scole of clergye,
And if it lyke to this compaignye
I wol yow of a somonour telle a game.
Pardee, ye may wel knowe by the name 1280
That of a somonour may no good be sayd.
I praye that noon of you be yvele apayd,—
A somonour is a rennere up and doun
With mandementz for fornicacioun,
And is y-bet at every townes ende.'
   Oure Hoost tho spak, ' A, sire, ye
      sholde be hende
And curteys, as a man of youre estaat,

In compaignye ; we wol have no debaat !
Telleth youre tale, and lat the Somonour
     be.'
   ' Nay,' quod the Somonour, ' lat hym
     seye to me   1290
What so hym list,—whan it comth to
     my lot,
By God ! I shal hym quiten every grot !
I shal hym tellen which a greet honóur
It is to be a flaterynge lymytour ;
And his office I shal hym telle y-wis.'
   Oure Hoost answerdé, ' Pees ! namoore
     of this ! '
And after this he seyde unto the Frere,
' Tel forth youre tale, my leevé maister
     deere.'

FRIAR'S TALE

Heere bigynneth The Freres Tale

Whilom ther was dwellynge in my
     contree
An erchédekene, a man of heigh degree,
That boldély dide execucioun   1301
In punysshynge of fornicacioun,
Of wicchécraft, and eek of bawderye,
Of diffamacioun and avowtrye,
Of chirché-revés, and of testamentz,
Of contractes, and of lakke of sacramentz,
And eek of many another manere cryme,
Which nedeth nat rehercen for this tyme ;
Of usure, and of symonye also.   1309
But certés, lecchours dide he grettest wo ;
They sholdé syngen if that they were hent ;
And smalé tytheres weren foule y-shent ;
If any persone wolde upon hem pleyne
Ther myghte asterte hym no pecunyal
     peyne.
For smalé tithés, and for smal offrynge,
He made the peple pitously to synge,
For er the bisshope caughte hem with
     his hook,

   1294, 1295. Between these lines E⁶ wrongly
insert 1307, 1308.
   The Freres Tale. Two Latin stories, one of a
wicked seneschal, the other of a lawyer, making
the same points as this, were printed by Thomas
Wright, and have been reprinted in Part 1. of
the Chaucer Society's *Originals and Analogues.*
We may be sure that the setting of this story is
entirely Chaucer's own.

They weren in the erchédeknes book ;
And thanne hadde he, thurgh his juris-
     diccioun,
Power to doon on hem correccioun.   1320
He hadde a somonour redy to his hond ;
A slyer boye was noon in Engelond ;
For subtilly he hadde his espiaille
That taughté hym whér hym myghte
     availle.
He koudé spare of lecchours oon or two,
To techen hym to foure and twenty mo ;
For thogh this somonour wood was as
     an hare,
To telle his harlotrye I wol nat spare,
For we been out of his correccioun,
They han of us no jurisdiccioun,   1330
Ne never shullen, terme of alle hir lyves.
   ' Peter ! so been the wommen of the
     styves,'
Quod the Somonour, ' y-put out of my
     cure ! '
   ' Pees ! with myschance and with
     mysáventure ! '
Thus seyde our Hoost, ' and lat hym
     telle his tale.
Now telleth forth, thogh that the
     Somonour gale ;
Ne spareth nat, myn owene maister deere.'
   This falsé theef, this somonour, quod
     the Frere,
Hadde alwey bawdés redy to his hond,
As any hauk to lure in Engelond,   1340
That tolde hym al the secree that they
     knewe,
For hire acqueyntance was nat come of
     newe ;
They weren his approwours prively.
He took hymself a greet profit therby ;
His maister knew nat alwey what he wan.
Withouten mandément, a lewéd man
He koude somne, on peyne of Cristés curs,
And they were glade to fillé wel his purs,
And make hym greté feestés atte nale ;
And right as Judas haddé purses smale, 1350
And was a theef, right swich a theef was he.
His maister hadde but half his duétee.
He was, if I shal yeven hym his laude,
A theef, and eek a somnour, and a baude.
He hadde eek wenches at his retenue

         1323. *subtilly,* H *prively.*

That wheither that sir Robert, or sir
    Huwe,
Or Jakke, or Rauf, or whoso that it were
That lay by hem, they tolde it in his ere.
    Thus was the wenche and he of oon
      assent,   1359
And he wolde fecche a feynèd mandèment,
And somne hem to the chapitre bothè
    two,
And pile the man, and lete the wenchè go.
    Thanne wolde he seye, 'Freend, I
      shal for thy sake
Do striken thee out of oure lettres blake,
Thee thar namoore as in this cas travaille,
I am thy freend, ther I thee may availle.'
    Certeyn he knew of briberýes mo
Than possible is to telle in yerès two ;
For in this world nys doggè for the bowe
That kan an hurt deer from an hool y-
    knowe   1370
Bet than this somnour knew a sly lecchour,
Or an avowtier, or a paramour ;
And, for that was the fruyt of al his rente,
Therfore on it he sette al his entente.
    And so bifel that onès on a day
This somnour, ever waityng on his pray,
Rod forth to somne an old wydwe, a ribibe,
Feynynge a causè, for he woldè brybe,—
And happed that he saugh bifore hym ryde
A gay yeman, under a forest syde.   1380
A bowe he bar, and arwes brighte and
    kene ;
He hadde upon a courtèpy of grene,
An hat upon his heed with frenges blake.
    'Sire,' quod this somnour, 'hayl ! and
      wel atake !'
    'Welcome !' quod he, 'and every
      good felawe.
Wher rydestow, under this grene-wode
    shawe,'
Seydè this yeman ; 'wiltow fer to day ?'
    This somnour hym answerde and
      seydè, 'Nay,
Heere fastè by,' quod he, 'is myn entente
To ryden, for to reysen up a rente   1390
That longeth to my lordès duètee.'
    'Ártow thanne a bailly ?' 'Ye,' quod
    he,—

He dorstè nat, for verray filthe and shame,
Seye that he was a somonour, for the
    name.
    '*Depardieux !*' quod this yeman,
      'deerè broother !
Thou art a bailly, and I am another.
I am unknowen as in this contree ;
Of thyn acqueyntance I wolde prayè thee,
And eek of bretherhede, if that yow leste ;
I havè gold and silver in my cheste ;   1400
If that thee happe to comen in oure shire
Al shal be thýn, right as thou wolt desire.'
    '*Grantmercy !*' quod this somonour,
      'by my feith !'
Everych in ootheres hand his trouthè leith,
For to be swornè bretheren til they deye ;
In daliance they ryden forth hir weye.
    This somonour that was as ful of jangles
As ful of venym been thise waryangles,
And ever enqueryng upon every thyng ;
'Brother,' quod he, 'where is now youre
    dwellyng,   1410
Another day if that I sholde yow seche ?'
This yeman hym answerde, in softè
    speche :
'Brother,' quod he, 'fer in the north
    contree,
Where as I hope som tyme I shal thee see.
Er we departe I shal thee so wel wisse
That of myn hous ne shaltow never mysse.'
    'Now, brother,' quod this somonour,
      'I yow preye,
Teche me, whil that we ryden by the
    weye,—
Syn that ye been a baillif as am I,—
Som subtiltee, and tel me feithfully   1420
In myn office how I may moostè wynne,
And spareth nat for consclence ne synne,
But as my brother tel me how do ye.'
    'Now, by my trouthè, brother deere,'
      seydè he,
'As I shal tellen thee a feithful tale,
My wages been ful streitè and ful smale ;
My lord is hard to me and daungerous,
And myn office is ful laborous ;
And therfore by extorcions I lyve ;
For sothe, I take all that men wol me yeve,
Algate by sleyghtè, or by violence.   1431

1356. *sir Robert*, a priest, not a knig'<t.
. 1364. *thee*, E² *hire*.

1395. *deere*, H² *lieve*.
1406. *hir weye*, H³ *and pleye(n)*.

173

Fro yeer to yeer I wynne al my dispence ;
I kan no bettré tellé, feithfully.'
  'Now certés,' quod this somonour,
   'so fare I ;
I sparé nat to taken, God it woot,
But if it be to hevy or to hoot,
What I may gete in conseil privély ;
No maner conscïence of that have I ;
Nere myn extorcïoun I myghte nat lyven,
Nor of swiche japés wol I nat be shryven.
Stomak, ne conscïence, ne knowe I noon
I shrewe thise shrifté-fadres 'everychoon !
Wel be we met, by God and by Seint
   Jame !
But, leevé brother, tel me thanne thy
   name,'
Quód this somonour ; 'in this meené
   while.'
This yeman gan a litel for to smyle.
  'Brother,' quod he, 'wiltow that I
   thee telle ?
I am a feend ; my dwellyng is in helle,
And heere I ryde aboute my purchasyng,
To wite wher men wol yeve me anything.
My purchas is theffect of al my rente. 1451
Looke how thou rydest for the same
   entente.
To wynné good, thou rekkest never how ;
Right so fare I, for ryde I wolde right
   now
Unto the worldés endé for a preyé.'
  'A !' quod this somonour, '*benedicite !*
   what sey ye ?
I wende ye were a yeman trewély.
Ye han a mannés shape as wel as I,
Han ye a figure thanne determinat
In hellé, ther ye been in youre estat ?' 1460
  'Nay, certeinly,' quod he, 'ther have
   we noon,
But whan us liketh we kan take us oon,
Or ellés make yow semé we been shape
Somtymé lyk a man, or lyk an ape ;
Or lyk an angel kan I ryde or go.
It is no wonder thyng thogh it be so ;
A lowsy jogelour kan deceyvé thee,
And *pardee !* yet kan I moore craft than
   he.'
  'Why,' quod the somonour, ' ryde ye
   thanne or goon
In sondry shape, and nat alwey in oon ?'

  'For we,' quod he, 'wol us swiche
   formés make   1471
As moost able is oure preyés for to take.'
  'What maketh yow to han al this
   labour ?'
  'Ful many a cause, leevé sire
   somonour,'
Seydé this feend ; 'but allé thyng hath
   tyme ;
The day is short, and it is passéd pryme,
And yet ne wan I nothyng in this day ;
I wol entende to wynnyng if I may,
And nat entende our wittés to declare ;
For, brother myn, thy wit is al to bare 1480
To understonde, althogh I tolde hem thee.
But for thou axest why labouren we,—
For somtyme we been Goddés instrumentz,
And meenés to doon his comandémentz,
Whan that hym list, upon his creätures,
In divers art and in diverse figures.
Withouten hym we have no myght,
   certayn,
If that hym list to stonden ther agayn.
And somtyme, at oure prayere, han we leve
Oonly the body and nat the soulé greve ;
Witnesse on Job, whom that we diden wo ;
And somtyme han we myght of bothé
   two,
This is to seyn, of soule and body eke ;
And somtyme be we suffred for to seke
Upon a man and doon his soule unreste,
And nat his body, and al is for the beste.
Whan he withstandeth oure temptacïoun
It is a cause of his savacïoun,—
Al be it that it was nat oure entente
He sholde be sauf, but that we wolde
   hym hente,—   1500
And somtyme be we servant unto man,
As to the erchébisshope, Seint Dunstan ;
And to the Apostles servant eek was I.'
  'Yet tel me,' quod the somonour,
   'feithfully,
Make ye yow newé bodies thus alway
Of elementz ?'   The feend answerdé,
   'Nay,
Somtyme we feyne, and somtyme we aryse
With dedé bodyes, in ful sondry wyse,
And speke as renably and faire and wel,

1479. *wittes*, H *thinges.*
1486. *art*, H⁴ *act, actes.*

As to the Phitonissa dide Samuel ;   1510
And yet wol som men seye it was nat he.
I do no fors of youre dyvynytee,
But o thyng warne I thee, I wol nat jape,
Thou wolt algatès wite how we been
     shape,
Thou shalt herafterwardes, my brother
     deere,
Come there thee nedeth nat of me to leere,
For thou shalt by thyn owene experience
Konne in a chayer rede of this sentence
Bet than Virgilè while he was on lyve,
Or Dant also ; now lat us rydè blyve,   1520
For I wole holdè compaignye with thee
Til it be so that thou forsakè me.'
   ' Nay,' quod this somonour, ' that shal
     nat bityde !
I am a yeman knowen is ful wyde ;
My trouthè wol I holde as in this cas ;
For though thou were the devel, Sathanas,
My trouthè wol I holdè to my brother,
As I am sworn, and ech of us til oother,
For to be trewè brother in this cas ;
And bothe we goon abouten oure purchas.
Taak thou thy part, what that men wol
     thee yeve,   1531
And I shal myn,—thus may we bothè
     lyve,—
And if that any of us have moore than
     oother,
Lat hym be trewe and parte it with his
     brother.'
   ' I grauntè,' quod the devel, ' by my fey !'
And with that word they ryden forth
     hir wey,
And right at the entryng of the townès
     ende,
To which this somonour shoope hym for
     to wende,
They saugh a cart that charged was with
     hey,
Which that a cartere droof forth in his
     wey.   1540
Deepe was the wey, for which the cartè
     stood :
The cartere smoot and cryde as he were
     wood,

1510. *Phitonissa*, Pythoness, *i.e.* the Witch of
Endor.
   1518. *i.e.* be able to lecture on this theme.

' Hayt, Brok ! hayt, Scot ! what spare ye
     for the stones !
The feend,' quod he, ' yow fecchè, body
     and bones,
As ferforthly as ever were ye foled !
So muchè wo as I have with yow tholed !
The devel have al, bothe hors and cart
     and hey !'
This somonour seyde, ' Heere shal we
     have a pley ' ;
And neer the feend he drough, as noght
     ne were,
Ful privèly, and rownèd in his ere,   1550
' Herkne, my brother ! herkne, by thy
     feith !
Herestow nat how that the cartere seith ?
Hent it anon, for he hath yeve it thee,
Bothe hey and cart and eek his caples
     thre.'
   ' Nay,' quod the devel, ' God woot,
     never a deel.
It is nat his entente, trust thou me weel ;
Axe hym thyself, if thou nat trowest me,
Or ellès stynt a while, and thou shalt see.'
   This cartere thakketh his hors upon
     the croupe,
And they bigonnè drawen and to-stoupe.
' Heyt ! now,' quod he, ' ther Jhesu Crist
     yow blesse !   1561
And al his handwerk bothè moore and
     lesse !
That was wel twight, myn owene lyard
     boy !
I pray God savè thee ! and Seintè Loy !
Now is my cart out of the slow, *pardee !* '
   ' Lo, brother,' quod the feend, ' what
     tolde I thee ?
Heere may ye se, myn owene deerè
     brother,
The carl spak oon thing, but he thoghte
     another.
Lat us go forth abouten oure viage ;
Heere wynne I nothyng upon cariage.' 1570
   Whan that they coomen somwhat out
     of towne

1559. *thakketh*, smacks ; E² *taketh.*
1559. *hors*, plural.
1564. *pray*, E *pray to.*
1564. *thee*, H³ *thy* (the) *body.*
1564. *Seintè Loy*, St. Eligius.
1568. *thing*, om. E.

This somonour to his brother gan to
     rowne :
' Brother,' quod he, ' heere woneth an
     old rebekke
That hadde almoost as lief to lese hire
     nekke,
As for to yeve a peny of hir good.
I wole han twelf pens though that she be
     wood,
Or I wol sompne hire unto oure office,
And yet, God woot, of hire knowe I no
     vice ;
But, for thou kanst nat, as in this contree,
Wynné thy cost, taak heer ensample of
     me.'   1580
     This somonour clappeth at the wydwés
     gate :
' Com out,' quod he, ' thou oldé virytrate !
I trowe thou hast som frere or preest with
     thee.'
     ' Who clappeth ? ' seyde this wyf,
         ' *benedicitee !*
God save you, sire ! what is youre sweeté
     wille ? '
     ' I have,' quod he, ' of somonaunce a
     bille ;
Up peyne of cursyng looké that thou be
To-morn bifore the erchédeknes knee,
Tanswere to the court of certeyn thynges.'
     ' Now, Lord,' quod she, ' Crist Jhesu,
     kyng of kynges,   1590
So wisly helpé me, as I ne may !
I have been syk, and that ful many a day ;
I may nat go so fer,' quod she, ' ne ryde,
But I be deed, so priketh it in my syde.
May I nat axe a libel, sire somonour,
And answere there by my procúratour
To swich thyng as men wole opposen me ? '
     ' Yis,' quod this somonour, ' pay anon
     —lat se—
Twelf pens to me and I wole thee acquite.
I shal no profit han therby but lite,   1600
My maister hath the profit, and nat I.
Com of, and lat me ryden hastily ;
Gif me twelf pens, I may no lenger tarye ! '
     ' Twelf pens ! ' quod she, ' now lady,
     Seinté Marie !
So wisly help me out of care and synne,

1586. *somonaunce*, E *somonce*.
1587. *Up*, E *Upon*.

This wydé world thogh that I sholdé
     wynne,
Ne have I nat twelf pens withinne myn
     hoold ;
Ye knowen wel that I am poure and oold.
Kithé youre almesse on me, pouré wrecche.'
     ' Nay, thanne,' quod he, ' the foulé
     feend me fecche,   1610
If I thexcusé though thou shul be spilt ! '
     ' Allas ! ' quod she, ' God woot I have
     no gilt.'
     ' Pay me ! ' quod he, ' or by the sweete
     Seinte Anne,
As I wol bere awey thy newé panne
For dette which that thou owest me of
     old,—
Whan that thou madest thyn housbonde
     cokéwold
I payde at hoom for thy correccioun.'
     ' Thou lixt ! ' quod she, ' by my sava-
     cioun
Ne was I never er now, wydwe ne wyf,
Somoned unto youre court in al my lyf !
Ne never I nas but of my body trewe. 1621
Unto the devel, blak and rough of hewe,
Yeve I thy body and my panne also ! '
     And whan the devel herde hire cursen
     so
Upon hir knees, he seyde in this manere :
' Now, Mabély, myn owene moder deere,
Is this youre wyl in ernest that ye seyde ? '
     ' The devel,' quod she, ' so fecche hym
     er he deye,—
And panne and al, but he wol hym
     repente ! '
     ' Nay, oldé stot ! that is nat myn
     entente,'   1630
Quod this somonour, ' for to repenté me
For anythyng that I have had of thee ;
I wolde I hadde thy smok and every
     clooth.'
     ' Now, brother,' quod the devil, ' be
     nat wrooth :
Thy body and this panne been myne by
     right ;
Thou shalt with me to hellé yet to-nyght,
Where thou shalt knowen of oure privétee
Moore than a maister of dyvynytee.'
     And with that word this foulé feend hym
     hente.   1639

Body and soule he with the devel wente
Where as that somonours han hir heritage;
And God, that makéd after his ymage
Mankyndé, save and gyde us alle and
    some,
And leve thise somonours goodé men
    bicome !
  Lordynges, I koude han toold yow,
    quod this Frere,
Hadde I had leyser for this Somnour heere,
After the text of Cristé, Poul, and John,
And of oure othere doctours many oon,
Swiche peynés that youre herté myghte
    agryse ;
Al be it so no tongé may devyse—   1650
Thogh that I myghte a thousand wynter
    telle—
The peynes of thilké curséd hous of helle ;
But for to kepe us fro that curséd place
Waketh and preyeth Jhesu for his grace,
So kepe us fro the temptour Sathanas.
Herketh this word, beth war, as in this
    cas :
' The leoun sit in his awayt alway
To sle the innocent, if that he may.'
Disposeth ay youre hertés to withstonde
The feend, that yow wolde maké thral
    and bonde ;   1660
He may nat tempté yow over youre
    myght,
For Crist wol be youre champion and
    knyght ;
And prayeth that thise somonours hem
    repente
Of hir mysdedes, er that the feend hem
    hente !

The prologe of the Somonours Tale

  This Somonour in his styropes hyé
    stood.
Upon this Frere his herté was so wood,
That lyk an aspen leef he quook for ire.
  ' Lordynges,' quod he, ' but o thyng I
    desire,—
I yow biseke that of youre curteisye,

1663. H⁵ make the hit more direct, reading
this (oure) sompnour him repente, etc.
1665. *hye,* H *up he.*

N   177

Syn ye han herd this falsé Frere lye,   1670
As suffereth me I may my talé telle.
  ' This Freré bosteth that he knoweth
    helle,
And God it woot, that it is litel wonder ;
Frerés and feendés been but lyte asonder ;
For, *pardee !* ye han ofté tyme herd telle
How that a freré ravysshed was to helle
In spirit onés by a visioun ;
And as an angel ladde hym up and doun,
To shewen hym the peynés that ther
    were,
In al the placé saugh he nat a frere.   1680
Of oother folk he saugh ynowe in wo.
Unto this angel spak the freré tho :
  ' " Now, sire," quod he, " han frerés
    swich a grace
That noon of hem shal comé to this place ? "
  ' " Yis," quod this angel, " many a
    millioun " ;
And unto Sathanas he ladde hym doun,
And now hath Sathanas, seith he, a tayl,
Brodder than of a carryk is the sayl.
" Hold up thy tayl, thou Sathanas,"
    quod he,
" Shewe forth thyn ers, and lat the freré
    se   1690
Where is the nest of frerés in this place " ;
And er that half a furlong wey of space,
Right so as bees out swarmen from an
    hyve,
Out of the develes ers ther gonné dryve
Twénty thousand frerés in a route,
And thurgh-out hellé swarméden aboute,
And comen agayn as faste as they may
    gon,
And in his ers they crepten everychon ;
He clapte his tayl agayn and lay ful
    stille.
This frere, whan he hadde lookéd al his
    fille   1700
Upon the tormentz of this sory place,
His spirit God restoréd of his grace
Unto his body agayn, and he awook ;
But nathéles, for feré yet he quook,
So was the develes ers ay in his mynde ;
That is his heritage of verray kynde.
God save yow allé, save this curséd
    Frere !
My prologe wol I ende in this manere.'

SUMMONER'S TALE

Heere bigynneth The Somonour his Tale

Lordynges, ther is in Yorkshire, as I gesse,
A mersshy contree callèd Holdernesse, 1710
In which ther wente a lymytour aboute
To preche, and eek to begge, it is no doute.
And so bifel that on a day this frere
Hadde prechèd at a chirche in his manere,
And specially, aboven every thyng,
Excited he the peple in his prechyng
To trentals, and to yeve for Goddès sake,
Wherwith men myghtè hooly houses make,
Ther as divinè servyce is honóured,
Nat ther as it is wasted and devoured,
Ne ther it nedeth nat for to be yeve, 1721
As to possessioners that mowen lyve,
Thankèd be God! in wele and habun- daunce.
'Trentals,' seyde he, 'deliveren fro penaunce
Hir freendès soulès, as wel olde as yonge;
Ye, whan that they been hastily y-songe,
Nat for to holde a preest joly and gay;
He syngeth nat but o masse in a day.
Delivereth out,' quod he, 'anon, the soules!
Ful hard it is, with flesshhook or with oules 1730
To been y-clawèd, or to brenne, or bake;
Now spede yow hastily for Cristès sake.'
And whan this frere had seyd al his entente
With *qui cum patre*, forth his wey he wente.
. Whan folk in chirche had yeve him what hem lest,
He went his wey, no lenger wolde he reste.
With scrippe and tippèd staf, y-tukkèd hye,
In every hous he gan to poure and prye,
And beggeth mele, and chese, or ellès corn.
His felawe hadde a stafe tippèd with horn,

Summoner's Tale. The central incident of this was, no doubt, common property; but the setting of the tale must be Chaucer's.
1709. *Yorkshire, as,* H *Engelond.*
1737. *tipped,* H *pyked.*

A peyre of tables al of yvory, 1741
And a poyntel polysshed fetisly,
And wroote the namès alwey as he stood
Of allè folk that yaf hym any good,
Ascaunces that he woldè for hem prey.
'Yif us a busshel whetè, malt or reye,
A Goddès kechyl, or a trype of chese,
Or ellès what yow lyst, we may nat cheese;
A Goddès halfpeny, or a masse peny, 1749
Or yif us of youre brawn, if ye have eny;
A dagoun of youre blanket, leevè dame,
Oure suster deere,—lo heere I write youre name,—
Bacoun, or beef, or swich thyng as ye fynde.'
(A sturdy harlot wente ay hem bihynde,
That was hir hostès-man, and bar a sak,
And what men yaf hem leyde it on his bak.
And whan that he was out at dore anon,
He planed awey the namès everichon
That he biforn had writen in his tables.
He servèd hem with nyfles and with fables.
'Nay! ther thou lixt, thou Somonour!' quod the Frere. 1761
'Pees!' quod oure Hoost, 'for Cristès mooder deere;
Tel forth thy tale and spare it nat at al.'
So thryve I, quod this Somonour, so I shal!
So longe he wentè, hous by hous, til he
Cam til an hous ther he was wont to be
Refresshèd moore than in an hundred placis;
Syk lay the goodè man whos that the place is;
Bedrede upon a couchè lowe he lay.
'*Deus hic!*' quod he, 'O Thomas, freend, good day!' 1770
Seydè this frerè, curteisly and softe.
'Thomas,' quod he, 'God yeldè yow! ful ofte
Have I upon this bench faren ful weel;
Heere have I eten many a myrie meel';
And fro the bench he droof awey the cat,
And leyde adoun his potente and his hat,
And eek his scrippe, and sette hym softe adoun.
His felawe was go walkèd into toun,

Forth with his knave into that hostelrye
Where as he shoope hym thilkė nyght to
   lye.   1780
'O deerė maister,' quod this sikė man,
'How han ye farė sith that March bigan?
I saugh yow noght this fourtėnyght or
   moore.'
   'God woot,' quod he, 'laboured I
   have ful soore,
And specially for thy savacioun
Have I seyd many a precious orisoun ;
And for oure othere freendės, God hem
   blesse.
I have to day been at youre chirche at
   messe,
And seyd a sermoun after my symple wit,
Nat al after the text of hooly writ ;   1790
For it is hard to yow, as I suppose,
And therfore wol I teche yow al the glose.
Glosynge is a glorious thyng certeyn,
For lettre sleeth, so as we clerkės seyn.
There have I taught hem to be charitable,
And spende hir good ther it is resonable ;
And there I saugh oure dame,—a, where
   is she ?'
   'Yond, in the yerd, I trowė that
   she be,'
Seydė this man, 'and she wol come anon.'
   'Ey, maister, welcom be ye, by Seint
   John !'   1800
Seydė this wyf ; 'how fare ye, hertėly ?'
The frere ariseth up ful curteisly
And hire embraceth in his armes narwe,
And kiste hire sweete, and chirketh as a
   sparwe
Wíth his lyppės : 'Dame,' quod he,
   'right weel,
As he that is youre servant every deel.
Thankėd be God, that yow yaf soule and
   lyf,
Yet saugh I nat this day so fair a wyf
In al the chirchė, God so savė me !'
   'Ye, God amende defautės, sire,' quod
   she,   1810
'Algatės welcome be ye, by my fey !'
   '*Graunt mercy*, dame, this have I
   foundė alwey,
But of youre gretė goodnesse, by youre
   leve,
I woldė prey yow that ye nat yow greve,

I wole with Thomas speke a litel throwe ;
Thise curatz been ful necligent and slowe
To gropė tendrėly a conscience.
In shrift, in prechyng is my diligence,
And studie in Petrės wordės and in
   Poules.   1819
I walke, and fisshė cristen mennės soules,
To yelden Jhesu Crist his proprė rente.
To sprede his word is set al myn entente.'
   'Now, by youre leve, O deerė sire,'
   quod she,
'Chideth him weel, for, seintė Trinitee !
He is as angry as a pissėmyre,
Though that he have al that he kan desire,
Though I him wrye a-nyght and make
   hym warm,
And on hym leye my leg, outher myn arm,
He groneth lyk oure boor, lith in oure
   sty.
Oother desport ryght noon of hym have I,
I may nat plese hym in no maner cas.' 1831
   'O Thomas, *je vous dy*, Thomas !
   Thomas !
This maketh the feend, this mostė ben
   amended ;
Ire is a thyng that hyė God defended,
And therof wol I speke a word or two.'
   'Now, maister,' quod the wyf, 'er that
   I go,
What, wol ye dyne ? I wol go theraboute.'
   'Now, damė,' quod he, '*je vous dy
   sans doute*,
Have I nat of a capoun but the lyvere,
And of youre softė breed nat but a
   shyvere,   1840
And after that a rosted piggės heed,—
But that I nolde no beest for me werė
   deed,—
Thanne haddė I with yow hoomly suffi-
   saunce.
I am a man of litel sustenaunce.
My spirit hath his fostryng in the Bible,
The body is ay so redy and penyble
To wakė, that my stomak is destroyed ;
I prey yow, damė, ye be nat anoyed,
Though I so freendly yow my conseil
   shewe.
By God, I wolde nat telle it but a fewe !'
   'Now, sire,' quod she, 'but o word er
   I go :   1851

My child is deed withinne thise wykès two,
Soone after that ye wente out of this toun.'
'His deeth saugh I by revelacioun,'
Seith this frere, 'at hoom in oure dortour.
I dar wel seyn that er that half an hour
After his deeth, I saugh hym born to blisse
In my avisioun, so God me wisse !
So dide our sexteyn and oure fermerer,
That han been trewè frerès fifty yeer,—
They may now, God be thanked of his
  loone !   1861
Maken hir jubilee, and walke allone.
And up I roos, and al oure covent eke,
With many a tearè triklyng on my cheke,
Withouten noyse, or claterynge of bellès,
Te deum was oure song and no thyng
  elles ;
Save that to Crist I seyde an orisoun,
Thankynge hym of his revelacioun ;
For, sire and damè, trusteth me right weel,
Oure orisons been moore effectueel,   1870
And moore we seen of Cristès secree
  thynges,
Than burel folk, al though they weren
  kynges.
We lyve in poverte and in abstinence,
And burell folk in richesse and despence
Of mete and drynke, and in hir foul delit.
We han this worldès lust al in despit.
Lazar and Dives lyveden diversly
And diverse gerdoun hadden they ther-by.
Who-so wol preye he moot faste and be
  clene,
And fatte his soule and make his body
  lene.   1880
We fare as seith thapostle ; clooth and
  foode
Suffisen us, though they be nat ful goode ;
The clennesse and the fastynge of us freres
Maketh that Crist accepteth oure preyeres.
'Lo, Moyses fourty dayes and fourty
  nyght
Fasted, er that the heighè God of myght
Spak with hym in the mount of Synay.
With empty wombe, fastyngè many a
  day,
Receyvèd he the lawè that was writen
With Goddès fynger ; and Elye, wel ye
  witen,   1890
In mount Oreb, er he hadde any speche

With hyè God, that is oure lyvès leche,
He fasted longe, and was in contemp-
  launce.
'Aaron, that hadde the temple in
  governaunce,
And eek the othere preestès everichon,
Into the temple whan they sholdè gon
To preyè for the peple, and do servyse,
They nolden drynken in no maner wyse
No drynkè which that myghte hem
  dronkè make ;   1899
But there, in abstinencè preye and wake,
Lest that they deyden :—taak heede what
  I seye,—
But they be sobre that for the peple preyè,
War that !—I seye namoore,—for it
  suffiseth.
Oure Lord Jhesu, as hooly writ devyseth,
Yaf us ensample of fastynge and preyeres ;
Therfore we mendynantz, we sely freres,
Been wedded to povérte and continence,
To charite, humblesse, and abstinence,
To persecucioun for rightwisnesse,
To wepynge, misericordè and clennesse ;
And therfore may ye se that oure pre-
  yeres,—   1911
I speke of us, we mendynantz, we freres,—
Been to the hyè God moore acceptable
Than yourès with youre feestès at the table.
Fro Paradys first, if I shal nat lye,
Was man out chacèd for his glotonye,
And chaast was man in Paradys certeyn.
'But herknè, Thomas, what I shal the
  seyn,
I ne have no text of it, as I suppose,
But I shal fynde it in a maner glose,   1920
That specially oure sweetè Lord Jhesus
Spak this by frerès, whan he seydè thus :
'"Blessed be they that povere in
  spirit been,"—
And so forth al the gospel may ye seen
Wher it be likker oure professioun,
Or hirs that swymmen in possessioun,—
Fy on hire pompe and on hire glotonye !
And for hir lewèdnesse, I hem diffye !
'Me thynketh they been lyk Jovinyan,
Fat as a whale, and walkynge as a swan,
Al vinolent as botel in the spence.   1931

1929. *Jovinyan*, probably the mythical emperor of the *Gesta Romanorum*.

Hir preyere is of ful greet reverence
Whan they for soulès seye the Psalm of
     Davit,—
Lo, "buf" they seye, *cor meum eructavit*,—
Who folweth Cristes gospel, and his foore,
But we that humble been and chaast and
     poore,
Werkeris of Goddès word, not auditours?
Therfore, right as an hauk up at a sours
Up springeth into their, right so prayeres
Of charitable and chastè, bisy frères   1940
Maken hir sours to Goddès erès two.
Thomas, Thomas, so moote I ryde or go,—
And by that lord that clepid is Seint Yve !
Nere thou oure brother sholdestou nat
     thryve !
In our chapítrè praye we day and nyght
To Crist that he thee sendè heele and
     myght
Thy body for to weelden, hastily.'
    ' God woot,' quod he, ' no thyng therof
     feele I !
As help me Crist, as I, in fewè yeres,
Han spent upon diversè manere freres   1950
Ful many a pound, yet fare I never the bet.
Certeyn my good I have almoost biset,—
Farwel my gold, for it is al ago ! '
    The frere answerde, ' O Thomas, dos-
     tow so ?
What nedeth yow diversè frerès seche ?
What nedeth hym that hath a parfit leche
To sechen othere lechès in the toun ?
Youre inconstance is youre confusioun.
Holde ye thanne me, or ellès oure covent,
To praye for yow been insufficient ?   1960
Thomas, that japè nys nat worth a myte ;
Youre maladye is for we han to lyte.
A ! yif that covent half a quarter otes !
A ! yif that covent foure and twenty grotes!
A ! yif that frere a peny, and lat hym go !
Nay, nay, Thomas, it may no thyng be so !
What is a ferthyng worth parted in twelve?
Lo, ech thyng that is oned in it selve
Is moorè strong than whan it is to-scatered.
Thomas, of me thou shalt nat been y-
     flatered ;   1970
Thou woldest han oure labour al for noght ;
The hyè God, that al this world hath
     wroght,
Seith that the werkman worthy is his hyre.

Thomas, noght of youre tresor I desire,
As for my self, but that al oure covent
To preye for yow is ay so diligent,
And for to buylden Cristès owene chirche.
Thomas, if ye wol lernen for to wirche
Of buyldynge up of chirches, may ye fynde
If it be good in Thomas lyf of Inde.   1980
Ye lye heere ful of anger and of ire,
With which the devel set youre herte afyre,
And chiden heere the sely innocent,
Youre wyf, that is so meke and pacient ;
And therfore, Thomas, trowe me if thee
     leste,
Ne stryve nat with thy wyf, as for thy
     beste ;
And ber this word awey now, by thy feith,
Touchynge this thyng, lo what the wisè
     seith,
"Withinne thyn hous ne be thou no leoun ;
To thy subgitz do noon oppressioun,   1990
Ne makè thyne acqueyntis fro the flee."
And, Thomas, yet eft-soones I chargè thee,
Be war of yre that in thy bosom slepeth,
War fro the serpent that so slily crepeth
Under the gras and styngeth subtilly ;
Be war, my sone, and herkne paciently,
That twenty thousand men han lost hir
     lyves
For stryvyng with hir lemmans and hir
     wyves.
Now sith ye han so hooly, meke a wyf,
What nedeth yow, Thomas, to maken stryf?
Ther nys, y-wys, no serpent so cruél   2001
Whan man tret on his tayl, ne half so fel
As womman is, whan she hath caught an
     ire ;
Vengeance is thannè al that they desire.
Ire is a synne, oon of the gretè sevene,
Abhomynable unto the God of hevene,
And to hymself it is destruccioun.
This every lewèd viker, or persoun,
Kan seye, how ire engendreth homycide.
Ire is in sooth executour of pryde.   2010
I koude of ire seye so muchè sorwe
My talè sholdè lastè til tomorwe ;
And therfore preye I God, bothe day and
     nyght,

1980. *Thomas.* St. Thomas professed to be an
architect, but the palace he built for the Indian
king was in heaven.

An irous man God sende hym litel myght.
It is greet harme and certès greet pitee
To sette an irous man in heigh degree.
  ' Whilom ther was an irous potestat,
As seith Senek, that durynge his estaat
Upon a day out ryden knyghtès two ;
And as Fortúnè wolde that it were so
That oon of hem cam hoom, that oother
    noght.   2021
Anon the knyght bifore the juge is broght,
That seydè thus : " Thou hast thy felawe
    slayn,
For which I deme thee to the deeth
    certayn " ;
And to another knyght comanded he,
" Go lede hym to the deeth, I chargè
    thee ! "
And happed as they wentè by the weye,
Toward the placè ther he sholdè deye,
The knyght cam which men wenden had
    be deed.
Thanne thoughtè they it was the bestè
    reed,   2030
To lede hem bothè to the juge agayn.
They seiden, " Lord, the knyght ne hath
    nat slayn
His felawe ; heere he standeth hool alyve."
" Ye shul be deed," quod he, "so moot I
    thryve !
That is to seyn, bothe oon, and two, and
    thre."
And to the firstè knyght right thus spak
    he :
" I dampnèd thee, thou most algate be
    deed ;
And thou, also, most nedès lese thyn heed,
For thou art causè why thy felawe deyth";
And to the thriddè knyght right thus he
    seith :   2040
" Thou hast nat doon that I comanded
    thee " ;
And thus he dide doon sleen hem allè
    thre.
  ' Irous Cambises was eek dronkelewe
And ay delited hym to been a shrewe ;
And so bifel a lord of his meynee,

That lovèd vertuous moralitee,
Seyde on a day bitwene hem two right
    thus :
  ' " A lord is lost if he be vicius,
And dronkenesse is eek a foul record
Of any man, and namely in a lord.   2050
Ther is ful many an eye, and many an ere,
Awaityng on a lord, and he noot where.
For Goddès love drynk moore attemprely !
Wyn maketh man to lesen wrecchedly
His myndè and eek his lymès everichon."
  ' " The revers shaltou se," quod he anon,
" And preeve it by thyn owene experience,
That wyn ne dooth to folk no swich
    offence.
Ther is no wyn bireveth me my myght
Of hand, ne foot, ne of myne eyen sight " ;
And for despit he drank ful muchel moore,
An hondred part, than he hadde doon
    bifoore ;
And right anon, this irous, cursèd wrecche
Lèet this knyghtès sone bifore hym fecche,
Comandynge hym he sholde bifore hym
    stonde ;
And sodeynly he took his bowe in honde,
And up the streng he pullèd to his ere,
And with an arwe he slow the child right
    there.
" Now, wheither have I a siker hand or
    noon ? "
Quod he ; " is al my myght and mynde
    agon ?   2070
Hath wyn byrevèd me myne eyen sight ? "
What sholde I tellè thanswere of the
    knyght ?
His sone was slayn, ther is namoore to
    seye.
Beth war, therfore, with lordès how ye
    pleye.
Syngeth *Placebo*,—and I shal, if I kan,
But if it be unto a pourè man.
To a poure man men sholde his vices telle.
But nat to a lord, thogh he sholde go
    to helle.
  ' Lo, irous Cirus, thilkè Percien,
How he destroyed the ryver of Gysen, 2080
For that an hors of his was dreynt ther-
    inne,

2018. *Senek.* This story is told by Seneca, *De Ira*, i. 16, of Cn. Piso (T.)
2043. *Cambises.* This story is also in Seneca, iii. 14 ; it differs a little from one in Herodotus, Bk. iii. (T.)

2079. *Cirus.* See Herodotus, Bk. i., and Seneca, *De Ira*, both of whom call the river Gyndes.

Whan that he wentè Babiloigne to wynne.
He madè that the ryver was so smal
That wommen myghtè wade it over al.
   'Lo, what seyde he that so wel techè
      kan :
"Ne be no felawe to an irous man,
Ne with no wood man walkè by the weye,
Lest thee repente,"—ther is namoore to
      seye.'
   'Now, Thomas, leevè brother, lef thyn
      ire,
Thou shalt me fynde as just as is a squyre ;
Hoold nat the develes knyf ay at thyn
      herte,—   2091
Thyn angre dooth thee al to soorè
      smerte,—
But shewe to me al thy confessioun.'
   'Nay,' quod the sikè man, 'by Seint
      Symoun !
I have be shryven this day at my curat ;
I have hym toold hoolly al myn estat.
Nedeth namoore to speken of it, seith he,
But if me list, of myn humylitee.'
   'Yif me thanne of thy gold, to make
      oure cloystre,'
Quod he, 'for many a muscle and many
      an oystre,   2100
Whan othere men han ben ful wel at eyse,
Hath been oure foode, our cloystre for
      to reyse ;
And yet, God woot, unnethe the
      fundèment
Parfournèd is, ne of our pavèment
Nys nat a tyle yet withinne oure wones,—
By God, we owen fourty pound for stones !
   'Now help, Thomas ! for hym that
      harwed helle,
For ellès mostè we oure bookès selle ;
And if ye lakke oure predicacioun   2109
Thanne goth the world al to destruccioun.
For whoso wolde us fro this world bireve,
So God me savè, Thomas, by youre leve,
He wolde bireve out of this world the
      sonne ;
For who kan teche, and werchen, as we
      konne ?
And that is nat of litel tyme,' quod he,
'But syn that Elie was, or Elise,
Han frerès been,—that fynde I of record :

2116. *Elie*, E *Ennok*.

In charitee y-thanked be oure Lord !
Now, Thomas, helpe for seintè charitee ! '
And doun anon he sette hym on his
      knee.   .   2120
This sikè man wax wel ny wood for ire ;
He woldè that the frere had been on fire
With his false dissymulacioun.
   'Swich thyng as is in my possessioun,'
Quod he, 'that may I yeven, and noon
      oother.
Ye sey me thus, "that I am yourè
      brother"?'
   'Ye, certès,' quod the frere, 'trusteth
      weel,
I took oure dame oure lettre and oure
      seel.'
   'Now wel,' quod he, 'and somwhat
      shal I yeve   2129
Unto youre hooly covent whil I lyve,
And in thyn hand thou shalt it have anon,
On this condicioun, and oother noon ;
That thou departe it so, my leevè brother,
That every frere have also muche as
      oother ;
This shaltou swere on thy professioun,
Withouten fraud or cavillacioun.'
   'I swere it,' quod this frerè, 'by my
      feith ! '
And therwithal his hand in his he leith,—
'Lo heer my feith, in me shal be no lak.'
   'Now thanne, put in thyn hand doun
      by my bak,'   2140
Seydè this man, 'and gropè wel bihynde ;
Bynethè my buttok ther shaltow fynde
A thyng that I have hyd in pryvetee.'
   'A !' thoghte this frere, 'this shal go
      with me !'
And doun his hand he launcheth to the
      clifte,
In hopè for to fyndè there a yifte ;
And whan this sikè man feltè this frere
Aboute his tuwel gropè there and heere,
Amydde his hand he leet the frere a
      fart ;
Ther nys no capul drawynge in a cart 2150
That myghte have lete a fart of swich a
      soun.
   The frere up stirte, as dooth a wood
      leoun,—

2133. *leeve*, H⁶ *deere*.

'A! falsé cherl,' quod he, 'for Goddés
bones!
This hastow for despit doon for the nones;
Thou shalt abye this fart, if that I may!'
    His meynee, whiche that herden this
affray,
Cam lepynge in, and chacéd out the frere;
And forth he gooth with a ful angry
cheere,
And fette his felawe, ther as lay his stoor.
He lookéd as it were a wildé boor,—
He grynté with his teeth, so was he
wrooth; 2161
A sturdy paas doon to the court he gooth,
Wher as ther woned a man of greet
honour,
To whom that he was alwey confessour;
This worthy man was lord of that village.
This freré cam as he were in a rage,
Where as this lord sat etyng at his bord;
Unnethés myghte the freré speke a word,
Til atté laste he seydé, 'God yow see!'
    This lord gan looke and seidé,
      'Benedicitee! 2170
What, freré John, what maner world is
this?
I se wel that som thyng ther is amys;
Ye looken as the wode were ful of thevys;
Sit doun anon, and tel me what youre
grief is,
And it shal been amended, if I may.'
    'I have,' quod he, 'had a despit this
day,
God yeldé yow! adoun in youre village,
That in this world is noon so poure a page,
That he nolde have abhomynacioun 2179
Of that I have receyvéd in youre toun;
And yet ne greveth me no thyng so soore,
As that this oldé cherl, with lokkés hoore,
Blasphéméd hath oure hooly covent eke.'
    'Now, maister,' quod this lord, 'I yow
biseke'—
    'No "maister," sire,' quod he, 'but
servitour,
Thogh I have had in scolé swich honour;
God liketh nat that "Raby" men us calle,
Neither in market ne in youre largé halle.'
    'No fors,' quod he, 'but tel me al
youre grief.'

2172. *se wel that som,* E *trowe som maner.*

'Sire,' quod this frere, 'an odious
meschief 2190
This day bityd is to myn ordre and me;
And so *par consequéns* in ech degree
Of hooly chirché; God amende it soone!'
    'Sire,' quod the lord, 'ye woot what
is to doone;
Distempre yow noght, ye be my confes-
sour;
Ye been the salt of the erthe and the
savour;
For Goddés love youre pacience ye
holde;
Tel me youre grief'; and he anon hym
tolde,
As ye han herd biforn, ye woot wel
what.
    The lady of the hous al stillé sat 2200
Til she had herdé what the freré sayde;
'Ey! Goddés mooder,' quod she,—
      'blisful mayde!
Is ther oght ellés? Telle me feithfully.'
    'Madame,' quod he, 'how thynké ye
hereby?'
    'How that me thynketh?' quod she;
      'so God me speede!
I seye, a cherle hath doon a cherlés dedc.
What sholde I seye? God lat hym
never thee,
His siké heed is ful of vanytee;
I holde hym in a manere frenésye.'
    'Madame,' quod he, 'by God I shal
nat lye, 2210
But I on oother wise may be awreke,
I shal disclaundre hym, over al ther I
speke,—
This falsé blasphemour that chargéd me
To parté that wol nat departed be,—
To every man ylaché, with meschaunce!'
    The lord sat stille, as he were in a
traunce,
And in his herte he rolléd up and doun
'How hadde the cherl ymaginacioun,
To shewé swich a probleme to the frere?
Never erst er now herd I of swich
mateere; 2220
I trowe the devel putte it in his mynde.
In ars-metriké shal ther no man fynde,
Biforn this day of swich a questioun.

2211. *wise,* E² *weyes.*

Certès, it was a shrewed conclusioun,
That everyman sholde have yliche his part,
As of the soun or savour of a fart.
O vilè proudè cherl ! I shrewe his face !
Lo, sirès,' quod the lord, with hardè grace,
' Who herd ever of swich a thyng er now ?
" To every man ylikè,"—tel me how ?
It is an inpossíble, it may nat be. 2231
Ey, nycè cherl? God lete thee never thee !
The rumblynge of a fart, and every soun,
Nis but of eir reverberacioun,
And ever it wàsteth, litel and litel awey.
Ther is no man kan demen, by my fey !
If that it were departed equally.
What, lo, my cherl, lo, yet how shrewèdly,
Unto my confessour to day he spak ;
I holde hym, certeyn, a demonyak. 2240
Now ete youre mete, and lat the cherl go
pleye.
Lat hym go honge hymself a devel weye ! '

The wordes of the lordes Squier and his kervere for départynge of the fart on twelve

Now stood the lordès Squier at the bord,
That karf his mete, and herdè, word by
word,
Of allè thyngès whiche that I have sayd ;
' My lord,' quod he, ' be ye nat yvele
apayd,
I koudè tellè for a gownè-clooth
To yow, sir frerè, so ye be nat wrooth,
How that this fart sholde evene y-delèd be
Among youre covent, if it lykèd me.' 2250
' Tel,' quod the lord, ' and thou shalt
have anon
A gownè-clooth, by God, and by Seint
John !'
' My lord,' quod he, ' whan that the
weder is fair,
Withouten wynd, or perturbynge of air,
Lat brynge a cartèwheel into this halle,—
But lookè that it have his spokès alle,—
Twelve spokès hath a cartwheel comunly ;
And bryng me thanne twelf frerès,—
woot ye why ?

For thritten is a covent, as I gesse ;
The cónfessour heere, for his worthynesse,
Shal parfourne up the nombre of his
covent. 2261
Thanne shal they knelè doun, by oon
assent,
And to every spokès ende, in this manere,
Ful sadly leye his nosè shal a frere.
Youre noble cónfessour there, God hym
save !
Shal holde his nose upright under the nave.
Thanne shal this cherl, with bely stif
and toght
As any tabour, hyder been y-broght,
And sette hym on the wheel right of this
cart, 2269
Upon the nave, and make hym lete a fart,
And ye shul seen, up peril of my lyf,
By preevè which that is demonstratif,
That equally the soun of it wol wende,
And eke the stynk, unto the spokès ende,—
Save that this worthy man, youre con-
fessour,
By cause he is a man of greet honour,
Shal have the firstè fruyt, as resoun is.
The noble usage of frerès yet is this,
The worthy men of hem shul first be
served,— 2279
And certeinly, he hath it weel disserved,
He hath to day taught us so muchel good
With prechyng in the pulpit ther he stood,
That I may vouchèsauf, I sey for me,
He hadde the firstè smel of fartès three,
And so wolde al the covent hardily ;
He bereth hym so faire and hoolily.'
The lord, the lady, and alle men save
the frere,
Seyden that Jankyn spak in this matere
As wel as Euclide, or Protholomee :
Touchynge this cherl, they seyden, sub-
tiltee 2290
And heigh wit made hym speken as he
spak ;
He nys no fool, ne no demonyak ;
And Jankyn hath y-wonne a newe gowne.
My tale is doon,—we been almoost at
towne.

2224. H⁶ read *who schulde make a demonstra-cioun.*
2227. *vile*, H⁶ *nyce.*

2272. *preeve which*, H *verray proef.*
2289. *Protholomee*, Ptolemy.
2294. *at towne*, Sittingbourne.

GROUP E

Heere folweth The Prologe of the Clerkes Tale of Oxenford

'SIRE Clerk of Oxenford,' oure Hostè sayde,
'Ye ryde as coy and stille as dooth a mayde,
Were newè spousèd, sittynge at the bord ;
This day ne herd I of youre tonge a word.
I trowe ye studie aboutè som sophyme ;
But Salomon seith "every thyng hath tyme."
For Goddès sake ! as beth of bettre cheere !
It is no tymè for to studien heere ;
Telle us som myrie talè, by youre fey !
For what man that is entred in a pley,　10
He nedès moot unto the pley assente ;
But precheth nat, as frerès doon in Lente,
To make us for oure oldè synnès wepe,
Ne that thy talè make us nat to slepe.-
Telle us som murie thyng of áventúres,—
Youre termès, youre colóurs, and youre figúres
Keepe hem in stoor til so be ye endite
Heigh style, as whan that men to kyngès write ;
Speketh so pleyn at this tyme, I yow preye,　19
That we may understondè what ye seye.'
This worthy clerk benignèly answérde,
'Hostè,'quod he, 'I am under youre yerde,
Ye han of us, as now, the governance,
And therefor wol I do yow obeisance
As fer as resoun axeth hardily.
I wol yow telle a talè which that I
Lernèd at Padwè of a worthy clerk,
As prevèd by his wordès and his werk ;
He is now deed and naylèd in his cheste,
I prey to God so yeve his soulè reste !　30
' Frauncèys Petrak, the lauriat poete,
Hightè this clerk whos rethorikè sweete
Enlumyned al Ytaille of poetrie,—

19. *I*, E² *we.*
27. *Lernèd at Padwè.* Petrarch was at Arqua, near Padua, from Jan. to Sept. 1373, and Chaucer may easily have visited him on his Genoese mission of that year.
29. *deed.* Petrarch died in 1374.

As Lynyan dide of philosophie,
Or lawe, or oother art particuler,—
But deeth, that wol nat suffre us dwellen heer,
But as it were a twynklyng of an eye,
Hem bothe hath slayn, and allè shul we dye.
But forth to tellen of this worthy man
That taughtè me this tale, as I bigan,　40
I seye that first with heigh stile he enditeth,
Er he the body of his talè writeth,
A prohemye, in which discryveth he
Pemond, and of Salucès the contree ;
And speketh of Apennyn, the hillès hye
That been the boundès of West Lumbardye,
And of Mount Vesulus in special,
Where as the Poo out of a wellè smal
Taketh his firstè spryngyng and his sours,
That estward ay encresseth in his cours　50
To Emeleward, to Ferrare and Venyse,—
The which a longe thyng werè to devyse,
And trewèly, as to my juggèment,
Me thynketh it a thyng impertinent,
Save that he wole convoyen his mateere ;
But this is his talè which that ye may heere.'

CLERK OF OXFORD'S TALE

Heere bigynneth The Tale of the Clerk of Oxenford

PART I

Ther is, at the West sydè of Ytaille,
Doun at the roote of Vesulus the colde,

34. *Lynyan*, an Italian jurist, who died in 1383.
44. *Pemond*, Piedmont.
44. *Salucès*, Saluzzo.
47. *Mount Vesulus*, Monte Viso.
51. *To Emeleward*, *i.e.* towards the district traversed by the old *Via Aemiliana.*
56. *this is*, E² *this.*
The Tale of the Clerk. This is for the most part a close rendering of the Latin version of the Tale of Griselda, written by Petrarch after reading Boccaccio's story in the *Decamerone.* Chaucer's chief departures from Petrarch are pointed out in the notes,

A lusty playne, habundant of vitaille,
Where many a tour and toun thou mayst
    biholde   60
That founded were in tyme of fadrès olde,
And many another delitáble sighte,
And Salucès this noble contree highte.

A markys whilom lord was of that lond,
As were his worthy eldrès hym bifore,
And obeisant and redy to his hond
Were alle his ligès, bothe lasse and moore.
Thus in delit he lyveth, and hath doon
    yoore,
Biloved and drad, thurgh favour of
    Fortune,   69
Bothe of his lordès and of his commune.

Therwith he was, to speke as of lynage,
The gentilleste y-born of Lumbardye ;
A faire persone, and strong, and yong
    of age,
And ful of honour and of curteisye ;
Discreet ynogh his contree for to gye,—
Save in somme thyngès that he was to
    blame,—
And Walter was this yongè lordès name.

    I blame him thus, that he considered
    noght
In tymè comynge what hym myghte
    bityde ;   79
But in his lust present was al his thoght,
As for to hauke and hunte on every syde,
Wel ny alle othere curès leet he slyde ;
And eek he nolde, and that was worst of
    alle,
Weddè no wyf, for noght that may bifalle.

Oonly that point his peplè bar so soore
That flokmeele on a day they to hym
    wente,
And oon of hem that wisest was of
    loore,—

Or ellès that the lord best wolde assente
That he sholde telle hym what his peplè
    mente,
Or ellès koude he showe wel swich
    mateere,—   90
He to the markys seyde as ye shul heere :

'O noble markys, youre humanitee
Asseureth us and yeveth us hardinesse
As ofte as tyme is of necessitee
That we to yow mowe telle oure hevy-
    nesse.
Accepteth, lord, now for youre gentillesse,
That we with pitous herte unto yow
    pleyne,
And lat youre erès nat my voys desdeyne.

Al have I noght to doone in this mateere
Moore than another man hath in this place,
Yet for as muche as ye, my lord so deere,
Han alwey shewèd me favour and grace,
I dar the bettrè aske of yow a space
Of audience, to shewen oure requeste,
And ye, my lord, to doon right as yow
    leste ;

For certès, lord, so wel us liketh yow
And al youre werk, and ever han doon,
    that we
Ne koudè nat us-self devysen how
We myghtè lyven in moore felicitee,
Save o thyng, lord, if it youre willè be, 110
That for to been a wedded man yow leste ;
Thanne were youre peple in sovereyn
    hertès reste.

Boweth youre nekke under that blisful yok
Of soveraynètee, noght of servyse,
Which that men clepeth spousaille or
    wedlok,
And thenketh, lord, among youre thoghtès
    wyse,
How that oure dayès passe in sondry wyse,
For thogh we slepe, or wake, or rome,
    or ryde,
Ay fleeth the tyme, it nyl no man abyde ;

78. *considered*, E³ *considereth.* We may quote
the original of this stanza to show how close
Chaucer keeps to his text : 'vir insignis nisi
quod, præsenti sua sorte contentus, incuriosissimus
futurorum erat. Itaque venatui aucupioque de-
ditus sic illis incubuerat ut alia pene cuncta
negligeret ; quodque in primis ægre populi fere-
bant ab ipsis quoque conjugii consiliis abhor-
reret.'

113. Chaucer here transfers Petrarch's epithets.
'Collumque non liberum modo sed imperiosum
legitimo subjicias jugo' is the Latin.

And thogh youre grené youthé floure as
yit,   120
In crepeth age alwey, as stille as stoon,
And Deeth manaceth every age and smyt
In ech estaat, for ther escapeth noon ;
And al so certein as we knowe echoon
That we shul deye, as uncerteyn we alle
Been of that day whan deeth shal on us
falle.

  ' Accepteth thanne of us the trewe
  entente
That never yet refuséden thyn heeste,
And we wol, lord, if that ye wole assente,
Chese yow a wyf in short tyme atté leeste,
Born of the gentilleste and of the meeste
Of al this land, so that it oghté seme
Honour to God and yow, as we kan
deeme.

Delivere us out of al this bisy drede,
And taak a wyf, for hyé Goddés sake ;
For if it so bifelle, as God forbede !
That thurgh youre deeth youre lyné
sholdé slake,
And that a straungé súccessour sholde take
Youre heritage, O, wo were us alyve !
Wherfore we pray you hastily to wyve.' 140

  Hir meeké preyere, and hir pitous
  cheere,
Madé the markys herté han pitee.
' Ye wol,' quod he, ' myn owéne peplé
deere,
To that I never erst thoughté streyné me.
I me rejoyséd of my libertee,
That seeldé tyme is founde in mariage ;
Ther I was free, I moot been in servage ;

But nathélees, I se youre trewe entente,
And trust upon youre wit, and have
doon ay ;
Wherfore, of my free wyl, I wole assente
To weddé me as soone as ever I may.   151
But ther as ye han profréd me this day
To chesé me a wyf, I yow relesse
That choys, and prey yow of that profré
cesse,

For, God it woot, that children ofté been
Unlyk hir worthy eldrés hem bifore ;

Bountee comth al of God, nat of the streen
Of which they been engendred and y-bore.
I truste in Goddés bontee, and therfore
My mariage, and myn estaat and reste,
I hym bitake,—he may doon as hym leste.

Lat me allone in chesynge of my wyf—
That charge upon my bak I wol endure ;
But I yow preye, and charge upon youre lyf,
That what wyf that I take, ye me assure
To worshipe hire, whil that hir lyf may dure,
In word and werk, bothe heere and
everywheere,
As she an emperourés doghter weere ;

And forthermoore, this shal ye swere,
that ye
Agayn my choys shul neither grucche ne
stryve ;   170
For sith I shal forgoon my libertee
At youre requeste, as ever moot I thryve !
Ther as myn herte is set, ther wol I wyve ;
And, but ye wole assente in this manere,
I prey yow speketh namoore of this matere.'

  With hertely wyl they sworen and
  assenten
To al this thyng, ther seydé no wight nay ;
Bisekynge hym of grace, er that they
wenten,
That he wolde graunten hem a certein day
Of his spousaille, as soone as ever he may :
For yet alwey the peplé somwhat dredde
Lest that this markys no wyf woldé wedde.

  He graunted hem a day, swich as hym
  leste,
On which he wolde be wedded sikerly,
And seyde he dide al this at hir requeste ;
And they, with humble ententé, buxomly,
Knelynge upon hir knees ful reverently,
Hym thonken alle ; and thus they han
an ende
Of hire entente, and hoom agayn they
wende.

  And heer-upon he to his officerés   190
Comaundeth for the festé to purveye ;
And to his privee knyghtés and squierés

174. *And but ye wole*, etc., not in Latin.

Swich chargé yaf as hym liste on hem leye ;
And they to his comandément obeye,
And ech of hem dooth al his diligence
To doon unto the feesté reverence.

PART II

Noght fer fro thilké paleys honurable
Ther as this markys shoope his mariage,
There stood a throop, of sité delitable,
In which that pouré folk of that village
Hadden hir beestés and hir herbergage,
And of hire labour tooke hir sustenance,
After the erthé yaf hem habundance. 203

Among thise pouré folk ther dwelte a man
Which that was holden pourest of hem
    alle, —
But hyé God som tymé senden kan
His grace into a litel oxés stalle ;
Janicula, men of that throope hym calle ;
A doghter hadde he fair ynogh to sighte,
And Grisildis this yongé mayden highte.

But for to speke of vertuous beautee
Thanne was she oon the faireste under
    sonne,
For pouréliche y-fostred up was she ;
No likerous lust was thurgh hire herte
    y-ronne,
Wel ofter of the welle than of the tonne
She drank, and for she woldé vertu plese
She knew wel labour, but noon ydel ese.

But thogh this maydé tendre were of age,
Yet in the brest of hire virginitee   219
Ther was enclosèd rype and sad corage,
And in greet reverence and charitee
Hir oldé, pouré fader fostred shee ;
A fewé sheepe, spynnynge, on feeld she
    kepte,
She woldé noght been ydel til she slepte.

And whan she homward cam she woldé
    brynge
Wortés, or othere herbés, tymés ofte,
The whiche she shredde and seeth for hir
    lyvynge,

215-220. Chaucer's addition.

And made hir bed ful harde and no thyng
    softe ;
And ay she kepte hir fadres lyf on-lofte,
With everich obeisaunce and diligence
That child may doon to fadres reverence.

Upon Grisilde, this pouré creäture,
Ful ofté sithe this markys sette his eye
As he on huntyng rood paráventure ;
And, whan it fil that he myghte hire espye,
He noght with wantowne lookyng of folye
His eyén caste on hire, but in sad wyse
Upon hir chiere he gan hym ofte avyse,

Commendynge in his herte hir womman-
    hede,   239
And eek hir virtu, passynge any wight
Of so yong age, as wel in chiere as dede ;
For thogh the peplé have no greet insight
In vertu, he considerèd ful right
Hir bountee, and disposéd that he wolde
Wedde hire oonly, if ever he weddé sholde.

The day of weddyng cam, but no wight kan
Tellé what womman that it sholdé be ;
For which merveillé wondred many a man,
And seyden, whan they were in privétee,
'Wol nat oure lord yet leve his vanytee ?
Wol he nat wedde ? allas ! allas ! the while !
Why wole he thus hymself and us bigíle ? '

But náthélees this markys hath doon make,
Of gemmés, set in gold and in asure,
Broochés and ryngés, for Grisildis sake ;
And of hir clothyng took he the mesure
Bý a mayde lyke to hire of stature,
And eek of othere ornementés alle
That unto swich a weddyng sholdé falle.

The time of undern of the samé day
Approcheth, that this weddyng sholdé be,
And al the paleys put was in array,   262
Bothe hall and chambrés, ech in his degree ;
Houses of office stuffèd with plentee,
Ther maystow seen of deyntéuous vitaille
That may be founde as fer as last Ytaille.

233. *sette*, E *casts*.
238. *gan*, H⁶ wolde.
249-252. Chaucer's addition.
263-266. Chaucer's addition.

This roial markys richély arrayed,
Lordès and ladyes in his compaignye,
The whiché to the feesté weren y-prayed,
And of his retenue the bachelrye,   270
With many a soun of sondry melodye,
Unto the village of the which I tolde,
In this array the righté wey han holde.

Grisilde of this, God woot, ful innocent,
That for hire shapen was al this array,
To fecchen water at a welle is went,
And cometh hoom as soone as ever she
     may ;
For wel she hadde herd seyd that thilké day
The markys sholdé wedde, and if she
     myghte   279
She woldé fayn han seyn som of that sighte.

She thoghte, ' I wole with othere maydens
     stonde,
That been my felawes, in oure dore and se
The markysesse, and therfore wol I fonde
To doon at hoom as soone as it may be
The labour which that longeth unto me ;
And thanne I may at leyser hire biholde
If she this wey unto the castel holde.'

And as she wolde over hir thresshfold gon
The markys cam, and gan hire for to calle ;
And she set doun hir water pot anon   290
Biside the thresshfold in an oxès stalle,
And doun upon hir knes she gan to falle,
And with sad contenancé kneleth stille
Til she had herd what was the lordès will.

This thoghtful markys spak unto this mayde
Ful sobrely, and seyde in this manere :
' Where is youre fader, Grisildis ? ' he
     sayde ;
And she with reverence, in humble cheere,
Answerdé, ' Lord, he is al redy heere ' ;
And in she gooth withouten lenger lette,
And to the markys she hir fader fette.   301

He by the hand thanne took this oldé man,
And seydé thus, whan he hym hadde asyde,
' Janicula, I neither may ne kan
Lenger the plesance of myn herté hyde.

If that thou vouchésauf, what-so bityde,
Thy doghter wol I take, er that I wende,
As for my wyf unto hir lyvés ende.

Thou lovest me, I woot it wel certeyn,
And art my feithful ligé man y-bore,   310
And all that liketh me, I dar wel seyn.
It liketh thee, and specially therfore,
Tel me that poynt that I have seyd bifore,
If that thou wolt unto that purpos drawe,
To také me as for thy sone-in-lawe.'

This sodeyn cas this man astonyed so
That reed he wax, abayst, and al quakyng
He stood ; unnethès seyde he wordès mo,
But oonly thus : ' Lord,' quod he, ' my
     willyng   319
Is as ye wole, ne ayeynes youre likyng
I wol no thyng, ye be my lord so deere ;
Right as yow lust governeth this mateere.'

' Yet wol I,' quod this markys softély,
' That in thy chambre, I, and thou,
     and she,
Have a collacioun, and wostow why ?
For I wol axe if it hire willé be
To be my wyf, and reule hire after me ;
And al this shal be doon in thy presence,
I wol noght speké out of thyn audience.'

And in the chambre whil they were
     aboute   330
Hir tretys, which as ye shal after heere,
The peple cam unto the hous with-oute,
And wondred hem in how honeste
     manere,
And tentifly, she kepte hir fader deere ;
But outrély Grisildis wondré myghte,
For never erst ne saugh she swich a sighte.

No wonder is thogh that she were astoned
To seen so greet a gest come in that place ;
She never was to swiché gestés woned,
For which she lookèd with ful palé face.
But, shortly forth this talé for to chace,   341
Thise arn the wordès that the markys sayde
To this benigné, verray, feithful mayde :

267. *richely,* H² *really* (royally).
281 *sqq.* The form of the soliloquy is Chaucer's.
290-294. Chaucer's addition.

334. *tentifly,* H *tendurly.*
340. Chaucer's conventional addition.
341. *tale,* H⁶ *matiere.*

'Grisilde,' he seyde, 'ye shal wel understonde
It liketh to youre fader and to me
That I yow wedde; and eek it may so stonde,
As I suppose, ye wol that it so be;
But thise demandès axe I first,' quod he,
'That sith it shal be doon in hastif wyse,
Wol ye assente or ellès yow avyse?   350

I seye this, be ye redy with good herte
To al my lust, and that I frely may
As me best thynketh do yow laughe or smerte,
And never ye to grucche it nyght ne day?
And eek whan I sey "ye" ne sey nat "nay,"
Neither by word, ne frownyng contenance?
Swere this, and heere I swere oure alliance.'

Wondrynge upon this word, quakynge for drede,
She seydè, 'Lord, undigne and unworthy
Am I to thilke honóur that ye me beede;
But as ye wole youreself, right so wol I, 361
And heere I swere that never willyngly
In werk, ne thoght, I nyl yow disobeye,
For to be deed, though me were looth to deye!'

'This is ynogh, Grisildè myn,' quod he,
And forth he gooth with a ful sobrè cheere
Out at the dore, and after that cam she,
And to the peple he seyde in this manere:
'This is my wyf,' quod he, 'that standeth heere;   369
Honoureth hire, and loveth hire, I preye,
Whoso me loveth; ther is namoore to seye.'

And for that nothyng of hir oldè gere
She sholdè brynge into his hous, he bad
That wommen sholde dispoillen hire right there;
Of which thise ladyes werè nat right glad
To handle hir clothès wher-inne she was clad;
But nathèlees this maydè, bright of hewe,
Fro foot to heed they clothèd han al newe.

375, 376. Chaucer here varies needlessly from Petrarch.

Hir heris han they kembd, that lay untressed
Ful rudèly, and with hir fyngres smale 380
A corone on hire heed they han y-dressed,
And sette hire ful of nowches grete and smale.
Of hire array what sholde I make a tale?
Unnethe the peple hire knew for hire fairnesse,
Whan she translated was in swich richesse.

This markys hath hire spousèd with a ryng,
Broght for the samè cause, and thanne hire sette
Upon an hors snow-whit and wel amblyng,
And to his paleys, er he lenger lette,
With joyful peplè that hire ladde and mette,   390
Convoyèd hire, and thus the day they spende
In revel til the sonnè gan descende;

And, shortly forth this talè for to chace,
I seye that to this newè markysesse
God hath swich favour sent hire of his grace,
That it ne semèd nat by liklynesse
That she was born and fed in rudènesse,
As in a cote, or in an oxè stalle,
But norissed in an emperourès halle.

To every wight she woxen is so deere
And worshipful, that folk ther she was bore,   401
And from hire birthè knewe hire yeer by yeere,
Unnethè trowèd they, but dorste han swore
That to Janicle of which I spak bifore
She doghter nere, for, as by conjecture,
Hem thoughte she was another creäture;

For though that ever vertuous was she,
She was encressèd in swich excellence
Of thewès goode, y-set in heigh bountee,
And so discreet and fair of eloquence,   410
So benigne, and so digne of reverence,
And koudè so the peplès herte embrace,
That ech hire lovede that lookèd on hir face.

Noght oonly of Saluces in the toun
Publicèd was the bountee of hir name.
But eek biside in many a regioun,
If oon seide wel, another seyde the same.
So spradde of hirè heighe bountee the fame
That men and wommen, as wel yonge as
    olde,
Goon to Saluce upon hire to bihold.   420

Thus Walter lowely—nay, but roially—
Wedded with fortunat honestètee,
In Goddès pees lyveth ful esily
At hoom, and outward grace ynogh had he;
And for he saugh that under lowe degree
Was oftè vertu hid, the peple hym heelde
A prudent man, and that is seyn ful seelde.

Nat oonly this Grisildis thurgh hir wit
Koude al the feet of wyfly homlynesse,
But eek, whan that the cas requirèd it,   430
The commune profit koudè she redresse;
Ther nas discord, rancour, ne hevynesse,
In al that land, that she ne koude apese,
And wisely brynge hem alle in reste
    and ese.

Though that hire housbonde absent were
    anon,
If gentil men or othere of hire contree
Were wrothè, she wolde bryngen hem a ton;
So wise and rypè wordès haddè she,
And juggèmentz of so greet equitee,
That she from hevene sent was, as men
    wende,   440
Peplè to save and every wrong tamende.

Nat longè tyme after that this Grisild
Was wedded, she a doghter hath y-bore,
Al had hire levere have born a knavè child.
Glad was this markys and the folk ther-
    fore,
For though a maydè child coome al bifore,
She may unto a knavè child atteyne,
By liklihede, syn she nys nat bareyne.

PART III

Ther fil, as it bifalleth tymès mo,
Whan that this child had soukèd but a
    throwe,   450

415. *bountee,* E *beautee.*

This markys in his hertè longeth so
To tempte his wyf, hir sadnesse for to
    knowe,
That he ne myghte out of his hertè throwe
This merveillous desir his wyf tassaye;
Nedelees, God woot, he thoghte hire for
    taffraye.

He hadde assayèd hire ynogh bifore,
And foond hire ever goode, — what
    neded it
Hire for to tempte, and alwey moore and
    moore?
Though som men preise it for a subtil wit,
But as for me, I seye that yvele it sit   460
To assaye a wyf whan that it is no nede,
And putten hire in angwyssh and in drede.

For which this markys wroghte in this
    manere;
He cam allone a nyght, ther as she lay,
With stiernè face and with ful trouble
    cheere,
And seydè thus: 'Grisilde,' quod he,
    'that day
That I yow took out of youre poure array
And putte yow in estaat of heigh
    noblesse,—
Ye have nat that forgeten, as I gesse?

I seye, Grisilde, this present dignitee   470
In which that I have put yow, as I trowe,
Maketh yow nat forgetful for to be
That I yow took in poure estaat ful lowe;
For any wele ye moot youreselven knowe;
Taak heede of every word that I yow seye,
Ther is no wight that hereth it but we
    tweye.

Ye woot youreself wel how that ye cam
    heere
Into this hous, it is nat longe ago,
And though to me that ye be lief and
    deere,
Unto my gentils ye be no thyng so;   480
They seyn to hem it is greet shame and wo
For to be subgetz, and been in servage,   ·
To thee, that born art of a smal village;

460. Chaucer is here much more emphatic than
Petrarch.

And namely sith thy doghter was y-bore
Thise wordès han they spoken, doutèlees ;
But I desire, as I have doon bifore,
To lyve my lyf with hem in reste and pees ;
I may nat in this caas be recchèlees,
I móot doon with thy doghter for the beste,
Nat as I wolde, but as my peplè leste ; 490

And yet, God woot, this is ful looth to me ;
But nathèlees withoutè yóure wityng
I wol nat doon, but this wol I,' quod he,
' That ye to me assente, as in this thyng.
Shewe now youre pacïence in youre werkyng,
That ye me highte and swore in youre village,
That day that makèd was oure mariage.'

    Whan she had herd al this she noght ameved,
Neither in word, or chiere, or countenaunce,
For as it semèd she was nat agreved. 500
She seydè, ' Lord, al lyth in youre plesaunce ;
My child and I, with hertely obeisaunce,
Been yourès al, and ye mowe save or spille
Youre owene thyng ; werketh after youre wille.

    Ther may no-thyng, God so my soulè save !
Liken to yow that may displesè me ;
Ne I desirè no-thyng for to have,
Ne dredè for to leese, save oonly yee ;
This wyl is in myn herte, and ay shal be.
No lengthe of tyme, or deeth, may this deface, 510
Ne chaunge my corage to another place.'

    Glad was this markys of hire answeryng,
But yet he feynèd as he were nat so ;
Al drery was his cheere and his lookyng,
Whan that he sholde out of the chambrè go,
Soone after this, a furlong wey or two,
He privèly hath toold al his entent
Unto a man, and to his wyf hym sente.

A maner sergeant was this privee man,
The which that feithful ofte he founden hadde 520
In thyngès grete, and eek swich folk wel kan
Doon execucïoun in thyngès badde ;
The lord knew wel that he hym loved and dradde :
And whan this sergeant wiste his lordès wille,
Into the chambre he stalkèd hym ful stille.

    ' Madame,' he seyde, ' ye moote foryeve it me,
Though I do thyng to which I am constreynèd ;
Ye been so wys, that ful wel knowè ye
That lordès heestès mowe nat been y-feyned :
They mowe wel been biwaillèd and compleynèd, 530
But men moote nede unto hire lust obeye,
And so wol I ; ther is namoore to seye.

    This child I am comanded for to take,'—
And spak namoore but out the child he hente
Despitously, and gan a cheerè make
As though he wolde han slayn it er he wente.
Grisildis moot al suffren and consente ;
And as a lamb she sitteth meke and stille,
And leet this crueel sergeant doon his wille.

    Suspecious was the diffame of this man,
Suspect his face, suspect his word also, 541
Suspect the tyme in which he this bigan ;
Allas, hir doghter that she lovèd so,
She wende he wolde han slawen it right tho ;
But nathèlees she neither weepe ne syked,
Consentynge hire to that the markys lyked ;

    But attè laste to speken she bigan,
And mekèly she to the sergeant preyde,

546. *Consentynge*, Hᵈ *Conformyng.*

So as he was a worthy gentil man,
That she moste kisse hire child er that it
   deyde.   550
And in hir barm this litel child she leyde
With ful sad face, and gan the child to
   blisse,
And lulled it, and after gan it kisse ;

And thus she seyde in hire benigné voys,
'Fareweel, my child, I shal thee never
   see !
But sith I thee have markéd with the croys,
Of thilké Fader, blessed moote he be,
That for us deyde up on a croys of tree.
Thy soulé, litel child, I hym bitake,   559
For this nyght shaltow dyen for my sake.'

I trowe that to a norice in this cas
It had been hard this reuthé for to se ;
Wel myghte a mooder thanne han cryd,
   allas !
But nathéless, so sad stidefast was she,
That she enduréd al adversitee,
And to the sergeant mekély she sayde,
'Have heer agayn youre litel yongé
   mayde ;

Gooth now,' quod she, 'and dooth my
   lordés heeste ;
But o thyng wol I prey yow of youre grace,
That, but my lord forbad yow, atté leeste
Burieth this litel body in som place   571
That beestés, ne no briddés, it to-race ' ;
But he no word wol to that purpos seye,
But took the child and wente upon his
   weye.

This sergeant cam unto his lord ageyn,
And of Grisildis wordés and hire cheere
He tolde hym point for point, in short
   and pleyn,
And hym presenteth with his doghter
   deere.
Somwhat this lord hath routhe in his
   manere,
But nathélees his purpos heeld he stille, 580

554-560. Chaucer's addition, though Petrarch
mentions the signing with the cross.
567. This pretty line is Chaucer's addition.

As lordés doon whan they wol han hir
   wille ;

And bad his sergeant that he pryvély
Sholdé this child ful softé wynde and
   wrappe
With allé circumstances, tendrely,
And carie it in a cofre, or in a lappe ;
But, upon peyne his heed of for to swappe,
That no man sholdé knowe of his entente,
Ne whenne he cam, ne whider that he
   wente ;

But at Boloigné to his suster deere,
That thilké tyme of Panik was countesse,
He sholde it take, and shewe hire this
   mateere,   591
Bisekynge hire to doon hire bisynesse
This child to fostre in allé gentillesse ;
And whos child that it was he bad hir hyde
From every wight for oght that may bityde.

The sergeant gooth, and hath fulfild
   this thyng ;
But to this markys now retourné we,
For now gooth he ful faste ymaginyng
If by his wyvés cheere he myghté se,
Or by hire word aperceyvé, that she   600
Were chaungéd ; but he never hire koudé
   fynde
But ever in oon yliké sad and kynde,

As glad, as humble, as bisy in servyse,
And eek in love, as she was wont to be,
Was she to hym in every maner wyse ;
Ne of hir doghter noght a word spak she.
Noon accident for noon adversitee
Was seyn in hire, ne never hir doghter
   name
Ne nempnéd she, in ernest nor in game.

PART IV

In this estaat ther passéd been foure yeer
Er she with childé was ; but, as God wolde,

581. Chaucer's comment.
589. *Boloigne*, Bologna.
590. *Panik*, E⁵ *Pavyk, Pavie ;* 'Comiti de
Panico' in Petrarch.
607-609. An unhappy translation of Petrarch's
'nunquam siue ex proposito siue incidenter nomen
eius ex ore matris auditum.'

A knavé child she bar by this Walter,
Ful gracious and fair for to biholde ;
And whan that folk it to his fader tolde,
Nat oonly he, but al his contree, merye
Was for this child, and God they thanke
     and herye.

Whan it was two yeer old, and fro the brest
Departed of his norice, on a day
This markys caughté yet another lest
To tempte his wyf yet ofter, if he may.   620
O, nedelees was she tempted in assay !
But wedded men ne knowé no mesure
Whan that they fynde a pacient creature !

    'Wyf,' quod this markys, 'ye han
     herd er this
My peplé sikly berth oure mariage,
And namely sith my sone y-boren is,
Now is it worse than ever in al oure age.
The murmure sleeth myn herte and my
     corage ;
For to myne erés comth the voys so smerte
That it wel ny destroyéd hath myn herte.

    ' Now sey they thus : "Whan Walter
     is agon   631
Thanne shal the blood of Janicle succede,
And been oure lord, for oother have we
     noon " ;
Swiche wordés seith my peplé, out of drede,
Wel oughte I of swich murmur taken heede,
For certeinly I dredé swich sentence,
Though they nat pleyn speke in myn
     audience.

I woldé lyve in pees, if that I myghte,
Wherfore I am disposéd outrély,
As I his suster servédé by nyghte,   640
Right so thenke I to serve hym pryvély.
This warne I yow, that ye nat sodeynly
Out of youreself for no wo sholde outreye—
Beth pacient, and ther-of I yow preye.'

    ' I have,' quod she, ' seyd thus, and
     ever shal,
I wol no thyng, ne nyl no thyng, certayn,
But as yow list ; naught greveth me at al

     621-623. Chaucer's comment.

Though that my doughter and my sone
     be slayn
At youre comandément ; this is to sayn,
I have noght had no part of children
     tweyne,   650
But first siknesse and after wo and peyne.

Ye been oure lord, dooth with youre
     owene thyng
Right as yow list,—axeth no reed at me,
For as I lefte at hoom al my clothyng
Whan I first cam to yow, right so,' quod she,
' Lefte I my wyl, and al my libertee,
And took youre clothyng ; wherfore I
     yow preye,
Dooth youre plesaunce, I wol youre lust
     obeye.

And certés, if I haddé prescience
Youre wyl to knowe er ye youre lust me
     tolde,   660
I wolde it doon withouten necligence ;
But now I woot youre lust and what ye
     wolde,
Al youre plesancé ferme and stable I holde;
For wiste I that my deeth wolde do yow ese,
Right gladly wolde I dyen, yow to plese ;

Deth may noght maké no comparisoun
Unto youre love'; and whan this markys say
The constance of his wyf, he caste adoun
His eyén two, and wondreth that she may
In pacienceé suffre al this array ;   670
And forth he goth with drery contenance,
But to his herte it was ful greet plesance.

    This ugly sergeant, in the samé wyse
That he hire doghter caughté, right so he,
Or worsé, if men worsé kan devyse,
Hath hent hire sone that ful was of beautee.
And ever in oon so pacient was she
That she no chieré maade of hevynesse,
But kiste hir sone, and after gan it blesse ;

Save this : she preydé hym, that, if he
     myghte,   680
Hir litel sone he wolde in erthé grave,
His tendré lymés, delicaat to sighte,

667. *youre*, Corp.² *our*, supported by Petrarch's
' nec mors ipsa *nostro* fuerit par amori.'

Fro fowelės and fro beestės for to save ;
But she noon answere of hym myghtė have;
He wente his wey, as hym nothyng ne
   roghte,
But to Boloigne he tendrely it broghte.

This markys wondred ever lenger the
   moore
Upon hir pacience, and if that he
Ne haddė soothly knowėn ther-bifoore
That parfitly hir children lovėd she,   690
He wolde have wend that of som subtiltee,
And of malice, or for crueel corage,
That she haddesuffrėd this with sad visage;

But wel he knew, that next hymself, certayn
She loved hir children best in every wyse.
But now of wommen wolde I axen fayn
If thise assayės myghtė nat suffise ?
What koude a sturdy housbonde moore
   devyse
To preeve hire wyfhod and hir stedefast-
   nesse,   699
And he continuynge ever in sturdinesse ?

But ther been folk of swich condicioun
That whan they have a certein purpos take,
They kan nat stynte of hire entencioun,
But, right as they were bounden to that
   stake,
They wol nat of that firstė purpos slake.
Right so this markys fulliche hath purposed
To tempte his wyf as he was first disposed.

He waiteth, if by word or contenance,
That she to hym was changėd of corage ;
But never koude he fyndė variance :   710
She was ay oon in herte and in visage,
And ay the forther that she was in age
The moorė trewe, if that it were possfble,
She was to hym in love, and moore penyble;

For which it semėd thus that of hem two
Ther nas but o wyl, for as Walter leste,
The samė lust was hire plesance also ;
And, God be thankėd, al fil for the beste.
She shewėd wel, for no worldly unreste
A wyf, as of hirself, no thing ne sholde   720
Wille in effect, but as hir housbonde wolde.

696. It is Chaucer who addresses the query to *women*.

The sclaundre of Walter ofte and wydė
   spradde,
That of a crueel herte he wikkedly,
For he a pourė womman wedded hadde,
Hath mordred bothe his children privėly.
Swich murmure was among hem comunly.
No wonder is, for to the peplės ere
Ther cam no word but that they mordred
   were ;

For which, where-as his peplė ther-bifore
Hadde loved hym wel, the sclaundre of
   his diffame   730
Made hem that they hym hatedė therfore.
To been a mordrere is an hateful name,
But nathėlees, for ernest ne for game,
He of his crueel purpos noldė stente ;
To tempte his wyf was set al his entente.

Whan that his doghter twelf yeer was
   of age
He to the court of Rome, in subtil wyse
Enformėd of his wyl, sente his message,
Comaundynge hem swiche bullės to devyse
As to his crueel purpos may suffyse,   740
How that the pope, as for his peplės reste,
Bad hym to wedde another, if hym leste.

I seye, he bad they sholdė countrefete
The popės bullės, makynge mencioun
That he hath leve his firstė wyf to lete,
As by the popės dispensacioun,
To styntė rancour and dissencioun
Bitwixe his peple and hym ; thus seyde
   the bulle,
The which they han publicėd attė fulle.

The rudė peple, as it no wonder is,   750
Wenden ful wel that it hadde be right so ;
But whan thise tidynges cam to Grisildis
I deemė that hire hertė was ful wo ;
But she—ylikė sad for evermo—
Disposėd was, this humble creäture
The adversitee of Fortune al tendure,

Abidynge ever his lust and his plesance
To whom that she was yeven herte and al,
As to hire verray worldly suffisance.   759

754. *sad*, constant ; Petrarch's ' inconcussa.'

But, shortly if this storie I tellen shal,
This markys writen hath in special
A lettre, in which he sheweth his entente,
And secreely he to Boloigne it sente.

To the erl of Panyk, which that haddè tho
Wedded his suster, preyde he specially
To bryngen hoom agayn his children two
In honurable estaat al openly;
But o thyng he hym preyéde outrely,
That he to no wight, though men wolde
     enquere,   769
Sholdè nat tellè whos children they were

But seye, the mayden sholde y-wedded be
Unto the markys of Saluce anon.
   And as this erl was preyéd, so dide he ;
For at day set he on his wey is goon
Toward Saluce, and lordès many oon
In riche array, this mayden for to gyde,
Hir yongè brother ridynge hire bisyde.

Arrayéd was toward hir mariage
This fresshè maydè ful of gemmès cleere.
Hir brother, which that seven yeer was
     of age,   780
Arrayéd eek ful fressh in his manere ;
And thus in greet noblesse and with glad
     cheere,
Toward Saluces shapynge hir journey,
Fro day to day they ryden in hir wey.

PART V

   Among al this, after his wikke usage,
This markys, yet his wyf to temptè moore,
To the utterestè preeve of hir corage,
Fully to han experience and loore
If that she were as stidefast as bifoore,
He on a day, in open audience,   790
Ful boistously hath seyd hire this sentence :

' Certès, Grisilde, I hadde ynogh plesance
To han yow to my wyf for youre goodnesse,
As for youre trouthe and for youre obeis-
     ance,

Noght for youre lynage, ne for youre
     richesse :
But now knowe I in verray soothfastnesse
That in greet lordshipe, if I wel avyse,
Ther is greet servitute, in sondry wyse.

I may nat doon as every plowman may,—
My peplè me constreyneth for to take   800
Another wyf, and crien day by day,
And eek the popè, rancour for to slake,
Consenteth it, that dar I undertake ;
And trewèliche thus muche I wol yow seye,
My newè wyf is comynge by the weye.

Be strong of herte, and voyde anon hir place,
And thilkè dowere that ye broghten me,
Taak it agayn, I grauntè it of my grace.
Retourneth to youre fadrès hous,' quod he,
' No man may alwey han prosperitee.   810
With evene herte I redè yow tendure
This strook of Fortune or of áventure.'

And she answerde agayn in pacience :
' My lord,' quod she, ' I woot and wiste
     alway
How that bitwixen youre magnificence
And my povertè no wight kan ne may
Maken comparisoun, it is no nay ;
I ne heeld me never digne in no manere
To be youre wyf, no, ne youre chamberere ;

And in this hous ther ye me lady maade,   820
The heighè God take I for my witnesse,
And also wysly he my soulè glaade !
I never heeld me lady, ne maistresse,
But humble servant to youre worthynesse,
And ever shal, whil that my lyf may dure,
Aboven every worldly creäture.

That ye so longe, of youre benignitee,
Han holden me in honour and nobleye,
Where as I was noght worthy for to bee,
That thonke I God, and yow, to whom I
     preye   .   830
Foryelde it yow ; ther is namoore to seye ;
Unto my fader gladly wol I wende
And with hym dwelle unto my lyvès ende.

764. *Panyk*, E⁵ *Pavyk, Pavie.*
770. *they*, E *that they.*
777. *hire bisyde*, H⁵ *by hir syde.*

808. *I grauntè it of my grace.* Petrarch only
has ' dotem tuam referens.'
811, 812. Chaucer's expansion of ' æqua mente.'

197

Ther I was fostréd of a child ful smal,
Til I be deed my lyf ther wol I lede,
A wydwé clene, in body, herte and al ;
For sith I yaf to yow my maydenhede,
And am youre trewé wyf, it is no drede,
God shildé swich a lordés wyf to take   839
Another man to housbonde or to make ;

And of youre newé wyf God of his grace
So graunté yow wele and prosperitee ;
For I wol gladly yelden hire my place,
In which that I was blisful wont to bee ;
For sith it liketh yow, my lord,'quod shee,
' That whilom weren al myn hertés reste,
That I shal goon, I wol goon whan yow leste.

But ther as ye me profré swich dowaire
As I first broghte, it is wel in my mynde
It were my wrecchéd clothés, no thyng faire,
The whiche to me were hard now for to
    fynde.   851
O goodé God, how gentil and how kynde
Ye seméd by youre speche and youre visage
The day that makéd was oure mariage !

But sooth is seyd, algate I fynde it trewe,
For in effect it preevéd is on me,
Love is noght oold as whan that it is newe!
But certés, lord, for noon adversitee,
To dyén in the cas, it shal nat bee   859
That ever in word or werk I shal repente
That I yow yaf myn herte in hool entente.

My lord, ye woot that in my fadrés place
Ye dide me streepe out of my pouré weede,
And richély me cladden of youre grace.
To yow broghte I noght ellés, out of drede,
But feith and nakednesse and maydenhede ;
And heere agayn my clothyng I restoore,
And eek my weddyng ryng, for evermore.

The remenant of youre jueles redy be   869
In-with youre chambré, dar I saufly sayn.
Naked out of my fadrés hous,' quod she,
' I cam and naked moot I turne agayn ;
Al youre plesancé wol I folwen fayn ;

But yet I hope it be nat youre entente
That I smoklees out of youre paleys wente.

Ye koude nat doon so dishoneste a thyng,
That thilké wombe in which youre children
    leye
Sholdé biforn the peple, in my walkyng,
Be seyn al baré, wherfore I yow preye,
Lat me nat lyk a worm go by the weye.
Remembre yow, myn owene lord, so deere,
I was youre wyf, though I unworthy weere ;

Wherfore in gerdoun of my maydenhede
Which that I broghte, and noght agayn I
    bere,
As vouchethsauf to yeve me to my meede
But swich a smok as I was wont to were,
That I ther-with may wrye the wombe of
    here
That was youre wyf ; and heer take I my
    leeve
Of yow, myn owene lord, lest I yow greve.'

' The smok,' quod he, ' that thou hast on
    thy bak,   890
Lat it be stille, and bere it forth with thee.'
But wel unnethés thilké word he spak,
But wente his wey, for routhe and for pitee.
   Biforn the folk hirselven strepeth she,
And in her smok, with heed and foot al
    bare,
Toward hir fader hous forth is she fare.

The folk hire folwé wepynge in hir weye,
And Fortune ay they cursen as they goon ;
But she fro wepyng kepte hire eyén dreye,
Ne in this tymé word ne spak she noon.
   Hir fader, that this tidynge herde anoon,
Curseth the day and tymé that nature
Shoope hym to been a lyvés creature ;

For out of doute this oldé pouré man
Was ever in suspect of hir mariage ;
For ever he deméd, sith that it bigan,
That whan the lord fulfild hadde his corage,
Hym woldé thynke it were a disparage
To his estaat, so lowé for talighte,
And voyden hire as soone as ever he
    myghte.   910

836-840. Expanded from Petrarch's 'Felix semper et honorabilis vidua, quæ viri talis uxor fuerim.'
853-860. Chaucer's addition.
866. *nakednesse*, H² *mekenes*.

888. *and heer*, etc., Chaucer's addition.

Agayns his doghter hastiliche goth he,
For he by noyse of folk knew hire
    comynge,
And with hire oldė coote, as it myghte be,
He covered hire ful sorwefully wepynge ;
But on hire body myghte he it nat brynge,
For rudė was the clooth and moore of age
By deyės fele than at hire mariage.

    Thus with hire fader, for a certeyn space,
Dwelleth this flour of wyfly pacĭence,   919
That neither by hire wordės ne hire face,
Biforn the folk, ne eek in hire absence,
Ne shewėd she that hire was doon offence ;
Ne of hire heighe estaat no remembraunce
Ne haddė she, as by hire contenaunce.

No wonder is, for in hire grete estaat,
Hire goost was ever in pleyn humylitee ;
No tendrė mouth, noon hertė delicaat,
No pompė, no semblant of roialtee ;
But ful of pacient benyngnytee,
Discreet and pridėlees, ay honurable, 930
And to hire housbonde ever meke and
    stable.

    Men speke of Job, and moost for his
    humblesse,
As clerkės, whan hem list, konne wel
    endite,
Namely of men, but as in soothfastnesse,
Though clerkės preisė wommen but a lite,
Ther kan no man in humblesse hym
    acquite
As wommen kan, ne kan been half so
    trewe
As wommen been, but it be falle of newe.

PART VI

Fro Boloigne is this erl of Panyk come,
Of which the fame up sprang to moore
    and lesse,   940
And to the peplės erės, alle and some,
Was kouth eek that a newė markysesse

915-917. Chaucer's perverse expansion of
'attritam senio.'
932-938. Chaucer's addition, in apparent forget-
fulness that it is a Clerk who is speaking.

He with hym broghte, in swich pompe
    and richesse,
That never was ther seyn with mannės eye
So noble array in al West Lumbardye.

    The markys, which that shoope and
    knew al this,
Er that this erl was come, sente his message
For thilkė sely, pourė Grisildis ;
And she with humblėherte and glad visage,
Nat with no swollen thoght in hire corage,
Cam at his heste, and on hire knees hire
    sette,   951
And reverently and wisely she hym grette.

'Grisilde,' quod he, 'my wyl is, outrely,
This mayden, that shal wedded been to me,
Receivėd be to-morwe as roially .
As it possíble is in myn hous to be,
And eek that every wight in his degree
Have his estaat in sittyng and servyse
And heigh plesaunce as I kan best devyse.

I have no wommen suffisaunt, certayn, 960
The chambrės for tarraye in ordinaunce
After my lust, and therfore wolde I fayn
That thyn were al swich manere govern-
    aunce ;
Thou knowest eek of old al my plesaunce ;
Thogh thyn array be badde and yvel biseye,
Do thou thy devoir at the leestė weye.'

    'Nat oonly, lord, that I am glad,' quod
    she,
'To doon youre lust, but I desire also
Yow for to serve and plese in my degree
Withouten feyntyng, and shal evermo ;
Ne never for no welė, ne no wo,   971
Ne shal the goost withinne myn hertė
    stente
To love yow best, with al my trewe
    entente.'

And with that word she gan the hous to
    dighte,
And tables for to sette and beddės make,
And peynėd hire to doon al that she
    myghte,
Preyynge the chambrėrės for Goddės sake

To hasten hem, and fastė swepe and shake;
And she the moostė servysable of alle
Hath every chambre arrayėd and his halle.

Abouten undern gan this erl alighte 981
That with him broghte thise noble children tweye,
For which the peplė ran to seen the sighte
Of hire array, so richėly biseye;
And thanne at erst amongės hem they seye,
That Walter was no fool, thogh that hym leste
To chaunge his wyf, for it was for the beste;

For she is fairer, as they deemen alle,
Than is Grisilde, and moorė tendre of age,
And fairer fruyt bitwene hem sholdė falle,
And moorė plesant, for hire heigh lynage;
Hir brother eek so faire was of visage
That hem to seen the peple hath caught plesaunce,
Commendynge now the markys governaunce.—

Auctor. 'O stormy peple! unsad, and ever untrewe!
Ay undiscreet, and chaungynge as a vane,
Delitynge ever in rumbul that is newe;
For lyk the moone ay wexė ye and wane!
Ay ful of clappyng, deere ynogh a jane!
Youre doom is fals, youre constance yvele preeveth, 1000
A ful greet fool is he that on yow leeveth.'

Thus seyden saddė folk in that citee
Whan that the peplė gazėd up and doun,—
For they were glad, right for the noveltee,
To han a newė lady of hir toun.
Namoore of this make I now mencioun,
But to Grisilde agayn wol I me dresse,
And telle hir constance and hir bisynesse.—

Ful bisy was Grisilde in every thyng
That to the feestė was apertinent; 1010
Right noght was she abayst of hire clothyng,

Thogh it were rude and somdeel eek to-rent,
But with glad cheerė to the gate is went
With oother folk to greete the markysesse,
And after that dooth forth hire bisynesse.

With so glad chiere his gestės she receyveth,
And konnyngly, everich in his degree,
That no defautė no man aperceyveth,
But ay they wondren what she myghtė bee
That in so poure array was for to see, 1020
And koudė swich honóur and reverence,
And worthily they preisen hire prudence.

In al this meenė-whilė she ne stente
This mayde, and eek hir brother, to commende
With al hir herte, in ful benyngne entente,
So wel that no man koude hir pris amende;
But attė laste whan that thise lordės wende
To sitten doun to mete, he gan to calle
Grisilde, as she wás bisy in his halle.

'Grisilde,' quod he, as it were in his pley,
'How liketh thee my wyf, and hire beautee?'
'Right wel,' quod she, 'my lord, for in good fey
A fairer saugh I never noon than she;
I prey to God yeve hire prosperitee;
And so hope I that he wol to yow sende
Plesance ynogh unto youre lyvės ende.

O thyng biseke I yow, and warne also,
That ye ne prikkė with no tormentynge
This tendrė mayden, as ye han doon mo; 1040
For she is fostrėd in hire norissynge
Moore tendrely, and, to my supposynge,
She koudė nat adversitee endure
As koude a pourė fostrėd creature.'

And whan this Walter saugh hire pacience,
Hir gladė chiere, and no malice at al,
And he so ofte had doon to hire offence
And she ay sad and constant as a wal,
Continuynge ever hire innocence overal,

993. *the peple.* Petrarch merely says 'erantque qui dicerent.' The next two stanzas are Chaucer's addition (marked *Auctor* in E³), inserted in revising the tale.

1039. *mo*, more, others; cp. Petrarch 'ne hanc illis aculeis agites, quibus alteram agitasti.' Even now she will not say 'me.'

This sturdy markys gan his hertė dresse
To rewen upon hire wyfly stedfastnesse.

' This is ynogh, Grisildė myn,' quod he,
' Be now namoore agast, ne yvele apayed ;
I have thy feith and thy benyngnytee,
As wel as ever womman was, assayed,
In greet estaat and pourėliche arrayed.
Now knowe I, goodė wyf, thy stedfast-
    nesse ' ;
And hire in armės took, and gan hire kesse.

And she for wonder took of it no keepe,
She herdė nat what thyng he to hire seyde,
She ferde, as she had stert out of a sleepe,
Til she out of hire mazėdnesse abreyde. 1061
' Grisilde,' quod he, ' by God that for us
    deyde,
Thou art my wyf, ne noon oother I have,
Ne never hadde, as God my soulė save !

This is thy doghter, which thou hast
    supposed
To be my wyf,—that oother feithfully
Shal be myn heir, as I have ay purposed ;
Thou bare hym in thy body trewėly ;
At Boloigne have I kept hem privėly.
Taak hem agayn, for now maystow nat seye
That thou hast lorn noon of thy children
    tweye ;   1071

And folk that ootherweys han seyd of me,
I warne hem wel that I have doon this deede
For no malice, ne for no crueltee,
But for tassaye in thee thy wommanheede,
And nat to sleen my children, God forbeede !
But for to kepe hem pryvėly and stille
Til I thy purpos knewe and al thy wille.'

Whan she this herde, aswownė doun she
    falleth   1079
For pitous joye, and after hire swownynge
She bothe hire yongė children to hire
    calleth,
And in hire armės, pitously wepynge,
Embraceth hem, and tendrėly kissynge,
Ful lyk a mooder, with hire saltė teeres
She bathėd bothe hire visage and hire
    heeres.

1056. *goodė*, H⁸ *dere.*
1084. *Ful lyk a mooder*, Chaucer's phrase.

O which a pitous thyng it was to se
Hir swownyng, and hire humble voys to
    heere !
' *Graunt mercy*, lord ! that thanke I yow,'
    quod she,
' That ye han savėd me my children deere.
Now rekke I never to been deed right
    heere,   1090
Sith I stonde in youre love and in youre
    grace.
No fors of deeth, ne whan my spirit pace !

O tendre, O deere, O yongė children myne!
Youre woful mooder wendė stedfastly
That crueel houndės, or som foul vermyne,
Hadde eten yow ; but God, of his mercy,
And youre benyngnė fader, tendrėly
Hath doon yow kept '—and in that samė
    stounde
Al sodeynly she swapte adoun to grounde ;

And in hire swough so sadly holdeth she
Hire children two, whan she gan hem
    tembrace,
That with greet sleighte, and greet
    difficultee
The children from hire arm they goone
    arace.
O many a teere on many a pitous face
Doun ran, of hem that stooden hire bisyde;
Unnethe abouten hire myghte they abyde!

Walter hire gladeth, and hire sorwė slaketh;
She riseth up, abaysėd, from hire traunce,
And every wight hire joye and fecstė
    maketh,   1109
Til she hath caught agayn hire contenaunce.
Walter hire dooth so feithfully plesaunce
That it was deyntee for to seen the cheere
Bitwixe hem two, now they been met yfeere.

Thise ladyes, whan that they hir tymė saye,
Han taken hire and into chambrė gon,
And strepen hire out of hire rude array,
And in a clooth of gold that brightė shoon,
With a coroune of many a richė stoon

1086-1113. Chaucer's addition.
1088. *that thankė I you*, H⁶ *God thank it
(thankė) you, God I thank it (thank) you.*

201

Upon hire heed, they into halle hire
    broghte,   1119
And ther she was honúrèd as hire oghte.

Thus hath this pitous day a blisful ende,
For every man and womman dooth his
    myght
This day in murthe and revel to dispende,
Til on the welknè shoon the sterrès lyght;
For more solempne in every mannès syght
This festé was, and gretter of costage,
Than was the revel of hire mariage.

Ful many a yeer in heigh prosperitee
Lyven thise two in concord and in reste,
And richèly his doghter maryed he   1130
Unto a lord, oon of the worthieste
Of al Ytaille; and thanne in pees and reste,
His wyvès fader in his court he kepeth,
Til that the soule out of his body crepeth.

His sone succedeth in his heritage
In reste and pees after his fader day,
And fortunat was eek in mariage ;
Al putte he nat his wyf in greet assay.
This world is nat so strong, it is no nay,
As it hath been of oldè tymès yoore ;   1140
And herkneth what this auctour seith
    therfoore.

This storie is seyd, nat for that wyvès
    sholde
Folwen Grisilde as in humylitee,
For it were inportáble, though they
    wolde,—
But for that every wight in his degree
Sholdè be constant in adversitee
As was Grisildè, therfore Petrak writeth
This storie, which with heigh stile he
    enditeth ;

For sith a womman was so pacient   1149
Unto a mortal man, wel moore us oghte
Receyven al in gree that God us sent,
For greet skile is he preevè that he wroghte.

1124. *lyght,* H⁴ *bright.*
1140. *of,* H⁶ *in.*
1141. *this auctour,* Petrarch, who added the
moralizing of the next three stanzas to Boccaccio's
tale.

But he ne tempteth no man that he boghte,
As seith Seint Jame, if ye his pistel rede.
He preeveth folk al day, it is no drede,

And suffreth us, as for oure exercise,
With sharpè scourges of adversitee
Ful oftè to be bete in sondry wise,
Nat for to know oure wyl, for certès he,
Er we were born, knew al oure frelètee ;
And for oure beste is al his governaunce ;
Lat us thanne lyve in vertuous suffraunce.

But o word, lordynges, herkneth, er I go :
It were ful hard to fyndè now-a-dayes
In al a toun Grisildis thre or two ;
For if that they were put to swiche assayes,
The gold of hem hath now so badde alayes
With bras, that thogh the coynè be fair at eye
It woldè rather breste a-two than plye ;

For which heere, for the Wyvès love of
    Bathe,—   1170
Whos lyf and al hire sectè God mayntene
In heigh maistrie, and ellès were it scathe,—
I wol with lusty hertè, fressh and grene,
Seyn yow a song, to gladè yow, I wene ;
And lat us stynte of ernestful matere :
Herkneth my song that seith in this manere.

Lenvoy de Chaucer

Grisilde is deed, and eek hire pacience,
And bothe atonès buryed in Ytaille ;
For which I crie in open audience,
No wedded man so hardy be tassaille   1180
His wyvès pacience in hope to fynde
Grisildis, for in certein he shal faille !

O noble wyvès, ful of heigh prudence,
Lat noon humylitee youre tongè naill,
Ne lat no clerk have cause or diligence
To write of yow a storie of swich mervaille
As of Grisildis pacient and kynde,
Lest *Chichivache* yow swelwe in hire
    entraille !

1163. *But o word.* What follows is all Chaucer's.
Its unsuitablenesse to the Clerk has often been
noticed.
1188. *Chichivache,* the lean cow who fed on
patient wives, while her mate Bycorne grew fat on
humble husbands. A corruption of *chichefache,*
lean-faced.

Folweth Ekko, that holdeth no silence,
But ever answereth at the countretaille.
Beth nat bidaffèd for youre innocence, 1191
But sharply taak on yow the governaille.
Emprenteth wel this lessoun in youre mynde
For commune profit sith it may availle.

Ye archiwyvès stondeth at defense,
Syn ye be strong as is a greet camaille,
Ne suffreth nat that men yow doon offense;
And sklendrè wyvès, fieble, as in bataille,
Beth egre as is a tygrè yond in Ynde; 1199
Ay clappeth as a mille, I yow consaille;

Ne dreed hem nat, doth hem no reverence,
For though thyn housbonde armèd be in
    maille,
The arwès of thy crabbèd eloquence
Shal perce his brest, and eek his aventaille.
In jalousie I rede eek thou hym bynde,
And thou shalt make hym couche as
    dooth a quaille.

If thou be fair, ther folk been in presence
Shewe thou thy visage and thyn apparaille;
If thou be foul, be fre of thy dispence, 1209
To gete thee freendès ay do thy travaille;
Be ay of chiere, as light as leef on lynde,
And lat hym care and wepe, and wryng
    and waille!

The Prologe of the Marchantes Tale

'Wepyng and waylyng, care and oother
    sorwe
I knowe ynogh, on even and a-morwe,'
Quod the Marchant, 'and so doon othere mo
That wedded been, I trowe that it be so;
For wel I woot it fareth so with me.
I have a wyf, the worstè that may be,
For thogh the feend to hire y-coupled were,
She wolde hym overmacche, I dar wel
    swere.   1220
What sholde I yow reherce in special
Hir hye malice? She is a shrewe at al.
Ther is a long and largè difference
Bitwix Grisildis gretè pacience,
And of my wyf the passyng crueltee.
Were I unbounden, al so moot I thee!

I woldè never eft comen in the snare.
We wedded men lyven in sorwe and care.
Assayè who so wole and he shal fynde 1229
I seyè sooth, by Seint Thomas of Ynde!
As for the moorè part, I sey nat alle;
God shildè that it sholdè so bifalle!
    'A! good sire Hoost! I have y-
    wedded bee
Thise monthès two, and moorè nat, *pardee!*
And yet, I trowè, he that al his lyve
Wyflees hath been, though that men wolde
    him ryve
Unto the herte, ne koude in no manere
Tellen so muchel sorwe as I now heere
Koude tellen of my wyvès cursednesse!'
    'Now,' quod our Hoost, 'Marchant,
    so God yow blesse!   1240
Syn ye so muchel knowen of that art,
Ful hertèly I pray yow telle us part.'
    'Gladly,' quod he, 'but of myn owenè
    soore,
For soory herte, I tellè may namoore.'

MERCHANT'S TALE

Heere bigynnèth The Marchantes Tale

Whilom ther was dwellynge in Lum-
    bardye
A worthy knyght that born was of Pavye,
In which he lyved in greet prosperitee;
And sixty yeer a wyflees man was hee,
And folwed ay his bodily delyt
On wommen ther as was his appetyt, 1250
As doon thise foolès that been seculeer;
And whan that he was passèd sixty yeer,
Were it for hoolynesse or for dotage
I kan nat seye, but swich a greet corage
Haddè this knyght to been a wedded man
That day and nyght he dooth al that he
    kan
Tespien where he myghtè wedded be;
Preyinge oure Lord to granten him that he

The Marchantes Tale. The Pear-tree incident
in this story is the subject of the ninth novel of
the seventh day in Boccaccio's *Decamerone*, and
is found also in a collection of Latin fables by one
Adolphus, written in 1315, and elsewhere. It has
probably an Eastern origin.
1248. *sixty*, H² *fourty*; so H in 1252.

Mighte onės knowe of thilkė blisful lyf 1259
That is bitwixe an housbonde and his wyf,
And for to lyve under that hooly bond
With which that first God man and
     womman bond.
' Noon oother lyf,' seyde he, ' is worth a
     bene,
For wedlok is so esy, and so clene,
That in this world it is a paradys ';
Thus seyde this oldė knyght, that was so
     wys.
     And certeinly, as sooth as God is kyng,
To take a wyf it is a glorious thyng,
And namely whan a man is oold and hoor,—
Thanne is a wyf the fruyt of his tresor,—
Thanne sholde he take a yong wyf and a feir,
On which he myghte engendren hym an
     heir,
And lede his lyf in joye and in solas ;
Where as thise bachelėris synge, ' Allas ! '
Whan that they fynden any adversitee
In love, which nys but childyssh vanytee ;
And trewėly it sit wel to be so
That bacheleris have often peyne and wo ;
On brotel ground they buylde, and brotel-
     nesse   1279
They fyndė whan they wenė sikernesse.
They lyve but as a bryd, or as a beest,
In libertee and under noon arreest,
Ther as a wedded man, in his estaat,
Lyveth a lyf blisful and ordinaat,
Under this yok of mariage y-bounde.
Wel may his herte in joye and blisse ha-
     bounde,
For who kan be so buxom as a wyf ?
Who is so trewe and eek so ententyf
To kepe hym, syk and hool, as is his make?
For wele or wo she wole hym nat forsake ;
She nys nat wery hym to love and serve,
Thogh that he lye bedredė til he sterve.
     And yet somme clerkės seyn it nys nat so,
Of whiche he, Theofraste, is oon of tho.
What force though Theofrastė listė lye ?
' Ne take no wyf,' quod he, ' for hous-
     bondrye,
As for to spare in houshold thy dispence ;
A trewė servant dooth moore diligence

Thy good to kepė, than thyn owenė wyf,
For she wol claymė half part al hir lyf; 1300
And if that thou be syk, so God me save !
Thy verray freendės, or a trewė knave,
Wol kepe thee bet than she, that waiteth ay
After thy good, and hath doon many a day ;
And if thou take a wyf unto thyn hoold,
Ful lightly maystow been a cokėwold.'
This sentence, and an hundred thyngės
     worse,
Writeth this man, ther God his bonės corse !
But take no kepe of al swich vanytee ;
Deffiė Theofraste and herkė me.   1310
     A wyf is Goddės yiftė verraily ;
Alle othere manere yiftės hardily,
As londės, rentės, pasture, or commune,
Or moeblės, alle been yiftės of Fortune,
That passen as a shadwe upon a wal ;
But dredėlees, if pleynly speke I shal,
A wyf wol laste and in thyn hous endure,
Wel lenger than thee list, parãventure.
     Mariage is a ful greet sacrement ;
He which that hath no wyf I holde hym
     shent ;   1320
He lyveth helplees and al desolat,—
I speke of folk in seculer estaat ;
And herkė why, I sey nat this for noght,
That womman is for mannės helpe y-
     wroght.
The hyė God whan he haddė Adam maked,
And saugh him al allonė, bely naked,
God of his gretė goodnesse seydė than,
' Lat us now make an helpe unto this man,
Lyk to hymself '; and thanne he made
     him Eve.   1329
Heere may ye se, and heer by may ye preve,
That wyf is mannės helpe and his confort,
His Paradys terrestre, and his disport ;
So buxom and so vertuous is she,
They mostė nedės lyve in unitee.
O flessh they been, and o flessh, as I gesse,
Hath but oon herte in wele and in distresse.
     A wyf ! a ! Seintė Marie, *benedicite*,
How myghte a man han any adversitee
That hath a wyf ? Certės, I kan nat seye.
The blissė which that is bitwixe hem
     tweye   1340
Ther may no tongė telle or hertė thynke.
If he be poure she helpeth hym to swynke,

1273. *joye*, H *mirthe*.
1294. *Theofraste*. See Wife of Bath's Tale, ll.
235, 671.

1316. *dredelees*, H⁵ *drede not*.

She kepeth his good and wasteth never
    a deel ;
Al that hire housbonde lust hire liketh
    weel ;
She seith not onės, 'nay,' whan he
    seith, 'ye.'
'Do this,' seith he ; 'Al redy, sire,' seith
    she.
O blisful ordre of wedlok precious !
Thou art so mùrye, and eek so vertuous,
And so commended and apprevèd eek,
That every man that halt hym worth a
    leek,   1350
Upon his barė knees, oughte, al his lyf,
Thanken his God that hym hath sent a
    wyf ;
Or ellès preye to God hym for to sende
A wyf, to laste unto his lyvès ende ;
For thanne his lyf is set in sikernesse ;
He may nat be deceyvèd, as I gesse,
So that he werke after his wyvès reede.
Thanne may he boldely kepen up his heed,
They been so trewe, and therwithal so
    wyse ;
For which, if thou wolt werken as the
    wyse,   1360
Do alwey so as wommen wol thee reede.
    Lo, how that Jacob, as thise clerkès
    rede,
By good conseil of his mooder Rebekke,
Boondė the kydès skyn aboute his nekke,
Thurgh which his fadrès benysoun he
    wan.
    Lo Judith, as the storie tellė kan,
By wys conseil she Goddès peple kepte,
And slow hym Olofernus, whil he slepte.
    Lo Abigayl, by good conseil how she
Savèd hir housbonde, Nabal, whan that he
Sholde han be slayn ; and looke Ester
    also,   1371
By good conseil delyvered out of wo
The peple of God, and made hym Mar-
    dochee
Of Assuere enhauncèd for to be.
    Ther nys no thyng in gree superlatyf,
As seith Senek, above an humble wyf.

Suffre thy wyvès tonge, as Catoun bit,
She shal comande, and thou shalt suffren it,
And yet she wole obeye of curteisye ;
A wyf is kepere of thyn housbondrye. 1380
Wel may the sikė man biwaille and wepe,
Ther as ther nys no wyf the hous to kepe.
I warnė thee if wisely thou wolt wirche,
Love wel thy wyf, as Crist lovèd his
    chirche.
If thou lovest thyself thou lovest thy wyf.
No man hateth his flessh, but in his lyf
He fostreth it, and therfore bidde I thee
Cherisse thy wyf, or thou shalt never
    thee.
Housbonde and wyf, what so men jape
    or pleye,
Of worldly folk holden the siker weye ; 1390
They been so knyt ther may noon harm
    bityde,
And namély upon the wyvès syde ;
For which this Januarie, of whom I tolde,
Considered hath, inwith his dayès olde,
The lusty lyf, the vertuous quyete,
That is in mariágė hony sweete ;
And for his freendès on a day he sente,
To tellen hem theffect of his entente.
    With facė sad his tale he hath hem
    toold.   1399
He seydė, ' Freendès, I am hoor and oold,
And almoost, God woot, on my pittès
    brynke ;
Upon the soulė somwhat moste I thynke.
I have my body folily despended ;
Blessèd be God ! that it shal been
    amended,
For I wol be certeyn a wedded man,
And that anoon, in al the haste I kan.
Unto som maydė, fair and tendre of age,
I prey yow shapeth for my mariage
Al sodeynly, for I wol nat abyde ;
And I wol fonde tespien on my syde 1410
To whom I may be wedded hastily ;
But for as muche as ye been mo than I,
Ye shullen rather swich a thyng espyen
Than I, and where me best were to allyen.

1366. *storie*, E⁴ *storie eek*.
1375. Glossed in E and Heng. : 'Seneca: Sicut
nichil est superius (om. E) benigna conjuge, ita
nihil crudelius est infesta muliere.'

1377. Glossed, 'Cato : Uxoris linguam, si
frugi est, ferre memento.'
1387. *bidde*, H *warne*.
1390. *siker*, H *righte*.
1408. *shapeth*, H *helpith*.

But o thyng warne I yow, my freendès
　deere,
I wol noon oold wyf han in no manere.
She shal nat passè twenty yeer certayn,
Oold fissh and yongè flessh wolde I
　have fayn.
Bet is,' quod he, ' a pyk than a pykerel,
And bet than olde boef is the tendrè veel.
I wol no womman thritty yeer of age,—
It is but benèstraw and greet forage ;
And eek thise oldè wydwès, God it woot,
They konne so muchel craft on Wadès
　boot,
So muchel broken harm, whan that hem
　leste,
That with hem sholde I never lyve in
　reste ;
For sondry scolès maken sotile clerkis.
Womman of manye scolès half a clerk is ;
But certeynly a yonge thyng may men gye,
Right as men may warm wex with handès
　plye.　　　　　　　　　1430
Wherfore I sey yow pleynly in a clause,
I wol noon oold wyf han right for this
　cause ;
For if so were that I hadde swich mys-
　chaunce
That I in hire ne koude han no plesaunce,
Thanne sholde I lede my lyf in avoutrye,
And go streight to the devel, whan I dye ;
Ne children sholde I none upon hire
　geten ;
Yet were me levere houndès had me eten,
Than that myn heritágè sholde falle
In straungè hand, and this I telle yow alle.
I dotè nat ; I woot the causè why　1441
Men sholdè wedde, and forthermoore
　woot I
Ther speketh many a man of mariage,
That woot namoore of it than woot my
　page,
For whichè causès man sholde take a wyf.
Siththè he may nat lyven chaast his lyf,
Take hym a wyf with greet devocioun,

By cause of leveful procreacioun
Of children, to thonóur of God above,
And nat oonly for paramour or love ;　1450
And for they sholdè leccherye eschue,
And yelde hir dettès whan that they
　ben due ;
Or for that ech of hem sholde helpen
　oother
In meschief, as a suster shal the brother,
And lyve in chastitee ful holily ;
But, sirès, by youre leve, that am nat I,
For, God be thankèd, I dar make avaunt,
I feele my lymès stark and suffisaunt
To do al that a man bilongeth to ;　1459
I woot my-selven best what I may do.
Though I be hoor, I fare as dooth a tree
That blosmeth, er that fruyt y-woxen bee ;
And blosmy tree nys neither drye ne deed.
I feele me nowhere hoor but on myn heed ;
Myn herte and alle my lymès been as
　grene
As laurer thurgh the yeer is for to sene ;
And syn that ye han herd al myn entente,
I prey yow to my wyl ye wole assente.'
　Diversè men diversèly hym tolde
Of mariágè manye ensamples olde.　1470
Somme blamèd it, somme preysèd it
　certeyn,
But attè lastè, shortly for to seyn,
As al day falleth altercacioun
Bitwixen freendès in disputisoun,
Ther fil a stryf bitwixe his bretheren two,
Of whiche that oon was clepèd Placebo,
Justinus soothly callèd was that oother.
　Placebo seyde, ' O Januarie brother,
Ful litel nede hadde ye, my lord so deere,
Conseil to axe of any that is heere,　1480
But that ye been so ful of sapience
That yow ne liketh, for youre heighe
　prudence,
To weyven fro the word of Salomon.
This word seyde he unto us everychon,
'Wirk allè thyng by conseil,' thus seyde he,
' And thannè shaltow nat repentè thee ' ;
But though that Salomon spak swich
　a word,
Myn owenè deerè brother, and my lord,
So wysly God my soulè brynge at reste,

1417. *twenty*, H⁴ *sixtene*.
1418. *fayn*, H⁴ *ful fayn*, Pet. *certayn*.
1421. *thritty*, H³ *twenty*.
1424. *on Wades boot.* The legend of Wade and
his adventures in his boat Guingelot has perished.
1446. H⁴ *If he ne* (om. Corp.³) *may not chast
be by his life.*

1455. *holily*, H⁴ *hevenly*.
1477. *called*, H⁵ *cleped*.

I holde youre owene conseil is the beste ;
For, brother myn, of me taak this motyf,
I have now been a court-man al my lyf,
And, God it woot, though I unworthy be,
I havè stonden in ful greet degree
Abouten lordès of ful heigh estaat ;
Yet hadde I never with noon of hem
    debaat ;
I never hem contraried trewèly.
I woot wel that my lord kan moore
    than I ;
What that he seith I holde it ferme and
    stable ;   1499
I seye the same, or ellès thyng semblable.
A ful greet fool is any conseillour,
That serveth any lord of heigh honóur,
That dar presume, or ellès thenken it,
That his conseil sholde passe his lordès wit.
Nay, lordès been no foolès, by my fay !
Ye han youreselven shewèd heer to-day
So heigh sentence, so holily and weel,
That I consente and conferme everydeel
Youre wordes alle, and youre opinioun.
By God, ther nys no man in al this toun,
Ne in Ytaillè, koudè bet han sayd.   1511
Crist halt hym of this conseil wel apayd ;
And trewèly it is an heigh corage,
Of any man that stapen is in age,
To take a yong wyf ; by my fader kyn,
Youre hertè hangeth on a joly pyn !
Dooth now in this matiere right as yow leste,
For, finally, I holde it for the beste.'
  Justinus, that ay stillè sat and herde,
Right in this wise to Placebo answerde: 1520
' Now, brother myn, be pacient I preye,
Syn ye han seyd, and herkneth what I seye.
  ' Senek among his othere wordès wyse
Seith that a man oghte hym right wel avyse
To whom he yeveth his lond or his catel ;
And syn I oghte avysè me right wel
To whom I yeve my good awey fro me,
Wel muchel moore I oghte avysèd be
To whom I yeve my body for alwey.
I warne yow wel, it is no childès pley 1530
To take a wyf withoute avysèment.
Men moste enquerè, this is myn assent,
Wher she be wys, or sobre, or dronkèlewe,
Or proud, or ellès ootherweys a shrewe,

A chidestere, or a wastour of thy good,
Or riche, or poore, or ellès mannyssh wood.
Al be it so that no man fynden shal
Noon in this world that trotteth hool in al,
Ne man ne beest, which as men koude
    devyse,
But nathèlees it oghte ynough suffise 1540
With any wyf, if so were that she hadde
Mo goodè thewès than hire vices badde ;
And al this axeth leyser for tenquere,—
For, God it woot, I have wept many a teere
Ful pryvèly, syn I have had a wyf.
Preyse who-so wole a wedded mannès lyf,
Certein I fynde in it but cost and care,
And observance of allè blisses bare ;
And yet, God woot, my neighèbores aboute,
And namèly of wommen many a route, 1550
Seyn that I have the moostè stedefast wyf,
And eek the mekeste oon that bereth lyf;
But I woot best where wryngeth me my sho.
Ye mowe, for me, right as yow liketh do.
Avyseth yow, ye been a man of age,
How that ye entren into mariage,
And namely with a yong wyf and a fair.
By hym that madè water, erthe, and air,
The yongeste man that is in al this route
Is bisy ynough to bryngen it aboute 1560
To han his wyf allonè ; trusteth me,
Ye shul nat plesen hire fully yerès thre,—
This is to seyn, to doon hire ful plesaunce.
A wyf axeth ful many an observaunce.
I prey yow that ye be nat yvele apayd.'
  ' Wel,' quod this Januarie, ' and hastow
    sayd ?
Straw for thy Senek, and for thy provérbes !
I countè nat a panyer ful of herbes
Of scolè termès ; wyser men than thow,
As thou hast herd, assenteden right now
To my purpos. Placebo, what sey ye ?'
  ' I seye it is a cursèd man,' quod he,
' That letteth matrimoignè sikerly ! '
And with that word they rysen sodeynly,
And been assented fully that he sholde
Be wedded whanne hym list and where
    he wolde.
  Heigh fantasye and curious bisynesse
Fro day to day gan in the soule impresse
Of Januarie, aboute his mariáge.   1579
Many fair shape and many a fair visage

1495. *heigh*, H² *gret*.
1503. *ellès*, H⁴ *oones*.

1548. *observance*, E⁶ *observances*.

Ther passeth thurgh his herté nyght by
    nyght,
As whoso tooke a mirour polisshed bryght
And sette it in a commune market-place,
Thanne sholde he se ful many a figure pace
By his mirour ; and in the samé wyse
Gan Januarie inwith his thoght devyse
Of maydens whiche that dwellen hym
    bisyde.
He wisté nat wher that he myghte abyde,
For, if that oon have beaute in hir face,
Another stant so in the peples grace   1590
For hire sadnesse and hire benyngnytee,
That of the peple grettest voys hath she ;
And somme were riche, and hadden
    baddé name ;
But nathélees, bitwixe ernest and game,
He atté laste apoynted hym on oon,
And leet alle othere from his herté goon,
And chees hire of his owene auctoritee ;
For love is blynd al day, and may nat see.
And whan that he was in his bed y-broght
He purtreyed in his herte and in his thoght
Hir fresshé beautee, and hir agé tendre, 1601
Hir myddel smal, hire armés longe and
    sklendre,
Hir wisé governaunce, hir gentillesse,
Hir wommanly berynge, and hire sadnesse.
And whan that he on hire was condescended
Hym thoughte his choys myghté nat
    ben amended ;
For whan that he hym self concluded hadde,
Hym thoughte ech oother mannés wit so
    badde
That inpossíble it weré to repplye   1609
Agayn his choys,—this was his fantasye.
His freendés sente he to, at his instaunce,
And preyéd hem to doon hym that ples-
    aunce,
That hastily they wolden to hym come ;
He wolde abregge hir labour, alle and some;
Nedeth namoore for hym to go ne ryde,
He was apoynted ther he wolde abyde.
    Placebo cam, and eek his freendés
    soone,
And alderfirst he bad hem alle a boone,
That noon of hem none argumentés make
Agayn the purpos which that he hath take,
Which purpos was plesant to God, seyde he,
And verray ground of his prosperitee.

He seyde ther was a mayden in the toun,
Which that of beautee haddé greet renoun,
Al were it so she were of smal degree,
Suffiseth hym hir yowthe, and hir beautee ;
Which mayde, he seyde, he wolde han
    to his wyf,
To lede in ese and hoolynesse his lyf ;
And thankéd God that he myghte han
    hire al,   1629
Thát no wight his blissé parten shal ;
And preydé hem to laboure in this nede
And shapen that he faillé nat to spede ;
For thanne he seyde his spirit was at ese.
' Thanne is,' quod he, ' no-thyng may me
    displese,
Save o thyng priketh in my conscience,
The which I wol reherce in youre presence.
    ' I have,' quod he, ' herd seyd, ful
    yoore ago,
Ther may no man han parfite blissés two,—
This is to seye, in erthe and eek in hevene,—
For though he kepe hym fro the synnés
    sevene,   1640
And eek from every branche of thilké tree,
Yet is ther so parfit felicitee
And so greet ese and lust in mariáge,
That ever I am agast now in myn age,
That I shal ledé now so myrie a lyf,
So delicat, withouten wo and stryf,
That I shal have myn hevene in erthé heere ;
For sith that verray hevene is boght so
    deere,
With tribulacioun and greet penaunce,
How sholde I thanne, that lyve in swich
    plesaunce   1650
As allé wedded men doon with hire wyvys,
Come to the blisse ther Crist eterne on
    lyve ys ?
This is my drede, and ye my bretheren
    tweye,
Assoilleth me this questioun, I preye.'
    Justinus, which that hated his folye,
Answerde anon right in his japerye ;
And for he wolde his longé tale abregge,
He woldé noon auctoritee allegge,
But seydé, ' Sire, so ther be noon obstácle
Oother than this, God of his hygh myrácle,
And of his mercy, may so for yow wirche
That er ye have youre right of hooly chirche,
Ye may repente of wedded mannés lyf,

In which ye seyn ther is no wo ne
   stryf ;
And ellès, God forbedè, but he sente
A wedded man hym gracè to repente
Wel oftè rather than a sengle man ;
And therfore, sire,—the bestè reed I
   kan,—
Dispeire yow noght, but have in youre
   memorie,   1669
Paraunter she may be youre purgatorie ;
She may be Goddès meene, and Goddès
   whippe !
Thanne shal youre soulè up to hevene
   skippe
Swifter than dooth an arwe out of the bowe.
I hope to God herafter shul ye knowe
That ther nys no so greet felicitee
In mariage, ne never mo shal bee,
That yow shal lette of youre savacioun,
So that ye use, as skile is and resoun,
The lustès of youre wyf attemprely,   1679
And that ye plese hire nat to amorously,
And that ye kepe yow eek from oother
   synne.
My tale is doon, for my witte is thynne ;
Beth nat agast her-of, my brother deere,
But lat us waden out of this mateere.
(The Wyf of Bathe, if ye han understonde,
Of mariágè, which ye have on honde,
Declarèd hath ful wel in litel space.)
Fareth now wel, God have yow in his
   grace.'
   And with this word this Justyn and his
     brother
Han take hir leve, and ech of hem of
   oother ;   1690
For whan they saughe that it moste
   needis be,
They wroghten so, by sly and wys tretee,
That she, this mayden, which that Mayus
   hightè,
As hastily as ever that she myghte,
Shal wedded be unto this Januarie.
I trowe it were to longè yow to tarie,
If I yow tolde of every scrit and bond
By which that she was feffed in his lond,
Or for to herknen of hir riche array.
But finally y-comen is the day   1700
That to the chirchè bothè be they went,
For to receyve the hooly sacrement.

Forth comth the preest, with stole aboute
   his nekke,
And bad hire be lyk Sarra and Rebekke
In wysdom and in trouthe of mariáge,
And seyde his orisons as is uságe,
And croucheth hem and bad God sholde
   hem blesse,
And made al siker ynogh with hoolynesse.
   Thus been they wedded with solemp-
     nitee,
And at the feestè sitteth he and she,   1710
With othere worthy folk, up on the deys.
Al ful of joye and blisse is the paleys,
And ful of instrumentz, and of vitaille
The mostè deyntéuous of all Ytaille.
Biforn hem stoode swich instrumentz of
   soun
That Orpheus, ne of Thebès Amphioun,
Ne maden never swich a melodye.
   At every cours thanne cam loud
     mynstralcye
That never trompèd Joab for to heere,
Nor he Theodomas yet half so cleere 1720
At Thebès, whan the citee was in doute.
Bacus the wyn hem skynketh al aboute,
And Venus laugheth upon every wight,
For Januarie was bicome hir knyght,
And woldè bothe assayen his coráge
In libertee, and eek in mariáge ;
And with hire fyrbrond in hire hand aboute
Daunceth biforn the bryde and al the
   route ;
And certeinly I dar right wel seyn this
Yménëus, that god of weddyng is,   1730
Saugh never his lyf so myrie a wedded
   man.
Hoold thou thy pees, thou poete Marcian,—
That writest us that ilkè weddyng murie
Of hire Philologie and hym Mercurie,
And of the songès that the Muses songe,—
To smal is bothe thy penne and eek thy
   tonge,
For to descryven of this mariáge,

1722. Cp. *Hous of Fame*, l. 1245, on which
Professor Skeat points out that Chaucer takes his
mention of Theodamas from Statius, *Thebaid*,
viii. 343.
1732. *Marcian*, Martianus Capella, a writer of
the 5th century, whose *De Nuptiis Philologiae et
Mercurii* was a treatise on the liberal arts in nine
books.

Whan tendrė youthe hath wedded stoup-
     yng age ;
Ther is swich myrthe that it may nat be
     writen.   1739
Assayeth it youre self, thanne may ye witen
If that I lye or noon in this matiere.
    Mayus, that sit with so benyngne a chiere,
Hire to biholde it semed faïrye.
Queene Ester looked never with swich
     an eye
On Assuer, so meke a look hath she.
I may yow nat devyse al hir beautee,
But thus muche of hire beautee telle I may,
That she was lyk the brightė morwe of May
Fulfild of allė beautee and plesaunce. 1749
    This Januarie is ravysshed in a traunce
At every tyme he lookėd on hir face ;
But in his herte he gan hire to manace,
That he that nyght in armės wolde hire
     streyne
Harder than ever Parys dide Eleyne ;
But nathėlees yet hadde he greet pitee
That thilkė nyght offenden hire moste he;
And thoughte, ' Allas ! O tendrė creäture !
Now woldė God ye myghtė wel endure
Al my corage, it is so sharpe and keene !
I am agast ye shul it nat susteene ;   1760
But God forbede that I dide al my myght,
Now woldė God that it were woxen nyght,
And that the nyght wolde lasten evermo.
I wolde that al this peple were ago ! '
And finally he dooth al his labóur,
As he best myghtė, savynge his honóur,
To haste hem fro the mete in subtil wyse.
    The tymė cam that resoun was to ryse,
And after that men daunce and drynken
     faste,   1769
And spices al aboute the hous they caste,
And ful of joye and blisse is every man,—
All but a squyer hightė Damyan,
Which carf biforn the knyght ful many a
     day.
He was so ravysshed on his lady May
That for the verray peyne he was ny wood.
Almoost he swelte and swownėd ther he
     stood,
So soore hath Venus hurt hym with hire
     brond
As that she bar it daunsynge in hire hond ;
And to his bed he wente hym hastily.

Namoore of hym as at this tyme speke I,
But there I lete hym wepe ynogh and
     pleyne   1781
Til fresshė May wol rewen on his peyne.
    O perilous fyr that in the bedstraw
     bredeth !
O famulier foo, that his servyce bedeth !
O servant traytour, falsė, hoomly hewe,
Lyk to the naddre in bosom, sly, untrewe,
God shilde us allė from youre áqueyntance !
O Januarie, dronken in plesance
In mariáge, se how thy Damyan,   1789
Thyn owenė squier and thy bornė man,
Entendeth for to do thee vileynye !
God grauntė thee thyn hoomly fo tespye,
For in this world nys worsė pestilence
Than hoomly foo al day in thy presence !

    Parfournėd hath the sonne his ark
     diurne,
No lenger may the body of hym sojurne
On thorisonte, as in that latitude.
Night with his mantel, that is derk and rude,
Gan oversprede the hemysperie aboute,
For which departed is this lusty route 1800
Fro Januarie, with thank on every syde.
Hoom to hir houses lustily they ryde,
Where-as they doon hir thyngės as hem
     leste,
And, whan they sye hir tymė, goon to reste.
    Soone after that, this hastif Januarie
Wolde go to bedde, he wolde no lenger
     tarye.
He drynketh ypocras, clarree and vernáge,
Of spices hoote, tencreessen his coráge ;
And many a letuarie hath he ful fyn
Swiche as the cursėd monk, Daun
     Constantyn,   1810
Hath writen in his book, *De Coitu ;*
To eten hem alle he nas no thyng eschu ;
And to his privee freendės thus seyde he :
' For Goddės love, as soone as it may be,
Lat voyden al this hous in curteys wyse ' ;
And they han doon right as he wol devyse.
Men drynken and the travers drawe anon ;
The bryde was broght a-bedde as stille
     as stoon,
And whan the bed was with the preest
     y-blessed,

1810. *Daun Constantyn,* a monk of Monte
Cassino. Cp. Gen. Prologue, 433.

Out of the chambre hath every wight hym
    dressed ;   1820
And Januarie hath faste in armes take
His fresshe May, his paradys, his make.
He lulleth hire, he kisseth hire ful ofte,
With thikke brustles of his berd unsofte,
Lyk to the skyn of houndfyssh, sharpe as
    brere ;
For he was shave al newe in his manere.
He rubbeth hire aboute hir tendre face
And seyde thus, 'Allas ! I moot trespace
To yow, my spouse, and yow greetly
    offende,   1829
Er tyme come that I wil doun descende ;
But nathelees, considereth this,' quod he,
' Ther nys no werkman, whatsoever he be,
That may bothe werke wel and hastily.
This wol be doon at leyser parfitly,
It is no fors how longe that we pleye ;
In trewe wedlok coupled be we tweye,
And blessed be the yok that we been inne !
For in oure actes we mowe do no synne.
A man may do no synne with his wyf,
Ne hurte hymselven with his owene knyf ;
For we han leve to pleye us, by the lawe.'
Thus laboureth he til that the day gan dawe,
And thanne he taketh a sope in fyne clarree,
And upright in his bed thanne sitteth he ;
And after that he sang ful loude and cleere,
And kiste his wyf, and made wantowne
    cheere.
He was al coltissh, ful of ragerye,
And ful of jargon as a flekked pye.
The slakke skyn aboute his nekke shaketh
Whil that he sang, so chaunteth he and
    craketh ;   1850
But God woot what that May thoughte
    in hire herte
Whan she hym saugh up-sittynge in his
    sherte,
In his nyght-cappe, and with his nekke
    lene !
She preyseth nat his pleyyng worth a bene.
    Thanne seide he thus, 'My reste wol
    I take ;
Now day is come, I may no lenger wake ' ;
And doun he leyde his heed and sleepe til
    pryme.
And afterward, whan that he saugh his
    tyme,

Up ryseth Januarie, but fresshe May   1859
Heeld hire chambre unto the fourthe day,
As usage is of wyves, for the beste ;
For every labour som tyme moot han reste,
Or elles longe may he nat endure ;
This is to seyn, no lyves creature,
Be it of fyssh, or bryd, or beest, or man.
    Now wol I speke of woful Damyan,
That langwissheth for love, as ye shul heere ;
Therfore I speke to hym in this manere.

    I seye, O sely Damyan, allas !   1869
Andswere to my demaunde as in this cas.
How shaltow to thy lady, fresshe May,
Telle thy wo ?   She wole alwey seye nay.
Eek if thou speke, she wol thy wo biwreye.
God be thyn helpe, I kan no bettre seye.
    This sike Damyan in Venus fyr
So brenneth, that he dyeth for desyr ;
For which he putte his lyf in aventure.
No lenger myghte he in this wise endure,
But prively a penner gan he borwe,   1879
And in a lettre wroot he al his sorwe,—
In manere of a compleynte or a lay,—
Unto his faire, fresshe lady May ;
And in a purs of sylk, heng on his sherte,
He hath it put and leyde it at his herte.
    The moone, that at noon was thilke day
That Januarie hath wedded fresshe May
In two of Tawr, was into Cancre glyden,
So longe hath Mayus in hir chambre byden,
As custume is unto thise nobles alle.
A bryde shal nat eten in the halle   1890
Til dayes foure, or thre dayes atte leeste,
Y-passed been ; thanne lat hire go to feeste.
The fourthe day compleet fro noon to noon,
Whan that the heighe masse was y-doon,
In halle sit this Januarie and May,
As fressh as is the brighte someres day ;
And so bifel, how that this goode man
Remembred hym upon this Damyan,
And seyde, 'Seynte Marie ! how may
    this be
That Damyan entendeth nat to me ?   1900
Is he ay syk ? or how may this bityde ?'
His squieres, whiche that stooden ther
    bisyde,

1887. *In two of Tawr.* The moon could pass
through Taurus and Gemini into Cancer in four
days.

Excusèd hym by cause of his siknesse,
Which letted hym to doon his bisynesse,—
Noon oother causè myghtè make hym
    tarye.
  ' That me forthynketh,' quod this
    Januarie,
' He is a gentil squier, by my trouthe !
If that he deyde, it werè harm and routhe ;
He is as wys, discreet, and eek secree,
As any man I woot, of his degree ;   1910
And therto manly and eek servysable,
And for to been a thrifty man right able ;
But after mete, as soone as ever I may,
I wol myself visite hym, and eek May,
To doon hym al the confort that I kan ' ;
And for that word hym blessèd every man,
That of his bountee and his gentillesse
He woldè so conforten in siknesse
His squier, for it was a gentil dede.
' Dame,' quod this Januarie, ' taak good
    hede   1920
At after mete ye with youre wommen alle,
Whan ye han been in chambre out of
    this halle,
That allè ye go se this Damyan.
Dooth hym disport, he is a gentil man,
And telleth hym that I wol hym visite,
Have I no thyng but rested me a lite ;
And spede yow fastè, for I wole abyde
Til that ye slepè fastè by my syde ' ;
And with that word he gan unto hym calle
A squier, that was marchal of his halle,
And tolde hym certeyn thyngès, what he
    wolde.   1931
  This fresshè May hath streight hir wey
    y-holde,
With alle hir wommen, unto Damyan.
Doun by his beddès sydè sit she than,
Confortynge hym as goodly as she may.
This Damyan, whan that his tyme he say,
In secree wise, his purs and eek his bille,
In which that he y-writen hadde his wille,
Hath put into hire hand, withouten moore,
Save that he siketh wonder depe and soore,
And softèly to hire right thus seyde he :
' Mercy ! and that ye nat discovere me,
For I am deed, if that this thyng be kyd.'
This purs hath she inwith hir bosom hyd,
And wente hire wey—ye gete namoore
    of me ;

But unto Januarie y-comen is she
That on his beddès sydè sit ful softe.
He taketh hire and kisseth hire ful ofte,
And leyde hym doun to slepe, and that
    anon.   1949
She feynèd hire as that she mostè gon
Ther as ye woot that every wight moot
    neede ;
And whan she of this bille hath taken
    heede,
She rente it al to cloutès attè laste,
And in the pryvee softèly it caste.
  Who studieth now, but fairè, fresshè
    May ?
Adoun by oldè Januarie she lay,
That sleep til that the coughe hath hym
    awaked.
Anon he preyde hire strepen hire al naked,
He wolde of hire, he seyde, han som
    plesaunce ;
And seyde hir clothès dide hym encom-
    braunce.   1960
And she obeyeth, be hire lief or looth ;
But, lest that precious folk be with me
    wrooth,
How that he wroghte I dar nat to yow telle,
Or wheither hire thoughte it paradys or
    helle ;
But heere I lete hem werken in hir wyse,
Til evensong rong, and than they moste
    aryse.
  Were it by destynee or àventure,
Were it by influence or by nature,   1968
Or constellacioun, that in swich estaat
The hevene stood, that tymè fortunaat
Was, for to putte a bille of Venus werkes
(For allè thyng hath tyme, as seyn thise
    clerkes)
To any womman for to get hire love,
I kan nat seye ; but gretè God above
That knoweth that noon act is causèlees,
He deme of al, for I wole holde my pees ;
But sooth is this, how that this fresshè May
Hath takè swich impressioun that day,
For pitee of this sikè Damyan,   1979
That from hire hertè she ne dryvè kan
The remembrancè, for to doon hym ese.
' Certeyn,' thoghte she, ' whom that this
    thyng displese

    1966. *than,* E⁵ *that.*

I rekkė noght, for heere I hym assure
To love hym best of any creäture,
Though he namoorė haddė than his sherte.'
Lo, pitee renneth soone in gentil herte !
  Heere may ye se how excellent franchise
In wommen is, whan they hem narwe avyse.
Som tyrant is, as ther be many oon,   1989
That hath an herte as hard as any stoon,
Which wolde han lat hym storven in the
      place,
Wel rather than han graunted hym hire
      grace ;
And hem rejoysen in hire crueel pryde,
And rekkė nat to been an homycide.
  This gentil May, fulfillėd of pitee,
Right of hire hand a lettrė madė she,
In which she graunteth hym hire verray
      grace.
Ther lakketh noght, oonly but day and
      place
Wher that she myghte unto his lust suffise,
For it shal be right as he wole devyse ; 2000
And whan she saugh hir tyme, upon a day,
To visitė this Damyan gooth May,
And sotilly this lettrė doun she threste
Under his pilwe, rede it if hym leste !
She taketh hym by the hand and harde
      hym twiste,
So secrėly that no wight of it wiste,
And bad hym been al hool ; and forth
      she wente
To Januarie, whan that he for hire sente.
  Up riseth Damyan the nextė morwe ;
Al passėd was his siknesse and his sorwe.
He kembeth hym, he preyneth hym and
      pyketh,   2011
He dooth al that his lady lust and lyketh;
And eek to Januarie he gooth as lowe
As ever dide a doggė for the bowe.
He is so plesant unto every man,—
For craft is al, whoso that do it kan,—
That every wight is fayn to speke hym good,
And fully in his lady grace he stood.
Thus lete I Damyan aboute his nede,
And in my talė forth I wol procede.   2020
  Somme clerkės holden that felicitee
Stant in delit, and therfore certeyn he,

2014. *for the bowe*, a dog used in shooting.
2018. *lady*, the possessive case.
2021. *Somme clerkes.* Cp. General Prologue,
337, 338.

This noble Januarie with al his myght,
In honeste wyse, as longeth to a knyght,
Shoope hym to lyvė ful deliciously.
His housynge, his array, as honestly
To his degree was makėd as a kynges.
Amongės othere of his honeste thynges
He made a gardyn wallėd al with stoon.
So fair a gardyn woot I nowher noon,   2030
For out of doute, I verraily suppose
That he that wroot the Romance of the Rose
Ne koude of it the beautee wel devyse ;
Ne Priapus ne myghtė nat suffise,
Though he be god of gardyns, for to telle
The beautee of the gardyn, and the welle,
That stood under a laurer, alwey grene.
Ful oftė tyme he Pluto, and his queene
Proserpina, and al hire fairye,
Disporten hem and maken melodye   2040
Aboute that welle, and dauncėd as men
      tolde.
  This noble knyght, this Januarie the
      olde,
Swich deyntee hath in it to walke and pleye
That he wol no wight suffren bere the keye,
Save he hymself, for of the smale wykėt
He baar alwey of silver a clykėt,
With which, whan that hym leste, he it
      unshette ;
And whan he woldė paye his wyf hir dette
In somer sesoun, thider wolde he go,
And May his wyf, and no wight but
      they two,   2050
And thyngės whiche that were nat doon
      a bedde
He in the gardyn parfourned hem and
      spedde ;
And in this wysė many a murye day
Lyvėd this Januarie and fresshė May ;
But worldly joyė may nat alwey dure
To Januarie, ne to no creäture.

O sodeyn hape! O thou Fortune instable!
Lyk to the scorpion so deceyvable
That flaterest with thyn heed whan thou
      wolt stynge ;
Thy tayl is deeth, thurgh thyn envenym-
      ynge !   2060
O brotil joye ! O sweetė venym queynte !
O monstrė, that so subtilly kanst peynte
Thy yiftės, under hewe of stidefastnesse,

That thou deceyvest bothe moore and lesse,
Why hastow Januarie thus deceyved,
That haddest hym for thy ful freend
    receyved?
And now thou hast biraft hym bothe his
    eyen,
For sorwe of which desireth he to dyen.

Allas! this noble Januarie free,
Amydde his lust and his prosperitee,   2070
Is woxen blynd, and that al sodeynly!
He wepeth and he wayleth pitously,
And therwithal the fyr of jalousie—
Lest that his wyf sholde falle in som folye—
So brente his herte, that he wolde fayn
That som man bothe hym and hire had
    slayn;
For neither after his deeth nor in his lyf,
Ne wolde he that she were love ne wyf,
But ever lyve as wydwe in clothes blake,
Soul as the turtle that lost hath hire make.
But atte laste, after a monthe or tweye,
His sorwe gan aswage, sooth to seye,
For whan he wiste it may noon oother be
He paciently took his adversitee,
Save, out of doute, he may nat forgoon
That he nas jalous evermoore in oon.
Which jalousye it was so outrageous,
That neither in halle, nyn noon oother hous,
Ne in noon oother place never-the-mo,
He nolde suffre hire to ryde or go,   2090
But if that he had hond on hire alway;
For which ful ofte wepeth fresshe May,
That loveth Damyan so benyngnely
That she moot outher dyen sodeynly,
Or elles she moot han hym as hir leste;
She wayteth whan hir herte wolde breste.
Upon that oother syde Damyan
Bicomen is the sorwefulleste man
That ever was, for neither nyght ne day
Ne myghte he speke a word to fresshe May,
As to his purpos, of no swich mateere,   2101
But if that Januarie moste it heere,
That hadde an hand upon hire evermo;
But nathelees, by writyng to and fro,
And privee signes, wiste he what she mente,
And she knew eek the fyn of his entente.

O Januarie! what myghte it thee availle

2106. *fyn*, sum

Thogh thou myghtest se as fer as shippes
    saille?
For al-so good is blynd deceyved be   2109
As to be deceyved whan a man may se.
Lo Argus, which that hadde an hondred
    eyen,
For al that ever he koude poure or pryen,
Yet was he blent, and, God woot, so
    been mo,
That wenen wisly that it be nat so;
'Passe-over is an ese,'—I sey namoore.

This fresshe May, that I spak of so
    yoore,
In warm wex hath emprented the clyket
That Januarie bar of the smale wyket,
By which into his gardyn ofte he wente;
And Damyan, that knew al hire entente,
The cliket countrefeted pryvely.   2121
Ther nys namoore to seye; but hastily
Som wonder by this clyket shal bityde,
Which ye shul heeren, if ye wole abyde.

O noble Ovyde! ful sooth seystou,
    God woot,
What sleighte is it, thogh it be long and
    hoot,
That he nyl fynde it out in som manere.
By Piramus and Tesbee may men leere,
Thogh they were kept ful longe streite
    overal,
They been accorded, rownynge thurgh
    a wal,   2130
Ther no wight koude han founde out
    swich a sleighte.

But now to purpos,—er that dayes eighte
Were passed er the monthe of Juyn bifille,
That Januarie hath caught so greet a wille,
Thurgh eggyng of his wyf, hym for to pleye
In his gardyn, and no wight but they
    tweye,
That in a morwe unto this May seith he,
'Rys up, my wyf, my love, my lady free!
The turtle voys is herd, my dowve sweete,
The wynter is goon with alle his reynes
    weete;

2133. *Juyn*, MSS. *Juyl*, but see l. 2222; the mistake may be Chaucer's.
2138. January had been reading the *Song of Solomon*.

Com forth now with thyne eyen columbyn !
How fairer been thy brestes than is wyn !
The gardyn is enclosed al aboute ;
Com forth, my whitė spousė ! out of doute
Thou hast me wounded in myn herte, O
     wyf !
No spot of thee ne knew I al my lyf ;
Come forth, and lat us taken som disport ;
I chees thee for my wyf and my confort !'
Swiche oldė lewėd wordės used he.
    On Damyan a signė madė she,   2150
That he sholde go biforn with his clikėt.
This Damyan thanne hath openėd the
     wykėt,
And in he stirte, and that in swich manere
That no wight myght it se, neither y-heere ;
And stille he sit under a bussh anon.
    This Januarie, as blynd as is a stoon,
With Mayus in his hand and no wight mo,
Into his fresshė gardyn is ago,
And claptė to the wyket sodeynly.
    'Now, wyf,' quod he, 'heere nys but
     thou and I,   2160
That art the creäture that I best love ;
For, by that Lord that sit in hevene above,
Levere ich hadde to dyen on a knyf,
Than thee offendė, trewė, deerė wyf.
For Goddės sakė, thenk how I thee chees
Noght for no coveitisė doutėlees,
But oonly for the love I had to thee ;
And though that I be oold and may nat
     see,
Beth to me trewe, and I shal telle yow
     why.
Thre thyngės, certės, shal ye wynne therby ;
First, love of Crist, and to yourself honour,
And al myn heritagė, toun and tour ;
I yeve it yow ; maketh chartres as yow leste.
This shal be doon tomorwe er sonnė reste,
So wisly God my soulė brynge in blisse !
I prey yow first in covenat ye me kisse,
And though that I be jalous, wyte me
     noght.
Ye been so depe enprented in my thoght,
That whan that I considere youre beautee,
And therwithal the unlikly elde of me,
I may nat, certės, though I sholdė dye,
Forbere to been out of youre compaignye ;

For verray love this is, withouten doute.
Now kys me, wyf, and lat us rome aboute.'
    This fresshė May, whan she thise wordės
     herde,
Benyngnėly to Januarie answerde ;
But first and forward, she bigan to wepe ;
'I have,' quod she, 'a soulė for to kepe
As wel as ye, and also myn honóur ;
And of my wyfhod thilkė tendrė flour   2190
Which that I have assurėd in youre hond,
Whan that the preest to yow my body
     bond ;
Wherfore I wole answere in this manere,
Bý the leve of yow, my lord so deere ;
I prey to God that never dawe the day
That I ne sterve, as foule as womman may,
If ever I do unto my kyn that shame,
Or ellės I empeyrė so my name,
That I be fals ; and if I do that lakke,
Do strepė me, and put me in a sakke,   2200
And in the nextė ryver do me drenche,—
I am a gentil womman and no wenche !
Why speke ye thus ? But men been ever
     untrewe,
And wommen have repreve of yow ay
     newe.
Ye han noon oother contenance, I leeve,
But speke to us of untrust and repreeve.'
And with that word she saugh wher Damyan
Sat in the bussh, and coughen she bigan,
And with hir fynger signės madė she
That Damyan sholde clymbe upon a tree
That chargėd was with fruyt, and up he
     wente ;   2211
For verraily he knew al hire entente,
And every signė that she koudė make
Wel bet than Januarie, hir owenė make ;
For in a lettrė she hadde toold hym al
Of this matérė, how he werchen shal ;
And thus I lete hym sitte upon the pyrie,
And Januarie and May romyngė myrie.
    Bright was the day, and blew the firma-
     ment ;   2219
Phebus of gold doun hath his stremės sent
To gladen every flour with his warmnesse.
He was that tyme in Geminis, as I gesse,
But litel fro his declynacioun

2222. The sun would pass from Gemini into
Cancer about June 11 or 12, attaining at that time
its greatest northern declination.

Of Cancer, Jovis exaltacioun ;
And so bifel, that brighte morwe tyde,
That in that gardyn, in the ferther syde,
Pluto, that is the kyng of faïrye,
And many a lady in his compaignye,
Folwynge his wyf, the queene Proserpyne,
Ech after oother, right as ony lyne,— 2230
Whil that she gadered floures in the mede,
In Claudyan ye may the stories rede,
How in his grisely carte he hire sette.
This kyng of fairye thanne adoun hym sette
Upon a bench of turves, fressh and grene,
And right anon thus seyde he to his queene :
'My wyf,' quod he, ' ther may no wight seye nay,
Thexperience so preveth every day
The tresons whiche that wommen doon to man. 2239
Ten hondred thousand [tales] tellen I kan
Notable of youre untrouthe and brotil-nesse.
O Salomon ! wys, and richest of richesse,
Fulfild of sapience and of worldly glorie,
Ful worthy been thy wordes to memorie
To every wight that wit and reson kan !
Thus preiseth he yet the bountee of man :
' Amonges a thousand men yet foond I oon,
But of wommen alle foond I noon.'
' Thus seith the kyng that knoweth youre wikkednesse,
And Jhesus *filius* Syrak, as I gesse, 2250
Ne speketh of yow but seelde reverence.
A wylde fyr and corrupt pestilence,
So falle upon youre bodyes yet to-nyght !
Ne se ye nat this honurable knyght ?
By-cause, allas ! that he is blynd and old
His owene man shal make hym cokewold.
Lo, heere he sit, the lechour, in the tree !
Now wol I graunten of my magestee
Unto this olde, blynde, worthy knyght,
That he shal have ageyn his eyen syght,
Whan that his wyf wold doon hym vileynye.
Thanne shal he knowen al hire harlotrye
Bothe in repreve of hire and othere mo.'
' Ye shal ?' quod Proserpyne ; ' and wol ye so ?

Now by my moodres sires soule ! I swere
That I shal yeven hire suffisant answere,
And alle wommen after, for hir sake,
That though they be in any gilt y-take,
With face boold they shulle hemself excuse,
And bere hem doun that wolden hem accuse ; 2270
For lakke of answere noon of hem shal dyen.
Al hadde man seyn a thyng with bothe his eyen,
Yit shul we wommen visage it hardily,
And wepe, and swere, and chide subtilly.
So that ye men shul been as lewed as gees.
What rekketh me of youre auctoritees ?
' I woot wel that this Jew, this Salomon,
Foond of us wommen fooles many oon,
But though that he ne foond no good womman, 2279
Yet hath ther founde many another man
Wommen ful trewe, ful goode and vertuous ;
Witnesse on hem that dwelle in Cristes hous ;
With martirdom they preved hire con-stance.
The Romayn Geestes eek make remem-brance
Of many a verray trewe wyf also ;
But, sire, ne be nat wrooth,—al be it so,
Though that he seyde he foond no good womman,
I prey yow take the sentence of the man,
He mente thus, that in sovereyn bontee
Nis noon but God that sit in Trinitee. 2290
Ey, for verray God, that nys but oon,
What make ye so muche of Salomon ?
What though he made a temple, Goddes hous ?
What though he were riche and glorious ?
So made he eek a temple of false goddis.
How myghte he do a thyng that moore forbode is ?
Pardee ! as faire as ye his name emplastre
He was a lecchour and an ydolastre,
And in his elde he verray God forsook ;
And if that God ne hadde, as seith the book, 2300

2232. *In Claudyan*, *i.e.* in the *De Raptu Proserpinae.*
2247. See Ecclesiastes vii. 29.

2265. *moodres sires soule, i.e.* Saturn's, but *sires* is probably a blunder for *Ceres.*

Y-sparèd for his fadres sake, he sholde
Have lost his regnè rather than he wolde.
I sette right noght, of al the vileynye
That ye of wommen write, a boterflye !
I am a womman, nedès moot I speke,
Or ellès swellè til myn hertè breke ;
For sithen he seyde that we been jangler-
    esses,
As ever hool I mootè brouke my tresses !
I shal nat sparè for no curteisye
To speke hym harm that wolde us vil-
    eynye !'   2310
    ' Dame,' quod this Pluto, 'be no lenger
        wrooth,
I yeve it up ! but sith I swoor myn ooth
That I wolde graunten hym his sighte
    ageyn,
My word shal stonde, I warnè yow certeyn.
I am a kyng, it sit me noght to lye !'
    'And I,' quod she, ' a queene of faïery !
Hir answere shal she have, I undertake.
Lat us namoorè wordès heer-of make,
For sothe I wol no lenger yow contrarie.'
    Now lat us turne agayn to Januarie, 2320
That in the gardyn with his fairè May
Syngeth ful murier than the papèjay :
' Yow love I best, and shal, and oother
    noon.'
So longe aboute the aleyes is he goon,
Til he was come agayns thilkè pyrìe
Where as this Damyan sitteth ful myrìe,
Anheigh among the fresshè levès grene.
    This fresshè May, that is so bright and
        sheene,
Gan for to syke and seyde, ' Allas, my
        syde !
Now, sire,' quod she, ' for aught that may
    bityde,   2330
I moste han of the perès that I see,
Or I moot dye, so soorè longeth me
To eten of the smalè perès grene.
Help, for hir love that is of hevenè queene !
I telle yow wel, a womman in my plit
May han to fruyt so greet an appetit
That she may dyen, but she of it have.'
    ' Allas !' quod he, ' that I ne had heer
        a knave
That koudè clymbe ! Allas, allas !' quod he,
' That I am blynd !' ' Ye, sire, no fors,'
    quod she ;   2340

' But wolde ye vouchè-sauf, for Goddès
    sake,
The pyrie in with youre armès for to take,—
For wel I woot that ye mystrustè me,—
Thanne sholde I clymbè wel ynogh,'
    quod she,
' So I my foot myghte sette upon youre
    bak.'
    ' Certès,' quod he, ' theron shal be no
        lak,
Mighte I yow helpen with myn hertè
    blood !'
He stoupeth doun, and on his bak she stood,
And caughte hire by a twiste, and up she
    gooth,—
Ladyes, I prey yow that ye be nat wrooth,
I kan nat glose, I am a rudè man,— 2351
And sodeynly anon this Damyan
Gan pullen up the smok, and in he throng.
    And whan that Pluto saugh this gretè
        wrong,
To Januarie he yaf agayn his sighte,
And made hym se as wel as ever he myghte ;
And whan that he hadde caught his sighte
    agayn,
Ne was ther never man of thyng so fayn ;
But on his wyf his thoght was evermo.
Up to the tree he castè his eyen two, 2360
And saugh that Damyan his wyf had dressed
In swich manere it may nat been expressed,
But if I woldè speke uncurteisly ;
And up he yaf a roryng and a cry,
As dooth the mooder whan the child shal
    dye.
' Out ! helpe ! allas ! harrow !' he gan to
    crye ;
' O strongè lady, stoorè, what dostow ?'
    And she answerdè, ' Sire, what eyleth
        yow ?
Have pacience and resoun in youre mynde.
I have yow holpe on bothe youre eyen
    blynde,—   2370
Up peril of my soule, I shal nat lyen,—
As me was taught to heelè with youre
    eyen,
Was no thyng bet to makè yow to see
Than strugle with a man upon a tree.
God woot, I dide it in ful good entente.'
    ' Strugle,' quod he, ' ye, algate in it
        wente !

God yeve yow bothe on shamès deth to
    dyen !
He swyvèd thee ; I saugh it with myne
    eyen ;
And ellès be I hangèd by the hals ! '
    ' Thanne is,' quod she, ' my medicynè
        fals,   2380
For certeinly, if that ye myghtè se,
Ye wolde nat seyn this wordès unto me ;
Ye han som glymsyng, and no parfit sighte.'
    ' I se,' quod he, 'as wel as ever I myghte,
Thonkèd be God ! with bothe myne eyen
    two,
And, by my trouthe, me thoughte he
    dide thee so.'
    ' Ye mazè, mazè, goodè sire,' quod she ;
' This thank have I for I have maad yow
    see.
Allas ! ' quod she, ' that ever I was so
    kynde.'
    ' Now, dame,' quod he, ' lat al passe
    out of mynde.   2390
Com doun, my lief, and if I have myssayd,
God helpe me so, as I am yvele apayd.
But, by my fader soule ! I wende han seyn
How that this Damyan hadde by thee
    leyn,
And that thy smok hadde leyn upon his
    brest.'
    ' Ye, sire,' quod she, ' ye may wene as
    yow lest,
But, sire, a man that waketh out of his
    sleepe,
He may nat sodeynly wel taken keepe
Upon a thyng, ne seen it parfitly,
Til that he be adawèd verraily.   2400
Right so a man that longe hath blynd y-be,
Ne may nat sodeynly so wel y-se,
First whan his sighte is newè come ageyn,
As he that hath a day or two y-seyn.
Til that youre sighte y-satled be a while,
Ther may ful many a sightè yow bigile.
Beth war, I prey yow, for, by hevenè kyng,

    2405. *y-satled*, H⁵ *y-stablid*.

Ful many a man weneth to seen a thyng,
And it is al another than it semeth.
He that mysconceyveth, he mysdemeth,'—
And with that word she leepe doun fro
    the tree.   2411
    This Januarie, who is glad but he ?
He kisseth hire and clippeth hire ful ofte,
And on hire wombe he stroketh hire ful
    softe ;
And to his palays hoom he hath hire lad.
Now, goodè men, I pray yow to be glad.
Thus endeth heere my tale of Januarie.
God blesse us, and his mooder Seintè
    Marie !

    ' Ey, Goddès mercy,' seyde oure Hostè
    tho,
' Now swich a wyf, I pray God kepe me
    fro !   2420
Lo, whichè sleightès and subtilitees
In wommen been ! for ay as bisy as bees
Been they, us sely men for to deceyve ;
And from a sooth ever wol they weyve.
By this Marchauntès tale it preveth weel ;
But doutèlees, as trewe as any steel
I have a wyf, though that she pourè be ;
But of hir tonge a labbyng shrewe is she ;
And yet she hath an heepe of vicès mo,
Therof no fors, lat alle swiche thyngès
    go ;
But wyte ye what ? In conseil be it seyd,
Me reweth soore I am unto hire teyd ;
For, and I sholdè rekenen every vice
Which that she hath, y-wis I were to nyce ;
And causè why, it sholde reported be,
And toold to hire of somme of this meynee,
Of whom it nedeth nat for to declare
(Syn wommen konnen outen swich chaf-
    fare),
And eek my wit suffiseth nat therto, 2439
To tellen al, wherfore my tale is do.'

    2419. E heads this *The Prologe of the Squierès
Tale*, printing with it the first eight lines of Group
F. Camb., Corp. and Lansd. omit.

TALES OF THE FOURTH DAY

GROUP F

Words of the Host to the Squire

'SQUIER, come neer, if it youre willè be,
And sey somwhat of love ; for certès ye
Konnen theron as muche as any man.'
 ' Nay, sire,' quod he, ' but I wol seye
  as I kan
With hertly wyl,—for I wol nat rebelle
Agayn youre lust. A talè wol I telle.
Have me excusèd, if I speke amys,
My wyl is good, and lo, my tale is this.'

SQUIRE'S TALE

Heere bigynneth The Squieres Tale

At Sarray, in the land of Tartarye,
Ther dwelte a kyng that werreyèd Russye,
Thurgh which ther dydè many a doughty
 man.   II
This noble kyng was clepèd Cambyuskan,
Which in his tyme was of so greet renoun
That ther was nowher in no regioun
So excellent a lord in allè thyng.
Hym lakkèd noght that longeth to a kyng;
As of the secte of which that he was born,
He kepte his lay, to which that he was
 sworn ;
And therto he was hardy, wys, and riche,
Pitous and just, and evermore yliche ; 20
Sooth of his word, benigne and honurable,

Of his coráge as any centre stable ;
Yong, fressh, and strong, in armès desirous
As any bacheler of al his hous.
A fair persone he was, and fortunat,
And kepte alwey so wel roial estat
That ther was nowher swich another man.
 This noble kyng, this Tartre Cambyus-
  kan,
Haddè two sones on Elpheta his wyf,
Of whichè the eldeste hightè Algarsyf ; 30
That oother sone was clepèd Cambalo.
A doghter hadde this worthy kyng also
That yongest was, and hightè Canacee,
But for to tellè yow al hir beautee
It lyth nat in my tonge, nyn my konnyng;
I dar nat undertake so heigh a thyng ;
Myn Englissh eek is insufficient ;
It mostè been a rethor excellent,
That koude his colours longynge for that
 art,
If he sholde hire discryven every part ; 40
I am noon swich, I moot speke as I kan,
 And so bifel that whan this Cambyuskan
Hath twenty wynter born his diademe,
As he was wont fro yeer to yeer, I deme,
He leet the feeste of his nativitee
Doon cryen thurghout Sarray his citee,
The last Idus of March after the yeer.
 Phebus, the sonne, ful joly was and
  cleer,
For he was neigh his exaltacioun
In Martès face, and in his mansioun 50
In Aries, the colerik hootè signe.
Ful lusty was the weder and benigne,
For which the foweles agayn the sonnè
 sheene,
What for the sesoun and the yongè grene,
Ful loudè songen hire affecciouns,

---

1. *Squier*, H *Sir Squier ;* Heng., Pet. *Sire Frankeleyn.* Camb., Corp. and Lansd. omit these lines.
 2. *sey somwhat of love*, H *say us a tale.*
Squire's Tale. Keightley in his *Tales and Popular Fictions* (1834) suggested that the local colour of this Tale was derived from Marco Polo, and Col. Yule notes that Cambyuscan is only a corruption of Chinghiz (or 'the great') Khan. Dr. Skeat has quoted passages from Marco Polo's description of Kublai Khan as the sources of some of Chaucer's lines, but the resemblances are not at all close. On magic horses, rings and mirrors Mr. Clouston has written a whole book for the Chaucer Society.
 16. *longeth*, H⁵ *longed.*

31. *Cambalo.* Keightley suggests that the name was taken from Kublai Khan's capital, Cambaluc.
 47. *The last Idus*, March 15. On this day the sun would be in the 4th degree of Aries, approaching his highest exaltation in the 19th degree. The first ten degrees of Aries were called the face of Mars.

Hem semed han geten hem protecciouns
Agayn the swerd of wynter, keene and
    coold.
    This Cambyuskan—of which I have
      yow toold—
In roial vestiment sit on his deys,
With diademe, ful heighe in his paleys, 60
And halt his feeste so solempne and so
    ryche,
That in this worlde was ther noon it lyche;
Of which, if I shal tellen al tharray,
Thanne wolde it occupie a someres day;
And eek it nedeth nat for to devyse
At every cours the ordre of hire servyse.
I wol nat tellen of hir strange sewes,
Ne of hir swannes, ne of hire heronsewes.
Eek in that lond, as tellen knyghtes olde,
Ther is som mete that is ful deynte holde 70
That in this lond men recche of it but smal;
Ther nys no man that may reporten al.
    I wol nat taryen yow, for it is pryme,
And for it is no fruyt, but los of tyme;
Unto my firste I wole have my recours.
    And so bifel that after the thridde cours,
Whil that this kyng sit thus in his nobleye,
Herknynge his mynstralles hir thynges pleye
Biforn hym at the bord deliciously,
In at the halle dore, al sodeynly,   80
Ther cam a knyght upon a steede of bras,
And in his hand a brood mirour of glas;
Upon his thombe he hadde of gold a ring,
And by his syde a naked swerd hangyng;
And up he rideth to the heighe bord.
In al the halle ne was ther spoken a word,
For merveille of this knyght; hym to
    biholde
Ful bisily ther wayten yonge and olde.
    This strange knyght that cam thus
      sodeynly,
Al armed, save his heed, ful richely,   90
Saleweth kyng and queene, and lordes alle,
By ordre, as they seten in the halle,
With so heigh reverence and obeisaunce,
As wel in speche as in contenaunce,
That Gawayn, with his olde curteisye,
Though he were comen ageyn out of fairye,
Ne koude hym nat amende with a word;
And after this, biforn the heighe bord,
He with a manly voys seith his message
After the forme used in his langage,   100

Withouten vice of silable, or of lettre;
And for his tale sholde seme the bettre,
Accordant to his wordes was his cheere,
As techeth art of speche hem that it leere.
Al be it that I kan nat sowne his stile,
Ne kan nat clymben over so heigh a style,
Yet seye I this, as to commune entente,
Thus muche amounteth al that ever he
    mente,
If it so be that I have it in mynde.
    He seyde, 'The kyng of Arabe and of
      Inde,   110
My lige lord, on this solempne day
Saleweth yow, as he best kan and may,
And sendeth yow, in honour of youre feeste,
By me, that am al redy at youre heeste,
This steede of bras, that esily and weel
Kan in the space of o day natureel,—
This is to seyn, in foure and twenty
    houres,—
Wher so yow lyst, in droghte or elles
    shoures,
Beren youre body into every place   119
To which youre herte wilneth for to pace,
Withouten wem of yow, thurgh foul or fair;
Or, if yow lyst to fleen as hye in the air
As dooth an egle whan hym list to soore,
This same steede shal bere yow evermoore,
Withouten harm, til ye be ther yow leste,
Though that ye slepen on his bak, or reste;
And turne ageyn with writhyng of a pyn.
He that it wroghte koude ful many a gyn.
He wayted many a constellacioun
Er he had doon this operacioun,   130
And knew ful many a seel, and many a bond.
    'This mirrour eek, that I have in myn
      hond,
Hath swich a myght that men may in it see
Whan ther shal fallen any adversitee
Unto youre regne, or to youreself also,
And openly who is youre freend or foo;
And over al this, if any lady bright
Hath set hire herte on any maner wight,
If he be fals she shal his tresoun see,
His newe love, and al his subtiltee,   140
So openly that ther shal no thyng hyde.
Wherfore, ageyn this lusty someres tyde,
This mirour and this ryng that ye may see
He hath sent to my lady Canacee,
Youre excellente doghter that is heere.

'The vertu of the ryng, if ye wol heere,
Is this, that if hire lust it for to were
Upon hir thombe, or in hir purs it bere,
Ther is no fowel that fleeth under the hevene
That she ne shal wel understonde his
     stevene,   150
And knowe his menyng openly and pleyn,
And answere hym in his langage ageyn ;
And every gras that groweth upon roote
She shal eek knowe and whom it wol do
     boote,
Al be his woundès never so depe and
     wyde.
  'This naked swerd that hangeth by my
     syde
Swich vertu hath that what man so ye smyte,
Thurghout his armure it wol kerve and
     byte,
Were it as thikke as is a branchèd ook ;
And what man that is wounded with the
     strook   160
Shal never be hool, til that yow list of grace
To stroke hym with the plat in thilkè place
Ther he is hurt ; this is as muche to seyn,
Ye mootè with the plattè swerd ageyn
Strìke hym in the wounde and it wol close.
This is a verray sooth, withouten glose,
It failleth nat whil it is in youre hoold.'
     And whan this knyght hath thus his
     talè toold,
He rideth out of halle, and doun he lighte.
His steedè, which that shoon as sonnè
     brighte,   170
Stant in the court as stille as any stoon.
This knyght is to his chambrè lad anoon,
And is unarmed and unto mete y-set.
     The presentes been ful roially y-fet,—
This is to seyn, the swerd and the mirour,—
And born anon into the heighè tour,
With certeine officers ordeyned therfore ;
And unto Canacee this ryng was bore
Solempnèly, ther she sit at the table ;
But sikerly, withouten any fable,   180
The hors of bras, that may nat be remewed,
It stant as it were to the ground y-glewed;
Ther may no man out of the place it dryve
For noon engyn of wyndas ne polyve ;
And causè why? for they kan nat the craft ;
And therfore in the place they han it laft,

Til that the knyght hath taught hem the
     manere
To voyden hym, as ye shal after heere.
     Greet was the prees that swarmeth to
     and fro   189
To gauren on this hors that stondeth so ;
For it so heigh was, and so brood and long,
So wel proporcionèd for to been strong,
Right as it were a steede of Lumbardye ;
Ther-with so horsly, and so quyk of eye,
As it a gentil Poilleys courser were ;
For certès, fro his tayl unto his ere,
Nature ne art ne koude hym nat amende
In no degree, as al the peple wende.
But evermoore hir moostè wonder was
How that it koudè go, and was of bras !
It was of fairye, as al the peple semed.   201
Diversè folk diversèly they demed ;
As many heddes as manye wittes ther been.
They murmureden as dooth a swarm of
     been,
And maden skiles after hir fantasies,
Rehersynge of thise oldè poetries ;
And seyde that it was lyk the Pegasee,
The hors that haddè wyngès for to flee ;
Or elles it was the Grekès hors, Synoun,
That broghtè Troiè to destruccioun,   210
As men may in thise oldè geestès rede.
     'Myn herte,' quod oon, 'is evermoore
     in drede ;
I trowe som men of armès been ther-inne,
That shapen hem this citee for to wynne;
It were right good that al swich thyng
     were knowe.'
     Another rownèd to his felawe lowe,
And seyde, 'He lyeth ! it is rather lyk
An apparence, y-maad by som magyk ;
As jogelours pleyen at thise feestès grete.'
Of sondry doutès thus they jangle and trete,
As lewèd peple demeth comunly   221
Of thyngès that been maad moore subtilly
Than they kan in hir lewednesse compre-
     hende,
They demen gladly to the badder ende.
     And somme of hem wondred on the
     mirour
That born was up into the hyè tour,

195. *Poilleys*, Apulian.
201. *the peple*, E² *al the peple*.
217. *it*, H⁶ *for it*.
226. *hyè*, H⁶ *maistre*.

165. *strìke*, H⁵ *stroke*.

221

How men myghte in it swiché thyngès se.
Another answerde and seyde it myghte
　　wel be
Naturelly, by composiciouns
Of angles, and of slye reflexiouns ;　230
And seyden that in Romé was swich oon.
They speken of Alocen and Vitulon,
And Aristotle, that writen in hir lyves
Of queynté mirours, and of prospectives,
As knowen they that han hir bookès herd.
　　And oother folk han wondred on the
　　swerd
That woldé percen thurghout every thyng ;
And fille in speche of Thelophus the kyng,
And of Achilles with his queynté spere,
For he koude with it bothé heele and dere,
Right in swich wise as men may with the
　　swerd　　　　　　　　　241
Of which right now ye han youre-selven
　　herd.
They speken of sondry hardyng of metal,
And speke of medicynès therwithal,
And how and whanne it sholde y-harded be,
Which is unknowe, algatès unto me.
　　Tho speeké they of Canacëes ryng,
And seyden alle that swich a wonder thyng
Of craft of ryngès herde they never noon ;
Save that he Moyses and kyng Salomon
Hadden a name of konnyng in swich art ;
Thus seyn the peple and drawen hem
　　apart.
　　But nathélees somme seiden that it was
Wonder to maken of fern-asshen glas,
And yet nys glas nat lyk asshen of fern,
But for they han i-knowen it so fern
Therfore cesseth hir janglyng and hir
　　wonder.
　　As sooré wondren somme on cause of
　　thonder,
On ebbe, on flood, on gossomer, and on
　　myst,　　　　　　　　　259
And on alle thyng til that the cause is wyst,
Thus jangle they, and demen and devyse,
Til that the kyng gan fro the bord aryse.

Phebus hath laft the angle meridional,
And yet ascendynge was the beest roial,
The gentil Leon, with his Aldrian,
Whan that this Tartré kyng Cambyuskan
Roos fro his bord, ther as he sat ful hye.
Toforn hym gooth the loudé mynstralcye
Til he cam to his chambre of parementz ;
Ther as they sownen diverse instrumentz
That it is lyk an hevene for to heere.　271
Now dauncen lusty Venus children deere,
For in the Fyssh hir lady sat ful hye,
And looketh on hem with a freendly eye.
　　This noble kyng is set up in his trone ;
This strangé knyght is fet to hym ful soone,
And on the daunce he gooth with Canacee.
Heere is the revel and the jolitee
That is nat able a dul man to devyse ;　279
He moste han knowen love and his servyse,
And been a feestlych man, as fressh as May,
That sholdé yow devysen swich array.
　　Who koudé tellé yow the forme of
　　daunces
So unkouthe, and so fresshé contenaunces,
Swich subtil lookyng and dissymulynges
For drede of jalouse mennes aperceyv-
　　ynges ?
No man but Launcelet, and he is deed.
Therfore I passe of al this lustiheed ;
I sey namoore, but in this jolynesse
I lete hem til men to the soper dresse.
　　The styward byt the spices for to hye,
And eek the wyn, in al this melodye.
The usshers and the squiers been y-goon,
The spices and the wyn is come anoon.
They ete and drynke, and whan this hadde
　　an ende,
Unto the temple, as reson was, they wende.
　　The service doon they soupen al by day ;
What nedeth yow rehercen hire array ?
Éch man woot wel that a kyngès feeste　299
Hath plentee to the mooste and to the leeste,
And deyntees mo than been in my knowyng.
　　At after soper gooth this noble kyng
To seen this hors of bras, with all the
　　route
Of lordès and of ladyes hym aboute.

231. *in Rome*, an allusion to the wizardries
attributed to Virgil.
232. *Alocen and Vitulon.* Alhazen was an
Arab astronomer of the 11th century, and Vitellio
a Polish one of the 13th.
238. *Thelophus*, Telephus of Mysia, wounded
and healed by the spear of Achilles.

263. *angle meridional.* The southern angle
answered to the time from 10 A.M. to noon.
265. *Aldrian*, or Aldiran, the star marking the
Lion's fore-paws.
273. *the Fyssh.* Venus is 'exalted' in Piscis.

Swich wondryng was ther on this hors of
    bras
That syn the grete sege of Troie was,—
Ther as men wondreden on an hors also,—
Ne was ther swich a wondryng as was tho.
But fynally, the kyng axeth this knyght
The vertu of this courser, and the myght,
And preyde hym to telle his governaunce.
   This hors anoon bigan to trippe and
    daunce
Whan that this knyght leyde hand upon
    his reyne,
And seyde, 'Sire, ther is namoore to seyne,
But whan yow list to ryden anywhere
Ye mooten trille a pyn, stant in his ere,
Which I shal telle yow bitwix us two.
Ye moote nempne hym to what place also,
Or to what contree, that yow list to ryde;
And whan ye come ther as yow list abyde,
Bidde hym descende, and trille another
    pyn,—   321
For therin lith theffect of al the gyn,—
And he wol doun descende and doon youre
    wille,
And in that place he wol stonde stille.
Though al the world the contrarie hadde
    y-swore,
He shal nat thennes been y-drawe ne y-bore;
Or, if yow liste bidde hym thennes goon,
Trille this pyn, and he wol vanysshe anoon
Out of the sighte of every maner wight,
And come agayn, be it by day or nyght, 330
Whan that yow list to clepen hym ageyn
In swich a gyse as I shal to yow seyn,
Bitwixe yow and me, and that ful soone.
Ride whan yow list, ther is namoore to
    doone.'
   Enformed whan the kyng was of that
    knyght,
And hath conceyved in his wit aright
The manere and the forme of al this thyng,
Ful glad and blithe this noble doughty kyng
Repeireth to his revel as biforn.
   The brydel is unto the tour y-born 340
And kept among his jueles leeve and deere,
The hors vanysshed, I noot in what manere,
Out of hir sighte,—ye gete namoore of me;
But thus I lete in lust and jolitee
This Cambyuskan his lordes festeiynge,
Til wel ny the day bigan to sprynge.

[PART II]

   The norice of digestioun, the sleepe,
Gan on hem wynke, and bad hem taken
    keepe
That muchel drynke and labour wolde
    han reste;
And with a galpyng mouth hem alle he
    keste, 350
And seyde, it was tyme to lye adoun,
For blood was in his domynacioun.
'Cherisseth blood, natures freend,' quod he.
They thanken hym galpynge, by two, by
    thre,
And every wight gan drawe hym to his reste,
As sleepe hem bad; they tooke it for the
    beste.
   Hire dremes shul nat been y-toold for me;
Ful were hire heddes of fumositee,
That causeth dreem, of which ther nys no
    charge.
They slepen til that it was pryme large, 360
The mooste part, but it were Canacee.
She was ful mesurable, as wommen be;
For of hir fader hadde she take leve
To goon to reste, soone after it was eve.
Hir liste nat appalled for to be,
Ne on the morwe unfeestlich for to se,
And slepte hire firste sleepe and thanne
    awook;
For swich a joye she in hir herte took,
Bothe of hir queynte ryng and hire mirour,
That twenty tyme she changed hir colour,
And in hire sleepe, right for impressioun
Of hire mirour, she hadde a visioun.
Wherfore er that the sonne gan up glyde
She cleped on hir maistresse hire bisyde,
And seyde that hire liste for to ryse.
   Thise olde wommen that been gladly
    wyse,
As is hire maistresse, answerde hire anon,
And seyde, 'Madame, whider wil ye goon
Thus erly, for the folk been alle on reste?'
   'I wol,' quod she, 'arise,—for me leste
No lenger for to slepe, — and walke
    aboute.' 381

---

352. *blood*, etc. The blood was supposed to be
'in domination' from 9 P.M. to 3 A.M.
360. *pryme large*, full prime, *i.e.* 9 A.M.

Hire maistresse clepeth wommen a
   greet route,
And up they rysen, wel a ten or twelve ;
Up riseth fresshè Canacee hir-selve,
As rody and bright as dooth the yongè sonne
That in the Ram is foure degrees up ronne.
Noon hyer was he whan she redy was,
And forth she walketh esily a pas,
Arrayed after the lusty sesoun soote   389
Líghtly, for to pleye and walke on foote,
Nat but with fyve or sixe of hir meynee,
And in a trench, forth in the park, gooth
   she.
The vapour, which that fro the erthè glood,
Madè the sonne to semè rody and brood,
But nathèlees it was so fair a sighte
That it made alle hire hertès for to lighte,—
What for the sesoun, and the morwènynge,
And for the foweles that she herdè synge ;
For right anon she wistè what they mente
Right by hir song, and knew al hire entente.

The knottè why that every tale is toold,
If it be taried til that lust be coold
Of hem that han it after herkned yoore,
The savour passeth ever lenger the moore,
For fulsomnesse of his prolixitee ;
And by the samè resoun thynketh me,
I sholdè to the knotte condescende
And maken of hir walkyng soone an ende.
   Amydde a tree fordrye, as whit as chalk,
As Canacee was pleyyng in hir walk,   410
Ther sat a faucon over hire heed ful hye,
That with a pitous voys so gan to crye
That all the wode resounèd of hire cry.
Y-beten hath she hir-self so pitously
With bothe hir wyngès til the redè blood
Ran endèlong the tree ther as she stood,
And ever in oon she cryde alwey and
   shrighte,
And with hir beek hir-selven so she prighte,
That ther nys tygre, ne noon so crueel beest,
That dwelleth outher in wode or in forest,
That noldè han wept, if that he wepè koude,
For sorwe of hire, she shrighte alwey so
   loude ;
For ther nas never yet no man on lyve,—

If that I koude a faucon wel discryve,—
That herde of swich another of fairnesse,
As wel of plumage as of gentillesse
Of shape, and al that myghte y-rekened be.
A faucon peregryn thanne semèd she
Of fremdè land, and evermoore, as she
   stood,
She swowneth now and now for lakke of
   blood,   430
Til wel neigh is she fallen fro the tree.
   This fairè kyngès doghter, Canacee,
That on hir fynger baar the queyntè ryng,
Thurgh which she understood wel every
   thyng
That any fowel may in his leden seyn,
And koude answere hym in his ledene
   ageyn,
Hath understondè what this faucon seyde,
And wel neigh for the routhe almoost she
   deyde ;
And to the tree she gooth ful hastily,
And on this faukon looketh pitously,   440
And heeld hir lappe abrood, for wel she
   wiste
The faukon mostè fallen fro the twiste,
Whan that it swownèd next, for lakke of
   blood.
A longè while to wayten hire she stood,
Til attè laste she spak in this manere
Unto the hauk, as ye shal after heere :
   ' What is the cause, if it be for to telle,
That ye be in this furial pyne of helle ? '
Quod Canacee unto the hauk above.   449
' Is this for sorwe of deeth, or los of love?
For, as I trowè, thise been causes two
That causen moost a gentil hertè wo.
Of oother harm it nedeth nat to speke,
For ye youre-self upon your-self yow wreke,
Which proveth well that outher love or
   drede
Moot been enchesoun of youre cruel dede,
Syn that I see noon oother wight yow chace.
For love of God, as dooth youre-selven
   grace,
Or what may been youre helpe ; for West
   nor Est

---

386. *fourè* (H⁴ *ten*), cp. l. 51 and note. At its
rising on the 16th March the sun would be passing
from the 4th degree to the 5th.

428. *peregryn*, the pilgrim falcon, so called
because it keeps away from its nest.
436. *answere*, E *answeren*.
455. *love*, H⁵ *ire*.

Ne saugh I never, er now, no bryd ne
    beest   460
That ferdė with hymself so pitously.
Ye sle me with youre sorwe, verrailly ;
I have of yow so greet compassioun.
For Goddės love, com fro the tree adoun ;
And, as I am a kyngės doghter trewe,
If that I verraily the causė knewe
Of youre disese, if it lay in my myght,
I wolde amenden it er it were nyght,
As wisly helpe me gretė God of kynde !
And herbės shal I right ynowe y-fynde
To heelė with youre hurtės hastily.'   471
  Tho shrighte this faucon yet moore
    pitously
Than ever she dide, and fil to groundeanon,
And lith aswownė, deed, and lyk a stoon,
Til Canacee hath in hire lappe hire take
Unto the tyme she gan of swough awake ;
And after that she of hir swough gan breyde
Right in hir haukės ledene thus she seyde :
' That pitee renneth soone in gentil herte,
Feelynge his similitude in peynės smerte,
Is prevėd al day, as men may it see,   481
As wel by werk as by auctoritee ;
For gentil hertė kitheth gentillesse.
I se wel that ye han of my distresse
Compassioun, my fairė Canacee,
Of verray wommanly benignytee
That nature in youre principles hath set ;
But for noon hopė for to fare the bet,
But for to obeye unto youre hertė free,
And for to maken othere be war by me,
As by the whelpe chasted is the leoun, 491
Right for that cause and that conclusioun,
Whil that I have a leyser and a space,
Myn harm I wol confessen, er I pace.'
And ever whil that oon hir sorwe tolde
That oother weepe as she to water wolde,
Til that the faucon bad hire to be stille,
And, with a syk, right thus she seyde hir
    wille.
  ' Ther I was bred, allas ! that hardė
    day,—   499
And fostred in a roche of marbul gray
So tendrėly that no thyng eylėd me,—
I nystė nat what was adversitee
Til I koude flee ful hye under the sky—
Tho dwelte a tercėlet me fastė by,

That semėd welle of allė gentillesse ;
Al were he ful of tresoun and falsnesse,
It was so wrappėd under humble cheere,
And under hewe of trouthe in swich manere,
Under plesance, and under bisy peyne,
That I ne koude han wend he koudė feyne,
So depe in greyn he dyėd his coloures.
Right as a serpent hit hym under floures
Til he may seen his tymė for to byte,
Right so this god of love, this ypocryte,
Dooth so his cerymonyes and obeisaunces,
And kepeth in semblant alle his obser-
    vaunces
That sowneth into gentillesse of love.
As in a toumbe is al the faire above,
And under is the corps, swich as ye woot,
Swich was the ypocrite, bothe coold and
    hoot,   520
And in this wise he servėd his entente,
That save the feend, noon wistė what he
    mente
Til he so longe hadde wopen and com-
    pleyned,
And many a yeer his service to me feyned,
Til that myn herte, to pitous and to nyce,
Al innocent of his corouned malice,
For-ferėd of his deeth, as thoughtė me,
Upon his othės and his seurėtee,
Graunted hym love upon this condicioun,
That evermoore myn honour and renoun
Were savėd, bothė privee and apert : 531
This is to seyn, that after his desert,
I yaf hym al myn hertė and my thoght,—
God woot, and he, that otherwisė noght,—
And took his herte in chaunge for myn
    for ay ;
But sooth is seyd, goon sithen many a day,
" A trewe wight and a theef thenken nat
    oon " ;
And whan he saugh the thyng so fer y-goon
That I hadde graunted hym fully my love,
In swich a gyse as I have seyd above, 540
And yeven hym my trewė herte as fre
As he swoor he yaf his hertė to me ;
Anon this tigre ful of doublenesse
Fil on his knees with so devout hum-
    blesse,

472. *yet*, om. H².

510. *I ne*, H⁵ *no wight.*
515. *obeisaunces*, H *observaunce*, reading in
next line, *Under subtil colour and aqueyntaunce.*

With so heigh reverence, and, as by his
   cheere,
So lyk a gentil lovere of manere,
So ravysshed, as it seméd, for the joye,
That never Jason, ne Parys of Troye,—
Jason ? Cértés, ne noon oother man
Syn Lameth was, that alderfirst bigan 550
To loven two, as writen folk biforn ;
Ne never, syn the firsté man was born,
Ne koudé man, by twenty thousand part,
Countrefeté the sophymes of his art,
Ne weré worthy unbokelen his galoche
Ther doublenesse or feynyng sholde
   approche,
Ne so koude thanke a wight as he dide me !
His manere was an hevene for to see
Til any womman, were she never so wys,
So peynted he, and kembde at point-
   devys, 560
As wel his wordés as his contenaunce ;
And I so loved hym for his obeisaunce,
And for the trouthe I deméd in his herte,
That if so were that any thyng hym smerte,
Al were it never so lite, and I it wiste,
Me thoughte I felté deeth myn herté twiste;
And shortly, so ferforth this thyng is went,
That my wyl was his willés instrument,—
This is to seyn, my wyl obeyed his wyl
In allé thyng, as fer as resoun fil, 570
Kepynge the boundés of my worshipe ever;
Ne never hadde I thyng so lief, ne lever,
As hym, God woot ! ne never shal namo.
This lasteth lenger than a yeer or two
That I supposéd of hym noght but good ;
But finally thus, atté laste it stood,
That Fortune woldé that he mosté twynne
Out of that placé which that I was inne.
Wher me was wo, that is no questioun ;
I kan nat make of it discripsioun, 580
For o thyng dare I tellen boldély,
I knowe what is the peyne of deeth ther-by;
Swich harme I felte for he ne myghte
   bileve !
So on a day of me he took his leve,
So sorwful eek that I wende verraily
That he had felt as muché harm as I,

Whan that I herde hym speke and saugh
   his hewe ;
But nathélees I thoughte he was so trewe,
And eek that he repairé sholde ageyn
Withinne a litel whilé, sooth to seyn, 590
And resoun wolde eek that he mosté go
For his honóur, as ofte it happeth so,
That I made vertu of necessitee,
And took it wel, syn that it mosté be.
As I best myghte I hidde fro hym my sorwe
And took hym by the hond, Seint John to
   borwe,
And seyde hym thus : "Lo, I am yourés al ;
Beth swich as I to yow have been and shal."
What he answerde it nedeth noght reherce ;
Who kan sey bet than he, who kan do
   werse ? 600
Whan he hath al i-seyd, thanne hath he
   doon.
"Therfore bihoveth hire a ful long spoon
That shal ete with a feend," thus herde I
   seye ;
So atté laste he mosté forth his weye,
And forth he fleeth til he cam ther hym
   leste,
Whan it cam hym to purpos for to reste.
I trowe he haddé thilké text in mynde,
That "Allé thyng repeirynge to his kynde
Gladeth hymself,"—thus seyn men, as I
   gesse.
Men loven of propré kynde newefangel-
   nesse, 610
As briddés doon that men in cages fede ;
For though thou nyght and day take of
   hem hede,
And strawe hir cagé faire, and softe as silk,
And yeve hem sugre, hony, breed and milk,
Yet right anon as that his dore is uppe,
He with his feet wol spurne adoun his cuppe,
And to the wode he wole, and wormés ete ;
So newéfangel been they of hire mete
And loven novelrie of propré kynde,
No gentillesse of blood ne may hem
   bynde. 620
'So ferde this tercélet, allas, the day !
Though he were gentil born, fressh and gay,
And goodlich for to seen, humble and free.
He saugh upon a tyme a kyté flee,

548. *Jason*, E² *Troilus*, an impossible reading.
550. *Lameth*, Genesis iv. 19.
583. *he*, E *I*
585. *sorwful*, E⁶ *sorwefully*.

601. *i-seyd*, H⁵ *wel seyd*.
602. *hire*, H⁴ *him*.

And sodeynly he loved this kyte so
That al his love is clene fro me ago,
And hath his trouthe falsed in this wyse.
Thus hath the kyte my love in hire servyse,
And I am lorn withouten remedie.'   629
And with that word this faucon gan to crie,
And swowned eft in Canacees barm.

Greet was the sorwe for the haukes harm
That Canacee and alle hir wommen made;
They nyste how they myghte the faucon
    glade,
But Canacee hom bereth hire in hir lappe,
And softely in plastres gan hire wrappe,
Ther as she with hire beek hadde hurt hir-
    selve.
Now kan nat Canacee but herbes delve
Out of the ground, and make salves newe
Of herbes preciouse, and fyne of hewe,   640
To heelen with this hauk; fro day to nyght
She dooth hire bisynesse and al hir myght,
And by hire beddes heed she made a mewe,
And covered it with veluettes blewe,
In signe of trouthe that is in wommen sene,
And al withoute the mewe is peynted grene,
In which were peynted alle thise false
    fowles,
As beth thise tidyves, tercelettes and owles;
And pyes, on hem for to crie and chyde,
Right for despit, were peynted hem bisyde.

Thus lete I Canacee, hir hauk kepyng,
I wol namoore as now speke of hir ryng
Til it come eft to purpos for to seyn
How that this faucon gat hire love ageyn,
Repentant, as the storie telleth us,
By mediacioun of Cambalus,
The kynges sone, of whiche I yow tolde;
But hennes-forth I wol my proces holde
To speken of aventures and of batailles,
That never yet was herd so greet mer-
    vailles.   660
First wol I telle yow of Cambyuskan,
That in his tyme many a citee wan;
And after wol I speke of Algarsif,
How that he wan Theodera to his wif,
For whom ful ofte in greet peril he was,
Ne hadde he ben holpe by the steede of
    bras;
And after wol I speke of Cambalo,

That faught in lystes with the bretheren two
For Canacee, er that he myghte hire wynne;
And ther I lefte I wol ageyn bigynne.   670

[PART III]

Appollo whirleth up his chaar so hye,
Til that the god Mercurius hous, the slye—
.   .   .   .

Heere folwen the wordes of the Frankelyn
to the Squier, and the wordes of the
Hoost to the Frankelyn

' In feith, Squier, thow hast thee wel
    y-quit
And gentilly, I preise wel thy wit,'
Quod the Frankeleyn, 'considerynge thy
    yowthe
So feelyngly thou spekest, sire, I allowe the,
As to my doom ther is noon that is heere
Of eloquence that shal be thy peere,
If that thou lyve ! God yeve thee good
    chaunce,
And in vertu sende thee continuaunce;   680
For of thy speche I have greet deyntee.
I have a sone, and, by the Trinitee !
I hadde levere than twenty pound worth
    lond,
Though it right now were fallen in myn
    hond,
He were a man of swich discrecioun
As that ye been ; fy on possessioun,
But if a man be vertuous withal !
I have my sone snybbed and yet shal,
For he to vertu listeth nat entende,   689
But for to pleye at dees, and to despende
And lese al that he hath, is his usage ;
And he hath levere talken with a page
Than to comune with any gentil wight,
There he myghte lerne gentilesse aright.'
' Straw for youre "gentillesse," ' quod
    our Hoost.
' What ! Frankeleyn, *pardee*, sire, wel
    thou woost
That ech of yow moot tellen atte leste
A tale or two, or breken his biheste.'
' That knowe I wel, sire,' quod the
    Frankeleyn,
' I prey yow haveth me nat in desdeyn   700
Though to this man I speke a word or two.'

649, 650. These two lines are reversed in the
six MSS.; Camb.⁴ omitting *And*.   672. The 'half-told' tale breaks off here.

'Telle on thy tale, withouten wordès
   mo !'
'Gladly, sire Hoost,' quod he, 'I wole
   obeye
Unto your wyl; now herkneth what I seye.
I wol yow nat contrarien in no wyse
As fer as that my wittès wol suffyse ;
I prey to God that it may plesen yow,
Thanne woot I wel that it is good ynow.'

The Prologe of the Frankeleyns Tale

Thise oldè, gentil Britons, in hir dayes,
Of diverse áventurès maden layes,   710
Rymeyèd in hir firstè Briton tonge,
Whiche layès with hir instrumentz they
   songe,
Or ellès redden hem for hir plesaunce,
And oon of hem have I in rémembraunce,
Which I shal seyn with good wyl as I kan.
   But, sires, by-cause I am a burel man,
At my bigynnyng first I yow biseche,
Have me excusèd of my rudè speche.
I lernèd never rethoric certeyn ;
Thyng that I speke it moot be bare and
   pleyn.   720
I sleepe never on the Mount of Pernaso,
Ne lernèd Marcus Tullius Scithero.
Colours ne knowe I none, withouten drede,
But swichè colours as growen in the mede,
Or ellès swichè as men dye or peynte.
Colours of rethoryk been me to queynte ;
My spirit feeleth noght of swich mateere,
But if yow list my talè shul ye heere.

FRANKLIN'S TALE

Heere bigynneth The Frankeleyns Tale

In Armorik, that callèd is Britayne,
Ther was a knyght that loved and dide
   his payne   730
To serve a lady in his bestè wise ;
And many a labour, many a greet emprise,

He for his lady wroghte, er she were wonne ;
For she was oon the faireste under sonne,
And eek therto come of so heigh kynrede,
That wel unnethès dorste this knyght, for
   drede,
Telle hire his wo, his peyne, and his
   distresse ;
But attè laste she for his worthynesse,
And namely for his meke obeÿsaunce,
Hath swich a pitee caught of his penaunce,
That pryvély she fil of his accord,   741
To take hym for hir housbonde and hir lord,
Of swich lordshipe as men han over hir
   wyves,
And for to lede the moore in blisse hir lyves,
Of his free wyl he swoor hire as a knyght,
That never in al his lyf he, day ne nyght,
Ne sholde upon hym takè no maistrie
Agayn hir wyl, ne kithe hire jalousie ;
But hire obeye and folwe hir wyl in al,
As any lovere to his lady shal,   750
Save that the name of soveraynètee,
That wolde he have, for shame of his degree.
   She thankèd hym and with ful greet
   humblesse,
She seydè, 'Sire, sith of youre gentillesse
Ye profre me to have so large a reyne,
Ne woldè never God bitwixe us tweyne,
As in my gilt, were outher werre or stryf.
Sire, I wol be youre humble, trewè wyf ;
Have heer my trouthe, til that myn hertè
   breste' ;
Thus been they bothe in quiete and in reste.
   For o thyng, sirès, saufly dar I seye, 761
That freendès everych oother moot obeye,
If they wol longè holden compaignye.
Love wol nat been constreynèd by maistrye.
Whan maistrie comth, the god of love,
   anon,
Beteth his wynges and, farewel, he is gon !
Love is a thyng as any spirit free.
Wommen of kynde desiren libertee,
And nat to been constreynèd as a thral ;
And so doon men, if I sooth seyen shal.
Looke, who that is moost pacient in love,
He is at his avantage al above.
Pácience is an heigh vertú, certeyn,
For it venquysseth, as thise clerkès seyn,
Thyngès that rigour sholdè never atteyne ;

---

714. *oon of hem*, etc. This distinct statement (cp. l. 813) leaves no doubt that this tale follows, probably with some closeness, a French or Breton story, unluckily now lost.
721. To disprove his claim of lack of letters he quotes Persius (Prol. l. 2).

739. *namely*, especially.

For every word men may nat chide or
　　pleyne.
Lerneth to suffre, or elles so moot I goon,
Ye shul it lerne, wher-so ye wole or noon;
For in this world, certein, ther no wight is
That he ne dooth, or seith, som tyme amys.
Irè, siknesse, or constellacioun,　　　781
Wyn, wo, or chaungynge of complexioun,
Causeth ful ofte to doon amys or speken.
On every wrong a man may nat be wreken;
After the tymé moste be temperaunce
To every wight that kan on governaunce;
And therfore hath this wisè, worthy
　　knyght,—
To lyve in esè,—suffrance hire bihight,
And she to hym ful wisly gan to swere
That never sholde ther be defaut in here.
　　Heere may men seen an humble, wys
　　accord;　　　　791
Thus hath she take hir servant and hir
　　lord,—
Servant in love, and lord in mariage,—
Thanne was he bothe in lordshipe and
　　servage.
Servagè? nay, but in lordshipe above;
Sith he hath both his lady and his love;
His lady, certès, and his wyf also,
The which that lawe of love acordeth to;
And whan he was in this prosperitee　799
Hoom with his wyf he gooth to his contree,
Nat fer fro Pedmark, ther his dwelling was,
Wher as he lyveth in blisse and in solas.
　　Who koudè telle, but he hadde wedded
　　be,
The joye, the ese, and the prosperitee
That is bitwixe an housbonde and his wyf?
　　A yeer and moore lastèd this blisful lyf,
Til that the knyght of which I speke of thus,
That of Kayrrud was cleped Arveragus,
Shoope him to goon and dwelle a yeer or
　　tweyne　　　809
In Engèlond, that cleped was eek Briteyne,
To seke in armès worshipe and honour,
For al his lust he sette in swich labour;
And dwellèd there two yeer,—the book
　　seith thus.
　　Now wol I stynten of this Arveragus,

801. *Pedmark*, Penmark, on the west coast of
Brittany.
808. *Kayrrud*, the Red City.

And speken I wole of Dorigene his wyf,
That loveth hire housbonde as hire hertès
　　lyf;
For his absencè wepeth she and siketh,
As doon thise noble wyvès, whan hem
　　liketh;
She moorneth, waketh, wayleth, fasteth,
　　pleyneth;　　　819
Desir of his presence hire so distreyneth,
That al this wydè world she sette at noght.
Hire freendès, whiche that knewe hir hevy
　　thoght,
Conforten hire in al that ever they may.
They prechen hire, they telle hire, nyght
　　and day,
That causèlees she sleeth hirself, allas!
And every confort possible in this cas
They doon to hire with all hire bisynesse,
Al for to make hire leve hire hevynesse.
　　By proces, as ye knowen everichoon,
Men may so longè graven in a stoon　830
Til som figúre therinne emprented be.
So longe han they conforted hire, til she
Receyvèd hath, by hope and by resoun,
The emprentyng of hire consolacioun,
Thurgh which hir gretè sorwè gan aswage;
She may nat alwey duren in swich rage.
　　And eek Arveragus in al this care
Hath sent hire lettres hoom of his welfare;
And that he wol come hastily agayn;
Or ellès hadde this sorwe hir hertè slayn.
　　Hire freendès sawe hir sorwè gan to
　　slake,　　　841
And preyède hir on knees, for Goddès
　　sake,
To come and romen hire in compaignye,
Awey to dryve hire derkè fantasye;
And finally she grauntèd that requeste,
For wel she saugh that it was for the beste.
　　Now stood hire castel fastè by the see,
And often with hire freendès walketh shee,
Hire to disporte upon the bank an heigh,
Where as she many a shipe and bargè seigh
Seillynge hir cours, where as hem listè go;
But thanne was that a parcel of hire wo,
For to hirself ful ofte 'Allas!' seith she,
'Is ther no shipe, of so manye as I se,
Wol bryngen hom my lord? Thanne were
　　myn herte
Al warisshed of his bittrè peynès smerte.'

Another tyme ther wolde she sitte and
    thynke,
And caste hir eyen dounward fro the
    brynke;
But whan she saugh the grisly rokkès blake,
For verray feere so wolde hir hertè quake
That on hire feet she myghte hire noght
    sustene ;   861
Thanne wolde she sitte adoun upon the
    grene,
And pitously into the see biholde,
And seyn right thus, with sorweful sikès
    colde,
' Eternè God, that thurgh thy purvei-
    aunce,
Ledest the world by certein governaunce,
In ydel, as men seyn, ye nothyng make ;
But, Lord, thise grisly, feendly, rokkès
    blake,
That semen rather a foul confusioun
Of werk than any fair creacioun   870
Of swich a parfit wys God, and a stable,—
Why han ye wroght this werk unresonable?
For by this werk south, north, ne west,
    ne est,
Ther nys y-fostred man, ne bryd, ne beeste;
It dooth no good, to my wit, but anoyeth;
Se ye nat, Lord, how mankynde it de-
    stroyeth?
An hundred thousand bodyes of mankynde
Han rokkès slayn, al be they nat in mynde,
Which mankynde is so fair part of thy werk,
That thou it madest lyk to thyn owene merk.
' Thanne semèd it ye haddo a greet
    chiertee   881
Toward mankynde, but how thanne may
    it bee,
That ye swiche meenès make it to de-
    stroyen,
Whiche meenès do no good, but ever
    anoyen ?
I woot wel clerkès wol seyn as hem leste,
By argumentz, that al is for the beste,
Though I ne kan the causes nat y-knowe;
But, thilkè God that madè wynd to blowe,
As kepe my lord ; this is my conclusioun.
To clerkes lete I al disputisoun ;   890
But woldè God that alle thise rokkès blake
Were sonken into hellè for his sake.
Thise rokkès sleen myn hertè for the feere. '

Thus wolde she seyn with many a pitous
    teere.
    Hire freendès sawe that it was no disport
To romen by the see, but disconfort,
And shopen for to pleyen somwher elles.
They leden hire by ryveres, and by welles,
And eek in othere places delitables ;
They dauncen, and they pleyen at ches
    and tables.   900
    So on a day, right in the morwe tyde,
Unto a gardyn that was ther bisyde,
In which that they hadde maad hir or-
    dinaunce
Of vitaille, and of oother purveiaunce,
They goon and pleye hem al the longè day ;
And this was on the sixtè morwe of May,
Which May hadde peynted with his softè
    shoures
This gardyn, full of levès and of floures,
And craft of mannès hand so curiously
Arrayèd hadde this gardyn, trewèly,   910
That never was ther gardyn of swich prys
But if it were the verray Paradys.
The odour of flourès and the fresshè sighte
Woldè han makèd any hertè lighte
That ever was born, but if to greet siknesse,
Or to greet sorwè, helde it in distresse ;
So full it was of beautee with plesaunce.
    At after dyner gonnè they to daunce,
And synge also, save Dorigen allone,
Which made alwey hir compleint and hir
    moone,   920
For she ne saugh hym on the dauncè go
That was hir housbonde, and hir love also;
But nathèlees she moste a tyme abyde
And with good hopè lete hir sorwe slyde.
    Upon this daunce, amongès othere men,
Dauncèd a squier biforn Dorigen,
That fressher was, and jolyer of array,
As to my doom, than is the monthe of May ;
He syngeth, daunceth, passynge any man
That is, or was, sith that the world bigan.
Therwith he was, if men sholde hym
    discryve,   931
Oon of the bestè farynge man on lyve,
Yong, strong, right vertuous, and riche
    and wys,
And wel biloved, and holden in greet prys.
And, shortly, if the sothe I tellen shal,
Unwityng of this Dorigen at al,

This lusty squier, servant to Venus,
Which that y-clepéd was Aurelius,
Hadde loved hire best of any creature
Two yeer and moore, as was his áventure;
But never dorste he tellen hire his
    grevaunce;   941
Withouten coppe he drank al his penaunce.
He was despeyréd, nothyng dorste he seye,
Save in his songés somwhat wolde he wreye
His wo, as in a general compleynyng;
He seyde he lovede, and was biloved no
    thyng.
Of swich matéré made he manye layes,
Songés, compleintés, roundels, virelayes;
How that he dorsté nat his sorwe telle,
But langwissheth as a furye dooth in helle;
And dye he moste, he seyde, as dide Ekko
For Narcisus, that dorste nat telle hir wo.
In oother manere than ye heere me seye
Ne dorst he nat to hire his wo biwreye,
Save that paráventure somtyme at daunces,
Ther yongé folk kepen hir observaunces,
It may wel be he lookéd on hir face
In swich a wise as man that asketh grace;
But no thyng wisté she of his entente;
Nathelees it happéd, er they thennés wente,
By-causé that he was hire neighébour, 961
And was a man of worshipe and honour,
And hadde y-knowen hym of tymé yoore,
They fille in speche, and forthé, moore
    and moore,
Unto this purpos drough Aurelius.
And whan he saugh his tyme he saydé thus:
    'Madame,' quod he, 'by God that
    this world made,
So that I wiste it myghte youre herté glade,
I wolde that day that youre Arveragus
Wente over the see, that I, Aurelius, 970
Hadde went ther never I sholde have
    come again;
For wel I woot my servyce is in vayn,
My gerdoun is but brestyng of myn herte.
Madamé, reweth upon my peynés smerte,
For with a word ye may me sleen or save;
Heere at youre feet God wolde that I
    were grave!
I ne have, as now, no leyser moore to
    seye,—

950. *furye*, Heng.⁴ *fuyre, firs*, perhaps a better
reading.

Have mercy, sweete, or ye wol do me deye!'
She gan to looke upon Aurelius:
'Is this your wyl,' quod she, 'and sey ye
    thus?   980
Never erst,' quod she, 'ne wiste I what
    ye mente;
But now, Aurelie, I knowe youre entente,
By thilké God that yaf me soule and lyf!
Ne shal I never been untrewé wyf,
In word ne werk, as fer as I have wit,
I wol been his to whom that I am knyt!
Taak this for fynal answere, as for me';
But after that in pley thus seydé she:
    'Aurelie,' quod she, 'by heighé God
    above!
Yet wolde I graunté yow to been youre love,
Syn I yow se so pitously complayne. 991
Looké, what day that endélong Britayne,
Ye remoeve alle the rokkés, stoon by stoon,
That they ne letté shipe ne boot to goon,—
I seye whan ye han maad the coost so clene
Of rokkés, that ther nys no stoon y-sene,
Thanne wol I love yow best of any man.
Have heer my trouthe, in al that ever I
    kan.'
    'Is ther noon oother grace in yow?'
    quod he.
    'No, by that Lord,' quod she, 'that
    makéd me!   1000
For wel I woot that it shal never bityde.
Lat swiché folies out of youre herté slyde;
What deyntee sholde a man han in his lyf
For to go love another mannés wyf,
That hath hir body whan so that hym
    lyketh?'
Aurelius ful ofté sooré siketh.
Wo was Aurelie, whan that he this herde,
And with a sorweful herte he thus answerde:
    'Madame,' quod he, 'this were an in-
    possible!   1009
Thanne moot I dye of sodeyn deth horrible!'
And with that word he turnéd hym anon.
Tho come hir othere freendés many oon.
And in the aleyes romeden up and doun,
And no thyng wiste of this conclusioun;
But sodeynly bigonné revel newe,
Til that the brighté sonné lost his hewe,
For thorisonte hath reft the sonne his
    lyght,—
This is as muche to seye, as it was nyght;

And hoom they goon in joye and in solas,
Save oonly wrecche Aurelius, allas ! 1020
He to his hous is goon with sorweful herte ;
He seeth he may nat fro his deeth asterte,
Hym seméd that he felte his herté colde.
Up to the hevene his handés he gan holde,
And on his knowés bare he sette hym
    doun,
And in his ravyng seyde his orisoun.
For verray wo out of his wit he breyde,
He nysté what he spak, but thus he seyde.
With pitous herte his pleynt hath he bigonne
Unto the goddes, and first unto the sonne.
    He seyde, 'Appollo, god and governour,
Of every plaunté, herbé, tree and flour,
That yevest after thy declinacioun
To ech of hem his tyme and his sesoun,
As thyn herberwé chaungeth lowe or
    heighe ;
Lord Phebus, cast thy merciable eighe
On wrecche Aurelie, which that am but
    lorn !
Lo, lord, my lady hath my deeth y-sworn
Withouté gilt, but thy benignytee
Upon my dedly herte have som pitee ; 1040
For wel I woot, lord Phebus, if yow lest
Ye may me helpen, save my lady, best.
Now vouchethsauf that I may yow devyse
How that I may been holpen and in what
    wyse.
    'Youre blisful suster, Lucina the sheene,
That of the see is chief goddesse and
    queene,—
Though Neptunus have deitee in the see,
Yet emperisse aboven hym is she,—
Ye knowe wel, lord, that right as hir desir
Is to be quyked, and lightned of youre fir,
For which she folweth yow ful bisily, 1051
Right so the see desireth naturelly
To folwen hire, as she that is goddesse,
Bothe in the see and ryveres moore and
    lesse.
Wherfore, lord Phebus, this is my requeste,
Do this mirácle, or do myn herté breste ;
That now next at this opposicioun,
Which in the signe shal be of the Leoun,
As preieth hire so greet a flood to brynge,
That fyve fadme at the leeste it over-
    sprynge   1060

1045. *Lucina*, or Diana, the moon.

The hyeste rokke in Armorik Briteyne ;
And lat this flood enduré yerés tweyne,
Thanne certés to my lady may I seye,
"Holdeth youre heste, the rokkés been
    aweye."
'Lord Phebus, dooth this miracle for me ;
Preye hire she go no faster cours than ye ;
I seyé, preyeth your suster that she go
No faster cours than ye thise yerés two ;
Thanne shal she been evene atté fulle
    alway,
And spryng-flood lasté bothé nyght and
    day ;   1070
And, but she vouchésauf in swich manere
To graunté me my sovereyn lady deere,
Prey hire to synken every rok adoun
Into hir owene dirké regioun
Under the ground, ther Pluto dwelleth
    inne,
Or never-mo shal I my lady wynne.
Thy temple in Delphos wol I barefoot
    seke,—
Lord Phebus, se the teeris on my cheke,
And of my peyne have som compassioun !'
And with that word in swowne he fil adoun,
And longé tyme he lay forth in a traunce.
    His brother, which that knew of his
    penaunce,
Up caughte hym, and to bedde he hath
    hym broght.
Dispeyréd in this torment and this thoght,
Lete I this woful creäturé lye ;
Chese he, for me, wher he wol lyve or dye.
    Arveragus with heele and greet honour,
As he that was of chivalrie the flour,
Is comen hoom, and othere worthy men.
O, blisful artow now, thou Dorigen ! 1090
That hast thy lusty housbonde in thyne
    armes,
The fresshé knyght, the worthy man of
    armes,
That loveth thee as his owene hertés lyf.
Nothyng list hym to been ymaginatyf,
If any wight had spoke, whil he was oute,
To hire of love ; he hadde of it no doute.
He noght entendeth to no swich mateere,
But daunceth, justeth, maketh hire good
    cheere ;

1074. Under her name of Hecate Diana ruled
also in the underworld.

And thus in joye and blisse I lete hem
    dwelle,
And of the sike Aurelius wol I telle.　1100
  In langour and in torment furyus,
Two yeer and moore, lay wrecche Aurelyus
Er any foot he myghte on erthe gon ;
Ne confort in this tyme hadde he noon,
Save of his brother, which that was a clerk.
He knew of al this wo and al this werk ;
For to noon oother creäture, certeyn,
Of this matere he dorste no word seyn ;
Under his brest he baar it moore secree
Than ever dide Pamphilus for Gala-
    thee.　　　　　　　　　　　1110
His brest was hool withoute for to sene,
But in his herte ay was the arwe kene ;
And wel ye knowe that of a sursanure
In surgerye is perilous the cure,
But men myghte touche the arwe, or come
    therby.
  His brother weepe and wayled pryvely,
Til atte laste hym fil in remembraunce
That whiles he was at Orliens in Fraunce,—
As yonge clerkes, that been lykerous
To reden artes that been curious,　　1120
Seken in every halke and every herne
Particuler sciénces for to lerne,—
He hym remembred that, upon a day,
At Orliens in studie a book he say
Of magyk natureel, which his felawe,
That was that tyme a bacheler of lawe,—
Al were he ther to lerne another craft,—
Hadde pryvely upon his desk y-laft,
Which book spak muchel of the operaciouns
Touchynge the eighte and twenty man-
    siouns　　　　　　　　　　1130
That longen to the moone, and swich folye
As in oure dayes is nat worth a flye,—
For hooly chirches feith, in oure bileve,
Ne suffreth noon illusion us to greve ;
And whan this book was in his remem-
    braunce,
Anon for joye his herte gan to daunce,
And to hymself he seyde pryvely,
' My brother shal be warisshed hastily,
For I am siker that ther be sciénces　1139
By whiche men maken diverse apparences,

1110. *Pamphilus*, etc., a reference to the poem
Pamphilus de Amore, of which Galatea was the
heroíne.

Swiche as thise subtile tregetoures pleye.
For ofte at feestes have I wel herd seye
That tregetours withinne an halle large
Have maad come in a water and a barge,
And in the halle rowen up and doun.
Somtyme hath semed come a grym leoun,
And somtyme floures sprynge as in a mede ;
Somtyme a vyne, and grapes white and rede;
Somtyme a castel, al of lym and stoon,
And whan hem lyked voyded it anoon,—
Thus semed it to every mannes sighte.　1151
Now thanne conclude I thus, that if I
    myghte
At Orliens som old felawe y-fynde,
That hadde these moones mansions in
    mynde,
Or other magyk natureel above,
He sholde wel make my brother han his
    love ;
For with an apparence a clerk may make,
To mannes sighte, that alle the rokkes blake
Of Britaigne weren y-voyded everichon,
And shippes by the brynke comen and gon ;
And in swich forme enduren a wowke or
    two.　　　　　　　　　　1161
Thanne were my brother warisshed of his
    wo ;
Thanne moste she nedes holden hire
    biheste,
Or elles he shal shame hire atte leeste.'
  What sholde I make a lenger tale of
    this ?
Unto his brotheres bed he comen is,
And swich confort he yaf hym for to gon
To Orliens, that he up stirte anon,
And on his wey forthward thanne is he fare
In hope for to been lissed of his care.
  Whan they were come almoost to that
    citee,　　　　　　　　　　1171
But if it were a two furlong or thre,
A yong clerk romynge by hymself they
    mette,
Which that in Latyn thriftily hem grette,
And after that he seyde a wonder thyng:
'I knowe,' quod he, 'the cause of youre
    comyng,'—
And er they ferther any foote wente,
He tolde hem al that was in hire entente.
  This Briton clerk hym asked of felawes

1161. *wowke* (week), Heng.[2] *day*, Corp.[3] *yeer*.

The whiche that he had knowe in oldė
   dawes ;   1180
And he answerde hym that they dedė were,
For which he weep ful oftė many a teere.
  Doun of his hors Aurelius lighte anon,
And forth with this magicien is he gon
Hoom to his hous, and maden hem wel
  at ese ;
Hem lakkėd no vitaille that myghte hem
  plese,
So wel arrayėd hous as ther was oon
Aurelius in his lyf saugh never noon.
  He shewed hym, er he wentė to sopeer,
Forestės, parkės ful of wildė deer ;   1190
Ther saugh he hertės with hir hornės hye,
The gretteste that were ever seyn with
  eye,—
He saugh of hem an hondred slayn with
  houndes,
And somme with arwės blede of bittrė
  woundes.
He saugh, whan voyded were thise wildė
  deer,
Thise fauconers upon a fair ryver,
That with hir haukės han the heroun slayn.
Tho saugh he knyghtės justyng in a playn,
And after this he dide hym swich ples-
  aunce   1199
That he hym shewed his lady on a daunce,
On which hymself he dauncėd, as hym
  thoughte ;
And whan this maister that this magyk
  wroughte
Saugh it was tyme, he clapte his handės
  two,
And, farewel ! al oure revel was ago.
And yet remoeved they never out of the
  hous
Whil they saugh al this sightė merveillous ;
But in his studie, ther as his bookės be,
They seten stille, and no wight but they
  thre.
  To hym this maister callėd his squier,
And seyde hym thus : 'Is redy oure soper?
Almoost an houre it is, I undertake, 1211
Sith I yow bad oure soper for to make,
Whan that thise worthy men wenten with
  me
Into my studie, ther as my bookės be.'

    1205. *was ago*, Corp.³ *is y-do.*

'Sire,' quod this squier, 'whan it liketh
  yow
It is al redy, though ye wol right now.'
' Go we thanne soupe,' quod he, ' as for
  the beste ;
This amorous folk somtymė moote han
  hir reste.'
  At after soper fille they in tretee
What sommė sholde this maistrės gerdoun
  be   1220
To remoeven alle the rokkės of Britayne,
And eek from GeROunde to the mouth of
  Sayne.
  He made it straunge, and swoor, so
  God hym save !
Lasse than a thousand pound he wolde
  nat have,
Ne gladly for that somme he wolde nat
  goon.
Aurelius, with blisful herte anoon,
Answerdė thus : ' Fy on a thousand
  pound !
This wydė world, which that men seye
  is round,
I wolde it yeve, if I were lord of it !
This bargayn is ful dryve, for we been
  knyt   1230
Ye shal be payėd trewely, by my trouthe,
But looketh now, for no necligence or
  slouthe
Ye tarie us heere no lenger than to morwe.'
  ' Nay,' quod this clerk, ' have heer my
  feith to borwe.'
  To bedde is goon Aurelius whan hym
  leste,
And wel ny al that nyght he hadde his
  reste.
What for his labour, and his hope of
  blisse,
His woful herte of penaunce hadde a lisse.
  Upon the morwe, whan that it was day,
To Britaigne tookė they the rightė way,—
Aurelius and this magicien bisyde ;   1241
And been descended ther they wolde abyde;
And this was, as thise bookės me remembre,
The coldė, frosty sesoun of Decembre.
  Phebus wox old, and hewėd lyk latoun,
That in his hootė declynacioun
Shoon as the burnėd gold, with stremės
  brighte ;

But now in Capricorn adoun he lighte,
Where as he shoon ful pale, I dar wel seyn.
The bittré frostés with the sleet and reyn
Destroyéd hath the grene in every yerd ;
Janus sit by the fyr with double berd,
And drynketh of his bugle horn the wyn ;
Biforn hym stant brawn of the tuskéd swyn,
And '*Nowel*' crieth every lusty man.
   Aurelius in al that ever he kan
Dooth to his maister chiere and reverence,
And preyeth hym to doon his diligence
To bryngen hym out of his peynés smerte,
Or with a swerd that he wolde slitte his
      herte.   1260
   This subtil clerk swich routhe had of
      this man,
That nyght and day he spedde hym that
      he kan
To wayten a tyme of his conclusioun,
This is to seye, to maken illusioun
By swich an apparence or jogelrye,—
I ne kan no termés of astrologye,—
That she and every wight sholde wene
      and seye
That of Britaigne the rokkés were aweye,
Or ellés they were sonken under grounde.
So atté laste he hath his tyme y-founde
To maken his japés and his wrecchednesse
Of swich a supersticious cursednesse.
His tables Tolletanés forth he brought
Ful wel corrected, ne ther lakkéd nought,
Neither his collect, ne his expans yeeris,
Né his rootés, ne his othere geeris,
As been his centris, and his argumentz,
And his proporcioneles convenientz
For his equacïons in every thyng ;   1279
And by his eighté speere in his wirkyng
He knew ful wel how fer Alnath was shove
Fro the heed of thilke fixe Aries above,
That in the nynté speere considered is ;

1248. *in Capricorn.* This would be on Dec. 13.
1273. *tables Tolletanes,* the astronomical tables,
drawn up by order of Alphonso X. of Castille,
and primarily adapted to the city of Toledo.
1275. *collect,* a table of a planet's motion during
a round number of years, as opposed to the *expans,*
or separate, years.
1280. *And by his eighte speere.* The astrologer
was calculating the precession of the equinoxes
by the distance between the true equinoctial
point—the head of the fixed Aries—and the nearest
convenient bright star, for which Alnath was
chosen.

Ful subtilly he kalkuléd al this.
   Whan he hadde founde his firsté
      mansioun,
He knew the remenaunt by proporcioun,
And knew the arisyng of his mooné weel,
And in whos face, and terme, and every-
      deel,
And knew ful weel the moonés mansioun
Acordaunt to his operacioun ;   1290
And knew also his othere observaunces,
For swiche illusiouns and swiche mes-
      chaunces
As hethen folk useden in thilké dayes ;
For which no lenger makéd he delayes ;
But thurgh his magik for a wyke or tweye
It semed that alle the rokkés were aweye.
   Aurelius, which that yet despeired is
Wher he shal han his love or fare amys,
Awaiteth nyght and day on this myrácle ;
And whan he knew that ther was noon
      obstácle,   1300
That voyded were thise rokkés everychon,
Doun to his maistrés feet he fil anon,
And seyde, ' I, woful, wrecche Aurelius,
Thanké yow, lord, and lady myn, Venus,
That me han holpen fro my carés colde ' ;
And to the temple his wey forth hath he
      holde,
Where as he knew he sholde his lady see ;
And whan he saugh his tyme anon right hee,
With dredful herte and with ful humble
      cheere,   1309
Salewed hath his sovereyn lady deere.
   ' My righté lady,' quod this woful man,
' Whom I mooste drede, and love as I
      best kan,
And lothest were of al this world displese,
Nere it that I for yow have swich disese
That I moste dyen heere at youre foot anon ;
Noght wolde I telle how me is wo bigon,
But certés, outher moste I dye or pleyne.
Ye sle me giltélees for verray peyne,
But of my deeth thogh that ye have no
      routhe,
Avyseth yow, er that ye breke youre
      trouthe.   1320
Repenteth yow, for thilké God above,
Er ye me sleen by-cause that I yow love,
For, madame, wel ye woot what ye han
      hight,—

235

Nat that I chalange anythyng of right,
Of yow, my sovereyn lady, but youre
   grace,—
But in a gardyn yond, at swich a place,
Ye woot right wel what ye bihighten me,
And in myn hand youre trouthé plighten ye
To love me best,—God woot ye seydé so,
Al be that I unworthy be therto.   1330
Madame, I speke it for the honour of yow,
Moore than to save myn hertés lyf right now,
I have do so as ye comanded me,
And, if ye vouchésauf, ye may go see.
Dooth as yow list, have youre biheste in
   mynde,
For, quyk or deed, right there ye shal me
   fynde.
In yow lith al to do me lyve or deye,—
But wel I woot the rokkés been aweye.'
   He taketh his leve and she astonied
   stood ;
In al hir facé nas a drope of blood,   1340
She wendé never han come in swich a
   trappe !
'Allas !' quod she, 'that ever this sholde
   happe,
For wende I never by possibilitee,
That swich a monstre or merveille myghté
   be ;
It is agayns the proces of nature.'
And hoom she goth a sorweful creäture,—
For verray feere unnethé may she go.
She wepeth, wailleth al a day or two,
And swowneth, that it routhé was to see ;
But why it was to no wight toldé shee,   1350
For out of towne was goon Arveragus.
But to hirself she spak, and seydé thus,
With facé pale and with ful sorweful cheer,
In hire compleynt as ye shal after heere.
   'Allas !' quod she, 'on thee, Fortune,
   I pleyne,
That unwar wrappéd hast me in thy cheyne,
For which tescapé woot I no socour,
Save oonly deeth or ellés dishonour.
Oon of thise two bihoveth me to chese,
But nathélees yet have I levere lese   1360
My lif, than of my body have a shame,
Or knowe myselven fals, or lese my name ;

1355. As noted in E, the stories referred to in this wearisome complaint are all taken from St. Jerome's treatise, *Contra Jovinianum* (ch. 41. § 306 *sqq.* in Migne).

And with my deth I may be quyt, y-wis ;
Hath ther nat many a noble wyf er this,
And many a mayde, y-slayn hir self, allas !
Rather than with hir body doon trespas ?
   'Yis, certés, lo, thise stories beren
   witnesse
Whan Thretty Tirauntz ful of cursednesse
Hadde slayn Phidoun, in Atthenés, at feste,
They comanded his doghtres for tareste,
And bryngen hem biforn hem in despit,
Al naked, to fulfille hir foul delit ;
And in hir fadrés blood they made hem
   daunce
Upon the pavement,—God yeve hem mys-
   chaunce !
For which thise woful maydens, ful of drede,
Rather than they wolde lese hir mayden-
   hede
They prively been stirt into a welle,
And dreynte hemselven, as the bookés telle.
   'They of Mecené leete enquere and seke,
Of Lacedomye, fifty maydens eke,   1380
On whiche they wolden doon hir lecherye,
But was ther noon of al that compaignye
That she nas slayn, and with a good entente
Chees rather for to dyé, than assente
To been oppressed of hir maydenhede.
Why sholde I thanne to dyé been in drede?
   'Lo, eek the tiraunt Aristóclides,
That loved a mayden heet Stymphalides,
Whan that hir fader slayn was on a nyght,
Unto Dianés temple goth she right,   1390
And hente the ymage in hir handés two,
Fro which ymagé wolde she never go :
No wight ne myghte hir handes of it arace
Til she was slayn, right in the selvé place.
   'Now sith that maydens hadden swich
   despit
To been defouled with mannés foul delit,
Wel oghte a wyf rather hirselven slee
Than be defouléd, as it thynketh me.
   'What shal I seyn of Hasdrubalés wyf
That at Cartage birafte hirself hir lyf?   1400
For whan she saugh that Romayns wan the
   toun,
She took hir children alle, and skipte adoun
Into the fyr, and chees rather to dye
Than any Romayn dide hire vileynye.

1379. *Mecene*, Messenia.
1387. *Aristoclides*, tyrant of Orchomenus.

'Hath nat Lucresse y-slayn hirself, allas!
At Romé, whan [that] she oppresséd was
Of Tarquyn? for hire thoughte it was a
   shame
To lyven whan she haddé loste hir name.
   'The sevene maydens of Melesie, also,
Han slayn hemself for verray drede and wo,
Rather than folk of Gawle hem sholde
   oppresse,—
Mo than a thousand stories, as I gesse,
Koude I now telle as touchynge this
   mateere.
   'Whan Habradate was slayn, his wyf
   so deere
Hirselven slow, and leet hir blood to glyde
In Habradates woundés depe and wyde,
And seyde, "My body, at the leesté way,
Ther shal no wight defoulen, if I may."
   'What sholde I mo ensamples heer-of
   sayn?
Sith that so manye han hemselven slayn 1420
Wel rather than they wolde defoulé be,
I wol conclude that it is bet for me
To sleen myself than been defoulé thus.
I wol be trewe unto Arveragus,
Or rather sleen myself in some manere,
As dide Democionés doghter deere
By-cause that she wolde nat defoulé be.
O Cedasus, it is ful greet pitee
To reden how thy doghtren deyde, allas!
That slowe hemself for swich a manere
   cas.   1430
As greet a pitee was it, or wel moore,
The Theban mayden that for Nichanore
Hirselven slow, right for swich manere wo.
Another Theban mayden dide right so.
For oon of Macidonye hadde hire oppressed
She with hir deeth hir maydenhede re-
   dressed.
What shal I seye of Nicerates wyf,
That for swich cas birafte hirself hir lyf?
How trewe eek was to Alcebiades

His love, that rather for to dyen chees 1440
Than for to suffre his body unburyed be?
Lo, which a wyf was Alcesté,' quod she.
   'What seith Omer of goode Penalopee?
Al Grecé knoweth of hire chastitee.
Pardee, of Laodomya is writen thus,
That whan at Troie was slayn Protheselaus,
No lenger wolde she lyve after his day.
The same of noble Porcia telle I maye;
Withouté Brutus koudé she nat lyve,
To whom she hadde al hool hir herté yive.
The parfit wyfhod of Arthemesie   1451
Honuréd is thurgh al the Barbarie.
O Teuta, queene, thy wyfly chastitee
To allé wyvés may a mirour bee.
The samé thyng I seye of Bilyea,
Of Rodogone, and eek Valeria.'
   Thus pleynéd Dorigene a day or tweye,
Purposynge ever that she woldé deye;
But nathélees upon the thriddé nyght 1459
Hoom cam Arveragus, this worthy knyght,
And askéd hire why that she weepe so soore,
And she gan wepen ever lenger the moore.
   'Allas!' quod she, 'that ever I was
   born!
Thus have I seyd,' quod she, 'thus have
   I sworn,'—
And toold hym al, as ye han herd bifore,
It nedeth nat reherce it yow namoore.
   This housbonde, with glad chiere, in
   freendly wyse,
Answerde and seyde as I shal yow devyse,
'Is ther oght ellés, Dorigen, but this?'
   'Nay, nay,' quod she, 'God helpe me
   so as wys!   1470
This is to muche, and it were Goddés wille.'
   'Ye, wyf,' quod he, 'lat sleepen that
   is stille,
It may be wel, paráventure, yet to day;
Ye shul youre trouthé holden, by my fay!
For God so wisly have mercy upon me,
I hadde wel levere y-stikéd for to be,
For verray love which that I to yow have,
But if ye sholde youre trouthé kepe and
   save!

1409. *Melesie*, Milesia.
1414. *Habradate*. See Xenophon, *Cyropedia*,
lib. vii., for the story of Abradates and Panthea.
1426. *Demociones doghter*. On the death of
her betrothed, Leosthenes, she killed herself
rather than take another as husband.
1432. *Nichanore*, refused by the Theban maiden
because he was her conqueror.
1437. *Nicerates wyf*, at the time of the Thirty
Tyrants.

1451. *Arthemesie*, of Caria, wife of Mausolus,
whose tomb she built.
1453. *Teuta*, Queen of Illyria.
1454, 1455. Bilia was the wife of Duilius, consul
260 B.C.; Rhodogone, daughter of Darius, killed
her nurse for suggesting a second marriage.

Trouthe is the hyeste thyng that man may
     kepe,'—   1479
But with that word he brast anon to wepe,
And seyde, 'I yow forbede, up peyne of
     deeth,
That never whil thee lasteth lyf ne breeth,
To no wight telle thou of this áventure,—
As I may best I wol my wo endure,—
Ne make no contenance of hevynesse
That folk of yow may demen harm or gesse.'
     And forth he cleped a squier and a mayde;
'Gooth forth, anon, with Dorigen,' he
     sayde,
'And bryngeth hire to swich a place, anon.'
They take hir leve and on hir wey they gon,
But they ne wisté why she thider wente :
He noldé no wight tellen his entente.
     Paráventure an heepe of yow, y-wis,
Wol holden hym a lewéd man in this,
That he wol putte his wyf in jupartie.
Herkneth the tale, er ye upon hire crie ;
She may have bettré fortune than yow
     semeth ;
And, whan that ye han herd the talé,
     demeth.
     This squier, which that highte Aurelius,
On Dorigen that was so amorus,   1500
Of áventuré happéd hire to meete
Amydde the toun, right in the quykkest
     strete,
As she was bown to goon the wey forth right
Toward the gardyn, ther as she had hight ;
And he was to the gardynward also ;
For wel he spyéd whan she woldé go
Out of hir hous to any maner place ;
But thus they mette, of áventure or grace,
And he saleweth hire with glad entente ;
And askéd of hire whiderward she wente ;
And she answérdé, half as she were mad,
' Unto the gardyn, as myn housbonde bad,
My trouthé for to holde, allas ! allas !'
     Aurelius gan wondren on this cas,
And in his herte hadde greet compassioun
Of hire and of hire lamentacioun,
And of Arveragus, the worthy knyght,
That bad hire holden al that she had hight,
So looth hym was his wyf sholde breke hir
     trouthe ;

1481. *of*, om. E.
1503. *bown*, ready.

And in his herte he caughte of this greet
     routhe,   1520
Considerynge the beste on every syde,
That fro his lust yet were hym levere abyde,
Than doon so heigh a cherlyssh wrecched-
     nesse
Agayns franchise and allé gentillesse ;
For which in fewé wordés seyde he thus :
' Madame, seyeth to youre lord, Arver-
     agus,
That sith I se his greté gentillesse ;
To yow, and eek I se wel youre distresse,
That him were levere han shame,—and
     that were routhe,—
Than ye to me sholde breké thus youre
     trouthe,   1530
I have wel levere ever to suffre wo,
Than I departe the love bitwix yow two.
I yow relesse, madame, into youre hond,
Quyt every surément and every bond
That ye han maad to me as heer biforn,
Sith thilké tymé which that ye were born.
My trouthe I plighte, I shal yow never
     repreve
Of no biheste, and heere I take my leve,
As of the treweste and the besté wyf,
That ever yet I knew in al my lyf.   1540
But every wyf be war of hire biheeste ;
On Dorigene remembreth, atté leeste.
Thus kan a squier doon a gentil dede
As wel as kan a knyght, withouten drede.'
     She thonketh hym upon hir knees al
     bare,
And hoom unto hir housbonde is she fare,
And tolde hym al, as ye han herd me sayd ;
And be ye siker he was so weel apayd
That it were inpossíble me to wryte.
What sholde I lenger of this cas endyte ?
     Arveragus and Dorigene his wyf   1551
In sovereyn blissé leden forth hir lyf ;
Never eft ne was ther angre hem bitwene.
He cherisseth hire, as though she were a
     queene,
And she was to hym trewe for evermoore.
Of thisé folk ye gete of me namoore.
     Aurelius, that his cost hath all forlorn,
Curseth the tyme that ever he was born.
' Allas !' quod he, 'allas, that I bihighte
Of puréd gold a thousand pound of wighte
Unto this philosophre ! How shal I do ?

238

I se namoore but that I am fordo ;
Myn heritagé moot I nedés selle,
And been a beggere ; heere may I nat dwelle
And shamen al my kynrede in this place,
But I of hym may geté bettre grace ;
But nathélees I wole of hym assaye
At certeyn dayés, yeer by yeer, to paye,
And thanke hym of his greté curteisye.
My trouthé wol I kepe, I wol nat lye.' 1570
  With herté soor he gooth unto his cofre,
And broghté gold unto this philosophre,
The value of fyve hundred pound, I gesse,
And hym bisecheth, of his gentillesse,
To graunte hym dayés of the remenaunt,
And seydé, 'Maister, I dar wel make avaunt
I faillé never of my trouthe as yit,
For sikerly my detté shal be quyt
Towardés yow, however that I fare
To goon a-begged in my kirtle bare ; 1580
But wolde ye vouchésauf, upon seuretee,
Two yeer, or thre, for to respiten me,
Thanne were I wel, for ellés moot I selle
Myn heritage ; ther is namoore to telle.'
  This philosophre sobrely answerde,
And seydé thus, whan he thise wordés
    herde :
' Have I nat holdé covenant unto thee ?'
' Yes, certés, wel and trewély,' quod he.
' Hastow nat had thy lady as thee liketh?'
' No, no,' quod he, and sorwefully he siketh.
' What was the causé ; tel me if thou kan.'
Aurelius his tale anon bigan,
And tolde hym al, as ye han herd bifoore ;
It nedeth nat to yow reherce it moore.
  He seide, ' Arveragus, of gentillesse,
Hadde levere dye in sorwe and in distresse,

Than that his wyf were of hir trouthé fals' ;
The sorwe of Dorigen he tolde hym als,—
How looth hire was to been a wikked wyf,
And that she levere had lost that day hir lyf,
And that hir trouthe she swoor thurgh
    innocence, 1601
She never erst herd speke of apparence ;
' That made me han of hire so greet pitee,
And right as frely as he sente hire me,
As frely sente I hire to hym ageyn ;
This is al and som, ther is namoore to seyn.'
  This philosophre answérde, ' Leevé
    brother,
Everich of yow dide gentilly til other ;
Thou art a squier, and he is a knyght,
But God forbedé, for his blisful myght, 1610
But if a clerk koude doon a gentil dede,
As wel as any of yow, it is no drede.
' Sire, I releessé thee thy thousand pound
As thou right now were cropen out of the
    ground,
Ne never er now ne haddest knoweh me ;
For, sire, I wol nat taken a peny of thee
For al my craft, ne noght for my travaille.
Thou hast y-payéd wel for my vitaille ;
It is ynogh, and farewel, have good day ! '
And took his hors, and forth he goth his way.

Lordynges, this questioun, thanne,
    wolde I aske now, ⊦ 1621
Which was the moosté fre, as thynketh
    yow ?
Now telleth me, er that ye ferther wende.
I kan namoore, my tale is at an ende.

1620. Chaucer has forgotten that Aurelius came
to the philosopher, not the philosopher to Aurelius.

SECOND NUN'S TALE

The Prologe of the Seconde Nonnes Tale

THE ministre and the norice unto vice
Which that men clepe in Englissh ydelnesse,

Seconde Nonnes Tale, a translation, at first
close, afterwards free, of the life of St. Cecilia in
the *Legenda Aurea* of Jacobus de Voragine.
The stanzas on idleness were probably suggested
by the Prologue of the French translator, Jehan

That porter at the gate is of delices,
To eschue, and by hire contrarie hire
  oppresse,—
That is to seyn, by leveful bisynesse,—
Wel oghten we to don al oure entente,
Lest that the feend thurgh ydelnesse us
  hente,

de Vignay, but in the Tale Chaucer follows the
Latin.
  3. *porter*, as in the *Roman de la Rose*.

For he that with his thousand cordes slye
Continuelly us waiteth to biclappe,　　　9
Whan he may man in ydelnesse espye,
He kan so lightly cacche hym in his trappe,
Til that a man be hent right by the lappe,
He nys nat war the feend hath hym in
　　honde :
Wel oghte us werche, and ydelnesse
　　withstonde.

And though men dradden never for to dye,
Yet seen men wel by resoun, doutelees,
That ydelnesse is roten slogardye,
Of which ther never comth no good
　　encrees ;
And seen that slouthe hir holdeth in a lees
Oonly to slepe and for to ete and drynke,
And to devouren al that othere swynk.　21

And for to putte us fro swich ydelnesse,
That cause is of so greet confusioun,
I have heer doon my feithful bisynesse,
After the Legende, in translacioun,
Right of thy glorious lif and passioun,
Thou with thy gerland wroght with rose
　　and lilie,—
Thee, meene I, mayde and martir, seint
　　Cecilie.

Invocacio ad Mariam

And thow that flour of virgines art alle,
Of whom that Bernard list so wel to write ;
To thee, at my bigynnyng, first I call,　31
Thou confort of us wrecches, do me endite
Thy maydens deeth, that wan thurgh
　　hire merite,
The eternel lyf, and of the feend victorie
As man may after reden in hire storie.

Thow mayde and mooder, doghter of
　　thy sone,
Thow welle of mercy, synful soules cure,
In whom that God, for bountee, chees to
　　wone,
Thow humble, and heigh over every
　　creature,　　　39

36-56. These three stanzas are partly a translation of some of the first twenty-one lines of
Dante's *Paradiso*, Cant. 33, or perhaps of some
Latin prayer or hymn which Dante may have
imitated.

Thow nobledest so ferforth oure nature,
That no desdeyn the Makere hadde of kynde
His sone in blood and flessh to clothe
　　and wynde.

Withinne the cloistre blisful of thy sydis
Took mannes shape the eterneel Love
　　and Pees,
That of the tryne compas lord and gyde is,
Whom erthe, and see, and hevene, out
　　of relees,
Ay heryen ; and thou virgine wemmelees
Baar of thy body, and dweltest mayden
　　pure,
The creatour of every creature.

Assembled is in thee magnificence,　　50
With mercy, goodnesse, and with swich
　　pitee,
That thou, that art the sonne of excellence,
Nat oonly helpest hem that preyen thee,
But often tyme, of thy benygnytee,
Ful frely, er that men thyn help biseche,
Thou goost biforn and art hir lyves leche.

Now help, thow meeke and blisful faire
　　mayde,
Me flemed wrecche in this desert of galle ;
Thynk on the womman Cananee, that sayde
That whelpes eten somme of the crommes
　　alle　　　60
That from hir lordes table been y-falle,
And though that I, unworthy sone of Eve,
Be synful, yet accepte my bileve.

And for that feith is deed withouten werkis,
So, for to werken, yif me wit and space,
That I be quit fro thennes that moost
　　derk is.
O thou that art so fair and ful of grace,
Be myn advocat in that heighe place,
Theras withouten ende is songe Osanne,
Thow Cristes mooder, doghter deere of
　　Anne !　　　70

And of thy light my soule in prison lighte,
That troubled is by the contagioun

62. *sone of Eve.* The phrase (cp. l. 78, *reden
that I write*) shows that this legend was not
written as one of the Canterbury Tales.

Of my body, and also by the wighte
Of erthely lust and fals affeccioun !
O havene of refut, O salvacioun
Of hem that been in sorwe and in distresse,
Now helpe, for to my werk I wol me dresse !

Yet preye I yow that reden that I write,
Foryeve me that I do no diligence
This ilkė storie subtilly to endite,   80
For bothe have I the wordės and sentence
Of hym that at the seintės reverence
The storie wroot, and folwen hire legende ;
I pray yow that ye wole my werk amende.

Interpretacio nominis Cecilie

First wolde I yow the name of Seinte
    Cecile
Expowne, as men may in hir storie see.
It is to seye in Englissh 'hevenes lilie,'
For purė chaastnesse of virginitee,
Or for she whitnesse hadde of honestee,
And grene of conscience, and of good fame
The sootė savour, lilie was hir name ; 91

Or Cecile is to seye 'the wey to blynde,'
For she ensample was by good techynge ;
Or ellės Cecile, as I writen fynde,
Is joynėd by ·a manere conjoynynge
Of 'hevene' and 'lia,' and heere, in
    figurynge,
The 'hevene' is set for thoght of hoolynesse
And 'lia' for hire lastynge bisynesse.

Cecile may eek be seyd in this manere
'Wantynge of blyndnesse,' for hir gretė
    light   100
Of sapience, and for hire thewės cleere ;
Or ellės, loo, this maydens namė bright
Of 'hevene' and 'leos' comth, for which
    by right
Men myghte hire wel the hevene of peple
    calle,
Ensample of goode and wisė werkės alle.

For 'leos' ' 'peple' in Englissh is to seye ;
And right as men may in the hevene see

87. *hevenes lilie,* 'cœli lilia.'
92. *the wey to blynde,* 'cæcis via.'
103. *leos,* Gk. λεώς.

R   241

The sonne, and moone, and sterrės,
    every weye,
Right so men goostly in this mayden free
Syen of feith the magnanymytee,   110
And eek the cleernesse hool of sapience,
And sondry werkes brighte of excellence.

And right so as thise philosophres write
That hevene is swift, and round, and eek
    brennýnge,
Right so was fairė Cecilie the white,
Ful swift and bisy ever, in good werkýnge ;
And round and hool in good persėverýnge,
And brennynge ever in charite ful brighte :
Now have I yow declarėd what she highte.

Here bigynneth The Seconde Nonnes Tale of the lyf of Seinte Cecile

This mayden bright, Cecile, as hir lif
    seith,   120
Was comen of Romayns and of noble
    kynde,
And from hir cradel up fostred in the feith
Of Crist, and bar his gospel in hir mynde.
She never cessėd, as I writen fynde,
Of hir preyere, and God to love and drede,
Bisekynge hym to kepe hir maydenhede.

And whan this mayden sholde unto a man
Y-wedded be, that was ful yong of age,
Which that y-clepėd was Valerian,
And day was comen of hir marriage,   130
She ful devout and humble in hire corage,
Under hir robe of gold that sat ful faire,
Hadde next hire flessh y-clad hire in an
    haire ;

And whil the organs maden melodie,
To God allone in hertė thus sang she :
'O Lord, my soule and eek my body
    gye
Unwemmėd, lest that I confounded be';
And for his love that dyde upon a tree,
Every secónde or thriddė day she faste
Ay biddynge in hire orisons ful faste.   140

The nyght cam, and to beddė moste
    she gon

With hire housbonde, as ofte is the manere,
And pryvély to hym she seyde anon,
' O sweete and wel-biloved spousé deere,
Ther is a conseil, and ye wolde it heere,
Which that right fayn I wolde unto yow
    seye,
So that ye swere ye shul it nat biwreye.'

Valerian gan faste unto hire swere
That for no cas, ne thyng that myghté be,
He sholdé never mo biwreyen here ;   150
And thanne at erst to hym thus seydé she :
' I have an aungel which that loveth me,
That with greet love, wher so I wake or
    sleepe,
Is redy ay my body for to kepe ;

And if that he may feelen, out of drede,
That ye me touche or love in vileynye,
He right anon wol sle yow with the dede,
And in youre yowthé thus ye sholden dye ;
And if that ye in clené love me gye,
He wol yow loven as me for youre clennesse,
And shewen yow his joye and his
    brightnesse.'   161

Valerian, corrected as God wolde,
Answerde agayn, ' If I shal trusten thee
Lat me that aungel se, and hym biholde,
And if that it a verray angel bee,
Thanne wol I doon as thou hast prayéd me ;
And if thou love another man, for sothe,
Right with this swerd thanne wol I sle
    yow bothe !'

Cecile answerde anon right in this wise :
' If that yow list, the angel shul ye see,
So that ye trowe in Crist, and yow baptize.
Gooth forth to *Via Apia*,' quod shee,
' That fro this toun ne stant but milés three,
And to the pouré folkés that ther dwelle
Sey hem right thus as that I shal yow telle.

' Tell hem that I, Cecile, yow to hem
    sente

142. *as ofte is the manere*, Chaucer's tag. Cp. *and ye wolde it heere*, l. 145 ; *wher so I wake or sleepe*, l. 153, and many more.
172. *Via Apia.* Chaucer seems to take this as the name of a place. The Latin says ' the third milestone on the Appian road.'

To shewen yow the goode Urban the olde,
For secree needés, and for good entente ;
And whan that ye Seint Urban han biholde,
Telle hym the wordés whiche that I yow
    tolde,   180
And whan that he hath purgéd yow fro
    synne,
Thanne shul ye see that angel, er ye
    twynne.'

Valerian is to the place y-gon,
And right as hym was taught by his
    lernynge,
He foond this hooly olde Urban anon,
Among the seintés buryeles lotynge ;
And he anon, withouten tariynge,
Dide his messáge ; and whan that he it
    tolde,
Urban for joye his handés gan up holde ;

The teeris from his eyen leet he falle.   190
' Almyghty Lord !   O Jhesu Crist,'
    quod he,
' Sower of chast conseil, hierde of us alle,
The fruyt of thilké seed of chastitee
That thou hast sowe in Cecile, taak to thee !
Lo, lyk a bisy bee, withouten gile,
Thee serveth ay thyn owene thral Cecile ;

For thilké spousé that she took right now,
Ful lyk a fiers leoun, she sendeth heere
As meke as ever was any lamb, to yow' :
And with that word anon ther gan appere
An oold man, clad in whité clothés cleere,
That hadde a book with lettre of gold,
    in honde,
And gan bifore Valerian to stonde.

Valerian, as deed, fil doun for drede
Whan he hym saugh, and he up hente
    hym tho,
And on his book right thus he gan to rede :
' O Lord, o feith, o God, withouten mo ;
O Cristendom, and Fader of alle also,
Aboven alle, and over alle, everywhere' ;
Thise wordés al with gold y-writen were.

195. *bisy bee*, Latin : 'apis argumentosa,' a delightful phrase for Cecilia.
208. *O Cristendom*, Latin : 'unum baptisma.'

Whan this was rad, thanne seyde this
    olde man,   211
'Leevestow this thyng ; or no ? Sey ye
    or nay.'
'I leeve al this thyng,' quod Valerian,
'For oother thyng than this, I dar wel say,
Under the hevene no wight thynke may.'
Tho vanysshed this olde man, he nyste
    where,
And Pope Urban hym cristned right there.

Valerian gooth hoom and fynt Cecile
Withinne his chambre with an angel
    stonde.
This angel hadde of roses and of lilie   220
Córones two, the which he bar in honde ;
And first to Cecile, as I understonde,
He yaf that oon, and after gan he take
That oother to Valerian, hir make.

'With body clene, and with unwemméd
    thoght,
Kepeth ay wel thise córones,' quod he ;
'Fro paradys to yow have I hem broght,
Ne never mo ne shal they roten bee,
Ne lese hir sooté savour, trusteth me ;
Ne never wight shal seen hem with his eye,
But he be chaast and haté vileynye ;   231

And thow, Valerian, for thow so soone
Assentedest to good conseil also,
Sey what thee list, and thou shalt han
    thy boone.'
'I have a brother,' quod Valerian tho,
'That in this world I love no man so ;
I pray yow that my brother may han grace
To knowe the trouthe, as I do in this place.'

The angel seyde, 'God liketh thy requeste,
And bothé with the palm of martirdom
Ye shullen come unto his blissful feste' ;
And with that word Tiburce his brother
    com,
And whan that he the savour undernom
Which that the roses and the lilies caste,
Withinne his herte he gan to wondre faste ;

And seyde, 'I wondre, this tyme of the yeer,
Whennés that sooté savour cometh so

241. *unto his blissful feste*, 'ad Dominum.'

Of rose and lilies that I smellé heer ;
For though I hadde hem in myne handés
    two   249
The savour myghte in me no depper go ;
The sweeté smel that in myn herte I fynde
Hath chaungéd me al in another kynde.'

Valerian seyde, 'Two córones han we,
Snow white and rosé reed, that shynen
    cleere,
Whiche that thyne eyen han no myght
    to see ;
And as thou smellest hem thurgh my
    preyere,
So shaltow seen hem, leevé brother deere,
If it so be thou wolt, withouten slouthe,
Bileve aright and knowen verray trouthe.'

Tiburce answerdé, 'Seistow this to me
In soothnesse, or in dreem I herkné this ?'
'In dremés,' quod Valerian, 'han we be
Unto this tymé, brother myn, y-wis ;
But now at erst in trouthe our dwellyng is.'
'How woostow this,' quod Tiburce, 'in
    what wyse ?'
Quod Valerian, 'That shal I thee devyse.

The aungel of God hath me the trouthe
    y-taught,
Which thou shalt seen, if that thou wolt
    reneye
The ydoles, and be clene, and ellés naught.'
(And of the myracle of thise córones tweye,
Seint Ambrose in his preface list to seye,—
Solempnély this noble doctour deere
Commendeth it, and seith in this manere :

'The palm of martirdom for to receyve
Seinté Cecile, fulfild of Goddés yifte,
The world and eek hire chambre gan she
    weyve ;
Witnesse Tyburcés and Valerians shrifte,
To which God of his bountee woldé shifte
Córones two of floures wel smellynge,
And made his angel hem the córones
    brynge ;   280

The mayde hath broght thise men to
    blisse above ;

251. 'Ita sum refectus.'

The world hath wist what it is worth
    certeyn,
Devocioun of chastitee to love.')
Tho shewèd hym Cecile, al open and pleyn,
That alle ydoles nys but a thyng in veyn ;
For they been dombe and therto they
    been deve,
And chargèd hym his ydoles for to leve.

' Who so that troweth nat this, a beest
    he is,'
Quod tho Tiburce, 'if that I shal nat lye,'
And she gan kisse his brest that herdè this,
And was ful glad he koudè trouthe espye.
' This day I takè thee for myn allye,'
Seydè this blissful, fairè maydè, deere,
And after that she seyde as ye may heere :

' Lo, right so as the love of Crist,' quod she,
' Made me thy brotheres wyf, right in
    that wise
Anon for myn allye heer take I thee,
Syn that thou wolt thyne ydolès despise ;
Go with thy brother now, and thee baptise,
And make thee clene so that thou mowe
    biholde   300
The angeles face, of which thy brother
    tolde.'

Tiburce answerde and seydè, ' Brother
    dere,
First tell me whider I shal, and to what
    man ? '
' To whom ? ' quod he ; ' com forth with
    right good cheere ;
I wol thee lede unto the Pope Urban.'
' Til Urban, brother myn Valerian ? '
Quod tho Tiburce ; ' woltow me thider
    lede ?
Me thynketh that it were a wonder dede.

Ne menestow nat Urban,' quod he tho,
' That is so oftè dampnèd to be deed,   310
And woneth in halkes alwey to and fro,
And dar nat onès puttè forth his heed ?
Men sholde hym brennen in a fyr so reed,
If he were founde, or that men myghte
    hym spye,
And we also to bere hym compaignye ;

292. ' Hodie te fateor meum esse cognatum,' I
own you are really of my kin.

And whil we seken thilke divinitee,
That is y-hid in hevene pryvèly,
Algate y-brend in this world shul we be !'
    To whom Cecile answerdè boldèly,
' Men myghten dreden wel and skilfully
This lyf to lese, myne owene deerè brother,
If this were lyvynge oonly, and noon
    oother ;

But ther is bettre lif in oother place,
That never shal be lost, ne drede thee
    noght,
Which Goddès sone us toldè thurgh his
    grace ;
That Fadrès sone hath allè thyng y-wroght,
And al that wroght is with a skilful thoght
The Goost, that fro the Fader gan procede,
Hath sowled hem, withouten any drede.

By word and by myrácle, Goddès sone,
Whan he was in this world, declarèd heere
That ther was oother lyf ther men may
    wone.'
To whom answerde Tiburce, ' O suster
    deere,
Ne seydestow right now in this manere,
" Ther nys but o God, lord in soothfast-
    nesse,"—
And now of three how maystow bere
    witnesse ? '

' That shal I tellè,' quod she, 'ere I go.
Right as a man hath sapiences three,
Memorie, engyn, and intellect also,
So in o beynge of divinitee   340
Thrè persónès may ther right wel bee ' ;
Tho gan she hym ful bisely to preche
Of Cristès come, and of his peynès teche ;

And many pointès of his passioun,
How Goddès sone in this world was
    withholde
To doon mankyndè playn remissioun,
That was y-bounde in synne and carès
    colde ;
Al this thyng she unto Tiburce tolde,

322. ' Si hæc sola esset vita.'
346. Hitherto Chaucer has translated literally,
only eking out his stanzas with tags ; he now
begins to abridge, at the same time adding stanzas
of his own.

And after this Tiburce in good entente
With Valerian to Pope Urban he wente,

That thanked God, and with glade herte
    and light,   351
He cristned hym, and made hym in that
    place
Parfit in his lernyngè, Goddès knyght ;
And after this Tiburcè gat swich grace
That every day he saugh in tyme and space
The aungel of God, and every maner boone
That he God axèd, it was sped ful soone.

It were ful hard by ordre for to seyn
How manye wondres Jhesus for hem
    wroghte ;   359
But attè laste, to tellen short and pleyn,
The sergeantz of the toun of Rome hem
    soghte,
And hem biforn Almache, the Prefect,
    broghte,
Which hem apposed, and knew al hire
    entente,
And to the ymage of Juppiter hem sente ;

And seydè, ' Whoso wol nat sacrifise,
Swape of his heed; this my sentencè heer !'
Anon thise martirs that I yow devyse,
Oon Maximus, that was an officer
Of the Prefectes, and his corniculer,
Hem hente, and whan he forth the
    seintès ladde,   370
Hymself he weepe for pitee that he hadde.

Whan Maximus had herd the seintès
    loore,
He gat hym of the tormentourès leve,
And ladde hem to his hous, withoutè moore,
And with hir prechyng, er that it were eve,
They gonnen fro the tormentours to reve,
And fro Maxime, and fro his folk echone,
The falsè feith, to trowe in God allone.

Cecilè cam, whan it was woxen nyght,
With preestès, that hem cristned all y-feere ;
And afterward, whan day was woxen light,
Cecile hem seyde with a ful stedefast cheere,

' Now, Cristès owene knyghtès, leeve,
    and deere,
Cast alle awey the werkès of derknesse,
And armeth yow in armure of brightnesse.

Ye han, for sothe, y-doon a greet bataille,
Youre cours is doon, youre feith han ye
    conserved.
Gooth to the corone of lyf, that may nat
    faille ;
The rightful Jugè, which that ye han served,
Shal yeve it yow, as ye han it deserved ' ;
And whan this thing was seyd as I devyse,
Men ledde hem forth to doon the sacrefise.

But whan they weren to the place
    y-broght, —
To tellen shortly the conclusioun, —
They nolde encense ne sacrifise right noght,
But on hir knees they setten hem adoun
With humble herte and sad devocioun,
And losten bothe hir hevedes in the place ;
Hir soulès wenten to the kyng of grace.

This Maximus, that saugh this thyng
    bityde,   400
With pitous teeris tolde it anon right,
That he hir soulès saugh to hevene glyde,
With aungels ful of cleernesse and of light ;
And with his word converted many a wight,
For which Almachius dide hym so to-bete,
With whippe of leed, til he his lif gan lete.

Cecile hym took, and buryed hym anon
By Tiburce and Valerian softèly
Withinne hire buriyng-place under the
    stoon ;
And after this Almachius hastily   410
Bad his ministres fecchen openly
Cecile, so that she myghte in his presence
Doon sacrifice, and Juppiter encense ;

But they, converted at hir wisè loore,
Wepten ful soore, and yaven ful credence
Unto hire word, and cryden moore and
    moore,
' Crist, Goddès sone, withouten difference
Is verray God, this is al oure sentence,

---

360. *attè lastè.* The offence alleged in the
Legend is the burial of the bodies of martyrs.

409. Added.

That hath so good a servant hym to serve;
This with o voys we trowen, thogh we
  sterve!'   420

Almachius that herde of this doynge
Bad fecchen Cecile that he myghte hire see;
And alderfirst, lo this was his axynge,
'What maner womman artow?' tho
  quod he.
'I am a gentil womman born,' quod she.
'I axé thee,' quod he, 'though it thee
  greeve,
Of thy religioun, and of thy bileeve.'

'Ye han bigonne youre question folily,'
Quod she, 'that wolden two answeres
  conclude
In o demande; ye axéd lewedly.'   430
Almache answerde unto that similitude,
'Of whennés comth thyn answering so
  rude?'
'Of whennés?' quod she, whan that
  she was freyned;
'Of conscience, and of good feith
  unfeyned.'

  Almachius seyde, 'Ne takestow noon
    heede
Of my powér?' And she answerde hym
  this:
'Youre myght,' quod she, 'ful litel is to
  dreede,
For every mortal mannés power nys
But lyke a bladdre, ful of wynd, y-wys;
For with a nedles poynt whan it is blowe
May al the boost of it be leyd ful lowe.'

'Ful wrongfully bigonné thow,' quod he,
'And yet in wrong is thy perséveraunce;
Wostow nat how oure myghty princes free
Han thus comanded and maad ordinaunce,
That every Cristen wight shal han
  penaunce,
But if that he his Cristendom withseye;
And goon al quit, if he wole it reneye?'

'Yowre princes erren, as youre nobleye
  dooth,'   449
Quod tho Cecile, 'and with a wood sentence
Ye make us gilty, and it is nat sooth;

For ye that knowen wel oure innocence,—
For as muche as we doon a reverence
To Crist, and for we bere a Cristen name,—
Ye putte on us a cryme, and eek a blame;

But we, that knowen thilké namé so
For vertuous, we may it not withseye.'
Almache answerde, 'Chees oon of thisé
  two,—
Do sacrifice, or Cristendom reneye, 459
That thou mowe now escapen by that weye.'
At which the hooly blisful fairé mayde
Gan for to laughe, and to the jugé sayde,

'O jugé, confus in thy nycétee!
Woltow that I reneyé innocence,
To maké me a wikked wight?' quod she.
Lo, he dissymuleth heere in audience,
He stareth, and woodeth in his adver-
  tence.
  To whom Almachius, 'Unsely wrecche!
Ne woostow nat how far my myght may
  strecche?

Han noght oure myghty princes to me
  yeven,   470
Ye, bothé power and auctoritee
To maken folk to dyen or to lyven?
Why spekestow so proudly thanne to me?'
  'I speké noght but stedfastly,' quod she,
'Nat proudly, for, I speke as for my syde,
We haten deedly thilké vice of pryde;

And if thou dredé nat a sooth to heere,
Thanne wol I shewe al openly by right
That thou hast maad a ful gret lesyng heere.
Thou seyst thy princes han thee yeven
  myght   480
Bothe for to sleen and for to quyken a wight;
Thou that ne mayst but oonly lyf bireve,
Thou hast noon oother power, ne no leve:

But thou mayst seyn thy princes han
  thee maked
Ministre of deeth, for if thou speke of mo,
Thou lyest, for thy power is ful naked!'
'Do wey thy booldnesse!' seyde Alma-
  chius tho,
'And sacrifie to oure goddés er thou go!

I recché nat what wrong that thou me
 profre,
For I can suffre it as a philosophre,   490

But thilké wrongés may I nat endure,
That thou spekest of oure goddés heere,'
 quod he.
 Cecile answerde, ' O nycé creature !
Thou seydest no word syn thou spak to me
That I ne knew therwith thy nycétee,
And that thou were in every maner wise
A lewéd officer and a veyn justise !

Ther lakketh no thyng to thyne outter eyen
That thou nart blynd, for thyng that we
 seen alle
That it is stoon,—that men may wel
 espyen,—   500
That ilké stoon a god thow wolt it calle.
I rede thee, lat thyn hand upon it falle,
And taste it wel, and stoon thou shalt it
 fynde,
Syn that thou seest nat with thyne eyen
 blynde.

It is a shamé that the peple shal
So scorné thee, and laughe at thy folye ;
For communly men woot it wel overal
That myghty God is in his hevenés hye,
And thise ymáges, wel thou mayst espye,
To thee, ne to hemself, mowen noght
 profite,   510
For in effect they been nat worth a myte.'

Thise wordés and swiche other seydé she ;
And he weex wrooth, and bad men
 sholde hir lede
Hom til hir house, and ' In hir hous,'
 quod he,
' Brenne hire right in a bath of flambes
 rede ' ;
And as he bad, right so was doon in dede,
For in a bath they gonne hire fasté shetten,
And nyght and day greet fyre they under
 betten.

The longé nyght, and eek a day also,
For al the fyr, and eek the bathés heete,

489-497. Chaucer's addition.
505-511. Added.

She sat al coold and felte of it no wo ;
It made hire nat a dropé for to sweete ;
But in that bath hir lyf she mosté lete,
For he, Almachius, with ful wikke entento
To sleen hire in the bath his sondé sente.

Thre strokés in the nekke he smoot hire
 tho,
The tormentour, but for no maner chaunce
He myghté noght smyt al hir nekke atwo ;
And for ther was that tyme an ordinaunce,
That no man sholde doon men swich
 penaunce   530
The ferthe strook to smyten, softe or soore,
This tormentour ne dorsté do namoore ;

But half deed, with hir nekke y-corven
 there,
He lefte hir lye, and on his wey is went.
 The Cristen folk which that aboute hire
 were,
With sheetés han the blood ful faire y-hent.
Thre dayés lyvéd she in this torment,
And never cesséd hem the feith to teche
That she hadde fostred ; hem she gan to
 preche ;   539

And hem she yaf hir moebles, and hir thyng,
And to the Pope Urban bitook hem tho,
And seyde, ' I axéd this at hevene kyng,
To han respit thre dayés and namo,
To recomende to yow, er that I go,
Thise soulés, lo, and that I myghte do
 werche
Heere of myn hous perpetuelly a cherche.'

Seint Urban, with his deknés, privély
The body fette, and buryed it by nyghte
Among his other seintés honestly.
Hir hous the chirche of Seinte Cecilie
 highte ;   550
Seint Urban halwéd it, as he wel myghte,
In which, into this day, in noble wyse,
Men doon to Crist and to his seinte servyse.

  *The prologe of the Chanons Yemannes
   Tale*

Whan toold was al the lyf of Seinte
 Cecile,

535, 536. Added.

Er we hadde riden fully fyvė mile,
At Boghton-under-Blee, us gan atake
A man that clothėd was in clothės blake,
And undernethe he had a white surplys ;
His hackeney, which that was al pomely
     grys,
So swattė that it wonder was to see ;   560
It semed as he had prikėd milės three.
The hors eek that his Yeman rood upon
So swattė that unnethė myghte it gon ;
Aboute the peytrel stood the foom ful hye,
He was of foom al flekkėd as a pye.
A male tweyfoold upon his croper lay,
It semėd that he caried lite array.
Al light for somer rood this worthy man,
And in myn hertė wondren I bigan
What that he was, til that I understood   570
How that his cloke was sowėd to his hood,
For which, whan I hadde long avysėd me,
I demėd hym som Chanoun for to be.
His hat heeng at his bak doun by a laas,
For he hadde riden moore than trot or
     paas ;
He hadde ay prikėd lik as he were wood.
A clotė-leef he hadde under his hood
For swoot, and for to kepe his heed from
     heete ;
But it was joyė for to seen hym swete !
His forheed dropped as a stillatorie   580
Were ful of plantayne and of paritorie ;
And whan that he was come he gan to crye,
'God save,' quod he, 'this joly compaignye !
Faste have I prikėd,' quod he, 'for youre
     sake,
By-causė that I woldė yow atake
To riden in this myrie compaignye.'
His Yeman eek was ful of curteisye,
And seydė, 'Sires, now in the morwė tyde,
Out of youre hostelrie I saugh you ryde,
And warnėd heer my lord, and my
     soverayn,   590
Which that to ryden with yow is ful fayn,
For his desport ; he loveth daliaunce.'
   'Freend, for thy warnyng God yeve thee
     good chaunce !'
Thanne seyde oure Hoost, 'for certės it
     wolde seme

Thy lord were wys, and so I may wel deme ;
He is ful jocunde also, dar I leye !
Can he oght telle a myrie tale or tweye,
With which he gladė may this com-
     paignye ? '
   ' Who, sire ? my lord ? ye, ye, withouten
     lye !   599
He kan of murthe, and eek of jolitee
Nat but ynough ; also, sire, trusteth me,
And ye hym knewė as wel as do I,
Ye woldė wondre how wel and craftily
He koudė werke, and that in sondry wise.
He hath take on hym many a greet emprise,
Which were ful hard for any that is heere
To brynge about, but they of hym it leere.
As hoomely as he rit amongės yow,
If ye hym knewe it wolde be for youre prow ;
Ye woldė nat forgoon his áqueyntaunce
For muchel good, I dar leye in balaunce
Al that I have in my possessioun.
He is a man of heigh discrecioun ;
I warne yow wel, he is a passyng man.'
   'Wel,' quod oure Hoost, ' I pray thee
     tel me than
Is he a clerk or noon ? Telle what he is.'
   ' Nay, he is gretter than a clerk, y-wis,'
Seydė this Yeman, 'and in wordės fewe,
Hoost, of his craft somwhat I wol yow
     shewe.   619
   ' I seye, my lord kan swich subtilitee,—
But al his craft ye may nat wite at me,
And somwhat helpe I yet to his wirkyng,—
That al this ground on which we been
     ridyng,
Til that we come to Caunterbury toun,
He koude al clenė turne it up-so-doun,
And pave it al of silver and of gold.'
   And whan this Yeman hadde this tale
     y-told
Unto oure Hoost, he seydė, ' *Benedicitee !*
This thyng is wonder merveillous to me,
Syn that thy lord is of so heigh prudence,
By cause of which men sholde hym
     reverence,   631
That of his worshipe rekketh he so lite.
His overslopė nys nat worth a myte,
As in effect, to hym, so moot I go !
It is al baudy and to-tore also.
Why is thy lord so sluttissh, I the preye,

555. *fyve mile*, i.e. from Ospringe.
573. *som Chanoun.* The description accords
with that of a 'black Augustinian.'

603. *craftily*, H⁶ *thriftily.*

And is of power bettré clooth to beye,—
If that his dede accordé with thy speche ?
Tellé me that, and that I thee biseche.'
   ' Why ? ' quod this Yeman, ' wherto axe
      ye me ?   640
God help me so, for he shal never thee !—
But I wol nat avowé that I seye,
And therfore keepe it secree, I yow
     preye,—
He is to wys, in feith, as I bileeve ;
That that is overdoon it wol nat preeve
Aright ; as clerkés seyn, it is a vice.
Wherfore in that I holde hym lewed and
     nyce ;
For whan a man hath over-greet a wit,
Ful oft hym happeth to mysusen it.
So dooth my lord, and that me greveth
     soore.   650
God it amende ! I kan sey yow namoore.'
   ' Ther-of no fors, good Yeman,' quod
     oure Hoost,
' Syn of the konnyng of thy lord thow woost,
Telle how he dooth, I pray thee hertély,
Syn that he is so crafty and so sly ;
Where dwellé ye, if it to tellé be ? '
   ' In the suburbés of a toun,' quod he,
' Lurkynge in hernés, and in lanés blynde,
Where as thise robbours and thise theves
     by kynde,
Holden hir pryvee fereful residence, 660
As they that dar nat shewen hir presence ;
So faren we, if I shal seye the sothe.'
   ' Now,' quod oure Hoost, ' yet lat me
     talke to the ;
Why artow so discoloured of thy face ? '
   ' Peter ! ' quod he, ' God yeve it hardé
   * grace,
I am so uséd in the fyr to blowe,
That it hath chaungéd my colóur, I trowe.
I am nat wont in no mirour to prie,
But swynké soore, and lerné multiplie ;
We blondren ever, and pouren in the fir,
And for al that we faille of our desir, 671
For ever we lakken oure conclusioun.
To muchel folk we doon illusioun,
And borwé gold, be it a pound or two,
Or ten, or twelve, or manye sommés mo,
And make hem wenen, at the leesté weye,
That of a pound we koudé maké tweye ;
Yet is it fals ; but ay we han good hope

It for to doon and after it we grope ;
But that sciénce is so fer us biforn   680
We mowen nat, al though we hadde it
     sworn,
It over-take, it slit awey so faste.
It wole us maken beggers atté laste.'

   Whil this Yeman was thus in his talkyng
This Chanoun drough hym neer, and herde
     al thyng
Which this Yeman spak, for suspecioun
Of mennés speche ever haddé this
     Chanoun ;
For Catoun seith that he that gilty is
Demeth alle thyng be spoke of hym, y-wis.
That was the cause he gan so ny hym drawe
To his Yeman, to herknen al his sawe,
And thus he seyde unto his Yeman tho :
   ' Hoold thou thy pees, and spek no
     wordés mo !
For if thou do, thou shalt it deere abye !
Thou sclaundrest me, heere in this
     compaignye,
And eek discoverest that thou sholdest
     hyde.'
   ' Ye ? ' quod our Hoost, ' telle on what
     so bityde ;
Of al his thretyng rekké nat a myte ! '
   ' In feith,' quod he, ' namoore I do
     but lyte.'
   And whan this Chanoun saugh it wolde
     nat be,   700
But his Yeman wolde telle his pryvétee,
He fledde awey for verray sorwe and
     shame.
   ' A ! ' quod the Yeman, ' heere shal
     arise a game ;
Al that I kan anon now wol I telle,
Syn he is goon,—the foulé feend hym
     quelle !
For never heer-after wol I with hym meete,
For peny ne for pound, I yow biheete !
He that me broghté first unto that game,
Er that he dye, sorwe have he and shame ;
For it is ernest to me, by my feith ! 710
That feele I wel, what so any man seith.
And yet for al my smert, and al my grief,

688. *Catoun : De Morib.* i. 17 : ' Conscius ipse
sibi de se putat omnia dici.'
690. *That was the cause,* H⁵ *By cause of
that.*

249

For al my sorwe, labour, and meschief,
I koude never leve it in no wise.
Now wolde God, my witte myghte suffise
To tellen al that longeth to that art ;
And nathelees yow wol I tellen part ;
Syn that my lord is goon I wol nat spare ;
Swich thyng as that I knowe I wol declare.'

CANON'S YEOMAN'S TALE

Heere bigynneth the Chanouns Yeman his Tale

[PART 1]

With this Chanoun I dwelt have seven
yeer,   720
And of his science am I never the neer ;
Al that I hadde I have y-lost ther-by,
And, God woot, so hath many mo than I.
Ther I was wont to be right fressh and gay
Of clothyng and of oother good array,
Now may I were an hose upon myn heed ;
And wher my colour was bothe fressh
and reed,
Now is it wan and of a leden hewe,—
Who so it useth, soore shal he rewe,—
And of my swynk yet blered is myn eye ; 730
Lo, which avantage is to multiplie !
That slidynge science hath me maad so
bare,
That I have no good wher that ever I fare ;
And yet I am endetted so ther-by,
Of gold that I have borwed, trewely,
That whil I lyve I shal it quite never,—
Lat every man be war by me for ever.
What maner man that casteth hym ther-to,
If he continue, I holde his thrift y-do ;
For, so helpe me God, ther-by shal he
nat wynne,   740
But empte his purs, and make his wittes
thynne ;
And whan he thurgh his madnesse and folye
Hath lost his owene good thurgh jupartye,
Thanne he exciteth oother folk ther-to,
To lesen hir good, as he hymself hath do ;
For unto shrewes joye it is and ese,
To have hir felawes in peyne and disese,—
Thus was I ones lerned of a clerk.
Of that no charge, I wol speke of oure werk.
Whan we been there as we shul exercise

Oure elvysshe craft, we semen wonder wise,
Oure termes been so clergial and so
queynte ;
I blowe the fir til that myn herte feynte.
What sholde I tellen eche proporcioun
Of thynges whiche that we werche upon ;
As on fyve or sixe ounces, may wel be,
Of silver, or som oother quantitee ;
And bisye me to telle yow the names
Of orpyment, brent bones, iren squames,
That into poudre grounden been ful smal ?
And in an erthen pot how put is al,   761
And salt y-put in, and also papeer,
Biforn thise poudres that I speke of heer,
And wel y-covered with a lampe of glas ;
And muchel oother thyng which that
ther was,
And of the pot and glasses enlutyng,
That of the eyr myghte passe out no thyng,
And of the esy fir, and smart also,
Which that was maad, and of the care and wo
That we hadden in oure matires sublymyng,
And in amalgamyng and calcenyng   771
Of quyk-silver, y-clept mercurie crude ;
For alle oure sleightes we kan nat conclude.
Oure orpyment and sublymed mercurie,
Oure grounden litarge eek on the porfurie,
Of ech of thise of ounces a certeyn,
Noght helpeth us, oure labour is in veyn ;
Ne eek oure spirites ascencioun,
Ne oure matires that lyen al fix adoun,
Mowe in oure werkyng no thyng us availle ;
For lost is al oure labour and travaille,   781
And al the cost, a twenty devel way,
Is lost also, which we upon it lay.
Ther is also ful many another thyng
That is unto oure craft apertenyng,*
Thogh I by ordre hem nat reherce kan,
By-cause that I am a lewed man,
Yet wol I telle hem as they come to mynde,
Thogh I ne kan nat sette hem in hir
kynde,—
As boole armonyak, vertgrees, boras,   790
And sondry vessels maad of erthe and glas ;
Oure urynals, and our descensories,
Violes, crosletz, and sublymatories,
Cucurbites, and alambikes eek,
And othere swiche, deere ynough a leek ;

790. *boole armonyak*, astringent earth, from Armenia.

Nat nedeth it for to reherce hem alle,—
Wátres rubifiyng, and bolés galle,
Arsenyk, sal armonyak, and brymstoon ;
And herbés koude I telle eek many oon,
As egremoyne, valerian, and lunárie, 800
And othere swiche, if that me listé tarie ;
Oure lampés brennyng bothé nyght and
   day,
To brynge aboute oure purpos if we may ;
Oure fourneys eek of calcinacioun,
And of watrés albificacioun,
Unslekkéd lym, chalk, and gleyre of an ey,
Poudrés diverse, asshes, donge, pisse, and
   cley,
Cered pokettes, sal-peter and vitriole,
And diverse firés maad of wode and cole ;
Sal-tartre, alkaly and sal-preparat ;   810
And combust matires, and coagulat ;
Cley maad with hors and mannés heer,
   and oille
Of tartre, alum, glas, berme, wort and
   argoille,
Resalgar, and oure matires enbibyng,
And eek of oure matires encorporyng,
And of oure silver citrinacioun,
Oure cémentyng and fermentacioun,
Oure yngottés, testés, and many mo.
   I wol yow telle as was me taught also
The fouré spirites and the bodies sevene,
By ordre, as ofte I herde my lord hem
   nevene.   821
   The firsté spirit quyk-silver called is,
The seconde orpyment, the thridde, y-wis,
Sal-armonyak, and the ferthe brymstoon.
The bodyes sevene eek, lo, hem heere
   anoon !
   Sol gold is, and Luna silver we threpe,
Mars iren, Mercurie quyk-silver we clepe,
Saturnus leed, and Juppiter is tyn,
And Venus coper, by my fader kyn.
   This curséd craft whoso wol exercise 830
He shal no good han that hym may suffise ;
For al the good he spendeth ther-aboute
He lesé shal ; ther-of have I no doute.
Whoso that listeth outen his folie,
Lat hym come forth and lerné multiplie ;
And every man that oght hath in his cofre,
Lat hym appiere and wexe a philosophre ;
Ascauncé that crafte is so light to leere !
Nay, nay, God woot, al be he monk or frere,

Preest or chanoun, or any oother wyght, 840
Though he sitte at his book bothe day
   and night
In lernyng of this elvysshe nycé loore,
Al is in veyn, and, *parde*, muchel moore !
To lerne a lewéd man this subtiltee,—
Fy ! spek nat ther-of, for it wol nat bee ;
And konne he letterure, or konne he noon,
As in effect he shal fynde it al oon ;
For bothé two, by my salvacioun,
Concluden in multiplicacioun
Ylíké wel, whan they han al y-do,— 850
This is to seyn, they faillen bothé two.
   Yet forgat I to maken rehersaille
Of watrés corosif, and of lymaille,
And of bodies mollificacioun,
And also of hire induracioun,
Oillés, ablucions, and metal fusible,—
To tellen al wolde passen any bible
That owher is ; wherfore, as for the beste,
Of alle thise namés now wol I me reste,
For as I trowe I have yow toold ynowe 860
To reyse a feend, al looke he never so rowe.
   A ! nay ! lat be ; the philosophres stoon,
Elixer clept, we sechen faste echoon,
For hadde we hym, thanne were we siker
   ynow ;
But, unto God of hevene I make avow,
For al oure craft, whan we han al y-do,
With al oure sleighte, he wol nat come us to.
He hath y-made us spenden muchel good,
For sorwe of which almoost we wexen
   wood,   869
But that good hopé crepeth in oure herte,
Supposynge ever, though we soré smerte,
To be releevéd by hym afterward.
Swich supposyng and hope is sharpe and
   hard ;
I warne yow wel it is to seken ever ;
That *futur temps* hath maad men to dis-
   sever,
In trust ther-of, from al that ever they
   hadde.
Yet of that art they kan nat wexen sadde,
For unto hem it is a bitter-sweete,—
So semeth it,—for nadde they but a sheete,
Which that they myghté wrappe hem
   inne at nyght,   880
And a brat to walken inne by day-lyght,

881. *brat*, cloak ; H⁶ *bak*, back-cloth.

They wolde hem selle, and spenden on
　this craft ;
They kan nat styntè til no thyng be laft ;
And evermoorè, where that ever they goon,
Men may hem knowè by smel of brymstoon.
For al the world they stynken as a goot ;
Hir savour is so rammyssh and so hoot
That though a man a milè from hem be
The savour wole infecte hym, trustè me.
Lo thus by smellyng, and threedbare
　array,　　890
If that men liste, this folk they knowè may;
And if a man wole aske hem pryvèly,
Why they been clothèd so unthriftily,
They right anon wol rownen in his ere
And seyn, that if that they espièd were,
Men wolde hem slee by-cause of hir science.
Lo, thus this folk bitrayen innocence !
　Passe over this, I go my tale unto.
Er that the pot be on the fire y-do,
Of metals with a certeyn quantitee　900
My lord hem trempreth, and no man but
　he,—
Now he is goon I dare seyn boldèly,—
For as men seyn he kan doon craftily,
Algate I woot wel he hath swich a name,
And yet ful oft he renneth in a blame ;
And wite ye how?　Ful ofte it happeth so
The pot to-breketh, and farewel, al is go.
Thise metals been of so greet violence
Oure wallès mowe nat make hem
　resistence,　　909
But if they weren wroght of lym and stoon,
They percen so, and thurgh the wal they
　goon,
And somme of hem synken into the
　ground,—
Thus han we lost by tymès many a pound,—
And somme are scatered al the floor aboute,
Somme lepe into the roof, withouten doute.
Though that the feend noght in oure
　sighte hym shewe,
I trowe he with us be, that ilkè shrewe !
In hellè, where that he is lord and sire,
Nis ther moore wo, ne moore rancour,
　ne ire.　　919
Whan that oure pot is broke, as I have
　sayd,
Every man chit and halt hym yvele apayd.

919. H⁵ *Nis ther no more wo, ne anger, ne ire.*

Somme seyde it was along on the fir
　makyng,
Somme seydè nay, it was on the blowyng,—
Thanne was I fered, for that was myn office.
　‘ Straw ! ’ quod the thriddè, ‘ ye been
　lewed and nyce,
It was nat trempèd as it oghtè be.’
　‘ Nay,’ quod the fourthè, ‘ stynt and
　herknè me ;
By-cause our fir ne was nat maad of beech,
That is the cause, and oother noon, so
　theech.’
I kan nat telle wheron it was along,　930
But wel I woot greet strif us is among.
　‘ What ! ’ quod my lord, ‘ ther is
　namoore to doone ;
Of thise perils I wol be war eft-soone.
I am right siker that the pot was crased ;
Be as be may, be ye no thyng amased.
As usage is, lat swepe the floor as swithe,
Plukke up your hertès and beeth glad
　and blithe ! ’
The mullok on an heepe i-swepèd was,
And on the floor y-cast a canèvas,　939
And al this mullok in a syve y-throwe,
And sifted and y-pikèd many a throwe.
　‘ *Pardee !* ’ quod oon, ‘ somwhat of
　oure metal
Yet is ther heere, though that we han
　nat al.
Al though this thyng myshappèd have as
　now,
Another tyme it may be wel ynow.
Us mostè putte oure good in áventure ;
A marchant, *pardee !* may nat ay endure,
Trusteth me wel, in his prosperitee.
Somtyme his good is drenchèd in the see,
And somtyme comth it sauf unto the londe.’
　‘ Pees ! ’ quod my lord, ‘ the nexte
　tyme I shal fonde　951
To bryngen oure craft al in another plite ;
And but I do, sires, lat me han the wite ;
Ther was defaute in somwhat, wel I woot.’
　Another seyde the fir was over hoot ;
But, be it hoot or coold, I dar seye this,
That we concluden evermoore amys.
We faille of that which that we wolden
　have,
And in oure madnesse evermoore we rave ;

941. *y-pikèd*, picked over ; H⁵ *y-plukkèd.*

And whan we been togidrės everichoon
Every man semeth a Salomon ;   961
But al thyng which that shyneth as the gold,
Nis nat gold, as that I have herd it told ;
Ne every appul that is fair at eye
Ne is nat good, what so men clappe or crye.
Right so, lo, fareth it amongės us :
Hė that semeth the wiseste, by Jhesus,
Is moost fool, whan it cometh to the preef;
And he that semeth trewest is a theef.
That shul ye knowe, er that I fro yow
     wende,   970
By that I of my tale have maad an ende.

[PART II]

Ther is a Chanoun of Religioun
Amongės us wolde infecte al a toun.
Thogh it as greet were as was Nynyvee,
Rome, Alisaundre, Troye, and othere
     three.
His sleightės and his infinit falsnesse
Ther koudė no man writen, as I gesse,
Though that he lyvė myghte a thousand
     yeer.
In al this world of falshede nis his peer,
For in his termės so he wolde hym
     wynde,   980
And speke his wordės in so sly a kynde,
Whanne he communė shal with any wight,
That he wol make hym doten anon right,
But it a feend be, as hymselven is.
Ful many a man hath he bigiled er this,
And wole, if that he lyvė may a while ;
And yet men ride and goon ful many a mile
Hym for to seke and have his aqueyntaunce,
Noght knowynge of his falsė governaunce ;
And if yow list to yeve me audience, 990
I wol it tellė heere in youre presence.

     But, worshipful chanouns religious,
Ne demeth nat that I desclaundre youre
     hous,
Although my talė of a chanoun bee ;
Of every ordrė som shrewe is, *pardee*,
And God forbede that al a compaignye
Sholde rewe o singuleer mannės folye.
To sclaundre yow is no thyng myn entente,
But to correcten that is mys, I mente.
This talė was nat oonly toold for yow, 1000

     978. *lyvė myghtė*, Hᵉ *mighte lyven.*

But eek for othere mo ; ye woot wel how
That among Cristės apostellės twelve
Ther nas no traytour but Judas hymselve.
Thanne why sholde al the remenant have
     a blame,
That giltlees were ? By yow I seye the
     same,
Save oonly this, if ye wol herkne me, —
If any Judas in youre covent be,
Remoeveth hym bitymės, I yow rede,
If shame, or los, may causen any drede,
And beeth no thyng displesėd, I yow
     preye,   1010
But in this cas herketh what I shal seye.

     In Londoun was a preest, an annuėleer,
That ther-inne dwellėd haddė many a yeer,
Which was so plesaunt and so servysable
Unto the wyf, where as he was at table,
That she wolde suffre hym no thyng for
     to paye
For bord ne clothyng, wente he never so
     gaye ;
And spendyng silver hadde he right ynow.
Ther-of no fors, I wol procede as now,
And tellė forth my tale of the chanoun
That broghtė this preest to confusioun.
     This falsė chanoun cam upon a day
Unto this preestės chambre, wher he lay,
Bisechynge hym to lene hym a certeyn
Of gold, and he wolde quite it hym ageyn.
' Leene me a marc,' quod he, ' but dayės
     three,
And at my day I wol it quiten thee ;
And if so be that thow me fyndė fals
Another day, do hange me by the hals.'
     This preest hym took a marc, and that
     as swithe,   1030
And this chanoun hym thankėd oftė sithe,
And took his leve, and wentė forthe his
     weye,
And at the thriddė day broghte his moneye,
And to the preest he took his gold agayn,
Wher-of this preest was wonder glad and
     fayn.
' Certės,' quod he, ' no thyng anoyeth me
To lene a man a noble, or two, or thre,

1012. *an*, om. E.
1012. *annuėleer*, a priest employed to sing
anniversary masses for the dead.

253

Or what thyng were in my possessioun,
Whan he so trewe is of condicioun   1039
That in no wise he breké wole his day;
To swich a man I kan never seye nay.'
  'What!' quod this chanoun, 'sholde
      I be untrewe?
Nay, that were thyng y-fallen al of newe.
Trouthe is a thyng that I wol ever kepe,
Unto that day in which that I shal crepe
Into my grave, or ellis, God forbede!
Bileveth this, as siker as the Crede.
God thanke I, and in good tymé be it sayd,
That ther was never man yet yvele apayd
For gold ne silver that he to me lente;
Ne never falshede in myn herte I mente;
And, sire,' quod he, 'now of my
      pryvétee,—
Syn ye so goodlich han been unto me,
And kithéd to me so greet gentillesse,—
Somwhat to quyté with youre kyndénesse
I wol yow shewe, and if yow list to leere.
I wol yow teché pleynly the manere
How I kan werken in philosophie;
Taketh good heede ye shul wel seen at eye
That I wol doon a maistrie er I go.'   1060
  'Ye,' quod the preest, 'ye, sire, and
      wol ye so?
Marie! ther-of I pray yow hertély.'
  'At youre comandément, sire, trewély,'
Quod the chanoun, 'and ellis God
      forbeede.'
  Loo, how this theef koude his servicé
      beede!
Ful sooth it is that swiche profréd servyse
Stynketh, as witnessen thise oldé wyse;
And that ful soone I wol it verifie
In this chanoun, roote of alle trecherie,
That ever moore delit hath and glad-
      nesse,—   1070
Swiche feendly thoughtés in his herte
      impresse,—
How Cristés peple he may to meschief
      brynge.
God kepe us from his false dissymulynge!
  Noght wisté this preest with whom
      that he delt,
Ne of his harm comynge he no thyng felte.
O sely preest, O sely innocent!
With coveitise anon thou shalt be blent.
O gracélees, ful blynd is thy conceite,

No thyng ne artow war of the deceite
Which that this fox y-shapen hath for thee;
His wily wrenchés thou ne mayst nat flee;
Wherfore, to go to the conclusioun
That refereth to thy confusioun,
Unhappy man, anon I wol me hye
To tellen thyn unwit and thy folye,
And eek the falsnesse of that oother
      wrecche,
As ferforth as my konnyngé may strecche.
  This chanoun was my lord, ye wolden
      weene—
Sire Hoost, in feith, and by the hevenes
      queene,
It was another chanoun and nat hee,   1090
That kan an hundred foold moore subtiltee.
He hath bitrayéd folkés many tyme;
Of his falshede it dulleth me to ryme.
Éver whan I speke of his falshede,
For shame of hym my chekés wexen rede;
Algatés they bigynnen for to glowe,
For reednesse have I noon, right wel I
      knowe,
In my visagé; for fumés diverse
Of metals, whiche ye han herd me reherce,
Consumed and wasted han my reedénesse.
Now taak heede of this chanons cursed-
      nesse.   1101
  'Sire,' quod he to the preest, 'lat youre
      man gon
For quyk-silver, that we hadde it anon,
And lat hym bryngen ounces two or three,
And whan he comth, as fasté shal ye see
A wonder thyng which ye saugh never
      er this.'
  'Sire,' quod the preest, 'it shal be
      doon y-wis.'
He bad his servant fecchen hym this thyng,
And he al redy was at his biddyng,   1109
And wente hym forth, and cam anon agayn
With this quyk-silver, soothly for to
      sayn;
And toke thise ounces thre to the chanoun,
And he hem leydé faire and wel adoun,
And bad the servant colés for to brynge,
That he anon myghte go to his werkynge.
  The colés right anon weren y-fet,
And this chanoun took out a crossélet
Of his bosom, and shewed it to the preest.

1111. *soothly*, H⁸ *schortly*.

'This instrument,' quod he, 'which that
    thou seest,   .
Taake in thyn hand and put thy self therinne
Of this quyk-silver an ounce, and heer
    bigynne,   1121
In the name of Crist, to wexe a philosofre.
Ther been ful fewe to whiche I woldé profre
To shewen hem thus muche of my science :
For ye shul seeñ heer by experience,
That this quyk-silver wol I mortifye,
Right in youre sighte anon, I wol nat lye,
And make it as good silver and as fyn,
As ther is any in youre purse or myn,   1130
Or ellés where, and make it malliable ;
And ellés holdeth me fals and unable
Amongés folk for ever to appeere.
I have a poudre heer, that coste me deere,
Shal make al good, for it is cause of al
My konnyng, which that I yow shewen
    shal.
Voydith youre man and lat hym be
    ther-oute,
And shette the doré, whils we been aboute
Oure pryvétee, that no man us espie,
Whilés we werke in this philosophie.'
    Al as he bad fulfillé d was in dede ;   1140
This ilké servant anonright out yede,
And his maister shetté the dore anon,
And to hire labour spedily they gon.
    This preest at this cursé d chanouns
        biddýng
Upon the fir anon setté this thyng,
And blew the fir and bisyed hym ful faste;
And this chanoun into the crosselet cast
A poudre,—noot I wher-of that it was
Y-maad, outher of chalk, outher of glas,
Or somwhat ellés, was nat worth a flye,—
To blynde with the preest, and bad hym hye
The colés for to couchen al above
The crosselet ; 'For in tokenyng I thee
    love,'
Quod this chanoun, 'thyne owene handés
    two
Shul werche al thyng which shal heer
    be do.'
    'Graunt mercy !' quod the preest,
        and was ful glad,
And couchéd colés as that chanoun bad ;
And while he bisy was, this feendly
    wrecche,

This false chanoun,—the foulé feend hym
    fecche !—   1159
Out of his bosom took a bechen cole,
In which ful subtilly was maad an hole,
And therinne put was of silver lemaille
An ounce, and stoppéd was withouten faille
The hole with wex, to kepe the lemaille in ;
And understondeth, that this falsé gyn
Was nat maad ther, but it was maad bifore ;
And othere thyngés I shal tellen moore
Herafterward, whiche that he with hym
    broghte ;
Er he cam there, hym to bigile he thoghte;
And so he dide, er that they wente
    atwynne ;   1170
Til he had tervéd hym, he koude nat
    blynne.
It dulleth me, whan that I of hym speke ;
On his falshedé fayn wolde I me wreke,
If I wiste how, but he is heere and there,
He is so variaunt, he abit nowhere.
    But taketh heede now, sires, for
        Goddés love !
He took this cole of which I spak above,
And in his hand he baar it pryvély,
And whyles the preest couchédé bisily
The colés, as I toldé yow er this,   1180
This chanoun seydé, 'Freend, ye doon
    amys,
This is nat couchéd as it oghté be ;
But soone I shal amenden it,' quod he.
'Now lat me medle ther-with but a while,
For of yow have I pitee, by Seint Gile !
Ye been right hoot, I se wel how ye swete ;
Have heer a clooth, and wipe awey the
    wete.'
And whylés that the preest wipéd his face,
This chanoun took his cole with hardé
    grace,   1189
And leyde it above, upon the myddéward
Of the crosselet, and blew wel afterward,
Til that the colés gonné fasté brenne.
    'Now yeve us drynké,' quod the
        chanoun thenne,
'As swithe al shal be wel, I undertake.
Sitté we doun, and lat us myrie make' ;

1171. *tervéd*, stripped. Dr. Skeat's restoration
for the common reading *ternéd.*
1189. *with hardé* (Camb. *sory*) *grace*, H⁶ *I
schrewe his faas.*

And whan that this chanonès bechen cole
Was brent, al the lemaille out of the hole
Into the crosselet fil anon adoun,
And so it mostè nedès, by resoun,   1199
Syn it so evene aboven couchèd was ;
But ther-of wiste the preest no thyng, alas !
He demèd alle the coles ylichè good,
For of that sleighte he no thyng under-
stood ;
And whan this alkamystre saugh his
tyme,—
' Ris up,' quod he, ' sire preest, and
stonde by me,
And for I woot wel ingot have ye noon,
Gooth walketh forth, and brynge us a
chalk stoon,
For I wol make it of the samè shape
That is an ingot, if I may han hape ;
And bryngeth eek with yow a bolle or a
panne   1210
Ful of water, and ye shul se wel thanne
How that oure bisynesse shal thryve and
preeve ;
And yet, for ye shul han no mysbileeve,
Ne wrong conceite of me in youreabsence,
I ne wol nat been out of youre presence,
But go with yow, and come with yow
ageyn.'
The chambrè dorè, shortly for to seyn,
They openèd andshette, and went hir weye,
And forth with hem they carieden the keye,
And coome agayn withouten any delay.
What sholde I tarien al the longè day ?
He took the chalk and shoope it in the
wise
Of an ingot, as I shal yow devyse.
   I seye, he took out of his owene sleeve
A teyne of silver—yvele moot he cheeve !—
Which that ne was nat but an ounce of
weighte ;
And taketh heede now of his cursed
sleighte.
   He shoope his ingot in lengthe and
eek in breede
Óf this teyne, withouten any drede,
So slyly that the preest it nat espide,   1230
And in his sleve agayn he gan it hide,
And fro the fir he took up his mateere
And in thyngot putte it with myrie cheere,
And in the water-vessel he it caste,

Whan that hym luste, and bad the preest
as faste,
' Look what ther is, put in thin hand
and grope,
Thow fyndè shalt ther silver, as I hope.'
What, devel of hellè ! sholde it ellis be ?
Shavyng of silver silver is, *parde!*   1239
He putte his hand in, and took up a teyne
Of silver fyn, and glad iñ every veyne
Was this preest, when he saugh that it
was so.
' Goddès blessyng, and his moodres also,
And allè halwès, have ye, sire chanoun !'
Seydè this preest, ' and I hir malisoun !
But, and ye vouchèsauf to techen me
This noble craft and this subtilitee,
I wol be youre in al that ever I may.'
   Quod the chanoun, ' Yet wol I make
assay   1249
The seconde tyme, that ye may taken heede
And been expert of this, and in youre neede
Another daye assaye in myn absence
This disciplyne, and this crafty science.
Lat take another ouncè,' quod he tho,
' Of quyk-silver, withouten wordès mo,
And do therwith as ye han doon er this
With that oother, which that now silver is.'
   This preest hym bisieth in al that he kan
To doon as this chanoun, this cursèd man,
Comanded hym, and faste he blew the fir,
For to come to theffect of his desir ;   1261
And this chanoun, right in the meenè
while,
Al redy was the preest eft to bigile,
And for a contenaunce in his hand he bar
An holwè stikkè,—taak kepe and be
war,—
In the ende of which an ouncè and namoore
Of silver lemaille put was (as bifore
Was in his cole) and stoppèd with wex weel,
For to kepe in his lemaille every deel. 1269
And whil this preest was in his bisynesse,
This chanoun with his stikkè gan hym
dresse
To hym anon, and his poudrè caste in
As he did er,—the devel out of his skyn
Hym terve, I pray to God, for his falshede !
For he was ever fals in thoght and dede,—
And with this stikke, above the crossèlet,

1274. *terve*, Hᵉ *torne, turne* ; see l. 1171.

That was ordeynèd with that falsè get,
He stired the colès, til relentè gan
The wex agayn the fir, as every man,
But it a fool be, woot wel it moot nede; 1280
And al that in the stikkè was out yede,
And in the crosselet hastily it fel.
　Nów, good sires, what wol ye bet
　　than wel?
Whan that this preest thus was bigiled
　ageyn,
Supposynge noght but treuthè, sooth to
　seyn,
He was so glad that I kan nat expresse
In no manere his myrthe and his gladnesse;
And to the chanoun he profred eftsoone
Body and good. 'Ye,' quod the chanoun
　soone,
'Though poure I be, crafty thou shalt
　me fynde ; 1290
I warnè thee yet is ther moore bihynde.
Is ther any coper her-inne?' seyde he.
' Ye,' quod the preest, 'sire, I trowe
　wel ther be.'
' Ellès go bye us som, and that as swithe.
Now, goodè sire, go forth thy wey and
　hy the.'
He wente his wey, and with the coper cam,
And this chanoun it in his handès nam,
And of that coper weyed out but an ounce.
Ál to symple is my tonge to pronounce,
As ministre of my wit, the doublenesse 1300
Of this chanoun, roote of alle cursednesse.
He semed freendly to hem that knewe
　hym noght,
But he was feendly bothe in werk and
　thoght.
It weerieth me to telle of his falsnesse,
And nathèlees yet wol I it expresse
To that entent men may be war therby,
And for noon oother causè, trewèly.
　He puttè the ounce of coper in the
　　crosselet,
And on the fir as swithe he hath it set,
And caste in poudre, and made the preest
　to blowe, 1310
And in his werkyng for to stoupè lowe,
As he dide er, and al nas but a jape.
Right as hym liste the preest he made
　his ape ;
And afterward in the ingot he it caste,

And in the pannè putte it at the laste,
Of water. In he putte his owene hand ;
And in his sleve, as ye biforen-hand
Herdè me telle, he hadde a silver teyne ;
He slyly tooke it out,—this cursèd heyne,—
Unwityng this preest of his falsè craft, 1320
And in the pannès botme he hath it laft,
And in the water rombleth to and fro,
And wonder pryvèly took up also
The coper teyne, noght knowyngè this
　preest,
And hidde it, and hym hentè by the breest,
And to hym spak and thus seyde in his game,
' Stoupeth adoun, by God, ye be to blame,
Helpeth me now, as I dide yow whil-eer,
Putte in youre hand, and looketh what
　is theer.'
　This preest took up this silver teyne
　　anon, 1330
And thannè seyde the chanoun, 'Lat us gon
With thise thre teynès whiche that we han
　wroght
To som goldsmyth, and wite if they been
　ought ;
For, by my feith, I noldè for myn hood,
But if they werè silver fyn and good,
And that as swithè preevèd it shal bee.'
　Unto the goldsmyth with thise teynès
　　three
They wente, and putte thise teynès in
　assay
To fir and hamer; myghte no man seye nay,
But that they weren as hem oghtè be. 1340
　This sottèd preest, who was gladder
　　than he?
Was never brid gladder agayn the day,
Ne nyghtyngale in the sesoun of May,
Nas never man that lustè bet to synge,
Ne ladye lustier in carolynge,
Or, for to speke of love and wommanhede,
Ne knyght in armes to doon an hardy dede
To stonden in gracè of his lady deere,
Than haddè this preest this soory craft
　to leere ; 1349
And to the chanoun thus he spak and seyde :
' For love of God, that for us allè deyde,
And as I may deserve it unto yow,
What shal this receite costè, telleth now?'
　' By oure lady,' quod this chanoun,
　　' it is deere,

8   257

I warne yow wel, for save I and a frere
In Engèlond ther kan no man it make.'
  'No fors,' quod he, 'now, sire, for
    Goddès sake,
What shal I payè? Telleth me, I preye.'
  'Y-wis,' quod he, 'it is ful deere, I seye.
Sire, at o word, if that thee list it have,
Ye shul paye fourty pound, so God me
    save ;   1361
And nere the freendshipe that ye dide er this
To me ye sholdè payè moore, y-wis.'
  This preest the somme of fourty pound
    anon
Of noblès fette, and took hem everichon
To this chanoun, for this ilkè receit.
Al his werkyng nas but fraude and deceit.
  'Sire preest,' he seyde, 'I kepè han
    no loos
Of my craft, for I wolde it kept were cloos,
And, as ye love me, kepeth it secree ; 1370
For, and men knewen al my soutiltee,
By God, they wolden han so greet envye
To me, by cause of my philosophye,
I sholde be deed ; ther were noon oother
    weye.'
  'God it forbeedè,' quod the preest ;
    ' what say ye?
Yet hadde I levere spenden al the good
Which that I have,—and ellès wexe I
    wood !—
Than that ye sholden falle in swiche
    mescheef.'
  'For youre good wyl, sire, have ye
    right good preef,'
Quod the chanoun, ' and farewel, *grant*
  mercy ! '   1380
He wente his wey and never the preest
    hym sy
After that day; and whan that this preest
    sholde
Maken assay at swich tyme as he wolde
Of this receit, farwel, it wolde nat be !
Lo, thus byjapèd and bigiled was he.
Thus maketh he his introduccioun,
To bryngè folk to hir destruccioun.

  Considereth sires, how that in ech estaat,
Bitwixè men and gold ther is debaat
So ferforth, that unnethè is ther noon. 1390
This multiplying blent so many oon,

That, in good feith, I trowè that it bee
The causè grettest of swich scarsetee.
Philosophres speken so mystily
In this craft, that men kan nat come therby,
For any wit that men han now-a-dayes.
They mowe wel chiteren as doon these
    jayes,
And in hir termès sette hir lust and peyne,
But to hir purpos shul they never atteyne.
A man may lightly lerne, if he have aught,
To multiplie, and bryngè his good to
    naught.   1401
Lo, swich a lucre is in this lusty game
A mannès myrthe it wol turne unto grame,
And empten also grete and hevye purses,
And maken folk for to purchacen curses
Of hem that han hir good therto y-lent.
O fy, for shamè ! they that han been brent,
Allas ! kan they nat flee the firès heete ?
Ye that it use I redè ye it leete,
Lest ye lese al, for 'bet than never is late';
Never to thryvè were to long a date. 1411
Though ye prolle ay, ye shul it never fynde,
Ye been as boold as is Bayard the blynde,
That blondreth forth and peril casteth
    noon.
He is as boold to renne agayn a stoon,
As for to goon bisidès in the weye.
So faren ye that multiplie, I seye ;
If that youre eyen kan nat seen aright,
Looke that youre myndè lakkè noght his
    sight,
For though ye looken never so brode, and
    stare,   1420
Ye shul nat wynne a myte on that chaffare,
But wasten al that ye may rape and renne.
Withdraweth the fir, lest it to fastè
    brenne,—
Medleth namoorè with that art, I mene
For, if ye doon, youre thrift is goon ful clene:
And right as swithe, I wol yow tellen heere,
What philosophres seyn in this mateere.
  Lo, thus seith Arnold of the Newè-Toun,
As his *Rosarie* maketh mencioun ;
He seith right thus, withouten any lye, 1430
Ther may no man mercurie mortifie,
But it be with his brother knowlechyng.

1413. *Bayard*, a typical name for a horse.
1428. *Arnold of the Newe-Toun*, Arnoldus de
Villanova, a philosophical physician of the 13th
century.

258

How that he which that first seydè this
    thyng
Of philosophres fader was, Hermes ;
He seith how that the dragon doutèlees
Ne dyeth nat, but if that he be slayn
With his 'brother'; and that is for to sayn
By the dragon Mercurie, and noon oother,
He understood, and brymstoon by his
    brother,
That out of Sol and Luna were y-drawe ;
'And therfore,' seydè he, 'taak heede
    to my sawe ;   1441
Lat no man bisye hym this arte for to seche,
But if that he thentencioun and speche
Of philosophres understondè kan ;
And, if he do, he is a lewèd man,
For this science and this konnyng,' quod he,
' Is of the secree of secrees, *pardee*.'
Also ther was a disciple of Plato
That on a tymè seydè his maister to,
As his book *Senior* wol bere witnesse, 1450
And this was his demande, in soothfast-
    nesse,
' Telle me the namè of the privee stoon.'
   And Plato answerde unto hym anoon,
' Takè the stoon that *Titanos* men name '—

1434. *Hermes, i.e.* Hermes Trismegistus.
1435. *the dragon*, Mercury.
1440. *Sol and Luna, i.e.* gold and silver.
1447. The allusion is to the pseudo-Aristotelian
Secreta Secretorum.
1450. *his book Senior*. 'The book alluded to is
printed in the *Theatrum Chemicum* under this
title : "Senioris Zadith fil.   Hamuelis tabula
chemica."   The story which follows of Plato and
his disciples is there told, with some variations,
of Solomon ' (Tyrwhitt). Dr. Skeat notes that
the name Plato occurs three times only a few
lines below, which explains Chaucer's mistake.

' Which is that ? ' quod he. '*Magnasia*
    is the same,'
Seydè Plato.   ' Ye, sire, and is it thus ?
This is *ignotum per ignocius*.
What is Magnasia, good sire, I yow preye ?'
' It is a water that is maad, I seye,
Of elementès fourè,' quod Plato.   1460
' Telle me the rootè, good sire,' quod
    he tho,
' Of that water, if it be yourè wille.'
' Nay, nay,' quod Plato, ' certein that
    I nylle ;
The philosophres sworn were everychoon
That they sholden discovere it unto noon,
Ne in no book it write in no manere,
For unto Crist it is so lief and deere,
That he wol nat that it discovered bee,
But where it liketh to his deitee
Man for tenspire, and eek for to deffende
Whom that hym liketh ; lo, this is the
    ende.'   1471
Thanne conclude I thus, sith that God
    of hevene
Ne wil nat that the philosophres nevene
How that a man shal come unto this
    stoon,
I rede as for the bestè lete it goon ;
For who so maketh God his adversarie,
As for to werken anythyng in contrarie
Of his wil, certès never shal he thryve,
Thogh that he multiplie terme of his lyve ;
And there a poynt ; for ended is my tale.
God sende every trewe man boote of his
    bale. *Amen.*   1481

1461. *rootè*, H⁶ *roche*.

GROUP H

Words of Divers of the Pilgrims

Woot ye nat where ther stant a litel toun,
Which that y-clepèd is Bobbe-up-and-
    doun,
Under the Blee in Caunterbury weye ?

2. *Bobbe-up-and-doun*, usually identified with
Harbledown, but in the parish of Thannington
there is a field of 'Up-and-Down' which, if,
as is probable, the old Canterbury road took a
somewhat different direction from the modern
one, may be the site intended.
3. *the Blee*, Blean forest.

Ther gan oure Hoostè for to jape and pleye,
And seydè, 'Sires, what ! Dun is in the
    Myre !
Is ther no man for preyere ne for hyre,
That wole awake oure felawe al bihynde ?
A theef myght hym ful lightly robbe and
    bynde.

5. *Dun is in the Myre* (the horse is stuck), the
name of an old game in which the company had
to extricate a wooden ' Dun ' from an imaginary
slough.

See how he nappeth ! see how, for cokkès
   bones !
As he wol fallè fro his hors atones.   10
Is that a Cook of Londoun? with
   meschaunce !
Do hym come forth, he knoweth his
   penaunce,
For he shal telle a talè, by my fey !
Although it be nat worth a botel hey.
Awake, thou Cook,' quod he, ' God yeve
   thee sorwe !
What eyleth thee to slepè by the morwe ?
Hastow had fleen al nyght, or artow
   dronke ?
Or hastow with som quene al nyght
   y-swonke,
So that thou mayst nat holden up thyn
   heed ?'
   This Cook, that was ful pale and no
     thyng reed,   20
Seyde to oure Hoost, ' So God my soulè
   blesse,
As ther is falle on me swich hevynesse,
Noot I nat why, that me were levere slepe
Thán the bestè galon wyn in Chepe.'
   ' Wel,' quod the Maunciple, ' if it may
     doon ese
To thee, sire Cook, and to no wight displese
Which that heere rideth in this com-
   paignye,
And that oure Hoost wole of his curteisye,
I wol as now excuse thee of thy tale,
For, in good feith, thy visage is ful pale,
Thyne eyen daswen eek, as that me
   thynketh,   31
And wel I woot thy breeth ful sourè
   stynketh,
That sheweth wel thou art nat wel disposed ;
Of me certeyn thou shalt nat been y-glosed.
See how he ganeth, lo, this dronken wight !
As though he woldè swolwe us anonright.
Hoold cloos thy mouth, man, by thy fader
   kyn !
The devel of hellè sette his foot ther-in !
Thy cursèd breeth infectè wole us alle.
Fy, stynkyng swyn ! fy, foulè moote thou
   falle !   40
A ! taketh heede, sires, of this lusty man !
Now, sweete sire, wol ye justen attè fan ?

Therto me thynketh ye been wel y-shape !
I trowè that ye dronken han wyn ape,
And that is whan men pleyen with a straw.'
   And with this speche the Cook wax
     wrooth and wraw,
And on the Manciple he gan noddè faste
For lakke of speche, and doun the hors
   hym caste,
Where as he lay till that men up hym took.
This was a fair chyvachee of a Cook.   50
Allas ! he naddè holde hym by his ladel !
And er that he agayn were in his sadel
Ther was greet showvyng, bothè to and fro,
To lifte hym up, and muchel care and wo,
So unweeldy was this sory, pallèd goost.
And to the Manciplè thanne spak oure
   Hoost :
   ' By-causè drynke hath dominacioun
Upon this man, by my savacioun,
I trowe, he lewedly wolde telle his tale,
For were it wyn, or oold or moysty ale,
That he hath dronke, he speketh in his
   nose,   61
And fneseth faste, and eek he hath the pose.
He hath also to do moore than ynough
To kepe hym and his capul out of slough ;
And if he fallè from his capul eftsoone,
Thanne shal we allè have ynogh to doone,
In liftyng up his hevy, dronken cors ;
Telle on thy tale, of hym make I no fors.
   ' But yet, Manciple, in feith thou art
     to nyce,
Thus openly repreve hym of his vice;   70
Another day he wole, peráventure,
Reclaymè thee and bryngè thee to lure,—
I meene, he spekè wole of smalè thynges
As for to pynchen at thy rekenynges :
That were nat honeste, if it cam to preef.'
   ' No,' quod the Manciple, ' that were
     a greet mescheef !
So myghte he lightly brynge me in the snare,
Yet hadde I levere payen for the mare
Which he rit on, than he sholde with me
   stryve.   79
I wol nat wratthe hym, al so moot I thryve !
That that I spake I seyde it in my bourde ;
And wite ye what? I have heer in a gourde

44. *wyn ape.* The lion, ape, sheep, and pig
represented degrees of drunkenness ; the ape
answering to the ' joyous' stage, an unkind jest
at the cook's sullenness.

260

A draghte of wyn, ye, of a ripé grape,
And right anon ye shul seen a good jape.
This Cook shal drynke ther-of, if that I may.
Up peyne of deeth, he wol nat seye me nay.'
  And certeynly, to tellen as it was,
Of this vessel the Cook dranke faste, allas !
What neded hym ? he drank ynough
      biforn ;   89
And whan he haddé pouped in this horn,
To the Manciple he took the gourde agayn ;
And of that drynke the Cook was wonder
      fayn,
And thankéd hym in swich wise as he
      koude.
  Thanne gan oure Hoost to laughen
      wonder loude,
And seyde, ' I se wel it is necessarie,
Where that we goon, good drynke we
      with us carie,
For that wol turné rancour and disese
Tacord and love, and many a wrong apese.
  ' O thou Bacus ! y-blessed be thy name !
That so kanst turnen ernest into game,
Worshipe and thank be to thy deitee !
Of that mateere ye gete namoore of me ;
Telle on thy tale, Manciple, I thee preye.'
  ' Wel, sire,' quod he, ' now herkneth
      what I seye.'

MANCIPLE'S TALE

Heere bigynneth The Manciples Tale of
the Crowe

Whan Phebus dwelled heere in this
      erthe adoun,
As oldé bookés maken mencioun,
He was the moosté lusty bachiler
In al this world, and eek the best archer.
He slow Phitoun, the serpent, as he lay
Slepynge agayn the sonne upon a day,
And many another noble worthy dede
He with his bowé wroghte, as men may
      rede.

Manciple's Tale. 'The fable of the Crow,
which is the subject of the Manciple's Tale, has
been related by so many authors from Ovid down
to Gower that it is impossible to say whom
Chaucer principally followed' (Tyrwhitt).
105. *erthe*, E *world.*
109. *Phitoun*, Python.

Pleyen he koude on every mynstralcie,
And syngen, that it was a melodie
To heeren of his cleeré voys the soun.
Certés the kyng of Thebés, Amphioun,
That with his syngyng walléd that citee,
Koude never syngen half so wel as hee.
Therto he was the semeliesté man   119
That is, or was, sith that the world bigan.
What nedeth it his fetures to discryve,
For in this world was noon so fair on lyve.
He was ther-with fulfild of gentillesse,
Of honour, and of parfit worthynesse.
  This Phebus that was flour of bachilrie,
As wel in fredom as in chivalrie,
For his desport, in signe eek of victorie
Of Phitoun, so as telleth us the storie,
Was wont to beren in his hand a bowe.
  Now hadde this Phebus in his hous a
      crowe   130
Which in a cage he fostred many a day,
And taughte it speken, as men teche a jay.
Whit was this crowe as is a snow-whit
      swan,
And countrefete the speche of every man
He koudé, whan he sholdé telle a talé ;
Ther-with in al this world no nyghtyngale
Ne koudé, by an hondred thousand deel,
Syngen so wonder myrily and weel.
  Now hadde this Phebus in his hous a wyf,
Which that he lovede mooré than his lyf,
And nyght and day dide ever his diligence
Hir for to plese, and doon hire reverence ;
Save oonly, if the sothe that I shal sayn,
Jalous he was and wolde have kept hire fayn,
For hym were looth byjapéd for to be ;
And so is every wight in swich degree ;
But all in ydel, for it availleth noght.
A good wyf that is clene of werk and thoght
Sholde nat been kept in noon awayt,
      certayn ;
And trewély the labour is in vayn   150
To kepe a shrewé, for it wol nat bee.
This holde I for a verray nycetee,
To spillé labour for to kepé wyves ;
Thus writen oldé clerkés in hir lyves.
  But now to purpos, as I first bigan ;
This worthy Phebus dooth all that he kan
To plesen hire, wenynge by swich
      plesaunce,

147. *in ydel*, H⁴ *for nought.*

And for his manhede and his governaunce,
That no man sholde han put hym from
　　hire grace ;　　　159
But God it woot, ther may no man embrace
As to destreyne a thyng which that nature
Hath natureelly set in a creature.
　Taak any bryd, and put it in a cage,
And do al thyn entente, and thy corage,
To fostre it tendrely with mete and drynke
Of allé deyntees that thou kanst bithynke,
And keepe it al so clenly as thou may,
Al though his cage of gold be never so gay,
Yet hath this brid by twenty thousand foold
Levere in a forest, that is rude and coold,
Goon eté wormés and swich wreeched-
　　nesse ;
For ever this brid wol doon his bisynesse
To escape out of his cagé, if he may ;
His libertee this brid desireth ay.
　Lat take a cat, and fostre hym wel
　　with milk
And tendré flessh, and make his couche
　　of silk,
And lat hym seen a mous go by the wal,
Anon he weyveth milk, and flessh, and al,
And every deyntee that is in that hous,
Swich appetit he hath to ete a mous.　180
Lo, heere hath lust his dominacioun,
And appetit fleemeth discrecioun.
　A she-wolf hath also a vileyns kynde ;
The lewedesté wolf that she may fynde,
Or leest of reputacioun, that wol she take
In tymé whan hir lust to han a make.
　Alle thise ensamples speke I by thise
　　men
That been untrewe, and no thyng by
　　wommen ;
For men han ever a likerous appetit,
On lower thyng to parfourne hir delit　190
Than on hire wyvés, be they never so faire,
Ne never so trewé, ne so debonaire ;
Flessh is so newéfangel, with meschaunce !
That we ne konne in no thyng han
　　plesaunce,
That sowneth into vertu, any while.
　This Phebus, which that thoghte upon
　　no gile,
Deceyvéd was for al his jolitee,
For under hym another haddé shee,
A man of litel reputacioun,

Nat worth to Phebus in comparisoun ;　200
The moore harm is, it happeth ofté so,
Of which ther cometh muchel harm and wo.
　And so bifel, whan Phebus was absent,
His wyf anon hath for hir lemman sent.
' Hir lemman ? ' certés this is a knavyssh
　　speche !
Foryeveth it me, and that I yow biseche.
　The wisé Plato seith, as ye may rede,
' The word moot nede accordé with the
　　dede ' ;
If men shal tellé properly a thyng　209
The word moot cosyn be to the werkyng.
I am a boystous man ; right thus seye I,
Ther nys no differencé trewély
Bitwixe a wyf that is of heigh degree,
If of hire body dishoneste she bee,
And a pouré wenche, oother than this,—
If it so be they werké both amys,—
But that the gentile in hire estaat above,
She shal be cleped his ' lady,' as in love ;
And for that oother is a poure womman,
She shal be cleped his ' wenche,' or his
　　' lemman,'　220
And God it woot, myn owene deeré brother,
Men leyn that oon as lowe as lith that
　　oother.
　Right so bitwixe a titleless tiraunt
And an outlawe, or a theef erraunt,
The same I seye, ther is no difference,—
To Alisaundré was toold this sentence,—
That for the tiraunt is of gretter myght
By force of meynee, for to sleen doun right,
And brennen hous and hoom, and make
　　al playn,
Lo, therfore is he cleped a ' capitayn ' ;　230
And for the outlawe hath but smal meynee,
And may nat doon so greet an harm as he,
Ne brynge a contree to so greet mescheef,
Men clepen hym an ' outlawe,' or a ' theef ' ;
But for I am a man noght textueel,
I wol noght telle of textés never a deel ;
I wol go to my tale as I bigan.
Whan Phebus wyf had sent for hir lemman,
Anon they wroghten al hire lust volage.
　The whité crowe that heeng ay in the
　　cage　240

207. *The wisé Plato*, quoted from Boethius,
Bk. iii. prose 12. Cp. General Prologue, ll. 741,
742.

Biheeld hire werk and seydė never a word ;
And whan that hoom was come Phebus,
   the lord,
This crowė sang 'Cokkow ! Cokkow !
   Cokkow ! '
   'What ! bryd,' quod Phebus, ' what
      song syngestow ?
Ne were thow wont so myrily to synge
That to myn herte it was a rejoysynge
To heere thy voys ? Allas ! what song
     is this ? '
   ' By God !' quod he, ' I syngė nat amys.
Phebus,' quod he, ' for al thy worthynesse,
For al thy beautee and thy gentilesse,   250
For al thy song and al thy mynstralcye,
For al thy waityng, blerėd is thyn eye
With oon of litel reputacioun,
Noght worth to thee as in comparisoun
The montance of a gnat, so moote I thryve !
For on thy bed thy wyf I saugh hym swyve. '
   What wol ye moore ?   The crowe anon
     hym tolde
By saddė tokenes, and by wordės bolde,
How that his wyf had doon hire lecherye,
Hym to greet shame and to greet vileynye,
And tolde hym ofte he saugh it with his
     eyen.   261
This Phebus gan aweyward for to wryen,
And thoughte his sorweful hertė brast
   atwo ;
His bowe he bente, and sette ther-inne
   a flo,
And in his ire his wyf thanne hath he
   slayn,—
This is theffect, ther is namoore to sayn ;
For sorwe of which he brak his mynstralcie,
Bothe harpe, and lute, and gyterne, and
   sautrie,
And eek he brak his arwes and his bowe,
And after that thus spak he to the crowe :
   ' Traitour,' quod he, ' with tonge of
     scorpioun   271
Thou hast me broght to my confusioun.
Allas ! that I was wroght ! why nere I
   deed ?
O deerė wyf ! O gemme of lustiheed !
That were to me so sad, and eek so trewe,
Now listow deed, with facė pale of hewe,
Ful gyltėles,—that dorste I swere, y-wys !
O rakel hand ! to doon so foule amys.

O trouble wit ! O irė, recchėles !
That unavysėd smyteth giltėles !   280
O wantrust ! ful of fals suspecioun,
Where was thy wit and thy discrecioun ?
O every man, be war of rakelnesse,
Ne trowe no thyng withouten strong
   witnesse.
Smyt nat to soone, er that ye witen why ;
And beeth avysėd wel and sobrely,
Er ye doon any execucioun
Upon youre irė for suspecioun !
Allas ! a thousand folk hath rakel ire
Fully fordoon, and broght hem in the
   mire !   290
Allas ! for sorwe I wol myselven slee.'
   And to the crowe, ' O falsė theef ! '
     seyde he,
' I wol thee quite anon thy falsė tale.
Thou songė whilom lyk a nyghtyngale ;
Now shaltow, falsė theef, thy song forgon,
And eek thy whitė fetherės everichon ;
Ne never in al thy lif ne shaltou speke ;
Thus shal men on a traytour been awreke.
Thou, and thyn of-spryng, ever shul be
   blake,
Ne never sweetė noysė shul ye make,   300
But ever crie agayn tempest and rayn,
In tokenynge that thurgh thee my wyf is
   slayn.'
And to the crowe he stirte, and that anon,
And pulled his whitė fetherės everychon,
And made hym blak, and refte hym all
   his song,
And eek his speche, and out at dore hym
   slong,
Unto the devel, which I hym bitake !
And for this caas been allė crowės blake.
   Lordynges, by this ensample I yow
     preye,   309
Beth war, and taketh kepė what I seye ;
Ne telleth never no man in yourė lyf
How that another man hath dight his wyf ;
He wol yow haten mortally, certeyn.
Daun Salomon, as wisė clerkės seyn,
Techeth a man to kepen his tonge weel ;
But as I seyde, I am noght textueel,
But nathėlees, thus taughtė me my dame :

300. *noyse,* E *voys.*
310. *I seye,* H⁴ *ye seye.*
316. *textueel,* H⁴ *texted (text) wel.*

'My sone, thenk on the crowe, on
   Goddès name ;
My sone, keepe wel thy tonge and keepe
   thy freend ;   319
A wikked tonge is worsè than a feend ;
My sonè, from a feend men may hem blesse ;
My sone, God of his endelees goodnèsse
Wallèd a tonge with teeth and lippès eke,
For man sholde hym avysè what he speeke ;
My sone, ful oftè for to muchè speche
Hath many a man been spilt, as clerkès
   teche,
Bút for litel speche avysèly
Is no man shent, to spekè generally.
My sone, thy tongè sholdestow restreyne
At allè tymes, but whan thou doost thy
   peyne   330
To speke of God, in honour and preyere.
The firstè vertu, sone, if thou wolt leere,
Is to restreyne and kepè wel thy tonge ;
Thus lernè children whan that they been
   yonge.
My sone, of muchel spekyng yvele avysed,
Ther lassè spekyng haddè ynough suffised,
Comth muchel harm, thus was me toold
   and taught ;
In muchel spechè synnè wanteth naught.
Wostow wher-of a rakel tongè serveth ?
Right as a swerd for-kutteth and forkerveth

An arm atwo, my deerè sone, right so
A tongè kutteth freendshipe al atwo.
A jangler is to God abhomynable.
Reed Salomon, so wys and honurable,
Reed David in his Psalmès, reed Senekke.
My sone, spek nat, but with thyn heed
   thou bekke ;
Dissimule as thou were deef, if that thou
   heere
A jangler speke of perilous mateere.
The Flemyng seith, and lerne it if thee leste,
That ''litel janglyng causeth muchel
   rest.''   350
My sone, if thou no wikked word hast seyd,
Thee thar nat dredè for to be biwreyd ;
But he that hath mysseyd, I dar wel sayn,
He may by no wey clepe his word agayn.
Thyng that is seyd is seyd, and forth it
   gooth,
Though hym repente, or be hym leef or
   looth.
He is his thral to whom that he hath sayd
A tale of which he is now yvele apayd.
My sone, be war, and be noon auctour newe
Of tidynges, wheither they been false or
   trewe ;   360
Wher so thou come, amongès hye or lowe,
Kepe wel thy tonge, and thenk upon the
   crowe.'

GROUP I

*Heere folweth the Prologe of the Persons
Tale*

  By that the Maunciple hadde his tale
   al ended
The sonnè fro the south lyne was descended
So lowè that he ne nas nat to my sighte
Degreës nyne-and-twenty as in highte ;
[Foure] of the clokke it was tho, as I gesse,
For ellevene foot, or litel moore or lesse,
My shadwe was at thilkè tyme, as there,
Of swiche feet as my lengthè parted were
In sixe feet equal of proporcioun.

Ther-with the moonès exaltacioun,   10
I meene *Libra*, alwey gan ascende,
As we were entryng at a thropès ende ;
For which our Hoost, as he was wont to gye,
As in this caas, oure joly compaignye,
Seyde in this wisè, 'Lordynges everichoon,
Now lakketh us no talès mo than oon ;
Fulfilled is my sentence and my decree ;
I trowe that we han herd of ech degree.
Almoost fulfild is al myn ordinaunce ;
I pray to God so yeve hym right good
   chaunce   20
That telleth this tale to us lustily.

1. *the Maunciple.* According to the notes of
time some other tales must have intervened, and
Manciple is only the guess of the copyists.
5. *Foure.* The MSS. read *Ten*, which accords
with neither line 4 nor line 72.
7. *as there, i.e.* in that latitude ; H *of the yere.*

10, 11. *the moonès exaltacioun, I meene Libra.*
It seems best to suppose with Tyrwhitt that *the
moones* is a blunder for *Saturnes*, Taurus being
the exaltation of the moon, and *Libra* of Saturn.
H reads *In mena* for *I meene. In meene* (in the
middle of) has been suggested as a possible reading.

'Sire Preest,' quod he, 'artow a vicary,
Or arte a Person? sey sooth, by thy fey!
Be what thou be, ne breke thou nat oure
    pley,
For every man save thou hath toold his tale.
Unbokele, and shewe us what is in thy
    male;
For trewely, me thynketh by thy cheere,
Thou sholdest knytte up wel a greet
    mateere.
Telle us a fable anon, for cokkes bones!'
    This Persoune answerde al atones, 30
'Thou getest fable noon y-toold for me,
For Paul, that writeth unto Thymothee,
Repreveth hem that weyveth soothfast-
    nesse,
And tellen fables and swich wrecched-
    nesse.
Why sholde I sowen draf out of my fest,
Whan I may sowen whete, if that me lest?
For which I seye, if that yow list to heere
Moralitee and vertuous mateere,
And thanne that ye wol yeve me audience,
I wol ful fayn, at Cristes reverence, 40
Do yow plesaunce leefful, as I kan;
But, trusteth wel, I am a southren man,
I kan nat geeste "*rum, ram, ruf,*" by lettre;
Ne, God woot, rym holde I but litel bettre;
And therfore, if yow list,—I wol nat
    glose,—
I wol yow telle a myrie tale in prose,
To knytte up al this feeste, and make an
    ende;
And Jhesu, for his grace, wit me sende
To shewe yow the wey, in this viage,
Of thilke parfit, glorious pilgrymage, 50
That highte Jerusalem celestial;
And if ye vouchesauf, anon I shal
Bigynne upon my tale, for whiche I preye
Telle youre avys.   I kan no bettre seye.
    'But nathelees this meditacioun
I putte it ay under correccioun
Of clerkes, for I am nat textueel.
I take but the sentence, trusteth weel;
Therfore I make a protestacioun
That I wol stonde to correccioun.' 60
    Upon this word we han assented soone,

43. *geeste*, etc., tell tales in alliterative metres like the northern poets.
58. *the* (om. E) *sentence*, the meaning as opposed to the letter.

For as us semed, it was for to doone,
To enden in som vertuous sentence,
And for to yeve hym space and audience;
And bede oure Hoost he sholde to hym seye
That alle we to telle his tale hym preye.
    Oure Hooste hadde the wordes for us
    alle:
'Sire Preest,' quod he, 'now faire yow
    bifalle!
Sey what yow list, and we wol gladly heere';
And with that word, he seyde in this
    manere: 70
'Telleth,' quod he, 'youre meditacioun;
But hasteth yow, the sonne wole adoun.
Beth fructuous, and that in litel space,
And to do wel, God sende yow his grace.'

PARSON'S TALE

Heere bigynneth the Persouns Tale

JER. VI. *State super vias, et videte, et interrogate de semitis antiquis, quæ sit via bona, et ambulate in ea; et invenietis refrigerium animabus vestris.*

[75] Oure sweete Lord God of hevene, that no man wole perisse, but wole that we comen alle to the knoweleche of hym and the blissful lif that is perdurable, amonesteth us by the prophete Jeremie, and seith in this wyse: 'Stondeth upon the weyes, and seeth, and axeth of olde pathes, that is to seyn of olde sentences, which is the goode wey, and walketh in that wey, and ye shal fynde refresshynge for youre soules.'
    Manye been the weyes espirituels that leden folk to oure Lord Jhesu Crist, and to the regne of glorie; [80] of whiche weyes ther is a ful noble wey, and a covenable, which may nat fayle to man, ne to womman, that thurgh synne hath mysgoon fro the righte wey of Jerusalem celestial, and this

Parson's Tale. The treatise on the Deadly Sins and their cure which is wedged into this account of Penitence is taken from the *Somme de Vices et de Vertus* of Frère Lorens, a thirteenth century writer. Chaucer's authorship of these sections has been doubted, perhaps needlessly; but the sermon is unmercifully long.
Jer. vi., v. 16.
75. *that no man wole perisse*, who desires to destroy no man.

wey is cleped penitence; of which man sholde gladly herknen and enquere with al his herte to wyten what is penitence, and whennes it is cleped penitence, and in how manye maneres been the acciouns or werkynges of penitence, and how manye speces ther been of penitence, and whiche thynges apertenen and bihoven to penitence, and whiche thynges destourben penitence.

Seint Ambrose seith that penitence is the pleynynge of man for gilt that he hath doon and namoore to do any thyng for which hym oghte to pleyne; [85] and som doctour seith, ' Penitence is the waymentynge of man that sorweth for his synne, and pyneth hym self for he hath mysdoon.' Penitence with certeyne circumstances is verray repentance of a man that halt hym self in sorwe and oother peyne for his giltes; and for he shal be verray penitent, he shal first biwaylen the synnes that he hath doon and stidefastly purposen in his herte to have shrift of mouthe and to doon satisfaccioun, and never to doon thyng for which hym oghte moore biwayle or to compleyne, and continue in goode werkes, or elles his repentance may nat availle; for, as seith Seint Ysidre, ' He is a japer and a gabber and no verray repentant that eftsoone dooth thyng for which hym oghte repente.' [90] Wepynge, and nat for to stynt to do synne, may nat avaylle; but nathelees men shal hope that at every tyme that man falleth, be it never so ofte, that he may arise thurgh penitence, if he have grace; but certeinly it is greet doute, for, as seith Seint Gregorie, unnethe ariseth he out of his synne that is charged with the charge of yvel usage; and therfore repentant folk that stynte for to synne, and forlete synne er that synne forlete hem, hooly chirche holdeth hem siker of hire savacioun. And he that synneth and verraily repenteth hym in his laste ende, hooly chirche yet hopeth his savacioun, by the grete mercy of oure Lord Jhesu Crist for his repentaunce; but taak the siker wey.

85. *shrift of mouthe*, verbal confession.
85. *Seint Ysidre*, St. Isidore.

[95] And now sith I have declared yow what thyng is penitence, now shul ye understonde that ther been thre acciouns of penitence. The firste accioun of penitence is that a man be baptized after that he hath synned. Seint Augustyn seith, ' But he be penytent for his olde synful lyf, he may nat bigynne the newe clene lif'; for certes, if he be baptized withouten penitence of his olde gilt, he receyveth the mark of baptesme, but nat the grace, ne the remission of his synnes, til he have repentance verray. Another defaute is this, that men doon deedly synne after that they han receyved baptesme. [100] The thridde defaute is that men fallen in venial synne after hir baptesme fro day to day. Ther-of seith Seint Augustyn that penitence of goode and humble folk is the penitence of every day.

The speces of penitence been thre. That oon of hem is solempne, another is commune, and the thridde is privee. Thilke penance that is solempne is in two maneres; as to be put out of hooly chirche in Lente for slaughtre of children, and swich maner thyng. Another thyng is whan a man hath synned openly, of which synne the fame is openly spoken in the contree, and thanne hooly chirche by juggement destreyneth hym for to do open penaunce. [105] Commune penaunce is that preestes enjoynen men in certeyn caas, as for to goon peraventure naked in pilgrimages, or bare-foot. Pryvee penaunce is thilke that men doon alday for privee synnes, of whiche they shryve hem prively, and receyve privee penaunce.

Now shaltow understande what is bihovely and necessarie to verray perfit penitence. And this stant on thre thynges: Contricioun of herte, Confessioun of mouth, and Satisfaccioun; for which seith Seint John Crisostom, ' Penitence destreyneth a man to accepte benygnely every peyne that hym is enjoyned with contricioun of herte, and shrift of mouth, with satisfaccioun, and in werkynge of alle manere humylitee'; [110] and this is

105. *naked*, *i.e.* without upper garments.

fruytful penitence agayn thre thynges in whiche we wratthe oure Lord Jhesu Crist. This is to seyn, by delit in thynkynge, by reccheleesnesse in spekynge, and by wikked synful werkynge ; and agayns thise wikkede giltes is penitence, that may be likned unto a tree.

The roote of this tree is contricioun, that hideth hym in the herte of hym that is verray repentaunt, right as the roote of a tree hydeth hym in the erthe. Of the roote of contricioun spryngeth a stalke, that bereth braunches and leves of confessioun, and fruyt of satisfaccioun. [115] For which Crist seith in his gospel, 'Dooth digne fruyt of penitence'; for by this fruyt may men knowe this tree, and nat by the roote that is hyd in the herte of man, ne by the braunches, ne by the leves of confessioun ; and therfore oure Lord Jhesu Crist seith thus, ' By the fruyt of hem ye shul knowen hem.' Of this roote eek spryngeth a seed of grace, the which seed is mooder of sikerness, and this seed is egre and hoot. The grace of this seed spryngeth of God thurgh remembrance of the day of doome and on the peynes of helle. Of this matere seith Salomon, that in the drede of God man forleteth his synne. [120] The heete of this seed is the love of God, and the desiryng of the joye perdurable. This heete draweth the herte of a man to God, and dooth hym haten his synne ; for soothly ther is no thyng that savoureth so wel to a child as the milk of his norice, ne no thyng moore abhomynable than thilke milk whan it is medled with oother mete. Right so the synful man that loveth his synne, hym semeth that it is to him moost sweete of any thyng ; but fro that tyme that he loveth sadly oure Lord Jhesu Crist, and desireth the lif perdurable, ther nys to him no thyng moore abhomynable ; [125] for soothly the lawe of God is the love of God. For which David the prophete seith, ' I have loved thy lawe, and hated wikkednesse and hate ; he that loveth God kepeth his lawe and his word.' This tree saugh the prophete Daniel in spirit upon the avysioun of Nabugodonosor, whan he conseiled hym to do penitence. Penaunce is the tree of lyf to hem that it receyven, and he that holdeth hym in verray penitence is blessed, after the sentence of Salomon.

In this penitence or contricioun man shal understonde foure thynges ; that is to seyn, what is contricioun, and whiche been the causes that moeven a man to contricioun, and how he sholde be contrit, and what contricioun availleth to the soule. Thanne is it thus that contricioun is the verray sorwe that a man receyveth in his herte for his synnes, with sad purpos to shryve hym and to do penaunce, and nevermoore to do synne ; [130] and this sorwe shal been in this manere, ay seith Seint Bernard ; it shal been hevy and grevous, and ful sharpe and poynant in herte. First, for man hath agilt his Lord and his Creatour, and moore sharpe and poynaunt for he hath agilt hys Fader celestial, and yet moore sharpe and poynaunt for he hath wrathed and agilt hym that boghte hym, which with his precious blood hath delivered us fro the bondes of synne, and fro the crueltee of the devel, and fro the peynes of helle.

The causes that oghte moeve a man to contricioun been sexe. First, a man shal remembre hym of his synnes ; but looke he that thilke remembraunce ne be to hym no delit by no wey, but greet shame and sorwe for his gilt ; for Job seith, synful men doon werkes worthy of confessioun. [135] And therfore seith Ezechie, 'I wol remembre me alle the yeres of my lyf in bitternesse of myn herte.' And God seith in the Apocalipse, ' Remembreth yow fro whennes that ye been falle ' ; for biforn that tyme that ye synned ye were the children of God, and lymes of the regne of God ; but for youre synne ye been woxen thral and foul, and membres of the feend, hate of aungels,

<hr>

125. *in spirit upon the avysioun of,* E *in the avysioun of the kyng.*
125. *Nabugodonosor,* Nebuchadnezzar.

sclaunde of hooly chirche, and foode of the false serpent, perpetueel matere of the fir of helle; and yet moore foul and abhomynable, for ye trespassen so ofte tyme as dooth the hound that retourneth to eten his spewyng; and yet be ye fouler for youre longe continuyng in synne and youre synful usage, for which ye be roten in youre synne as a beest in his dong. [140] Swiche manere of thoghtes maken a man to have shame of his synne and no delit, as God seith by the prophete Ezechiel, 'Ye shal remembre yow of youre weyes and they shuln displese yow.' Soothly synnes been the weyes that leden folk to helle.

The seconde cause that oghte make a man to have desdeyn of synne is this, that, as seith Seint Peter, 'Who-so that dooth synne is thral of synne'; and synne put a man in greet thraldom, and therfore seith the prophete Ezechiel, 'I wente sorweful in desdayn of my self'; and certes, wel oghte a man have desdayn of synne and withdrawe hym from that thraldom and vileynye. And lo, what seith Seneca in this matere? He seith thus: 'Though I wiste that God —neither God ne man—ne sholde never knowe it, yet wolde I have desdayn for to do synne.' [145] And the same Seneca also seith, 'I am born to gretter thynges than to be thral to my body, or than for to maken of my body a thral'; ne a fouler thral may no man ne womman maken of his body than for to yeven his body to synne. Al were it the fouleste cherl, or the fouleste womman that lyveth, and leest of value, yet is he thanne moore foule and moore in servitute. Ever fro the hyer degree that man falleth, the moore is he thral, and moore to God and to the world vile and abhomynable. O goode God! wel oghte man have desdayn of synne, sith that thurgh synne ther he was free now is he maked bonde; [150] and therfore seyth Seint Augustyn, 'If thou hast desdayn of thy servant, if he agilte or synne, have thou thanne desdayn that thou thyself sholdest do synne; take reward of thy value, that thou ne be to foul to thyself.' Allas! wel oghten they thanne have desdayn to been servauntz and thralles to synne, and soore been ashamed of hemself, that God of his endelees goodnesse hath set hem in heigh estaat, or yeven hem wit, strengthe of body, heele, beautee, prosperitee, and boghte hem fro the deeth with his herte blood, that they so unkyndely agayns his gentilesse quiten hym so vileynsly, to slaughtre of hir owene soules. [155] O goode God! ye wommen that been of so greet beautee, remembreth yow of the proverbe of Salomon, he seith, 'Likneth a fair womman that is a fool of hire body lyk to a ryng of gold that were in the groyn of a sowe, for right as a sowe wroteth in everich ordure, so wroteth hire beautee in the stynkynge ordure of synne.'

The thridde cause that oghte moeve a man to contricioun is drede of the day of doome and of the horrible peynes of helle; for as Seint Jerome seith, 'At every tyme that me remembreth of the day of doome, I quake, [160] for whan I ete, or drynke, or what so that I do, ever semeth me that the trompe sowneth in myn ere, "Riseth up, ye that been dede, and cometh to the juggement."' O goode God! muchel oghte a man to drede swich a juggement, ther as we shullen been alle, as Seint Poul seith, biforn the seete of oure Lord Jhesu Crist, wher as he shal make a general congregacioun, wher as no man may been absent, for certes there availleth noon essoyne, ne excusacioun. [165] And nat oonly that oure defautes shullen be jugged, but eek that alle oure werkes shullen openly be knowe. And as seith Seint Bernard, 'Ther ne shal no pledynge availle, ne sleighte; we shullen yeven rekenynge of everich ydel word; ther shul we han a juge that may nat been deceyved ne corrupt.' And why? for certes alle oure thoghtes been discovered as to hym; ne for preyere, ne for meede, he shal nat been corrupt. And therfore seith Salomon, 'The wratthe of God ne wol nat spare no wight for preyere ne for yifte'; and therfore, at the day of doom ther nys noon hope to escape.

Wherfore, as seith Seint Anselm, 'Ful greet angwyssh shul the synful folk have at that tyme. [170] Ther shal the stierne and wrothe juge sitte above, and under hym the horrible put of helle open to destroyen hym that moot biknowen his synnes, whiche synnes openly been shewed biforn God and biforn every creature; and in the left syde mo develes than herte may bithynke, for to harye and drawe the synful soules to the peyne of helle; and withinne the hertes of folk shal be the bitynge conscience, and withoute forth shal be the world al brennynge.' Whider shal thanne the wrecched synful man flee to hiden hym? Certes, he may nat hyden hym,—he moste come forth and shewen hym; for certes, as seith Seint Jerome, 'The erthe shal casten hym out of hym, and the see also, and the eyr also, that shal be ful of thonder clappes and lightnynges.'

[175] Now soothly, who so wel remembreth hym of thise thynges, I gesse that his synne shal nat turne hym to delit, but to greet sorwe, for drede of the peyne of helle. And therfore seith Job to God, 'Suffre, Lord, that I may awhile biwaille, and wepe, er I go withoute, returnyng to the derke lond, covered with the derknesse of deeth, to the lond of mysese and of derknesse, where as is the shadwe of deeth, where as ther is noon ordre or ordinaunce, but grisly drede that ever shal laste.' Loo, heere may ye seen that Job preyde respit a while to biwepe and waille his trespas, for soothly oon day of respit is bettre than al the tresor of this world; and forasmuche as a man may acquiten hymself biforn God by penitence in this world, and nat by tresor, therfore sholde he preye to God to yeve hym respit a while to biwepe and biwaillen his trespas; [180] for certes, al the sorwe that a man myghte make fro the bigynnyng of the world nys but a litel thyng at regard of the sorwe of helle.

The cause why that Job clepeth helle 'the lond of derknesse': understondeth that he clepeth it londe or erthe, for it is stable and never shal faille; dirk, for he that is in helle hath defaute of light material, for certes, the derke light that shal come out of the fyr that ever shal brenne shal turne hym al to peyne that is in helle, for it sheweth hym to the horrible develes that hym tormenten; 'covered with the derknesse of deeth'; that is to seyn, that he that is in helle shall have defaute of the sighte of God; for certes, the sighte of God is the lyf perdurable. [185] The 'derknesse of deeth' been the synnes that the wrecched man hath doon, whiche that destourben hym to see the face of God, right as dooth a derk clowde bitwixe us and the sonne. 'Lond of misese,' by-cause that ther been thre maneres of defautes agayn thre thynges that folk of this world han in this present lyf; that is to seyn, honours, delices, and richesses. Agayns honour have they in helle shame and confusioun; for wel ye woot that men clepen honour the reverence that man doth to man; but in helle is noon honour ne reverence, for certes, namoore reverence shal be doon there to a kyng than to a knave. For which God seith by the prophete Jeremye, 'Thilke folk that me despisen shul been in despit.' [190] Honour is eek cleped greet lordshipe. Ther, shal no wight serven oother but of harm and torment. Honour is eek cleped greet dignytee and heighnesse, but in helle shul they been al fortroden of develes. And God seith, 'The horrible develes shulle goon and comen upon the hevedes of the dampned folk'; and this is forasmuche as the hyer that they were in this present lyf, the moore shulle they been abated and defouled in helle.

Agayns the richesses of this world shul they han mysese of poverte; and this

185. *despisen*, H *displesen*.

poverte shal been in foure thynges. In defaute of tresor, of which that David seith, 'The riche folk that embraceden and oneden al hire herte to tresor of this world, shul slepe in the slepynge of deeth, and no thyng ne shal they fynden in hir handes of al hir tresor.' And mooreover the mysese of helle shal been in defaute of mete and drinke, [195] for God seith thus by Moyses, 'They shul been wasted with hunger, and the briddes of helle shal devouren hem with the bitter deeth, and the galle of the dragon shal been hire drynke, and the venym of the dragon hire morsels.' And forther-over hire mysese shal been in defaute of clothyng, for they shulle be naked in body, as of clothyng, save the fyr in which they brenne, and othere filthes; and naked shul they been of soule, as of alle manere vertues which that is the clothyng of the soule. Where been thanne the gaye robes, and the softe shetes, and the smale shertes? Loo, what seith God of hem by the prophete Ysaye? That under hem shul been strawed motthes, and hire covertures shulle been of wormes of helle. And forther-over hir mysese shal been in defaute of freendes, for he nys nat poure that hath goode freendes; but there is no frend; [200] for neither God, ne no creature, shal been freend to hem; and everich of hem shal haten oother with deedly hate. The sones and the doghtren shullen rebellen agayns fader and mooder, and kynrede agayns kynrede, and chiden and despisen everich of hem oother bothe day and nyght, as God seith by the prophete Michias. And the lovynge children, that whilom loveden so flesshly everich oother, wolden everich of hem eten oother, if they myghte; for how sholden they love togidre in the peyne of helle, whan they hated ech of hem oother in the prosperitee of this lyf? For truste wel, hir flesshly love was deedly hate, as seith the prophete David, 'Whoso that loveth wikkednesse he hateth his soule'; [205] and whoso hateth his owene

195. the bitter deeth, H bitter teeth.

soule, certes, he may love noon oother wight in no manere; and therfore in helle is no solas, ne no freendshipe, but ever the moore flesshly kynredes that been in helle, the moore cursynges, the more chidynges, and the moore deedly hate ther is among hem.

And forther-over they shul have defaute of alle manere delices; for certes delices been after the appetites of the five wittes, as sighte, herynge, smellynge, savorynge, and touchynge: [210] but in helle hir sighte shal be ful of derknesse and of smoke, and therfore ful of teeres, and hir herynge ful of waymentynge and of gryntynge of teeth, as seith Jhesu Crist. Hir nose-thirles shullen be ful of stynkynge stynk; and, as seith Ysaye the prophete, hir savoryng shal be ful of bitter galle; and touchynge of al hir body y-covered with fir that never shal quenche, and with wormes that never shul dyen, as God seith by the mouth of Ysaye. And forasmuch as they shul nat wene that they may dyen for peyne, and by hir deeth flee fro peyne, that may they understonden by the word of Job, that seith, 'Ther as is the shadwe of deeth.' Certes a shadwe hath the liknesse of the thyng of which it is shadwe, but shadwe is nat the same thyng of which it is shadwe. Right so fareth the peyne of helle; it is lyk deeth for the horrible angwissh; and why? For it peyneth hem ever as though they sholde dye anon, but certes, they shal nat dye, for as seith Seint Gregorie, 'To wrecche caytyves shal be deeth withoute deeth, and ende withouten ende, and defaute withoute failynge, [215] for hir deeth shal alwey lyven and hir ende shal evermo bigynne, and hir defaute shal nat faille'; and therfore seith Seint John the Evaungelist, 'They shullen folwe deeth and they shul nat fynde hym, and they shul desiren to dye and deeth shal flee fro hem.'

And eek Job seith that in helle is noon ordre of rule, and al be it so that God hath creat alle thynges in right ordre and no thyng withouten ordre, but alle thynges been ordeyned and nombred; yet nathelees, they that been dampned been no thyng in the ordre, ne holden noon ordre, for the erthe ne shal bere hem no fruyt, [220] for, as the prophete David seith, 'God shal destroie the fruyt of the erthe as fro hem, ne water ne shal yeve hem no moisture, ne the eyr no refresshyng, ne fyr no light.' For as seith Seint Basilie, 'The brennynge of the fyr of this world shal God yeven in helle to hem that been dampned, but the light and the cleernesse shal be yeven in hevene to his children, right as the goode man yeveth flessh to his children and bones to his houndes.' And for they shullen have noon hope to escape, seith Seint Job atte laste, that ther shal horrour and grisly drede dwellen withouten ende.

Horrour is alwey drede of harm that is to come, and this drede shal ever dwelle in the hertes of hem that been dampned; and therfore han they lorn al hire hope for sevene causes. [225] First, for God that is hir juge shal be withouten mercy to hem, and they may nat plese hym ne noon of his halwes; ne they ne may yeve no thyng for hir raunsoun; ne they have no voys to speke to hym; ne they may nat fle fro peyne; ne they have no goodnesse in hem that they mowe shewe to delivere hem fro peyne. And therfore seith Salomon, 'The wikked man dyeth, and whan he is deed he shal have noon hope to escape fro peyne.' Whoso thanne wolde wel understande these peynes and bithynke hym weel that he hath deserved thilke peynes for his synnes, certes, he sholde have moore talent to siken and to wepe, than for to syngen and to pleye, for as that seith Salomon, 'Whoso that hadde the science to know the peynes that been establissed and ordeyned for synne, he wolde make sorwe.' [230] Thilke science, as seith Seint Augustyn, maketh a man to waymenten in his herte.

The fourthe point that oghte maken a man to have contricioun is the sorweful remembraunce of the good that he hath left to doon heere in erthe, and eek the good that he hath lorn. Soothly, the goode werkes that he hath [left], outher they been the goode werkes that he hath wroght er he fel into deedly synne, or elles the goode werkes that he wroghte while he lay in synne. Soothly, the goode werkes that he dide biforn that he fil in synne been al mortefied and astoned, and dulled, by the ofte synnyng. The othere goode werkes that he wroghte while he lay in deedly synne, thei been outrely dede as to the lyf perdurable in hevene.

[235] Thanne thilke goode werkes that been mortefied by ofte synnyng, whiche goode werkes he dide whil he was in charitee, ne mowe never quyken agayn withouten verray penitence; and ther-of seith God by the mouth of Ezechiel, 'That if the rightful man returne agayn from his rightwisnesse and werke wikkednesse, shal he lyve? Nay, for alle the goode werkes that he hath wroght ne shul never been in remembrance, for he shal dyen in his synne.' And upon thilke chapitre seith Seint Gregorie thus: 'That we shulle understonde this principally, that whan we doon deedly synne it is for noght thanne to rehercen or drawen into memorie the goode werkes that we han wroght biforn'; [240] for certes, in the werkynge of the deedly synne ther is no trust to no good werk that we han doon biforn, that is for to seyn, as for to have therby the lyf perdurable in hevene; but nathelees, the goode werkes quyken agayn and comen agayn and helpen and availlen to have the lyf perdurable in hevene whan we han contricioun. But soothly, the goode werkes that men doon whil they been in deedly synne, forasmuch as they were doon in deedly synne, they may never quyke agayn; for certes, thyng that never hadde lyf may never quykene; and nathelees, al be it that they ne availle noght to han the lyf perdurable,

yet availlen they to abregge of the peyne of helle, or elles to geten temporal richesse, or elles that God wole the rather enlumyne and lightne the herte of the synful man to have repentaunce. [245] And eek they availlen for to usen a man to doon goode werkes that the feend have the lasse power of his soule. And thus the curteis Lord Jhesu Crist wole that no good werk be lost, for in somwhat it shal availle. But, forasmuche as the goode werkes that men doon whil they been in good lyf been al mortefied by synne folwynge, and eek sith that alle the goode werkes that men doon whil they been in deedly synne been outrely dede, for to have the lyf perdurable, wel may that man that no good werk ne dooth synge thilke newe Frenshe song, '*Jay tout perdu—mon temps et mon labour.*'

For certes synne bireveth a man bothe goodnesse of nature and eek the goodnesse of grace ; [250] for soothly, the grace of the Hooly Goost fareth lyk fyr that may nat been ydel, for fyr fayleth anoon as it forleteth his wirkynge ; and right so grace fayleth anoon as it forleteth his werkynge. Then leseth the synful man the goodnesse of glorie that oonly is bihight to goode men that labouren and werken. Wel may he be sory thanne that oweth al his lif to God, as longe as he hath lyved and eek as longe as he shal lyve, that no goodnesse ne hath to paye with his dette to God, to whom he oweth al his lyf ; for, trust wel, he shal yeven acountes, as seith Seint Bernard, of alle the goodes that han be yeven hym in this present lyf, and how he hath hem despended ; noght so muche that ther shal nat perisse an heer of his heed, ne a moment of an houre ne shal nat perisse of his tyme, that he ne shal yeve of it a rekenyng.

[255] The fifthe thyng that oghte moeve a man to contricioun is remembrance of the passioun that oure Lord Jhesu Crist suffred for oure synnes, for, as seith

245. *thilke newe Frenshe song.* Quoted again in the *Fortune*, l. 7.

Seint Bernard, 'Whil that I lyve I shal have remembrance of the travailles that oure Lord Crist suffred in prechyng, his werynesse in travaillyng, his temptaciouns whan he fasted, his longe wakynges whan he preyde, his teeres whan that he weepe for pitee of good peple, the wo and the shame and the filthe that men seyden to hym, of the foule spittyng that men spitte in his face, of the buffettes that men yaven hym, of the foule mowes and of the repreves that men to hym seyden, of the nayles with whiche he was nayled to the croys, and of al the remenaunt of his passioun that he suffred for my synnes and no thyng for his gilt.'

[260] And ye shul understonde that in mannes synne is every manere of ordre or ordinaunce turned up-so-doun. For it is sooth that God and resoun and sensualitee and the body of man been ordeyned that everich of thise foure thynges sholde have lordshipe over that oother ; as thus : God sholde have lordshipe over resoun, and resoun over sensualitee, and sensualitee over the body of man ; but soothly, whan man synneth al this ordre or ordinaunce is turned up-so-doun. And therfore thanne, forasmuche as the resoun of man ne wol nat be subget ne obeisant to God, that is his lord by right, therfore leseth it the lordshipe that it sholde have over sensualitee, and eek over the body of man. [265] And why ? For sensualitee rebelleth thanne agayns resoun, and by that wey leseth resoun the lordshipe over sensualitee and over the body, for, right as resoun is rebel to God, right so is bothe sensualitee rebel to resoun and the body also.

And certes, this disordinaunce and this rebellioun oure Lord Jhesu Crist aboghte upon his precious body ful deere ; and herkneth in which wise. For as muche thanne as resoun is rebel to God, therfore is man worthy to have sorwe and to be deed. This suffred oure Lord Jhesu Crist for man, after that he hadde be bitraysed of his disciple, and distreyned

and bounde, so that his blood brast out
at every nayl of his handes, as seith
Seint Augustyn. [270] And forther-over
for as muchel as resoun of man ne wol
nat daunte sensualitee whan it may,
therfore is man worthy to have shame,
and this suffred oure Lord Jhesu Crist
for man whan they spetten in his visage.
And forther-over for as muchel thanne
as the caytyf body of man is rebel bothe
to resoun and to sensualitee, therfore is
it worthy the deeth, and this suffred oure
Lord Jhesu Crist for man upon the croys,
where as ther was no part of his body
free withouten greet peyne and bitter
passioun.

And al this suffred Jhesu Crist that
never forfeted, and therfore resonably
may be said of Jhesu in this manere:
' To muchel am I peyned for the thynges
that I never deserved, and to muche
defouled for shendshipe that man is
worthy to have.' And therfore may the
synful man wel seye, as seith Seint
Bernard, ' Acursed be the bitternesse of
my synne, for which ther moste be
suffred so muchel bitternesse ' ; [275] for
certes, after the diverse discordaunces
of oure wikkednesses was the passioun of
Jhesu Crist ordeyned in diverse thynges,
as thus ; certes, synful mannes soule is
bitraysed of the devel by coveitise of
temporeel prosperitee, and scorned by
deceite whan he cheseth flesshly delices,
and yet is it tormented by inpacience of
adversitee, and by-spit by servage and
subjeccioun of synne, and atte laste it is
slayn fynally. For this disordinaunce of
synful man was Jhesu Crist first bitraysed,
and after that he was bounde that cam
for to unbynden us of synne and of
peyne. Thanne was he by-scorned that
oonly sholde han been honoured in alle
thynges and of alle thynges. Thanne
was his visage, that oghte be desired to
be seyn of al mankynde, in which visage
aungels desiren to looke, vileynsly bispet ;
[280] thanne was he scourged that no
thyng hadde agilt ; and finally thanne

275. *by-spit*, E *dispeir*.

was he crucified and slayn. Thanne
was acompliced the word of Ysaye,
' He was wounded for oure mysdedes and
defouled by oure felonies.' Now, sith
that Jhesu Crist took upon hymself the
peyne of alle oure wikkednesses, muchel
oghte synful man wepen and biwayle
that for his synnes Goddes sone of
hevene sholde al this peyne endure.

The sixte thyng that oghte moeve a
man to contricioun is the hope of thre
thynges ; that is to seyn, foryifnesse of
synne, and the yifte of grace wel for to
do, and the glorie of hevene, with which
God shal gerdone a man for his goode
dedes.

And, for as muche as Jhesu Crist
yeveth us thise yiftes of his largesse, and
of his sovereyn bountee, therfore is he
cleped *Jhesus Nazarenus, rex Judæorum.*
[285] *Jhesus* is to seyn saveour, or
salvacioun, on whom men shul hope to
have foryifnesse of synnes, which that is
proprely salvacioun of synnes ; and therfore seyde the aungel to Joseph, ' Thou
shalt clepen his name Jhesus that shal
saven his peple of hir synnes.' And
heer-of seith Seint Peter, ' Ther is noon
oother name under hevene that is yeve
to any man by which a man may be
saved,' but oonly Jhesus. *Nazarenus* is
as muche for to seye as florisshynge, in
which a man shal hope that he that
yeveth hym remissioun of synnes shal
yeve hym eek grace wel for to do, for in
the flour is hope of fruyt in tyme comynge,
and in foryifnesse of synnes, hope of
grace wel for to do. ' I was atte dore
of thyn herte,' seith Jhesus, ' and cleped
for to entre ; he that openeth to me shal
have foryifnesse of synne ; [290] I wol entre
into hym by my grace and soupe with
hym (by the goode werkes that he shal
doon, whiche werkes been the foode of
God), and he shal soupe with me ' (by
the grete joye that I shal yeven hym).

Thus shal man hope for his werkes of
penaunce that God shal yeven hym his
regne, as he bihooteth hym in the gospel.
Now shal a man understonde in which

manere shal been his contricioun. I seye that it shal been universal and total. This is to seyn, a man shal be verray repentaunt for alle his synnes that he hath doon in delit of his thoght, for delit is ful perilous. For ther been two manere of consentynges; that oon of hem is cleped consentynge of affeccioun, whan a man is moeved to do synne, and deliteth hym longe for to thynke on that synne, and his resoun aperceyveth it wel that it is synne agayns the lawe of God, and yet his resoun refreyneth nat his foul delit or talent, though he se wel apertly that it is agayns the reverence of God; although his resoun ne consente noght to doon that synne in dede, [295] yet seyn somme doctours that swich delit that dwelleth longe it is ful perilous, al be it never so lite. And also a man sholde sorwe namely, for al that ever he hath desired agayn the lawe of God with perfit consentynge of his resoun, for ther-of is no doute that it is deedly synne in consentynge; for certes, ther is no deedly synne that it nas first in mannes thought, and after that in his delit and so forth into consentynge, and into dede. Wherfore, I seye that many men ne repenten hem never of swiche thoghtes and delites, ne never shryven hem of it, but oonly of the dede of grete synnes outward; wherfore, I seye that swiche wikked delites and wikked thoghtes been subtile bigileres of hem that shullen be dampned.

[300] Moore-over, man oghte to sorwe for his wikkede wordes, as wel as for his wikkede dedes; for, certes, the repentaunce of a synguler synne, and nat repente of alle his othere synnes, or elles repenten hym of alle his othere synnes and nat of a synguler synne, may nat availle. For certes, God Almyghty is al good, and therfore he foryeveth al, or elles right noght. And heer-of seith Seint Augustyn, I wot certeynly that God is enemy to everich synnere, and how thanne he that observeth o synne, shal he have foryifnesse of the remenaunt of his othere synnes? Nay.

[305] And forther-over contricioun sholde be wonder sorweful and angwissous, and therfore yeveth hym God pleynly his mercy, and therfore 'whan my soule was angwissous with-inne me, I hadde remembrance of God, that my preyere myghte come to hym.' Forther-over contricioun moste be continueel, and that man have stedefast purpos to shriven hym, and for to amenden hym of his lyf; for, soothly, whil contricioun lasteth man may ever have hope of foryifnesse, and of this comth hate of synne, that destroyeth synne bothe in him-self and eek in oother folk, at his power; for which seith David, 'Ye that loven God, hateth wikkednesse,' for, trusteth wel, to love God is for to love that he loveth and hate that he hateth.

The laste thyng that man shal understonde in contricioun is this, 'Wher-of avayleth contricioun?' I seye that som tyme contricioun delivereth a man fro synne; of which that David seith, 'I seye,' quod David, that is to seyn, 'I purposed fermely to shryve me, and thow, Lord, relesedest my synne.' [310] And right so as contricioun availleth noght withouten sad purpos of shrifte, if man have oportunitee, right so litel worth is shrifte or satisfaccioun withouten contricioun. And moore-over contricioun destroyeth the prisoun of helle, and maketh wayk and fieble alle the strengthes of the develes, and restoreth the yiftes of the Hooly Goost and of alle goode vertues; and it clenseth the soule of synne and delivereth the soule fro the peyne of helle, and fro the compaignye of the devel, and fro the servage of synne, and restoreth it to alle goodes espirituels, and to the compaignye and communyoun of hooly chirche.

And forther-over it maketh hym that whilom was sone of ire to be sone of grace, and alle thise thynges been preved by hooly writ, and therfore he that wolde sette his entente to thise thynges, he were ful wys, for, soothly, he ne sholde nat

310. *entente*, H *herte*.

274

thanne in al his lyf have corage to synne, but yeven his body and al his herte to the service of Jhesu Crist, and ther-of doon hym hommage; [315] for soothly oure sweete Lord Jhesu Crist hath spared us so debonairly in our folies, that if he ne hadde pitee of mannes soule a sory song we myghten alle synge.

Explicit prima pars penitentie. Et sequitur secunda pars eiusdem

The seconde partie of penitence is confessioun that is signe of contricioun. Now shul ye understonde what is confessioun, and wheither it oghte nedes be doon or noon, and whiche thynges been covenable to verray confessioun.

First shaltow understonde that confessioun is verray shewynge of synnes to the preest; this is to seyn 'verray,' for he moste confessen hym of alle the condiciouns that bilongen to his synne, as ferforth as he kan; [320] al moot be seyd and no thyng excused, ne hyd, ne for-wrapped, and noght avaunte thee of thy goode werkes. And forther-over it is necessarie to understonde whennes that synnes spryngen, and how they encreessen, and whiche they been.

Of the spryngynge of synnes seith Seint Paul in this wise, that 'Right as by a man synne entred first into this world, and thurgh that synne deeth; right so thilke deeth entred into alle men that synneden'; and this man was Adam, by whom synne entred into this world whan he brak the comaundementz of God. And therfore, he that first was so myghty that he sholde nat have dyed, bicam swich oon that he moste nedes dye, wheither he wolde or noon, and al his progenye in this world that in thilke man synneden.

[325] Looke, that in thestaat of innocence, whan Adam and Eve naked weren in Paradys and no thyng ne hadden shame of hir nakednesse, how that the serpent, that was moost wily of alle

320. *thee of thy*, H⁵ *him of his.*

othere beestes that God hadde maked, seyde to the womman, 'Why comaunded God to yow ye sholde nat eten of every tree in Paradys?' The womman answerde, 'Of the fruyt,' quod she, 'of the trees in Paradys we feden us, but soothly, of the fruyt of the tree that is in the myddel of Paradys God forbad us for to ete, and nat touchen it, lest peraventure we sholde dyen.' The serpent seyde to the womman, 'Nay, nay, ye shul nat dyen of deeth; for sothe, God woot that what day that ye eten ther-of youre eyen shul opene, and ye shul been as goddes, knowynge good and harm.'

The womman thanne saugh that the tree was good to feedyng, and fair to the eyen, and delitable to the sighte. She took of the fruyt of the tree, and eet it, and yaf to hire housbonde, and he eet, and anoon the eyen of hem bothe openeden; [330] and whan that they knewe that they were naked they sowed of fige leves a maner of breches, to hiden hire members.

There may ye seen that deedly synne hath first suggestioun of the feend, as sheweth heere by the naddre, and afterward the delit of the flessh, as sheweth heere by Eve, and after that the consentynge of resoun, as sheweth heere by Adam. For trust wel, though so were that the feend tempted Eve, that is to seyn the flessh, and the flessh hadde delit in the beautee of the fruyt defended, yet certes til that resoun, that is to seyn Adam, consented to the etynge of the fruyt, yet stood he in thestaat of innocence. Of thilke Adam tooke we thilke synne original, for of hym flesshly descended be we alle, and engendred of vile and corrupt mateere; and whan the soule is put in oure body, right anon is contract original synne, and that that was erst but oonly peyne of concupiscence is afterward both peyne and synne; [335] and therfore be we alle born sones of wratthe and of dampnacioun perdurable, if it nere baptesme that we receyven, which bynymeth us the culpe. But for sothe the peyne dwelleth with us as to temptacioun, which peyne highte concupiscence. And this concupiscence whan it is wrongfully disposed or ordeyned in man it maketh hym coveite by coveitise of flessh, flesshly synne by sighte of his eyen as to ertthely thynges, and eek coveitise of hynesse by pride of herte.

Now, as for to speken of the firste coveitise, that is concupiscence after the lawe of oure membres that weren lawefulliche y-maked and by rightful juggement of God. I seye, forasmuche as man is nat obeisaunt to God, that is his Lord, therfore is the flessh to hym disobeisaunt thurgh concupiscence, which yet is cleped norrissynge of synne, and occasion of synne. Therfore al the while that a man hath in hym the peyne of concupiscence it is impossible but he be tempted somtime and moeved in his flessh to synne, [340] and this thyng may nat faille as longe as he lyveth. It may wel wexe fieble and faille by vertu of baptesme, and by the grace of God thurgh penitence, but fully ne shal it never quenche, that he ne shal som tyme be moeved in hymself, but if he were al refreyded by siknesse, or by malefice of sorcerie, or colde drynkes. For lo, what seith Seint Paul, 'The flessh coveiteth agayn the spirit, and the spirit agayn the flessh; they been so contrarie and so stryven that a man may nat alwey doon as he wolde.' The same Seint Paul after his grete penaunce in water and in lond ;—in water by nyght and by day, in greet peril and in greet peyne ; in lond, in famyne, in thurst, in coold, and cloothlees, and ones stoned almoost to the deeth,—yet seyde he, 'Allas ! I caytyf man, who shal delivere me fro the prisoun of my caytyf body?' [345] And Seint Jerome, whan he longe tyme hadde woned in desert, where as he hadde no compaignye but of wilde beestes, where as he ne hadde no mete but herbes, and water to his drynke, ne no bed but the naked erthe, for which his flessh was blak as an Ethiopeen for heete, and ny destroyed for coold, yet seyde he that the brennynge of lecherie

boyled in al his body ; wherfore, I woot wel sykerly, that they been deceyved that seyn that they ne be nat tempted in hir body. Witnesse on Seint Jame the Apostel, that seith that every wight is tempted in his owene concupiscence, that is to seyn, that everich of us hath matere and occasioun to be tempted of the norissynge of synne that is in his body. And therfore seith Seint John the evaungelist, 'If that we seyn that we beth withoute synne, we deceyve us selve, and trouthe is nat in us.'

[350] Now shal ye understonde in what manere that synne wexeth and encreesseth in man. The firste thyng is thilke norissynge of synne of which I spak biforn, thilke flesshly concupiscence; and after that comth the subjeccioun of the devel, this is to seyn the develes bely, with which he bloweth in man the fir of flesshly concupiscence ; and after that a man bithynketh hym wheither he wol doon, or no, thilke thing to which he is tempted. And thanne, if that a man withstonde and weyve the firste entisynge of his flessh, and of the feend, thanne is it no synne ; and if it so be that he do nat so, thanne feeleth he anoon a flambe of delit, and thanne is it good to be war and kepen hym wel, or elles he wol falle anon into consentynge of synne ; and thanne wol he do it, if he may have tyme and place. [355] And of this matere seith Moyses, by the devel, in this manere : The feend seith, 'I wole chace and pursue the man by wikked suggestioun, and I wole hente hym by moevynge and stirynge of synne; I wol departe my prise, or my praye, by deliberacioun, and my lust shal been accompliced in delit ; I wol drawe my swerd in consentynge,'— for certes, right as a swerd departeth a thyng in two peces, right so consentynge departeth God fro man,—'and thanne wol I sleen hym with myn hand in dede of synne' ; thus seith the feend; for certes, thanne is a man al deed in soule. And thus is synne accompliced

by temptacioun, by delit, and by consentynge, and thanne is the synne cleped actueel.

Forsothe synne is in two maneres, outher it is venial, or deedly synne. Soothly, whan man loveth any creature moore than Jhesu Crist oure Creatour, thanne is it deedly synne. And venial synne is it, if man love Jhesu Crist lasse than hym oughte. Forsothe the dede of this venial synne is ful perilous, for it amenuseth the love that men sholde han to God moore and moore. [360] And therfore if a man charge hymself with manye swiche venial synnes, certes, but if so be that he som tyme descharge hym of hem by shrifte, they mowe ful lightly amenuse in hym al the love that he hath to Jhesu Crist ; and in this wise skippeth venial into deedly synne, for certes, the moore that a man chargeth his soule with venial synne, the moore is he enclyned to fallen into deedly synne. And therfore lat us nat be necligent to deschargen us of venial synnes, for the proverbe seith that 'manye smale maken a greet.' And herkne this ensample ; a greet wawe of the see comth somtyme with so greet a violence that it drencheth the shipe ; and the same harm dooth som tyme the smale dropes of water that entren thurgh a litel crevace into the thurrok, and in the botme of the shipe, if men be so necligent that they ne descharge hem nat by tyme. And therfore, although ther be a difference bitwixe thise two causes of drenchynge, algates the shipe is dreynt. [365] Right so fareth it somtyme of deedly synne, and of anoyouse veniale synnes, whan they multiplie in a man so greetly that thilke worldly thynges that he loveth, thurgh whiche he synneth venyally, is as greet in his herte as the love of God, or moore. And therfore the love of every thyng that is nat biset in God, ne doon principally for Goddes sake, al though that a man love it lasse than God, yet is it venial synne, and deedly synne whan

the love of any thyng weyeth in the herte of man as muchel as the love of God, or moore. Deedly synne, as seith Seint Augustyn, is ' whan a man turneth his herte fro God, which that is verray sovereyn bountee, that may nat chaunge, and yeveth his herte to thyng that may chaunge and flitte ' ; and certes, that is every thyng, save God of hevene. For sooth is that if a man yeve his love, the which that he oweth al to God with al his herte, unto a creature, certes as muche as he yeveth of his love to thilke creature, so muche he bireveth fro God, [370] and therfore dooth he synne, for he that is dettour to God ne yeldeth nat to God al his dette, that is to seyn, al the love of his herte.

Now, sith man understondeth generally which is venial synne, thanne is it covenable to tellen specially of synnes whiche that many a man peraventure ne demeth hem nat synnes, and ne shryveth hem nat of the same thynges, and yet nathelees they been synnes. Soothly, as thise clerkes writen, this is to seyn, that at every tyme that a man eteth or drynketh moore than suffiseth to the sustenaunce of his body, in certein he dooth synne ; and eek whan he speketh moore than nedeth it is synne ; eke whan he herkneth nat benignely the compleint of the poure ; eke whan he is in heele of body and wol nat faste whan hym oghte faste, withouten cause resonable ; eke whan he slepeth moore than nedeth, or whan he comth by thilke enchesoun to late to chirche, or to othere werkes of charite ; [375] eke whan he useth his wyf withouten sovereyn desir of engendrure, to the honour of God, or for the entente to yelde to his wyf the dette of his body ; eke whan he wol nat visite the sike and the prisoner, if he may ; eke if he love wyf or child, or oother worldly thyng, moore than resoun requireth ; eke if he flatere or blandise moore than hym oghte, for any necessitee ; eke if he amenuse or withdrawe the

370. *hym oghte*, H⁶ *other folk (other men)*.

almesse of the poure; eke if he appar-ailleth his mete moore deliciously than nede is, or ete to hastily, by likerous-nesse; eke if he tale vanytees at chirche, or at Goddes service, or that he be a talker of ydel wordes, of folye, or of vileynye,—for he shal yelden acountes of it at the day of doome; eke whan he biheteth or assureth to do thynges that he may nat perfourne; eke whan that he by lightnesse or folie mysseyeth or scorneth his neighebore; [380] eke whan he hath any wikked suspecioun of thyng ther he ne woot of it no sooth-fastnesse; thise thynges and mo withoute nombre been synnes, as seith Seint Augustyn.

Now shal men understonde that al be it so that noon erthely man may eschue alle venial synnes, yet may he refreyne hym by the brennynge love that he hath to oure Lord Jhesu Crist, and by preyeres and confessioun and othere goode werkes, so that it shal but litel greve; for, as seith Saint Augustyn, 'If a man love God in swich manere that al that ever he dooth is in the love of God, and for the love of God verraily, for he brenneth in the love of God, looke, how muche that a drope of water that falleth in a fourneys ful of fyr anoyeth or greveth, so muche anoyeth a venial synne unto a man that is perfit in the love of Jhesu Crist.' [385] Men may also refreyne venial synne by receyvynge worthily of the precious body of Jhesu Crist; by receyvyng eek of hooly water, by almes-dede, by general confessioun of *Confiteor* at masse, and at complyn, and by blessynge of bisshopes and of preestes and oothere goode werkes.

Sequitur de septem peccatis mortalibus et eorum dependenciis et speciebus

Now is it bihovely thyng to telle

Sequitur de septem peccatis. At this point Chaucer begins to follow the *Somme de Vices et de Vertus* of Frère Lorens, altering, however, his arrangement, and with less close logical coherence.

whiche been the deedly synnes, this is to seyn chieftaynes of synnes. Alle they renne in o lees, but in diverse maneres. Now been they cleped chieftaynes, for-as-muche as they been chief, and spryngen of alle othere synnes. Of the roote of thise sevene synnes thanne is pride, the general roote of alle harmes, for of this roote spryngen certein braunches, as ire; envye; accidie, or slewthe; avarice, or coveitise, to commune understondynge; glotonye, and lecherye. And everich of thise chief synnes hath his braunches and his twigges as shal be declared in hire chapitres folwynge.

De Superbia

[390] And thogh so be that no man kan outrely telle the nombre of twigges and of the harmes that cometh of pride, yet wol I shewe a partie of hem, as ye shul understonde. Ther is inobedience, avauntynge, ypocrisie, despit, arrogance, inpudence, swellynge of herte, insolence, elacioun, inpacience, strif, contumacie, presumpcioun, irreverence, pertinacie, veyne glorie and many another twig that I kan nat declare. Inobedient is he that disobeyeth for despit to the comandementz of God and to his sovereyns and to his goostly fader. Avauntour is he that bosteth of the harm or of the bountee that he hath doon. Ypocrite is he that hideth to shewe hym swich as he is, and sheweth hym swich as he noght is. [395] Despitous is he that hath desdeyn of his neighebore, that is to seyn of his evene Cristene, or hath despit to doon that hym oghte to do. Arrogant is he that thynketh that he hath thilke bountees in hym that he hath noght, or weneth that he sholde have hem by his desertes, or elles he demeth that he be that he nys nat. Inpudent is he that for his pride hath no shame of his synnes. Swellynge of herte is whan a man rejoyseth hym of

385. *as ire*, etc. These are really treated separately, and not as branches of Pride.

harm that he hath doon. Insolent is he that despiseth in his juggement alle othere folk, as to regard of his value, and of his konnyng, and of his spekyng, and of his beryng. [400] Elacioun is whan he ne may neither suffre to have maister ne felawe. Inpacient is he that wol nat been y-taught ne undernome of his vice, and by strif werreieth trouthe wityngly, and deffendeth his folye. Contumax is he that thurgh his in- dignacioun is agayns everich auctoritee or power of hem that been his sovereyns. Presumpcioun is whan a man under- taketh an emprise that hym oghte nat do, or elles that he may nat do, and this is called surquidie. Irreverence is whan men do nat honour there as hem oghte to doon, and waiten to be reverenced. Pertinacie is whan man deffendeth his folies, and trusteth to muchel in his owene wit. [405] Veyneglorie is for to have pompe and delit in his temporeel hynesse, and glorifie hym in this worldly estaat. Janglynge is whan men speken to muche biforn folk, and clappen as a mille, and taken no kepe what they seye.

And yet is ther a privee spece of pride that waiteth first to be salewed er he wole salewe, al be he lasse worth than that oother is, peraventure; and eek he waiteth or desireth to sitte, or elles to goon above hym in the wey, or kisse pax, or been encensed, or goon to offryng biforn his neighebore, and swiche semblable thynges, agayns his duetee, peraventure, but that he hath his herte and his entente in swich a proud desir to be magnified and honoured biforn the peple.

Now been ther two maneres of pride. That oon of hem is withinne the herte of man and that oother is withoute, [410] of whiche soothly thise forseyde thynges, and mo than I have seyd, apertenen to pride that is in the herte of man, and that othere speces of pride been withoute;

but natheles that oon of thise speces of pride is signe of that oother, right as the gaye leefsel atte taverne is signe of the wyn that is in the celer. And this is in manye thynges, as in speche and con- tenaunce, and in outrageous array of clothyng; for certes, if ther ne hadde be no synne in clothyng, Crist wolde nat so soone have noted and spoken of the clothyng of thilke riche man in the gospel. And as seith Seint Gregorie, 'That precious clothyng is cowpable for the derthe of it, and for his softenesse and for his strangenesse and degisynesse, and for the superfluitee, and for the inordinat scantnesse of it.'

[415] Allas! may men nat seen as in oure dayes the synful costlewe array of clothynge, and namely in to muche superfluite, or elles in to desordinat scantnesse?

As to the firste synne, in superfluitee of clothynge, which that maketh it so deere to harm of the peple, nat oonly the cost of embrowdynge, the degise, endentynge, barrynge, owndynge, palynge, wyndynge or bendynge, and semblable wast of clooth in vanitee, but ther is also costlewe furrynge in hir gownes, so muche pownsonynge of chisel to maken holes, so muche daggynge of sheres; forth-with the superfluitee in lengthe of the forseide gownes, trailynge in the dong, and in the mire, on horse and eek on foote, as wel of men as of wommen, that al thilke trailyng is verraily as in effect wasted, consumed, thredbare, and roten with donge, rather than it is yeven to the poure, to greet damage of the forseyde poure folk. [420] And that in sondry wise; this is to seyn, that the moore that clooth is wasted, the moore it costeth to the peple for the scantnesse. And forther-over if so be that they wolde yeven swich powsoned and dagged clothyng to the poure folk, it is nat convenient to were for hire estaat, ne suffisant to beete hire necessitee

405. *privee spece*, secret kind. This section is Chaucer's addition.

410. On the subject of clothes, Chaucer greatly expands his original.

to kepe hem fro the distemperance of the firmament.

Upon that oother side to speken of the horrible disordinat scantnesse of clothyng as been thise kutted sloppes, or haynselyns, that thurgh hire shortnesse ne covere nat the shameful membres of man, to wikked entente. Allas! somme of hem shewen the boce of hir shape, and the horrible swollen membres, that semeth lik the maladie of hirnia, in the wrappynge of hir hoses; and eek the buttokes of hem faren as it were the hyndre part of a she ape in the fulle of the moone. [425] And mooreover the wrecched swollen membres that they shewe thurgh the degisynge, in departynge of hire hoses in whit and reed, semeth that half hir shameful privee membres weren flayne. And if so be that they departen hire hoses in othere colours, as is whit and blak, or whit and blew, or blak and reed, and so forth, thanne semeth it as by variaunce of colour that half the partie of hire privee membres were corrupt by the fir of Seint Antony, or by cancre, or by oother swich meschaunce. Of the hyndre part of hir buttokes it is ful horrible for to see, for certes, in that partie of hir body ther as they purgen hir stynkynge ordure, that foule partie shewe they to the peple prowdly in despit of honestitee, the which honestitee that Jhesu Crist and his freendes observede to shewen in hir lyve. [430] Now of the outrageous array of wommen, God woot that though the visages of somme of hem seme ful chaast and debonaire, yet notifie they in hire array of atyr likerousnesse and pride. I sey nat that honestitee in clothynge of man or womman is uncovenable, but certes the superfluitee or disordinat scantitee of clothynge is reprevable. Also the synne of aornement, or of apparaille, is in thynges that apertenen to ridynge,—as in to manye delicat horses that been hoolden for delit, that been so faire, fatte, and costlewe, and also to

many a vicious knave that is sustened by cause of hem; in to curious harneys, as in sadeles, in crouperes, peytrels, and bridles covered with precious clothyng, and riche barres, and plates of gold, and of silver; for which God seith, by Zakarie the prophete, 'I wol confounde the rideres of swiche horses.' [435] This folk taken litel reward of the ridynge of Goddes sone of hevene and of his harneys whan he rood upon the asse, and ne hadde noon oother harneys but the poure clothes of his disciples, ne we ne rede nat that ever he rood on oother beest. I speke this for the synne of superfluitee, and nat for resonable honestitee, whan reson it requireth.

And forther, certes, pride is greetly notified in holdynge of greet meynee whan they be of litel profit, or of right no profit; and namely whan that meynee is felonous and damageous to the peple, by hardynesse of heigh lordshipe, or by wey of offices; for certes, swiche lordes sellen thanne hir lordshipe to the devel of helle, whanne they sustenen the wikkednesse of hir meynee. [440] Or elles whan this folk of lowe degree, as thilke that holden hostelries, sustenen the thefte of hire hostilers, and that is in many manere of deceites. Thilke manere of folk been the flyes that folwen the hony, or elles the houndes that folwen the careyne. Swich forseyde folk stranglen spiritually hir lordshipes, for which thus seith David the prophete, 'Wikked deeth moote come upon thilke lordshipes, and God yeve that they moote descenden into helle al doun, al doun; for in hire houses been iniquitees and shrewednesses, and nat God of hevene.' And certes, but if they doon amendement, right as God yaf his benysoun to Pharao by the service of Jacob, and to Laban by the service of Joseph, right so God wol yeve his malisoun to swiche lordshipes as sustenen

440. *Pharao . . . Jacob.* All the seven MSS. have the names in this order, so it may be Chaucer's mistake.

the wikkednesse of hir servauntz, but if they come to amendement.

Pride of the table appeereth eek ful ofte ; for certes, riche men been cleped to festes and poure folk been put awey and rebuked. [445] Also in excesse of diverse metes and drynkes, and namely swiche manere bake-metes and disshmetes, brennynge of wilde fir, and peynted and castelled with papir, and semblable wast, so that it is abusioun for to thynke. And eek in to greet preciousnesse of vessel and curiositee of mynstralcie, by whiche a man is stired the moore to delices of luxurie. If so be that he sette his herte the lasse upon oure Lord Jhesu Crist, certeyn it is a synne ; and certeinly the delices myghte been so grete in this caas that man myghte lightly falle by hem into deedly synne.

The especes that sourden of pride, soothly, whan they sourden of malice ymagined, avised, and forncast, or elles of usage, been deedly synnes, it is no doute ; and whan they sourden by freletee unavysed and sodeynly withdrawen ageyn, al been they grevouse synnes, I gesse that they ne been nat deedly.

[450] Now myghte men axe wher-of that pride sourdeth and spryngeth, and I seye, somtyme it spryngeth of the goodes of nature, and somtyme of the goodes of fortune, and somtyme of the goodes of grace. Certes, the goodes of nature stonden outher in goodes of body or in goodes of soule. Certes, goodes of body been heele of body, as strengthe, delivernesse, beautee, gentrie, franchise ; goodes of nature of the soule been good wit, sharpe understondynge, subtil engyn, vertu natureel, good memorie ; goodes of fortune been richesse, hyghe degrees of lordshipes, preisynges of the peple ; [455] goodes of grace been science, power to suffre spiritueel travaille, benignitee, vertuous contemplacioun, withstondynge of temptacioun, and semblable thynges ; of whiche forseyde goodes, certes, it is a ful greet folye a man to priden hym in

any of hem alle. Now as for to speken of goodes of nature ; God woot that somtyme we han hem in nature as muche to oure damage as to oure profit. As for to speken of heele of body, certes, it passeth ful lightly, and eek it is ful ofte enchesoun of the siknesse of oure soule ; for, God woot, the flessh is a ful greet enemy to the soule, and therfore the moore that the body is hool the moore be we in peril to falle. Eke for to pride hym in his strengthe of body, it is an heigh folye, for certes, the flessh coveiteth agayn the spirit, and ay the moore strong that the flessh is, the sorier may the soule be, [460] and over al this, strengthe of body and worldly hardynesse causeth ful ofte many a man to peril and meschaunce. Eek for to pride hym of his gentrie is ful greet folie, for ofte tyme the gentrie of the body binymeth the gentrie of the soule, and eek we ben alle of o fader and of o mooder, and alle we been of o nature, roten and corrupt, bothe riche and poure. Forsothe o manere gentrie is for to preise—that apparailleth mannes corage with vertues and moralitees and maketh hym Cristes child ; for truste wel, that over what man that synne hath maistrie he is a verray cherl to synne.

Now been ther generale signes of gentillesse, as eschewynge of vice and ribaudye and servage of synne, in word, in werk, and contenaunce, [465] and usynge vertu, curteisye, and clennesse, and to be liberal, that is to seyn, large by mesure, for thilke that passeth mesure is folie and synne. Another is to remembre hym of bountee that he of oother folk hath receyved. Another is to be benigne to his goode subgetis, wherfore seith Senek, ' Ther is no thing moore covenable to a man of heigh estaat, than debonairetee and pitee ' ; and therfore thise flyes that men clepeth bees, whan they maken hir kyng,. they chesen oon that hath no prikke wherwith he may stynge.

Another is, a man to have a noble

herte, and a diligent to attayne to heighe vertuoose thynges. Now certes, a man to pride hym in the goodes of grace is eek an outrageous folie, for thilke yifte of grace that sholde have turned hym to goodnesse and to medicine, turneth hym to venym and to confusioun, as seith Seint Gregorie. [470] Certes also, who-so prideth hym in the goodes of fortune, he is a ful greet fool, for somtyme is a man a greet lord by the morwe, that is a caytyf and a wrecche er it be nyght; and somtyme the richesse of a man is cause of his deth; somtyme the delices of a man is cause of the grevous maladye thurgh which he dyeth. Certes, the commendacioun of the peple is somtyme ful fals and ful brotel for to triste,—this day they preyse, tomorwe they blame; God woot, desir to have commendacioun of the peple hath caused deeth to many a bisy man.

Remedium contra peccatum Superbie

[475] Now sith that so is that ye han understonde what is pride, and whiche been the speces of it, and whennes pride sourdeth and spryngeth, now shul ye understonde which is the remedie agayns the synne of pride; and that is humylitee or mekenesse, that is a vertu thurgh which a man hath verray knoweleche of hymself, and holdeth of hymself no pris ne deyntee, as in regard of his desertes, considerynge ever his freletee.

Now been ther thre maneres of humy-litee; as humylitee in herte, and another humylitee in his mouth, the thridde in his werkes.

The humilitee in herte is in foure maneres. That oon is whan a man holdeth hymself as noght worth biforn God of hevene. Another is, whan he ne despiseth noon oother man. [480] The thridde is whan he rekketh nat though men holde hym noght worth.

470. *Remedium.* In the *Somme de Vices*, etc., the remedies and the sins are kept apart. Chaucer brings each remedy after its sin.

The ferthe is whan he nys nat sory of his humiliacioun.

Also the humilitee of mouth is in foure thynges; in attempree speche, and in humblesse of speche; and whan he biknoweth with his owene mouth that he is swich as hym thynketh that he is in his herte; another is whan he preiseth the bountee of another man and no thyng therof amenuseth.

Humilitee eek in werkes is in foure maneres; the firste is whan he putteth othere men biforn hym; the seconde is to chese the loweste place over al; the thridde is gladly to assente to good conseil; the ferthe is to stonde gladly to the award of his sovereyns, or of hym that is in hyer degree. Certein this is a greet werk of humylitee.

Sequitur de Invidia

After pride wol I speken of the foule synne of envye, which is, as by the word of the philosophre, sorwe of oother mannes prosperitee; and after the word of Seint Augustyn, it is sorwe of oother mannes wele and joye of othere mennes harm. [485] This synne is platly agayns the Hooly Goost. Al be it so that every synne is agayns the Hooly Goost, yet nathelees for-as-muche as bountee aperteneth proprely to the Hooly Goost, and envye comth proprely of malice, therfore it is proprely agayn the bountee of the Hooly Goost.

Now hath malice two speces, that is to seyn, hardnesse of herte in wikkednesse, or elles the flessh of man is so blynd that he considereth nat that he is in synne, or rekketh nat that he is in synne, which is the hardnesse of the devel.

That oother spece of malice is whan a man werreyeth trouthe, whan he woot that it is trouthe, and eek whan he wer-reyeth the grace that God hath yeve to his neighebore; and al this is by envye. Certes thanne is envye the worste synne that is; for soothly alle othere synnes been somtyme oonly agayns o special vertu, but certes, envye is agayns alle vertues, and agayns alle goodnesses, for it is sory of alle the bountees of his neighebore ; and in this manere it is divers from alle othere synnes ; [490] for wel unnethe is ther any synne that it ne hath som delit in itself, save oonly envye, that ever hath in itself angwissh and sorwe.

The speces of envye been thise ; ther is first, sorwe of oother mannes goodnesse and of his prosperitee ; and prosperitee is kyndely matere of joye ; thanne is envye a synne agayns kynde. The seconde spece of envye is joye of oother mannes harm ; and that is proprely lyk to the devel, that ever rejoyseth hym of mannes harm.

Of thise two speces comth bakbityng, and this synne of bakbityng, or detraccion, hath certeine speces, as thus ; som man preiseth his neighebore by a wikke entente, for he maketh alwey a wikked knotte atte laste ende, alwey he maketh a 'but' atte laste ende,—that is digne of moore blame than worth is al the preisynge. [495] The seconde spece is that if a man be good, and dooth or seith a thing to good entente, the bakbiter wol turne all thilke goodnesse up-so-doun, to his shrewed entente. The thridde is to amenuse the bountee of his neighebore. The fourthe spece of bakbityng is this, that if men speke goodnesse of a man, thanne wol the bakbiter seyn, ' Pardee ! swich a man is yet bet than he,' in dispreisynge of hym that men preise.

The fifte spece is this, for to consente gladly and herkne gladly to the harm that men speke of oother folk ; this synne is ful greet and ay encreeseth after the wikked entente of the bakbiter.

After bakbityng cometh grucchyng or murmuracioun, and somtyme it spryngeth of inpacience agayns God, and somtyme agayns man.

[500] Agayns God it is whan a man gruccheth agayn the peynes of helle, or agayns poverte, or loss of catel, agayn reyn or tempest, or elles gruccheth that shrewes han prosperitee, or elles for that goode men han adversitee ; and alle thise thynges sholde men suffre paciently, for they comen by the rightful juggement and ordinance of God. Somtyme comth grucching of avarice, as Judas grucched agayns the Magdaleyne, whan she enoynte the heved of oure Lord Jhesu Crist with hir precious oynement. This maner murmure is swich as whan man gruccheth of goodnesse that hymself dooth, or that oother folk doon of hir owene catel.

Somtyme comth murmure of pride, as whan Simon the Pharisee grucched agayn the Magdaleyne, whan she approched to Jhesu Crist and weepe at his feet for hire synnes. [505] And somtyme grucchyng sourdeth of envye, whan men discovereth a mannes harm that was pryvee, or bereth hym on hond thyng that is fals.

Murmure eek is ofte amonges servantz, that grucchen whan hir sovereyns bidden hem doon leveful thynges ; and, for-as-muche as they dar nat openly withseye the comaundementz of hir sovereyns, yet wol they seyn harm, and grucche and murmure prively, for verray despit, whiche wordes men clepen 'the develes *Pater noster*,' though so be that the devel ne hadde never *Pater noster*, but that lewed folk yeven it swich a name. Somtyme grucchyng comth of ire, or prive hate that norisseth rancour in herte, as afterward I shal declare. [510] Thanne cometh eek bitternesse of herte, thurgh which bitternesse every good dede of his neighebor semeth to hym bitter and unsavory. Thanne cometh discord that unbyndeth alle manere of freendshipe. Thanne comth scornynge of his neighebor, al do he never so weel. Thanne comth accusynge, as whan man seketh occasioun to anoyen his neighebor, which that is lyk to the craft of the devel, that waiteth bothe nyght and day to accusen us alle. Thanne comth malignitee, thurgh which a man anoyeth his neighebor prively, if he may ; and if he noght may, algate his wikked wil ne shal nat wante, as for to

505. *withseye*, contradict ; H *withstonde*.
505. *folk . . . name*, H *men calle it so.*

brennen his hous pryvely, or empoysone or sleen his beestes, and semblable thynges.

[515] *Remedium contra peccatum Invidie*

Now wol I speke of the remedie agayns this foule synne of envye. First is the lovynge of God principal, and lovyng of his neighebor as hymself, for soothly that oon ne may nat been withoute that oother. And truste wel, that in the name of thy neighebore thou shalt understonde the name of thy brother; for certes alle we have o fader flesshly, and o mooder, that is to seyn, Adam and Eve; and eek o Fader espiritueel, and that is God of hevene. Thy neighebore artow holden for to love and wilne hym alle goodnesse, and therfore seith God, 'Love thy neighebore as thyselve'; that is to seyn, to salvacioun of lyf and of soule. And moore-over thou shalt love hym in word, and in benigne amonestynge and chastisynge, and conforten hym in his anoyes, and preye for hym with al thyn herte. And in dede thou shalt love hym in swich wise that thou shalt doon to hym in charitee as thou woldest that it were doon to thyn owene persone; [520] and therfore thou ne shalt doon hym no damage in wikked word, ne harm in his body, ne in his catel, ne in his soule by entissyng of wikked ensample; thou shalt nat desiren his wyf, ne none of his thynges. Understoood eek, that in the name of neighebor is comprehended his enemy. Certes man shal loven his enemy by the comandement of God, and soothly, thy freend shaltow love in God. I seye, thyn enemy shaltow love for Goddes sake by his comandement; for if it were reson that a man sholde haten his enemy, forsothe God nolde nat receyven us to his love, that been his enemys. Agayns thre manere of wronges that his enemy dooth to hym he shal doon thre thynges, as thus: [525] agayns hate and rancour of herte, he shal love hym in herte; agayns chidyng and wikkede

wordes, he shal preye for his enemy; and agayn wikked dede of his enemy, he shal doon hym bountee; for Crist seith, 'Loveth youre enemys, and preyeth for hem that speke yow harm, and eek for hem that yow chacen and pursewen, and dooth bountee to hem that yow haten." Loo, thus comaundeth us oure Lord Jhesu Crist to do to oure enemys, for soothly nature dryveth us to loven oure freendes, and *parfey*, oure enemys han moore nede to love than oure freendes; and they that moore nede have, certes, to hem shal men doon goodnesse; and certes, in thilke dede have we remembrance of the love of Jhesu Crist that deyde for his enemys. And, in as muche as thilke love is the moore grevous to perfourne, in so muche is the moore gretter the merite, and therfore the lovynge of oure enemy hath confounded the venym of the devel; [530] for, right as the devel is disconfited by humylitee, right so is he wounded to the deeth by love of oure enemy. Certes thanne is love the medicine that casteth out the venym of envye fro mannes herte. The speces of this paas shullen be moore largely in hir chapitres folwynge declared.

Sequitur de Ira

After envye wol I discryven the synne of ire; for soothly whoso hath envye upon his neighebor anon he wole comunly fynde hym a matere of wratthe in word, or in dede, agayns hym to whom he hath envye. And as wel comth ire of pride as of envye, for soothly he that is proude or envyous is lightly wrooth.

[535] This synne of ire, after the discryvyng of Seint Augustyn, is wikked wil to been avenged by word or by dede. Ire, after the philosophre, is the fervent blood of man y-quyked in his herte, thurgh which he wole harm to hym that he hateth. For certes, the herte of man, by eschawfynge and moevynge of his blood, wexeth so trouble that he is out of alle juggement of resoun.

284

But ye shal understonde that ire is in two maneres; that oon of hem is good and that oother is wikked. The goode ire is by jalousie of goodnesse, thurgh which a man is wrooth with wikkednesse, and agayns wikkednesse; and therfore seith a wys man, that ire is bet than pley. [540] This ire is with debonairetee, and it is wrooth withouten bitternesse, nat wrooth agayns the man, but wrooth with the mysdede of the man, as seith the prophete David, *Irascimini, et nolite peccare.*

Now understondeth that wikked ire is in two maneres, that is to seyn, sodeyn ire, or hastif ire withouten avisement and consentynge of resoun. The menyng and the sens of this is, that the resoun of man ne consente nat to thilke sodeyn ire; and thanne it is venial. Another ire is ful wikked, that comth of felonie of herte, avysed and cast biforn with wikked wil to do vengeance, and therto his resoun consenteth; and soothly this is deedly synne. This ire is so displesant to God that it troubleth his hous and chaceth the Hooly Goost out of mannes soule, and wasteth and destroyeth the liknesse of God, that is to seyn, the vertu that is in mannes soule, [545] and put in hym the liknesse of the devel, and bynymeth the man fro God that is his rightful lord. This ire is a ful greet plesaunce to the devel, for it is the develes fourneys that is eschawfed with the fir of helle. For certes, right so as fir is moore mighty to destroyen erthely thynges than any oother element, right so ire is myghty to destroyen alle spiritueel thynges.

Looke how that fir of smale gleedes, that been almoost dede under asshen, wollen quike agayn whan they been touched with brymstoon. Right so ire wol evermo quyken agayn whan it is touched by the pride that is covered in mannes herte; for certes, fir ne may nat comen out of no thyng, but if it were first in the same thyng natureelly, as fir is drawen out of flyntes with steel. [550] And, right so as pride is ofte tyme matere of ire, right so is rancour norice and keper of ire. Ther is a maner tree, as seith Seint Ysidre, that whan men maken fire of thilke tree and covere the coles of it with asshen, soothly the fir of it wol lasten al a yeer or moore, and right so fareth it of rancour; whan it is ones conceyved in the hertes of som men, certein it wol lasten peraventure from oon Estre day unto another Estre day and moore; but certes, thilke man is ful fer fro the mercy of God in thilke while.

In this forseyde develes fourneys ther forgen thre shrewes: Pride, that ay bloweth and encreesseth the fir by chidynge and wikked wordes; [555] thanne stant Envye, and holdeth the hoote iren upon the herte of man with a peire of longe toonges of long rancour; and thanne stant the synne of Contumelie or strif and cheeste, and batereth and forgeth by vileyns reprevynges. Certes, this cursed synne anoyeth bothe to the man hymself and eek to his neighebore. For soothly, almoost al the harm that any man dooth to his neighebore comth of wratthe; for certes, outrageous wratthe dooth al that ever the devel hym comaundeth: for he ne spareth neither Crist, ne his sweete mooder. And in his outrageous anger and ire, allas! allas! ful many oon at that tyme feeleth in his herte ful wikkedly both of Crist and of alle his halwes.

[560] Is nat this a cursed vice? Yis, certes. Allas! it bynymeth from man his wit and his resoun and al his debonaire lif espiritueel, that sholde kepen his soule.

Certes it bynymeth eek Goddes due lordshipe, and that is mannes soule and the love of his neighebores. It stryveth eek alday agayn trouthe. It reveth hym the quiete of his herte and subverteth his soule.

Of ire comen thise stynkynge engendrures; first, hate, that is oold wratthe; discord, thurgh which a man forsaketh his olde freend that he hath lovede ful longe; and thanne cometh werre, and every manere of wrong that man dooth to his neighebore in body, or in catel. Of this cursed synne of ire cometh eek manslaughtre, and understonde wel that homycide, that is manslaughtre, is in diverse wise. Som manere of homycide is spiritueel, and som is bodily.

[565] Spiritueel manslaughtre is in sixe thynges. First, by hate, as Seint John seith, 'He that hateth his brother is homycide.' Homycide is eek by bakbitynge; of whiche bakbiteres seith Salomon, that they han two swerdes with whiche they sleen hire neighebores; for soothly as wikke is to bynyme his good name, as his lyf. Homycide is eek in yevynge of wikked conseil by fraude, as for to yeven conseil to areysen wrongful custumes and taillages, of whiche seith Salomon : ' Leoun rorynge and bere hongry been like to the crueel lordshipes in withholdynge or abreggynge of the shepe (or the hyre), or of the wages of servauntz, or elles in usures or in withdrawynge of the almesse of poure folk.' For which the wise man seith, 'Fedeth hym that almoost dyeth for honger'; for soothly, but if thow feede hym, thou sleest hym. And alle thise been deedly synnes. [570] Bodily manslaughtre is whan thow sleest him with thy tonge in oother manere, as whan thou comandest to sleen a man, or elles yevest hym conseil to sleen a man.

Manslaughtre in dede is in foure maneres. That oon is by lawe, right as a justice dampneth hym that is coupable to the deeth; but lat the justice be war that he do it rightfully, and that he do it nat for delit to spille blood, but for kepynge of rightwisenesse. Another homycide is that is doon for necessitee, as whan o man sleeth another in his defendaunt, and that he ne may noon ootherwise escape from his owene deeth; but certeinly, if he may escape withouten manslaughtre of his adversarie and sleeth hym, he dooth synne, and he shal bere

penance as for deedly synne. Eek if a man, by caas or aventure, shete an arwe, or caste a stoon, with which he sleeth a man, he is homycide. [575] Eek if a womman by necligence overlyeth hire child in hir slepyng, it is homycide and deedly synne. Eek whan man destourbeth concepcioun of a child, and maketh a womman outher bareyne by drynkynge venemouse herbes thurgh which she may nat conceyve, or sleeth a child by drynkes, or elles putteth certeine material thynges in hire secree places to slee the child, or elles dooth unkyndely synne by which man or womman shedeth hire nature, in manere or in place ther as a child may nat be conceived, or elles if a woman have conceyved and hurt hirselfe, and sleeth the child, yet it is homycide. What seye we eek of wommen that mordren hir children for drede of worldly shame? Certes, an horrible homicide! Homycide is eek if a man approcheth to a womman by desir of lecherie, thurgh which the child is perissed, or elles smyteth a womman wityngly, thurgh which she leseth hir child. Alle thise been homycides and horrible deedly synnes.

[580] Yet comen ther of ire manye mo synnes, as wel in word, as in thoght and in dede, as he that arretteth upon God, or blameth God of thyng of which he is hymself gilty, or despiseth God, and alle his halwes, as doon thise cursede hasardours in diverse contrees. This cursed synne doon they whan they feelen in hir hertes ful wikkedly of God and of his halwes; also whan they treten unreverently the sacrament of the auter,— thilke synne is so greet that unnethe may it been releessed, but that the mercy of God passeth alle his werkes, it is so greet, and he so benigne.

Thanne comth of ire attry angre, whan a man is sharpely amonested in his shrifte to forleten his synne, thanne wole he be angry and answeren hokerly and angrily, and deffenden or excusen

575. *by drynkes*, E adds *wilfully*.

his synne by unstedefastnesse of his flessh ; or elles he dide it for to holde compaignye with his felawes ; or elles he seith, the fend enticed hym ; [585] or elles he dide it for his youthe ; or elles his compleccioun is so corageous that he may nat forbere ; or elles it is his destinee, as he seith, unto a certain age ; or elles, he seith, it cometh hym of gentillesse of his auncestres ; and semblable thynges. Alle this manere of folk so wrappen hem in hir synnes that they ne wol nat delivere hemself ; for soothly no wight that excuseth hym wilfully of his synne may nat been delivered of his synne, til that he mekely biknoweth his synne.

After this thanne cometh sweryng, that is expres agayn the comandement of God ; and this bifalleth ofte of anger and of ire. God seith, 'Thow shalt nat take the name of thy Lord God in veyn,' or in ydel. Also oure Lord Jhesu Crist seith, by the word of Seint Mathew, 'Ne wol ye nat swere in alle manere ; neither by hevene, for it is Goddes trone ; ne by erthe, for it is the bench of his feet ; ne by Jerusalem, for it is the citee of a greet kyng ; ne by thyn heed, for thou mayst nat make an heer whit ne blak ; [590] but seyeth by youre word, "ye, ye," and "nay, nay" ; and what that is moore it is of yvel,' seith Crist. For Cristes sake, ne swereth nat so synfully, in dismembrynge of Crist by soule, herte, bones, and body ; for certes it semeth that ye thynke that the cursede Jewes ne dismembred nat ynough the preciouse persone of Crist, but ye dismembre hym moore. And if so be that the lawe compelle yow to swere, thanne rule yow after the lawe of God in youre sweryng, as seith Jeremye, 4° c°, Thou shalt kepe thre condicions ; 'thou shalt swere in trouthe, in doom, and in rightwisnesse' ; this is to seyn, thou shalt swere sooth ; for every lesynge is agayns Crist, for Crist is verray trouthe.

And thynk wel this, that every greet swerere, nat compelled lawefully to swere, the wounde shal nat departe from his hous whil he useth swich unleveful sweryng. Thou shalt sweren eek in doom, whan thou art constreyned by thy domesman to witnessen the trouthe. [595] Eek thow shalt nat swere for envye, ne for favour, ne for meede, but for rightwisnesse, and for declaracioun of it, to the worshipe of God, and helpyng of thyne evene Cristene. And therfore, every man that taketh Goddes name in ydel, or falsly swereth with his mouth, or elles taketh on hym the name of Crist, to be called a Cristene man, and lyveth agayns Cristes lyvynge and his techynge, alle they taken Goddes name in ydel.

Looke eek, what Seint Peter seith, *Actuum* 4°, *Non est aliud nomen sub celo*, etc. : 'Ther nys noon oother name,' seith Seint Peter, 'under hevene yeven to men, in which they mowe be saved' ; that is to seyn, but the name of Jhesu Crist. Take kepe eek how that the name of Crist so precious is, as seith Seint Paul *ad Philipenses* 2°, *In nomine Jhesu*, etc. : that 'in the name of Jhesu every knee of hevenely creatures, or erthely, or of helle, sholden bowe' ; for it is so heigh and so worshipful that the cursede feend in helle sholde tremblen to heeren it y-nempned. Thanne semeth it that men that sweren so horriblely by his blessed name, that they despise hym moore booldely than dide the cursede Jewes, or elles the devel, that trembleth whan he heereth his name. [600] Now certes, sith that sweryng, but if it be lawefully doon, is so heighly deffended, muche worse is forsweryng falsly, and yet nedelees.

What seye we eek of hem that deliten hem in sweryng and holden it a gentrie or a manly dede to swere grete othes ? And what of hem that of verray usage ne cesse nat to swere grete othes, al be the cause nat worth a straw ? Certes, it is horrible synne. Swerynge sodeynly, withoute avysement, is eek a synne.

590. *dismembrynge*, *i.e.* the swearing by Christ's different members ; cp. *Pardoner's Tale*, ll. 474, 475.

But lat us go now to thilke horrible sweryng of adjuracioun and conjuracioun, as doon thise false enchauntours or nigromanciens, in bacyns ful of water, or in a bright swerd, in a cercle, or in a fir, or in a shulder-boon of a sheepe ! I kan nat seye but that they doon cursedly and damnablely agayns Crist, and al the feith of hooly Chirche.

[605] What seye we of hem that bileeven in divynailes, as by flight or by noyse of briddes, or of beestes, or by sort, by geomancie, by dremes, by chirkynge of dores, or crakynge of houses, by gnawynge of rattes, and swich manere wrecchednesse ? Certes, al this thyng is deffended by God, and by al hooly Chirche ; for which they been acursed til they come to amendement, that on swich filthe setten hire bileeve. Charmes for woundes or maladie of men, or of beestes, if they taken any effect, it may be peraventure that God suffreth it, for folk sholden yeve the moore feith and reverence to his name.

Now wol I speken of lesynges, which generally is fals signyficacioun of word, in entente to deceyven his evene Cristene. Some lesynge is, of which ther comth noon avantage to no wight ; and som lesynge turneth to the ese and profit of o man, and to disese and damage of another man. [610] Another lesynge is for to saven his lyf or his catel. Another lesynge comth of delit for to lye, in which delit they wol forge a long tale and peynten it with alle circumstaunces, where al the ground of the tale is fals. Som lesynge comth for he wole sustene his word ; and som lesynge comth of reccheleesnesse withouten avisement ; and semblable thynges.

Lat us now touche the vice of flaterynge, which ne comth nat gladly, but for drede, or for coveitise. Flaterye is generally wrongful preisynge. Flatereres been the develes norices, that norissen his children with milk of losengerie. Forsothe Salomon seith that flaterie is wors than detraccioun, for somtyme detraccion maketh an hauteyn man be the moore

humble, for he dredeth detraccion ; but certes, flaterye, that maketh a man to enhauncen his herte and his contenaunce. [615] Flatereres been the develes enchauntours, for they make a man to wene of hymself be lyk that he nys nat lyk ; they been lyk to Judas, that bitraysed [God, and thise flatereres bitraysen] a man to sellen hym to his enemy, that is to the devel. Flatereres been the develes chapelleyns, that syngen ever *Placebo.* I rekene flaterie in the vices of ire, for ofte tyme if o man be wrooth with another, thanne wole he flatere som wight to sustene hym in his querele.

Speke we now of swich cursynge as comth of irous herte. Malisoun generally may be seyd every maner power or harm. Swich cursynge bireveth man fro the regne of God, as seith Seint Paul. [620] And ofte tyme swich cursynge wrongfully retorneth agayn to hym that curseth, as a bryd that retorneth agayn to his owene nest. And over alle thyng men oghten eschewe to cursen hire children, and yeven to the devel hire engendrure, as ferforth as in hem is ; certes it is greet peril and greet synne.

Lat us thanne speken of chidynge and reproche, whiche been ful grete woundes in mannes herte, for they unsowen the semes of freendshipe in mannes herte. For certes, unnethes may a man pleynly been accorded with hym that hath hym openly revyled and repreved in disclaundre. This is a ful grisly synne, as Crist seith in the gospel. And taak kepe now, that he that repreveth his neighebor, outher he repreveth hym by som harm of peyne that he hath on his body, as, 'mesel !' 'croked harlot !' or by som synne that he dooth. [625] Now if he repreve hym by harm of peyne, thanne turneth the repreve to Jhesu Crist, for peyne is sent by the rightwys sonde of God, and by his suffrance, be it meselrie, or mayme, or maladie. And if he repreve hym uncharitably of synne, as 'thou

---

615. *I rekene flaterie*, etc., Chaucer's unhappy defence of the digression in the *Somme*.

dronkelewe harlot!' and so forth, thanne aperteneth that to the rejoysynge of the devel, that ever hath joye that men doon synne.

And certes chidynge may nat come but out of a vileyns herte, for after the habundance of the herte speketh the mouth ful ofte. And ye shul understonde that. Looke by any wey whan any man shal chastise another, that he be war from chidynge and reprevynge; for trewely, but he be war, he may ful lightly quyken the fir of angre, and of wratthe, which that he sholde quenche, and peraventure sleeth hym which that he myght chastise with benignitee. For as seith Salomon, 'The amyable tonge is the tree of lyf'; that is to seyn, of lyf espiritueel, and soothly, a deslavee tonge sleeth the spirites of hym that repreveth and eek of hym that is repreved. [630] Loo, what seith Seint Augustyn, 'Ther is no thyng so lyk the develes child as he that ofte chideth.' Seint Paul seith eek, 'A servant of God bihoveth nat to chide.' And how that chidynge be a vileyns thyng bitwixe alle manere folk, yet is it, certes, moost uncovenable bitwixe a man and his wyf; for there is never reste; and therfore seith Salomon, 'An hous that is uncovered in reyn and droppynge and a chidynge wyf been lyke.' A man that is in a droppynge hous in manye places, though he eschewe the droppynge in o place, it droppeth on hym in another place; so fareth it by a chydynge wyf; but she chide hym in o place, she wol chide hym in another; and therfore, 'Bettre is a morsel of breed with joye than an hous ful of delices with chidynge,' seith Salomon. Seint Paul seith, 'O ye wommen, be ye subgetes to youre housbondes, as bihoveth in God, and ye men loveth youre wyves.' *Ad Colossenses* 3°.

[635] Afterward speke we of scornynge, which is a wikked synne, and namely whan he scorneth a man for his goode werkes; for certes, swiche scorneres faren lyk the foule tode that may nat endure to smelle the soote savour of the vyne whanne it florissheth. Thise scorneres been partyng-felawes with the devel, for they han joye whan the devel wynneth, and sorwe whan he leseth; they been adversaries of Jhesu Crist, for they haten that he loveth, that is to seyn, salvacioun of soule.

Speke we now of wikked conseil, for he that wikked conseil yeveth is a traytour; he deceyveth hym that trusteth in hym, *ut Achitofel ad Absolonem.* But nathelees yet is his wikked conseil first agayn hymself. [640] For, as seith the wise man, 'Every fals lyvynge hath his propertee in hymself, that he that wole anoye another man, he anoyeth first hymself.' And men shul understonde that man shal nat taken his conseil of fals folk, ne of angry folk, or grevous folk that loven specially to muchel hir owene profit; ne to muche worldly folk; namely in conseilynge of soules.

Now comth the synne of hem that sowen and maken discord amonges folk; which is a synne that Crist hateth outrely; and no wonder is; for he deyde for to make concord. And moore shame do they to Crist, than dide they that hym crucifiede; for God loveth bettre that freendshipe be amonges folk than he dide his owene body, the which that he yaf for unitee. Therfore been they likned to the devel, that ever been aboute to maken discord.

Now comth the synne of double tonge swiche as speken faire byforn folk and wikkedly bihynde, or elles they maken semblant as though they speeke of good entencioun or elles in game and pley, and yet they speke of wikked entente.

[645] Now comth biwreying of conseil, thurgh which a man is defamed; certes, unnethe may he restoore the damage.

Now comth manace, that is an open folye, for he that ofte manaceth, he threteth moore than he may perfourne ful ofte tyme.

Now cometh ydel wordes, that is with-

U   289

outen profit of hym that speketh tho wordes, and eek of hym that herkneth tho wordes. Or elles ydel wordes been tho that been nedelees, or withouten entente of natureel profit. And al be it that ydel wordes been somtyme venial synne, yet sholde men douten hem, for we shul yeve rekenynge of hem bifore God.

Now comth janglynge, that may nat been withoute synne. And as seith Salomon, it is a synne of apert folye, [650] and therfore a philosophre seyde, whan men axed hym how that men sholde plese the peple, and he answerde, ' Do manye goode werkes and spek fewe jangles.'

After this comth the synne of japeres, that been the develes apes, for they maken folk to laughe at hire japerie as folk doon at the gawdes of an ape. Swich japes deffendeth Seint Paul. Looke, how that vertuouse wordes and hooly woordes conforten hem that travaillen in the service of Crist, right so conforten the vileyns wordes and knakkes of japeris hem that travaillen in the service of the devel. Thise been the synnes that comen of the tonge, that comen of ire, and of othere synnes mo.

Sequitur remedium contra peccatum Ire

The remedie agayns ire is a vertu that men clepen mansuetude, that is debonairetee, and eek another vertu that men callen pacience, or suffrance.

[655] Debonairetee withdraweth and refreyneth the stirynges and the moevynges of mannes corage in his herte, in swich manere that they ne skippe nat out by angre ne by ire.

Suffrance suffreth swetely alle the anoyaunces and the wronges that men doon to man outward. Seint Jerome seith thus of debonairetee, that it dooth noon harm to no wight, ne seith, ne for noon harm that men doon or seyn he ne eschawfeth nat agayns his resoun. This

650. *that is debonairetee*, Cam. *that Jhon de Bonania clepith debonayretee.*

vertu som tyme comth of nature, for, as seith the philosophre, ' A man is a quyk thyng, by nature debonaire and tretable to goodnesse' ; but whan debonairetee is enformed of grace, thanne is it the moore worth.

Pacience, that is another remedie agayns ire, is a vertu that suffreth swetely every mannes goodnesse, and is nat wrooth for noon harm that is doon to hym. [660] The philosophre seith that pacience is thilke vertu that suffreth debonairely alle the outrages of adversitee and every wikked word. This vertu maketh a man lyk to God, and maketh hym Goddes owene deere child, as seith Crist ; this vertu disconfiteth thyn enemy, and therfore seith the wise man, ' If thow wolt venquysse thyn enemy, lerne to suffre.' And thou shalt understonde that man suffreth foure manere of grevances in outward thynges ; agayns the whiche foure he moot have foure manere of paciences.

The firste grevance is of wikkede wordes ; thilke suffrede Jhesu Crist withouten grucchyng, ful paciently, whan the Jewes despised and repreved hym ful ofte. Suffre thou therfore paciently ; for the wise man seith, ' If thou stryve with a fool, though the fool be wrooth or though he laughe, algate thou shalt have no reste.'

[665] That oother grevance outward is to have damage of thy catel. Theragayns suffred Crist ful paciently, when he was despoyled of al that he hadde in this lyf, and that nas but his clothes.

The thridde grevance is a man to have harm in his body. That suffred Crist ful paciently in al his passioun.

The fourthe grevance is in outrageous labour in werkes. Wherfore I seye that folk that maken hir servantz to travaillen to grevously, or out of tyme, as on haly dayes, soothly they do greet synne. Heer-agayns suffred Crist ful paciently and taughte us pacience, whan he baar upon his blissed shulder the croys, upon which he sholde suffren despitous deeth.

Heere may men lerne to be pacient; for certes noght oonly Cristen men been pacient for love of Jhesu Crist and for gerdoun of the blisful lyf that is perdurable, but certes the olde payens that never were Cristene, commendeden and useden the vertu of pacience.

[670] A philosophre upon a tyme, that wolde have beten his disciple for his grete trespas, for which he was greetly amoeved, and broghte a yerde to scourge the child; and whan this child saugh the yerde, he seyde to his maister, 'What thenke ye to do?' 'I wol bete thee,' quod the maister, 'for thy correccioun.' 'Forsothe,' quod the child; 'ye oghten first correcte youreself, that han lost al youre pacience for the gilt of a child.' 'Forsothe,' quod the maister, al wepynge, 'thow seyst sooth; have thow the yerde, my deere sone, and correcte me for myn inpacience.' Of pacience comth obedience, thurgh which a man is obedient to Crist and to alle hem to whiche he oghte to been obedient in Crist. [675] And understond wel that obedience is perfit whan that a man dooth gladly and hastily, with good herte, entierly, al that he sholde do. Obedience generally is to perfourne the doctrine of God and of his sovereyns, to whiche hym oghte to ben obeisaunt in alle rightwisnesse.

Sequitur de Accidia

After the synne of envye and of ire, now wol I speken of the synne of accidie; for envye blyndeth the herte of man, and ire troubleth a man, and accidie maketh hym hevy, thoghtful and wrawful. Envye and ire maken bitternesse in herte, which bitternesse is mooder of accidie and bynymeth hym the love of alle goodnesse. Thanne is accidie the angwissh of troubled herte; and Seint Augustyn seith, it is anoy of goodnesse and joye of harm. Certes this is a dampnable synne, for it dooth wrong to Jhesu Crist, in as muche as it bynymeth the service that men oghte doon to Crist with alle diligence, as seith Salomon. [680] But accidie dooth no swich diligence. He dooth alle thyng with anoy, and with wrawnesse, slaknesse, and excusacioun, and with ydelnesse, and unlust; for which the book seith, 'Accursed be he that dooth the service of God necligently.'

Thanne is accidie enemy to everich estaat of man; for certes the estaat of man is in thre maneres. Outher it is thestaat of innocence, as was thestaat of Adam biforn that he fil into synne; in which estaat he was holden to wirche, as in heriynge and adowrynge of God. Another estaat is estaat of synful men, in which estaat men been holden to laboure in preiynge to God for amendement of hire synnes, and that he wole graunte hem to arysen out of hir synnes. Another estaat is thestaat of grace, in which estaat he is holden to werkes of penitence; and certes to alle thise thynges is accidie enemy and contrarie, for he loveth no bisynesse at al. [685] Now certes this foule sinne, accidie, is eek a ful greet enemy to the liflode of the body, for it ne hath no purveaunce agayn temporeel necessitee, for it forsleweth and forsluggeth, and destroyeth alle goodes temporeles by reccheleesnesse.

The fourthe thyng is, that accidie is lyk to hem that been in the peyne of helle, by-cause of hir slouthe and of hire hevynesse; for they that been dampned been so bounde that they ne may neither wel do, ne wel thynke. Of accidie comth first, that a man is anoyed and encombred for to doon any goodnesse, and maketh that God hath abhomynacion of swich accidie, as seith Seint John.

Now cometh slouthe, that wol nat suffre noon hardnesse ne no penaunce; for soothly, slouth is so tendre and so delicat, as seith Salomon, that he wol nat suffre noon hardnesse, ne penaunce, and therfore he shendeth al that he dooth. Agayns this roten-herted synne of accidie and slouthe sholde men exercise hemself to doon goode werkes, and manly and

685. *sinne*, E *swyn.*

291

vertuously cacchen corage wel to doon, thynkynge that oure Lord Jhesu Crist quiteth every good dede, be it never so lite. [690] Usage of labour is a greet thyng, for it maketh, as seith Seint Bernard, the laborer to have stronge armes, and harde synwes; and slouthe maketh hem feble and tendre. Thanne comth drede to bigynne to werke anye goode werkes; for certes he that is enclyned to synne, hym thynketh it is so greet an emprise for to undertake to doon werkes of goodnesse, and casteth in his herte that the circumstaunces of goodnesse been so grevouse and so chargeaunt for to suffre, that he dar nat undertake to do werkes of goodesse, as seith Seint Gregorie.

Now comth wanhope, that is despeir of the mercy of God, that comth somtyme of to muche outrageous sorwe, and somtyme of to muche drede, ymaginynge that he hath doon so muche synne that it wol nat availlen hym, though he wolde repenten hym and forsake synne; thurgh which despeir or drede he abaundoneth al his herte to every maner synne, as seith Seint Augustin. [695] Which dampnable synne, if that it continue unto his ende, it is cleped synnyng in the Hooly Goost. This horrible synne is so perilous, that he that is despeired, ther nys no felonye ne no synne that he douteth for to do, as sheweth wel by Judas.

Certes, aboven alle synnes thanne is this synne moost displesant to Crist and moost adversarie.

Soothly, he that despeireth hym is lyke the coward champioun recreant that seith 'creaunt' withoute nede. Alas! alas! nedeles is he recreaunt and nedelees despeired. Certes, the mercy of God is ever redy to the penitent, and is aboven alle his werkes. [700] Allas! kan a man nat bithynke hym on the gospel of Seint Luc xv., where as Crist seith that as wel shal ther be joye in hevene upon a synful man that dooth penitence, as upon nynety and nyne rightful men that never ne dede synne, ne neden no penitence.

Looke forther in the same gospel, the joye and the feeste of the goode man that hadde lost his sone, whan his sone with repentaunce was retourned to his fader. Kan they nat remembren hem eek, that, as seith Seint Luc xxiii., how that the theef that was hanged bisyde Jhesu Crist seyde, 'Lord, remembre of me, whan thow comest into thy regne.' 'Forsothe,' seyde Crist, 'I seye to thee, to day shaltow been with me in paradys.' Certes, ther is noon so horrible synne of man that it ne may in his lyf be destroyed by penitence, thurgh vertu of the passion and of the deeth of Crist. [705] Allas! what nedeth man thanne to been despeired, sith that his mercy so redy is and large? Axe and have.

Thanne cometh sompnolence, that is sloggy slombrynge, which maketh a man be hevy and dul in body and in soule. And this synne comth of slouthe. And certes, the tyme that by wey of resoun men sholde nat slepe, that is by the morwe, but if ther were cause resonable; for soothly the morwe tyde is moost covenable a man to sey his preyeres, and for to thynken on God, and for to honoure God, and to yeven almesse to the poure, that first cometh in the name of Crist. Lo, what seith Salomon? 'Whoso wolde by the morwe awaken and seke me, he shal fynde.' [710] Thanne cometh necligence or reccheleesnesse, that rekketh of no thyng; and how that ignoraunce be mooder of alle harm, certes necligence is the norice. Necligence ne dooth no fors, whan he shal doon a thyng, wheither he do it weel or baddely.

Of the remedie of thise two synnes, as seith the wise man, that he that dredeth God he spareth nat to doon that him oghte doon, and he that loveth God he wol doon diligence to plese God by his werkes, and abaundone hymself, with al his myght, wel for to doon. Thanne comth ydelnesse that is the yate of alle harmes. An ydel man is lyk to a place that hath no walles; the develes may entre on every syde and sheten at hym at discovert, by temptacion on every syde. [715] This ydelnesse is the thurrok of alle wikked and vileyns thoghtes and of alle jangles, trufles, and of alle ordure. Certes, the hevene is yeven to hem that wol labouren, and nat to ydel folk. Eek David seith, that they ne been nat in the labour of men, ne they shul nat been whipped with men, that is to seyn in purgatorie ; certes thanne semeth it they shul be tormented with the devel in helle, but if they doon penitence.

Thanne comth the synne that men clepen *tarditas*, as whan a man is to laterede or tariynge, er he wole turne to God; and certes that is a greet folie. He is lyk to hym that falleth in the dych, and wol nat arise. And this vice comth of a fals hope, that he thynketh that he shal lyve longe ; but that hope faileth ful ofte.

[720] Thanne comth lachesse ; that is he that whan he biginneth any good werk, anon he shal forleten it, and stynten, as doon they that han any wight to governe and ne taken of hym namoore kepe, anon as they fynden any contrarie or any anoy. Thise been the newe sheepherdes that leten hir sheepe wityngly go renne to the wolf, that is in the breres, or do no fors of hir owene governaunce. Of this comth poverte and destruccioun, bothe of spiritueel and temporeel thynges. Thanne comth a manere cooldnesse, that freseth al the herte of a man. Thanne comth undevocioun, thurgh which a man is blent, as seith Seint Bernard, and hath swich langour in soule, that he may neither rede ne singe in hooly chirche, ne heere, ne thynke of no devocioun, ne travaille with his handes in no good werk, that it nys hym unsavory and al apalled. Thanne wexeth he slough and slombry, and soone wol be wrooth, and soone is enclyned to hate and to envye. [725] Thanne comth the synne of worldly sorwe, swich as is cleped *tristicia*, that sleeth man, as Seint Paul seith. For certes, swich sorwe werketh to the deeth of the soule and of the body also, for

ther-of comth that a man is anoyed of his owene lif; wherfore swich sorwe shorteth ful ofte the lif of man, er that his tyme be come by wey of kynde.

Remedium contra peccatum Accidie

Agayns this horrible synne of accidie, and the branches of the same, ther is a vertu that is called *fortitudo*, or strengthe ; that is, an affeccioun thurgh which a man despiseth anoyouse thinges. This vertu is so myghty and so vigorous that it dar withstonde myghtily, and wisely kepen hym self fro perils that been wikked, and wrastle agayn the assautes of the devel ; [730] for it enhaunceth and enforceth the soule, right as accidie abateth it, and maketh it fieble ; for this *fortitudo* may endure by long suffraunce the travailles that been covenable.

This vertu hath manye speces, and the firste is cleped magnanimitee, that is to seyn greet corage ; for certes ther bihoveth greet corage agains accidie lest that it ne swolwe the soule by the synne of sorwe, or destroye it by wanhope. This vertu maketh folk to undertake harde thynges and grevouse thynges by hir owene wil, wisely and resonably. And for as muchel as the devel fighteth agayns a man moore by queyntise and by sleighte than by strengthe, therfore men shal withstonden hym by wit and by resoun and by discrecioun.

Thanne arn ther the vertues of feith and hope in God, and in his seintes, to acheve and accomplice the goode werkes, in the whiche he purposeth fermely to continue. [735] Thanne comth seuretee, or sikernesse, and that is whan a man ne douteth no travaille in tyme comynge of the goode werkes that a man hath bigonne. Thanne comth magnificence, that is to seyn whan a man dooth and perfourneth grete werkes of goodnesse ; and that is the ende why that men sholde do goode werkes ; for in the acomplissynge of grete goode werkes lith the grete gerdoun. Thanne is ther con-staunce, that is stablenesse of corage; and this sholde been in herte by stedefast feith, and in mouth, and in berynge, and in chiere, and in dede. Eke ther been mo speciale remedies agains accidie in diverse werkes, and in consideracioun of the peynes of helle, and of the joyes of hevene, and in trust of the grace of the Holy Goost, that wole yeve hym myght to perfourne his goode entente.

Sequitur de Avaricia

After accidie wol I speke of avarice and of coveitise, of which synne seith Seint Paule that the roote of alle harmes is coveitise. *Ad Thimotheum* vi. [740] For soothly, whan the herte of a man is confounded in itself, and troubled, and that the soule hath lost the confort of God, thanne seketh he an ydel solas of worldly thynges.

Avarice, after the descripcion of Seint Augustyn, is likerousnesse in herte to have erthely thynges. Som oother folk seyn that avarice is for to purchacen manye erthely thynges, and no thyng yeve to hem that han nede. And understoond that avarice ne stant nat oonly in lond ne catel, but somtyme in science and in glorie, and in every manere of outrageous thyng is avarice and coveitise.

And the difference bitwixe avarice and coveitise is this; coveitise is for to coveite swiche thynges as thou hast nat, and avarice is for to withholde and kepe swiche thynges as thou hast withoute rightful nede. [745] Soothly this avarice is a synne that is ful dampnable, for al hooly writ curseth it, and speketh agayns that vice, for it dooth wrong to Jhesu Crist; for it bireveth hym the love that men to hym owen, and turneth it bakward agayns alle resoun, and maketh that the avaricious man hath moore hope in his catel than in Jhesu Crist, and dooth moore observance in kepynge of his tresor than he dooth to service of Jhesu Crist. And therfore seith Seint Paul, *ad Ephesios* v., that an avaricious man is the thraldom of ydolatrie.

What difference is betwixe an ydolastre and an avaricious man? but that any ydolastre peraventure ne hath but o mawmet or two and the avaricious man hath manye; for certes, every floryn in his cofre is his mawmet. [750] And certes, the synne of mawmettrie is the firste thyng that God deffended in the ten comaundmentz, as bereth witnesse *Exodi* capitulo xx. 'Thou shalt have no false goddes bifore me, ne thou shalt make to thee no grave thyng.' Thus is an avaricious man that loveth his tresor biforn God an ydolastre, thurgh this cursed synne of avarice.

Of coveitise comen thise harde lordshipes thurgh whiche men been distreyned by taylages, custumes, and cariages, moore than hire duetee or resoun is; and eek they taken of hire bonde-men amercimentz, whiche myghten moore resonably ben cleped extorcions than amercimentz. Of whiche amercimentz and raunsonynge of bondemen somme lordes stywardes seyn that it is rightful, for as muche as a cherl hath no temporeel thyng that it ne is his lordes, as they seyn; but certes thise lordshipes doon wrong that bireven hire bonde folk thynges that they never yave hem. *Augustinus de Civitate Dei*, libro ix. [755] Sooth is that the condicioun of thraldom and the firste cause of thraldom is for synne. *Genesis* ix.

Thus may ye seen that the gilt disserveth thraldom, but nat nature; wherfore thise lordes ne sholde nat muche glorifien hem in hir lordshipes, sith that by natureel condicioun they been nat lordes of thralles, but that thraldom comth first by the desert of synne. And forther-over ther as the lawe seith that temporeel goodes of boonde folk been the goodes of hir lordshipes, ye, that is for to understonde, the goodes of the empereur, to deffenden hem in hir right, but nat for to robben

750. *the firste thyng.* The 1st and 2nd commandments were reckoned by the Roman Church as one, the 10th being divided.

hem ne reven hem. And therfore seith Seneca, 'Thy prudence sholde lyve benignely with thy thralles'; [760] thilke that thou clepest thy thralles been Goddes peple, for humble folk been Cristes freendes, they been contubernyal with the Lord.

Thynk eek that of swich seed as cherles spryngeth, of swich seed spryngen lordes. As wel may the cherl be saved as the lord; the same deeth that take the cherl, swich deeth taketh the lord; wherfore I rede, do right so with thy cherl as thou woldest that thy Lord dide with thee, if thou were in his plit. Every synful man is a cherl to synne. I rede thee, certes, that thou, lord, werke in swiche wise with thy cherles that they rather love thee than drede. I woot wel ther is degree above degree, as reson is, and skile it is that men do hir devoir ther as it is due; but certes, extorcions and despit of youre underlynges is dampnable.

[765] And forther-over understoond wel that thise conquerours, or tirauntz, maken ful ofte thralles of hem that been born of as roial blood as been they that hem conqueren. This name of thraldom was never erst kowth, til that Noe seyde that his sone Canaan sholde be thral to his bretheren for his synne. What seye we thanne of hem that pilen and doon extorcions in hooly chirche? Certes, the swerd that men yeven first to a knyght, whan he is newe dubbed, signifieth that he sholde deffenden hooly chirche, and nat robben it ne pilen it; and who so dooth is traitour to Crist. And, as seith Seint Augustyn, they been the develes wolves that stranglen the sheepe of Jhesu Crist, and doon worse than wolves; for, soothly, whan the wolf hath ful his wombe he stynteth to strangle sheepe, but soothly, the pilours and destroyours of Goddes hooly chirche ne do nat so, for they ne stynte never to pile.

[770] Now, as I have seyd, sith so is

765. *thraldom*, H² *cherldom.*

that synne was first cause of thraldom, thanne is it thus, that thilke tyme that al this world was in synne, thanne was al this world in thraldom and subjeccioun; but certes, sith the time of grace cam, God ordeyned that som folk sholde be moore heigh in estaat and in degree, and som folk moore lough, and that everich sholde be served in his estaat and his degree; and therfore in somme contrees, ther they byen thralles, whan they han turned hem to the feith, they maken hire thralles free out of thraldom. And therfore certes the lord oweth to his man that the man oweth to his lord. The pope calleth hymself servaunt of the servauntz of God; but for-as-muche as the estaat of hooly chirche ne myghte nat han be, ne the commune profit myghte nat han be kept, ne pees and reste in erthe, but if God hadde ordeyned that som men hadde hyer degree and som men lower, therfore was sovereyntee ordeyned to kepe and mayntene and deffenden hire underlynges or hire subgetz, in resoun, as forforth as it lith in hire power, and nat to destroyen hem ne confounde.

[775] Wherfore I seye, that thilke lordes that been lyk wolves that devouren the possessiouns or the catel of poure folk wrongfully, withouten mercy or mesure, they shul receyven, by the same mesure that they han mesured to poure folk, the mercy of Jhesu Crist, but if it be amended.

Now comth deceite bitwixe marchaunt and marchaunt. And thow shalt understonde that marchandise is in manye maneres; that oon is bodily, and that oother is goostly, that oon is honeste and leveful, and that oother is deshoneste and unleveful. Of thilke bodily marchandise that is leveful and honeste is this, that there as God hath ordeyned that a regne or a contree is suffisaunt to hym-self, thanne is it honeste and leveful that of habundaunce of this contree that men helpe another contree that is moore nedy; and therfore ther moote been marchantz to bryngen fro that o contree to that oother hire marchandises.

[780] That oother marchandise, that men haunten with fraude and trecherie and deceite, with lesynges and false othes, is cursed and dampnable.

Espiritueel marchandise is proprely symonye, that is, ententif desir to byen thyng espiritueel, that is thyng that aperteneth to the seintuarie of God, and to cure of the soule. This desir, if so be that a man do his diligence to parfournen it, al be it that his desir ne take noon effect, yet is it to hym a deedly synne, and if he be ordred he is irreguleer. Certes symonye is cleped of Simon Magus, that wolde han boght for temporeel catel the yifte that God hadde yeven by the Hooly Goost to Seint Peter and to the Apostles. And therfore understoond that bothe he that selleth and he that beyeth thynges espirituels been cleped symonyals, be it by catel, be it by procurynge, or by flesshly preyere of his freendes, flesshly freendes, or espiritueel freendes. [785] Flesshly in two maneres; as by kynrede, or othere freendes; soothly, if they praye for hym that is nat worthy and able, it is symonye, if he take the benefice; and if he be worthy and able ther nys noon.

That oother manere is whan a man or womman preyen for folk to avauncen hem oonly for wikked flesshly affeccioun that they have unto the persone, and that is foul symonye. But certes in service for which men yeven thynges espirituels unto hir servantz it moot be understonde that the service moot been honeste, and elles nat; and eek that it be withouten bargaynynge, and that the persone be able; for, as seith Seint Damasie, 'Alle the synnes of the world at regard of this synne arn as thyng of noght, for it is the gretteste synne that may be, after the synne of Lucifer and Antecrist'; for by this synne God forleseth the chirche and the soule that he boghte with his precious blood by hem that yeven chirches to hem that

been nat digne, [790] for they putten in theves that stelen the soules of Jhesu Crist and destroyen his patrimoyne. By swiche undigne preestes and curates han lewed men the lasse reverence of the sacramentz of hooly chirche, and swiche yeveres of chirches putten out the children of Crist, and putten into the chirche the develes owene sone. They sellen the soules that lambes sholde kepen, to the wolf that strangleth hem; and therfore, shul they never han part of the pasture of lambes, that is the blisse of hevene.

Now comth hasardrie, with his apurtenaunces, as tables and rafles, of which comth deceite, false othes, chidynges, and alle ravynes, blasphemynge and reneiynge of God, and hate of his neighebores, wast of goodes, mysspendynge of tyme, and somtyme manslaughtre. Certes, hasardours ne mowe nat been withouten greet synne whil thay haunte that crafte. [795] Of avarice comen eek lesynges, thefte, fals witnesse, and false othes; and ye shul understonde that thise been grete synnes, and expres agayn the comaundementz of God, as I have seyd. Fals witnesse is in word and eek in dede. In word, as for to bireve thy neighebores goode name by thy fals witnessyng, or bireven hym his catel or his heritage by thy fals witnessyng, whan thou for ire, or for meede, or for envye, berest fals witnesse, or accusest hym, or excusest hym, by thy fals witnesse, or elles excusest thyself falsly. Ware yow questemongeres and notaries. Certes, for fals witnessyng was Susanna in ful gret sorwe and peyne, and many another mo. The synne of thefte is eek expres agayns Goddes heeste, and in two maneres, corporeel and espiritueel. Corporel, as for to take thy neighebores catel agayn his wyl, be it by force or by sleighte, be it by met or by mesure, [800] by stelyng eek of false enditementz upon hym, and in borwynge of thy neighebores catel, in entent never to payen it agayn, and semblable thynges.

Espiritueel thefte is sacrilege, that is to seyn, hurtynge of hooly thynges, or of thynges sacred to Crist, in two maneres ; by reson of the hooly place, as chirches or chirche-hawes, for which every vileyns synne that men doon in swiche places may be cleped sacrilege, or every violence in the semblable places. Also they that withdrawen falsly the rightes that longen to hooly chirche. And pleynly and generally, sacrilege is to reven hooly thyng fro hooly place, or unhooly thyng out of hooly place, or hooly thyng out of unhooly place.

Relevacio contra peccatum Avaricie

Now shul ye understonde that the releevynge of avarice is misericorde and pitee largely taken. And men myghten axe why that misericorde and pitee is releevynge of avarice. [805] Certes, the avaricious man sheweth no pitee ne misericorde to the nedeful man, for he deliteth hym in the kepynge of his tresor and nat in the rescowynge ne releevynge of his evene Cristene ; and therfore speke I first of misericorde.

Thanne is misericorde, as seith the philosophre, a vertu by which the corage of man is stired by the mysese of hym that is mysesed ; upon which misericorde folweth pitee in parfournynge of charitable werkes of misericorde. And certes, thise thynges moeven a man to misericorde of Jhesu Crist, that he yaf hymself for oure gilt, and suffred deeth for misericorde, and foryaf us oure originale synnes, and therby relessed us fro the peynes of helle, and amenused the peynes of purgatorie by penitence, and yeveth grace wel to do, and atte laste the blisse of hevene. [810] The speces of misericorde been, as for to lene and for to yeve, and to foryeven and relesse, and for to han pitee in herte, and compassioun of the meschief of his evene Cristene, and eek to chastise there as nede is.

Another manere of remedie agayns avarice is resonable largesse, but soothly heere bihoveth the consideracioun of the grace of Jhesu Crist and of his temporeel goodes, and eek of the goodes perdurables that Crist yaf to us, and to han remembrance of the deeth that he shal receyve, he noot whanne, where, ne how ; and eek that he shal forgon al that he hath, save oonly that he hath despended in goode werkes.

But, for as muche as som folk been unmesurable, men oughten eschue fool-largesse, that men clepen wast. Certes, he that is fool-large ne yeveth nat his catel, but he leseth his catel. Soothly what thyng that he yeveth for veyne glorie, as to mynstrals and to folk, for to beren his renoun in the world, he hath synne ther-of, and noon almesse. [815] Certes he leseth foule his good that ne seketh with the yifte of his good no thyng but synne. He is lyk to an hors that seketh rather to drynken drovy or trouble water, than for to drynken water of the clere welle. And for as muchel as they yeven ther as they sholde nat yeven, to hem aperteneth thilke malisoun that Crist shal yeven at the day of doome to hem that shullen been dampned.

Sequitur de Gula

After avarice comth glotonye, which is expres eek agayn the comandement of God. Glotonye is unmesurable appetit to ete or to drynke, or elles to doon ynogh to the unmesurable appetit and desordeynee coveitise to eten or to drynke. This synne corrumped al this world, as is wel shewed in the synne of Adam and of Eve. Looke, eek, what seith Seint Paul of glotonye. [820] 'Manye,' seith Seint Paul, 'goon, of whiche I have ofte seyd to yow, and now I seye it wepynge, that been the enemys of the croys of Crist, of whiche the ende is deeth, and of whiche hire wombe is hire God, and hire glorie in confusioun of hem that so devouren erthely thynges.' He that is usaunt to this synne of glotonye

820. *devouren*, H³ *saueren*.

297

he ne may no synne withstonde; he moot been in servage of alle vices, for it is the develes hoord ther he hideth hym and resteth.

This synne hath manye speces. The firste is dronkenesse, that is the horrible sepulture of mannes resoun, and therfore whan a man is dronken he hath lost his resoun, and this is deedly synne. But soothly, whan that a man is nat wont to strong drynke, and peraventure ne knoweth nat the strengthe of the drynke, or hath feblesse in his heed, or hath travailed, thurgh which he drynketh the moore, al be he sodeynly caught with drynke, it is no deedly synne, but venyal. The seconde spece of glotonye is, that the spirit of a man wexeth al trouble, for dronkenesse bireveth hym the discrecioun of his wit. [825] The thridde spece of glotonye is whan a man devoureth his mete, and hath no rightful manere of etynge. The fourth is, whan thurgh the grete habundaunce of his mete, the humours in his body been destempred. The fifthe is forgetelnesse by to muchel drynkynge, for which somtyme a man forgeteth er the morwe what he dide at even, or on the nyght biforn.

In oother manere been distinct the speces of glotonye, after Seint Gregorie. The firste is for to ete biforn tyme to ete; the seconde is whan a man get hym to delicaat mete or drynke; the thridde is whan men taken to muche over mesure; the fourthe is curiositee with greet entente to maken and apparaillen his mete; the fifthe is for to eten to gredily. [830] Thise been the fyve fyngres of the develes hand, by whiche he draweth folk to synne.

Remedium contra peccatum Gule

Agayns glotonye is the remedie abstinence, as seith Galien; but that holde I nat meritorie, if he do it oonly for the heele of his body. Seint Augustyn wole that abstinence be doon for vertu and with pacience. 'Abstinence,' he seith,

'is litel worth, but if a man have good wil ther-to, and but it be enforced by pacience and by charitee, and that men doon it for Godes sake, and in hope to have the blisse of hevene.'

The felawes of abstinence been attemperaunce, that holdeth the meene in alle thynges; eek shame, that eschueth alle deshonestee; suffisance, that seketh no riche metes ne drynkes, ne dooth no fors of to outrageous apparailynge of mete; mesure also, that restreyneth by resoun the deslavee appetit of etynge; sobrenesse also, that restreyneth the outrage of drynke; [835] sparynge also, that restreyneth the delicaat ese to sitte longe at his mete and softely, wherfore som folk stonden, of hir owene wyl, to eten at the lasse leyser.

Sequitur de Luxuria

After glotonye thanne comth lecherie, for thise two synnes been so ny cosyns, that ofte tyme they wol nat departe. God woot this synne is ful displesaunt thyng to God, for he seyde hymself, 'Do no lecherie'; and therfore he putte grete peynes agayns this synne in the olde lawe. If womman thral were taken in this synne, she sholde be beten with staves to the deeth; and if she were a gentil womman, she sholde be slayn with stones; and if she were a bisshoppes doghter, she sholde been brent, by Goddes comandement. Fortherover, by the synne of lecherie God dreynte al the world at the diluge, and after that he brente five citees with thonder leyt and sank hem into helle.

[840] Now lat us speke thanne of thilke stynkynge synne of lecherie that men clepe avowtrie of wedded folk; that is to seyn, if that oon of hem be wedded, or elles bothe. Seint John seith that avowtiers shullen been in helle in a stank brennynge of fyr and of brymston. In fyr for lecherie, in brymston for the stynk of hire ordure. Certes, the brekynge of this sacrement is an horrible thyng; it

was maked of God hymself in paradys, and confermed by Jhesu Crist, as witnesseth Seint Mathew in the gospel : 'A man shal lete fader and mooder and taken hym to his wif, and they shullen be two in o flessh.' This sacrement bitokneth the knyttynge togidre of Crist and of hooly chirche. And nat oonly that God forbad avowtrie in dede, but eek he comanded that thou sholdest nat coveite thy neighebores wyf. [845] In this heeste, seith Seint Augustyn, is forboden alle manere coveitise to doon lecherie. Lo, what seith Seint Mathew in the gospel ; that who-so seeth a womman to coveitise of his lust, he hath doon lecherie with hire in his herte. Heere may ye seen that nat oonly the dede of this synne is forboden, but eek the desir to doon that synne.

This cursed synne anoyeth grevousliche hem that it haunten. And first to hire soule, for he obligeth it to synne and to peyne of deeth that is perdurable. Unto the body anoyeth it grevously also, for it dreyeth hym, and wasteth, and shenteth hym, and of his blood he maketh sacrifice to the feend of helle ; it wasteth his catel and his substaunce. And certes if it be a foul thyng a man to waste his catel on wommen, yet is it a fouler thyng whan that for swich ordure wommen dispenden upon men hir catel and substaunce. [850] This synne, as seith the prophete, bireveth man and womman hir goode fame, and al hire honour, and it is ful plesaunt to the devel ; for ther-by wynneth he the mooste partie of this world ; and, right as a marchant deliteth hym moost in chaffare that he hath moost avantage of, right so deliteth the fend in this ordure.

This is that oother hand of the devel with five fyngres to cacche the peple to his vileynye. The firste fynger is the fool lookynge of the fool womman, and of the fool man, that sleeth right as the basilicok sleeth folk by the venym of his sighte ; for the coveitise of eyen folweth the coveitise of the herte. The seconde fynger is the vileyns touchynge in wikked

manere ; and therfore, seith Salomon that whoso toucheth and handleth a womman he fareth lyk hym that handleth the scorpioun that styngeth and sodeynly sleeth thurgh his envenymynge ; as who-so toucheth warm pych, it shent his fyngres. [855] The thridde is foule wordes, that fareth lyk fyr, that right anon brenneth the herte. The fourthe fynger is the kissynge ; and trewely he were a greet fool that wolde kisse the mouth of a brennynge ovene, or of a fourneys. And moore fooles been they that kissen in vileynye, for that mouth is the mouth of helle ; and namely thise olde dotardes holours, yet wol they kisse, though they may nat do, and smatre hem. Certes, they been lyk to houndes, for an hound whan he comth by the roser, or by othere [bushes], though he may nat pisse, yet wole he heve up his leg and make a contenaunce to pisse. And for that many man weneth that he may nat synne, for no likerousnesse that he dooth with his wyf, certes, that opinioun is fals ; God woot a man may sleen hymself with his owene knyf and make hymselven dronken of his owene tonne. [860] Certes, be it wyf, be it child, or any worldly thyng that he loveth biforn God, it is his mawmet, and he is an ydolastre. Man sholde loven his wyf by discrecioun, paciently and atemprely, and thanne is she as though it were his suster.

The fifthe fynger of the develes hand is the stynkynge dede of leccherie. Certes, the five fyngres of glotonie the feend put in the wombe of a man, and with his five fyngres of lecherie he gripeth hym by the reynes for to throwen hym into the fourneys of helle, ther as they shul han the fyr and the wormes that ever shul lasten, and wepynge and wailynge, sharpe hunger and thurst, and grymnesse of develes that shullen al to-trede hem, withouten respit and withouten ende.

[865] Of leccherie, as I seyde, sourden

855. *bushes*, Tyrwhitt's emendation for *beautes* of the MSS.

diverse speces, as fornicacioun that is bitwixe man and womman that been nat maried, and this is deedly synne and agayns nature. Al that is enemy and destruccioun to nature is agayns nature. *Parſay*, the resoun of a man telleth eek hym wel that it is deedly synne, for as muche as God forbad leccherie. And Seint Paul yeveth hem the regne, that nys dewe to no wight but to hem that doon deedly synne. Another synne of leccherie is to bireve a mayden of hir maydenhede, for he that so dooth, certes, he casteth a mayden out of the hyeste degree that is in this present lif, and bireveth hire thilke precious fruyt that the book clepeth the 'hundred fruyt.' I ne kan seye it noon oother weyes in Englissh, but in Latyn it highte *Centesimus fructus*. [870] Certes, he that so dooth is cause of manye damages and vileynyes, mo than any man kan rekene, right as he somtyme is cause of alle damages that beestes don in the feeld that breketh the hegge or the closure, thurgh which he destroyeth that may nat been restoored. For certes, namoore may maydenhede be restoored than an arm that is smyten fro the body may retourne agayn to wexe. She may have mercy, this woot I wel, if she do penitence; but never shal it be that she nas corrupt.

And, al be it so that I have spoken somwhat of avowtrie, it is good to shewen mo perils that longen to avowtrie, for to eschue that foule synne. Avowtrie in Latyn is for to seyn, approchynge of oother mannes bed, thurgh which that whilom weren o flessh abawndone hir bodyes to othere persones. [875] Of this synne, as seith the wise man, folwen manye harmes. First, brekynge of feith; and certes, in feith is the keye of Cristendom, and whan that feith is broken and lorn, soothly, Cristendom stant veyn and withouten fruyt. This synne is eek a thefte; for thefte generally is for to reve a wight his thyng agayns his wille. Certes this is the fouleste thefte that may be, whan a womman steleth hir

body from hir housbonde and yeveth it to hire holour to defoulen hire, and steleth hir soule fro Crist, and yeveth it to the devel. This is a fouler thefte than for to breke a chirche and stele the chalice, for thise avowtiers breken the temple of God spiritually, and stelen the vessel of grace, that is the body and the soule, for which Crist shal destroyen hem, as seith Seint Paul.

[880] Soothly of this thefte douted Joseph, whan that his lordes wyf preyed hym of vileynye, whan he seyde, 'Lo, my lady, how my lord hath take to me under my warde al that he hath in this world, ne no thyng of his thynges is out of my power, but oonly ye, that been his wyf; and how sholde I thanne do this wikkednesse and synne so horrible agayns God, and agayns my lord? God it forbeede!' Allas! al to litel is swich trouthe now y-founde.

The thridde harm is the filthe thurgh which they breken the comandement of God and defoulen the auctour of matrimoyne, that is, Crist. For certes, in so muche as the sacrement of mariage is so noble and so digne, so muche is it gretter synne for to breken it; for God made mariage in paradys, in the estaat of innocence, to multiplye mankynde to the service of God; and therfore is the brekynge moore grevous; of which brekynge comen false heires ofte tyme, that wrongfully ocupien folkes heritages. And therfore wol Crist putte hem out of the regne of hevene, that is heritage to goode folk. [885] Of this brekynge comth eek ofte tyme that folk unwar wedden or synnen with hire owene kynrede, and namely thilke harlottes that haunten bordels of thise fool wommen, that mowe be likned to a commune gonge, where as men purgen hire ordure.

What seye we eek of putours that lyven by the horrible synne of putrie, and constreyne wommen to yelden to hem a certeyn rente of hire bodily puterie,—ye, somtyme of his owene wyf, or his child, as doon this bawdes. Certes, thise been cursede synnes. Understoond eek, that avowtrie is set gladly in the ten comandementz bitwixe thefte and manslaughtre, for it is the gretteste thefte that may be, for it is thefte of body and of soule; and it is lyk to homycide, for it kerveth atwo and breketh atwo hem that first were maked o flessh, and therfore by the olde lawe of God they sholde be slayn. But nathelees, by the lawe of Jhesu Crist, that is lawe of pitee, whan he seyde to the wommman that was founden in avowtrie, and sholde han been slayn with stones after the wyl of the Jewes, as was hir lawe, 'Go,' quod Jhesu Crist, 'and have namoore wyl to synne,' or wille namoore to do synne. [890] Soothly, the vengeaunce of avowtrie is awarded to the peynes of helle, but if so be that it be destourbed by penitence.

Yet been ther mo speces of this cursed synne, as whan that oon of hem is religious, or elles bothe, or of folk that been entred into ordre, as subdekne, or dekne or preest, or hospitaliers, and ever the hyer that he is in ordre the gretter is the synne. The thynges that gretly agreggen hire synne is the brekynge of hire avow of chastitee, whan they receyved the ordre. And forther-over, sooth is, that hooly ordre is chief of al the tresorie of God, and his especial signe and mark of chastitee, to shewe that they been joyned to chastitee, which that is moost precious lyf that is. And thise ordred folk been specially titled to God, and of the special meignee of God, for which, whan they doon deedly synne, they been the special traytours of God and of his peple, for they lyven of the peple to preye for the peple, and while they been suche traytours her preyers availle not to the peple.

[895] Preestes been aungeles as by the dignitee of hir mysterye, but forsothe Seint Paul seith, that Sathanas transformeth hym in an aungel of light. Soothly, the preest that haunteth deedly synne, he may be likned to the aungel of derknesse transformed in the aungel of light; he semeth aungel of light, but forsothe he is aungel of derknesse. Swiche preestes been the sones of Helie, as sheweth in the book of Kynges, that they weren the sones of Belial, that is the devel. 'Belial' is to seyn 'withouten juge,' and so faren they; hem thynketh they been free and han no juge, namoore than hath a free bole, that taketh which cow that hym liketh in the town. So faren they by wommmen, for right as a free bole is ynough for al a toun, right so is a wikked preest corrupcion ynough for al a parisshe, or for al a contree.

[900] Thise preestes, as seith the book, ne konne nat the mysterie of preesthode to the peple, ne God ne knowe they nat; they ne holde hem nat apayd, as seith the book, of soden flessh that was to hem offred, but they tooke by force the flessh that is rawe. Certes, so thise shrewes ne holden hem nat apayed of roosted flessh and sode flessh with which the peple fedden hem in greet reverence, but they wole have raw flessh of folkes wyves and hir doghtres. And certes, thise wommen that consenten to hire harlotrie doon greet wrong to Crist and to hooly chirche and alle halwes, and to alle soules; for they bireven alle thise hym that sholde worshipe Crist and hooly chirche, and preye for cristene soules. And therfore han swiche preestes, and hire lemmanes eek that consenten to hir leccherie, the malisoun of al the court cristiene, til they come to amendement.

The thridde spece of avowtrie is som tyme bitwixe a man and his wyf; and that is whan they take no reward in hire assemblynge but oonly to hire flesshly delit, as seith Seint Jerome; [905] and ne rekken of no thyng but that they been assembled. By-cause that they been maried al is good ynough, as thynketh to hem. But in swich folk hath the devel power, as seyde the aungel Raphael to Thobie, for in hire assemblynge they putten Jhesu Crist out of hire herte, and yeven hem-self to alle ordure.

The fourthe spece is the assemblee of hem that been of hire kynrede, or of hem that been of oon affynytee, or elles with hem with whiche hir fadres or hir kynrede han deled in the synne of lecherie. This synne maketh hem lyk to houndes that taken no kepe to kynrede. And certes, parentele is in two maneres, outher goostly or flesshly : goostly, as for to deelen with his godsibbes ; for, right so as he that engendreth a child is his flesshly fader, right so is his godfader his fader espiritueel ; for which a womman may in no lasse synne assemblen with hire godsib than with hire owene flesshly brother.

[910] The fifthe spece is thilke abhomynable synne of which that no man unnethe oghte speke ne write, nathelees it is openly reherced in holy writ. This cursednesse doon men and wommen in diverse entente, and in diverse manere, but though that hooly writ speke of horrible synne, certes hooly writ may nat been defouled, namoore than the sonne that shyneth on the mixen.

Another synne aperteneth to leccherie that comth in slepynge ; and this synne cometh ofte to hem that been maydenes, and eek to hem that been corrupt. And this synne men clepen polucioun, that comth in thre maneres. Somtyme of langwissynge of body, for the humours been to ranke and habundaunt in the body of man ; somtyme of infermetee, for the fieblesse of the vertu retentif, as phisik maketh mencioun ; somtyme for surfeet of mete and drynke ; and somtyme of vileyns thoghtes that been enclosed in mannes mynde whan he gooth to slepe, which may nat been withoute synne ; for which men moste kepen hem wisely, or elles may men synnen ful grevously.

Remedium contra peccatum Luxurie

[915] Now comth the remedie agayns leccherie, and that is generally chastitee and continence, that restreyneth alle the desordeynee moevynges that comen of flesshly talentes. And ever the gretter merite shal he han that moost restreyneth the wikkede eschawfynges of the ordure of this synne , and this is in two maneres ; that is to seyn, chastitee in mariage, and chastitee of widwehode. Now shaltow understonde that matrimoyne is leefful assemblynge of man and of womman, that receyven, by vertu of the sacrement, the boond thurgh which they may nat be departed in al hir lyf, that is to seyn, whil that they lyven bothe. This, as seith the book, is a ful greet sacrement ; God maked it, as I have seyd, in paradys, and wolde hymself be born in mariage ; and, for to halwen mariage, he was at a weddynge, where as he turned water in to wyn, which was the firste miracle that he wroghte in erthe biforn his disciples.

[920] Trewe effect of mariage clenseth fornicacioun and replenysseth hooly chirche of good lynage, for that is the ende of mariage ; and it chaungeth deedly synne into venial synne bitwixe hem that been y-wedded, and maketh the hertes al oon of hem that been y-wedded, as wel as the bodies. This is verray mariage that was establissed by God, er that synne bigan, whan natureel lawe was in his right poynt in paradys, and it was ordeyned that o man sholde have but o womman, and o womman but o man, as seith Seint Augustyn, by manye resouns.

First, for mariage is figured bitwixe Crist and holy chirche ; and that oother is, for a man is heved of a womman,—algate by ordinaunce it sholde be so. For, if a womman hadde mo men than oon, thanne sholde she have moo hevedes than oon, and that were an horrible thyng biforn God ; and eek a womman ne myghte nat plese to many folk at oones. And also ther ne sholde never be pees ne reste amonges hem, for everich wolde axen his owene thyng ; and forther-over no man ne sholde knowe his owene engendrure, ne who sholde have his heritage, and the womman sholde been the lasse biloved fro the tyme that she were conjoynt to many men.

[925] Now comth how that a man sholde bere hym with his wif; and namely in two thynges, that is to seyn, in suffraunce and reverence, as shewed Crist whan he made first womman. For he ne made hire nat of the heved of Adam, for she sholde nat clayme to greet lordshipe; for ther as the womman hath the maistrie she maketh to muche desray. Ther neden none ensamples of this, the experience of day by day oghte suffise. Also certes, God ne made nat womman of the foot of Adam, for she ne sholde nat been holden to lowe, for she kan nat paciently suffre. But God made womman of the ryb of Adam for womman sholde be felawe unto man. Man sholde bere hym to his wyf in feith, in trouthe, and in love, as seith Seint Paul, that a man sholde loven his wyf as Crist loved hooly chirche, that loved it so wel that he deyde for it; so sholde a man for his wyf, if it were nede.

[930] Now how that a womman sholde be subget to hire housbonde, that telleth Seint Peter. First, in obedience. And eek, as seith the decree, a womman that is wyf, as longe as she is a wyf, she hath noon auctoritee to swere, ne bere witnesse, withoute leve of hir housbonde, that is hire lord,—algate he sholde be so by resoun. She sholde eek serven hym in alle honestee, and been attempree of hire array. I woot wel that they sholde setten hire entente to plesen hir housbondes, but nat by hire queyntise of array. Seint Jerome seith that wyves that been apparailled in silk and in precious purpre ne mowe nat clothen hem in Jhesu Crist. What seith Seint John eek in thys matere? Seint Gregorie eek seith that no wight seketh precious array, but oonly for veyne glorie to been honoured the moore biforn the peple. [935] It is a greet folye, a womman to have a fair array outward and in hir-self foul inward.

A wyf sholde eek be mesurable in lookynge, and in berynge, and in lawghynge, and discreet in all hire wordes and hire dedes and aboven alle worldly thyng she sholde loven hire housbonde with al hire herte, and to hym be trewe of hir body. So sholde an housbonde eek be to his wyf, for, sith that al the body is the housbondes, so sholde hire herte been, or elles ther is bitwixe hem two, as in that, no parfit mariage.

Thanne shal men understonde that for thre thynges a man and his wyf flesshly mowen assemble. The firste is in entente of engendrure of children, to the service of God, for certes that is the cause final of matrimoyne. [940] Another cause is to yelden everich of hem to oother the dette of hire bodies, for neither of hem hath power over his owene body. The thridde is for to eschewe leccherye and vileynye. The ferthe is forsothe deedly synne. As to the firste, it is meritorie; the seconde also, for, as seith the decree, that she hath merite of chastitee that yeldeth to hire housbonde the dette of hir body, ye, though it be agayn hir likynge and the lust of hire herte. The thridde manere is venyal synne, and trewely scarsly may ther any of thise be withoute venial synne, for the corrupcioun and for the delit. The fourthe manere is for to understonde if they assemble oonly for amorous love, and for noon of the fore-seyde causes, but for to accomplice thilke brennynge delit, they rekke never how ofte, soothly it is deedly synne, and yet with sorwe somme folk wol peynen hem moore to doon than to hire appetit suffiseth.

The seconde manere of chastitee is for to been a clene wydewe and eschue the embracynges of man and desiren the embracynge of Jhesu Crist. [945] Thise been tho that han been wyves and han forgoon hire housbondes, and eek wommen that han doon leccherie and been releeved by penitence. And certes, if that a wyf koude kepen hire al chaast, by licence of hir housbonde, so that she yeve never noon occasion that he agilte, it were to hire a greet merite. Thise manere wommen that observen chastitee moste be clene in herte, as wele as in body and in thoughte, and mesurable in clothynge and in contenaunce, abstinent in etynge and drynkynge, in spekynge and in dede. They been the vessel, or the boyste of the blissed Magdelene, that fulfilleth hooly chirche of good odour.

The thridde manere of chastitee is virginitee, and it bihoveth that she be hooly in herte, and clene of body; thanne is she spouse to Jhesu Crist, and she is the lyf of angeles. She is the preisynge of this world, and she is as thise martirs in egalitee. She hath in hire that tonge may nat telle, ne herte thynke. [950] Virginitee baar oure Lord Jhesu Crist, and virgine was hym-selve.

Another remedie agayns leccherie is specially to withdrawen swiche thynges as yeve occasion to thilke vileynye, as ese, etynge and drynkynge; for certes, whan the pot boyleth strongly the beste remedie is to withdrawe the fyr. Slepynge longe in greet quiete is eek a greet norice to leccherie.

Another remedie agayns leccherie is that a man or a womman eschue the compaignye of hem by whiche he douteth to be tempted, for al be it so that the dede is withstonden, yet is ther greet temptacioun. Soothly, a whit wal, although it ne brenne noght fully by stikynge of a candele, yet is the wal blak of the leyt. Ful ofte tyme [955] I rede, that no man truste in his owene perfeccioun, but he be stronger than Sampsoun, and hoolier than Danyel, and wiser than Salomon.

Now after that I have declared yow as I kan the sevene deedly synnes, and somme of hire braunches and hire remedies, soothly, if I koude, I wolde telle yow the ten comandementz; but so heigh a doctrine I lete to divines; nathelees I hope to God they been touched in this tretice, everich of hem alle.

Sequitur secunda pars Penitencie

Now, for as muche as the seconde partie of penitence stant in confessioun of mouth, as I bigan in the firste chapitre, I seye, Seint Augustyn seith, 'Synne is every word and every dede, and al that men coveiten agayn the lawe of Jhesu Crist; and this is for to synne in herte, in mouth, and in dede, by thy five wittes, that been sighte, herynge, smellynge, tastynge or savourynge, and feelynge.'

[960] Now is it good to understonde the circumstaunces that agreggeth muchel every synne. Thow shalt considere what thow art that doost the synne; wheither thou be male or femele, yong or oold, gentil or thral, free or servant, hool or syk, wedded or sengle, ordred or unordred, wys or fool, clerk or seculeer; if she be of thy kynrede, bodily or goostly, or noon; if any of thy kynrede have synned with hire or noon, and manye mo thinges.

Another circumstaunce is this, wheither it be doon in fornicacioun, or in avowtrie, or noon, incest or noon, mayden or noon, in manere of homicide or noon, horrible grete synnes or smale, and how longe thou hast continued in synne. The thridde circumstaunce is the place ther thou hast do synne, wheither in oother mennes hous or in thyn owene, in feeld or in chirche or in chirchehawe, in chirche dedicaat or noon; [965] for if the chirche be halwed, and man or womman spille his kynde in-with that place, by wey of synne or by wikked temptacioun, the chirche is entredited til it be reconsiled by the bysshope; and the preest that dide swich a vileyne, to terme of al his lif he sholde namoore synge masse; and if he dide, he sholde doon deedly synne at every time that he so songe masse. The fourthe circum-staunce is, by whiche mediatours or by whiche messagers, as for enticement or for consentement to bere compaignye with felaweshipe,—for many a wrecche,

304

for to bere compaignye, wil go to the devel of helle,—wher-fore they that eggen or consenten to the synne been parteners of the synne and of the dampnacioun of the synnere.

The fifthe circumstance is, how manye tymes that he hath synned, if it be in his mynde, and how ofte that he hath falle ; [970] for he that ofte falleth in synne he despiseth the mercy of God and encreesseth hys synne, and is unkynde to Crist, and he wexeth the moore fieble to withstonde synne and synneth the moore lightly. And the latter ariseth, and is the moore eschew for to shryven hym, namely to hym that is his con-fessour ; for which that folk whan they falle agayn in hir olde folies, outher they forleten hir olde confessours al outrely, or elles they departen hir shrift in diverse places, but soothly swich departed shrift deserveth no mercy of God of his synnes. The sixte circumstaunce is, why that a man synneth, as by whiche temptacioun, and if hymself procure thilke temptacioun, or by the excitynge of oother folke ; or if he synne with a womman by force, or by hire owene assent, or if the womman maugree hir hed hath been afforced or noon, this shal she telle ; for coveitise, or for poverte, and if it was hire pro-curynge or noon, and swiche manere harneys.

[975] The seventhe circumstaunce is, in what manere he hath doon his synne, or how that she hath suffred that folk han doon to hire, and the same shal the man telle pleynly with alle circumstaunces, and wheither he hath synned with comune bordel wommen or noon, or doon his synne in hooly tymes or noon, in fastynge tymes or noon, or biforn his shrifte, or after his latter shrifte, and hath peraventure broken therfore his penance enjoyned ; by whos helpe and whos conseil, by sorcerie or craft,—al moste be toold. Alle thise thynges, after that they been grete or smale,

engreggen the conscience of man. And eek the preest, that is thy juge, may the bettre been avysed of his juggement in yevynge of thy penaunce, and that is after thy contricioun. [980] For under-stond wel that after tyme that a man hath defouled his baptesme by synne, if he wole come to salvacioun, ther is noon other wey but by penitence, and shrifte, and satisfaccioun ; and namely by the two, if ther be a confessour to which he may shriven hym, and the thridde, if he have lyf to parfournen it.

Thanne shal man looke and considere that if he wole maken a trewe and a profitable confessioun ther moste be foure condiciouns. First, it moot been in sorweful bitternesse of herte, as seyde the kyng Ezechiel to God, 'I wol remembre me alle the yeres of my lif in bitternesse of myn herte.'ʼ This con-dicioun of bitternesse hath fyve signes. The firste is, that confessioun moste be shamefast, nat for to covere ne hyden his synne, for he hath agilt his God and defouled his soule ; [985] and ther-of seith Seint Augustyn, 'The herte travailleth for shame of his synne, and for he hath greet shamefastnesse he is digne to have greet mercy of God.' Swich was the confessioun of the puplican that wolde nat heven up his eyen to hevene, for he hadde offended God of hevene ; for which shamefastnesse he hadde anon the mercy of God. And ther-of seith Seint Augustyn that swich shamefast folk been next foryevenesse and remissioun.

Another signe is humylitee in con-fessioun, of which seith Seint Peter, 'Humbleth yow under the myght of God.' The hond of God is myghty in confessioun, for ther-by God foryeveth thee thy synnes, for he allone hath the power. And this humylitee shal been in herte and in signe outward ; for right as he hath humylitee to God in his herte ; right so sholde he humble his body out-ward to the preest that sit in Goddes

965. *wil*, E *shal*.
970. *departed shrift*, cp. 1006-11.
980. *Ezechiel*, Hezekiah.

X   305

place. [990] For which in no manere, sith that Crist is sovereyn and the preest meene and mediatour bitwixe Crist and the synnere, and the synnere is the laste by wey of resoun, thanne sholde nat the synnere sitte as heighe as his confessour, but knele biforn hym or at his feet, but if maladie destourbe it; for he shal nat taken kepe, who sit there, but in whos place that he sitteth. A man that hath trespased to a lord and comth for to axe mercy and maken his accord and set him doun anon by the lord, men wolde holden hym outrageous and nat worthy so soone for to have remissioun ne mercy.

The thridde signe is, how that thy shrift sholde be ful of teeris, if man may; and if man may nat wepe with his bodily eyen, lat hym wepe in herte. Swich was the confessioun of Seint Peter, for after that he hadde forsake Jhesu Crist he wente out and weepe ful bitterly. [995] The fourthe signe is, that he ne lette nat for shame to shewen his confessioun; swich was the confessioun of the Magdelene, that ne spared for no shame of hem that weren atte feeste for to go to oure Lord Jhesu Crist and biknowe to hym hire synnes. The fifthe signe is, that a man or a womman be obeisant to receyven the penaunce that hym is enjoyned for his synnes, for certes Jhesu Crist for the giltes of a man was obedient to the deeth.

The seconde condicion of verray confession is that it be hastily doon; for certes, if a man hadde a deedly wounde, ever the lenger that he taried to warisshe hymself the moore wolde it corrupte and haste hym to his deeth, and eek the wounde wolde be the wors for to heele; and right so fareth synne that longe tyme is in a man unshewed.

[1000] Certes a man oghte hastily shewen his synnes for manye causes; as for drede of deeth that cometh ofte sodenly, and is in no certeyn what tyme it shal be, ne in what place; and eek the drecchynge of o synne draweth in another; and eek the lenger that he tarieth the ferther he is fro Crist. And if he abide to his laste day scarsly may he shryven hym, or remembre hym of his synnes, or repenten hym for the grevous maladie of his deeth. And for as muche as he ne hath nat in his lyf herkned Jhesu Crist whanne he hath spoken, he shal crie to Jhesu Crist at his laste day and scarsly wol he herkne hym.

And understond that this condicioun moste han foure thynges. Thi shrift moste be purveyed bifore and avysed, for wikked haste dooth no profit; and that a man konne shryve hym of his synnes, be it of pride, or of envye, and so forth, of the speces and circumstances; and that he have comprehended in hys mynde the nombre and the greetnesse of his synnes, and how longe that he hath leyn in synne; [1005] and eek that he be contrit of his synnes, and in stidefast purpos, by the grace of God, never eft to falle in synne; and eek that he drede and countrewaite hymself that he fle the occasiouns of synne to whiche he is enclyned.

Also thou shalt shryve thee of alle thy synnes to o man, and nat a parcel to o man and a parcel to another; that is to understonde in entente to departe thy confessioun as for shame or drede, for it nys but stranglynge of thy soule. For certes Jhesu Crist is entierly al good; in hym nys noon inperfeccioun, and therfore outher he foryeveth al parfitly, or never a deel. I seye nat that if thow be assigned to the penitauncer for certein synne that thow art bounde to shewen hym al the remenaunt of thy synnes of whiche thow hast be shryven to thy curaat, but if it like to thee of thyn humylitee; this is no departynge of shrifte. Ne I seye nat, ther as I speke of divisioun of confessioun, that if thou have licence for to shryve thee to a discreet and an honeste preest, where thee liketh, and by licence of thy curaat, that thow ne mayst wel shryve thee to him of alle thy synnes; [1010] but lat no blotte be bihynde, lat no synne been

untoold, as fer as thow hast remembraunce. And whan thou shalt be shryven
to thy curaat telle hym eek alle the
synnes that thow hast doon syn thou
were last y-shryven; this is no wikked
entente of divisioun of shrifte.

Also, the verray shrifte axeth certeine
condiciouns. First, that thow shryve
thee by thy free wil, noght constreyned,
ne for shame of folk, ne for maladie, ne
swiche thynges, for it is resoun that he
that trespasseth by his free wyl, that by
his free wyl he confesse his trespass; and
that noon oother man telle his synne
but he hymself; ne he shal nat nayte
ne denye his synne, ne wratthe hym
agayn the preest for his amonestynge to
leve synne.

The seconde condicioun is, that thy
shrift be laweful, that is to seyn that
thow that shryvest thee, and eek the
preest that hereth thy confessioun, been
verraily in the feith of hooly chirche,
[1015] and that a man ne be nat despeired
of the mercy of Jhesu Crist as Caym or
Judas. And eek a man moot accusen
hymself of his owene trespas, and nat
another, but he shal blame and wyten
hymself and his owene malice of his
synne and noon oother; but nathelees if
that another man be occasioun or enticere
of his synne, or the estaat of a persone
be swich thurgh which his synne is
agregged, or elles that he may nat pleynly
shryven hym but he telle the persone
with which he hath synned, thanne may
he telle; so that his entente ne be nat
to bakbite the persone, but oonly to
declaren his confessioun.

Thou ne shalt nat eek make no lesynges
in thy confessioun for humylitee, peraventure to seyn that thou hast doon synnes
of whiche that thow were never gilty.
[1020] For Seint Augustyn seith, ' If
thou by cause of thyn humylitee makest
lesynges on thyself, though thow ne were
nat in synne biforn, yet artow thanne in
synne thurgh thy lesynges.' Thou most
eek shewe thy synne by thyn owene
propre mouth, but thow be woxe dowmb,

and nat by no lettre, for thow that hast
doon the synne thou shalt have the shame
therfore. Thow shalt nat eek peynte
thy confessioun by faire subtile wordes,
to covere the moore thy synne, for thanne
bigilestow thyself and nat the preest;
thow most tellen it pleynly, be it never
so foul ne so horrible.

Thow shalt eek shryve thee to a preest
that is discreet to conseille, and eek thou
shalt nat shryve thee for veyne glorie,
ne for ypocrisye, ne for no cause, but
oonly for the doute of Jhesu Crist and
the heele of thy soule. Thow shalt nat
eek renne to the preest sodeynly to tellen
hym lightly thy synne, as who so telleth
a jape or a tale, but avysely, and with
greet devocioun.

[1025] And, generally, shryve thee ofte.
If thou ofte falle, ofte thou arise by confessioun, and though thou shryve thee
ofter than ones of synne of which thou
hast be shryven, it is the moore merite.
And, as seith Seint Augustyn, thow shalt
have the moore lightly relesyng and grace
of God bothe of synne and of peyne.
And certes, oones a yeere atte leeste wey
is it laweful for to been housled, for
certes, oones a yeere alle thynges renovellen.

Now have I toolde you of verray confessioun, that is the seconde partie of
penitence.

*Explicit secunda pars penitencie et
sequitur tercia pars eiusdem*

The thridde partie of penitence is satisfaccioun and that stant moost generally
in almesse, and in bodily peyne. [1030]
Now been ther thre manere of almesses:
contricioun of herte, where a man offreth
hymself to God; another is to han pitee
of defaute of his neighebores; and the
thridde is in yevynge of good conseil and
comfort, goostly and bodily, where men
han nede, and namely in sustenaunce of
mannes foode. And tak kepe that a
man hath nede of thise thinges generally,
he hath nede of foode, he hath nede of

clothyng and herberwe, he hath nede of charitable conseil and visitynge in prisone and in maladie, and sepulture of his dede body. And if thow mayst nat visite the nedeful with thy persone, visite hym by thy message and by thy yiftes. Thise been generally almesses or werkes of charitee of hem that han temporeel richesses or discrecioun in conseilynge. Of thise werkes shaltow heren at the day of doome.

Thise almesses shaltow doon of thyne owene propre thynges, and hastily and prively if thow mayst ; [1035] but nathe-lees if thow mayst nat doon it prively, thow shalt nat forbere to doon almesse though men seen it, so that it be nat doon for thank of the world, but oonly for thank of Jhesu Crist ; for, as witness-eth Seint Mathew, *capitulo* v., ' A citee may nat been hyd that is set on a montayne, ne men lighte nat a lanterne and put it under a busshel, but men sette it on a candlestikke to yeve light to the men in the hous ; right so shal youre light lighten bifore men, that they may seen youre goode werkes and glorifie youre Fader that is in hevene.'

Now as to speken of bodily peyne ; it stant in preyeres, in wakynges, in fast-ynges, in vertuouse techinges of orisouns.

And ye shul understonde that orisouns or preyeres is for to seyn a pitous wyl of herte that redresseth it in God, and expresseth it by word outward to re-moeven harmes, and to han thynges espiritueel and durable, and somtyme temporele thynges, of whiche orisouns, certes, in the orison of the *Pater noster* hath Jhesu Crist enclosed moost thynges. [1040] Certes, it is privyleged of thre thynges in his dignytee, for which it is moore digne than any oother preyere : for that Jhesu Crist hymself maked it ; and it is short, for it sholde be koud the moore lightly, and for to withholden it the moore esily in herte, and helpen hym self the ofter with the orisoun, and for a man sholde be the lasse wery to seyen it, and for a man may nat excusen hym to

lerne it, it is so short and so esy ; and for it comprehendeth in itself alle goode preyeres.

The exposicioun of this hooly preyere that is so excellent and digne, I bitake to thise maistres of theologie, save thus muchel wol I seyn, that whan thow prayest that God sholde foryeve thee thy giltes as thou foryevest hem that agilten to thee, be ful wel war that thow be nat out of charitee. This hooly orisoun amenuseth eek venyal synne, and therfore it aperteneth specially to penitence.

[1045] This preyere moste be trewely seyd, and in verray feith, and that men preye to God ordinatly and discreetly and devoutly, and alwey a man shal putten his wyl to be subget to the wille of God. This orisoun moste eek been seyd with greet humblesse and ful pure honesty, and nat to the anoyaunce of any man or womman. It moste eek been continued with the werkes of charitee. It avayleth eek agayn the vices of the soule, for, as seith Seint Jerome, ' By fastynge been saved the vices of the flessh, and by preyere the vices of the soule.'

After this thou shalt understonde that bodily peyne stant in wakynge ; for Jhesu Crist seith, ' Waketh and preyeth that ye ne entre in wikked temptacioun.' [1050] Ye shul understanden also, that fastynge stant in thre thynges : in forber-ynge of bodily mete and drynke, and in forberynge of worldly jolitee, and in forberynge of deedly synne, this is to seyn, that a man shal kepen hym fro deedly synne with al his myght.

And thou shalt understanden eek that God ordeyned fastynge ; and to fastynge appertenen foure thinges : largenesse to poure folk, gladnesse of herte espiritueel, nat to been angry ne anoyed ne grucche for he fasteth, and also resonable houre for to ete by mesure, that is for to seyn, a man shal nat ete in untyme, ne sitte the lenger at his table to ete for he fasteth.

Thanne shaltow understonde that

bodily peyne stant in disciplyne or techynge by word and by writynge or in ensample; also in werynge of heyres, or of stamyn, or of haubergeons on hire naked flessh, for Cristes sake, and swiche manere penaunces. But war thee wel that swiche manere penaunces on thy flessh ne make thee nat or angry or anoyed of thy self; for bettre is to caste awey thyn heyre, than for to caste awey the swetnesse of Jhesu Crist. And therfore seith Seint Paul, 'Clothe yow, as they that been chosen of God, in herte, of misericorde, debonairetee, suffraunce,' and swiche manere of clothynge, of whiche Jhesu Crist is moore apayed than of heyres or haubergeons or hauberkes.

[1055] Thanne is discipline eek in knokkynge of thy brest, in scourgynge with yerdes, in knelynges, in tribulacions, in suffrynge paciently wronges that been doon to thee, and eek in pacient suffraunce of maladies, or lesynge of worldly catel, or of wyf, or of child, or othere freendes.

Thanne shaltow understonde whiche thynges destourben penaunce; and this is in foure maneres; that is, drede, shame, hope, and wanhope, that is, desperacioun. And for to speke first of drede, for which he weneth that he may suffre no penaunce. Theragayns is remedie for to thynke that bodily penaunce is but short and litel, at regard of the peynes of helle, that is so crueel and so long that it lasteth withouten ende.

[1060] Now again, the shame that a man hath to shryven hym, and namely thise ypocrites that wolden been holden so parfite that they han no nede to shryven hem. Agayns that shame sholde a man thynke that by wey of resoun that he that hath nat been shamed to doon foule thinges, certes hym oghte nat been ashamed to do faire thynges, and that is confessioun. A man sholde eek thynke that God seeth and woot alle his thoghtes and alle his werkes; to hym

may no thyng been hyd ne covered. Man sholden eek remembren hem of the shame that is to come at the day of doome to hem that been nat penitent and shryven in this present lyf; for alle the creatures in erthe and in helle shullen seen apertly al that they hyden in this world.

[1065] Now for to speken of the hope of hem that been necligent and slowe to shryven hem; that stant in two maneres. That oon is that he hopeth for to lyve longe and for to purchacen muche richesse for his delit, and thanne he wol shryven hym, and as he seith, hym semeth thanne tymely ynough to come to shrifte. Another is surquidrie, that he hath in Cristes mercy. Agayns the firste vice, he shal thynke that oure lif is in no sikernesse, and eek that alle the richesses in this world ben in aventure and passen as a shadwe on the wal; and, as seith Seint Gregorie, that it aperteneth to the grete rightwisnesse of God, that never shal the peyne stynte, of hem that never wolde withdrawen hem fro synne hir thankes, but ay continue in synne, for thilke perpetueel wil to do synne shul they han perpetueel peyne.

[1070] Wanhope is in two maneres: the firste wanhope is in the mercy of Crist; that oother is that they thynken that they ne myghte nat longe persevere in goodnesse. The firste wanhope comth of that he demeth that he hath synned so greetly, and so ofte, and so longe leyn in synne, that he shal nat be saved. Certes, agayns that cursed wanhope sholde he thynke that the passion of Jhesu Crist is moore strong for to unbynde than synne is strong for to bynde. Agayns the seconde wanhope he shal thynke that as ofte as he falleth he may arise agayn by penitence; and though he never so longe have leyn in synne, the mercy of Crist is alwey redy to receiven hym to mercy. Agayns the wanhope that he demeth that he sholde nat longe persevere in goodnesse, he shal thynke that the feblesse of the devel may no thyng doon but if men wol suffren hym, [1075] and eek he shal han strengthe of the helpe of God, and of al hooly chirche, and of the proteccioun of aungels, if hym list.

Thanne shal men understonde what is the fruyt of penaunce ; and, after the word of Jhesu Crist, it is the endelees blisse of hevene. Ther joye hath no contrarioustee of wo, ne grevaunce ; ther alle harmes been passed of this present lyf ; ther as is the sikernesse fro the peyne of helle ; ther as is the blisful compaignye that rejoysen hem evermo everich of otheres joye ; ther as the body of man, that whilom was foul and derk, is moore cleer than the sonne ; ther as the body, that whilom was syk, freele, and fieble, and mortal, is inmortal and so strong and so hool that ther may no thyng apeyren it ; ther as ne is neither hunger, thurst, ne coold, but every soule replenyssed with the sighte of the parfit knowynge of God.

[1080] This blisful regne may men purchace by poverte espiritueel, and the glorie by lowenesse, the plentee of joye by hunger and thurst, and the reste by travaille, and the lyf by deeth and mortificacioun of synne.

Here taketh the Makere of this Book his Leve

Now preye I to hem alle that herkne this litel tretys or rede, that if ther be any thyng in it that liketh hem, that ther-of they thanken oure Lord Jhesu Crist, of whom procedeth al wit and al goodnesse ; and if ther be any thyng that displese hem, I preye hem also that they arrette it to the defaute of myn unkonnynge, and nat to my wyl, that wolde ful fayn have seyd bettre if I hadde had konnynge ; for oure boke seith, 'Al that is writen is writen for oure doctrine,' and that is myn entente.

Wherfore I biseke yow mekely, for the mercy of God, that ye preye for me that Crist have mercy on me and foryeve me my giltes, [1085] and namely of my translaciouns and enditynges of worldly vanitees the whiche I revoke in my Retracciouns ; as is the book of Troylus ; the book also of Fame ; the book of the xxv Ladies ; the book of the Duchesse ; the book of Seint Valentynes day, of the Parlement of Briddes ; the Tales of Canterbury,—thilke that sownen in to synne ; the book of the Leoun ; and many another book, if they were in my remembrance ; and many a song and many a leccherous lay, that Crist, for his grete mercy, foryeve me the synne.

But of the translacioun of Boece *De Consolacione* and othere bookes of Legendes of Seintes, and omelies and moralitee, and devocioun, that thanke I oure Lord Jhesu Crist, and his blisful mooder and alle the Seintes of hevene, [1090] bisekynge hem that they from hennes forth unto my lyves ende sende me grace to biwayle my giltes and to studie to the salvacioun of my soule ; and graunte me grace of verray penitence, confessioun and satisfaccioun, to doon in this present lyf, thurgh the benigne grace of hym that is Kyng of Kynges, and Preest over alle Preestes, that boghte us with the precious blood of his herte, so that I may been oon of hem at the day of doome that shulle be saved. *Qui cum Patre et Spiritu Sancto vivis et regnas Deus per omnia secula. Amen.*

Heere is ended the book of the Tales of Canterbury, compiled by Geffrey Chaucer, of whos soule Jhesu Crist have mercy. Amen.

1085. *my Retracciouns*, apparently a formal document.
1086. *the book of the xxv Ladies*, the ' Legend of Good Women ' ; Lans. xv., H xxix.
1087. *the book of the Leoun*, lost—probably a translation from Machault.
1087. *another book*, H² *other bokes*.
1087. *remembrance*, H *mynde or remembraunce*.
1088. *of Legendes of*, H *of consolacioun and of Legendes of lyves of*.

EARLIER MINOR POEMS

THE DETHE OF BLAUNCHE THE DUCHESSE

I HAVE gret wonder, by this lyghte,
How that I lyve, for day ne nyghte
I may slepé wel neigh noght ;
I have so many an ydel thoght,
Purely for defaute of slepe,
That, by my trouthe, I take no kepe
Of no thyng how hit cometh or gooth,
Ne me nis no thyng leef nor looth.
Al is y-liché good to me,—
Joye or sorwe, wherso hit be,— 10
For I have felyng in no thyng,
But as it were, a maséd thyng
Alway in poynt to falle a-doun ;
For sorwful ymagynacioun
Is alway hoolly in my mynde.
    And wel ye woot agaynès kynde
Hit were to liven in this wyse,
For Nature woldé nat suffyse
To noon erthly crëature
Not long tymé to endure 20
Withoute slepe, and been in sorwe ;
And I ne may, no nyght ne morwe,
Slepe ; and this melancolye
And drede I havé for to dye,
Defaute of slepe and hevynesse,
Hath sleyn my spirit of quyknesse
That I have lost al lustihede.
Suche fantasyes been in myn hede
So I noot what is best to do.
    But men myghte axé me why so 30
I may not slepe, and what me is ?
But nathéless, who aské this
Leseth his asking trewély.
My selven can not tellé why
The sothe ; but trewely, as I gesse,

I holdé hit ben a siknesse
That I have suffred this eight yere,
And yet my boote is never the nere ;
For ther is phisicien but oon
That may me hele ; but that is doon. 40
Passe we over until eft ;
That wil not be, moot nede be left ;
Our first matere is good to kepe.
    So whan I saw I might not slepe
Til now late, this other nyght
Upon my bedde I sat upryght
And bad oon reché me a book,
A romaunce, and he hit me took
To rede, and dryve the nyght away ;
Fór me thoghte it bettre play 50
Then playen either at chesse or tablés.
    And in this book were writen fablés
That clerkès hadde, in oldé tyme,
And other poets, put in ryme
To rede, and for to be in mynde
Whyl men loved the lawe of kynde.
This book ne spak but of such thynges
Of quenès livès, and of kynges
And many other thyngès smale.
Amonge al this I fond a tale 60
That me thoghte a wonder thyng.
    This was the tale : There was a kyng
That highté Seys, and hadde a wyf,
The besté that mighte beré lyf ;
And this quene highté Alcyone.
So hit befill, thereafter sone
This kyng wolde wenden over see.
To tellen shortly, whan that he
Was in the see, thus in this wyse,
Swich a tempest gan to ryse 70
That brak hir mast and made it falle,
And clefte hir ship, and dreinte hem alle,
That never was foundé, as it telles,
Bórd ne man, ne nothyng elles.
Right thus this kyng Seys loste his lyf.

31-96. Tn. omits these lines ; F has them in a later hand.

311

Now for to speken of his wyf.
This lady, that was left at home,
Hath wonder that the king ne come
Home, for it was a longè terme.
Anon hir hertè bigan to erme,   80
And for that hir thoghte evermo
It was not wel,—he dweltè so.
She longèd so after the kyng,
That certes, it were a pitous thyng
To telle hir hertely sorwful lyf
Thát she had, this noble wyf;
For him she lovèd alderbest!
Anon she sente bothe eest and west
To seke him, but they foundè nought.
    ' Alas,' quoth she, 'that I was wrought!
I make avowe to my god here,   91
But I mowe of my lordè here,
And wher my lord, my love, be deed,
Certes, I nylle never etè breed.'
    Swich sorw this lady to hir took,
That trewely I, which made this book,
Had swich pitè and swich rowthe
To rede hir sorwe, that by my trowthe,
I ferde the worsè al the morwe
After, to thenken on hir sorwe.   100
    So whan this lady coude heere no
            word
That no man myghtè fynde hir lord,
Ful oft she swouned, and seyde, 'Alas!'
For sorwè ful neigh wood she was,
Ne she koude no reed but oon;
But doun on knees she sat anoon
And wepte, that pitè was to here.
    ' A! mercy! swetè ladi dere!'
Quod she to Juno, hir goddesse;
' Helpe me out of this distresse,   110
And yeve me grace my lord to se
Sóone, or wite wher-so he be,
Or how he fareth, or in what wyse,
And I shal make yow sacrifyse,
And hoolly youres become I shal
With good wil, body, herte, and al;
And but thow wilt this, ladi swete,
Send me grace to slepe, and mete
In my slepe som certeyn sweven,

80. *erme*, Ten Brink and Skeat's emendation of *yerne* of MSS.
82. *he dwelte*, Skeat's emendation of *her thought* of the MSS., repeated from l. 81.
87. All MSS. read *For him alas she*, etc.
91-94. All place these couplets in reverse order.

Wher-through that I may knowen even
Whether my lord be quyk or deed.'   121
    With that word she heng doun the heed
And fil a-swown, as colde as ston.
Hir women caughte her up anon,
And broghten hir in bed al nakèd,
And she, forwepèd and forwakèd,
Was wery, and thus the dedè sleep
Fil on hir, or she tokè keep,
Through Juno that had herd hir bone,
That madè hir to slepè sone;   130
For as she prayde, right so was don
In dede, for Juno right anon
Calledè thus hir messagere
To do hir erande, and he com nere.
Whan he was come, she bad him thus:
' Go bet,' quod Juno, 'to Morpheus,—
Thou knowest him wel, the god of sleep,—
Now understond wel, and tak keep;
Sey thus, on my halfe, that he
Go faste in-to the gretè se,   140
And bid him that, on allè thyng,
He take up Seys body the kyng,
That lyeth ful pale and no-thyng rody.
Bid him crepe in-to the body
And doo hit goon to Alcyone
The quenè, ther she lyeth allone,
And shewe hir shortly—hit is no nay!—
How hit was dreynt this other day,
And doo the body speke right soo,
Right as hit was woned to doo   150
The whylès that hit was alyve.
Goo now faste, and hy the blyve!'
    This messager took leve and wente
Upon his wey, and never ne stente,
Til he com to the derke valeye
That stant betwixè rochès tweye,
Ther never yet grew corn ne gras,
Ne tre, ne no thyng that ought was,
Bést ne man, ne no wight elles,
Save ther were a fewè welles   160
Came rennyng fro the cliffes a-doun,
That made a deedly, slepyng soun,
And ronnen doun right by a cave
That was under a rokke y-grave
Amidde the valey, wonder depe.

133. *messagere, i.e.* Iris.
136. *Go bet*, lit. go better, *i.e.* fast.
142. *He*, etc.; F Tn. B. *That he*, etc
158. *no thyng*. All read *nought*.
159. *no wight*. All read *nought*.

Ther this goddès laye and slepe,—
Morpheus, and Eclympasteyre,
That was the god of slepès heyre,
That sleepe and dide noon other werk.
  This cavè was also as derk   170
As hellè pit over-al aboute.
They had good leyser for to route,
To envye who might slepè beste.
Some henge hir chyn upon hir breste
And slepte upright, hir heed y-hede,
And some laye naked in hir bedde
And slepè whyles the dayès laste.
  This messager com fleyng faste   178
And cried, 'O, hoo! a-wak anoon!'
Hit was for noght, ther herde him noon,
'A-wak!' quod he, 'who is it lyth there!'
And blew his horne right in hir ere,
And cried, 'A-waketh!' wonder hye.
This god of slepe, with his oon ȳe
Cast up, axed, 'Who clepèth there?'
'Hit am I,' quod this messagere,
'Juno bad thou shuldest goon,'—
And tolde him what he shuldè doon
As I have tolde yow here-to-fore,
Hit is no need reherse hit more;   190
And went his wey whan he hadde sayd.
  Anoon this god of slepe a-brayd
Out of his slepe, and gan to goon,
And dide as he hadde bede him doon;
Took up the dreyntè body sone
And bar hit forth to Alcyone,
His wyf the quene, ther-as she lay,
Right even a quarter before day,
And stood right at hir beddès feete,
And callèd hir right as she heete   200
By name, and seyde, 'My swetè wyf,
Awak! let be your sorwful lyf!
For in your sorwe ther lyth no reed;
For certes, swete, I am but deed,
Ye shul me never on lyve y-se,
But, good swete hertè, [for] that ye
Burie my body, swich a tyde
Ye mowe hit fyndè the see besyde,
(And far-wel, swete, my worldès blisse!)

I prayè god your sorwè lisse;   210
To litel whyl our blissè lasteth!'
  With that hir eyen up she casteth
And saw noght. 'Allas!' quod she for
    sorwe,
And deyde within the thriddè morwe.
But what she sayde more in that swow
I may not tellè yow as now,
Hit were to longè for to dwelle,
My first matere I wil yow telle,
Wherfor I havè told this thyng
Of Alcyone and Seys the kyng.   220
  For thus moche dar I sayè wel,
I had be dolven everydel,
And deed, right throgh defaute of sleepe,
Gif I nadde red and takè keepe
Of this talè next befor;
And I wol tellè yow wherfor;
For I ne might, for bote ne bale,
Slepe, or I hadde red this tale
Of this dreyntè Seys the kyng
And of the goddès of slepyng.   230
  Whan I hadde red this talè wel,
And over-loked hit everydel,
Me thoghtè wonder if hit were so,
For I hadde never herd speke, or tho,
Of no goddès that koudè make
Men to sleepe, ne for to wake;
For I ne knewe never God but oon,
And in my game I sayde anoon,—
And yet me lyst right evel to pleye,—
'Rather than that I shuldè deye   240
Throgh defaute of slepyng thus
I wolde yive thilkè Morpheus
Or his goddessè, dame Juno,
Or som wight elles, I ne roghtè who,
To make me sleepe and have som reste,—
I wil yive him the alder-beste
Yift that ever he abood his lyve.
And here on warde, right now, as blyve,
If he wol make me slepe a lite,
Of downe of purè dowvès white   250
I wil yive him a fether-bed,
Rayèd with golde, and right wel cled
In fyn blak satyn *doutremere*,
And many a pilwe, and every berc
Of clothe of Reynes, to slepè softe;
Him thar not nede to turnen ofte.

167. *Eclympasteyre*. Meaning and derivation
doubtful—represents perhaps *Icelon plastera* or
Icelon Phobetora, cp. Ovid. *Met.* xi. 640.
  181. *who is*, etc. F omits *it*; Tn. inserts
that after *it*; Th. *who lyeth*.
  206. *for that*. All om. *for*; B om. *hertè* also.
  207. *swich a*. All read *for swich a*.

255. *Rennes*, in Brittany. Linen is still made
there.

And I wol yive him al that fallès
To a chambre ; and al his hallès
I wol do peynte with purè golde,
And tapite hem ful many folde   260
Of oo sute : this shal he have
If I wiste wher were his cave,
If he kan make me sleepè sone,
As did the goddesse quene Alcyone ;
And thus this ilkè god, Morpheus,
May wynne of me mo feès thus
Than ever he wan ; and to Juno,
That is his goddesse, I shal so do,
I trowe, that she shal holde hir payd.
    I hadde unneth that word y-sayd   270
Right thus as I have told it yow,
That sodeynly, I nistè how,
Swich a lust anoon me took
To sleep, that right upon my book
I fil asleepe, and therwith even
Me mette so ynly swete a sweven,
So wonderful, that never yit
I trowè no man hadde the wit
To konnè wel my sweven rede.
No, not Joseph, with-outè drede,   280
Of Egipte, he that reddè so
The kyngès metyng, Pharao,   -
No more than koude the leste of us ;
Ne nat skarsly Macrobeus,
He that wroot al thavisioun
That he mette, kyng Scipioun,
The noble man, the Affrikan,—
Swichè mervayles, fortunèd than,—
I trowe, a-rede my dremès even.   289
Lo, thus hit was, this was my sweven.

The Dream

    Me thoghtè thus,—that hit was May,
And in the dawenyng I lay,
(Me mette thus,) in my bed al naked,
And lokèd forth, for I was wakèd
With smalè foulès a gret hepe,
That had affrayed me out of my slepe
Through noyse and swetnesse of her song.
And as me mette they sate a-mong
Upon my chambre roof wyth-oute
Upon the tyles over al a-boute,   300
And songen, everich in his wyse,

The mostè solempnè servyse
By note, that ever man, I trowe,
Hadde herd ; for som of hem songe lowe
Som hye, and al of oon acorde.
To tellè shortly, at oo worde,
Was never herd so swete a steven,—
But hit hadde be a thyng of heven,—
So mery a soun, so swete entunes,
That certes, for the toune of Tewnes,   310
I nolde but I hadde herd hem synge,
For al my chambre gan to rynge
Through syngyng of hir armonye.
For instrument nor melodye
Was nowher herd yet half so swete,
Nor of acordè half so mete ;
For ther was noon of hem that feynèd
To synge, for ech of hem him peynèd
To fynde out mery crafty notes ;
They ne sparèd not hir throtes.   320
    And sooth to seyn my chambre was
Ful wel depeynted, and with glas
Were al the wyndowes wel y-glasèd
Ful clere, and nat an hole y-crasèd,
That to beholde hit was gret joye ;
For hoolly al the storie of Troye
Was in the glasyng y-wroght thus,
Of Ector, and of kyng Priamus ;
Of Achilles, and of Lamedon,
And eke of Medea and of Jasoun ;   330
Of Paris, Eleyne, and of Lavyne ;
And alle the walles with colours fyne
Were peynted, bothè text and glose,
And al the Romaunce of the Rose.
    My wyndowes weren shet echon
And through the glas the sunnè shon
Upon my bed with bryghtè bemès,
With many gladè, gilden stremès ;
And eek the welken was so fair,—
Blew, bryght, clerè was the air,   340
And ful attempre forsothe hit was ;
For nother to cold nor hoot it nas,
Ne in al the welkene was a clowde.
    And as I lay thus, wonder lowde
Me thoghte I herde an huntè blowe,
Tassaye his horn, and for to knowe
Whether hit were clere, or hors of soune.
    And I herde goyng, bothe up and doune ;

---

284. *Macrobius*, famous in the Middle Ages for his commentary on Cicero's *Somnium Scipionis*.

310. *Tewnes*, Tunis.
329. *of Lamedon.* All read *of kynge Lamedon*, caught from line above.

Men, hors, houndes, and other thyng,
And al men speken of huntyng ;   350
How they wolde slee the hert with
   strengthe,
And how the hert hadde upon lengthe
So moche embosed, I not now what.
  Anoon right whan I herdé that
How that they wolde on huntyng goon,
I was right glad and up anoon,
Took my hors and forth I wente
Out of my chambre, I never stente
Til I com to the feld withoute.
Ther overtok I a gret route   360
Of huntes and eek of foresteres,
With many relayes and lymeres,
And hyed hem to the forest faste,
And I with hem. So at the laste
I askéd oon, ladde a lymere,
' Say, felow, who shal hunté here ? '
Quod I ; and he answerde ageyn,
' Sir, themperour Octovyen,'
Quod he, ' and is heer fasté by.'
' A goddes half, in good tyme ! ' quod I.
' Go we faste ! ' and gan to ryde.   371
Whan we came to the forest syde
Every man dide right anoon
As to huntyng fil to doon.
  The mayster-hunte anoon, foot-hoot,
With a gret horné blew three mot
At the uncouplyng of his houndés.
With-inne a whyl the hert y-founde is,
Y-halowed and rechaséd faste
Longé tymé ; so at the laste   380
This hert rused and stal away
Fro alle the houndes a prevy way.
The houndes had overshete hym alle,
And were on a defaute y-falle.
Therwyth the hunté wonder faste
Blew a ' forloyn ' at the laste.
  I was go walkéd fro my tree,
And as I wente ther cam by me
A whelp, that fawned me as I stood,
That hadde y-folwed and koude no good.
Hit com and crepte to me as lowe   391
Right as hit haddé me y-knowe,
Heeld doun his heed and joyned his erés,

And leyde al smothé doun his herés.
I wolde have kaught hit, and anoon
Hit fleddé, and was fro me goon ;
And I him folwed, and hit forth wente
Doun by a floury grené wente
Ful thikke of gras, ful softe and sweete,
With flourés fele, faire under feete,   400
And litel used, hit seméd thus ;
For bothé Flora and Zephirus,
They two that maké flourés growe,
Had mad hir dwellyng ther, I trowe ;
For hit was oon to be-holde,
As though the erthe envyé wolde
To be gayer than the heven,
To have mo flourés sithés seven
As in the welkné sterrés be.
Hit had forgete the povertee   410
That wynter, through his coldé morwés,
Had made hit suffren, and his sorwés,
Al was for-geten, and that was sene,
For al the wode was waxen grene ;
Swetnesse of dewe hadde mad hit waxe.
  Hit is no need eek for to axe
Wher ther were many grené grevés,
Or thikke of trees, so ful of levés ;
And every tree stood by him-selve,
Fro other wel ten feet or twelve.   420
So greté trees, so huge of strengthe,
Of fourty, or fifty fadme lengthe,
Clene withouté bough or stikke,
With croppés brode and eek as thikke,—
They weré nat an ynche a-sonder,—
That hit was shadwe over al under ;
And many an hert and many an hynde
Was bothe before me and be-hynde.
Of founés, sourés, bukkés, doés,
Was ful the wode ; and many roés,   430
And many squirellés, that sete
Ful heigh upon the trees and ete,
And in hir maner madé festés.
Shortly, hit was so ful of bestés,
That though Argus, the noble countour,

368. *Octovyen*, a favourite character in the Carlovingian romances. There is a M. Engl. metrical romance *Octavian Imperator*. He was an Emperor of Rome who married Floraunce, daughter of Dagabars (*i.e.* Dagobert), king of France.

408. *sithes seven*. The MSS. read *swiche seven*, which makes no sense. The reading suggested, ' seven times more flowers than there are stars in heaven,' agrees with the ' d'estre miex estelée ' in the *Rom. de la Rose* (ll. 8465-8468), from which these lines are copied.
435. *Argus*, Algus the Arab mathematician, *fl.* early in the 9th cent.; cp. *New Engl. Dict.* s.v. Algorism. Through his treatise on Algebra the Arabic or ' new ' numerals became known in Europe.

Sete to rekene in his countour,
And rekene with his figures ten—
For by tho figures new al ken,
If they be crafty, rekene and noumbre
And telle of every thinge the noumbre,—
Yet sholde he fayle to rekene even   441
The wondres me mette in my sweven.
     But forth they romed right wonder faste
Doun the wode ; so at the laste
I was war of a man in blak,
That sat, and hadde y-turned his bak
To an ooke, an hugé tree.
     'Lord!' thoghte I, 'who may that
     be ?
What ayleth hym to sitten here ?'
Anoon right I wenté nere ;   450
Than fond I sitte even upright
A wonder wel-farynge knyght,—
By the maner me thoughté so,—
Of good mochel, and right yong therto,
Of the age of four and twenty yeer,
Upon his berde but litel heer,
And he was clothéd al in blake.
     I stalkéd even unto his bake,
And ther I stood as stille as ought,
That, sooth to saye, he saw me nought ;
For why he heng hys heed adoun,   461
And with a deedly, sorwful soun
He made of ryme ten vers or twelve
Of a Compleynt to him-selve,
The mosté pitee, the mosté routhe,
That ever I herde ; for by my trouthe,
Hit was gret wonder that Nature
Myght suffren any creature
To have swich sorw, and be not deed.
Ful pitous, pale, and no-thyng reed   470
He sayde a lay, a maner song,
Withouté note, withouté song ;
And was this, for ful wel I kan
Reherse hit—right thus hit began.—

I have of sorwé so grete woon
That joyé gete I never noon,
Now that I see my lady bright,
Which I have loved with al my myght,
Is fro me deed and is a-goon.

445. John of Gaunt, who was, however, twenty-
nine when his wife died ; cp. l. 455.
479. Th. wrongly inserts *And thus in sorowe
lefte me alone* after this line.

Allas, Deeth, what ayleth thee   480
  That thou noldest have taken me,
  Whan thou toke my lady sweete
That was so fayr, so fresh, so fre,
  So good, that men may wel se
  Of al goodnesse she had no meete.

     Whan he hadde mad thus his com-
     playnte,
His sorwful herté gan fasté faynte,
And his spirites wexen dede ;
The blood was fled for puré drede   489
Doun to his herté, to make hym warme ;
For wel hit feled the herte hadde harme ;
To wite eke why hit was a-drad
By kynde, and for to make hit glad ;
For hit is membre principal
Of the body ; and that made al
His hewé chaunge, and wexé grene,
And pale, for ther no blood was sene
In no maner lyme of his.
     Anoon therwith whan I saw this,
He ferde thus evel ther he seet,   500
I went and stood right at his feet,
And gretté hym, but he spak noght,
But argued with his owné thoght
And in his wit disputéd faste,
Why and how his lyf myght laste,—
Hym thought his sorwés were so smerte
And lay so colde upon his herte ;
So, through his sorw and hevy thoght,
Made hym that he herde me noght
For he had wel-nygh lost his mynde   510
Thogh Pan, that men clepe god of
     kynde,
Were for his sorwés never so wrooth.
     But at the last, to sayn right sooth,
He was war of me how I stood
Before hym, and did of myn hood,
And hadde y-gret hym as I best coude.
Debonayrly, and no thyng loude,
He sayde, 'I prey the be not wrooth ;
I herde thee not, to seyn the sooth,
Ne I saw thee not, sir, trewély.'   520
     'A ! goodé sir, no fors,' quod I,
'I am right sory if I have ought
Destroubled yow out of your thought ;
For-yive me, if I have mis-take.'
     'Yis, thamendes is light to make,'

Quod he, ' for ther lyth noon ther-to,
Ther is no thyng missayd nor do.'
  Lo ! how goodly spak this knyght,
As hit hadde been a-nother wyght.
He made hit nouther tough ne queynte,
And I saw that, and gan me aqueynte   531
With hym, and fond hym so tretable,
Right wonder skilful and reasonable,
As me thoghte, for al his bale ;
A-noon right I gan fynde a tale
To hym, to loke wher I might ought
Have moré knowyng of his thought.
  ' Sir,' quod I, ' this game is doon ;
I holdé that this hert be goon ;
Thise huntés conne hym nowher see.'   540
  ' I do no fors therof,' quod he,
' My thought is ther-on never a del.'
  ' Bi our Lord ! ' quod I, ' I trowe yow
        wel,
Right so me thinketh bi your chere.
But, sir, oo thyng, wol ye here ?
Me thinketh in gret sorwe I yow see ;
But certés, siré, if that ye
Wolde ought discuré me your wo
I wolde, as wis God helpe me so,
Amende hit, if I can or may.   550
Ye mowé preve hit bi assay,
For, by my trouthe, to make yow hool,
I wol do al my power hool ;
And telleth me of your sorwés smerte,
Paraunter hit may ese your herte,
That semeth ful seke under your side.'
  With that he loked on me aside,
As who sayth, ' Nay, that wol not be.'
  ' Graunt mercy ! goodé frend,' quod he,
' I thanke the that thou woldest so,   560
But hit may never the rather be do.
No man may my sorwé glade
That maketh my hewe to falle and fade,
And hath myn understondyng lorn,
That me is wo that I was born !
May noght make my sorwés slyde,—
Nought al the remedies of Ovyde ;
Ne Orpheus, god of melodye ;
Ne Dedalus, with his playés slye ;
Ne hele me may no phisicien,   570
Noght Ypocras, ne Galyen ;

Me is wo that I lyve hourés twelve,
But who so wol assay hym-selve,
Whether his herté can have pite
Of any sorwe, lat hym see me.
I, wrecche, that deeth hath mad al naked
Of all the blisse that ever was makéd ;
Y-worthé worste of allé wightes,—
That hate my dayés and my nightes ;
My lyf, my lustés, be me lothe   580
For al welfare, and I be wrothe.
The puré Deeth is so ful my fo
That I wolde deye,—hit wol not so ;
For whan I folwe hit, hit wol flee ;
I wolde have hym, hit nyl nat me.
This is my peyne wythouté reed,
Alway deyinge and be not deed,
That Cesiphus, that lyth in helle,
May not of moré sorwé telle ;
And who-so wiste al, bi my trouthe,   590
My sorwé, but he haddé routhe
And pité of my sorwés smerte,
That man hath a feendly herte ;
For who so seeth me first on morwe
May seyén he hath met with Sorwe,
For I am Sorwe, and Sorwe is I.
  ' Allas ! and I wol telle the why ;
My song is turnéd to pleynyng,
And al my laughter to wepyng,
My gladé thoghtes to hevynesse,   600
In travaile is myn ydelnesse,
And eek my reste ; my wele is wo,
My good is harm, and ever mo
In wrathe is turnéd my pleying,
And my delit in-to sorwyng.
Myn hele is turned in-to seekuesse,
In drede is al my sykernesse ;
To derke is turnéd al my light,
My wit is foly, my day is night,
My love is hate, my sleep wakyng,   610
My mirthe and melés is fastyng,
My countenaunce is nycete,
And al abaved wher-so I be.
My pees, in pledyng, and in werre.
Allas ! how myghte I faré werre ?
  ' My boldnesse is turnéd to shame,
For fals Fortune hath pleyd a game
Atte chess with me,—allas ! the while !

569. *his playés slye*, his ingenious contrivances,
i.e. his artificial wings.
  571. *Ypocras*, Hippocrates.

588. *Cesiphus*, Sisyphus.
598. *song*. All read *sorowe*, a contamination
from l. 596.

The trayteresse fals, and ful of gyle,
That al behoteth, and no thyng halt, 620
She goth upright, and yet she halt,
That baggeth foule, and loketh faire,
The dispitousè debonaire !
That scorneth many a crëature.
An ydole of fals portrayture
Is she, for she wol sonè wrien.
She is the monstres heed y-wrien,
As filthè over y-strawed with flourès.
Hir mostè worship and hir flour is
To lyen, for that is hir nature ; 630
With-outè feythe, lawe, or mesure,
She is fals ; and ever laghyng
With oon eye, and that other wepyng.
That is broght up she set al doun ;
I likne hir to the scorpioun,
That is a fals, flateryng beste,
For with his heed he maketh feste,
But, al amydd his flaterynge,
With his taylè he wol stynge
And envenyme ; and so wol she. 640
She is thenvyousè Charite,
That is ay fals, and semeth weel,
So turneth she hir falsè wheel
Aboute, for hit is no thyng stable,
Now by the firè, now at table ;
For many oon hath she thus y-blent.
She is pley of enchauntèment,
That semeth oon, and is not so.
The falsè theef ! what hath she do,
Trowest thou ? By our Lord, I wol thee
        seye. 650
    'Atte ches with me she gan to pleye ;
With hir falsè draughtes dyvers
She stal on me, and took my fers ;
And whan I saw my fers aweye,
Allas ! I couthe no lenger pleye,
But seydè, " Far-wel, swete, y-wys !
And far-wel al that ever ther is ! "
Ther-with Fortunè seyde, " Chek heer ! "
And " Mate ! " in the myd poynt of the
        chekkere,
With a poune erraunt, allas ! 660
Ful craftier to pley she was
Than Athalus that made the game

First of the ches, so was his name.
But God wolde, I had oones or twyes
Y-coud and knowe the jeupardyes
That coude the Grek Pithagores,
I shulde have pleyde the bet at ches,
And kept my fers the bet ther-by.
    'And thogh whereto ? For trewèly
I holde that wysh nat worth a stree ! 670
Hit had be never the bet for me,
For Fortune can so many a wyle,
Ther be but fewe can hir begyle,
And eek she is the las to blame ;
My-self I wolde have do the same,
Before God, hadde I been as she.
She oghte the more excusèd be
For this. I say yet more ther-to,—
Hadde I be God and myghte have do
My willè, whan my fers she caughte, 680
I wolde have drawe the samè draughte.
For, also wys God yive me reste !
I dar wel swere, she took the beste.
    ' But through that draughte I havè lorn
My blisse. Allas ! that I was born,
For evermore I trowe trewèly,
For al my wil, my lust hoolly
Is turnèd ; but yet, what to doone ?
Be our Lorde ! hit is to deyè soone,
For no thyng I leve hit noght, 690
But lyve and deye right in this thoght.
For there nis planete in firmament
Ne in ayre, ne in erthe, noon element
That they ne yive me a yift echoon
Of wepyng, whan I am alloon.
For whan that I avise me wel,
And be-thenke me every-del,
How that ther lyth in rekenyng
In my sorwè for no thyng ;
And how ther leveth no gladnesse 700
May gladdè me of my distresse,
And how I have lost suffisance,
And ther-to I have no plesance,
Than may I say I have right noght.
And whan al this falleth in my thoght,
Allas, than am I overcome !
For that is doon is not to come :
I have more sorwè than Tantale ! '

---

651. *Atte.* All read *At the.*
662. *Athalus.* The reputed inventor of Chess.
According to Warton *Attalus Philometer*, King
of Pergamus, is meant. This whole passage is
imitated from the *Rom. de la Rose*, ll. 6644-6881.

665. *jeupardyes*, problems ; O.F. *jeu parti*, a
divided game.
681. *the same draughte*, move at chess.
698, 699. In my account with sorrow there lies
to my credit no amount at all.

And whan I herde hym telle this tale
Thus pitously, as I yow telle,   710
Unnethé myghte I lenger dwelle,
Hit dide myn herté so moché wo.
  ' A, good sir !' quod I, 'say not so !
Have som pite on your nature,
That forméd yow to creature.
Remembre yow of Socrates,
For he ne counted nat three strees
Of noght that Fortune coudé do.'
  ' No,' quod he, ' I can not so.'
  ' Why so, sir ? yis, pardé !' quod I ;
' Ne say noght soo, for trewély,   721
Thogh ye had lost the ferses twelve,
And ye for sorwe mordred your selve,
Ye sholde be dampned in this cas
Bi as good right as Medea was,
That slow hir children for Jason ;
And Phyllis also for Demophon
Heng hir-selfe, so weylaway !
For he had broke his termé day
To come to hir.   Another rage   730
Had Dydo, the quene eek of Cartage,
That slow hir self, for Eneas
Was fals ;—which a foole she was.
And Ecquo died, for Narcisus
Noldé nat love hir ; and right thus
Hath many another foly don.
And for Dalida dyed Sampson,
That slow hym-self with a pilere,—
But ther is no man a-lyvé here
Wolde for a fers maké this wo !'   740
  ' Why so !' quod he, ' hyt ys nat so ;
Thou wost ful lytel what thou menest ;
I have lost moré than thow wenest.'
  ' Lo, sey, how that may be ?' quod I ;
' Good sir, tel me al hoolly
In what wyse, how, why, and wherfore,
That ye have thus your blissé lore.'
  ' Blythly,' quod he ; 'com sit adoun !
I telle the upon a condicioun
That thou shalt hooly with al thy wit   750

720. *sir.* All read *good syr*, contamination
with *quod* in line above.
722. *the ferses twelve*, *i.e.* 'all the pieces except the king, which could not be taken.' (Skeat.)
727. Phyllis committed suicide from fear that
Demophon had forgotten her, and was changed
into a tree. Demophon was a son of Theseus.
734. *Ecquo*, Echo. All these examples occur
in the *Roman de la Rose.*
737. *Dalida*, Delilah.

Do thyn entent to herkene hit.'
  ' Yis, sir !'
                ' Swere thy trouthe ther-to.'
  ' Gladly.'
                ' Do than holde her-to.'
  ' I shal, right blythly, so God me save !
Hoolly with al the wit I have
Here yow as wel as I kan.'
  ' A Goddes half !' quod he, and began:
' Sir,' quod he, ' sith first I kouthe
Have any maner wit fro youthe,
Or kyndély understondyng   760
To comprehende in any thyng
What love was in myn owné wit,
Dredeles I have ever yit
Be tributary and yiven rente
To love, hooly with goode entente,
And through plesaunce become his thral
With good wil, body, herte, and al.
Al this I putte in his servage,
As to my lorde, and dide homage,
And ful devoutly I prayde hym to,   770
He shulde besette myn herté so,
That hit plesancé to hym were,
And worship to my lady dere.
  ' And this was longe, and many a
          yeer,
Or that myn herté was set owher,
That I dide thus, and nysté why,
I trowe, hit cam me kyndély.
Peraunter I was therto most able,
As a whyt wal or a table,
For hit is redy to cacche and take   780
Al that men wil therynné make,
Whethir-so men wil portreye or peynte,
Be the werkés never so queynte.
  ' And thilké tyme I ferde right so
I was ablé to have lernéd tho,
And to have kenned as wel or better
Paraunter other art or letter,
But for love cam first in my thought,
Therfore I forgat hit nought.
I chees love to my firsté craft,   790
Therfore hit is with me laft.
For why ? I took hit of so yong age
That malice haddé my corage
Nat that tyme turnéd to no thyng,
Through to mochel knowlechyng.
For that tyme Youthé, my maistresse,
Governéd me in ydelnesse,

319

For hit was in my firstė youthe,
And tho ful litel good I couthe,
For al my werkės were flittynge　　800
That tyme, and thoghtės varyinge,
Al were to me ylychė good,
That I knew tho, but thus hit stood.
　'Hit happed that I cam on a day
In-to a place ther that I say
Trewly the fayrest companye
Of ladyes, that ever man with ÿe
Had seen to-gedres in oo place.
Shal I clepe hyt hap, other grace
That broghte me ther? Nay, but
　　Fortune,　　810
That is to lyen ful comune,—
The falsė trayteresse, pervers !
God wolde I coudė clepe hir wers !
For now she worcheth me ful wo,
And I wol tellė sone why so.
　'Among these ladies thus echoon,
Soth to seyėn, I sawgh oon
That was lyk noon of the route,
For I dar swere, withoutė doute,
That as the someres sonnė bryght　　820
Is fairer, clerer, and hath more lyght
Than any other planete in heven,
The monė, or the sterrės seven ;
For al the worldė so had she
Surmounted hem alle of beaute,
Of maner, and of comlynesse,
Of stature, and of wel set gladnesse,
Of goodlihede, so wel be-seye,—
Shortly, what shal I more seye ?
By God, and by his halwės twelve,　　830
Hit was my swete, ryght as hir-selve !
She had so stedfast countenaunce,
So noble port and meyntenaunce.
And love, that had wel herd my bone,
Had espyėd me thus sone,
That she ful sonė, in my thoght,
As helpe me God, so was y-caught
So sodenly, that I ne took
No maner counseyl, but at hir look
And at myn hertė ; for-why, hir ÿen　　840
So gladly, I trow, myn hertė syen,
That purely tho myn ownė thoght
Seyde hit were beter serve hir for noght

798. John of Gaunt was married at nineteen.
828. *so.* All read *and so,* caught from the line above.
830. By Christ and His twelve apostles.

Than with a-nother to be wel.
And it was sooth, for everydel
I wil a-noon right telle the why.
　'I saw hir daunce so comlily,
Carole and synge so swetėly,
Laughe and pleye so womanly,
And lokė so debonairly,　　850
So goodly speke, and so friendly,
That certes, I trowe that ever-more
Nas seyn so blisful a tresore,
For every heer on hir hede,
Soth to seyn, it was not rede,
Ne nouther yelw, ne broun it nas,
Me thoghtė most lyk gold it was.
　'And whiche ÿen my lady hadde !
Debonair, goodė, glade, and sadde,
Symple, of goode mochel, noght to wyde,
Ther-to hir look nas not a-syde,　　861
Ne overthwert, but beset so wel,
Hit drew and took up everydel
Alle that on hir gan be-holde.
Hir ÿen semed anoon she wolde
Have mercy,—foolės wenden so,—
But hit was never the rather do.
Hit nas no countrefeted thyng,
Hit was hir ownė pure lokyng,
That the goddessė, dame Nature,　　870
Had made hem opene by mesure,
And close ; for were she never so glad
Hir lokyng was not foly sprad,
Ne wildėly, thogh that she pleyde ;
But ever me thoghte hir ÿen seyde,
" By God, my wrathe is al for-yive ! "
　'Therwith hir liste so wel to live,
That dulnesse was of hir a-drad.
She nas to sobre, ne to glad.
In allė thyngės more mesure　　880
Had never, I trowė, creature.
But many oon with hir loke she herte,
And that sat hir ful lyte at herte,
For she knew no-thyng of hir thoght,
But whether she knew, or knew it noght,
Algate she ne roghte of hem a stree !
To gete hir love noo ner nas he
That woned at home, than he in Ynde,
The formest was alway behynde.
But goodė folke, over al other,　　890
She loved as man may do his brother,
Of whiche love she was wonder large
In skilful places that berė charge.

‘ But which a visage had she ther-to !
Allas, myn herte is wonder wo
That I ne can discryven hit !
Me lakketh bothe English and wit
For to un-do hit at the fulle,
And eek my spirits be so dulle
So greet a thyng for to devyse.   900
I have no wit that can suffise
To comprehenden hir beautè,
But thus moche dar I seyn, that she
Was, rody, fresh, and lyvely hewed ;
And every day hir beautè newed ;
And negh hir face was alder-best ;
For certès, Nature had swich lest
To make that fair, that trewly she
Was hir cheef patron of beautè,
And cheef ensample of al hir werke,   910
And moustre ; for be hit never so derke,
Me thynketh I se hir ever-mo ;
And yet, more-over, thogh allè tho
That ever lyved were now a-lyve,
They ne sholde have foundè to diskryve
In al hir face a wikked signe ;
For hit was sad, symple, and benygne.
‘ And which a goodly, softè speche
Had that swete, my lyvès leche !
So friendly and so wel y-grounded,   920
Up al resoun so wel y-founded,
And so tretable to al gode,
That I dar swere wel by the rode,
Of eloquence was never founde
So swete a sownyngè facounde,
Ne trewer tongèd, ne scornèd lasse,
Ne bet coude hele ; that by the masse
I durste swere, thogh the pope hit songe,
That ther was never yet through hir tonge
Man ne woman gretly harmèd,   930
As for hir ther was al harm hyd ;
Ne lassè flateryng in hir worde,
That purèly hir symple recorde
Was foundè as trewe as any bonde,
Or trouthe of any mannès honde.
Ne chyde she koudè never a del,
That knoweth al the world ful wel.
‘ But swich a fairnesse of a nekke
Had that swete, that boon nor brekke

Nas ther non senè that mys-sat ;   940
Hit was smothe, streght, and purè flat,
Wyth-outen hole ; nor canel boon,
As be semynge, had she noon.
Hir throte, as I have now memoire,
Semèd a round tour of yvoire,
Of good gretnesse, and noght to grete.
‘ And godè, fairè, White, she hete,—
That was my lady namè ryght,—
She was bothe faire and bryght,
She haddè not hir namè wrong.   950
Right fairè shuldrès, and body long,
She hadde, and armès, every lith
Fattyssh, flesshy, not greet therwith ;
Right whitè handes, and naylès rede,
Roundè brestes ; and of good brede
Hir hippès were, a streight flat bak.
I knew on hir non other lak,
That al hir lymmes nere pursewing,
In as fer as I had knowyng.
‘ Therto she coudè so wel pleye,   960
Whan that hir lyste, that I dar seye
That she was lyk to torchè bright
That every man may take of light
Ynogh, and hit hath never the lesse.
‘ Of maner and of comlynesse,
Right so ferde my lady dere,
For every wyght of hir manere
Myght cacche ynogh, if that he wolde,
If he had ÿen hir to be-holde ;
For I dar swere wel if that she   970
Hadde among ten thousand be,
She woldè have be, at the leste,
A cheef mirour of al the feste,
Thogh they had stonden in a rowe,
To mennès ÿen that coude have knowe.
For wher-so men had pleyed or wakèd,
Me thoghte the felawship as naked
Withouten hir, that saw I ones,
As a coroune withoutè stones.
Trewly she was to myn ÿe   980
The soleyn fenix of Arabye,
For ther lyveth never but oon ;
Ne swich as she ne knew I noon.
‘ To speke of goodnesse ; trewly she

904. All read *white, rody,* etc. Skeat omits
white, for it spoils the point of l. 948 and the metre
of this line.
915. All omit *They,* which is necessary to the
syntax.

941. All read *white, smothe,* etc.; cp. l. 904 note.
Skeat here omits *pure.*
942. All read *or.*
947. A reference to the name of the Duchess,
viz. Blaunche.
958. All read *pure sewing.*

Hadde as moche debonairtè
As ever hadde Hester in the Bible,
And more, gif morè were possible.
And soth to seynè, therwyth-al
She had a wyt so genèral,
So hool enclyned to allè gode,   990
That al hir wyt was set, by the rode,
With-oute malyce upon gladnesse ;
And ther-to I saw never yet a lesse
Harmful than she was in doyng.
I sey nat that she ne had knowyng
Whàt harm was, or ellès she
Had coud no good, so thynketh me.
   'And trewly, for to speke of trouthe,
But she hadde had, it hadde be routhe.
Therof she had so moche hir del,   1000
And I dar seyn, and swere hit wel,
That Trouthe hym-self, over al and al,
Had chose his maner principal
In hir, that was his restyng-place.
Ther-to she hadde the mostè grace
To have stedfast perseveraunce
An esy, atempre governaunce,
That ever I knew, or wystè yit,
So purè, suffraunt, was hir wyt.
And resoun gladly she understood ;   1010
Hit folowed wel she coudè good.
She usèd gladly to do wel :
These were hir maners everydel.
   'Therwith she lovèd so wel right,
She wrong do woldè to no wyght ;
Nò wyght myghte do hir no shame,
She loved so wel hir ownè name.
Hir luste to holde no wyght in honde,
Ne, be thou siker, she wolde not
      fonde
To holdè no wyght in balaunce   1020
By half word, ne by countenaunce,
But if men wolde upon hir lye ;
Ne sende men in-to Walakye,
To Pruyse, and in-to Tartarye,
To Alysaundre, ne in-to Turkye ;
And bidde hym faste, anoon that he
Go hoodles in-to the dryè se,

And come hoom by the Carrenare ;
And seyè, "Sir, be now right ware
That I may of yow herè seyn   1030
Worship, or that ye come ageyn !"
She ne usèd no suche knakkès smale.
   'But wherfor that I telle my tale ?
Right on this same, as I have seyd,
Was hoolly al my lovè leyd,
For certès, she was, that swetè wyf
My suffisauncè, my lust, my lyf,
Myn hap, myn hele, and al my blisse,
My worldes welfare, and my [goodè lisse,]
And I hoolly hirs, and everydel.'   1040

   'By our Lord,' quod I, 'I trowe yow
      wel !
Hardely, your love was wel beset,
I not how ye myghte have do bet.'
   'Bet ? ne noght so wel !' quod he.
   'I trowe hit, sir,' quod I, 'parde !'
   'Nay, leve hit wel !'
              'Sire, so do I ;
I leve yow wel, that trewèly
Yow thoghtè that she was the beste,
And to be-holde the alderfayreste,   1049
Who so had loked hir with your eyen '—
   'With myn ? nay, allè that hir seyen
Seyde, and sworen hyt was so.
And thogh they ne hadde, I woldè tho
Have lovèd best my lady fre,
Thogh I haddè had al the beautè
That ever haddè Alcipyades,
And al the strengthe of Ercules,
And therto haddè the worthynesse
Of Alysaundre, and al the rychesse
That ever was in Babyloyne,   1060
In Cartage, or in Macedoyne,
Or in Rome, or in Nynyvè ;
And therto also as hardy be
As was Ector, so have I joye,
That Achilles slow at Troye,—
And ther-for was he slayn also
In a temple, for bothè two
Were slayn, he and Antylegyus,

---

986. *Hester*, Esther.
1024. *Pruyse*, Prussia.
1027. *the dryè se.* According to Mr. Brae
(Appendix to his ed. of Chaucer's *Astrolabe*, p.
101) this refers to the variable Lake Czirknitz,
near Laibach, N.E. of Trieste, which is sometimes dry.

1028. Mr. Brae suggests that this is the Gulf
of Carnaro or Quarnaro in the Adriatic to which
Dante refers ; cp. *Inf.* ix. 113. It is within 40
miles of Lake Czirknitz.
1039. *goodè lisse.* All read *goddesse.* Skeat
lisse.
1056. *Alcipyades*, Alcibiades.
1068. *Antylegyus*, Antilochus.

And so seyth Dares Frigius,
For lové of Polixena,— 1070
Or ben as wys as Mynerva,
I wolde ever, withouté drede,
Have loved hir, for I mosté nede !
'"Nede !" nay, trewly, I gabbé
now,—
Noght "nede," and I wol tellé how,
For of good wille myn herte it wolde,
And eek to love hir I was holde,
As for the faireste and the beste.
'She was as good, so have I reste,
As ever was Penelope of Grece, 1080
Or as the noble wyf Lucrece,
That was the beste,—he telleth thus
The Romayn, Tytus Lyvyus,—
She was as good, and no thyng lyke,
Thogh hir stories be autentyke ;
Algate she was as trewe as she.
'But wherfor that I tellé the
Whan I first my lady say ?
I was right yong, soth to say,
And ful greet need I hadde to lerne 1090
Whan my herté woldé yern
To love, it was a greet emprise ;
But as my wyt coude beste suffise,
After my yongé, childly wyt,
Withoute drede, I be-setté hit
To love hir in my besté wyse,
To do hir worship, and the servise.
That I coude tho, by my trouthe,
Withouté feynyng, outher slouthe,
For wonder fayn I wolde hir se. 1100
'So mochel hit amended me,
That whan I saw hir first a-morwe,
I was warished of al my sorwe
Of al day after, til hit were eve ;
Me thoghté no-thyng myghte me greve,
Were my sorwés never so smerte ;
And yet she syt so in myn herte,
That by my trouthe, I noldé noght,
For al this worlde, out of my thoght
Levé my lady ; no, trewély !' 1110

1069. Dares Phrygius, the Trojan priest of Vulcan, in whose name the popular spurious history of Troy was written by a Roman after the fall of Rome. The reference here, however, is to the mediæval version of the story, written by Guido delle Colonne, which was based on Benoit de Sainte-Maure's *Roman de Troie*.
1089. Possibly, as Skeat thinks, *the* has been omitted before *soth*, but cp. l. 1180.

'Now, by my trouthé, sir,' quod I,
'Me thynketh ye have such a chaunce,
As shrift wythouté répentaunce.'
'"Répentaunce !" nay, fy !' quod he,
'Shulde I now repenté me
To love ? nay, certés, than were I wel
Wers than was Achitofel,
Or Anthenor, so have I joye,
The traytour that betrayséd Troye,
Or the falsé Genellon, 1120
He that purchased the treson
Of Rowland and of Olyvere.
Nay, whil I am a-lyvé here
I nyl foryete hir, never mo !'
'Now, goodé siré,' quod I tho,
'Ye han wel told me her-before,
Hit is no need to reherse hit more
How ye sawe hir first, and where ;
But wolde ye telle me the manere
To hir which was your firsté speche,—
Therof I woldé yow be-seche,— 1131
And how she knewé first your thoght,
Whether ye lovéd hir or noght,
And telleth me eek what ye have lore,
I herde yow tellé herbefore.'
'Ye,' seyde he, 'thou nost what
thou menest ;
I have lost moré than thou wenest.'
'What los is that ?' quod I tho ;
'Nyl she not love yow ? is hit so ?
Or have ye oght doon amys, 1140
That she hath left yow ? is it this ?
For Goddés lové, telle me al.'
'Be-fore God,' quod he, 'and I shal.
I sayé right as I have seyd,
On hir was al my lové leyd,
And yet she nyste it never a del
Noght longé tymé, leve it wel !
For be right siker, I dursté noght,
For al this worlde, tel hir my thoght,
Ne I wolde have wratthed hir trewély.
For wostow why ? she was lady 1151
Of the body,—she had the herte,
And who hath that may not asterte.
'But, for to kepe me fro ydelnesse,

1120. *Genellon*, one of Charlemagne's officers, whose treachery caused the defeat at Roncevaux and the death of Roland.
1122. *Rowland and Oliver*, the two most celebrated of Charlemagne's knights.
1146. All read *not never*.

Trewly I did my besynesse
To makė songes, as I best coude ;
And oftė tyme I song hem loude,
And madė songes thus a greet del,
Al thogh I coude not make so wel
Songės, ne knowė the art al   1160
As coudė Lamekes sone, Tubal,
That fond out first the art of songe ;—
For as his brothres hamers ronge
Upon his anvelt up and doun
Therof he took the firstė soun ;
But Grekės seyn Pictagoras,
That he the firstė fynder was
Of the art, *Aurora* telleth so ;
But therof no fors, of hem two.
Algatės, songės thus I made   1170
Of my felyng, myn herte to glade.
And lo ! this was the alther-firste,—
I not wher it were the werste.
Lorde, hyt maketh myn hertė lyght
Whan I thenke on that swetė wyght
That is so semely on to see ;
And wisshe to God it myght so bee
    That she wolde holde me for hir knyght,
    My lady that is so fair and bright !

    ' Now have I told the, soth to saye,
My firstė song.   Upon a daye   1181
I be-thoghtė me what wo
And sorwė that I suffrėd tho
For hir, and yet she wyste it noght,
Ne telle hir durste I nat my thoght.
Allas ! thoghte I, I can no reed ;
And but I telle hir I nam but deed,
And if I telle hir, to seye right sooth,
I am a-dred she wol be wrooth.
Allas ! what shal I thannė do ?   1190
    ' In this debat I was so wo,
Me thoghte myn hertė braste a-tweyn !
So at the lastė, soth to sayn,
I be-thoghte me that Nature
Ne formėd never in crėature
So mochė beautė, trewėly,
And bountė, wyth-oute mercy.

1161. *Tubal*, an error for Jubal, ' the father of all such as handle the harp and organ.'
1166. *Pictagoras*, Pythagoras.
1168. *Aurora*, a Latin metrical version of parts of the Bible allegorised by Petrus de Riga, Canon of Rheims, in the 12th century.
1172. *the alther-firste*. All omit *the*, but the rime proves the necessity of the demonstrative.

    ' In hope of that my tale I tolde
With sorwe, as that I never sholde
For nedės ; and, maugree my heed,   1200
I moste have told hir or be deed.
I not wel how that I began,
Ful evel rehersen hit I can,
And eek, as helpe me God, with-al
I trowe hit was in the dismal
That was the ten woundes of Egipte,
For many a word I over-skipte
In my tale, for purė fere
Lest my wordės mys-set were ;
With sorwful herte, and woundės dede,
Softe, and quakyng for purė drede   1211
And shame, and styntyng in my tale
For ferdė, and myn hewe al pale,
Ful ofte I wex bothe pale and reed ;
Bowyng to hir, I heng the heed,
I durste nat onės loke hir on,
For wit, manere, and al was goon.
I seydė " Mercy ! " and no more.
Hit nas no game, hit sat me sore.
    ' So at the lastė, sooth to seyn,   1220
Whan that myn herte was come ageyn,
To tellė shortly al my speche,
With hool herte I gan hir beseche
That she wolde be my lady swete ;
And swor, and gan hir hertely hete
Ever to be stedfast and trewe,
And love hir alwey freshly newe,
And never other lady have,
And al hir worship for to save
As I best coude,—I swor hir this,—   1230
" For youres is al that ever ther is
For evermore, myn hertė swete !
And never to false yow, but I mete,
I nyl, as wys God helpe me so ! "
    ' And whan I hadde my tale y-do,
God wot she acounted nat a stree
Of al my tale, so thoghtė me.
To tellė shortly, right as it is,
Trewly hir answere hit was this ;
I can not now wel counterfete   1240
Hir wordės, but this was the grete
Of hir answere : she saydė, " Nay ! "
Al-outerly.   Allas ! that day
The sorwe I suffred and the wo,

1205. *dismal*, on an evil day ; Anglo-French *dis mal* (Lat. *dies mali*). The form of the word caused it to be used as an adjective later.

That trewly Cassandra, that so
Bewaylèd the destruccioun
Of Troyè and of Ilioun,
Had never swich sorwe as I tho.
I durste no morè say ther-to
For purè fere, but stal away ; 1250
And thus I lyved ful many a day,
That trewèly, I hadde no need,
Ferther than my beddès heed,
Never a day to sechè sorwe ;
I fond hit redy every morwe,
For why I loved hir in no gere.
  ' So hit befel another yere,
I thoughtè ones I woldè fonde
To do hir knowe and understonde
My wo ; and she wel understood 1260
That I ne wilned no thyng but good,
And worship, and to kepe hir name
Over allè thyng, and drede hir shame,
And was so besy hir to serve,
And pite were I shuldè sterve,
Sith that I wilned noon harm y-wys.
  ' So whan my lady knew al this,
My lady yaf me al hoolly
The noble yift of hir mercy,
Savyng hir worship by al weyes ; 1270
Dredles, I mene noon other weyes.
And therwith she yaf me a ryng,
I trowe hit was the firstè thyng ;
But if myn hertè was y-waxe
Glad, that is no need to axe !
As helpe me God, I was as blyve
Reysèd, as fro dethe to lyve,
Of al happès the alder-beste,
The gladdest, and the moste at reste.
For trewèly that swetè wyght 1280
Whan I hadde wrong and she the right,
She wolde alway so goodèly
For-yeve me so debonairly !
In alle my youthe, in allè chaunce
She took me in hir governaunce.
  ' Therwyth she was alway so trewe
Our joye was ever y-lichè newe,
Our hertès wern so even a payre
That never nas that oon contraire
To that other, for no wo ; 1290
For sothe y-liche they suffred tho
Oo blysse, and eek oo sorwè bothe ;

1261. *thyng*. All read *thynges*, unidiomatically.

Y-liche they were bothe gladde and wrothe,
Al was us oon withoutè were.
And thus we lyved ful many a yere
So wel, I can nat tellè how.'
  ' Sir,' quod I, ' wher is she now ? '
' " Now ! " ' quod he, and stynte anoon.
Therwith he wex as deed as stoon
And seyde, ' Allas, that I was bore ! 1300
That was the los, that her-before
I toldè the that I hadde lorn ;
Bethenk how I seyde herbeforn ;
" Thow wost ful litel what thou menest ;
I have lost morè than thou wenest ! "
God wot, allas ! right that was she ! '
  ' Allas ! sir, how ? what may that be ? '
' She ys deed ! '
                    ' Nay ! '
                              ' Yis, by my trouthe ! '
  ' Is that your los ? by God, hit is
routhe ! '
And with that wordè right anoon 1310
They gan to strake forth ; al was doon
For that tyme, the hert-huntyng.

  With that me thoghtè that this kyng
Gán homwardès for to ryde,
Unto a place was ther besyde,
Which was from us but a lyte ;
A long castel with wallès white
Be Seynt Johan ! on a richè hil,
As me mette ; but thus hyt fil.
  Ryght thus me mette, as I yow telle, 1320
That in the castell ther was a belle,
As hit hadde smyten hourès twelve.

Therewyth I a-wook my selve
And fond me lying in my bed ;
And the book that I hadde red,
Of Alcyone and Seys the kyng,
And of the goddès of slepyng,
I fond it in myn honde ful even.
  Thoghte I, ' This is so queynt a sweven,
That I wol, be processe of tyme, 1330
Fonde to putte this sweven in ryme
As I can best ' ; and that anoon.
This was my sweven ; now hit is doon !

1314. All read *Gan homward*, which seems
to make the line too short.
1317. *A long castel*, presumably Windsor.

325

THE COMPLEYNTE UNTO PITE

*Complainte of the Deathe of Pitie, in
Stowe's hand.*

PITÈ that I have sought so yore ago
With hertė sore and ful of besy peyne,
That in this worlde was never wight so wo
With-outė dethe ; and if I shal not feyne,
My purpos was to Pite to compleyne
Upon the crueltee and tirannye
Of Love, that for my trouthė doth me dye.

And when that I, by lengthe of certeyn
      yeres,
Had evere in oon a tymė sought to speke,
To Pite ran I, al bespreynt with teres,   10
To preyen hir on Crueltee me a wreke ;
But er I myght with any worde out-breke,
Or tellen any of my peynės smerte,
I fond hir deed and buried in an herte.

Adoun fel I when that I saugh the herse,
Deed as a stoon, whyl that the swogh me
      laste ;
But up I roos with colour ful dyverse,
And pitously on hir myn eyen I casté,
And ner the corps I gan to presen faste,
And for the soule I shoop me for to
      preye ;   20
I nas but lorne, ther was no more to sey.

Thus am I slayn sith that Pitè is deed ;
Allas the day ! that ever hit shulde falle !
What maner man dar now holde up his
      heed ?
To whom shal any sorwful hertė calle ?
Now Crueltee hath cast to sleen us alle,
In ydel hope, folk redėlees of peyne,—
Sith she is deed, to whom shul we com-
      pleyne ?

But yet encreseth me this wonder newe,   29
That no wight woot that she is deed but I ;
So mony men as in her tyme hir knewe,
And yet she dyėd not so sodeynly ;
For I have sought hir ever ful besily
Sith I first haddė wit or mannės mynde ;
But she was deed er that I coude hir fynde.

Aboute hir herse ther stoden lustily,
Withouten any wo, as thoughtė me,
Bountee parfit, wel-armed and richėly,
And fresshė Beautee, Lust and Jolitee,
Assured Maner, Youthe and Honestee,   40
Wisdom, Estaat, and Dreed, and Govern-
      aunce,
Confedred bothe by bonde and alliaunce.

A compleynte hadde I writen in myn
      hond,
For to have put to Pite as a bille ;
But whan I al this companye ther fond,
That rather wolden al my causė spille
Than do me help, I held my pleyntė stille ;
For to tho folk, with-outen any faile,
Withoutė Pite may no bille availe.

Then leve I al thise vertues, sauf Pitè,   50
Kepyng the corps, as ye have herd me seyn,
Cofedred alle by bonde of Cruelte,
And ben assented that I shal be sleyn.
And I have put my Compleynte up ageyn ;
For to my foes my bille I dar not shewe,
Theffect of which seith thus in wordės fewe.

The Bille

Humblest of herte, highest of reverence,
Benygnė flour, coroune of vertues alle !
Sheweth un-to your rial excellence
Your servaunt, if I durstė me so calle,   60
His mortal harm in which he is y-falle ;
And noght al only for his evel fare,
But for your renoun, as he shal declare.

Hit stondeth thus, your contraire
      Crueltee
Allyed is ageynst your regalye,
Under colour of womanly Beautee,—
For men ne shulde not knowe hir
      tirannye,—
With Bountee, Gentilesse, and Curtesye,
And hath depryvėd yow now of your place,
That highte 'Beautee apertenant to
      Grace.'   70

21. *nas.* All read *was.*

41. All omit *and* after *Estaat;* Ten Brink supplies it.
67. All omit *ne*, which Ten Brink supplies.

For kyndly, by your heritagé right,
Ye been annexéd ever unto Bountee,
And verrayly ye oughté do your myght
To helpé Trouthe in his adversitee.
Ye been also the coroune of Beautee,
And certes, if ye wanten in thise tweyne
The world is lore; ther nis no more to seyne.

Eek what availeth Maner and Gentilesse
Withouté you, benygné creature !
Shal Crueltee be your governeresse ?　　8o
Allas ! what herté may hit long endure ?
Wherfor but ye the rather také cure
To breké that perilous alliaunce,
Ye sleen hem that ben in your obeisaunce.

And further over, if ye suffre this,
Your renoun is fordo than in a throwe ;
Ther shal no man wite wel what Pite is.
Allas! that your renoun shoulde be so lowe;
Ye be than fro your heritage y-throwe
By Crueltee, that occupieth your place,　90
And we despeired that seken to your grace.

Have mercy on me, thou serenous quene,
That you have sought so tenderly and yore,
Let som streem of your light on me be sene,
That love and drede yow ever lenger the
　　　more ;
For, sothly for to seyne, I bere the sore,
And though I be not cunnyng for to pleyne,
For Goddés love, have mercy on my peyne !

My peyne is this, that what-so I desire, 99
That have I not, ne no thing lyk therto ;
And ever set Desire myn herte on fire,
Eek on that other syde where-so I go.
What maner thinge that may encrese my wo
That have I redy, unsoght, everywhere,
Me ne lakketh but my deth, and than my
　　　bere.

What nedeth to shewé parcel of my
　　　peyne,
Sith every wo that herté may be-thynke,
I suffre ?　And yet I dar not to you pleyne,
For wel I woot, although I wake or wynke,
Ye rekké not whether I flete or synke 110

92. *serenous*, Mr. Liddell's emendation for
herenus, heremus, and *vertuouse*, of the MSS.
105. All omit *ne*.

But nathéles, my trouthe I shal sustene
Unto my deth, and that shal wel be sene.

This is to seyne, I wol be yourés ever ;
Though ye me slee by Crueltee your fo,
Algate my spirit shal never dissever
Fro your servyse, for any peyne or wo !
Sith ye be deed,—allas ! that hit is so !—
Thus for your deth I may wel wepe and
　　　pleyne
With herté sore, and ful of besy peyne !

*Here endeth the exclamacion of the Deth
　　　of Pyte.*

CHAUCER'S A B C

*Incipit carmen secundum ordinem
　　Litterarum alphabeti.*

AL myghty and al mercyable Queene,
To whom that al this world fleeth for socour
To have relees of sinne, of sorwe, and teene !
Glorious Virgine, of allé flourés flour,
To thee I flee confounded in errour.
Help, and releeve, thou mihti debonayre,
Have mercy on my perilous langour !
Venquisshed me hath my cruel adversaire.

Bountee so fix hath in thyn herte his
　　　tente,
That wel I wot, thou wolt my socour be ;
Thou canst not warne him that with good
　　　entente　　　　　　　　　　　　11
Axeth thyn helpe, thyn herte is ay so free !
Thou art largesse of pleyn felicitee,
Haven of refute, of quiete, and of reste.
Loo ! how that theevés seven chasen mee !
Help ! Lady bryght, er that my ship to-
　　　breste !

Comfort is noon, but in you, Ladi deere !
For loo, my sinne and my confusioun,
Which oughten not in thy presence appeere,
Han take on me a grevous accioun　　　　20
Of verrey right and desperacioun !
And as bi right they mighten wel susteene
That I were worthy my dampnacioun,
Nere merci of you, blisful hevené Queene !

Doute is ther noon, Queen of miseri-
　　　corde,
That thou nart cause of grace and merci
　　　here ;

God vouchèd-sauf thurgh thee with us to accorde.

For certès, Crystès blisful mooder dere,
Were now the bowè bent in swich manere
As it was first, of justice and of ire, 30
The rightful God nolde of no mercy here ;
But thurgh thee han we grace as we desire.

Ever hath myn hope of refut been in thee,
For heer-biforn ful ofte in many a wyse
Hast thou to misericorde resceyvèd me ;
But merci, Lady at the grete assyse,
Whan we shul come bifore the hye justyse !
So litel fruit shal thanne in me be founde
That, but thou er that day me wel chastyse,
Of verrey right my werk wol me confounde.

Fleeyng, I flee for socour to thy tente 41
Me for to hide from tempest ful of dreede,
Biseeching you that ye you not absente
Though I be wikke ; O help yit at this neede !
Al have I ben a beste in wille and deede,
Yit, Lady, thou me clothè with thy grace.
Thyn enemy and myn, Lady, tak heede,
Un-to my deth in poynt is me to chace !

Glorious mayde and moder which that never 49
Were bitter, neither in erthè nor in see,
But ful of swetnesse and of merci, ever,
Help that my Fader be not wroth with me !
Spek thou, for I ne dar not him y-see,
So have I doon in erthe, allas the while !
That certès, but if thou my socour be
To stynk eterne he wol my gost exile !

He vouchèd-sauf, tel him, as was his wille
Bicome a man to have our alliaunce,
And with his precious blood he wrot the bille
Up-on the crois as general acquitaunce
To every penitent in ful creaunce. 61
And therfor, Lady bright, thou for us praye !
Thanne shalt thou bothè stinte al his grevaunce,
And make our foo to failen of his praye.

I wot it wel thou wolt ben our socour,
Thou art so ful of bountee in certeyn ;
For whan a soulè falleth in errour
Thi pitee goth and haleth him ageyn.
Thanne makest thou his pees with his sovereyn,
And bringest him out of the crooked strete.

Who-so thee loveth he shal not love in veyn : 71
That shal he fynde as he the lyf shal lete.
Kalenderès enlumynèd ben they
That in this world ben lighted with thy name,
And who-so goth to yow the rihtè wey,
Him thar not drede in soulè to be lame.
Now, Queen of comfort ! sith thou art that same
To whom I sechè for my medicyne,
Lat not my foo no more my wounde entame,
Myn hele in-to thyn hand al I resigne. 80

Lady, thi sorwè kan I not portreye
Under the cros, ne his grevous penaunce,
But for your bothès peynès I yow preye,
Lat not our alder foo make his bobaunce
That he hath in his listès of mischaunce
Cònvict that ye bothe have boughts so dere.
As I seide erst, thou ground of our substaunce
Continue on us thy pitous eyen clere.

Moises that saugh the bush with flaumès rede 89
Brenninge, of whichè never a stikkè brende,
Was signe of thyn unwemmèd maidenhede ;
Thou art the bush on which ther gan descende
The Holy Goost, the which that Moyses wende
Had ben a-fyr ; and this was in figure.
Now, Lady, from the fyr thou us defende
Which that in helle eternally shal dure.

Noble princesse that never haddest pere !
Certès, if any comfort in us be
That cometh of thee, thou Cristès moder deere,
We han noon other melodye or glee 100
Us to rejoyse in our adversitee,
Ne advócat noon that wol and dar so preye
For us, and that for litel hire as ye,
That helpen for an Ave Marie or tweye.

O verrey light of eyen that ben blynde !
O verrey lust of labour and distresse !
O tresorere of bountee to mankynde !
Thee whom God ches to moder for humblesse !
From his ancille he madè thee maistresse
Of hevene and erthe, our bille up for to bede. 110

This world awaiteth ever on thy goodnesse,
For thou ne failest never wight at nede.

Purpos I have sum tymé for to enquere
Wherfore and why the Holy Gost the
  soughte,
Whan Gabriellés vois cam to thyn ere;
He not to werre us swich a wunder
  wroughte,
But for to save us that he sithen boughte ;
Than needeth us no wepen us for to save,
But oonly ther we did not as us oughte,—
Do penitence, and merci axe and have. 120

Queen of comfort ! yit whan I me bi-
  thinke
That I agilt have bothé him and thee,
And that my soule is wurthi for to sinke,
Allas ! I caitif, whider may I flee ?
Who shal un-to thi Sone my mené bee ?
Who, but thy-self, that art of pitee welle ?
Thou hast more reuthe on our adversitee
Than in this world mighte any tungé telle.

Redressé me, moder, and me chastise,
For certeynly my Fadres chastisynge 130
That dar I nought abiden in no wise,
So hidous is hys rightful rekenynge.
Moder, of whom our merci gan to sprynge,
Beth ye my juge and eek my soulés leche,
For ever in you is pitee haboundynge
To eche that wol of pitee you bÌseche.

Both is that God ne granteth no pitee
With-outé thee ; for God, of his goodnesse,
Foryiveth noon, but it like un-to thee ;
He hath thee makéd vicaire and
  maistresse 140
Of al the world, and eek governeresse
Of hevene, and he represseth his justise
After thy wille, and therfore in witnesse,
He hath thee crounéd in so ryal wise.

Temple devout, ther God hath his
  wonynge
Fro which these misbileved deprivéd
  been,
To you my soulé penitent I brynge.
Resceyvé me,—I can no ferther fleen.
With thornés venymous, O hevené Queen !
For which the erthe acurséd was ful yore.
I am so wounded as ye may wel seen 151
That I am lost almost, it smert so sore.

Virgine, that art so noble of apparaile,
And ledest us in-to the hyé tour

Of paradys, thou me wisse and counsaile
How I may have thy grace and thy socóur,
Al have I ben in filthe and in erróur.
Lady, un-to that court thou me ajourne
That clepéd is thy bench, O freshé flour
Ther as that merci evere shal sojourne. 160

Xristus, thi sone, that in this world
  alighte
Up-on the cros to suffre his passioun,
Eek suffréd that Longiús his herté prihte,
And made his herté blood to renne adoun,
And al was this for my salvacioun,
And I to hym am fals and eek unkynde,
And yit he wol not my dampnacioun ;
This thanke I you, socour of al mankynde !

Ysaac was figure of his deth certeyn,
That so fer forth his fader wolde obeye, 170
That him ne rouhté no thing to be slayn ;
Right soo thy Sone lust as a lamb to deye.
Now, Lady ful of mercy ! I you preye,
Sithe he his mercy mesuréd so large,
Be ye not skant, for alle we singe and seye
That ye ben from vengeauncé ay oure targe.

Zacharie you clepeth the opené welle,
To wasshé sinful soule out of his gilt ;
Therfore this lessoun ought I wel to telle,
That nere thy tender herte we weren spilt.
Now, Lady brihté, sith thou canst and wilt,
Ben to the seed of Adam merciable,
So bring us to that palais that is bilt
To penitents that ben to mercy able.

  Amen.

Explicit carmen.

THE COMPLEYNTE OF MARS

The Proem

'GLADETH, ye foulés, of the morwé
  gray !
Lo, Venus, risen among you rowés rede !
And flourés fresshe, honoureth ye this day ;
For when the sonne uprist, then wol ye
  sprede.

163. All read *And* at the beginning of this line,
destroying the syntax of the stanza. It is clearly
caught from the lines below. All read *pihte* for
prighte, which is Skeat's suggestion ; *pihte* does
not mean ' pierced.'
2. *Venus*, the planet which sometimes rises in
the morning.

But ye lovers, that lye in any drede,
Fleéth, lest wikked tongés yow espye!
Lo yond the sonne, the candel of jelosye!

' Wyth terés blewe, and with a
    wounded herte,
Taketh your leve; and with Seynt John
    to borwe,   9
Apeseth somwhat of your sorwés smerte,
Tyme cometh eft that cesé shal your
    sorwe;
The gladé nyght is worth an hevy morwe!'
(Seynt Valentyne! a foul thus herde I synge
Upon thy day, er sonné gan up-sprynge.)

Yet sang this foul, ' I rede yow alle a-
    wake,
And ye that han not chosen in humblé wyse,
With-out repentyng cheseth yow your
    make;
And ye that han ful chosen as I devyse,
Yet at the leste renoveleth your servyse;
Confermeth hit perpetuely to dure,   20
And paciently taketh your aventure.'

And for the worship of this highé feste,
Yet wol I, in my briddés wisé, synge
The sentence of the compleynt at the leste
That woful Mars made atté departynge
Fro fresshé Venus, in a morwenynge
Whan Phebus, with his firy torchés rede,
Ransakéd every lover in his drede.

Whilom the thriddé hevenés lord above,
As wel by hevenysh revolucioun   30
As by desert, hath wonne Venus, his love,
And she hath take him in subjeccioun,
And as a maistresse taught him his lessoun,
Commaundyng him that never, in her
    servyse,
He nere so bold no lover to despyse.

For she forbad him jelosye at alle,
And crueltee, and bost, and tyrannye;
She made hym at hir lust so humble and
    talle,
That when hir deyned caste on hym her ŷe,
He took in pacience to lyve or dye;   40

And thus she brydeleth him in hir manere,
With no-thing but with scourgyng of hir
    chere.

Who regneth now in blissé but Venus,
That hath this worthy knyght in govern-
    aunce?
Who syngeth now but Mars, that serveth
    thus   ·
The fairé Venus, causer of plesaunce?
He bynt him to perpetual obeisaunce,
And she bynt hir to loven him for ever,
But so be that his trespas hit dissever.

Thus be they knyt, and regnen as in
    heven   50
Be lokyng most; til hit fil on a tyde
That by her bothe assent was set a steven
That Mars shal entre, as fast as he may
    glyde,
Into hir nexté paleys, and abyde,
Walkyng his cours til she hadde him a-take;
And he preyde hir to haste hir for his sake.

Then seyde he thus, ' Myn hertés lady
    swete
Ye knowé wel my myschef in that place;
For sikerly, til that I with yow mete,
My lyf stant ther in áventure and grace, 60
But when I se the beautee of your face,
Ther nis no dreed of deth may do me smerte,
For al your lust is esé to myn herte.'

She hath so gret compassion of hir knyght
That dwelleth in solitudé til she come,—
For hit stood so, that ilké tyme, no wyght
Counseyléd hym, ne seyde to him wel-
    come,—
That nygh her wit for sorwe was overcome;
Wherfore she spedde hir as faste in her weye
Almost in oon day as he dide in tweye.   70

The greté joye that was betwix hem two
When they be met, ther may no tungé telle;
Ther is no more, but unto bed they go;
And thus in joye and blisse I let hem dwelle;
This worthi Mars, that is of knyghthod
    welle,

9. *Seynt John*, the apostle of truth.
31. All read *his* except Harl., which omits the word.

62. *nis.* All read *is.*
70. The orbit of Venus is smaller than that of Mars, so her apparent motion is twice as great.

The flour of faimes lappeth in his armès,
And Venus kisseth Mars, the god of armès.

Sojourned hath this Mars of which I rede
In chambre amyd the paleys, privèly,
A certeyn tymè, til him fel adrede,   80
Through Phebus, that was comen hastèly
Within the paleys gatès, sturdèly,
With torche in honde, of which the
    stremès bryghte
On Venus chambre knokeden ful lighte.

The chambre ther as lay this fresshè
    quene
Depeynted was with whitè bolès grete,
And by the light she knew, that shoon
    so shene,
That Phebus cam to brenne hem with his
    hete ;
This sely Venus, nygh dreynt in terès wete,
Enbraceth Mars, and seyde, 'Alas, I dye !
The torch is come that al this world wol
    wrie.'   91

Up stertè Mars, hym listè not to slepe,
When he his lady herdè so compleyne,
But for his nature was not for to wepe,
Instede of terès, from his eyen tweyne
The firy sparkès brosten out for peyne ;
And hente his hauberk, that lay hym besyde.
Flee wolde he not, ne myghte him-selven
    hyde.

He throweth on his helm of hugè wyghte,
And girt him with his swerde ; and in
    his honde   100
His myghty spere, as he was wont to fighte
He shaketh so that almost hit to-wonde.
Ful hevy was he to walken over londe,
He may not holde with Venus companye,
But bad her fleen, lest Phebus hir espye.

O woful Mars ! alas ! what mayst thou
    seyn,
That in the paleys of thy disturbaunce
Art left behynde in peril to be sleyn ?
And yet ther-to is double thy penaunce,
For she that hath thyn herte in govern-
    aunce   110

Is passèd halfe the stremès of thyn ÿen ;
That thou nere swift wel mayst thou wepe
    and crien.

Now fleeth Venus un-to Cylenius tour,
With voidè cours, for fere of Phebus light,
Alas ! and ther ne hath she no socour,
For she ne fond ne saugh no maner wyght ;
And eek as ther she had but litil myght ; ·
Wher-for her-selven for to hyde and save,
Within the gate she fledde in-to a cave.

Derk was this cave, and smokyng as
    the helle,   120
Not but two pas within the gate hit stood ;
A naturel day in derk I lete her dwelle.
Now wol I speke of Mars, furious and wood.
For sorwe he wolde have seen his hertè
    blood ;
Sith that he myghte don her no companye,
He ne roghtè not a mytè for to dye.

So feble he wex for hete and for his wo
That nygh he swelt, he myghte unnethe
    endure,
He passeth but oo steyre in dayès two,
But nathèles for al his hevy armure,
He foloweth hir that is his lyvès cure ; 131
For whos departyng he toke gretter ire
Thannè for al his brennyng in the fire.

After he walketh softèly a pas,
Compleynyng, that it pite was to here ;
He seyde, ' O lady bryght, Venus ! alas !
That ever so wyde a compas ys my spere !
Alas ! when shal I mete yow, hertè dere ?
This twelftè day of April I endure,
Through jelous Phebus, this mysaventure.'

Now God helpè sely Venùs, al a-lone ! 141
But, as God wolde, hit happèd for to be
That while that Venus weping made her
    mone

112. *Cylenius*, Mercury, born on Mt. Cyllene
in Arcadia. The Tower of Cyllenium, *i.e.* mansion of Mercury, is the sign Gemini into which
Venus now passes.
119. *cave*, according to Skeat a translation of
the technical Latin astrological term *puteus*.
The *putei* in Gemini are the degrees numbered
2, 12, 17, 26, 30. So Venus was now in the
second degree of the sign.
139. On 12th April the sun entered Taurus.

86. *white boles*, the sign of Taurus, in which
both Mars and Venus now are.

Cylenius, ridyng in his chevauche
Fro Venus valance, myghte his paleys se,
And Venus he salueth, and maketh chere,
And her receyveth as his frend ful dere.

Mars dwelleth forth in his adversitè,
Compleynyng ever in on hir departynge,
And what his compleynt was, remem-
    breth me,   150
And therfor in this lusty morwenynge,
As I best can, I wol it seyn and synge,
And after that I wol my levè take ;
And God yeve every wyght joye of his
    make !

THE COMPLEYNTE OF MARS

The Proem

The ordre of compleynt requireth skil-
    fully,
That if a wyght shal pleynè pitously
Ther mot becausè wherfor that men pleyne ;
Or men may deme he pleyneth folily,
And causèles ; alas, that am not I !
Wherfor the ground and cause of al my
    peyne,   160
So as my troublèd wit may hit ateyne,
I wol reherse ; not for to have redresse,
But to declare my ground of hevynesse.

I

The firstè tyme, alas ! that I was wroght,
And for certeyn effectès hider broght,
By him that lordeth ech intelligence,
I yaf my trewè servise and my thoght,
For ever-more,—how dere I have it
    boght !—
To hir, that is of so gret excellence
That what wyght that first sheweth his
    presence   170
When she is wroth and taketh of hym no
    cure,
He may not longe in joye of love endure.

This is no feynèd mater that I telle ;
My lady is the verrey sours and welle
Of beaute, lust, fredom, and gentilnesse,
Of riche aray,—how derè men it selle !—
Of al disport in which men frendly dwelle,
Of love and pley, and of benigne humblesse,
Of soune of instruments of al swetnesse,
And therto so wel fortunèd and thewèd
That through the world hir goodnesse is
    y-shewed.   181

What wonder is then, thogh that I besette
My servise on suche oon that may me knette
To wele or wo, sith hit lyth in her myght ?
Therfor my herte for ever I to her hette,
Ne trewly for my dethe I shal not lette
To ben her trewest servaunt, and her
    knyght.
I flater noght, that may wite every wyght,
For this day in hir servise shal I dye ;
But gracè be, I se hir never with ÿe.   190

II

To whom shal I then pleyne of my
    distresse ?
Who may me helpe ?   Who may my harm
    redresse ?
Shal I compleyne unto my lady fre ?
Nay, certes ! for she hath such hevynesse
For fere, and eek for wo, that, as I gesse,
In litil tyme it wol her banè be.
But were she sauf, it were no fors of me !
Alas ! that ever lovers mote endure,
For love, so many a perilous aventure !

For thogh so be that lovers be as trewe
As any metal that is forgèd newe,   201
In many a cas hem tydeth oftè sorwe.
Somtyme hir ladies will not on hem rewe ;
Somtymè if that Ielosie hit knewe,
They myghten lightly leye hir heed to
    borwe ;
Somtyme envyous folke with tungès horwe
Depraven hem ; alas ! Whom may they
    plese ?
But he be fals, no lover hath his ese !

But what availeth suche a long sermoun
Of áventures of lovè up and doun ?   210

145. *valance*, according to Skeat, is either the
Fr. *fallance, faillance*, failure, and an exact
translation of the Latin astrological term *detrimentum*, or it is *avalance*, a translation of the
Latin *occasus*, an alternative expression for the
same thing. The *detrimentum* is the sign of the
Zodiac opposite the planet's mansion, and is here
equivalent to Aries.

I wol returne and speken of my peyne ;
The poynt is this of my destruccioun,—
My rightè lady, my salvacyoun,
Is in affray, and not to whom to pleyne.
O hertè swete ! O lady sovereyne !
For your disese wel oghte I swoune and
    swelte,
Thogh I non other harm ne dredè felte.

III

To what fyn made the God that sit so hye,
Be-nethen him love other companye,
And streyneth folk to love malgrè hir hede,
And then hir joye, for oght I can espye, 221
Ne lasteth not the twynkelyng of an ÿe ;
And somme han never joye til they be dede.
What meneth this? what is this mystihede?
Wherto constreyneth he his folk so faste
Thyng to desyrè, but it sholdè laste ?

And thogh he made a lover love a thyng,
And maketh it semè stedfast and duryng,
Yet putteth he in it such mysaventure
That restè nis ther noon in his yevyng ; 230
And that is wonder that so just a kyng
Doth such hardnessè to his creature.
Thus, whether lovè breke, or ellès dure,
Algatès he that hath with love to done
Hath ofter wo then changèd is the mone.

Hit semeth he hath to lovers enmyte,
And lyk a fissher, as men alday may se,
Baiteth his angle-hook with som plesaunce,
Til mon ya fish is wood, til that he be 239
Sesèd ther-with ; and then at erst hath he
Al his desire, and ther-with al myschaunce ;
And thogh the lynè breke, he hath pen-
    aunce,
For with the hook he wounded is so sore
That he his wages hath for ever-more.

IV

The broche of Thebès was of such a
    kynde ;

245. *The broche of Thebes* or magic bracelet
(cp. *Thebais* of Statius, Bk. ii.) was made by
Vulcan for Harmonia, a daughter of Mars and
Venus, in order to bring an evil fate on her and
all later possessors of it.

So ful of rubies, and of stonès Inde,
That every wyght that sette on hit an ÿe,
He wende anon to worthe out of his
    mynde,—
So sore the beautè wold his hertè bynde,—
Til he hit hadde him thoghte he mostè dye,
And whan that hit was his, then sholde
    he drye   251
Such wo for drede, ay while that he hit
    hadde,
That welnygh for the fere he sholdè madde.

And whan hit was fro his possessioun
Then hadde he double wo and passioun,
For he so fair a tresor had forgo ;
But yet this broche, as in conclusioun,
Was not the cause of this confusioun ;
But he that wroghte hit enfortuned hit so
That every wyght that hadde hit sholde
    have wo ;   260
And therfor in the worcher was the vyce,
And in the covetour that was so nyce.

So fareth hit by lovers and by me ;
For thogh my lady have so gret beautè
That I was mad til I had gete hir grace,
She was not cause of myn adversitè,
But he that wroghte hir, also mot I thee,
That puttè such a beaute in hir face,
That madè me coveten and purchace 269
Myn ownè deth ; him wyte I that I dye,
And myn unwit that ever I clomb so hye.

V

But to yow, hardy knyghtès of renoun,
Syn that ye be of my divisioun,—
Al be I not worth to so grete a name,
Yet seyn these clerkès I am your patroun,—
Ther-for ye oghte have som compassioun
Of my disese, and take hit noght a-game,
The proudest of yow may be mad ful tame.
Wherfor I prey yow of your gentilesse,
That ye compleynè for myn hevynesse. 280

And ye, my ladies, that ben trewe and
    stable,
By way of kynde, ye oghten to been able
To have pitè of folk that been in peyne ;

246. *Inde* is an adjective ; cp. *Romaunt of the
Rose*, l. 67.

Now have ye cause to clothe yow in sable;
Sith that your emperice, the honorable,
Is desolat, wel oghte ye to pleyne;
Now sholde your holy teres falle and reyne.
Alas! your honour and your emperice,
Nigh deed for drede, ne can hir not chevise!

Compleyneth eek, ye lovers, al in-fere,
For hir that with unfeyned humble chere
Was ever redy to do yow socour;   292
Compleyneth hir that ever hath had yow
    dere;
Compleyneth beaute, fredom, and manere;
Compleyneth hir that endeth your labour;
Compleyneth thilke ensample of al honour,
That never dide but al gentilesse;
Kytheth therfor on hir som kyndenesse!

A COMPLEYNTE TO HIS LADY

I

THE longe nightes, whan every creature
Shulde have hir rest in somwhat, as by
    kynde,
Or elles ne may hir lif nat long endure,
Hit falleth most into my woful mynde
How I so fer have broght myself behynde,
That, sauf the deeth, ther may no-thyng
    me lisse,
So desespaired I am from alle blisse.

This same thoght me lasteth til the morwe
And from the morwe forth til hit be eve;
Ther nedeth me no care for to borwe,   10
For bothe I have good leyser and good leve;
Ther is no wyght that wol me wo bereve
To wepe y-nogh, and wailen al my fille;
The sore spark of peyne now doth me spille.

II

This Love, that hath me set in swich
    a place
That my desir wol never he fulfille,
For neither pitee, mercy, neither grace,

Can I nat fynde; and yit my sorwful
    herte,
For to be deed, I can hit nought arace;
The more I love, the more she doth me
    smerte.   20
Through which I see, withoute remedye
That from the deeth I may no wyse
    asterte;

.   .   .   .   .   .

III

Now sothly, what she hight I wol reherse.
Hir name is Bountee, set in womanhede,
Sadnesse in youthe and Beautee
    prydelees
And Plesaunce, under governaunce
    and drede;
Her surname is eek Faire Rewthelees,
The Wyse, y-knit un-to Good Aventure,
That, for I love hir, she sleeth me
    giltelees.   30
Hir love I best, and shal, whyl I may dure,
Bet than my-self an hundred thousand
    deel,
Than al this worldes richesse or creature.
Now hath not Love me bestowed weel
To love ther I never shal have part?
Allas! right thus is turned me the wheel,
Thus am I slayn with Loves firy dart.
I can but love hir best, my swete fo;
Love hath me taught no more of his art
But serve alwey, and stinte for no wo.   40

IV

In my trewe and careful herte ther is
So moche wo, and [eek] so litel blis
    That wo is me that ever I was bore;

2, 3. Shirley, *theyre* for *hir*.
15-43. This passage is in *terza rima*, the first example of the measure in English literature.
16. Shirley omits *he*.

23. It is possible that another line to rime with l. 22 is missing here.
24. Skeat thinks two lines have fallen out before this, forming the opening to this section, but it is more probable that l. 24, which is not necessary to the sense, has been inserted. Shirley or his author-ity has tried to reduce this passage of *terza rima* to a series of eight-line stanzas. He divides at l. 23, l. 32, and l. 41; the last stanza, being hard to amend, had to remain with nine lines.
39. This line seems to be a syllable short.
41. So Shirley, who first wrote *In my trewe* *hert*, etc., and then corrected *hert* into *and*. The line is probably corrupt. Ed. 1561 omits *and*.
42. Shirley omits *eek*, which Skeat supplies.

For al that thyng which I desyre I mys,
And al that ever I woldė not, y-wys,
　That findė I redy to me evermore ;
And of al this I not to whom me pleyne.
　For she that mightė me out of this brynge
　Ne recchcth nought whether I wepe
　　or synge ; 49
So litel rewthe hath she upon my peyne.

Allas ! whan slepyng-tyme is, than I wake,
Whan I shuldė daunce, for ferė than I
　　quake ;
This hevy lif I ledė for your sake
Thogh ye ther-of in no wyse hedė take,
My hertės lady, and hool my lyvės quene !
　For trewly dorste I seye, as that I fele,
　Me semeth that your swetė herte of stele
Is whettėd now ageynės me to kene.

My derė herte and best belovėd fo,
Why liketh yow to do me al this wo, 60
　What have I doon that greveth yow, or
　　sayd,
But for I serve and love yow and no mo ?
And whilst I lyve I wol ever do so ;
　And therfor, swetė, ne beth nat yvel
　　apayd.
For so good and so fair as ye be
Hit werė right gret wonder but ye haddė
　Of allė servantes, bothe of goode and
　　baddė ;
And leest worthy of alle hem, I am he.

But never-the-les, my rightė lady swete,
Thogh that I be unconnyng and unmete
　To serve, as I coude best, ay your
　　hynesse. 71
Yit is ther fayner noon, that woldė I hete,
Than I, to do yow ese, or ellės bete
　What so I wiste that were to your
　　[distresse] ;

And haddė I myght as good as I have wille
Than shuldė ye fele wher it were so
　or noon ;
For in this worldė lyvyng is ther noon
That fayner wolde your hertės wil fulfille.

For bothe I love and cek dredeyow so sore,
And algates moot, and have doon yow,
　ful yore, 80
That bettrė loved is noon, ne never shal ;
And yit I wolde beseche yow of no more,
But leveth wel, and be not wrooth ther-fore,
　And lat me serve yow forth ; lo, this is al !
For I am not so hardy, ne so wood,
　For to desire that ye shulde lovė me ;
　For wel I wot, allas ! that may nat be ;
I am so litel worthy, and ye so good.

For ye be oon the worthiest on-lyve
And I the most unlikly for to thryve ; 90
Yit for al this witeth ye right wele
That ye ne shul me from your servyce dryve
That I nil ay, with alle my wyttės fyve,
　Serve yow trewly, what wo so that I fele.
For I am set on yow in swich manere,
　That, thogh ye never wil upon me rewe,
　I moste yow love, and beėn ever as trewe
As any man can, or may, on-lyvė [here].

But the morė that I love yow, goodly free,
The lassė fynde I that ye loven me ; 100
　Allas ! whan shal that hardė wyt amende ?
Wher is now al your wommanly pitee,
Your gentilesse and your debonairtee
　Wil ye no-thyng ther-of upon me spende ?
And so hool, swete, as I am yourės al,
　And so gret wil as I have yow to serve,
　Now, certės, and ye letė me thus sterve,
Yit have ye wonnė ther-on but a smal.

Fór at my knowyng, I do nought why,
And this I wol beseche yow hertėly, 110

44-46. Cp. *Parl. Foules*, ll. 90, 91, and *Compl. of Pite*, ll. 99-104.
47. Cp. *Anelida*, l. 237.
51. Shirley inserts *lo* before *than*.
51. This stanza is different in form from those that precede and follow it.
53. Shirley inserts *lo* after *lede*.
65. *fair* seems here to be dissyllabic as in A.S.
72. Shirley, *noon fayner*.
74. Shirley, *to youre hyenesse*, caught from l. 71. Skeat reads *to yow distresse*. Perhaps *that* was

not in the original text and *wiste* was pronounced as a dissyllable.
91. Skeat inserts *now* before *witeth*, but the whole poem is experimental, and possibly this line is as Chaucer wrote it. Cp. ll. 39, 109, and 116. In all a heavy stress on the first syllable lends dramatic value to the line.
93. Shirley, *ne wil*.
98. *here* supplied by Skeat.
99. Shirley, *But the more*, etc. Skeat omits *But*.

That, ther ever ye fyndė, whil ye lyve,
A trewer servant to yow than am I,
Leveth thanne, and sleeth me hardėly
And I my deeth to yow wol al foryive.
And if ye fynde no trewer verėly
  Will ye suffrė than that I thus spille,
  And for no maner gilt but my good wille?
As good wer thanne untrewe as trewe to be.

But I, my lyf and deeth, to yow obeye,
And with right buxom herte hooly I preye
  As is your mostė plesure, so doth by me ;
Wel lever is me liken yow and dye   122
Than for to anythyng or thynke or seye
  That myghtė yow offende in any tyme.
And ther-for, swete, rewe on my peynės
    smerte
And of your gracė granteth me som
    drope ;
For ellės may me laste ne blis, ne hope,
Ne dwellen in my troublė careful herte.

THE COMPLEYNTE OF FAIRE ANELIDA AND FALSE ARCITE

THOU fersė God of armės, Mars the rede,
That in the frosty contree callėd Trace,
Within thy grisly temple ful of drede,
Honóured art, as patroun of that place !
With thy Bellona, Pallas, ful of grace !
Be present, and my song contynue and gye.
At my begynnyng thus to the I crye.

For hit ful depe is sonken in my mynde,
With pitous herte, in Englysh for tendyte
This oldė storie, in Latyn which I fynde, 10
Of quene Anelyda and fals Arcite,
That eldė, which that al can frete and
    bite,—

111. Shirley, *whyles*.
115. Shirley, *no trewer so verrayly*. Ed. 1561 *no trewer verėly*, a false rime.
119-128. This stanza is only found in the Philipps MS., and I take the text from Skeat. I am doubtful of its authenticity.
1-70. These first ten stanzas are based on the *Teseide*, i. and ii.
1. *Mars the redė*, 'O Marte rubicondo,' *Tes.* i. 3.
2. *Trace*, Thrace.

As hit hath fretėn mony a noble storie,—
Hath nygh devourėd out of our memórie.

Be favorable eek, thou Polýmnyá,
On Párnaso that with thy sustrės glade,
By Elicon, not fer from Cirreá,
Syngest with vois memorial in the shade,
Under the laurer, which that may not fade,
And do that I my shippe to haven wynne.
First folwe I Stace, and after him Corynne.

[*The Story*]

When Theseús, with werrės longe and
    grete,   22
The asprė folk of Cithe hadde overcome,
With laurer crounėd, in his char, gold bete,
Home to his contrė houses is y-come ;
For which the peple, blisful al and somme,
So crydėn, that un-to the sterres hit wente,
And him to honouren dide al bir entente.

Beforn this duke, in signe of hy victórie,
The trompės come, and in his baner large,
The ymáge of Mars ; and in tokenýng of
    glórie,   31
Men myghtė seen of tresor mony a charge,
Mony a bright helm, and mony a spere
    and targe,
Mony a fresh knyght, and mony a blis-
    ful route,
On hors, and fote, in al the felde aboute.

Ipolita, his wyf, the hardy quene
Of Cithia, that he conquérėd hadde,
With Emelye her yongė suster shene,

15. *Polymnya*, Πολυμνία, one of the nine Muses.
16. *Parnaso*, Mount Parnassus.
17. *Elicon*, Mount Helicon in Bœotia, but Chaucer seems to have confused it with the Castalian spring. Cp. *H. of F.* l. 522, and *Troil.* iii. 1809.
17. *Cirrea*, Cirra, an ancient town near Delphi at the foot of Parnassus.
21. *Stace*, Statius, whose *Thebaid* is the source of some of the following stanzas.
21. *Corynne*, Corinnus, who is said to have written an account of the Trojan war in Doric Greek.
23. *Cithe*, Scythia.
24. Cp. *Kn. T.* 169, 121.
30, 31. Cp. *Ibid.* 117, 118.
36, 37. Cp. *Ibid.* 23, 24.
38. Cp. *Ibid.* 114.

Faire in a char of golde he with hym ladde,
That al the ground aboute her char she
    spradde   40
With brightnesse of the beautee in her face,
Fulfillèd of largesse and of al grace.

With his tryúmph, and laurer-crounèd
    thus,
In al the floure of fortunès yevynge,
Lete I this noble prince, this Thesëus,
Toward Athénès in his wey ridynge,
And founde I wol in shortly for to brynge
The slyé wey of that I gan to write,
Of quene Anélida and fals Arcite.

Mars, which that through his furious
    course of yre,   50
The oldè wrath of Juno to fulfille,
Hath set the peplès hertès bothe on fire
Of Thebes and Grece, eche other for to kille
With blody speres, ne restèd, never stille,
But throng now her, now ther, among hem
    bothe,
That everych other slough, so were they
    wrothe.

For when Amphiorax and Tydëus,
Ipomedon, Parthonopee also
Were dede, and slawen proud Campanëus,
And when the wrecchèd Thebans bretheren
    two   60
Were slayn, and kyng Adrastus home a-go,
So desolat stood Thebès and so bare,
That no wyght coude remédie of his fare.

And when that oldè Creon gan espye
How that the blood roial was broght adoun,
He held the cite by his tyrannye,
And dide the gentils of that regioun
To ben his frendes, and wonnèn in the toun. ·

50-70. Cp. *Teseide*, ii. st. 10-12.
57. *Amphiorax*, Amphiaraus, swallowed up by
the earth at the siege of Thebes.
57. *Tydeus*, married a daughter of Adrastus.
58. *Ipomedon*, Hippomedon, one of the
'Septem contra Thebas,' as also was *Parthonopee*
(Parthenopæus), and *Campaneus* (Capaneus)
who was struck with lightning by Jupiter.
59. Cx. *slayn and proud*; rest *slayn proud*.
60. *i.e.* Eteocles and Polynices, who caused the
war.
61. *Adrastus*, King of Argos, who assisted his
son-in-law Polynices.

So, what for love of him, and what for awe,
The noble folk wer to the toune y-drawe.

Among al these, Anélida the quene   71
Of Ermony was in that toune duellynge,
That fairer was then is the sonnè shene ;
Throughout the world so gan her namè
    sprynge,
That her to seen had every wyght likýnge ;
For, as of trouthè, ther is noon her liche,
Of al the women in this worldè riche.

Yong was this quene, of twenty yeer
    of elde,
Of mydel stature, and of swich fairnesse,
That Nature had a joye hir to beholde ;   80
And for to speken of her stidfastnesse,
She passed hath Penelope and Lucresse,
And shortly, yf she shal be comprehended,
In her ne myghtè nothing been amended.

This Theban knyght [Arcite] eek, soth
    to seyn,
Was yonge, and ther-withal a lusty knyght,
But he was double in love, and nothyng
    pleyn,
And subtil in that crafte over any wyght,
And with his cunnyng wan this lady bright :
For so ferforth he can hir trouthe assure,   90
That she him trust over any creature.

What shulde I seyn ? She lovede
    Arcitè so
That when that he was absent any throwe,
Anon hir thoghte hir hertè brast a-two ?
For in hir sight to hir he bar him lowe,
So that she wende have al his herte y-knowe ;
But he was fals, hit nas but feynèd chere,—
As nedeth not to men such craft to lere !

But nathéles ful mychel besynesse
Hadde he, er that he myghte his lady wynne,
And swor he woldè dyèn for distresse,   101
Or from his wyt, he seyde, he woldè twynne.

72. *Ermony*, Armenia.
76. So Lt. ; the rest *is ther;* perhaps Chaucer
wrote *nis ther*.
82. *Lucresse*, Lucretia.
85. Skeat inserts *Arcite*.
91. Skeat reads *trust;* B Lt. F H D Cx.
trusted; Ha. Tn. *trusteth*.

Z   **337**

Alas the while! for hit was routhe and synne,
That she upon his sorwès woldè rewe,
But nothyng thenketh the fals as doth the
    trewe.

Hir fredom fond Arcite in swich manere,
That al was his that she hath, moche or lyte;
Ne to no crëature ne made she chere,
Ferther than that it lykède to Arcite;
Ther was no lak with which he myghte
    hir wyte,   110
She was so ferforth yeven him to plese,
That al that lykède him it dide hir ese.

Ther nas to hir no maner lettre y-sent
That touchèd love, from eny maner wyght,
That she ne shewed hit him er hit was
    brent;
So pleyn she was, and dide hir fullè myght,
That she nyl hiden nothyng from her
    knyght,
Lest he of any untrouth hir upbreyde;
Withoutè bode his hestè she obeyde.   119

And eek he made him jelous over here,
That what that eny man hadde to hir seyd,
Anoon he woldè preyèn hir to swere
What was that word, or make him evel
    apaid;
Then wendè she out of her wyt have brayd,
But al this nas but sleight and flaterie;
Withoutèn love, he feynèd jelousye.

And al this took she so debonairly,
That al his wylle, hir thoghte hit skilful
    thyng;
And ever the lenger she loved him tenderly,
And dide him honour as he were a kyng. 130
Hir herte was to him wedded with a ring;
So ferforth upon trouthe is hir entente,
That wher he goth, hir hertè with him wente.

When she shal ete, on him is so hir
    thoght,
That wel unnethe of metè took she kepe;
And whan that she was to her restè broght,
On him she thoghte alwey til that she sleep;
When he was absent, prevèly she weep.
Thus lyveth fair Anelida the quene,   139
For fals Arcite, that dide her al this tene.

This fals Arcite, of his newfangelnesse,
For she to him so lowly was and trewe,
Took lessè deyntee for her stedfastnesse,
And saw another lady, proud and newe,
And right anon he claddè him in hir
    hewe,—
Wot I not whether in whitè, rede, or
    grene,—
And falsèd fair Anelida the quene.

But nathèlesse, gret wonder was hit noon
Thogh he were fals, for hit is kynde of man, 150
Sith Lamek was, that is so longe agoon,
To been in love as fals as ever he can;
He was the firstè fader that began
To lovèn two, and was in bigamye.
And he found tentès first, but if men lye.

This fals Arcitè somwhat moste he feyne
When he was fals, to covere his traitorye,
Right as an hors, that can both bite and
    pleyne;
For he bar hir on honde of trecherye,
And swoor he coude her doublenesse espye,
And al was falsnes that she to him mente;
Thus swoor this theef, and forth his way
    he wente.   161

Alas! what hertè myghte endurèn hit,
For routhe or wo, hir sorwè for to telle?
Or what man hath the cunnyng or the wyt?
Or what man myghte within the chambre
    duelle,
If I to him rehersèn shal the helle
That suffreth fair Anelida the quene
For fals Arcite, that dide her al this tene?

She wepeth, waileth, swouneth pitously,
To groundè deed she falleth as a stoon;
Al crampissheth hir lymès crokedly; 171
She speketh as hir wyt were al agoon;
Other colour then asshen hath she noon,
Non other word she speketh moche or lyte,
But 'Mercy! cruel hertè myn, Arcite!'

And thus endureth, til she was so
    mate

146. But not blue, the colour of constancy.
174. All read *speketh she.*

338

That she ne hath foot, on which she may
   sustene,
But forth, languisshing evere in this estate,
Of which Arcite hath nother routhe ne
   tene;
His herte is elléswher so newe and grene,
That on hir wo ne deyneth him not to
   thinke,   181
Him rekketh never wher she flete or synke.

His newé lady holdeth him so narwé
Up by the brydel, at the stavés ende,
That every word he dradde hit as an arwé;
Hir daunger made him bothé bowe and
   bende,
And as hir listé, made him turne or wende;
For she ne graunted him in her lyvynge
No gracé, why that he hath lust to synge;

But drof him forth, unnethé liste hir
   knowe   190
That he was servaunt to her ladishippe;
But lest that he wer proude, she helde
   him lowe.
Thus serveth he, withoutén fee or shipe
She sent him now to londé, now to shippe,
And for she yaf him daunger al his fille,
Therfor she hadde him at her owné wille.

Ensample of this, ye thrifty wymmen,
   alle,
Take here of Anelida and fals Arcite,
That for hir liste him ' deré herté ' calle,
And was so meke, therfor he loved hir lyte;
The kynde of mannés herte is to delyte 201
In thyng that straunge is, also God me
   save !
For what he may not gete, that wolde he
   have

Now turne we to Anelida ageyn,
That pyneth day be day in languisshyng :
But when she saw that hir ne gat no geyn,
Upon a day, ful sorwfully wepyng,
She caste hir for to make a compleynyng;
And with her owné hond she gan hit wryte,
And sente it to her Theban knyght Arcite.

<hr>

183. A metaphor borrowed from a horse lightly
harnessed to the pole of a cart.
191. All read *unto*.

[*The Compleynt of Faire Anelyda upon
Fals Arcyte*]

(*Proem*)

So thirleth with the poynt of remem-
   brance,   211
The swerd of sorwe, y-whet with fals
   plesaunce,
Myn herté bare of blis, and blak of hewe,
That turnéd is to quakyng al my daunce,
My suretè in a-whapéd countenaunce,
   Sith hit availeth not for to ben trewe :
   For who-so trewest is, hit shall hir rewe
That serveth love, and doth hir observaunce
   Alwey to oon, and chaungeth for no
   newe.

(*Strophe*)

I wot my-self as wel as any wyght, 220
For I loved oon with al my herte and myght,
   More then my-self an hundred thousand
   sithe,
And calléde him my hertés lyf, my knyght,
And was al his, as fer as hit was right ;
   And whan that he was glad, than was
   I blithe,
   And his disesé was my deeth as swythe,
And he ageyn his trouthe me haddé plight,
   For ever-more, his lady me to kythe.

Now is he fals, alas ! and causéles,
And of my wo he is so routhéles, 230
   That with a worde him list not onés deyne
To bringe ageyn my sorwful herte in pees,
For he is caught up in another lees ;
   Right as him list, he laugheth at my
   peyne,
   And I ne can myn herté not restreyne
That I ne love him alwey nathéles,
   And of al this I noot to whom me pleyne.

And shal I pleyne (alas ! the hardé
   stounde)   238
Unto my foo, that yaf my herte a wounde,
   And yet desireth that myn harm be more?
Nay, certés ! ferther wol I never founde
Non other help my sorès for to sounde ;
   My desteny hath shapen hit ful yore,
   I wil non other medecyne ne lore,

<hr>

229. F B H *Allas now hath he left me
causeles*.

I wil ben ay ther I was onès bounde ;
That I have seid, be seid for evermore.

Alas ! wher is become your gentilesse?
Your wordès ful of plesaunce and hum-
   blesse ?
Your observaunces in soo low manere ?
And your awayting, and your besynesse, 250
Upon me, that ye callède your maistresse,
Your sovereyn lady in this world here?
Alas ! and is ther now nother word ne
   chere,
Ye vouchèsauf upon myn hevynesse ?
Alas ! your love, I bye hit al to dere !

Now certès, swetè, thogh that ye
Thus causèles the cause be,
   Of my dedlý adversité,
Your manly resoun oghte it to respyte,
To slee your frend, and namely me, 260
That never yet in no degrè
   Offended yow, as wisly he,
That al wot, out of wo my soulè quyte.

But for I was so pleyne, Arcite,
In alle my werkès, muche and lite,
   And so besý yow to delyte, —
Myn honour save, —meke, kynde, and fre,
   Therfor ye putte on me this wyte :
And of me recchè not a myte,
Thogh that the swerde of sorwè byte 270
My woful hertè, through your cruelté.

My swetè foo, why do ye so, for shame?
And thenkè ye that furtherèd be your
   name,
To love a-newe, and ben untrewè? Nay !
And puttè you in sclaunder now and blame,
And do to me adversitee and grame,
   That love you most—God, wel thou
      wost !—alway ?
And come ageyn, and be al pleyn som
   day,
And then shal this, that hath be mys,
   be game,
And al foryivè, whyl I lyvè may.   280

264-266. F B Tn. H D Lt. Ff.—
    But for I shewed you, Arcite,
    All that men wolde to me wryte,
    And was so besy, etc.
279. F B H *And turne al this . . . to.*

(*Antistrophe*)
Lo, hertè myn, al this is for to seyn,
As whether shal I preye or ellès pleyn ?
   Which is the wey to doon yow to be
     trewe ?
For either mot I have yow in my cheyn,
Or with the dethe ye mot departe us tweyn ;
   Ther ben non other menè weyès newe,
   For, God so wisly upon my soulè rewe,
As verily ye sleen me with the peyn ;
   That may ye see unfeynèd of myn hewe.

For thus ferforth have I my deeth y-soght,
My-self I mordrè with my prevy thoght ; 291
   For sorwe and routhe of your unkyndè-
     nesse,
I wepe, I wake, I faste ; al helpeth noght ;
I weyvè joy that is to speke of oght,
   I voydè companye, I flee gladnesse ;
   Who may avaunte hir bet of hevynesse
Then I ? And to this plyte have ye me
   broght,
   Withoutè gilt,—me nedeth no witnesse.

And sholde I preye, and weyvè woman-
   hede ?   299
Nay ! rather deeth, then do so cruel dede,
   And axè mercy, causèles,—what nede?
And if I pleynè what lyf that I lede,
Than wol ye laugh ; I know it out of drede ;
   And if I unto you myn othès bede
For myn excuse, a scorn shal be my mede,
   Your cherè floureth, but it wol not sede,
Ful longe agoon I oghte have takè hede.

For thogh I haddè yow to-morwe ageyn,
I myghte as wel holde Avèrill fro reyn,
   As holdè yow to makè yow stedfast. 310
Almyghty God, of trouth the sovèreign !
Wher is the trouthe of man ? who hath it
   sleyn ?
   Who that hem lovèth, shal hem fynde
     as fast
   As in a tempest is a roten mast.
Is that a tamè best, that is ay feyn
   To renne away, when he is leest agast ?

290. Harl. Cx. omit this stanza. All read
soght.
303. F B Tn. Lt. Ff. H *Yow rekketh not that ;*
D *You rekke not that.*

Now mercy, swete, if I mysseye !
Have I seyd oght amys, I preye ?
I noot, my wit is al aweye.
I fare as doth the songe of *Chauntepleure;*
  For now I pleyne, and now I pleye, 321
I am so maséd that I deye,
Arcite hath born awey the keye
Of al my worlde, and my good aventure.

For in this worlde nys crëature,
Walkynge, in more discomfiture,
  Then I, ne moré sorwe endure ;
And if I slepe a furlong wey or tweye,
  Than thinketh me, that your figure
Before me stant clad in asure,   330
  To profren eft a newe assure,
For to be trewe, and mercy me to preye.

The longé nyght, this wonder sight I
  drye,
And on the day for this afray I dye,
And of al this right noght, ywys, ye recche ;
Ne nevermo myn ÿen two be drye,
And to your routhe and to your trouthe
  I crie !
But, welawey ! to fer be they to fecche,
Thus holdeth me my destynee a wrecche,
But me to rede out of this drede, or gye,
Ne may my wit, so weyke is hit, not
  strecche.   341

(Conclusion)

Then ende I thus, sith I may do no more,—
I yeve hit up for now and evermore ;
For I shal never eft putten in balaunce
My sekernes, ne lerne of love the lore ;
But as the swan, I have herd seye ful yore,
Ayeyns his deeth shal singen his penaunce,
So singe I here the destyny or chaunce,
How that Arcite, Anelida so sore
Had thirléd with the poynt of remem-
  braunce.   350

[The Story continued]

Whan that Anelida, this woful quene,
Hath of her handé writen in this wyse,

320. *Chauntepleure,* the name of a famous
poem of the 13th century addressed to those who
sing in this world but shall weep in the next.
331. F B H *To swere yet.*
351. This stanza is found only in Tn. D Fl.
and Lt.

With facé deed, betwyxé pale and grene,
She fel a-swowe ; and sith she gan to rise,
And unto Mars avoweth sacrifise
Within the temple, with a sorwful chere,
That shapen was, as ye shal after here.

  .   .   .

THE PARLEMENT OF FOULES

Here begynyth the Parlement of Foulys

The Proem

THE lyf so short, the craft so long to lerne,
Thassay so hard, so sharp the conquerynge,
The dredful joye, alwey that slit so yerne ;
Al this mene I be love, that my felyng
A-stonyeth with his wondyrful werkyng,
So sore y-wis, that whan I on hym thynke
Nat wot I wel wher that I flete or synke.

For al be that I knowe not Love in dede,
Ne wot how that he quyteth folk hir hyre,
Yit happeth me ful ofte in bokés rede 10
Of his myraclés and his cruel yre ;
Ther rede I wel he wol be lord and syre,
I dar nat seyn, his strokés been so sore,
But God save swich a lord ! I sey no more.

Of usage, what for lust and what for lore,
On bokés rede I ofte, as I yow tolde.
But wherfor that I speke al this ? Not yore
Agon, it happéd me for to be-holde   18
Up-on a bok, was write with lettrés olde ;
And ther-upon, a certeyn thing to lerne,
The longé day ful faste I radde and yerne.

For out of oldé feldés, as men seith,
Cometh al this newé corn from yeer to
  yere ;
And out of oldé bokes, in good feith,
Cometh al this newé science that men lere.
But now to purpos as of this matere,—
To redé forth it gan me so delyte,
That al the day me thoughté but a lyte.

This bok, of which I maké mencioun,
Entitled was al thus as I schal telle,   30

357. Lt. Th. *may plainly.*
1. Hippocrates' first aphorism :—
  ὁ βίος βραχύς, ἡ δὲ τέχνη μακρή.

' Tullyus, of the Dreem of Scipioun.'
Chapitrès it hadde sevene, of hevene and helle
And erthe, and soulés that therynnè dwelle,
Of whiche, as shortly as I can it trete,
Of his sentence I wol you seyn the grete.

First, telleth it, whan Scipioun was come
In Affrik, how he mettè Massynisse
That him for joye in armès hath y-nome.
Than telleth he hir speche, and al the blisse   39
That was betwix hem til the day gan misse,
And how his auncestre, African so dere,
Gan in his slep that nyght to him appere.

Than telleth it, that from a sterry place,
How African hath him Cartagè shewèd,
And warnèd him be-fore of al his grace,
And seyd him, what man lerèd other lewèd
That loveth comun profit, wel y-thewèd,
He shulde in-to a blisful placè wende,
Ther as joye is that last with-outen ende.

Than axède he if folk that heer been dede   50
Han lyf and dwellyng in another place.
And African seyde, ' Ye, withoutè drede,'
And that our present worldès lyvès space
Nis but a maner deth, what wey we trace,
And rightful folk shul gon after they dye
To hevene ; and shewède him the Galaxye.

Than shewede he hym the litel erthe that here is, —
At regard of the hevenès quantitè, —
And after shewede he hym the nynè sperès,
And after that the melodye herde he   60
That cometh of thilkè sperès thryès three,
That welle is of musik and melodye
In this world heer, and cause of armonye.

Than bad he him, syn erthè was so lyte,
And ful of torment and of hardè grace,
That hene schulde him in the world delyte.
Thanne tolde he him in certeyn yerès space
That every sterre shulde come into his place
Ther it was first, and al shulde out of mynde
That in this world is don of al mankynde.

Than praydè him Scipioun to telle hym al
The weye to come in-to that hevenè blisse ;
And he seyde, ' Know thy-self first immortál,
And loke ay besily thow werche and wysse
To comoun profit, and thow shalt not myssc
To comén swiftly to that placé dere
That ful of blysse is and of soulés clere.

' But brekers of the lawè, soth to seyn,
And lecherous folk, after that they be dede,
Shul whirle a-boutè the erthe alwey in peyne,   80
Til many a world be passèd, out of drede,
And than, for-yeven alle hir wikked dede,
Than shul they come in-to that blysful place,
To which to comén God thee sende his grace ! '

The day gan failen, and the derkè nyght,
That reveth bestès from hir besynesse,
Beraftè me my book for lakke of lyght,
And to my bed I gan me for to dresse,
Fulfild of thought and besy hevynesse ;   89
For bothe I haddè thyng which that I nolde,
And ek I ne haddè that thyng that I wolde.

But fynally, my spirit at the laste,
For-wery of my labour al the day,
Took rest, that madè me to slepè faste ;
And in my sleep I mette, as that I lay,
How African right in the same aray
That Scipioun him saw before that tyde
Was come and stood right at my beddès syde.

31. Marcus Tullius Cicero, whose *Somnium Scipionis* was originally included in the *De Re-publica*, Bk. vi.
36. *Scipioun*, P. Cornelius Scipio Æmilianus Africanus Minor, who won the third Punic War. He went in 150 B.C. to meet Masinissa, King of Numidia, who had received many favours from 'his auncestre' Africanus Major.
61, 62. An allusion to the so-called 'harmony of the spheres' which arose from the supposed connection between the number of the planets and the number of musical notes in the scale. Cp. Shak. *M. of V.* v. 60.
80. *whirle a-boute*, 'volutantur,' Cicero.
85 f. Cp. *Inferno*, ii. 1-3.

Lo giorno se n' andava, e l' aer bruno
Toglieva gli animai, che sono in terra
Dalle fatiche loro.

90. Cp. Boethius, Bk. iii. pr. 3.

The wery hunter, slepyng in his bed,
To wode ayein his myndė goth anoon ; 100
The jugė dremeth how his plees ben sped ;
The carter dremeth how his carte is goon ;
The riche of gold ; the knyght fight with
his foon ;
The sykė met he drynketh of the tonne ;
The lover met he hath his lady wonne.

Can I not seyn if that the causė were
For I hadde red of African beforn,
That madė me to mete that he stood there,
But thus seyde he : ' Thou hast thee so
wel born
In lokyng of myn oldė book to-torn, 110
Of which Macrobie roghtė not a lyte,
That somdel of thy labour wolde I quyte.'

Cytherea, thou blisful lady swete,
That with thy fyrbrond dauntest whom
thee lest,
And madest me this sweven for to mete,
Be thou my helpe in this, for thow mayst
best
As wisly as I say the north-north-west,
Whan I began myn sweven for to wryte ;
So yif me myght to ryme it and endyte.

The Story

This forseyd African me hente a-noon,
And forth-with him unto a gate me broghte
Right of a park, wallėd with grenė stoon ;
And over the gate with lettrės large
y-wroghte
There werėn vers y-writen, as me thoghte,
On eyther syde of ful gret difference,
Of which I shal now seyn the pleyn
sentence.

' Thurgh me men goon in-to that blisful
place
Of hertės hele and dedly woundės cure ;
Thurgh me men gon un-to the welle of
Grace

99. Cp. Claudian, *In Sextum Consulatum
Honorii Augusti Præfatio*, ll. 3-10.
109. Cp. *Inferno*, i. 83.
113. *Cytherea*, Venus.
117. A reference to the planet Venus. *say*, saw.
127. Cp. *Inferno*, iii. 1 ff.

Ther grene and lusty May shal ever
endure ; 130
This is the wey to al good aventure ;
Be glad, thow reder and thy sorwe of-caste.
Al open am I, pas in and sped the
faste ! '

' Thurgh me men gon,' than spak that
other syde,
' Unto the mortal strokes of the spere
Of which Disdayn and Daunger is the gyde,
Ther never tre shal fruyt ne levės bere.
This streem you ledeth to the sorwful were
Ther as the fish in prison is al drye ;
The schewyng is only the remedye.' 140

Thise vers of gold and blak y-writen
were,
The whiche I gan a-stonied to be-holde ;
For with that oon encresėde ay my fere,
And with that other gan myn hertė bolde ;
That oon me hette, that other dide me
colde ;
No wit hadde I, for errour, for to chese
To entre or fleen, or me to save or lese.

Right as be-twixėn adamauntės two
Of even myght a pece of yrėn set, 149
That hath no myght to mevė to ne fro,—
For what that oon may hale that other let,—
Ferde I, that nystė whether me was best
To entre or leve, til African, my gyde,
Me hente, and shoof in at the gatės wyde.

And seyde, ' It stondeth writen in thy
face
Thyn errour, though thou telle it not to me,
But dred thee not to come in-to this place,
For this writyng nis no thyng ment by thee,
Ne by noon, but he Lovės servaunt be,
For thou of love hast lost thy tast, I gesse,
As seek man hath of swete and bitternesse.

' But nathėles, al-though that thou be
dulle, 162
Yit that thou canst not do, yit mayst thou se,
For many a man that may not stonde a
pulle,
It liketh him at wrastlyng for to be,
And demėn yit wher he do bet or he ;

343

And, if thou haddest cunnyng for tendite,
I shal thee shewe mater of to write.'

With that my hond in his he took a-noon,
Of which I comfort caughte, and wente
    in faste ;   170
But Lord ! so I was glad and wel begoon !
For overal wher that I myn eyén caste
Were treës clad with leves that ay shal
    laste,
Eche in his kynde, of colour fresch and
    grene
As emeraude, that joye it was to sene.

The bildere ook and eek the hardy asshe ;
The piler elm, the cofre unto careyne ;
The boxtree piper; holm to whippés lasshe ;
The saylyng firr ; the cipres, deth to
    pleyne ;
The sheter ew ; the asp for shaftés pleyne ;
The olyve of pees, and eek the drunken
    vyne ;   181
The victor palm, the laurer to devyne.

A garden saw I ful of blosmy bowés
Up-on a river in a grené mede,
There as ther swetnesse evermore y-now is ;
With flourés whité, blewé, yelwe, and rede,
And coldé wellé-stremés, no-thyng dede,
That swommen ful of smalé fischés lighte,
With fynnés rede and scalés silver-brighte.

On every bough the briddés herde I
    synge,   190
With voys of nungel in her armonye ;
Som besyede hem hir briddés forth to
    brynge.
The litel conyes to hir pley gunne hye ;
And further al aboute I gan aspye
The dredful roo, the buk the hert and
    hynde,
Squerels and bestés smale of gentil kynde.

169 f. Cp. *Inferno*, iii. 19.
176 ff. Cp. *Faery Queene*, I. i. 8, 9. The above
is based on *Teseide*, xi. 22-24, and *R. de la R.*
1338-1368.
    177. *piler elm*, Spenser ' vine-prop elm.'
    178. *piper*, *i.e.* used for pipes or horns.
    180. *sheter ew*, because used for bows.
    182. *to devyne*, because used for divination.
    183-259. Cp. *Teseide*, vii. st. 51-60 ; also *Kingis Quair*, st. 31-33, 152, 153.

Of instruments of strengés in acord
Herde I so pleye a ravisshyng swetnesse,
That God, that maker is of al and Lord,
Ne herdé never beter, as I gesse ;   200
Therwith a wynd, unnethe it myghte be
    lesse,
Made in the levés grene a noysé softe,
Acordant to the foulés songe on-lofte.

The air of that place so attempré was
That never was grevaunce of hoot ne cold ;
There wex eek every holsom spice and gras ;
Ne no man may ther wexé seek ne old,
Yit was ther joyé more a thousand fold
Than man can telle ; ne never wolde it
    nyghte,
But ay cleer day to any mannés sighte.   210

Under a tre beside a welle, I say
Cupide our lord his arwés forge and file
And at his fet his bowe al redy lay,
And Wille his doghter temprede al this while
The hedés in the welle ; and with hir wyle
She couchéde hem after as they shuldé
    serve,
Som for to slee, and som to wounde and
    kerve.

Tho was I war of Plesaunce anon-right,
And of Aray and Lust and Curtesye,   219
And of the Craft that can and hath the
    myght
To doon be force a wyght to doon folye ;
Disfigurat was she, I nyl not lye ;
And by him-self, under an ok I gesse,
Saw I Delyt that stood with Gentilesse.

I saw Beauté, withouten any atyr ;
And Youthé, ful of game and Jolyté ;
Fool-hardinesse, Flatery and Desyr,
Messagerye and Mede and other three,—
Hir namés shal not here be told for me,—
And upon pilers grete of Jasper longe,   230
I saw a temple of bras y-founded stronge.

Aboute the temple daunsédén alwey
Wommen y-nowe, of whiché somme ther
    were
Faire of hem-self, and somme of hem
    were gay ;

In kirtels, al disshevelé wente they
   there,—
That was hir office alwey, yeer be yere,—
And on the temple of dovés white and
   faire
Saw I sittyngé many an hundred peire.

Be-fore the temple dore, ful soberly,
Dame Pees sat with a curteyn in hir
   hond,   240
And hir besydé, wonder discretly,
Dame Paciencé sittyng ther I fond
With facé pale, up-on an hille of sond ;
And aldernext within and eek with-oute,
Beheste and Art, and of hir folk a route.

Within the temple, of syghés hote as
   fyr
I herde a swogh that gan abouté renne ;
Whiche syghés were engendred with
   desyr
That maden every auter for to brenne
Of newé flaume ; and wel espyed I
   thenne   250
That al the cause of sorwés that they
-   drye
Com of the bitter goddesse Jelousye.

The god Priapus saw I as I wente
Within the temple, in sovereyn placé
   stonde
In swich aray as whan the asse him
   shente,
With cry by nyght, and with his ceptre
   in honde.
Ful besily men gunne assaye and fonde
Up-on his hede to sette, of sondry hewe
Garlondés ful of freshé flourés newe. 259

And in a privee corner in desporte
Fond I Venus and hir portére Richesse,
That was ful noble and hauteyn of hir
   porte ;
Derk was that place, but afterward
   lightnesse
I saw a lyte, unnethe it myghte be lesse,
And on a bed of golde she lay to reste
Til that the hoté sonné gan to weste.

Hir gilté herés with a golden thred
Y-bounden were, untrussed as she lay,
And naked fro the breste unto the hed
Men myghte hir seen ; and sothly for to
   say,   270
The remenaunt was wel keveréd to my
   pay,
Right with a subtil kerchef of Valence,
Ther nas no thikker cloth of no defence.

The placé yaf a thousand savours swote,
And Bachus, god of wyn, sat hir besyde,
And Sereis next, that doth of hungir
   bote ;
And as I seyde, amyddés lay Cypride,
To whom, on knees two yongé folkés cryde
To ben hir help ; but thus I let hir lye,
And ferther in the temple I gan espye 280

That, in dispit of Diané the chaste,
Ful many a bow y-broke heng on the wal,
Of maydens swiche as gunne hir tymés
   waste
In hir servyse ; and peynted overal
Ful many a story of which I touché shal
A fewe, as of Calyxte and Athalante,
And many a mayde of which the name I
   wante :

Semyramus, Candace and Herculés,
Biblis, Dido, Thisbé, and Piramus,
Tristram, Isoude, Paris, and Achillés, 290
Eleyné, Cleopatre, and Troilus,
Silla, and eek the moder of Romulus,—

272. *Valence*, probably Valence near Lynos,
where silk is still made. Boccaccio has ' Testa,
tanta sottil.'
276. *Sereis*, Ceres.
277. *Cypride*, *i.e.* Venus, because of her worship in Cyprus.
281-294. Cp. *Teseide*, vii. st. 61, 62.
286. *Calixte*, daughter of Lycaon, King of
Arcadia, and mother of Arcas, changed by Juno
from jealousy into a she-bear, and raised to
heaven by Jupiter as Ursa Major.
288. *Semyramus*, Semiramis, Queen of As-
syria.
288. *Candace*, an Indian queen loved by Alexander the Great.
290. *Tristram, Isoude*, Tristran (or Tristan)
and Ysolde (Ysolt) of French mediæval romance.
292. *Silla*, Scylla, daughter of Nisus, who for
love of Minos cut off her father's hair, on which his
life depended, and was turned into the bird Ciris.
292. *moder of Romulus*, Ilia or Rhea Silvia,
daughter of Numitor.

255. Cp. Ovid, *Fasti*, i. 415.
260-280. Cp. *Teseide*, vii. st. 63-66.

Alle these were peynted on that other
    syde,
And al hir love and in what plyt they
    dyde.   .

    Whan I was come ayen un-to the
      place
That I of spak, that was so swote and
    grene,
Forth welk I tho my-selven to solace.
Tho was I war wher that ther sat a
    quene
That as of light the somer-sunné shene
Passeth the sterre, right so over mesure 300
She fairer was than any creature.

    And in a launde upon an hille of
      flourés
Was set this noblé goddessé Nature.
Of braunchés were hir hallés and hir
    bourés
Y-wrought after hir craft and hir mesure ;
Ne there nas foul that cometh of engen-
    drure,
That they ne weré prest in hir presence,
To take hir doom and yeve hir audience.

    For this was on Seynt Valentynés
      day,
Whan every bryd cometh ther to chese
    his make,   310
Of every kyndé that men thynké may ;
And that so huge a noysé gan they maké,
That erthe and eyr and tre and every
    lake
So ful was, that unnethé was there space
For me to stonde, so ful was al the
    place.

    And right as Aleyn, in the Pleynt of
      Kynde,
Devyseth Nature of aray and face,
In swich aray men myghtén hir ther
    fynde.
This noble empéressé, ful of grace,
Bad every foul to take his owné place, 320

As they were wont alwey fro yeer to yere
Seynt Valentynés day to stonden there.

    That is to seyn, the foulés of ravyne
Were hyest set, and than the foulés
    smale,
That eten as hem nature wolde enclyne,
As worm or thyng, of whiche I telle no
    tale ;
And water-foul sat lowest in the dale,
But foul that lyveth by seed sat on the
    grene,
And that so fele that wonder was to sene.

    There myghté men the royal egle fynde,
That with his sharpé look perséth the
    sonne ;   331
And other eglés of a lower kynde,
Of whiche that clerkés wel devysé cunne.
Ther was the tyraunt with his fethrés donne
And greye, I mene the goshauk that doth
    pyne
To bryddés for his outrageous ravyne.

    The gentil faucon that with his feet
    distreyneth   .
The kyngés hond ; the hardy sperhauk
    eke,   338
The quaylés foo ; the merlion that peyneth
Hym-self ful ofte the larké for to seke ;
There was the douvé, with hir eyén meke ;
The jalous swan, ayens his deth that
    syngeth ;
The oule eke, that of deth the bodé
    bryngeth ;

    The crane the gëaunt, with his trompés
    soune ;
The theef the chough, and eek the
    jangelyng pye ;
The scornynge jay ; the elés foo, the
    heroune ;
The falsé lapwyng, ful of trecherye ;
The staré, that the counseyl can be-wrye ;
The tamé ruddok, and the coward kyte ;
The cok, that orloge is of thorpés lyte ;

---

316. A reference to the *Planctus Naturæ* of
Alanus de Insulis, or Alain Delille, a poet of the
12th century.
319. MSS. unanimous as to this line.

342, 343. From Alanus ; cp. *Anglo-Latin
Satirical Poets*, vol. ii. p. 74 (Record Series).
Most of the natural history of this whole passage
comes from him.

The sparwé, Venus sone ; the nyhtyn-
gale, 351
That clepeth forth the grené levés newe ;
The swalow, mortrer of the flyés smale,
That maken hony of flourés fresshe of
hewe ;
The wedded turtel, with hire herté trewe,
The pecok, with his aungels fethrés
bright ;
The fesaunt, scorner of the cok by nyght ;

The waker goos ; the cukkow ever un-
kynde ;
The popynjay, ful of delicasye ; 359
The draké, stroyer of his owné kynde ;
The stork, the wreker of avouterye ;
The hoté cormeraunt of glotenye ;
The raven wys ; the crow, with vois of care ;
The throstel old ; the frosty feldéfare.

What shulde I seyn ? Of foulés every
kynde
That in this world han fethrés and stature,
Men myghtén in that place assembled fynde
Before the noble goddessé Nature.
And everich of hem did his besy cure
Benygnély to chese or for to take 370
By hir acord his formel or his make.

But to the poynt,—Nature held on
hir hond
A formel egle, of shap the gentiléste
That ever she a-mong hire werkés fond ;
The moste benygné and the goodliéste ;
In hir was every vertu at his reste
So ferforth, that Nature hir-selfe hadde
blisse
To loke on hir and ofte hir bek to kisse.

Nature, the vicaire of the almyghty
Lord,
That hoot, cold, hevy, light, and moist,
and dreye 380
Hath knyt, with evené noumbrés of a-cord,
In esy vois began to speke and seye,
' Foulés, tak hede of my sentence, I preye,

351. The sparrow was sacred to Venus.
361. Cp. Neckam, *Liber de Naturis Rerum*
(Ed. Wright, lib. i. c. 64).
363. *with vois of care*, a mistranslation of
Virgil, *Georg.* i. 388.

And, for your ese in furtheryng of your nede,
As faste as I may speke I wol me speede.

' Ye know wel how seynt Valentynés day,
By my statut and through my governaunce,
Ye comen for to chese—and flee your
way—
Your makés, as I prike yow with plesaunce;
But nathéles my rightful ordénaunce 390
May I nat lete for al this world to wynne,
That he that most is worthy shal begynne.

' The tercel egle, as that ye knowén wel,
The foul royal, a-bove yow in degree,
The wyse and worthy, secree, trewe as stel,
The which I have y-formed, as ye may see,
In every part as it best liketh me,—
Hit nedeth not his shap yow to devyse,—
He shal first chese and spekén in his gyse.

' And after him by order shul ye chese,
After your kyndé, everich as yow lyketh,
And as your hap is shul ye wynne or lese ;
But which of yow that lové most entriketh
God sende him hir that sorest for him
syketh.'
And therwithal the tercel gan she calle,
And seyde, ' My sone, the choys is to
thee falle.

' But nathéles, in this condicioun
Mot be the choys of everich that is here,
That she a-gree to his eleccioun,
Who-so he be that shuldé be hir fere ; 410
This our usage alwey from yeer to yere,
And who-so may at this tyme have his grace,
In blisful tyme he com into this place.'

With hed enclynéd and with humblé
chere
This royal tercel spak, and taried nought :
' Un-to my sovereyn lady, and nought
my fere—
I chese, and chese with wille and herte
and thought,
The formel on your hond, so wel y-wrought,
Whos I am al and ever wol hir serve, 419
Do what hir list, to do me live or sterve.

411. *This*=this is. Cp. ll. 620, 649; also *K. T.*
233 and 885.

347

'Besechyng hir of mercy and of grace,
As she that is my lady sovereyne ;
Or let me dyė present in this place ;
For certės, longe I may nat live in payne,
For in myn herte is corven every veyne;
And havyng réward only to my trouthe,
My derė herte have of my wo som routhe !

'And if that I to hir be founde untrewe,
Disobeysaunt, or wilful negligent,
Avauntour, or in proces love anewe,   430
I preye to yow this be my jugėment,
That with these foulės be I al to-rent,
That ilkė day that ever she me fynde
To hir untrewe, or in my gilt unkynde.

'And, syn that noon loveth hir so wel as I,
Al be she never of lovė me behette,
Than oughtė she be myn thourgh hir mercy,
For other bond can I noon on hir knette ;
Ne never for no wo ne shal I lette   439
To serven hir, how fer so that she wende ;
Say what yow list, my tale is at an ende.'

Right as the fresshė, redė rosė newe
A-yen the somer sonnė coloured is,
Right so for shame al wexėn gan the hewe
Of this formeL   Whan she herde al this,
She neyther answerdė 'Wel,' ne seyde
    amys,
So sore abasshed was she, til that Nature
Seyde, 'Doughter, dred yow nought, I
    yow assure.'

Another tercel egle spak anoon,
Of lower kynde, and seyde, 'That shal
    not be !   450
I love hir bet than ye do, by Seynt John !
Or attė leste I love as wel as ye,
And lenger have servėd hir in my degree ;
And if she shulde have loved for long
    lovyng,
To me allone hadde been the guerdonyng.

'I dar eek seyn, if she me fyndė fals,
Unkynde, janglere, or rebel any wyse,
Or jalous, do me hangen by the hals !
And, but I berė me in hir servyse,   459
As wel as that my wit can me suffyse,

445. A short line, but so in all MSS. Perhaps
hadde herd is the true reading.

Fro poynt to poynt hir honour for to save,
Tak she my lif and al the good I have.'

The thriddė tercel egle answėrdė tho,
'Now, sirs, ye seen the litel leyser here,
For every foul cryeth out to ben a-go
Forth with his make, or with his lady dere,
And eek Nature hir-self ne wol not here,
For tarying here, not half that I wolde seye,
And but I speke I mot for sorwė deye.

'Of long servyse avaunte I me nothing
But as possible is me to deye to-day   471
For wo, as he that hath ben languysshyng
Thise twenty winter, and wel happen may
A man may servėn bet and more to pay
In half a yer, although it were no more
Than som man doth that hath servėd ful
    yore.

'I ne sey not this by me, for I ne can
Don no servyse that may my lady plese ;
But I dar seyn I am hir trewest man,   479
As to my dom, and feynest wolde hir ese ;
At shortė wordės, til that deth me sese,
I wol ben hirės, whether I wake or wynke,
And trewe in al that hertė may bethynke.'

Of al my lyf syn that day I was born
So gentil ple in love or other thyng
Ne herdė never no man me beforn,
Who-so that haddė leyser and cunnyng
For to reherse hir chere and hir spekyng :
And from the morwė gan this spechė laste
Til dounward drow the sonnė wonder faste.

The noyse of foulės for to ben delyverėd
So loudė rong, 'Have doon and let us
    wende !'
That wel wende I the wode hadde al to-
    shyverėd.
'Come of !' they cryde, 'allas, ye wil
    us shende !
Whan shal your cursed pleyng have an
    ende ?
How shulde a jugė eyther party leve
For yee or nay, with-outen any preve ?'

The goos, the cokkow, and the dokė
    also,

348

So cryden, 'Kek, kek!' 'Kokkow!'
'Quek, quek!' hye,   499
That thurgh myn eres the noysé wenté tho.
The goos seyde, 'Al this nys not worth
 a flye!
But I can shape hereof a remedye,
And I wol sey my verdit faire and swythe,
For water-foul, who-so be wrooth or
 blythe.'

'And I for worm-foul!' quod the fol
 cokkow;
'And I wol of myn owne autorité,
For comun sped take on the chargé now,—
For to delyvere us is gret charité.'
'Ye may abyde a whilé yet, *pardé!*'
Seidé the turtil, 'if it be your wille   510
A wight may speke, him were as fayr be
 stille.'

'I am a seed-foul, oon the unworthieste,
That wot I wel, and litel of cunnynge,
But bet is that a wyghtés tongé reste,
Than entrémetén him of swiche doynge
Of which he neyther redé can, ne synge;
And who-so doth, ful foule himself acloyeth,
For office uncommytted ofte anoyeth.'

Naturé, which that alway hadde an ere
To murmur of the lewédnes behynde,   520
With facound voyse seyde, 'Hold your
 tungés there!
And I shal sone, I hope, a conseyl fynde,
Yow to delyvere, and fro this noyse un-
 bynde.
I juge, of every flok men shal oon calle
To seyn the verdit for yow foulés alle.'

Assentéd were to this conclusioun
The briddés alle; and foulés of ravyne
Han chosen first, by playn eleccioun,
The tercelet of the faucon, to diffyne   529
Al hir sentence as him list to termyne;
And to Nature him gonnén to presente,
And she accepteth him with glad entente.

The tercelet seidé then in this manère:
'Ful hard were hit to prevén by resoun
Who loveth best this gentil formel here,
For everich hath swich replicacioun

That noon by skillés may be brought a-
 doun;
I can not se that arguments avayle;
Than semeth hit ther musté be batayle.'

'Al redy!' quod these eglés tercels
 tho.   540
'Nay, sirs,' quod he, 'if that I dorste
 it seye
Ye doon me wrong, myn tale is not y-do,
For sirs, ne taketh nought a-gref, I preye,
It may not gon, as ye wolde, in this weye;
Oure is the voys that han the charge in
 honde,
And to the jugés dome ye moten stonde;

'And therfor, pes! I seye, as to my wit,
Me woldé thynke how that the worthieste
Of knyghthode, and lengest hath uséd hit,
Moste of estat, of blod the gentileste,   550
Were sittyngest for hir, if that hir leste,
And of these thre she wot hir-self, I trowe,
Which that he be, for hit is light to knowe.'

The water-foulés han her hedés leyd
Togedre, and of a short avysément,
Whan everich hadde his largé golee seyd,
They seyden sothly, al by oon assent,
How that the 'goos, with hir facoundé gent,
That so desyreth to pronounce our nede,
Shal telle our tale,' and preyden 'god hir
 spede.'   560

And for these water-foulés tho began
The goos to speke, and in hir kakelynge
She seydé, 'Pees! now tak keep every man,
And herkeneth which a resoun I shal
 brynge;
My wit is sharp, I love no taryinge;
I seye, I rede him, though he were my
 brother,
But she wol love him let him take another.'

'Lo here! a perfit resoun of a goos!'
Quod tho the sperhauke, 'never mot she
 the!
Lo, sich it is to have a tungé loos!   570
Now pardé, fool, yet were it bet for the
Han holde thy pes, than shewed thy
 nyceté!

It lyth nat in his wit, né in his wille,
But sooth is seyd, "a fool can noght be
    stille."'

The laughter aroos of gentil foulés alle,
And right a-noon the seed-foul chosen hadde
The turtel trewe, and gunne hir to hem calle
And preyden hir to seyn the sothé sadde
Of this matere, and askéd what she radde.
And she answérde, that pleynly hir entente
She woldé shewe, and sothly what she
    mente.   581

  'Nay, god forbede a lover shuldé
    chaunge!'
The turtel seyde, and wex for shamé red;
'Though that his lady ever more be
    straunge,
Yet let him serven hir til he be deed.
Forsothe I preysé noght the goosés reed,
For though she deyede I wol non other
    make,
I wol ben hires til that the deth me take!'

  'Wel bourdéd,' quod the doké, 'by my
    hat!
That men shul lovèn alwey, causéles, 590
Who can a resoun fynde, or wit in that?
Daunceth he mury that is myrthéles?
Who shuldé recche of that is recchéles?
Ye, kek!' yit seyde the gos, ful wel
    and fayre,
'There been mo sterrés, god wot, than a
    payre!'

  'Now fy, cherl!' quod the gentil tercélet,
'Out of the donghil com that word ful right,
Thou canst not see what thyng is wel be-set;
Thow farest by love as oulés doon by light,
The day hem blent, but wel they sen by
    nyght;   600
Thy kynde is of so lowe a wrechednesse,
That what love is thow canst nat see ne
    gesse.'

  Tho gan the cukkow put him forth in
    prees

For foul that eteth worm, and seydé blythe,
'So I,' quod he, 'may have my make in
    pees
I recché nat how longé that ye stryve;
Lat ech of hem be soleyn al hir lyve;
This is my reed, syn they may not acorde,
This shorté lessoun nedeth not recorde.'

  'Ye! have the glotoun fild y-nogh his
    paunche,   610
Than are we wel,' seydé the merlioun;
'Thow mordrer of the heysugge on the
    braunche
That broghte thee forth! thou [rewthélees]
    glotoun!
Live thou soleyn, wormés corrupcioun!
For no fors is of lakke of thy nature!
Go, lewéd be thou, while the world may
    dure!'

  'Now pees,' quod Nature, 'I comaundé
    here!
For I have herd al your opynyoun,
And in effect yet be we never the nere;
But fynally, this my conclusioun,— 620
That she hir-self shal han the eleccioun
Of whom hir list, who-so be wrooth or
    blythe,
Him that she cheseth, he shal hir han as
    swythe;

  'For syn it may not here discusséd be
Who loveth hir best, as seyde the tercélet,
Than wol I don hir this favour, that she
Shal han right him on whom hir herte is
    set,
And he hir that his herte hath on hir knet,
Thus juge I, Nature, for I may not lye
To non estat, I have non othir ÿe. 630

  'But as for conseyl for to chese a make,
If I were Resoun, certés than wolde I
Conseylé yow the royal tercel take,
As seyde the tercélet ful skylfully,
As for the gentilest and most worthy
Which I have wrought so wel to my
    plesaunce
That to yow oughté been a suffisaunce.'

574. Cp. 'A fool's bolt is soon shot,' *As You Like It*, v. 4, 67, and *Henry V.* iii. 7, 132.
594. So Ha., except that it reads *Za queke.*

613. Skeat's emendation for *rrewful* of most MSS. Gg. *reufulles*; P. *rowthfull.*

With dredful vois the formel hir
  answerde :
' Myn rightful lady, goddesse of Nature,
Soth is that I am ever under your yerde,
Like as is everich other creature,   641
And mot ben yourès whil my lyf may dure ;
And therfor graunteth me my firstè bone,
And myn entent I wol yow seyn right sone.'

    ' I graunte it yow,' quod she, and right
      a-non
This formel egle spak in this degre :
' Almyghty quene, unto this yer be gon
I askè réspit for to a-visè me,
And after that to have my choys al fre ;
This al and som that I wol speke and
    seye ;
Ye gete no more al-though ye do me deye.

    ' I wol not servèn Venus ne Cupide,
For sothe as yet, by no manèrè weye.'
' Now, syn it may non otherweys betyde,'
Quod tho Nature, ' here is no more to
    seye ;
Than wolde I that these foulès were a-weye,
Ech with his make, for tarying lenger
    here,'—
And seyde hem thus, as ye shul after here.

    ' To you speke I, ye tercelets,' quod
      Nature,
' Beth of good herte and serveth, alle thre ;
A yeer nis nat so longè to endure,   661
And ech of yow peyne him in his degrè
For to do well ; for, God wot, quit is she
Fro you this yeer ; what after so be-falle ;
This entremès is dressèd for you alle.'

    And whan this werk al broght was to
      an ende,
To every foulè Nature yaf his make
By even acorde, and on hir wey they wende ;
And, Lord, the blisse and joyè that they
    make !
For ech gan other in his wyngès take, 670
And with hir nekkès ech gan other wynde,
Thankyng alwey the noble quene of kynde.

But first were chosen foulès for to synge,
As, yeer be yere, was alwey hir usance
To synge a roundel at hir departynge,
To don to Nature honour and plesaunce.
The note, I trowe, y-makèd was in
    Fraunce ;
The wordès were swiche as ye may here
    fynde
The nextè vers, as I now have in mynde.

' Now welcom, somer, with thy sonnè softe,
That hast this wintrès weders over-
    shake   681
And driven a-wey the longè nyghtès blake ;

Seynt Valentyn, that art ful hy on lofte,
Thus syngèn smalè foulès for thy sake
    Now welcom, somer, with thy sonnè
      softe,
    That hast this wintrès weders over-
      shake.

Wele han they causè for to gladèn ofte,
Sith ech of hem recoverèd hath his make ;
Ful blisful mowe they ben when they
    awake.
    Now welcom, somer, with thy sonnè
      softe,   690
    That hast this wintrès weders over-
      shake
    And driven a-wey the longè nyghtès
      blake ;'

And with the showtyng whan the song
    was do
That foulès madèn at hir flight awey,
I wook, and other bokès tok me to,
To rede up-on ; and yet I rede alwey ;
In hope y-wys to redè so sum day,
That I shall metè somthyng for to fare
The bet ; and thus to rede I nyl not spare.

675. *roundel*, also called *triolet* in its oldest
form, a short poem in which the first line or lines
recur in the middle and at the end.
676. All but Gg. om. second *to*.
685 f. These lines are not repeated either here
or at l. 690 ff. in Gg. and Jo., the only MSS.
which give the roundel. In Jo the first three lines
are wanting altogether.

BOECE

INCIPIT LIBER BOECII DE CONSOLA-
CIONE PHILOSOPHIE

'*Carmina qui quondam studio florente
peregi.*'—Metrum 1

ALLAS ! I, wepynge, am constreyned to
bygynnen vers of sorwful matere, that
whilom in florysschyng studie made delitable ditees.　For lo ! rendynge Muses
of poetes enditen to me thynges to ben
writen, and drery vers of wrecchidnesse
weten my face with verray teres.

At the leeste, no drede ne myghte
overcomen tho Muses, that thei ne were
felawes, and folwyden my wey (that is to
seyn, whan I was exiled).　They that
weren glorie of my youthe, whilom weleful and grene, conforten nowe the sorwful
wyerdes of me, olde man.　For eelde is
comyn unwarly uppon me, hasted by the
harmes that y have, and sorwe hath
comandid his age to ben in me. [5]
Heeris hore arn schad over-tymeliche
up-on myn heved, and the slakke skyn
trembleth of myn emptid body.

Thilke deth of men is weleful that ne
comyth noght in yeeris that ben swete,
but cometh to wrecches often yclepid.
Allas ! allas ! with how deef an ere deth,
cruwel, turneth awey fro wrecches, and
nayteth to closen wepynge eien.　Whil
fortune, unfeithful, favourede me with

For the relation of MSS. see Introduction.
Abbreviations—C₁, Camb. Univ. Libr. Ii. i.
38 ; A₂, Brit. Mus. Additional 16,165 ; H, Brit.
Mus. Harleian 2421 ; Cx., Caxton's Ed. ; B.,
Bodleian Libr., Bodley 797 ; C₂, Camb. Univ.
Libr. Ii. 3. 21 ; A₁, Brit. Mus. Add. 10,340 ; Hn.,
the Hengwrt Fragment, MS. Peniarth 393 ;
Com., the fragment of a commentary in Bodl.
MS. Auct. F. 3. 5 ; Fr., Bibl. Nat. Fonds Franç.
1079, or French text in general ; L, Bibl. Nat.
Fonds Lat. 18,424 (French and Latin parallel
text) ; Lat., Latin text of Obbarius, Jena 1843 ;
Aq., the so-called Aquinas Commentary.
4. *wyerdes*, 'fata.'

lyghte goodes, the sorwful houre (that is
to seyn, the deth) hadde almoost dreynt
myn heved.　But now, for fortune
cloudy hath chaunged hir deceyvable
chere to me ward, myn unpietous lif
draweth along unagreable duellynges in
me. [10]

O ye, my frendes, what, or wher-to
avaunted ye me to be weleful ? For he
that hath fallen stood noght in stedefast
degre.

'*Hec dum mecum tacitus.*'—Prosa 1

In the mene while that I, stille, re-
cordede these thynges with my-self, and
merkid my weply compleynte with office
of poyntel, I sawe, stondynge aboven the
heighte of myn heved, a womman of ful
greet reverence by semblaunt, hir eien
brennynge and cleer seynge over the
comune myghte of men ; with a lifly
colour and with swich vigour and strengthe
that it ne myghte nat ben emptid, al
were it so that sche was ful of so greet
age that men ne wolden not trowen in no
manere that sche were of our elde. [15]
The stature of hire was of a doutous
jugement, for som-tyme sche constreyned
and schronk hir-selven lik to the comune
mesure of men, and som-tyme it semede
that sche touchede hevene with the
heighte of here heved ; and whan sche
hef hir heved heyere, sche percede the
selve hevene so that the sighte of men
lokynge was in ydel.

Hir clothes weren makid of right delye
thredes and subtile craft, of perdurable
matere, the whiche clothes sche hadde

10. *unpietous*, 'impia.'　C₁ H Cx. A₂ omit *in
me.*
11. *what* here, as often, is Chaucer's translation of 'quid,' 'why.'
18. Supply 'with' before *subtile.*　In the Latin
the beaute belongs to the next sentence, 'Quarum
speciem,' etc.

woven with hir owene handes, as I knewe wel aftir by hir-selve declarynge and schewynge to me the beaute. The whiche clothes a derknesse of a for-leten and despised elde hadde duskid and dirked, as it is wont to dirken besmokede ymages. In the nethereste hem or bordure of thise clothes, men redden y-woven in a Grekissch P (that signifieth the lif actif) ; [20] and aboven that lettre, in the heieste bordure, a Grekyssh T (that signifieth the lif contemplatif). And bytwixen thise two lettres ther were seyn degrees nobly y-wrought in manere of laddres, by whiche degrees men myghten clymben fro the nethereste lettre to the uppereste.

Natheles handes of some men hadden korve that cloth by violence and by strengthe, and everich man of hem hadde boren awey swiche peces as he myghte geten. And for sothe this forseide womman bar smale bokis in hir right hand, and in hir left hand sche bar a ceptre. And whan she saughe thise poetical Muses aprochen aboute my bed and enditynge wordes to my wepynges, sche was a litil amoeved, and glowede with cruel eighen. [25] 'Who,' quod sche, 'hath suffred aprochen to this sike man thise comune strompettis of swich a place that men clepen the theatre ; the whiche not oonly ne asswagen noght his sorwes with none remedies, but thei wolden fedyn and noryssen hym with sweete venym. For sothe thise ben tho that with thornes and prikkynges of talentes or affeccions, whiche that ne bien nothyng fructifyenge nor profitable, destroyen the corne plentyvous of fruytes of resoun. For thei holden hertes of men in usage, but thei delyvre noght folk fro maladye. But yif ye muses hadden with-drawen fro me with youre

flateries, any unkunnynge and unprofitable man as men ben wont to fynde comonly among the peple, I wolde wene suffre the lasse grevosly ; [30] for-whi, in swych an unprofitable man, myne ententes weren nothyng endamaged. But ye with-drawen me this man, that hath ben noryssed in the studies or scoles of Eleaticis and of Achademycis in Grece. But goth now rather awey, ye mermay denes, whiche that ben swete til it be at the laste, and suffreth this man to be-cured and heeled by myne muses (that is to seyn, by noteful sciences). And thus this companye of Muses, I-blamed, casten wrothly the chere dounward to the erthe, and, schewing by rednesse hir schame, thei passeden sorwfully the thresschefolde. And I, of whom the sighte, ploungid in teeres, was dirked so that y ne myghte noght knowen what that womman was of so imperial auctorite, [35] I wax al abayssched and astoned, and caste my syghte doun to the erthe, and bygan, stille, for to abide what sche woolde doon aftirward. Tho com sche ner, and sette her doun uppon the uttereste corner of my bed ; and sche, byholdynge my chere that was cast to the erthe hevy and grevous of wepynge, compleynede, with thise wordis that I schal seyn, the perturbacion of my thought.

' *Heu quam precipiti mersa profundo.*'
Metrum 2

'Allas how the thought of this man, dreynt in overthrowynge depnesse, dulleth and for-leteth his propre clernesse, myntynge to gon in-to foreyne dirknesses as ofte as his anoyos bysynes waxeth withoute mesure, that is dryven with werldly wyndes. This man, that whilom was fre, to whom the hevene was opyn and knowen, and was wont to gon in hevenliche pathes, [40] and saughe the lyghtnesse of the rede sonne, and saughe the sterres of the coolde mone, and whiche sterre in hevene useth wandrynge recourses

20, 21. P, T, *i.e.* Πρακτική, Θεωρητική, referring to the two divisions of philosophy.
23. C₁ A₂ H read *or* for first *and.*
27. C₁ A₂ read *cornes.*
27. *plentyvous of fruytes,* 'uberem fructibus.'
29. 'Hominum mentes adsuefaciunt morbo, non liberant.' But Chaucer has mistranslated, 'Tiennent les pensees des hommes en costume et ne les delivrent pas de maladie.'

39. C₂ A₁ com. *dryven to and fro.*

I-flyt by diverse speeris, this man, over-comere, hadde comprehendid al this by nombres (of acontynge in astronomye). And, over this, he was wont to seken the causes whennes the sounynge wyndes moeven and bysien the smothe watir of the see ; and what spirit turneth the stable hevene ; and why the sterre ariseth out of the rede est, to fallen in the westrene wawes ; and what attemprith the lusty houres of the firste somer sesoun, that highteth and apparaileth the erthe with rosene floures ; [45] and who maketh that plentyvous autumpne in fulle yeris fletith with hevy grapes. And eek this man was wont to tellen the diverse causes of nature that weren yhidde. Allas ! now lyth he emptid of lyght of his thoght, and his nekke is pressyd with hevy cheynes, and bereth his chere enclyned adoun for the grete weyghte, and is con-streyned to loken on the fool erthe !

'Set medicine inquit tempus.'—Prosa 2

'But tyme is now,' quod sche, 'of medicyne more than of compleynte.' Forsothe thanne sche, entendynge to me ward with al the lookynge of hir eien, seyde :—[50] 'Art nat thou he,' quod sche, 'that whilom, norissched with my melk and fostred with myne metes, were escaped and comyn in-to corage of a parfit man. Certes I yaf the swiche armures that, yif thou thi-selve ne haddest first cast hem a-wey, they schulden han defended the in sekernesse that mai nat ben overcomyn. Knowestow me nat? Why arttow stille? Is it for schame or for astonynge? It were me levere that it were for schame, but it semeth me that astonynge hath oppresside the.' [55] And whan she say me nat oonly stille, but withouten office of tunge and al dowmbe, sche leyde hir hand sooftly uppon my breest, and seide :

'Here nys no peril,' quod sche, 'he is fallen in-to a litargye, whiche that is a comune seknesse to hertes that been desceyved. He hath a litil foryeten hym-selve, but certes he schal lightly remembren hymself, yif it so be that he hath knowen me or now ; and that he may so doon, I will wipe a litil his eien that ben dirked by the cloude of mor-tel thynges.' [60] Thise woordes seide sche, and with the lappe of hir garne-ment, yplited in a frownce, sche dryede myn eien, that weren fulle of the wawes of my wepynges.

'Tunc me discussa.'—Metrum 3

Thus, whan that nyght was discussed and chased a-wey, dirknesses forleten me, and to myn eien repeyred ayen hir firste strengthe. And ryght by ensaumple as the sonne is hydd whan the sterres ben clustred (that is to seyn, when sterres ben covered with cloudes) by a swyft wynd that hyghte Chorus, and that the firmament stant dirked with wete plowngy cloudes, and that the sterres nat apeeren upon hevene, so that the nyght semeth sprad upon erthe : yif thanne the wynde that hyghte Boreas, I-sent out of the kaves of the cuntre of Trace, betith this nyght (that is to seyn, chaseth it a-wey), [65] and discovereth the closed day, thanne schyneth Phebus I-schaken with sodeyn light, and smyteth with his beemes in merveylynge eien.

'Haut aliter tristicie.'—Prosa 3

Ryght so, and noon other wise, the cloudes of sorwe dissolved and doon a-wey, I took hevene, and resceyved mynde to knowe the face of my fisycien ; so that I sette myne eien on hir and fastned my lookynge. I byholde my noryce, Philosophie, in whoos houses I

---

42. *I-flyt by diverse speeris*, 'flexa, i.e. mota, per varios orbes,' refers to the ancient theory of direct and retrograde planetary motions; cp. *Astr.* II. concl. 35.

49. C₁ A₂ H Cx. B A₁ read *foul erthe*; Lat. 'stolidam terram'; Fr. 'la fole terre.'

63. *sterres ben clustred*, literal rendering of 'sidera glomerantur.'

68. *I took hevene*, Fr. 'ie pris le ciel,' a literal translation of 'hausi cœlum' (! looked up).

hadde conversed and hauntyd fro my youthe; and I seide thus: 'O thou maystresse of alle vertues, descended from the sovereyne sete, whi arttow comen in-to this solitarie place of myn exil? Artow comen for thou art maad coupable with me of false blames?' [70] 'O I!' quod sche, 'my nory, schulde I forsake the now, and schulde I nat parten with the, by comune travaile, the charge that thow hast suffred for envye of my name? Certes it nere nat leveful ne syttynge thyng to philosophie, to leten with-outen companye the weye of hym that is innocent. Schulde I thanne redowte my blame, and agrysen as though ther were by-fallen a newe thyng? For trowestow that philosophie be now alder-ferst assailed in periles by folk of wykkide maneris? Have I noght stryven with ful greet strif in olde tyme, byfor the age of my Plato, ayens the foolhardynesse of folye? [75] And eek, the same Plato lyvynge, his mayster Socrates desserved victorie of unryghtful deth in my presence. The heritage of the whiche Socrates (the heritage is to seyn, the doctryne of the whiche Socrates in his opinyoun of felicite, that I clepe welefulnesse) whan that the peple of Epycuriens and Stoyciens and many othre enforceden hem to gon ravyssche everyche man for his part (that is to seyn that everych of hem wolde drawen to the deffense of his opinyoun the wordes of Socrates), they as in partye of hir preye to-drowen me, cryinge and debatyng ther ayens, and korven and to-rente my clothes that I hadde woven with myn handes; and with the cloutes that thei hadden arased out of my clothes, thei wenten a-wey wenynge that I hadde gon with hem every del. [80] In whiche Epycuriens and Stoyciens for as myche as ther semede some traces or steppes of myn abyte, the folie of men wenynge tho Epycuryens and Stoyciens my familiers pervertede some thurw the errour of the wikkide or unkunnynge multitude of hem. (This is to seyn, that, for they semeden philoso-phres, thei weren pursued to the deth and slayn.) So yif thou ne hast noght knowen the exilynge of Anaxogore, ne the enpoisonynge of Socrates, ne the turmentes of Zeno, for they weren straungiers, yit myghtestow han knowen the Seneciens, and the Canyos, and the Soranas, of whiche folk the renoun is neyther over-oold ne unsollempne. [85] The whiche men no thyng elles broght hem to the deeth, but oonly for thei weren enformyd of myne maneris, and semyde moost unlyk to the studies of wykkid folk. And for-thi thou ought-est noght to wondren thoughe that I, in the byttere see of this lif, be fordryven with tempestes blowynge aboute. In the whiche this is my moste purpoos, that is to seyn to displesen to wikkide men. Of whiche schrewes al be the oost nevere so greet, it is to despise; for it nys nat governyd with no ledere (of resoun), but it is ravyssched oonly by fleetynge errour folyly and lightly; and yif they som-tyme, makynge an oost ayens us, assayle us as strengere, our ledere draweth to-gidre his richesses in-to his tour, and they ben ententyf aboute sar-pleris or sachelis, unprofitable for to taken. [90] But we that ben heighe above, syker fro alle tumolte and wood noyse, warnstoryd and enclosed in swiche a paleys whider as that chaterynge or anoyinge folye ne may nat atayne, we scorne swyche ravyneres and henteres of fouleste thynges.

'*Quisquis composito.*'—Metrum 4

Who-so it be that is cleer of vertue, sad and wel ordynat of lyvynge, that hath put under fote the proude weerdes and loketh, up-right, up-on either fortune, he may holden his chere undesconfited.

84. *Anaxogore*, like *Canyos* (and *Soranas?*) below, owes its form to the Latin text.
85. *the Seneciens*, etc., *i.e.* men like Seneca, Canius, and Soranus. *Seneciens* is probably due to Fr. 'Seneciens.'
92. *cleer of vertue*, 'serenus' glossed 'clarus virtute.'

The rage ne the manaces of the see, commoevynge or chasynge upward hete fro the botme, ne schal nat moeve that man. Ne the unstable mowntaigne that highte Visevus, that writhith out thurw his brokene chemeneyes smokynge fieres, ne the wey of thonder leit, that is wont to smyten hye toures, ne schal nat moeve that man. Whar-to thanne, o wrecches, drede ye tirauntes that ben wode and felenous withouten ony strengthe? [95] Hope aftir no thyng, ne drede nat; and so schaltow desarmen the ire of thilke unmyghty tiraunt. But who so that, qwakynge, dredeth or desireth thyng that nys noght stable of his ryght, that man that so dooth hath cast awey his scheeld, and is remoeved from his place, and enlaceth hym in the cheyne with whiche he mai ben drawen.

'Sentis ne inquit.'—Prosa 4

'Felistow,' quod sche, 'thise thynges, and entren thei aughte in thy corage? Artow like an asse to the harpe? Why wepistow, why spillestow teeris? Yif thou abidest after helpe of thi leche, the byhoveth discovre thy wownde.'

Tho I, that hadde gaderyd strengthe in my corage, answeride and seide: 'And nedeth it yit,' quod I, 'of rehersynge or of ammonicioun? [100] And scheweth it nat y-noghe by hym-selve the sharpnesse of fortune, that waxeth wood ayens me? Ne moeveth it nat the to seen the face or the manere of this place? Is this the librarye whiche that thou haddest chosen for a ryght certein sege to the in myn hous, there as thow disputedest ofte with me of the sciences of thynges touchynge dyvinyte and mankynde? Was thanne myn habit swiche as it is now? Was my face or my chere swyche as now whan I soghte with the

the secretis of nature, whan thow enformedest my maneris and the resoun of al my lif to the ensaumple of the ordre of hevene? Is noght this the gerdouns that I referre to the, to whom I have ben obeisaunt? [105]

Certes thou confermedest by the mouth of Plato this sentence, that is to seyne that comune thynges or comunalites weren blisful yif they that hadden studied al fully to wysdom governeden thilke thynges; or elles yif it so befille that the governours of comunalites studieden to geten wysdom. Thou seidest eek by the mouth of the same Plato that it was a necessarie cause wise men to taken and desire the governance of comune thynges, for that the governementz of cites, I-lefte in the handes of felonous turmentours citezeens, ne schulde noght bryngen in pestilence and destruccioun to good folk. And therfore I, folwynge thilke auctorite, desired to putten forth in execucion and in acte of comune administracioun thilke thynges that I hadde lernyd of the among my secre restyng-whiles. [110]

Thow and god, that putte the in the thoughtes of wise folk, ben knowynge with me that no thyng ne brought me to maistrie or dignyte but the comune studie of alle goodnesse. And therof cometh it that bytwixen wikkid folk and me han ben grevous discordes, that ne myghte nat ben relessed by preyeris; for this liberte hath fredom of conscience, that the wraththe of more myghty folk hath alwey ben despised of me for savacioun of right. How ofte have I resisted and withstonden thilke man that highte Conigaste, that made alwey assawtes ayens the prospere fortunes of pore feble folk! How ofte eek have I put of or cast out hym Trygwille, provost of the kyngis hous, bothe of the wronges that

---

93. *hete*, 'æstum,' which means 'surge' here; cp. 255.

97. *his*, its. Chaucer follows L., 'estables [et Fr.] de son droit,' not Lat. 'stabilis suique iuris.'

98. *an asse to the harpe*, the Greek proverb ὄνος λύρας, through Lat. 'asinus ad lyram.'

105. *Is noght this*, etc., 'Hæccine præmia referimus tibi?'

108. *wise men*, etc., gerundive idiom, *i.e.* 'for wise,' etc.

111. *ben knowynge*, etc., 'mihi conscii,' but Fr. 'consachables avecques moi.'

112. *for this*, etc., should be *and, for this*, etc.

he hadde bygunne to doon, and ek fully performed ! [115] How ofte have I covered and defended by the auctorite of me put ayens perils (that is to seyn, put myn auctorite in peril for) the wrecche pore folk, that the covetise of straungiers unpunyschid tormentyde alwey with myseses and grevances out of nombre !

Nevere man ne drow me yit fro right to wrong. Whan I say the fortunes and the richesses of the peple of the provinces ben harmed or amanuced outher be pryve rauynes or by comune tributes or cariages, as sory was I as they that suffriden the harm. (Glosa. Whan that Theoderic, the kyng of Gothes, in a dere yeer, hadde his gerneeris ful of corn, and comaundede that no man schulde byen no coorn til his corn were soold, and that at grevous dere prys, Boece with-stood that ordenaunce and overcome it, knowynge al this the kyng hym-selve. [120] Coempcioun is to seyn comune achat or beyinge to-gidre, that were establissed up-on the peple by swiche a manere imposicioun, as whoso boughte a busschel corne, he most yyve the kyng the fyfte part.) Textus. Whan it was in the sowre hungry tyme, ther was establissed or cryed grevous and unplitable coempcioun, that men sayen wel it schulde gretly tormenten and endamagen al the provynce of Campayne, I took stryf ayens the provost of the pretorie for comune profit ; and, the kyng knowynge of it, overcom it, so that the coempcioun ne was nat axid ne took effect. Paulyn, a conseiller of Rome, the richesses of the whiche Paulyn the howndes of the paleys (that is to seyn the officeres) wolden han devoured by hope and covetyse, yit drowe I hym out of the jowes of hem that gapeden. And for as moche as the peyne of the accusacioun ajugid byforn ne schulde noght sodeynli henten ne punyssche wrongfully Albyn, a conseiller

of Rome, I putte me ayens the hates and indignacions of the accusour Cyprian. [125] Is it not thanne I-noghe sene, that I have purchaced grete discordes ayens my-self? But I oughte be the more asseured ayens alle othere folk, that, for the love of rightwisnesse, I ne reservede nevere no thyng to my selve to hem ward of the kyngis halle, by whiche I were the more syker. But thurw the same accusours accusynge I am condempned. Of the nombre of whiche accusours, oon Basilius, that whilom was chased out of the kyngis servyse, is now compelled in accusynge of my name for nede of foreyne moneye. Also Opilion and Gaudencius han accused me, al be it so that the justise regal hadde whilom demed hem bothe to gon in-to exil for hir trecheries and frawdes withouten nombre, [130] to whiche juggement they nolden nat obeye, but defendeden hem by the sikernesse of holi houses (that is to seyn, fledden into seynte warie) ; and whan this was aperceyved to the kyng, he comandide that, but they voydide the cite of Ravenne by certeyn day assigned, that men scholde marken hem in the forheved with an hoot iren and chasen hem out of towne. Now what thyng semyth myghte ben likned to this cruelte? For certes thilke same day was resceyved the accusynge of myn name by thilke same accusours. What may ben seyd her-to? Hath my studie and my kunnynge disserved thus? Or elles the forseyde dampnacioun of me —made that hem ryghtfulle accusours or no? Was noght fortune aschamed of this? [135] Certes, al hadde noght fortune ben aschamed that innocence was accused, yit oughte sche han hadde schame of the fylthe of myn accusours. But axestow in somme of what gylt I am

127. *to hem ward* is due to a mistranslation of 'vers' in 'vers ceus du paliz roial'; Lat. 'apud aulicos.'
129. *for nede*, etc., 'alieni æris necessitate.'
132. C₂ C₁ A₂ Cx. B *of the town.*
133. A₂ A₁ *seemeth the ;* B *seemeth you ; likned* should be 'added,' 'posse adstrui.' Chaucer has understood Fr. 'pareille,' p. part. of 'pareiller' (adstruere), as that of *pareiller*, 'to liken.'

116. C₁ Cx. B C₂ read *tormentyden.*
119, 120 refer to what precedes, 121 to what follows.

accused? Men seyn that I wolde saven the companye of the senatours. And desirestow to heren in what manere? I am accused that I schulde han disturbed the accusour to beren lettres, by whiche he scholde han maked the senatours gylty ayens the kynges real maieste. O Maystresse, what demestow of this? Schal I forsake this blame, that y ne be no schame to the? Certes I have wolde it (that is to seyn the savacioun of the senat), ne schal I nevere letten to wilne it; and that I confesse and am aknowe; but the entente of the accusour to ben distorbed schal cese. [140] For shal I clepe it thanne a felonye or a synne, that I have desired the savacioun of the ordre of the senat? And certes yit hadde thilke same senat don by me thurw hir decretes and hir jugementes as thoughe it were a synne and a felonye (that is to seyn, to wilne the savacioun of hem). But folye, that lyeth alwey to hym-selve, may noght chaunge the merite of thynges, ne I trowe nat by the jugement of Socrates, that it were leveful to me to hide the sothe, ne assente to lesynges. But certes, how so evere it be of this, I putte it to gessen or prisen to the jugement of the and of wys folk. Of whiche thyng all the ordenaunce and the sothe, for as moche as folk that been to comen aftir our dayes schullen knowen it, I have put it in scripture and in remembraunce. [145] For touchynge the lettres falsly maked by whiche lettres I am accused to han hoped the fredom of Rome, what aperteneth me to speken ther-of? Of whiche lettres the fraude hadde ben schewed apertely, yif I hadde had liberte for to han used and ben at the confessioun of myn accusours, the whiche thyng in alle nedes hath greet strengthe. For what other fredom mai men hopen? Certes I wolde that som other fredom myghte ben hoped; I wolde thanne han answeryd

by the wordys of a man that hyghte Canyus. For whan he was accused by-fore Gaius Cesar, Germaynes sone, that he was knowynge and consentynge of a coniuracioun ymaked ayens hym, this Canyus answeride thus: "Yif I hadde wyst it, thou haddest noght wyst it." In whiche thyng sorwe hath noght so dullid my wyt, that I pleyne oonly that schrewed folk apparailen felonyes ayens vertu; but I wondre gretly how that thei may performe thynges that thei han hoped for to doon. [150] For-why to wylne schrewydnesse—that cometh per-aventure of our defaute; but it is lyk a monstre and a merveyle, how that, in the presente sight of god, may ben acheved and performed swiche thynges as every felonous man hath conceyved in his thoght ayens innocentes. For whiche thynge oon of thy familiers noght unskil-fully axed thus: "Yif god is, whennes comen wikkide thyngis? And yif god ne is, whennes comen gode thynges?" But al hadde it ben leveful that felonous folk, that now desiren the blood and the deeth of alle gode men and ek of al the senat, han wilned to gon destroyen me, whom they han seyn alwey bataylen and defenden gode men and eek al the senat, yit hadde I nought disservyd of the faderes (that is to seyn, of the senatours) that they schulden wilne my destruccioun. Thow remembrest wel, as I gesse, that whan I wolde doon or seyn any thyng, thow thi-selve alwey present reuledest me. [155] Atte cite of Verone, whan that the kyng, gredy of comune slaughtre, caste hym to transporten up-on al the ordre of the senat the gilt of his real maieste, of whiche gilt that Albyn was accused, with how gret sykernesse of peril to me defended I al the senat! Thow woost wel that I sey sooth, ne I ne avawntede me nevere in preysynge of my-selve. For alwey whan any wyght

140. *and that I confesse*, etc., should be *Shal I confesse?* 'Fatebimur?'
147. *in alle nedes*, 'omnibus negotiis,' 'en toutez besoingnes.' Chaucer read 'besoignes' (besognes) as *besoings* (besoins).

153. *to gon destroyen*, 'perditum ire,' 'aler destruire.'
156. *the gilt*, etc., 'maiestatis crimen,' 'le blasme de la royal maieste.'

resceyveth precious renoun in avauntynge hym-selve of his werkes, he amenuseth the secre of his conscience. But now thow mayst wel seen to what eende I am comen for myn innocence ; I resceyve peyne of fals felonye for guerdoun of verrai vertue. And what opene confessioun of felonye hadde evere juges so accordaunt in cruelte (that is to seyn, as myn accusynge hath) that either errour of mannys wit, or elles condicion of fortune, that is uncerteyn to alle mortel folk, ne submyttede some of hem (that is to seyn, that it ne enclynede some juge to have pite or compassioun)? [160] For al-thoughe I hadde ben accused that I wolde brenne holi houses and straungle preestis with wykkid sweerd, or that I hadde greythed deth to alle gode men, algates the sentence scholde han punysshed me present, confessed or convict. But now I am remuwed fro the cite of Rome almost fyve hundred thowsand paas, I am withoute deffense dampnyd to proscripcion and to the deth for the studie and bountes that I have doon to the senat. But O wel ben thei wurthy of meryte ! (As who seith, nay.) Ther myghte nevere yit noon of hem ben convicte of swiche a blame as myn is. Of whiche trespas myne accusours sayen ful wel the dignete ; the whiche dygnyte, for thei wolden derken it with medlynge of some felonye, they bare me on hande and lieden that I hadde pollut and defouled my conscience with sacrilegie for covetise of dignyte. And certes thou thi-selve, that art plaunted in me, chacedest out of the sege of my corage alle covetise of mortel thynges, ne sacrilege hadde no leve to han a place in me byforn thyne eien. [165] For thow droppiddest every day in myn eris and in my thought thilke comaundement of Pittagoras, that is to seyn men schal serven to god, and noght to goddes.

Ne it was noght convenient ne no nede to taken help of the fouleste spirites—I, that thow hast ordeyned and set in swiche excellence, that thou makedest me lyk to god. And over this, the right clene secre chaumbre of myn hous (that is to seyn my wif), and the companye of myne honeste freendes, and my wyves fadir, as wel holi as worthy to ben reverenced thurw his owene dedes, defenden me fro alle suspecioun of swiche blame. But O malice ! For they that accusen me taken of the, philosophie, feith of so greet blame, for they trowen that I have had affinyte to malefice or enchauntement, bycause that I am replenysshid and fulfild with thy techynges, and enformed of thi maneris. And thus it suffiseth nat oonly that thi reverence ne avayle me nat, but that thow of thy free wil rather be blemessched with myne offencioun. [170] But certes to the harmes that I have ther bytideth yit this encrees of harm, that the gessynge and the jugement of moche folk loken no thyng to the desertes of thynges, but oonly to the aventure of fortune ; and jugen that oonly swiche thynges ben purveied of god, whiche that temporel welefulnesse commendeth. (Glose. As thus : that yif a wyght have prosperite, he is a good man and worthy to han that prosperite ; and who-so hath adversite, he is a wikkid man, and god hath forsake hym, and he is worthy to han that adversite. This is the opinyoun of some folk.) Textus. And ther-of cometh that good gessynge, first of alle thynge, forsaketh wrecches. Certes it greveth me to thynke ryght now the diverse sentences that the peple seith of me. [175] And thus moche I seie, that the laste charge of contrarious fortune is this :

167. For *was* C₁ A₂ H B read *is ;* C₂ omits.
168. *the right clene*, etc., ' penetral innocens domus,' *i.e.* ' my unblemished private life.' Chaucer translates a gloss, ' uxor.'
170. *of thy free wil*, ' ultro,' *i.e.* ' for thy part ' ; but Fr. ' de ton gre.'
171. *bytideth.* Chaucer has read ' accedit ' as ' accidit.'

157. *the secre*, etc., ' se probantis conscientiæ secretum (*sc.* pretium).' The same mistake occurs in Fr.
164. For *lieden* H Cx. read *seyden,* B *seyden* corrected in same hand from *leyden.*

that whan that eny blame is leid upon a caytif, men wenen that he hath desservyd that he suffreth. And I, that am put a-wey fro gode men, and despoyled of dignytes, and defouled of myn name by gessynge, have suffride torment for my gode dedes. Certes me semyth that I se the felonous covynes of wykkid men habounden in joye and in gladnesse ; and I se that every lorel schapeth hym to fynde out newe fraudes for to accuse good folk ; and I se that goode men ben overthrowen for drede of my peril, and every luxurious turmentour dar doon alle felonye unpunysschyd, and ben excited ther-to by yiftes ; and innocentes ne ben noght oonly despoiled of sikernesse, but of defence ; and ther-fore me lyst to crie to god in this manere : ' [180]

' *O stelliferi conditor orbis.*'—Metrum 5

' O thow makere of the wheel that bereth the sterres, whiche that art festnyd to thi perdurable chayer, and turnest the hevene with a ravysschynge sweighe, and constreynest the sterres to suffren thi lawe ; so that the moone som-tyme, schynynge with hir fulle hornes metynge with alle the beemes of the sonne hir brothir, hideth the sterres that ben lasse, and som-tyme, whan the moone pale with hir derke hornes aprocheth the sonne, leeseth hir lyghtes ; and that the eve sterre, Hesperus, whiche that in the first tyme of the nyght bryngeth forth hir colde arysynges, cometh eft ayen hir used cours, and is pale by the morwe at rysynge of the sonne, and is thanne clepid Lucyfer ! Thow re-streynest the day by schortere duellynge in the tyme of coold wynter, that maketh the leeves falle. Thow devydest the swyfte tydes of the nyght, whan the

hote somer is comen. [185] Thy myghte attempreth the variauntes sesouns of the yer, so that Zephirus, the debonere wynd, bryngeth ayen in the first somer sesoun the leeves that the wynd that hyghte Boreas hath reft awey in autumpne (that is to seie, the laste ende of somer) ; and the seedes that the sterre that highte Aucturus saugh, ben waxen heye cornes whan the sterre Syrius eschaufeth hem. Ther nys no thyng unbounde from his olde lawe, ne for-leteth the werk of his propre estat. O governour, governynge alle thynges by certein ende, whi refusestow oonly to governe the werkes of men by duwe manere ? Why suffrestow that slydynge fortune turneth so grete enterchaungynges of thynges ; so that anoyous peyne, that scholde duweliche punysche felons, punysscheth innocentes ? [190] And folk of wikkide maneres sitten in heie chayeres ; and anoyinge folk treden, and that unrightfully, on the nekkes of holi men ; and vertue, cleer and schynynge naturely, is hidde in derke derknesses ; and the rightful man bereth the blame and the peyne of the feloun ; ne the for-swerynge, ne the fraude covered and kembd with a false colour, ne anoieth nat to schrewes ? The whiche schrewes, whan hem list to usen hir strengthe, they reioyssen hem to putten undir hem the sovereyne kynges, whiche the peple withowten nombre dreden. O thou, what so evere thou be that knyttest alle boondes of thynges, loke on thise wrecchide erthes. We men, that ben noght a foul partie, but a fair partie of so greet a werk, we ben turmented in this see of fortune. Thow governour withdraughe and restreyne the ravysschynge flodes, and fastne and ferme ¦ thise erthes stable with thilke boond by whiche thou governest the hevene that is so large.' [195]

181. *wheel*, etc., ' stelliferi orbis,' ' la roe qui porte les estoiles.'
181. *festnyd*, ' nexus' variant of Lat. text for *nixus*.
183. *cometh eft*, etc., *i.e.* returns in the op-posite direction.

186. C₂ A₂ H B *in the laste ende.*
187. For *saugh*, ' vidit,' Hn. reads *sewgh*, Cx. *sewe*, B *sowyn.*
189. *slydynge fortune*, ' lubrica fortuna.'

' Hec ubi continuato dolore delatraui.'—

Prosa 5

Whan I hadde, with a contynuel sorwe, sobbyd or borken out thise thynges, sche, with hir cheere pesible and no thyng amoeved with my compleyntes, seide thus : 'Whan I saugh the,' quod sche, 'sorwful and wepynge, I wiste anoon that thow were a wrecche and exiled ; but I wyste nevere how fer thyn exil was yif thy tale ne hadde schewid it me. But certes, al be thow fer fro thy cuntre, thou nart nat put out of it, but thow hast fayled of thi weye and gon a-mys. And yif thou hast levere for to wene that thow be put out of thy cuntre, thanne hastow put out thy-selve rather than ony other wyght hath. For no wyght but thy-selve myghte nevere han doon that to the. [200] For yif thow remembre of what cuntre thow art born, it nys nat governed by emperoures, ne by gouvernement of multitude, as weren the cuntrees of hem of Atthenes ; but o lord and o kyng, and that is god, is lord of thi cuntre, whiche that reioisseth hym of the duellynge of his citezeens, and nat for to putten hem in exil ; of the whiche lord it is a sovereyn fredom to ben governed by the brydel of hym and obeye to his justice. Hastow foryeten thilke ryghte oolde lawe of thi citee, in the whiche cite it is ordeyned and establysschid, that what wyght that hath levere founden ther-in his sete or his hous than elles where, he may nat ben exiled by no ryght fro that place ? For who-so that is contened in-with the palays and the clos of thilke cite, ther nys no drede that he mai deserve to ben exiled ; but who that leteth the wil for to enhabyten there, he for-leteth also to deserve to ben citezen of thilke cite. [205] So that

I seie that the face of this place ne moeveth me noght as mochel as thyn owene face, ne I ne axe nat rather the walles of thy librarye, apparayled and wrought with yvory and with glas, than after the sete of thi thought, in whiche I put noght whilom bookes, but I putte that that maketh bokes wurthy of prys or precyous, that is to seyn the sentence of my bookes.

And certeynly of thy dessertes bystowed in comune good thow hast seyd soth, but after the multitude of thy gode dedes thou hast seyd fewe. And of the honestete or of the falsnesse of thynges that ben opposed ayens the, thow hast remembred thynges that ben knowen to alle folk. And of the felonyes and fraudes of thyn accusours, it semeth the have touched it for sothe ryghtfully and schortly, al myghten tho same thynges betere and more plentevously ben couth in the mouth of the peple that knoweth all this. [210] Thow hast eek blamed gretly and compleyned of the wrongful dede of the senat, and thow hast sorwyd for my blame, and thow hast wepen for the damage of thi renoun that is apayred ; and thi laste sorwe eschaufede ayens fortune and compleyndest that guerdouns ne ben nat eveneliche yolden to the dessertes of folk. And in the lattre eende of thy wode muse, thow preydest that thilke pees that governeth the hevene schulde governe the erthe.

But for that many tribulacions of affeccions han assailed the, and sorwe and ire and wepynge to-drawen the diversely, as thou art now feble of thought, myghtyere remedies ne schullen noght yit touchen the. For wyche we wol usen somdel lyghtere medicynes, so that thilke passiouns that ben waxen hard in swellynge by perturbacions flowynge in to thy thought, mowen waxen esy and softe to resceyven the

196. *borken*, 'delatravi'; A₁ A₂ H Cx. read *broken*; B *spoken.*

201. *emperoures* is due to the Fr. trans. of 'imperio,' 'par empire ne par commandement.'

202. MSS. *that is lord* (B *he is lord*).

204. C₁ A₂ H Cx. A₁ Hn. omit *and the clos.*

208. *dessertes*, etc., 'de tuis in commune bonum meritis.'

212. *compleyndest*, subject omitted as often ; cp. 49, '*bereth.*'

strengthe of a more myghty and more egre medicyne, by an esyere touchynge. [215]

' Cum Phebi radiis grave Cancri sidus inestuat.'—Metrum 6

Whan that the hevy sterre of the Cancre eschaufeth by the bemes of Phebus (that is to seyn, whan that Phebus the sonne is in the sygne of the Cancre), who-so yeveth thanne largely his seedes to the feeldes that refusen to resceyven hem, lat hym gon, be-giled of trust that he hadde to his corn, to accornes of okes. Yif thow wolt gadere vyolletes, ne go thow nat to the purpre wode whan the feeld, chirkynge, agryseth of cold by the felnesse of the wind that hyghte Aquilon. Yif thou desirest or wolt usen grapes, ne seek thou nat with a glotonous hand to streyne and presse the stalkes of the vyne in the first somer sesoun ; for Bachus, the god of wyn, hath rather yyven his yiftes to autumpne (the lattere ende of somer). God tokneth and assigneth the tymes, ablynge hem to hir propre office, ne he ne suffreth nat the stowndes whiche that hym-self hath devyded and constreyned to ben I-medled to-gidre. [220] And for-thy he that forleteth certein ordenaunce of doynge by overthrowynge wey, he hath no glad issue or ende of his werkes.

' Primum igitur paterisne me pauculis rogacionibus.'—Prosa 6

First wiltow suffre me to touche and assaye the staat of thi thought by a fewe demaundes, so that I may understande what be the manere of thi curacioun ? '

'Axe me,' quod I, 'at thi wille what thou wolt, and I schal answere.' Tho seyde sche thus : 'Whethir wenestow,' quod sche, 'that this world be governed by foolyssche happes and fortunows, or elles wenestow that ther be inne it ony gouvernement of resoun ? '

'Certes,' quod I, 'I ne trowe nat in no manere that so certeyn thynges schulden be moeved by fortunows [folie] ; [225] but I woot wel that god, makere and maister, is governour of his werk, ne nevere nas yit day that myghte putte me out of the sothnesse of that sentence.'

'So it is,' quod sche, 'for the same thyng songe thow a litil here by-forn, and by-wayledest and by-weptest, that oonly men weren put out of the cure of god ; for of alle othere thynges thou ne doutedest the nat that they nere governed by resoun. But owgh I wondre gretly, certes, whi that thou art sik, syn that thow art put in so holsome a sentence : but lat us seken deppere ; I coniecte that ther lakketh y not what. But sey me this : syn that thow ne doutest noght that this world be governed by god, with whiche governayles takestow heede that it is governed ? '

'Unnethes,' quod I, 'knowe I the sentence of thy questioun, so that I ne may nat yit answeren to thy demandes.' [230]

'I nas nat desseyved,' quod sche, 'that ther ne faileth som-what, by whiche the maladye of perturbacion is crept in to thi thought, so as [thorw] the strengthe of the palys chynynge [and] open. But sey me this : remembrestow what is the ende of thynges, and whider that the entencion of alle kende tendeth ?'

'I have herd tolde it som-tyme,' quod I, 'but drerynesse hath dulled my memorie.'

'Certes,' quod sche, 'thou wost wel whennes that alle thynges bien comen and proceded ? '

'I woot wel,' quod I, and answerede that god is bygynnynge of al. [235]

225. Instead of *folie* all MSS. read *fortune*. But Lat. 'fortuita temeritate' and Fr. 'fortunele folie' point to *folie* as the word Chaucer used.

228. *owgh*, 'papae.'

229. *y not what*, 'nescio quid'; L. 'ie ne sce quoi.'

231. *so as*, etc., 'velut hianti valli robore'; the MSS. omit *thorw* and read *is open* instead of *and open*. The correction, justified by the Lat. and Fr. versions, is necessary to the sense.

216. *hevy sterre*, ' grave Cancri sidus.'

221. *by overthrowynge wey*, 'præcipiti via.'

'And how may this be,' quod sche, 'that, syn thow knowest the bygynnynge of thynges, that thow ne knowest nat what is the eende of thynges? But swiche ben the customes of perturbaciouns, and this power they han, that they mai moeve a man from his place (that is to seyn, fro the stabelnesse and perfeccion of his knowynge); but certes, thei mai nat al arrace hym, ne aliene hym in al. But I wolde that thou woldest answere to this : Remembrestow that thow art a man?'

'Whi schulde I nat remembren that?' quod I.

'Maystow noght telle me thanne,' quod sche, 'what thyng is a man?'

'Axestow me nat,' quod I, 'whethir that I be a resonable mortel beste? I woot wel, and I confesse wel that I am it.' [240]

'Wystestow nevere yit that thow were ony othir thyng?' quod sche.

'No,' quod I.

'Now woot I,' quod sche, 'other cause of thi maladye, and that ryght greet : thow hast left for-to knowen thy-selve what thou art. Thurw whiche I have playnly fownde the cause of thi maladye, or elles the entree of recoverynge of thyn hele. For-why, for thow art confunded with foryetynge of thi-self, for-thi sorwestow that thou art exiled fro thy propre goodes; and for thow ne woost what is the eende of thynges, for-thy demestow that felouns and wikkide men ben myghty and weleful; [245] and for thow hast foryeten by whiche governementes the werld is governed, for-thy weenestow that thise mutacions of fortunes fleten withouten governour. Thise ben grete causes, noght oonly to maladye, but certes gret causes to deth. But I thanke the auctour and the makere of hele, that nature hath nat al forleten the.

I have gret noryssynge of thy hele, and that is, the sothe sentence of governance of the world, that thou by-levest that the governynge of it is nat subgit ne underput to the folye of thise happes aventurous, but to the resoun of god. And ther-fore doute the nothing, for of this litel spark thine heet of lijf schal shine.

But for as moche as it is nat tyme yet of fastere remedies, and the nature of thoughtes desceyved is this, that, as ofte as they casten awey sothe opynyouns, they clothen hem in false opynyouns, [250] of the whiche false opynyouns the derknesse of perturbacion waxeth up, that confowndeth the verray insyghte— that derknesse schal I assaie som-what to maken thynne and wayk by lyghte and meneliche remedies; so that, aftir that the derknesse of desceyvynge desyrynges is doon away, thow mowe knowe the schynynge of verraye light.

' *Nubibus atris condita.*'—Metrum 7

The sterres, covred with blake cloudes, ne mowen yeten a-doun no lyght. Yif the truble wynd that hyghte Auster, turnynge and wallwynge the see, medleeth the heete (that is to seyn, the boylynge up fro the botme), the wawes, that whilom weren clere as glas and lyk to the fayre bryghte dayes, withstant anon the syghtes of men by the filthe and ordure that is resolved. [255] And the fleetynge streem, that royleth doun diversely fro heye montaygnes, is areestid and resisted ofte tyme by the encountrynge of a stoon that is departed and fallen fro some roche. And for-thy, yif thou wolt loken and demen soth with cleer lyght, and hoolden the weye with a ryght path, weyve thow joie, dryf fro the drede, fleme thow hope, ne lat no sorwe aproche (that is to seyn, lat non of thise passiouns overcomen the or blenden the). For

243. *Thurw whiche*, etc., 'quare plenissime . . . inveni'; Fr. 'par quoy (for *pourquoi*) ie ai plainement (i.e. *pleinement*, mistaken by Chaucer for O.F. *plainement*, ouvertement) trouvee,' etc.

246. *fortunes*, 'fortunarum'; found only in C_1 Cx.; others *fortune*.

248. *noryssynge*, 'fomentum'; found only in Cx.; B *trust*; others *noryssynges*.

251. Before *that derknesse* all MSS. insert *and*.

257. C_2 A_1 Hn. *thise foure passiouns*.

cloudy and derk is thilke thoght, and bownde with bridelis, where as thise thynges reignen.'

EXPLICIT LIBER PRIMUS

INCIPIT LIBER SECUNDUS

' *Postea paulisper conticuit.*'—Prosa 1

After this sche stynte a lytel ; and after that sche hadde gadrede by atempre stillenesse myn attencioun (as who so myghte seyn thus : after thise thynges sche stynte a litil, and whan sche aperceyved by atempre stillenesse that I was ententyf to herkne hire), sche bygan to speke on this wyse : ' If I,' quod sche, ' have undirstonden and knowen outrely the causes and the habyt of thy maladye, thow languyssest and art deffeted for desir and talent of thi rather fortune. [260] Sche (that ilke Fortune) oonly, that is chaunged, as thow feynest, to the ward, hath perverted the cleernesse and the estat of thi corage. I understonde the fele folde colours and desceytes of thilke merveylous monstre (Fortune) and how sche useth ful flaterynge famylarite with hem that sche enforceth to bygyle, so longe, til that sche confounde with unsuffrable sorwe hem that sche hath left in despeir unpurveied. And yif thou remembrest wel the kynde, the maneris, and the desserte of thilke fortune, thou shalt wel knowe that, as in hir, thow nevere ne haddest ne hast ylost any fair thyng. But, as I trowe, I schal nat greetly travailen to don the remembren on thise thynges. [265] For thow were wont to hurtlen hir with manly woordes whan sche was blaundyssching and present, and pursuydest hir with sentences that weren drawen out of myn entre (that is to seyn, of myn enformacion).

264. *as in hir, i.e.* as far as she is concerned.
266. C₂ Hn. Cx. *hurtelyn and despysen;* Lat. 'incessere'; Fr. 'assaillir.'
267. *entre*, cp. Aq., 'aditu id est de nostra informatione.' The received text has simply *adyto*.

But no sodeyn mutacioun ne bytideth noght with-outen a manere chaungynge of corages ; and so is it by-fallen that thou art a litil departed fro the pees of thi thought.

But now is tyme that thou drynke and a-taste some softe and delitable thynges, so that whanne thei ben entred with-ynne the, it mowen maken wey to strengere drynkes of medycines. Com now forth, therfore, the suasyoun of swetnesse rethorien, whiche that goht oonly the righte wey while sche forsaketh nat myn estatutes. And with Rethorice com forth Musice, a damoysele of our hous, that syngeth now lightere moedes or prolacions, now hevyere. [270] What eyleth the, man ? What is it that hath cast the in-to moornynge and in-to wepynge ? I trow that thou hast seyn some newe thyng and unkouth. Thou wenest that fortune be chaunged ayens the ; but thow wenest wrong, yif thou that wene : alway tho ben hir maneres. Sche hath rather kept, as to the ward, hir propre stablenesse in the chaungynge of hir-self. Ryght swiche was sche whan sche flateryd the and desseyved the with unleful lykynges of false weleful-nesse. Thou hast now knowen and ateynt the doutous or double visage of thilke blynde goddesse (Fortune). [275] Sche, that yit covereth and wympleth hir to other folk, hath schewyd hir every del to the. Yif thou approvest here and thynkest that sche is good, use hir maneris and pleyne the nat ; and yif thou agrisest hir false trecherie, despise and cast awey hir that pleyeth so harmfully. For sche, that is now cause of so mochel sorwe to the, scholde ben cause to the of pees and of joye. Sche hath forsaken the, forsothe, the whiche that nevere man mai ben siker that sche ne schal forsaken hym. (Glose. But natheles some bookes han the texte thus : for-

270. *moedes or prolacions,* ' modos '; but probably due to some gloss.
277. *use hir maneris,* ' utere moribus.'
280. *some bookes, i.e.* the French text.

sothe sche hath forsaken the, ne ther nys no man siker that sche hath nat forsake.) [280] Holdestow thanne thilke weleful-nesse precious to the, that schal passen? And is present Fortune dere-worth to the, whiche that nys nat feithful for to duelle, and whan sche goth awey that sche bryngeth a wyght in sorwe? For syn sche may nat ben with-holden at a mannys wille, sche maketh hym a wrecche when sche departeth fro hym. What other thyng is flyttynge Fortune but a maner schewynge of wrecchidnesse that is to comen? Ne it suffiseth nat oonly to loken on thyng that is present byforn the eien of a man; but wisdom loketh and mesur-eth the ende of thynges. And the same chaungynge from oon in-to another (that is to seyn, fro adversite in-to prosperite), maketh that the manaces of Fortune ne ben nat for to dreden, ne the flaterynges of hir to ben desired. Thus, at the laste, it byhoveth the to suffren wyth evene wil in pacience al that is doon in-with the floor of Fortune (that is to seyn, in this world), syn thou hast oonys put thy nekke undir the yok of hir. [285] For yif thow wilt writen a lawe of wend-ynge and of duellynge to Fortune, whiche that thow hast chosen frely to ben thi lady, artow nat wrongful in that, and makest Fortune wroth and aspre by thyn impacience? And yit thow mayst nat chaungen hir. Yif thou committest and be-takest thi seyles to the wynd, thow shalt ben shoven, nat thider that thow woldest, but whider that the wynd shouveth the. Yif thow castest thi seedes in feeldes, thou sholdest han in mynde that the yeres ben amonges outher-while plentevous and outher-while bareyne. Thou hast by-taken thi-self to the governaunce of Fortune and for-thi it byhoveth the to ben obeisaunt to the maneris of thi lady. Enforcestow the to aresten or withholden the swyft-nesse and the sweighe of hir turnynge wheel? O thow fool of alle mortel foolis! Yif Fortune bygan to duelle stable, she cessede thanne to ben Fortune. [290]

'*Hec cum superba.*'—Metrum 1

Whan Fortune with a proud ryght hand hath turned hir chaungynge stowndes, sche fareth lyke the maneres of the boylynge Eurippe. (Glosa. Eurippe is an arm of the see that ebbeth and floweth, and som-tyme the streem is on o side, and som-tyme on the tothir.) Textus. She cruel (Fortune) casteth adoun kynges that whilom weren y-dradd; and sche, desceyvable, enhaunceth up the humble chere of hym that is discounfited. Ne sche neither heereth, ne rekketh of wrecchide wepynges; and she is so hard that sche leygheth and scorneth the wepynges of hem, the whiche sche hath maked wepe with hir free wille. Thus sche pleyeth, and thus sche proeveth hir strengthes, and scheweth a greet wonder to alle hir servauntes yif that a wyght is seyn weleful and overthrowe in an houre. [295]

'*Vellem autem pauca.*'—Prosa 2

Certes I wolde pleten with the a fewe thynges, usynge the woordes of Fortune. Take hede now thy-selve, yif that sche asketh ryght: "O thou man, wherfore makestow me gylty by thyne every dayes pleynynges? What wrong have I don the? What godes have I byreft the that weren thyne? Stryf or pleet with me byforn what juge that thow wolt of the possessioun of rychesses or of dignytees; and yif thou maist schewen me that ever any mortel man hath resceyved ony of tho thynges to ben hise in propre, thanne wil I graunte freely that thilke thynges weren thyne whiche that thow axest.

Whan that nature brought the foorth out of thi modir wombe, I resceyved the nakid and nedy of alle thynges, and I norissched the with my richesses, and was redy and ententyf thurwe my favour

295. *in an houre, i.e.* in one hour.
296. *asketh ryght,* 'ius postulet.'
297. C₁ Cx. A₂ read *gyltyf.*
299. *ever* goes with *any,* 'cuiusquam.'

to sustene the [300]—and that maketh the now inpacient ayens me; and I envyrounde the with al the habundaunce and schynynge of alle goodes that ben in my ryght. Now it liketh me to withdrawe myn hand. Thow hast had grace as he that hath used of foreyne goodes; thow hast no ryght to pleyne the, as though thou haddest outrely forlorn alle thy thynges. Why pleynestow thanne? I have doon the no wrong. Richesses, honours, and swiche othere thinges ben of my right. My servauntes knowen me for hir lady; they comen with me, and departen whan I wende. I dar wel affermen hardely that, yif tho thynges of whiche thow pleynest that thou hast for-lorn [hem] hadden ben thyne, thow ne haddest nat lorn hem. Schal I thanne, oonly, be defended to usen my ryght? Certes it is leueful to the hevene to maken clere dayes, and after that to coveren the same dayes with dirke nyghtes. [305] The yeer hath eek leve to apparaylen the visage of the erthe, now with floures, and now with fruyt, and to confownden hem som-tyme with reynes and with coldes. The see hath eek his ryght to ben som-tyme calm and blaundysschyng with smothe watir, and som-tyme to ben horrible with wawes and with tempestes. But the covetise of men, that mai nat be stawnched,—schal it bynde me to ben stidfast, syn that stidfastnesse is uncouth to my maneris? Swiche is my strengthe, and this pley I pleye continuely. I torne the whirlynge wheel with the turnynge sercle; I am glad to chaungen the loweste to the heyeste, and the heyeste to the loweste. Worth up yif thow wolt, so it be by this lawe, that thow ne holde nat that I do the wrong, though thow descende a-down whan the resoun of my pley axeth it. [310] [Wystestow nat thanne my maneris?] Wystestow nat how Cresus, kyng of Lydyens, of whiche kyng Cirus was ful

sore agast a lytil byforn,—that this rewliche Cresus was caught of Cirus and lad to the fyer to ben brend; but that a rayn descendede down fro hevene that rescowyde hym. And is it out of thy mynde how that Paulus, consul of Rome, whan he had taken the kyng of Percyens, weep pitously for the captivyte of the selve kyng. What other thynge bywaylen the cryinges of tragedyes but oonly the dedes of fortune, that with unwar strook overturneth the realmes of greet nobleye? (Glose. Tragedye is to seyn a dite of a prosperite for a tyme, that endeth in wrecchidnesse.) Textus. [315] Lernedest nat thow in Greek whan thow were yong, that in the entre or in the seler of Juppiter ther ben cowched two tonnes; the toon is ful of good, and the tother is ful of harm. What ryght hastow to pleyne, yif thou hast taken more plentevously of the gode side (that is to seyn of my richesses and prosperites)? And what ek yif y ne be nat al departed fro the? What eek yif my mutabilite yeveth the ryghtful cause of hope to han yit bettere thynges? Natheles dismaye the nat in thi thought; and thow that art put in the comune realme of alle, desire nat to lyven by thyn oonly propre ryght.

'Si quantas rapidis.'—Metrum 2

Though Plente (that is, goddesse of rychesses) hielde a-doun with ful horn, and withdraweth nat hir hand, as many richesses as the see torneth upward sandes whan it is moeved with ravysshynge blastes, [320] or elles as manye rychesses as ther schynen bryghte sterres in hevene on the sterry nyghtes; yit for all that mankynde nolde nat cese to wepe wrecchide pleyntes. And al be it so that god resceyveth gladly hir preiers,

304. *hem*, supplied from Fr. B omits *of*, and for *that thou hast* reads *to have*.
311. *Wystestow*, etc. Supplied from Lat. and Fr.; probably omitted by Adam Scrivener.

313. *kyng of Percyens* (should be *kyng Perses*), 'regis Persi'; but Fr. 'le roy de Perse.'
316. *seler*, possibly a mistake for *selle*, 'limine'; Fr. 'sueil.'
319. *desire nat*, 'desideres vivere'; but cp. variant in Notker, 'ne desideres v.'

and yyveth hem, as fool large, moche gold, and apparayleth coveytous folk with noble or cleer honours; yit semeth hem haven I-geten no thyng, but alwey hir cruel ravyne, devourynge al that they han geten, scheweth othere gapynges (that is to seyn, gapyn and desiren yit after mo rychesses). What brydles myghte withholden to any certeyn ende the disordene covetise of men, whan evere the rather that it fletith in large yiftes, the more ay brenneth in hem the thurst of havynge? Certes he that qwakynge and dredful weneth hym-selven nedy, he ne lyveth never-mo ryche." [325]

'*Hiis igitur si pro se.*'—Prosa 3

Therfore, yif that fortune spake with the for hir-self in this manere, for-sothe thow ne haddest noght what thou myghtest answere. And yif thow hast any thyng wher-with thow mayst right-fully defenden thi compleynte, it be-hoveth the to schewen it, and I wol yyve the space to tellen it.'

'Certeynly,' quod I thanne, 'thise ben faire thynges and enoynted with hony swetnesse of Rethorik and Musike; and oonly whil thei ben herd thei ben delycious, but to wrecches it is a deppere felyng of harm. (This is to seyn, that wrecches felen the harmes that thei suffren more grevously than the remedies or the delices of thise wordes mowen gladen or conforten him.) So that, whanne thise thynges stynten for to soune in eris, the sorwe that is in-set greveth the thought.' [330]

'Right so it is,' quod sche. 'For thise ben yit none remedies of thy maladye, but they ben a maner norissch-ynges of thi sorwe, yit rebel ayen thi curacioun. For whan that tyme is, I schal moeve and adiust swiche thynges

that percen hem-selve depe. But natheles that thow schalt noght wilne to leten thi-self a wrecche, hastow foryeten the nowmbre and the maner of thi wele-fulnesse? I holde me stille how that the sovereyn men of the city token the in cure and in kepynge, whan thow were orphelyn of fader and of modir, and were chose in affynite of prynces of the cite; and thow by-gonne rather to ben leef and deere than for to been a neyghebour, the whiche thyng is the moste precyous kinde of any propinquyte or alliaunce that mai ben. [335] Who is it that ne seide tho that thow neere right weleful, with so gret a nobleye of thi fadres-in-lawe, and with the chastete of thy wyf, and with the oportunyte and noblesse of thyne masculyn children (that is to seyn, thy sones)? And over al this—me list to passen of comune thynges—how thow haddest in thy youthe dignytees that weren wernd to oolde men. But it deliteth me to comen now to the synguler uphepynge of thi welefulnesse. Yif any fruyt of mortel thynges mai han any weyghte or pris of welefulnesse, myghtestow evere forgeten, for any charge of harm that myghte byfalle, the remembraunce of thilke day that thow seye thi two sones maked conseileris, and I-ladde to-gidre fro thyn hous under so greet assemble of senatours and under the blithnesse of peple; [340] and whan thow saye hem set in the court in hir chayeres of dignytes? Thow, rethorien or pronouncere of kynges preysynges, desservedst glorie of wit and of eloquence when thow, syttynge bytwixen thi two sones conseylers, in the place that highte Circo, fulfildest the abydynge of the multitude of peple that was sprad abouten the with so large preysynge and laude as men syngen in victories. Tho yave

323. *scheweth*, etc., 'pandit i.e. manifestat alios hiatos.'
328. *it is*, *i.e.* there is. C₂ Hn. A₁ A₂ H omit *it*.
332. C₂ Hn. A₁ C₁ omit *and adiust*: B *and* aiuse; Fr. 'aiusterai.'
336. *neere*, C₂ *were*.
336. *fadres-in-lawe*, 'socerorum.'
337. *over al this*, etc., 'Praetereo (libet enim praeterire conmunia) sumptas,' etc., misread as 'Praeterea (libet praeterire,' etc., so that *how* depends on *I holde me stille* in 334.
340. *under*, 'sub frequentia,' etc.
343. MSS. *and fulfildest*.

thow woordes to Fortune, as I trowe, (that is to seyn, tho feddestow fortune with glosynge wordes and desceyvedest hir) whan sche accoyede the and norysside the as hir owne delices. Thow bare awey of Fortune a yifte (that is to seye swich guerdoun) that sche nevere yaf to prive man. [345] Wiltow therfore leye a reknynge with Fortune? Sche hath now twynkled first upon the with a wikkid eye. If thow considere the nowmbre and the maner of thy blisses and of thy sorwes, thou mayst noght forsaken that thow nart yit blisful. For yif thou therfore wenest thi-self nat wele-ful, for thynges that tho semeden joyeful ben passed, ther nys nat why thow sholdest wene thi-self a wrecche; for thynges that semen now sory passen also. Artow now comen first, a sodeyn gest, into the schadowe or tabernacle of this lif? Or trowestow that any stedfastnesse be in mannes thynges, whan ofte a swyft hour dissolveth the same man (that is to seyn, whan the soule departeth fro the body). [350] For al though that selde is ther any feith that fortunes thynges wollen dwellen, yet nathelees the laste day of a mannes lif is a maner deth to fortune, and also to thilke that hath dwelt. And therfore what wenestow thar rekke, yif thow forleete hir in deyinge, or elles that sche (Fortune) forleete the in fleynge awey?

'*Cum primo polo.*'—Metrum 3

Whan Phebus (the sonne) bygynneth to spreden his clernesse with rosene chariettes, thanne the sterre, y-dymmed, paleth hir white cheeres by the flambes of the sonne that overcometh the sterre lyght. (This to seyn, whan the sonne is rysen, the day-sterre waxeth pale, and leeseth hir lyght for the grete bryght-nesse of the sonne.) Whan the wode waxeth rody of rosene floures in the fyrst somer sesoun thurw the breeth of the wynd Zephirus that waxeth warm, yif the cloudy wynd Auster blowe felliche, than goth awey the fairnesse of thornes. [355] Ofte the see is cleer and calm with-out moevynge flodes, and ofte the horrible wynd Aquylon moeveth boylynge tem-pestes, and overwhelveth the see. Yif the forme of this world is so seeld stable, and yif it torneth by so manye entre-chaungynges, wiltow thanne trusten in the tumblynge fortunes of men? Wiltow trowen on flyttynge goodes? It is certeyn and establissched by lawe perdurable, that nothyng that is engendred nys sted-fast ne stable.'

'*Tum ego vera inquam.*'—Prosa 4

Thanne seide I thus: 'O norice of alle vertues, thou seist ful sooth; ne I mai noght forsake the ryght swyfte cours of my prosperite (that is to seyn, that prosperite ne be comen to me wonder swyftli and sone); but this is a thyng that greetly smerteth me whan it remem-breth me. [360] For in alle adversites of fortune the moost unseely kynde of contrarious fortune is to han ben weleful.' 'But that thow,' quod sche, 'abyest thus the torment of thi false opynioun, that maistow nat ryghtfully blamen ne aretten to thynges. (As who seith, for thow hast yit manye habundances of thynges.) Textus. For al be it so that the ydel name of aventurous welefulnesse moeveth the now, it is leveful that thow rekne with me of how many grete thynges thow hast yit plente. And therfore yif that thilke thyng that thow haddest for moost precyous in al thy rychesse of fortune be kept to the yit by the grace of god unwemmed and undefouled, [365] maistow thanne pleyne ryghtfully upon

344. *as hir owne delices*, 'ut suas delicias' (as her darling).
349. *schadowe or tabernacle*, 'in . . . scenam'; Fr. 'en la cortine et en l'ombre.' But 'taber-naculum' and 'umbra' are common mediæval glosses of 'scena.'
352. *thar rekke* (A *thar*, B *ther*, others *dar*. Perhaps read *the* before *thar*, cp. D 329, Boece 1001), *i.e.* What do you think you need care, etc.

364. *grete*, found only in C₂ Hn.

the mescheef of fortune, syn thow hast yit thi beste thynges? Certes yit lyveth in good poynt thilke precyous honour of mankynde, Symacus, thi wyves fader, whiche that is a man maked al of sapience and of vertu, the whiche man thow woldest byen redyly with the pris of thyn owene lif. He bywayleth the wronges that men don to the, and nat for hym-self; for he lyveth in sikernesse of anye sentences put ayens hym. And yit lyveth thi wyf, that is a-tempre of wyt and passynge othere wommen in clennesse of chastete; and, for I wol closen schortly hir bountes, sche is lyk to hir fadir. I telle the wel that sche lyveth, loth of this lyf, and kepeth to the oonly hir goost, and is al maat and overcomen by wepynge and sorwe for desir of the; [370] in the whiche thyng oonly I moot graunten that thi welefulnesse is amenused. What schal I seyn eek of thi two sones con-seylours, of whiche, as of children of hir age, ther shyneth the liknesse of the wit of hir fadir or of hir eldefader ! And syn the sovereyne cure of al mortel folk is to saven hir owene lyves, O how weleful artow, if thow knowe thy goodes ! For yit ben ther thynges dwelled to the ward that no man douteth that they ne be more derworthe to the than thyn owene lif. And for-thy drye thi teeris, for yit nys nat every fortune al hateful to the ward, ne over greet tempest hath nat fallen upon the, [375] whan that thyne ancres clyven faste, that neither wolen suffren the counfort of this tyme present ne the hope of tyme comyng to passen ne to faylen.'

'And I preie,' quod I, 'that faste mote thei halden; for, whiles that thei halden, how so ever that thynges been, I shal wel fleetyn forth and escapyn; but thou mayst wel seen how grete apparailes and array that me lakketh, that ben passed awey fro me.'

'I have somwhat avaunced and for

thred the,' quod sche, 'yif that thow anoye nat, ne forthynke nat of al thy fortune. (As who seith, I have som-what comforted the, so that thou tempeste the nat thus with al thy fortune, syn thow hast yit thy beste thynges.) [380] But I mai nat suffren thi delices, that pleyn-est so wepynge and angwysschous for that ther lakketh som-what to thy wele-fulnesse. For what man is so sad or of so parfite welefulnesse, that he ne stryveth or pleyneth on some halfe ayen the qualite of his estat? For-why ful anguysschous thing is the condicioun of mannes goodes; for eyther it cometh nat altogidre to a wyght, or elles it ne last nat perpetuel. For som man hath gret rychesse, but he is aschamed of his ungentil lynage; and som man is renomyd of noblesse of kyn-rede, but he is enclosed in so greet angwyssche of nede of thynges that hym were levere that he were unknowe; and som man haboundeth bothe in rychesse and noblesse, but yit he bewayleth his chaste lyf, for he ne hath no wyf; [385] and som man is wel and selyly y-maried, but he hath no children, and norissheth his rychesses to the eyres of straunge folk; and som man is gladed with children, but he wepeth ful sory for the trespas of his sone or of his doughter. And for this ther ne accordeth no wyght lyghtly to the condicioun of his fortune; for alwey to every man ther is in som-what that, unassayed, he woot nat, or elles he dredeth that he hath assaied. And adde this also, that every weleful man hath a ful delicaat feelynge; so that, but yif alle thynges byfalle at his owene wil, for he [is] inpacient or is nat used to have noon adversite, anoon he is throwen adoun for every litil thyng. [390] And ful litel thynges ben tho that withdrawen the somme or the perfeccioun

---

372. *of whiche, i.e.* in whom, ' es quiex.'
373. *ben dwelled*, have remained ; A₁ *ben dwellyng.*

381. *delices*, ' delicias tuas,' effeminacy ; cp. 344.
384. *angwyssche of nede*, etc., 'angustia rei familiaris'; Fr. 'angoisse de povrete.'
389. *ther is in* (B *ther is in hym*, A *ther is inmest*), *i.e.* something is therein that, etc.
390. *is inpacient*, ' is ' is found only in Cx. A₂.

of blisfulnesse fro hem that been most fortunat. How manye men trowestow wolde demen hemself to ben almoste in hevene, yif thei myghten atayne to the leste partye of the remenaunt of thi fortune? This same place that thow clepest exil is contre to hem that enhabiten here, and forthi no-thyng wrecchide but whan thou wenest it. (As who seith, thow thi-self, ne no wyght ellis, nis a wrecche but whanne he weneth hym self a wrech by reputacion of his corage.) And ayenward, alle fortune is blisful to a man by the aggreablete or by the egalyte of hym that suffreth it. [395] What man is that that is so weleful that nolde chaunge his estat whan he hath lost pacience? The swetnesse of mannes welefulnesse is spraynd with many bitternesses; the whiche welefulnesse although it seme swete and joieful to hym that useth it, yit mai it nat ben withholden that it ne goth away whan it wole. Thanne is it wele seene how wrecchid is the blisfulnesse of mortel thynges, that neyther it dureth perpetuel with hem that every fortune resceyven agreablely or egaly, ne it deliteth nat in al to hem that ben angwyssous.

O ye mortel folk, what seeke ye thanne blisfulnesse out of your-self whiche that is put in your-self? Errour and folie confoundeth yow. I schal schewe the shortly the poynt of soverayn blisfulnesse. Is there any thyng more precyous to the than thi-self? [400] Thow wolt answere, "nay." Thanne, yif it so be that thow art myghty over thyself (that is to seyn, by tranquillite of thi soule), than hastow thyng in thi powere that thow noldest nevere leesen, ne fortune may nat bynymen it the. And that thow mayst knowe that blisfulnesse ne mai nat standen in thynges that ben fortunous and temporel, now undirstond and gadere it togidre thus : yif blisfulnesse be the soverayn

good of nature that lyveth by resoun, ne thilke thyng nys nat soverayn good that may ben taken awey in any wise (for more worthy thyng and more dygne is thilke thyng that mai nat ben take awey) ; than scheweth it wel that the unstablenesse of fortune may nat atayne to receyven verray blisfulnesse. [405] And yit more over, what man that this towmblynge welefulnesse ledeth, eyther he woot that it is chaungeable, or eller he woot it nat. And yif he woot it nat, what blisful fortune may ther ben in the blyndnesse of ignoraunce? And yif he woot that it is chaungeable, he mot alwey ben adrad that he ne lese that thyng that he ne douteth nat but that he may leseen it (as who seith he mot bien alwey agast lest he lese that he woot wel he may lese it) ; for whiche the contynuel drede that he hath, ne suffreth hym nat to ben weleful, or elles yif he lese it, he weneth to ben despised and forleten. Certes eek that is a ful litel good that is born with evene herte whan it is lost (that is to seyn that men do no more force of the lost than of the havynge). [410] And for as moche as thow thi-self art he to whom it hath be schewed and proved by ful many demonstracyons, as I woot wele, that the soules of men ne mowen nat deyen in no wyse ; and ek syn it is cleer and certeyne that fortunous welefulnesse endeth by the deth of the body; it mai nat be douted that, yif that deth may take awey blisfulnesse, that al the kynde of mortel thynges ne descendeth into wrecchidnesse by the ende of the deth. And syn we knowe wel that many a man hath sought the fruyt of blysfulnesse, nat oonly with suffrynge of deeth, but eek with suffrynge of peynes and tormentes, how myghte thanne this present lif make men blisful, syn that whanne thilke selve lif is ended it ne maketh folk no wrechches? [415]

393. *and forthi*, etc., should be *and forthi nothyng is wrecched*, etc. But some Latin texts read 'nihil miserum' for 'nihil est miserum.'

395. *by the aggreablete*, etc., according to the equanimity with which one takes it.

406. *ledeth*, 'vehit.'

410. *lost, i.e.* loss.

413. *al the kynde*, etc., mistranslation of 'omne mortalium genus.'

' *Quisquis volet perhennem caulus.*'—
Metrum 4

What maner man stable and war, that
wol fownden hym a perdurable seete,
and ne wol noght ben cast doun with the
lowde blastes of the wynd Eurus, and wole
despice the see manasynge with flodes ;
lat hym eschuwen to bilde on the cop of
the mountaigne, or in the moyste sandes ;
for the felle wynd Auster tormenteth the
cop of the mountaigne with alle hise
strengthes, and the lause sandes refusen
to beren the hevy weyghte. And for-thi,
yif thou wolt fleen the perilous aventure
(that is to seyn, of the werld) have mynde
certeynly to fycchen thin hous of a myrie
site in a low stoon. For al-though the
wynd troublynge the see thondre with
overthrowynges, thou, that art put in
quiete and weleful by strengthe of thi
palays, schalt leden a cler age, scornynge
the woodnesses and the ires of the
eyr. [420]

' *Set cum racionum iam in te.*' ‑‑
Prosa 5

But for as mochel as the norisschynges
of my resouns descenden now into the, I
trowe it were tyme to usen a litel strengere
medicynes. Now undirstand heere ; al
were it so that the yiftes of fortune ne
were noght brutel ne transitorie, what is
ther in hem that mai be thyn in any tyme,
or elles that it nys fowl, yif that it be
considered and lookyd perfitely ? Richesses ben they preciouse by the nature of
hem-self, or elles by the nature of the ?
What is most worth of rychesses ? Is it
nat gold or myght of moneye assembled ?
Certes thilke gold and thilke moneye
schyneth and yeveth bettre renoun to
hem that dispenden it than to thilke folk

that mokeren it ; for avaryce maketh
alwey mokereres to ben hated, and
largesse maketh folk cleer of renoun.
[425] For, syn that swiche thyng as is
transferred fro o man to an othir ne may
nat duellen with no man, certes thanne
is thilke moneye precyous whan it is
translated into other folk and stynteth
to ben had by usage of large yyvynge of
hym 'that hath yeven it. And also yif al
the moneye that is over-al in the world
were gadryd to-ward o man, it scholde
make alle othere men to be nedy as of
that. And certes a voys al hool (that is
to seyn with-outen amenusynge) fulfilleth
to-gydre the herynge of moche folk.
But certes your rychesses ne mowen
noght passen unto moche folk withouten
amenusynge ; and whan they ben apassed,
nedes they maken hem pore that forgoon
tho rychesses. O streyte and nedy clepe
I this richesse, syn that many folk mai
nat han it al, ne al mai nat comen to o
man without pouert of alle othere folke.
[430] And the schynynge of gemmes, that
I clepe precyous stones, draweth it nat
the eighen of folk to hem-ward (that is to
seyn for the beautes) ? But certes, yif
ther were beaute or bountee in the
schynynge of stones, thilke clernesse is
of the stones hem-selve, and nat of men ;
for whiche I wondre gretly that men
merveylen on swiche thynges. For-whi
what thynge is it that, yif it wanteth
moevynge and joynture of soule and
body, that by right myghte semen a fair
creature to hym that hath a soule of
resoun ? For al be it so that gemmes
drawen to hem-self a litel of the laste
beaute of the world thurw the entente of
hir creatour and thurw the distinccioun of
hem-self, yit, for as mochel as thei ben
put under your excellence, thei ne han
nat desserved by no way that ye schulde
merveylen on hem. [435] And the beaute
of feeldes, deliteth it nat mochel unto you ?'

---

419. *of a myrie site* (C₁ H B *cite*, A₂ *cytee*, Hn.
Cx. *sele*) should follow *aventure*, 'sortem sedis
amœnæ.'
420. *a cler age*, 'duces serenus ævum,' misread as ' duces serenum ævum.'
422. *Now undirstand heere*, mistranslation of
' Or entens ici' (Lat. 'age').

428. *a voys*, etc., 'vox quidem tota pariter
multorum replet auditum.'
434. Chaucer means *moevynge of soule and
joynture of body*. '*a fair creature*,' etc., should be
fair to a creature that hath a soule and resoun.

Boece. 'Why schulde it nat deliten us, syn that it is a ryght fayr porcioun of the ryght fair werk (that is to seyn, of this worlde)? And right so ben we gladed som-tyme of the face of the see whan it is cleer; and also merveylen we on the hevene, and on the sterres, and on the sonne, and on the moone.'

Philosophie. 'Aperteneth,' quod sche, 'any of thilke thynges to the? Why darstow glorifye the in the shynynge of any swiche thynges? Artow distyng-wed and embelysed by the spryngynge floures of the first somer sesoun, or swelleth thi plente in fruites of somer? Whi artow ravyssched with idel joies? Why enbracest thow straunge goodes as they weren thyne? [440] Fortune schal nevere maken that swiche thynges ben thyne that nature of thynges hath maked foreyne fro the. Soth is that, withouten doute, the fruites of the erthe owen to be to the noryssynge of beestis; and yif thow wilt fulfille thyn nede after that it suffiseth to nature, thanne is it no nede that thow seke aftir the superfluyte of fortune. For with ful fewe thynges and with ful litel thynges nature halt hir apayed; and yif thow wolt a-choken the fulfillynge of nature with superfluytees, certes thilke thynges that thow wolt thresten or powren in-to nature schulle ben unjoyeful to the, or elles anoyous. Wenestow eek that it be a fair thyng to schyne with diverse clothynge? [445] Of whiche clothynge yif the beaute be aggre-able to loken uppon, I wol merveylen on the nature of the matiere of thilke clothes, or elles on the werkman that wroughte hem. But also a long route of meyne, maketh that a blisful man? The whiche servantes yif thei ben vicyous of condy-ciouns, it is a gret charge and a destruccioun to the hous, and a gret enemy to the lord hym-self; and yif

they ben gode men, how schal straunge or foreyne goodnesse ben put in the nowmbre of thi richesses? So that by alle thise forseide thynges it es cleerly schewed, that nevere oon of thilke thynges that thou acountedest for thyne goodes nas nat thi good.

In the whiche thynges yif ther be no beaute to ben desired, why scholdestow ben sory yif thou leese hem, or whi scholdestow reioysen the for to holden hem? [450] For yif thei ben faire of hir owene kynde, what aperteneth that to the? For als so wel scholde they han ben fayre by hem-selve, though thei were departed fro alle thyne rychesses. For-why fair ne precyous were thei nat for that thei comen among thi rychesses; but for they semeden fair and precyous, therfore thou haddest levere rekne hem among thi rychesses. But what desires-tow of fortune with so greet a noyse and with so greet a fare? I trowe thou seeke to dryve a-wey nede with habundaunce of thynges, but certes it turneth to you al in the contrarie. For-why certes it nedeth of ful manye helpynges to kepyn the diversite of precious ostelementes; and sooth it is that of many thynges han they nede, that many thynges han; and ayenward of litel nedeth hem that mesureth hir fille after the nede of kynde, and nat after the oultrage of covetyse. [455] Is it thanne so, that ye men ne han no propre good I-set in you, for whiche ye mooten seke outward your goodes in foreyne and subgit thynges? So is thanne the condicion of thynges turned up so doun, that a man, that is a devyne beest be meryte of his resoun, thynketh that hym-self nys neyther fair ne noble but it be thurw possessioun of ostelementes that ne han no soules. And certes alle othere thynges ben apayed of hir owene beautes, but ye men that ben semblable to god by your resonable thought, desiren to apparailen your excellent kynde

445. *a-choken the fulfillynge,* 'urgere satie-tatem.'

445. *to the* should be *to her.*

447. *vicyous of condyciouns,* 'vitiosi moribus.'

448. *a gret enemy,* 'forment anemie,' 'vehe-menter inimica'; *enemy* is here adj.

456. *subgit,* 'sepositis,' probably misread as 'suppositis.'

458. *apayed of, i.e.* satisfied with.

of the loweste thynges; ne ye undir-standen nat how greet a wrong ye don to your creatour. For he wolde that mankynde were moost wurthy and noble of any othere erthly thynges, and ye thresten a-doun yowre dignytes bynethen the loweste thynges. [460] For yif that al the good of every thyng be more precyous than is thilke thyng whos that the good is, syn ye demen that the fowleste thynges ben your goodes, thanne submitten ye and putten your-selven undir the fouleste thynges by your estima-cioun; and certes this betydeth nat withouten your desert. For certes swiche is the condicioun of alle mankynde, that oonly whan it hath knowynge of it-self, thanne passeth it in noblesse alle othere thynges; and whan it forletith the knowynge of it-self thanne it is brought by-nethen alle beestes. For-whi alle othere lyvynge beestes han of kynde to knowe nat hem-self; but whan that men leeten the knowynge of hem-self, it cometh hem of vice. But how broode scheweth the errour and the folie of yow men, that wenen that anythyng mai ben apparailed with straunge apparailementes! But for-sothe that mai nat be don. [465] For yif a wyght schyneth with thynges that ben put to hym (as thus, yif thilke thynges schynen with whiche a man is aparayled), certes thilke thynges ben comended and preysed with whiche he is apparayled; but natheles, the thyng that is covered and wrapped under that duelleth in his felthe.

And I denye that thilke thyng be good that anoyeth hym that hath it. Gabbe I of this? Thow wolt sey "nay." Certes rychesses han anoyed ful ofte hem that han tho rychesses, syn that every wikkid schrewe, and for his wikkidnesse is the

more gredy aftir othir folkes rychesses wher so evere it be in ony place, be it gold or precyous stones; and weneth hym oonly most worthy that hath hem. [470] Thow thanne, that so bysy dredest now the swerd and the spere, yif thou haddest entred in the path of this lif a voyde weyfarynge man, thanne woldestow syngen by-for the theef. (As who seith, a pore man that bereth no rychesse on hym by the weie may boldely synge byforn theves, for he hath nat where-of to be robbed.) O precyous and ryght cleer is the blisfulnesse of mortel rychesses, that, whan thow hast geten it, thanne hastow lorn thi sikernesse!

'Felix nimium prior etas.'—Metrum 5

Blisful was the firste age of men. They heelden hem apayed with the metes that the trewe feeldes broughten forth. They ne destroyeden ne des-seyvede nat hem-self with outrage. They weren wont lyghtly to slaken hir hungir at even with accornes of ookes. [475] They ne coude nat medle the yift of Bachus to the cleer hony (that is to seyn, they coude make no pyment or clarree), ne they coude nat medle the bryghte fleeses of the contre of Seryens with the venym of Tyrie (this is to seyn, thei coude nat deyen white fleeses of Syrien contre with the blood of a maner schelle-fyssche that men fynden in Tyrie, with whiche blood men deyen purpre). They slepen holsome slepes uppon the gras, and dronken of the rennynge watres, and layen undir the schadwes of the heye pyn trees. Ne no gest ne straunger ne karf yit the heye see with oores or with schipes; ne thei ne hadden seyn yit none newe stroondes to leden marchandise into diverse contrees. Tho weren the cruele clariouns ful hust and ful stille. Ne blood I-schad by egre hate ne hadde nat

---

463. *han . . . to knowe*, 'ceteris animantibus natura est ignorare sese,' with 'natura' read as abl. *cometh hem*, 'leur vint'; cp. *Bk. of Du.*, 778.

470. *and for his wikkidnesse*, etc. (C₁ Hn. A₂ A₁ omit *is*, B *of his wikkidnesse is the more*, etc., C₃ *is for his wikkidnesse the more*, etc.), *i.e.* even for his wickedness, etc.

474-484. Also translated in *The Former Age*.
476. *fleeses of the*, etc., 'vellera serum' (cp. Verg. *Georg.* ii. 121), 'les toisons des Sirians,' *i.e.* silks of Syria. *venym of Tyrie*, 'Tyrio veneno' (cp. *Georg.* ii. 465).

deyed yit armures. [480] For wher-to or which woodnesse of enemys wolde first moeven armes, whan thei seyen cruele wowndes ne none medes be of blood I-shad. I wolde that our tymes sholde torne ayen to the oolde maneris! But the anguysschous love of havynge brenneth in folk more cruely than the fyer of the mountaigne of Ethna that ay brenneth. Allas! what was he that first dalf up the gobbettes or the weyghtes of gold covered undir erthe and the precyous stones that wolden han be hydd? He dalf up precious periles. (That is to seyn, that he that hem first up dalf, he dalf up a precious peril for-why, for the preciousnesse of swich thyng hath many man ben in peril.)

' Quid autem de dignitatibus.'—Prosa 6

But what schal I seye of dignytes and of powers, the whiche ye men, that neither knowen verray dignyte ne verray powere, areysen hem as heyghe as the hevene? [485] The whiche dignytees and powyeres yif thei comen to any wikkid man, thei doon as greet damages and destrucciouns as doothe the flaumbe of the mountaigne Ethna whan the flaumbe walweth up, ne no deluge ne doth so cruele harmes. Certes the remembreth wel, as I trowe, that thilke dignyte that men clepyn the Imperie of consulers, the whiche that whilom was begynnynge of fredom, yowr eldren coveyteden to han don awey that dignyte for the pride of the consulers. And ryght for the same pride yowr eldres by-forn that tyme hadden doon awey out of the cite of Rome the kynges name (that is to seyn, thei nolden han no lengere no kyng).

But now, if it so be that dignytees and poweris ben yyven to gode men, the whiche thyng is ful selde, what aggreable thynges is ther in the dignytees or powyers but oonly the goodnesse of folk that usen hem? And therfore it is thus that honour ne cometh nat to vertu for

cause of dignyte, but, ayenward, honour cometh to dygnite for cause of vertu. [490] But whiche is thilke your derworthe power that is so cleer and so requerable? O ye erthliche bestes considere ye nat over whiche thyng that it semeth that ye han power? Now yif thou saye a mows among othere mys that chalanged to hym-self ward ryght and power over alle othere mys, how gret scorn woldestow han of it! (Glosa. So fareth it by men; the body hath power over the body.) For yif thou looke wel upon the body of a wyght, what thyng shaltow fynde more freele than is mankynde; the whiche men ful ofte ben slayn by bytynge of smale flyes, or elles with the entrynge of crepynge wormes in-to the pryvetees of mannes body? [495] But wher schal men fynden any man that mai exercen or haunten any ryght up-on another man, but oonly on his body, or elles up-on thynges that ben lowere than the body, the whiche I clepe fortunous possessiouns? Maystow evere have any comaundement over a free corage? Maystowe remuwen fro the estat of his propre reste a thought that is clyvynge togidre in hym self by stedfast resoun? As whilom a tyraunt wende to confownde a fre-man of corage, and wende to constreyne hym by torment to maken hym discoveren and accusen folk that wisten of a coniuracioun (whiche I clepe a confederacye) that was cast ayens this tyraunt; but this freman boot of his owene tonge, and caste it in the visage of thilk wode tyraunt. So that the tormentes that this tyraunt wende to han maked matere of cruelte, this wise man maked it matere of vertu. [500] But what thing is it that a man may doon to an other man, that he ne may resceyven the same thyng of other folk in hym-self?

491. *But whiche is*, etc., 'mais quiex est,' *i.e* but what is, etc.
491. *over whiche thyng*, etc., 'consideratis, quibus qui præsidere videamini.'
498. *As whilom*, 'cum' temporal; but probably Fr. 'comme' was misunderstood.
500. *tormentes* . . . *it*, 'les torments . . . li sages homs le (L. les) fist estre.'

(Or thus : what may a man don to folk, that folk ne may don hym the same?) I have herd told of Busyrides, that was wont to sleen his gestes that herberweden in his hous, and he was slayn hym-self of Ercules that was his gest. Regulus hadde taken in bataile manye men of Affryke and cast hem in-to feteres, but sone ther after he most yyve hise handes to ben bownde with the cheynes of hem that he hadde whilom overcomen. Wenestow thanne that he be myghty that hath no power to doon a thyng that othere ne mai doon in hym that he doth in othere? [505] And yit moreover, yif it so were that thise dygnytes or poweris hadden any propre or naturel goodnesse in hem-self, nevere nolde they comen to schrewes. For contrarious thynges ne ben nat wont to ben I-felaschiped togydre. Nature refuseth that contrarious thynges ben I-joygned. And so, as I am in certeyn that ryght wykkyd folk han dignytees ofte tyme, thanne scheweth it wel that dignytees and poweres ne ben nat gode of hir owene kynde, syn that they suffren hem-selve to cleven or joynen hem to schrewes. And certes the same thyng mai I most digneliche juggen and seyn of alle the yiftes of fortune that most plentevously comen to schrewes. Of the whiche yiftes I trowe that it oughte ben considered, that no man douteth that he ne is strong in whom he seeth strengthe ; [510] and in whom that swyftnesse is, sooth it is that he is swyft ; also musyke maketh mucisyens, and phisyk maketh phisicyeens, and rethoryke, rethoriens. For-why the nature of every thyng maketh his proprete, ne it is nat entremedlyd with the effect of contrarious thynges, and of wil it chaseth out thynges that to it ben contrarie. But certes rychesse mai nat restreyne avarice unstaunched ; ne power ne maketh nat a man myghty over hym-selve, whiche that vicyous lustes holden destreyned with cheynes that ne mowen nat ben unbownden. And dignytees that ben yyven to schrewide folk nat oonly ne maketh hem nat digne, but it scheweth rather al opynly that they been unworthy and undigne. And whi is it thus? Certes for ye han joie to clepen thynges with false names, that beren hem al in the contrarie ; the whiche names ben ful ofte reproved by the effect of the same thynges ; [515] so that thise ilke rychesses ne oughten nat by ryghte to ben cleped rychesses, ne swyche power ne aughte nat ben clepyd power, ne swiche dignyte ne aughte nat ben clepyd dignyte. And at the laste, I may conclude the same thyng of alle the yyftes of fortune, in whiche ther nys no thyng to ben desired, ne that hath in hym-selve naturel bownte, as it is ful wel yseene. For neither thei ne joygnen hem nat alwey to gode men, ne maken hem alwey gode to whom they been I-ioyned.

' Novimus quantas dederit.'—Metrum 6

We han wel knowen how many grete harmes and destrucciouns weren I-doon by the emperour Nero. He leet brennen the cite of Rome, and made sleen the senatours ; and he cruel whilom sloughe his brothir, and he was maked moyst with the blood of his modir (that is to seyn, he leet sleen and slitten the body of his modir to seen wher he was conceyved) ; [520] and he lookede on every halve uppon hir cold deed body, ne no teer ne wette his face, but he was so hardherted that he myghte ben domesman or juge of hir dede beaute. And natheles yit governed this Nero by septre alle the peples that Phebus (the sonne) may seen,

502. *Busyrides,* rather 'Busirus,' as in B. 3293 ; but Aq. has 'Busirides.'
505. *Wenestow . . . othere,* nonsense, due either to mistranslation of 'de faire que' ('efficere ne'), or to text-corruption, *a thyng* belonging after *2nd to doon.*
512. *of wil,* 'ultro, *i.e.* sponte'; C₂ A₁ *as of wil,* A₂ *offt times,* Cx. omits *and . . . contrarie.*

514. *dignytees . . . it,* 'dignete (L. dignites) . . . fait elle (L. font elle)'; cp. 449.
514. *that beren hem* goes with *thynges, i.e.* which behave in just the opposite way.
519. *We han,* etc., 'nouimus.'
519. *made sleen,* 'fist ocire.'

comynge fro his uttreste arysynge til he hidde his bemes undir the wawes. (That is to seyn he governede al the peples by ceptre imperiale that the sonne goth aboute from est to west.) And ek this Nero governyde by ceptre all the peples that ben undir the colde sterres that highten the vij Tryones. (This is to seyn he governede alle the peples that ben under the partye of the north.) And eek Nero governede alle the peples that the vyolent wynd Nothus scorklith, and baketh the brennynge sandes by his drye heete (that is to seyn, al the peple in the south). [525] But yit ne myghte nat al his heie power torne the woodnesse of this wikkid Nero. Allas! it is grevous fortune as ofte as wikkid sweerd is joyned to cruel venym (that is to seyn, venymows cruelte to lordschipe).'

'*Tum ego scis inquam.*'—Prosa 7

Than seyde I thus: 'Thow woost wel thi - selve that the covetise of mortel thynges ne hadden nevere lordschipe of me, but I have wel desired matere of thynges to done (as who seith, I desirede to have matiere of governaunce over comunalites), for vertue stille sholde nat elden (that is to seyn that, list that, or he waxe oold, his vertu, that lay now ful stille, ne schulde nat perysshe un-exercised in governaunce of comune, for whiche men myghten speken or wryten of his gode governement).'

'For sothe,' quod sche, 'and that is a thyng that mai drawen to govern-aunce swiche hertes as ben worthy and noble of hir nature, [530] but natheles it may nat drawen or tollen swiche hertes as ben I-brought to the ful per-feccioun of vertue, that is to seyn, covetise of glorie and renoun to han wel adminystred the comune thynges, or doon gode desertes to profyt of the

comune. For see now and considere how litel and how voyde of alle prys is thylk glorye. Certeyn thyng is, as thou hast leerned by the demonstracioun of astronomye, that al the envyrounynge of the erthe aboute ne halt but the resoun of a prykke at regard of the gretnesse of hevene; that is to seyn that, yif ther were maked comparysoun of the erthe to the gretnesse of hevene, men wolde juggen in al that the erthe heelde no space. Of the whiche litel regioun of this world, the ferthe partye is enhabited with lyvynge beestes that we knowen, as thou hast thy-selve leerned by Tholome that proveth it. [535] And yif thow haddest withdrawen and abated in thy thought fro thilke ferthe partie as moche space as the see and the mareys contene and overgoon, and as moche space as the regioun of drowghte overstreccheth (that is to seyn sandes and desertes), wel un-nethe sholde ther duellen a ryght streyte place to the habitacioun of men. And ye thanne, that ben envyrouned and closed with-ynne the leeste prykke of thilke prykke, thynken ye to manyfesten or publisschen your renoun and doon yowr name for to be born forth? But yowr glorye that is so narwe and so streyt I-thrungen into so litel bowndes, how mochel conteneth it in largesse and in greet doynge? And also set this therto: that manye a nacioun, diverse of tonge and of maneris and ek of resoun of hir lyvynge, ben enhabited in the cloos of thilke lytel habitacle; [540] to the whiche nacyons, what for difficulte of weyes, and what for diversite of langages, and what for defaute of un-usage and entre-comunynge of marchandise, nat oonly the names of synguler men ne may nat strecchen, but eek the fame of citees ne may nat strecchen. At the laste,

528. *for, i.e.* that.
529. *i.e.* lest his virtue should perish, etc. For and *that* C₁ reads *it*, Cx. A₂ omit.

533. *halt,* etc., *i.e.* is accounted but a point in comparison with, etc.
535. *Tholome, i.e.* Ptolemy.
541. *defaute of un-usage,* etc., mixture of 'insolentia, i.e. inconsuetudine (*unusage*) commercii' (*entrecomunynge*) and 'par faute de (*defaute of*) acoustumance de mercheandise' (*of marchandise*).

certes, in the tyme of Marcus Tulyus, as hym-selve writ in his book, that the renoun of the comune of Rome ne hadde nat nat yit passid ne clomben over the mountaigne that highte Caucasus; and yit was thilke tyme Rome wel waxen and greetly redouted of the Parthes, and eek of the othere folk enhabitynge aboute. Seestow nat thanne how streyte and how compressid is thilke glorie that ye travailen aboute to schewe and to multeplye? [545] May thanne the glorie of a synguler Romeyn strecchen thider as the fame of the name of Rome may nat clymben ne passen? And ek seestow nat that the maneris of diverse folk and ek hir lawes ben discordaunt among hem-selve, so that thilke thyng that som men juggen worthy of preysynge, other folk juggen that it is worthy of torment? And therof comyth it that, though a man delyte hym in preysynge of his renoun, he ne mai nat in no wyse bryngen forthe ne spreden his name to many manere peples. And therfore every maner man aughte to ben apayed of his glorie, that is publysschid among his owene neyghebours; and thilke noble renoun schal ben restreyned withynne the boundes of o manere folk. But how many a man, that was ful noble in his tyme, hath the wrecchid and nedy foryetynge of writeris put out of mynde and doon awey; [550] al be it so that, certes, thilke wrytynges profiten litel, the whiche writynges long and dirk eelde doth awey, both hem and ek hir auctours! But yow men semeth to geten yow a perdurablete, whan ye thynken that in tyme comynge your fame schal lasten. But natheles yif thow wolt maken com-parysoun to the endles spaces of eternyte, what thyng hastow by whiche thow mayst reioisen the of long lastynge of thi name? For yif ther were makyd comparysoun of the abydynge of a moment to ten thowsand wynter, for as

mochel as bothe two spaces ben endyd, for yit hath the moment som porcioun of it, although it litel be. But natheles thilke selve nowmbre of yeeris, and eek as many yeris as ther-to mai be multiplyed, ne mai nat certes be comparysoned to the perdurablete that is endlees; [555] for of thinges that han ende may ben maked comparysoun, but of thynges that ben withouten ende to thynges that han ende may be makid no comparysoun. And for-thi is it that, al-though renome, of as longe tyme as evere the list to thynken, were thought to the regard of eternyte, that is unstaunchable and infynyt, it ne sholde nat only semen litel, but pleynliche ryght noght. But ye men, certes, ne konne doon no thyng aryght, but yif it be byfore the audience of the peple and for idel rumours; and ye forsaken the grete worthynesse of concience and of vertu, and ye seeken yowr gerdouns of the smale wordes of straunge folk. Have now (here and undirstand) in the lyghtnesse of swiche pryde and veyne glorye how a man scornede festyvaly and myriely swich vanyte. [560] Whilom ther was a man that hadde assaiede with stryvynge wordes another man, the whiche, nat for usage of verray vertu but for proud veyn glorie, had taken upon hym falsly the name of a philosophre. This rather man that I spak of thoughte he wolde assaie where he thilke were a philosophre or no; that is to seyn, yif that he wolde han suffride lyghtly in pacience the wronges that weren doon unto hym. This feynede philosophre took pacience a litel while; and whan he hadde resceyved wordes of outrage, he, as in stryvynge ayen and reioysynge of hym-self, seide at the laste ryght thus: "undirstondistow nat that I am a philosophre?" The tother man

543. *that the renoun*, 'that' is often thus used before a direct quotation.
552. *yow men*, etc. (Cx. A₁ *ye men semen*), i.e. it seems to you that, etc.

554. *bothe two*, A₁ Hn. Cx. *bothe tho*; C₂ *bothe the. for yit*, i.e. yet.
560. *Have now*, etc., 'Accipe' and 'Or recoit et entent.'
562. *where*, i.e. whether.
564. *took pacience*, 'il prist vn petit en soi (L omits) pacience.'

377

answerede ayen ful bytyngely and seyde: "I hadde wel undirstonden it yif thou haddest holde thi tonge stille." But what is it to thise noble worthy men? —for, certes, of swych folk speke I that seken glorie with vertue—What is it,' quod sche; 'what atteyneth fame to swiche folk, whan the body is resolved by the deeth at the laste? [565] For if it so be that men dyen in all (that is to seyen, body and soule), the whiche thing our reson defendeth us to byleeven, thanne is ther no glorie in no wyse; for what schulde thilke glorie ben, whan he, of whom thilke glorie is seyd to be, nys ryght naught in no wise? And yif the soule, whiche that hath in hym-self science of gode werkes, unbownden fro the prysone of the erthe, weendeth frely to the hevene, despiseth it nat thanne al erthly ocupacioun; and, beynge in hevene, reioyseth that it is exempt fro alle erthly thynges? (As who seith, thanne rekketh the soule of noon othir thyng, ne of renoun of this world.) [570]

' *Quicumque solam mente.*'—Metrum 7

Who so that with overthrowynge thought oonly seketh glorie of fame, and weneth that it be sovereyn good, lat hym looke upon the brode schewynge contrees of the hevene, and upon the streyte sete of this erthe; and he shal be asschamed of the encres of his name, that mai nat fulfille the litel compas of the erthe. O! what coveyten proude folk to lyften up hir nekkes on idel in the dedly yok of this world? For al though that renoun y-sprad, passynge to ferne peples, goth by diverse tonges; and al-though that greet houses or kynredes shynen with cleer titles of honours; yit natheles deth despiseth al heye glorie of fame, and deth wrappeth to gidre the heyghe heved and the lowe, and maketh egal and evene the heygheste to the loweste. [575] Where wonen now the bones of trewe Fabricius? What is now Brutus or

stierne Caton? The thynne fame yit lastynge of here idel names is marked with a fewe lettres. But al-thoughe that we han knowen the fayre wordes of the fames of hem, it is nat yyven to knowen hem that ben dede and consumpt. Liggeth thanne stille, al outrely unknowable, ne fame maketh yow nat knowe. And yif ye wene to lyve the longere for wynd of yowr mortel name whan o cruel day schal ravyssche yow, than is the seconde deth duellynge unto yow.' (Glose. The first deeth he clepeth here departynge of the body and the soule, and the seconde deth he clepeth as here the styntynge of the renoun of fame.) [580]

' *Set ne me inexorabile.*'—Prosa 8

'But for as mochel as thow schalt nat wenen,' quod sche, 'that I bere an untretable batayle ayens fortune, yit somtyme it by-falleth that sche desceyvable desserveth to han ryght good thank of men. And that is whan sche hir-self opneth, and whan sche discovereth hir frownt and scheweth hir maneris. Peraventure yit undirstandestow nat that I schal seie. It is a wonder that I desire to telle, and for-thi unnethe may I unplyten my sentence with wordes. For I deme that contrarious Fortune profiteth more to men than Fortune debonayre. For alwey, whan Fortune semeth debonayre, thanne sche lieth, falsly byhetynge the hope of welefulnesse; but forsothe contraryous Fortune is alwey sothfast, whan sche scheweth hir-self unstable thurw hir chaungynge. [585] The amyable Fortune desceyveth folk; the contrarie Fortune techeth. The amyable Fortune byndeth with the beaute of false goodes the hertes of folk that usen hem; the contrarye Fortune unbyndeth hem by the knowynge of freel welefulnesse. The amyable

---

570. C₂ Hn. Cx. *rekketh the sowle of no glorye of renoun.* A₁ omits from *As who* to *this world.*

578. *Liggeth thanne*, etc., 'jacetis,' read as imperative on account of Fr. 'Donques gesiez vous.'

581-614. A₁ omits, beginning again at II, met. 1.

581. *bere . . . batayle*, 'gerere bellum.'

Fortune maystow seen al-wey wyndy and flowynge, and evere mysknowynge of hir-self; the contrarie Fortune is atempre and restreyned and wys thurw exercise of hir adversite. At the laste, amyable Fortune with hir flaterynges draweth myswandrynge men fro the sovereyne good; the contrarious Fortune ledeth ofte folk ayen to sothfast goodes, and haleth hem ayen as with an hook. Wenestow than that thow augghtest to leeten this a litel thyng, that this aspre and horrible Fortune hath descovered to the the thoughtes of thi trewe freendes. [590] For-why this ilke Fortune hath departed and uncovered to the bothe the certein visages and eek the doutes visages of thi felawes. Whan she departed awey fro the, she took awey hir freendes and lefte the thyne freendes. Now whanne thow were ryche and weleful, as the semede, with how mochel woldestow han bought the fulle knowynge of thys (that is to seyn, the knowynge of thyne verray freendes)? Now pleyne the nat thanne of rychesse y-lorn, syn thow hast fownden the moste precyous kynde of rychesses, that is to seyn, thi verray freendes.

'*Quod mundus stabili fide.*'—Metrum 8

That the world with stable feyth varieth accordable chaungynges; that the contrarious qualites of elementes holden among hemself allyaunce perdurable; [595] that Phebus, the sonne, with his goldene chariet bryngeth forth the rosene day; that the moone hath comaundement over the nyghtes, whiche nyghtes Esperus, the eve sterre, hath brought; that the see, gredy to flowen, constreyneth with a certein eende his floodes, so that it is nat leveful to strecche his brode termes or bowndes uppon the erthes (that is to seyn, to coveren al the erthe)—al this accordaunce of thynges is bounde with love, that governeth erthe and see, and

588. *exercise*, 'exercitatione,' *i.e.* experience.
595. *varieth*, etc., 'concordes variat vices.'
597. B *gredy constreyneth to flowen.*

hath also comandement to the hevene. And yif this love slakede the bridelis, alle thynges that now loven hem to-gidres wolden make batayle contynuely, and stryven to fordo the fassoun of this world, the which they now leden in accordable feith by fayre moevynges. This love halt togidres peples joyned with an holy boond, and knytteth sacrement of mariages of chaste loves; and love enditeth lawes to trewe felawes. [600] O weleful were mankynde, yif thilke love that governeth hevene governede yowr corages.'

EXPLICIT LIBER SECUNDUS

INCIPIT LIBER TERTIUS

'*Iam cantum illa.*'—Prosa 1

By this sche hadde ended hir song, whan the swetnesse of here dite hadde thurw perced me, that was desyrous of herknynge, and I a-stoned hadde yit streyghte myn eres (that is to seyn, to herkne the bet what sche wolde seye). So that a litel herafter I seide thus: 'O thow that art sovereyne confort of angwyssous corages, so thow hast remounted and norysshed me with the weyghte of thi sentences and with delyt of thy syngynge; so that I trowe nat nowe that I be unparygal to the strokes of Fortune (as who seith, I dar wel now suffren alle the assautes of Fortune and wel defende me fro hir). And tho remedies whiche that thou seydest her byforn that weren ryght scharpe, nat oonly that I ne am agrisen of hem now, but I, desiros of herynge, axe gretly to heren tho remedies.' [605]
Thanne seyde sche thus: 'That feeled

598. *hath comandement to*, 'imperitans celo,' 'commandant au ciel.'
598. *loven hem to-gidres*, 's'entreaiment,' *i.e.* love one another. *contynuely*, 'continuo'; rather, 'straightway.'
600. B A₂ *the sacr.*, Cx. *mariage.*
605. *that weren* (C₂ A₁ om. *that*), omitted subject as in 629.

I ful wel,' quod sche, 'whan thow ententyf and stille ravysschedest my wordes, and I abood til that thou haddest swich habite of thi thought as thou hast now, or elles til that I my-self hadde maked to the the same habite, whiche that is a more verray thyng. And certes the remenant of thynges that ben yet to seie ben swiche, that first whan men tasten hem, they ben bytynge; but whan they ben resceyved with-ynne a wyght, thanne ben thei swete. But for thou seyst that thow art so desyrous to herkne hem, with how greet brennynge woldestow glowen, yif thow wistest whider I wol leden the!'

'Whider is that?' quod I.

'To thilke verraye welefulnesse,' quod sche, 'of whiche thyn herte dremeth; [610] but forasmoche as thi syghte is ocupyed and destourbed by imagynacoun of erthly thynges, thow mayst nat yit seen thilke selve welefulnesse.'

'Do,' quod I, 'and schewe me what is thilke verray welefulnesse, I preie the, withoute taryinge.'

'That wol I gladly do,' quod sche, 'for the cause of the. But I wol first marken the by woordes, and I wol enforcen me to enforme the thilke false cause of blisfulnesse that thou more knowest; so that whanne thow hast fully byhoolden thilke false goodes and torned thin eighen to the tother syde, thow mowe knowe the cleernesse of verray blisfulnesse.'

'*Qui serere ingenuum.*'—Metrum 1

'Who-so wole sowe a feld plentevous, let hym first delyvren it of thornes, and kerve asondir with his hook the busschches and the feern, so that the corn may comen hevy of erys and of greynes.

606. *whiche that*, etc., 'quod est verius.'
612. *Do and schewe*, 'Fac . . . et demonstra,' 'Fai . . . et demonstre.'
613. *for the cause of the*, *i.e.* for thy sake.
613. *marken the*, 'je te senefierai'; *the* dative.
613. *that thou more*, etc., *i.e.* which thou art more familiar with.

[615] Hony is the more swete, if mouthes han first tasted savours that ben wykke. The sterres schynen more aggreablely whan the wynd Nothus leteth his plowngy blastes; and aftir that Lucifer, the day-sterre, hath chased awey the dirke nyght, the day the fairere ledeth the rosene hors of the sonne. And ryght so thow, by-hooldyng first the false goodes, bygyn to withdrawe thy nekke fro the yok of erthely affeccions; and afterward the verray goodes schullen entren into thy corage.'

'*Cum defixo paululum.*'—Prosa 2

Tho fastnede sche a litel the syghte of hir eyen, and withdrowghe hir ryght as it were into the streyte seete of here thought, and bigan to speke ryght thus: 'Alle the cures,' quod sche, 'of mortel folk, whiche that travailen hem in many manere studies, gon certes by diverse weyes; but natheles thei enforcen hem alle to comyn oonly to oon ende of blis-fulnesse. [620] And blisfulnesse is swiche a good, that who-so that hath geten it, he ne may over that nothyng more desire. And this thyng forsothe is the soverayn good that conteneth in hym-self alle maner goodes; to the whiche goode if ther fayled any thyng, it myghte nat ben sovereyn good, for thanne wer ther som good out of thilke sovereyn good, that myghte ben desired. Now is it cleer and certeyne thanne, that blisfulnesse is a parfyt estat by the congregacioun of alle goodes; the whiche blisfulnesse, as I have seyd, alle mortel folk enforcen hem to geten by diverse weyes. For-why the covetise of verray good is naturely I-plauntyd in the hertes of men, but the myswandrynge errour mysledeth hem into false goodes. [625] Of the whiche men, some of hem wenen that sovereyn good be to lyven with-oute nede of any thyng, and travaylen hem to ben

616. *mouthes han*, etc., 'si malus ora (mis-construed as nom.) prius sapor edat.'
617. *hors*, horses.

habundaunt of rychesses. And some othere men demen that sovereyn good be for to be ryght digne of reverence, and enforcen hem to ben reverenced among hir neyghbours by the honours that thei han I-geten. And some folk ther ben that holden that ryght heye power be sovereyn good, and enforcen hem for to reignen or elles to joygnen hem to hem that reignen. And it semeth to some other folk, that noblesse of renoun be the sovereyn good, and hasten hem to geten hem gloryouse name by the artes of werre or of pees. And many folk mesuren and gessen that the sovereyne good be joye and gladnesse, and wenen that it be ryght blisful thyng to plowngen hem in voluptuous delyt. [630] And ther ben folk that entrechaungen the causes and the endes of thyse forseyde goodes, as they that desiren rychesses to han power and delites, or elles they desiren power for to have moneye or for cause of renoun. In thise thynges and in swiche other thynges is torned al the entencioun of desyrynges and werkes of men; as thus: noblesse and favour of peple whiche that yyveth to men, as it semeth hem, a maner cleernesse of renoun; and wyf and children, that men desiren for cause of delyt and myrynesse. But for-sothe freendes schulde nat ben rekned among the goodes of fortune, but of vertu, for it is a ful hooly maner thyng; alle thise othere thinges for-sothe ben taken for cause of power or elles for cause of delyt. [635] Certes now am I redy to referren the goodes of the body to thise forseide thynges aboven; for it semeth that strengthe and gretnesse of body yyven power and worthynesse, and that beaute and swyftnesse yyven noblesse and glorie of renoun; and heele of body semeth yyven delyt. In alle thise thynges it semeth oonly that blisfulnesse is desyred; for-why thilk thing that every man desireth moost over alle thynges

he demeth that it be the sovereyn good; but I have diffyned that blisfulnesse is the sovereyn good; for whiche every wyght demeth that thilke estat that he desireth over alle thynges, that it be blisfulnesse. Now hastow thanne byforn thyne eien almest al the purposede forme of the welefulnesse of mankynde; that is to seyn rychesses, honours, power, glorie, and delites. [640] The whiche delit oonly considered Epicurus, and juggid and establissyde that delyt is the soverayn good, for as moche as alle othere thynges, as hym thoughte, byrefte awey joye and myrthe from the herte. But I retorne ayen to the studies of men, of whiche men the corage alwey rehercheth and seketh the sovereyne good, al be it so that it be with a dyrkyd memorie; but he not by whiche path, ryght as a dronke man not nat by whiche path he may retourne hom to his hous. Semeth it thanne that folk foleyen and erren, that enforcen hem to have nede of no thyng? Certes ther nys noon other thyng that mai so wel performe blisfulnesse, as an estat plentevous of alle godes, that ne hath nede of noon other thyng, but that it is suffisant of hym-self un-to hym-self. [645] And foleyen swiche folk, thanne, that wenen that thilke thyng that is ryght good, that it be eek ryght worthy of honour and of reverence? Certes, nay. For that thyng nys neither foul ne worthy to ben despysed that wel neyghe al the entencioun of mortel folk travaylen for to geten it. And power, aughte nat that ek to ben rekned amonge goodes? What elles? For it nys nat to wene that thilke thyng that is most worthy of alle thynges be feble and withoute strengthe. And cleernesse of renoun, aughte that to ben despysed? Certes ther may no man for-

632. *is torned*, mistranslation of 'versatur'; also in Fr. 'est tournee.'
635. *freendes* '(genus) amicorum,' hence the *it* below.

*640. *purposede* (*i.e.* proposed) should precede *byforn thyne eien*: misreading of Aq. 'habes ante oculos propositam formam humane,' etc.
641. *byrefte awey*, etc., should be *broughte* . . . *to the herte*; 'afferre' misread as 'auferre.'
642. *rehercheth and seketh*, 'repetit'; *rehercheth* is probably due to *studies*, 'studia' (which here means 'efforts').

sake, that alle thyng that is right excellent and noble, that it ne semeth to ben ryght cleer and renomed. For certes it nedeth nat to saie that blisfulnesse [ne] be angwyssous ne drery, ne subgit to grevaunces ne to sorwes ; syn that in ryght litele thynges folk seken to haven and to usen that may delyten hem. [650] Certes thise ben thise thinges that men wolen and desiren to geten, and for this cause desiren they rychesses, dignytes, reignes, glorie, and delices ; for ther-by wenen they to han suffysaunce, honour, power, renoun, and gladnesse. Thanne is it good that men seken thus, by so manye diverse studies. In whiche desir it mai lyghtly be schewyd how greet is the strengthe of nature. For how so that men han diverse sentences and discordynge, algates men accorden alle in lovynge the eende of good.

'*Quantas rerum flectat.*'—Metrum 2

It likethe me to schewe by subtil soong, with slakke and delytable sown of strenges, how that Nature, myghty, enclyneth and flytteth the governementes of thynges ; and by whiche lawes sche, purveiable, kepith the grete world ; and how sche, byndynge, restreyneth alle thynges by a boond that may nat be unbownde. [655] Al be it so that the lyouns of the contre of Pene beren the fayre chaynes, and taken metes of the handes of folk that yeven it hem, and dreden hir stourdy maistres of whiche thei ben wont to suffre betynges ; yif that hir horrible mouthes ben by-bled (that is to seyn, of beestes devoured), hir corage of tyme passed, that hath ben idel and rested, repeireth ayen, and thei roren grevously, and remembren on hir nature, and slaken hir nekkes from hir cheynes unbownde ; and hir mayster fyrst, to-torn with bloody

tooth, assaieth the wode wratthes of hem (this to seyn thei freten hir maister). And the janglynge brid that syngeth on the heighe braunches (that is to seyn, in the wode), and after is enclosed in a streyte cage, al thoughe that the pleyinge bysynes of men yeveth hem honyed drynkes and large metes with swete studyes, yit natheles yif thilke bryd skippynge out of hir streyte cage seith the agreable schadwes of the wodes, sche defouleth with hir feet hir metes I-schad, and seketh mornynge oonly the wode, and twytereth desyrynge the wode with hir swete voys. [660] The yerde of a tree, that is haled a-doun by myghty strengthe, boweth redily the crop adown ; but yif the hand of hym that it bente leet it goon ageyn, anoon the crop loketh upryght to hevene. The sonne, Phebus, that falleth at even in the westrene wawes, retorneth ayen eft sones his cart, by a pryve path, there as it is wont aryse. Alle thynges seken ayen to hir propre cours, and alle thynges reioysen hem of hir retornynge ayen to hir nature. Ne noon ordenaunce is by-taken to thynges, but that that hath joyned the endynge to the bygynnynge, and hath maked the cours of it-self stable (that it chaunge nat from his propre kynde).

'*Vos quoque terrena animalia.*'—
Prosa 3

Certes also ye men, that ben erthliche beestes, dremen alwey your bygynnynge, al thoughe it be with a thynne ymaginacioun ; and by a maner thought, al be it nat clerly ne parfitely, ye loken from afer to thilke verray fyn of blisfulnesse. [665] And therfore naturel entencioun ledeth yow to thilke verray good, but many maner errours mystorneth yow ther fro. Considere now yif that by thilke thynges by whiche a man weneth

---

654. *slakke and delytable*, etc., 'lentis fidibus' and '*par sons delitables.*' *slakke* is probably Adam's mistake for *wakke* or *waike* (*i.e.* soft), the usual gloss for *lentus*.
656. *Pene*, 'Pœni leones.'

658. *assaieth*, 'imbuit.' Perhaps we should read *apaieth*.
659. *hem.* Cp. the similar transition to plu. in Tales, F 610 ff., where this passage is quoted.
659. *out of hir*, etc., to end of prose, missing in Hn. C₂ A₁ H Cx. *studye*.

to geten hym blisfulnesse, yif that he mai comen to thilk ende that he weneth to come by nature. For yif that moneye, or honours, or thise othere forseyde thynges, brynge to men swiche a thyng that no good ne fayle hem ne semeth faile, certes thanne wol I graunte that they ben maked blisful by thilke thynges that thei han geten. But yif it so be that thilke thynges mowen nat performen that they byheten, and that there be defaute of manye goodis, scheweth it nat thanne clerly that false beaute of blysfulnesse is known and ataynt in thilke thynges. First and forward thow thi-self, that haddest haboundances of rychesses nat longe agoon, I aske yif that, in the habowndance of alle swiche rychesses, thow were nevere angwyssous ne sory in thy corage of any wrong or grevance that by-tydde the on any side?' [670]

'Certes,' quod I, 'it ne remembreth me nat that evere I was so fre of my thought that I ne was alwey in angwyse of som-what.'

'And was nat that,' quod sche, 'for that the lakkide somwhat that thow woldest nat han lakkid, or elles thou haddest that thow noldest nat han had?'

'Ryght so is it,' quod I.

'Than desiredest thow the presence of the toon and the absence of the tothir?'

'I graunte wel,' quod I.

'For-sothe,' quod sche, 'thanne nedeth ther som-what that every man desireth?'

'Yee, ther nedeth,' quod I.

'Certes,' quod sche, 'and he that hath lak or nede of aught nys nat in every wey suffisant to hym-self?'

'No,' quod I. [675]

'And thow,' quod sche, 'in al the plente of thy richesses haddest thilke lakke of suffisaunce?'

'What elles?' quod I.

'Thanne mai nat richesses maken that a man nys nedy, ne that he be suffisaunt to hym-self; and yit that was

it that thei byhighten, as it semeth. And eek certes I trow that this be gretly to considere, that moneye ne hath nat in his owene kynde that it ne mai ben bynomen of hem that han it, maugre hem.'

'I byknowe it wel,' quod I.

'Whi sholdestow nat byknowen it,' quod sche, 'whan every day the strengere folk bynymen it fro the feblere, maugre hem? For whennes comen elles thise foreyne compleyntes or quereles of pledynges but for that men axen hir moneye that hath ben bynomen hem by force or by gyle, and alwey maugre hem?' [680]

'Right so is it,' quod I.

'Than,' quod sche, 'hath a man nede to seken hym foreyne help by whiche he may defenden his moneye?'

'Who mai seie nay?' quod I.

'Certes,' quod sche, 'and hym nedide noon help yif he ne hadde no moneye that he myghte leese.'

'That is douteles,' quod I.

'Than is this thyng torned into the contrarie,' quod sche; 'for rychesses, that men wenen scholde maken suffisaunce, they maken a man rather have nede of foreyne help. Whiche is the maner or the gyse,' quod sche, 'that rychesse mai dryve awey nede? Riche folk, mai they neyther han hungir ne thurst? Thise riche men, may they fele no cold on hir lymes in wynter? But thow wolt answeren that ryche men han Inoghe wher-with thei mai staunchen hir hungir, and slaken hir thurst, and don awey cold. [685] In this wise mai nede be conforted by richesses, but certes nede mai nat al outrely be doon awey; for thoughe this nede that is alwey gapynge and gredy, be fulfild with richesses and axe any thyng, yit duelleth

677. *byhighten, i.e.* promised.
680. *foreyne compleyntes,* etc., 'forenses querimoniæ' (*i.e.* public appeals) and 'complaintez de plaiz.'
686. *and axe any thyng* (Cx. H omit *axe*) should follow *gredy; i.e.* is always asking for something. *yit duelleth,* etc., *i.e.* the need of food, drink, etc., always remains to be filled.

670. C inserts *that,* Cx. H *the* after *aske.*
673. C₁ B H Cx. *desirest.*

thanne a nede that myghte be fulfild. I holde me stille and telle nat how that litel thyng suffiseth to nature ; but certes to avarice Inowghe suffiseth nothyng. For syn that rychesse ne mai nat al doon awey nede, but richesses maken nede, what mai it thanne be that ye wenen that richesses mowen yyven yow suffisaunce ?

' Quamvis fluente dives.'—Metrum 3

Al weere it so that a riche coveytous man hadde a ryver or a goter fletynge al of gold, yit sholde it nevere staunchen his covetise ; and thoughe he hadde his nekke charged with precyous stones of the rede see, and thoughe he do ere his feeldes plentevous with an hundred oxen, nevere ne schal his bytynge bysynesse forleeten hym whil he lyveth, ne the lyghte richesses ne schal nat beren hym companye whan he is deed. [690]

' Set dignitatibus.'—Prosa 4

But dignytees, to whom thei ben comen, make they hym honourable and reverent? Han thei nat so gret strengthe that thei may putten vertus in the hertes of folk that usen the lordschipes of hem, or elles may they don awey the vices ? Certes thei ben nat wont to don awey wikkidnesse, but thei ben wont rather to schewen wykkydnesse. And ther-of cometh it that y have right gret disdayn that dignytes ben yyven ofte to wikkide men. For which thyng Catullus clepid a consul of Rome that hyghte Nomyus " postum " or " boch " (as who seith, he clepid hym a congregacioun of vices in his brest, as a postum is ful of corrupcioun), al were this Nomyus set in chayere of dygnite. Sestow nat thanne how grete vylenye dignytes don to wikkide men ? Certes unworthynesse of wikkide men schulde ben the lesse I-sene if thei neere renomed of none honours. [695] Certes thou thi-self ne myghtest nat ben broght, with as many perils as thow myghtest suffren, that thow woldest beren the magistrat with Decorat (that is to seyn, that for no peril that myghte byfallen the by offence of the kyng Theodorik, thou noldest nat be felawe in 'governaunce with Decorat), whan thow seye that he hadde wikkide corage of a likerous schrewe and of an accusour. Ne I ne mai nat for swiche honours juggen hem worthy of reverence that I deme and holde unworthy to han thilke same honours. Now yif thow seie a man that were fulfild of wysdom, certes thou ne myghtest nat deme that he were unworthy to the honour or elles to the wisdom of whiche he is fulfild ?'

'No,' quod I.

'Certes dignytees,' quod sche, 'aperteignen properly to vertu, and vertu transporteth dignyte anoon to thilke man to whiche sche hir-self is conioigned. [700] And for as moche as honours of peple ne mai nat maken folk digne of honour, it is wel seyn cleerly that thei ne han no propre beaute of dignyte. And yet men aughten taken more heede in this. For yif a wykkyd wyght be in so mochel the fowlere and the more out-cast that he is despysed of moost folk, so as dignyte ne mai nat maken schrewes worthy of no reverence, than maketh dignyte schrewes rather so much more despised than preysed, the whiche schrewes dignyte scheweth to moche folk ; and forsothe nat unpunyssched (that is for to

688. *what, i.e.* why, 'quid.'
689. C₂ A₁ Hn. omit *or a goter.* The 2nd clause is inaccurately translated and should be, following Fr.: *and hepede richesses that yit sholde nevere,* etc.
690. *do ere, i.e.* have his fields plowed.
691. *Han thei nat,* etc., 'Num vis ea est magistratibus,' should be *Han lordschipes nat,* etc. . . . *of folk that usen hem.* For *nat,* cp. 105.
694. *Nomyus* (A₁ *vonnus*), Catullus (*Carm.* 52) alludes to Nonius Struma. Some Boethius MSS. read *Nomium.*

696. *beren,* 'gerere' (cp. 581) ; *magistrat* (O.F. magistrat), 'magistratum' ; *i.e.* hold office.
702. C₁ A₂ H Cx. B omit *wykkyd* and *the fowlers and* and *so much more* ; C₂ A₁ Hn. omit *in* before *so mochel* ; C₂ Hn. A₂ B place *the whiche . . . folk* after *reverence* ; A₁ alters the passage.
702. *so as, i.e.* since.

seyn that schrewes revengen hem ayen-ward uppon dignytes), for thei yelden ayen to dignytees as greet gerdoun, whan they by-spotten and defoulen dignytes with hir vylenye. And for as mochel as thou mow knowe that thilke verray reverence ne mai nat comen by thise schadwy transitorie dignytes, undir-stond now thus: [705] yif that a man hadde used and had manye maner dignytees of consules, and weere comen peraventure among straunge nacions, scholde thilke honour maken hym wor-schipful and redouted of straunge folk ? Certes yif that honour of peple were a natureel yifte to dignytes, it ne myghte nevere cesen no where amonges no maner folk to don his office ; right as fyer in every contre ne stynteth nat to eschaufen and to ben hoot. But for as mochel as for to be holden honourable or reverent ne cometh nat to folk of hir propre strengthe of nature, but oonly of the false opynyoun of folk (that is to seyn, that weenen that dignytees maken folk digne of honour), anoon therfore, whan that thei comen there as folk ne knowen nat thilke dignytees, hir honours van-ysschen a-way, and that anoon. But that is amonges straunge folk, maystow seyn. Ne amonges hem ther thei weren born, ne duren nat thilke dignytes al-wey ? [710] Certes the dignyte of the provostrye of Rome was whilom a greet power ; now nys it no thyng but an idel name, and the rente of the senatorie a greet charge. And yif a wyght whilom hadde the office to taken heede to the vitayles of the peple, as of corn and othere thynges, he was holden amonges grete ; but what thyng is now more out cast than thilke provostrye ? And, as I have seyd a litel here byforn, that thilke thyng that hath no propre beute of hym-self resceyveth somtyme prys and

schynynge, and som-tyme leeseth it, by the opinyoun of usaunces. Now yif that dignytes thanne ne mowen nat make folk digne of reverence, and if that dignytees waxen foule of hir wil by the filthe of schrewes, and yif dignytees leesen hir schynynge by chaungynge of tymes, and yif thei waxen fowle by estimacioun of peple, what is it that they han in hem-self of beaute that oughte ben desired ? [715] (As who seith noon.) Thanne ne mowen they yeven no beaute of dignyte to noone othere.

' Quamvis se Tirio.'—Metrum 4

Al be it so that the proude Nero, with al his wode luxure, kembde hym and apparayled hym with faire purpres of Tyrie and with white peerles, algates yit throf he haatful to alle folk (this is to seyn that, al was he byhated of alle folk, yit this wikkide Nero hadde gret lord-schipe), and yaf whilom to the reverentes senatours the unworschipful seetis of dignytees. (Unworschipful seetes he clepeth here, for that Nero, that was so wikkide, yaf tho dignytees.) Who wolde thanne resonably wenen that blisfulnesse were in swiche honours as ben yyven by vycious schrewes ? [720]

' An vero regna.'—Prosa 5

But regnes and familiarites of kynges, mai thei maken a man to ben myghti ? How elles, whan hir blisfulnesse dureth perpetuely ? But certes the olde age of tyme passed, and ek of present tyme now, is ful of ensaumples how that kynges han chaungyd into wrecchidnesse out of hir welefulnesse. O, a noble thyng and a cleer thyng is power that is nat fownden myghty to kepe it-self ! And yif that power of remes be auctour and makere of blisfulnesse, yif thilke power lakketh

---

710. *weren born,* i.e. spring. *ne duren nat,* ' Num,' etc.
711. *rente,* tax.
712. *grete,* great people.
713. *that* formally introduces the quoted statement as in 543.

713. *of usaunces,* 'utentium,' is possibly ' des usans ' mistaken for ' des usances ' ; it should be ' of hem that usen hem.'
720. C_1 Hn. H *to* for *by.*
721. *How elles,* etc., glossed *yronice* in C_1.

on any syde, amenuseth it nat thilke blisfulnesse and bryngeth in wrecchidnesse? But yit, al be it so that the remes of mankynde strecchen brode, yit moot ther nede ben moche folk over whiche that every kyng ne hath no lordschipe ne comaundement. [725] And certes uppon thilke syde that power fayleth, whiche that maketh folk blisful, ryght on the same syde noun-power entreth undir-nethe, that maketh hem wrecches. In this manere thanne moten kynges han more porcioun of wrecchidnesse than of welefulnesse. A tyraunt, that was kyng of Sysile, that hadde assayed the peril of his estat, schewede by simylitude the dredes of remes by gastnesse of a swerd that heng over the heved of his familyer. What thyng is thanne this power, that mai nat doun awey the bytynges of bysynesse, ne eschewe the prykkes of drede? And certes yit wolde thei lyven in sykernesse, but thei may nat, and yit they glorifien hem in hir power. [730] Holdestow thanne that thilke man be mighty, that thow seest that he wolde doon that he may nat doon? And holdestow thanne hym a myghti man, that hath envyrowned his sydes with men of armes or sergeantes, and dredeth more hem that he maketh agast thanne thei dredden hym, and that is put in the handes of hise servauntes for he scholde seme myghty? But of familiers or servantes of kynges, what scholde I telle the any thyng, syn that I my-self have schewyd the that rewmes hem-self ben ful of greet feblesse? The whiche familyeres certes the real power of kynges, in hool estat and in estaat abated, ful ofte throweth adoun. Nero constreynede Senek, his familyer and his mayster, to chesen on what deeth he wolde deye. [735] Antonyus comaundede that knyghtes slowen with here swerdes Papynian, his famylier, whiche Papynian

that had ben long tyme ful myghty amonges hem of the court. And yet certes thei wolden bothe han renounced hir power; of whiche two Senek enforcede hym to yeven to Nero his richesses, and also to han gon into solitarie exil. But whan the grete weyghte (that is to seyn of lordes power or of fortune) draweth hem that schullen falle, neither of hem ne myghte don that he wolde. What thyng is thanne thilke powere, that though men han it, yit thei ben agast; and whanne thou woldest han it, thou nart nat siker; and yif thou woldest forleeten it, thow mayst nat eschuen it? But whethir swiche men ben freendes at nede, as ben conseyled by fortune and nat be vertu? [740] Certes swiche folk as weleful fortune maketh frendes, contraryous fortune maketh hem enemys. And what pestilence is more myghty for to anoye a wyght than a famylier enemy?

'Qui se volet esse potentem.'—Metrum 5

Who so wol ben myghti he moot daunten his cruel corages, ne putte nat his nekke, overcomen, undir the foule reynes of leccherie. For al be it so that thi lordschipe strecche so fer that the contre of Ynde quaketh at thy comaundementes or at thi lawes, and that the last ile in the see that highte Tyle be thral to the, yit yif thou maist nat putten awey thi foule dirke desires, and dryven out fro the wrecchide compleyntes, certes it nys no power that thow hast. [745]

'Gloria vero quam fallax.'—Prosa 6

But glorie, how deceyvable and how foul is it ofte! For which thyng nat unskilfully a tragedien (that is to seyn a makere of dytees that highten tragedies) cride and seide: "O glorie, glorie,"

---

726. *noun-power*, impotence.

733. *familiers or servantes*, Fr. 'familieres,' and Lat. 'familiaribus' read as 'famularibus.'

736. *Antonyus*, mistake of some Latin texts for *Antoninus*, i.e. Caracalla.

738. *hem that schullen*, etc., 'ipsos casuros.'

739. Should be, *But whether* (introducing simple direct question) *swiche freendes as ben conciled* ('conciliat') *by fortune, and not by vertu, ben a help* ('auxilio' dat. not abl.)?

745. *Tyle*, Ultima Thule.

746. Cp. Euripides, *Androm.* 319.

quod he, "thow nart nothyng elles to thousandes of folk but a greet swellere of eres!" For manye han had ful greet renoun by the false opinyoun of the peple, and what thyng mai ben thought foulere than swiche preysynge? For thilke folk that ben preysed falsly, they mote nedes han schame of hire preysynges. And yif that folk han geten hem thonk or preys-ynge by here dissertes, what thyng hath thilke pris echid or encresed to the conscience of wise folk, that mesuren hir good, nat by the rumour of the peple, but by sothfastnesse of conscience? And yif it seme a fair thyng a man to han encreced and sprad his name, thanne folweth it that it is demed to ben a foul thyng yif it ne be yspradde and encreced. [750] But, as I seide a litel here byforn, that syn ther moot nedes ben many folk to whiche folk the renoun of a man ne mai nat comen, it byfalleth that he that thow wenest be glorious and renomed semeth in the nexte partie of the erthes to ben withouten glorie and withouten renoun. And certes amonges thise thynges I ne trowe nat that the pris and the grace of the peple nys neyther worthi to ben remembred, ne cometh of wys juge-ment, ne is ferme perdurably.

But now of this name of gentilesse, what man is it that ne may wele seen how veyn and how flyttynge a thyng it is? For yif the name of gentilesse be referred to renoun and cleernesse of lynage, thanne is gentil name but a foreyne thyng (that is to seyn to hem that gloryfien hem of hir lynage). [755] For it semeth that gentilesse be a maner preisynge that cometh of the dessertes of auncestres; and yif preisynge make gentilesse, thanne mote they nedes ben gentil that been preysed. For whiche thing it folweth that yif thou ne have no gentilesse of thi-self (that is to seyn prys that cometh of thy deserte), foreyne gen-tilesse ne maketh the nat gentil. But

certes yif ther be ony good in gentilesse, I trowe it be al only this, that it semeth as that a maner necessite be imposed to gentil men for that thei ne schulde nat owtrayen or forlyven fro the vertus of hir noble kynrede.

' Omne hominum genus in terris.'—
Metrum 6

Alle the lynage of men that ben in erthe ben of semblable byrthe ; on allone is fadir of thynges, on allone mynystreth alle thynges. He yaf to the sonne his bemes, he yaf to the moone hir hornes, he yaf the men to the erthe, he yaf the sterres to the hevene. [760] He encloseth with membres the soules that comen from his heye sete. Thanne comen alle mortel folk of noble seed. Why noysen ye or bosten of your eldres ? For yif thow loke youre bygynnyng, and god your auctour and yowr makere, thanne nis ther none for-lyved wyght or on-gentil but if he noryssche his corage un-to vices and forleten his propre byrthe.

' Quid autem de corporibus.'—Prosa 7

But what schal I seye of delyces of body, of which delices the desirynges ben ful of anguyssch, and the fulfillynges of hem ben ful of penance? How grete seknesses and how grete sorwes un-suffrable, ryght as a maner fruyte of wykkidnesse, ben thilke delices wont to bryngen to the bodyes of folk that usen hem ! Of whiche delices I not what joie mai ben had of here moevynge, [765] but this woot I wel, that who-so-evere wol remembren hym of hise luxures, he schal wel undirstonden that the issues of delices ben sorweful and sorye. And yif thilke delices mowen maken folk blisful, thanne by the same cause moten thise beestis ben clepid blisful, of whiche beestes al the entencioun hasteth to ful-

751. *as I seide . . . that,* cp. 713.
753. *I ne trowe nat,* etc., due to 'ne . . . quidem' in 'popularem gratiam ne commemora-tione quidem dignam puto.'

758. *owtrayen or forlyven,* 'degenerent'; *owtrayen,* 'go to excess,' does not seem happy.
762. Hn. Cx. H B *yif ye loke.*

fille here bodily jolyte. And the gladnesse of wyf and children were an honest thyng, but it hath ben seyd that it is overmochel ayens kynde that children han ben fownden tormentours to here fadris I not how manye ; of whiche children how bytynge is every condicioun, it nedeth nat to tellen it the that hast or this tyme assayed it, and art yit now angwysshous. In this approve I the sentence of my disciple Euridippis, that seide that he that hath no children is weleful by infortune. [770]

' *Habet hoc voluptas.*'—Metrum 7

Every delit hath this, that it angwissch-eth hem with prykkes that usen it. It resembleth to thise flyenge flyes that we clepen ben ; that, aftir that the be hath sched hise agreable honyes, he fleeth awey, and styngeth the hertes of hem that ben y-smyte, with bytynge over-longe haldynge.

' *Nichil igitur dubium.*'—Prosa 8

Now is it no doute thanne that thise weyes ne ben a maner mysledynges to blisfulnesse, ne that they ne mowen nat leden folk thider as thei byheten to leden hem. But with how grete harmes thise forseide weyes ben enlaced, I schal schewe the shortly. For-why yif thou enforcest the to assemble moneye, thow must byreven hym his moneye that hath it ; [775] and yif thow wolt schynen with dignytees, thow must bysechen and supplyen hem that yyven tho dignytees ; and yif thow coveytest be honour to gon byfore othere folk, thow schalt defoule thi-self thurw humblesse of axynge.

---

767. *jolyte*, 'lasciviam,' variant for 'lacunam.'
768. *but it hath*, etc., 'sed nimis e (Aq. extra) natura dictum est, nescio quem filios invenisse tortores,' mistranslated. By omitting *that it is* we get a possible version.
770. H *Euripides*, cp. *Androm.* 394.
772. *bytynge*, etc., 'tenaci morsu.'
773. *to blisfulnesse* should follow *weyes*.
774. *shortly*, briefly.

Yif thou desirest power, thow schalt, be awaytes of thy subgetis, anoyously ben cast undir by manye periles. Axestow glorye ? Thow shalt so bien distract by aspere thynges that thow schalt forgon sykernesse. And yif thow wolt leden thi lif in delyces, every wyght schal despysen the and for-leeten the, as thow that art thral to thyng that is right foul and brutyl (that is to seyn, servaunt to thi body). [780] Now is it thanne wel yseyn how litil and how brotel possessioun thei coveyten that putten the goodes of the body aboven hir owene resoun. For maystow surmounten thise olifauntes in gretnesse or weighte of body ? Or maistow ben strengere than the bole ? Maystow ben swyftere than the tigre ? Byhoold the spaces and the stablenesse and the swyft cours of the hevene, and stynt som-tyme to wondren on foule thynges. The whiche hevene certes nys nat rathere for thise thynges to ben won-dryd upon, than for the resoun by whiche it is governed. [785] But the schynynge of thi forme (that is to seyn, the beaute of thi body), how swyftly passynge is it, and how transitorie !

Certes it is more flyttynge than the mutabilite of floures of the somer sesoun. For so as Aristotle telleth, that if that men hadden eyghen of a beeste that highte lynx, so that the lokynge of folk myghte percen thurw the thynges that withstonden it, who-so lokide thanne in the entrayles of the body of Alcibiades, that was ful fair in the superfice withoute, it schulde seme ryght foul. And for-thi yif thow semest fair, thy nature ne maketh nat that, but the deceyvaunce or the feblesse of the eighen that loken. [790] But preise the goodes of the body as mochil as evere the lyst, so that thowe knowe algatis that, what-so it be (that is to seyn, of the godes of the body) whiche that thou wondrist uppon, mai ben

---

778. *awaytes*, 'insidiis.'
778. *anoyously ben cast undir by*, 'obnoxius subjacebis' mistranslated.
787. *lynx*, Lynceis oculis ; but Fr. 'yeulz de lins.' Aq. quotes Isidor, *de lince*.

destroied or dissolvid by the heete of a fevere of thre dayes. Of alle whiche forseide thynges y mai reducen this schortly in a somme : that thise worldly goodes, whiche that ne mowen nat yeven that they by-heeten, ne ben nat parfite by the congregacioun of alle goodis ; that they ne ben nat weyes ne pathes that bryngen men to blisfulnesse, ne maken men to ben blisful.

'*Heu que miseros tramite.*'—Metrum 8

Allas ! whiche folie and whiche ignorance mysledeth wandrynge wrecchis fro the path of verray good ! Certes ye ne seke no gold in grene trees, ne ye gadere nat precyous stones in the vynes, ne ye ·ne hiden nat yowr gynnes in heye mountaignes to kacchen fyssche of whiche ye mai maken riche festes. [795] And if yow liketh to hunt to roos, ye ne gon nat to the foordes of the watir that highte Tyrene. And over this, men knowen wel the krikes and the cavernes of the see yhidde in the flodes, and knowen ek whiche watir is moost plentevous of white peerlis, and knowen whiche watir haboundeth moost of reed purpre (that is to seyn, of a maner schelle fyssche with whiche men deien purpre), and knowen whiche strondes habounden most of tendre fysches, or of scharpe fyssches that hyghten echynnys. But folk suffren hem-selve to ben so blynde, that hem ne reccheth nat to knowe where thilke goodes ben yhidd whiche that thei coveyten, but ploungen hem in erthe, and seken there thilke good that surmounteth the hevene that bereth the sterris. What preyere mai I make, that be digne to the nyce thoughtes of men ? [800] But I preie that thei coveyten rychesses and honours. So that, whanne thei han geten tho false goodes with greet travaile, that ther-by they mowen knowen the verray goodes.

'*Hactenus mendacis formam.*'—Prosa 9

It suffiseth that I have schewyd hiderto the forme of fals welefulnesse, so that yif thou loke now cleerly, the ordre of myn entencioun requireth from hennes forth to schewe the verray welefulnesse.'

'For sothe,' quod I, 'I se wel now that suffisaunce may· nat comen by rychesses, ne power by remes, ne reverence by dignites, ne gentilesse by glorie, ne joie be delices.'

'And hastow wel knowen the causes,' quod sche, 'whi it is ?'

'Certes me semeth,' quod I, 'that y see hem ryght as thoughe it were thurw a litil clyfte, but me were levere to knowen hem more opynly of the.' [805]

'Certes,' quod sche, 'the resoun is al redy. For thilke thyng that symply is o thyng with outen ony devysioun, the errour and folie of mankynde departeth and divideth it, and mysledeth it and transporteth from verray and parfit good to godes that ben false and imparfit. But seye me this. Wenestow that he that hath nede of power, that hym ne lakketh nothyng ?'

'Nay,' quod I.

'Certes,' quod sche, 'thou seyst aryght ; for if it so be that ther is a thyng that in any partie be feblere of power, certes, as in that, it moot needes be nedy of foreyne help.'

'Ryght so is it,' quod I.

'Suffisaunce and power ben thanne of o kynde ?' [810]

'So semeth it,' quod I.

'And demestow,' quod sche, 'that a thyng that is of this manere, that is to seyn suffisaunt and mighty, oughte ben despised, or ellis that it be right digne of reverence aboven alle thynges ?'

---

796. *foordes*, 'Tyrrhena vada.'
797. *krikes*, inlets.
800. *What preyere*, etc., 'Quid imprecer,' but 'Quelle priere puis je faire,' etc.
800. *nyce*, foolish.

801. *ther-by*, not in original.
802. *the verray welefulnesse, the* is the article.
806. *al redy*, 'promptissima.'
808. *Wenestow*, etc., rather *Wenestow that he that ne lakketh nothyng hath nede of power!*

'Certes,' quod I, 'it nys no doute that it nys right worthy to ben reverenced.'

'Lat us,' quod sche, 'adden thanne reverence to suffisaunce and to power, so that we demen that thise thre thynges be al o thyng?'

'Certes,' quod I, 'lat us adden it, yif we wiln graunten the sothe.' [815]

'What demestow thanne,' quod sche, 'is that a dirk thyng and nat noble that is suffisaunt, reverent, and myghty; or elles that it is ryght noble and ryght cleer by celebrete or renoun? Considere thanne,' quod sche, 'as we han grauntide her-by-fore, that he that ne hath nede of no thyng and is moost myghty and moost digne of honour, if hym nedeth any cleernesse of renoun, whiche clernesse he myght nat graunten of hym-self; so that for lak of thilke cleernesse he myghte seme the feblere on any side, or the more out-cast.' (Glose. This to seyn, nay; for who-so that is suffisaunt, myghty, and reverent, clernesse of renoun folweth of the forseyde thynges, so that there ne be amonges hem no difference; he hath it al redy of his suffysaunce.)

'I mai nat,' quod I, 'denye it, but I moot granten, as it is, that this thyng be ryght celebrable by clernesse of renoun and noblesse.' [820]

'Thanne folweth it,' quod sche, 'that we adden clernesse of renoun to the thre forseyde thynges, so that there ne be amonges hem no difference.'

'This is a consequence,' quod I.

'This thyng thanne,' quod sche, 'that ne hath nede of no foreyne thyng, and that may don alle thynges by hise strengthis, and that is noble and honour-able, nys nat that a myry thyng and a joyful?'

'But whennes,' quod I, 'that any

sorwe myghte comen to this thyng that is swiche, certes I mai nat thynke.'

'Thanne mote we graunten,' quod sche, 'that this thing be ful of gladnesse, if the forseide thynges ben sothe; [825] and certes also mote we graunten that suffisaunce, power, noblesse, reverence, and gladnesse be oonly diverse by names, but hir substaunce hath no diversite.'

'It moot nedly ben so,' quod I.

'Thilke thyng thanne,' quod sche, 'that is oon and symple in his nature, the wikkidnesse of men departeth it and divideth it; and whanne thei enforcen hem to gete partie of a thyng that ne hath no part, thei ne geten hem neyther thilke partie that is noon, ne the thyng al hool that thei ne desire nat.'

'In whiche manere?' quod I.

'Thilke man,' quod sche, 'that seketh richesse to fleen poverte, he ne travaileth hym nat for to geten power, for he hath lever to ben dirk and vyl; [830] and eek withdraweth from hym-self manye naturel delites, for he nolde leese the moneie that he hath assembled. But certes in this manere he ne geteth hym nat suffisance, that power forletteth, and that moleste prikketh, and that filthe maketh out-caste, and that dirknesse hideth. And certes he that desireth oonly power, he wasteth and scatereth rychesse, and despyseth delices and eek honour that is withoute power, ne he ne preiseth glorie no thyng. Certes thus seestow wel that manye thynges failen to hym, for he hath som tyme defaute of manye necessites, and manye anguysshes byten hym; and whan he ne mai nat do tho defautes awey, he for-letith to ben myghty, and that is the thyng that he moost desireth. [835] And ryght thus mai I make semblable resouns of honour, and of glorie, and of delyces; for so as every of thise forseide thinges is the same that thise othere thynges ben (that is to seyn, al oon thyng), who-so that

---

817. *i.e.* Consider whether he who nedes nothing and is myghty and honoured, needs fame. The *that* seems to be used as in 713.

821. *that we adden*, etc., 'ut claritudinem superioribus tribus nihil differre fateamur.' Chaucer's incorrect version is due to Fr.

822. C₃ A₁ omit *is* after *this*.

830. *dirk and vyl*, 'vilis obscurusque.'

832. *maketh out-caste*, 'abicit.'

835. C₁ A₂ H *the defautes*.

evere seketh to geten that oon of thise, and nat that othir, he ne geteth nat that he desireth.'

'What seystow thanne, yif that a man coveyte to geten alle thise thynges togidre?'

'Certes,' quod sche, 'I wolde seye, that he wolde geten hym sovereyn blisfulnesse ; but that schal he nat fynde in tho thynges that I have schewed that ne mowen nat yeven that thei byheeten?'

'Certes no,' quod I. [840]

'Thanne,' quod sche, 'ne scholde men nat by no weye seken blisfulnesse in siche thynges as men wenen that they ne mowen yeven but o thyng sengly of al that men seken?'

'I graunte wel,' quod I, 'ne no sothere thyng ne may be seyd.'

'Now hastow thanne,' quod sche, 'the forme and the causes of false welefulnesse. Now torne and flytte the eighen of thi thought, for ther shaltow seen anoon thilke verray blisfulnesse that I have be-hyght the.'

'Certes,' quod I, 'it is cler and opene, though it were to a blynd man ; [845] and that schewedestow me ful wel a litel her byforn, whan thow enforcedest the to schewe me the causes of the fals blisfulnesse. For, but if I be begiled, thanne is thilke the verray perfit blisfulnesse that perfitly maketh a man suffisaunt, myghty, honourable, noble, and ful of gladnesse. And for thow schalt wel knowe that I have wel undirstonden thise thinges withynne myn herte, I knowe wel that thilke blisfulnesse that may verrayly yeven on of the forseyde thynges, syn thei ben alle oon —I knowe dowtelees that thilke thyng is the ful blysfulnesse.'

'O my nory,' quod sche, 'by this opynyoun I seie thow art blisful, yif thow putte this therto that I schal seyn.'

'What is that?' quod I. [850]

Philosophie. 'Trowestow that ther be any thyng in this erthly, mortel, toumblynge thynges that may brynge this estat?'

'Certes,' quod I, 'y trowe it nought ; and thow hast schewyd me wel that over thilke good ther nys no thyng more to ben desired.'

'Thise thynges thanne,' quod sche, (that is to seyn, erthly suffysaunce, and powere, and swiche thynges) outher thei semen lyknesse of verray good, or elles it semeth that thei yeve to mortel folk a maner of goodes that ne be nat perfyt. But thilke good that is verray and perfyt that mai thei nat yeven.' [855]

'I accorde me wel,' quod I.

'Thanne,' quod sche, 'for as moche as thou hast knowen whiche is thilke verray blisfulnesse, and eek whiche thilke thynges ben that lyen falsly blisfulnesse (that is to seyn, that be deceyte semen verray goodes), now byhoveth the to knowe whennes and where thow mowe seke thilke verrai blisfulnesse.'

'Certes,' quod I, 'that desire I gretly and have abyden longe tyme to herkne it.'

'But for as moche,' quod sche, 'as it liketh to my disciple Plato, in his book of *In Thymeo*, that in ryght litel thynges men schulde byseche the help of god, [860] what juggestow that be now to done, so that we may desserve to fynde the seete of thilk sovereyn good?'

'Certes,' quod I, 'y deme that we schul clepe to the fadir of alle goodes, for withouten hym is ther no thyng founded aryght.'

'Thow seyst aryght,' quod sche, and bygan anoon to syngen right thus :

839. *What seystow?* 'Quid igitur? inquam.' So also Fr. *yif that*, etc., is assigned to Philosophy in Obbarius' text, but early MSS. and translations take it as Chaucer does.

840. *but that schal he nat*, etc., 'num . . . reperiet,' etc., cp. 691, 710. The subject of *ne mowen* is omitted. B.'s reading, *they* for *ne*, is probably a scribe's correction.

845. Some phrase like *to the othere part*, 'in adversum,' has probably dropped out after *thought*.

851. *this*, these. *toumblynge*, 'caducis,' as in 357, 406.

856. *lyen*, counterfeit.

860. *In Thymeo*, rather *in the Timeus* (cp. *Tim.* 27 c.)

'*O quam perpetua.*'—Metrum 9

'O thow fadir, soowere and creatour of hevene and of erthes, that governest this world by perdurable resoun, that comaundest the tymes to gon from syn that age hadde bygynnynge; thow that duellest thi-selve ay stedefast and stable, and yevest alle othere thynges to ben meved, [865] ne foreyne causes necesseden the nevere to compoune werk of floterynge matere, but oonly the forme of sovereyn good I-set with-in the withoute envye, that moevede the frely. Thow, that art althir-fayrest, berynge the faire world in thyn thought, formedest this world to the lyknesse semblable of that faire world in thy thought. Thou drawest alle thyng of thy sovereyn ensaumpler and comaundest that this world, parfytely ymakid, have frely and absolut hise parfyte parties. Thow byndest the elementis by nombres proporcionables, that the coolde thinges mowen accorde with the hote thinges, and the drye thinges with the moyste; that the fuyer, that is purest, fleigh nat over-heye, ne that the hevynesse drawe nat adoun over-lowe the erthes that ben ploungid in the watris. [870] Thow knyttest togidere the mene soule of treble kynde moevynge alle thingis, and divydest it by membrys accordynge; and whan it is thus divyded [and] it hath assembled a moevynge in-to two rowndes, it gooth to torne ayen to hym-self, and envyrouneth a ful deep thought and turneth the hevene by semblable ymage. Thow by evene lyke causes enhauncest the soules and the lasse lyves; and, ablynge hem heye by lyghte waynes or cartes, thow sowest hem in-to hevene and in-to erthe. [875] And whan thei ben convertyd to the by thi benygne lawe, thow makest hem retourne ayen to the by ayen-ledynge fyer. O fadir, yyve thou to the thought to steyen up in-to thi streyte seete; and graunte hym to environe the welle of good; and, the lyght I-founde, graunte hym to fycchen the clere syghtes of his corage in the; and skatere thou and to-breke the weyghtes and the cloudes of erthly hevynesse; and schyn thou by thi bryghtnesse, for thou art cleernesse, thow art pesible reste to debonayre folk; thow thi-self art bygynnynge, berere, ledere, path and terme; to looke on the, that is our ende. [880]

'*Quoniam igitur que sit.*'—Prosa 10

For as moche thanne as thow hast seyn which is the fourme of good that nys nat parfit, and whiche is the forme of good that is parfit, now trowe I that it were good to schewe in what this perfeccioun of blisfulnesse is set. And in this thing I trowe that we schulde first enquere for to witen, yf that any swich maner good as thilke good that thou hast dyffinysshed a litel here-byforn (that is to seyn sovereyn good) may be founde in the nature of thinges, for that veyn ymagynacioun of thought desceyve us nat, and put us out of the sothfastnesse of thilke thinge that is summytted to us. But it may nat be denyed that thilke good ne is, and that it nys ryght as a welle of alle goodes. For alle thing that is cleped inparfyt is proevid inparfit be the amenusynge of perfeccioun or of thing that is parfit. [885] And herof cometh it that in every thing general, yif that men seen any thing that is inparfit, certes in thilke general ther moot ben som thing that is parfit. For yif so be that perfeccioun is don awey, men may nat thinke ne say

864. C₂ A₁ Hn. omit *soowere and;* H Cx. *sovereigne and.*
866. *frely.* Not in Latin or French.
868. *Thou drawest . . . ensaumpler,* precedes *Thow that art,* etc., in Latin and French. Perhaps displaced by an early scribe; if so, the reading of A₁, *and commaundedest,* is correct.
869. *nombres proporcionables,* numerical proportions.
871. 'Quæ cum secta duos motum glomeravit in orbes, In semet reditura meat mentemque profundam circuit, et simili convertit imagine cælum.'

875. *heye,* to rise.
877. *environe,* 'lustrare' (to look upon), Fr. 'auirouner.'

fro whennes thilke thing is that is cleped inparfyt. For the nature of thinges ne took nat hir begynnynge of thinges amenused and inparfit, but it procedith of thinges that ben alle hole and ab-solut, and descendith so doun into uttereste thinges and in-to thinges empty and withouten fruyt. But, as I have schewid a litel here byforn that yif ther be a blisfulnesse that be freel and veyn and inparfyt, ther may no man doute that ther nys som blisfulnesse that is sad, stede-fast, and parfyt.'

'This is concluded,' quod I, 'feermely and soothfastly.' [89c]

'But considere also,' quod sche, 'in whom this blisfulnesse enhabiteth. The comune accordaunce and conceyt of the corages of men proveth and graunteth that god, prince of alle thinges, is good. For, so as no thyng mai ben thought betere than god, it mai nat ben douted thanne that he that no thinge nys betere, that he nys good. Certes resoun scheweth that god is so good that it proeveth by verray force that parfyt good is in hym. For yif god nys swyche, he ne mai nat be prince of alle thinges; [895] for certes som-thing possessyng in it-self parfyt good schulde be more worthy than god, and it scholde semen that thilke were first and eldere than god. For we han schewyd apertely that alle thinges that ben parfyt ben first er thynges that ben inparfit; and for-thy, for as moche as that my resoun or my proces ne go nat awey withouten an ende, we owe to graunte that the sovereyn god is right ful of sovereyn parfit good. And we han establissched that the sovereyne good is verray blisfulnesse. Thanne moot it nedis be that verray blisfulnesse is set in sovereyn god.' [900]

'This take I wel,' quod I, ' ne this ne mai nat be withseid in no manere.'

'But I preye the,' quod sche, 'see now how thou mayst proeven holily and

withoute corrupcioun this that I have seid, that the sovereyn god is ryght ful of sovereyne good.'

' In whiche manere?' quod I.

'Wenestow aught,' quod sche, 'that the prince of alle thynges have I-take thilke sovereyne good any-wher out of hym-self, of whiche sovereyne good men proeveth that he is ful; ryght as thou myghtest thynken that god, that hath blisfulnesse in hym-self, and thilk blisful-nesse that is in hym, were divers in substaunce? [905] For yif thow wene that god have resseyved thilke good out of hym-self, thow mayst wene that he that yaf thilke good to god be more worth than is god. But I am beknowe and confesse, and that ryght dignely, that god is ryght worthy aboven alle thinges. And yif it so be that this good be in hym by nature, but that it is dyvers from him by wenynge resoun, syn we speke of god prynce of alle thynges, — feyne who so feyne mai—who was he that hath con-ioyned thise divers thynges togidre? And eek at the laste se wel that a thing that is divers from any thing, that thilke thing nys nat that same thing fro whiche it is undirstonden to be diverse. Thanne folweth it that thilke thing that by his nature is divers from sovereyn good, that that thyng nys nat sovereyn good. [910] But certes it were a felenous cursydnesse to thinken that of hym that no thing nys more worth. For alwey, of alle thinges, the nature of hem may nat ben betere thanne his begynnynge. For whiche I mai concluden by ryght verray resoun that thilke that is begynnynge of alle thinges, thilke same thing is sovereyn good in his substaunce.'

'Thow hast seyd ryghtfully,' quod I.

'But we han graunted,' quod sche, ' that the sovereyn good is blisfulnesse.'

'That is sooth,' quod I. [915]

---

904. Chaucer and one of French MSS. omit ' vel ita naturaliter habere.' Add, therefore, after *ful; or wenestow that he hath it naturely in himself.*

912. C₁ H Cx. A₂ *hir beginnynge,* and rightly, but probably a correction.

894. *that no thinge,* etc., *i.e.* to whom nothing is superior.

901. *take,* ' accipio '; Fr. ' recoif.'

'Thanne,' quod sche, 'moten we nedes granten and confessen that thilke same sovereyn good be god?'

'Certes,' quod I, 'y ne may nat denye, ne withstonde the resouns purposed; and I se wel that it folweth by strengthe of the premisses.'

'Loke now,' quod sche, 'yif this be proevid yet more fermely thus that there ne mowen not ben two sovereyn goodis that ben divers among hem-self. For certes the goodis that ben divers among hem-self, that oon is nat that that that othir is; thanne mowen neither of hem ben parfit, so as eyther of hem lakketh to othir. But that that nys nat parfit, men mai seen apertely that it nys not sovereyn. [920] The thinges thanne that ben sovereynly gode ne mowe by no weie be divers. But I have wel concluded that blisfulnesse and god ben the sovereyn good; for whiche it mote nedes be that sovereyne blisfulnesse is sovereyn devynite.'

'No thing,' quod I, 'nys more soth-faste than this, ne more ferme by resoun, ne a more worthy thing than god mai not ben concluded.'

'Upon thise thynges thanne,' quod sche, 'ryght as thise geometriens whan thei han schewed her proposicions ben wont to bryngen yn thinges that thei clepen porismes or declaracions of for-seide thinges, right so wol I yeve the here as a corolarie or a meede of coroune. For-why for as moche as by the getynge of blisfulnesse men ben makid blisful, and blisfulnesse is dyvinite, than is it manifest and opene that by the getynge of dyvinite men ben makid blisful. [925] Right as by the getynge of justice [men ben maked just], and be the getynge of sapience thei ben maked wise, ryght so nedes by the semblable resoun, whan they han geten dyvinite thei ben maked goddes. Thanne is every blisful man

god. But certes by nature ther nys but o god; but by the participacioun of dyvinite ther ne let ne distourbeth no thyng that ther ne ben many goddis.'

'This ys,' quod I, 'a fair thing and a precious, clepe it as thou wilt, be it corolerie, or porisme, or mede of coroune, or declarynges.'

'Certes,' quod sche, 'no thing nys fairere than is the thing that by resoun schulde ben addide to thise forseide thinges.' [930]

'What thing?' quod I.

'So,' quod sche, 'as it semeth that blisfulnesse conteneth many thinges, it weere for to witen whether that alle thise thinges maken or conioynen as a maner body of blisfulnesse by diversite of parties or membres, or elles yif any of alle thilke thinges ben swich that it acomplise by hymself the substaunce of blisfulnesse, so that alle thise othere thynges ben referrid and brought to blisfulnesse (that is to seyn, as to the cheef of hem).'

'I wolde,' quod I, 'that thow madest me clerly to undirstonde what thou scist, and that thou recordidest me the for-seide thinges.'

'Have I not jugged,' quod sche, 'that blisfulnesse is good?' [935]

'Yys for sothe,' quod I, 'and that sovereyn good.'

'Adde thanne,' quod sche, 'thilke good that is maked [of] blisfulnesse to alle thise forseide thinges. For thilke same blisfulnesse that is demed to ben sovereyn suffisaunce, thilke selve is sovereyn power, sovereyn reverence, sovereyn clernesse or noblesse, and sovereyn delyt. What seistow thanne of all thise thinges, that is to seyn, suffisaunce, power, and alle thise othere thinges,—ben thei thanne as membris of blisfulnesse, or ben they reffered and brought to sovereyne good ryght as alle thinges that ben brought to the cheef of hem?'

'I undirstonde wel,' quod I, 'what

918. *thus that*, *i.e.* from the fact that.
919. *neither*, often plural in Middle-English.
924. *as*, as it were.
924. *meede of coroune*, 'loier de coroune.'
926. *men . . . just*, MSS. omit; supplied from French.

928. *let*, hindereth.
937. *of*, MSS. omit; supplied from French.

thou purposest to seke, but I desire for to herkne that thow schewe it me.' [940]

' Tak now thus the discrecioun of this questioun,' quod sche ; ' yif alle thise thinges,' quod sche, ' weren membris to felicite, thanne weren thei dyverse that on fro that othir. And swich is the nature of parties or of membres, that diverse membris compounen a body.'

' Certes,' quod I, ' it hath wel ben schewyd here byforn that alle thise thinges ben al o thyng.'

' Thanne ben thei none membres,' quod sche, ' for elles it schulde seme that blisfulnesse were conioyned al of o membre allone ; but that is a thing that mai not ben don.'

' This thing,' quod I, 'nys not doutous ; but I abide to herknen the remenaunt of the question.' [945]

' This is opene and cler,' quod sche, ' that alle othere thinges ben referrid and brought to good. For therfore is suffi- saunce requerid, for it is demyd to ben good ; and for-thy is power requirid, for men trowen also that it be good ; and this same thing mowen we thinken and coniecten of reverence, and of noblesse, and of delyt. Thanne is sovereyn good the somme and the cause of al that oughte ben desired ; for-why thilke thing that with-holdeth no good in it selve, ne semblance of good, it mai not wel in no manere be desired ne requerid. [950] And the contrarie ; for thoughe that thinges by here nature ne ben not gode, algates yif men wene that ben gode, yet ben thei desired as though that thei were verrayliche gode ; and ther-fore is it that men oughte to wene by ryghte that bounte be the sovereyn fyn and the cause of alle the thinges that ben to requiren. But certes thilke that is cause for which men requiren any thing, it semeth that thilke same thing be moost desired. As thus : yf that a wyght wolde ryden for cause of hele, he ne desireth not so mochel the

moevyng to ryden, as the effect of his hele. Now thanne, syn that alle thynges ben required for the grace of good, thei ne ben not desired of alle folk more than the same good. [955] But we han grauntide that blisfulnesse is that thing, for whiche that alle thise othere thinges ben desired ; thanne is it thus that certes oonly blysfulnesse is requered and desired. By whiche thing it scheweth cleerly that of good and of blisfulnesse is al on and the same substaunce.'

' I se nat,' quod I, ' wherfore that men myghten discorden in this.'

' And we han schewed that god and verray blisfulnesse is al o thing.'

' That is sooth,' quod I.

' Thanne mowen we concluden sykerly, that the substaunce of god is set in thilke same good, and in noon other place. [960]

' *Nunc omnes pariter venite capti.*'—
Metrum 10

Cometh alle to gidre now, ye that ben ykaught and ybounde with wikkide cheynes by the desceyvable delyt of erthly thynges enhabitynge in yowr thought ! Her schal ben the reste of your labours, her is the havene stable in pesible quiete ; this allone is the open refut to wreches. (Glose. This to seyn, that ye that ben combryd and disseyvid with worldly affeccions, cometh now to this sovereyn good, that is god, that is refut to hem that wolen come to hym.) Textus. Alle the thinges that the ryver Tagus yyveth yow with his goldene gravelis, or elles alle the thinges that the ryver Herinus yeveth with his rede brinke, [965] or that Indus yyveth, that is next the hote partie of the world, that medleth the grene stones with the white, ne scholden not

940. *that*, Fr. ' que ' (how).
941. *Tak now*, ' accipe.'
942. *a body*, one body.
951. Hn. ends with ' *yit ben they.*'

954. *moevyng to ryden*, movement of riding.
955. *for the grace*, etc., ' gratia boni.'
961. C₂ A₁ *O cometh.*
965. *Herinus*, Hermus.
966. *grene stones . . . white*, glossed *smarag-dus* (emeralds) and *margarites* (pearls) in C₁ C₂ A₂.

cleren the lookynge of your thought, but hiden rather your blynde corages withynne here derknesse. Al that liketh yow here, and exciteth and moeveth your thoughtes, the erthe hath norysschid it in his lowe caves. But the schynynge by whiche the hevene is governed and whennes that it hath his strengthe, that eschueth the derke overthrowynge of the soule; and who so evere may knowen thilke light of blisfulnesse, he schal wel seyn that the white beemes of the sonne ne ben nat cleer.' [970]

'*Assencior inquam cuncta.*'—Prosa 11

'I assente me,' quod I, 'for alle thise thinges ben strongly bounden with ryght ferme resouns.'

'How mychel wiltow preysen it,' quod sche, 'yif that thow knowe what thilke good is?'

'I wol preyse it,' quod I, 'be pris withouten ende, yif it schal betyde me to knowe also to gedre god that is good.'

'Certes,' quod sche, 'that schal I do the be verray resoun, yif that tho thinges that I have concluded a litel here byforn duellen only in hir first grauntynge.'

'Thei dwellen graunted to the,' quod I. (This to seyn as who seith, 'I graunte thi forseide conclusyouns.') [975]

'Have I nat schewed the,' quod sche, 'that the thinges that ben required of many folk ne ben not verray goodis ne parfite; for thei ben divers that on fro that othir. And so as iche of hem is lakkynge to othir, thei han no power to bryngen a good that is ful and absolut. But thanne at erste ben thei verraye good, whan thei ben gadred togidere alle in-to o forme and in-to oon werkynge. So that thilke thing that is suffisaunce, thilke same be power, and reverence, and noblesse, and myrthe. And for sothe, but yif alle thise thinges ben alle o same

thing, thei ne han not wherby that the mowen be put in the nombre of thinges that oughten ben required or desired.' [980]

'It is schewyd,' quod I, 'ne herof mai ther no man douten.'

'The thinges thanne,' quod sche, 'that ne ben none goodis whan thei ben diverse, and whanne thei bygynnen to ben al o thing, thanne ben thei goodes, — ne cometh it hem nat thanne by the getynge of unyte that thei ben maked goodes?'

'So it semeth,' quod I.

'But alle thing that is good,' quod sche, 'grauntestow that it be good by the participacioun of good, or no?'

'I graunte it,' quod I.

'Thanne mustow graunten,' quod sche, 'by semblable resoun that oon and good be o same thing; [985] for of thinges of whiche that the effect nys nat naturely divers, nedes the substaunce moot be oo same thing.'

'I ne may nat denye it,' quod I.

'Hastow nat knowen wel,' quod sche, 'that alle thing that is hath so longe his duellynge and his substaunce as longe as it is oon? But whanne it forletith to be oon, it moot nedys deien and corrumpen to gidres?'

'In whiche manere?' quod I.

'Ryght as in beestis,' quod sche, 'whanne the body and the soule ben conioyned in oon and dwellen to gidre, it is cleped a beeste; and whanne her unyte is destroyed be the disseveraunce the toon fro the tothir, thanne scheweth it wel that it is a deed thing, and that it nys no lengere no beeste. [990] And the body of a wyght, while it duelleth in oo fourme be coniunccion of membris, it is wel seyn that it is a figure of mankynde; and yif the parties of the body ben so devyded and disseverid the ton fro the tother that thei destroyen unite, the body forletith to ben that it was beforn. And who so wolde renne in the same

---

970. *overthrowynge*, 'ruinas.'
972. *preysen*, prize.
973. *also to gedre*, 'aussi ensemble,' at the same time.

983. *cometh it hem*, 'leur avient'; cp. 463.
988. *to gidres*, at once.
990. *no beeste*, a beast.
991. *figure of mankynde*, 'humaine figure.'

manere be alle thinges, he scholde seen that withouten doute every thing is in his substaunce as longe as it is oon ; and whanne it forletith to ben oon, it dyeth and peryssheth.'

' Whanne I considere,' quod I, ' manye thinges, I se noon other.'

' Is ther any thing thanne,' quod sche, ' that, in as moche as it lyveth naturely, that forletith the talent or the appetyt of his beynge and desireth to come to deth and to corrupcioun ? ' [995]

' Yif I considere,' quod I, ' the beestes that han any maner nature of wyllynge and of nyllynge, I ne fynde no beeste, but if it be constreyned fro withoute-forth that forletith or despiseth the entencion to lyven and to duren ; or that wole, his thankes, hasten hym to dyen. For every beest travaileth hym to defende and kepe the savacion of his lif, and eschueth deeth and destruccioun. But certes I doute me of herbes and of trees (that is to seyn, that I am in a doute of swiche thinges as herbes or trees), that ne han no felyng soules (ne no naturel werkynges servynge to appetites as beestes han), whether thei han appetyt to duellen and to duren.' [1000]

' Certes,' quod sche, ' ne therof thar the nat doute. Now looke upon thise herbes and thise trees. They wexen first in suche places as ben covenable to hem, in which places thei mowen nat sone deye ne dryen, as longe as hir nature mai defenden hem. For some of hem waxen in feeldis, and some in mountaynes, and othere waxen in mareys, and othre cleven on roches, and some wexen plentyvous in soondes ; and yif any wyght enforce hym to bere hem in-to other places, thei wexen drye. [1005] For nature yeveth to every thing that that is convenient to hym, and travailleth that they ne deie nat, as longe as thei han power to duellen and to lyven. What wiltow seyn of this, that thei drawen alle here norysschynges by here rootes, ryght as thei hadden here mouthes y-plounged withynne

997. *his thankes*, voluntarily.

the erthes, and sheden be hir maryes hir wode and hir bark ? And what wyltow seyn of this, that thilke thing that is ryght softe, as the marie is, that it is alwey hyd in the seete al with-inne, and' that it is defended fro withoute by the stedfastnesse of wode ; and that the outreste bark is put ayens the distemperaunce of the hevene as a·deffendour myghty to suffren harm ? And thus certes maistow wel seen how greet is the diligence of nature ; [1010] for alle thinges renovelen and publysschen hem with seed y-multiplied, ne ther nys no man that ne woot wel that they ne ben ryght as a foundement and edifice for to duren, noght oonly for a tyme, but ryght as for to dure perdurably by generacion. And the thinges eek that men wenen ne haven none soules, ne desire thei nat iche of hem by semblable resoun to kepyn that that is his (that is to seyn, that is accordynge to hir nature in conservacioun of hir beynge and endurynge)? For wherfore ellis bereth lightnesse the flaumbes up, and the weyghte presseth the erthe adoun, but for as moche as thilke places and thilke moevynges ben covenable to everyche of hem ? And for-sothe every thing kepeth thilke that is accordynge and propre to hym, ryght as thinges that ben contrarious and enemys corrumpen hem. [1015] And yet the harde thinges, as stones, clyven and holden here parties togidre ryght faste and harde, and defenden hem in withstondynge that thei ne departe nat lyghtly atwynne. And the thinges that ben softe and fletynge, as is watir and eyr, thei departen lyghtly and yeven place to hem that breken or divyden hem ; but natheles they retorne sone ageyn into the same thinges fro whennes thei ben arraced ; but fyer fleeth and

1007. *sheden* ; perhaps *sheden* should be *spreden*, 'espandent.'
1008. C₂ A₃ H Cx. *that is alwey*.
1010. *myghty*, etc., Aq. 'patiens mali, i.e. potens mala sustinere.'
1011. *renovelen and publysschen*, 'renouvellent' and 'propagentur.'
1012. C₂ *is hirs*, possibly right ; cp. Fr. 'leur,' and pronouns of following gloss.

refuseth alle dyvisioun. I trete not now here of willeful moevynges of the soule that is knowyng, but of the naturel entencioun of thinges, as thus: [1020] ryght as we swolwen the mete that that we resseyven and ne thinke nat on it, and as we drawen our breeth in slepynge that we witen it nat while we slepyn. For certes in the beestis the.love of hire lyvynges ne of hire beynges ne cometh not of the wilnynges of the soule, but of the bygynnynges of nature. For certes, thurw constreynynge causes, wil desireth and embraceth ful ofte tyme the deeth that nature dredeth. (That is to seyn as thus: that a man may be constreyned so, by som cause, that his wille desireth and taketh the deeth whiche that nature hateth and dredeth ful sore.) And somtyme we seen the contrarye, as thus: that the wil of a wyght distourbeth and constreyneth that that nature desireth and requirith alwey, that is to seyn the werk of generacioun, by whiche generacioun only duelleth and is susteyned the longe durablete of mortel thinges. [1025] And thus this charite and this love, that every thing hath to hym-self, ne cometh not of the moevynge of the soule, but of the entencioun of nature. For the purveaunce of god hath yeven to thinges that ben creat of hym this, that is a ful grete cause to lyven and to duren, for whiche they desiren naturely here lif as longe as evere thei mowen. For which thou mayst not drede be no manere that alle the thinges that ben any where, that thei ne requiren naturely the ferme stablenesse of perdurable duellynge, and eek the eschuynge of destruccioun.'

'Now confesse I wel,' quod I, 'that y see wel now certeynly withouten doutes the thinges that whilom semeden uncerteyn to me.'

'But,' quod sche, 'thilke thing that desireth to be and to duelle perdurably, he desireth to ben oon. [1030] For yif

that oon were destroyed certes beynge schulde ther noon duellen to no wyght.'

'That is sooth,' quod I.

'Thanne,' quod sche, 'desiren alle thinges oon.'

'I assente,' quod I.

'And I have schewed,' quod sche, 'that thilke same oon is thilke that is good.'

'Ye forsothe,' quod I.

'Alle thinges thanne,' quod sche, 'requiren good; and thilke good thow mayst descryven ryght thus: good is thilk thing that every wyght desireth.' [1035]

'Ther ne may be thought,' quod I, 'no more verraye thing. For eyther alle thinges ben referrid and brought to noght, and floteren withouten governour, despoyled of oon as of hire propre heued; or elles, yif ther be any thing to whiche that alle thinges tenden and hyen to, that thing muste ben the sovereyn good of alle goodes.'

Thanne seide sche thus: 'O my nory,' quod sche, 'I have greet gladnesse of the, for thow hast fycched in thyn herte the myddel sothfastnesse, that is to seyn, the prykke. But this thing hath ben discoveryd to the in that thow seydest that thow wisteth not a litel her byforn.'

'What was that?' quod I.

'That thou ne wistest noght,' quod sche, 'whiche was the ende of thinges. [1040] And certes that is the thyng that every wyght desireth; and for as mochel as we han gadrid and comprehendid that good is thilke thing that is desired of alle, thanne mote we nedys confessen that good is the fyn of alle thinges.'

'*Quisquis profunda.*'—Metrum 11

Whoso that seketh sooth by a deep thought, and coveyteth not to ben disseyvid by no mys-weyes, lat hym rollen

1036. *oon,* unity.
1037. *the myddel sothfastnesse,* 'mediæ veritatis notam.' The gloss is due to note in Aq.
1039. *But this thing* should be *But in this thing,* and *in that* should be *that that* to give sense of Latin and French.
1042. *mis-weyes,* bypaths.

and trenden withynne hymself the lyght of his ynwarde sighte ; and let hym gaderyn ayein, enclynynge in-to a compas, the longe moevynges of his thoughtes ; and let hym techyn his corage that he hath enclosid and hid in his tresors, al that he compasseth or secheth fro withoute. And thanne thilke thing, that the blake cloude of errour whilom hadde y-covered, schal lighte more clerly than Phebus hymself ne schyneth. [1045] (Glosa. Who so wol seke the depe ground of soth in his thought, and wil nat ben disseyvid by false proposicouns that goon amys fro the trouthe, lat hym wel examine and rolle withynne hym-self the nature and the propretes of the thing ; and let him yet eft sones examine and rollen his thoughtes by good deliberacion or that he deme, and lat hym techyn his soule that it hath, by naturel principles kyndeliche yhyd with-ynne it-self, al the trouthe the whiche ymagineth to ben in thinges withoute. And thanne al the derknesse of his mysknowynge shall seen more evydently to the sighte of his undirstondynge than the sonne ne semeth to the sighte withoute-forth.) [1050] For certes the body, bryngynge the weighte of foryetynge, ne hath nat chased out of your thought al the cleernesse of your knowyng ; for certeynli the seed of soth haldeth and clyveth within yowr corage, and it is a-waked and excited by the wynde and by the blastes of doctrine. For wherfore elles demen ye of your owene wil the ryghtes, whan ye ben axid, but if so were that the norysschynges of resoun ne lyvede y-plounged in the depe of your herte ? (This to seyn, how schulde men deme the sothe of any thing that wer axid, yif ther nere a rote of sothfastnesse that were y-plounged and hyd in the naturel principles, the whiche sothfastnesse lyvede within the depnesse of the thought ?) And if it so be that the Muse and the

doctrine of Plato syngeth soth, al that every wyght leerneth, he ne doth no thing elles thanne but recordeth, as men recorden thinges that ben foryeten.' [1055]

' Tunc ego Platoni inquam.'—Prosa 12

Thanne seide I thus : ' I accorde me gretly to Plato, for thou recordist and remembrist me thise thinges yet the seconde tyme ; that is to seye, first whan I loste my memorie be the contagious coniunccioun of the body with the soule, and eftsones aftirward, whan y lost it confounded by the charge and be the burdene of my sorwe.'

And thanne seide sche thus : ' Yif thow loke,' quod sche, ' first the thynges that thou hast graunted, it ne schal nat ben ryght fer that thow ne schalt remembren thilke thinges that thou seidest that thou nystist nat.'

' What thing ?' quod I.

' By whiche governement,' quod sche, ' that this world is governed.'

' Me remembreth it wel,' quod I ; ' and I confesse wel that I ne wyste it nat. [1060] But al be it so that I see now from afer what thou purposist, algates I desire yit to herknen it of the more pleynly.'

' Thou ne wendest nat,' quod sche, ' a litel here byforn, that men schulde doute that this world nys governed by god.'

' Certes,' quod I, ' ne yet ne doute I it naught, ne I nyl nevere wene that it were to doute ' (as who seith, ' but I woot wel that god gouverneth this world ') ; ' and I schal schortly answeren the be what resouns I am brought to this. This world,' quod I, ' of so manye and diverse and contraryous parties, ne myghte nevere han ben assembled in o forme, but yif ther ne were oon that conioyned so manye diverse thinges ; [1065] and the same diversite of here

1050. *seen* (B has *be*) seems to mean ' appear ' ; cp. *Legend of G. W.* 156, *Gen. and Ex.* 1923 (Morris).

1058. *it ne schal nat*, etc., *i.e.* thou shalt not be far from remembering.
1064. *answeren*, ' exponam ' ; Fr. ' espondrai, read as *respondrai*.

natures, that so discorden the ton fro that other, most departen and unioynen the thinges that ben conioynid, yif ther ne were oon that contenyde that he hath conioynid and ybounden. Ne the certein ordre of nature schulde not brynge forth so ordene moevynges by places, by tymes, by doynges, by spaces, by qualites, yif ther ne were on, that were ay stedfaste duellynge, that ordeynide and disponyde thise diversites of moevynges. And thilke thing, what-so-evere it be, by whiche that alle thinges ben y-maked and I-lad, y clepe hym " god," that is a word that is used to alle folk.' [1070]

Thanne seide sche : ' Syn thou feelist thus thise thinges,' quod sche, ' I trowe that I have litel more to done that thou, myghty of welefulnesse, hool and sound, ne see eftsones thi contre.

' But let us loken the thinges that we han purposed here-byforn. ' Have I nat nombrid and seid,' quod sche, ' that suffisaunce is in blisfulnesse ? and we han accorded that god is thilke same blisfulnesse ? '

' Yis forsothe,' quod I.

' And that to governen this world,' quod sche, ' ne schal he nevere han nede of noon help fro with-oute ? For elles, yif he hadde nede of any help, he ne schulde nat have no ful suffisaunce?' [1075]

' Yys thus it moot nedes be,' quod I.

' Thanne ordeyneth he be hym-self alone alle thinges ? ' quod sche.

' That may noght ben denyed,' quod I.

' And I have schewyd that god is the same good ? '

' It remembreth me wel,' quod I.

' Thanne ordeigneth he alle thinges by thilke good,' quod sche, ' syn he, whiche that we han accordid to ben good, governeth alle thinges by hym-self; and he is as a keye and a styere, by whiche

that the edifice of this world is kept stable and withouten corrumpynge ? '

' I accorde me greetly,' quod I. ' And I aperceyvede a litil here byforn that thow woldest seyn thus, al be it so that it were by a thynne suspecioun.' [1080]

' I trowe it wel,' quod sche ; ' for, as I trowe, thou ledist now more ententyfliche thyn eyen to loken the verray goodes. But natheles the thing that I schal telle the yet ne scheweth not lesse to loken.

' What is that ? ' quod I.

' So as men trowen,' quod sche, ' and that ryghtfully, that god governeth alle thinges by the keye of his goodnesse, and alle thise same thinges, as I have taught the, hasten hem by naturel entencioun to come to good, ther ne may no man douten that thei ne ben governed voluntariely, and that they ne converten hem of here owene wil to the wil of here ordeynour, as thei that ben accordynge and enclynynge to here governour and here kyng.'

' It moot nedes be so,' quod I, ' for the reame ne schulde nat seme blisful yif ther were a yok of mysdrawynges in diverse parties, ne the savynge of obedient thynges ne scholde nat be.' [1085]

' Thanne is ther no thyng,' quod sche, ' that kepith his nature, that enforceth hym to gon ayen god.'

' No,' quod I.

' And yif that any thing enforcede hym to withstonde god, myghte it avayle at the laste ayens hym that we han graunted to ben almyghty be the ryght of blisfulnesse ? '

' Certes,' quod I, ' al outrely it ne myghte nat avaylen hym.'

' Thanne is ther no thing,' quod she, ' that either wole or mai with-stonden to this sovereyn good.'

' I trow nat,' quod I.

' Thanne is thilke the sovereyn good,'

1067. *Ne the certein*, etc., should be ' *The ordre of nature ne schoulde not procede certeinly and unfolden so ordene*,' etc.

1077. *the same good*, ' ipsum bonum,' ' biens meismes.'

1079. *keye* ' clavus ' read as ' clavis,' or ' clos ' as ' clef.'

1082. *scheweth*, etc., is no less evident.

1085. *yif ther were*, etc., *i.e.* if it were a restraining of the refractory elements and not a preserving of the harmonious ones.

quod sche, 'that alle thinges governeth strongly and ordeyneth hem softly?' [1090]

Thanne seide I thus: 'I delite me,' quod I, 'nat oonly in the eendes or in the somme of resouns that thou hast concluded and proved, but thilke woordes that thou usest deliten me moche more. So that, at the laste, foolis that somtyme reenden grete thinges oughten ben asschamid of hem-self.' (That is to seyn, that we foolis that reprehenden wikkidly the thinges that touchin godis governaunce, we aughten ben asschamid of our-self; as I, that seide that god refuseth oonly the werkis of men and ne entremittith nat of it.)

'Thow hast wel herd,' quod sche, 'the fables of the poetis, how the geaunttis assaileden hevene with the goddis, but for-sothe the debonayre force of god disposide hem as it was worthy (that is to sey, destroyden the geauntes, as it was worthy.) [1095] But wiltow that we ioynen to-gidres thilke same resouns, for paraventure of swiche coniunccioun may sterten up som fair sparcle of soth?'

'Do,' quod I, 'as the list.'

'Wenestow,' quod sche, 'that god ne be almyghty?—No man is in doute of it?'

'Certes,' quod I, 'no wyght ne douteth it, yif he be in his mynde.'

'But he,' quod sche, 'that is almyghti —ther nys no thyng that he ne may?'

'That is sooth,' quod I.

'May god don evel?' quod sche.

'Nay for-sothe,' quod I.

'Thanne is evel no thing,' quod sche, 'syn that he ne may not don evel, that mai doon alle thinges.' [1100]

'Scornestow me,' quod I,—(or elles, 'Pleyestow or disseyvistow me,')—'that hast so wovven me with thi resouns the hous of Didalus, so entrelaced that it is unable to ben unlaced—thow that other-

while entrist ther thow issist, and other while issest ther thow entrest? Ne fooldist thou nat to-gidre (by replicacioun of wordes) a manere wondirful cercle or envirounynge of the simplicite devyne? For certes a litel here byforne, whanne thou bygunne at blisfulnesse, thou seidest that it is sovereyn good, and seidest that it is set in sovereyn god; and seidest that god hym-self is sovereyn good, and that good is the ful blisfulnesse; [1105] for whiche thou yave me as a covenable yifte, that is to seyn, that no wyght is blisful, but yif he be god also ther-with. And seidest eke that the forme of good is the substaunce of god and of blisfulnesse; and seidest that thilke same oon is thilke same good that is required and desired of al the kynde of thinges. And thou provedest in disputynge that god governeth alle the thinges of the world by the governementis of bounte; and seidest that alle thinges wolen obeyen to hym; and seidest that the nature of yvel nys no thing. And thise thinges schewedest thou, naught with noone resouns y-taken fro withouten, [1110] but by proeves in cercles and homliche knowen, the whiche proeves drawen to hem-self heer feyth and here accord everiche of hem of othir.'

Thanne seide sche thus: 'I ne scorne the nat, ne pleie, ne disceyve the; but I have schewed the the thing that is grettest over alle thinges, by the yifte of god that we whilome prayeden. For this is the forme of the devyne substaunce, that is swiche that it ne slideth nat in-to uttreste foreyne thinges, ne ne resceyveth noone straunge thinges in hym; but ryght as Parmanydes seide in Greec of thilke devyne substaunce—he seide thus: that thilke devyne substaunce tornith the

1091. H Cx. A₂ *the resouns;* C₁ *the* inserted later (?).

1095. *with the goddis,* against the gods. Probably due to misreading 'ou les dieux' as 'aux diex.'

1101. *Didalus,* Dedalus.

1106. *as,* as it were.

1106. *covenable yifte,* probably misreading of 'coronable don' (correlarium).

1111. *proeves in cercles,* etc., 'insitis et domesticis probationibus'; *in cercles* is due to gloss on *insitis* in Aq., and *known* to Fr. 'conneus' (? conseus) translating 'domesticis.'

1115. *Parmanydes,* Parmenides.

2 D

world and the moevable cercle of thinges, while thilke devyne substaunce kepith it-self withouten moevynge. [1115] (That is to seyn that it ne moeveth nevere mo, and yet it moeveth alle othere thinges.) But natheles, yif I have styred resouns that ben nat taken from withouten the compas of the thing of whiche we treten, but resouns that ben bystowyd withinne that compas, ther nys nat why that thou schuldest merveillen, sith thow hast lernyd by the sentence of Plato that nedes the wordis moot nedes be cosynes to the thinges of whiche thei speken.

' Felix qui potuit.'—Metrum 12

Blisful is that man that may seen the clere welle of good! Blisful is he that mai unbynden hym fro the boondes of the hevy erthe! The poete of Trace (Orpheus), that whilome hadde ryght greet sorwe for the deth of his wyf, aftir that he hadde makid by his weeply songes the wodes moevable to renne, [1120] and hadde makid the ryveris to stonden stille, and hadde maked the hertes and the hyndes to joynen dreedles here sydes to cruel lyouns (for to herknen his song), and hadde maked that the hare was nat agast of the hound, whiche was plesed by his song; so, whanne the moste ardaunt love of his wif brende the entrayles of his breest, ne the songes that hadden overcomen alle thinges ne mighten nat asswagen hir lord (Orpheus). He pleynid hym of the hevene goddis that weren cruel to hym. He wente hym to the houses of helle, and ther he tempride his blaundysschinge songes by resounynge strenges, [1125] and spak and song in wepynge al that evere he hadde resceyved and lavyd out of the noble welles of his modir (Calliope), the goddesse. And he song, with as mochel as he myghte of wepynge, and with as moche as love, that doublide his sorwe, myghte yeve hym and teche hym, and he commoevde the helle, and requyred and bysoughte by swete preyere the lordes of soules in helle of relessynge (that is to seyn, to yelden hym his wyf). Cerberus, the porter of helle, with hise thre hevedes was caught and al abasschid for the newe song. And the thre goddesses, furiis and vengeresses of felonyes, that tormenten and agasten the soules by anoy, woxen sorweful and sory, and wepyn teeris for pite. Tho was nat the heved of Ixion y-tormented by the overthrowynge wheel. [1130] And Tantalus, that was destroied by the woodnesse of long thurst, despyseth the floodes to drynken. The foul that highte voltor, that etith the stomak or the gyser of Tycius, is so fulfild of his song that it nil eten ne tiren no more. At the laste the lord and juge of soules was moevid to misericordes, and cryede: "We ben overcomen," quod he; "yeve we to Orpheus his wif to beren hym compaignye; he hath wel y-bought hire by his faire song and his ditee. [1135] But we wolen putten a lawe in this and covenaunt in the yifte; that is to seyn that, til he be out of helle, yif he loke byhynde hym, that his wyf schal comen ageyn unto us." But what is he that may yeven a lawe to loverys? Love is a grettere lawe and a strengere to hymself (thanne any lawe that men mai yyven). Allas! whanne Orpheus and his wyf weren almost at the termes of the nyght (that is to seyn, at the laste boundes of helle), Orpheus lokede abakward on Erudyce his wif, and lost hire, and was deed. This fable apertenith to yow alle, who so evere desireth or seketh to lede his thought in-to the sovereyn day (that is to seyn, in-to cleernesse of sovereyn good). [1140] For who so that evere be so overcomen that he ficche his eien in-to the put of helle (that is to seyn, who so sette his thoughtes in erthly thinges), al that evere he hath drawen of the noble good celestial he

1117. *styred*, 'agitavimus.'
1123. *ne the songes*, not even the songs.
1125. *lavyd*, 'puisie.'

1129. *by anoy*, rather *anoyous soules*, 'sontes.'
1136. *covenaunt*, 'covenances.'
1137. *men mai yyven*, one may give.
1139. *and was deed*, and she was dead.

lesith it, whanne he looketh the helles (that is to seyn, in-to lowe thinges of the erth).'

EXPLICIT LIBER TERCIUS

INCIPIT LIBER QUARTUS

' *Hec cum philosophia dignitate vultus.'*—
Prosa 1

Whanne Philosophie hadde songen softly and delitably the forseide thinges kepynge the dignyte of hir cheere and the weyghte of hir wordes, I, thanne, that ne hadde nat al outrely foryeten the wepynge and the moornynge that was set in myn herte, for-brak the entencioun of hir that entendede yit to seyn some othere thinges. ' O,' quod I, ' thou that art gyderesse of verray light, the thinges that thou hast seid me hidir-to ben to me so cleer and so schewynge by the devyne lookynge of hem, and by thy resouns, that they ne mowen nat ben overcomen. [1145] And thilke thinges that thou toldest me, al be it so that I hadde whilom foryeten hem for the sorwe of the wrong that hath ben don to me, yet natheles thei ne weren not al outrely un-knowen to me. But this same is namely a ryght grete cause of my sorwe : that so as the governour of thinges is good, yif that the eveles mowen ben by any weyes, or elles yif that evelis passen with-outen punysschynge. The whiche thing oonly how worthy it is to ben wondrid uppon, thou considerest it wel thi-selve certeynly. But yit to this thing ther is yit another thing I-ioyned more to ben wondrid uppon : [1150] for felonye is emperisse, and floureth ful of richesses, and vertu is nat al oonly withouten meedes, but it is cast undir and fortroden undir the feet of felonous folk, and it

1142. *helles*, ' inferos.'
1145. C₂ Cx. A₃ *the resouns.*
1148. *yif that . . . or yif that, i.e.* how that
. . . or how that.

abyeth the tormentes in stede of wikkide felouns. Of alle whiche thinges ther nys no wyght that may merveillen y-nowghe, ne compleyne that swiche thinges ben don in the reigne of god, that alle thinges woot and alle thinges may and ne wole nat but oonly gode thinges.'

Thanne seide sche thus : ' Certes,' quod sche, ' that were a greet merveille and abaysschinge withouten ende, and wel more horrible than alle monstres, yif it were as thou wenest ; that is to seyn, that in the ryght ordene hous of so mochel a fadir and an ordeynour of meyne, that the vesselis that ben foule and vyl schulden ben honoured and heryed, and the precious vesselis schulden ben defouled and vyl. [1155] But it nys nat so. For yif the thinges that I have concludid a litel here byforn ben kept hoole and unaraced, thou schalt wel knowe by the auctorite of god, of the whos regne I speke, that certes the gode folk ben alwey myghty and schrewes ben alwey outcast and feble ; ne the vices ben nevere mo with-outen peyne, ne the vertus ben nat withouten mede ; and that blisfulnesses comen alwey to good folk, and infortune comith alwey to wykkide folk. [1160] And thou schalt wel knowe manye thinges of this kynde, that schullen cesen thi pleyntis and strengthen the with stedfaste sadnesse. And for thou hast seyn the forme of the verray blisfulnesse by me that have whilom y-schewid it the, and thow hast knowen in whom blisfulnesse is y-set, alle thingis y-treted that I trowe ben necessarie to putten forth, I schal schewe the the weye that schal bryngen the ayen unto thyn hous ; and I schal fycchen fetheris in thi thought, by whiche it mai areisen in heighte ; so that, alle tribu-laciouri I-don awey, thow, by my gyding and by my path and by my sledys, shalt mowen retourne hool and sownd in-to thi contree. [1165]

1151. *abyeth the tormentes*, ' supplicia luit.'
1161. *sadnesse*, firmness.
1164. *fetheris*, wings.
1165. *sledys*, ' vehiculis,' ' voiturez.'

' Sunt etenim penne volucres michi.'—
Metrum 1

'I have, for-thi, swifte fetheris that surmounten the heighte of the hevene. Whanne the swifte thoght hath clothid it-self in tho fetheris, it despiseth the hateful erthes, and surmounteth the rowndenesse of the gret ayr ; and it seth the clowdes byhynde his bak, and passeth the heighte of the regioun of the fir, that eschaufeth by the swifte moevynge of the firmament, til that he aryseth hym in-to the houses that beren the sterres, and ioyneth his weies with the sonne, Phebus, and felawschipeth the weie of the olde colde Saturnus ; and he, I-maked a knyght of the clere sterre (that is to seyn, whan the thought is makid godis knyght by the sekynge of cleer trouthe to comen to the verray knowleche of god) [1170] —and thilke soule renneth by cercle of the sterres in alle the places there as the schynnynge nyght is y-painted (that is to sey, the nyght that is cloudeles ; for on nyghtes that ben cloudeles it semeth as the hevene were peynted with diverse ymages of sterres). And whan the thought hath don there I-noghe, he schal forleten the laste hevene, and he schal pressen and wenden on the bak of the swifte firmament, and he schal be makid parfit of the worschipful lyght of god. There halt the lord of kynges the septre of his myght and a-temprith the governementes of the world, [1175] and the schynynge juge of thinges, stable in hym-self, governeth the swifte wayn (that is to seyn, the circuler moevynge of the sonne). And yif thi wey ledeth the ayein so that thou be brought thider, thanne wiltow seye that that is the contre that thou requerest, of

whiche thou ne haddest no mynde—"but now it remembreth me wel, here was I born, her wol I fastne my degree (here wol I duelle)." But yif the liketh thanne to looken on the derknesse of the erthe that thou hast forleten, thanne schaltow seen that these felouns tirantes, that the wrecchide peple dredeth now, schullen ben exiled fro thilke faire contre.'

' Tum ego pape ut magna.'—Prosa 2

Thanne seide I thus : ' Owh ! I wondre me that thow byhctist me so grete thinges. [1180] Ne I ne doute nat that thow ne maist wel performe that thow behetist ; but I preie the oonly this, that thow ne tarie nat to telle me thilke thinges that thou hast moevid.'

' First,' quod sche, 'thow most nedes knowen that good folk ben alwey strong and myghti, and the schrewes ben feble, and desert and naked of alle strengthes. And of thise thinges certes everiche of hem is declared and schewed by othere. For so as good and yvel ben two contraries, yif so be that good be stedfast, thanne scheweth the feblesse of yvel al opynly ; and if thow knowe clerly the freelnesse of yvel, the stedfastnesse of good is knowen. [1185] But for as moche as the fey of my sentence schal ben the more ferme and haboundant, I wil gon by the to weye and by the tothir, and I wil conferme the thinges that ben purposed, now on this side and now on that side. Two thinges ther ben in whiche the effect of alle the dedes of mankynde standeth, that is to seyn, wil and power ; and yif that oon of thise two faileth, ther nys nothing that may be doon. For yif that wille lakketh, ther nys no wyght that undirtaketh to done that he wol nat doon ; and yif power faileth, the wil nys but in idel and stant for naught. [1190] And therof cometh it that yif thou see a

1166. *for-thi*, C₂ A₁ *forsothe.*
1168. Ptolemy's system of the universe is here referred to.
1169. C₁ A₂ Cx. B H omit *hym* ; A₁ *hir* (*soule* is represented by the feminine pronoun after 1168 in A₁).
1170. C₂ A₁ read *that* for *whan* and omit *cleer.*
1174. *worschipful lyght*, A₁ *dredeful clerenesse.*

1177. *fastne my degree*, ' sistam gradum.'
1181. *that thou*, etc. ; *me* is the antecedent of *that.*
1182. *naked*, ' desuner,' misread as ' desnuez.'

wyght that wolde geten that he mai not geten, thow maist nat douten that power ne faileth hym to have that he wolde.'

'This is open and cler,' quod I, 'ne it ne mai nat be denyed in no manere.'

'And yif thou se a wyght,' quod sche, 'that hath doon that he wolde doon, thow ne wil nat douten that he ne hath had power to doon it?'

'No,' quod I.

'And in that that every wyght may, in that men may holden hym myghti?' (As who seith, in so moche as man is myghty to doon a thing, in so mochel men halt hym myghti; and in that he ne mai, in that men demen hym to ben feble.) [1195]

'I confesse it wel,' quod I.

'Remembreth the,' quod sche, 'that I have gaderid and I-schewid by forseide resouns that al the entencioun of wil of mankynde, whiche that is lad by diverse studies, hasteth to comen to blisfulnesse.'

'It remembreth me wel,' quod I, 'that it hath ben schewed.'

'And recordeth the nat thanne,' quod sche, 'that blisfulnesse is thilke same good that men requiren? so that whanne that blisfulnesse is required of alle, that good also is required and desired of alle?' [1200]

'It ne recordeth me noght,' quod I, 'for I have it gretly alwey ficched in my memorie.'

'Alle folk thanne,' quod sche, 'good and eek badde, enforcen hem withoute difference of entencioun to comen to good.'

'This is a verray consequence,' quod I.

'And certein is,' quod sche, 'that by the getynge of good men ben y-makid gode.'

'This is certein,' quod I.

'Thanne geten gode men that thei desiren?'

'So semeth it,' quod I.

'But wikkide folk,' quod sche, 'yif

thei geten the good that thei desiren, thei ne mowe nat ben wikkid.' [1205]

'So is it,' quod I.

'Than so as the ton and the tothir,' quod sche, 'desiren good, and the gode folk geten good and not the wikkide folk, than is it no doute that the gode folk ne ben myghty and wikked folk ben feble.'

'Who so that evere,' quod I, 'douteth of this, he ne mai nat considere the nature of thinges ne the consequence of resouns.'

'And over this,' quod sche, 'if that ther ben two thinges that han o same purpos by kynde, and that oon of hem pursuweth and performeth thilke same thing by naturel office, and that oother mai nat doon thilke naturel office, but folweth, by other manere than is covenable to nature, hym that acomplisseth his purpos kyndely, [1210] and yit he ne acomplisseth nat his owene purpos— whether of thise two demestow for more myghti?'

'Yif that I coniecte,' quod I, 'that thou wilt seie, algates yit I desire to herkne it more pleynly of the.'

'Thou nilt nat thanne denye,' quod sche, 'that the moevement of goynge nys in men by kynde?'

'No for sothe,' quod I.

'Ne thou doutest nat,' quod sche, 'that thilke naturel office of goinge ne be the office of feet?'

'I ne doute it nat,' quod I.

'Thanne,' quod sche, 'yif that a wight be myghti to moeve, and goth uppon hise feet, and another, to whom thilke naturel office of feet lakketh, enforceth hym to gone crepinge uppon his handes, whiche of thise two oughte to ben holden the more myghty by right?' [1215]

'Knyt forth the remenaunt,' quod I, 'for no wight ne douteth that he that mai gon by naturel office of feet ne be more myghty than he that ne may nat.'

'But the soverein good,' quod sche,

1201. H Cx. omit *gretly* (not found in Latin and French).

1206. *the ton*, etc., 'utrique,' 'li un et li autre.'
1207. *mai nat*, is not able.
1208. *han o same purpos*, have the same function to perform.
1212. *yif that*, although.

'that is eveneliche purposed to the good folk and to badde, the gode folk seken it by naturel office of vertus, and the schrewes enforcen hem to getin it by diverse coveytise of erthly thinges, whiche that nys noon naturel office to gete thilke same soverein good. Trowestow that it be any other wise?'

'Nai,' quod I, 'for the consequence is opene and schewynge of thinges that I have graunted, that nedes good folk moten be myghty, and schrewes feble and unmyghti.' [1220]

'Thou rennist aryght byforn me,' quod sche, 'and this is the jugement (that is to sein, I juge of the), ryght as thise leches ben wont to hopin of sike folk, whan thei aperceyven that nature is redressed and with-stondeth to the maladye. But for I se the now al redy to the undirstondynge, I schal schewe the more thikke and contynuel resouns. For loke now, how greetly scheweth the feblesse and infirmite of wikkid folk, that ne mowen nat comen to that hir naturel entencioun ledeth hem; and yit almost thilke naturel entencioun constreyneth hem. And what were to demen thanne of schrewes, yif thilk naturel help hadde forleten hem, the whiche naturel help of entencioun goth alwey byforn hem and is so gret that unnethe it mai ben overcome. [1225] Considere thanne how gret defaute of power and how gret feblesse ther is in wikkide felonous folke. (As who seith the grettere thing that is coveyted and the desir nat acomplissed, of the lasse myght is he that coveyteth it and mai nat acomplisse; and for-thi philosophie seith thus be sovereyn good.) Ne schrewes requeren not lighte meedes ne veyne games, whiche thei ne mai nat

folwen ne holden; but thei failen of thilke somme and of the heighte of thinges (that is to seyn sovereyn good). Ne these wrecches ne comen nat to the effect of sovereyn good, the whiche thei enforcen hem oonly to geten by nyghtes and dayes. [1230] In the getyng of whiche good the strength of good folk is ful wel yseene. For ryght so as thou myghtest demen hym myghty of goinge that goth on his feet til he myghte comen to thilke place fro the whiche place ther laye no weie forthere to be gon, ryght so mostow nedes demen hym for ryght myghty, that geteth and atteyneth to the ende of alle thinges.that ben to desire, by-yonde the whiche ende ther nys no thing to desire. Of the whiche power of good folk men mai conclude that the wikkide men semen to be bareyne and naked of alle strengthe. For whi forleten thei vertus and folwen vices? Nys it nat for that thei ne knowen nat the godes? But what thing is more feble and more caytif than is the blyndnesse of ignorance? [1235] Or elles thei knowen ful wel whiche thinges that thei oughten folwe, but lecherie and covetise overthroweth hem mys-torned. And certes so doth distempraunce to feble men, that ne mowen nat wrastlen ayen the vices. Ne knowen thei nat thanne wel that thei forleten the good wilfully, and turnen hem wilfully to vices? And in this wise thei ne forleten nat oonly to ben myghti, but thei forleten al outrely in any wise for to been. For thei that forleten the comune fyn of alle thinges that ben, thei forleten also therwith-al for to been. [1240] And peraventure it scholde seme to som folk that this were a merveile to seien, that schrewes, whiche that contenen the more partie of men, ne ben nat ne han no beynge; but yit natheles it is so, and thus stant this thing. For thei that ben schrewes I denye nat that they ben schrewes, but I denye, and seie simply and pleynly, that thei ne ben nat, ne han no beynge. For

---

1220. *schewynge*, perhaps error for 'sewing.'
1221. *jugement*, 'jugemens' ('indicium' read as 'iudicium').
1222. *redressed*, rather *addressed*, 'erectæ.'
1224. *to that*, to that to which.
1225. C₁ A₂ H B omit *alwey*; C₂ *awey*.
1227. *be sovereyn good*, in respect to the chief good.
1228. *games*, A₁ H *gaines*, 'præmia levia et ludicra, i.e. jocosa.'

1236. *mys-torned*, 'transversos,' 'les en destourne.'

right als thou myghtest seyn of the careyne of a man, that it were a deed man, but thou ne myghtest nat symply callen it a man ; so graunte I wel for-sothe that vicyous folk ben wikkid, but I ne may nat graunten absolutly and symply that thei ben. For thilke thing that with-holdeth ordre and kepeth nature, thilke thing is, and hath beinge ; [1245] but what thing that faileth of that (that is to seyn, he that forleteth naturel ordre), he forleteth thilke beinge that is set in his nature. But thow wolt seyn that schrewes mowen. Certes, that ne denye I nat ; but certes hir power ne desscendeth nat of strengthe, but of feblesse. For thei mowen don wikkydnesses, the whiche thei ne myghten nat don yif thei myghten duellen in the forme and in the doynge of good folk. And thilke power scheweth ful evidently that they ne mowen ryght nat. For so as I have gadrid and proevid a litil byforn that evel is nawght, and so as schrewes mowen oonly but schrewednesses, this conclusion is al cler, that schrewes ne mowen ryght nat, ne han no power. [1250] And for as moche as thou undir-stonde which is the strengthe of this power of schrewes, I have diffinysched a litil her-byforn that no thing is so myghti as sovereyn good ? '

' That is soth,' quod I.

' And thilke same sovereyn good may don noon yuel ? '

' Certes no,' quod I.

' Is ther any wyght thanne,' quod sche, ' that weneth that men mowen don alle thinges ? '

' No man,' quod I, ' but yif he be out of his wyt.'

' But certes schrewes mowen don evel ? ' quod sche.

' Ye ; wolde god,' quod I, ' that thei ne myghten don noon ! '

' Thanne,' quod sche, ' so as he that is myghty to doon oonly but goode thinges

mai doon alle thinges, and thei that ben myghti to doon yvele thinges ne mowen nat alle thinges, [1255] thanne is it open thing and manyfest that thei that mowen doon yvele ben of lasse power. And yit to proeve this conclusioun ther helpeth me this, that I have schewed here-byforn, that alle power is to be noumbred among thinges that men oughten requere ; and I have schewed that alle thinges that oughten ben desired ben referred to good, ryght as to a maner heighte of hir nature. But for to mowen don yvel and felononye ne mai nat ben referrid to good. Thanne nys nat yvel of the nombre of thinges that oughten ben desired. But alle power aughte ben desired and required. [1260] Thanne is it open and cler that the power ne the mowynge of schrewes nis no power. And of alle thise thinges it scheweth wel that the gode folk ben certeinli myghty, and the schrewes doutelees ben unmyghty. And it is cler and opene that thilke sentence of Plato is verray and soth, that seith that oonly wise men may doon that thei desiren, and schrewes mowen haunten that hem liketh, but that thei desiren (that is to seyn, to come to sovereyn good), thei ne han no power to acomplissen that. For schrewes don that hem lyst whan, by tho thinges in whiche thei deliten, thei wenen to ateynen to thilke good that thei desiren ; but thei ne geten nat ne ateyne nat therto, for vices ne comen nat to blisfulnesse. [1265]

' *Quos vides sedere celsos.*'—Metrum 2

Who so that the coverturis of hir veyn apparailes myghte strepen of thise proude kynges, that thow seest sitten an hye in here chayeres, gliterynge in schynynge purpre, envyrowned with sorwful armures manasyng with cruel mowth, blowynge by woodnesse of herte,

1245. *with-holdeth*, retains.
1248. H Cx: A₂ B *wickidnes.*
1249. H Cx. A₂ B A₁ *schrewdenes.*
1251. H Cx. A₂ B *understondis.*

1256. *yit*, moreover.
1261. *mowynge*, H Cx. A₂ A₁ *moevyng.*
1267. *sorwful armures*, ' tristis armis.'
1267. *blowynge*, panting.

he schulde seen thanne that thilke lordis berin withynne hir corages full streyte cheynes. For lecherye tormenteth hem on that o side with gredy venymes; and trowblable ire, that areyseth in hem the floodes of trowblynges, tormenteth upon that othir side hir thought; or sorwe halt hem wery and I-cawght, or slidynge and desceyvynge hope turmenteth hem. And therfore, syn thow seest on heved (that is to seyn, o tiraunt) beren so manye tyranyes, than doth thilke tyraunt nat that he desireth, [1270] syn he is cast doun with so manye wikkide lordes (that is to seyn, with so manye vices that han so wikkidly lordschipes over hym).

' *Videsne igitur quanto.*'—Prosa 3

Seestow nat thanne in how greet filthe thise schrewes been I-wrapped, and with which clernesse thise gode folk schynen? In this scheweth it wel that to good folk ne lakketh nevere mo hir meedes, ne schrewes ne lakken nevere mo turmentes, for of alle thinges that ben I-doon, thilke thing for which any thing is doon, it semeth as by ryght that thilke thing be the mede of that; as thus: yif a man renneth in the stadye (or in the forlonge) for the corone, thanne lith the mede in the coroune for which he renneth. [1275] And I have schewed that blisfulnesse is thilke same good for which that alle thinges ben doon; thanne is thilke same good purposed to the werkes of mankynde right as a comune mede, which mede ne may nat ben disseveryd fro good folk. For no wight as by ryght, fro thennesforth that hym lakketh goodnesse, ne schal ben cleped good. For whiche thing folk of gode maneres, hir medes ne forsaken hem never mo. For al be it so that schrewes waxen as wode as hem lyst ayein good folk, yit natheles the coroune of wise men ne schal nat fallen ne faden; [1280] for foreyne schrewed-

nesse ne bynymeth nat fro the corages of good folk hir propre honour. But yif that any wyght reioysede hym of goodnesse that he hadde taken fro withoute (as who seith, yif any man hadde his goodnesse of any other man than of hymself), certes he that yaf hym thilke goodnesse, or elles som other wyght, myghte benymen it hym. But for as moche as to every wyght his owene propre bounte yeveth hym his mede, thanne at erste schal he failen of mede whan he forletith to ben good. And at the laste, so as alle medes ben requirid for men wenen that thei ben gode, who is he that nolde deme that he that is ryght myghti of good were partlees of the mede? And of what mede schal he ben gerdoned? Certes of ryght fair mede and ryght greet aboven alle medes. [1285] Remembre the of thilke noble corrolarie that I yaf the a litel here-byforn, and gadre it togidre in this manere: so as god hymself is blisfulnesse, thanne is it cler and certein that alle gode folk ben I-maked blisful for thei ben gode; and thilke folk that ben blisful it accordeth and is covenable to ben goddes. Thanne is the mede of good folk swych that no day ne schal empeiren it, ne no wikkidnesse schal derkne it, ne power of no wyght ne schal nat amenusen it, that is to seyn, to ben maked goddes. And syn it is thus (that gode men ne failen nevere mo of hir mede), certes no wise man ne may doute of the undepartable peyne of schrewes (that is to seyn, that the peyne of schrewes ne departeth nat from hemself nevere mo). For so as good and yvel, and peyne and mede ben contrarie, it moot nedes ben that, ryght as we seen betyden in guerdoun of gode, that al so moot the peyne of yvel answere by the contrarie partie to schrewes. [1290] Now thanne so as bounte and pruesse ben the mede to good folk, also is schrewidnesse it-self

1268. *gredy venymes*, 'avidis venenis.'
1269. C₁ A₂ H Cx. B *flood*.
1277. *werkes*, actions.

1281. C₂ *reioyse*, A₁ *reioyseth*.
1284. A₁ *wolde deme*; cp. 336.
1288. *that is to seyn*, etc., appositive to *mede*.
1291. *also*, so.

torment to schrewes. Thanne who so that evere is entecchid or defowled with peyne, he ne douteth nat that he nys entecchid and defowled with yvel. Yif schrewes thanne wol preysen hem-self, may it semen to hem that thei ben with-outen parti of torment, syn thei ben swiche that the uttreste wikkidnesse (that is to seyn wikkide thewes, which that is the uttereste and the worst kynde of schrewednesse) ne defouleth ne en-teccheth nat hem oonly, but enfecteth and envenymeth hem greetly? And also loke on schrewes, that ben the contrarie partie of gode men, how gret peyne felaw-schipith and folweth hem! [1295] For thou hast lerned a litil here-byforn that alle thing that is and hath beynge is oon, and thilke same oon is good : than is this the consequence, that it semeth that al that is and hath beynge, is good. (This is to seyn as who seith that beinge and unite and goodnesse is al oon.) And in this manere it folweth thanne that alle thing that fayleth to ben good, it stynteth for to be and for to han any beynge. Wherfore it is that schrewes stynten for to ben that thei weeren. But thilke othir forme of mankynde (that is to seyn the forme of the body withowte) scheweth yit that thise schrewes weren whilom men. [1300] Wherfore whan thei ben perverted and turned in-to malice certes thanne have thei for-lorn the nature of mankynde. But so as oonly bownte and prowesse may enhawnsen every man over othere men, than moot it nedes be that schrewes, whiche that schrewednesse hath cast out of the condicion of mankynde, ben put undir the merit and the dissert of men. Than betidith it that, yif thou seest a wyght that be transformed in-to vices, thow ne mayst nat wene that he be a man. For if he be ardaunt in avaryce, and that he be a ravynour by violence of

foreyne richesse, thou schalt seyn that he is lik to the wolf ; and if he be felonows and withoute reste, and exercise his tonge to chidynges, thow schalt likne hym to the hownd ; [1305] and if he be a pryve awaytour y-hid, and reioiseth hym to ravyssche be wiles, thou schalt seyn hym lik to the fox whelpes ; and yif he be distempre, and quakith for ire, men schal wene that he bereth the corage of a lyoun ; and yif he be dredful and fleynge, and dredith thinges that ne aughte nat to ben dredd, men schal holden hym lik to the hert ; and yf he be slow, and astonyd, and lache, he lyveth as an asse ; yif he be lyght and unstedfast of corage, and chaungith ay his studies, he is likned to briddes ; and if he be ploungid in fowle and unclene luxuris, he is withholden in the foule delices of the fowle sowe. [1310] Than folweth it that he that for-leteth bounte and prowesse, he forletith to ben a man ; syn he ne may nat passe in-to the condicion of god, he is torned in-to a beeste.

' *Vela Naricii ducis.*'—Metrum 3

Eurus, the wynd, aryved the sayles of Ulixes, duc of the cuntre of Narice, and his wandrynge shippes by the see, into the ile ther-as Cerces, the faire goddesse, dowhter of the sonne, duelleth, that medleth to hir newe gestes drynkes that ben touchid and makid with enchaunte-mentes. And aftir that hir hand, myghti over the erbes, hadde chaunged hir gestes into diverse maneres, that oon of hem is coverid his face with forme of a boor ; the tother is chaungid in-to a lyoun of the contre Marmoryke, and his nayles and his teth waxen, [1315] that oother of hem is newliche chaunged in-to a wolf, and howleth whan he wolde wepe ; that

1292. *entecchid or defowled*, 'afficitur.'
1294. *ne defouleth*, etc., 'non afficit modo verum etiam vehementer inficit.' Chaucer has confused *afficit* and *inficit*.
1300. *othir*, 'reliqua,' *i.e.* the human form left to them.

1304. *foreyne richesse*, another's goods.
1306. *wiles*, C₂ H *whiles*.
1306. *seyn hym lik*, pronounce him like.
1309. *astonyd*, 'stupidus.'
1309. *studies*, purposes.
1313. *drynkes*, etc., 'pocula tacta carmina,' and 'beuvages fez (facta ?) par enchantemens.'

other goth debonayrely in the hows as a tigre of Inde. But al be it so that the godhede of Mercurie, that is cleped the bridde of Arcadye, hath had merci of the duc Ulixes, bysegid with diverse yveles, and hath unbownden hym fro the pestilence of his oostesse, algates the rowerys and the maryneres hadden by this I-drawen in-to hir mouthes and dronken the wikkide drynkes. Thei that weren woxen swyn, hadden by this I-chaunged hir mete of breed for to eten akkornes of ookes. Noon of hir lymes duelleth with hem hool, but thei han lost the voys and the body; [1320] oonly hir thought duelleth with hem stable, that wepeth and by-wayleth the monstruous chaungynge that thei suffren. O over lyght hand !' (As who seith : ' O feble and light is the hand of Circes the enchaunteresse, that chaungith the bodyes of folk in-to beestes, to regard and to comparysoun of mutacioun that is makid by vices !') ' Ne the herbes of Circes ne ben nat myghty. For al be it so that thei mai chaungen the lymes of the body, algates yit thei may nat chaungen the hertes. For with-inne is I-hidd the strengthe and the vygour of men, in the secre tour of hir hertes, (that is to seyn the strengthe of resoun) ; but thilke venym of vices to-drawen a man to hem more myghtely than the venym of Circes. For vices ben so cruel that they percen and thurw passen the corage withinne ; [1325] and, thoughe thei ne anoye nat the body, yit vices wooden to destroyen men by wounde of thought.'

' *Tum ego fateor inquam.*'—Prosa 4

Thanne seide I thus : ' I confesse and I am a-knowe it,' quod I, ' ne I ne se nat that men may seyn as by ryght that schrewes ne ben chaunged in-to beestes by the qualite of hir soules, al be it so

that thei kepin yit the forme of the body of mankynde ; but I nolde nat of schrewes, of whiche the thought crwel woodeth alwey into destruccion of gode men, that it were leveful to hem to don that.'

' Certes,' quod sche, ' ne it is nat leveful to hem, as I schal wel schewen the in covenable place. But natheles, yif so were that thilke that men wenen ben leveful to schrewes were by-nomyn hem, so that they ne myghte nat anoyen or doon harm to gode men, certes a gret partie of the peyne to schrewes scholde ben alegged and releved. [1330] For al be it so that this ne seme nat credible thing peraventure to some folk, yit moot it nedes be that schrewes ben more wrecches and unsely, when thei mai doon and performe that thei coveyten, than yif that thei ne myghte nat acomplissen that thei coveiten. For yif it so be that it be wrecchidnesse to wilne to doon yvel, thanne is more wrecchidnesse to mowe don yvel, withoute whiche mowynge the wrecchid wil scholde langwisse withouten effect. Thanne syn that everiche of thise thinges hath his wrecchidnesse (that is to seyn, wil to don yvel and power to don yvel), it moot nedes be that thei (schrewes) ben constreyned by thre unselynesses, that wolen, and mowen, and performen felonyes and schrewednesses.' [1335]

' I acorde me,' quod I ; ' but I desire gretly that schrewes losten sone thilke unselynesses, that is to seyn, that schrewes weren despoyled of mowynge to don yvel.'

' So schollen thei,' quod sche, ' sonnere peraventure than thou woldest, or sonnere than they hem-selve wene. For ther nis no thing so late, in so schorte bowndes of this lif, that is long to abyde, nameliche

---

1317. *Mercurie*, etc., Aq. ' sed licet numen, i.e. dietas arcadis, i.e. mercuri . . . qui dicitur ales quod,' etc. (*ales* read as *bridde*).
1327. *am a-knowe it*, acknowledge it.
1327. *as by ryght*, justly.

1335. *thre*, C₂ H Cx. *the*, A₂ *theyr.*
1335. *unselynesses*, B H Cx. A₂ *unselynesse.*
1336. B H Cx. *unselynesse*; *thilke* is Fr. ' ceste' (' hoc '), which refers to the last-named of the three misfortunes.
1337. *wene.* A₁ adds *to lakken mowynge to done yvel*, which is in Latin but not in French.
1338. *late*, slow moving.
1338. *to abyde*, gerundive, *i.e.* that one has long to wait for it.

to a corage immortel. Of whiche schrewes the grete hope and the heye compassynges of schrewednesses is ofte destroyed by a sodeyn ende, or thei ben war; and that thing establisseth to schrewes the ende of hir schrewednesses. [1340] For yf that schrewednesse makith wrecchis, than mot he nedes ben moost wrecchide that lengest is a schrewe. The whiche wikkide schrewes wolde I demen althermost unsely and kaytifs, yif that hir schrewednesse ne were fynissched at the leste weye by the owtreste deth; for yif I have concluded soth of the unselynesse of schrewednesse, thanne schewith it clerly that thilke wrecchidnesse is withouten ende the whiche is certein to ben perdurable.'

'Certes,' quod I, 'this conclusion is hard and wondirful to graunte; but I knowe wel that it accordeth moche to the thinges that I have grauntid herebiforn.'

'Thou hast,' quod sche, 'the ryght estimacion of this. [1345] But who so evere wene that it be an hard thing to accorde hym to a conclusioun, it is ryght that he schewe that some of the premysses ben false, or elles he mot schewe that the collacioun of proposicions is nat sped-ful to a necessarie conclusioun; and yif it ne be nat so, but that the premisses ben y-grauntid, ther nys nat why he scholde blame the argument. For this thing that I schal telle the now ne schal nat seme lesse wondirful, but of the thingis that ben taken also it is necessarie.' (As who seith, it folweth of that which is purposed byforn.)

'What is that?' quod I.

'Certes,' quod sche, 'that is that thise wikkid schrewes ben more blisful, or elles lasse wrecches, that abyen the tormentes that thei han desservid, than if no peyne of justice chastisede hem. [1350] Ne this ne seie I nat now for that any man myghte thinke that the maneris of schrewes ben coriged and chastised by vengeaunce and thei ben brought to the

ryghte weye by the drede of the torment, ne for that they yeven to other folk ensaumple to fleen fro vices; but I undirstonde yit in another manere that schrewes ben more unsely whan thei ne ben nat punyssched, al be it so that ther ne be hadde no resoun or lawe of correccioun, ne noon ensample of lokynge.'

'And what manere schal that be,' quod I, 'other than hath ben told herbyforn?'

'Have we nat thanne graunted,' quod sche, 'that good folk ben blisful and schrewes ben wrecches?'

'Yis,' quod I. [1355]

'Thanne,' quod sche, 'yif that any good were added to the wrecchidnesse of any wyght, nis he nat more blisful than he that ne hath no medlynge of good in his solitarie wrecchidnesse?'

'So semeth it,' quod I.

'And what seistow thanne,' quod sche, 'of thilke wrecche that lakketh alle goodes, (so that no good nys medlyd in his wrecchidnesse,) and yit over al his wikkidnesse, for which he is a wrecche, that ther be yit another yvel anexed and knyt to hym—schal nat men demen hym more unsely thanne thilke wrecche of whiche the unselynesse is relevid by the participacioun of som good?'

'Why sholde he nat?' quod I.

'Thanne certes,' quod sche, 'han schrewes, whan thei ben punyschid, somwhat of good anexid to hir wrecchidnesse, [1360] that is to seyn, the same peyne that thei suffren, which that is good by the resoun of justice; and whanne thilke same schrewes ascapen withouten torment, than han they somwhat more of yvel yit over the wikkidnesse that thei han don, that is to seyn, defaute of peyne, whiche defaute of peyne thou hast grauntid is yvel for the disserte of felonye?'

'I ne may nat denye it,' quod I.

'Moche more thanne,' quod sche, 'ben

1348. *taken*, 'sumpta.'

1354. *ensample of lokynge*, example for consideration. But perhaps read *lokynge of ensample* as in Latin and French.

schrewes unsely whan thei ben wrongfully delivred fro peyne, thanne whan thei ben punyschid by ryghtful vengeaunce. But this is opene thing and cleer, that it is ryght that schrewes ben punyschid, and it is wikkidnesse and wrong that thei escapen unpunyschid.' [1365]

'Who myghte denye that?' quod I.

'But,' quod sche, 'may any man denye that al that is ryght nis good, and also the contrarie, that al that is wrong is wikke?'

'Certes,' quod I, 'thise thinges ben clere ynowe, and that we han concluded a lytel here-byforn. But I preye the that thow telle me, yif thow accordest to leten no torment to the soules aftir that the body is ended by the deeth?' (This is to seyn, 'Undirstondestow aught that soules han any torment aftir the deeth of the body?')

'Certes,' quod sche, 'ye, and that ryght greet. Of whiche soules,' quod sche, 'I trowe that some ben tormented by asprenesse of peyne, [1370] and some soules, I trowe, ben exercised by a purgynge mekenesse; but my conseil nys nat to determyne of thise peynes. But I have travailed and told yit hider-to for thou scholdest knowe the mowynge of schrewes, whiche mowynge the semeth to ben unworthy, nis no mowynge; and ek of schrewes, of whiche thou pleynedest that they ne were nat punysschid, that thow woldest seen that thei ne were nevere mo withouten the tormentes of hir wikkidnesse; and of the licence of mowynge to don yvel that thou preyedest that it myghte sone ben ended, and that thou woldest fayn lernen that it ne sholde nat longe endure; and that schrewes ben more unsely yif thei were of lengere durynge, and most unsely yif thei weren perdurable. [1375] And aftir this I have

schewyd the that more unsely ben schrewes whan thei escapen withouten hir ryghtful peyne, thanne whan thei ben punyschid by ryghtful veniaunce; and of this sentence folweth it that thanne ben schrewes con- streyned at the laste with most grevous torment, whan men wene that thei ne ben nat punyssched.'

'Whan I considere thi resouns,' quod I, 'I ne trowe nat that men seyn any thing more verrayly. And yif I turne ayein to the studies of men, who is he to whom it sholde seme, that he ne scholde nat oonly leven thise thinges, but ek gladly herkne hem?'

'Certes,' quod sche, 'so it is. [1380] But men may nat, for they have hir eien so wont to the derknesse of erthly thinges that they ne may nat lyften hem up to the light of cler sothfastnesse, but thei ben lyk to briddes of whiche the nyght lightneth hir lokynge and the day blendith hem. For whan men loke nat the ordre of thinges, but hir lustes and talentes, they wene that either the leve or the mowynge to don wikkidnesse, or elles the scapynge withouten peyne be wele- ful. But considere the jugement of the perdurable lawe. For yif thou conferme thi corage to the beste thinges, thow ne hast noon nede of no juge to yeven the prys or mede; for thow hast joyned thi- self to the most excellent thing. And yif thow have enclyned thi studies to the wikkide thinges, ne seek no foreyne wrekere out of thi-self; for thow thi-self hast thrist thiself in-to wikke thinges: [1385] ryght as thow myghtest loken by diverse tymes the fowle erthe and the hevene, and that alle othere thinges stynten fro withoute (so that thow nere neyther in hevene ne in erthe, ne saye no thyng more); thanne scholde it semen to the, as by oonly resoun of lokynge, that thow

---

1367. C₁ H Cx. omit *a lytel.*
1369. *This is,* C₁ A₁ *This,* Cx. *That is.*
1371. *purgynge mekenesse,* 'purgatoria cle- mentia.'
1374. *and that thow woldest,* etc., should be *that thow woldest lernen,* etc. One of the French MSS. has the same mistake.

1382. C₁ H *hir talentes.*
1385. H Cx. A₂ B A₁ *wicked thinges.*
1386. *ryght as,* just as if.
1386. *and that, that* serves to repeat the preceding particle.
1386. *stynten,* preterite.
1386. C₁ H Cx. A₂ A₁ omit *nere . . . erthe.*

were now in the sterres, and now in the erthe. But the peple ne lokith nat on these thinges. What thanne? Schal we thanne approchen us to hem that I have schewed that thei ben lyke to beestes? And what wyltow seyn of this: yif that a man hadde al forlorn his syghte, and hadde foryeten that he evere sawhe, and wende that no thing ne faylede hym of perfeccioun of mankynde; now we that myghten sen the same thinges—wolde we nat wene that he were blynd? [1390] Ne also ne accordith nat the peple to that I schal seyn, the whiche thing is sustenyd by as stronge foundementes of resouns, that is to seyn, that more unsely ben they that doon wrong to othere folk, than they that the wrong suffren.'

'I wolde here thilke same resouns,' quod I.

'Denyestow,' quod sche, 'that all schrewes ne ben worthy to han torment?'

'Nay,' quod I.

'But,' quod sche, 'I am certein by many resouns that schrewes ben unsely.'

'It accordeth,' quod I.

'Thanne ne dowtestow nat,' quod sche, 'that thilke folk that ben worthy of torment, that they ne ben wrecches?' [1395]

'It accordeth wel,' quod I.

'Yif thou were thanne I-set a juge or a knowere of thinges, whethir trowestow that men scholden tormenten, hym that hath don the wrong or elles hym that hath suffred the wrong?'

'I ne doute nat,' quod I, 'that I nolde doon suffisaunt satisfaccioun to hym that hadde suffrid the wrong, by the sorwe of hym that hadde doon the wrong.'

'Thanne semeth it,' quod sche, 'that the doere of wrong is more wrecche than he that hath suffride wrong?'

'That folweth it wel,' quod I.

'Than,' quod sche, 'by thise causes and by othere causes that ben enforced by the same roote, that filthe or synne be

the propre nature of it maketh men wrecches; and it scheweth wel that the wrong that men doon nis nat the wrecchid-nesse of hym that resceyveth the wrong, but wrecchidnesse of hym that dooth the wrong. [1400] But certes,' quod sche, 'thise oratours or advocattes don al the contrarie; for thei enforcen hem to com-moeve the juges to han pite of hem that han suffrid and receyved the thinges that ben grevous and aspre, and yit men scholden more ryghtfully han pite of hem that doon the grevances and the wronges: the whiche schrewes it were a more covenable thing that the accusours or advocattes, nat wrooth but pytous and debonayre, ledden the schrewes that han don wrong to the jugement, ryght as men leden syke folk to the leche, for that thei sholden seken out the maladyes of synne by torment. And by this covenant, eyther the entent of the deffendours or advocates sholde fayle and cesen in al, or elles, yif the office of advocates wolde betre profiten to men, it scholde be torned into the habyte of accusacioun. [1405] (That is to seyn thei scholden accuse schrewes, and nat excusen hem.) And eek the schrewes hem-self, yif it were leveful to hem to seen at any clifte the vertu that thei han forleten, and sawen that they scholden putten adoun the filthes of hir vices by the tormentes of peynes, they ne aughten nat, ryght for the recompensacioun for to geten hem bounte and prowesse whiche that thei han lost, demen ne holden that thilke peynes weren tormentes to hem; and eek thei wolden refuse the attend-aunce of hir advocattes, and taken hem-self to hir juges and to hir accusours. For whiche it betydeth that, as to the wise folk, ther nis no place y-leten to hate (that is to seyn that hate ne hath no place among wise men); for no wyght nil haten gode men, but yif he were over mochel a

---

1390. *wolde we nat,* 'num videntes eadem caecos putaremus?' Chaucer follows the French in taking 'videntes' with 'putaremus.'
1398. *That folweth it wel,* 'ce s'ensuit bien.'
1399. *that filthe,* etc., in Latin and French

depends on *roote* ('radice'). Omitting *and* before *it scheweth* the sense becomes clear.
1405. C₁ A₃ H Cx. B omit *deffendours or* and *sholde fayle and.*

fool, and for to haten schrewes it nis no resoun. [1410] For ryght so as langwissynge is maladye of body, ryght so ben vices and synne maladye of corage ; and so as we ne deme nat that they that ben sike of hir body ben worthy to ben hated, but rather worthy of pite ; wel more worthy nat to ben hated, but for to ben had in pite, ben thei of whiche the thoughtes ben constreyned by felonous wikkidnesse, that is more crwel than any langwissynge of body.

' *Quid tantos Iuvat.*'—Metrum 4

What deliteth yow to exciten so grete moevynges of hatredes, and to hasten and bysien the fatal disposicioun of your deth with your propre handes (that is to seyn, by batayles or contek)? For yif ye axen the deth, it hasteth hym of his owene wil, ne deth ne taryeth nat his swifte hors. [1415] And the men that the serpentes, and the lyoun, and the tigre, and the bere, and the boor, seken to sleen with hir teeth, yit thilke same men seken to sleen everiche of hem oothir with swerd. Lo, for hir maneres ben diverse and discordaunt, thei moeven unryghtful oostes and cruel batayles, and wilnen to perise by entrechaungynge of dartes ! But the resoun of cruelte nis nat i-nowhe ryghtful. Wiltow thanne yelden a covenable gerdoun to the dissertes of men ? Love ryghtfully gode folk, and have pite on schrewes.'

' *Hic ego video inquam.*'—Prosa 5

' Thus se I wel,' quod I, ' eyther what blisfulnesse or elles what unselynesse is establisshid in the dissertes of gode men and of schrewes. [1420] But in this ilke fortune of peple I se somwhat of good and somwhat of yvel. For no wise man hath nat levere ben exiled, pore and nedy

and nameles, thanne for to duellen in his cyte, and flouren of rychesses, and be redowtable by honour and strong of power. For in this wise more clerly and more witnesfully is the office of wise men y-treted, whanne the blisfulnesse and the pouste of gouvernours is, as it were, I-schadde among peples that ben neyghbors and subgites ; syn that namely prisown, lawe, and thise othere tormentes of laweful peynes ben rather owed to felonus citezeins, for the whiche felones citezeens the peynes ben establisschid than for good folk.' [1425]

' Thanne I merveile me gretely,' quod I, ' why that the thinges ben so mys entrechaunged that tormentes of felonyes pressen and confounden good folk, and schrewes ravysschen medes of vertu (and ben in honours and in gret estates). And I desire eek for to witen of the what semeth the to be the resoun of this so wrongful a confusioun ; for I wolde wondre wel the lasse, yif I trowede that alle thise thinges weren medlede by fortunows hap. But now hepith and encreseth myn astonyenge god governour of thinges, that, so as god yeveth ofte tymes to gode men godes and myrthes, and to schrewes yvelis and aspre thinges, and yeveth ayeinward to good folk hardenesses, and to schrewes he graunteth hem hir wil and that they desiren — [1430] what difference thanne may ther be bytwixen that that god doth and the hap of fortune, yif men ne knowe nat the cause why that it is ?'

' Ne it nis no merveile,' quod sche, ' thowh that men wenen that ther be somwhat foolisshe and confus, whan the resoun of the ordre is unknowe. But although that thou ne knowe nat the cause of so gret a disposicioun, natheles for as moche as god the gode governour atempreth and gouverneth the world, ne doute the nat that alle thinges ne ben don aryght.'

1414. *What*, why.
1414. *hasten and bysien*, 'haster' and 'sollicitare.'
1415. *hors*, horses.
1416. *serpentes*, rather ' *serpent.*'
1421. *fortune of peple*, 'fortuna populari.'

1424. *wise men*, rather *wisdom*, ' sapientiæ.'
1424. *subgites* not in Latin or French.
1429. *that, so as god*, etc., who, since he, etc.

'*Si quis Arcturi sidera.*'—Metrum 5

'Who so that ne knowe nat the sterres of Arctour, y-torned neyghe to the sovereyne centre or poynt (that is to seyn y-torned neyghe to the sovereyne pool of the firmament), and wot nat why the sterre Boetes passeth or gadreth his waynes, and drencheth his late flaumbes in the see, [1435] and whi that Boetes, the sterre, unfooldeth hise overswifte arysynges, thanne schal he wondryn of the lawe of the heye eyr; and eek yif that he knowe nat why that the hornes of the fulle mone waxen pale and infect by bowndes of the derk nyght, and how the mone derk and confus discovereth the sterres that sche hadde covered by hir clere vysage. The comune errour moeveth folk, and maketh weery hir basyns of bras by thikke strokes. (That is to seyn, that ther is a maner peple that highte Coribandes, that wenen that whan the mone is in the eclips that it be enchaunted, and therfore for-to rescowe the mone thei betyn hir basyns with thikke strokes.) Ne no man ne wondreth whanne the blastes of the wynd Chorus beten the strondes of the see by quakynge floodes; [1440] ne no man ne wondrith whan the weighte of the snowh, I-hardid by the cold, is resolvyd by the brennynge hete of Phebus, the sonne; for her seen men redily the causes. But the causes y-hidd (that is to seyn, in hevene) trowblen the brestes of men. The moevable peple is astoned of alle thinges that comen seelde and sodeynly in our age; but yif the trubly errour of our ignoraunce departed fro us, so that we wisten the causes why that swiche thinges bytyden, certes thei scholde cesen to seme wondres.'

'*Ita est inquam.*'—Prosa 6

'Thus it is,' quod I. 'But so as thou hast yeven or byhyght me to unwrappen

1434. *sterres of Arctour,* '*Arcturi sidera,' i.e.* Ursa Major.
1435. *passeth or gadreth,* 'legat'; *gadreth* is incorrect. Bootes apparently pass·s Ursa Major.
1438. *maketh,* they make (*folk* is singular).
1439. *Coribandes,* not in Latin; Fr. 'li coribant.'

the hidde causes of thinges, and to discovere me the resouns covered with derknes, I preie the that thou devyse and juge me of this matere, and that thou do me to undirstonden it. For this miracle or this wonder trowbleth me ryght gretly.'

And thanne sche, a litel what smylinge, seide: [1445] 'Thou clepist me,' quod sche, 'to telle thing that is gretteste of alle thingis that mowen ben axed, and to the whiche questioun unnethes is ther aught I-nowgh to laven it. (As who seith, unnethes is ther suffisauntly any thing to answeren parfitly to thy questioun.) For the matere of it is swich, that whan o doute is determined and kut awey, ther waxen othere doutes withoute nombre, ryght as the hevedes wexen of Idre (the serpent that Hercules slowh). Ne ther ne were no manere ne noon ende, but if that a wyght constreynede tho doutes by a ryght lifly and quyk fir of thought (that is to seyn, by vigour and strengthe of wit). For in this matere men weren wont to maken questiouns of the symplicite of the purveaunce of god, and of the ordre of destyne, and of sodeyn hap, and of the knowynge and predestinacioun devyne, and of the liberte of fre wil; [1450] the whiche thinges thou thi-self aperceyvest wel of what weighte thei ben. But for as moche as the knowynge of thise thinges is a maner porcioun of the medycyne to the, al be it so that I have litil tyme to doon it, yit natheles y wol enforcen me to schewe somwhat of it. But although the noryssynges of dite of musyk deliteth the, thou most suffren and forberen a litel of thilke delit, whil that I weve to the resouns y-knyt by ordre.'

'As it liketh to the,' quod I, 'so do.'

Tho spak sche ryght as by an other bygynnynge, and seide thus: 'The engendrynge of alle thinges,' quod sche, 'and alle the progressiouns of muable nature, and al that moeveth in any manere, taketh hise causes, his ordre, and his formes, of the stablenesse of the devyne thought. [1455] And thilke devyne thought

1453. *dite of musyk,* 'musici carminis.'

that is I-set and put in the tour (that is to seyn, in the heighte) of the simplicite of god, stablissith many maner gises to things that ben to done; the whiche manere whan that men looken it in thilke pure clennesse of the devyne intelligence, it is y-cleped purveaunce; but whanne thilke manere is referred by men to things that it moeveth and disponyth, than of olde men it was clepyd destyne. The whiche thinges yif that any wyght loketh wel in his thought the strengthe of that oon and of that oothir, he schal lyghtly mowen seen that thise two things ben dyvers. For purveaunce is thilke devyne resoun that is establissed in the sovereyn prince of thinges, the whiche purveaunce disponith alle thinges; but destyne is the disposicioun and ordenance clyvyng to moevable thinges, by the whiche disposicion the purveaunce knytteth alle thingis in hir ordres; [1460] for purveaunce enbraceth alle thinges to hepe, al-thoghe that thei ben diverse and although thei ben infinit. But destyne certes departeth and ordeyneth alle thinges singulerly and devyded in moevynges, in places, in formes, in tymes. As thus: lat the unfoldynge of temporel ordenaunce, assembled and oonyd in the lokynge of the devyne thought, be cleped purveaunce; and thilke same assemblynge and oonynge, devyded and unfolden by tymes, lat that ben called destyne. And al be it so that thise thinges ben diverse, yit natheles hangeth that oon of that oother; for-whi the ordre destynal procedith of the simplicite of purveaunce. [1465] For ryght as a werkman that aperceyveth in his thought the forme of the thing that he wol make, and moeveth the effect of the work, and ledith that he hadde lookid byforn in his thought symplely and presently, by temporel ordenaunce; certes ryght so god disponith in his purveaunce singulerly and stablely the thinges that ben to doone; but he amyni-

streth in many maneris and in diverse tymes by destyne thilke same thinges that he hath disponyd. Thanne, whethir that destyne be exercised outhir by some devyne spirites, servantes to the devyne purveaunce, or elles by some soule, or elles by alle nature servynge to god, or elles by the celestial moevynges of sterres, or elles by vertu of aungelis, or elles by divers subtilite of develis, or elles by any of hem, or elles by hem alle; the destinal ordenaunce is y-woven and acomplissid. Certes it is opene thing that the purveaunce is an unmoevable and symple forme of thinges to doone; [1470] and the moevable bond and the temporel ordenaunce of thinges whiche that the devyne symplicite of purveaunce hath ordeyned to doone, that is destyne. For whiche it is that alle thinges that ben put undir destyne ben certes subgites to purveaunce, to whiche purveaunce destyne itself is subgit and under. But some thinges ben put undir purveaunce, that sourmounten the ordenance of destyne; and tho ben thilke that stablely ben I-fycchid neyghe to the first godhede. They surmounten the ordre of destynal moevablete. For ryght as cerklis that tornen aboute a same centre or aboute a poynt, thilke cerkle that is innerest or most withinne ioyneth to the symplesse of the myddle, [1475] and is, as it were, a centre or a poynt to that othere cerklis that tornen abouten hym; and thilke that is utterest, compased by a largere envyrownynge, is unfolden by largere spaces, in so moche as it is ferthest fro the myddel symplicite of the poynt; and yif ther be any thing that knytteth and felawschipeth hym-self to thilke myddel poynt, it is constreyned in-to simplicite (that is to seyn, into unmoevablete), and it ceseth to ben schad and to fleten diversely. Ryght so, by semblable reson, thilke thing that departeth ferrest fro the first thought of god, it is unfolden and summittid to grettere bondes of destyne; and in so moche is the thing more fre and laus fro destyne, as it axeth and hooldeth hym neer to thilke centre of thingis (that

1458. *of olde men, i.e.* by the ancients.
1460. C₁ B A₂ H Cx. add *certes* before *destyne.*
1464. *be cleped*, C₂ A₁ *is.*
1467. *ledith . . . by temporel ordenaunce*, through processes in time.

is to seyn, god) ; [1480] and yif the thing clyveth to the stedfastnesse of the thought of god and be withoute moevynge, certes it surmounteth the necessite of destyne. Thanne ryght swich comparysoun as is of skillynge to undirstondyng, and of thing that ys engendrid to thing that is, and of tyme to eternite, and of the cercle to the centre ; ryght so is the ordre of moevable destyne to the stable symplicite of purve-aunce. Thilke ordenaunce moveth the hevene and the sterres, and atemprith the elementes to-gidre amonges hem-self, and transformeth hem by entrechaungeable mutacioun. And thilke same ordre neweth ayein alle thinges growynge and fallynge adoun, by semblable progressions of sedes and of sexes (that is to seyn, mal and femele). [1485] And this ilke ordre constreyneth the fortunes and the dedes of men by a bond of causes nat able to ben unbownde ; the whiche destynal causes, whan thei passen out of the bygynnynges of the unmoevable purve-aunce, it moot nedes be that thei ne be nat mutable. And thus ben the thinges ful wel I-governed yif that the symplicite duellynge in the devyne thoght scheweth forth the ordre of causes unable to ben I-bowed. And this ordre constreyneth by his propre stablete the moevable thingis, or elles thei scholden fleten folyly. For whiche it es that alle thingis' semen to ben confus and trouble to us men, for we ne mowen nat considere thilke orde-naunce. [1490] Natheles the propre maner of every thing, dressynge hem to gode, disponith hem alle ; for ther nys no thing doon for cause of yvel, ne thilk thing that is doon by wikkid folk nys nat doon for yvel, the whiche schrewes, as I have schewed ful plentyvously, seken good, but wikkid errour mystorneth hem ; ne the ordre comynge fro the poynt of sovereyn good ne declyneth nat fro his bygynnynge.

But thou mayst seyn, "What unreste may ben a worse confusioun than that gode men han som tyme adversite and som tyme prosperite, and schrewes also han now thingis that they desiren and now thinges that thei haten ?" Whethir men lyven now in swich holnesse of thought (as who seith, ben men now so wyse) that swiche folk as thei demen to ben gode folk or schrewes, that it moste nedes ben that folk ben swiche as thei wenen ? But in this manere the domes of men discorden, that thilke men that som folk demen worthy of mede, other folk demen hem worthy of torment. [1495] But lat us graunten, I pose, that som man may wel demen or knowen the good folk and the badde ; may he thanne knowen and seen thilke innereste atempraunce of corages as it hath ben wont to ben seyd of bodyes ? (As who seith, may a man speken and determinen of atempraunce in corages, as men were wont to demen or speken of complexions and atempraunces of bodies?) Ne it ne is nat an unlike miracle to hem that ne knowen it nat (as who seith, but it is lik a mervayle or miracle to hem that ne knowen it nat) whi that swete thinges ben covenable to some bodies that ben hole, and to some bodies byttere thinges ben covenable ; [1500] and also why that some syk folk ben holpen with lyghte medicynes, and some folk ben holpen with sharpe medicynes. But natheles the leche, that knoweth the manere and the atempraunce of hele and of maladye, ne merveyleth of it no-thyng. But what othir thing semeth hele of corages but bounte and prowesse ? And what othir thing semeth maladye of corages but vices ? Who is elles kepere of good or dryvere awey of yvel but god, governour and lechere of thoughtes ? The whiche god, whan he hath byholden from the hye tour of his purveaunce, he knoweth what

1480. C₁ A₂ H Cx. *to god.*
1482. *skillynge*, 'ratiocinatio.'
1485. *sexes*, Fr. 'sexes,' 'fetuum' confused with *secus* (*sexus*).
1487. *whan thei passen*, 'cum' causal con-strued as 'cum' temporal.
1492. *poynt*, centre.

1493. *What unreste*, etc., 'Quæ, tu inquies, potest ulla iniquior confusio?' Chaucer began with Fr. 'Mais tu diras,' and then turned to Latin, construing 'inquies' as a noun.
1494. *Whethir men*, etc., do men, etc.
1499. *lik a mervayle*, rather *a lik mervayle*.

is covenable to every wight, and lenyth hem that he woot that is covenable to hem. [1505] Lo herof comyth and herof is don this noble miracle of the ordre destynal, whan god, that al knoweth, dooth swiche thing, of whiche thing unknowynge folk ben astonyd. But for to constreyne (as who seith, but for to comprehende and to telle) a fewe thingis of the devyne depnesse, the whiche that mannys resoun may undirstonde, thilke man that thou wenest to ben ryght just and ryght kepynge of equite, the contrarie of that semeth to the devyne purveaunce, that al woot. And Lucan, my famylier, telleth that the victorious cause likide to the goddes, and the cause overcomen likide to Catoun. Thanne what so evere thou mayst seen that is doon in this world unhopid or unwened, certes it is the ryghte ordre of thinges; but as to thi wikkid opynioun, it is a confusioun. [1510] But I suppose that som man be so wel I-thewed that the devyne jugement and the jugement of mankynde accorden hem to gidre of hym; but he is so unstidfast of corage that, yif any adversite come to hym, he wol forleten peraventure to continue innocence, by the whiche he ne may nat withholden fortune. Thanne the wise dispensacion of god sparith hym, the whiche man adversite myghte enpeyren; for that god wol nat suffren hym to travaile, to whom that travaile nis nat covenable. Another man is parfit in alle vertus, and is an holi man and neigh to god, so that the purveaunce of god wolde deme that it were a felonie that he were touched with any adversites; so that he wol nat suffre that swich a man be moeved with any bodily maladye. [1515] But so as seyde a philosophre, the more excellent by me,—he seyde in Grec that "vertues han edified the body of the holi man." And ofte tyme it be-tydeth that the somme

of thingis that ben to done is taken to governe to good folk, for that the malice haboundaunt of schrewes scholde ben abated. And god yeveth and departeth to other folk prosperites and adversites, I-meddled to hepe aftir the qualite of hir corages, and remordith some folk by adversite, for thei ne scholden nat waxen proude by long welefulnesse; and other folk he suffreth to ben travailed with harde thinges, for that thei scholden confermen the vertues of corage by the usage and the exercitacioun of pacience. [1520] And other folk dreden more than thei oughten the whiche thei myghte wel beren, and thilke folk god ledeth in-to experience of hem-self by aspre and sorweful thingis. And many othir folk han bought honourable renoun of this world by the prys of glorious deth; and som men, that ne mowen nat ben overcomen by torment, han yeven ensample to other folk that vertu mai nat ben overcomyn by adversites.

And of alle thise thinges ther nis no doute that thei ne ben doon ryghtfully and ordeynly, to the profit of hem to whom we seen thise thingis betyde. For certes, that adversite cometh somtyme to schrewes and somtyme that that they desiren, it comith of thise forseyde causes. [1525] And of sorweful thingis that betyden to schrewes certes no man ne wondreth; for alle men wenen that thei han wel desservid it, and that thei ben of wykkid meryt. Of whiche schrewes the torment som-tyme agasteth othere to don felonyes, and som-tyme it amendeth hem that suffren the tormentes; and the prosperite that is yeven to schrewes scheweth a gret argument to good folk what thing thei scholde demen of thilke welefulnesse, the whiche prosperite men seen ofte serven to schrewes. In the whiche thing I trowe that god dispenseth. For peraventure the nature of som man is so overthrowynge to yvel,

1507. *to constreyne*, rather *to speke schortly of.*
1509. *Lucan*, v. *Pharsalia* i. 128.
1510. *but as to*, etc., rather *but to thi opinion it is a wikked confusion.*
1512. *continue* should be *haunten* or *usen,* 'colere'; Fr. 'coutiuer' read as *continuer.*

1517. *taken*, entrusted.
1526. *of wykkid meryt*, 'male meritos,' 'de mauuaise merite.'

and so uncovenable, that the nedy poverte of his houshold myghte rather egren hym to don felonyes ; and to the maladye of hym god putteth remedye to yeven hym rychesses. [1530] And som othir man byholdeth his conscience defouled with synnes, and makith comparysoun of his fortune and of hym-self, and dredith peraventure that his blisfulnesse, of whiche the usage is joyeful to hym, that the lesynge of thilke blisfulnesse ne be nat sorwful to hym ; and therfore he wol chaunge his maneris, and, for he dredith to lesen his fortune, he forletith his wikkidnesse. To other folke is welefulnesse I-yeven unworthely, the whiche overthroweth hem in-to destruccioun, that thei han disservid ; and to som othir folk is yoven power to punysshen, for that it schal be cause of contynuacioun and exercisynge to good folk, and cause of torment to schrewes. [1535] For so as ther nis noon alliaunce bytwixe good folk and schrewes, ne schrewes ne mowen nat acorden among hem - self. And whi nat ? For schrewes discorden of hem-self by hir vices, the whiche vices al to-reenden her consciences, and doon ofte time thinges the whiche thingis, whan thei han doon hem, they demen that tho thinges ne scholden nat han ben doon. For whiche thing thilke sovereyne purveaunce hath makid ofte tyme fair myracle, so that schrewes han maked schrewes to ben gode men. For whan that some schrewes seen that they suffren wrongfully felonyes of othere schrewes, they wexen eschaufed in-to hate of hem that anoyed hem, and retornen to the fruyt of vertu, whan thei studien to ben unlyk to hem that thei han hated. Certis oonly this is the devyne myght to the whiche myghte yvelis ben thanne gode whan it useth the yvelis covenably and draweth out the effect of any good. [1540] (As who seith that yvel is good

1529. *uncovenable*, rather *outragtous*, 'inportuna,' probably read as *inoportuna*.
1535. *contynuacioun*, 'coutumance' ('exercitium'), read as *continuance*.
1537. H Cx. A₁ omit *fair* before *myracle*.
1539. *whan*, 'dum.'
1540. *any good*, 'aucun bien.'

only to the myghte of god, for the myght of god ordeyneth thilke yvel to good.)

For oon ordre enbraseth alle thinges, so that what wyght that departeth fro the resoun of thilke ordre which that is assigned to hym, algatis yit he slideth in-to an othir ordre ; so that no thing is leveful to folye in the reaume of the devyne purveaunce (as who seith, no thing nis withouten ordenaunce in the reame of the devyne purveaunce), syn that the ryght strong god governeth alle thinges in this world. For it nis nat leveful to man to comprehenden by wit, ne unfolden by word, alle the subtil ordenaunces and disposicionis of the devyne entente. For oonly it owghte suffise to han lokid that god hym-self, makere of alle natures, ordeineth and dresseth alle thingis to gode ; [1545] whil that he hasteth to withholden the thingis that he hath makid into his semblaunce (that is to seyn, for to withholden thingis in-to gode, for he hym-self is good), he chasith out alle yvel fro the boundes of his comynalite by the ordre of necessite destinable. For whiche it folweth that, yif thou loke the purveaunce ordeynynge the thinges that men wenen ben outraious or haboundaunt in erthis, thou ne schalt nat seen in no place no thing of yvel. But I se now that thou art charged with the weyghte of the questioun, and wery with lengthe of my resoun, and that thou abydest som swetnesse of songe. Tak thanne this drawght, and, whanne thou art wel reffressched and refect, thou schalt be more stedfast to stye in-to heyere questions or thinges. [1550]

' Si vis celsi iura.'—Metrum 6

Yif thou, wys, wilt demen in thi pure thought the ryghtes or the lawes of the heye thondrere (that is to seyn, of god), loke thou and byhoold the heightes of the sovereyn hevene. Ther kepin the sterres, be ryghtful alliaunce of thinges,

1544. *man*, A₁ *to no man*; C₁ H Cx. A₂ B *men*.
1550. *or thinges*, A₂ H *of thinges*; C₂ A₁ omit.

hir oolde pees. The sonne, I-moevid by his rody fyr, ne distorbeth nat the colde cercle of the mone. Ne the sterre yclepid the Bere, that enclyneth his ravysschynge coursis abowte the sovereyn heighte of the world—ne the same sterre Ursa nis nevere mo wasschen in the depe westrene see, ne coveyteth nat to deeyen his flaumbes in the see of the occian, although it see othere sterres I-plowngid in the see. And Hesperus the sterre bodith and telleth alwey the late nyghtes, and Lucyfer the sterre bryngeth ayein the clere day. [1555]

And thus maketh Love entre-chaunge-able the perdurable courses; and thus is discordable bataile y-put out of the contre of the sterres. This accordaunce atempryth by evenelyke maneres the elementes, that the moiste thingis, stryvynge with the drye thingis, yeven place by stoundes; and that the colde thingis joynen hem by feyth to the hote thingis; and that the lyghte fyr ariseth in-to heighte, and the hevy erthes avalen by her weyghtes. By thise same causes the floury yer yeldeth swote smelles in the first somer sesoun warmynge; and the hote somer dryeth the cornes; and autumpne comith ayein hevy of apples; and the fletyng reyn by-deweth the wynter. This a-tempraunce norysscheth and bryngeth forth alle thinges that brethith lif in this world; [1560] and thilke same attempraunce, ravysschynge, hideth and bynymeth, and drencheth undir the laste deth, alle thinges I-born.

Among thise thinges sitteth the heye makere, kyng and lord, welle and bygynnynge, lawe and wys juge to don equite, and governeth and enclyneth the brydles of thinges. And tho thinges that he stireth to gon by moevynge, he with-draweth and aresteth, and affermeth the moevable or wandrynge thinges. For

yif that he ne clepide nat ayein the ryght goynge of thinges, and yif that he ne constreynede hem nat eftsones into roundnesses enclyned, the thingis that ben now contynued by stable ordenaunce, thei scholden departen from hir welle (that is to seyn, from hir bygynnynge), and failen (that is to seyn, tornen into noght). This is the comune love to alle thingis, and alle thinges axen to ben holden by the fyn of good. [1565] For elles ne myghten they nat lasten yif thei ne comen nat eftsones ayein, by love retorned, to the cause that hath yeven hem beinge (that is to seyn, to god).

'*Iam ne igitur vides.*'—Prosa 7

Sestow nat thanne what thing folweth alle the thingis that I have seyd?'

'What thing?' quod I.

'Certes,' quod sche, 'al outrely that alle fortune is good.'

'And how may that be?' quod I.

'Now undirstand,' quod sche, 'so as al fortune, whethir so it be joyeful fortune or aspre fortune, is yeven eyther bycause of gerdonynge or elles of exercisyng of good folk, or elles bycause to punysschen or elles chastisen schrewes; thanne is alle fortune good, the whiche fortune is certeyn that it be either ryghtful or elles profitable.' [1570]

'Forsothe this is a ful verray resoun,' quod I; 'and yif I considere the purveaunce and the destyne that thou taughtest me a litel here byforn, this sentence is sustenyd by stedfast resouns. But yif it like unto the, lat us nombren hem amonges thilke thingis, of whiche thow seydest a litel here byforn that thei ne were nat able to ben wened to the peple.'

'Why so?' quod sche.

1555. *bodith*, etc., 'seras nuntiat umbras.'
1556. *the perdurable*, C₁ H Cx. omit *the*; perhaps the original reading was *her*, Fr. 'leur.'
1560. *brethith*, A₁ *bredith*; C₂ A₂ Cx. *berith*.
1562. *Among thise thinges*, 'interea,' read as 'inter ea'; so also in French.

1564. *roundnesses enclyned*, 'flexos orbes.' 'rondeces flechiez.'
1564. *that ben now contynued*, etc., 'Quæ nunc stabilis continet ordo'; 'continet' as *continuit* (or through Fr. 'contenuez'), and 'ordo' as ablative through 'par ordenance estable.' A₂ *conteyned*, probably a correction.

'For that the comune word of men,' quod I, 'mysuseth this manere speche of fortune, and seyn ofte tymes that the fortune of som wyght is wikkid.'

'Woltow thanne,' quod sche, 'that I approche a litil to the wordis of the peple, so that it seme nat to hem that I be over-moche departed fro the usage of man-kynde?'

'As thou wilt,' quod I.

'Demestow nat,' quod sche, 'that alle thing that profiteth is good?' [1575]

'Yis,' quod I.

'And certes thilke thing that exerciseth or corrigith profitith?'

'I confesse it wel,' quod I.

'Thanne is it good,' quod sche.

'Whi nat?' quod I.

'But this is the fortune,' quod sche, 'of hem that eyther ben put in vertu and batayllen ayein aspre thingis, or elles of hem that eschuen and declynen fro vices and taken the weye of vertu.'

'This ne mai I nat denye,' quod I.

'But what seistow of the merye fortune that is yeven to good folk in guerdoun? Demeth aught the peple that it is wikkid?'

'Nay forsothe,' quod I; 'but thei demen, as it soth is, that it is ryght good.' [1580]

'And what seistow of that othir fortune,' quod sche, 'that, although it be aspre and restreyneth the schrewes by ryghtful torment, weneth aught the peple that it be good?'

'Nay,' quod I, 'but the peple demeth that it is moost wrecchid of alle thingis that mai ben thought.'

'War now and loke wel,' quod sche, 'lest that we, in folwynge the opynioun of the peple, have confessid and con-cluded thing that is unable to be wened to the peple?'

'What is that?' quod I.

'Certes,' quod sche, 'it folweth or comith of thingis that ben grauntid that alle fortune, what so evere it be, of hem that ben eyther in possessioun of vertu, or

in the encres of vertu, or elles in the purchasynge of vertu, that thilke fortune is good; and that alle fortune is ryght wikkid to hem that duellen in schrewid-nesse.' (As who seith: 'And thus weneth nat the peple.') [1585]

'That is soth,' quod I, 'al be it so that no man dar confessen it ne by-knowen it.'

'Whi so?' quod sche; 'for ryght as the stronge man ne semeth nat to abaissen or disdaignen as ofte tyme as he herith the noyse of the bataile, ne also it ne semeth nat to the wise man to beren it grevously as ofte as he is lad into the stryf of fortune. For, bothe to the to man and eek to the tothir thilke difficulte is the matere, to the to man of encres of his glorious renoun, and to the tothir man to confermen his sapience (—that is to seyn the asprenesse of his estat). For therfore it is called " vertu," for that it sustenith and enforceth by hise strengthes that it nis nat overcomen by adversites. Ne certes thou, that art put in the encres or in the heyghte of vertu, ne hast nat comen to fleten with delices, and for to welken in bodily lust; [1590] thou sowest or plawntest a ful egre bataile in thy corage ayeins every fortune. For that the sorwful fortune ne confownde the nat, ne that the myrie fortune ne corrumpe the nat, ocupye the mene by stidefast strengthes. For al that evere is undir the mene, or elles al that overpasseth the mene, despyseth welefulnesse (as who seith, it is vycious), and ne hath no mede of his travaile. For it is set in your hand (as who seith, it lyth in your power) what fortune yow is levest (that is to seyn good or yvel). For alle fortune that semeth scharp or aspre, yif it ne exercise nat the good folk ne chastiseth the wikkide folk, it punysseth. [1595]

1587. *semeth*, 'debet' read as *decet*.
1590. *encres*, *heyghte*, 'provectu,' 'hautece.'
1591. *sowest or plawntest*, 'conseritis' (prœ-lium).
1595. *yif it ne*, etc., should be *yif it ne exer-cise ne chastiseth, it punysseth*. The translation combines two variant readings of the Latin.

'*Bella bis quinis.*'—Metrum 7

The wrekere Attrides (that is to seyn, Agamenon), that wrought and contynued the batailes by x yer, recovered and purgide in wrekynge, by the destruccioun of Troye, the loste chaumbris of mariage of his brothir. (That is to seyn that he, Agamenon, wan ayein Eleyne that was Menelaus wif his brothir.) In the mene while that thilke Agamenon desirede to yeven sayles to the Grykkyssche naveye, and boughte ayein the wyndes by blood, he unclothide hym of pite of fadir; and the sory preest yeveth in sacrifyinge the wrecchide kuttynge of throte of the doughter. (That is to seyn that Agamenon leet kutten the throte of his doughter by the preest, to maken alliaunce with his goddes, and for to han wynd with whiche he myghte wenden to Troye.) [1600]

Ytakus (that is to seyn Ulixes) bywepte his felawes I-lorn, the whiche felawes fyerse Poliphemus, ligginge in his grete cave, had fretyn and dreynt in his empty wombe. But natheles Poliphemus, wood for his blynde visage, yald to Ulixes ioye by his sorwful teres. (This is to seyn that Ulixes smoot out the eye of Poliphemus, that stood in his forheed, for whiche Ulixes hadde ioye whan he say Poliphemus wepynge and blynd.)

Hercules is celebrable for his harde travaile. He dawntide the proude Centauris (half hors, half man), and he byrafte the dispoilynge fro the cruel lyoun (that is to seyn, he slouhe the lyoun and rafte hym his skyn); he smot the briddes that hyghten Arpiis with certein arwes; [1605] he ravysschide applis fro the wakynge dragoun, and his hand was the more hevy for the goldene metal; he drowh Cerberus (the hound of helle) by his treble cheyne; he, overcomer, as it is seyd, hath put an unmeke lord foddre to his crwel hors (this to seyn that Hercules slowh Diomedes, and made his hors to freten hym); and he, Hercules, slowh Idra the serpent, and brende the venym; and Acheleous the flod, defowled in his forheed, dreynte his schamefast visage in his strondes (that is to seyn that Achaleous coude transfiguren hym-self into diverse liknesse, and, as he faught with Hercules, at the laste he torned hym in-to a bole, and Hercules brak oon of his hornes, and he for schame hidde hym in his ryver); [1610] and he, Hercules, caste adoun Antheus the geaunt in the strondes of Libye; and Kacus apaysede the wratthes of Evander (this to seyn that Hercules slouh the monstre Kacus, and apaysed with that deth the wratthe of Evander); and the bristilede boor markide with scornes the scholdres of Hercules, the whiche scholdres the heye cercle of hevene sholde thriste; and the laste of his labours was that he susteynede the hevene uppon his nekke unbowed; and he disservide eftsones the hevene to ben the pris of his laste travaile.

Goth now thanne, ye stronge men, ther as the heye wey of the greet ensaumple ledith yow. [1615] O nyce men! why nake ye your bakkes? (As who seith, "O ye slowe and delicat men! whi flee ye adversites, and ne fyghte nat ayeins hem by vertu, to wynnen the mede of the hevene?") For the erthe overcomen yeveth the sterres. (This to seyn that whan that erthly lust is overcomyn, a man is makid worthy to the hevene.)'

EXPLICIT LIBER QUARTUS

INCIPIT LIBER QUINTUS

'*Dixerat orationisque cursum.*'—Prosa 1

Sche hadde seyd, and tornede the cours of hir resoun to some othere thingis to

1596. *recovered,* etc., 'recouura' ('piavi'), and Latin gloss 'purgavit ulciscendo.'
1598. *pite of fadir,* 'pietatem paternam' (in gloss).
1598. *yeveth in sacrifyinge,* etc., 'Foederat natæ jugulum.'
1598. *kuttynge of throte* is due to a note in Aq.
1601. *empty,* rather *grete.*
1604. *dispoilynge,* rather *spoil.*

1613. *scornes,* flecks of foam, 'spumia.'
1615. *the cours,* C₁ C₂ by *cours.*
1618. *resoun,* 'orationis' read as *rationis.*

ben treted and to ben Ispedd. Than seide I, 'Certes ryghtful is thin amones-tynge and ful digne by auctorite. But that thou seydest whilom that the questioun of the devyne purveaunce is enlaced with many othere questiouns, I undirstande wel and prove it by the same thing. But I axe yif that thou wenest that hap be anything in any weys; and yif thou wenest that hap be anything, what is it?' [1620]

Thanne quod sche, 'I haste me to yelden and assoilen to the the dette of my byheste, and to schewen and openen the wey, by whiche wey thou maist comen ayein to thi contre. But al be it so that the thingis whiche that thou axest ben ryght profitable to knowe, yit ben thei divers somwhat fro the path of my purpos; and it is to douten that thou ne be makid weery by mys-weyes, so that thou ne maist nat suffise to mesuren the ryghte weie.'

'Ne doute the ther-of no thing,' quod I; 'for for to knowen thilke thingis to-gidre, in the whiche thinges I delite me gretly,—that schal ben to me in stede of rest, syn it nis nat to douten of the thingis folwynge, whan every syde of thi disputesioun schal han ben stedfast to me by undoutous feyth.' [1625]

'Thanne,' seide sche, 'that manere wol I don the,' and bygan to speken ryght thus: 'Certes,' quod sche, 'yif any wyght diffynisse hap in this manere, that is to seyn that "hap is a bytydynge I-brought forth by foolisshe moevynge and by no knyttynge of causes," I conferme that hap nis ryght naught in no wise; and I deme al outrely that hap nis, ne duelleth but a voys (as who seith, but an idel word), withouten any significacioun of thing summitted to that voys. For

what place myght ben left or duellynge to folie and to disordenaunce, syn that god ledeth and constreyneth alle thingis by ordre? For this sentence is verray and soth, that "no thing hath his beynge of naught," to the whiche sentence noon of thise oolde folk ne withseide nevere; [1630] al be it so that they ne undirstoden ne meneden it nat by god prince and bygynnere of wirkynge, but thei casten as a maner foundement of subiect material (that is to seyn, of the nature of alle resouns). And yif that any thing is woxen or comen of no causes, thanne schal it seme that thilke thing is comen or woxen of nawght; but yif this ne mai nat ben don, thanne is nat possible that hap be any swich thing as I have diffynysschid a litel here byforn.'

'How schal it thanne be?' quod I. 'Nys ther thanne no thing that by right may ben clepid other hap or elles aventure of fortune; or is ther awght, al be it so that it is hidd fro the peple, to whiche thing thise wordes ben covenable?'

'Myn Aristotles,' quod sche, 'in the book of his Phisic diffynysseth this thing by schort resoun, and nyghe to the sothe.'

'In whiche manere?' quod I. [1635]

'As ofte,' quod sche, 'as men don any thing for grace of any other thing, and an other thing than thilke thing that men entenden to don bytideth by some causes, it is clepid "hap." Ryght as a man dalf the erthe bycause of tylyinge of the feld, and founde ther a gobet of gold bydolven; thanne wenen folk that it is byfalle by fortunous bytydynge. But forsothe it nis nat of naught, for it hath his propre causes, of whiche causes the cours unforseyn and unwar semeth to han makid hap. For yif the tiliere of the feeld ne dulve nat in the erthe, and yif the hidere of the gold ne hadde hyd the gold in thilke place, the gold ne hadde nat ben founde. Thise ben thanne the

1618. *ful digne*, etc., 'dignissima auctoritate' misconstrued.
1619. *by the same thing*, rather *by the thing itself*, i.e. by experience.
1620. *in any weys*, at all.
1625. *knowen . . . togidre*, 'agnoscere' ends first clause, 'simul cum' begins the second one. Chaucer took 'agnoscere simul' together.
1628. *thing summitted*, 'rei subiectæ.'

1631. *by god*, in respect to god.
1631. *as*, as it were.
1635. *thing*, C₂ A₁ omit.
1639. *dulve*, pret. subj. of *deluen*.

causes of the abregginge of fortuit hap, the whiche abreggynge of fortuit hap cometh of causes encontrynge and flowynge togidre to hem-self, and nat hy the entencioun of the doere. [1640] For neither the hidere of the gold ne the delvere of the feeld ne undirstoden nat that the gold sholde han ben founde; but, as I seide, it bytidde and ran togidre that he dalf there as that oothir had hid the gold. Now mai I thus diffinysshen "hap": hap is an unwar betydinge of causes assembled in thingis that ben doon for som oothir thing; but thilke ordre, procedinge by an uneschuable byndinge to-gidre, whiche that descendeth fro the welle of purveaunce, that ordeyneth alle thingis in hir places and in hir tymes, makith that the causes rennen and assemblen togidre.

. '*Rupis Achemenie.*'—Metrum 1

Tigrys and Eufrates resolven and springen of o welle in the cragges of the roche of the contre of Achemenye, ther as the fleinge bataile ficcheth hir dartes retorned in the breestis of hem that folwen hem. [1645] And sone aftir the same ryverys, Tigris and Eufrates, unioignen and departen hir watres. And if thei comen togidre, and ben assemblid and clepid togidre into o course, thanne moten thilke thingis fleten togidre whiche that the watir of the entrechaungynge flood bryngeth. The schippes and the stokkes, araced with the flood, moten assemblen; and the watris I-medled wrappeth or emplieth many fortunel happes or maneris; the whiche wandrynge happes natheles thilke enclynynge lowenesse of the erthe and the flowinge ordre of the slydinge watir governeth. Right so fortune, that

semeth as it fletith with slakid or ungoverned bridles, it suffreth bridelis (that is to seyn, to ben governed), and passeth by thilke lawe (that is to seyn, by the devyne ordenaunce).' [1650]

'*Animadverto inquam.*'—Prosa 2

'This undirstonde I wel,' quod I, 'and I accorde me that it is ryght as thou seist, but I axe yif ther be any liberte of fre wille in this ordre of causes that clyven thus togidre in hem-self. Or elles I wolde witen yif that the destinal cheyne constrenith the moevynges of the corages of men.'

'Yis,' quod sche, 'ther is liberte of fre wil. Ne ther ne was nevere no nature of resoun that it ne hadde liberte of fre wil. For every thing that may naturely usen resoun, it hath doom by whiche it discernith and demeth every thing; thanne knoweth it by it-self thinges that ben to fleen and thinges that ben to desiren. [1655] And thilke thing that any wight demeth to ben desired, that axeth or desireth he; and fleeth thilke thing that he troweth be to fleen. Wherfore in alle thingis that resoun is, in hem also is liberte of willynge and of nillynge. But I ne ordeyne nat (as who seith, I ne graunte nat) that this liberte be evenelyk in alle thinges. For-why in the sovereynes devynes substaunces (that is to seyn in spirites) jugement is more cleer, and wil nat I-corrumped, and myght redy to speden thinges that ben desired. But the soules of men moten nedes be more fre whan thei loken hem in the speculacioun or lokynge of the devyne thought; [1660] and lasse fre whan thei slyden in-to the bodyes; and yit lasse fre whan thei ben gadrid to gidre and comprehended in erthli membres. But the laste servage is whan that thei ben yeven to vices and han I-falle fro the possessioun of hir propre resoun.

1639. *abregginge of fortuit hap*, 'fortuiti compendii' (accidental gain) glossed 'fortuiti eventus'; Fr. 'l'abregement du cas fortunel' with wrong meaning of *compendium*, which Chaucer follows.

1641. *undirstoden* (C₂ *undirstonden*, but probably a correction), 'intendit,' Fr. 'entendirent,' which Chaucer misunderstood.

1645. *the fleinge bataile*, etc., i.e. in Parthia.

1650. *passeth*, moves along.

1660. *loken hem* (C₁ A₂ him), 'conservant,' Fr. 'se gardent' mistranslated.

For aftir that thei han cast awey hir eyghen fro the lyght of the sovereyn sothfastnesse to lowe thingis and derke, anon thei derken by the cloude of ignoraunce and ben troubled by felonous talentes; to the whiche talentes whan thei approchen and assenten, thei hepen and encrecen the servage whiche thei han joyned to hem-self; and in this manere thei ben caytifs fro hir propre liberte. The whiche thingis natheles the lokynge of the devyne purveaunce seth, that alle thingis byholdeth and seeth fro eterne, and ordeyneth hem everiche in here merites as thei ben predestinat; and it is seid in Greke that "alle thinges he seeth and alle thinges he herith." [1665]

' Puro clarum lumine.'—Metrum 2

Homer with the hony mouth (that is to seyn, Homer with the swete ditees) singeth that the sonne is cler by pure light; natheles yit ne mai it nat, by the infirme light of his bemes, breken or percen the inward entrayles of the erthe or elles of the see. So ne seth nat god, makere of the grete werld. To hym, that loketh alle thinges from an hey, ne withstondeth no thinges by hevynesse of erthe, ne the nyght ne withstondeth nat to hym by the blake cloudes. Thilke god seeth in o strok of thought alle thinges that ben, or weren, or schollen comen; and thilke god, for he loketh and seeth alle thingis alone, thou maist seyn that he is the verrai sonne.'

' Tum ego en inquam.'—Prosa 3

Thanne seide I, 'Now am I confowndide by a more hard doute than I was.'
'What doute is that?' quod sche, 'for certes I coniecte now by whiche thingis thou art trubled.' [1670]
'It semeth,' quod I, 'to repugnen and

1663. *talentes,* 'affectibus.'
1665. *in Greke,* Homer, *Il.* iii. 277; *Odys.* xii. 323.
1666. 'Puro clarum lumine Phœbum Meiliflu canit oris Homerus.'

to contrarien gretly, that god knoweth byforn alle thinges and that ther is any fredom of liberte. For yif it so be that god loketh alle thinges byforn ne god ne mai nat ben desceyved in no manere, thanne moot it nedes ben that alle thinges betyden the whiche that the purveaunce of god hath seyn byforn to comen. For whiche, yif that god knoweth byforn nat oonly the werkes of men, but also hir conseilles and hir willes, thanne ne schal ther be no liberte of arbitre; ne certes ther ne may be noon other dede, ne no wil, but thilke whiche that the devyne purveaunce, that ne mai nat ben disseyved, hath felid byforn. [1675] For yif that thei myghten writhen awey in othere manere than thei ben purveyed, thanne ne sholde ther be no stedefast prescience of thing to comen, but rather an uncerteyn opynioun; the whiche thing to trowen of god, I deme felonye and unleveful. Ne I ne proeve nat thilke same resoun (as who seith, I ne allowe nat, or I ne preyse nat, thilke same resoun) by whiche that som men wenen that thei mowe assoilen and unknytten the knotte of this questioun. For certes thei seyn that thing nis nat to comen for that the purveaunce of god hath seyn byforn that it is to comen, but rathir the contrarie; and that is this: that, for that the thing is to comen, that therfore ne mai it nat ben hidd fro the purveaunce of god; and in this manere this necessite slideth ayein into the contrarie partie: [1680] ne it ne byhoveth nat nedes that thinges betiden that ben I-purveied, but it byhoveth nedes that thinges that ben to comen ben I-purveied: but, as it were, y travailed (as who seith, that thilke answere procedith ryght as though men travaileden or weren besy) to enqueren the whiche thing is cause of the whiche thing, as

1671 ff. Cp. *Troilus,* iv. 967-1078.
1677. *proeve,* wrong meaning of 'probo'; Fr. 'loe'; cp. Chaucer's gloss.
1681. *nedes,* necessarily.
1682. *y travailed,* MSS. *ytravailed* (H Cx. *travailed*), cp. *Troilus,* v. 1009; Fr. 'nous trauaillons,' both incorrect translations of 'laboretur.' Cp. Chaucer's gloss.

whethir the prescience is cause of the necessite of thinges to comen, or elles that the necessite of thinges to comen is cause of the purveaunce. But I ne enforce me nat now to schewen it, that the bytidynge of thingis I-wyst byforn is necessarie, how so or in what manere that the ordre of causes hath it-self; although that it ne seme naught that the prescience bringe in necessite of bytydinge to thinges to comen. [1685] For certes yif that any wyght sitteth, it byhoveth by necessite that the opynioun be soth of hym that coniecteth that he sitteth; and ayeinward also is it of the contrarie: yif the opinioun be soth of any wyght for that he sitteth, it byhoveth by necessite that he sitte. Thanne is here necessite in the toon and in the tothir; for in the toon is necessite of syttynge, and certes in the tothir is necessite of soth. But therfore sitteth nat a wyght for that the opynioun of the sittynge is soth, but the opinioun is rather soth for that a wyght sitteth byforn. And thus, althoughe that the cause of the soth cometh of that other side (as who seith, that althoughe the cause of soth cometh of the sittynge, and nat of the trewe opinioun), algates yit is ther comune necessite in that oon and in that othir. [1690] Thus scheweth it that y may make semblable skiles of the purveaunce of god and of thingis to comen. For althoughe that for that thingis ben to comen therfore ben thei purveied, and nat certes for thei be purveied therfore ne bytide thei nat; natheles byhoveth it by necessite that eyther the thinges to comen ben I-purveied of god, or elles that the thinges that ben I-purveyed of god betyden. And this thing oonly suffiseth I-now to destroien the fredom of oure arbitre (that is to seyn, of our fre wil). But certes now scheweth it wel how fer fro the sothe and how up-so-doun is this thing that

we seyn, that the betydynge of temporel thingis is cause of the eterne prescience. [1695] But for to wenen that god purveieth the thinges to comen for thei ben to comen, —what oothir thing is it but for to wene that thilke thinges that bytiden whilom ben causes of thilke soverein purveaunce that is in god? And her-to I adde yit this thing: that ryght as whanne that I woot that a thing is, it byhoveth by necessite that thilke selve thing be: and eek whan I have knowen that any thing schal betyden, so byhovith it by necessite that thilke same thing betide: so folweth it thanne that the betydynge of the thing that I wyste byforn ne may nat ben eschued. And at the laste, yif that any wyght wene a thing to ben oothir weyes than it is, it nis nat oonly unscience, but it is desceyvable opynioun ful divers and fer fro the sothe of science. Wherfore, yif any thing be so to comen that the betidynge of it ne be nat certein ne necessarie, who mai witen byforn that thilke thing is to comen? [1700] For ryght as science ne may nat ben medled with falsnesse (as who seith, that yif I woot a thing, it ne mai nat ben fals that I ne woot it), ryght so thilke thing that is conceyved by science may ben noon other weies than as it is conceyved. For that is the cause why that science wanteth lesynge (as who seith, why that wytynge ne resceyveth nat lesynge of that it woot); for it byhoveth by necessite that every thing be ryght as science comprehendeth it to be. What schal I thanne seyn? In whiche manere knoweth god byforn the thinges to comen, yif thei ne ben nat certein? For yif that he deme that thei ben to comen uneschewably, and so may be that it is possible that thei ne schollen nat comen, god is disseyved. [1705] But not oonly to trowe that god is disseyved, but for to speke it with mouthe, it is a felonous synne. But yif that god woot that ryght so as thinges ben to comen, so schollen they comen, so that

1684. *I ne enforce me nat* should be *I enforce me.* Ch. and Fr. translate 'non nitamur' a variant of 'nos nitamur.'
1691. *skiles*, arguments.

1701. *that I ne woot it.* The 'ne' is due to the negative in the main clause.

he wite egaly (as who seith, indifferently) that thingis mowen ben doon or elles nat I-doon, what is thilke prescience that ne comprehendeth no certein thing ne stable? Or elles what difference is ther bytwixe the prescience and thilke jape-worthi devynynge of Tyresie the divynour, that seide, "Al that I seie," quod he, "either it schal be or elles it schal nat be?" Or elles how mochel is worth the devyne prescience more than the opinioun of mankynde, yif so be that it demeth the thinges uncertayn, as men doon, of the whiche domes of men the betydinge is nat certein? But yif so be that noon uncertein thing ne mai ben in hym that is certein welle of alle thinges, than is the betydinge certein of thilke thingis whiche he hath wist byforn fermely to comen. [1710] For whiche it folweth that the fredom of the conseiles and of the werkis of mankynde nis noon, syn that the thought of god, that seeth alle thinges withouten errour of falsnesse, byndeth and constreyneth hem to a bytidynge by necessite. And yif this thing be oonys I-grauntid and resceyved (this is to seyn, that ther nis no fre wil), thanne scheweth it wel how gret destruccioun and how gret damages ther folwen of thingis of man-kynde. For in idel ben ther thanne purposed and byhyght medes to good folk, and peynes to badde folk, syn that no moevynge of fre corage voluntarie ne hath nat disservid hem (that is to seyn neither mede ne peyne). And it scholde seme thanne that thilke thing is alther-worst whiche that is now demed for alther-moost just and moost ryghtful, that is to seyn that schrewes ben punys-schid or elles that good folk ben I-gerdoned. [1715] The whiche folk, syn that hir propre wil ne sent hem nat to the toon ne to that othir (that is to seyn neither to good ne to harm), but [ther] constreyneth hem certein necessite of thingis to comen; thanne ne schulle ther nevere be, ne nevere were,

vice ne vertu, but it scholde rather ben confusion of alle dissertes medlid with-outen discrecioun. And yit ther folweth anothir inconvenient, of the whiche ther ne mai be thought no more felonous ne more wikke, and that is this: that, so as the ordre of thingis is I-led and cometh of the purveaunce of god, ne that no thing is leveful to the conseiles of mankynde (as who seith that men han no power to don no thing ne wilne no thing), thanne folweth it that oure vices ben referrid to the makere of alle good (as who seith, thanne folweth it that god oughte han the blame of our vices, syn he constreyneth us by necessite to doon vices). [1720]

Than nis ther no resoun to han hope in god, ne for to preien to god. For what scholde any wyght hopen to god, or why scholde he preien to god, syn that the ordenaunce of destyne, the whiche that mai nat ben enclyned, knytteth and streyneth alle thingis that men mai desiren? Thanne scholde ther be don awey thilke oonly alliaunce bytwixen god and men, that is to seyn, to hopen and to preien. But by the pris of ryghtwis-nesse and of verray mekenesse we disserven the gerdon of the devyne grace whiche that is inestimable (that is to seyn, that it is so greet that it ne mai nat ben ful I-preysed). And this is oonly the manere (that is to seyn, hope and preieris) for whiche it semeth that men mowen spekyn with god, and by resoun of supplicacion be conioyned to thilke cleernesse that nis nat aprochid no rather or that men byseken it and impetren it. [1725] And yif men ne wene nat that hope ne preieres ne han no strengthis by the necessite of thingis to comen I-resceyved, what thing is ther thanne by whiche we mowen ben conioyned and clyven to thilke sovereyne

1708. *Tyresie*, Tiresias; cp. 84.
1711. *nis noon*, 'est nulle,' is no freedom.
1713. *purposed*, offered.
1716. *ther*, supplied from Fr.

1717. *inconvenient*, 'desconvenue,' inconveni-ence.
1725. *oonly the manere . . . for whiche*, the only way . . . by which.
1725. *no rather or*, 'prius quoque,' which Chaucer has wrongly connected with 'inaccessæ luci,' should be *and rather or*, i.e. even before.
1726. *I-resceyved*, conceded.

prince of thingis? For whiche it by-hoveth by necessite that the lynage of mankynde, as thou songe a litel here byforn, be departed and unioyned from his welle, and failen of his bygynnynge (that is to seyn, god).

'*Quenam discors.*'—Metrum 3

What discordable cause hath to-rent and unioyned the byndynge or the alliaunce of thingis (that is to seyn, the coniunccions of god and of man)? Whiche god hath establisschid so grete bataile bytwixen these two sothfast or verreie thinges (that is to seyn, bytwyxen the purveaunce of god and fre wil) that thei ben singuler and dyvided, ne that they ne wole nat ben medled ne couplid togidre. But ther nis no discord to the verray thinges, but thei clyven alwey certein to hem-self. [1730] But the thought of man, confownded and over-throwen by the derke membres of the body, ne mai nat be fyr of his derked lookynge (that is to seyn, by the vigour of his insyghte while the soule is in the body) knowen the thynne subtile knyt-tynges of thinges. But wherfore eschaufeth it so by so gret love to fynden thilke notes of soth I-covered? (That is to seyn, wherfore eschaufeth the thought of man by so gret desir to knowen thilke notificaciouns that ben I-hid undir the covertures of soth?) Woot it aught thilke thing that it angwisshous desireth to knowe? (As who seith, nay; for no man ne travaileth for to witen thingis that he wot. And therfore the texte seith thus:) [1735] But who travaileth to wite thingis I-knowe? And yif that he ne knoweth hem nat, what sekith thilke blynde thoght? What is he that desireth any thyng of which he wot right nought?

(As who seith, who so desireth any thing, nedes somwhat he knoweth of it, or elles he coude nat desiren it.) Or who may folwen thinges that ne ben nat I-wist? And thoughe that he seke tho thingis, wher schal he fynde hem? What wyght that is al unkunnynge and ignoraunt may knowe the forme that is I-founde? [1740] But whanne the soule byholdeth and seeth the heye thought (that is to seyn, god), thanne knoweth it togidre the somme and the singularites (that is to seyn the prin-ciples and everyche by hym-self). But now, while the soule is hidd in the cloude and in the derknesse of the membres of the body, it ne hath nat al foryeten itself, but it withholdeth the somme of thinges and lesith the singularites. Thanne who so that sekith sothnesse, he nis in neyther nother habite, for he not nat al, ne he ne hath nat al foryeten; but yit hym re-membreth the somme of thinges that he withholdeth, and axeth conseile, and re-tretith deepliche thinges I-seyn by-forn (that is to seyn, the grete somme in his mynde). So that he mowe adden the parties that he hath foryeten to thilke that he hath withholden.' [1745]

'*Tum illa vetus inquit hec est.*'—Prosa 4

Than seide sche 'This is,' quod sche, 'the olde questioun of the purveaunce of god. And Marcus Tullius, whan he devyded the divynaciouns (that is to seyn, in his book that he wrot of dyvynaciouns), he moevede gretly this questioun; and thou thiself hast y-sought it mochel, and outrely, and longe. But yit ne hath it nat ben determined, ne I-sped fermely ne diligently of any of yow. And the cause of this derknesse and of this difficulte is, for that the moevynge of the resoun of mankynde ne may nat moeven to (that is to seyn, applien or joignen to) the sim-plicite of the devyne prescience; the

---

1728. Chaucer's glosses here are derived mainly from Fr.
1730. *But ther nis,* etc., 'An nulla est,' etc. 'An' read as 'ac,' or perhaps gloss is Aq. 'An est nota solutionis.' Similarly, *But whanne,* etc. 1741.

1743. *neyther nother,* neutro.'
1744. *retretith* (A₁ A₂ *tretith*), 'retraite,' 're-tractans.'
1746. *devyded* ('distribuit'), C₂ H *devynede;* Cx. *distribuyd* (from rubric?).

whiche symplicite of the devyne prescience, yif that men myghte thinken it
in any manere (that is to seyn, that yif
men myghten thinken and comprehenden
the thinges as god seeth hem), thanne ne
scholde ther duelle outrely no doute.
[1750] The whiche resoun and cause of
difficulte I schal assaye at the last to
schewe and to speden, whanne I have
first I-spendid and answerd to the resouns
by whiche thou art y-moeved.   For I
axe whi thou wenest that thilke resouns
of hem that assoilen this questioun ne be
nat speedful I-now ne sufficient ; the
whiche solucioun, or the whiche resoun,
for that it demeth that the prescience nis
nat cause of necessite to thinges to comen,
than weneth it nat that fredom of wil be
distorbed or y-let be prescience.   For ne
drawestow nat argumentes fro elles where
of the necessite of thingis to comen (as
who seith, any oothir wey than thus) but
that thilke thinges that the prescience
woot byforn ne mowen nat unbetyde ?
[1755] (That is to seyn, that thei moten
betide.)   But thanne, yif that prescience
ne putteth no necessite to thingis to
comen, as thou thi-self hast confessed it
and byknowen a litel here byforn, what
cause or what is it (as who seith, ther
may no cause be) by whiche that the endes
voluntarie of thinges myghten be constreyned to certein bytydynge ?   For by
grace of possessioun, so that thou mowe
the betere undirstonde this that folweth,
I pose that ther ne be no prescience.
Thanne axe I,' quod sche, ' in as moche
as aperteneth to that, scholden thanne
thingis that comen of fre wil ben constreyned to bytyden by necessite ? '
' Nay,' quod I.
' Thanne ayeinward,' quod sche, ' I
suppose that ther be prescience, but
that it ne putteth no necessite to thingis ;

thanne trowe I that thilke selve fredom
of wil schal duellen al hool and absolut
and unbounden.   But thou wolt seyn
that, al be it so that prescience nis nat
cause of the necessite of tydynge to
thingis to comen, algatis yit it is a sign
that the thingis ben to bytyden by necessite. [1760]   By this manere thanne,
althoughe the prescience ne hadde nevere
I-ben, yit algate or at the leste wey it is
certein thing that the endes and by-
tydinges of thingis to comen scholden
ben necessarie.   For every signe scheweth
and signifieth oonly what the thing is,
but it ne makith nat the thing that it
signifieth.   For whiche it byhoveth first
to schewen that no thing ne bytideth that
it ne betideth by necessite, so that it mai
apiere that the prescience is signe of this
necessite ; or elles, yif ther nere no necessite, certes thilke prescience ne myghte
nat ben signe of thinge that nis nat.
But certes, it is now certein that the
proeve of this, y-susteyned by stedfast
resoun, ne schal nat ben lad ne proeved
by signes, ne by argumentes I-taken fro
withoute, but by causes covenable and
necessarie. [1765]   But thou mayst seyn,
" How may it be that the thingis ne betyden nat that ben I-purveied to comen ? "
But certes ryght as we trowen that tho
thingis whiche that purveaunce woot byforn to comen, ne ben nat to bytiden.
But that ne scholde we nat demen ; but
rathir, althoughe that thei schal betyden,
yit ne have thei no necessite of hir kynde
to betyden.   And this maystow lyghtly
aperceyven by this that I schal seyn.
For we seen many thingis whan thei ben
don byforn oure eyen, ryght as men seen
the cartere worken in the tornynge and
in atemprynge or adressynge of hise cartes
or chariottes. [1770]   And by this manere
(as who seith, maistow undirstonden) of
alle othere werkmen.   Is ther thanne
any necessite (as who seith, in our look-

1751. *I-spendid*, etc., 'expendero' (I shall
have considered), 'respondu.'
1755. *For ne drawestow nat*, etc., 'Num enim
tu aliunde,' etc.
1757. *possessioun* (H Cx. *position*), 'positionis
gratia' should be *position*; but Fr. 'possion'
(sic), L. 'position.'

1765. *argumentis I-taken*, etc., 'petitis extrin-
secus argumentis.'
1766. *But certes*, etc., the answer to the preceding question.
1770. *cartere, cartes*, charioteer, chariots.

ynge) that constreynith or compelleth any of thilke thingis to ben don so?'

'Nay,' quod I, 'for in idel and in veyn were al the effect of craft, yif that alle thingis weren moeved by constreynynge (that is to seyn, by constreinynge of our eyen or of our sighte).'

'The thingis thanne,' quod sche, 'that, whan men doon hem, ne han no necessite that men doon hem, eek the same thingis, first er thei ben don, thei ben to comen withoute necessite. For-why ther ben some thingis to betyden, of whiche the eendes and the bytydynges of hem ben absolut and quit of alle necessite. [1775] For certes I ne trow nat that any man wolde seyn thus: that tho thingis that men don now, that thei ne weren to bytiden first or thei weren I-doon; and thilke same thinges, al-thoughe that men hadden I-wyst hem byforn, yit thei han fre bytydynges. For right as science of thingis present ne bryngith in no necessite to thingis that men doon, right so the prescience of thinges to comen ne bryngith in no necessite to thinges to bytiden. But thou maist seyn that of thilke same it is I-douted, as whethir that of thilke thingis that ne han noon issues and bytidynges necessaries, yif therof mai ben any prescience; for certes thei semen to discorden. For thou wenest, yif that thingis ben I-seyn byfore, that necessite folwith hem; [1780] and yif necessite faileth hem, thei ne myghten nat ben wist byforn, and that nothing may be comprehended by science but certein; and yif tho thinges that ne han no certein bytydingis ben I-purveied as certein, it scholde ben dirknesse of opinioun, nat sothfastnesse of science. And thou wenest that it be dyvers fro the holnesse of science that any man schol deme a thing to ben otherwyse than it is it-self. And the cause of this errour is that of alle the thingis that every wyght hath I-knowe, thei wenen that tho thingis ben I-knowe al only by the strengthe and by the nature of the thinges that ben I-wyst or

1781. *but certein*, but certainty; cp. 1711, 1717.

I-knowe. And it is al the contrarye; for al that evere is I-knowe, it is rather comprehendid and knowen, nat aftir his strengthe and his nature, but aftir the faculte (that is to seyn, the power and the nature) of hem that knowen. [1785] And, for that this schal mowen schewen by a schort ensaumple, the same rowndnesse of a body, otherweys the sighte of the eighe knoweth it, and otherweys the touchynge. The lookynge, by castynge of his bemys, waiteth and seeth fro afer al the body togidre, withoute moevynge of it-self; but the touchynge clyveth and conioyneth to the rounde body, and moeveth aboute the envyrounynge, and comprehendeth by parties the roundnesse. And the man hym-self, ootherweys wit byholdeth hym, and ootherweys ymaginacioun, and otherweyes resoun, and ootherweies intelligence. For the wit comprehendith withoute-forth the figure of the body of the man that is establisschid in the matere subgett; [1790] but the ymaginacioun comprehendith oonly the figure withoute the matere; resoun surmountith ymaginacioun and comprehendith by an universel lokynge the comune spece that is in the singuler peces; but the eighe of the intelligence is heyere, for it surmountith the envyrounynge of the universite, and loketh over that bi pure subtilte of thought thilke same symple forme of man that is perdurablely in the devyne thought. In whiche this oughte gretly to ben considered, that the beyeste strengthe to comprehenden thinges enbraseth and contienith the lowere strengthe; but the lowere strengthe ne ariseth nat in no manere to the heyere strengthe. For wit ne mai no thing comprehende out of matere ne the ymaginacioun loketh nat the universels speces, ne resoun ne

1786. *schal mowen schewen*, may be made clear.
1789. *wit*, 'sensus.'
1790. *ymaginacioun*, 'imaginatio.'
1791. *resoun*, 'ratio.'
1791. *spece*, 'speciem.'
1792. *singuler peces*, 'singularibus.
1792. *eighe of the intelligence*, 'intelligentiæ oculus.'

taketh nat the symple forme so as intelligence takith it; but intelligence, that lookith al aboven, whanne it hath comprehendeth the forme, it knoweth and demyth alle the thinges that ben undir that foorme. [1795] But sche knoweth hem in thilke manere in the whiche it comprehendeth thilke same symple forme that ne may nevere ben knowen to noon of that othere (that is to seyn, to none of the thre forseyde strengthis of the soule). For it knoweth the universite of resoun, and the figure of ymaginacioun, and the sensible material conceyved by wit; ne it ne useth nat nor of resoun ne of ymaginacioun ne of wit withoute-forth; but it byholdeth alle thingis, so as I schal seie, by a strook of thought formely withoute discours or collacioun. Certes resoun, whan it lokith any thing universel, it ne useth nat of ymaginacioun, nor of wit; and algates yit it comprehendith the thingis ymaginable and sensible. For resoun is she that diffynyscheth the universel of here conceyte ryght thus :— Man is a resonable two-foted beest. [1800] And how so that this knowyngeisuniversel, yit is ther no wyght that ne wot wel that a man is a thing ymaginable and sensible; and this same considereth wel resoun; but that nis nat by ymaginacioun nor by wit, but it lookith it by resonable concepcioun. Also ymaginacioun, albeit so that it takith of wit the bygynnynges to seen and to formen the figures, algates althoughe that wit ne were nat present, yit it envyrowneth and comprehendith alle thingis sensible; nat by resoun sensible of demynge, but by resoun ymaginatyf. Seestow nat thanne that alle the thingis in knowynge usen more of hir faculte or of hir power than thei don of the faculte or power of thingis that ben I-knowe? Ne that nis nat wrong; for so as every jugement is the dede or the doyng of hym that demeth, it byhoveth that every wyght performe the werk and his entencioun, nat of foreyne power, but of his propre power. [1805]

' Quondam porticus attulit.'—Metrum 4

The porche (that is to seyn a gate of the toun of Athenis there as philosophris hadden hir congregacioun to desputen)— thilke porche broughte somtyme olde men, ful dirke in hir sentences (that is to seyn philosophris that hyghten Stoycenis), that wenden that ymages and sensibilities (that is to seyn, sensible ymaginaciouns or ellis ymaginaciouns of sensible thingis) weren enprientid in-to soules fro bodyes withoute-forth; (as who seith that thilke Stoycenis wenden that sowle had ben nakid of it-self, as a mirour or a clene parchemyn, `so that alle figures most first comen fro thingis fro withoute in-to soules, and ben emprientid in-to soules); ryght as we ben wont somtyme by a swift poyntel to fycchen lettres emprientid in the smothnesse or in the pleynesse of the table of wex or in parchemyn that ne hath no figure ne note in it. (Glose. But now argueth Boece ayens that opynioun and seith thus:) [1810] But yif the thryvynge soule ne unpliteth no thing (that is to seyn, ne doth no thing) by his propre moevynges, but suffrith and lith subgit to the figures and to the notes of bodies withoute-forth, and yeldith ymages ydel and vein in the manere of a mirour, whennes thryveth thanne or whennes comith thilke knowynge in our soule, that discernith and byholdith alle thinges? And whennes is thilke strengthe that byholdeth the singuler thinges? Or whennes is the strengthe that devydeth thinges I-knowe; and thilke strengthe that gadreth togidre the thingis devyded; and the strengthe that chesith his entrechaunged wey? For somtyme it hevyth up the heued (that is

1798. *formely*, 'formaliter.'
1803. *nat by resoun*, etc., mistranslation of ' non sensibili sed imaginaria ratione (method) Judicandi.'

1805. *the werk and his entencioun*, 'suam operam.'
1813. *his entrechaunged wey*, ' alternumque legens iter.'

to seyn that it hevyth up the entencioun to ryght heye thinges), and som tyme it descendith in-to ryght lowe thinges ; and whan it retorneth in-to hym-self it reproveth and destroyeth the false thingis by the trewe thinges. [1815] Certes this strengthe is cause more efficent, and mochel more myghty to seen and to knowe thinges, than thilke cause that suffrith and receyveth the notes and the figures empressid in manere of matere. Algatis the passion (that is to seyn the suffraunce or the wit) in the quyke body goth byforn, excitynge and moevynge the strengthes of the thought.   Ryght so as whan that cleernesse smyteth the eyen and moeveth hem to seen, or ryght so as voys or soun hurteleth to the eres and commoeveth hem to herkne ; than is the strengthe of the thought I-moevid and excited, and clepith forth to semblable moevyngis the speces that it halt withynne it-self, and addith tho speces to the notes and to the thinges withoute-forth, and medleth the ymagis of thinges withoute-forth to the foormes I-hidd withynne hym-self. [1820]

' Quod si in corporibus sentiendis.'—
Prosa 5

But what yif that in bodyes to ben feled (that is to seyn, in takynge of know-lechynge of bodily thinges), and albeit so that qualites of bodies that ben obiect fro withoute-forth moeven and ental-enten the instrumentes of the wittes, and albeit so that the passioun of the body (that is to seyn, the wit or the suff-raunce) goth to-forn the strengthe of the wirkynge corage, the whiche passioun or suffraunce clepith forth the dede of the thought in hym-self and moeveth and exciteth in this mene-while the formes

that resten within-forth—and yif that in sensible bodies, as I have seid, our corage nis nat y-taught or empriented by passioun to knowe thise thinges, but demeth and knoweth of his owne strengthe the passioun or suffrance subiect to the body, [1825] moche more than the thingis that ben absolut and quit fro alle talentes or affecciouns of bodyes (as god or his aungelis) ne folwen nat in discernynge thinges obiect fro withoute-forth, but thei acomplissen and speden the dede of hir thought.   By this resoun thanne ther comen many maner knowynges to dyverse and differynge substaunces.   For the wit of the body, the whiche wit is naked and despoiled of alle oothre knowynges,— thilke wit cometh to beestis that ne mowen nat moeven hem-self her and ther, as oistres and muscles and oothir swich schelle fyssche of the see, that clyven and ben norisschid to roches.   But the ymaginacioun cometh to remuable bestis, that semen to han talent to fleen or to desiren any thing.   But resoun is al oonly to the lynage of mankynde, ryght as intelligence is oonly the devyne nature. [1830] Of whiche it folweth that thilke knowynge is more worth than thise oothre, syn it knoweth by his propre nature nat oonly his subget (as who seith, it ne knoweth nat al oonly that apertenith properly to his knowinge) but it knoweth the subiect of alle othre knowynges.   But how schal it thanne be, yif that wit and ymaginacioun stryven ayein resonynge, and seyn that, of thilke universel thinges that resoun wenith to seen, that it nis ryght naught ?   For wit and ymaginacioun seyn that that that is sensible or ymaginable, it ne mai nat ben universel.   Thanne is either the jugement of resoun soth ne that ther nis no thing sensible ; or elles, for that resoun woot wel that many thinges ben subiect to wit and to ymaginacioun, thanne is the

1816. *in manere of matere.* Construe with *receyveth.*
1818. *hurteleth,* C₁ A₃ *hurteth,* H Cx. *hurleth.*
1821. *But what yif that,* 'Quod si.'
1821. *and albeit so that,* 'quamuis'; *and* is a strengthening particle, *i.e.* even though ; likewise in *and if,* 1825.

1825. *y-taught or empriented,* 'insignitur'; the rest of the phrase is from the Fr., hence the confusion.
1806. *thinges* is object of *folwen.*
1833. *that that is,* that what is.

432

concepcioun of resoun veyn and fals, whiche that lokith and comprehendith that that is sensible and singuler as universel. [1835] And yif that resoun wolde answere ayein to thise two (that is to seyn, to wit and to ymaginacioun), and seyn, that sothly sche hir-selve (that is to seyn, resoun) lokith and comprehendith, by resoun of universalite, bothe that that is sensible and that that is ymaginable; and that thilke two (that is to seyn, wit and ymaginacioun) ne mowen nat strecchen ne enhaunsen hem-self to knowynge of universalite, for that the knowynge of hem ne mai exceden ne surmounten the bodily figures: certes of the knowynge of thinges, men oughten rather yeven credence to the more stidfast and to the more parfit jugement. In this manere stryvynge thanne we that han strengthe of resonynge and of ymagynynge and of wit (that is to seyn, by resoun and by imagynacioun and by wit)—we scholde rathir preise the cause of resoun (as who seith, than the cause of wit and of ymaginacioun). [1840]

Semblable thing is it, that the resoun of mankynde ne weneth nat that the devyne intelligence byholdeth or knoweth thingis to comen, but ryght as the resoun of mankynde knoweth hem. For thou arguist and seist thus: that if it ne seme nat to men that some thingis han certeyn and necessarie betydynges, thei ne mowen nat ben wist byforn certeinly to betyden, and thanne nis ther no prescience of thilke thinges; and yif we trowe that prescience be in thise thingis, thanne is ther nothing that it ne bytydeth by necessite. But certes yif we myghten han the jugement of the devyne thoght, as we ben parsoners of resoun, ryght so as we han demyd that it byhovith that ymaginacioun and wit ben bynethe resoun, ryght so wolde we demen that it were ryghtfull thing, that mannys resoun oughte to summytten it-self and to ben bynethe the devyne thought. [1845] For whiche yif

1836. The apodosis begins with *certes*, 1838.
1844. *parsoners of*, sharers in.

2 F

that we mowen (as who seith that, if that we mowen, I conseile that) we enhaunse us in-to the heighte of thilke soverein intelligence; for ther schal resoun wel seen that that it ne mai nat byholden in it-self. And certes that is this, in what manere the prescience of god seeth alle thinges certeins and diffinyssched, althoughe thei ne han no certein issues or bytydyngis; ne this nis noon opinioun, but it is rather the simplicite of the sovereien science, that nis nat enclosed nor I-schet withinne none boundes.

<hr/>

'Quam variis figuris.'—Metrum 5

The beestes passen by the erthes be ful diverse figures. For some of hem han hir bodyes straught, and crepyn in the dust, and drawen aftir hem a traas or a furwe I-contynued (that is to sein, as naddres or snakes); [1850] and oothre beestis, by the wandrynge lyghtnesse of hir wynges beten the wyndes, and overswymmen the spaces of the longe eir by moyst fleynge; and oothere bestes gladen hem self to diggen hir traas or hir steppys in the erthe with hir goinges or with hir feet, and to gon either by the grene feeldes, or elles to walken undir the wodes. And al be it so that thou seest that thei alle discorden by diverse foormes, algatis hir faces enclyned hevyeth hir dulle wittes. Only the lynage of man heveth heyest his heie heved, and stondith light with his upryght body, and byholdeth the erthes undir hym. And, but yif thou, erthly man, waxest yvel out of thi wit, this figure amonesteth the, that axest the hevene with thi ryghte visage, and hast areised thi forheved to beren up an hye thi corage, [1855] so that thi thought ne be nat I-hevyed ne put lowe undir fote, syn that thi body is so heyghe areysed.

1849. This metre is very badly translated.
1850. *passen by*, 'passent . . . par,' 'permeant.'
1851. *by the wandrynge*, etc., 'alarum levitas vaga.'
1851. *moyst fleynge*, 'liquido volatu.'
1852. *to walken undir*, etc., 'subire siluas.'

'Quoniam igitur uti paulo ante.'—Prosa 6

Therfore thanne, as I have schewed a litel here byforne that alle thing that is I-wist nis nat knowen by his nature propre, but by the nature of hem that comprehenden it, lat us loke now, in as mochil as it is leveful to us (as who seith, lat us loke now as we mowen) whiche that the estat is of the devyne substaunce; so that we mowe eek knowen what his science is. The comune jugement of alle creatures resonables thanne is this: that god is eterne. Lat us considere thanne what is eternite; for certes schal schewen us togidre the devyne nature and the devyne science. [1860] Eternite thanne is parfit possessioun and al-togidre of lif interminable. And that schewethe more cleerly by the compary-soun or collacioun of temporel thinges. For alle thing that lyveth in tyme, it is present, and procedith fro preterites into futures (that is to seyn, fro tyme passed into tyme comynge), ne ther nis nothing establisshed in tyme that mai enbrasen togidre al the space of his lif. For certis yit ne hath it nat taken the tyme of tomorwe, and it hath lost that of yister-day. And certes in the lif of this dai ye ne lyve no more but right as in this moevable and transitorie moment. [1865] Thanne thilke thing that suffreth temporel condicioun, althoughe that it nevere bygan to be, ne thoughe it nevere ne cese for to be, as Aristotile demed of the world, and althoghe that the lif of it be strecchid with infinite of tyme; yit algatis nis it nat swich thing that men mighten trowen by ryghte that it is eterne. For althoughe that it comprehende and em-brase the space of lif infinit, yit algatis ne enbraseth it nat the space of the lif altogidre; for it ne hath nat the futuris that ne ben nat yit, ne it ne hath no lengere the preterites that ben I-doon or I-passed. But thilke thing thanne that hath and comprehendith togidre al the

plente of the lif interminable, to whom ther ne faileth naught of the future, and to whom ther nis noght of the preteryt escaped nor I-passed, thilke same is I-witnessed and I-proevid by right to ben eterne; [1870] and yit it byhovith by necessite that thilke thing be alwey present to hym-self, and compotent (as who seith, alwey present to hym-selve, and so myghty that al be right at his plesaunce), and that he have al present the infinite of the moevable tyme. Wherfore som men trowen wrongfully that, when thei heren that it semede to Plato that this world ne hadde nevere bygynnynge of tyme, ne that it nevere schal han failynge, thei wenen in this manere that this world be makid coeterne with his makere. (As who seith, thei wene that this world and god ben makid togidre eterne, and that is a wrongful wenynge.) For other thing is it to ben I-lad by lif interminable, as Plato grauntide to the world, and oothir is it to enbrace togidre al the presence of the lif intermynable, the whiche thing it is cleer and manyfest that it is propre to the devyne thought. [1875] Ne it ne scholde nat semen to us that god is eldere than thinges that ben I-maked by quantite of tyme, but rather by the proprete of his simple nature. For this ilke infinit moevynge of temporel thinges folweth this presentarie estat of the lif unmoevable; and, so as it ne mai nat contrefetin it, ne feynen it, ne be evene lik to it, for the immoevablete (that is to sein, that is in the eternite of god), it faileth and fallith into moevynge fro the simplicite of the presence of god, and discresith into the infinit quantite of future and of preterit. And so as it ne mai nat han togidre al the plente of the lif, algates yit for as moche as it ne ceseth nevere for to ben in som manere, it semyth somdel to us that it folwith and resemblieth thilke thing that it ne mai nat atayne to, ne

1860. *nature* and *science* are the subjects of *schewen*.

1877. *folweth*, 'imitatur.'
1878. *discresith* (C₂ A₁ H Cx. A₂ B *disencre-seth*), 'descraist.'

fulfillen; and byndeth it - self to som maner presence of this litle and swift moment, the whiche presence of this litle and swift moment, [1880] for that it bereth a maner ymage or liknesse of the ai duellynge presence of god, it grauntith to swich manere thinges as it betydith to, that it semeth hem that thise thinges han I-ben and ben. And for that the presence of swiche litel moment ne mai nat duelle, therfore it ravysschide and took the infynit wey to tyme (that is to seyn, by successioun). And by this manere is it I-doon, for that it sholde contynue the lif in goinge, of the whiche lif it myght nat enbrace the plente in duellinge. And for-thi yif we wollen putten worthi names to thinges and folwen Plato, lat us seyen thanne sothly that god is "eterne," and that the world is "perpetuel." Thanne, syn that every jugement knoweth and comprehendith by his owne nature thinges that ben subgect unto hym, ther is sothly to god always an eterne and presentarie estat ; [1885] and the science of hym that overpasseth alle temporel moevement duelleth in the simplicite of his presence, and embraceth and considereth alle the infynit spaces of tymes preterites and futures, and lokith in his simple knowynge alle thingis of preterit ryght as thei weren I-doon presently ryght now. Yif thou wolt thanne thinken and avise the prescience by whiche it knoweth alle thinges, thou ne schalt naught demen it as prescience of thinges to comen, but thou schalt demen more ryghtfully that it is science of presence or of instaunce that nevere ne faileth. For whiche it nis nat y-cleped "previdence," but it sholde rathir ben clepid "purveaunce," that is establisshed ful fer fro ryght lowe thinges, and byholdeth fro afer alle thinges, right as it were fro the heye heighte of thinges. [1890]

Why axestow thanne, or whi desputestow thanne, that thilke thingis ben doon by necessite whiche that ben y-seyn and knowen by the devyne sighte, syn

1888. *avise*, consider.

that forsothe men ne maken nat thilke thingis necessarie whiche that thei seen ben I-doon in hir sighte ? For addith thi byholdynge any necessite to thilke thinges that thou byholdest present ?'

'Nay,' quod I.

Philosophie. 'Certes thanne, yif men myghte maken any digne comparysoun or collacioun of the presence devyne and of the presence of mankynde, ryght so as ye seen some thinges in this temporel present, ryght so seeth god alle thinges by his eterne present. [1895]

Wherfore this devyne presence ne chaungeth nat the nature ne the proprete of thinges, but byholdeth swiche thingis present to hymward as thei shollen betyde to yowward in tyme to comen. Ne it ne confowndeth nat the jugementes of thingis ; but by o sight of his thought ne knoweth the thinges to comen, as wol necessarie as nat necessarie. Ryght so as whan ye seen togidre a man walke on the erthe and the sonne arisen in the hevene, albeit so that ye seen and byholden the ton and the tothir togidre, yit natheles ye demen and discerne that the toon is voluntarie and the tother is necessarie. Ryght so thanne the devyne lookynge, byholdynge alle thinges undir hym, ne trowbleth nat the qualite of thinges that ben certeinly present to hymward ; but, as to the condicioun of tyme, forsothe thei ben futur. [1900] For which it folweth that this nis noon opynioun, but rathir a stidfast knowynge I-strengthid by soothnesse that, whan that god knoweth any thing to be, he ne unwot not that thilke thing wanteth necessite to be. (This is to sein that whan that god knoweth any thing to betide, he wot wel that it ne hath no necessite to betyde.) And yif thou seist here that thilke thing that god seeth to

1895. *presence* both times seems to be a mistake for *presente* ; Lat. 'presentis,' Fr. 'present.'
1896. *presence* should be *prescience*, 'prænotio,' 'prescience.' In 1931 H reads *prescience* for *presence*, and similarly H Cx. in 1932 have *prescience* for *presence*.
1900. *trowbleth*, 'perturbat' ; Fr. 'trouble,' L 'destourbe.'
1902. *ne unwot not*, 'non nesciat.'

betide, it ne may nat unbytide (as who seith, it moot bytide), and thilke thing that ne mai nat unbytide, it mot bytiden by necessite, and that thou streyne me to this name of necessite, certes I wol we confessen and byknowen a thing of ful sad trouthe. But unnethe schal ther any wight mowe seen it or come therto, but yif that he be byholdere of the devyne thought. [1905] For I wol answeren the thus: that thilke thing that is futur, whan it is referred to the devyne knowynge than is it necesserie; but certis whan it is undirstonden in his owene kynde, men seen it outrely fre and absolut fro alle necessite.

For certes ther ben two maneris of necessites: that oon necessite is symple, as thus; that it byhovith by necessite that alle men ben mortal or dedly; anothir necessite is condicionel, as thus: yif thou wost that a man walketh, it byhovith by necessite that he walke. Thilke thing thanne that any wight hath I-knowe to be, it ne mai ben noon oothir weys thanne he knowith it to be. [1910] But this condicion draweth nat with hir thilke necessite simple; for certes this necessite condicionel—the propre nature of it ne makith it nat, but the adieccioun of the condicioun makith it. For no necessite ne constreyneth a man to gon that goth by his propre wil, al be it so that whan he goth that it is necessarie that he goth. Ryght on this same manere thanne, yif that the purveaunce of god seeth any thyng present, than moot thilke thing ben by necessite, althoghe that it ne have no necessite of his owne nature. But certes the futures that bytiden by fredom of arbitrie, god seth hem alle togidre presentes. Thise thinges thanne, yf thei ben referrid to the devyne sighte, than ben they maked necessarie by the condicioun of the devyne knowynge. [1915] But certes yif thilke thingis ben considered by hem-self, thei ben absolut of necessite,

and ne forleten nat ne cesen nat of the liberte of hir owne nature. Thanne certes withoute doute alle the thinges shollen ben doon whiche that god woot byforn that thei ben to comen. But some of hem comen and bytiden of fre arbitrie or fre wil, that, al be it so that thei bytiden, yit algates ne lese thei nat hir propre nature in beinge; by the whiche first, or that thei weren I-don, thei hadden power noght to han bytyd.'

'What is this to seyn thanne,' quod I, 'that thinges ne ben nat necesserie by hir propre nature, so as thei comen in alle maneris in the liknesse of necessite by the condicioun of the devyne science?'

'This is the difference,' quod sche, 'that tho thinges that I purposide the a litel her byforn (that is to seyn, the sonne arysynge and the man walkynge), that ther whiles that thilke thinges ben I-doon, they ne myghte nat ben undoon; [1920] natheles that oon of hem, or it was I-doon, it byhovide by necessite that it was I-doon, but nat that oothir. Ryght so is it here, that the thinges that god hath present withoute doute thei shollen ben. But some of hem descendith of the nature of thinges (as the sonne arysynge); and some descendith of the power of the doeris (as the man walkynge). Thanne seide I no wrong that, yif that thise thinges ben referred to the devyne knowynge, thanne ben thei necessarie; and yif thei ben considered by hem-self, than ben thei absolut fro the boond of necessite. Right so as alle thingis that apiereth or scheweth to the wittes, yif thou referre it to resoun, it is universel; and yif thou loke it or referre it to itself, than is it singuler. But now yif thou seist thus: that, "If it be in my power to chaunge my purpos, than schal I voiden the purveaunce of god, whan peraventure I schal han chaungid the thingis that he knoweth byforn," [1925] thanne schal I answeren the thus: "Certes thou maist wel chaungen

1914. *presentes* (C₂ A₂ H B *present*); Lat. 'presentes,' Fr. 'presens.' Chaucer probably carried over the French adjective.

1919. C₁ B H Cx. omit *the* before *condicioun*.
1924. *alle thingis*, 'tout'; perhaps therefore the 'it's ('le') that follow.

thi purpos; but for as mochel as the present sothnesse of the devyne purveaunce byholdeth that thou maist chaunge thi purpos, and whethir thou wolt chaunge it or no, and whiderward that thou torne it, thou ne maist nat eschuen the devyne prescience, ryght as thou ne maist nat fleen the sighte of the present eye, althoghe that thou torne thiself by thi fre wil into diverse accions." But thou maist sein ayein: "How schal it thanne be— schal nat the devyne science ben chaunged by my disposicioun whan that I wol o thing now and now anothir; and thilke prescience—ne semeth it nat to entrechaunge stoundis of knowynge?"' (As who seith, ne schal it nat seme to us that the devyne prescience entrechaungith hise diverse stoundes of knowynge, so that it knowe som-tyme o thyng, and somtyme the contrarie?) [1930]

'No,' quod I.

'No forsothe,' quod sche, 'for the devyne sighte renneth to-forn, and seeth alle futures, and clepith hem ayen, and retorneth hem to the presence of his propre knowynge; ne he ne entrechaungith nat, so as thou wenest, the stoundes of foreknowynge, as now this, now that; but he ay duellynge cometh byforn, and enbraseth at o strook alle thi mutaciouns. And this presence to comprehenden and to seen alle thingis—god ne hath nat taken it of the bytidynge of thinges to come, but of his propre symplicite. And herby is assoiled thilke thing that thou puttest a litel here byforn, that is to seyn,

that it is unworthy thing to seyn that our futures yeven cause of the science of god. For certis this strengthe of the devyne science, whiche that embraseth alle thinges by his presentarie knowynge, establissheth manere to alle thinges, and it ne oweth nawht to lattere thinges. [1935] And syn that thise thinges ben thus (that is to seyn, syn that necessite nis nat in thinges by the devyne prescience), thanne is ther fredom of arbitre, that duelleth hool and unwemmed to mortal men; ne the lawes ne purposen nat wikkidly medes and peynes to the willynges of men, that ben unbownden and quyt of all necessite; and god, byholdere and forwytere of alle thingis, duelleth above, and the present eternite of his sighte renneth alwey with the diverse qualite of our dedes, dispensynge and ordeynynge medes to gode men and tormentes to wikkide men. Ne in ydel ne in veyn ne ben ther put in god hope and preyeris, that ne mowen nat ben unspedful ne withouten effect whan they been ryghtful.

'Withstond thanne and eschue thou vices; worschipe and love thou vertues; areise thi corage to ryghtful hopes; yilde thou humble preieres an heyghe. [1940] Gret necessite of prowesse and vertu is encharged and comaunded to yow, yif ye nil nat dissimulen; syn that ye worken and don (that is to seyn, your dedes or your werkes) byforn the eyen of the juge that seeth and demeth alle thinges.'

EXPLICIT LIBER BOECII.

1930. *stoundes*, 'vices.'
1933. *presence to comprehenden*, etc., 'presence de . . . comprehendre,' *i.e.* power to comprehend things in present time.

1935. *manere*, 'modum,' 'propre maniere'; rather *bownd*.
1935. *lattere thinges*, 'posterioribus.'

TROILUS AND CRISEYDE

BOOK I

THE doublé sorwe of Troilus to tellen,
That was the king Priámus' sone of
  Troye,
In loving how his áventurés fellen
Fro wo to wele, and after out of joye,
My purpos is, or that I parté fro ye.—
Thesiphoné, thou help me for t' endite
Thise woful vers, that wepen as I write !

To thee clepe I, thou Goddesse of
  tormént,   8
Thou cruel Furie, sorwing evere in peyne !
Help me that am the sorwful instrument
That helpeth lovers, as I can, to pleyne !
For wel sit it, the sothé for to seyne,
A woful wight to han a drery fere,
And to a sorwful tale, a sory chere !

For I, that God of Lovés servants serve,
Ne dar to Love for myn unliklinesse
Preyen for sped, al sholde I therfor sterve,
So fer am I from his help in derknésse :
But nathéles, if this may don gladnésse
Unt' any lover and his cause availe,   20
Have he my thank, and myn be this
  travaile !

But ye lovéres, that bathen in gladnésse,
If any drope of pité in you be,
Remembreth you on passéd hevinesse
That ye han felt, and on th' adversité
Of other folk ; and thenketh how that ye
Han felt that Lové dorsté you displese,
Or ye han wonne him with too gret an
  ese.

And preyéth for hem that ben in the cas
Of Troilus, as ye may after here,   30
That Love hem bringe in hevené to solás ;

And ek for me preyéth to God so dere
That I have might to shewe in som manére
Swich peyne and wo as Lovès folk endure,
In Troilus' unsely áventure.

And biddeth ek for hem that ben de-
  speyred
In love, that neveré n'il recoveréd be,
And ek for hem that falsly ben apeyred
Thorugh wikked tongés, be it he or she :
Thus biddeth God for his benignété   40
So graunte hem soone out of this world
  to pace,
That ben despeyréd out of Lovès grace.

And biddeth ek for hem that ben at ese
That God hem graunte ay good per-
  sévéraunce,
And sende hem might hir ladies so to plese
That it to Love be worship and plesaunce.
For so hope I my soulé best t'avaunce,
To preye for hem that Lovès servants be,
And write hir wo, and live in charité,

And for to have of hem compassioun   50
As though I were hir owné brother dere.—
Now herkneth with a good entencioun,
For now wol I gon streight to my matére,
In which ye may the doublé sorwes here
Of Troilus in loving of Criseyde,
And how that she forsook him or she
  deyde.

—It is wel wist how that the Grekés
  stronge
In armés with a thousand shippés wente
To Troyéwardés, and the cité longe

For relations of MSS. and letters by which
they are quoted, see Introduction.
  6. *Thesiphoné*, Tisiphone.
  21. *he*, i.e. Love.

  44. *a In love, that God hem graunte pér-
severaunce.*
  45. *ladies*, a and others *loves*.
  47. *f avaunce*, J Cp. Cl. *avaunce*.
  52. *herkneth*. Shows that *Troilus* was written
for recitation. See I. 450 ; ii. 30, 1751 ; iii. 499,
1332. But see later, v. 270.

Assegéden wel ten yer or they stente,   60
And in diversé wise and oon entente
The ravisshing to wreken of Eleyne
By Paris don, they wroughten al hir peyne.

Now fil it so, that in the town ther was
Dwelling a lord of gret auctorité,
A gret devyn that clepéd was Calcas,
That in sciénce so expert was, that he
Knew wel that Troyé sholde destroyéd be
By answer of his God, that highté thus,
Daun Phebus, or Appollo Delphicus.   70

So when that Calcas knew by calculinge,
And ek by answer of this Appollo,
That Grekés sholden swich a peplé bringe
Thorugh which that Troyé mosté be for-do,
He caste anon out of the town to go ;
For wel wiste he by sort that Troyé sholde
Destroyéd ben, ye, woldé who-so n'olde.

For-which for to departen softély
Took purpos ful this fór-knowingé wise,
And to the Grekés oost ful privily   80
He stal anon ; and they in curteys wise
Him deden bothé worship and servíse,
In trust that he hath konning hem to rede
In every peril which that is to drede.

The noise up ros, whan it was first aspyed
Thorugh al the town, and generaly was
    spoken,
That Calcas traytour fled was and allyed
With hem of Grece ; and casten to ben
    wroken
On him that falsly hadde his feyth so
    broken,
And seyden he and al his kyn at onés   90
Ben worthy for to brennen fel and bonés.

Now haddé Calcas left in this mischaunce,
Al unwist of this false and wikked dede,
His doughter, which that was in gret
    penaunce ;

For of her lif she was ful sore in drede
As she that n'isté what was best to rede ;
For bothe a widwé was she, and alone
Of any frend, to whom she dorste her
    mone.

Criseydé was this lady name al right :
As to my dom in al Troyés cité   100
N'as non so fair ; for, passing every
    wight,
So angelik was hir natíf beauté,
That lik a thing inmortal seméd she,
As is an hevenissh parfit créatúre
That down were sent in scorning of natúre.

This lady, which that herde al-day at ere
Her fadres shame, his falsnesse and tresoún,
Wel nigh out of her wit for sorwe and fere,
In widwes habit large of samyt broun,
On knees she fil biforn Ectór a-doun   110
With pitous vois, and tendrely wepínge
His mercy bad, her-selven éxcusinge.

Now was this Ector pitous of natúre,
And saw that she was sorwfully bigon,
And that she was so fair a créatúre ;
Of his goodnésse he gladéd her anon,
And seydé, ' Lat your fadres treson gon
Forth with mischaunce ! And ye yourself
    in joye
Dwelleth with us whil you good list in
    Troye !

' And al th' honóur that men may don you
    have,   120
As ferforth as your fader dwelléd here,
Ye shul han, and your body shal men save
As fer as I may aught enquere and here.'
And she him thankéd with ful humblé
    chere,

60. *wel*, H₄ γ *nigh*.
71. *that*, ay *this*.
83. *a Hopyng in hym (good ?) kunnyng hem to rede*. Boc. Da lui sperando sommo e buon consiglio.
85. *The noise up ros*, α *Gret rumour gan (was)*. Boc. Fu rumor grande.
87. γ insert *fals* after *traytour*.
93. *Al unwist*, α *Unknowing*.

101. *passing*, α *over* (H₄ omits).
104. *is*, ay *doth*.
106. *herde al-day*, γ and others *al-day herde*.
109. *large*, J G H₈ H₃ *blak*.
111. *a With chere and voys ful pytous, and wepynge*. Boc. E lagrimosa . . . e con voce e con vista assai pietosa.
118. *Forth with mischaunce*, α *To sory hap*.
123. *and*, γ and others *or*.
124. *a thanked ofte in humble chere*. Boc.
    Ella di questo il ringrazio assai
    E più volea.

And ofter wolde and it had ben his wille,
And took her leve, and hom, and held
    her stille.

And in her hous sh' abood with swich
    meyné
As til her honour nedè was to holde,
And whil she was dwellinge in that cité
Kepte her estat, and bothe of yonge and
    olde   130
Ful wel beloved, and wel men of her
    tolde.
But whether that she children hadde or non,
I rede it nat ; therfor I lete it gon.

The thingès fellen as they don of werre
Bytwixen hem of Troye and Grekès ofte ;
For som day boughten they of Troye it
    derre,
And eft the Grekès founden nothing softe
The folk of Troye. And thus Fortúne
    on-lofte,
And under eft, gan hem to wheelen bothe
After her cours, ay whil they weren
    wrothe.   140

But how this town com to destruccioun
Ne falleth naught to purpos me to telle,
For it were here a long digressioun
Fro my matére, and for you long to dwelle.
But the Trojánès gestès, as they felle,
In Omer, or in Dares, or in Dite,
Who-so that can may rede hem as they
    write.

But though that Grekès hem of Troyè
    shetten,
And hir cité bysegèd al aboute,
Hir olde uságè n'oldè they nat letten 150
As for t' honoure hir Goddès ful devoute ;

But aldermost in honour, out of doute,
They hadde a relik, heet Palladion,
That was hir trust aboven everychon.

And so bifil whan comen was the time
Of Apéril, when clothèd is the mede
With newè grene, of lusty Ver the prime,
And swotè smelling flourès white and rede,
In sondry wises shewèd, as I rede,
The folk of Troye hir observaunces olde,
Palladionès festè for to holde.   161

And to the temple in al hir bestè wise
In general ther wentè mony a wight
To herknen of Palladion servíse ;
And namèly so mony a lusty knight,
So mony a lady fressh and mayden bright,
Ful wel arayèd bothè meste and leste,
Ye, bothé for the seson and the feste.

Among thise othrè folk was Criseydà
In widwes habit blak ; but nathéles,   170
Right as our firstè lettre is now an A,
In beauté first so stood she makèlés :
Her goodly loking gladèd al the prees :
N'as neverè seyn thing to ben praysèd derre,
Nor under cloudè blak so bright a sterre,

As was Criseyde, as folk seyde everychone
That her behelden in her blakè wede.
And yit she stood ful lowe and stille alone
Behinden othrè folk in litel brede   179
And nigh the dore, ay under shamès drede,
Simple of atir and debonaire of chere,
With ful assurèd loking and manére.

This Troilus, as he was wont to gide
His yongè knightès, ladde hem up and doun
In th'ilkè largè temple on every side,
Biholding ay the ladies of the toun,
Now here, now there ; for no devocioun

132. This may be due to Chaucer's mis-reading
Boccaccio, who says 'she had no need to care
for son or daughter.'
140. J and others *ay whil that they were wrothe.*
143. *For it were here,* so β ; *a For-why it were ;*
γ *For it were.*
144. *for you long to dwelle,* so H₂ (see *H.F.*
i. 252); rest var.
145. *Trojánes,* so P H₂ R ; Cl. *Troiane ;* rest
Troian.
146. *Dares* and *Dite,* Dares and Dictys, supposed writers on the Trojan war.
151. *a goddes and to loute.*

153. *Palladion,* the Palladium or sacred image
of Pallas.
156. *Aperil,* a *Apparaille* (possibly intended
as a pun. See iii. 353).
158. *smelling,* so a Cx. D ; J and others *smellen.*
Boc. Riveste i prati d' erbette e di fiori.
167. Jo. *the* before *meste* and *leste ; a Ful wel
biseyn the meste, mene and leste ;* γ *Ful wel
arayed bothe moste, meyne and leste.*
174. *nevere seyn,* so a Cx. Ad. H₂ ; J and
others *nevere yet seyn.*
183. *This,* a *Daun.*

Hadde he to non, to reven him his reste,
But gan to preyse and lakken whom him
    leste.

And in his walk ful faste he gan to wayten
If knight or squiér of his companýe   191
Gan for to sike or lete his ýen bayten
On any woman that he coude espýe :
He woldé smile and holden it folýe,
And seye him thus, ' God wot, she slepeth
    softe
For love of thee, whan thou tornest ful ofte!

' I have herd told, pardieux, of your livínge,
Ye lovers, and your lewéd óbservauncés,
And which a labour folk han in winnínge
Of love, and in the keping which dout-
    aunces ;   200
And whan your preye is lost, wo and pen-
    aunces !
O verray foolés, nyce and blynd ben ye !
Ther n'is nat oon can war by other be !'

And with that word he gan caste up the
    browe
Ascaunces, 'Lo ! is this nat wisly spoken?'
At which the God of Love gan loken rowe
Right for despit, and shop for to ben wroken:
He kidde anon his bowé n'as nat broken !
For sodeinly he hitte him at the fulle ;
And yit as proud a pecok can he pulle !

O blindé world ! O blinde entencioun ! 211
How often falleth al th' effect contraire
Of surquidrye and foul presumpcioun ;
For caught is proud, and caught is de-
    bonaire !
This Troilus is clomben on the staire,
And litel weneth that he mot descenden !
But alday faileth thing that foolés wenden !

As proudé Bayard ginneth for to skippe
Out of the wey, so priketh him his corn,

Til he a lasshe have of the longé whippe,
Than thenketh he, ' Though I praunce al
    beforn   221
First in the trais, ful fat and newé shorn,
Yit am I but an hors, and horses lawe
I mot endure and with my ferés drawe.'

So ferde it by this fierse and proudé knight :
Though he a worthy kingés soné were,
And wendé no thing haddé had swich might
Ayein his wil, that sholde his herté stere,
Yit with a look his herté wex a-fere,   229
That he that now was most in pride above
Wex sodeinly most subget unto Love.

For-thy ensaumplé taketh of this man,
Ye wisé, proude, and worthy folkés alle,
To scornen Love, which that so sooné can
The fredom of your hertés to him thralle !
For evere it was, and evere it shal bifalle,
That Love is he that allé thing may binde ;
For may no man for-do the lawe of kinde.

That this be soth, hath provéd, and doth yit.
For this, trowe I, ye knowen, alle or some:
Men reden nat that folk han gretter wit   241
Than they that han ben most with love
    y-nome ;
And strengest folk ben therwith overcome,
The worthieste and grettest of degree :
This was, and is, and yit men shal it see.

And trewéliche it sit wel to be so ;
For alderwisest han therwith ben plesed,
And they that have ben aldermost in wo,
With love have ben confórted most and
    eséd ;
And ofte it hath the cruel herte apeséd,   250
And worthy folk maad worthier of name,
And causeth most to dreden vice and shame.

Now, sith it may nat goodly be withstonde,
And is a thing so vertuous in kinde,
Refuseth nat to Love for to be bonde,
Sin, as him-selven list, he may you binde,
The yerde is bet that bowen wol and winde,

195. *softe*, J Cx. G S *ful softe*.
198. *lewed*, γ om.
202, 203. α reads :
    O verrey folys ! may ye no thing see ?
    Kan non of yow y-war by other be?
208, 209. α reads :
    Yes, certein, Loves bowe was not y-broken !
    For, by myn heed, he . . .
215 *This*, α *Dawn*.

224. *with*, α *as*.
227. *swich*, R G H₃ S *swich* α.
229, 231. *wex*, so H₄ G D ; others *wax*.
237. *alle*, J and others *al*.
257. α *Betir is the wand*.

Than that that brest ; and therfor I you rede
To folwen Love, that you so wel can lede.

But for to tellen forth in special   260
As of this kingés sone of which I tolde,
And leten other thing collateral,
Of him thinke I my talé forth to holde,
Bothe of his joye and of his carès colde ;
And al his werk as touching this matére,
For I it gan, I wil ther-to refere.

Within the temple he wente him forth, pleyinge,
This Troilus, of every wight aboute ;
On this lady, and now on that lokínge,
Whe'r-so she were of towne or of withoute ;
And upon cas bifil that thorugh a route 271
His ýe percéd, and so depe it wente,
Til on Criseyde it smot, and ther it stente.

And sodeinly he wex ther-with astonéd,
And gan her bet beholde in thrifty wise.
'O mercy, God !' thoughte he, 'wher hastow wonéd,
That art so fair and goodly to devise ?'
Ther-with his herté gan to sprede and rise ;
And softe he sikéd lest men mighte him here,   279
And caughte ayein his firsté pleying cherc.

She n'as nat with the leste of her statúre ;
But alle her limès so wel answeringe
Werén to wommanhode, that créatúre
N'as neveré lassé mannissh in seminge ;
And ek the puré wise of her movinge
Shewédé wel that men mighte in her gesse
Honour, estat, and wommanly noblesse.

To Troilus right wonder wel with-alle
Gan for to like her moving and her chere,
Which somdel deignous was ; for she let falle   290
Her look a lite aside in swich manére

Ascaunces, 'What ! may I nat stonden here ?'
And after that her loking gan she lighte,
That neveré thoughte him sen so good a sighte.

And of her look, in him ther gan to quiken
So gret desir, and swich affeccioun,
That in his hertés botmé gan to stiken
Of her his fixe and depe inpressioun ;
And, though he erst had pouréd up and doun,   299
He was tho glad his hornés in to shrinke :
Unnethès wiste he how to loke or winke !

Lo ! he, that leet him-selven so conninge,
And scornéd hem that Lovés peynés dryèn,
Was ful unwar that Love had his dwellinge
Within the subtil stremés of her ýen,
That sodeynly him thoughte he felté dyen,
Right with her look, the spirit of his herte.—
Blesséd be Love, that can thus folk converte !

She, this in blak, liking to Troilus   309
Over allé thing, he stood for to beholde ;
Ne his desir, ne wher-for he stood thus,
He neither cheré madé, ne word tolde ;
But, from a-fer his maner for to holde,
On other thing som time his look he caste,
And eft on her, whil that servisé laste.

And after this, nat fullich al a-whaped,
Out of the temple al esiliche he wente,
Repenting him that he had evere y-japed
Of Lovés folk, lest fully the descente
Of scorn fille on him-self ; but what he mente,   320
Lest it were wist on any maner side,
His wo he gan dissimulen and hide.

Whan he was fro the templé thus departed,
He streight anon unto the paleys torneth,
Right with her look thorugh-shoten and thorugh-darted,
Al feyneth he in lust that he sojorneth ;
And al his chere and speche also he borneth,

259. β *Love* ; γ *him* ; α *Now folweth him.*
261. G γ omit *As.*
263. *forth,* Cl. H₁ *for* ; S *forth for* ; G omits.
264. *joye,* J G Cl. *joyes.*
279. *he,* so α G ; β γ omit.
286. α *She shewed.*
288. *To,* so J H₃ γ ; rest *Tho.*

307. *of,* γ *in.*
324. α β *the* (Boc.) ; Cx. γ *his.*

And ay of Lovès servants every while
Himself to wrye, at hem he gan to smile,

And seydè, 'Lord ! so ye live al in lest, 330
Ye lovers !   For the conningeste of yow
That serveth most ententifliche and best,
Him tit as often harm ther-of as prow :
Your hire is quit ayein, ye, God wot how !
Naught wel for wel, but scorn for good
    servíse !
In feith your ordre is rulèd in good wise !

'In noun-certeyn ben alle your óbservaunces
But it a fewè sely pointès be ;   338
Ne no thing asketh so grete áttendaunces
As doth your lay, and that knowe allè ye.
But that is nat the worste, as mote I thè !
But, tolde I you the worstè point, I leve,
Al seyde I soth, ye wolden at me greve.

' But tak this : that ye lovers ofte eschue
Or ellès don of good entencíoun,
Ful ofte thy lady wol it mis-construe,
And deme it harm by her opiníoun ;
And yit if she for other enchesoun
Be wroth, than shaltow han a groin anon !
Lord, wel is him that may ben of you oon!'

But for al this, whan that he saw his time, 351
He held his pees ; non other boote him
    gainede ;
For Love began his fetherès so to lime,
That wel unnethe until his folk he fainede
That othrè bisy nedès him destrainede ;
For wo was him, that what to don he n'iste,
But bad his folk to gon wher that hem liste.

And whan that he in chaumbrè was allone,
He down upon his beddès feet him sette ;
And first he gan to sike, and eft to grone, 360
And thoughte ay so on her withouten lette,
That, as he sat and wook, his spirit mette
That he her saw in temple, and al the wise
Right of her look ; and gan it newe avise.

Thus gan he make a mirrour of his minde,
In which he saw al hoolly her figúre,

And that he wel coude in his hertè finde !
It was to him a right good áventure
To love swich oon ; and if he dede his cure
To serven her, yit mighte he falle in grace,
Or ellès for oon of her servants pace.   371

Imaginínge that travàile nor grame
Ne mightè for so goodly oon be lorn
As she, ne him for his desir no shame,
Al were it wist, but in pris and up-born
Of allè lovers wel more than biforn,—
Thus argumented he in his ginnínge,
Ful unavisèd of his wo comínge.

Thus took he purpos Lovès craft to suwe,
And thoughte he woldè werken privèly 380
First for to hiden his desir in muwe
From every wight y-born al outrèly,
But he mighte aught recoverèd ben ther-by ;
Remembring him, that love too wide y-
    blowe
Yelt bittrè fruit, though swetè seed be sowe.

And over al this, ful muchel more he
    thoughte,
What for to speke, and what to holden
    inne ;
And what to arten her to love he soughte,
And on a song anon right to beginne, 389
And gan loude on his sorwè for to winne ;
For with good hope he gan fullíche assente
Criseydè for to love, and naught repente.

And of his song, not only the senténce
As writ myn auctour callèd Lollius,
But pleynly, save our tongès difference,
I dar wel seyn, in al that Troilus
Seyde in his song, lo, every word right thus
As I shal seyn ! And, who-so list it here,
Lo, next this vers he may it finden here.

381. *for to*, so S H₃ Ad. ; others *to*.
386. *ful muchel*, so H₄ R ; γ *yet muche(l)*;
J and others *muchel*.
393. In Boccaccio Troilus merely gives way to
singing in light-heartedness. Chaucer makes
Troilus compose a song (ll. 400-420) which is a
translation of Petrarch's 88th Sonnet.
393. *a And of this song, not only his sentence.*
394. *Lollius*, i.e. Boccaccio (see v. 1653). Why
Chaucer always refers to Boccaccio as Lollius, is
still a mystery.
399. *he*, J *ye*.

338. β *fewè sely* ; others *sely fewe*.
345. *Or elles don*, α *For good, or don*.
347. *by*, so β ; others *in*.
363. *in*, so α ; Cx. om. *in* ; R *at* ; Cl. *a* ; others
and.

' If no love is, O God, what fele I so?   400
And if love is, what thing and which
     is he ?
If love be good, from whennès com'th
     my wo ?
If it be wikke, a wonder thinketh me
Whenne every torment and adversité
That com'th of him may to me savory
     thinke ;
For ay thurste I the more that ich it drinke.

' And if that at myn ownè lust I brenne,
From whennès com'th my wailing and my
     pleynte ?
If harm agree me, wher-to pleyne I thenne?
I n'ot, ne why unwery that I feynte.   410
O quikè deth ! O swetè harm so queynte !
How may of thee in me swich quantité,
But if that I consentè that it be ?

' And if that I consente, I wrongfully
Compleyne, y-wis.—Thus possèd to and
     fro,
Al sterèles with-in a boot am I
A-midde the see betwixen windès two
That in contrárie stonden everè mo.
Allas ! What is this wonder maladye?   419
For hete of cold, for cold of hete, I dye !'

And to the God of Love thus seydè he
With pitous vois, ' O Lord, now yourès is
My spirit which that oughtè yourès be !
You thanke I, Lord, that han me brought
     to this !
But whether goddesse or wommán, y-wis,
She be, I n'ot, which that ye do me serve ;
But as her man I wol ay live and sterve.

' Ye stonden in her ỳen mightily,
As in a place unto your vertu digne,
Wherfórè, Lord, if my servíse or I   430
May liken you, so beth to me benigne ;
For myn estat roiál here I resigne
Into her hand, and with ful humblè chere
Bicome her man, as to my lady dere.'

In him ne deynèd sparen blood roiál
The fir of lovè,—wher-fro God me blesse !

406. *ich it drinke*, so J Cx. γ ; *a* R G I *drinke.*
430. *Lord,* S *O lord ;* Cl. S₂ *my lord.*
436. *wher-fro,* J S Cl. *the wherfro ;* H₅ H₁ *ye wherfro.*

Ne him forbar in no degree for al
His vertu or his excellent prowesse,
But held him as his thral lowe in destresse,
And brende him so in sondry wise ay newe,
That sexty time a day he lost his hewe.   441

So mochel day fro day his ownè thought,
For lust, to her gan quiken and encresse,
That everich other charge he sette at
     nought ;
For-thy ful ofte, his hotè fir to cesse,
To seen her goodly look he gan to presse ;
For ther-by to ben esèd wel he wende.
And ay the neer he was, the more he
     brende ;

For ay the neer, the fir the hotter is :   449
This, trowe I, knoweth al this companỳe.
But were he fer or ner, I dar seye this,—
By night or day for wisdom or folỳe
His hertè, which that is his brestès ỳe,
Was ay on her, that fairer was to sene
Than everè was Eleyne or Polyxene.

Ek of the day ther passèd nought an houre
That to him-self a thousand time he seyde,
' Good goodly, whom to serven I labóure
As I best can, now woldè God, Criseyde,
Ye wolden on me rewe, or that I deydè !   460
My derè herte, allas, myn hele and hewe
And lif is lost, but ye wol on me rewe !

Alle othrè dredès weren from him fledde
Both of th' assege and his savacioun,
N' in his desir none othrè sounès bredde
But arguments to his conclusioun,
That she on him wolde han compassioun,
And he to ben her man, whil he may
     dure :
Lo, here his lif, and from the deth his
     cure !

442. α β *day fro day* (Boc. di giorno in giorno) ;
γ *day by day.*
457. *That.* We should expect *But.*
458. *whom* (?), all *to whom ; to* (after *whom*),
so D.
458. *laboure,* G A Cl. *and laboure.*
465. *his,* so α β H₁ ; G γ *him.*
465. *sounes,* so H₄ R and others ; J and others
sownes.
466. *his,* D H₁ CL *this.*
469. *his,* J and others *is.*

ıe sharpė shourės felle of armės preve 470
ıat Ector or his othrė brethren diden,
ı made him only ther-for onės meve ;
ıd yit was he, wher-so men wente or riden,
ıunde oon the beste and lengest time
       abiden
ıer peril was, and dide ek swich travaile
  armės, that to thenke it was mervaile.

ıt for non hate he to the Grekės hadde,
ı also for the rescous of the toun,
ı made him thus in armės for to madde,
ıt only, lo, for this conclusioun,   480
ı liken her the bet for his renoun :
ıo day to day in armės so he spedde
ıat alle the Grekės as the deth him dredde.

ıd fro this forth tho refte him Love his
       sleep,
ıd made his mete his foo ; and ek his sorwe
ın multiplýė, that, who-so took keep,
ı shewėd in his hewe on eve and morwe.
ıerfore a title he gan him for to borwe
ıf other siknesse, lest men of him wende
ıat th' hotė fir of love so sore him
       brende ;   490

ıd seyde he hadde a fevere, and ferde amis.
ıt how it was, certeyn, I can not seye,—
ı that his lady understood not this,
ır feynėd her she n'iste,—oon of the
       tweye !
ıt wel rede I, that by no maner weye
ıe semėd it as that she of him roughte,
ır of his peyne, or what-so-evere he
       thoughte.

ıt thennė feltė Troilus swich wo
ıhat he was wel nigh wood ; for ay his drede
ı'as this, that she som wight had lovėd so
ıat nevere of him she wolde han taken
       hede.   501

For that, him thoughte he feltė his hertė
       blede ;
Ne of his wo ne durste he not biginne
To tellen her, for al this world to winne.

But, whan he hadde a spacė from his care,
Thus to him-self ful ofte he gan to pleyne :
He seyde, ' O fool, now artow in the snare,
That whilom japedest at Lovės peyne !
Now artow hent ! Now gnaw thyn ownė
       cheyne !
Thou were ay wont ech lover to reprende 510
Of thing, fro which thou canst thee not
       defende.

' What wol now every lover seyn of thee,
If this be wist, but evere in thyn absence
Laughen in scorn and seyn, " Lo, ther
       go'th he
That is the man of so gret sapience
That held us lovers leest in reverence !
Now, thankėd God, he may go in the
       daunce
Of hem that Love list feblėly t'avaunce !"

' But, O thou woful Troilus, God wolde,
Sith thou most loven thorugh thy destinė,
That thou biset were on swich oon that
       sholde   521
Knowe al thy wo, al lakkėd her pitė !
But al-so cold in love towárdės thee
Thy lady is, as frost in winter moone ;
And thou for-don, as snow in fir is soone.

' God wolde, I were arivėd in the port
Of deth, to which my sorwė wol me lede !
A, Lord, to me it were a gret confort !
Than were I quit of languisshinge in
       drede !
For, be myn hiddė sorwe y-blowe on
       brede,   530
I shal bejapėd ben a thousand time
More than that fool of whos folý men rime.

471. *or*, R Cl. *and* (Boc.)
483. a β *alle the* (H₄ *alle*); G J γ *the.*
487. a β *on eve ;* γ *bothe eve.*
490. S₁ D *so sore him brende ;* Ad. *him for*
rnde ; rest *him brende.*
496. a β *as that* (P H₂ *as*); G γ *that.*
498. *thenne* (?), all *than*(*ne*) ; Ad. *han.* Boc.
quinci sentia Troilo *tal dolore.* All except H₂
ı insert *this* before *Troilus.*

502. a β *For that ;* J G *For that cause ;* γ
For which.
510. β *to reprehende* (*reprende*) ; rest omit *to.*
515. *so,* J D *the.*
518. *feblely t'avaunce ;* J and others *febly for*
t'avaunce.
530. *be* (Boc.) ; *by,* Cx. G S₁ Cl. Cp.
532. *that,* Cx. R *a.*

'But now, help, God! and ye, swetè
    for whom
I pleyne y-caught, ye, neverè wight so
    faste,
O mercy, derè herte, and help me from
The deth! For I, whil that my lif may
    laste,
More than my lif wol love you to my laste.
And with som frendly look gladdeth me,
    swete,
Though neverè no thing more ye me
    bihete!'—

Thise wordès, and ful many another mo
He spak, and callèd evere in his com-
    pleynte   541
Her namè, for to tellen her his wo,
Til nigh that he in saltè terès dreynte.
Al was for naught: she herdè not his
    pleynte;
And whan that he bethoughte on that
    folýe,
A thousand fold his wo gan multiplýe.

Bi-wailing in his chambrè thus allone,
A frend of his, that callèd was Pandáre,
Com onès in unwar, and herde him grone,
And saw his frend in swich distresse and
    care: 550
'Allas!' quod he, 'who causeth al this
    fare?
O mercy, God! what unhap may this mene?
Han now thus sonè Grekès maad you lene?

'Or hastow som remors of conscience,
And art now falle in som devocioun,
And wailest for thy sinne and thyn offence,
And hast for ferdè caught attricioun?
God save hem that bi-segèd han our toun,
That so can leye our jolité on presse, 559
And bringe our lusty folk to holinesse!'

These wordès seyde he for the nonès alle,
That with swich thing he mighte him
    angry maken,
And with an anger don his sorwè falle
As for the time, and his coráge awaken:
But wel wiste he, as fer as tongès spaken,
Ther n'ns a man of gretter hardinesse
Than he, ne more desirèd worthinesse.

'What cas,' quod Troilus, 'or what
    áventúre
Hath guided thee to see my languisshinge
That am refús of every créatúre?   570
But for the love of God, at my preyínge
Go henne away, for certès my deyínge
Wol thee disese, and I mot nedès deye:
Therfor go wey, there n'is no more to seye!

'But if thou wene I be thus sik for drede,
It is not so; and therfor scorn me nought.
Ther is another thing I take of hede
Wel more than aught that Grekès han
    yit wrought,
Which cause is of my deth for sorwe and
    thought.
But though that I now telle it thee ne leste,
Be thou naught wroth: I hide it for the
    beste.'   581

This Pandar that nigh malt for wo and
    routhe
Ful oftè seyde, 'Allas! what may this be?
Now frend,' quod he, 'if everè love or
    trouthe
Hath been, or is, betwixen thee and me.
Ne do thou neverè swich a cruelté
To hidè fro thy frend so gret a care!
Wostow not wel that it am I, Pandáre?

'I woldè parten with thee al thy peyne
If it be so I do thee no comfórt,   590
As it is frendès right, soth for to seyne,
To entréparten wo, as glad desport.

533. *ye*,] Cp. *the*.
534. *ye*,] Cp. *the*.
537. *my lif*, P *my lyf* (Boc. Che t' ama più che
la sua vita assai); H₂ *my silf*; H₄ corrupt; J
and others *my-self*.
539. *no thing more*, γ *more thing*.
540. *mo*, so a; others *to(o)*.
546. *thousand*, H₄ *hundred* (Boc. in cento).
559. *That so*, H₂ Cl. H₁ *And so*.
559. *on presse*, a *in presse*.

563. *his sorwe falle*, R S γ *his wo to falle*.
566. *a man*, J *no man*.
569. *my languisshinge*, J and others *me languisshing*.
576. *scorn me nought*, J and others *scorne(s)
nought*.
585. *or is*, J and others *or this*.
589. *wolde*, so D S₂ Dg.; rest *wil, wol, wo's
wele*.

I have, and shal, for trewe or fals report,
In wrong and right, y-loved thee al my
    live :
Hyd not thy wo fro me, but tel it blive.'

Than gan this sorwful Troilus to sike,
And seyde him thus : 'God leve it be
    my beste
To telle it thee, for sith it may thee like
Yit wol I telle it, though myn hertè breste :
And wel wot I, thou mayst do me no reste.
But lest thou deme I trustè not to thee,
Now herknè, frend, for thus it stant with
    me.—   602

' Lo, Love, ayeins the whiche who-so de-
    fendeth
Himselven most, him altherlest availeth,
With desespair so sorwfully m' offendeth,
That streight unto the deth myn hertè
    saileth :
Ther-to desir so brenningly m' assaileth,
That to be slayn it were a gretter joye   608
To me than king of Grecè ben and Troye !

' Suffiseth this, my fullè frend Pandáre,
That I have seyd, for now wostow my wo.
And for the love of God, my coldè care
So hyd it wel !   I tolde it nevere to mo,
For harmès mighten folwen, mo than
    two,
If it were wist.—But be thou in gladnésse,
And let me sterve, unknowe, of my des-
    tresse !'

' How hast thou thus unkindély and longe
Hid this fro me ? thou fool !' quod
    Pandarus.
' Paraunter thou mayst after swich oon
    longe,
That myn avys anon may helpen us.'   620
' This were a wonder thing !' quod Troilus.

' Thou coudest nevere in love thy-selven
    wisse :
How devel mayst thou than bringè me to
    blisse !'

' Ye, Troilus, now herknè,' quod Pandáre,
' Though I be nice !   It happeth often so
That oon that exces doth ful yvelè fare,
By good counseil can kepe his frend therfro.
I have myselven seyn a blind man go,
Ther-as he fel that coudè loken wyde :
A fool may eek a wis-man oftè gyde.   630

' A wheston is no kerving instrument,
But yit it maketh sharpè kerving toles ;
And ther thou wost that I have aught
    miswent,
Eschewe thou that, for swich thing to
    thee scole is :
Thus often wisè men ben war by foles.
If thou so do, thy wit is wel bewared :
By his contrárie is every thing declared.

' For how mighte everè swetnesse han
    ben knowe   638
To him that neverè tasted bitternesse ?
Ne no man wot what gladnesse is, I trowe,
That neverè was in sorwe or som destresse :
Eek whyt by blak, by shame ek worthinesse,
Ech set by other more for' other semeth :
As men may see, and so the wise it demeth.

' Sith thus of two contraries is o lore,
And that I have in love so ofte assayed
Grevaunces, m' oughtè connen wel the more
Counseilen thee of that thou art amayed ;
And ek thee n' oughtè not ben yvele apayed
Though I desirè with thee for to berè   650
Thyn hevy charge : it shal thee lessè dere.

602. *herkne*, J and others *herke*.
603. *Lo, Love* (?), all *Love*.
605. *sorwfully*, J and others *sorwfull(*).
613. *I tolde*, Cl. *I telle* ; H⁵ *and telle* ; J omits
it after *tolde*.
613. H₄ *nevere to no mo* ; Cx. *nevere no mo* ;
rest *nevere to mo.* (Read ? *nevere mo* or *nevere
o mo.* See l. 675, where G has *never to moo*.)
619. *mayst*, γ *might(est*).

623. *How devel mayst thou than*, so P H₂ Cx. ;
S₁ *devel than* ; R *me than* ; J and rest om. *than* ;
G H₅ *del(l)* for *devel*.
628. *myselven seyn*, γ insert *eek* before or after
seyn.
640. *wot what gladnesse is*, so a β ; R Cx. H₃
γ *may be inly* (R *veryly*) *glad.*
646. *And that I have* (?), P H₂ *That y have* ;
rest *I that have.*
647. *Grevaunces*, etc., P H₂ *me oght* ; S₃ Dg.
I oght ; rest *oughti(e*). All except H₂ H₄ Cx. insert *and* before *wel.*
649. *And ek thee* (*me*) *oughte not*, so β ; a *And
ek thou oughtest* ; γ *Eh thee ne oughte not.*

'I wot wel that it fareth thus by me,
As to thy brother Paris an herdesse,
Which that y-clepèd was Oénone,
Wrot in a compleynt of her hevynesse :
Ye saw the lettrè that she wrot, I gesse ?'
'Nay, neverè yit, y-wis,' quod Troilus.
'Now,' quod Pandárè, 'herkneth, it
    was thus.——   658

'"Phebus, that first fond art of medicine,"
Quod she, "and coude in every wightès care
Remédie and reed by herbès he knew fine,
Yit to himself his conning was ful bare ;
For Love hadde him so bounden in a snare,
Al for the doughter of the King Amete,
That al his craft ne coude his sorwes bete."

'Right so fare I, unhappily for me :
I love oon best, and that me smerteth sore ;
And yet paraunter can I reden thee,   668
And not myself : reprevè me no more !
I have no cause, I wot wel, for to sore
As doth a hauk that listeth for to pleye ;
But to thyn help yit somwhat can I seye.

'And of oo thing right siker maystow be,
That certein, for to dyen in the peyne,
That I shal neverè mo discoveren thee ;
Ne, by my trouthe, I kepè not restreyne
Thee fro thy love, though that it were
    Eleyne
That is thy bròther wyf, if ich it wiste :
Be what she be, and love her as thee liste !

'Therfore, as frend, fulliche in me assure,
And tel me plat now what is th' enchesoun
And final cause of wo that ye endure ;   682
For douteth no thing, myn entencioun
N' is not to you of reprehencioun
To spèke as now, for no wight may bireve
A man to love, til that him list to leve.

'And witeth wel, that bothè two ben
    vices,——

Mistrusten alle, or ellès allè leve ;
But wel I wot the mene of it no vice is,
For for to tristen som wight is a preve 690
Of trouthe, and for-thy wolde I fayn re-
    meve
Thy wronge conceyt, and do thee som
    wight triste
Thy wo to telle ; and tel me, if thee liste.

'The wisè seyth, "Wo him that is allone,
For, and he falle, he hath non help to rise";
And sith thou hast a felaw, tel thy mone ;
For this n' is not, certéyn, the nextè wise
To winnen love, as techen us the wise,——
To walwe and wepe as Niobè the quene,
Whos terès yit in marbel ben y-sene. 700

'Lat be thy weping and thy drerinesse,
And lat us lissen wo with other speche,
So may thy woful timè semè lesse.
Delytè not in wo thy wo to seche,
As don thise foolès that hir sorwes eche
With sorwè, whan they have misáventure,
And listè not to seche hem other cure.

'Men seyn, "To wrecche is consolacioun
To have another felaw in his peyne."
That oughtè wel ben our opinioun, 710
For, bothè thou and I, of Love we pleyne !
So ful of sorwe am I, soth for to seyne,
That certeynly no morè hardè grace
May sitte on me, for-why thèr is no space !

'If God wile, thou art not agast of me,
Lest I wolde of thy lady thee bigile !
Thou wost thy-self whom that I love, pardé,
As I best can, gon sithen longè while.
And sith thou wost I do it for no wile, 719
And seyst I am he that thou trustest most,
Tel me somwhat, sin al my wo thou wost.'

Yit Troilus for al this no word seyde,
But longe he lay as stille as he ded were ;
And after this with siking he abreyde,
And to Pandárès vois he lente his ere,

654. *Oenone*, see Ovid, *Heroid.* v.
658. *Now*, P H₂ Cl. *No.*
661. *he*, γ *she.*
681. *And tel me plat now*, P H₂ G γ om.
now.
681. G Cl. *thyn enchesoun.*
682. *final*, G J H₂ γ *finally.*

690. *For for to*, so H₄ J G H₁ ; rest *For to.*
719. *wile*, so a γ ; J and others *gile.*
720. *seyst*, γ *sith(en).*
725. *Pandáres*, so P H₂ G R ; rest *Pandarus.*
725. *lente*, P H₂ G *bente* ; H₄ *laide.*

448

ind up his yen caste he, that in fere
Vas Pandarus, lest that in frenèsye
Ie sholdè falle, or ellès soonè dye ;

ind cri'de ' A-wak ' ful wonderliche and
    sharpe ;
What ! slombrestow as in a litargye? 730
)r artow lyk an assè to an harpe,
Chat hereth soun, whan men the strengès
    plye,
3ut in his minde of that no melodýe
May sinken, him to gladden, for that he
5o dul is of his bestialitè ?'

And with that Pandar of his wordès stente;
And Troilus yit him no word answèrde,
For-why to tellen was not his entente   738
To nevere no man, for whom that he so ferde.
For it is seyd, men maketh ofte a yerde
With which the maker is himself y-beten
In sundry maner, as thise wisè treten.

And namèliche in his counsèil tellínge :
That toucheth love, that oughtè ben secrè,
For of himself it wol ynough out-springe,
But-if that it the bet govèrned be ;
Eek somtime it is craft to semè flee
For thing which in effect men huntè faste.—
Al this gan Troilus in his hertè caste.   749

But nathèles whan he had herd him crye
' Awak ! ' he gan to sikè wonder sore,
And seydè, ' Frend, though that I stillè lye,
I am not deef. Now pees, and cry no more,
For I have herd thy wordès and thy lore;
But suffrè me my mischief to biwailen,
For thy provèrbès may me naught availen !

' Nor other curè canst thou non for me :
Eek I n'il not be curèd : I wol deye !
What knowe I of the quenè Niobe !
Lat be thine olde ensaumples, I thee
    preye !'   760

' No !' quod tho Pandarus, ' Therfore I seye,
Swich is delit of folès to biwepe
Hir wo, but seken botè they ne kepe !

' Now knowe I, that ther reson in thee
    faileth !
But tel me, if I wistè what she were
For whom that thee al this misaunter aileth,
Dorstestow that I tolde her in her ere
Thy wo, sith thou darst not thyself for fere,
And her besoughte on thee to han som
    routhe ?'—
' Why, nay !' quod he, ' by God and by
    my trouthe !'   770

' What ! not as bisily,' quod Pandarus,
' As though myn ownè lyf lay on this nede?'
' No, certès, brother !' quod this Troilus.
' And why ?'—' For that thou sholdest
    neverè spede.'—
' Wost thou that wel ?'—' Ye, that is out
    of drede !'
Quod Troilus. ' For al that evere ye conne,
She n'il to no swich wrecche as I ben wonne!'

Quod Pandarus, ' Allas ! what may this be,
That thou despeyrèd art thus causèles ?
What ! liveth not thy lady, bendistè !   780
How wostow so that thou art gracèles ?
Swich yvel is not alwey bootèles.
Why, put not impossíblè thus thy cure,
Sith thing to come is ofte in áventure.

' I grauntè wel that thou endurest wo
As sharp as doth he, Ticius, in helle,
Whos stomak foulès tiren everè mo
That highten voltourès, as bookès telle ;
But I may not endurè that thou dwelle
In so unskilful an opinioun   790
That of thy wo is no curacioun.

' But onès n'iltow, for thy coward herte
And for thyn ire and folissh wilfulnesse,

737. MSS. vary—some *word* for *thing*.
739. MSS. vary. H₄ R Cx. *Nevere to no man,
for whom he so ferde ; a² To no man, for-why that
he so ferde* (read *nevere* for *no !*).
747. *it is craft*, so a Cx. H₂ ; rest *it is a craft.*
748. *For thing*, γ *Fro thing*. (See ii. 194, 868.)
749. *in his hertè*, H₄ H₂ omit *his*.
753. *am*, J G *nam*.
757. *Nor*, J and others *For*.

761. *tho*, all omit except H₄ S γ⁴.
764. *ther reson*, so H₄ G R J Cp. H₁ ; rest
omit *ther.*
767. *Dorstestow*, so G R Cl. H₁ ; rest *dorst thou.*
767. *tolde her*, so H₄ G H₃ H₃ ; P H₂ R Cx.
tolde it ; rest *tolde* (Cl. *tellè*).
773. *No, certes, brother, a Why, no, pardè, sir.*
780. *bendistè*, so J Cp. H₁ ; others *benedicitè.*
786. *Ticius*, Tityus. Ovid, *Met.* iv. 456 ;
Boethius iii. met. 12.

For wantrust, tellen of thy sorwes smerte,
Ne to thyn owné help do bisinesse
As muche as speke a reson more or lesse,
But li'st as he that list of no thing recche !
What woman coudé lové swich a wrecche ?

'What may she demen other of thy deth,
If thou thus dye, and she n'ot why it is,
But that for fere is yolden up thy breth,
For Grekés han besegéd us, y-wis ?   802
Lord, which a thonk than shaltow han
    of this !
Thus wol she seyn, and al the toun at ones,
"The wrecche is ded, the devil have his
    bones !"

'Thou mayst allone here wepe and crye
    and knele ;
But love a woman that she wot it nought,
And she wol quite it that thou shalt not
    fele,—
Unknowe, unkist, and lost, that is
    unsought.
What ! many a man hath love ful dere
    y-bought,   810
Ye, twenty winter, that his lady wiste,
That neveré yit his lady mouth he kiste !

'What ! sholde he therfor fallen in despair,
Or be recréant for his owné tene,
Or slen himself, al be his lady fair ?
Nay, nay ! but evere in oon be fressh
    and grene
To serve and love his deré hertés quene,
And thenke it is a guerdon, her to serve,
A thousand fold more than he can deserve !'

And of that word took hedé Troilus,   820
And thoughte anon what foly he was inne,
And how that soth him seydé Pandarus,
That for to slen himself mighte he not winne,
But bothé don unmanhod and a sinne,
And of his deth his lady naught to wite ;
For of his wo, God wot, she knew ful lite.

And with that thought he gan ful soré sike,
And seyde, 'Allas ! what is me best to do ?'
To whom Pandáre answerdé, 'Yif thee like,
The beste is that thou tellé me thy wo ;
And have .my trouthé, but thou finde it so
I be thy bote or that it be ful longe,   832
To peces do me drawe, and sithen honge !'

'Ye, so seystow !' quod Troilus tho,
    'Allas !
But, God wot, it is naught the rather so !
Ful hard were it to helpen in this cas ;
For wel finde I that Fortune is my fo,
Ne alle the men that riden conne or go
May of her cruel wheel the harm with-
    stonde ;
For as her list, she pley'th with free and
    bonde.'   840

Quod Pandarus, 'Than blamestow Fortúne
For thou art wroth : ye, now at erst I see !
Wostow not wel that Fortune is commúne
To every maner wight in som degree ?
And yit thou hast this confort, lo, pardé !
That as her joyés moten overgon,
So mote her sorwes passen everychon.

'For if her wheel stinte any thing to torne,
Than cesséd she Fortúne anon to be.
Now, sith her wheel by no way may sojorne,
What wostow, if her mutabilité   851
Right as thy-selven list wol don by thee,
Or that she be not fer fro thyn helpínge ?
Paraunter thou hast causé for to singe !

'And therfor wostow what I thee
    beseche ?
Lat be thy wo and torning to the grounde ;
For who-so list have heling of his leche,
To him bihoveth first unwrye his wounde.
To Cerberus in helle ay be I bounde,
Al were it for my suster al thy sorwe,   860
By my wil she sholdé be thyn to-morwe !

794. *For, a And.*
796. *speke a reson, a speke o word (ye).*
803. *than, J and others omit.*
808. *it, γ omits.*
811. *Ye, so S ; H₄ Ya ; rest omit ; P Ad. or
(er) that ; Cx. ne wiste ; G not wiste.*
820. *And, γ omits.*

830. *thy wo, so a² J G H₅ A ; γ and others al
thy wo.*
831. *finde it, γ it finde.*
834. *seystow, γ thou seyst.*
857. *heling, G J Cl. helping.*
858. *unwrye, J γ unwre.*
860. *Al (γ), all omit first Al ; P H₂ corrupt.*
861. *sholdé be thyn, P inserts al before thyn :
Jo. γ inserts al before be.*

'Look up, I seye, and tel me what she is
Anon, that I may gon aboute thy nede.
Knowe ich her aught? For my love, tel
    me this!
Than wolde I hopen rather for to spede.'
Tho gan the veyne of Troilus to blede,
For he was hit, and wex al red for shame.
'A ha!' quod Pandar, 'here biginneth
    game!'

And with that word he gan him for to shake,
And seydė, 'Thef, thou shalt her namė
    telle!'   870
But tho gan sely Troilus for to quake
As though men sholde han led him into
    helle,
And seyde, 'Allas! of al my wo the welle,
Than is my swetė fo callėd Criseyde!'
And wel nigh with the word for fere he
    deyde.

And whan that Pandar herde her namė
    nevene,
Lord! he was glad, and seydė, 'Frend
    so dere,   877
Now fare aright! for Jovės name in hevene,
Love hath bi-set thee wel! Be of good chere!
For of good namė, wisdom, and manére
She hath y-nough, and ek of gentilesse.
If she be fair, thou wost thyself, I gesse!

'N' I neverė saw a morė bountevous
Of her estat, n' a gladder, ne of speche
A frendlier, n' a morė gracious
For to do wel, ne lasse had nede to seche
What for to don; and al this bet to eche
In honour to as fer as she may strecche,
A kingės hertė sem'th by heres a wrecche.

'And for-thy look of good confórt thou be;
For certeinly, the firstė point is this   891

Of noblė corage and wel ordeynė,—
A man to have pes with himself, ywis.
So oughtest thou; for nought but good it is
To loven wel and in a worthy place:
Thee oughtė not to clepe it hap, but grace.

'And also thenk, and therwith gladdė thee,
That sith thy lady vertuous is al,
So folweth it that ther is som pité
Amongės alle thise othre in general: 900
And for-thy see that thou in special
Requerė naught that is ayein her name,
For vertu streccheth not himself to shame.

'But wel is me that everė I was born,
That thou biset art in so good a place;
For by my trouthe, in love I dorste han
    sworn
Thee sholdė nevere han tid thus fair a grace.
And wostow why? For thou were wont
    to chace
At Love in scorn, and for despit him calle
"Seint Idiot, lord of thise foolės alle."   910

'How often hastow maad thy nicė japes,
And seyd, that "Lovės servants every-
    chone
Of nicetė ben verray Goddės apės;
And somė woldė monche hir mete allone
Ligging a-bedde and make hem for to grone;
And som," thou seydest, "had a blanchė
    fevere,
And preydest God he sholdė neverė kevere.

'"And some of hem toke on hem for
    the cold
More than y-nough," so seydestow ful ofte;
"And some han feynėd oftė time and
    told   920
How that they waken whan they slepen
    softe;

865. *rather,* P H₉ H₃ Cl. H₁ *the rather(e).*
875. *the word,* H₄ R Cx. H₁ *that word.*
880. *name, wisdom,* R γ insert *and* before *wisdom.*
883. *N' I nevere saw,* so P H₂ Jo. H₁; H⁴ R Cx. D *Ne nevere saw I;* G H₃ Cp. Cl. *Ne nevere saw.*
884. *n' a,* Cl. *ne a;* Cp. *na;* G *non;* rest *ne.*
890-896. All MSS. except P H₂ H₄ (and Jo. in later hand on margin) omit this stanza; Cx. omits it, but Th. has it.

892. *and wel ordeynė,* so P H₂; J Th. *and wel ordeyne the;* H₄ *thou ordeyne the.*
893. *A man,* } H₄ omit.
896. *Thee,* J H₄ *Men.*
904. *that evere I was born,* R *that evere was I;* G S Ad. Cp. H₁ *that evere that I was born.*
907. *nevere han tid,* G H₅ J *nevere in love han tid.*
907. *thus fair,* a R Cx. D Cl. *so fair.*
914. *monche,* so a; rest *muche, mucche, muchche, meche.*

And thus they wolde han brought hemself a-lofte,
But nathéles were under at the laste ! "
Thus seydestow, and japèdest ful faste.

' Yit seydestow that " for the moré part,
These lovers woldé speke in general,
And thoughten that it was a siker art
For failing for t' assayen over-al ! "
Now may I jape of thee, if that I shal !
But nathéles, though that I sholdé deye, 930
That thou art non of tho, I dorsté seye.

' Now beet thy brest, and sey to God of Love,
" Thy gracé, Lord ! for now I me repente
If I mis-spak, for now myself I love."
Thus sey with al thyn herte in good en-
tente ! '
Quod Troilus, ' A, Lord ! I me consente,
And preye to thee my japès thou forgive,
And I shal neverémoré whil I live.'

' Thou seyst wel,' quod Pandáre, ' and now I hope
That thou the Goddès wraththe hast al apesed ; 940
And sithen thou hast wopen many a drope,
And seyd such thing wherwith thy god is plesed,
Now woldé neveré God but thou were esed !
And thenk wel, she of whom rist al thy wo,
Her-after may thy confort ben also.

' For th'ilké grounde that ber'th the wedès wikke
Ber'th eek these holsom herbés as ful ofte ;
And next the foulé netlé, rough and thikke,
The rosé waxeth sweté, smothe, and softe ;
And next the valey is the hil o-lofte ; 950
And next the derké night, the gladdé morwe ;
And also joye is next the fyn of sorwe.

' Now looké that a-tempré be thy bridel,
And for the beste ay suffré to the tide,
Or ellés al our labour is on ydel :
He hasteth wel that wisly can abide.
Be diligent, and trewe, and ay wel hide :
Be lusty, free, persévere in thy servíse,
And al is wel, if thou werke in this wise.

' But he that parted is in every place 960
Is nowher hool, as writen clerkès wise.
What wonder is, though swich oon have no grace ?
Eek wostow how ? It far'th of som servíse,
As plante a tree, or herbe, in sondry wise,
And on the morwé pulle it up as blive !
No wonder is, though it may neveré thrive.

' And sith that God of Love hath thee bestowed
In placé digne un-to thy worthinesse,
Stond fasté, for to good port hastow rowed !
And of thy-self for any hevinesse 970
Hope alwey wel ; for, but-if drerinesse
Or over-haste our bothé labour shende,
I hope of this to maken a good ende.

' And wostow why ? I am the lesse a-fered
Of this matéré with my necé trete,
For this have I herd seyd of oldé lered :
Was neveré man nor woman yit begete
That was unapt to suffré lovés hete—
Celestial, or ellés love of kinde.
For-thy som grace I hope in her to finde. 980

' And for to speke of her in special,
Her beauté to bithenken and her youthe,
It sit her naught to be celestial
As yit, though that her listé bothe and couthe :
But trewély it sate her wel right nouthe
A worthy knight to loven and cheríce ;
And, but she do, I holde it for a vice !

924. *japedest*, P H₂ Cx. Ad. *ympedist (impedest).*
926. *lovers,* P H₂ *faitours.*
938. *whil I live,* a³ *whil that I live.*
939. *Panddre,* so a R Cx. D ; rest *Pandarus.*
947. *as ful ofte,* P H₂ *and* (for *as*) ; Cx. omit *as.*
948. *And next,* so S ; rest omit *And.*
949. *The rose waxeth swete,* a *The lilie wexith whil(e)* ; J D γ insert *and* before *smothe.*

953. *Now looke that,* H₂ *Look that thou* ; Ph. *Look thou that* ; G *wel* (for *be*).
960. *parted,* γ *departed.*
962, 966. *What wonder is, No wonder is,* G *ist* (for *is*).
972. *bothe,* H₄ *botheres* ; D *bother* ; G Ad. *bothis.*
976. *of olde lered,* so a³ R ; Cx. *oft of lered* ; H₂ *and lered* ; G *of leryd* ; rest *of wise lered.*
984. *though that,* J γ *if that* ; R *as that* ; G *that.*

'Wherfore I am, and wol be, ay redy
To peyné me to do you this servíse ;
For bothé you to plesé, this hope I,   990
Herafterward ; for ye be bothé wise,
And conne it counseil kepe in swich a wise
That no man shal the wiser of it be ;
And so we may be gladed allé three.

'And, by my trouthe, I have right now
    of thee
A good conceit in my wit, as I gesse !
And what it is, I wil now that thou see.—
I thenké, sith that Love of his goodnésse
Hath thee converted out of wikkednesse,
That thou shalt be the besté post, I leve, 1000
Of al his lay, and most his foos ay greve.

'Ensamplé why, see now these greté
    clerkes,
That erren aldermost ayein a lawe,
And ben converted from hir wikked werkes
Thorugh grace of God that list hem to
    him drawe,—
Than arn they folk that han most God in
    awe,
And strengest feithéd ben, I understonde,
And conne an errour alderbest with-
    stonde.'

Whan Troilus had herd Pandáre, assented
To ben his helpe in loving of Criseyde, 1010
Wex off his wo, as who seith, untor-
    mented ;
But hotter wex his love ; and than he seyde
With sobré chere, although his herté
    pleyde :—
'Now blisful Venus help, or that I sterve,
Of thee, Pandáre, I may som thank
    deserve !

'But, deré frend, how shal my wo be lesse
Til this be don ? And good, ek tel me this,

How wiltow seyn of me and my destresse ?
Lest she be wroth, this drede I most y-wis,
Or n'il not here or trowén how it is. 1020
Al this drede I ; and ek for the manére
Of thee, her eem, she n'il no swich thing
    here.'

Quod Pandarus, 'Thou hast a ful gret care
Lest that the cherl may falle out of the
    mone !
Why, Lord ! I hate of thee thy nicé fare !
Why, entrémete of that thou hast to done !
For Goddés love, I biddé thee a bone :
So lat m' alone, and it shal be thy beste !'—
'Why, frend,' quod he, 'now do right
    as thee leste ! 1029

'But herké, Pandar, oo word ; for I n'olde
That thou in me wendest so gret folýe,
That to my lady I desiren sholde
That toucheth harm or any vilanye ;
For dredéles me weré leveré dye
Than she of me aught ellés understoode
But that that mighté sounen in-to goode.'

Tho lough this Pandar, and anon
    answérde,
'And I thy borw, fy ! no wight doth but so !
I roughté naught though that she stood
    and herde 1039
How that thou seyst ! But far-wel, I wol go.
A-dieu ! be glad ! God spede us bothé two !
Yif me this labour and this bisinesse,
And of my speed be thyn al the swetnesse !'

Tho Troilus gan doun on knees to falle,
And Pandar in his armés henté faste,
And seydé, 'Now, fy on the Grekés alle !
Yit, pardé, God shal helpe us at the laste !
And dredéles, if that my lif may laste,
And God to-forn, lo, some of hem shal
    smerte ; 1049
And yit m' athinketh, this avaunt m'
    asterte !

'Now, Pandarus, I can no moré seye
But, thou wis, thou wost, thou mayst,
    thou art al !

988. *Wherfore*, P H₂ G H₃ Cx. *Therfore*.
988. *be ay redy*, G H₂ Cx. *be al redy* ; P *alwey
be redy* ; H₃ *al day be redy*.
990. *this*, so P H₃ G J R H₃ D ; rest *thus*.
992. *conne it*,] *konne a*.
995. *And*, J *Now* ; Cl. *For*.
1001. *foos ay greve*, so R J S ; a³ G H₃ Cx. D
foes (*fois, foos*) *greve* ; γ (except D) *foos to greve*.
1003. *erren*, P H₂ G Cx. *are* (*arn*).
1017. *And good, ek tel*, P H₂ *And eek now tel*.

1038. *fy !* G om. ; Jo. *for* ; R *whi*.
1043. *al the*,] γ *al that*.
1050. *this avaunt*, H₂ γ *that this avaunt*.
1051. *Now, Pandarus*, P H₃ γ *Now, Pandare*.

453

My lif, my deth, hool in thyn hond I leye!
Help now!'—Quod he, 'Yis, by my
    trouthe I shal!'—
'God yelde thee, frend! And this in
    special,'
Quod Troilus, 'that thou me recomaunde
Til her that may me to the deth comaunde!'

This Pandarus, tho désirous to serve
His fullé frend, tho seyde in this manére;
'Far-wel, and thenk I wil thy thank
    deserve!   1060
Have here my trouthe, and that thou
    shalt wel here!'
And wente his wey, thenking on this
    matére,
And how he best mighte her beseche of
    grace,
And finde a timé ther-to and a space.

For every wight that hath an hous to founde
Ne renneth not the werk for to beginne
With rakel hond; but he wol bide a
    stounde,
And sende his hertés line out fro withinne
How alderfirst his purpos for to winne.

1058. *tho*, H₄ *ful.*
1059. *tho*, γ⁵ *than.*
1064. *space*, J γ *place.*
1069. *How* (?), all omit (but necessary to the
sense as well as metre?).

Al this tho Pandar in his herté thoughte,
And caste his werk ful wisly or he wroughte.

But Troilus lay tho no lenger doun,   1072
But up anon up-on his stedé bay,
And in the feld he pleydé the lióun.
Wo was that Greek that with him mette
    a-day!
And in the toun his maner tho forth ay
So goodly was, and gat him so in grace
That ech him lovede that lokéd on his face.

For he bicom the frendliesté wight,   1079
The gentilleste and ek the mosté free,
The thriftieste and oon the besté knight,
That in his timé was or mighté be.
Dede were his japés and his crueltȩ́,
His hyé port and his manére estraunge;
And ech of tho gan for a vertu chaunge.

Now let us stinte of Troilus a stounde,
That fareth lik a man that hurt is sore
And is somdel of aking of his wounde
Y-lisséd wel, but heléd no del more.
And, as an esy pacient, the lore   1090
Abit of him that go'th about his cure;
And thus he drieth forth his aventúre.

1070. *Al this tho*, so H₄; rest omit *tho.*
1075. *a-day*, so J and others; rest *that day.*
1078. *on*, a H₂ Cx. *in.*
1092. *drieth*, P H₂ H₅ Cx. A S *driveth.*

BOOK II

OUT of thise blaké wawés for to saile,
O wind, O wind, the weder ginneth clere:
For in this see the boot hath swich
    travaile,
Of my conníng that unnethe I it stere.
This see clepe I the tempestous matére
Of desespeyr that Troilus was inne;
But now of hope the kalendés biginne.

O lady myn, that calléd art Cleó,
Thou be my speed fro this forth, and my
    muse,
To rimé wel this book til I have do!   10

1. R omits ll. 1-49.
4. *conníng*, J and others *com(m)ing.*

Me nedeth here non other art to use;
For-why to every lover I m' excuse,
That of no sentément I this endite,
But out of Latin in my tonge it write.

Wherfore I n'il have neither thank ne
    blame
Of al this werk, but preye you mekély
Disblameth me if any word be lame;
For as myn auctour seydé, so seye I.
Ek though I speke of love unfelingly,
No wonder is; for it no thing of-newe
    is,   20
A blind man can-not juggen wel in hewes.

21. *man*, J H₅ *wight;* H³ *knight.*

Ye knowe ek, that in forme of speche is
    chaunge
Withinne a thousand yeer, and wordès tho
That hadden pris, now wonder nice and
    straunge
Us thinketh hem; and yit they spake
    hem so,
And spedde as wel in love as men now do:
Ek for to winnen love in sondry ages,
In sondry londès sondry ben uságes.

And for-thy if it happe in any wise,
That here be any lover in this place   30
That herkneth, as the story can devise
How Troilus com til his lady grace,
And thenketh, 'so n'olde I not love
    purcháce,'
Or wondreth on his speche or his doínge,
I n'ot; but it is me no wonderínge.

For every wight which that to Romè went
Halt not oo path, ne alwey oo manére;
Ek in som lond were al the gamé shent,
If that men ferde in love as men don
    here,
As thus,—in open doing or in chere,   40
In visitinge, in forme, or seyde hir sawes:
For-thy men seyn, ech contré hath his
    lawes.

Ek scarsly ben ther in this placè three
That han in love seyd lik, and don in al,
For to thy purpos this may likè thee,
And thee right nought, yit al is seyd or
    shal;
Ek some men grave in tree, some in ston
    wal,
As it bitit.—But, sin I have begonne,
Myn auctour shal I folwen, if I conne.   49

—In May that moder is of monthès glade,
That fresshè flourès, blewè, white, and
    rede,

Ben quike a-gayn, that winter dedé made,
And ful of bawme is fleting every mede:
Whan Phebus doth his brightè bemès
    sprede
Right in the whitè Bole, it so betidde
As I shal singe, on Mayès day the
    thridde,

That Pandarus, for al his wisè speche,
Felte ek his part of lovès shotès kene,
That, coude he nevere so wel of loving
    preche,
It made his hewe a-day ful oftè grene.   60
So shoop it, that him fil that day a tene
In love, for which in wo to bedde he
    wente,
And made, or it was day, ful many a
    wente.

The swalwè Proigné, with a sorwful lay,
Whan morwè com, gan make her way-
    mentínge
Why she forshapen was; and everè lay
Pandare a-bedde, half in a slomberínge,
Til she so nigh him made her cheterínge
How Terèus gan forth his suster take,   69
That with the noise of her he gan awake,

And gan to calle and dresse him up to rise,
Remembring him his erand was to doone
From Troilus, and ek his grete emprise;
And caste, and knew in good plit was
    the moone
To don viage, and took his wey ful soone
Unto his neces paleys ther biside.—
Now Janus, God of Entré, thou him gide!

Whan he was come unto his neces place,
'Wher is my lady?' to her folk quod
    he;
And they him tolde, and he forth in gan
    pace,   80
And fond two othrè ladies sete and she
Withinne a pavéd parlour; and they three

22. *Ye*, J H₅ H₃ S Cx. *I.*
22. *that*, a³ *this.*
29. a² insert stanza 7 before stanza 5.
35. *wonderínge*, so H₃ Cl.; a³ *wondur thyng*;
J and others *wondrínge.*
37. *ne*, so a β; J H₃ *nor*; γ *or.*
39. *men*, so a β; Cx. γ *they.*
42. *seyn*, H₄ Cl. *seyth.*
47. *some men*, a² omit *men.*
51. *white*, J γ *and white.*

62. *in wo*, J *for wo*; a² *ful wo.*
64. *Proigné.* See *L.G.W.* vii.
69. *Terèus*, so H₄ R Cx.; a² *Thereus*; J
Tereux; γ *Tireux.*
71. *dresse*, J *dressed*; a² *dressyn.*
71. *up*, J γ; a β omit.
78. *neces*, J R Cx. H₃ *nece.*

Herden a mayden reden hem the geste
Of al the sege of Thebès, whil hem 'leste.

Quod Pandarus, 'Madámè, God you see,
With al your book and al the com-
panýe ! '—
'Ey, unclè, now welcóme y-wis ! ' quod she ;
And up she ros, and by the hond in hye
She took him faste, and seydè, ' This
night thrye—   89
To goodè mote it torne !—of you I mette.'
And with that word she doun on bench
him sette.

' Ye, necè, ye shal farè wel the bet,
If God wile, al this yer ! ' quod Pandarus ;
' But I am sory that I have you let
To herken of your book ye preisen thus.
For Goddès love, what seith it ? Tel it us !
Is it of love ? O, som good ye me lere ! '
' Uncle ! ' quod she, ' your maistresse is
not here ! '

With that they gonnen laughe ; and tho
she seyde,   99
'This rómaunce is of Thebès, that we rede ;
And we han herd how that King Laius
deyde
Thorugh Edippus his sone, and al that dede ;
And here we stinten at thise lettres rede,
How that the bisshop, as the book can telle,
Amphiorax, fil thorugh the groundè to
helle.'

Quod Pandarus, 'Al this knowe I my-selve,
And al th' assege of Thebès, and the care ;
For herof ben ther makèd bookès twelve.
But lat be this, and tel me how ye fare. 109
Do wey your barbe, and shewe your facè
bare.
Do wey your book : ris up, and lat us
daunce,
And lat us don to May som óbservaunce ! '

'Ey, God forbedè ! ' quod she, ' Be ye
mad ?
Is that a widwes lif, so God you save ?
By God, ye maken me right sore adrad !
Ye ben so wilde, it semeth as ye rave !
It satè me wel bet, ay in a cave
To bidde and rede on holy seintès lives !
Lat maydens gon to daunce, and yongè
wives ! '

' As everè thrive I,' quod this Pandarus,
' Yit coude I telle a thing to do you
pleye ! '—   121
' Now, uncle derè,' quod she, ' telle it us
For Goddès love ! Is than the sege aweye ?
I am of Grekès fer'd so that I deye ! '—
' Nay, nay ! ' quod he, ' As everè mote I
thrive,
It is a thing wel bet than swichè five ! '

' Ye, holy God ! ' quod she, ' What thing
is that ?
What ! bet than swichè five ? Ey, nay,
y-wis !
For al this world ne can I redè what
It sholdè ben ! Som jape I trowe is this !
And, but your-selven telle us what it is, 131
My wit is for t'arede it al too lene ;
As help me God, I n'ot not what ye
mene ! '—

' And I your borw, ne neverè shal for me
This thing be told to you, so mote I thrive ! '
' And why so, uncle myn ? Why so ? '
quod she.—
' By God,' quod he, ' that wol I telle as
blive !
For prouder womman is ther non on-live,
And ye it wiste, in al the town of Troye :
I japè naught, so everè have I joye ! ' 140

83. *the geste, a⁵ al the geste.*
84. *Of al the sege* (T).   All omit *al.*
86. *your book, γ your fayre book.*
87. *now, γ myn.*
104. *How that, so S Ad. ; rest omit that.*
105. *Amphiorax,* Amphiaraus.   See v. 1500;
A. *and A.* 57 ; C.T. D 741.
110. *barbe,* J G H₅ H₃ R Cx. *wimpel.*

115. *By God,* etc., *a⁵ (i.e.* P H₂ G H₃ H₄) ⅟₂
maken me by Joves sore adrad.
116. *as,* R H₃ Cl. *that.*
117. *in a,* J and others *in.*
119. *maydens gon to, a⁵ maydenes go daunce*
123. *the sege, γ th' assege.*
124. *fer'd so,* so R Cx. ; J *fered so ; γ so fer(e)d :*
others var.
133. *n'ot not,* so H₃ γ ; α β om. *not.*   G R
insert *as* before *I.*
134. *for me,* so a⁵ γ⁶ ; J R Cx. H₃ S₂ Dg. *quod I.*
140. *so,* H₄ γ *as.*

Tho gan she wondren moré than biforn
A thousand fold, and down her yen caste ;
For neveré sith the time that she was born
To knowé thing desiréd she so faste.
And with a sik she seyde him at the laste,
' Now, unclé min, I n'il you not displese,
Nor axen more that may do you disese.'

So after this with many wordés glade,
And frendly talés, and with mery chere,
Of this and that they pley'de, and gonnen
   wade   150
In many an uncouth glad and deep matere,
As frendés don, whan they be met i-fere ;
Til she gan axen him how Ector ferde,
That was the townés wal and Grekés
   yerde.

' Ful wel, I thanke it God,' quod Pandarus,
' Save in his arm he hath a litel wounde ;
And ek his fresshé brother Troilus,
The wisé worthy Ector the secounde,
In whom that allé vertu list abounde,
As allé trouthe and allé gentilesse, 160
Wisdom, honóur, fredom, and worthi-
   nesse.'

' In good feith, em,' quod she, ' that
   liketh me !
They faren wel, God save hem bothé two !
For trewéliche I holde it gret deynté,
A Kingés sone in armés wel to do,
And ben of good condiciouns therto ;
For gret powér and moral vertu here
Is selde y-seyn in o persóne i-fere.'

' In good feith, that is soth,' quod
   Pandarus ;
' But, by my trouthe the king hath sonés
   tweye,   170
That is to mene, Ector and Troilus,
That certeinly, though that I sholdé deye,
They ben as voide of vices, dar I seye,

As any men that live under the sonne :
Hir might is wide y-knowe, and what they
   conne.

' Of Ector nedeth no thing for to telle :
In al this world ther n'is a bettré knight
Than he, that is of worthinessé welle ;
And he wel moré vertu hath than might.
This knoweth many a wis and worthy wight.
The samé pris of Troilus I seye : 181
God help me so, I knowe not swiché
   tweye ! '—

' By God,' quod she, ' of Ector that is soth ;
Of Troilus the samé thing trowe I,
For dredéles men telleth that he doth
In armés day by day so worthily,
And ber'th him here at hom so gentilly
To every wight, that allé pris hath he
Of hem that me were levest preiséd be.'

' Ye seye right soth, y-wis ! ' quod
   Pandarus,   190
' For yesterday who-so had with him been,
Mighté han wondred upon Troilus ;
For neveré yit so thikke a swarm of been
Ne fleigh, as Grekés for him gonné fleen ;
And thorugh the feld in every wightés ere
Ther n'as no cry but " Troilus is there ! "

' Now here, now there he hunted hem so
   faste,
Ther n'as but Grekés blood and Troilus :
Now him he hurte, and him al doun he
   caste :   199
Ay wher he wente, it was arrayéd thus :
He was hir deth, and sheld and lif for us ;
That, as that day, ther dorsté non with-
   stonde,
Whil that he held his blody swerd in honde.

174. *live*, so J and others ; a² Cl. *liveth*; others *liven* ; H₄ *lyven under sonne*.
176. *nedeth no thing*, so a² J Cx. H₃ ; H₄ G *nedith (it) no(ugh)t* ; γ *nedeth it no more*.
182. *God help me so*, J *so helpe me god*; G *so god helpe me*.
185. *telleth*, so J etc. ; others *telle, tellen*.
188. *alle*, J etc. *al*; Ph. G *al the*; Cx. *overal*.
192. *Mighte*, γ *He mighte*.
194. *for him*, J Cp. and others ; rest *fro him* (see i. 748).
199. *him . . . him*, H₅ H₃ γ² *hem . . . hem*.

141. *more*, H₄ G *wel more*.
143. *time*, H₄ G *tid*.
143. *that*, R Cx. omit.
144. *thing*, a² Cx. *a thing*.
147. *Nor*, a² To ; R Cx. *Ne*.
166. *of good condiciouns* ; read (?) *good of con-diciouns*.
170. *trouthe*, a² *heed*.

'Therto he is the frendliesté man
Of gret estat, that evere I saw my live,
And, wher him list, best felawshipé can
To swich as him think'th ablé for to
    thrive.'—
And with that word tho Pandarus, as blive,
He took his leve and seyde, 'I wol go
    henne.'—
'Nay, blame have I, myn uncle,' quod
    she thenne.   210

'What aileth you to be thus wery sone,
And naméliche of wommen ? Wol ye so !
Nay, sitteth down ! By God, I have to done
With you, to speke of wisdom, or ye go !'
And every wight that was about them tho,
That herdé that, gan fer awey to stonde,
Whil they two hadde al that hem liste on
    honde.

Whan that her tale al brought was to an ende
Of her estat and of her governaunce,   219
Quod Pandarus, 'Now is it time I wende !
But yit, I seye, arise and lat us daunce,
And cast your widwes habit to mischaunce !
What list you thus your-self to disfigúre,
Sith you is tid so glad an aventúre ?'—

'A ! wel bithought ! For love of God,'
    quod she,
'Shal I not witen what ye mene of this ?'—
'No, this thing axeth leiser,' tho quod he,
'And ek me woldé muché greve, y-wis,
If I it tolde and ye it toke amis.
Yit were it bet my tongé for to stille   230
Than seye a soth that were a yeins your wille.

'For, necé, by the Goddessé Minerve,
And Jupiter that mak'th the thonder ringe,
And by the blisful Venus that I serve,
Ye ben the woman in this world livínge,
Withouten paramours, to my witínge,

That I best love and lothest am to greve :
And that ye witen wel your-self, I leve.'

'Y-wis, myn uncle,' quod she, 'graunt
    mercy !
Your frendship have I founden everé yit :
I am to no man holden trewély   241
So muche as you, and have so litel quit :
And with the grace of God, emforth my wit,
As in my gilt I shal you nevere offende :
And if I have or this, I wol amende !

'But, for the love of God, I you biseche,
As ye ben he that I most love and triste,
Lat be to me your fremdé maner speche,
And sey to me your necé what you liste.'—
And with that word her uncle anon her kiste,
And seydé, 'Gladly, levé necé dere !   251
Tak it for gode that I shal seye you
    here !'—

With that she gan her ÿen down to caste ;
And Pandarus to coughé gan a lite,
And seydé, 'Nece, alwey, lo ! to the laste,
How-so it be that some men hem delite
With subtil art hir talés for t' endite,
Yit for al that, in hir entencioun,
Hir tale is al for som conclusioun.

'And sithen th'ende is every talés strengthe,
And this matére is so bihovély,   261
What sholde I peynte or drawén it on
    lengthe
To you that ben my frend so feithfully ?'—
And with that word he gan right inwardly
Biholden her and loken on her face,
And seyde, 'On swich a mirour godé
    grace !'—

Than thoughte he thus : 'If I my tale endite
Aught harde, or make a proces any while,
She shal no savour han therin but lite,
And trowe I wolde her in my wil bigile :
For tendré wittés wenen al be wile   271

209. *I wol,* G Cx. H₂ D *he wolde.*
215. *tho,* so a J etc. ; others *to, too, two.*
217. *al that hem liste,* J *al this matere.*
217. *on honde,* γ *in honde.*
220. *is it time,* so H₂ G H₃ ; S₁ *time is that* ;
J γ *is time.* J D *io* (for *I*).
221. *I seye, arise,* J *ariseth, I seye.* J γ⁵ omit *and.*
224. *so glad,* so a β : γ *thus faire.*
226. *not,* aᵇ *now.*

239. *myn,* H₂ γ omit.
248. *fremde,* so A D only ; J *friende* ; others var. *frende, frendly,* etc.
252. *for gode,* so G H₃ etc. ; J etc. *for good.*
253. *ÿen down to,* J R H₂ *look down for to.*
257. *for t' endite,* a etc. *to endite.*

Wher-as they can not pleynlich under-
    stonde :
For-thy her wit to serven wol I fonde.'—

And lokèd on her in a bisy wise ;
And she was war that he biheld her so,
And seydè, ' Lord ! so fastè ye m' avise !
Say ye me nevere or now ?   What sey ye ?
    No ? '—
' Yis, yis ! ' quod he, ' and bet wol, or I go !
But, by my trouthe, I thoughtè now if ye
Be fortunat, for now men shal it see.   280

' For t' every wight som goodly áventure
Som time is shape, if he it can receiven ;
And if that he wol take of it no cure
Whan that it com'th, but wilfulliche it
    weiven,
Lo, neither cas ne fortune him deceiven,
But right his ownè slouthe and wrecched-
    nesse :
And swich a wight is for to blame, I gesse !

' Good áventure, O belè nece, have ye
Ful lightly founden, and ye conne it take !
And, for the love of God and ek of me,
Cache it anon, lest áventurè slake !   291
What sholde I lenger proces of it make ?
Yif me your hond ; for in this world is non,
If that you list, a wight so wel bi-gon.

' And sith I speke of good intencioun,
As I to you have told wel her-biforn,
And love as wel your honour and renoun
As crèature in al this world y-born,
By alle the oothès that I have you sworn,
And ye be wroth therfóre, or wene I lye,
Ne shal I neverè see you eft with ỳe !   301

' Beth not agast, ne quaketh not !   Wher-
    to ?
Ne chaungeth naught for ferè so your hewe!
For hardily the werste of this is do ;
And though my tale as now be to you newe,
Yit trist alwey ye shal me findè trewe ;
And were it thing that me thoughte
    únsittínge,
To you wolde I no swichè talès bringe.'—

286. *owne*, γ *verray.*
292. *of it*, a² H₄ Cx. H₃ *to you* ; R om.

' Now, my goode em, for Goddès love I
    preye,'   309
Quod she, ' Com off, and tel me what it is !
For bothe I am agast what ye wol seye,
And ek me longeth it to wite, y-wis ;
For whether it be wel or be amis,
Sey on !   Lat me not in this ferè dwelle !'—
' So wil I don: now herkneth ! I shal telle !

' Now, necè myn, the kingès derè sone,
The goodè, wisè, worthy, fresshe, and free,
Which alwey for to do wel is his wone,
The noble Troilus, so loveth thee,   319
That, but ye helpe, it wil his banè be.
Lo, here is al !   What sholde I morè seye ?
Do what you list, to make him live or deye !

' But if ye lete him deyen, I wil sterve :
Have here my trouthè, nece, I n'il not lyen,
Al sholde I with this knif my throtè
    kerven !'—
With that the terès braste out of his ỳen,
And seyde,—' If that ye don us bothè dyen
Thus giltéles, than have ye fisshèd faire !
What mendè ye, though that we bothe a-
    paire ?   329

' Allas ! he which that is my lord so dere,
That trewè man, that noble gentil knight,
That naught desireth but your frendly
    chere,
I see him deyèn, ther he go'th up right
And hasteth him with al his fullè might
For to be slayn, if his fortúne assente.
Allas, that God you swich a beauté sente !

' If it be so that ye so cruel be   337
That of his deth you listè not to recche,
(That is so trewe and worthy as we see),
No more than of a japer or a wrecche,—
If ye be swich, your beauté may not strecche
To make amendes of so crúel a dede !
Avisèment is good bifore the nede !

309. *my,* γ⁸ omits.
329. *though,* J H₁ *if.*
331. *gentil,* a⁶ *worthy* ; Cx. omits.
335. *his fortúne,* G H₃ Cl. *fortune wolde*) ;
H₅ *his fortune wolle.*
338. *you,* J and others *ye.*
339. *we,* so a β ; G γ *ye.*
342. *a,* R H₃ omit.

'Wo worth the fairé gemmé vertules !
Wo worth that herbe also that doth no bote !
Wo worth that beauté that is routhéles !
Wo worth that wight that tret ech under-
    fote !
And ye that ben of beauté crop and rote,
If therwithal in you ther be no routhe,   349
Than is it harm ye liven by my trouthe !

'And also thenk wel that it is no gaude ;
For me were leveré thou and I and he
Were hangéd, than I sholdé be his baude,
As hye, as men mighte on us allé see !
I am thyn em : the shamé were to me
As wel as thee, if that I sholde assente
Thorugh myn abet, that he thyn honour
    shente.

'Now understond, for I you naught requere
To bindé you to him thorugh no biheste,
But only that ye make him bettré chere
Than ye han don or this, and moré feste,
So that his lif be savéd at the leste :   362
This' al and som, and pleynly our entente :
God help me so, I neveré other mente.

'Lo, this requeste is not but skile y-wis ;
Ne doute of reson, pardé, is ther non.
I sette the wersté : that ye dredé this,
Men woldé wondren sen him come and gon ;
And ther-ayeins answére I thus anon,   369
That every wight, but he be fool of kinde,
Wol deme it love of frendship in his minde.

'What ! Who wil demen, though he see a
    man
To temple go, that he th' imágés eteth ?
Thenk ek how wel and wisly that he can
Govérne him-self, that he no thing
    forgeteth,
That wher he com'th he pris and thank
    him geteth ;
And ek therto, he shal come here so selde,
What fors were it, though al the town
    behelde ?

'Swich love of frendés regn'th in al this
    toun ;
And wrye you in that mantel everé mo !
And, God so wis be my savacioun,   381
As I have seyd, your best is to do so.
But, goodé nece, alwey to stinte his wo,
So lat your daunger sucred ben a lite,
That of his deth ye be not for to wite.'—

Criseydé, which that herde him in this wise,
Thoughte, 'I shal felen what he mene,
    y-wis !'—
'Now, em,' quod she, 'what woldé ye
    devise ?
What is your reed I sholdé don of this ?'—
'That is wel seyd !' quod he, 'Certein
    best is,   390
That ye him love ayein for his lovínge,
As love for love is skilful guerdonínge.

'Thenk ek how eldé wasteth every houre
In ech of you a party of beauté ;
And therfor, or that agé thee devoure,
Go love, for, old, ther wil no wight of thee !
Lat this provérbe a lore unto you be :
Too late y-war ! quod Beauté, whan it
    paste :
And Eldé daunteth Daunger at the laste !

'The kingés fool is wont to cryén loude,
Whan that him think'th a womman ber'th
    her hye,   401
"So longé mote ye live, and allé proude,
Til crowés feet be growe under your ýe,
And sende you thanne a mirour in to prye,
In which that ye may see your face a-
    morwe !"
I biddé wisshé you no moré sorwe !'—

With this he stinte, and caste adoun the hed ;
And she began to breste a-wepe anon,

349. *If,* J Cl. *And.*
349. *ther,* J G *ne ;* a Cx. Cp. omit.
351. *that it is,* so J H₂ G H₅ S ; H₁ *that is ;*
rest (*that*) *this is.*
369. *And,* R only ; rest omit.

379. *in,* so P H₂ R Cx. S₁ ; G *thour ;* J etc.
omit. (See *C.T.* B 776.)
380. *wrye,* a² *covere ;* γ *wire.*
383. *goode nece, alwey,* γ³ *alwey, good(e) nece.*
384. *So,* a³ omit.
385. *not for to,* a² *nothing to ;* Cx. H₁ Cl.
no(ugh)t to.
387. *he,* H₄ G H₃ Cx. *ye.*
403. *he growe,* so J R γ ; a β *be waxe.*
406. *I,* γ³ *Nece, I.*

And seyde, ' Allas, for wo !   Why n'ere
    I ded ?   409
For of this world the feith is al a-gon !
Allas ! What sholden straungé to me don,
Whan he that for my besté frend I wende,
Ret me to love, and sholde it me defende ?

' Allas ! I wolde han trusted, doutéles,
That if that I thorugh my disáventure
Had lovéd outher him or Achillés,
Ector, or any mannés créatúre,
Ye n'olde han had no mercy ne mesure
On me, but alwey had me in repreve !   419
This falsé world, allas, who may it leve ?

' What ! Is this al the joye and al the feste?
Is this your red ?   Is this my blisful cas ?
Is this the verray mede of your biheste ?
Is al this peynted proces seyd, allas,
Right for this fyn ?   O Lady myn, Pallas,
Thou in this dredful cas for me purveye,
For so astonéd am I that I deye !'

With that she gan ful sorwfully to sike.—
' A ! may it be no bet?' quod Pandarus ;
' By God I shal no more come here this
    wike,
And God to-forn, that am mistrusted thus !
I see wel that ye setté lite of us,   432
Or of our deth !   Allas, I woful wrecche !
Mighte he yit live, of me were naught to
    recche !

' O cruel God, O díspitousé Marte !
O Furies three of helle, on you I crye !
So lat me nevere out of this hous departe,
If that I menté harm or vilanye !
But sith I see my lord mot nedés dye,
And I with him, here I me shrive, and seye
That wikkedly ye don us bothé deye !   441

' But sith it liketh you that I be ded,
By Neptunus, that God is of the see,
Fro this forth shal I neveré eté bred
Til I myn owné herté blood may see !
For certein I wol deye as sone as he.'—
And up he sterte, and on his wey he raughte,
Til she agayn him by the lappé caughte.

432. *wel*, γ^β *ful wel.*
434. *were*, so J H₄ R Cx. H₃ ; others *is.*

Criseydé, which that wel nigh starf for fere,
So as she was the ferfullesté wight   450
That mighté be, and herde ek with her ere
And saw the sorwful ernest of the knight,
And in his prayér ek saw non unright,
And for the harm that mighte ek fallé more,
She gan to rewe and drede her wonder sore,

And thoughté thus : ' Unhappés fallen
    thikke
Alday for love, and in swich maner cas
As men ben cruel in hemself and wikke ;
And if this man slee here himself, allas,
In my presénce, it n'il be no solás !   460
What men wolde of it deme I cannot seye :
It nedeth me ful sleighly for to pleye !'—

And with a sorwful sik she seydé thrye,
' A ! Lord ! What me is tid a sory chance !
For myn estat li'th in a jupartye,
And ek myn emés lif is in baláunce !
But nathéles with Goddés governaunce
I shal so don, myn honour shal I kepe,
And ek his lif !'—and stinté for to wepe.

' Of harmés two the lesse is for to chese :
Yit have I leveré maken him good chere
In honour, than myn emés lif to lese !   472
Ye seyn, ye nothing ellés me requere ?'—
' No, wis,' quod he, ' myn owné necé
        dere !'—
' Now wel !' quod she, ' and I wol do
    my peyne !
I shal myn herte ayein my lust constreyne,

' But that I n'il not holden him in honde ;
Ne love a man ne can I naught, ne may
Ayeins my wil ; but ellés wil I fonde,   479
Myn honour sauf, plese him fro day to day.
Ther-to n'olde I not onés have seyd nay,
But-that I drede as in my fantasye ;
But, cessé cause, ay cesseth maladye !

454. *harm that mighte ek, α³ J harm ek that might.*
457. *and*, α³ R Cx. omit.
460. *nil*, so α³ J ; others *wil, wol.*
465. *lith in a*, so H₂ H₄ H₃ R ; *lith in*, J P
G H₅ Cx. ; γ *lith now in* (Cl. *now lith in*).
467. *Goddes*, H₂ H₄ H₃ H₅ D *gode (good).*
478, 479. α^b read : *Ne love no (a) man, that can
no wight ne may Ayeins his wil.*
482. *drede*, Cp. *dredde.*

'But here I make a protestacioun,
That in this proces if ye depper go,
That certeinly for no savacioun
Of you, though that ye sterven bothe two,
Though al the world on oo day be my fo,
Ne shal I nevere of him han other routhe!'
'I granté wel,' quod Pandar, 'by my
    trouthe!   490

'But may I trusté wel to you,' quod he,
'That of this thing that ye han hight me here
Ye wol it holden trewély to me?'—
'Ye, doutéles,' quod she, 'myn unclé
    dere!'—
'Ne that I shal han cause in this matére,'
Quod he, 'to pleyne, or ofter you to preche?'
'Why, no, pardé! What nedeth moré
    speche?'

Tho fillen they in othré talés glade,
Til at the laste, 'O goode em,' quod she tho,
'For love of God which that us bothé
    made,
Tel me how first ye wisten of his wo!   501
Wot non of it but ye?'—He seydé,
    'No!'—
'Can he wel speke of love?' quod she;
    'I preye,
Tel me; for I the bet me shal purveye.'—

Tho Pandarus a litel gan to smile,
And seydé, 'By my trouthe I shal you telle!
This other day, not gon ful longé while,
With-in the paleis gardin, by a welle,
Gan he and I wel half a day to dwelle,
Right for to speken of an ordinaunce   510
How we the Grekés mighten disavaunce.

Sone after that bigonné we to lepe,
And casten with our dartés to and fro,
Til at the laste he seyde he woldé slepe;
And on the gres a-doun he leyde him tho;
And I afer gan romen to and fro,

Til that I herde, as that I welk allone,
How he bigan ful wofully to grone.

'Tho gan I stalke him softély behinde;
And, sikerly the sothé for to seyne   520
As I can clepe ayein now to my minde,
Right thus to Love he gan him for to
    pleyne:
He seydé, "Lord, have routhe upon my
    peyne!
Al have I ben rebél in myn entente,
Now, mea culpa, Lord, I me repente!

'"O God, that at thy disposicioun
Ledest the fyn, by justé púrveyaunce,
Of every wight, my lowe confessioun   528
Accepte in gré, and send me swich penaunce
As liketh thee; but from desésperaunce,
That may my gost departe awey fro thee,
Thou be my sheld, for thy benignété!

'"For certés, Lord, so sore hath she me
    wounded,
That stood in blak, with loking of her ÿen,
That to myn hertés botme it is y-sounded,
Thorugh which I wot that I mot nedés dyen.
This is the worste: I dar me not biwryen;
And wel the hotter ben the gledés rede,
That men hem wryen with asshen pale and
    dede."   539

'With that he smot his hed a-doun anon,
And gan to muttre, I n'ot what trewély;
And I with that gan stille awey to gon,
And leet ther-of as no-thing wist had I,
And com ayein a-non, and stood him by,
And seyde, "Awak, ye slepen al too longe!
It semeth not that Lové doth you longe,

'"That slepen so that no man may you
    wake!
Who say everé or this so dul a man?"
"Ye, frend," quod he, "do ye your hedés
    ake

491. *to you*, γ⁸ *ther-to*.
493. *to*, so P H₉ H₅; others *unto*.
500. *love of God*, H₄ *the love*; H₅ Cx. γ⁸ *his love*.
504. *me shal*, a³ etc. *shal me*.
508. *With-in*, γ⁸ *In-with*.
516. *I afer*, so J R only; P H₂ *yn a fere* (!); H₄ G H₅ etc. *after*; γ⁸ *ther-after*.

521. *now*, so J H₄ etc.; a⁴ R Cx. A omit.
523. *routhe upon*, J R Cl. *routhe on*; H₄ G H₅ *mercy on* (*of*).
539. *wryen*; J H₁ *wrren*.
548. *evere or this*, G *or this evere* (*read ? evere sey or*).

For love, and lat me liven as I can !" 550
But though that he for wo was pale and wan,
Yit made he tho as fressh a countenaunce
As though he sholde have led the newé
    daunce !

' This passéd forth, til now this other day
It fil that I com roming al allone
Into his chaumbre, and fond how that he
    lay
Upon his bed.   But man so soré grone
Ne herde I nevere.   And what that was
    his mone
Ne wiste I not ; for, as I was comínge,
Al sodeynly he left his cómpleynínge ; 560

' Of which I took som-what suspecioun ;
And ner I com and fond he wepté sore ;
And, God so wis be my savacioun,
As nevere of thing hadde I no routhé more ;
For neither with engíne ne with no lore
Unnethés mighte I fro the deth him kepe,
That yit fele I myn herté for him wepe.

' And God wot, neveré sith that I was born
Was I so besy no man for to preche, 569
Ne neveré was to wight so depe y-sworn,
Or he me tolde who mighté ben his leche !
But now to you rehersen al his speche,
Or alle his woful wordés for to soune,
Ne bid me naught, but ye wol see me
    swoune !

' But for to save his lif, and ellés nought,
And to non harm of you, thus am I driven.
And for the love of God that us hath
    wrought,
Swich chere him doth, that he and I may
    liven !
Now have I plat to you myn herté shriven ;
And sith ye wot that myn entente is clene,
Tak hede ther-of, for I non yvel mene. 581

' And right good thrift, I preye to God,
    have ye,
That have swich oon y-caught withouté net !
And, be ye wis as ye be fair to see,

Wel in the ring than is the ruby set !
Ther weré neveré two so wel y-met !
When ye ben his al hool as he is youre,
Ther mighty God yit graunte us see that
    houre !'—   588

' Nay, therof spak I not, aha !' quod she,
' As help me God, ye shenden every del !'
' A ! mercy, deré nece !' anon quod he,
' What-so I spak, I menté not but wel,
By Mars, the God that helméd is of stel !
Now beth not wroth, my blood, my necé
    dere !'
' Now wel !' quod she, ' foryeven be it
    here !'

With this he took his leve and hom he
    wente ;
And, Lord, so he was glad and wel bigon !
Criseyde aros, no lenger she ne stente,
But streight into her closet wente anon, 599
And sette her doun as stille as any ston,
And every word gan up and doun to winde
That he had seyd, as it com her to minde ;

And was somdel astonéd in her thought
Right for the newé cas.   But whan that she
Was ful aviséd, tho fond she right nought
Of peril, why she oughte aferéd be ;
For man may love, of possibilité,
A womman, so his herté may to-breste,
And she not love ayein, but-if her leste.

But as she sat allone and thoughté thus,
Ascry aros at scarmuch al withoute, 611
And men cri'de in the strete, ' See, Troilus
Hath right now put to flight the Grekés
    route !'
With that gan al her meyné for to shoute,
' A ! Go we see ! Caste up the latis wide !
For thorugh this strete he mot to paleys ride ;

588. *yit graunte us see*, so G H₅ R, etc. ; J Cp.
graunte us see ; a² us graunte to see.
591. *A, γ⁸ O.*
597. *And, a⁴ Ye ; R Cx. H₃ A.*
597. *so, a² γ⁶ omit ; G H₅ how.*
603. *was, a⁵ wex.*
606. *aferéd be, a R Cx. aferd to be.*
611. *Ascry, H₄ G Th' ascry.*
615. *latis*, so H₂ only ; P H₄ G Cx. *satis* ; J etc.
yates.

551. *wo,* J G *love.*
568. *nevere sith that,* J R *that nevere sith.*
579. *shriven,* J P *I-shriven.*

' For other wey is fro the yaté non
Of Dardanus, ther open is the cheyne ! '
With that com he and al his folk anon
An esy pas, riding in routés tweyne,   620
Right as his happy day was, soth to seyne,
For-which, men seith, may not distorbéd be
That shal bitiden of necessité.

This Troilus sat on his bayé stede,
Al arméd save his hed ful richély ;
And wounded was his hors, and gan to
    blede,
On which he rod a pas ful softély.
But swich a knightly sighté trewély
As was on him, was not withouten faile
To loke on Mars, that God is of bataile !

So lik a man of armés and a knight   631
He was to sen, fulfil'd of heigh prowesse ;
For bothe he hadde a body and a might
To don that thing, as well as hardinesse ;
And ek to sen him in his gere him dresse,
So fressh, so yong, so weldy seméd he,
It was an hevene upon him for to see !

His helm to-hewén was in twenty places,
That by a tissu heng his bak bihinde ;
His sheld to-dasshéd was with swerdes and
    maces,   640
In which men mighté many an arwé finde
That thirléd haddé horn and nerf and rinde ;
And ay the peplé cri'de, ' Here com'th
    our joye !
And next his brother, holder up of Troye ! '

For which he wex a litel red for shame,
Whan he the peple upon him herdé cryen,
That to beholde it was a noblé game,
How sobreliche he casté doun his yen.
Criseyde anon gan al his chere aspyen,
And let so softe it in her herté sinke   650
That to her-self she seyde, ' Who yaf me
    drinke ? '

For of her owné thought she wex al red.
Remembring her right thus, ' Lo, this is he
Which that myn unclé swer'th he mot be
    ded
But I on him have mercy and pité ' ;
And with that puré thought for-shaméd, she
Gan in her hed to pulle, and that as faste,
Whil he and al the peplé for-by paste ;

And gan to caste and rollen up and doun
Within her thought his excellent prowésse,
And his estat, and also his renoun,   661
His wit, his shap, and ek his gentilesse ;
But most her favour was, for his distresse
Was al for her, and thoughte it was a routhe
To slen swich oon, if that he menté trouthe.

Now mighté som envíous jangle thus :
' This was a sodein love !   How mighte
    it be,
That she so lightly lovéd Troilus
Right for the firsté sighté ? '—Ye, pardé !
Now, who-so seith so, mote he neveré thé !
For every thing a ginning hath it nede   671
Or al be wrought, withouten any drede.

For I seye not that she so sodeinly
Yaf him her love, but that she gan encline
To like him first ; and I have told you
    why ;
And after that, his manhod and his pine
Made love within her herté for to mine :
For-which by proces and by good servise
He gat her love, and in no sodein wise.

And also blisful Venus, wel arrayed,   680
Sat in her seventhé hous of hevené tho,
Disposéd wel, and with aspéctés payed,
To helpen sely Troilus of his wo ;
And, soth to seyn, she n'as not al a fo
To Troilus in his nativité :
God wot that wel the soner speddé he !

617. *is,* J Cl. *is ther. fro,* γ *to.*
636. *weldy, so* a γ ; β *worthy.*
640. *swerdes,* a² H₂ *swerd.*
642. *horn and,* a² *bothe.*
646. *he the peple,* etc., a⁵ *he so herde the peple*
on him cryen.
648. *down,* a⁵ R *adoun.*
649. *Criseyde anon, so* a² R ; rest *Criseyde,*
Criseyda.
650. *it,* J H₄ Ad. Cp. omit.

656. (?) MSS. var. ; a² *And for that thought*
puré ashamyd she ; G J etc. γ *And with that*
thought (J *word) for puré* (a)*shaméd she.*
670. *seith,* J H₂ *seyde.*
670. *mote he nevere,* a⁵ *nevere mote he.*
671. *a,* G R *of.*
677. *within,* R Cx. *in.*
677. *herte, so* a² Cx. H₃ S₂ Dg. ; R *inwardly* ;
rest omit.
679. *gat,* a⁵ *was.*

Now lat us stinte of Troilus a throwe,
That rideth forth ; and let us tornè faste
Unto Criseyde, that heng her hed ful lowe,
Ther-as she sat allone, and gan to caste 690
Wher-on she wolde apoynte her at the laste,
If it so were her em ne woldè cesse
For Troilus upon her for to presse.

And, Lord ! so she gan in her herte arguwe
In this matére of which I have you told ;
And what to don best were, and what
      t' eschuwe,
That plited she ful ofte in many fold :
Now was her hertè warm, now was it cold ;
And what she thoughtè som-what shal I
      write,
As to myn auctour listeth for t' endite. 700

She thoughtè first that Troilus' persóne
She knew by sighte, and ek his gentilesse ;
And also thoughte, ' It werè not to done
To graunte him love ; yit for his worthi-
      nesse
It were honóur, with pley and with
      gladnésse,
In honesté with swich a lord to dele,
For myn estat, and also for his hele.

' Ek wel wot I my kingès sone is he,
And sith he hath to see me swich delit,
If I wolde outrèliche his sightè flee, 710
Paraunter he mighte have me in despit,
Thorugh which I mightè stonde in worsè
      plit :
Now were I wis, me hatè to purchace
Withoutè nede, ther I may stonde in grace ?

' In every thing I wot ther li'th mesúre :
For though a man forbedè dronkenesse,
He naught forbet, that every crèature
Be drinkèles for alwey, as I gesse ;
Ek sith I wot for me is his distresse,

I oughtè not for that thing him despise,
If it be so, he men'th in goodè wise. 721

' And ek I knowe, of longè time agon,
His thewès goode, and that he is not nice.
N'avauntour, seith men, certeyn, he is
      non ;
Too wis is he to don so gret a vice ;
Ne als I n'il him neverè so cheríce
That he may make avaunt by justè cause ;
He shal me neverè binde in swich a clause.

' Now sette a cas, the hardest is, y-wis :
Men mighten demen that he loveth me.
What dishonour to myn estat is this ? 731
May ich him lette of that ? Why nay,
      pardé !
I knowe also, and alday here and see,
Men loven wommen al biside hir leve ;
And whan hem list no morè, lat hem leve !

' Ek wot I wel he worthy is to have
Of wommen in this world the thriftieste,
As ferforth as she may her honour save ;
For out and out he is the worthieste, 739
Save only Ector, which that is the beste ;
And yit his lif li'th al now in my cure !
But swich is love, and ek myn áventure !

' Ne me to love, a wonder is it nought ;
For wel wot I myself, so God me spede,
Al wolde I that no man wiste of my
      thought,
I am oon of the fairest out of drede
And goodliestè, who-so taketh hede ;

694. *And,* J H₄ A.
694. *so,* H₄ G *how.*
694. *herte,* so a² J R H₃ S₂ Dg. ; rest *thought.*
696. *t'eschuwe,* so a⁴ Cx. S₂ Dg. ; rest *eschewe.*
697. *many,* G H₃ R Cx. H₂ S *many a.*
701. *first,* so a³ J R ; G H₅ *ek this;* Cx. H₃ γ⁸ *wel.*
703. *And also thoughte,* etc., so H₄ J R ; a⁴ *And seyde thus, ' Al were it not,* etc. ; Cx. H₃ β *And thus she seyde, ' Al were it not,* etc.

720. *oughte,* so J H₂ H₄ R ; rest *n'oughte.*
721. *If it be,* so J H₄ R ; rest *Sith it is.*
726. *als,* J G H₅ *also.*
734, 735. *al biside,* etc. a⁴ (and Ad. altered) *al this toun aboute Be they the wers ! Why nay, withouten doute !* (Boc.)
735. *love,* so J H₄ H₃ R Cx. ; γ *bileve.* (See l. 686.)
736, 737. *Ek wot I,* etc., so J H₄ R ; rest *I thenke ek how he able is for to have, Of al this noble toun the thriftieste* (γ⁸ insert *ilke* before *noble*).
738. *As ferforth as she may,* so J H₄ R ; a⁴ *That womman is, so she;* Cx. H₃ γ³ *To ben his love, so she.*
741. *li'th al now,* so J ; MSS. var. order.
745. *no man,* γ⁷ *noon.*
746. *of,* a² Cx. H₃ γ⁴ omit (read *? That I am oon the fairest*).
746. *out of,* a³ Cx. *withouten.*

And so men seyn in al the town of Troye.
What wonder is, though he of me have
    joye?

'I am myn ownė womman, wel at ese,
I thanke it God, as after myn estat,   751
Right yong, and stonde untey'd in lusty lese,
Withouten jalousye or swich debat :
Shal non housbóndė seyn to me "Chek-
    mat!"
For either they ben ful of jalousye,
Or maisterful, or loven novelrye.

'What shal I don? To what fyn live I
    thus ?
Shal I not love, in cas if that me leste ?
What, pardé ! I am not religious !
And though that I myn hertė sette at reste
Upon this knight that is the worthieste, 761
And kepe alwey myn honour and my name,
By allė right it may do me no shame !'

But right as whan the sonnė shineth brighte
In March that chaungeth oftė time his face,
And that a cloude is put with wind to flighte,
Which oversprat the sonne as for a space,
A cloudy thought gan thorugh her soulė
    pace,
That overspradde her brightė thoughtės
    alle,
So that for fere almóst she gan to falle.

That thought was this : 'Allas ! sith I am
    free,   771
Sholde I now love, and putte in jupartye
My sikernesse, and thrallen liberté ?
Allas ! how dorste I thenken that folýe ?
May I not wel in other folk aspye
Hir dredful joye, hir cónstreynt, and hir
    peyne ?
Ther loveth non that she n'ath why to
    pleyne !

'For love is yit the mostė stormy lif,
Right of himself, that everė was bigonne ;
For everė som mistrust or nicė strif   780
Ther is in love, som cloude is over that
    sonne ;
Therto we wrecched wommen nothing
    conne
Whan us is wo, but wepe, and sitte and
    thinke :
Our wreche is this, our ownė wo to drinke.

'Also these wikked tongės ben so prest
To speke us harm, ek men ben so untrewe,
That, right anon as cessėd is hir lest,
So cesseth love, and forth to love a-newe !
But harm y-don is don, who-so it rewe !
For though these men for love hem first to-
    rende,   790
Ful sharp biginning breketh ofte at ende.

'How oftė time hath it y-knowėn be,
The tresoun that to wommen hath be do !
To what fyn is swich love, I can not see,
Or wher becom'th it whan it is a-go ;
Ther is no wight that wot, I trowė so,
Wher it becom'th : lo, no wight on it
    sporneth :
That erst was no thing, into nought it
    torneth.

'How bisy, if I love, ek mostė I be
To plesen hem that jangle of love and
    demen,   800
And coye hem, that they seyn non harm of
    me ;
For, though ther be no causė, yit hem semen
Al be for harm that folk hir frendės quemen ;
And who may stoppen every wikked tonge,
Or soun of bellės whil that they be ronge ?'

And after that her thought began to clere,
And seyde, 'He which that nothing under-
    taketh,
Nothing acheveth, be him loth or dere.'

749. *is*, so J etc. : a³ etc. *is it* ; G *ist.*
751. *after*, J R *of* ; Cx. *for.*
758. *if*, J *be* ; a³ omit.
759. *pardė*, J γ *pardieux.*
759. *not*, H₃ Cx. *no.*
761. *Upon this knight*, J *unwist of him.*
768. *soule*, so J G γ ; a³ R Cx. H₃ *herte.*
775. *in*, J *by.*
777. *why*, so G Ad. only ; J *wer* (!) ; rest *wey.*
(*Wey*, meaning *wer*, may be the correct reading.)

781. *that*, G Cx. *the.*
783. *wepe and sitte*, a⁵ Cx. *sitte (and) wepe.*
784. *to*, G R H₂ *we.*
792. *hath it y-knowen be*, so Cx. H₃ γ ; a³ J R *may men rede and see.*
800. *demen*, so a ; J and others *dremen.*
801. *that*, γ omit.
808. *acheveth*, γ *n'acheveth.*

And with another thought her hertè
   quaketh ;
Than slepeth hope, and after drede
   awaketh ;   810
Now hot, now cold ; but thus betwixè tweye
She rist her up, and wente her for to pleye.

A-doun the stayre anon right tho she wente
Into the gardin, with her neces three ;
And up and doun they maden many a wente,
Flexippe and she, Tarbe and Antigone,
To pleyèn, that it joyè was to see ;
And other of her wommen, a gret route,
Her folwed in the gardin al aboute.

This yerd was large, and railèd alle th'
   aléyes,   820
And shad wed wel with blosmy bowès grene ;
Y-benchèd newe, and sonded alle the weyes,
In which she walketh arm in arm bitwene ;
Til at the laste Antigonè the shene
Gan on a Trojan lay to singen clere,
That it an hevenè was her vois to here.

She seyde, 'O Love, to whom I have and
   shal
Ben humblè subgit, trewe in myn entente
As I best can, to you, Lord, give ich al
For everè mo myn hertès lust to rente !   830
For neverè yit thy gracè no wight sente
So blisful cause as me, my lif to lede
In allè joye and seurté, out of drede.

'Ye, blisful God, han me so wel biset
In love, y-wis, that al that bereth lif
Imaginen ne coude how to be bet ;
For, Lord, withouten jalousye or strif,
I lovè oon which is most éntentif

To serven wel, unwery or unfeyned,
That everè was, and leest with harm disteyned.   840

'As he that is the welle of worthinesse,
Of trouthè ground, mirour of goodlihed,
Of wit Apollo, ston of sikernesse,
Of vertu rote, of lust findére and hed,
Thorugh which is allè sorwe fro'me ded,—
Y-wis, I love him best, so doth he me :
Now good thrift have he, wher-so that
   he be !

'Whom sholde I thanken but you, God
   of Love,
Of al this blisse, in which to bathe I ginne ?
And thankèd be ye, Lord, for that I love !
This is the rightè lif that I am inne,   851
To flemen allè maner vice and sinne !
This doth me so to vertu for t' entende,
That day by day I in my wil amende.

'And who-so seith that for to love is vice,
Or thraldom, though he fele in it distresse,
He outher is envious or right nice,
Or is unmighty, for his shrewèdnesse,
To love.   Lo, swichè maner folk, I gesse,
Defamen Love, as nothing of him knowe :
They speken, but they benten nevere his
   bowe !   861

'What ! Is the sonnè wers of kindè right,
Though that a man, for feblesse of his
   yèn,
May not endure on it to see for bright ?
Or love the wers, though wrecches on it
   cryen ?
No wele is worth, that may no sorwè dryen ;
And for-thy, who that hath a hed of verre,
For cast of stonès war him in the werre !

'But I with al myn herte and al my might,
As I have seyd, wol love unto my laste   870
My derè herte, and al myn ownè knight ;
In which myn hertè growèn is so faste,

812. *wente her*, J G² *wente*.
813. *A-doun*, J H₄ R *And doun*.
814. *the*, J R *her*; a² *a*.
815. *they*, γ⁶ *ther*; H₃ *the*.
816. *and she*, γ⁶ *she*.
821. *blosmy*, H₄ Cx. H₃ *blosmed* (see *Rom. Rose*, 108).
822. *Y-benched*, P R H₅ γ⁶ *And benched*.
825. *lay*, so a⁵ J R ; Cx. H₃ γ¹ *song*.
834. *Ye*, J Cx. and others *The*.
834. *han*, J Cx. *hath*.
835. *al*, H₄ H₁ *alle*.
835. *bereth*, P H₄ R *beryn*.
837. *or*, J *and*.
838. *which is most*, so a² J H₅ Cx. D Cl. ; G R H₃ S S₂ *which that is most* ; H₄ A H₁ Cp *which that most is*.

840. *disteyned*, so G R Cp. and others ; J and others *distreyned*.
843. *sikernesse*. J H₄ Cx. S H₁ Cl. *secrenesse*.
850. *ye*, a² J G² *thou*.
859. *Lo*, so J H₁ R ; rest *For*.
868. *For*, so J H₄ R D ; others *Fro*.

And his in me, that it shal everè laste :
Al dredde I first to love him to biginne,
Now wot I wel ther is no peril inne !'

And of her song right with that word she
   stente ;
And therwithal, 'Now, necè,' quod
   Criseyde,
'Who made this song now with so good
   entente ?'
Antigonè answèrde anon and seyde,
'Madame, y-wis, the goodliestè mayde
Of gret estat in al the toun of Troye, 881
And let her lif in most honóur and joye.'

'For-sothè so it semeth by her song !'
Quod tho Criseyde, and gan ther-with to
   site,
And seydè, 'Lord, is ther such blisse among
These lovers, as they connè faire endite ?'
'Ye, wis !' quod fresshe Antigonè the white,
'For alle the folk that han or ben on-live
Ne connè wel the blisse of love discrive.

'But wenè ye that every wrecchè wot   890
The parfit blisse of lovè ? Nay, y-wis !
They wenen al be love, if oon be hot !
Do wey, do wey, they wot no thing of this !
Men mosten axe at seintès, if it is
Aught fair in hevenè, (why ? for they
   can telle !)
And axen fendes if it be foul in helle.'

Criseydè therto no-thing her answèrde,
But seyde, 'Y-wis, it wol be night as faste !'
But every word which that she of her herde,
She gan to prenten in her hertè faste ;   900
And ay gan love her lassè for t' agaste

Than it dide erst, and sinken in her herte,
That she wex somwhat able to converte.

The dayès honour, and the hevenès ÿe,
The nightès fo, (al this clepe I the sonne)
Gan westren faste, and dounward for to
   wrye,
As he that hadde his dayès cours y-ronne ;
And whitè thingès gan to waxen donne
For lak of light, and sterrès for t' apere,
That she and alle her folk in wente i-fere.

So whan it likèd her to gon to reste,   911
And voided werèn tho that voiden oughte,
She seydè that to slepen wel her leste :
Her women sone unto her bed her broughte.
Whan al was hust tho lay she stille and
   thoughte
Of al this thing ; the maner and the wise
Reherse it nedeth nought, for ye ben wise !

A nightingale upon a cedrè grene
Under the chambrè wal ther-as she lay,
Ful loudè song ayein the monè shene,   920
Paraunter, in his briddès wise, a lay
Of lovè which that made his hertè gay ;
Him herkned she so longe in good entente,
That at the laste the 'dedè slep her hente.

And as she slep, anon right tho her mette
How that an egle, fetherèd whit as bon,
Under her brest his longè clawès sette,
And out her hertè rente, and that anon,
And dide his herte into her brest to gon ;
Of which she nought agroos, ne no-thing
   smerte ;   930
And forth he fleigh, with hertè left for
   herte.

Now lat her slepe, and we our talès holde
Of Troilus, that is to paleis riden

874. *dredde*, J etc. *drede.*
878. *now with*, so J H₄ R H₃ γ (exc. Cl.); others *with.*
879. *answèrde anon*, J *anon answerde* ; G³ omit *anon.*
884. *site* (Ṭ), all *sike, syke.* (Skeat's emendation is here adopted, to avoid the assonant rhyme.)
891. *Nay*, so a β ; J γ *Why, nay.*
896. *axen*, J G² *axeth.*
896. *if it be*, so a β ; J H₃ γ *is it.*
897. *therto no-thing her*, so a β (var. order, J *nothing therto her*) ; Cx. H₃ γ *unto that purpos nought* (S *lyte*).
901. *love*, J P omit ; G *sche.*

908. *gan to waxen*, so a β ; Cx. H₃ γ *wexen dimme and.*
910. *in*, so J H₅ R H₃ γ ; a³ G Cx. *hom.*
912. *tho*, H₄ γ *they.*
914. *unto*, γ *til.*
922. *which that*, etc., so a β (a² *her* for *his*) ; Cx. H₃ γ *that made her herte fressh and gay.*
923. *Him*, so J H₄ R H₅ ; a³ *Her* ; others *That.*
924. *That*, a etc. *Til.*
928. *rente*, H₅ H₃ γ *he rente.*

Fro th' ilké scarmuch of the whiche I tolde,
And in his chambré sit and hath abiden,
Til two or three of his messáges yeden
For Pandarus, and soughten him so faste,
Til they him founde and broughte him at
    the laste.

This Pandarus com leping in at ones, 939
And seydé thus, 'Who hath ben wel y-bete
To-day, with swerdés and with slingé-
    stones,
But Troilus, that hath caught him an hete !'
And gan to jape, and seydé, 'Lord, ye
    swete !
But ris and lat us soupe and go to reste !'
And he answérdé, 'Do we as thee leste !'

With al the hasté goodly that they mighte,
They speddehem fro thesoper and to bedde ;
And every wight out at the dore him dighte,
And wher him liste upon his wey him
    spedde :
But Troilus, that thoughte his herté bledde
For wo, til that he herdé som tidínge, 951
He seydé, 'Frend, shal I now wepe or singe?'

Quod Pandarus, 'Be stille, and lat me slepe,
And don thy hood ; thy nedés speddé be !
And chees if thou wolt daunce, or singe,
    or lepe !
At shorté wordés, thou shalt trúste in me !
Siré, my necé wol don wel by thee
And love thee best, by God and by my
    trouthe, 958
But lak of púrsuit make it in thy slouthe !

'For thus ferforth have I thy werk bigonne
Fro day to day, til this day by the morwe
Her love of frendship have I to thee wonne,

934. *th' ilke* (?), all *the.*
937. *so*, γ *ful.*
943. *ye*, a² γ⁴ *so ye.*
945. *answérde*, H₃ γ⁷ *answerde him.*
947. *and to*, so J H₄ G² R Cx. H₃ ; a² *to her ;*
γ⁷ *unto.*
949. *him spedde*, γ³ *he spedde.*
950. *that*, γ⁸ omits.
953. *Be*, so J R Cx. H₃ ; rest *Ly.*
955. *daunce, or singe*, so J D a³ ; R *daunce, singe ;*
H₄ G² Cx. H₃ *singe, daunce ;* γ *singe or daunce.*
956. *truste in*, so J etc. ; a³ *trust to ;* γ *trowe.*
957. *Sire*, Cx. *And* (read ? *And sir*).
960. *have I*, J *I have I* (!) ; H₃ γ *I have.*

And therto hath she leyd her feith to borwe :
Algate a foot is hameled of thy sorwe !'—
What sholde I lenger sermoun of it holde ?
As ye han herd bifore, al he him tolde.

But right as flourés, thorugh the cold of night
Y-closéd, stouping on hir stalkés lowe,
Redressen hem ayein the sonné bright, 969
And spreden on hir kindé cours by rowe,
Right so gan tho his ÿen up to throwe
This Troilus, and seyde, 'O Venus dere,
Thy might, thy grace, y-heried be it here !

And to Pandáre he held up bothe his
    hondes,
And seydé, 'Lord, al thyn be that I have !
For I am hool : al brosten be my bondes !
A thousand Troyés who-so that me yave,
Ech after other, God so wis me save,
Ne mighté me so gladen ; lo, myn herte !
It spredeth so for joye, it wol to-sterte !

'But, Lord, how shal I don ?   How shal
    I liven ? 981
Whan shal I next my deré herté see ?
How shal this longé time awey be driven,
Til that thou be ayein at her fro me ?
Thou mayst answére, "Abid, abid !"
    But he
That hangeth by the nekké, soth to seyne,
In gret disese abideth for the peyne !'

'Al esily, now, for the love of Marte !'
Quod Pandarus, 'for every thing hath
    time : 989
So longe abid, til that the night departe,
For al so siker as thou li'st here by me,
And God to-forn, I wol be ther at prime ;
And for-thy, werk somwhat as I shal seye,
Or on som other wight this chargé leye !

'For, pardé, God wot, I have everé yit
Ben redy thee to serve ; and to this night

963. *therto*, γ⁶ *also.*
965. *lenger*, J R *long(e).*
967. *the*, J a² H₅ omit.
967. *of*, G H₅ omit ; D *on.*
968. *stouping*, so H₄ ; a² *stoupyn* ; J and others
stoupen.
977. *Troyes* (Boc.), γ⁴ *Troians.*
978. *so wis me*, J R *so my soule.*

Have I not feynéd, but emforth my wit
Don al thy lust, and shal with al my might
Do now as I shal seyn, and fare aright ;
And if thou n'ilt, wite al thy-self thy care !
On me is nought along thyn yvel fare ! 1001

' I wot wel that thou wiser art than I
A thousand fold ; but if I were as thou,
God help me so, as I wolde outrély
Right of myn owné hond write her right now
A lettre, in which I wolde her tellen how
I ferde amis, and her biseche of routhe :
Now help thy-self, and leve it not for
　　　slouthe !

' And I my-self shal therwith to her gon ;
And, whan thou wost that I am with her
　　　there, 1010
Worth thou upon a courser right anon,
Ye hardily, right in thy besté gere,
And rid forth by the place, as nought ne
　　　were ;
And thou shalt finde us, if I may, sittínge
At som windówe, into the strete lokínge.

' And, if thee list, than maystow us saluwe ;
And upon me mak thou thy countenaunce ;
But by thy lif be war that thou eschuwe
To tarien ought !　God shilde us fro mis-
　　　chaunce !
Rid forth thy wey, and hold thy govern-
　　　aunce ! 1020
And we shal speke of thee somwhat, I trowe,
Whan thou art gon, to don thine erés glowe !

' Touching thy lettré, thou art wis y-nough :
I wot thou n'ilt it dignéliche endite,
As make it with these argumentés tough :

Ne scrivenly ne craftily thou write ;
Beblotte it with thy terés ek a lite :
And if thou write a goodly word al softe,
Though it be good, reherce it not too ofte !

' For though the besté harpour upon live
Wolde on the besté sounéd joly harpe 1031
That everé was, with alle his fingres five,
Touche ay oo streng, or ay oo werblé harpe,
Al were his nailés pointed nevere so sharpe,
It sholdé maken every wight to dulle
To here his glee, and of his strokés fulle.

' Ne jompre ek no discordaunt thing i-fere,
As thus, to usen termés of phisik
In lovés termés : hold of thy matére 1039
The forme alwey, and do that it be lik :
For, if a peyntour woldé peynte a pik
With asses feet, and hede it as an ape,
It cordeth nought ; so n'ere it but a jape !'

This counseil likéd wel to Troilus ;
But as a dredful lover seyde he this :
' Allas ! my deré brother Pandarus,
I am ashaméd for to write, y-wis,
Lest of myn innocence I seyde a-mis,
Or that she n'olde it for despit receyve :
Than were I ded, ther mighte it nothing
　　　weyve !' 1050

To that Pandáre answérdé, ' Yif thee lest.
Do that I seye, and lat me therwith gon :
For, by that Lord that forméd est and west,
I hope of it to bringe answére anon
Right of her hond !　And if that thou
　　　n'ilt non,
Lat ben !　And sory mote he ben his live,
A yeins thy lust that helpeth thee to thrive !'

Quod Troilus, ' Depardieux, I assente !
Sith that thee list, I wol arise and write '

1005. *Right of,* J γ⁶ *Of.*
1005. *right now,* a⁵ Cx. *now.*
1008. *not for slouthe,* a² R Cx. H₃ *for no slouthe.*
1009. *shal,* γ⁶ *wol.*
1010. *that,* so H₅ R Cx. γ⁶ ; rest omit.
1011. *Worth thou,* so a² γ⁶ ; H₃ *Lepe thou ;* rest *Worth(e).*
1017. *mak thou,* so H₄ H₅ γ⁶ ; H₂ R *thou make ;* rest *make.*
1018. *that thou,* Cx. H₃ γ⁶ *and faste.*
1024. *digneliche,* so a² H₃ γ ; J *clerkissly ;* Cx. *clerkly ;* H₄ *clergaly ;* R *papally ;* G² *digneliche ne mystiliche* (read ? *deynousliche*).
1025. *As,* a⁵ *Or ;* H₄ *Ne ;* G *As to.*

1026. *scrivenly,* so H₅ R Cx. ; J H₄ *scrive isshli(che) ;* others *scrivenissh.*
1026. *thou,* so J H₄ G² H₃ ; R omits ; Cx. *it ;* a² γ *thou it.*
1034. *Al were,* so R only ; rest *Were.*
1042. *hede,* J *hewede.*
1044. *to,* J Cx. H₃ omit ; γ⁶ *unto.*
1045. *dredful,* J *dred.*
1045. *seyde he,* so H₄ G² ; R *seyde ;* J a² H₃ γ kr *seyde.*
1055. *Right,* γ⁶ omit (see l. 1005).

And blisful God preye ich with good
    entente,   1060
The viage and the lettre I shal endite,
So spede it ! And thou, Mínerva, the white,
Yif thou me wit my lettré to devise ! '
And sette him doun and wrot right in this
    wise.

First, he gan her his righté lady calle,
His hertès lif, his lust, his sorwes leche,
His blisse, and ek these othré termés allé
That in swich cas ye lovers allé seche ;
And in ful humblé wise as in his speche
He gan him recomaunde unto her grace :
To telle al how, it axeth muchel space.

And after this ful lowly he her preyde 1072
To be not wroth, though he of his folýe
So hardy was to her to write ; and seyde
That love it made, or ellés moste he dye ;
And pitously gan mercy for to crye ;
And after that he seyde, and leigh ful loude,
Him-self was litel worth, and lesse he
    coude ;

And that she sholde han his conning ex-
    cused,
That litel was ; and ek he dredde her so ;
And his unworthinesse he ay acused ; 1081
And after that than gan he telle his wo ;
But that was infinit for ay and o ;
And how he wolde in trouthe alwey him
    holde ;
And his adieux he made, and gan it folde.

And with his salté terès gan he bathe
The ruby in his signet, and it sette
Upon the wax deliverliche and rathe ;

Therwith a thousand timés, or he lette,
He kisté tho the lettré that he shette,
And seydé, ' Lettre, a blisful destiné 1091
Thee shapen is : my lady shal thee see ! '

This Pandar up therwith, and that be-time
On morwe, and to his necés paleis sterte,
And seidé, ' Slepé ye, and it is prime ? '
And gan to jape, and seidé thus : ' Myn
    herte,
So fressh is it though lové do it smerte,
I may not slepen nevere a Mayés morwe !
I have a joly wo, a lusty sorwe ! ' 1099

Criseydé, whan that she her unclé herde,
With dredful herte, and désirous to here
The cause of his comíngé, thus answérde :
' Now by your fey, myn unclé,' quod she,
    ' dere,
What maner wind gideth you hider here ?
Tel us your joly wo and your penaunce !
How ferforth be ye put in lovés daunce ? '

' By God,' quod he, ' I hoppe alwey
    behinde ! '
And she to laughe, as though her herté brest.
Quod Pandarus, ' Loke alwey that ye finde
Game in myn hood !   But herkneth if you
    lest.—   1110
Ther is right now come into toune a gest,
A Grek espye, and telleth newé thingès,
For-which come I to tellé you tidínges.

' Into the gardin go w', and ye shal here
Al privély of this a long sermoún.'—
With that they wenten arm in arm i-fere
Into the gardin fro the chaumbré doun ;

1060. *with,* a² *in.*
1065. *he gan,* a² *gan he.*
1068. *ye,* so H₄ R G² ; J *the ;* a² γ *these.*
1079. *And that she sholde,* Cx. S *And preyde
her ;* H₅ *Beseching her.*
1083. *infinit,* H₂ *infynyte* (later) ; H₄ *infenit ;*
G *enfeyned ;* H₅ *infinyth ;* P (later) J Cx. γ
endeles.
1083. *for ay and o,* so H₂ (later) H₄ G² J R ;
P (later) Cx. γ *withouten ho.*
1084. *how,* Cx. γ *seyde.*
1085. *And his adieux he made,* etc., so R, and
a² G² (*adew* and omitting *he*) ; H₄ *And thus an
eend made,* etc. ; J Cx. γ *And redde it over and
gan the lettré folde.*

1091. *Lettre,* G omits ; J R *I wis.*
1093. *up therwith,* Cx. γ *took the lettre.*
1095. Cx. γ read : *And faste he swor that it
was passed prime.*
1097. *is it,* J Cx. γ *it is.*
1097. *though lové do it,* Cx. γ *although it sore.*
1104. *wind,* so a³ R Cx. ; others *windes.*
1104. *you hider,* so a² only ; others *you, now,
now you, you now.*
1108. *as though,* so a² H₈ R S ; H₄ G *and
though*(te) ; Cx. D *hir thought ;* J Ad. γ³ *it
thought ;* S₂ Dg. *yet if.*
1109. *alwey that ye,* so J H₄ Cx. H₅ H₈ S ; G
R *that ye alwey ;* a² γ³ *alwey ye.*
1113. *For-which,* J H₄ *For-why ;* R *for-
thy.*
1113. *come I,* Cx. γ³ *I come.*
1113. *tidínges,* R γ³ *newe tidinges.*

And whan that he so fer was, that the soun
Of that he spak ther no man heren mighte,
He seide her thus, and out the lettré plighte:

'Lo, he that is al hoolly yourès free   1121
Him recomaundeth lowly to your grace,
And sent to you this lettré here by me :
Aviseth you on it whan ye han space,
And of som goodly answer you purcháce,
Or, help me God so, pleynly for to seyne,
He may not longé liven for the peyne !'—

Ful dredfully tho gan she stonden stille,
And took it nought, but al her humblé chere
Gan for to chaunge ; and seidé, 'Scrit ne
        bille,   1130
For love of God, that toucheth swich matére
Ne bring me non ; and also, unclé dere,
To myn estat have more reward, I preye,
Than to his lust !   What sholde I moré
        seye ?

'And loketh now if this be resonáble,
And letteth not for favour ne for slouthe
To seyn a soth !   Now were it covenáble
To myn estat, by God and by your trouthe,
To taken it, or to han of him routhe,
In harming of my-self, or in repreve ?   1140
Ber it ayein, for Him that ye on leve !'—

This Pandarus gan on her for to stare,
And seidé, ' Now is this the mosté wonder
That evere I say !   Lat be this nicé fare !
To dethé mote I smiten be with thonder,
If, for the cité which that stondeth yonder,
To you a lettré wolde I bringe or take,
To harm of you !   What list you thus to
        make ?   1148

' But thus ye faren wel nigh alle and some,
That he that most desireth you to serve,
Of him ye recché leest wher he bicome,

And whether that he live or ellès sterve !
But, for al that that evere I may deserve,
Refuse it not !' quod he, and hente her
        faste,
And in her bosom doun the lettré thraste.

And seide her, ' Cast it now awey anon,
That folk may sen and gauren on us
        tweye !'
Quod she, ' I can abide til they be gon !'
And gan to smile, and seide him, ' Em,
        I preye   1159
Swich answer as you list your-self purveye ;
For trewély I n'il no lettré write !'—
' No ? than wol I,' quod he, ' so ye endite !'

Therwith she lough, and seidé, 'Go we
        dine !'
And he gan at him-self to japé faste,
And seidé, ' Nece, I have so gret a pine
For love, that everich other day I faste !'
And gan his besté japés forth to caste,
And made her so to laughe at his folýe,
That she for laughter wendé for to dye.

And whan that she was comén into halle,
' Now em,' quod she, ' we wol go dine
        anon !'   1171
And gan some of her wommen for to calle,
And streight into her chaumbré gan she
        gon ;
But of her bisinessé this was oon
Amongès othré thingès, out of drede,
Ful privély this lettré for to rede.

Avisèd word by word in every line,
And fond no lak, she thoughte he coudé
        good,
And up it putte, and wente her in to dine :
But Pandarus, that in a study stood,   1180
Or he was war, she took him by the hood,

1119. *Of that he spak, a⁵ Of his wordes.* ther,
so J S only ; H₃ D Cp. etc. *spake* (for *spak*).
1119. *herun,* R *hit herun.*
1123. *sent to you,* so a² only ; J etc. *sente you ;*
others *sent you.*
1125. *of,* a² G² omit.
1130. *Scrit,* J Cx. *Script.*
1143. *moste,* γ *grettest.*
1148. *to,* G γ *it.*

1155. *down the lettre,* etc., H₄ R Cx., and J S
(*he thraste*), and a² (*caste*) ; G² γ *the lettre down
he thraste* (Dg. *caste*).
1156. *Cast it now,* a⁵ S ; J *Cast it ;* R *Cast it
not ;* Cx. *Cast it faste ;* γ *Now cast it.*
1164. *he,* J R *Pandare ;* G *Pandarus.* R *at
himself gan iape faste.*
1172. *for to,* so J G ; a² Cx. omit ; H₄ H₃ *it
to ;* R *gan she ;* γ⁵ *to her.*
1174. *bisinesse.* Cp. *bisinesses.*
1181. *him,* D γ³ omit ; R *tho.*

And seidė, 'Ye were caught or that ye
  wiste !'
'I vouchė sauf !' quod he, 'Do what
  you liste !'

Tho wesshen they, and sette hem doun,
  and ete ;
And after noon ful sleighly Pandarus
Gan drawe him to the window next the
  strete,
And seidė, 'Nece, who hath arayėd thus
The yonder hous that stant afor-yein us ?'
'Which hous ?' quod she, and com for to
  biholde,   1189
And knew it wel, and whos it was him tolde ;

And fillen forth in speche of thingės smale,
And seten in the window bothė tweye.
Whan Pandarus saw time unto his tale,
And say wel that hir folk were alle aweye,
'Now, necė myn, tel on !' quod he, 'I seye,
How liketh you the lettrė that he wrot ?
Can he theron ? For by my trouthe I n'ot !'

Therwith al rosy hewėd tho wex she,
And gan to humme, and seidė, 'So I
  trowe !'—
'Aquite him wel, for Goddės love !' quod
  he.   1200
'My-self to-medės wol the lettrė sowe !'
And held his hondės up, and fel on knowe ;
'Now, goodė Necė, be it nevere so lite,
Yif me the labour it to sowe and plite.'

'Ye, for I can so write,' quod she tho,
'And eek I n'ot what that I sholde him seye.'
'Nay, necė,' quod Pandárė, 'sey not so !
Yit at the lestė thanketh him, I preye,
Of his good-wil, and doth him not to deye !
Now, for the love of me, my necė derė,
Refuseth not at this time my preyére !'   1211

'Depardieux,' quod she, 'God leve al be
  wel !
God help me so, this is the firstė lettre
That evere I wrot, ye, al or any del !'—
And int' a closet for t' avise her bettre
She went allone, and gan her herte unfettre
Out of Disdeynės prison but a lite,
And sette her doun, and gan a lettrė write ;

Of which to telle in short is myn entente
Th' effect, as fer as I can understonde.—
She thankėd him of al that he wel mente
Towárdės her, but holden him in honde
She n'oldė nought, ne make her selven
  bonde   1223
In love ; but as his suster him to plese
She wolde ay fain, to don his herte an ese.

She shette it, and to Pandar in gan gon
Ther-as he sat and lokėd into strete,
And doun she sette her by him, on a ston
Of jaspre, upon a quisshin gold y-bete,
And seide, 'As wisly help me God the grete,
I neverė dide a thing with morė peyne
Than writen this, to which ye me con-
  streyne !'   1232

And took it him.—He thankėd her, and
  seide,
'God wot, of thing ful oftė loth bigonne
Com'th endė good ! And necė myn,
  Criseyde,
That ye to him of hard now ben y-wonne,
Oughte he be glad, by God and yonder
  sonne,
For-why men seith, "Impressióunės lighte
Ful lightly ben ay redy to the flighte." 1239

'But ye han pley'd the tirant ny too longe,
And hard was it your hertė for to grave,
Now stint, that ye no lenger on it honge,
(Al woldė ye the forme of daunger save),
But hasteth you to don him joyė have ;

1189. *com,* so a³ Cx.; others *gan.*
1193. *unto,* H₄ *on to ;* J G² Cl *to.*
1195. *seye,* R *preye.*
1196. *he wrot,* so a²; others *ye wot(e).*
1202. *fel,* γ *sat.*
1205. *Ye, for I can so write,* H₅ *Ful febly can
I write.* (The meaning of the text is not evident.)
1206. *that,* so P R only.
1206. *him,* Cx. γ⁶ *to him.*
1209. *and,* J G² Cx. O.
1210. *me,* J G² *god.*
1211. *time,* J a³ G *tid(e).*

1215. *int',* a² *in.*
1217. *Disdeynes,* a³ Cx. *disdeynous.*
1225. *ay,* γ' omit.
1227. *into strete,* so J Cp. ; Cl. *into a strete ;*
R *to the strete ;* a⁶ etc. *into the strete.*
1229. *gold,* P H₄ *with gold ;* H₂ R Cx. *of gold.*
1240. *the,* γ omit.

For trusteth wel too longe y-don hardnésse
Causeth despit ful ofté for distresse.'—

And right as they declaméd this matére,
Lo, Troilus, right at the stretés ende,
Com riding with his tenthé some i-fere
Al softély, and thíderward gan bende 1250
Ther-as they sete, as was his wey to wende
To paleis-ward; and Pandar him espi'de,
And seidé, ' Nece, y-see who com'th here
    ride !

' O flee not in (he seeth us, I suppose),
Lest he may thinken that ye him eschuwe !'
' Nay, nay !' quod she, and wex as red as
    rose.
With that he gan her humblély saluwe
With dredful chere, and ofte his hewés
    muwe ;
And up his look debónerly he caste,
And bekkéd on Pandáre, and forth he paste.

God wot if he sat on his hors aright, 1261
Or goodly was biseyn that ilké day !
God wot whe'r he was lik a manly knight !
What sholde I drecche, or telle of his array?
Criseydé, which that alle these thingés say,
To telle in short, her likéd al in-fere,
His person, his array, his look, his chere,

His goodly maner, and his gentilesse
So wel, that neveré sith that she was born
Ne haddé she swich routhe of his distresse ;
And, how-so she hath hard ben her-biforn,
To God hope I she hath now caught a
    thorn, 1272
She shal not pulle it out this nexté wike !
God send mo swiché thornés on to pike !

Pandáré, which that stood her fasté by,
Felte iren hot, and he bigan to smite ;
And seidé, ' Nece, I preye you hertély,
Tel me that I shal axen you a lite :
A womman that were of his deth to wite,

Withoute his gilt, but for her lak of routhe,
Were it wel don ?'—Quod she, ' Nay, by
    my trouthe !' 1281

' God help me so,' quod he, ' ye sey me
    soth !
Ye felen wel your-self that I not·lye !
Lo, yond he rit !'—' Ye,' quod she, ' so
    he doth.'—
' Wel,' quod Pandáre, 'as I have told you
    thrye,
Lat be your nicé shame and your folýe,
And spek with him in esing of his herte '
Lat nicété not do you bothé smerte !'

But theron was to heven and to done ! 1289
' Consideréd allé thing it may not be.—
And why for speche?—And it were ek
    too sone
To graunte him yit so gret a liberté.'
For pleinly her entente, as seidé she,
Was for to love him unwist, if she mighte,
And guerdone him with no-thing but with
    sighte.

But Pandarus thoughte, ' It shal not be so ;
If that I may, this nice opinioun
Shal not ben holden fully yerés two !'—
What sholde I make of this a long sermóun ?
He moste assente on that conclusioun 1300
As for the time ; and when that it was
    eve,
And al was wel, he ros and took his leve.

And on his wey ful faste homward he
    spedde,
And right for joye he felte his herté daunce :
And Troilus he fond allone a-bedde,
That lay, as don these lovers, in a traunce
Bi-twixen hope and derk desésperaunce ;
But Pandarus, right at his in-cominge,
He song, as who seith, ' Somwhat I thee
    bringe !'

1247. *declamed*, a³ etc. *declared.*
1253. *y-see,* J R *se;* H₄ omits ; G Cx. *lo.*
1257. *humblely,* a³ γ⁶ *humbly to.*
1258. *muwe,* a² G etc. *newe.*
1270. *swich,* R *swich a.*
1272. *I,* so R γ⁵ only ; rest omit. H₅ *Thorow good hope.*

1280. *lak of,* γ⁴ *lakked.*
1283. *not,* a³ *ne.*
1291. *speche,* γ⁶ *shame.*
1292. *yit,* so J G² Cx. ; rest omit.
1306. *these,* J *the;* G *ye.* (See L 1068.)
1309. *Somwhat I thee,* so R only ; S₁ *Sumquhat now I;* Th. *Lo, sumwhat I;* rest *somwhat I.*

And seydė, 'Who is in his bed so sone
'Y-buried thus?'—'It am I, frend!' quod
he.   1311
'Who? Troilus? Nay, help me so the
mone,'
Quod Pandarus, 'thou shalt arise and see
A charmė that was right now sent to thee,
The whichė can thee hele of thyn accėsse
So thou thy-self do forth thy bisinesse.'

'Ye, thorugh the might of God!' quod
Troilus.—
And Pandarus gan him the lettrė take,
And seidė, 'Pardé, God hath holpen us!
Have here a light, and look on al this
blake!'   1320
Lord, oftė gan the hertė glade and quake
Of Troilus, whil that he gan it rede,
So as the wordės yave him hope and drede.

But finaly he took al for the beste
That she him wrot; for somwhat he beheld
On which he thoughte he mighte his
       hertė reste,
Al coverėd she the wordės under sheld.
Thus to the morė worthy part he held,
That, what for hope and Pandarus' biheste,
His gretė wo foryede he at the leste.   1330

But, as we may alday our-selven see,
Thorugh morė wode or col, the morė fir,
Right so, encresseth hope, of what it be,
Therwith ful ofte encresseth ek desir:
Or, as an ook com'th of a litel spir,
So thorugh this lettrė which that she him
       sente,
Encressen gan desir, of which he brente.

Wherfore I seye alwey that day and night
This Troilus gan to desiren more
Than he dide erst, thorugh hope, and
       dide his might   1340

To pressen on, as by Pandárės lore,
And writen to her of his sorwes sore:
Fro day to day he let it not refreyde,
That by Pandáre he somwhat wrot or seyde;

And dide also his othrė óbservaunces
That til a lover longeth in this cas;
And, after-that his dees tornėd on chaunces,
So was he outher glad or seide 'Allas!'
And held, after his gestės, ay his pas;
And after swiche answérės as he hadde,
So were his dayės sory outher gladde. 1351

But to Pandáre alwey was his recours;
And pitously gan ay unto him pleyne,
And him bisoughtė reed or som socours;
And Pandarus, that say his wodė peyne,
Wex wel ny ded for routhė, soth to seyne,
And bisily with al his hertė caste
Som of his wo to sleen, and that as faste;

And seydė, 'Lord, and frend, and brother
       dere,   1359
God wot that thy disesė doth me wo!
But, wilt thou stinten of this woful chere,
And by my trouthe, or it be dayės two,
And God to-forn, yit shal I shape it so
That thou shalt come into a certein place,
Ther-as thou mayst thy-self preye her of
       grace.

'And certeinly, I n'ot if thou it wost,
But tho that ben expert in love it seye,
It is oon of the thingės fortherėth most,
A man to have a leiser for to preye,   1369
And siker place his wo for to biwreye;
For in good herte it mot som routhe impresse
To here and see the giltles in distresse.

'Paraunter thenkestow "Though it be so
That Kindė wolde hir don for to biginne

1315. *thee hele,* so R only; others *helen thee.*
1316. *So thou thy-self do forth,* so R only;
α J Cx. *So that thou do forth(with);* γ *If thou
do forthwith al.*
1321. *Lord,* so α³ J G²; R Cx. γ⁸ *But.*
1323. *and,* α³ γ *or.*
1326. *which he,* J γ *which him.*
1333. *encresseth,* so J G²; others *encres of*
(read? *encresse*).

1341. *Pandárės,* J etc. *Pandarus.*
1344. *he somwhat wrot,* so R S only; J *he
som wrot;* α⁵ Cx. *somwhat he wrot;* γ⁸ *he wrot
somwhat.*
1347. *his,* γ⁸ *thise.*
1353. *ay unto,* J Cx. S; H₄ G² etc. *ay to;* α²
alwey to; γ⁴ *ay til him to.*
1354. *or,* α⁵ R Cx.; J omits; γ *and.*
1365. *preye her,* γ *her preye.*
1374. *wolde her don for,* so J H₄ R and Cx.
(omit *her*); others var.

To han a maner routhe upon my wo,
Seith Daunger, Nay, thou shalt me neveré
    winne !
So rewleth her her hertés gost withinne,
That, though she bendé, yit she stant on
    rote :
What in effect is this unto my bote ? "

'Thenk her-ayeins, whan that the sturdy
    ook,   1380
On which men hakketh ofté for the nones,
Receivéd hath the happy falling strook,
The greté sweigh doth it come al at ones,
As don these rokkés or these milné-stones ;
For swifter cours com'th thing that is of
    wighté,
Whan it descendeth, than don thingés
    lighte.

' But reed that boweth doun for every blast
Ful lightly, cessé wind, it wol arise ;
But so wil not an ook whan it is cast.—
It nedeth me not longé thee forbise. 1390
Men shal rejoysen of a gret emprise,
Achevéd wel, and stant withouten doute,
Al han men been the lenger ther-aboute.

' But, Troilus, now tel me, if thee lest,
A thing which that I shal now axen thee :
Which is thy brother that thou lovest beste,
As in thy verray hertés privété ?'   1397
' Y-wis, my brother Deiphebus,' quod he.—
Quod Pandarus, ' Or hourés twyés twelve,
He shal thee ese, unwist of it him-selve.

'Now lat m'allone, and werken as I may !'
Quod he; and to Deiphébus wente he tho,
Which hadde his lord and greté frend ben
    ay ;
Save Troilus no man he lovéd so.
To telle in short, withouten wordés mo,

Quod Pandarus, ' I preye you that ye be
Frend to a causé which that toucheth me.'

' Yis, pardé ! ' quod Deiphébus, ' wel thou
    wost,
In al that evere I may, and God to-fore,
Al n'ere it but for man I lové most,   1410
My brother Troilus.   But sey wherfóre
It is ; for sith the day that I was bore
I n'as, ne neveré mo to ben I thinke,
Ayeins a thing that mighté thee for-thinke.'

Pandáré gan him thanke, and to him seydé,
' Lo, sire, I have a lady in this toun,
That is my nece, and calléd is Criseyde,
Which some men wolden don oppressioun,
And wrongfully han her possessioun ; 1419
Wherfore I of your lordship you biseche
To ben our frend, withouten moré speche.'

Deiphébus him answérde, ' O, is not this
That thou spek'st of to me thus strangély
Criséÿda, my frend ! '—He seidé, ' Yis.'
'Than nedeth,' quod Deiphébus, ' hardily
No more of this, for trusteth wel that I
Wol ben her champioun with spere and
    yerde :
I roughté not though alle her foos it herde.

' But tel me how—thou wost of this
    matére—   1429
It mighté best availen ! '—' Now lat see ! '
Quod Pandarus, ' If ye my lord so dere
Wolden as now do this honoúr to me
And preyén her to-morwé, lo, that she
Come unto you her pleintés to devise,
Her adversaries wolde of it agrise.

' And if I moré dorsté preye as now,
And chargen you to han so gret travaile
To han some of your brethren here with
    you

1376. *Nay,* J omits ; a² *than.*
1383. *doth,* J G² *makith.*
1383. *it,* G γ *it to.*
1383. *come,* a² G Cx. *falle.*
1387. *But,* so a β ; H₄ *As* ; γᵇ *And* ; γ² *For.*
1387. *for,* so J P H₄ γ ; H₂ G Cx. H₃ *with* ; R *fro.*
1390. *longe thee,* γ *thee longe to.*
1394. *now,* so β ; a² S A omit : γ *yet* (H₁ *that*).
1395. so J ; others var.
1399. *Quod Pandarus,* R Cx. γᵇ *Now quod Pandaré.*

1412. *the,* P γ² *that.*
1423. *thus,* H₄ R Cx. Cl. *so.*
1426. *of this,* γᵇ *to speke.*
1429. *how thou,* so J H₄ G² Ad. ; a² R Cx. *how for thou* ; γ *thou that.*
1429. *of,* H₄ R Cx. omit ; γ *al.*
1430. *It,* H₄ omits ; Cx. *I* ; γᵇ *How I.*
1430. *mighté,* R Cx. *mighté her.*
1433. *And,* so J H₄ G² ; rest *To.*
1436. *preye,* Cx. γᵇ *preye you.*

That mighten in her causé bet availe, 1439
Than wot I wel she mighté neveré faile
For to ben holpen, what at your instaunce,
What with her othré frendés governaunce.'

Deiphébus, which that comen was of kinde
To alle honoúr and bounté to consente,
Answérde, 'It shal be don! And I can finde
Yit gretter help to this, in myn entente !
What wiltow seyn, if for Eleyne I sente
To speke of this?   I trowe it be the beste ;
For she may leden Paris as her leste. 1449

'Of Ector, which that is my lord, my brother,
It nedeth nought to preye him frend to be ;
For I have herd him, oo time and ek other,
Speke of Criseydé swich honoúr, that he
May seyn no bet ; swich hap to him hath
          she,
It nedeth nought his helpés moré crave :
He shal be swich, right as we wol him have.

'Spek thou thy-self also to Troilus
On my bihalve, and prey him with us
          dine.'—   1458
'Sire, al this shal be don !' quod Pandarus ;
And took his leve, and neveré gan to fine,
But to his neces hous, as streight as line,
He com ; and fond her fro the mete arise ;
And sette him doun, and spak right in this
          wise.—

He seide, 'O verray God, so have I ronne !
Lo, necé myn, see ye not how I swete ?
I n'ot whe'r ye the moré thank me conne !
Be ye not war how falsé Poliphete
Is now about eft-sonés for to plete,   •
And bringe on you advócacyés newe ?'—
'I ?   No !' quod she, and chaungéd al
          her hewe.   1470

'What?   Is he more abouté me to drecche
And do me wrong?   What shal I don, allas?

Yit of him-selven nothing wolde I recche,
N'ere it for Antenor and Eneás,
That ben his frendés in swich maner cas.
But, for the love of God, myn uncle dere,
No fors of that, lat him have al i-fere !

'Withouten that, I have y-nough for us.'—
' Nay,' quod Pandáre, 'it shal no-thing be
          so ;
For I have ben right now at Deiphebus,
At Ector and mine othré lordés mo, 1481
And shortly makéd ech of hem his fo ;
That by my thrift he shal it neveré winne,
For aught he can, whan that so he biginne.'

And, as they casten what was best to done,
Deiphébus, of his owné curtesýe,
Com her to preye, in his propré persóne,
To holde him on the morwé companýe
At diner, which she n'oldé not denye,
But goodly gan to his preyére obeye. 1490
He thankéd her, and wente upon his weye.

Whan this was don, this Pandar up anon,
To telle in short, and forth he gan to wende
To Troilus, as stille as any ston ;
And al this thing he tolde him word and
          ende,
And how that he Deiphébus gan to blende,
And seide him, ' Now is time, if that thou
          conne,
To bere thee wel tomorwe, and al is wonne.

' Now spek, now prey, now pitously com·
          pleyne !
Let not for nicé shame, or drede, or
          slouthe !   1500
Som time a man mot telle his owné peyne !
Bileve it, and she shal han on thee routhe ;
Thou shalt be savéd by thy feith in trouthe !
But wel wot I that thou art now in drede,
And what it is I leye I can a-rede !

' Thou thinkest now, " How sholde I don
          al this ?

1439. *in*, Cx. omits ; *y⁸ to.*
1442. *governaunce, a²* Cx. R *sustenaunce.*
1447. *for Eleyne I*, so J H₄ Cx. S Ad. Du. ;
rest *I for Eleyne.*
1455. *more*, so J G² ; H₄ *more to (a² us more
help to)* ; γ *for to.*
1466. *whe'r*, P G² *wher* ; J *whar* ; others
whether.

1473. *him-selven* (?), all *him-self(e)* ; J *him-self
right* ; G *himself yit.*
1473. *wolde*, Cp. H₁ *ne wolde.*
1482. *maked*, so J Cp. etc. ; others *mad(e).*
1500. *Let, a³* R Cx. *Leve.*
1504. *that*, so J G³ S H₃ ; rest omit.
1504. *in*, H₄ *a* ; H₂ R Cx. *in a.*

For by my cherès mosten folk espye
That for her love is that I fare amis ; 1508
Yit hadde I levere unwist for sorwè dye."—
Now think not so, for thou dost gret folýe ;
For I right now have founden oo manére
Of sleightè, for to coverèn al thy cherè.

'Thou shalt gon over night, and that as blive,
Unto Deiphébus' hous, as thee to pleye,
Thy maladye awey the bet to drive,
For-why thou semest sik, soth for to seye.
Sone after that, doun in thy bed thee leye,
And sey thou mayst no lenger up endure,
And·ly right there, and byd thyn aventure.

'Sey that thy fevere is wont thee for to take   1520
The samè time, and lasten til a-morwe ;
And lat see now how wel thou canst it make,
For, pardé, sik is he that is in sorwe !
Go now, farwel ! and, Venus here to borwe,
I hope, and thou this purpos holdè ferme,
Thy gracè she shal fully ther confernie !'

Quod Troilus, 'Y-wis, thou nedéles
Counseilest me that siklich I me feyne,
For I am sik in ernest doutéles,   1529
So that wel nigh I stervè for the peyne !'
Quod Pandarus, 'Thou shalt the bettrè pleyne,
And hast the lassè nede to contrefete,
For him men demen hot, that men seen swete !

'Lo, hold thee at thy tristè clos, and I
Shal wel the deer unto thy bowè drive !'
Ther-with he took his leve al softély.
And Troilus to paleis wentè blive,
So glad ne was he nevere in al his live ;
And to Pandárès reed gan al assente, 1539
And to Deiphébus' hous at night he wente.

What nedeth you to tellen al the chere
That Deiphebus unto his brother made,
Or his accésse, or his sikly manére ;
How men gan him with clothès for to lad :
Whan he was leyd ; and how men wold him glade ?
But al for nought : he held forth ay the wise
That ye han herd Pandáre or this devise.

But certein is, or Troilus him leyde,
Deiphébus had him preyéd over night 154
To ben a frend and helping to Criseyde :
God wot that he it graunted anon right.
To ben her fullè frend with al his might
But swich a nedè was to preye him thenne,
As for to bidde a wood man for to renne !

The morwen com, and neighen gan the time
Of mel-tid, that the fairè Queene Eleyne
Shoop her to ben an houre after the prime
With Deiphebus, to whom she n'oldè feyne :
But as his suster, homly, soth to seyne,
She com to diner in her pleyne ententè :
But God and Pandar wiste al what this mente.   1561

Com ek Criseyde, al innocent of this,
Antigoné, her suster Tarbe also.—
But flee we now prolixité best is,
For love of God, and lat us fastè go
Right to th' effect, withouten talès mo
Why al this folk assembled in this place :
And lat us of hir saluíngès pace !   1568

Gret honour dide hem Deiphebus certéyne,
And feddehem wel withal that mightè like ;
But everè-mo 'Allas !' was his refréyne,
'My godè brother Troilus, the sike,
Li'th yit !' And therwithal he gan to sike,
And after that he peynéd him to glade
Hem as he mighte, and cherè good he made.

1507. *cherès*, J *teres* ; α³ R Cx. *chere.*
1513. *as blive*, so α³ Cx. S ; J etc. *bylyve* ; others *blyve.*
1517. *Sone*, α² Cl. *So* ; γ *And.*
1526. *fully ther*, J R *thee fully ther* ; G Cx. *thee fully.* Cx. *In* and G *Thyn* for *Thy.*
1532. *nedè to*, H₂ H₁ *nede.*
1539. *Pandárès*, so H₄ G D ; others *Pandarus.*

1543. *sikly*, J etc. *siklich(e).*
1549. *had him preyed*, J G³ H₃ *hadde (y) preyd him.*
1550. *a frend*, J G² *good frend* ; S₁ *good lord.*
1551. *it*, J G² H₃ omit.
1553. *was*, so α⁴ γ³ ; J S₁ *was it* ; Cx. Ad. 1h. *it was* ; G *was for* ; R *was that.*
1557. *Shoop*, γ³ *Shapè(e)*
1561. *al.*, α² R Cx. *non.*
1561. *this*, α² *it.*
1575. *he made*, α³ R Cx. G *hem made.*

Compleynèd ek Eleyne of his siknésse
So feithfully, that pité was to here ;
And every wight gan waxen for accesse
A leche anon, and seide, ' In this manére
Men curen folk.'—' This charme I wol
     thee lere.'   1580
But ther sat oon, al list her not to teche,
That thoughtè, ' Best coude I yit ben his
     leche ! '

After compleynte, him gonnen they to
     preise,
As folk don yit, whan som wight hath
     bigonne
To preise a man, and up with pris him reise
A thousand fold yit hyèr than the sonne :
' He is, he can, that fewè lordès conne ! '
And Pandarus, of that they wolde afferme,
He nought forgat hir preising to conferme.

Herde alwey this Criseydè wel y-nough,
And every word gan for to notifye ;   1591
For which with sobrè chere her hertè lough ;
For who is it that n'olde her glorifye
To mowèn swich a knight do live or dye ?
But al passe I, lest ye too longè dwelle,
For for oo fyn is al that evere I telle.

The timè com fro diner for to rise ;
And as hem oughte arisen everychon,
And gonne a while of this and that devise.
But Pandarus brak al this speche anon,
And seidè to Deiphébus, ' Wol ye gon,
If it your willè be, as I you preyde,   1602
To speke here of the nedès of Criseyde ? '

Eleynè, which that by the hond her held,
Took first the tale, and seidè, ' Go we blive ! '
And goodly on Criseydè she biheld,

And seidè, ' Jovès, lat him neverè thrive
That doth you harm, and bring him sone
     of live !
And yeve me sorwè, but he shal it rewe
If that I may, and allè folk be trewe ! '   1610

' Tel thou thy neces cas,' quod Deiphebus
To Pandarus, ' for thou canst best it telle.'—
' My lordès and my ladies, it stant thus :
What sholde I lenger,' quod he, ' do you
     dwelle ? '—
He rong hem out a proces lik a belle
Upon her fo, that hightè Poliphete,
So hèynous, that men mighte on it spete.

Answérde of this ech wers of hem than other,
And Poliphete they gonnen thus to warien,
' An-hongèd be swich oon, were he my
     brother,   1620
And so he shal, for it ne may not varien ! '
What sholde I lenger in this talè tarien ?
Pleinlich, at onès, allè they her highten
To ben her frend in al that evere they
     mighten.

Spak than Eleyne and seidè, ' Pandarus,
Wot ought my lord my brother this matére,
I mene Ectór ?   Or wot it Troilus ? '
He seidè, ' Ye !   But wol ye now me here ?
Me thinketh this, sith Troilus is here, 1629
It werè good, if that ye wolde assente,
She tolde her-self him al this, or she wente.

' For he wol have the more her grief at herte
By causè, lo, that she a lady is,
And, by your leve, I wol but in right sterte
And do you wite, and that anon y-wis,
If that he slepe, or wile ought here of this.'
And in he lep, and seide him in his ere,
' God have thy soule !   Y-brought have
     I thy bere ! '

1577. *that pite*, J *it pite*; Th. *that it pete*; G² *a pete it.*
1585. *up*, H₄ γᵝ omit.
1587. *he can*, J Cx. *that can.*
1590. *alwey this*, Cx. *al this*; γᵝ *al this thing.*
1591. *for*, J Cx. D Cl. omit.
1593. *it that*, so J G only; R Du. Dg. *that that*; H₂ *he that* ; rest *that.*
1593. *n'olde*, *y ne wolde.*
1594. *do*, J aᵝ *to.*
1596. *For for*, so βγ; a² *For* ; J H₄ G² *But for.*
1598. *arisen*, a² Cx. *they risen.*
1602. *If it*, Cx. γᵝ *If.*

1616. *Upon*, J H₄ G² R *Unto.*
1619. *gonnen*, a³ R Cx. *gan.*
1621. *it*, aᵝ Cl. *he.*
1623. *at ones alle*, so a³ only ; rest *al(le) at ones.*
1624. *frend*, so β; a² S *frendes* ; γᵝ *help(e).*
1629. *this, sith*, so R Cx. H₁ etc.; a² *sith that* ; J Cp. Cl. etc. *this, sith that.*
1630. *good*, R *right good.*
1634. *in right*, so J G R etc. ; H₄ Cx. *in* ; a² Cl. etc. *right in.*
1637. *lep*, γ *lepte.*

To smilen gan of this tho Troilus,
And Pandarus withouten rekéninge   1640
Out wente anon t' Eleyne and Deiphebus,
And seide hem, 'So ther be no taryínge
Ne moré prees, he wol wel that ye bringe
Criseyde anon, my lady, that is here,
And as he may endure he wol her here.

'But wel ye wot the chaumbré n'is but
    lite,
And fewé folk may lightly make it warm.
Now loketh ye, for I wol han no wite
To bringe in prees that mighté don him
    harm
Or him disesen, for my bettré arm !— 1650
Whe'r it be bet sh' abidé til eft-sones :
Now loketh ye that knowén what to done
    is.

'I seye for me, best is, as I can knowe,
That no wight in ne wendé but ye tweye,
But it were I ; for I can in a throwe
Reherse her cas, unlik that she can seye :
And after this she may him onés preye
To ben good lord in short, and take her
    leve ;   1658
This may not muchel of his ese him reve.

'And ek, for she is straunge, he wol forbere
His esé, which that him thar not for you ;
Ek other thing, that toucheth not to here,
He wol you telle—I wot it wel—right
    now,
That secret is and for the tounés prow.'
And they, that knowen no-thing of his
    entente,
Withouten more to Troilus in wente.

Eleyne in al her goodly softé wise
Gan him salue, and wommanly to pleye,
And seide, 'Y-wis, ye mote algate arise !
Now, fairé brother, be al hool, I preye !'
And gan her arm right over his shulder
    leye ;   1671
And him with al her wit to réconforte,
As she best coudé, she gan him desporte.

So after this quod she, 'We you biseke,
My deré bróther Deiphebus and I,
For love of God—and so doth Pandar
    eke—
To ben good lord and frend right hertély
Unto Criseydé, which that certeinly   1678
Receiveth wrong, as wot wel here Pandáre,
That can her cas wel bet than I declare.'

This Pandarus gan newe his tonge affile,
And al her cas reherse, and that anon.
Whan it was seid, sone after in a while,
Quod Troilus, 'As sone as I may gon,
I wol right fayn with al my might ben
    oon,
Have God my trouthe, her causé to
    sustene.'
'Now good thrift have ye !' quod Eleyne
    the Queene.

Quod Pandarus, 'And it your willé be,
That she may take her leve or that she
    go—'
'O, ellés God forbedé,' tho quod he, 1690
'If that she vouché-sauf for to do so !'
And with that word quod Troilus, 'Ye two,
Deiphébus and my suster, leef and dere,
To you have I to speke of oo matére,

'To ben avisé d of your reed the bettre ';
And fond as hap was at his beddés heed

1639. *gan of this*, so H₄ Cx. S ; others *of this gan.*
1644. *anon*, so R Cx. ; rest omit (γ *Criseyda*).
1645. *her here*, so R ; H₂ Cx. *yow here ;* rest *here* (γ etc. *enduren*).
1646. *n'is*, J *nye ;* rest *is.*
1651. *abidé*, so J H₄ G³ Cx. ; others *bide.*
1654. *ye*, J *we.*
1662. *to here*=to her.
1663. *you*, so a² J etc.; H₄ R G *it ;* γ⁵ *me.*
1665. *knowen no-thing*, so J H₄ G² ; *knewe no-thing*, R S ; Ad. Du. *nothing knowe ; nothing knewe*, a² Cx. γ⁶.
1665. *his*, γ *this.*
1666. *wente*, so H₄ Cx. R ; rest *they wente* (G *sche wente*).

1669. *algate*, γ⁶ *alweyes.*
1673. *him*, γ *him to.*
1674. *So*, Cx. *Sone.*
1687. *Now*, so S only. (See l. 847.)
1687. *Eleyne*, J *Elena ;* H₄ *Helena ;* R *Heleyn tho.*
1688. *And*, J G² S *Yif.*
1690. *O*, a² G H₃ etc. *Or ;* H₄ R omit ; Cx. *Now.*
1690. *tho*, a² Cx. etc. *it tho.*
1691. *she*, J R *ye ;* G² *thou.*
1693. *leef ;* H₂ *leve.*

The copy of a tretis and a lettre
That Ector hadde him sent, to axen reed
If swich a man was worthy to ben deed,
Wot I not who : but in a grislich wise
He preyèd hem anon on it avise.   1701

Deiphébus gan this lettrè to unfolde
In ernest gret ; so dide Eleyne the Queene ;
And roming outward, faste it gan biholde,
Dounward a steire, and in an herber grene
This ilkè thing they redden hem bitwene ;
And largèly the mountaunce of an houre
They gonne on it to reden and to poure.

Now lat hem rede, and tornè we anon
To Pandarus, that gan ful fastè prye 1710
That al was wel ; and out he gan to gon
Into the gretè chaumbre, and that in hye,
And seidè, ' God save al this companye !
Com, necè myn, my lady Queene Eleyne
Abideth you, and ek my lordès tweyne.

Ris, tak with you your nece Antigone
Or whom you list,—or no fors, hardily :
The lassè pres, the bet.—Com forth with
    me ;
And lokè that ye thonken humblèly 1719
I em allè three ; and whan ye may goodly
Your timè see, taketh of hem your leve,
Lest we too longe his restès him bireve.'

Al innocent of Pandarus' entente,
Quod tho Criseydè, ' Go we, uncle dere !'
And arm in arm inward with him she wente,
Avisèd wel her wordès and her chere ;
And Pandarus in ernestful manére 1727
Seide, ' Allè folk, for Goddès love I preye,
Stinteth right here, and softèly you pleye.

Avisèth you what folk ben here withinne,
And in what plit oon is, God him amende !'

And inward, thus : ' Ful softèly biginne,
Nece, I conjure ; and heyly you defende,
On His half which that soule us allè sende,
And in the vertu of coróunès tweyne,
Sle not this man, that hath for you this
    peyne !

' Fy on the devil ! Think which oon he is,
And in what plit he li'th ! Com off anon !
Thenk al swich taried tidè, lost it is !
That wol ye bothè seyn whan ye ben oon !
Secoundèly ther yit devineth non   1741
Upon you two : com off now, if ye conne !
Whil folk is blent, lo, al the time is wonne !

' In titeringe, in púrsuit, and delayes,
The folk devine at wagging of a stre ;
That, though ye wolde han, after, merie
    dayes,
Than dar ye nought ; and why ? For
    she and she
Spak swich a word : thus lookèd he and he !
Lest time I loste, I dar nought with you
    dele :   1749
Com off therfóre, and bringeth him to hele !'

But now to you, ye lovers that ben here,
Was Troilus not in a cankerdort,
That lay, and mightè whispring of hem
    here,
And thoughte, ' O Lord, right now
    renneth my sort,
Fully to deye, or han anon confórt !'
And was the firstè time he sholde her
    preye
Of love : O mighty God, what shal he seye ?

1699. *was*, J *war* ; H₄ G *werr*.
1701. *anon on*, Cx. *bothe anon on* ; S *bothe*
n ; J G² *faste on*.
1705. *and in*, so J H₄ G² R ; Cx. *and into* ; rest
ito.
1707. *mountaunce*, J etc. *mountenaunce*.
1715. *lordes*, H₄ R *ladies* (!).
1729. *vou*, J H₄ G Cx. *ye*.

1733. *Nece*, J H₄ G O *nece*.
1734. *half which that*, so Cx. S etc.; R H₃
behalf that ; J H₄ etc. *half that*.
1735. *in the*, J H₄ etc. *in*.
1739. *tide, lost it is*, so a² and Cx. (omit *it*) ;
J and others *tid(e), but lost it (n)is*.
1741. *Secoundèly*, H₄ Cx. (*And*) *sikerly*.
1744. *in*, so a³ Cx. ; R *and in* ; J G *y and*.
1746. *That*, γ *And*.
1749. *Lest*, so H₂ H₅ R ; J etc. *Las*.
1752. *cankerdort*, so a³ Cx. ; J etc. *cankedort*.
1756. *And*, H₄ *And it*.
1757. *O*, a² J *A*.

BOOK III

O BLISFUL light, of which the bemès clere
Adorneth al the thriddè hevenè faire !
O sonnès lief, O Jovès daughter dere,
Plesaunce of love, O goodly debonaire,
In gentil hertes ay redy to repaire !
O verray cause of hele and of gladnesse,
Y-heried be thy might and thy goodnesse !

In hevene and helle, in erthe and salté see
Is felt thy might ; if that I wel discerne,
As man, brid, best, fissh, herbe, and grenè
     tree   10
Thee fele in timès with vapóur eterne,
God loveth, and to lovè wol not werne ;
And in this world no livès créatúre,
Withouten love, is worth, or may endure.

Ye Jovès first to th'ilke effectès glade,
Thorugh whiche that thingès liven alle
     and be,
Commoeveden, and amorous him made
On mortal thing ; and as you list ay ye
Yeve him in love ese or adversité,   19
And in a thousand formès down him sente
For love in erthe, and whom you list he
     hente.

Ye fiersè Mars apaisen of his ire,
And as you list ye maken hertès digne ;
Algatès, hem that ye wol sette a-fire,
They dreden shame, and vices they resigne ;
Ye don hem curteis ben, fresshe and
     benigne ;
And heighe or lowe, after a wight en-
     tendeth,
The joyès that he hath your might him
     sendeth.

Ye holden regne and hous in unité ;
Ye sothfast cause of frendship ben also ;
Ye knowe al th'ilkè coverèd qualité   31

Of thingès which that folk on wondren
     so,
Whan they can not construe how it may jo
She loveth him, or why he loveth here,
As why this fissh, and not that, com'th to
     were.

Ye folk a lawe han set in univers ;
And this knowe I by hem that lovers be.
That who-so striveth with you hath the
     wers.
Now, lady bright, for thy benignité,
At reverence of hem that serven thee,   40
Whos clerk I am, so techeth me devise
Some joye of that is felt in thy servise.

Ye in my naked hertè sentément
In-hielde, and do me shewe of thy swet-
     nesse !—
Caliopé, thy vois be now présént,
For now is nede ! Sestow not my destresse,
How I mot telle anon-right the gladnesse
Of Troilus, to Venus heryinge ?
To which gladnésse, who nede hath, God
     him bringe !

—Lay al this menè whilè Troilus   5
Recording his lessóun in this manére :
'Ma fey !' thoughte he, 'thus wol I sey
     and thus ;
Thus wol I pleyne unto my lady dere ;
That word is good, and this shal be my
     chere ;
This n'il I not foryeten in no wise.'
God leve him werken as he can devise !

And, Lord, so that his hertè gan to quappe,
Hering her come, and shorté for to sik ;
And Pandarus, that ledde her by the
     lappe,
Com neer, and gan in at the curtein pike
And seidè, 'God do bote on allè sike !
See who is here you comen to visite !
Lo, here is she that is your deth to wite

1. R omits ll. 1-49. This apostrophe to Venus,
as planet and goddess of love, is adapted by
Chaucer from a speech of Troilus in *Filostrato*.
5. *ay* ; *a²* Cx. H₃ omit.
17. *him* (?) (Boc.), all *hem*.
28. *him*, H₂ Cx. *hym* ; H₄ omits ; Ph. *hyt* ;
rest *it*.

49. *gladnésse*, γ³ omits.
53, 54. J H₅ invert ; R omits l. 53.
58. *shorte*, J R Cx. *sor(e)*.

Therwith it seméd as he wepte almost.
'Ha a!' quod Troilus so reufully,
'Whe'r me be wo, O mighty God, thou
   wost!
Who is al there? I see nought trewély.'
·Sir,' quod Criseyde, 'it is Pandáre and I.'
'Ye, sweté herte? Allas, I may not rise
To knele and do you honour in som wise.'

And dresséd him upwárd; and she right
   tho   71
Gan bothe her handés softe upon him leye :
'O, for the love of God, do ye not so
To me!' quod she, 'ey! what is this to
   seye?
Sir, comen am I to you for causes tweye,—
First, you to thanke, and of your lordship
   eke
Continuance I woldé you biseke.'

This Troilus, that herde his lady preye
Of lordship him, wex neither quik ne ded,
Ne mighte a word for shamé to it seye, 80
Although men sholdé smiten off his hed ;
But, Lord, so he wex sodeinlíché red,
And sire, his lesson that he wendé konne
To preyén her was thorugh his wit y-ronne.

Criseyde al this aspi'dé wel y-nough,
For she was wis, and lovede him nevere the
   lasse,
Al n'ere he malapert, or made it tough,
Or was too bold to singe a fool a masse.
But whan his shamé gan somwhat to passe,
His wordés, as I may my rimés holde, 90
I wol you telle, as techen bokés olde.

In chaungéd vois right for his verray drede,
Which vois ek quook, and therto his manére
Goodly abayst, and now his hewés rede,
Now pale, unto Criseyde, his lady dere,
With look down-cast and humblé yolden
   chere,—

Lo, th' alderfirsté word that him asterte'
Was, twyés, 'Mercy, mercy, sweté herte !

And stinte a while ; and, whan he mighte
   out-bringe,   99
The nexté word was, 'God wot, for I have,
As ferforthliche as I have had konnínge,
Ben yourés al, God so my soulé save,
And shal til that I, woful wight, be grave !
And though I dar ne can unto you pleyne,
Y-wis I suffré not the lassé peyne.

'Thus muche as now, O wommanlíché wif,
I may out-bringe ; and if this you displese,
That shal I wreke upon myn owné lif
Right sone I trow, and do your herte an
   ese,
If with my deth your wreththe I may
   apese.   110
For, sithen ye han herd me somwhat seye,
Now recche I nevere how soné that I deye.'

Therwith his manly sorwé to biholde
It mighte have maad an herte of stoon to
   rewe ;
And Pandar wep as he to water wolde,
And pokéd evere his necé newe and newe,
And seidé, 'Wo bigon ben hertés trewe !
For love of God, mak of this thing an
   ende,
Or slee us bothe at-onés or ye wende !'

'Ey ! what?' quod she, 'by God and by
   my trouthe   120
I n'ot not what ye wilné that I seye.'—
'"Ey ! what?"' quod he, 'that ye han
   on him routhe,
For Goddés love ; and doth him not to
   deye.'—
'Now thanné thus,' quod she, 'I wolde
   him preye
To tellé me the fyn of his entente ;
Yit wiste I neveré wel what that he
   mente.'

66. *O mighty,* J Ph. R *almighty.*
80. *to it,* J R Cx. *to hir.*
83. *wendé ;* a² Cx. *wend had.*
84. *was,* γ⁸ *is.*
84. *wit ;* a² Cx. *herte.*
90. *wordés,* so a³ J Cx. S ; G² R *werkes ;* γ⁸
resons.
91. *wol yow,* Cp. H₁ Cl. *yow wol.*

101. *ferforth(liche),* so a β S ; γ⁸ *feithfully.*
104. *I ;* a³ R Cx. H₃ *I ne.*
110. *wreththe,* H₂ Cx. S γ⁸ *herte. I,* all
except a² G² S omit.
111. *For,* γ⁷ *But.*
119. *or ye,* H₄ γ⁷ *er (or) that ye ;* H₂ J Cx. *or
we.*

'What that I mene, O swetė hertė dere?'
Quod Troilus. 'O goodly fresshė free !
That with the stremės of your ẏen clere
Ye wolden frendly somtime on me see ; 130
And thanne agreėn that I may ben he,
Withouten braunche of vice in any wise,
In trouthe alwey to don you my servise

'As to my lady right and chief resort,
With al my wit and al my diligence ;
And I to han, right as you list, confórt,
Under your yerde, egal to myn offence,
As deth, if that I brekė your defence ;
And that you deignė me so muche honoúre,
Me to comanden aught in any houre ; 140

'And I to ben your verray humblė trewe,
Secret, and in my peynės pacient,
And everė mo desiren fresshly newe
To serve and ben y-likė diligent,
And with good herte al hoolly your talent
Receiven wel, how sorė that me smerte,—
Lo, this mene I, myn ownė swetė herte.'

Quod Pandarus, 'Lo, here an hard
    requeste,
And resonable a lady for to werne !
Now, necė myn, by natal Jovės feste, 150
Were I a god, ye shulden sterve as yerne,
That heren wel this man wol no thing
    yerne
But your honoúr, and sen him almost
    sterve,
And ben so loth to suffren him you serve !'

With that she gan her ẏen on him caste
Ful esily and ful debónerly,
Avising her, and hiede her not too faste
With nevere a word, but seide him
    sobrely,
'Myn honour sauf, I wol wel trewėly,
And in swich forme as he gan now devise,
Receiven him fullẏ to my servíse, 161

'Biseching him, for Goddės love, that he
Wolde, in honóur of trouthe and gentilesse,
As I wel mene, ek menė wel to me,
And myn honóur with wit and bisinesse
Ay kepe ; and if I may don him glad-
    nesse
From hennėsforth, ywis I n'il not feyne.—
Now beth al hool, no lenger that ye pleyne.

'But nathėles this warne I you,' quod she,
'A kingės sone although ye be y-wis, 170
Ye shal no more have sovėreynėtė
Of me in love than right in that cas is ;
N' I n'il forbere, if that ye don amis,
To wraththė you, and, whil that ye me
    serve,
Cherícė you right after ye deserve.

'And shortly, derė herte and al my knight,
Beth glad, and draweth you to lustinesse ;
And I shal trewėly with al my might
Your bittrė tornen al into swetnėsse ;
If I be she that may do you gladnėsse, 180
For every wo ye shal recovere a blisse.'—
And him in armės took, and gan him kisse.

Fil Pandarus on knees, and up his ẏen
To hevenė threw, and held his hondės
    hye :
'Inmortal God,' quod he, 'that mayst not
    dyen,
Cupide I mene, of this mayst glorifye ;
And Venus, thou mayst maken melodẏe ;
Withouten hond, me semeth that in toune
For this mirácle I here ech bellė soune !

'But ho ! no more as now of this matére,
For-why this folk wol comen up anon 191
That have the lettrė red : lo ! I hem here.
But I conjurė thee Criseyde, and—oon
And two—thee Troilus, whan thou mayst
    gon,
That at myn hous ye ben at my warnínge,
For I ful wel shal shapė your comínge ;

'And eseth ther your hertės right y-nough ;
And lat see which of you shal bere the belle

130. *frendly somtime*, H₄ γ⁸ *somtime frendly.*
136. *I*, γ⁸ omits.
139. *you*, so a² J G R S ; rest *ye.*
144. *y-like*, so a² Cx. H₃ ; J and others *ay y-like.*
157. *hiede her*, so a² Cx. ; others omit *her.*
158. *sobrely*, γ⁸ *softely.*
160. *And*, J *But.*
100. *he* ; J and others *ye.*

168. *lenger that ye*, a² R Cx. ; J G γ *lenger ye ne.*
188. *in*, γ⁸ *in the.*
189. *mirácle*, γ⁸ *merveille.*

To speke of love !'—and right therwith
    he lough,—   199
'For ther have ye a leiser for to telle.'—
Quod Troilus, 'How longe shal I dwelle
Or this be don ?' Quod he, 'Whan thou
    mayst rise,
This thing shal be right as I thee devise.'

With that, Eleyne and also Deiphebus
Tho comen upward right at the staires
    ende ;
And Lord, so tho gan gronen Troilus,
His brother and his suster for to blende.
Quod Pandarus, 'It time is that we wende :
Tak, nece myn, your leve at alle three,
And lat hem speke, and cometh forth
    with me.'   210

She took her leve at hem ful thriftily
As she wel coude ; and they her reverence
Unto the fulle diden hardily,
And speken wonder wel in her absence
Of her, in preising of her excellence,
Her governaunce, her wit ; and her manere
Commendeden, it joye was to here.

Now lat her wende unto her owne place,
And torne we to Troilus ayein,
That gan ful lightly of the lettre pace 220
That Deiphebus had in the gardin seyn ;
And of Eleyne and him he wolde feyn
Delivered ben, and seide that him leste
To slepe, and after-tales to han reste.

Eleyne him kiste and took her leve blive ;
Deiphebus ek ; and hom wente every
    wight ;
And Pandarus, as faste as he may drive,
To Troilus tho com, as line right ;
And on a pailet al that gladde night
By Troilus he lay, with blisful chere, 230
To tale ; and wel was hem they were i-fere.

Whan every wight was voided but they two,
And alle the dores weren faste y-shette—

To telle in short withoute wordes mo—
This Pandarus withouten any lette
Up-roos, and on his beddes side him sette,
And gan to speken in a sobre wise
To Troilus, as I shal you devise :   238

'Myn alderlevest lord and brother dere,
God wot, and thou, that it sat me so sore
When I thee saw so languisshing to-yere
For love, of which thy wo wex alwey more ;
That I with al my might and al my lore
Have evere sithen don my bisinesse
To bringe thee to joye out of distresse,

'And have it brought to swich plit as thou
    wost,
So that thorugh me thou stondest now
    in weye
To faren wel : I seye it for no bost,
And wostow why ? For, shame it is to seye,
For thee have I bigonne a game pleye 250
Which that I nevere don shal eft for other,
Although he were a thousand fold my
    brother ;

'That is to seyn, for thee am I becomen,
Betwixen game and ernest, swich a mene
As maken wommen unto men to comen :
Thou wost thy-selven what I wolde mene.
For thee have I my nece, of vices clene,
So fully maad thy gentilesse triste, 258
That al shal ben right as thy-selven liste.

'But God that al wot take I to witnesse,
That nevere I this for coveitise wroughte,
But only for t' abregge that distresse
For which wel nigh thou deydest, as me
    thoughte.
But, goode brother, do now as thee oughte
For Goddes love, and keep her out of blame ;
Sith thou art wis, so save alwey her name.

'For wel thou wost the name yit of here
Among the peple, as who seith, halwed is ;
For nevere was ther wight, I dar wel swere,

199. *and right,* J H₅ γ *a-right.*
203. *I thee,* so R ; a² Cx. *I* ; H₄ *thei* ; J G *thou wilt* ; H₅ *I woll* ; γ *I you.*
205. *right at* ; a² Cx. H₃ *at.*
206. *tho,* H₅ H₃ γ *than(ne).*
230. *blisful,* H₃ γ *merie.*

256. So α β ; γ *Alweye I nought, thou wost wel what I mene.*
266. *so save,* J G² *so kepe* ; γ *and save.*
267. *yet,* γ *as yet.*
269. So J H₄ G² S Cx. ; a² R γ *For that man is unbore.*

That everė wistė that she dide amis.　270
But wo is me, that I, that cause al this,
May thenken that she is my necė dere,
And I her em and trattor ek i-fere !

'And were it wist that I thorugh myn engýn
Had in my nece y-put this fantasye
To don thy lust and hoolly to ben thyn,
Why, al the peplė wolde upon it crye
And seyn that I the worstė trecherye
Dide in this cas that everė was bigonne,
And she fordon, and thou right naught
　　　y-wonne !　　　280

'Wherfor, or I wol further gon a pas,
Thee preye ich eft, although thou
　　　shuldest deye,
That privėtė go with us in this cas :
That is to seye, that thou us neverė wreyc;
And be not wroth though I thee oftė preye
To holden secrė swich an heigh matėre,
For skilful is, thou wost wel, my prayėre.

'And thenk what wo ther hath betid or this
For making of avauntės, as men rede,
And what mischaunce in this world yit
　　　ther is,　　　290
Fro day to day, right for that wikked dede;
For-which thise wisė clerkės that ben dede
Han everė thus provėrbėd to us yonge,
"The firstė vertu is to kepė tonge."

'And n'ere it that I wilne as now abregge
Defusioun of speche, I coude almost
A thousand oldė stories thee alegge
Of wommen lost thorugh fals and folis bost.
Provėrbės canst thyselve y-nowe and wost,
Ayeins that vicė, for to ben a labbe　300
　Though men soth seide as often as they
　　　gabbe.

'Oo tonge, allas, so often her-beforn
Hath maad ful many a lady bright of hewe
Seyn "weylawey the day that I was born !"
And many a maydės sorwė for to newe :
And for the morė part al is untrewe
That men of-yelpe, and it were brought
　　　to preve :
Of kindė non avauntour is to leve.

'Avauntour and a lier, al is on ;　300
As thus : I pose a womman graunteth me
Her love, and seith that other wol she non,
And I am sworn to holden it secrė,
And after I go telle it two or three ;
Y-wis, I am avauntour at the leste,
And lier, for I brekė my beheste.

'Now lokė than if they ben aught to blame?
Such maner folk, —what shal I clepe
　　　hem, what ?—
That hem avaunte of wommen, and by
　　　name,
That neverė yit behighte hem this ne
　　　that,
Ne knewe hem morė than myn oldė hat !
No wonder is, so god me sendė hele,　321
Though wommen dreden with us men to
　　　dele !

'I seye not this for no mistrust of you,
Ne for no wis-man, but for folės nice,
And for the harm that in the world is now
As wel for foly ofte as for malíce ;
For wel wot I in wisė folk that vice
No womman drat, if she be wel avised ;
For wisė ben by folės harm chastised.

'But now to purpos. Levė brother dere,
Have al this thing that I have seid in
　　　minde,　　　331
And kep thee clos, and be now of good
　　　chere,
For at thy day thou shalt me trewė findc.
I shal thy proces sette in swich a kinde,
And God to-forn, that it shal thee suffise,
For it shal ben right as thou wolt devise.

273. *trattor* (Ɣ), H₁ *tractor;* J and others *trait-our, tretour,* etc. (Boc. *trattator*).
277. *peple wolde upon it,* so a² J R Cx.; ɣ *world upon it wolde.*
280. *fordon,* so a β ; H₄ *forlorn;* G ɣ *forlost.*
282. So a β ; G ɣ *Yet eft I thee bieeche and fully seye.*
293. J H₄ R Cx. *Han write or this, as men yit teche us yonge.*
294. *The,* so a² R Cx. ; *That the,* H₄ H₃ H₃ ; rest *That.*
301. *Though men soth seide,* so a β ; ɣ *Alseyde men soth.*

302. *Oo,* H₄ Cx. *For* (*oo* probably means *one*).
303. *Hath maad ful,* so a β ; G ɣ *Hasten maad* (omit *ful*).
304. *Seyn,* so R Cx. H₃ S₂ Dg. ; rest *Seyde*.

' For wel I wot thou menest wel, pardé ;
Therfore I dar this fully undertake.
Thou wost ek what thy lady graunted thee,
And day is set the chartres up to make.
Have now good night, I may no lenger
    wake ;   341
And bid for me, sith thou art now in blisse,
That God me sendé deth or soné lisse !'

Who mighté tellen half the joye or feste
Which that the soule of Troilus tho felte,
Hering th'effect of Pandarus' beheste ?
His oldé wo that made his herté swelte
Gan tho for joyé wasten and to-melte ;
And al the richesse of his sikés sore   349
At-onés fledde, he felte of hem no more.

But right so as thise boltés and thise hayis,
That han in winter dedé ben and dreye,
Revesten hem in grené whan that May is,
Whan every lusty listeth best to pleye,
Right in that selvé wisé, soth to seye,
Wex sodeinly his herté ful of joye,
That gladder was ther neveré man in Troye.

And gan his look on Pandarus up-caste
Ful sobrely and frendly for to see,
And seidé, ' Frend, in Aperil the laste, 360
As wel thou wost, if it remembré thee,
How neigh the deth for wo thou foundé
    me,
And how thou didest al thy bisinesse
To knowe of me the cause of my distresse.

' Thou wost how longe ich it forbar to seye
To thee, that art the man that I best triste ;
And peril non was it to thee biwreye,
That wiste I wel : but tel me, if thee liste,
Sith I so loth was that thy-self it wiste,
How dorste I mo tellen of this matére, 370
That quaké now, and no wight may us
    here ?

' But nathéles by that God I thee swere
That as him list may al this world governe,
And if I lye, Achilles with his spere

Myn herté cleve, al were my lif eterne
As I am mortal, if I late or yerne
Wolde it biwreye, or dorste, or sholde
    konne,
For al the good that God made under
    sonne ;   378

' That rather dye I wolde, and détermine,
As thinketh me, now stokkéd in prisoun,
In wrecchednesse, in filthe, and in vermíne,
Captif to cruel King Agámenoun :
And this in alle the temples of this toun
Upon the Goddés alle I wol thee swere
To-morwé day, if that it lik'th thee here.

' And that thou hast so muche y-don for me
That I ne may it neveré mo deserve,
This knowe I wel, al mighte I now for
    thee
A thousand timés on a morwé sterve. 389
I can no more, but that I wol thee serve
Right as thy sclavé, whider so thou wende,
For everé-more unto my livés ende !

' But here with al myn herte I thee biseche
That nevere in me thou demé swich folýe
As I shal seyn : me thoughté by thy speche
That this which thou me dost for com-
    panýe,
I sholdé wene it were a bauderýe.
I am not wood, al if I lewéd be !
It is not oon, that wot I wel, pardé ! 399

' But he that go'th for gold or for richésse
On swich messágé, calle him as thee list ;
And this that thou dost, calle it gentilesse,
Compassioun, and felawship, and trist.
Departe it so, for widé-wher is wist
How that ther is diversité requered
Bitwixen thingés like, as I have lered.

' And that thou knowe I thenké not ne
    wene
That this servíse a shamé be or jape,
I have my fairé suster Polixene, 409
Cassandre, Eleyne, or any of the frape :
Al be she nevere so fairé or wel y-shape,

354. *listeth,* so α β ; γ *liketh.*
355. *to,* R Cx. γ *for to.*
359. *for to,* α⁵ H₃ Cx. *on(un) to.*
371. *wight,* J R Cx. *man.*

379. *That,* H₁ R Cx. S *But.*
399. *oon,* so J α² G² ; rest *so.*
411. *Al,* so R ; rest omit.

Tellė me which thou wilt of everychone
To han for thyn, and lat me thanne allone!

'But sith thou hast y-don me this servíse
My lif to save, and for non hope of mede,
So, for the love of God, this grete emprise
Parforme it out, for now is mostė nede ;
For heigh and lowe, withouten any drede,
I wol alwey thine hestės allė kepe :
Have now good night, and lat us bothė
    slepe.'   420

Thus held him ech of other wel apayed,
That al the world ne mighte it bet amende ;
And on the morwė, whan they were arayed,
Ech to his ownė nedės gan entende.
But Troilus, though as the fir he brende
For sharp desír of hope and of plesáunce,
He not forgat his wisė governaunce,

But in himself with manhod gan restreyne
Ech rakel dede and ech unbridled chere,
That allė tho that livėn, soth to seyne,   430
Ne sholde han wist by word or by manére
What that he mente, as touching this
    matére :
From every wight as fer as is the cloude
He was, so wel dissimulen he coude.

And al this whilė that I you devíse,
This was his lif : with al his fullė might
By day he was in Martės heigh servíse,
This is to seyn, in armès as a knight ;
And for the morė part the longė night   439
He lay and thoughtė how he mightė serve
His lady best, her thonk for to deserve.

I n'il not seyn that, though he lay ful softe,
That in his thought he n'as somwhat
    disesed,
Ne that he tornėd on his pilwes ofte,
And wolde of that he missėd han ben esed ;
But in swich cas men ben not alwey plesed,

For aught I wot, no morė than was he :
That can I deme of possibilité.

But certein is, to purpos for to go,   445
This menė while, as writen is in geste,
He saw his lady som-time ; and also
She with him spak whan that she dursie
    and leste ;
And by hir bothe avis, as was the beste,
Apointeden ful warly in this nede
In every thing how they wolden procede.

But it was spoken in so short a wise,
In swich await alwey, and in swich fere,
Lest any wight devinen or devise
Wolde on this thing, or to it leye an ere,
That al this world so lief to hem ne were
As Cupido wolde hem a spacė sende   451
To maken of hir speche aright an ende.

But th'ilkė litel that they spake or wroughte
His wisė gost took ay of al swich hede,
It semėd her he wistė what she thoughte
Withouten word, so that it was no nede
To bidde him aught to don, or aught
    forbede :
For which her thoughte that love, al
    come it late,
Of allė joye had opned her the yate.

And, shortly of this proces for to pace,   460
So wel his werk and wordės he bisette,
That he so ful stood in his lady grace
That twenty thousand timès or she lette
She thonkėd God she everė with hir
    mette,
So coude he him govérne in swich servise
That al the world ne mighte it bet devise.

For-why she fond him so discret in al,
So secret, and of swich obéisaunce,
That wel she felte he was to her a wal

412. *me ; γ omits.*
427. *wise,* so a β ; *γ gode.*
433. *From every wight,* a² G² *From ech in that.*
435. *this, γ the.*
439. *more,* a² G² R Cx. *moste.*
442. So J H₄ R S ; a² G² γ *N'il I not swere although.*
442. *ful,* so H₄ R ; rest omit.
445. *esed,* a² R γ *sesed.*

450. *This menė while ;* a² G² γ *That is this while.*
452. *and,* J and others *or.*
455. *In every thing,* so J H₄ R ; a² G² γ *as they dorste.*
459. *on this thing,* so J H₄ R S ; a² G² *in the speche ; γ of hem two.*
461. *As,* so J H₄ R ; a² G² γ *As that.*
461. *space,* so J a² G² H₄ ; R γ *grace.*
468. *her,* so J H₄ R ; a² G² γ *she.*

Of steel, and sheld from every displesaunce,
That to ben in his godè governaunce, 481
So wis he was, she was no more afered,—
I mene, as fer as oughtè ben requered.

And Pandarus, to quike alwey this fir,
Was evere y-likè prest and diligent ;
To ese his frend was set al his desir ;
He shof ay on ; he to and fro was sent ;
He lettres bar whan Troilus was absént ;
That neverè wight as in his frendès nede
Ne bar him bet to don his frend to spede.

But now paraunter som man waiten wolde
That every word or look, or sonde or chere
Of Troilus that I rehersen sholde   493
In al this while unto his lady dere :
I trowe it were a long thing for to here,
Or of what wight that stant in swich disjoint
His wordès alle or every look to-point !

For-sothe I have not herd it don or this
In storie non, ne no man here I wene !
And though I wolde, I coudè not y-wis ;
For ther was some epistel hem bitwene
That wolde, as seith myn auctour, wel
        contene   502
An hondred vers, of which him list not
        write ;
How sholde I than a line of it endite ?

But to the grete effect. Than seye I thus,
That—stonding in concord and in quiéte
Thise ilkè two, Criseyde and Troilus,
As I have seid, and in this timè swete,
Save only oftè mightè they not mete,
Ne leiser han hir spechè to fulfelle,— 510
That it bifel right as I shal you telle,

That Pandar, which that alwey dide his
        might
Right for the fin that I shal speke of here,
As for to bringen to his hous som night
His fairè nece and Troilus i-fere,
Wher-as at leiser al this heighe matére

Touching hir love were at the fulle up-
        bounde,
Had, as him thoughte, a timè to it founde.

For he with gret deliberacioun   519
Had every thing that ther-to mighte availe
Forncast and put in execucioun,
And neither left for cost ne for travaile.
Come if hem list, hem sholdè no thing
        faile ;
And for to ben in aught aspyèd there,
That wiste he wel an ímpossiblè were.

And dredèles it cler was in the wind
Of every pye, of every lettè-game.
Thus al is wel ; for al this world is blind
In this matérè, bothè wilde and tame !
This timber is al redy up to frame : 530
Us lakketh naught, but that we witen wolde
A certein houre in which she comen sholde !

And Troilus, that al this púrveyaunce
Knew at the fulle and waited on it ay,
Had her-upon ek maad his ordinaunce,
And foundè his causeānd ther-to al th'aray,
That if that he were missèd night or day
Ther-whil he was aboutè this servíse,
That he was gon to don his sacrifise,

And moste at swich a temple allonè wake,
Answérèd of Apollo for to be,   541
And first to sen the holy laurer quake
Or that Apollo spake out of the tree
To telle him whan the Grekès sholden
        flee,—
And for-thy lette him no man, God forbede,
But preye Apollo that he wolde him spede !

Now is ther litel morè for to done ;
But Pandar up, and (shortly for to seyne)

484. *this,* so J H₄ R ; *a² G² γ the.*
490. *to don his frend to spede,* so J H₄ R Cx.;
others *than he withouten drede.*
503. *An hondred vers,* so J H₄ R Cx. ; others
Neigh half this book.
508. *seid,* so J H₄ R Cx. ; others *told.*

518. *as him thoughte,* so J H₄ R Cx. S ; others
out of doute.
526. *And,* so Cx. S H₃ ; rest omit.
529. *wilde,* so J H₄ R Cx. S H₃; *a² G² γ
fremde.*
535. *his,* S H₃ γ *gret.*
537. *That if that.* γ *If that.*
543. *Apollo, a² G² the god (aught).*
544. *whan the Grekes, a² G² γ next whan
Grekes* (var.).
546. *that he wolde him spede,* so J H₄ R Cx. ;
others *helpen in this nede.*

Right sone upon the chaunging of the mone
Whan lightles is the world a night or
     tweyne,   550
And that the welken shop him for to reyne,
He streight a-morwe unto his nece wente :
Ye han wel herd the fin of his entente.

Whan he was come, he gan anon to pleye
As he was wont, and at him-self to jape ;
And finaliche he swor and gan her seye
By this and that, she sholde him not escape,
Ne make him lenger after her to gape,
But certeinly she moste by her leve   559
Come soupen in his hous with him at eve.

At which she lough, and gan her faste
     excusen,
And seide, 'It raineth : lo, how sholde
     I gon ?'—
'Lat be,' quod he, 'ne stond not thus to
     musen :
This mot be don : ye shal be ther anon !'—
So at the laste her-of they fille at oon,
Or elles, softe he swor her in her ere,
He wolde nevere comen ther she were.

And she a-game gan him for to roune,
And axed him if Troilus were there.   569
He swor her, 'nay, for he was out of toune,'
And seide, 'Nece, I pose that he were,
Thee thurfte nevere han the more fere ;
For, rather than men sholde him ther aspye,
Me were levere a thousand fold to dye.'

Not list myn auctour fully to declare
What that she thoughte whan he seide so,
That Troilus was out of toune y-fare,
As if he seide soth ther-of or no ;
But that she graunted with him for to go
Withoute await, sin he her that bisoughte,
And as his nece obeyed as her oughte.

But natheles yit gan she him biseche,   582
Although with him to gon it was no fere,
For to be war of goosissh peples speche

That dremen thinges whiche that nevere
     were,
And wel avise him whom he broughte there.
And seide him, 'Em, sin I moste on
     you triste,
Loke al be wel, for I do as you liste.'

He swor her this, by stokkes and by stones,
And by the Goddes that in hevene dwelle,
Or elles were him levere, fel and bones,   591
With Pluto King as depe ben in helle
As Tantalus !—What sholde I longe telle?
Whan al was wel, he roos and took his leve :
And she to soper com, whan it was eve,

With ek a certein of her owne men,
And with her faire nece Antigone
And other of her wommen nine or ten.
But who was glad now? Who, as trowen ye,
But Troilus, that stood and mighte it see   600
Thorugh-out a litel window in a stewe
Ther he bi-shet til midnight was in mewe,

Unwist of every wight but of Pandare ?
But now to purpos. Whan that she was
     come
With alle joye and alle frendes fare,
Her em anon in armes hath her nome,
And after to the soper, alle and some,
When time was, ful softe they hem sette :
God wot, ther was no deynte for to fette !

And after soper gonnen they to rise   610
At ese wel with hertes fresshe and glade ;
And wel was him that coude best devise
To liken her, or that her laughen made.
He song : she pleyde : he tolde tale of
     Wade.
But at the laste, as every thing hath ende,
She took her leve, and nedes wolde wende.

588. *for I do*, so J H₄ R Cx ; G² *γ and (a² I) do now.*
589. *this*, so J R G² ; Cx. *tho ;* a² H₄ D om. ; *γ yis.*
596. *With ek* (I), all *With.*
598. a² G² *And (of) her wommen wel (a) nin: or ten.*
599. *was*, a² G² *is.*
602. *til*, H₂ *tul ;* others *sin.*
604. *now to purpos*, so J H₄ R Cx. S ; a² G² *γ to the point now.*
614. *tale of Wade ;* see C.T. E 1424.

568. *And she a-game* (I), J R Cx. *And she againe* (H₄ *on game*) ; a³ G² *γ Sone after this she* (var.) See ll. 636, 648.
   579, 580. So J H₄ R Cx. S ; a² G² *γ*
     But that withoute await with him to go
     She graunted him . . .

But O Fortúne, executrice of wierdes !
O Influences of thise hevenės hye !
Soth is, that under God ye ben our hierdes,
Though to us beestės ben the causes wrye !
This mene I now, for she gan homward
     hye ;   621
But execut was al biside her leve
The Goddės wil ; for which she mostė bleve.

The bentė monė with her hornės pale,
Saturn, and Jove, in Cancro joinėd were,
That swich a reyn from hevenė gan avale
That every maner womman that was there
Had of that smoky reyn a verray fere ;
At which Pandáre tho lough, and seidė
     thenne,   629
' Now were it time a lady to gon henne !

' But, godė nece, if I mighte everė plese
You any thing, than preye ich you,' quod he,
' To don myn herte as now so gret an ese
As for to dwelle here al this night with me ;
For, necė, this' your ownė hous, pardé !
Now by my trouthe I seye it not a-game :
To wende as now, to me it were a shame.'

Criseydė, which that coude as muchė good
As half a world, took hede of his preyére ;
And sin it ron and al was on a flood,   640
She thoughte, 'as good chep may I dwellen
     here,
And graunte it gladly with a frendės chere
And have a thank, as grucche and than
     abide,
For hom to gon, it may not wel bi-tide.'

' I wol,' quod she, 'myn uncle lief and dere ;
Sin that you list, it skile is to be so ;
I am right glad with you to dwellen here ;
I seidė but a-game, I woldė go.'—   648
' Y-wis, graunt mercy, necė !' quod he tho ;
' Were it a-game or no, soth for to telle,
Now am I glad, sin that you list to dwelle.'

Thus al is wel.   But tho began aright
The newė joye and al the feste agayn ;

But Pandarus, if goodly had he might,
He wolde han hyėd her to beddė fayn ;
And seidė, ' Lord, this is a hugė rayn !
This were a weder for to slepen inne !
And that I rede us sonė to beginne !   658

' And, necė, wot ye wher I shal you leye ?
For-that we shal not liggen fer asonder,
And for ye neither shullen, dar I seye,
Herė no noise of reynės nor of thonder,
By God, right in my litė closet yonder ;
And I wol in that outer hous allone
Ben wardein of your wommen everychone.

' And in this middel chaumbrė that ye see
Shul alle your wommen slepen wel and
     softe,
And al withinnė shal your-selven be ;
And if ye liggen wel to-night come ofte,
And careth not what weder is a-lofte !   670
The wyn anon ; and whan so that you leste,
Than is it timė for to gon to reste.'

Ther n'is no morė ; but her-after sone,
The voidė dronke, and travers drawe anon,
Gan every wight that haddė naught to done
More in the place out of the chaumbrė gon.
And alwey in this menė while it ron,
And blew ther-with so wonderlichė loudė,
That wel nigh no man herėn other coude.

Tho Pandarus, her em, right as him oughte,
With wommen swiche as were her most
     aboute,   681
Ful glad unto her beddės side her broughte,
And took his leve, and gan ful lowė loute,
And seide her, ' At this closet dore withoute,
Right overthwart, your wommen liggen
     alle,
That whom you list of hem ye may her calle.'

So whan that she was in the closet leyd,
And alle her wommen forth by ordinaunce

623. *The*, γ⁵ *At the.*
635. *For, nece, this (is)*, so J H₄ R Cx. S : α²
G² γ *For why this is.*
636. *Now*, H₃ *And* ; γ⁷ *For.*

662. *Here no* (?), all *Herė(n).*
667. *alle*, so H₆ S Cx. ; rest omit. (Read ?
Shullen ; see l. 661.)
668. *al withinne*, so J H₄ R Cx. S ; α² γ *ther
I seyde* ; G² *ther besyden.*
672. So J H₄ R Cx. S H₃ (var.) ; α² G² γ⁷ *So
go we slepe, I trowe it be the beste* (var.)
677. So J H₄ R Cx. S ; α² G² γ⁸ *And evere mo
so sterneliche it ron.*

A-beddė werėn ther-as I have seyd,   689
Ther was no more to skippen ne to traunce,
But boden gon to beddė, with mischaunce,
If any man was stering any-where,
And lat hem slepen that a-beddė were.

But Pandarus, that wel coude ech a del
The oldė daunce, and every point ther-inne,
Whan that he saw that allė thing was wel,
He thoughte he wolde upon his werk
    biginne,
And gan the stewė dore al softe unpinne ;
And stille as stoon, withouten lenger lette,
By Troilus adoun right he him sette.   700

And, shortly to the point right for to gon,
Of al this thing he tolde him word and
    ende,
And seidė, ' Mak thee redy right anon,
For thou shalt into hevenė blissė wende ! '
' Now, seintė Venus, thou me gracė sende,'
Quod Troilus, ' for neverė yit no nede
Hadde ich or now, ne halvendel the drede!'

Quod Pandarus, ' Ne dred thee nevere a del,
For it shal ben right as thou wolt desire :
So thrive I, this night shal I make it wel,
Or casten al the gruel in the fire ! '—   711
' Yit, blisful Venus, this night thou m'
    enspire,'
Quod Troilus, ' as wis as I thee serve,
And everė bet and bet shal til I sterve.

' And if ich hadde, O Venus ful of mirthe,
Aspėctės baddė of Mars or of Saturne,
Or thou combust or let were in my birthe,
Thy fader prey al th'ilkė harm disturne
Of grace, and that I glad ayein may turne,
For love of him thou lovedest in the shawe,
I mene Adón, that with the boor was slawe.

' O Jove ek, for the love of fairė Európe
The whiche in forme of bole awey thou fette,
Now help ! O Mars, thou with thy blody
    cope,
For love of Cipris thou me naught ne lette !

692. *man*, so J H₄ Cx. a³ G² ; R S γ³ *wight*.
696. *saw*, a² G² *wiste*.
725. *Cipris*, Venus ; see v. 208.

O Phebus, thenk whan Dane her-selven
    shette
Under the barke, and laurer wex for drede ;
Yit for her love, O help now at this nede !

' Mercúrie, for the love of Hiersė eke,   729
For which Pallás was with Aglauros wroth,
Now help ! And ek Diane, I thee bisekc
That this viágė be not to thee loth !
O fatal sustren, whiche, or any cloth
Me shapen was, my destinė me sponne,
So helpeth to this werk that is begonne !'—

Quod Pandarus, ' Thou wrecched mouses
    herte !
Art thou agast so that she wol thee bite ?
Why, don this furrėd cloke upon thy sherte,
And folwė me, for I wol han the wite !   739
But bid, and lat me gon biforn a lite.'—
And with that word he gan undo a trappe,
And Troilus he broughte in by the lappe.

The sternė wind so loudė gan to route
That no wight other noisė mightė here ;
And they that layėn at the dore withoute
Ful sikerly they slepten alle i-fere ;
And Pandarus, with a ful sobrė chere,
Go'th to the dore anon withouten lette
Ther-as they laye, and softėliche it shette.

And, as he com ayeinward privėly,   750
His nece awook, and askėd, ' Who go'th
    there ? '—
' My derė necė,' quod he, ' it am I !
Ne wondreth not, ne have of it no fere.'—
And ner he com, and seyde her in her ere,
' No word, for love of God, I you biseche !
Lat no wight rise and herėn of our
    speche ! '

' What ! which way be ye comėn, ben-
    distė ? '
Quod she, ' and how thus unwist of hem
    alle ? '—

726. *Dane*, Daphne ; see *C.T.* 2062-2064.
729. *Hierse*, Herse, daughter of Cecrops, beloved by Mercury.
730. *Aglauros*, Herse's sister ; see Ovid, *Met.*
ii. 708-832.
733. *fatal sustren*, the three Fates.
757. *bendistė*, so J ; others *benedicitė*.
758. *thus*, R γ³ omit.

'Here at this lite trappé-dore,' quod he.—
Quod tho Criseydé, 'Lat me som wight
    calle !'—   760
'Ey ! God forbedé that it sholdé falle,'
Quod Pandarus, 'that ye swich foly
    wroughte !
They mighté demen that they nevere er
    thoughte !

'It n'is not good a sleping hound to wake,
Ne yeve a wight a causé to devine :
Your wommen slepen alle, I undertake,
So that for hem the hous men mighté mine,
And slepen wollen til the sonné shine !
And whan my tale y-brought is to an ende,
Unwist, right as I com, so wol I wende. 770

'Now, necé myn, ye shal wel understonde,'
Quod he, 'so as ye wommen demen alle,
That for to holden longe a man in honde
And him her lief and deré herté calle,
And maken him an howve above a calle,
I mene, as love another in this while,—
She doth herself a shame and him a gile.

'Now, wher-by that I tellé you al this :
Ye wot your-self as wel as any wight
How that your love al fully graunted is 780
To Troilus, the worthiesté knight
Oon of this world, and therto trouthe
    y-plight,
That, but it were on him along, ye n'olde
Him neveré falsen whil ye livén sholde.

'Now stant it thus : that sin I fro you wente,
This Troilus, right platly for to seyn,
Is thorugh a goter by a privé wente
Into my chaumbré come in al this reyn,
Unwist of every maner wight, certeyn,
Save of myself, as wisly have I joye, 790
And by that feith I shal Priám of Troye !

'And he is come in swich peyne and distresse
That, but he be al fully wood by this,
He sodeinly mot falle into woodnésse
But-if God helpe. And causé why this is,—
He seith him told is of a frend of his,

How that ye sholden love oon, hatte
    Horaste,
For sorwe of which this night shal ben
    his laste !'

Criseydé, which that al this wonder herde,
Gan therwithal aboute her herté colde, 800
And with a sik she sodeinly answérde,
'Allas, I wen'dé, who-so talés tolde,
My deré herté wolde me not holde
So lightly fals ! Allas, conceités wronge,
What harm they don, for now live I too
    longe !

'Horaste ! allas, and falsen Troilus !
I knowe him not, God help me so !'
    quod she.
'Allas, what wikked spirit tolde him thus ?
Now certés, em, to-morwe, and I him see,
I shal of that as ful excusen me 810
As everé didé womman, if him like.'
And with that word she gan ful soré sike.

'O God !' quod she, 'so worldly selinesse,
Which clerkés callen fals felicité,
Y-medled is with many a bitternesse !
Ful anguisshous than is, God wot,' quod
    she,
'Condicioun of veyn prosperité !
For either joyés comen not i-fere,
Or ellés no wight hath hem alwey here.

'O brotel wele ! O worldly joye un-
    stable !   820
With what wight so thou be or how thou
    pleye,
Either he wot that thou, joye, art muáble,
Or wot it not ; it mot be oon of tweye.
Now, if he wot it not, how may he seye
That he hath verray joye and selinesse,
That is of ignoraunce ay in derknésse ?

'Now, if he wot that joye is transitorie,
As every joye of worldly thing mot flee,

---

773. *holden longe*, so J H₄ R Cx. H₃ ; others *holde in love*.

797. *oon*, G γ *oon that*.
800. *therwithal*, a² G² γ *sodeinly*.
801. *sodeinly*, a² G² γ *sorwfully*.
810. *of that*, S γ *therof*.
813-836. Adapted from *Boethius* ii. prosa 4.
820. *O worldly*, so J H₄ R Cx ; a² G² γ *of mannes*.

Than every time he that hath in memórie,
The drede of lesing maketh him that he   830
May in no parfit selinessé be ;
And if to lese his joye he set a mite,
Than semeth it that joye is worth ful lite.

'Wherfor I wol define in this manére,
That trewély, for aught I can espye,
Ther is no verray wele in this world here.
But O thou wikked serpent jalousýe !
Thou misbelevéd envious folýe !
Why hastow Troilus maad to me untriste,
That neveré yit agilte him that I
        wiste ?'—   840

Quod Pandarus, 'Thus fallen is this cas—'
'Why ! uncle myn,' quod she, 'who tolde
        him this ?
Why doth my deré herté thus, allas ?'—
'Ye wot, ye necé myn,' quod he, 'what is.
I hope al shal be wel that is amis,
For ye may quenche al this if that you leste.
And doth right so : I holde it for the
        beste.'—

'So shal I don to-morwe, y-wis,' quod she,
'And God to-forn, so that it shal suffise.'—
'To-morwe ? allas, that were a fair !'
        quod he.   850
'Nay, nay, it may not stonden in this wise ;
For, necé myn, thus writen clerkés wise,
That peril is with drecching in y-drawe :
Nay, such abodés ben not worth a hawe !

'Nece, allé thing hath time, I dar avowe ;
For whan a chaumbre a-fire is, or au halle,
Wel more nede is, it sodeinly rescowe
Than to dispute and axe amongés alle
"How is this candel in the straw y-falle ?"
A ! bendisté ! for al among this fare   860
The harm is don, and far-wel feldéfare !

'And, necé myn, ne take it not a-grief :
If that ye suffre him al night in this wo,
God help me so, ye had him neveré lief !
That dar I seyn, now ther is but we two.
But wel I wot that ye wol not do so ;

Ye ben too wis to don so gret folýe
To putte his lif al night in jupartýe.'—

'Had ich him neveré lief ? By God, I wene
Ye haddé neveré thing so lief !' quod
        she. —   870
'Now, by my thrift,' quod he, 'that shal
        be sene !
For, sin ye maken this ensaumple of me,
If ich al night wolde him in sorwé see
For al the tresour in the town of Troye,
I biddé God I neveré mote have joye !

'Now, loké than, if ye that ben his love
Shall putte his lif al night in jupartye
For thing of naught, now by that God above
Not only this delay com'th of folýe
But of malíce, if that I shal not lye !   880
What ! platly, and ye suffre him in distresse,
Ye neither wisdom don ne gentilesse !'

Quod tho Criseydé, 'Wol ye don oo thing,
And ye therwith shal stinten his disese :
Have here and bereth him this blewé ring,
For ther is no thing mighte him bettré plese
Save I my-self, ne more his herte apese ;
And seye my deré herté, that his sorwe
Is causéles : that shal he seen to-morwe !'—

'A ring ?' quod he, 'ye, haselwodés
        shaken !   890
Ye, necé myn, that ring moste have a ston
That mighté dedé men a-livé maken ;
And swich a ring trowe I that ye have non !
Discrecioun out of your hed is gon :
That fele I now,' quod he, 'and that is
        routhe.
O time y-lost ! wel maystow corsen
        slouthe !

'Wot ye not wel that noble and heigh coráge
Ne sorweth not ne stinteth ek for lite ?
But, if a fool were in a jalous rage,
I n'oldé setten at his sorwe a mite,   900
But feffe him with a fewé wordés white
Another day whan that I mighté him finde !
But this thing stant al in another kinde.

838. *envious*, J γ⁴ *and envious.*
862. *ne*, a² Gᵈ J omit.

882. *wisdom*, a² G² γ *bounte.*
889. *causeles*, a² G² *nedeles.*
889. *he seen*, a² Gᵈ γ *be sene (seyn).*

' This is so gentil and so tendre of herte
That with the deth he wol his sorwes wreke ;
For, trusteth wel, how soré that him
    smerte,
He wol to you no jalous wordès speke.
And for-thy, nece, or ye his hertè breke,
So spek yourself to him of this matére ;
For with oo word ye may his hertè stere. 910

' Now have I told what peril he is inne ;
And his cominge unwist is t' every wight ;
And, pardé, harm may ther be non ne
    sinne ;
I wol my-self ben with you al this night.
Ye knowe ek how it is your ownè knight,
And that by right ye moste upon him triste,
And I al prest to fecche him whan you
    liste.'—

This accident so pitous was to here,
And ek so lik a soth at primé face,
And Troilus her knight to her so dere, 920
His privé coming, and the siker place,
That, though that she dide him as tho a
    grace,
Consideréd allè thingès as they stode,
No wonder is, sin she dide al for gode.

Criseyde answérde, ' As wisly God at reste
My soulè bringe, as me is for him wo !
And em, y-wis, fayn wolde I don the beste,
If that ich haddé gracè to do so.
But whether that ye dwelle or for him go,
I am, til God me bettrè mindé sende, 930
At Dulcarnon, right at my wittès ende.'—

Quod Pandarus, ' Ye, necè, wol ye here ?
Dulcarnon callèd is " fleeminge of
    wrecches " :
It semeth hard, for wrecches wol not lere
For   verray slouthe and othrè wilful
    tecches ;
This' seid by hem that ben not worth
    two fecches !

913. *And, γ Ne.*
931. *Dulcarnon* (from Arab. two - horned),
applied to Euclid i. 47. Here in the general sense
of difficulty or perplexity.
933. *fleeminge of wrecches*; a translation of
Fuga miserorum, or *Eleufuga*, applied to Euclid
i. 5, which Pandarus, perhaps purposely confuses
with the 47th proposition.

But ye ben wis ; and this matére on
    honde
N'is neither hard, ne skilful to with-
    stonde.'—

' Than, em,' quod she, ' doth her-of as
    you list !
But, or he come, I wol up first arise. 940
And, for the love of God, sin al my trist
Is on you two, and ye ben bothè wise,
So werketh now in so discreet a wise
That ich honoúr may have, and he ples-
    áunce,
For I am here as in your governaunce.'

' That is wel seid,' quod he, ' my necè
    dere ;
Ther good thrift on that wisè gentil hertè !
But liggeth stille and taketh him right
    here ;
It nedeth not no ferther for him sterte.
And ech of you ese othres sorwes smerte 950
For love of God ! And, Venus, I thee
    herie,
For sone hope I we shul ben allè merie !'—

This Troilus ful sone on knees him sette
Ful sobrèly, right by her beddès hed,
And in his bestè wise his lady grette.
But, Lord, so she wex sodeinlichè red !
Ne, though men sholden smiten off her
    hed,
She coudè not a word a-right out-bringe
So sodeinly, for his sodéin cominge !

But Pandarus, that so wel coudè fele 960
In every thing, to pleye anon bigan,
And seidè, ' Nece, see how this lord can
    knele
Now for your trouthe ! Y-see this gentil
    man !'
And with that word he for a quisshin ran,
And seidè, ' Kneleth now whil that you
    leste !
Ther God your hertès bringé sone at
    reste !'—

Can I not seyn, for she bad him not rise,
If sorwe it putte out of her rémembraunce,

937. *this matére, α² G² γ that we han.*

Or ellès that she took it in the wise
Of duèté as for his óbservaunce ; 970
But wel wot I she dide him this plesáunce,
That she him kiste, although she sightè
 sore,
Ánd bad him sitte a-doun withouten more.

Quod Pandarus, ' Now wol ye wel biginne!
Now doth him sittè, godè necè dere,
Upon your beddès side al ther withinne,
That ech of you the bet may other
 here !'—
And with that word he drow him to the fere,
And took a light, and fond his conte-
 naunce
As for to loke upon an old romaunce. 980

Criseydè, that was Troilus' lady right
And cleer stood on a ground of sikernesse,
Al thoughtè she her servaunt and her
 knight
Ne sholde of right non untrouthe in her
 gesse,
Yet nathèles, considerèd his distresse
And that love is in cause of swich folýe,
Thus to him spak she of his jalousýe :

' Lo, hertè myn, as woldè th' excellence
Of love, ayeins the whichè no man may
Ne oughte ek goodly maken résistence, 990
And ek because I feltè wel and say
Your gretè trouthe and servise every day,
And that your herte al myn was, soth to
 seyne,
This drof me for to rewe upon your peyne.

' And your goodnésse have I founde alwey
 yit,
Of which, my derè herte and al my knight,
I thonke it you as fer as I have wit,
Al can I not as muche as it were right ;
And I emforth my conning and my might
Have, and ay shal how sorè that me
 smerte, 1000
Ben to you trewe and hool with al myn
 herte ;

' And dredèles that shal be founde at preve !
But, hertè myn, what al this is to seyne
Shal wel be told, so that ye not you greve,
Though I to you right on your-self com-
 pleyne ;
For ther-with mene I finally the peyne
That halt your herte and myn in hevinesse
Fully to slen, and every wrong redresse.

' My godè myn, n'ot I for-why ne how
That jalousýe, allas, that wikked wivere,
So causèles is cropen into you, 1011
The harm of which I woldè fayn delivere.
Allas, that he, al hool, or of him slivere,
Sholde han his refut in so digne a place !
Ther Jove him sone out of your herte arace !

' But O thou Jove, O auctour of natúre !
Is this an honour to thy deitè,
That folk ungiltif suffren here injúre,
And who that giltif is, al quit go'th he ?
O were it leveful for to pleyne on thee, 1020
That undeservèd suffrest jalousýe,
Of that I wolde upon thee pleyne and crye !

' Ek al my wo is this, that folk now usen
To seyn right thus, "Ye, jalousye is love,"
And wolde a busshel venim al excusen
For-that oo greyn of love is in it shove !
But that wot heighè God that sit above,
If it be liker love, or hate and grame !
And after that it oughtè bere his name !

' But certein is, som maner jalousye 1030
Is excusáblè more than som, y-wis ;
As whan cause is, and som swich fantasye
With pietè so wel repressèd is
That it unnethè doth or seith amis,
But goodly drinketh up al his distresse :
And that excuse I for the gentilesse.

' And som so ful of furie is and despit
That it surmounteth his repressioun.
But, hertè myn, ye ben not in that plit,

971. *wot*, so J H₄ R ; Cx. *rede* ; others *finde*.
972. *sightè*, so J ; others *siked*.
979. *fond*, H₅ Cx. *feynede*.
989. *whiche*, so H₄ R Cx. a² G² ; J γ *whiche that*.

1011. *So*, so J H₄ R Cx ; others *Thus*.
1024. *Ye*, J and others *that*.
1026. *in*, γ *on*.
1028. *and grame*, so J H₄ ; others *or*.
1033. *pietè*, so J S Cp. H₁ only ; rest *pite*.
pete, etc.

496

That thanke I God ; for-which your
     passioun   1040
I wol not calle it but illusioun
Of hábundaunce of love and bisy cure,
That doth your herté this disese endure ;

' Of which I am right sory, but not wroth.
But, for my devoir and your hertés reste,
Whe'r so you list by ordal, or by oth,
By sort, or in what wisé so you leste,
For love of God, lat preve it for the beste !
And if that I be giltif, do me deye !
Allas, what mighte I moré don or seye?'—

With that a fewé brighté terés newe   1051
Out of her yen fille, and thus she seyde,
' Now God, thou wost in thought ne dede
     untrewe
To Troilus was neveré yit Criseyde ! '—
With that her hed doun in the bed she
     leyde,
And with the shete it wreigh, and sighté
     sore,
And held her pees : not oo word spak she
     more.

But now help God to quenchen al this sorwe!
So hope I that he shal, for he best may !
For I have seyn of a ful misty morwe
Folwen ful ofte a merie somer's day ;   1061
And after winter folweth grené May.
Men sen alday, and reden ek in stories,
That after sharpé shourés ben victóriés.

This Troilus whan he her wordés herde,
(Have ye no care !) him listé not to slepe ;
For it thoughte him no strokés of a yerde
To here or sen Criseyde his lady crepe,
But wel he felte aboute his herté crepe,
For every tere which that Criseyde asterte,
The crampe of deth, to streyne him by
     the herte.   1071

And in his minde he gan the time acorse
That evere he com ther, or that he was born ;
For now is wikké turnéd into worse,

And al the labour he hath don biforn
He wen'de it lost : he thoughte he n'as
     but lorn.
' O Pandarus,' thoughte he, ' allas, thy wile
Serveth of naught, so weylawey the
     while ! '—

And therwithal he heng adoun the hed,
And fil on knees, and sorwfulliche he
     sighte :   1080
What mighte he seyn ? He felte he n'as
     but ded ;
For wroth was she that sholde his sorwés
     lighte.
But nathéles, whan that he speken mighte,
Than seide he thus, ' God wot that of
     this game,
Whan al is wist, than am I not to blame ! '—

Therwith the sorwé so his herté shette
That from his yen fil ther not a tere ;
And every spirit his vigóur in-knette,
So they astonéd and oppresséd were ;   1089
The feling of his sorwe, or of his fere,
Or of aught ellés, fled was out of towne ;
And down he fil al sodeinliche a-swowne.

This was no litel sorwé for to see ;
But al was hust, for Pandar up as faste,
' O necé, pes, or we be lost ! ' quod he,
' Beth not agast ! ' But certein, at the laste,
For this or that, he into bedde him caste,
And seide, ' O thef, is this a mannés herte?'
And off he rente al to his baré sherte.

And seidé, ' Necé, but ye helpe us now,
Allas, your owné Troilus is lorn ! '   1101
' Y-wis, so wolde I, and I wisté how,
Ful fayn ! ' quod she : ' Allas, that I
     was born ! '—
' Ye, necé, wole ye pullén out the thorn
That stiketh in his herté,' quod Pandáre,
' Sey "al foryeve," and stint is al this
     fare ! '—

' Ye, that to me,' quod she, ' ful leveré were
Than al the good the sonne abouté go'th ! '
And therwithal she swor him in his ere,

1073. *evere*, so H₃ only.
1073. *or*, γ *and.*
1073. *that*, Cp. *that that.*
1073. *was*, H₃ *man was.*

1094. *But*, J Cx a² and others *For.*
1094. *for*, so H₄ G ; Cx. a² *but* ; J γ *and.*

'Y-wis, my deré herte, I am not wroth,
Have here my trouthe!' and many
     another oth;   1111
'Now spek to me, for it am I, Criseyde!'—
But al for naught: yit mighte he not
     abreyde.

Therwith his pous and paumès of his hondes
They gan to frote, and wete his temples
     tweyne;
And, to deliverén him fro bittré bondes,
She ofte him kiste; and, shortly for to
     seyne,   1117
Him to revoken she dide al her peyne.
And at the laste, he gan his breth to drawe,
And of his swough sone after that adawe,

And gan bet minde and reson to him take;
But wonder sore he was abayst, y-wis,
And with a sik, when he gan bet awake,
He seide, 'O mercy, God, what thing is
     this?'—
'Why do ye with your-selven thus amis?'
Quod tho Criseyde, 'Is this a mannés game?
'What, Troilus! wol ye do thus? For
     shame!'—

And therwithal her arm over him she leyde,
And al foryaf, and ofté time him keste.
He thonkéd her, and to her spak and seyde
As fil to purpos for his hertés reste; 1131
And she to that answérde him as her leste,
And with her goodly wordès him disporte
She gan, and ofte his sorwes to confórte.

Quod Pandarus, 'For aught I can espyen,
I nor this candel serven here of nought;
Light is not good for siké folkés ýen!
But for the love of God, sin ye be brought
In thus good plit, lat now non hevy thought
Ben hanging in the hertès of you tweye!'—
And bar his candel to the chiméneye. 1141

Sone after this, though it no nedé were,
Whan she swiche othés as her list devise

Had of him take, her thoughté tho no fere.
Ne cause ek non to bidde him thennés rise.
Yit lassé thing than othés may suffise
In many a cas; for every wight, I gesse,
That loveth wel, meneth but gentilesse!

But in effect she woldé wite anon   1149
Of what man, and ek wher, and also why
He jalous was, sin ther was causé non;
And ek the signé that he took it by,
This bad she him to telle her bisily,
Or ellés, certein, she bar him on honde
That this was don for malice, her to fonde.

Withouté moré, shortly for to seyne,
He moste obeye unto his lady heste;
And for the lassé harm he mosté feyne.
He seide her, 'whan she was at swich
     a feste,   1159
She mighte on him han lokéd at the leste—
N'ot I not what, at dere ynough a risshe.
As he that nedés moste a causé fisshe!

Criseyde answérdé, 'Swete, al were it so,
What harm was that, sin I non yvel mene?
For, by that God that wroughte us bothé
     two,
In allé thing is myn ententé clene!
Swiche arguments ne ben not worth a bene!
Wol ye the childissh jalous contrefete?
Now were it worthy that ye were y-bete!'—

Tho Troilus gan sorwfully to sike;   1170
Lest she be wroth, him thoughte his
     herté deyde;
And seide, 'Allas, upon my sorwés sike
Have mercy, sweté herté myn, Criseyde!
And if that in tho wordès that I seyde
Be any wrong, I wol no more trespace:
Do what you list, I am al in your grace!'—

Criseyde answérde, 'Of gilt misericorde!
This is to seyn, that I foryeve al this. 1178
And everé-mo on this night you recorde.
And beth wel war ye do no more amis!'—
'Nay, deré herté myn,' quod he, 'y-wis!'—

1115. *wete,* J H₄ R H₃ *ek.*
1127. a² G² *Wol Troilus do thus? Allas, for shame!*
1136. *I nor this candel,* a² G² γ *This light nor I* (var.)
1141. *his,* γ *the.*

1148. *wel,* a² *wel and.*
1163. *Criseyde,* a² G² γ *And she.*
1168. *jalous;* J and others *jalousie.*
1177. *Criseyde,* a² G² γ *And she.*

And now,' quod she, 'that I have don
   you smerte,
'oryeve it me, myn ownè swetè herte !'—

This Troilus, with blisse of that supprised,
'utte al in Goddès hond, as he that mente
Vo thing but wel ; and, sodeinly avised,
le her in armès fastè to him hentè.
\nd Pandarus, with a ful good entente,
.eyde him to slepe, and seyde, 'If ye
   ben wise,
Swowneth not now lest morè folk
   arise !'—   1190

Vhat mighte or may the sely larkè seye,
Vhan that the sperhauk hath it in his
   foot ?—
can no more, but of thise ilkè tweye,
'o whom this talè sucrè be or soot,
'hough that I tarie a yeer, som time I moot
\fter myn auctour tellen hir gladnésse
\s wel as I have told hir hevinesse.

:riseydè, which that felte her thus y-take,
\s writen clerkès in hir bokès olde,   1199
light as an aspen leef she gan to quake,
Vhan she him feltè her in his armès folde.
\nd Troilus, al hool of carès coldè,
ian thanken tho the brightè Goddès
   sevenè.—
'hus sondry peynès bringen folk in hevene.

'his Troilus in armès gan her streyne,
\nd seide, 'O swete, as everè mote I gon,
low be ye eaught !   Now is ther but
   we tweyne !
low yeldeth you, for other bote is non !'—
'o that Criseyde answérdè thus anon,
N' had I or now, my swetè hertè dere,
en yolde, y-wis I werè now not here !'—

'), soth is seid, that helèd for to be   1212
s of a fevere, or other gret siknésse,
[en mostè drinke, as men may alday see,
ul bittrè drinke ; and for to han gladnésse,

Men drinken oftè peyne and gret distresse :
I mene it here, as for this áventure
That thorugh a peyne hath founden al
   his cure.

And now swetnéssè semeth morè swete
That bitternesse assayèd was biforn ;   1220
For out of wo in blissè now they flete ;
Non swich they felten sin they werè born.
Now is this bet than bothè two be lorn !
For love of God, take every womman hede
To werken thus, whan it com'th to the nede!

Criseyde, al quit from every drede and tene,
As she that justè cause had him to triste,
Made him swich feste, it joyè was to sene,
Whan she his trouthe and clene ententè
   wiste ;   1229
And as aboute a tree with many a twiste
Bitrent and wryth the swotè wodèbinde,
Gan ech of hem in armès other winde.

And as the newe abaysèd nightingale
That stinteth first whan she biginneth singe,
Whan that she hereth any herdè tale,
Or in the hegges any wight steringe,
And after siker doth her vois out-ringe ;
Right so Criseydè, whan her dredè stente,
Opned her herte, and tolde al her entente.

And right as he that saw his deth y-shapen,
And deyen moste, in aught that he may
   gesse,   1241
And sodeinly rescous doth him escapen,
And from his deth is brought in sikernesse ;
For al this world, in swich presént glad-
   nésse
Is Troilus, and hath his lady swete.—
With worsè hap God lat us neverè mete !

Her armès smale, her streightè bak and
   softe,
Her sidès longè, flesshly, smothe, and white
He gan to stroke, and good thrift bad ful
   ofte
Her snowissh throte, her brestes rounde
   and lite :   1250

1202. *And,* γ *But.*
1203. *brightè,* γ *blitful.*
1211. *I werè now not here,* R Cx. H₃ H₅ *I n'*
ïd not now ben here.
1214. *alday,* α² G² γ *ofte(n).*

1222. *sin,* H₄ and others *sin that.*
1240. *saw,* J *seith ;* α² γ *seth.*
1241. *moste,* α² G γ *mot.*
1245. *Is,* α² G² γ *Was.*

499

Thus in this hevene he gan him to delite,
And therwithal a thousand time her kiste,
That what to don for joye unnethe he
    wiste.

Than seide he thus, ' O Love, O Charité !
Thy moder ek, Citherea the swete,
After thy-self next heriéd be she,
Venus mene I, the wel-willy planéte !
And next you, Imenéus, I thee grete !
For neveré man was to you Goddès holde
As I, that ye han brought fro carès colde.

'Benigné Love, thou holy bond of thinges,
Who-so wol grace, and list thee not hon-
    óuren,   1262
Lo, his desir wol flee withouten winges !
For n'oldestow of bounté hem socóuren
That serven best and most alwéy labóuren,
Yit were al lost, that dar I wel seyn, certes,
But-if thy gracé passéd our desertes.

' And, for thou me, that coudé leest deserve
Of hem that noumbred ben unto thy grace,
Hast holpen ther I likly was to sterve, 1270
And me bestowéd in so heigh a place
That th' ilké boundès may no blissé pace,
I can no more, but laude and reverence
Be to thy bounté and thyn excellence ! '—

And therwithal Criseyde anon he kiste,
Of which, certein, she feltè no disese !
And thus seide he, 'Now woldé God I
    wiste,
Myn hertè swete, how I you mightè plese !
What man,' quod he, 'was everè thus at ese
As I on whom the fairest and the beste 1280
That evere I say, deyneth her hertè reste ?

' Here may men see that mercy passeth
    right :
Th' experience of this is felt in me,
That am unworthy to you, lady bright,
But, hertè myn, of your benignété
So thenketh, though that I unworthy be,

Yit mot I nede amenden in som wise
Right thorugh the vertu of your heighe
    servíse.

' And for the love of God, my lady dere,
Sin God hath wrought me for I shal you
    serve,   1290
As thus he wol how that ye ben my stere
To do me live, if that you list, or sterve,
So techeth me how that I may deserve
Your thonk, so that I thorugh myn ignor-
    aunce
Ne do no thing that be you displesaunce.

' For certès, fresshé wommanlichè wif,
This dar I seye, that trouthe and diligence,
That shal ye finden in me al my lif ;
N' I wol not, certein, breken your defence ;
And if I do, présent or in absénce, 1300
For love of God lat slee me with the dede,
If that it like unto your wommanhede ! '

' Y-wis,' quod she, 'myn ownè hertès list,
My ground of ese, and al myn hertè dere,
Gramercy, for on that is al my trist !
But lat us falle awey fro this matére,
For this suffiseth which that seyd is here :
And at oo word, withouten répentaunce,
Welcome, my knight, my pees, my
    suffisaunce ! '—

Of hir delit or joyès oon the leste   1310
Were impossiblé to my wit to seye ;
But juggeth ye that han ben at the feste
Of swich gladnésse, if that hem listè pleye !
I can no more, but thus thise ilké tweye
That night betwixen drede and sikernesse,
They feltè in love the gretè worthinesse.

O blisful night, of hem so longe y-songht,
How blithe unto hem bothè two thou wert !
Why n'had I swich oon with my soule
    y-bought,
Ye, or the leestè joyè that was there ? 1320
Awey, thou foulé daunger and thou fer,

1258. *Imenéus,* Hymen.
1268. *coude leest,* H₃ γ *lest coude.*
1282. *this,* a³ G² γ *that.*
1284. *to you, lady bright,* a² G² γ *to so sweet
a wight.*

1291. *how,* so H₄ H₃ ; J R Cx. omit.
1291. a² G² γ *read (var.)* As thus I mene, *
wol ye ben my stere.*
1307. *this suffiseth which that ;* a² G² γ
suffiseth, this that.

And lat hem in this hevenė blissė dwelle,
That is so heigh that no man can it telle !

But how al-though I can not tellen al
As can myn auctour of his excellence,
Yit have I seid, and God to-forn, and shal
In every thing the gret of his sentence ;
And if that I, at lovės reverence,
Have anything in echèd for the beste,
Doth therwithal right as your-selven leste.

For minė wordès, here and every part,   1331
I speke hem alle under correcioun
Of you, that feeling han in lovės art,
And putte hem hool in your discrecioun
T'encresse or makė diminucioun
Of my langáge ; and that I you biseche.—
But now to purpos of my rather speche.

Thise ilkė two that ben in armės laft,
So loth to hem asonder gon it were,
That ech from other wen'dė ben biraft,   1340
Or ellės, lo, this was hir mostė fere,
Lest al this thing but nicė dremės were :
For-which ful ofte ech of hem seide, ' O
  swete,
Clippe ich you thus, or ellės ich it mete ?'

And Lord I so he gan goodly on her see
That nevere his look ne bleyntė from her
  face,
And seide, ' O derė hertė, may it be
That this be soth, that ye ben in this
  place ?'—
Ye, hertė myn, God thanke I of his grace !'
Quod tho Criseyde, and therwithal him
  kiste,   1350
That wher his spirit was, for joye he n'iste.

This Troilus ful ofte her yen two
Gan for to kisse, and seide, ' O yen clere,
It werė ye that wroughten me this wo,
Ye humblė nettės of my lady dere !

Though ther be mercy writen in your chere,
God wot, the text ful hard is, soth, to finde !
How coudė ye withouten bond me
  binde ?'—

Therwith he gan her faste in armės take,
And wel a thousand timės gan he sike,   1360
Not swichė sorwful sikės as men make
For wo, or ellės whan that folk ben sike,
But esy sikės, swiche as ben to like,
That shewėd his affeccioun withinne ;
Of swichė sikės coude he nothing blinne.

Sone after this they spake of sondry thinges
As fil to purpos of hir áventure,
And pleying entrechaungeden hir ringes,
Of which I can not tellen no scriptúre ;
But wel I wot a broche of gold azure,
In which a ruby set was lik an herte,   1371
Criseyde him yaf, and stak it on his sherte.

Lord, trowèn ye a coveitousė wrecche,
That blameth love and halt of it despit,
That of the pens that he can mokre and
  kecche
Was everė yit y-yeve him swich delit
As is in love in oo point in som plit ?
Nay, doutéles I for al-so God me save,
So parfit joyė may no nigard have !

They wol seye ' yis,' but, Lord, so that
  they lye,   1380
Tho bisy wrecchės, ful of wo and drede !
They clepen love a woodnesse or folýe,
But it shal falle hem as I shal you rede :
They shal forgon the white and ek the
  rede,
And live in wo.   Ther God yeve hem
  mischaunce,
And every lover in his trouthe avaunce I

As woldė God, thise wrecches that despise
Servíse of love hadde erės al-so longe
As haddė Mida, ful of coveitíse,
And therto dronken hadde as hote and
  stronge   1390

1323. *no man can it*, so J P H₄ R Cx. H₃ S ;
thers *al ne can I.*
1324. J R Cx. H₃ S have the two following
anzas (ll. 1324-1337) after l. 1414 ; H₄ has them
i *both* places.
1324. *But how al-though*, P G γ *But soth is,
tough* ; S H₅ (var.)
1327. *the gret of*, P G γ *al hoolly.*

1360. *thousand* (Boc.), P G γ *hundred.*
1365. *nothing*, so R ; H₅ A *nevere* ; J and
others *not, nought.* H₁ (only) *bilynne* (for *blinne*).
1389. *Mida*, Midas. See *C.T.* D 951.

As Crassus dide for his affectès wronge,
To techen hem that coveitise is vice,
And love is vertu, though men holde it
    nice !

Thise ilkè two of whiche that I you seye,
Whan that hir hertès ful assurèd were,
Tho gonnè they to speken and to pleye,
And ek rehersen how and whan and where
They knewe hem first, and every wo and
    fere   1398
That passèd was ; but al that hevinesse,
Y-thankèd God, was tornèd to gladnésse.

And everè mo, whan that hem fil to speke
Of any wo of swich a time a-gon,
With kissing al that talè sholdè breke,
And fallen in a newè joye anon,
And diden al hir might, sin they were oon,
For to recoverèn blisse and ben at ese,
And passèd wo with joyè countrepese.

Reson wol not now that I speke of sleep,
For it acordeth not to my matére :
God wot, they toke of that ful litel keep ! 1410
But lest this night that was to hem so dere
Ne sholde in veyn escape in no manére,
It was biset in joye and bisinesse
Of al that souneth into gentilesse.

Whan that the cok, comúne astrologer,
Gan on his brest to bete and after crowe,
And Lucifer, the dayès messager,
Gan for to rise and out her stremès throwe,
And estward roos, to him that coude it
    knowe,
Fortúna maior, that anon Criseyde   1420
With hertè soor to Troilus thus seyde :

'Myn hertès lif, my trist, and my plesáunce,
That I was born, allas ! what me is wo,

That day of us mot makè disseveraunce !
For time it is to rise and hennès go,
Or ellés I am lost for everémo !
O night, allas, why n'iltow over us hove
As longe as whan Almena lay by Jove ?

'O blakè night, as folk in bokès rede,
That shapen art by God this world to
    hide   1430
At certein timès with thy blakè wede,
That under that men mighte in reste abide,
Wel oughten beestès pleyne and folk thee
    chide,
That ther-as day with labour wolde us
    breste,
That thou thus fleest, and deynest us not
    reste !

'Thou dost, allas, too shortly thyn office,
Thou rakel night ! Ther God, makére of
    kinde,
For thou so downward hastest of malice,
Thee corse, and to our hemisperè binde,
That neverémo under the grounde thee
    winde !   1442
For, thorugh thy rakel hying out of Troye,
Have I forgon thus hastily my joye !'—

This Troilus, that with tho wordès felte
As thoughte him tho, for pietous distresse,
The bloody terès from his hertè melte,
As he that neverè yit swich hevinesse
Assayèd had out of so gret gladnesse,
Gan therwithal Criseyde, his lady dere,
In armès streyne, and seyde in this manére :

'O cruel day, accusour of the joye   1452
That love and night han stole and fastè
    y-wryen,
Acorsèd be thy coming into Troye,
For every bore hath oon of thy brightè
    yen !
Envious day, what list thee so t'espyen ?

1391. *Crassus*, M. Crassus, the triumvir, sur-
named *Dives*. When slain in battle (53 B.C.),
molten gold was poured into his mouth, by order
of Orodes, king of Parthia.

1392, 1393. *coveitise*, etc., P G γ *they ben in
the vice, And lovers nought, al-though they holde
hem nice*.

1394. *whiche*, γ *whom*.

1402. *wo*, γ *thing*.

1408. *not now*, so S ; Cx. *I now* ; rest omit *now*.

1415. *Whan that*, so J R Cx. H₃ S (see note,
l. 1324) ; others *But whan*.

1428. *Almena*, Alcmena, mother of Hercules
by Jupiter.

1431. *blake*, a² G² γ *derke*.

1438-1441. a² G² γ read :
    Thee for thyn haste and thyn unkinde vice
    So faste ay to our hemispere binde,
    That nevere more under the grounde thou winde !
    For now, for thou so hyest out of Troye,

What hastow lost ?   What sek'st thou in
   this place ?
Ther God thy light so quenchè for his grace !

' Allas, what han thise lovers thee agilt,
Despítous day ? Thyn be the pine of helle !
For many a lover hastow slayn, and wilt ;
Thy pouring in wol no-wher lete hem
   dwelle !   1460
What profrestow thy light here for to selle ?
Go selle it hem that smalè selès grave !
We wol thee not ! us nedeth no day have !'

And ek the sonnè, Titan, wolde he chide,
And seide, ' O fool, wel may men thee
   despise,
That hast al night the Dawing by thy side
And suffrest her so sone up fro thee rise,
For to disesen lovers in this wise !
What ! hold thy bed ther, thou, and ek
   thy Morwe !
I preye to God, so yeve you bothè
   sorwe !'   1470

Therwith ful sore he sighte, and thus he
   seyde,
' My lady right, and of my wele and wo
The verray rote, O goodly myn, Criseyde,
And shal I rise ? Allas, and shal I so ?
Now fele I that myn hertè mot a-two !
For how sholde I my lif an hourè save,
Sin that with you is al the joye ich have ?

' What shal I don ? For certès I n'ot how,
Ne whan, allas, I may the timè see
That in this plit I may be eft with you ! 1480
And of my lif, God wot how that shal be !
Sin that desir right now so streyneth me,
That I am ded anon but I retorne,
How sholde I longe, allas, fro you sojorne ?

' But nathéles, myn ownè lady bright,
Yit were it so that I wiste outrely

That I, your ownè servant and your knight,
Were in your herte y-shet as fermély
As ye in myn, (the whiche thing trewèly
Me leverè werè than thise worldès
   tweyne),   1490
Yit sholde I bet enduren al my peyne.'—

To that Criseyde answerdè thus anon,
And with a sik she seyde, ' O hertè dere,
The game, y-wis, so ferforth now is gon,
That erst shal Phebus fallen fro his spere,
And everich eglè ben the dowvès fere,
And every roche out of his placè sterte,
Or Troilus out of Criseydès hertè !

' Ye ben so depe in-with my herte y-grave,
That, though I wolde it torne out of my
   thought,   1500
As wisly verray God my soulè save,
To deyen in the peyne I coudè nought !
And, for the love of God that us hath
   wrought,
Lat in your brayn non other fantasýe
So crepè, that it causè me to dye !

' And that ye me wolde han as faste in minde
As I have you, that wolde I you bisèche ;
And if I wistè sothly that to finde,
God mightè not a point my joyès eche !
But hertè myn, withoutè morè speche, 1510
Beth to me trewe, or ellès were it routhe ;
For I am thyn, by God and by my trouthe !

' Beth glad for-thý, and live in sikernesse ;
Thus seide I nevere or now, ne shal to mo !
And if to you it were a gret gladnésse
To torne ayein sone after that ye go,
As fayn wolde I as ye that it were so,
As wisly God myn hertè bringe at reste !'—
And him in armès took and oftè kiste.

Ayein his wil, sin it mot nedès be, 1520
This Troilus up ros, and faste him cledde,
And in his armès took his lady free
An hundred time, and on his wey him
   spedde ;

1455. *in*, so H₄ R Cx. H₃ ; J and others omit.
1464. *wolde*, a² G² γ *gan*.
1466. *Dawing*, wife of Tithonus, whom Chaucer
here confuses with Titan.
1473. *verray*, a² G² γ *welle and* (*of*).
1474. *so*, Cl. D G *go*.
1477. *joye* (Boc.), so R H₃ ; J and others *lif*.
1482. *streyneth* (Boc.), γ *biteth, bitleth,
brenneth*.
1486. *Yit*, γ omit.

1487. *owne*, a² γ *humble*.
1488. *y-shet*, a² γ (*y-*)*set*. (See l. 1549.)
1492. *thus*, a² γ *right* ; G² *and that*.
1496. *dowves*, J H₄ R Cx. H₃ *hawkes*.
1517. *that*, J γ omit.

And, with swich vois as though his hertè
　　bledde,
He seidè, 'Far-wel, derè hertè swetè !
Ther God us grauntè sounde and sonè
　　mete !'—

To which no word for sorwè she answérde,
So sorè gan his parting her distreyne ;
And Troilus unto his paleys ferde
As wo-bigon asshe was, soth to seyne ; 1530
So harde him wrong of sharp desir the
　　peyne
For to ben eft ther he was in plesaúnce,
That it may nevere out of his rémem-
　　braunce.

Retornèd to his rèal paleys sone,
He softe into his bed gan for to slinke,
To slepè longe as he was wont to done.
But al for naught ; he may wel ligge and
　　winke,
But slep ne may ther in his hertè sinke,
Thinking how she, for whom desir him
　　brende,
A thousand fold was worth more than he
　　wen'de.　　　　　　　　　1540

And in his thought gan up and down to
　　winde
Her wordès alle and every countenaunce,
And fermèliche inpressen in his minde
The lestè point that to him was plesaúnce ;
And verrayliche of th' ilkè rémembraunce
Desir al newe him brende, and lust to brede
Gan more than erst, and yit took he non
　　hede.

Criseyde also, right in the selvè wise,
Of Troilus gan in her hertè shette
His worthinesse, his lust, his dedès
　　wise,　　　　　　　　　1550
His gentilesse, and how she with him
　　mette,
Thankìngè Love, he so wel her bisette ;
Desiring eft to han her hertè dere
In swich a plit, she dorstè make him chere.

Pandáre, a-morwè which that comen was
Unto his nece and gan her fairè grete,
Seide, 'Al this night so reynèd it, allas,
That al my drede is that ye, necè swete,
Han litel leiser had to slepe and mete :
Al night,' quod he, 'hath reyn so don me
　　wake,　　　　　　　　　1560
That som of us for gode his hed may ake !'

And ner he com, and seide, 'How stant
　　it now
This brightè morwè ? Nece, how can ye
　　fare ? '
Criseyde answérdè, 'Nevere the bet for
　　you,
Fox that ye ben ! God yeve your hertè care !
God help me so, ye causèd al this fare,
Trowe I,' quod she, 'for al your wordès
　　white !
O, who-so seeth you knowèth you ful
　　lite !'—

With that she gan her facè for to wrye
Al with the shete, and wex for shamè
　　red ;　　　　　　　　　1570
And Pandarus gan under for to prye,
And seidè, 'Nece, if that I shal be ded,
Have here a swerd, and smiteth off myn
　　hed !'
With that his arm al sodeinly he threste
Under her nekke, and at the laste her keste.

I passe al that which nedeth not to seye.
What ! God foryaf his deth, and she also
Foryaf, and with her unclè gan to pleye,
For other causè was ther non than so. 1579
But of this thing right to th'effect to go,
Whan timè was, hom til her housshe wente ;
And Pandarus hath hoolly his entente.

Now tornè we ayein to Troilus,
That restèles ful longe a-beddè lay,
And privèly sente after Pandarus
To him to come in al the haste he may.
He com anon, not onès seide he nay ;

1524. *vois as though*, γ *wordes as.*
1525. *dere*, H₃ γ *my dere.*
1548. *selvs*, so J R H₃ Cx. ; *rest same.*
1552. *he*, S *that he.*

1561. *his*, so H₃ ; J *hir*; H₄ R *our.* a² G² γ
That some of us, I trowe, hir hedes ake !
1563. *brighte*, a² G² γ *merie.*
1570. *Al with* (T), all *with.*
1570. *red*, so a² ; *rest al red.*
1576. *nedeth*, a² G² γ *chargeth.*

504

And Troilus ful sobrèliche he grette,
And down upon his beddès side him sette.

This Troilus, with al th'affeccioun   1590
Of frendès love, that hertè may devise,
To Pandarus on knowès fil adoun ;
And, or that he wolde off the place arise,
He gan him thonken in his bestè wise
A thousand time, and gan the day to blesse
That he was born to bringe him fro dis-
    tresse.

And seide, ' O frend of frendès alder-
    beste
That everè was, the sothè for to telle,
Thou hast in hevene y-brought my soule
    at reste
Fro Flegitoun, the fery flood of helle ; 1600
That, though I mightè a thousand timès selle
Upon a day my lif in thy servise,
It mightè not a mote in that suffise.

' The sonnè, which that al the world may see,
Saw neverè yit, my lif that dar I leye,
So inly fair and goodly as is she,
Whos I am al and shal til that I deye ;
And that I thus am hirès, dar I seye,
That thonkèd be the heighè worthinesse
Of Love, and ek thy kindè bisinesse !   1610

' Thus hastow me no litel thing y-yive,
For which to thee obligèd be for ay
My lif.   And why?   For thorugh thy help
    I live,
Or ellès ded had I ben mony a day ! '—
And with that word down in his bed he lay ;
And Pandarus ful sobrèliche him herde
Til al was seyd, and than he thus answèrde :

' My derè frend, if I have don for thee
In any cas, God wot, it is me lief ;
And am as glad as man may of it be, 1620
God help me so ! But tak it not a-grief :
For love of God, be war of this mischief,

That, ther-as now thou brought art in thy
    blisse,
That thou thy-self ne cause it not to misse.

' For of fortúnès sharp adversité
The worstè kinde of ínfortune is this :
A man to han ben in prosperité,
And it remembren whan it passèd is. 1628
Thou'rt wis y-nough, for-thy do not amis :
Be not too rakel, though thou sittè warme,
For if thou be, certein, it wol thee harme.

' Thou art at ese, and hold thee wel ther-inne ;
For also seur as red is every fir,
As gret a craft is kepè wel as winne.
Bridle alwey wel thy speche and thy desir,
For worldly joye halt not but by a wir :
That preveth wel, it brest alday so ofte ;
For-thy nede is to werken with it softe ! '—

Quod Troilus, ' I hope, and God to-forn,
My derè frend, that I shal so me bere,   1640
That in my gilt ther shal no thing be lorn,
N'I wol not rakle as for to greven here.
It nedeth not this mater oftè stere ;
For, wistestow myn hertè wel, Pandáre,
By God of this thou woldest litel care ! '

Tho gan he telle him of his gladè night,
And wher-of first his hertè dredde, and how ;
And seidè, ' Frend, as I am trewè knight,
And by that feith I shal to God and you,
I hadde it neverè half so hote as now ;
And ay the morè that desir me biteth 1651
To love her best, the more it me deliteth.

' I n'ot myself not wisly what it is ;
But now I fele a newè qualité,
Ye, al another than I dide or this.'—
Pandáre answérde, and seidè thus, that 'he
That onès may in hevenè blissè be,
He feleth other-weyès, dar I leye,
Than th' ilkè time he first herde of it seye.

This is oo word for al : this Troilus 1660
Was neverè ful to speke of this matére,

1595. *thousand,* a² G² γ *hundred* (γ *sithe* for
time).
1595. *day to,* a² G² γ *time.*
1600. *Flegitoun,* Phlegethon.
1617. *thus,* γ *him.*
1622. *For love of God,* a² G² γ *That I shal seyn.*

1643. *this mater,* etc., a² G² (var.) *al day this
thing to tere.*
1643. *stere,* so R Cx. H₃ (see iv. 1451) ; J and
others *tere.*
1645. *By God,* a² G² γ *God wot.*

And for to preisen unto Pandarus
The bounté of his righté lady dere,
And Pandarus to thanke and maken chere.
This tale ay was span-newé to biginne,
Til that the night departed hem a-
   twinne.—

Sone after this, for-that Fortúne it wolde,
Y-comén was the blisful timé sweté,   1668
That Troilus was warnéd that he sholdé,
Ther he was erst, Criseyde his lady mete ;
For which he felte his herte in joyé flete,
And feithfully gan alle the Goddés herie.
And lat see now, if that he can be merie !

And holden was the forme and al the wise
Of her comínge, and eek of his also,
As it was erst, which nedeth not devise.
But pleinly to th'effect right for to go,
In joye and seurté Pandarus hem two   1678
A-beddé broughté, whan hem bothé leste ;
And thus they ben in quiete and in reste.

Not nedeth it to you, sin they ben met,
To axe at me if that they blithé were ;
For if it erst was wel, tho was it bet
A thousand fold : this nedeth not t'en-
   quere.
Agon was every sorwe and every fere ;
And bothe, y-wis, they hadde, and so they
   wen'de,
As muché joye as herté may comprende.

This n'is no litel thing of for to seye :
This passeth every wit for to devise ; 1689
For ech of hem gan othres lust obeye :
Felicité, which that thise clerkés wise
Commenden so, ne may not here suffise :
This joyé may not writen be with inké :
This passeth al that herté may bi-thinke !

But cruel day (so weylawey the stounde !)
Gan for t'aproche as they by signés knewe,
For which hem thoughté felen dethés
   wounde.
So wo was hem, that chaungen gan hir
   hewe ;
And day they gonnen to despise al newe,
Calling it traitour, envious, and worse ; 1700
And bitterly the dayés light they corse.

Quod Troilus, ' Allas, now am I war,
That Pireis and the swifté stedés three,
Whiché that drawén forth the sonnés char,
Han gon som by-path in dispit of me :
That makéth it so soné day to be ;
And, for the sonne him hasteth thus to rise,
Ne shal I neveré don him sacrifise !'

But nedés day departe hem mosté sone ;
And whan hir speche y-don was and hir
   chere,   1713
They twinne anon as they ben wont to done,
And setten time of meting eft i-fere.
And many a night they wroughte in this
   manére,
And thus Fortúne a timé ledde in joye
Criseyde and eek this kingés sone of Troye.

In suffisaunce, in blisse, and in singinges
This Troilus gan al his lif to lede.   1717
He spendeth, jousteth, maketh festeyínges ;
He yeveth frely ofte, and chaungeth wede,
And held aboute him ay, withouten drede,
A world of folk, as com him wel of kinde.
The fresshest and the beste he coudé finde ;

That swich a vois of him was, and a
   stevene,
Throughout the world, of honour and
   largésse,
That it up-rong unto the yate of hevene.
And, as in love, he was in swich gladnésse,
That in his herte he deméd, as I gesse,
That ther n'is lover in this world at ese
So wel as he ; and thus gan love him plese.

The goodlihede or bounté which that
   kinde   1727
In any other lady hadde y-set
Can not the mountaunce of a knot.
   unbinde,
About his herte, of al Criseydés net.

1703. *Pireis*, H₃ *Pireys* ; H₄ Cx. *Pirers* ; others
Pirous Pirus, Pirora, etc. Piroeis, one of the
four horses of the Chariot of the Sun ; see Ovid.
Met. ii. 153.
1718. *festeyinges*, so S ; others *festynges,
festeynynges*, etc.
1720. *ay, withouten*, a² G³ *y alwey out of*
1723. *of him was, y was of him.*
1730. *bounté*, so J G³ A ; rest *beauté*.

He was so narwe y-maskéd and y-knet,
That it undon on any maner side,
That n'il not ben, for aught that may bitide !

And by the hond ful ofte he woldé take
This Pandarus, and into gardin lede,
And swich a feste and swich a proces
    make   1739
Him of Criseyde, and of her wommanhede,
And of her beauté, that withouten drede
It was an hevene his wordés for to here ;
And than he woldé singe in this manére :

'Love, that of erthe and see hath
    governaunce,
Love, that his hestés hath in hevenés hye,
Love, which that with an holsom álliaunce
Halt peples joinéd as him list hem gye,
Love, that enditeth lawe of companye,
And couplés doth in vertu for to dwelle,
Bind this acord that I have told and telle.

' That that the world, with feith which
    that is stable,   1751
Diverseth so his stoundés concordínge ;
That elements that ben so discordable
Holden a bond perpetuely durínge ;
That Phebus mot his rosy day forth bringe ;
And that the mone hath lordship over
    ·   the nightes :—
Al this doth Love, ay heried be his mightes !

' That that the see, that gredy is to flowen,
Constreineth to a certein endé so   1759
His flodés, that so fiersly they ne growen
To drenchen erthe and al for everé-mo ;
And if that Love aught lete his bridel go,
Al that now lov'th asonder sholdé lepe,
And lost were al, that Love halt now to-
    hepe.

' So woldé God, that auctour is of kinde,
That with his bond Love of his vertu liste

To cerclen hertés alle, and fasté binde,
That from his bond no wight the wey
    out wiste !
And hertés colde, hem wolde I that he twiste
To make hem love, and that hem liste
    ay rewe   1770
On hertés sore, and kepe hem that ben
    trewe ! '—

In allé nedés for the townés werre
He was, and ay the firste in armés dight,
And certeinly, but-if that bokés erre,
Save Ector, most y-drad of any wight ;
And this encres of hardinesse and might
Com him of love, his lady thank to winne,
That alteréd his spirit so withinne.

In time of trewe, on hawking wolde he ride,
Or ellés hunté boor, bere or lioun ;   1780
The smalé beestés leet he gon biside.
And, whan that he com riding to the toun,
Ful ofte his lady from her window doun,
As fressh as faucon comén out of muwe,
Ful redy was him goodly to saluwe.

And most of love and vertu was his speche,
And in despit hadde allé wrecchednesse ;
And doutéles, no nede was him biseche
T'honóuren hem that hadden worthínesse,
And esen hem that werén in distresse ;
And glad was he, if any wight wel ferde
That lover was, whan he it wiste or herde.

For, soth to seyn, he lost held every wight
But-if he were in Lovés heigh servíse,
I mené folk that oughte it ben of right.
And over al this, so wel coude he devíse
Of sentement, and in so uncouth wise
Al his array, that every lover thoughte
That al was wel, what-so he seide or
    wroughte.

And though that he be come of blood
    royál,   1800
Him liste of pride at no wight for to chace :
Benigne he was to ech in general,
For which he gat him thank in every place.
Thus woldé Love, y-heried be his grace,

1744. Troilus' Song of Love is taken from *Boethius* ii. metre 8. This song (1744-1771) is omitted in H₂, and inserted later in P.
1746. *whick that,* so J H₄ R ; H₅ *that which ;* rest *that.*
1748. *enditeth,* so J H₄ R G ; H₅ *endith ;* Cx. *endueth ;* rest *knetteth, kenneth,* etc. (Boethius, *dictat*).
1754. *Holden,* J and others *Holde in.*
1760. *fiersly,* R Cx. H₅ Cl. D *freshly.*

1782. *to the,* so a² Cx. ; H₅ *into the ;* A *to ;* J and others *in to.*

That pride, envýe, and ire, and avarice
He gan to flee, and everich other vice.

Thou Lady bright, the doughter to Dione,
Thy blinde and wingèd sone eek, daun
    Cupíde,
Ye sustren nine eek, that by Elicone
In hil Parnaso listen for t'abide,—   1810
That ye thus fer han deynèd me to gide,

    1805. *envye, and ire,* so J; a² R H₃ G² Cl.
omit *and;* Cx. Cp. H *and ire, envye.*

I can no more but, sin that ye wol wende,
Ye heried ben for ay, withouten ende !

Thorugh you have I seid fully in my song
Th'effect and joye of Troilus' servíse,
Al be that ther was som disese among,
As to myn auctour listeth to devise.
My thriddè book now ende ich in this
    wise;
And Troilus in lust and in quiéte   1819
Is with Criseyde, his ownè hertè swete.

BOOK IV

BUT al too litel, weylawey the while,
Lasteth such joye, y-thankèd be Fortune,
That semeth trewest whan she wil bigile
And can to folès so her song entune
That she hem hent and blent, traitour
    comune !
And whan a wight is from her wheel y-
    throwe,
Than laugheth she, and maketh him a
    mowe.

From Troilus she gan her brightè face
Awey to writhe, and took of him non
    hede,   9
But caste him clene out of his lady grace,
And on hir wheel she sette up Diomede ;
For-which right now myn hertè ginneth
    blede,
And now my penne, allas, with which I
    write,
Quaketh for drede of that I moste endite.

For how Criseydè Troilus forsook,
Or at the leeste, how that she was un-
    kinde,
Mot hennès-forth ben mater of my book,
As writen folk thorugh which it is in
    minde.
Allas ! that they sholde everè causè finde
To speke her harm ; and, if they on her
    lye,   20
Y-wis, hem-self sholde han the vilanye !

    1. R omits ll. 1-28.
    7. *a,* a² H₅ γ *the.*

O ye Herínès, Nightès doughtren three,
That endèles compleinen evere in peyne,
Megera, Alete, and eek Thesiphone !
Thou cruel Mars eek, fader to Quirine,
This ilkè ferthè book me helpeth fine,
So that the los of lif and love i-fere
Of Troilus be fully shewèd here.

—Ligging in ost, as I have seid or this,
The Grekès stronge aboutè Troyè toun, 30
Bifel that, whan that Phebus shining is
Upon the brest of Hercules' Lióun,
That Ector with ful many a bold baróun
Caste on a day with Grekès for to fighte
As he was wont, to greve hem what he
    mighte.

N'ot I how long or short it was bitwene
This purpos and that day they issen
    mente;
But on a day wel armèd, brighte and
    shene,
With spere in honde and biggè bowès
    bente,
Ector and many a worthy wight out-
    wente ; 40
And in the berd anon withouten lette
Hir fo-men in the feld hem fastè mette.

    22. *Herínès;* the Three Furies, Megæra,
Alecto, and Tisiphone. (See i. 6.)
    26. *This ilkè ferthè,* a² *This ferthè;* H₃ *This
fyfte and laste;* H₄ *This feerdè and laste.*
    29. *seid,* H₄ R Cx. H₃ *told.*
    37. *issen,* so J; P *issu;* H₃ *thus;* others
fighten, fouhten. (Boc. usci.)
    39, 40. H₅ S γ transpose ll. 39, 40.

The longe day, with speres sharpe y-
grounde,
With arwes, dartes, swerdes, maces felle,
They fighte, and bringen hors and man to
grounde,
And with hir axes out the braines quelle.
But in the laste shour, soth for to telle,
The folk of Troye hem-selven so mis-ledden
That with the wors at night homward they
fledden.

Atte whiche day was taken Antenore   50
Maugré Polydamas or Monestéo,
Santippé, Sarpedon, Polynestore,
Polyte, or eek the Trojan daun Riphéo
And othré lassé folk as Phebuséo ;
So that for harm that day the folk of Troye
Dredden to lese a gret part of hir joye.

But nathéles a trewe was ther take
At gret requeste, and tho they gonnen
trete
Of prisoneres a chaungé for to make,   59
And for the surplus yeven sommés grete.
This thing anon was couth in every strete
Bothe in th'assege, in towne, and every
where,
And with the firste it com to Calcas' ere.

When Calcas knew this tretis sholdé holde,
In consistórie among the Grekés sone
He gan in-thringé forth with lordés olde,
And sette him ther-as he was wont to
done ;
And with a chaungéd face hem bad a bone,
For love of God to don that reverence
To stinté noise and yeve him audience.   70

Than seide he thus, ' Lo, lordés mine, ich
was

Trojan, as it is knowén out of drede ;
And, if that you remembre, I am Calcas
That alderfirst yaf confort to your nede,
And toldé wel how that ye sholden spede :
For dredéles thorugh you shal in a stounde
Ben Troye y-brent and beten doun to
grounde.

' And in what forme and in what maner
wise
This toun to shende, and al your list
t'acheve,   79
Ye han or this wel herd me you devise :
This knowé ye, my lordés, as I leve.
And, for the Grekés werén me so leve,
I com my-self in my propré persóne,
To teche in this how you was best to done,

' Having unto my tresour ne my rente
Right no resport, to réspect of your ese.
Thus al my good I lefte, and to you wente,
Wening in this, my lordés, you to plese.
But al this los ne doth me no disese :
I vouché-sauf, as wisly have I joye,   90
For you to lese al that I have in Troye,

' Save of a doughter that I lefte, allas,
Sleping at home, whan out of Troye I sterte.
O sterne and cruel fader that ich was !
How mighte I have in that so hard an herte ?
Allas, I n'hadde y-brought her in her sherte !
For sorwe of which I wil not live to morwe,
But-if ye lordés rewe upon my sorwe.

' For, by that cause I say no time or now
Her to delivere, ich holden have my pes ;
But now or neveré, yif it like yow,   101
I may her have right soné doutéles.
O help and grace ! amongés al this pres
Rewe on this oldé caitif in distresse,
Sin I thorugh you have al this hevinesse !

' Ye have now caught and fetred in prisoún
Trojans y-nowe ; and if your willés be
My child with oon may have redempcioún,

50. *Atte*, so H₂ A ; others *At*.
51. *Maugré Polydamas or* ; H₃ *Palidomas
and alto* (Boc.)
53. *or*, H₃ *and* (Boc.)
54. *And*, a² *Or*.
55. *So that for harm that day*, H₃ *For al
Ector ; so that* (Boc.)
57, 58, 59. So J H₄ R Cx. S (var.) ; H₃ H₅ a² y
read (var.)
To (of) Priamus was yeve at his (gret, Grek, Grekes)
requeste
A time of trewe, and tho they gonnen trete
Hir prisoneres to chaungen, most and leste.
(Boc. Chiese Priamo triegua, e fugti data, etc.)

80. *me you*, γ *it me*.
87. *lefte*, so J H₃ Cx. A D ; others *leste, loste*
(Boc. lasciai).
89. *this*, so J H₃ Cx. ; a² H₃ *my* ; others *that*.
93. *Troye*, a² H₅ *toune*.
101. *yif*, so J H₃ H₄ ; D Cp. Cl. *if that*.

Now for the love of God and of bounté,
Oon of so fele, alas, so yeve him me !　110
What nede were it this prayèr for to werne,
Sin ye shal bothe han folk and toun as yerne?

'On peril of my lif I shal not lye,
Appollo hath me told it feithfully ;
I have eek founde it by astronomye,
By sort and by augúrie eek trewèly,
And dar wel seyn the time is fastè by
That fir and flaumbe on al the toun shal
　　　sprede ;
And thus shal Troyè torne in asshen dede.

'For, certein, Phebus and Neptúnus bothe
That makeden the wallès of the toun　121
Ben with the folk of Troye alwéy so wrothe,
They wol eft bringe it to confusioun
Right for despit of King Laméadoun :
Bi-cause he n'oldè payèn hem hir hire,
The toun shal yit be set upon a fire.'

Telling his tale alwey, this oldè greye,
Humble in his speche, and in his loking eke,
The saltè terès from his ýen tweye
Ful fastè ronnen doun by either cheke.　130
So longe he gan of socour hem biseke
That, for to hele him of his sikès sore,
They yave him Antenor withouten more.

But who was glad y-nough but Calcas tho !
And of this thing ful sone his nedès leyde
On hem that sholden for the tretis go,
And hem for Antenor ful oftè preyde
To bringen hom King Thoas and Criseyde :
And whan Priám his savè gardè sente,
Th'embassadours to Troyè streight they
　　　wente.　140

The cause y-told of hir comínge, the olde
Priam, the king, ful sone in general
Let her-upon his parlèment to holde,
Of which th'effect rehersen you I shal :

Th'embassadours ben answer'd for finál,
Th'exchaunge of prisoneres and al this nede
Hem liketh wel ; and forth in they procede.

This Troilus was present in the place,
Whan axèd was for Antenor Criseyde ;　149
For-which ful sonè chaungen gan his face
As he that with tho wordès wel neigh deyde,
But nathéles he no word to it seyde ;
Lest men sholde his affeccioun espye,
With mannès herte he gan his sorwè drye.

And ful of anguissh and of grisly drede
Abood what other lordès woldè seye ;
And if they woldè graunte, as God forbede,
Th'exchaunge of her, than thoughte he
　　　thingès tweye :
First how to save her honour, and what weye
He mightè best th'eschaunge of her with-
　　　stonde ;　160
Ful faste he caste how al this mightè stonde.

Lovè made him al prest to don her bide,
Or rather dyen than she sholdè go ;
But Reson seide him on that other side,
'Withoute assent of her ne do not so,
If thou debate it, lest she be thy fo,
And seyn that thorugh thy medling is
　　　y-blowe
Your bother love, ther it was erst unknowe.'

For-which he gan deliberèn for the beste,
That, though the lordès woldè that she
　　　wente,　170
He woldè lete hem grauntè what hem leste,
And telle his lady first what that they mente :
And whan that she had seid him her entente,
Therafter wolde he werken al-so blive,
Theigh al the world ayein it woldè strive.

Ector which that right wel the Grekès herde,
For Antenor how they wolde han Criseyde,
Gan it withstonde and sobreliche answérde :

121. *makeden*, so J R γ (exc. A Cl.); a² G² S
maden alle; H₃ H₄ Cx. A Cl. *maden.*
123. *They wol eft*, so J H₃ H₄ R Cx. ; others
That they wol.
132. *sikes*, so J H₃ H₄ R Cx. ; others *sorwes.*
137, 138. H₃ reads :
　　　And hem ful ofte specyally preyde
　　　For Antenor to bringe home Criseide.
139. *save garde*, a² G² *saf conduit hem.*

156. *other lordes wolde*, a² G² γ *lordes wolde*
(*un*)*to it.*
162. *made him*, so H₃ A ; rest *him made*
(read ? *Lo, Love* ; see i. 603).
163. *Or*, γ *And.*
166. *If thou debate (it) lest she*, so J H₃ H₄ R ;
a² G² γ *Lest for thy werk she wolde be.*
176. *right wel*, so Cx. S ; rest *wel.*

'Sirès, she n'is no prisoner,' he seyde;　179
' I n'ot on you who that this charge leyde ;
But on my part ye may eft-sone hem telle,
We usen here no wommen for to selle.'

The noise of peple up-stertè than at ones
As breme as blase of straw y-set on fire ;
For Infortúne it woldè for the nones,
They sholden hir confusioun desire.
' Ector !' quod they, ' What gost may you
　　enspire
This woman thus to shilde, and don us lese
Daun Antenor—a wrong wey now ye
　　chese—　　　189

' That is so wis and eek so bold baroun ?
And we han nede of folk as men may se.
He is eek oon the grettest of this toun !
O Ector, lat tho fantasyès be !
O King Priam !' quod they, ' thus siggen
　　we,
That al our vois is to forgon Criseyde.'
And to deliverèn Antenor they preyde.

O Juvenal, lord, soth is thy sentence :
That litel witen folk what is to yerne,
That they ne finde in hir desir offence ;
For cloude of errour letteth hem discerne
What best is.　And lo, here ensaumple as
　　yerne !　　　201
This folk desiren now deliverance
Of Antenor, that broughte hem to
　　mischance ;

For he was after traitour to the toun
Of Troye.　Alas, they quitte him out too
　　rathe !
O nicè world, lo, thy discrecioun !
Criseydè which that neverè dide hem scathe
Shal now no lenger in her blissè bathe ;
But Antenor, he shal come hom to toune,
And she shal out : thus seiden here and
　　houne.　　　210

For-which deliverèd was by parlèment
For Antenor to yelden out Criseyde,
And it pronouncèd by the president,

Altheigh that Ector nay ful oftè preyde;
That finaly, what wight that it withseyde,
It was for naught : it mostè ben and sholde,
For substance of the parlèment it wolde.

Departed out of parlèment echone,
This Troilus withoutè wordes mo
Into his chambrè speddè him faste, allone
But-if it were a man of his or two,　　221
The whiche he bad out fastè for to go,
Because he woldè slepen, as he seydè ;
And hastily upon his bed him leyde.

And as in winter levès ben biraft,
Ech after other, til the tree be bare,
So that ther n'is but bark and braunche
　　y-lafte,
Li'th Troilus biraft of ech welfare,
Y-bounden in the blakè bark of care,　229
Disposèd wood out of his wit to breyde,
So sore him sat the chaunging of Criseyde.

He rist him up, and every dore he shette
And window eek ; and tho this sorwful
　　man
Upon his beddès side adoun him sette,
Ful lik a ded imágè pale and wan ;
And in his brest the hepèd wo began
Outbreste, and he to werken in this wise
In his woodnèsse, as I shal you devise.

Right as the wildè bolè ginneth springe
Now here, now there, y-darted to the herte,
And of his deth roreth in cómpleinínge,
Right so gan he aboute the chambrè sterte,
Smiting his brest ay with hiš fistès smerte ;
His hed to walle, his body to the grounde
Ful ofte he swapte, himselven to confounde.

His ÿen two for pietè of herte,
Out stremèden as swiftè wellès tweye ;
The heighè sobbès of his sorwes smerte
His speche him raftè : unnethès mightè
　　he seye,　　　249

239. *ginneth*, so G²; P H₃ *ginn'th to ;* J and
others *biginneth*.
244. *to walle*, so R ; Cx. *to wallys ;* J and
others *to the wall(s)*.
246. *pietè*, so J H₂ S ; others *pite, pete*.
247. *Out stremeden as swifte*, P G² *So weß(t)en
that they semen*.

197. *soth, y trewe*.
200. *letteth hem,* so R ; H₃ Cx. *let hem to ;*
others *lat hem, ne lat hem, lat hem not*, etc.

'O deth, allas! why n'ilt thou do me deye?
A-corséd be that day which that Natúre
Shoop me to be a livés créature !'

But after, whan the furie, and al this rage
Which that his herté twiste and fasté
    threste,
By lengthe of timé somwhat gan aswage,
Upon his bed he leide him doun to reste.
But tho bigonne his terés more out-breste,
That wonder is the body may suffise
To half this wo which that I you devise.

Than seide he thus : 'Fortúne, allas the
    while !   260
What have I don ?   What have I thus
    a-gilt ?
How mightestow for routhé me bigile ?
Is ther no grace ?   And shal I thus be
    spilt ?
Shal thus Criseyde awey, for-that thou
    wilt ?
Allas, how mayst thou in thyn herté finde
To be to me thus cruel and unkinde ?

'Have I thee not honoúréd al my live,
As thou wel wost, above the Goddés alle?
Why wiltow me fro joyé thus deprive?
O Troilus, what may men now thee calle
But wrecche of wrecches, out of honour
    falle   271
Into misérie, in which I wol biwaile
Criseyde, allas, til that the breth me faile.

'Allas, Fortúne ! if that my lif in joye
Displeséd hadde unto thy foule envýe,
Why n'haddestow my fader king of Troye
Biraft the lif, or don my brethren dye,
Or slain myself that thus compleine and
    crye ?
I, combré-world, that may of no thing serve,
But alwey dye and neveré fully sterve !

'If that Criseyde alloné were me laft 281
Nought roughte I whiderward thou woldest
    stere ;

And her, allas, than hast thou me biraft !
But everémo, lo, this is thy manére
To reve a wight that most is to him dere,
To preve in that thy gerful violence !
Thus am I lost : ther helpeth no defence !

'O verray Lord, O Love ! O God, allas !
That knowest best myn herte and al my
    thought !   289
What shal my sorwful lif don in this cas
If I forgo that I so dere have bought ?
Sin ye Criseyde and me han fully brought
Into your grace, and bothe our hertés
    seled,
How may ye suffre, allas, it be repeled ?

'What shal I don ? I shal, whil I may dure
On live, in torment and in cruel peyne
This ínfortune or this disáventure
Allone as I was born, y-wis, compleyne ;
Ne neveré wol I sen it shine or reyne ;
But ende I wol, as Edippe in derknésse,
My sorwful lif, and deyen for distresse.

'O wery gost, that errest to and fro, 302
Why n'iltow flen out of the wofulléste
Body that everé mighte on groundé go ?
O soulé, lurking in this wo, unneste !
Fle forth out of myn herte and lat it
    breste,
And folwe alwey Criseyde thy lady dere
Thy righté place is now no lenger here.

'O woful ÿen two, sin your disport
Was al to seen Criseydes ÿen brighte, 310
What shal ye don, but for my dísconfort
Stonden for naught and wepen out your
    sighte ?
Sin she is queynt that wont was you to
    lighte,
In veyn fro this forth have ich ÿen tweye
I-forméd, sin your vertu is aweye.

295. γ read : *What I may don, I shal, whil I
may dure.* Boc. Che faro io . . .? Io pian-
gerò . . .
300, 301. P G² H₃ read :
Ne hevenes light (H₃ Ne see no light) ; and thus I in
    derknesse
My woful (H₃ sorwful) lif wol enden for (H₃ in) distresse.
306. P G² read :
    Fle forth anon, and do myn herte breste.

258. *wonder is*, P G² *wel unnethe* (Boc. appena).
280. *alwey*, γ *evere*.
282. *whiderward*, γ *whider*.
282. *woldest*, so H₄ R ; J and others *woldest me.*

' O my Criseyde, O lady sovêreyne
Of th' ilkè woful soulé that thus cryeth,
Who shal now yevè confort to my peyne?
Allas, no wight! But whan myn hertè
     dyeth,   319
My spirit which that so unto you hyeth
Receive in gre, for that shal ay you serve!
For-thy no fors is though the body sterve!

' O ye lovéres that heighe upon the wheel
Ben set of Fortune, in good áventure,
God levè that ye finde ay love of steel,
And longè mote your lif in joye endure!
But whan ye comen by my sepulture,
Remembreth that your felaw resteth there;
For I lovede eek, though I unworthy were.

' O olde, unholsom and mislivéd man,—
Calcas I mene,—allas, what aileth thee
To ben a Grek, sin thou art born Troján?
O Calcas, which that wilt my banè be,
In cursed timè was thou born for me!
As woldè blisful Jovè for his joye
That I thee haddè wher I wolde in Troye!'

A thousand sikès hotter than the glede
Out of his brest, ech after other, wente,
Medled with pleintès newe his wo to fede,
For which his woful terès neverè stente; 340
And shortly so his peinès him to-rente,
And wex so maat, that joyè nor penaunce
He feleth non, but li'th forth in a traunce.

Pandáre, which that at the parlément
Had herd what every lord and burges seyde,
And how ful graunted was by oon assent
For Antenor to yelden so Criseyde,
Gan wel neigh wood out of his wit to breyde;
So that for wo he n'istè what he mente,
But in a rees to Troilus he wente.   350

A certein knight, that for the timè kepte
The chambrè dore, undide it him anon;
And Pandar, that ful tendrelichè wepte,
Into his derkè chambrè stille as ston
Toward the bed gan softèly to gon,

So cónfus that he n'iste what to seye:
For verray wo his wit was neigh aweye.

And with his chere and loking al to-torn
For sorwe of this, and with his armès folden,
He stood this woful Troilus biforn,   360
And on his pitous face he gan biholden;
But, Lord, so oftè gan his hertè colden,
Seing his frend in wo, whos hevinesse
His hertè slough, as thoughte him, for
     distresse.

This woful wight, this Troilus, that felte
His frend Pandáre y-comen him to see,
Gan as the snow ayein the sonnè melte;
For-which this sorwful Pandar, of pité,
Gan for to wepe as tendreliche as he;
And spechèles thus ben thise ilkè tweye,
That neither mighte oo word for sorwè seye.

But at the laste this woful Troilus,   372
Neigh ded for smert, gan bresten out to
     rore,
And with a sorwful noise he seidè thus,
Among his sobbès and his sighès sore,
' Lo, Pandar, I am ded, withoutè more!
Hastow not herd at parlèment,' he seyde,
' For Antenor how lost is my Criseyde?'

This Pandarus, ful ded and pale of hewe,
Ful pitously answérde and seidè, ' Yis! 380
As wisly were it fals as it is trewe
That I have herd, and wot al how it is.
O mercy, God, who wolde han trowèd this!
Who wolde have wen'd that, in so litel a
     throwe,
Fortúne our joyè wolde han over-throwe!

' For in this world ther n'is no créature,
As to my doom, that everè saw ruíne
Straunger than this, thorugh cas or
     áventure.
But who may al eschewe or al devine?

---

317. *th' ilke*, H₃ Cx. *that*; γ *this*.
318. *my*, so P G² H₂ A D; rest *the*, *thy*, *your*.
347. *yelden*, P G² H₃ *chaungen*.

357. *neigh*, P G² H₃ S Cx. *al*; A *now*; D om.
358. *And*, P G² H₃ *But*.
359. *For sorwe of this*, P G² H₃ *Ny ded for wo*.
(H₃ omits l. 359.)
362. *But*, P G² H₃ *And*.
373. *Neigh ded for smert*, P G² H₃ *For cruel
herte* (G² *smert*).
384. *litel*, R *lite*.

Swich is the world! For-thy I thus define:
Ne trust no wight to finden in fortúne   391
Ay propreté; her yiftés ben commúne.

'But tel me this, why thou art now so mad
To sorwen thus. Why li'stow in this wise,
Sin thy desir al hoolly hastow had,
So that by right it oughte y-nough suffice?
But I, that neveré felte in my servíse
A frendly chere or looking of an ýe,
Lat me thus wepe and wailen til I dye!

'And over al this, as thou wel wost thy-
    selve,
This town is ful of ladies al aboute;   401
And, to my doom, fairer than swiché twelve
As evere she was, shal I finde in som route,
Ye, oon or two, withouten any doute.
For-thy be glad, myn owné deré brother!
If she be lost, we shal recovere another!

'What! God forbede alwey that ech
    plesáunce
In oo thing were, and in non other wight!
If oon can singe, another can wel daunce;
If this be goodly, that is glad and light;
And this is fair, and that can good a-right.
Ech for his vertu holden is for dere,   412
Bothe heroner and faucon for rivére!

'And ek, as writ Zanzis that was ful wis,
"The newé love out-chaseth ofte the olde,"
And upon newé cas li'th newe avís.
Thenk ek thy lif to savén artow holde!
Swich fir by proces mot of kindé colde;
For sin it n'is but casuel plesáunce,   419
Som cas shal putte it out of rémembraunce.

'For al-so seur as day com'th after night,
The newé love, laboúr or other wo,
Or ellés seldé seing of a wight,
Don olde affecciouns alle over-go.
And, for thy part, thou shalt han oon of tho
T'abreggé with thy bittré peinés smerte:
Absence of her shal drive her out of
    herte!'—

Thise wordés seide he for the nonés alle,
To helpe his frend, lest he for sorwé deyde;

410. *that,* γ *she.*
419. *n'is,* so H₄ R Cx.; J and others *is.*

For douteles, to don his wo to falle,   430
He roughté not what unthrift that he seyde.
But Troilus, that neigh for sorwé deyde,
Took litel hede of al that evere he mente;
Oon ere it herde, att'other out it wente.

But at the laste answérde and seidé, 'Frend,
This lechécraft, or heléd thus to be,
Were wel sittínge, if that I were a fend.
To traysen her that trewe is unto me!
I preye God, lat this conseil neveré thé;
But do me rather sterve anon right here,
Or I so do as thou me woldest lere!   441

'She that I serve, y-wis, what-so thou seye,
To whom myn herte enhabit is by right,
Shal han me hoolly heres til that I deye.
What! Pandarus, sin I have her bihight,
I wol not ben untrewé for no wight;
But as her man I wol ay live and sterve,
And neveré other créature serve!

'And ther thou seyst thou shalt as fairé finde
As she, lat be, mak no comparisoun   45
To créature y-formèd here by kinde!
O levé Pandar, in conclusioun,
I wol not ben of thyn opinioun
Touching al this; for-thy, I thee biseche.
So hold thy pees: thou sleest me with
    thy speche!

'Thou biddest me I sholdé love another
Al fresshly newe, and lat Criseydé go!
It li'th not in my powér, levé brother;
And though I mighte, I woldé not do so
But canstow pleyen raket, to and fro,
Netle in, dokke out, now this, now that
    Pandáre,
Now foulé falle her for thy wo that care'

'Thou farest ek by me, thou Pandarus,
As he that, whan a man is wo-bigon,
He com'th to him a pas and seith right thus

434. *att'other,* so P H₁; rest *at the other,*
that other, at other.
435. *laste,* so H₄ R H₁; others *last(e) he.*
438. *her,* so J P G² H₂ A D Cl.; rest *a wight.*
445. *What,* so J P G² H₂; rest *For.*
445. *her bihight,* so J P G² H₃; rest *trowth*
her hight (plight).
464. *man,* so α (= J P G² H₃); rest *wight.*

"Thenk not on smert, and thou shalt
   felé non !"
Thou most me first transmuwèn in a ston,
And revè me my passiounès alle,
Or thou so lightly do my wo to falle ! 469

'The deth may wel out of my brest departe
The lif, so longè may this sorwè mine ;
But fro my soulé shal Criseydès darte
Out neverè mo ; but doun with Proserpine,
Whan I am ded, I wol go wone in pine ;
And ther I wol eternaly compleyne
This wo, and how that twinnéd be we
   tweyne !

'Thou hast here maad an argument, for fyn,
How that it sholde a lassè peiné be
Criseydè to forgon, for she was myn,
And livede in ese and in felicité ! 480
Why gabbestow ? that seidest thus to me,
That "him is wors that is fro wele y-throwe,
Than he had erst non of that wele y-
   knowe !"

But sey me this : sin that thee think'th
   so light
To chaungè so in love ay to and fro,
Why hastow not don bisily thy might
To chaungen her that doth thee al thy wo?
Why n'iltow lete her from thy hertè go ?
Why n'iltow love another lady swete,
That may thyn hertè setten in quiéte? 490

If thou hast had in love ay yit mischaunce,
And canst it not yit fro thyn hertè drive,
, that have lived in lust and in plesáunce
With her as muche as crèature on-live,
How sholde I that foryete, and that so blive ?
) where hastow ben hid so longe in muwe,
That canst so wel and formaly arguwe !

Nay, Pandarus, naught worth is al thy red ;
But doutèles, for aught that may bifalle,

Withouten wordès mo, I wol be ded ! 500
O deth, that ender art of sorwès alle,
Com now, sin I so ofte after thee calle ;
For sely is that deth, soth for to seyne,
That, ofte y-cleped, com'th and endeth
   peyne !

'Wel wot I, whil my lif was in quiéte,
Or deth me slowe I wolde han yiven hire ;
But now his coming is to me so swete
That in this world I no thing so desire.—
O deth, sin with this sorwe I am on fire,
Thou outher do m' anon in terès drenche,
Or with thy coldè strok myn hetè quenche !

'Sin that thou sleest so fele in sondry wise
Ayeins hir wil, unpreyèd, day and night,
Do me at my requestè this servíse : 514
Deliverè now the world, than dostow right,
Of me that am the wofullestè wight
That everè was ; for time is that I sterve,
Sin in this world of right naught may I
   serve !'—

This Troilus in terès gan distille,
As licour out of alambic, ful faste ; 520
And Pandarus gan holde his tongè stille,
And to the groundè his ýen doun he caste.
But nathéles thus thoughte he at the laste,
'What, pardé, rather than my felaw deye,
Yit shal I somwhat more unto him seye !'

And seidè, ' Frend, sin thou hast swich
   distresse,
And sin thee list myn arguments to blame,
Why n'ilt thy-selven helpè to redresse,
And with thy manhod letten al this grame ?
To ravisshe her ne canstow not? for shame!
And outher lat her out of tounè fare 531
Or hold her stille, and lef this nicè care !

'Artow in Troye, and hast non hardiment
To take a womman which that loveth thee
And wolde her-selven ben of thyn assent ?

---

480. *livede*, G² R Cx. Cl. *live(n)*.
484. *sey me this*, so a ; rest *tel me now, tel me
his.*
492. *yit fro*, so a (H₂ om. *yit*) ; rest *out of.*
493. *have lived* (T), H₂ *have had* ; G *havede* ;
rst *lived(e)* (read ? *livede ay*, Boc.).
498. *Nay, Pandarus*, so a ; H₂ H₄ R Cx. S
Nay, nay, God wot ; γ *Nay, God wot.*
499. So a ; rest read *For which, for what that
vere may bifalle.*

506. *deth*, so a ; rest *thou.*
507. *his*, so a (H₂ omits) ; rest *thy.*
511. *hete*, so J H₄ R H₁ Cl. (Boc.) ; H₂ *herte
hete ;* rest *herte.*
515. *than*, so a A D ; rest *so.*
530. *To*, so J H₂ D Cx. Cl. ; rest *Go.*
532. *this nice care*, Cx. γ *thy nice fare.*

Now is not this a nicé vanité?
Ris up anon, and lat thy weping be,
And kith thou art a man; for in this houre
I wol be ded, or she shal bleven oure!'—

To this answérde him Troilus ful softe,
And seidé, 'Pardé, levé brother dere, 541
Al this have I my-selve y-thought ful ofte,
And moré thing than thou devisest here.
But why this thing is left, thou shalt wel
here;
And whan thou me hast yiven audience,
Ther-after maystow telle al thy senténce.

'First, sin thou wost this town hath al this
werre
For ravisshing of women so by might,
It sholdé not be suffred me to erre, 549
As it stant now, ne don so gret unright.
I sholde han also blame of every wight,
My fadres graunt if that I so withstood,
Sin she is chaungéd for the townés good.

'I have ek thought, so it were her assent,
To axe her at my fader of his grace;
Than thenke I, this were her accusé-
ment,
Sin wel I wot I may her not purcháce.
For sin my fader in so heigh a place
As parlément hath her eschaunge enseled
He n'il for me his honour he repeled. 560

'Yit drede I most her herté to perturbe
With violence, if I do swich a game;
For, if I wolde it openly disturbe,
It mosté be disclaundré to her name,
And me were leveré ded than her defame.
As n'oldé God but-if I sholdé have
Her honour leveré than my lif to save!

'Thus am I lost, for aught that I may see;
For certein is, sin that I am her knight,
I have her honour leveré yit than me 570
In every cas, as lover oughte of right.
Thus am I with desir and reson twight:
Desir for to disturben her me redeth,
And reson n'il not, so myn herté dredeth.'

560. *honour*, so a; rest *lettre*.
571. *In*, J H₂ H₅ *And in*.

Thus weping that he coudé neveré cesse,
He seide, 'Allas, how shal I, wrecché,
fare?
For wel fele I alwéy my love encresse,
And hope is lasse and lasse alwéy, Pandáre;
Encressen ek the causes of my care; 579
So weylawey, why n'il myn herté breste?
For-why in love is litel hertés reste!'—

Pandáre answérdé, 'Frend, thou mayst for
me
Don as thee list. But hadde ich it so hote,
And thyn estat, she sholdé go with me!
Though al this town cri'de on this thing
by note,
I n'olde sette at al the noise a grote!
For whan men han wel cried, than lat
hem roune!
For wonder last but nine night nevere in
toune!

'Deviné not in reson ay so depe
Ne preciously, but help thy-selve anon! 590
Bet is that other than thy-selvé wepe,
And namély sin ye two ben al oon!
Ris up, for by myn hed she shal not goon!
And rather be a lite in blame y-founde
Than sterve here as a gnat withouté
wounde!

'It is no rape in my dom, ne no vice,
Her to with-holden that thee loveth most.
Paraunter she may holden thee for nice
To lete her go thus to the Grekés oost. 599
Thenk ek Fortúne, as wel thy-selven wost.
Helpeth an hardy man to his emprise,
And fleeth fro wrecches for hir cowardise.

'And though thy lady wolde a lite her greve,
Thou shalt thy pees ful wel her-after make:

581. *For-why in love*, so J P G; H₂ H₅ *Fr whil I live*; rest read *For as in love ther is in litel reste*.
587. *lat hem roune*, so a; rest *wel they roun*.
588. *For*, so a D; Cl. A; rest *Ek*.
590. *preciously*, so a; R *preciently*; Cl. *curyously*; rest *curteysly*. (Boc. *sottilmente*.)
596. *rape in my dom*, so a; rest *no shame* (un)*to you (thee)*.
597. *thee loveth*, J *thee lovest*; others var.
601. *an*, so R Cx. S; rest omit.
602. *fleeth fro*, so a Cx.; rest *weyveth*.

But as for me, certéin, I can not leve
That she wolde it as now for yvel take.
Why sholdé thanne of-fér'd thyn herté
    quake?
Thenk how that Paris hath, that is thy
    brother,
A love; and why shaltow not have another?

' And Troilus, oo thing I dar thee swere :
That if Criseydé, which that is thy lief,   611
Now loveth thee as wel as thou dost here,
God help me so, she n'il not take a-grief
Theigh thou do bote anon in this mischief.
And if she wilneth fro thee forth to passe,
Than is she fals : so love her wel the lasse !

' For-thy tak herte, and thenk thus as a
    knight :
Thorugh love is broken alday every lawe.
Kith now somwhát thy corage and thy
    might,
Have mercy on thy-self for any awe.   620
Lat not this wrecched wo thyn herté gnawe,
But manly set the world on sixe and sevene,
And if thou deye a martir, go to hevene !

' I wol my-self ben with thee at this dede,
Though ich and al my kin upon a stounde
Shulle in a strete as doggés liggen dede,
Thorugh-girt with many a wide and blody
    wounde.
In every cas I wol a frend be found.   628
And if thee list here sterven as a wrecche,
Adieu, the devil have him that it recche !'—

This Troilus gan with tho wordés quiken,
And seidé, ' Frend, gramercy, ich assente.
But certeinly thou mayst not so me priken,
Ne peyné non ne may me so tormente,
That for no cas it is not myn entente,
At shorté wordés, though I deyén sholde,
To ravisshe her, but-if herselve it wolde.'

Pandáre answérde, ' Of that be as be may !
But tel me thanne, hastow her wil assayed,
That sorwest thus ?'   And he answérdé,
      ' Nay.'   640

' Wher-of artow,' quod Pandar, ' than
    amayed,
That n'ost not that she wol ben yvele apayed
To ravisshe her, sin thou hast not ben there,
But any aungel tolde it in thyn ere?

' For-thy ris up, as naught ne were, anon,
And wassh thy face, and to the king thou
    wende,
Or he may wondren why thou art thus gon.
Thou most with wisdom him and othré
    blende,
Or upon cas he may after thee sende   649
Or thou be war. And, shortly, brother dere,
Be glad, and lat me werke in this matére.

' For I shal shape it so, that sikerly
Thou shalt this night, som time in som
    manére,
Come speken with thy lady privély ;
And by her wordés ek and by her chere
Thou shalt ful sone apárceive and wel here
Al her entente, and of this cas the beste.
And far now wel, for in this point I reste.'—

The swifté Famé, which that falsé thinges
Egál reporteth lik the thingés trewe,   660
Was thorugh-out Troye y-fled with presté
    winges
Fro man to man, and made this tale al newe,
How Calcas' doughter with her brighté
    hewe,
At parlément, withouté wordés more,
Y-graunted was in chaunge of Antenore.

The whiché tale anon right as Criseyde
Had herd, she, which that of her father
    roughte
As in this cas right naught, ne whan he
    deyde,
Ful bisily to Jupiter bisoughte
Yeve him mischauncé that this tretis
    broughte ;   670
But, shortly, lest thise tales sothé were,
She dorste at no wight axen it for fere,

630. *have*, so a ; rest *spede*.
630. *it*, J and othern omit.
638. So a ; rest read ' *Why so mene I,*' *quod
Pandar, ' al this day.*'

644. *But any aungel*, so a ; rest *But if that
Jove.*
647. *why thou art thus*, so a (G *whedyr thou
art thus*) ; rest *whider thou art.*
657. *of*, S γ *in.*

As she that hadde her herte and al her minde
On Troilus biset so wonder faste,
That al this world ne mighte her love
    unbinde,
Ne Troilus out of her herté caste,
She wol ben his, whil that her lif may laste:
And thus she brenneth bothe in love and
    drede,
So that she n'isté what was best to rede.

But, as men sen in tounés al aboute,   680
That wommen usen frendés to visíte,
So to Criseyde of wommen com a route
For pitous joye, and wen'den her delíte,
And with hir talés, dere y-nough a mite,
Thise wommen whiche that in the cité
    dwelle,
They sette hem down, and seide as I shal
    telle.

Quod first that oon, 'I am glad, trewély,
Bicause of you that shal your fader see.'
Another seide, 'Y-wis, so n'am not I;
For al too litel hath she with us be.'   690
The thridde answérde, 'I hope, y-wis,
    · that she
Shal bringen us the pees on every side;
That, when she go'th, almighty God her
    gide!'

Tho wordés and tho womanisshé thinges
She herdé right as though she thennés were,
For al this while her herte on other thing is,
Although the body sat among hem there;
God wot her ádvertence is ellés where,
For Troilus ful faste her soulé soughte: 699
Withouté word alwéy on him she thoughte.

Thise wommen, that so wen'den her to plese,
Abouté naught thus gonne hir talés spende:
Swich vanité ne can don her non ese,
As she that al this mené whilé brende
Of other passioun than that they wen'de,
So that she felte almost her herté dye
For wo, and wery of that companye.

691. *The thridde answerde*, so a; rest *Quod (tho) the thridde*.
696. *al this while*, so a; rest *God it wot*.
698. So a; rest *Her advertence* (R Cx. *audience*) *is alwey elleswhere*.

For-which no lenger mighté she restreyne
Her terés, so they gonnen up to welle,
That yaven signés of the bittré peyne   710
In which her spirit was and mosté dwelle,
Remembring her from hevene into which
    helle
She fallen was, sin she forgo'th the sighte
Of Troilus; and sorwfully she sighte.

And th' ilké foolés, sitting her aboute,
Wen'den that she so wepte and sighté sore,
Bicausé that she sholdé from that route
Departe, and neveré pleyé with hem more.
And they that haddé knowén her of yore
Saye her so wepe, and thoughte it kindé-
    nesse;   720
And ech of hem wep ek for her distresse.

And bisily they gonnen her conforten
Of thing, God wot, on which she litel
    thoughte,
And with hir wordés wen'den her disporten,
And to be glad they often her bisoughte.
But swich an esé therwith they her
    wroughte,
Right as a man is eséd for to fele,
For ache of hed to clawen him on his hele!

But after al this nicé vanité
They toke hir leve, and hom they wenten
    alle.   730
Criseydé, ful of sorwful pieté
Into the chaumbre up wente out of the halle,
And on her bed for ded she gan to falle,
In purpos neveré thennés for to rise;
And thus she wroughte as I shal you devise.

The salté terés from her yen tweyne
Out-ronne as shour in Aperil ful swithe:
Her whité brest she bet, and for the peyne

708. ll. 708-714 are omitted in γ (= A D Cp. H₁ Cl. S₂).
716. *so wepte*, so Cx.; rest *wepte*.
731. *pieté*, so S Cp.; others *plite*, *pite*, etc.
736. a (J P G H₃) have this stanza here (Boccaccio's order); β (H₂ H₄ R Cx.) and γ (S A D Cp. H₁ Cl. S₂) have it after l. 756.
736. β γ read:
    Therwith the teres from hir yen two
    Doun fille . . .
737. *ful*, so G R; Cx. *doth*; rest omit. H₄ *shoures in Aprille swithe*.
738. *peyne*, β γ *wo*.

After the deth she cri'de a thousand sithe,
Sin he that wont her wo was for to lithe 740
She mot forgon ; for which disáventure
She held herself a fórlost crèature.

Her ounded heer, that sonnissh was of hewe
She rente, and ek her fingres longe and
    smale
She wrong ful ofte, and bad God on her
    rewe
And with the deth do bote upon her bale.
Her hewè, whilom bright that tho was pale,
Bar witnesse of her wo and her constreynte ;
And thus she spak, sobbing in her com-
    pleynte :

'Allas !' quod she, 'out of this regioun 750
I, woful wrecche and infortúnèd wight,
And born in cursèd constellacioun,
Mot gon, and thus departen fro my knight !
Wo worth that day, and namély that night,
On which I saw him first with yen tweyne,
That causeth me, and ich him, al this peyne !

'What shal he don? What shal I don also?
How shal I live, if that I from him twinne?
O derè herte ek, that I lovè so,
Who shal that sorwè slee that ye ben
    inne ?   760
O Calcas fader, thyn be al this sinne !
And cursèd be that day which that Argive
Me of her body bar to ben on-live !

' To what fin sholde I live and sorwè thus ?
How sholde a fissh withouté water dure ?
What is Criseydè worth from Troilus ?
How sholde a plaunte or other crèature
Livèn withoute his kindè noriture ?
For-which ful ofte a by-word here I seye,
That, "erthéles, mot grené soné deye." 770

' I shal don thus : sin nother swerd ne darte
Dar I non handlè for the cruelté,

754. β γ read :
    Wo worth, allas, that like dayes light.
757. β γ read :
    She seyde, ' How shal he don, and I also?
762, 763. β γ read :
    O moder myn, that cleped were Argyve,
    Wo worth that day that thou me bere on lyve.
770. *ertheles*, β γ *roteles*.

That ilkè day I shal from you departe,
If sorwe of that n'il not my bané be,
Ther shal no mete or drinkè come in me,
Til I my soule out of my brest unshethe ;
And thus myselven wol I do to dethe.

' And Troilus, my clothès everychon
Shal blakè ben, in tokening, hertè swete,
That I am as out of this world agon, 780
That wont was you to holden in quíéte ;
And of myn ordré, til that deth me mete,
The óbservaunces evere in your absence‸
Shal sorwè be, compleynte, and abstinence.

' Myn herte and ek the woful goost therinne
Biquethe I, with your spirit to compleyne
Eternaly, for they shul neverè twinne.
For theigh in erthe y-twinnèd be we tweyne,
Yit in the feld of pité, out of peyne,
Ther Pluto regneth, shal we ben i-fere, 790
As Orphèus with Euridíce, his fere.

' Thus hertè myn, for Antenor, allas,
I sonè shal be yolden, as I wene !
But how shal ye don in this woful cas ?
How shal your tendrè hertè this sustene ?
But hertè myn, foryet this sorwe and tene,
And me also ; for, sothly for to seye,
So ye wel fare, I recchè not to deye ! '—

How mighte it evere al red ben or y-songe
The pleyntè that she made in her
    distresse ?   800
I n'ot ; but, as for me, my litel tonge,
If I discrivè wolde her hevinesse,
It sholdè make her sorwè semè lesse
Than that it was, and childisshly deface
Her heighe compleynte ; and therfor ich
    it pace.

Pandáre,—which that sent fro Troilus
Was to Criseyde, as ye han herd devise
That for the beste it was acorded thus,
And he ful glad to don him this servíse,—

773. *I shal*, so α ; β *I mot* ; γ *that I.*
783. *observaunces*, so J only ; rest *observaunces.*
790. *Ther Pluto regneth*, β γ *That hight(e)*
Elysos.
793. *yolden*, β γ *chaunged.*
799. *al red*, so J H₃ only ; other (*y-*)*red.* (Boc.
narrare a pieno.)

Unto Criseyde, in a ful secré wise,   810
Ther-as she lay in torment and in rage,
Com her to telle al hoolly his message.

And fond that she herselven gan to trete
Ful pitously; for with her salté teres
Her brest, her face, y-bathéd was ful wete,
The mighty tresses of her sonnissh heres,
Unbroiden, hanging al aboute her eres:
Which yaf him verray signal of martíre
Of deth, which that for wo she gan desire.

Whan she him saw, she gan for shame anon   820
Her tery face atwixe her armés hide;
For which this Pandar is so wo-bigon
That in the chaumbre he mighte unnethe abide,
As he that pité felte on every side;
For if Criseyde had erst compleynéd sore,
Tho gan she pleyne a thousand timès more.

And in her aspré pleynté thus she seyde,
' Myn em, Pandáre, of joyés mo than two
Was causé causing first to me Criséyde,
That now transmuwéd ben in cruel wo: 830
Whe'r shal I seyn to you welcóme or no,
That alderfirst me broughte into servíse
Of love, allas, that endeth in swich wise?

' Endeth than love in wo?   Ye, or men lieth;
And every worldly joye, as thinketh me!
The ende of blisse, ay sorwe it occupieth!
And who-so troweth not that it so be,
Let him upon me, woful wrecche, y-see,
That my-self hate, and ay my burthe acorse,
Feling alwéy, fro wikke I go to worse! 840

' Who-so me seeth, he seeth sorwe al at ones,
And peyné, torment, pleynté, wo, dis- tresse!

819. *for wo she*, β γ *her herte*.
820. *shame*, so α: β γ *sorwe*. (Boc. per ver- gogna.)
823. *chaumbre*, β γ *hous*.
828, 829. β γ read:
    Pandáre first of joyes mo than two
    Was cause causing unto me, Criseyde.
835. *every worldly joye*, β γ *al(le) worldly blisse*.
842. *And peyne* (†) *all Peyne.*
842. P G Cx. R Cl. *and* before *distresse.*

Out of my sorwful body harm ther non is,
As anguissh, langour, cruel bitternesse,
Anoy, smert, dredé, furie, and ek síknesse!
I trowe, y-wis, from hevené terés reyne
For pité of myn aspre and cruel peyne!'—

' And thou, my suster, ful of dísconfort,'
Quod Pandarus, ' what thenkestow to do?
Why n'hastow to thyself ven som resport? 850
Why wiltow thus thyselve, allas, fordo?
Leve al this werk, and tak now hedé to
What I shal seyn, and herkne of good entente
This that by me thy Troilus thee sente.'

Tornéd her tho Criseyde, a wo makinge
So gret that it a deth was for to see.
' Allas!' quod she, ' what wordés may ye bringe?
What wil my deré herté seyn to me,
Which that I dredé neveré-mo to see?
Wil he han pleynte of terés or I wende? 860
I have y-nowe, if he ther-after sende!'

She was right swich to sen in her viságe
As is that wight that men on beré binde;
Her facé, lik of Paradis th'imáge,
Was al y-chaungéd in another kinde;
The pley, the laughter, men was wont to finde
In her, and othré joyés everychone
Ben fled; and thus for hem she li'th allone.

Aboute her yen two a purpré ring   869
Bitrent, in sothfast tokening of her peyne,
That to beholde it was a dedly thing;
For which Pandáre mighté not restreyne
The terés from his yen for to reyne.
But nathéles, as he best mighte, he seyde
From Troilus thise wordes to Criseyde:

' Lo, nece, I trowe wel ye han herd al how
The king with othré lordés for the beste
Hath maad th'eschaunge of Antenor and you,   878
That cause is of this wo and this unreste.
But how this cas doth Troilus moleste,

867. *othre*, α β *ek her.*
868. *for hem she lith*, α β *lith* (now) *Criseyde.*

That may no worldly mannès tongé seye,—
As he that shortly shapeth him to deye.

' For which we han so sorwed, he and I,
That into litel bothe it hadde us slawe,
But thorugh my conseil this day finaly
He somwhat hath fro weping him with-
    drawe ;
And semeth me that he desireth fawe
With you to ben al night, for to devise
Remédie in this, if ther were any wise.

' This', short and pleyn, th'effect of my
    messáge,   890
And ek the beste as my wit can comprende ;
For ye, that ben of torment in swich rage,
May to no long prológe as now entende.
And her-upon ye may answére him sende ;
And, for the love of God, my necè dere,
So lef this wo or Troilus be here ! '

' Gret is my wo,' quod she, and sightè sore,
As she that feleth dedly sharp distresse ;
' But yit to me his sorwe is muchè more,
That love him bet than he himself, I gesse.
Allas ! for me hath he swich hevinesse ?
Can he for me so pitously compleyne ?
Now, wis, his sorwè doubleth al my peyne !

' Grevous to me, God wot, is for to twinne,'
Quod she, ' but yit it harder is to me
To sen him in that wo that he is inne ;
For wel I wot, it wil my banè be,
And deye I wol in certein ! '—Tho quod
    she,
' But bid him come, or deth, that thus
    me threteth,
Drive out that goost which in myn hertè
    beteth.'   910

Thise wordès seid, she on her armès two
Fil gruf, and gan to wepen pitously.—
Quod Pandarus, ' Allas ! why do ye so,
Sin wel ye wot the time is fastè by

That he shal come ?   Aris up softèly,
That he you not biwopen thus y-finde,
But ye wol han him wood out of his minde !

' For wiste he that ye ferde in this manére,
He wolde himselven slee ; and if I wen'de
To han this fare, he sholdè not come here
For al the good that Priam may dispende ;
For to what fin he wolde anon pretende,
That wot I wel !   And therfor yit I seye,
Lat be this sorwe, or platly he wol deye !

' And shapeth you his sorwè for t'abregge
And not encresse, O levé necè swete !
Beth rather to him cause of flat than egge,
And with som wisdom ye his sorwè bete.
What helpeth it to wepen ful a strete,   929
Or though ye bothe in saltè terès dreynte ?
Bet is a time of cure ay than of pleynte !

' I menè thus : whan ich him hider bringe,
Sin ye ben wise and bothe of oon assent,
So shapeth, how distorbè this goínge,
Or come ayein sone after ye be went.
Wommen ben wise of short avisèment.
And lat sen how your wit shal now availe ;
And that that I can helpe, it shal not
    faile ! '

' Go,' quod Criseyde, ' and unclè, trewèly,
I shal don al my might, me to restreyne
Fro weping in his sighte ; and bisily,   941
Him for to glade, I shal don al my peyne,
And in my hertè seken every veyne.
If to this soor ther may be founden salve,
It shal not lakkè, certein, on myn halve ! '

Go'th Pandarus, and Troilus he soughte,
Til in a temple he fond him al allone,
As he that of his lif no lenger roughte ;
But to the pitous Goddès everychone
Ful tendrely he prey'de and made his
    mone,   950
To don him sone out of this world to pace ;
For wel he thoughte ther n'as non other
    grace.

---

882. γ read :
    For verray wo his wit is al aweye.
(Boc.) Il qual del tutto in duol ne vuol morire.
891. β γ read :
    As ferforth as my wit can (may) comprehende.
903. *Now, wis, his*, β γ *Y-wis, this.*

947. *al allone*, 10 J H₃ Cx. S Cp. ; rest *allone.*
950-952. P H₃ read :
    He faste made his compleynte and his mone,
    Beseking hem to sende him other grace,
    Or fro this world to don him sone pace.

And, shortly, al the sothé for to seye,
He was so fallen in despair that day,
That outrély he shoop him for to deye ;
For right thus was his argument alwey :—
He seide ' I n'am but lorn, so weylawey !
For al that com'th, com'th by necessité :
Thus, to be lorn, it is my destiné !

' For certeinly, this wot I wel,' he seide,
' That for-sight of divíne Púrveyaunce 961
Hath seyn alwéy me to forgon Criseyde,
Sin God seeth every thing, out of doutaunce,
And hem disponeth thorugh his ordinaunce,
In hir merítés sothly for to be,
As they shul comén by predestiné.

' But nathéles, allas, whom shal I leve ?
For ther ben greté clerkés many oon,
That destiné thorugh argumentés preve ;
And some men seyn that nedly ther is
　　　　noon, 970
But that free chois is yiven us everychoon.
O, weylawey ! So sleighe arn clerkés
　　　　olde,
That I n'ot whos opinioun I may holde.

' For some men seyn, if God seeth al biforn,
(Ne God may not deceivéd ben, parde !)
Than mot it fallen, though men hadde it
　　　　sworn,
That Púrveyaunce hath seyn biforn to be.
Wherfor I seye that from eterne if he
Hath wist bifore our thought ek as our
　　　　dede, 979
We han no free chois, as thise clerkés rede.

' For other thought nor other dede also
Mighte neveré be, but swich as Púrvey-
　　　　aunce,
Which may not ben deceivéd neveré mo,
Hath fel'd biforn withouten ignoraunce.
For, if ther mighté ben a variaunce
To writhen out fro Goddés púrveyinge,
Ther n'ere no prescience of thing cominge,

' But it were rather an opinioun
Unstedfast, and no certein forseínge ;
And certés that were an abusioun, 990
That God sholde han no parfit cleer witinge
More than we men that han doutous
　　　　weninge.
But swich an errour upon God to gesse
Were fals and foul, and wikked corsednesse.

' Ek this is an opinioun of some
That han hir top ful heighe and smothe
　　　　y-shore :
They seyn right thus, that thing is not to
　　　　come
For-that the Prescience hath seyn bifore
That it shal come ; but they seyn that,
　　　　therfore
That it shal come, therfore the Púrvey-
　　　　aunce 1000
Wot it biforn withouten ignoraunce.

' And in this maner this necessité
Retorneth in his part contrárie ageyn.
For nedfully bihov'th it not to be
That th'ilké thingés fallen in certéyn
That ben purvey'd ; but needly, as they
　　　　seyn,
Bihoveth it that thingés whiche that falle,
That they in certein ben purveyéd alle.

' I mene as though I labour'd me in this,
T'enqueren which thing cause of which
　　　　thing be : 1010
As whether that the prescience of God is
The certein cause of the necessité
Of thingés that to comén ben, pardé ;
Or if necessité of thing cominge
Be causé certein of the púrveyinge.

' But now n'enforce I me not in shewínge
How th'ordre of causes stant. But wel
　　　　wot I
That it bihoveth, that the bífallínge
Of thingés wisté bíforn certeinly
Be necessarie, al seme it not therby 1020
That prescience put falling necessaire
To thing to come, al fálle it foule or faire.

953. H₃ and H₄ omit ll. 953-1085 ; P inserts
them later. G omits ll. 953-1078. This passage
(not in Boccaccio) is taken for the most part from
Boethius, bk. v.
957. *I n'am*, J Cx. S D *I am* ; P H₂ γ *he n'as*.
957. *so*, so J R Cx. S D ; P H₂ γ omit.
984. *fel'd*, R Cx. *felt* ; D *felte*.

989. *Unstedfast*, so J P Cx. D ; rest *Uncertein*.
989. *certein*, so J P Cx. (D omit) ; rest *stedfast*.

' For if ther sit a man yond on a see,
Than by necessité bihoveth it
That certés thyn opinioun soth be,
That wenest or conjectest that he sit ;
And further over now ayeinward yit,
Lo, right so is it of the part contrárie,
As thus :—now herknè, for I wol not
    tarie.—

' I seye, that if th'opinioun of thee   1030
Be soth for-that he sit, than seye I this,
That he mot sitten by necessité,
And thus necessité in either is.
For in him nede of sitting is, y-wis,
And in thee nede of soth ; and thus, for-
    sothe,
Ther mot necessité ben in you bothe.

' But thou mayst seyn : the man sit not
    therfore
That thyn opinioun of sitting soth is,
But rather, for the man sit ther bifore,
Therfor is thyn opinioun soth, y-wis.   1040
And I seye, though the cause of soth of this
Com'th of his sitting, yit necessité
Is entrechaungèd bothe in him and thee.

' Thus in this samè wise, out of doutaunce,
I may wel maken, as it semeth me,
My resoninge of Goddès púrveyaunce
And of the thingès that to comèn be :
By whichè resons men may wel y-see
That th'ilkè thingès that in erthè falle,
That by necessité they comen alle.   1050

' For although that, for thing shal come,
    y-wis,
Therfore is it purveyèd, certeinly,
Not that it cometh for it purvey'd is,—
Yit nathèles bihov'th it nedfully
That thing to come be purvey'd trewèly :
Or ellès, thingès that purveyèd be,
That they bitiden by necessité.

' And this suffiseth right ynough, certeyn,
For to destroye our free chois every del !
But now is this abusioun, to seyn   1060

That falling of the thingès temporel
Is cause of Goddès prescience éternel.
Now trewèly that is a fals senténce,
That thing to come shul cause his pre-
    science !

' What mighte I wene, and I had swich a
    thought,
But that God púrvey'th thing that is to
    come
For that it is to come, and ellès nought ?
So mighte I wene that thingès alle and
    some,
That whilom ben bifalle and overcome,
Ben cause of th'ilkè sovereign Púrveyaunce
That forwot al withouten ignoraunce ! 1071

' And over al this, yit seye I more therto :
That, right as whan I wot ther is a thing,
Y-wis that thing mot needfully be so,—
Ek right so, whan I wot a thing coming,
So mot it come. And thus the bífalling
Of thingès that ben wist biforn the tide,
They mowe not ben eschuwèd on no
    side.'—

Than seide he thus, 'Almighty Jove in trone,
That wost of al this thing the sothfastnesse,
Rewe on my sorwe, and do me deyen sone,
Or bring Criseyde and me from this dis-
    tresse ! '
And whil he was in al this hevinesse,
Disputing with himself in this matére,
Com Pandar in, and seide as ye may here.

' O mighty God,' quod Pandarus, ' in trone !
Ey ! who say evere a wis-man faren so ?
Why, Troilus, what thenkestow to done ?
Hastow swich list to ben thyn ownè fo ?
What, pardé, yit is not Criseyde ago !   1090
Why list thee so thyself fordon for drede,
That in thyn hed thine ÿen semen dede ?

' Hastow not livèd of thy lif biforn
Withouten her, and ferd ful wel at ese ?
Artow for her and for non other born ?

1030. *that,* Cx. omits.
1038. *of sitting,* so P only ; rest *of his sitting.*
1048. *resons,* all *reson.*

1064. *shul,* so R Cx. ; P *shal ;* J and others *shulde, sholde.*
1065. P omits ll. 1065-1071.
1093. *of thy lif,* so J (P H₃ *al thy lif* ; G *of tyn in thyn lif*) ; β γ *many a yer.*

Hath Kinde y-wrought thee only her to
    plese ?
Canstow not thenken thus in thy disese,
That, on the dees right as thee fallen
    chaunces,
In love alsó ther come and gon plesaunces ?

' And yit this is my wonder most of alle ;
Why thou thus sorwest, sin thou n'ost not
    yit,   1101
Touching her going, how that it shal falle,
Ne, if she can herself disturben it,
Thou hast not yet assayéd al her wit.
A man may al by-time his nekké bede
Whan it shal off, and sorwen at the nede !

' For-thy tak hedé what I shal thee seye :
I have with her y-spoke and longe y-be,
So as acorded was bitwixe us tweye ;
And everémo me thinketh thus, that she
Hath somwhat in her hertés privété, 1111
Wher-with she can, if I shal right arede,
Stinte al this thing of which thou art in
    drede.

' For-which my conseil is, whan it is night,
Thou to her go and make of this an ende ;
And blisful Juno, thorugh her greté might,
Shal, as I hope, her grace unto us sende.
Myn herté seith, " certein, she shal not
    wende " ;
And for-thy put thyn herte a while in reste,
And hold thy purpos, for it is the beste.'—

This Troilus answérde, and sighté sore,
' Thou sey'st right wel, and I wil don
    right so.'   1122
And what him list he seidé to him more.
But whan that it was timé for to go,
Ful privély himself, withouten mo,
Unto her com, as he was wont to done ;
And how they wroughte, I shal you tellen
    sone.

Soth is, that whan they gonnen first to mete,
So gan the sorwe hir hertés for to twiste,
That neither of hem other mighté grete,
But hem in armés hente and softé kiste ;
The lassé woful of hem bothé n'iste 1131
What for to don, ne mighte a word out-
    bringe,
As I seide erst, for wo and for sobbinge.

The woful terés that they leten falle
As bittré weren, out of terés kinde,
For peyne, as is ligne aloés or galle :
So bittré terés wep not thorugh the rinde
The woful Mirra, writen as I finde ; 1139
That in this world ther n'is so hard an herte,
That n'olde han rewéd on hir peynés smerte.

But whan hir woful wery goostés tweyne
Retornéd ben ther-as hem oughté dwelle,
And that somwhat to weyken gan the peyne
By lengthe of pleynte, and ebben gan the
    welle
Of bittré terés, and the herte unswelle,
With broken vois, al hoors for-shright,
    Criseyde
To Troilus thise ilké wordés seyde : 1145

' O Jove, I deye, and mercy I beseche !
Help, Troilus !'—And therwithal her face
Upon his brest she leyde, and losté speche,
Her woful spirit from his propré place,
Right with the word, alwey o-point to pace.
And thus she li'th with hewés pale and
    grene,
That whilom fressh and fairest was to sene.

This Troilus, that on her gan biholde,
Cleping her name,—and she lay as for ded,
Withoute answére, and felte her limés
    colde,   1158
Her yen throwén upward to her hed,—
This sorwful man can now no maner red,

1097. *Canstow not thenken*, β γ *Lat be, and
thenk right* (var.).
1099. *In love also*, β γ *Right so in love.*
1100. *my*, S γ *a.*
1113. *Stinte al this thing*, β γ *Disturbe al
this.* (See l. 1103.)
1124. *But*, so a β (Boc.); S γ *And.*

1133. *What for to don*, so a Cx. ; β γ *Wher
that he was.*
1138, 1139. β γ read :
  So bittre teres wep not, as I finde,
  The woful Myrra through the bark and rinde.
1146. *bittre* (T), H₄ *the ;* H₃ om. ; J and others
hir(e). (Boc. Gli occhi dolenti per gli aspri disiri.)
See ll. 1136-1138 (Boc. Ch'amare fosser oltre lor
natura).

But ofté time her coldé mouth he kiste :
Whe'r him was wo, God and himself it
    wiste !

He rist him up, and long streight he her
    leyde ;
For signe of lif, for aught he can or may,
Can he non finde in no cas on Criseyde,
For which his song ful ofte is 'weylawey !'
And whan he saw that spechéles she lay,
With sorwful vois and herte of blisse al
    bare,
He seide how she was fro this world y-fare.

So after-that he longe had her compleyned,
His hondés wrong, and seid that was to
    seye,   1171
And with his terés salte his brest bi-reyned,
He gan the terés wipen off ful dreye,
And pitously gan for the soulé preye,
And seidé, 'Lord, that set art in thy trone,
Rewe ek on me, for I shal folwe her sone !'

She cold was, and withouten sentément
For aught he wiste, and breth ne felte
    he non ;
And that was him a preignant argument
That she was forth out of this world agon.
And whan he saw ther was non other won,
He gan her limés dresse in swich manére,
As men don folk that shul ben laid on bere.

And after this, with sterne and cruel herte,
His swerd anon out of the shethe he twighte,
Himself to sleen, how soré that him smerte,
So that his soule her soulé folwé mighte
Ther-as the doom of Minos wolde it dighte ;
Sin Love and cruel Fortune it ne wolde
That in this world he lenger liven sholde.

Than seide he thus, fulfil'd of heigh desdayn,
'O cruel Jove, and thou Fortúne adverse,
This' al and som : that falsly han ye slayn
Criseyde, and sin ye can do me no werse,
Fy on your might and werkés so diverse !
Thus cowardly ye shal me neveré winne :
Ther shal no deth me fro my lady twinne !

'For I this world, sin ye han slain her
    thus,
Wol lete, and folwe her spirit forth in hye :
Shal neveré lover seyn that Troilus   1200
Dar not for feré with his lady dye ;
For, certein, I wol bere her companye.
But sin ye n'il not suffre us liven here,
Yit suffreth that our soulés ben i-fere !

'And thou cité, which that I leve in wo,
And thou Priám, and brethren alle i-fere,
And thou, my moder, far-wel, for I go !
And Attropos, mak redy thou my bere !
And thou, Criseydé, sweté herté dere,
Receivé now my spirit !'—wolde he seye,
With swerd at herte, al redy for to deye,

But, as God wolde, of swough therwith
    she breyde,   1212
And gan to sike, and 'Troilus !' she cride,
And he answérdé, ' Herté myn, Criseyde,
Livé ye yit ?' and let his swerd doun glide.
' Ye, herté myn, y-thankéd be Cipride !'
Quod she ; and therwithal she soré sighte,
And he bigan confórte her as he mighte ;

Took her in armes two, and kiste her ofte,
And her to glade he dide al his entente :
For-which her goost, that flikeréd ay on
    lofte,   1221
Ayein into her herte al softé wente.
So at the laste, as that her ýe glente
Aside, anon she gan his swerd espye,
As it lay bare, and gan for feré crye,

And axéd him, why he it hadde out-drawe.
And Troilus anon the causé tolde,
And how himself therwith he wolde han
    slawe :
For which Criseyde upon him gan biholde,
And gan him in her armés fasté folde,   1230

1199. *forth in hye,* β γ *lowe or* (*and*) *hye.*
1208. So P H₂ β γ; J G read *Thou Attropos
that is* (G *art) ful redy here* (read ? *for I go To
Attropos that is ful redy here.* Boc. ch'io me
ne vo sotterra).
1214. *Herte;* β γ *Lady* (Boc. dolce mio disiro).
1218. *confórte,* β γ *to glade* (see l. 1220).
Boc. La conforto.
1222. β γ read :
     Into her woful herte ayein it wente.
1223. *So,* β γ *But.*

1167. *And,* β γ *But.*
1173. *ful,* so P β γ; J H₂ G *and.*
1183. *folk,* β γ *hem* (*him*).

And seide, 'O mercy, God, lo, which a
     dede !
Allas ! how neigh we weré bothé dede !

'Than if I n'haddé spoke, as gracé was,
Ye wolde han slain yourself anon ?' quod
     she.——
'Ye, doutéles !'—And she answérde,
     'Allas !
For by that ilké Lord that madé me,
I n'olde a forlong wey on-live han be
After your deth, to han ben crownéd quene
Of al the lond the sonne on-shineth shene ;

'But with this selven swerd, which that here
     is,   1240
My-selve I wolde han slawé !'—Quod she
     tho,
'But ho ! for we han right ynough of this,
And lat us rise and streight to beddé go,
And theré lat us speken of our wo ;
For, by the morter which that I see brenne,
Knowe I ful wel that day is not fer henne.'

Whan they were in hir bed in armés folden,
Nought was it lik the nightés her-biforn ;
For pitously ech other gan biholden,
As they that hadde hir joyés allé lorn,   1250
Seying, 'allas, that everé they were born !'
Til at the laste this woful wight, Criseyde,
To Troilus thise ilké wordés seyde :

'Lo, herté myn, wel wot ye this,' quod she,
'That, if a wight alwéy his wo compleyne
And seketh nought how holpen for to be,
It n'is but foly and encrees of peyne.
And sin that here assembled be we tweyne
To findé bote of wo that we ben inne,
It were al timé soné to biginne.   1260

'I am a woman, as ful wel ye wot ;
And as I am aviséd sodeinly,
So wol I telle it you whil it is hot.
Me thinketh thus : that nouther ye nor I
Oughte half this wo to maken skilfully ;

For ther is art y-nough for to redresse
That yit is mis, and sleen this hevinesse.

'Soth is, that wo the whiche that we ben
     inne,
For aught I wot, for nothing ellés is   1269
But for the causé that we shullen twinne :
Consideréd al, ther n'is no more amis.
But what is thanne a rémedie unto this,
But that we shape us soné for to mete !
This' al and som, my deré herté swete !

'Now, that I shal wel bringen it aboute
To come ayein sone after that I go,
Therof am I no maner thing in doute.
For, dredéles, withinne a wowke or two
I shal ben here ; and that it may be so,
By allé right, and in a wordés fewe,   1280
I shal you wel an hep of weyés shewe

'For-which I n'il not maken long sermoún,
For time y-lost may not recoveréd be ;
But I wol go right to conclusioun,
And to the beste, in aught that I can see.
And for the love of God, foryive it me
If I speke aught ayeins your hertés reste,
For trewély I speke it for the beste ;

'Making alwey a protestacioun,
That in effect this thing that I shal seye   1290
N'is but to shewén you my mocioun,
To finde unto our help the besté weye.
And taketh it non other wise, I preye :
For finaly what-so ye me comaunde,
That wol I don, for that is no demaunde.

'Now herkneth this : ye han wel under-
     stonde
My going graunted is by parlément
So ferforth that it may not ben withstonde
For al this world, as by my jugément.
And sin ther helpeth non avisément   1300
To letten it, lat it passe out of minde,
And lat us shape a bettré wey to finde.

1241. *slawe,* so G R ; rest *slain.*
1251. β γ read :
     Biwailing ay the day that they were born.
1252. *woful,* so a β S ; γ *sorweful.*

1284. *right to conclusioun,* β γ *to my con-*
clusioun.
1288. *speke,* J *seye* ; P *mene.*
1290. *in effect this thing,* β γ *now thise wordes*
whiche.
1294. *finaly,* H₃ β γ *in effect.*

'The soth is this, that twinning of us tweyne
Wol us disese and crueliche anoye,
But him bihoveth somtime han a peyne,
That serveth Love, if that he wol have joye.
And sin I shal no ferther out of Troye
Than I may ride ayein on half a morwe,
It oughte lasse causen us to sorwe :

'So as I shal not so ben hid in muwe,   1310
That day by day, myn owne herte dere,
(Sin wel ye wot that it is now a truwe,)
Ye shal ful wel al myn estat y-here.
And, or that trewe is don, I shall ben here,
And thus have ye bothe Antenor y-wonne
And me also. Beth glad now, if ye conne,

'And thenk right thus : "Criseyde is now
     agon,
But what! she shal come hastily ayeyn!"'—
'And whanne, allas !'—'By God, lo, right
    anon,
Or dayes ten, that dar I saufly seyn !   1320
And thanne atte erste shal ye ben so feyn
That we shul evere-mo togedere dwelle,
That al this world ne mighte our joye telle.

'I see that often, ther-as we ben now,
That for the beste, our conseil for to hide,
Ye speken not with me, nor I with yow
In fourtenight, ne see you go ne ride.
Mowen ye not ten dayes thanne abide
For myn honour in swich an aventure ?
Y-wis, ye mowen elles lite endure !   1330

'Ye knowe ek how that al my kin is here,
Only but-if that it myn fader be,
And ek mine othre thinges alle i-fere,
And namely, my dere herte, ye,
Whom that I n'olde leven for to see
For al this world, as muche as it hath space ;
Or elles see ich nevere Joves face !

'Why ! trowe ye my fader in this wise
Coveiteth so to see me, but for drede
Lest in this town that folkes me despise   1340
Bicause of him, for his unhappy dede?
What wot my fader what lif that I lede ?

1315. *thus,* β γ *than(ne).*
1328. *Mowen* (γ) all *May* (see 1330).
1336. *muche,* H₃ *brode;* β γ *wid(e).*

For if he wiste in Troye how wel I fare,
Us nedeth for my going naught to care.

'Ye sen that every day ek more and more
Men trete of pees, and it supposed is
That men the quene Eleyne shal restore,
And Grekes us restoren that is mis ;
So, though ther n'ere confort non but this,
That men purposen pees on every side,   1350
Ye may the bettre at ese of herte abide.

'For if that it be pees, myn herte dere,
The nature of the pees mot nedes drive
That men moste entrecomunen i-fere,
And to and fro ek ride and go as blive,
Alday as thikke as been flen from a hive,
And every wight han liberte to bleve
Wher-as him list the bet, withouten leve.

'And though so be that pees ther may be
    non,
Yit hider, though ther nevere pees ne were,
I moste come : for whider sholde I gon,   1361
Or how mischaunce sholde I dwellen there
Among tho men of armes evere in fere ?
For which, so wisly God my soule rede,
I can not sen wherof ye sholden drede.

'Have here another wey, if it so be
That al this thing ne may you not suffise.
My fader, as ye knowen wel, parde,
Is old, and elde is ful of coveitise ;   1369
And I right now have founden al the gise,
Withouten net wherwith I shal him hente.
And herkneth how, if that ye wol assente !

'Lo, Troilus, men seith that hard it is,
The wolf ful and the wether hool to have ;
This is to seyn, that men ful ofte, y-wis,
Mot spenden part the remenaunt for to save.
For ay with gold men may the herte grave
Of him that set is upon coveitise.
And how I mene, I shal it you devise.

'The moeble which that I have in this
    toun   1380
Unto my fader shal I take, and seye,
That right for trust and for savacioun
It sent is from a frend of his or tweye,
The whiche frendes fervently him preye

527

To senden after more, and that in hye,
Whil-that this town stant thus in jupartye;

'And that shal ben a hugé quantité,—
Thus shal I seyn;—but lest it folk espi'de,
This may be sent by no wight but by me.
I shal ek shewén him, if pees bitide   1390
What frendés that I have on every side
Toward the court, to don the wrathé pace
Of Priamus, and don him stonde in grace.

'So, what for oo thing and for other, swete,
I shal him so enchaunten with my sawes,
That right in hevene his soulé shal he
    mete !
For al Appollo, or his clerkes lawes
Or calculinge availeth not three hawes !
Desir of gold shal so his soulé blende,   1399
That, as me list, I shal wel make an ende !

'And if he wolde aught by his sort it preve
If that I lye, in certein I shal fonde
Distorben him and plukke him by the sleve
Making his sort, or beren him on honde
He hath not wel the Goddés understonde :
For Goddes speke in amphibologyes,
And for a soth they tellen twenty lyes !

'Ek dredé fond first Goddés, I suppose,—
Thus shal I seyn,—and ek his coward herte
Made him amis the Goddés text to glose
Whan he for-feréd out of Delphos sterte.
And, but I make him soné to converte,
And don my red withinne a day or tweye,
I wol to you obligé me to deye !'

And treweliche as writen wel I finde,
That al this thing was seid of good entente,
And that her herté trewé was and kinde
Towárdés him, and spak right as she mente,
And that she starf for wo neigh, whan she
    wente,   1419
And was in purpos everé to ben trewe :
Thus writen they that of her werkés knewe.

This Troilus with herte and erés spradde
Herde al this thing devisen to and fro ;

And verrayliche him seméd that he hadde
The selvé wit ; but yit to lete her go
His herté mis-foryaf him everé-mo.
But finaly he gan his herté wreste
To tristen her, and took it for the beste.

For which the greté furie of his penáunce
Was queynt with hope ; and therwith ben
    bitwene   1430
Bigan for joyé th'amoroúsé daunce.
And as the briddés, whan the sonne is shene,
Deliten in hir song in levés grene,
Right so the wordés that they spake i-fere
Delited hem, and made hir hertés clere.

But nathéles the wending of Criseyde,
For al this world, ne may out of his minde :
For-which ful ofte he pitousliche her
    prey'de
That of her herte he mighte her trewé
    finde,
And seyde her,—'Certés, if ye ben un-
    kinde,   1440
And but ye come at day set into Troye,
Ne shal I nevere have hele, honoúr, ne
    joye.

'For al-so soth as sonne uprist a-morwe,
And God ! so wisly thou me, woful
    wrecche,
To resté bringe out of this cruel sorwe,
I wil myselven slee if that ye drecche !
But of my deth though litel be to recche,
Yit, or that ye me causen so to smerte,
Dwel rather here, myn owné dere herte !

'For trewély, myn owné lady dere,   1450
Tho sleightés yit that I you heré stere ,
Ful shaply ben to failen alle i-fere ;
And thus men seith, that "oon thenketh
    the bere,
But al another thenketh his ledére !"
Your sire is wis : and seid is, out of drede,
"Men may the wise at-renne, and not
    at-rede !"

'It is ful hard to halten unespyed
Bifore a crepil, for he can the craft :
Your fader is in sleighte as Argus yed.   1459

1396. *soule*, H₄ S D H₁ Cl. *soule is.*
1409. *ek*, H₃ β γ *that.*
1415. *as*, J D *is.*

1449. *dere*, γ *swete.*

For, al be that his moeble is him biraft,
His oldé sleighte is yit so with him laft,
Ye shal not blende him for your womman-
    hede,
Ne feyne aright : and that is al my drede.

' I n'ot if pees shal everé-mo bitide ;
But, pees or no, for ernest ne for game,
I wot, sin Calcas on the Grekés side
Hath onés ben and lost so foule his name,
He dar no more come here ayein for
    shame :
For-which that wey, for aught I can espye,
To trusten on, n'is but a fantasye.   1470

' Ye shal eek sen, your fader shal you glose
To ben a wif, and as he can wel preche,
He shal som Grek so preyse and wel alose,
That ravisshen he shal you with his speche,
Or do you don by force as he shal teche ;
And Troilus, of whom he n'il have routhe,
Shal causéles so sterven in his trouthe !

' And over al this, your fader shal despise
Us alle, and seyn this cité n'is but lorn,
And that the segé neveré shal arise,   1480
For-why the Grekés han it allé sworn
Til we be slayn and doun our walles torn ;
And thus he shal you with his wordés fere,
That ay drede I that ye wol bleven there.

' Ye shal ek sen so many a lusty knight
Among the Grekés, ful of worthinesse,
And ech of hem with herté, wit, and might
To plesen you don al his bisinesse,
That ye shul dullen of the rudénesse
Of us sely Trojánes, but-if routhe   1490
Remordé you, or vertu of your trouthe.

' And this to me so grevous is to thinke
That fro my brest it wol the soulé rende ;
Ne, dredéles, in me ther can not sinke
A good opinioun, if that ye wende ;
For-why your fadres sleighté wol us shende :
And if ye gon, as I have told you yore,
So thenk I n'am but ded, withouté more !

' For-which, with humblé, trewe and
    pitous herte,   1499
A thousand timés mercy I you preye :
So reweth on mine aspré peynés smerte,
And doth somwhat as that I shal you seye,
And lat us stele awey bitwixe us tweye ;
And thenk that foly is, whan man may
    chese,
For accident his substaunce ay to lese.

' I mené thus : that sin we mowe or day
Wel stele awey and ben togedré so,
What wit were it to putten in assay,
In cas ye sholden to your fader go,
If that ye mighten come ayein or no ?   1510
Thus mene I, that it were a gret folýe
To putte that sikernesse in jupartye.

' And, vulgarly to speken of substaúnce
Of tresour, may we bothé with us lede
Y-nough to live in honour and plesaúnce,
Til into timé that we shal be dede ;
And thus we may eschewén al this drede :
For everich other wey ye can recorde,
Myn herte, y-wis, may therwith not acorde.

' And hardily ne dredeth no povérté,   1520
For I have kin and frendés ellés where
That, though we comén in our baré sherte,
Us sholdé neither lakken gold ne gere,
But ben honoúréd whil we dwelten there :
And go w' anon : for, as in myn entente,
This is the beste, if that ye wol assente.' —

Criseyde him, with a sik, right in this wise
Answérde, ' Y-wis, my deré herté trewe,
We may wel stele awey, as ye devise,   1529
Or finden swiche unthrifty weyés newe ;
But afterward ful sore it wol us rewe.
And, help me God so at my mosté nede,
As causéles ye suffren al this drede !

' For th'ilké day that I for cherisshinge,
Or drede of fader, or for other wight,
Or for estat, delit, or for weddínge
Be fals to you, my Troilus, my knight,
Satúrnés doughter, Juno, thorugh her
    might,

1490. *Trojánes* (?), all *Trojans* (read ? *As of us
ely Trojans*).
1493. *the,* β γ *my.*

1527. *kim,* H₃ γ omit.
1530. *Or,* γ *and.*

2 M   529

As wood as Athamanté do me dwelle
Eternaliche in Stix, the put of helle !   1540

'And this on every God celestial
I swere it you, and ek on ech Goddésse,
On every Nymphe and Deité infernal,
On Satiry and Fauny more and lesse,
That halvé Goddés ben of wildernesse ;
And Attropos my thred of lif to-breste
If I be fals !   Now trowe me if you leste !

'And thou, Simoys, that as an arwé clere
Thorugh Troye ay rennest downward to
        the see,   1549
Ber witnesse of this word that seid is here,
That th'ilké day that ich untrewé be
To Troilus, myn owné herté free,
That thou retorné backward to thy welle,
And I with body and soulé sinke in helle !

'But that ye speke, awey thus for to go
And leten alle your frendés, God forbede
For any womman that ye sholdé so !
And namély, sin Troye hath now swich
        nede
Of help. And ek of oo thing taketh hede :
If this were wist, my lif laye in balaúnce,
And your honóur : God shilde us fro
        mischaunce !   1561

'And if so be, herafter pees be take,—
As alday happeth, after anger, game,—
Why, Lord, the sorwe and wo ye wolden
        make,
That ye ne dorsté come ayein for shame !
And, or that ye juparten so your name,
Beth not too hastif in this hoté fare :
For hastif man ne wanteth neveré care !

'What trowén ye the peple ek al aboute
Wolde of it seye ? It is ful light t'arede !
They wolden seyn, and swere it out of
        doute,   1571
That love ne drof you not to do this
        dede,
But lust voluptuous and coward drede :

Thus were al lost, y-wis, myn herté dere,
Your honour, which that shineth now so
        clere.

'And also thenketh on myn honesté
That floureth yit : how foule I sholde it
        shende,
And with what filthe it spotted sholdé be,
If in this forme I sholdé with you wende.
Ne though I livede unto the worldés ende,
My namé sholde I nevere ayein ward winne :
Thus were I lost, and that were routhe
        and sinne.

'And for-thy slee with reson al this hete!
Men seyn "the suffrant overcom'th,"
        pardé ;
Ek, "who-so wol han lief, he lief mot lete."
Thus maketh vertu of necessité !
Be pacient, and thenk that lord is he
Of Fortune ay, that naught wol of her
        recche,
And she ne daunteth no wight but a
        wrecche !   1585

'And trusteth this : that certés, herté swete,
Or Phebus' suster, Lúcina the shene,
The Lioun passe out of this Ariete,
I wil ben here, withouten any wene.
I mene, as help me Juno, hevenés quene,
The tenthé day, but-if that deth m'assaile,
I wil you sen, withouten any faile.'—

'And now, so this be soth,' quod Troilus,
I shal wel suffre unto the tenthé day,
Sin that I see that nede it mot be thus.
But for the love of God, if it be may,   1600
So lat us stelen privéliche away !
For evere in oon, as for to live in reste,
Myn herté seith that it wol be the beste.'—

'O mercy, God, what lif is this !' quod she.
'Allas, ye slee me thus for verray tene !
I see wel now that ye mistrusten me,
For by your wordés it is wel y-sene !
Now, for the love of Cynthea the shene,

1549. *ay rennest*, so J H₃ A D ; *rennest* P G
R Cx. ; H₂ H₄ S Cp. H₁ Cl. S₂ *rennest ay.*
1562. *herafter pees be take*, so P ; rest *that
pees herafter take.*

1575. *shineth now*, so P H₃ ; rest *now shineth.*
1587. *Be pacient*, so P G H₃ R ; J and others
By patience.

Mistrust me not thus causéles, for routhe,
Sin to be trewe I have you plight my
     trouthe !   1610

' And thenketh wel, that somtime it is wit
To spende a time, a time for to winne.
Ne, pardé, lorn am I not fro you yit,
Though that we ben a day or two a-twinne.
Drif out the fantasyés you withinne,
And trusteth me, and leveth ek your sorwe,
Or, her my trouthe, I wil not live til morwe !

' For if ye wiste how sore it doth me smerte,
Ye woldé cesse of this : for God, thou wost
The puré spirit wepeth in myn herte   1620
To sen you wepen that I lové most,
And that I mot gon to the Grekés ost !
Ye, n'ere it that I wisté remedye
To come ayein, right here I woldé dye !

' But, certés, I am not so nice a wight
That I ne can imaginen a wey
To com ayein that day that I have hight.
For who may holde a thing that wol awey?
My fader nought, for al his queynté pley !
And by my thrift, my wending out of
     Troye   1630
Another day shal torne us al to joye !

' For-thy with al myn herte I you biseke,
If that you list don aught for my preyére
And for that love which that I love you eke,
That, or that I departé fro you here,
That of so good a confort and a chere
I may you sen, that ye may bringe at reste
Myn herté which that is o-point to breste.

' And over al this I preye you,' quod she tho,
' Myn owné hertés sothfast suffisaunce, 1640
Sin I am thyn al hool, withouten mo,
That whil that I am absent, no plesaúnce
Of other do me fro your rémembraunce ;
For I am evere a-gast, for-why men rede
That "love is thing ay ful of bisy drede."

' For in this world ther liveth lady non,
If that ye were untrewe (as God defende!),
That so bitraysèd were or wo-bigon
As I, that allé trouthe in you entende.

And doutéles, if-that I other wén'de,   1650
I n'ere but ded. And, or ye causé finde,
For Goddés love, so beth me not un-
     kinde ! '—

To this answérdé Troilus, and seyde,
' Now God, to whom ther n'is no thought
     y-wrye,
Me glade, as wis I nevere unto Criseyde,
Sin th'ilké day I saw her first with ye,
Was fals, ne neveré shal til that I dye !
At shorté wordés, wel ye may me leve :
I can no more, it shal be founde at
     preve ! '—   1659

' Gramercy, goodé myn, y-wis !' quod she,
' And blisful Venus, lat me neveré sterve
Or I may stonde of plesaunce in degree
To quite him wel, that so wel can deserve !
And whil that God my wit wil me con-
     serve,
I shal so don, so trewe I have you founde,
That ay honoúr to me-ward shal rebounde !

' For trusteth wel, that your estat reál,
Ne veyn delit, nor only worthinesse
Of you in werre or torney marcial,   · 1669
Ne pompe, array, nobléye, or ek richesse
Ne madé me to rewe on your distresse,
But moral vertu, grounded upon trouthe :
That was the cause I first had on you
     routhe !

' Ek gentil herte and manhod that ye hadde,
And that ye hadde, as me thoughte, in
     despit
Evéry thing that sounèd into badde,
As rudénesse and poeplissh appetit,
And that your reson bridleth you delit :
This made, aboven every créature
That I was youre, and shal whil I may
     dure.   1680

' And this may lengthe of yerès not fordo,
Ne rémuable Fortune it deface.
But Jupiter, that of his might may do
The sorwful to be glad, so yive us grace,
Or nightés ten, to meten in this place,

1654. *thought*, β γ *cause*.
1682. *it*, so S ; rest om.

531

So that it may your herte and myn
   suffise !
And far now wel, for time is that ye
   rise !'—

But after · that they longe y · pleynèd
   hadde,
And oftè kist, and streite in armès folde,
The day gan rise, and Troilus him
   cladde,   1690
And rewfully his lady gan biholde
As he that feltè dethès carès colde,

1688. *But*, S γ *And.*

And to her grace he gan him recomaunde.
Whe'r him was wo, this holde I no de-
   maundè !

For mannès hed imaginen ne can,
N'entendèment considere, or tongè telle
The cruel peynès of this woful man,
That passen every torment down in helle.
For whan he saw that she ne mightè dwelle,
Which that his soule out of his hertè rente,
Withoutè more out of the chaumbre he
   wente.   1701

1696. *or*, so J H₃; P β γ *ne.*
1697. *woful*, γ *sorwful.*

BOOK V

APROCHEN gan the fatal destiné
That Jovès hath in disposicioun,
And to you, angry Parcas, sustren three,
Committeth to don execucioun :
For which Criseydè moste out of the toun,
And Troilus shal dwellen forth in pine
Til Lachesis his thred no lenger twine.

The gold-ytressèd Phebus heighe on-lofte
Thryès hadde allè, with his bemès shene,
The snowès molte, and Zephirus as ofte   10
Y-brought ayein the tendrè levès grene,
Sin that the sone of Ecuba the quene
Bigan to love her first for whom his sorwe
Was al, that she departè sholde a-morwe.

Ful redy was at primè Diomede,
Criseyde unto the Grekès ost to lede,
For sorwe of which she feltè her hertè blede,
As she that n'istè what was best to rede.
And trewèly, as men in bokès rede,   19
Men wistè neverè womman han the care,
Ne was so loth out of a town to fare.

This Troilus, withouten reed or lore,
As man that hath his joyès ek forlore,
Was wayting on his lady everè more

3. *Parcas*, Fates.
7. *Lachesis*, one of the Fates.
8. *gold-ytressed* (?), all *gold(e)-tressed.*
9. *shene*, so H₂ H₄ R S ; J P *clene*; Cx. H₂ γ
clere.

As she that was the sothfast crop and more
Of al his lust or joyès her-bifore.
But Troilus ! now far-wel· al thy joye,
For shaltow neverè sen her eft in Troye !

Soth is, that whil he bood in this manère,
He gan his wo ful manly for to hide,   30
That wel unnethe it sene was in his chere ;
But at the yatè ther she sholde out-ride,
With certein folk he hovèd her t'abide,
So wo-bigon, al wolde he naught him
   pleyne,
That on his hors unnethe he sat for peynè.

For ire he quok, so gan his hertè gnawe,
Whan Diomede on horsè gan him dresse,
And seide unto himself this ilkè sawe,
'Allas !' quod he, 'thus foul a wrecched·
   nesse,
Why suffre ich it ?   Why n'il ich it re-
   dresse ?   40
Were it not bet at onès for to dye
Than everè more in langour thus to drye ?

'Why n'il I make at onès riche and porè
To have y-nough to do or-that she go ?
Why n'il I bringe al Troye upon a rorè ?
Why n'il I sleen this Diomede also ?
Why n'il I rather with a man or two
Stele her awey ?   Why wol I this endure ?
Why n'il I helpen to myn ownè cure ?'

532

But why he n'oldè don so fel a dede,   50
That shal I seyn, and why him liste it spare :
He hadde in herte alweyes a maner drede
Lest that Criseyde, in rumour of this fare,
Sholde han ben slayn : lo, this was al
     his care.
And ellès, certein, as I seidè yore,
He hadde it don, withouten wordès more.

Criseydè, whan she redy was to ride,
Ful sorwfully she sighte, and seide, 'Allas !'
But forth she mot, for aught that may bitide :
Ther n'is non other rémedie in this cas ;
And forth she rit ful sorwfulliche a pas.   61
What wonder is though that her sorè smerte,
Whan she forgo'th her ownè derè herte ?

This Troilus, in wise of curteisye,
With hauke on honde, and with a hugè
     route
Of knightès, rod and dide her companye,
Passing al the valéyè fer withoute ;
And ferther wolde han riden, out of doute,
Ful fayn ; and wo was him to gon so sone :
But torne he moste, and it was ek to done.

And right with that was Antenor y-come   71
Out of the Grekès ost ; and every wight
Was of it glad, and seide he was welcóme.
And Troilus, al n'ere his hertè light,
He peynèd him with al his fullè might
Him to with-holde of weping at the leste ;
And Antenor he kiste, and madè feste.

And therwithal he moste his levè take,
And caste his ye upon her pitously,   79
And neer he rod, his causè for to make,
To take her by the hond al sobrely ;
And, Lord, so she gan wepen tendrely !
And he ful softe and sleighly gan her seye,
'Now hold your day, and do me not to deye!'

With that his courser tornèd he aboute
With facè pale, and unto Diomede
No word he spak, ne non of al his route ;
Of which the sone of Tydèus took hede,

As he that coudè moré than the credè   89
In swich a craft, and by the reyne her hente ;
And Troilus to Troye homwárde he wente.

This Diomede that led her by the bridel,
Whan that he saw the folk of Troye aweye,
Thoughte, 'Al my labour shal not ben
     on ydel
If that I may, for somwhat shal I seye ;
For at the worste it may yit shorte our weye.
I have herd seyd ek, timès twyès twelve,
"He is a fool that wol foryete himselve." '

But nathéles thus thoughte he wel y-nough,
That 'certeinliche I am aboutè nought   100
If that I speke of love, or make it tough ;
For doutéles, if she have in her thought
Him that I gesse, he may not ben y-brought
So sone awey ; but I shal finde a mene,
That she not wite as yit shal, what I mene.'

This Diomede, as he that coude his good,
Whan timè was, gan fallen forth in speche
Of this and that, and axèd why she stood
In swich disese, and gan her ek biseche   109
That if that he encressè mighte or eche
With any thing her esè, that she sholde
Comaunde it him, and seide he don it wolde.

For treweliche he swor her, as a knight,
That ther n'as thing with which he mighte
     her plese
That he n'il don his herte and al his might
To don it, for to don her herte an ese ;
And preyèd her, she wolde her sorwe
     apese,
And seide, 'Y-wis, we Grekès can have
     joye
T'honóuren you, as wel as folk of Troye.'

He seide ek thus, 'I wot you thinketh
     straunge,—   120
No wonder is, for it is to you newe,—
Th'aqueyntaunce of thise Trojans for to
     chaunge
For folk of Grecè, that ye neverè knewe.

60, 61. So a β S ; H₃ γ transpose ll. 60, 61.
63. *dere,* γ *swete.* (See iv. 1449.)
67. *valéye ;* R *wallys* (read ? *The walles alle*).
valeye is a mistranslation of Boc. *vallo,* 'rampart.'
88. *sone of Tydeus,* Diomede.

107. *Whan time was,* γ *Whan this was don.*
115. *n'il,* H₄ R S γ *n'olde.*
122. *Trojans ;* H₂ H₄ D *Trojanes.*
122. *for to,* so G Cx. ; J and others *to.*

But woldé neveré God but-if as trewe
A Grek ye sholde amonge us allé finde
As any Trojan is, and ek as kinde.

'And by the cause I swor you right lo now
To be your frend, and helply to my might,
And for-that more acqueyntaunce ek of
    yow   129
Have ich had than another straunger wight,
So fro this forth, I preye you, day and night,
Comaundeth me, how soré that me smerte,
To don al that may like unto your herte ;

'And that ye me wolde as your brother
    trete,
And taketh not my frendship in despit ;
And, though your sorwes ben for thingés
    grete,
N'ot I not why, but out of more respit
Myn herte hath for t'amende it gret delit ;
And if I may your harmés not redresse,
I am right sory for your hevinesse.   140

'For though ye Trojans with us Grekés
    wrothe
Han many a day ben, alwey yit, pardé,
Oo God of love in soth we serven bothe.
And, for the love of God, my lady free,
Whom so ye hate, as beth not wroth with me;
For trewély ther can no wight you serve,
That half so loth your wraththé wolde
    deserve.

'And n'ere it that we ben so neigh the tente
Of Calcas, which that sen us bothé may,
I wolde of this you tell eal myn entente ;   150
But this' enseléd til another day.
Yif me your hond : I am, and shal be ay,
God help me so, whil that my lif may dure,
Your owne, aboven every créature !

'Thus seide I nevere or now to womman
    born ;
For, God myn herte as wisly gladé so,
I lovedé neveré womman her-biforn
As paramours, ne neveré shal no mo :
And for the love of God beth not my fo,
Al can I not to you, my lady dere,   160
Compleyne aright, for I am yit to lere.

'And wondreth not, myn owné lady bright,
Though that I speke of love to you thus
    blive ;
For I have herd or this of mony a wight,
Hath lovéd thing he neveré say his live :
Nor I am not of powér for to strive
Ayeins the God of Love, but him obeye
I wol alwéy ; and mercy I you preye.

'Ther ben so worthy knightés in this place,
And ye so fair, that everich of them alle   170
Wol peynen him to stonden in your grace ;
But mighté me so fair a gracé falle,
That ye me for your servant woldé calle,
So lowly ne so trewély you serve
N'il non of hem, as I shal, til I sterve.'—

Criseyde unto that purpos lite answerde,
As she that was with sorwe oppresséd so,
That in effect she nought his talés herde
But here and there, now here a word or two.
Her thoughte her sorwful herté brast a-two ;
For whan she gan her fader fer espye,   181
Wel neigh down off her hors she gan to sye.

But nathéles she thankéd Diomede
Of al his travaile and his goodé chere,
And that him liste his frendship her to
    bede ;
And she accepteth it in good manére,
And wol do fayn that is him lief and dere ;
And trusten him she wolde, and wel she
    mighte,
As seidé she.   And from her hors sh'
    alighte.   189

Her fader hath her in his armés nome,
And twenty time he kiste his doughter
    swete,
And seide, 'O deré doughter myn, wel-
    cóme !'
She seide ek, she was fayn with him to mete,
And stood forth muwét, milde, and man-
    suéte. —
But here I leve her with her fader dwelle,
And forth I wol of Troilus you telle.

To Troye is come this woful Troilus
In sorwe abovén allé sorwes smerte,

166. *Nor*, J H₄ H₃ ; S γ *Ek* ; rest *For*, *Ne.*

With felon look, and facé díspitous.   199
Tho sodeinly down from his hors he sterte,
And thorugh his paleis with a swollen herte
To chaumbrè wente : of no wight took he
    hede,
Ne non to him dar speke a word for drede.

And there his sorwes that he sparèd hadde
He yaf an issue large, and Deth he cri'de ;
And in his throwès frenètik and madde
He corseth Jove, Appollo, and ek Cupide,
He corseth Ceres, Bacus, and Cipríde,
His burthe, himself, his fate, and ek natúre,
And, save his lady, every créáture.   210

To bedde he go'th, and walweth there and
    torneth
In furie, as doth he, Ixion, in helle ;
And in this wise he neigh til day sojorneth.
But tho bigan his herte a lite unswelle
Thorugh terès, whiche that gonnen up to
    welle ;
And pitously he cri'de upon Criseyde,
And to himself right thus he spak and seyde :

' Where is myn ownè lady, lief and dere ?
Where is her whitè brest ?   Where is it,
    where ?   219
Where ben her armès and her ẏen clere,
That yesternight this timè with me were ?
Now may I wepe allonè many a tere,
And graspe aboute I may ; but in this place,
Saving a pilwe, I findè naught t'enbrace.

' How shal I don ?   Whan shal she come
    ayeyn ?
I n'ot, allas !   Why let ich her to go ?
As woldè God, ich hadde as tho ben slayn !
O hertè myn, Criseyde !   O swetè fo !
O lady myn, that I love and no mo,   229
To whom for everè mo myn herte I dowe !
See how I deye, ye n'il me not rescowe !

' Who seeth you now, my rightè lodè-sterre ?
Who sit right now or stant in your presénce ?

Who can confórten now your hertès werre ?
Now I am gon, whom yeve ye audience ?
Who spek'th for me right now in myn
    . absénce ?
Allas, no wight : and that is al my care ;
For wel I wot, as yvele as I ye fare !

' How sholde I thus ten dayès ful endure,   239
Whan I the firstè night have al this tene ?
How shal she don ek, sorwful créature ?
For tendrenesse how shal she ek sustene
Swich wo for me ? O pitous, pale, and grene
Shal ben your fresshè, wommanlichè face
For longing, or ye torne into this place ! '

And whan he fil in any slombèringes,
Anon biginne he sholdè for to grone,
And dremen of the dredfullestè thinges
That mightè ben : as, mete he were allone
In place horríblè making ay his mone,   250
Or meten that he was amongès alle
His enemies and in hir hondès falle.

And therwithal his body sholdè sterte,
And with the stert al sodeinly awake,
And swich a tremour fele aboute his herte,
That of the fere his body sholdè quake ;
And therwithal he sholde a noisè make,
And seme as though he sholdè fallè depe
From heighe on-lofte : and than he woldè
    wepe,

And rewèn on himself so pitously,   260
That wonder was to here his fantasye.
Another time he sholdè mightily
Confórte himself, and seyn it was folýe
So causèles swich dredè for to drye ;
And eft biginne his asprè peynès newe,
That every man mightè on his sorwes rewe.

Who coudè telle aright or ful discrive
His wo, his pleynte, his langour, and his
    pine ?
Nought alle the men that han or ben on-live !
Thou, reder, mayst thyself ful wel devine 270
That swich a wo my wit can not define :

211. *walweth*, so G H₄ Cx. ; J *whieleth* ;
others *weyleth*.
212. *Ixion.* See *Æneid*, vi. 601.
223. *graspe*, H₄ A *grope*.
224. *Saving*, so R ; rest *Save*.

242. *ek*, R γ *this*.
245. *longing*, S γ *langour*.
265. *peynes*, so H₃ ; J and others *sorwes*.
270. *Thou, reder ;* see i. 52 (note).   Chaucer
seems now to be writing for publication.

On ydel for to write it sholde I swinke,
Whan that my wit is wery it to thinke !

On hevené yit the sterrès were y-sene, ·
Although ful pale y-woxen was the mone,
And whiten gan the orisontè shene
Al estward, as it wont is for to done,
And Phebus with his rosy cartè sone
Gan after that to dresse him up to fare,
Whan Troilus hath sent after Pandáre. 280

This Pandar,—that of al the day biforn
Ne mighte han comèn Troilus to see,
Although he on his hed it hadde y-sworn,
For with the king Priám alday was he,
So that it lay not in his liberté
No-wher to gon,—but on the morwe he
     wente
To Troilus, whan that he for him sente.

For in his herte he coudé wel devine
That Troilus al night for sorwe wook ;
And that he woldè telle him of his pine, 290
This knew he wel y-nough, withouté book !
For-which to chaumbrè streight the wey
     he took,
And Troilus tho sobreliche he grette,
And on the bed ful sone he gan him sette.

' My Pandarus,' quod Troilus, ' the sorwe
Which that I drye, I may not longe endure :
I trowe I shal not liven til to-morwe ;
For-which I wolde alweys, on áventure,
To thee devisen of my sepulture
The forme ; and of my moeblè thou
     dispone   300
Right as thee semeth best is for to done.

' But of the fir and flaumbè funeral
In which my body brennen shal to glede,
And of the feste and pleyès palestral
At my vigfle, I preye thee, tak good hede
That that be wel ; and offré Mars my stede,
My swerd, myn helm ; and, levé brother
     dere,
My sheld to Pallas yif, that shineth clere.

' The poudre in which myn herte y-brend
     shal torne,

That preye I thee thou take, and ek
     conserve   310
It in a vessel, that men clep'th an urne,
Of gold ; and to my lady that I serve,
For love of whom thus pitousliche I sterve,
So yive it her, and do me this plesáunce
To preye her kepe it for a rémembraunce.

' For wel I felè, by my maladye
And by my dremès now and yore ago,
Al certeinly that I mot nedès dye :
The owle eek, which that hight Escaphilo,
Hath after me shright alle thise nightès
     two.   320
And, God Mercúrie, of me now woful
     wrecche
The soulé gide, and, whan thee list, it
     fecche ! '—

Pandáre answérde and seidè, ' Troilus,
My derè frend, as I have told thee yore,
That it is foly for to sorwen thus,
And causéles, for-which I can no more :
But who-so wol not trowen red ne lore,
I can not sen in him no remedye
But lete him worthen with his fantasye.

' But Troilus, I preye thee, tel me now 330
If-that thou trowe, or this, that any wight
Hath lovéd paramours as wel as thou ?
Ye, God wot ! And ful many a worthy
     knight
Hath his ladý forgon a fourtènight,
And he not yit made halvendel the fare !
What nede is thee to maken al this care ?

' Sin day by day thou mayst thy-selven see
That from his love, or ellès from his wif,
A man mot twinnen of necessité,
Ye, though he love her as his ownè lif ; 340
Yit n'il he with himself thus maken strif :
For wel thou wost, my levé brother dere,
That alwey frendès may not ben i-fere.

310. *ek*, so G ; J and others *it*.
311. *It in* (T), all *In*.
319. *Escaphilo*, Ascalaphus, whom Proserpine changed into an owl. See Ovid, *Met.* v. 539.
333. *ful*, so P R ; G *so* ; rest *fro* (A *for*).
334. *forgon*, so P R G ; Cx. *ben gon* ; A *gon yee* ; rest *gon.*

'How don thise folk that seen hir lovès
   wedded
By frendès might, as it bitit ful ofte,
And seen hem in hir spouses bed y-bedded?
God wot, they take it wisly, faire, and softe,
For-why good hope halt up hir herte on-
   lofte ;
And, for they can a time of sorwe endure,
As time hem hurt, a timè doth hem cure! 350

'So sholdestow endure and leten slide
The time, and fondè to be glad and light!
Ten dayès n'is so longè nought t'abide!
And sin she thee to comen hath bihight,
She n'il her hestè breken for no wight ;
For dred thee nought that she n'il finden
   weye
To come ayein, my lif that dorste I leye!

'Thy swevenès ek and al swich fantasye
Drif out, and lat hem faren to mischaunce ;
For they procede of thy maléncolye, 360
That doth thee fele in slepe al this penáunce.
A straw for allè swevenès signefiaunce!
God help me so, I counte hem nought a
   bene!
Ther wot no man aright what dremès mene!

'For prestès of the templè tellen this,
That dremès ben the revelaciouns
Of Goddès ; and as wel they telle, y-wis,
That they ben ínfernals illusiouns ;
And lechès seyn, that of complexiouns
Proceden they, or fast, or glotonye ; 370
Who wot in soth thus what they signéfye?

'Ek othrè seyn that thorugh impressiouns,
As, if a wight hath faste a thing in minde,
That therof comen swiche avisiouns ;
And othrè seyn, as they in bookès finde,
That, after timès of the yeer, by kinde
Men dreme, and that th'effect go'th by
   the mone :
But lef no drem, for it is nought to done!

'Wel worth of dremès ay thise oldè wives,
And treweliche ek augurie of thise foules 380
For fere of which men wenen lese hir lives,

As ravenès qualm, or shriking of thise
   oules!
To trowèn on it bothè fals and foul is :
Allas, allas, so noble a créature
As is a man shal dreden swich ordure!

'For-which with al myn herte I thee biseche,
Unto thyself that al this thou foryive :
And ris now up withoutè morè speche,
And lat us caste how forth may best be drive
This time, and ek how fresshly we may
   live   390
Whan that she com'th, the whiche shal be
   right sone :
God help me so, thy beste is thus to done.

'Ris, lat us speke of lusty lif in Troye
That we han lad, and forth the timè drive,
And eek of timè coming us rejoye,
That bringen shal our blissè now so blive ;
And langour of thise twyès dayès five
We shal therwith so fóryete or oppresse,
That wel unnethe it don shal us duresse.

'This town is ful of lordès al aboute, 400
And trewès lasten al this menè while :
Go we and pleye us in som lusty route
To Sarpedoun, not hennès but a mile :
And thus thou shalt the timè wel bigile,
And drive it forth unto that blisful morwe
That thou her see, that cause is of thy sorwe.

'Now ris, my derè brother Troilus!
For certès, it non honour is to thee
To wepe, and in thy bed to rouken thus ;
For treweliche of oo thing trustè me, 410
If thou thus ligge a day or two or three,
The folk wol seyn that thou for cowardise
Thee feynest sik, and that thou darst
   not rise!'—

This Troilus answérde, 'O brother dere,
This knowèn folk that han y-suffred peyne,
That, though he wepe and makè sorwful
   chere

398. *or*, so P R H₄ H₃; rest *our(e)*.
402. *and*, so R S ; rest omit.
403. *Sarpedoun.* See iv. 52.
409. *rouken*, so Cx. Th. ; J and others *louken*.
(See *Cant. Tales*, A 1308.)
412. *seyn*, S γ *wene*. (Boc. diria l' uom.)

362. *signefiaunce*, so J G A ; rest *signifiaunce*.

537

That feleth harm and smert in every veyne,
No wonder is ; and, though ich everè pleyne
Or alwey wepe, I n'am no thing to blame,
Sin I have lost the cause of al my game.

'But sin of finè force I mot arise,   421
I shal arise as sone as evere I may ;
And God, to whom my herte I sacrifise,
So sende us hastily the tenthè day !
For was ther neverè fowl so fayn of May
As I shal ben, whan that she com'th to
     Troye
That cause is of my torment and my joye.

'But whider is thy red,' quod Troilus,
'That we may pleye us best in al this toun ?'
'By God, my conseil is,' quod Pandarus,
'To ride and pleye us with King
     Sarpedoun.'   431
So longe of this they spaken up and doun,
Til Troilus gan at the laste assente
To rise, and forth to Sarpedoun they wente.

This Sarpedoun, as he that honorable
Was evere his live, and ful of heigh largesse,
With al that mighte y-servèd ben on table
That deyntè was, al coste it gret richesse,
He fedde hem day by day ; that swich
     noblesse,   439
As seyden bothe the meste and ek the leste,
Was nevere or that day wist at any feste.

Nor in this world ther is non instrument
Delicious through wind, or touche of corde,
As fer as any wight hath everè went,
That tongè telle or hertè may recorde,
That at the feste it n'as wel herd acorde;
N'of ladies ek so fair a companye
On daunce, or tho, was neverè seyn with yè.

But what availeth this to Troilus,   449
That for his sorwè nothing of it roughte?
For evere in oon his hertè pietus
Ful bisily Criseyde his lady soughte :
On her was evere al that his hertè thoughte,

Now this, now that, so faste imagininge,
That glade, y-wis, can him no festeyinge.

Thise ladies ek that at the festè ben,
Sin that he saw his lady was aweye,
It was his sorwe upon hem for to sen,
Or for to here on instrument so pleye :   459
For she that of his hertè ber'th the keye
Was absent, lo, this was his fantasye,
That no wight sholdè maken melodye.

Nor ther n'as houre of al the day or night,
Whan he was there-as no wight mighte
     him here,
That he ne seide, 'O lufsom lady bright,
How have ye faren sin that ye were here?
Welcome, y-wis, myn ownè lady dere !'
But weylawey, al this n'as but a mase :
Fortune his howve intendeth bet to glase!

The lettres ek that she of oldè time   470
Hadde him y-sent, he wolde allonè rede
An hundred sithe a-twixen noon and
     prime,
Refiguring her shap, her wommanhede,
Withinne his herte, and every word or dede
That passèd was. And thus he drof t'an
     ende
The ferthè day ; and thennès wolde he
     wende,

And seidè, 'Levè brother Pandarus,
Intendestow that we shal herè bleve
Til Sarpedoun wil forth congéyèn us ?   479
Yit were it fairer that we toke our leve.
For Goddès love, lat us now sone at eve
Our levè take, and homward lat us torne,
For treweliche I n'il not thus sojorne !'

Pandáre answèrdè, 'Be we comen hider
To fecchen fir, and rennen hom ayeyn?
God help me so, I can not tellen whider
We mightè gon, if I shal sothly seyn,
Ther any wight is of us morè fayn
Than Sarpedoun. And if we hennès hye
Thus sodeinly, I holde it vilanye,   490

421. *sin of finè force;* var. *sith(en), fin, of fors*
(read ? *sith in fin of fors*). Rawl. has two leaves
wanting (ll. 421 560).
436. *largesse,* S γ *prowesse.*
443. *of,* so P H₂ H₄ Cx. A Cp. ; H₃ S H₁ S₂
on; J G D Cl. *or.*

455. *festeyinge,* so J S only; rest *festeyng,
festyng(e), festenynge.* (See iii. 1718.)
476. *thennes wolde he,* so J P G H₃; Cx. corrupt. ; rest *seyde* (S *that*) *he wolde.*
478. *bleve,* so J S D Cp. H Cl. ; rest *bileve.*

'Sin that we seiden that we woldė bleve
With him a wowke; and now thus sodeinly
The ferthė day to take of him our leve,
He woldė wondren on it trewėly.
Lat us forth holde our purpos fermėly,
And sin that we bihighten him to bide,
Hold forward now, and after lat us ride.'

Thus Pandarus with allė peyne and wo
Made him to dwelle; and at the wikės
    ende,
Of Sarpedoun they toke hir levė tho,   500
And on hir wey they spedden hem to wende.
Quod Troilus, 'Now Lord me gracė sende,
That I may finden at myn hom-comínge
Criseydė come!' and ther-with gan he
    singe.

'Ye, haselwodė!' thoughtė this Pandáre,
And to himself ful softėliche he seyde,
'God wot, refreyden may this hotė fare
Or Calcas sendė Troilus Criseyde!'   508
But nathėles he japėd thus, and pley'de,
And swor, y-wis, his herte him wel bihighte
She woldė come as sone as evere she mighte.

Whan they unto the paleis were y-comen
Of Troilus, they down off horse alighte,
And to the chaumbre hir wey than han
    they nomen ;
And into timė that it gan to nighte
They gonnė speken of Criseyde the
    brighte ;
And after this, whan that hem bothė leste,
They spedde hem fro the soper unto reste.

On morwe, as sone as day bigan to clere,
This Troilus gan of his slep t'abreyde,   520
And to Pandáre, his ownė brother dere,
'For love of God,' ful pitousliche he seyde,
'As go we sen the paleis of Criseyde :
For sin we yit may han no morė feste,
So lat us sen her paleis at the leste!'

And therwithal, his meynė for to blende,
A cause he fond in townė for to go,
And to Criseydės hous they gonnė wende.
But, Lord, this sely Troilus was wo!   529
Him thoughte his sorwful hertė brast a-two;
For, whan he saw her dorės sperėd alle,
Wel nigh for sorwe adown he gan to falle.

Therwith whan he was war and gan
    biholde
How shet was every window of the place,
As frost, him thoughte, his hertė gan to
    colde ;
For-which with chaungėd dedlich palė face,
Withouten word he forth-by gan to pace ;
And, as God wolde, he gan so fastė ride,
That no wight of his contenaunce espi'de.

Than seide he thus : 'O paleis desolat,
O hous, of houses whilom best y-hight,
O paleis empty and disconsolat,
O thou lantérne of which queynt is the
    light,
O paleis, whilom day that now art night,
Wel oughtestow to falle, and I to dye,
Sin she is went that wont was us to gye!

'O paleis, whilom crowne of houses alle,
Enluminėd with sonne of allė blisse!
O ring, fro which the ruby is out-falle,
O cause of wo, that cause hast been of
    lisse!   550
Yit, sin I may no bet, fayn wolde I kisse
Thy coldė dorės, dorste I for this route :
And far-wel shrine, of which the seynt is
    oute!'

Ther-with he caste on Pandarus his ẏe,
With chaungėd face, and pitous to bi-
    holde ;
And, whan he mighte his time aright espye,
Ay as he rod, to Pandarus he tolde
His newė sorwe and ek his joyės olde
So pitously, and with so ded an hewe,
That every wight mighte on his sorwe
    rewe.   560

Fro thennėsforth he rideth up and down,
And everything com him to rémembraunce

495. *forth holde*, so Cx.; S γ *holde(n) forth*;
rest *holde.*
  496. *we*, so J G S A; H₃ *he*; rest *ye.*
  509. *pley'de*, so H₃ H₄; J and others *seyde.*
  516. *gonne*, so J ; rest omit.
  521. *Pandare*; J G H₂ *Pandarus.*
  523. *As*, Cl. *So*; J G P omit.

550. *hast*, J G *hath.*
550. *lisse*, so J Cx. S Cp.; H₂ *kisse*; rest *blisse.*

As he rod for-by places of the town
In which he whilom hadde al his ples-
    áunce.
' Lo, yonder saw I last my lady daunce !
And in that templé with her yen clere
Me caughté first my righté lady dere !

' And yonder have ich herd ful lustily
My deré herté laughe ! And yonder pleye
Saw I her onés ek ful bisily !   570
And yonder onés to me gan she seye,
"Now goodé sweté, love me wel, I
    preye !"
And yond so goodly gan she me biholde,
That to the deth myn herte is to her holde !

' And at that corner in the yonder hous
Herde I myn alderlevest lady dere
So wommanly with vois melodious
Singen so wel, so goodly and so clere,
That in my soulé yit me think'th ich here
The blisful soun ! And in that yonder
    place   580
My lady first me took unto her grace !'

Than thoughte he thus : ' O blisful Lord
    Cupíde,
Whan I the proces have in my memórie,
How thou me hast werréy'd on every
    side,
Men mighte a book make of it, lik a
    storie !
What nede is thee to seke on me victórie,
Sin I am thyn, and hoolly at thy wille ?
What joye hast thou thine owné folk to
    spille ?

' Wel hastow, Lord, y-wroke on me thyn
    ire,
Thou mighty God, and dredful for to
    greve !   590
Now mercy, Lord ! Thou wost wel I desire
Thy gracé most of allé lustés leve,
And live and deye I wol in thy bileve :
For which I n'axe in guerdon but oo bone,
That thou Criseyde ayein me sendé sone.

' Distreyne her herte as fasté to retorne
As thou dost myn to longen her to see :
Than wot I wel that she n'il not sojorne.
Now, blisful Lord, so cruel thou ne be
Unto the blood of Troye, I preyé thee,   600
As Juno was unto the blood Thebáne,
For which the folk of Thebés caughte hir
    bane !'

And after this he to the yatés wente
Ther-as Criseyde out-rod a ful good pas :
And up and down ther made he many a
    wente,
And to himself ful ofte he seide, ' Allas !
From hennés rod my blis and my solás !
As woldé blisful God now for his joye,
I mighte her sen ayein come into Troye !

' And to the yonder hil I gan her gide,   610
Allas, and there I took of her my leve !
And yond I saw her to her fader ride,
For sorwe of which myn herté wol to-cleve !
And hider hom I com whan it was eve ;
And here I dwelle out-cast from allé joye,
And shal, til I may sen her eft in Troye !'

And of himself imaginéd he ofte
To ben defet and pale, and waxen lesse
Than he was wont ; and that men seiden
    softe,
' What may it be ? Who can the sothe
    gesse,   620
Why Troilus hath al this hevinesse ?'
And al this n'as but his maléncolye,
That he hadde of himself swich fantasye.

Another time imaginen he wolde
That every wight that wenté by the weye
Had of him routhe, and that they seyen
    sholde,
' I am right sory Troilus wol deye.'   627
And thus he drof a day yit forth or tweye
As ye han herd : swich lif right gan he lede
As he that stood bitwixen hope and drede.

For-which him likéd in his songés shewe
Th'encheson of his wo as he best mighte,

---

565. S y read : *Lo, yonder* (Cl. *yonde*) *saw I
myn owne lady daunce.*
570. *bisily,* so P G H₃ R Cx. ; rest *blisfully.*
583. *my,* P H₄ Cx. S y omit.

598. *not,* J *so* (read ? *Than wot I wel she n't
not so sojorne*).
628. *yit,* J P G H₃ R H₄ omit.
629. *right,* J P G Cx. omit.

And make a song of wordès but a fewe,
Somwhat his woful hertè for to lighte ;
And whan he was from every mannès
    sighte,
With softè vois he of his lady dere
That absent was gan singe as ye may here :

' O sterre, of which I lost have al the
    light,
With hertè soor wel oughte I to biwaile
That everè derk in torment night by
    night,   640
Toward my deth with wind in stere I
    saile :
For-which the tenthè night if-that I faile
The giding of thy bemès brighte an houre,
My ship and me Caribdis wol devoure.'

This song whan he thus songen haddè, sone
He fil ayein into his sikès olde ;
And every night, as he was wont to done,
He stood the brightè monè to biholde,
And al his sorwe he to the monè tolde,
And seide, ' Y-wis, whan thou art hornèd
    newe,   .   650
I shal be glad, if al the world be trewe !

' I saw thy hornès oldè by the morwe
Whan hennès rod my rightè lady dere,
That cause is of my torment and my sorwe :
For-which, O brightè Lúcina the clere,
For love of God, ren faste aboute thy spere !
For, whan thy hornès newè ginnè springe,
Than shal she come that may my blisse
    bringe !'

The dayès more and lenger every night
Than they ben wont to ben, him thoughtè
    tho ;   660
And that the sonnè wente his cours unright
By lenger wey than it was wont to go ;
And seide, ' Y-wis, me dredeth everè mo
The sonnès sonè Pheton be on-live,
And that his fader carte amis he drive.'

Upon the wallès faste ek wolde he walke,
And on the Grekès oost he woldè see,

655. *Lúcina*, so Cx. Th.; J and others *La-*
t(h)ona. See iv. 1591.
664. *Pheton*, Phaeton. See *H. F.* 942.

And to himself right thus he woldè talke,
' Lo, yonder is myn ownè lady free !
Or ellès yonder ther the tentès be !   670
And thennès com'th this eir that is so swote,
That in my soule I fele it doth me bote !

'And, hardily, this wind, that more and more
Thus stoundèmele encresseth in my face,
Is of my lady's depè sikès sore !
I preve it thus, for in non other space
Of al this town, save only in this place,
Fele I no wind that souneth so lik peyne :
It seith, " Allas ! why twinnèd be we
    tweyne ? " '

This longè time he driveth forth right thus,
Til fully passèd was the ninthè night ;   681
And ay biside him was this Pandarus,
That bisily dide al his fullè might
Him to confórte and make his hertè light,
Yiving him hope alwéy, the tenthè morwe
That she shal come and stinten al his sorwe.

—Upon that other sidè was Criseyde,
With women fewe, among the Grekès
    stronge :
For-which ful ofte a day 'Allas !' she seyde,
' That I was born ! Wel may myn hertè
    longe   690
After my deth, for now live I too longe !
Allas, and I ne may it not amende,
For now is wors than everè yit I wen'de !

' My fader n'il for no thing do me grace
To gon ayein, for aught I can him quemen;
And, if so be that I my termè pace,
My Troilus shal in his hertè deme
That I am fals ; and so it may wel seme :
Thus shal I have unthank on every side.
That I was born, so weylawey the tide ! 700

' And if that I me putte in jupartye
To stele awey by night, and it bifalle
That I be caught, I shal be holde espye :
Or ellès, lo, this drede I most of alle,
If in the hondès of som wrecche I falle.
I n'am but lost, al be myn hertè trewe !
Now mighty God, thou on my sorwè rewe !'

695. *aught*, J and others *naught*.

Ful pale y-waxen was her brightė face,
Her limės lene, as she that al the day
Stood whan she dorste, and lokėd on the
    place   710
Ther she was born and ther she dwelt
    had ay ;
And al the night wepinge, allas, she lay.
And thus despeirėd out of allė cure,
She ledde her lif, this woful crėature.

Ful ofte a day she sighte ek for distresse,
And in herself she wente ay pórtreyinge
Of Troilus the gretė worthinesse,
And alle his goodly wordės récordinge
Sin first that day her love bigan to springe :
And thus she sette her woful herte a-fire 720
Thorugh rémembraunce of that she gan
    desire.

In al this world ther n'is so cruel herte
That her had herd compleynen in her
    sorwe,
That n'olde han wepen for her peynės
    smerte,
So tendrely she wep bothe eve and morwe :
Her nedėdė no terės for to borwe.
And this was yet the worste of al her peyne,
Ther was no wight to whom she dorste
    her pleyne.

Ful rewfully she lokėd upon Troye,   729
Biheld the tourės heighe and ek the halles :
'Allas!' quod she, 'the plesaunce and the
    joye,
The whiche that now al tornėd into galle is,
Have ich had ofte withinne tho yonder
    walles !
O Troilus, what dostow now ? ' she seyde :
'Lord, whether thou yit thenke upon
    Criseyde !

'Allas, I n'hadde y-trowėd on your lore,
And went with you, as ye me redde or this !
Than hadde I now not sikėd half so sore !
Who mighte have said that I had don amis
To stele awey with swich oon as he is? 740
But al too latė com'th the letuárie
Whan men the cors unto the gravė carie !

'Too late is now to speke of that matere :
Prudence, allas ! oon of thine yen three
Me lakkėd alwey or that I com here !
On timė passėd wel remembred me,
And present time ek coude ich wel y-see,
But futur time, or I was in the snare,
Coude I not see : that causeth now my care !

'But nathéles, bitidė what bitide,   750
I shal tomorwe at night, by est or west,
Out of this oost stele on som maner side,
And gon with Troilus wher-as him lest :
This purpos wol I holde, and this is best.
No fors of wikked tongės janglerye,
For evere on love han wrecches had envýe !

'For who-so wol of every word take hede,
Or rulen him by every wightės wit,
Ne shal he neverė thriven, out of drede :
For that that some men blamen everė yit,
Lo, other maner folk comenden it.   761
And as for me, for al swich variaunce,
Felicité clepe I my suffisaunce !

'For-which, withouten any wordės mo,
To Troye I wol, as for conclusioun.'—
But God it wot, or fully monthės two,
She was ful fer fro that entencioun !
For bothė Troilus and Troyės toun
Shal knottėles throughout her hertė slide :
For she wol take a purpos for t'abide. 770

—This Diomede, of whom you telle I gan,
Go'th now, withinne himself ay arguinge
With al the sleighte and al that evere he can,
How he may best with shortest taryinge
Into his net Criseydes hertė bringe.
To this entente he coudė neverė fine :
To fisshen her, he leyde out hook and line.

But nathéles wel in his herte he thoughte,
That she n'as not withoute a love in Troye :
For neverė sithen he her thennės broughtė
Ne coude he sen her laughe and maken
    joye.   781
He n'iste how best her hertė for t'acoye ;
But 'for t'assaye,' he seide, ' it nought ne
    greveth,
For he that nought n'assayeth, naught
    n'acheveth ! '

Yit seide he to himself upon a night,
' Now am I not a fool, that wot wel how
Her wo for love is of another wight ;
And her-upon to gon assaye her now,
I may wel wite, it n'il not ben my prow.
For wisė folk in bokės it expresse,   790
"Men shal not wowe a wight in hevinesse."

' But who-so mightė winnen swich a flour
From him for whom she morneth night
    and day,
He mightė seyn he were a conquerour ! '
And right anon, as he that bold was ay,
Thoughte in his hertė, ' Happe how happė
    may,
Al sholde I deye, I wol her hertė seche :
I shal no morė lesė but my speche ! '

This Diomede, as bokės us declare,
Was in his nedės prest and corageus,   800
With sternė vois and mighty limės square,
Hardy and testif, strong and chivalrus
Of dedės, lik his fader Tidėus ;
And some men seyn he was of tongė large,
And heir he was of Calidoyne and Arge.

Criseydė menė was of her statúre,
Therto of shap, of face, and ek of chere
Ther mightė be no fairer créature :
And oftė timė this was her manére
To gon y-tressėd with her herės clere   810
Down by her coler at her bak bihinde,
Whiche with a thred of gold she wolde
    binde :

And, save her browės joinėden i-fere,
Ther nas no lak in aught I can espyen.
But for to speken of her yen clere,
Lo, trewély, they writen that her syen,
That Paradys stood formėd in her yen ;
And with her richė beauté everė more
Strof love in her ay, which of hem was
    more.   819

She sobrė was, ek simple and wis withal,
The best y-norisshėd ek that mightė be,

And goodlich of her speche in general,
And charitable, estatly, lusty, free :
Ne neverė mo ne lakkėd pieté
Her tendrė hertė, sliding of coráge.
But trewély I can not telle her age.

And Troilus wel waxen was on highte,
And complet formėd by proporcioun
So wel that kinde it nought amendė mighte :
Yong, fressh, and strong, and hardy as
    lioun,   830
And trewe as steel in ech condicioun :
And oon the best entecchėd créature
That is, or shal, whil-that the world may
    dure.

And certeinliche in storie it is y-founde
That Troilus was nevere unto no wight,
As in his time, in no degré secoúnde
In durring don that longeth to a knight.
Al mighte a geaunt passen him of might,
His herte ay with the firste and with the
    beste   839
Stood paregal to durre-don that him leste.

—But for to tellen forth of Diomede.
It fil that after, on the tenthė day
Sin that Criseyde out of the cité yede,
This Diomede, as fressh as braunche in
    May,
Com to the tentė ther-as Calcas lay,
And feynėd him with Calcas han to done :
But what he mente, I shal you tellė sone.

Criseyde, at shortė wordės for to telle,
Welcomėd him, and down him by her sette ;
And he was the y-nough to maken dwelle !
And after this, withoutė longė lette   851
The spices and the wyn men forth hem fette ;

823. *And charitable* (?), all *Charitable* ; P *and* (before *estatly*) ; H₄ G H₃ R Cx. A D H₁ Cl. *and* (before *free*) ; P R *estatly* ; J etc. *esta(t)l(ı)ch(e)*.
824. *lakked piete*(?), all *lakked(e) her pite* (*pete*). (See iii. 1033 ; iv. 246 ; v. 1598.)
825. *Her tendre herte* (?), G *tendyr herte* ; P *Tendre hertis* ; H₃ *Thendere hertede* ; rest *Tendre herted*.
830. *and strong*, so S ; rest *strong*.
831. *And trewe* (?), all *Trewe*.
832. *And oon the* (?), H₁ *Oon the* ; rest *Oon of the*.
842. This line follows l. 770 in Boccaccio, who makes it the *fourth* day.

799-840. Much of this passage seems to have been taken direct from Benoît de Sainte More, *Roman de Troie*. It is remarkable that in these six stanzas there should be six defective or doubtful lines.
802. *and testif*, so S ; rest *testif*.

And forth they speke of this and that i-fere
As frendès don, of which som shal ye here.

He gan first fallen of the werre in speche
Bitwixe hem and the folk of Troyè toun ;
And of th'assege he gan her ek biseche
To telle him what was her opinioun.
Fro that demaunde he so descendeth doun
To axen her, if that her straungè thoughte
The Grekès gise, and werkès that they
      wroughte ;   861

And why her fader tarieth so longe
To wedden her unto som worthy wight.—
Criseydè, that was in her peynès stronge
For love of Troilus, her ownè knight,
As ferforth as she conning hadde or might
Answérde him tho ; but, as of his entente,
It seméd not she wistè what he mente.

But nathéles this ilkè Diomede
Gan in himself assure, and thus he seyde :
' If ich aright have taken of you hede, 871
Me thinketh thus, O lady myn Criseyde,
That, sin I first hond on your bridel leyde
Whan ye out-come of Troyè by the morwe,
Ne coude I neverè sen you but in sorwe.

' Can I not seyn what may the causè be,
But-if for love of som Trojàn it were ;
The whiche right sorè wolde athinken me,
That ye for any wight that dwelleth there
Sholde everè spille a quarter of a tere, 880
Or pitously yourselven so bigile :
For dredèles it is not worth the while.

' The folk of Troye, as who seith, alle and
     some
In prison ben, as ye yourselven see ;
Nor thennès shal not oon on-live come
For al the gold atwixen sonne and sea :
Trusteth right wel and understondeth me,
Ther shal not oon to mercy gon on-live,
Al were he lord of worldès twyès five !

' Swich wreche on hem for fecching of
     Eleyne   890
Ther shal bèn take or-that we hennès
    wende,

That Manès, whiche that Goddès ben of
    peyne,
Shal ben agast that Grekès wol hem shende,
And men shul drede, unto the worldès ende,
From hennèsforth to ravisshèn any quene,
So cruel shal our wreche on hem be sene !

' And but-if Calcas lede us with ambáges,
That is to seyn, with doublè wordès slye,
Swich as men clepe a word with two viságes,
Ye shal wel knowèn that I nought ne lye,
And al this thing right sen it with your ye,
And that anon, ye n'il not trowe how
    sone !   900
Now taketh hedè, for it is to done !

' What ! Wenè ye your wisè fader wolde
Have yeven Antenor for you anon,
If he ne wistè that the citè sholde
Destroyèd ben ? Why, nay, so mote I gon !
He knew ful wel ther shal not scapen oon
That Trojan is, and for the gretè fere
He durstè not ye dweltè lenger there. 910

' What wol ye morè, lufsom lady dere ?
Lat Troye and Trojan fro your hertè pace !
Drif out that bittrè hope, and mak good
    chere,
And clepe ayein the beautè of your face
That ye with saltè terès so deface,
For Troye is brought in swich a jupartye
That it to save is now no remedye !

' And thenketh wel, ye shal in Grekès finde
A morè parfit love, or it be night,
Than any Trojan is, and morè kinde, 920
And bet to serven you wol don his might ;
And if ye vouchèsauf, my lady bright,
I wol ben he to serven you myselve,
Ye, leverè than be king of Grecès twelve !'

And with that word he gan to waxen red,
And in his speche a litel wight he quook,
And caste aside a litel wight his hed,
And stinte a while. And afterward he
    wook,

880. *Sholde evere* (Y), all *Sholden*.
887. *right wel*, so Cx. S ; rest *wel*.

895. *ravisshen*, pronounce *rav'sshen*. (See
norisshed, l. 821.)
903. *to*, so Cx. ; H₄ *now to* ; G *not to* ; J and
others *for to*.
928. *he wook*, J and others *awook*.

And sobreliche on her he threw his look, 929
And seide, 'I am, al be it you no joye,
'As gentil man as any wight in Troye.

'For if my fader Tydèus,' he seyde,
'Y-livèd hadde, ich haddè ben, or this,
Of Calidoyne and Arge a king, Criseyde !
And so hope I that I shal yit, ywis !
But he was slayn, allas, the more harm is,
Unhappily at Thebès al too rathe,
Polymites and many a man to scathe.

'But, hertè myn, sin that I am your man, 939
And ye the firste of whom I sechè grace
To servè you as hertly as I can,
And everè shal whil I to live have space,
So, or that I departe out of this place,
That ye me grauntè that I may tomorwe
At bettrè leiser tellè you my sorwe !'

What sholde I telle his wordès that he
    seyde ?
He spak y-nough for oo day at the meste !
It preveth wel, he spak so that Criseyde
Graunted him on the morwe at his requeste
To have a spechè with her at the leste, 950
So that he n'oldè speke of swich matere :
And thus to him she seide, as ye may here,

As she that hadde her herte on Troilus
So fastè, that ther may it non arace ;
And straungèly she spak, and seidè thus :
'O Diomede, I love that ilkè place
Ther I was born ; and Jovès for his grace
Delivere it sone of al that doth it care !
God, for thy might, so leve it wel to fare !

'That Grekès wolde hir wraththe on Troyè
    wreke   960
If that they mighte, I knowe it wel, y-wis :
But it shal not bifallen as ye speke,
And God to-forn ! And ferther over this,
I wot my fader wis and redy is ;

And that he me hath bought, as ye me
    tolde,
So dere, I am the more unto him holde.

'That Grekès ben of heigh condicioun
I wot ek wel ; but, certein, men shal finde
As worthy folk withinnè Troyè toun, 969
As conning, and as parfit, and as kinde,
As ben bitwixen Orcadès and Inde ;
And that ye coudè wel your lady serve,
It trowe it wel, her thank for to deserve.

'But as to speke of love, y-wis,' she seyde,
'I hadde a lord, to whom I wedded was,
The whos myn herte al was til that he
    deyde ;
And other love, as help me now Pallas,
Ther in myn hertè n'is, ne neverè was.
And that ye ben of noble and heigh kinrédè,
I have wel herd it tellen, out of drede ; 980

'And that doth me to han so gret a wonder,
That ye wol scornen any woman so !
Ek, God wot, love and I be fer asonder :
I am disposèd bet, so mote I go,
Unto my deth to pleyne and maken wo :
What I shal after don, can I not seye ;
But treweliche, as yit, me list not pleye.

'Myn herte is now in tribulacioun,
And ye in armès bisy day by day :   989
Herafter, whan ye wonnen han the toun,
Paraunter thannè so it happen may,
That whan I see that neverè yit I say,
Than wol I werkè that I neverè wroughte !
This word to you y-nough suffisen oughte.

'To-morwe ek wol I speken with you fayn,
So that ye touchen nought of this matére ;
And whan you list, ye may come here ayeyn.
And, or ye gon, thus muche I seye you here :
As help me Pallas with her herès clere, 999
If that I sholde on any Grek han routhe,
It sholdè be yourselven, by my trouthe !

'I sey not therfor that I wol you love,
N'I sey not nay ; but in conclusioun,
I menè wel, by God that sit above !'

---

938. *Polymites*, Polynices. (See ll. 1488, 1507,
and l. 1498 note.)
940. *ye the*, so Cx.; P *ye be*; H₃ *bethe the*;
rest *ben the*.
944. *That ye*, S γ *Ye wol*.
949. *him*, so Cx.; rest omit.
950. *To have a speche with her*, so Cx.; rest
For to speken with him.

992. *neverè yit I*, so Cx. P H⁴; J *I neverè yit*;
others *I neverè(er)*, etc.

And therwithal she caste her yen doun,
And gan to sike, and seide, 'O Troyé toun,
Yit bidde I God, in quiete and in reste
I may thee sen, or do myn herté breste!'

But in effect, and shortly for to seye,
This Diomede al fresshly newe ayeyn   1010
Gan pressen on, and faste her mercy preye;
And after this, the sothé for to seyn,
Her glove he took, of which he was ful fayn:
And finaly, whan it was waxen eve,
And al was wel, he roos and took his leve.

The brighté Venus folwed and ay taughte
The wey ther brodé Phebus doun alighte,
And Cynthea her char-hors over-raughte
To whirle out of the Leoun, if she mighte,
And Signifer his candels sheweth brighte,
Whan that Criseyde unto her resté wente
Inwith her fadres fairé brighté tente,   1022

Retorning in her soule ay up and doun
The wordés of this sodein Diomede,
His grete estat, and peril of the toun,
And that she was allone and haddé nede
Of frendés help. And thus bigan to brede
The causes why, the sothé for to telle,
That she took fully purpos for to dwelle.

The morwé com, and gostly for to speke
This Diomede is come unto Criseyde;   1031
And, shortly, lest that ye my talé breke,
So wel he for himselven spak and seyde,
That alle her sikés sore adoun he leyde;
And finaly, the sothé for to seyne,
He refte her of the grete of al her peyne.

And after this the storie telleth us
That she him yaf the fairé bayé stede

The whiche he onés wan of Troilus;   1039
And ek a broche—and that was litel nede!—
That Troilus' was, she yaf this Diomede;
And ek, the bet from sorwe him to releve,
She made him were a pencel of her sleve.

I finde ek in the stories elléswhere,
Whan thorugh the body hurt was Diomede
Of Troilus, tho wep she many a tere,
Whan that she saw his widé woundés blede;
And that she took, to kepen him, good
        hede;
And, for to hele him of his sorwés smerte,
Men seyn—I n'ot—that she yaf him her
        herte.   1050

But trewély the storie telleth us,
Ther madé neveré woman moré wo
Than she, whan that she falséd Troilus.
She seyde, 'Allas! for now is clene ago
My name of trouthe in love for everémo!
For I have falséd oon the gentileste
That everé was, and oon the worthieste!

'Allas! of me, unto the worldés ende,
Shal neither ben y-writen nor y-songe
No good word, for thise bokés wol me
        shende.   1060
O, rolléd shal I ben on many a tonge:
Throughout the world my bellé shal be
        ronge!
And wommen most wol haté me of alle!
Allas, that swich a cas me sholdé falle!

'They wol seyn, in as muche as in me is,
I have hem don dishonour, weylawey!
Al be I not the firste that dide amis,
What helpeth that, to don my blame awey?
But, sin I see ther is no bettré wey,   1069
And that too late is now for me to rewe,
To Diomede algate I wol be trewe.

'But Troilus, sin I no bettré may,
And sin that thus departen ye and I,
Yet preye I God so yive you right good day
As for the gentilesté, trewély,
That everé I say, to serven feithfully,
And best can ay his lady honour kepe.'
And with that word she brast anon to wepe.

1019. See Cressida's promise, iv. 1592, and v.
1190.
1020. *Signifer*, the Zodiac.
1021. *reste*, H₃ S γ *bed(de)*; H₄ *chambir*.
1028. *causes*, so J P G (Boc.); rest *cause*.
1030. *gostly*, as her spiritual adviser.
1037. The incidents in the two following stanzas
seem to have been taken from Benoît, though the
Historia Troiana of Guido delle Colonne may
also have been consulted (see l. 1044). Chaucer
(or his audience, see *Prologue to Legend of Good
Women*) has evidently been dissatisfied with
Boccaccio's account of Cressida's faithlessness.
Cressida's complaint (ll. 1051 *seq.*) is probably
Chaucer's own. Chaucer returns to Boccaccio
at l. 1100.

1044. *the*, J and others omit.
1046. *wep*, so J G P; H₄ *wepe gan*; rest *wepti.*

'And certès, you ne haten shal I nevere,
And frendès love, that shal ye han of me,
And my good-word, al mighte I livèn evere!
And trewèliche, I woldè sory be   1082
For to sen you in any adversité:
And giltèles, I wot wel, I you leve:
But al shal passe!—And thus take I my
    leve.'

But trewély, how longe it was bitwene,
That she forsook him for this Diomede,
Ther n'is non auctour telleth it, I wene:
Take every man now to his bokès hede,
He shal no termè finden, out of drede;
For though that he bigan to wowe her sone,
Or he her wan, yit was ther more to done.

Ne me ne list this sely womman chide
Further than thilkè storie wol devise:
Her name, allas, publísshèd is so wide,
That for her gilt it oughte y-nough suffise:
And if I mighte excuse her any wise,
For she so sory was for her untrouthe,
Y-wis, I wolde excuse her yit for routhe.

—This Troilus, as I bifore have told,   1100
Thus driveth forth as wel as he hath might:
But often was his hertè hoot and cold,
And namèly that ilkè ninthè night,
Which on the morwè she had him bihight
To come ayein: God wot, ful litel reste
Hadde he that night: nothing to slepe
    him leste!

The laurer-crownèd Phebus with his hete
Gan, in his cours ay upward as he wente,
To warme of th' estè see the wawès wete,
And Nisus' doughter song with fressh
    entente,   1110
Whan Troilus his Pandar after sente,
And on the wallès of the town they pleyde,
To loke if they can sen aught of Criseyde.

Til it was noon they stoden for to see
Who that ther com; and every maner wight
That com fro fer, they seiden it was she,
Til that they couden knowèn him aright:
Now was his hertè dul, now was it light;
And thus bi-japèd, stonden for to stare
Aboutè naught this Troilus and Pandare!

To Pandarus this Troilus tho seyde,   1121
'For aught I wot, bifor noon sikerly
Into this towne com'th not here Criseyde.
She hath y-nough to donè, hardily,
To winnen from her fader, so trowe I.
Her oldè fader wol yit make her dine
Or-that she go: God yive his hertè pine!'

Pandáre answérde, 'It may wel be, certein;
And for-thy lat us dine, I thee biseche;
And after noon than maystow come
    ayein.'   1130
And hom they gon, withouten morè
    speche,
And come ayein. But longè may they
    seche
Or-that they finden that they after cape:
Fortúne hem bothè thenketh for to jape!

Quod Troilus, 'I see wel now that she
Is taried with her oldè fader so,
That, or she come, it wil neigh even be.
Com forth, I wol unto the yatè go.
Thise porters ben unconning everè mo,
And I wol don hem holden up the yate
As naught ne were, although she comè
    late.'   1141

The day go'th faste, and after that com'th
    eve,
And yit com nought to Troilus Criseyde.
He loketh forth by haye, by tree, by greve,
And fer his hed over the wal he leyde;
And at the laste he tornèd him and seyde,
'By God, I wot her mening now, Pandáre!
Almost, y-wis, al newè was my care!

'Now doutèles this lady can her good!
I wot she meneth riden privély,   1150

1081. *mighte*, J and others *sholde*.
1083. *any*, so H₄ Cx. S; rest omit.
1085. *But*, J H₃ Cl. *And*.
1094. *thilke* (?), Cl. *this*; rest *the*.
1095. *publísshed*, so H₃ Cx.; J and others *punisshed*.
1103. *ninthe*, J G H₂ *tenthe*.
1110. *Nisus' doughter*, Scylla, changed into a lark. See *L.G.W.* 1908.

1123. *here*, J and others omit.
1125. *winnen*, J Cl. *twinnen*.
1144. *haye* (?), all *heg(g)es*, *heg(g)s*. (See iii. 351.)

And I comende her wisdom, by myn hood!
She n'il not maken peplé nicély
Gaure on her whan she com'th; but softély
By night into the town she thenketh ride.
And, deré brother, thenk not long t'abide;

We have not ellés for to done, y-wis.—
And Pandarus, now wiltow trowen me?
Have here my trouthe, I see her! Yond
    she is!
Heve up thine ýen, man! Maystow not
    see?'   1159
Pandáre answérdé, 'Nay, so mote I thee!
Al wrong, by God! What seystow, man?
    Wher arte?
That I see yond n'is but a faré-carte!'

'Allas, thou sey'st ful soth!' quod Troilus.
'But, hardily, it n'is not al for nought
That in myn herte I now rejoisé thus:
It is ayeins som good I have a thought.
N'ot I not how, but sin that I was wrought
Ne felte I swich a confort, soth to seye!
She com'th to-night, my lif that dorste I
    leye!'

Pandáre answérde, 'It may be, wel
    y-nough!'   1170
And held with him of al that evere he leyde:
But in his herte he thoughte, and softé
    lough,
And to himself ful sobreliche he seyde:
'From hasel-wode ther joly Robin pleyde
Shal come al that that thou abidest here!
Ye, far-wel al the snow of ferné yere!'

The wardein of the yatés gan to calle
The folk whiche that withoute the yatés
    were,
And bad hem driven in hir beestés alle,
Or al the night they mosten bleven there.
And fer withinne the night, with many a
    tere,   1181
This Troilus gan homward for to ride,
For wel he seeth it helpeth nought t'abide.

But nathéles he gladded him in this:
He thoughte he misacounted hadde his day,
And seide, 'I understonden have amis;
'For th'ilké night I last Criseydé say,
She seide, "I shal ben here, if that I may,
Or that the mone, O deré herté swete,
The Lioun passe out of this Ariete." 1190

'For-which she may yit holde al her
    biheste.'—
And on the morwe unto the yate he wente,
And up and down, by weste and ek by este,
Upon the wallés made he many a wente,
But al for nought: his hope alwéy him
    blente.
For-which at night, in sorwe and sikéssore,
He wente him hom, withouten any more.

His hope al clene out of his herté fledde,
He n'hath wheron now lenger for to honge.
But for the peyne him thoughte his herté
    bledde,   1200
So were his throwés sharpe and wonder
    stronge.
For, whan he saw that she abood so longe,
He n'isté what he jugen of it mighté,
Sin she hath broken that she him bihighte.

The thriddé, ferthé, fifté, sixté day
After tho dayés ten of which I tolde,
Bitwixen hope and drede his herté lay,
Yit somwhat trusting on her hestés olde;
But whan he saw she n'olde her termé holde,
He can now sen non other remedye 1210
But for to shape him soné for to dye.

Therwith the wikked spirit (God us blesse!)
Which that men clepeth wodé Jalousye,
Gan in him crepe in al his hevinesse;
For-which, bicause he woldé soné dye,
He n'eet ne dronk for his maléncolye,
And ek from every companye he fledde:
This was the lif that al this time he ledde.

He so defet was, that no maner man
Unnethe him mighté knowé; ther he
    wente,   1220
So was he lene, and therto pale and wan

1151. *And I* (?), all *I*. (Boc. ed ia 'l commendo.)
1163. *ful*, S γ (exc. A) *right*.
1168. *soth to seye*, S γ (exc. A) *dar I seye*.
1171. *leyde* (?), all *seyde*. (See ll. 1169, 1304.)
1174-1176. In Boccaccio, 'From Etna the poor fellow expects a wind!'
1175. *that that*, so J P H₄ R CL; A *that at*; rest *that*.

1190. *this*, J H₃ R *his*; G *that*. (See iv. 1590.)
1213. *wode*, P H₃ D Cp. CL *the wode*.

And feblé, that he walketh by potente ;
And with his ire he thus himselven shente.
And who-so axéd him wherof him smerte,
He seide, his harm was al aboute his herte.

Priam ful ofte, and ek his moder dere,
His brethren and his sustren gonne him
    freyne
Why he so sorwful was in all his chere,
And what thing was the cause of al his
    peyne ;
But al for nought.   He n'olde his causé
    pleyne,   1230
But seide he felte a grevous maladye
Aboute his herte, and fayn he woldé dye.

So on a day he leyde him down to slepe :
And so bifil that in his slep him thoughte
That in a forest faste he welk to wepe
For love of her that him this peyné
    wroughte ;
And, up and down as he the forest soughte,
Him mette, he say a boor with tuskés grete,
That slep ayein the brighté sonnés hete ;

And by this boor, faste in her armés
    folde,   1240
Lay, kissing ay, his lady bright, Criseyde :
For sorwe of which, whan he it gan biholde,
And for despit, out of his slep he breyde,
And loude he cri'de on Pandarus, and
    seyde,
' O Pandarus, now knowe I crop and rote !
I n'am but ded, ther n'is non other bote !

' My lady bright, Criseyde, hath me
    bitrayed,
In whom I trusted most of any wight :
She ellèswhere hath now her herte apayed :
The blisful Goddès through hir greté might
Han in my drem y-shewéd it ful right ! 1251
Thus in my drem Criseyde I have
    biholde,'—
And al this thing to Pandarus he tolde.

' O my Criseyde, allas ! what subtilté,
What newé lust, what beauté, what sciénce,
What wraththe of justé cause han ye to me ?
What gilt of me, what fel experience

1240. *her*, H₄ Cl. *kis* ; P H₂ H₃ Cx. omit.

Hath fro me reft, allas, thyn ádvertence ?
O trust ! O feith ! O depé ássuraunce !
Who hath me reft Criseyde, al my ples-
    aunce ?

' Allas ! why let I you from hennès go, 1261
For which wel neigh out of my wit I breyde ?
Who shal now trowe on any othès mo ?
God wot, I wen'de, O lady bright, Criseyde,
That every word was gospel that ye seyde !
But who may bet bigilé, yif him liste,
Than he on whom men weneth best to triste ?

' What shal I don, my Pandarus ? Allas !
I felé now so sharpe a newé peyne, 1269
Sin that ther li'th no remedie in this cas,
That bet were it I with mine hondès tweyne
Myselven slow, alwey than thus to pleyne ;
For through the deth my wo sholde have
    an ende,
Ther every day with lif myself I shende.'

Pandáre answérde and seide, ' Allas the
    while
' That I was born ! Have I not seid or this,
That dremès many a maner man bigile ?
And why ? For folk expounden hem amis !
How darstow seyn that fals thy lady is 1279
For any drem, right for thyn owné drede ?
Lat be this thought, thou canst no dremès
    rede !

' Paraunter, ther thou dremest of this boor,
It may so ben that it may signéfye,
Her fader, which that old is and ek hoor,
Ayein the sonné li'th, o-point to dye,
And she for sorwé ginneth wepe and crye,
And kisseth him ther he li'th on the
    grounde :
Thus sholdestow thy drem a-right ex-
    pounde !'

' How mighte I thanné don,' quod Troilus,
' To knowe of this, ye, were it nevere so
    lite ?'—   1290
' Now seystow wisly !' quod this Pandarus.
' My red is this : sin thou canst wel endite,

1259. read ? *O depe feith ! O assuraunce !*
1266. *yif*, so J G H₄ ; H₃ D *if that* ; others *if.*
1270. *li'th*, S γ *is.*

That hastily a lettré thou her write,
Thorugh which thou shalt wel bringen it
　aboute,
To knowe a soth ther thou art now in doute.

'And see now why! for this I dar wel seyn;
That, if so is that she untrewé be,
I can not trowén she wol write ayeyn;
And, if she writé, thou shalt soné see
As whether she hath any liberté　　　1300
To come ayein, or ellés in som clause,
If she be let, she wol assigne a cause.

'Thou hast not writen her sin that she wente,
Nor she to thee; and this I dorsté leye,
Ther may swich causé ben in her entente,
That hardily thou wolt thyselven seye
That her abood the beste is for you tweye.
Now write her thanne, and thou shalt
　felé sone
A soth of al: ther n'is no more to done.'

Acorded ben to this conclusioun,　　　1310
And that anon, thise ilké lordés two;
And hastily sit Troilus adoun,
And rolleth in his herté to and fro
How he may best discriven her his wo.
And to Criseyde, his owné lady dere,
He wrot right thus, and seide as ye shal
　here.—

'Right fresshé flour, whos I ben have and
　shal,
Withouten part of ellés where servise,
With herté, body, lif, lust, thought, and al,
I, woful wight, in every humblé wise　　1320
That tongé telle or herté may devise,
As ofte as mater occupieth place,
Me recomaunde unto your noblé grace.

'Liketh it you to witen, sweté herte,
As ye wel knowe, how longé time agon
That ye me lefte in aspré peynés smerte
Whan that ye wente: of which yit boté non
Have I non had, but everé wors bigon

Fro day to day am I, and so mot dwelle,
Whil it you list, of wele and wo my welle!

'For-which to you, with dredful herté
　trewe,　　　1331
I write, as he that sorwé drif'th to write,
My wo that everich houre encresseth newe,
Compleyning as I dar or can endite.
And that defacéd is, that may ye wite
The terés whiche that fro mine ýen reyne,
That wolden speke if that they conde, and
　pleyne.

'You first biseche I, that your ýen clere,
To loke on this, defouléd ye not holde,
And over al this, that ye, my lady dere,　1340
Wol vouché-sauf this lettré to biholde:
And by the cause ek of my carés colde
That sleeth my wit, if aught amis m'asterte,
Foryive it me, myn owné sweté herte!

'If any servant dorste or oughte of right
Upon his lady pitously compleyne,
Than wene I that ich oughté ben that
　wight,
Consideréd this, that ye thise monthés
　tweyne
Han taried, ther ye seyden, soth to seyne,
But dayés ten ye n'olde in oost sojorne,—
But in two monthés yit ye not retorne.　1351

'But for as muche as me mot nedés like
Al that you list, I dar not pleyné more;
But humblély, with sorwful sikés sike,
You write ich mine unresty sorwes sore,
Fro day to day desiring everé more
To knowén fully, if your wille it were,
How ye han ferd and don whil ye be there;

'The whos welfare and hele ek God
　encresse　　　1359
In honour swich, that upward in degree
It growe alwey, so that it neveré cesse.
Right as your herte ay can, my lady free,
Devise, I preye to God so mote it be,
And grante it that ye sone upon me rewe
As wisly as in al I am you trewe!

1295. *ther thou art now*, J Cx. omit *now*; S γ
of that (H₂ *of which*) *thou art.*
1298. *she*, so J R Cx. G H₃; rest *that she.*
1299. *sone*, J and others *ful sone.*
1316. *shal*, so J P R Cx. G H₄; rest *may.*
1324. *it*, J and others omit.

1335. *And that*, J *And that it* (read ? *And
that*).
1365. *you*, J and others *to you*; Cx. *your.*

' And if you liketh knowèn of the fare
Of me, whos wo ther may no wit descrive,
I can no more, but, cheste of every care,
At writing of this lettre I was on-live,
Al redy out my woful gost to drive : 1370
Which I delay, and holde him yit in honde
Upon the sighte of mater of your sonde.

' Myn ÿen two, in veyn with whiche I see,
Of sorwful terès salte arn waxen welles :
My song, in pleynte of myn adversité :
My good, in harm : myn ese ek waxen
    helle is :
My joye, in wo : I can seye you nought
    elles,
But turnèd is, for which my lif I warie,
Evèrich joye or ese in his contrárie.

' Which with your coming hom ayein to
    Troye   1380
Ye may redresse, and, more a thousand sithe
Than evere ich hadde, encressen in me joye.
For was ther neverè hertè yit so blithe
To han his lif as I shal ben, as swithe
As I you see. And, though no maner
    routhe
Coummevè you, yit thenketh on your
    trouthe.

' And if so be my gilt hath deth deserved,
Or if you list no more upon me see,
In guerdon yit of that I have you served
Biseche I you, myn hertès lady free, 1390
That her-upon ye wolden writè me,
For love of God, my rightè lodè-sterre,
That deth may make an ende upon my
    werre !

' If other cause aught doth you for to
    dwelle,
That with your lettrè ye me réconforte !
For, though to me your absence is an helle,
With pacience I wol my wo conporte,
And with your lettre of hope I wol desporte.
Now writeth, swete, and lat me thus not
    pleyne :
With hope, or deth, delivereth me fro
    peyne !   1400

' Y-wis, myn ownè derè hertè trewe,
I wot that, whan ye next upon me see,
So lost have I myn hele and ek myn hewe,
Criseydè shal not connè knowèn me.
Y-wis, myn hertès day, my lady free,
So thursteth ay myn hertè to biholde
Your beauté, that my lif unnethe I holde.

' I sey no more, al have I for to seye
To you wel morè than I tellen may. 1409
But whether that ye do me live or deye,
Yit preye I God so yive you right good day !
And far'th wel, goodly fairè fresshè may,
As she that lif or deth me may comaunde !
And to your trouthe ay I me recomaunde

' With helè swich that, but ye yiven me
The samè hele, I shal non helè have !
In you li'th, whan you list that it so be,
The day on which me clothen shal my
    grave :
In you my lif, in you might for to save
Me from disese of allè peynès smerte ! 1420
And far'th now wel, myn ownè swetè
    herte ! '

This lettrè forth was sent unto Criseyde,
Of which her answer in effect was this :
Ful pitously she wrot ayein, and seyde,
That al-so sone as that she mighte, y-wis,
She woldè come, and mende al that was
    mis,
And finaly—she wrot and seide him
    thanne—
She woldè come, ye, but she n'istè whanne.

But in her lettrè made she swichè festes
That wonder was, and swer'th she lov'th
    him best :   1430
Of which he fond but botmèles bihestes.
But Troilus, thou mayst now, est or west,
Pipe in an ivy leef, if that thee lest !
Thus go'th the world ! God shilde us
    fro mischaunce,
And every wight that meneth trouthe
    avaunce !

Encressen gan the wo fro day to night
Of Troilus, for tarying of Criseyde,

1367. *wit*, G Cl. and others *wight* ; H₄ *man*.
1393. *That*, Cx. *Or* ; H₃ *The* ; Cl. Cp. *Ther*.

1413. *she*, Cx. S γ *ye*.

And lessen gan his hope and ek his might ;
For which al down he in his bed him leyde.
He n'eet, ne dronk, ne slep, ne no word
     seyde,   1440
Imagininge ay that she was unkinde ;
For-which wel neigh he wex out of his
     minde.

This drem, of which I told have ek biforn,
May nevere come out of his rémembraunce :
He thoughte ay wel he hadde his lady lorn,
And that that Jovés of his púrveyaunce
Him shewéd hadde in slep the signefiaunce
Of her untrouthe and his disáventure,
And that this boor was shewed him in
     figúre.   1449

For-which he for Sibille his suster sente,
That calléd was Cassandre ek al aboute ;
And al his drem he tolde her or he stente,
And her bisoughte assoilen him the doute
Of th'ilké strongé boor with tuskés stoute ;
And finaly withinne a litel stounde
Cassandre him gan right thus his drem
     expounde.

She gan first smile, and seide, 'O brother
     dere,
If thou a soth of this desirest knowe,
Thou most a fewe of oldé stories here,
To purpos how that Fortune overthrowe
Hath lordés olde : thorugh which, withinne
     a throwe,   1461
Thou wel this boor shal knowe, and of
     what kinde
He comén is, as men in bokés finde.

' Diané, which that wroth was and in ire
For Grekés n'olden don her sacrifise,
N'encéns upon her auter sette a-fire,
She, for-that Grekés gonne her so despise,
Vengéd her in a wonder cruel wise ;

For with a boor as gret as oxe in stalle
She made up-frete hir corn and vinés alle.

'To slee this boor was al the contré reysed,
Amongés whiche ther com, this boor to
     see,   1472
A mayde, oon of this world the best
     y-preysed ;
And Meleagré, lord of that contré,
He lovedé so this fresshé maydé free
That with his manhod, or he woldé stente,
This boor he slow, and her the hed he
     sente :

' Of which, as oldé bokés tellen us,
Ther ros a contek and a gret envýe.
And of this lord descended Tydéus   1480
By ligne, or ellés oldé bokés lye :
But how this Meleagré gan to dye
Thórugh his moder, wol I you not telle,
For al too long it weré for to dwelle.'

She tolde ek how Tydéus, or she stente,
Unto the strongé cité of Thebés
To cleymen kingdom of the cité wente
For his feláwé, daun Polymites,
Of which the brother, daun Ethiocles,
Ful wrongfully of Thebés held the
     strengthe :   1490
This toldé she by proces al by lengthe.

She tolde ek how Hemonides asterte,
Whan Tydéus slough fifty knightés stoute ;
She tolde ek alle the prophecies by herte,
And how the sevené kingés with bir route
Bisegéden the cité al aboute ;
And of the holy serpent, and the welle,
And of the Furies, al she gan him telle :

1440. *no word*, so H₄ R Cx.; G *no word he ne*
(om. *ne slep*); H₃ *worde ne*; rest *word(e)*.
1446. *that that*, so J P H₄ G Frag.; rest *that*.
(See iii. 1751, 1758.)
1447. *signefiaunce*, so J A; rest *signifiaunce*.
1449. *this*, H₃ S γ *the*.
1454. *th'ilke* (?), R *that*; Cx. *this*; A *a*; rest
the.
1457. The incidents in the following lines are
taken from Ovid and Statius. Chaucer returns
to Boccaccio at l. 1513.
1468. *Venged*, so H₂ only ; rest *Wrak*.

1473. *A mayde*, Atalanta.
1480. Tydeus was Meleager's brother. Chaucer's mistake may have been made on purpose ; or
it may be due to *Filostrato* vii. stanza 27, where
Troilus refers to Meleager as the ancestor of
Diomede.
1482. *gan to*, G *dude*.
1483. *Thórugh his*, H₂ *Thurgh* ; G *Of him* :
R *Thrugh out*.
1483. *his moder*, Althæa.
1498. The following argument of the twelve
books of Statius' *Thebais* is placed after this line
in all the MSS. except H₄ and Rawl. :—
     Associat profugum Tideo *primus* Polimitem ;
     Tiden legatum docet insidiasque *secundus* :
     Tercius Hemonidem canit et vates latitantes ;

Of Archimoris' burying and the pleyes,
And how Amphiorax fil thorugh the
    grounde ;   1500
How Tydeus was slayn, lord of Argeyes :
And how Ypomedon in litel stounde
Was dreynt, and ded Parthonope of
    wounde :
And also how Cappaneus the proude
With thonder-dint was slayn, that cri'de
    loude.

She gan ek telle him how that either brother,
Ethiocles and Polymite also,
Yit at a scarmuche ech of hem slough
    other,
And of Argives weping and hir wo :
And how the town was brent she tolde ek
    tho ;   1510
And so descendeth down from gestes olde
To Diomede : and thus she spak and tolde.

' This ilke boor bitokneth Diomede,
Tydeus sone, that doun descended is
Fro Meleagre, that made the boor to blede :
And thy lady, wher-so she be, y-wis,
This Diomede her herte hath, and she his.
Wep if thou wolt, or lef !   For out of doute
This Diomede is inne, and thou art oute ! '

' Thou seyst not soth,' quod he, ' thou
    sorceresse,   1520
With al thy false gost of prophecye !
Thou wenest ben a gret devineresse !
Now seestow not this fool of fantasye
That peyneth her on ladies for to lye !

Awey !' quod he, ' Ther Joves yive thee
    sorwe !
Thou shalt ben fals paraunter yit to-morwe !

' As wel thou mightest lyen on Alceste,
That was of creatures, but men lye,
That evere weren, kindest and the beste :
For whan her housband was in jupartye
To dye himself but-if she wolde dye,   1531
She ches for him to dye and gon to helle,
And starf anon, as us the bokes telle ! '

Cassandre go'th : and he with cruel herte
Foryat his wo for angre of her speche,
And from his bed al sodeinly he sterte,
As though al hool him hadde maad a leche.
And day by day he gan enquere and seche
A soth of this with al his fulle cure :
And thus he drieth forth his aventure.   1540

—Fortune, which that permutacioun
Of thinges hath, as it is her committed
By purveyaunce and disposicioun
Of heighe Jove, as regnes shal be flitted
Fro folk to folk, or whan they shal be
    smitted,
Gan pulle awey the fetheres brighte of Troye
Fro day to day, til they ben bare of joye.

Among al this, the fyn of the parodie
Of Ector gan aprochen wonder blive :   1549
The Fate wolde, his soule sholde unbodie,
And shapen hadde a mene it out to drive
Ayeins which fate him helpeth not to strive ;
But on a day to fighten gan he wende,
At which, allas, he caughte his lives ende.

For which me thinketh every maner wight
That haunteth armes oughte to biwaile
The deth of him that was so noble a
    knight ;
For, as he drough a king by th'aventaile,
Unwar of this, Achilles, thorugh the maile
And thorugh the body gan him for to rive :
And thus this worthy knight was brought
    of live.   1561

Quartus habet reges ineuntes prelia septem ;
Mox furie Lenne *quinto* narratur et anguis ;
Archimori bustum *sexto* ludique leguntur ;
Dat Graios Thebes et vatem *septimus* umbris ;
Octavo cecidit Tideus, spes, vita Pelasgis ;
Ypomedon *nono* moritur cum Parthonopeo ;
Fulmine percussus, *decimo* Capaneus superatur ;
Undecimo sese perimunt per vulnera fratres ;
Argiuam flentem narrat *duodenus* et ignem.

1502-1504. J G read :
    And how Ypomedon with blody wounde
    And ek Parthonope in litel stounde
    Ben slayn, and how Cappaneus the proude

1503. *ded*, Cp. *dede* (read ? *deyde Parthonope
of* . . .).
    1508. *Yit at*, so A ; rest *At.*
    1516. *wher-so*, Cl. *wher that* ; J and others
wher (read ? *And thus thy lady, wher she be,
y-wis*).
    1524. *That peyneth* (?), all *Peyneth.*

1527. *Alceste*, Alcestis.   See l. 1778, and
L.G.W. 432, etc.
    1532. *for him to dye and gon*, J G *to dye* (G
deth) *and ek to gon.*
    1543. *By*, S γ *Thorugh.*
    1558. This account of the death of Hector
seems to have been taken from Benoit.

For whom, as oldé bokés tellen us,
Was maad swich wo, that tonge it may not
    telle,
And namély, the sorwe of Troilus,
That next him was of worthinessé welle :
And in this wo gan Troilus to dwelle,
That, what for sorwe, and love, and for
    unreste,
Ful ofte a day he bad his herté breste.

But nathéles, though he gan him despeire,
And dredde ay that his lady was untrewe,
Yit ay on her his herté gan repeire ; 1571
And as thisc lovers don, he soughte ay
    newe
To gete ayein Criseydé bright of hewe,
And in his herte he wente her éxcusinge,
That Calcas causéd al her taryinge.

And ofté time he was in purpos grete
Himselven lik a pilgrim to disgise,
To sen her ; but he may not contrefete
To ben unknowe of folk that weren wise,
Ne finde excuse aright that may suffise,
If he among the Grekés knowén were :
For which he wep ful ofte, and many a
    tere. 1582

To her he wrot yit ofté time al newe
Ful pitously,—he lefte it not for slouthe,—
Biseching her that, sin that he was trewe,
That she wol come ayein and holde her
    trouthe :
For which Criseyde upon a day, for routhe
(I take it so,) touching al this matére
Wrot him ayein, and seide as ye may
    here.— 1589

' Cupídés sone, ensaumple of godlihede,
O swerd of knighthod, sours of gentilesse !
How mighte a wight, in torment and in
    drede
And heléles, you sende as yit gladnésse ?
I hertéles, I sik, I in distresse !
Sin ye with me, nor I with you may dele,
You neither sende ich herté may ne hele !

' Your lettres ful, the papir al y-pleynted,
Conceyved hath myn hertés pieté : 1598
I have ek seyn with terés al depeynted
Your lettre, and how that ye requeren me
To come ayein, which yit ne may not be :
But why, lest that this lettré founden were,
No mencioun ne make I now for fere.

' Grevous to me, God wot, is your unreste,
Your haste, and that the Goddés ordi-
    naunce,
It semeth not ye take it for the beste ;
Nor other thing n'is in your rémem-
    braunce,
As thinketh me, but only your plesaunce.
But beth not wroth, and that I you bifeche :
For that I tarie is al for wikked specbe. 1610

' For I have herd wel moré than I wen'de,
Touching us two how thingés han y-stonde,
Which I shal with dissimulinge amende.
And beth not wroth, I have ek understonde
How ye ne don but holden me in honde.
But now no fors : I can not in you gesse
But allé trouthe and allé gentilesse.

' Comén I wol ; but yit in swich disioynt
I stonde as now, that what yer or what day
That this shal be, that can I not a-poynt. 1620
But in effect, I preye you as I may
Of your good-word and of your frendship
    ay ;
For trewély, whil-that my lif may dure,
As for a frend ye may in me assure.

' Yet preye I you, on yvel ye ne take
That it is short which that I to you write.
I dar not, ther I am, wel lettres make,
Ne neveré yit ne coude I wel endite.
Ek gret effect men write in placé lite :
Th'entente is al, and not the lettres space.
And far'th now wel, God have you in his
    grace ! '— 1631

This Troilus this lettré thoughte al straunge
Whan he it saugh, and sorwfully he sighte :

1570. *dredde ay,* J P G H₃ *dred(d)e ;* H₄ *dredde evere.*
1577. *disgise,* J H₁ Cl. *degise.*
1582. *and,* G H₄ Cl. omit.
1590. Cressida's letter is not in Boccaccio.

1598. *pieté,* so J S Cp. ; R *privetee ;* rest *pit(e)\ pete.*
1618. *disioynt,* J and others *disioynte.*
1620. *a-poynt,* J *poynte ;* Cl. and others a-
(*p*)*oynte.* (See iii. 496, 497.)

Him thoughte it lik a kalendès of chaunge.
But finaly he ful ne trowèn mighte
That she ne wolde him holden that she
    highte ;
For with ful yvel wil list him to leve
That loveth wel, in swich cas, though him
    greve !

But nathèles men seyn that at the laste,
For anything, men shal the sothè see ! 1640
And swich a cas bitidde, and that as faste,
That Troilus wel understood that she
N'as not so kinde as that her oughtè be ;
And finaly he wot now, out of doute,
That al is lost that he hath ben aboute.

—Stood on a day in his maléncolye
This Troilus, and in suspicioun
Of her for whom he wen'dè for to dye :
And so bifel that thorugh-out Troyè toun,
As was the gise, y-born was up and doun 1650
A maner cote-armúre, as seith the storie,
Biforn Deiphébe in signe of his victórie :

The whichè cote, as telleth Lollius,
Deiphébe it haddè y-rent fro Diomede
The samè day.   And whan this Troilus
It saugh, he gan to taken of it hede,
Avising of the lengthe and of the brede
And al the werk.   But, as he gan biholde,
Ful sodeinliche his hertè gan to colde,

As he that on the coler fond withinne 1660
A broche, that he Criseydè yaf that morwe
That she from Troyè mostè nedès twinne,
In rémembraunce of him and of his sorwe.
And she him leyde ayein her feith to borwe
To kepe it ay !   But now ful wel he wiste,
His lady n'as no lenger on to triste.

He go'th him hom, and gan ful sonè sende
For Pandarus ; and al this newè chaunce
And of this broche he tolde him, word and
    ende,
Compleyning of her hertès variaunce, 1670
His longè love, his trouthe, and his
    penaúnce.
And after deth, withouten wordès more,
Ful faste he cri'de, his reste him to restore.

1653. *Lollius*, Boccaccio. (See i. 394 note.)

Than spak he thus, 'O lady bright,
    Criseyde,
Wher is your feith, and wher is your
    biheste ?
Wher is your love?   Wher is your trouthe?'
    he seyde ;
'Of Diomede have ye now al this feste !
Allas !   I wolde han trowèd at the leste
That, sin ye n'olde in trouthè to me stonde,
That ye thus n'olde han holden me in
    honde !   1680

'Who shal now trowe on any oothès mo ?
Allas !   I n'oldè nevere han wen'd or this
That ye, Criseydè, coude han changèd so,
Ne, but I hadde agilt and don amis,
So cruel wen'de I not your herte, y-wis,
To slee me thus !   Allas, your name of
    trouthe
Is now fordon : and that is al my routhe !

'Was ther non other broche you listè lete
To feffè with your newè love,' quod he, 1689
'But th'ilkè broche that I with terès wete
You yaf as for a rémembraunce of me ?
Non other cause, allas, ne hadden ye
But for despit, and ek for-that ye mente
Al outrely to shewèn your entente !

'Thorugh which I see that clene out of your
    minde
Ye han me cast !   And I ne can ne may,
For al this world, within myn hertè finde
T'unloven you a quarter of a day !
In cursed time I born was, weylawey, 1699
That you, that don me al this wo endure,
Yit love I best of any créature !

'Now God,' quod he, ' me sendè yit the
    grace.
That I may meten with this Diomede !
And trewèly, if I have might and space,
Yet shal I make, I hope, his sidès blede !
O God,' quod he, ' that oughtest taken hede
To furthren trouthe, and wrongès to puníce,
Why n'iltow don a vengeaunce on this vice?

'O Pandar, that in dremès for to triste
Me blamèd hast, and wont art ofte
    upbreyde,   1710

1674. *bright*, H₃ S γ *myn* (Boc.)

Now maystow sen thyself, if that thee liste,
How trewe is now thy necé bright,
   Criseyde !
In sondry formés, God it wot,' he seyde,
' The Goddés shewén bothé joye and tene
In slep, and by my drem it is now sene.

' And certeinly, withouté moré speche,
From hennésforth, as ferforth as I may,
Myn owné deth in armés wol I seche :
I recché not how soné be the day !
But trewély Criseydé, sweté may,   1720
Whom I have ay with al my might y-served,
That ye thus don, I n'have it not deserved !'

This Pandarus, that alle these thingés herde,
And wisté wel he seide a soth of this,
He not a word ayein to him answérde ;
For sory of his frendés sorwe he is,
And shaméd for his nece hath don amis ;
And stant, astoné of thise causes tweye,
As stille as ston : a word ne coude he seye.

But at the lasté thus he spak and seide : 1730
' My brother dere, I may do thee no more !
What sholde I seye ?   I hate, y-wis,
   Criseyde ;
And God wot, I wol hate her everémore !
And that thou me bisoughtest don of yore,
Having unto myn honour ne my reste
Right no reward, I dide al that thee leste.

' If I dide aught that mighté liken thee,
It is me lief.   And of this treson now,
God wot that it a sorwe is unto me !
And dredéles, for hertés ese of yow, 1740
Right fayn I wolde amende it, wiste I how.
And fro this world, almighty God I preye,
Delivere her sone ! I can no moré seye !'—

Gret was the sorwe and pleynte of Troilus.
But forth her cours Fortúne ay gan to holde :
Criseydé lov'th the sone of Tydéus,
And Troilus mot wepe in carés colde !
Swich is this world ! Who-so it can biholde,
In ech estat is litel hertés reste !
God leve us for to take it for the beste ! 1750

In many cruel bataille, out of drede,
Of Troilus, this ilké noblé knight,

As men may in thise oldé bokés rede,
Was sene his knighthod and his greté
   might.
And dredéles, his iré, day and night,
Ful cruély the Grekés ay aboughte,
And alwey most this Diomede he soughte.

And ofté time, I findé that they mette
With blody strokés and with wordés grete,
Assaying how hir sperés werén whette ; 1760
And God it wot, with many a cruel bete
Gan Troilus upon his helm to bete !
But nathéles, Fortúne it nought ne wolde,
Of othres hond that either deyé sholde.

—And if I hadde y-taken for to writen
Thé armés of this ilké worthy man,
Than wolde I of his bataillés enditen.
But for-that I to writen first bigan
Of his lovínge, I have seid as I can. 1769
His worthy dedés, who-so list hem here,
Red Dares : he can telle hem alle i-fere.

Biseching every lady bright of hewe
And every gentil woman, what she be,
That, al be that Criseydé was untrewe,
That for that gilt ye be not wroth with me :
Ye may her gilt in othré bokés see !
And gladlier I wol writé, yif you leste,
Penelopéés trouthe and goode Alceste !

N' I sey not this al-only for thise men ;
But most for wommen that bitrayséd be 1780
Thorugh falsé folk. God yive hem sorwe,
   amen !
That with hir greté wit and subtilté
Bitraysé you ! And this commeveth me
To speke ; and, in effect, you alle I preye,
Beth ware of men, and herkneth what I
   seye !

—Go, litel book ! Go, litel myn tragédie !
Ther God thy maker yit, or-that he dye,
So sendé might to make in som comédie !
But, litel book, no making thou n'envye,
But subgit be to allé poesye !   1790

1731. *do thee,* J Cl. *thee do.*

1761. *many a,* J and others *many.*
1769. *lovínge,* so S ; rest *love.* (See L. 1833.)
(Read ? *As of his love . . .*)
1775. *ye,* R S y *she.*
1776. *othre,* H₂ H₁ *othres.*

And kis the steppès wher-as thou seest pace
Virgíle, Ovíde, Omér, Lucán, and Stace !

And, for ther is so gret diversité
In Englissh and in writing of our tonge,
So prey to God that non miswrité thee,
Ne thee mismetré for defaute of tonge !
And, red wher-so thou be or ellès songe,
That thou be understondè God bisèche !—
But yet to purpos of my rather speche.

—The wraththe, as I bigan you for to seye,
Of Troilus the Grekès boughten dere ; 1801
For thousandès his hondès maden deye,
As he that was withouten any pere
Save Ector in his time, as I can here.
But weylawey, save only Goddès wille,
Ful pitously him slough the fierse Achille.

And whan that he was slayn in this manére
His lightè goost ful blisfully is went
Up to the holwnesse of the eightè spere,
In convers leting everich element :   1810
And ther he saugh with ful avisément
Th'erratik sterrès, herkning armonye
With sounès fulle of hevenissh melodye.

And down from thennès faste he gan avise
This litel spot of erthe that with the see
Enbracèd is, and fully gan despise
This wrecched world, and held al vanité
To réspect of the pleyne felicite
That is in hevene above. And at the laste,
Ther he was slayn his loking down he
    caste,   1820

And in himself he lough right at the wo
Of hem that wepen for his deth so faste,

And dampned al our werk, that folwen so
The blindè lust the whiche that may not
    laste,
And sholden al our herte on hevenè caste.
And forth he wentè, shortly for to telle,
Ther-as Mercúrie sorted him to dwelle.

Swich fyn hath tho this Troilus for love !
Swich fyn hath al his gretè worthinesse !
Swich fyn hath his estat réál above ! 1830
Swich fyn his lust, swich fyn hath his
    noblesse !
Swich fyn, this falsè worldès brotelnesse !—
And thus bigan his loving of Criseyde
As I have told, and in this wise he deyde.

—O yongè fresshè folkès, he or she,
In whiche ay love up-groweth with your
    age,
Repeireth hom fro worldly vanité !
And of your herte up-casteth the viságe
To th'ilkè God that after his imáge
You made ; and thinketh al n'is but a
    faire   1840
This world, that passeth sone as flourès
    faire !

And loveth Him, the whiche that right
    for love
Upon a cros, our soulès for to beye,
First starf, and roos, and sit in hevene
    above ;
For He n'il falsen no wight, dar I seye,
That wol his herte al hoolly on him leye !
And sin He best to love is, and most meke,
What nedeth feynèd lovès for to seke ?

Lo here, of payens corsèd oldè rites !
Lo here, what alle hir Goddès may
    availe !   1850
Lo here, thise wrecched worldès appetites !
Lo here, the fyn and guerdon for travaile
Of Jove, Appollo, of Mars, of swich
    rascaile !
Lo here, the forme of oldè clerkès speche
In poetrye, if ye hir bokès seche !

1791. *pace*, so P H₄ Cl. Th. only ; rest *space*.
1795. *prey to God*, so J P Cx.; others *prey I to God, prey I God, prey thy God*.
1798. *God bisèche*, so J R A Cp. Cl. ; others *God I (thee) bisèche*.
1806. *Ful pitously*, Cx. S γ *Dispitously*. (Boc. miseramente.)
1807. The following three stanzas are from the account of the death of Arcite in Boccaccio's *Teseide*. They are omitted in H₂ H₄, and inserted later in P.
1809. *eightè*, J *viij*; others *seventhe*. (Boc. Ver la concavita del cielo ottava.)
1810. Boc. Degli elementi i conuessi lasciando. (Possibly Chaucer uses *convers* here with the meaning of *convex*.)
1823. *folwen* (?), all *folweth*.
1824. *that*, J D *ne* ; H₂ Cl. omit.
1831. *hath*, H₄ omits.
1832. *this* (?), H₂ *hath this* ; H₄ *hath the* ; J and others *hath*.
1836. *ay*, so J P H₂ H₄ H₃ ; R Cx. S γ *that*.
1842. *the*, J and others omit.

—O moral Gowèr, this book I directe
To thee, and to thee, philosophical Strode,
To vouchen-sauf, ther nede is, to correcte,
Of your benignétés and zelès gode.—
And to that sothfast Crist, that starf on
    rode,   1860
With al myn herte, of mercy evere I preye,
And to the Lord right thus I speke and
    seye :

Thou oon, and two, and three, eterne on·
    live,
That regnest ay in three and two and oon,
Uncircumscript, and al mayst circumscrive,
Us from visible and invisible foon
Defénde! And to thy mercy, everichoon,
So make us, Jesus, for thy mercy digne,
For love of mayde and moder thyn benigne!

CHAUCER'S WORDS UNTO ADAM, HIS OWNE SCRY-VEYNE

ADAM SCRIVEYN, if ever it thee bifalle
Boece or Troylus for to writen newe,
Under thy long lokkes thou most have
    the scalle
But after my making thou write more
    trewe.
So ofte a daye I mot thy werk renewe,
Hit to correcte and eek to rubbe and
    scrape ;
And al is through thy negligence and
    rape.

THE HOUS OF FAME

FIRST BOOK

(*Proem*)

GOD turne us every dreem to gode !
For hit is wonder, be the Rode,
To my wyt, what causeth swevenes
Either on morwés, or on evenes ;
And why theffect folwéth of somme,
And of somme hit shal never come ;
Why that is an avisioun,
And this a revelacioun ;
Why this a dreem, why that a sweven,
And noght to every man liche even ;   10
Why this a fantom, why these oracles,
I noot : but who-so of these miracles
The causés knoweth bet then I,
Devyne he ; for I certeynly
Ne can hem noght, ne never thynke
To besily my wyt to swynke,
To knowe of hir signifiaunce

The gendrés neither the distaunce
Of tymès of hem, ne the causès,
Or why this morè then that cause is ;   20
As if folkès complexiouns
Make hem dreme of reflexiouns ;
Or ellès thus, as other sayn,
For to greet feblenesse of her brayn,
By abstinence, or by seeknesse,
Prisoun, stewe or greet distresse ;
Or ellès by disordynaunce,
Of naturel acustomaunce,
That somme men ben to curious
In studie, or melancolious ;   30
Or thus, so inly ful of drede,
That no man may him botè rede ;
Or ellès that devocioun
Of somme, and contemplacioun,
Causeth swichè dremès ofte ;

7. P *a visioun;* Cx. *that it is a visioun;* Th. *that it is.*
8. All insert *why,* caught from line above.
17. P Cx. Th. *significacions.*

18. Cx. Th. *dystinctions.*
19. P Cx. Th. insert *the* before *tymes.*
20. F B *For why.* All read *this is.*
26. P *stoe;* Cx. Th. *stryf* for *stewe.*
32. F B *bote bede.*

Or that the cruel lyf unsofte
Which these ilkè lovers leden,
That hopen over moche or dreden,
That purely hir impressiouns
Causeth hem have visiouns ;　　　40
Or if that spirits have the myght
To makè folk to dreme a-nyght ;
Or if the soule, of propre kynde,
Be so parfit as men fynde,
That hit forwot that is to come,
And that hit warneth alle and somme
Of everiche of her aventures,
By avisiouns, or by figures,
But that our flesh ne hath no myght
To understonden hit aright,　　　50
For hit is warnèd to derklý ;
But why the cause is, noght wot I.
Wel worthe, of this thyng, gretè clerkes,
That trete of that, and other werkes ;
For I of noon opinioun
Nil as now makè mencioun ;
But oonly that the holy rode
Turne us every dreem to gode ;
For never sith that I was born,
Ne no man ellès me beforn,　　　60
Mette, I trowè stedfastly,
So wonderful a dreem as I
The tenthè day [dide] of Decembre ;
The which, as I can now remembre,
I wol yow tellèn every dele.

(*The Invocation*)

But at my gynnyng, trusteth wel,
I'wol make invocacioun,
With special devocioun
Unto the god of slepè anoon,
That dwelleth in a cave of stoon,　　　70
Upon a streem that cometh fro Lete,
That is a flood of helle unswete,
Besyde a folk men clepe Cymérie ;
There slepeth ay this god unmerie,

With his slepy thousand sones,
That alway for to slepe hir wone is ;
That to this god, that I of rede,
Preye I, that he wol me spede,
My sweven for to telle aright,
If every dreem stonde in his myght ;　　　80
And he that mover is of al
That is and was, and ever shal,
So yive hem joyè that hit here,
Of alle that they dreme to-yere ;
And for to stonden alle in grace
Of hir loves, or in what place
That hem were levest for to stonde,
And shelde hem fro povérte and shonde,
And fro unhappe and ech disese,
And sende hem al that may hem plese,　　　90
That take hit wel and scorne hit noght,
Ne hit mysdemen in her thoght,
Through malicious entencioun.
And who-so, through presumpcioun,
Or hate, or scorne, or through envýe,
Dispit, or jape, or vilanýe,
Mysdeme hit, pray I Jèsus God,
That (dreme he barfoot, dreme he shod),
That every harm, that any man
Hath had sith the world began,　　　100
Befalle him thérof, or he sterve,
And graunt he mote hit ful deserve,
Lo ! with swich a conclusioun,
As hadde of his avisioun
Cresus, that was kyng of Lyde,
That high upon a gebet dyde !
This prayer shal he have of me ;
I am no bet in charité.
　　Now herkneth, as I have yow seyd,
What that I mette or I abreyd.　　　110

(*The Dream*)

Of Decembrè the tenthè day,
Whan hit was nyght, to slepe I lay,
Right ther as I was wonte to done,
And fil on slepè wonder sone,
As he that wery was for-go
On pilgrymagè mylès two
To the córseynt Lëonard,
To makè lythe of that was hard.
　　But as I sleep, me mette I was

---

40. F B *hem avisiouns.*
63. Willert reads *dide* for *now* of the MSS. P and Cx. wrongly insert *dide* before *I* in l. 62, having caught it from its right place in l. 63.
64. F *yow* for *now* ; Cx. omits *now.*
65. P Cx. omit this and next line.
69. *god of slepe,* Morpheus ; cp. *Dethe of the Duchesse,* l. 137, and *Metamorphoses,* xi. l. 592 ff.
71. *Lete,* Lethe.
73. *Cymérie,* Cimmeria.

105. *Cresus,* Crœsus, king of Lydia.
119. MSS. *slepte.* Cp. l. 438.

Withyn a temple y-mad of glas ; 120
In whiche ther weré mo ymáges
Of gold, stondynge in divers stages,
And mo riché tabernacles,
And with perré mo pynacles,
And mo curious portreytures,
And queynté maner of figúres
Of golde werke, then I sawgh ever.
But certeynly I nysté never
Wher that I was, but wel wyste I,
Hit was of Venus redély, 130
This temple ; for in portreyture,
I saw anoon right hir figure
Naked fletynge in a see.
And also on hir heed, pardé,
Hir rosé garlond white and reed,
And hir comb to kembe hir heed,
Hir dowvés, and daun Cupidó,
Hir blynde sone, and Vulcanó,
That in his fáce was ful broun.

But as I roméd up and doun, 140
I fond that on a walle ther was
Thus writen on a table of bras :
' I wol now synge, gif that I can,
The armés, and also the man,
That first cam, through his destinee,
Fúgitif of Troy contree,
In Itáile, with ful moche pyne,
Unto the strondés of Lavyne.'
And tho began the story anoon,
As I shal tellé you echoon. 150
First saw I the destruccioun
Of Troyé through the Greek Synoun,
[That] with his falsé forswerynge,
And his chere and his lesynge
Made the hors broght into Troye,
Through which Troyens loste al her joye.

And after this was grave, allas !
How Ilioun assailed was
And wonne, and kyng Priám y-slayn,
And Polites, his sone, certayne, 160
Dispitously of daun Pirrús.

And next that saw I how Venús,
Whan that she saw the castel brende,
Doun fro the hevene gan descende,
And bad hir sone Eneas flee ;
And how he fledde, and how that he
Escapéd was from al the pres,
And took his fader, Anchisés,
And bar him on his bakke away,
Crying, ' Allas, and welaway ! ' 170
The whiche Anchises in his honde
Bar the goddes of the londe,
Thilké that unbrendé were.

And I saw next in al this fere,
How Creusa, daun Eneas wyf,
Which that he lovéde as his lyf,
And hir yongé sone Iuló
And eek Ascanius alsó,
Fledden eek with drery chere,
That hit was pitee for to here ; 180
And in a forest as they wente,
At a turnynge of a wente,
How Creusa was y-lost, allas !
That deed,—ne wot I how—she was ;
How he hir soughte, and how hir
     gost
Bad hym to flee the Grekés ost,
And seyde, he moste into Itaile,
As was his destinee, sauns faille,
That hit was pitee for to here,
Whan hir spirit gan appere, 190
The wordés that to him she seyde,
And for to kepe hir sone him preyde.

Ther saw I graven eek how he,
His fader eek, and his meynee,
With his shippés gan to saile
Toward the contree of Itaile,
As streight as that they myghté go.

Ther saw I thee, cruel Juno,
That art daun Jupitérés wyf,
That hast y-hated, al thy lyf, 200
Al the Troyanyshé blood,
Renne and crye, as thou were wood,
On Eolus, the god of wyndes,
To blowen out of allé kyndes
So loudé that he shuldé drenche
Lord and lady, grome and wenche

135. P *Her roosgarland on her hede,* and om. next line ; Cx. *Rose garlondes swellynge as a mede, And also fleyng about her hede.*
143. Cx. *wold . . . now* and *I* ; F B *say* for *synge.*
148. *Lavyne,* Lavinium.
152. *Synoun,* Sinon ; cp. *Æn.* ii. l. 195.
153. All omit *That.*
158. *Ilioun,* Ilium.
161. *Pirrús,* Pyrrhus.

177. *Iuló,* Iulus, the same person as Ascanius ; cp. *Æn.* i. l. 267.
184. All MSS. read *not* (= *ne wot*).
196. P omits this line.
198. P Cx. Th. insert *eek* before *thee.*

Of al the Troyan nacioun,
Withoute any savacioun.
  Ther saw I swich tempeste arise,
That every hertë myghte agrise,   210
To see hit peynted on the walle.
  Ther saw I graven eek withalle,
Venus, how ye, my lady dere,
Wepyng with ful woful chere,
Prayen Jupiter on hye
To save and kepë that navye
Of the Troyan Eneás,
Sith that he hir sonë was.
  Ther saw I Jovës Venus kisse,
And graunted of the tempest lisse.   220
  Ther saw I how the tempest stente,
And how with allë pyne he wente,
And prevély took arryvage
In the contree of Cartage ;
And on the morwë, how that he
And a knyght hight Achaté,
Metten with Venus that day,
Goyng in a queynt array,
As she hadde ben an hunteresse,
With wynd blowynge upon hir tresse ;
How Eneas gan him to pleyne,   231
Whan that he knew hir, of his
      peyne ;
And how his shippés dreyntë were,
Or ellës lost, he nyste where ;
How she gan hym comfortë tho,
And bad hym to Cartagë go,
And ther his folk he shuldë fynde,
That in the see were left behynde.
  And, shortly of this thyng to pace,
She made Eneas so in grace   240
Of Dido, quene of that contré,
That, shortly for to tellen, she
Becam his love, and lete him do
Al that weddyng longeth to.
What shulde I spekë morë queynte,
Or peynë me my wordës peynte,
To speke of love ? hit wol not be ;
I can not of that faculté.
And eek to tellë the manere
How that they first aqueyntéd were,   250

Hit were a longe proces to telle,
And over long for you to dwelle.
  Ther saw I grave, how Eneas
Toldë Dido every cas,
That him tidde upon the see.
  And after gravë was, how she
Made of him, shortly, at a word,
Hir lyf, hir love, hir lust, hir lord ;
And dide him al the reverence,
And leyde on him al the dispence,   260
That any woman myghtë do,
Wényng hit hadde al be so,
As he hir swoor ; and hertly demedë
That he was good, for he swiche semedë.
  Allas, what harme doth apparence,
Whan hit is fals in existence !
For he to hir a traytour was ;
Wherfor she slow hir-self, allas !
  Lo, how a woman doth amys,
To love him that unknowën is !   270
For, by Cryst, lo ! thus it fareth ;
' Hit is not al gold that glareth.'
For, al-so brouke I wel myn heed,
Ther may be under goodliheed
Keverëd many a shrewëd vyce ;
Therfor be no wyght so nyce,
To take a love only for chere,
Or speche, or for frendly manere ;
For this shal every woman fynde,
That som man of his purë kynde   280
Wol shewën outward the faireste,
Til he have caught that what him
      leste ;
And thannë wol he causës fynde,
And swerën how she is unkynde,
Or fals, or prevy or double was.
Al this seye I be Eneás
And Dido, and hir nycë lest,
That lovëde al to sone a gest ;
Therfor I wol seye o proverbe,
That ' he that fully knoweth therbe   290
May saufly leye hit to his yë ' ;
Withoutë dreed, that is no lyë.
  But let us speke of Eneás,
How he betrayéde hir, allas !
And lefte hir ful unkyndély.

208. P *of hem savacon*; Cx. Th. *of her*
savacion.
226. *Achaté,* fidus Achates.
237. All read *he shulde his folk.*
244. F B *That that* for *Al that.*
250. F B *acqueyneden in fere.*

254. P *Tolde to.*
263. F B Th. *herby* for *hertly.*
271. P *For eny trust lo now*; Cx. *For every*
trust.
280-283. All omit except Th.

2 O

So whan she saw al-utterly,
That he wolde hir of trouthè faile,
And wendè fro hir to Itaile,
She gan to wringe hir hondès two.
'Allas!' quod she, 'what me is wo!   300
Allas! is every man thus trewe,
That every yeer wolde have a newe,
If hit so longè tymé dure?
Or ellès three, peraventure?
And thus, of oon he wolde have fame
In magnyfying of his name;
Another for frendship, seith he;
And yet ther shal the thriddè be,
That shal be taken for delyt,
Loo, or for syngular profit.'   310
   In swichè wordès gan to pleyne
Dido of hir gretè peyne,
As me mettè redèly;
Non other autour alegge I.
'Allas!' quod she, 'my swetè herte,
Have pitee of my sorwès smerte,
And slee me not! go noght awey!'
'O woful Dido, welaway!'
Quod she to hir selvè tho.
'O Eneás! what wil ye do!   320
O, that your lovè, ne your bonde,
That ye han sworn with your right honde,
Ne my cruel deeth,' quod she,
'May holdè you still heer with me!
O, haveth of my deeth pitee!
Y-wys, my derè hertè, ye
Knowen ful wel that never yit,
As fer-forth as I haddè wyt,
Agilte [I] you in thoght ne dede.
O men, have ye swich goodliheed   330
In speche, and never a deel of trouthe?
Allas, that ever haddè routhe
Any woman on any man!
Now see I wel, and tellè can,
We wrecched wymmen conne noon art;
For certeyn, for the morè parte,
Thus we be servèd everichone.
How sorè that ye men conne grone,
Anoon as we have you receyved,
Certeinly we ben deceyved;   340
For, though your love laste a sesoun,
Wayte upon the conclusioun,

305. F B *As thus.*
329. All omit *I.*
333. P Cx. Th. *a fals man.*

And eek how that ye détermynen,
And for the morè part diffynen.
'O, welawey that I was born!
For through you is my namè lorn,
And myn actès red and songe
Over al this londe, on every tonge.
O wikkè Famè! for ther nys
Nothyng so swift, lo, as she is!   350
O, sooth is, every thyng is wyst,
Though hit be keverèd with the myst.
Eek, thogh I myghte endurèn ever,
That I have doon rekever I never,
That I ne shal be seyd, allas,
Y-shamèd be through Enèas,
And that I shal thus jugèd be,—
"Lo, right as she hath doon, now she
Wol do eftsonès, hardily."
Thus seyth the peple prevèly.'   360
But that is doon nis not to done;
Al hir compleynt ne al hir mone,
Certeyn avayleth hir not a stre.
   And whan she wistè sothly he
Was forth unto his shippès goon,
She into hir chambre wente anoon,
And callèd on hir suster Anne,
And gan her to compleynè thanne;
And seydè, that she causè was,
That she first lovède him, alas,   370
And thus counseillèd hir therto.
But what! whan this was seyd and do,
She roof hir-selvè to the herte,
And deydè through the woundè smerte.
But al the maner how she deyde,
And al the wordès that she seyde,
Who-so to knowe hit hath purpos,
Rede Virgile in Enèidos,
Or the Epistle of Ovide,
What that she wroot or that she dide;
And nerè hit to long tendyte,   381
By God, I woldë hit here write.
   But, welaway! the harm, the routhe.
That hath betid for swich untrouthe,
As men may ofte in bokès rede,

347. F B *your* for *myn*; F B insert *al* before *myn.*
362. All read *But* before *Al,* caught from line above; P *compleynynge ne hir*; Cx. Th. *ne hir.*
370. All except Th. omit *him*; P Cx. *se hr first,* perhaps rightly.
381. B P Cx. *nerè it were*; F *nor hyt were.*

And al day seen hit yet in dede,
That for to thenken hit a tene is.
   Lo, Demophon, duk of Athenis,
How he forswor him ful falsly,
And trayèd Phillis wikkedly,   390
That kyngès doghter was of Trace,
And falsly gan his termè pace;
And when she wyste that he was fals,
She heng hir-selven by the hals,
For he hadde do hir swich untrouthe;
Loo! was not this a wo and routhe?
   Eek lo! how fals and recchèles
Was to Breseida Achillès,
And París to Enoné;
And Jason to Isiphilé;   400
And eft Jason to Medëá;
Ercúles to Dyanirá;
For he lefte hir for Iölé,
That made him cacche his deeth, pardé.
   How fals eek was he, Thesëus;
That, as the story telleth us,
How he betrayèd Adriáne;
The devel be his soulès bane!
For had he laughèd, had he loured,
He mostè have ben al devoured,   410
If Adriane ne haddè be.
And, for she hadde of him pitee,
She made him fro the deeth escape,
And he made hir a ful fals jape;
For after this, withyn a while,
He lefte hir slepyng in an ile,
Deserte alone, right in the se,
And stal away, and leet hir be;
And took hir suster Phedra tho
With him, and gan to shippè go.   420
And yet he hadde y-sworn to here,
On al that ever he myghtè swere,
That so she savède him his lyf,
He wolde have take hir to his wyf,
For she desirède nothing ellès,
In certeyn, as the book us tellès.
   But to excusen Eneás
Fulliche of his gretè trespas,

The book seyth Mercurie, sauns faile,
Bad him go into Itaile,   430
And leve Auffrikès regioun,
And Dido and hir fairè toun.
   Tho saw I grave how to Itaile
Daun Eneas is go to saile;
And how the tempest al began,
And how he loste his sterèsman,
Which that the stere, or he took keep,
Smot over bord, lo as he sleep.
   And also saw I how Sibyle
And Eneas, beside an yle,   440
To hellè wentèn, for to see
His fader Anchises the free,
How he ther fond Palínurus,
And also Dido, and Deiphebús,
And every torment eek in helle
Saw he, which is long to telle.
Which who-so willeth for to knowe,
He mostè redè many a rowe
On Virgile or on Claudian,
Or Dauntè, that hit tellè can.   450
   Tho saw I grave al tharivaile
That Eneas had in Itaile;
And with kyng Latyne his treté,
And alle the bataillès that he
Was at himself, and eek his knyghtès,
Or he hadde al y-wonne his rightès;
And how he Turnus refte his lyf,
And wan Lavyna to his wyf,
And al the mervelous signals
Of the goddès celestials;   460
How, mawgrè Juno, Eneás
For al hir sleighte and hir compas,
Achevèd al his aventure;
For Jupiter took of him cure,
At the prayere of Venús,—
The whiche I preye alway save us,
And us ay of our sorwès lighte!
   When I hadde seyèn al this sighte
In this noble temple thus,
'A, Lord!' thoughte I, 'that madest us,
Yet saw I never swich noblesse   471
Of ymages, ne swich richesse,

---

388. *Demophon* and the other false lovers
mentioned below are referred to in the *Heroides*,
Epistles ii. iii. v. vi. ix. x. xi.
398. *Breseida*, Briseis.
400. *Isiphilé*, Hypsipyle; cp. *L. of G. W.*
407. *Adriáne*, Ariadne.
428. Th. inserts *al* before *his*; F B *of al his trespas.*

429. *The book*, i.e. *Æn.* iv. 252 ff.
446. P Cx. *whyche no tonge can telle.*
449. *Claudian*, Claudius Claudianus wrote *De Raptu Proserpinæ* in the 4th century.
450. *Dauntè*, Dante in the *Inferno.*
453. *Latyne*, Latinus, king of the Rutuli.
458. *Lavyna*, Lavinia, daughter of Latinus.

As I saw gravèn in this chirche ;
But not woot I who dide hem wirche,
Ne wher I am, ne in what contree.
But now wol I go out and see,
Right at the wyket, yif I can
See o-wher any steryng man,
That may me tellé wher I am.'
   When I out of the dorès cam,   480
I faste aboutè me beholde.
Then sawgh I but a largé feld,
As fer as ever I myghté see,
Withouten toun, or hous, or tree,
Or bush, or gras, or erèd lond ;
For al the feld nas but of sonde,
As smal as man may see yet lye
In the desert of Lybye ;
Ne no maner crëature,

478. Th. *sterynge any.*

That is y-formèd by nature,   490
Ne saw I me to rede or wysse.
   'O Crist,' thoughte I, 'that art in blisse,
Fro fantom and illusioun
Me save !' and with devocioun
Myn ÿen to the heven I caste.
   Tho was I war lo ! at the laste,
That faste be the sonne, as hÿe
As kennè myghte I with myn ÿe,
Me thoughte I saw an egle sore,
But that hit semedè mochè more   500
Then I hadde any egle seyn.
But, this as sooth as deeth certeyn,
Hit was of gold, and shoon so bright,
That never saw men swich a sight,
But-if the heven hadde y-wonne
Al newe of gold another sonne ;
So shoon the eglès fethrès brighte,
And somwhat dounward gan hit lighte.

SECOND BOOK

(*Proem*)

Now herkneth every maner man,
That English understondè kan,
And listeth of my dreem to lere ;
For at the firstè shul ye here
So sely an avisyoun,
That Isayè ne Scipioun,
Ne kyng Nabugodonosor,
Pharo, Turnús, ne Elcanor,
Ne mettè swich a dreem as this.
Now fairè blisful, O Cipris,   10
So be my favour at this tyme !
And ye, me to endite and ryme
Helpeth, that on Parnaso dwelle,
By Elicon the clerè welle.
   O Thought, that wroot al that I mette,

4. F B Th. *For now at erste shal.*
6. *Isaye,* Isaiah. *Scipioun,* cp. *P. of Foules,*
l. 31 note.
7. *Nabugodonosor,* Nebuchadnezzar, a variant
of the *Vulgate* spelling Nabuchodonosor.
8. *Pharo,* Pharaoh. *Elcanor,* perhaps Elkanah
(*Vulgate* Elcana); cp. 1 Sam. i. 1.
10. *Cipris,* Venus; cp. *P. of Foules,* l. 277 note.
13. *Parnaso,* Parnassus.
14. *Elicon;* cp. *Anelida,* l. 17 note.
15. *Thought;* cp. *Inferno,* ii. 8 :—
      O mente, che scrivesti ciò ch' io vidi.
It here means memory.

And in the tresorie hit shette
Of my brayn ! now shal men se
If any vertu in thee be,
To tellén al my dreem aright ;
Now kythè thyn engyn and myght !   20

(*The Dream*)

   This egle of which I now have told,
That shoon with fethrès alle of gold,
Which that so hyè gan to sore,
I gan beholdè more and more,
To see her beautee and the wonder,
But never was ther dynt of thonder,—
Ne that thyng that men callé foudre,
That smyteth sone a tour to poudre,
And in his swiftè comyng brende,—
That so swythè gan descende,   30
As this foul when hit beholde,
That I a-roume was in the felde ;
And with his grymmè pawès stronge,
Withyn his sharpè naylès longe,
Me, fleynge, at a swappe he hente,
And with his sours a-geyn up wente,

20. P Th. insert *thy* before *myght.*
28. P Cx. Th. *smyte* for *smyteth*; F B *smote*
som tyme a toure of poudre.
30. P Cx. Th. insert *downward* after *gan.*

Me carying in his clawès starke,
As lightly as I were a larke,
How high, I cannot tellè yow,
For I cam up, I nystè how.   40
For so astonyèd and a-sweved
Was every vertu in my heved,
What with his sours and with my drede,
That al my felyng gan to dede ;
For why hit was to greet affray.
   Thus I long in his clawès lay,
Til at the laste he to me spak
In mannès vois, and seyde, ' Awak !
And be not so a-gaste, for shame ! '
And calledè me tho by my name.   50
And for I sholde the bet abreyde,
Me mette, ' Awak,' to me he seyde,
Right in the samè vois and stevene,
That useth oon I coudè nevene ;
And with that vois, soth for to seyne,
My myndè cam to me ageyn
For hit was goodly seyd to me,
So nas hit never wont to be.
   And herwithal I gan to stere,
And he me in his feet to bere,   60
Til that he felte that I hadde hete,
And felte eek tho myn hertè bete.
And tho gan he me to disporte,
And with wordès to comforte,
And saydè twyès, ' Seynte Marie !
Thou art noyous for to carie,
And nothyng nedith hit pardè
For, al-so wys God helpe me,
As thou noon harm shalt have of this ;
And this cas that betid thee is,   70
Is for thy lore and for thy prow,—
Let see ! darst thou yet lokè now ?
Be ful assurèd, boldèly,
I am thy frend.'   And therwith I
Gan for to wondren in my mynde.
' O God,' thoghte I, ' that madest kynde,
Shal I noon other weyès dye ?
Wher Joves wol me stellifye,
Or what thing may this signyfye ?
I neyther am Énok, ne Elýe,   80
Ne Romulus, ne Ganymede,
That was y-bore up, as men rede,

To hevene with daun Jupiter,
And made the goddès botèler.'
   Lo ! this was tho my fantasye !
But he that bar me gan espye
That I so thoghte, and seydè this :
' Thow demest of thy-self amys ;
For Jovès is not theraboute,—
I dar wel putte thee out of doute,—   90
To make of thee as yit a sterre.
But er I bere thee mochè ferre,
I wol thee tellè what I am,
And whider thou shalt, and why I cam
To donè this, so that thou take
Good herte, and not for ferè quake.'
' Gladly,' quod I. ' Now wel,' quod he :—
' First, I, that in my feet have thee,
Of which thou haste a feer and wonder,
Am dwellyng with the god of thonder,   100
Which that men callèn Jupiter,
That dooth me flee ful oftè fer
To do al his comaundèment.
And for this cause he hath me sent
To thee : now herkè, by thy trouthe !
Certeyn he hath of thee routhe,
That thou so longè trewèly
Hast servèd so ententifly
His blindè nevew Cupido,
Ánd fair [dame] Venús also,   110
Withoutè guerdoun ever yit,
And neverthelesse hast set thy wyt—
Although that in thy heed ful lyte is—
To makè bookès, songes, or dytees,
In ryme, or ellès in cadence,
As thou best canst in reverence
Of Love, and of his servants eke,
That have his servyse soght, and seke ;
And peynest thee to preyse his arte,
Although thou haddest never part ;   120
Wherfor, al-so God me blesse,
Jovès halt hit greet humblesse,
And vertu eek, that thou wolt make
A-nyght ful ofte thyn heed to ake,
In thy studie so thou writest,
And evermo of love enditest,
In honour of him and preisynges,
And in his folkès furtherynges,
And in hir matere al devysest,

49. Cx. Th. P *agast so*; F B omit *so*.
80. *Enok*, Enoch.
80. *Elýe*, Elias.

110. All omit *dame*. Skeat inserts *goddesse*
after *Venus*.
113. All read *lytel*.

565

And noght him nor his folk despisest,　130
Although thou maist go in the daunce
Of hem that him list not avaunce.
'Wherfor, as I seyde, y-wys,
Jupiter considereth wel this ;
And also, beau sir, other thynges ;
That is, that thou hast no tydynges
Of Lovès folk, if they be glade,
Ne of nothyng ellès that God made ;
And noght only fro fer contree,
That ther no tydyng cometh to thee,　140
But of thy verray neyghèbores
That dwellen almost at thy dores,
Thou herest neither that ne this ;
For when thy labour doon al is,
And hast y-maad thy rekenynges,
In stede of reste and newé thynges,
Thou gost hoom to thy hous anoon,
And, also domb as any stoon,
Thou sittest at another boke,
Til fully daswèd is thy looke,　150
And lyvest thus as an herèmyte,
Although thyn abstynence is lyte.
'And therfor Jovès, through his grace,
Wol that I bere thee to a place,
Which that hight the Hous of Fame,
To do thee som disport and game,
In som recompensacioun
Of labour and devocioun
That thou hast had, lo ! causéles,
To Cupido the recchèles.　160
And thus this god, through his merite,
Wol with som maner thyng thee quyte,
So that thou wolt be of good chere.
For trustè wel that thou shalt here,
When we be comèn ther I seye,
Mo wonder thyngès, dar I leye,
Of Lovès folkè mo tidynges,
Both sothè sawès and lesynges ;
And moo lovès newe begonne,
And longe y-servèd lovès wonne ;　170
And mo lovès casuellý
That been betid, no man wot why,
But " as a blynd man stert an hare " ;
And more jolytee and well-fare,
Whil that they fynden love of stele,
As thinketh hem, and over-al wele ;
Mo discords, and mo jelousýes,
Mo murmurs, and mo novelrýes,

134. F B omit *wel*.

And mo dissymulaciouns,
And feynèd reparaciouns ;　180
And mo berdès in two houres—
Withoutè rasour or sisoures—
Y-maad, then greynès be of sondes ;
And eek mo holdýng in hondes,
And also mo renovelaunces
Of olde forletèn aqueyntaunces ;
Mo lovè-dayès, and acordes,
Then on instruments ben cordes ;
And eek of lovès mo eschaunges,
Than ever cornès were in graunges ;　190
Unethè maistow trowen this ? "
Quod he. ' No, helpe me God so wys ! '
Quod I. ' No ? why ? ' quod he. ' For hit
Were impossible to my wyt,
Though that Fame hadde al the pies
In al a realme, and al the spies,
How that yet shè shulde here all this,
Or they espie hit.' ' O yis, yis ! '
Quod he to me, ' that can I preve
By resoun, worthy for to leve,　200
So that thou yeve thyn advertence
To understondè my sentence.
'First shalt thou herèn where she
　　dwelleth,
And so thyn ownè book hit telleth,
Hir paleys stant, as I shal seye
Right even a-myddès of the weye,
Betwixen hevene, erthe, and see ;
That whatsoever in al these three
Is spoken in privee or aperte,
The wey therto is so overte,　210
And stant eek in so juste a place,
That every soun mot to hit pace,
Or what so cometh fro any tonge,
Be hit rounèd, red, or songe,
Or spoke in suertee or in drede,
Certeyn hit mostè thider nede.
' Now herknè wel ; for-why I wille
Tellen thee a proprè skile,
And a worthy demonstracioun
In myn ymagynacioun.　220
' Geffrey, thou wost right wel this,

182. P inserts *any* before *rasour*.
187. P Cx. Th. insert *mo* before *acordes*, perhaps rightly.
192. Cx. Th. *So helpe.* P Cx. Th. *as* for *so*.
195. P Cx. Th. omit *that*.
219. F *worthe a ;* B *worth a.* Perhaps *worth a* is the true reading.
221. P Cx. Th. *wotest wel*.

That every kyndly thyng that is,
Hath a kyndly stede ther he
May best in hit conservèd be ;
Unto which place every thyng,
Through his kyndly enclynyng,
Moveth for to comèn to,
Whan that it is awey therfro ;
As thus, lo, thou maist al day see
That any thing that hevy be,   230
As stoon or leed, or thyng of wighte,
And ber hit never so hye on highte,
Lat go thyn hand, hit falleth doun.
   ' Right so seye I, by fire or soun,
Or smoke, or other thyngès lighte,
Alwey they seke upward on highte ;
Whil ech of hem is at his large,
Lyght thyng up, and dounward charge.
   ' And for this causè mayst thou see,
That every ryver to the see   240
Enclynèd is to go by kynde.
And by these skillès, as I fynde,
Hath fish dwellyng in floode and see,
And treès eek on erthè be.
Thus every thyng by this resoun
Hath his propre mansioun,
To which hit seketh to repaire,
Ther as hit shuldè not apaire.
Loo, this sentence is knowen couthe
Of every philosophrès mouthe,   250
As Aristotle and dan Platon,
And other clerkès many oon,
And to confirmè my resoun,
Thou wost wel this, that speche is soun,
Or ellès no ·man myghte hit here ;
Now herkne what I wol thee lere.
   ' Soun is noght but eyr y-broken,
And every spechè that is spoken,
Lowde or pryvee, foul or fair,
In his substaunce is but air ;   260
For as flaumbe is but lightèd smoke,
Right so soun is air y-broke.
But this may be in many wyse,
Of which I wil thee two devyse,
As soun that cometh of pipe or harpe.
For whan a pipe is blowèn sharpe,

The air is twyst with violence,
And rent : lo, this is my sentence ;
Eek, whan men harpè-stryngès smyte,
Whether hit be moche or lyte,   270
Lo, with the strook the air to-breketh ;
Right so hit breketh whan men speketh.
Thus wost thou wel what thyng is speche.
   ' Now hennèsforth I wol thee teche,
How every speche, or noise, or soun,
Through his multiplicacioun,
Thogh hit were pipèd of a mouse,
Moot nedès come to Famès House.
I preve hit thus—tak hedè now—
By experience ; for if that thou   280
Throwe in a water now a stoon,
Wel wost thou, hit wol make anoon
A litel roundel as a cercle,
Paraunter brood as a covercle ;
And right anoon thow shalt see weel,
That wheel wol cause another wheel,
And that the thridde, and so forth, brother,
Every cercle causyng other,
Broder than himselve was ;
And thus, fro roundel to compas,   290
Ech aboute other goynge,
Causèth of othrès sterynge,
And multiplying evermo,
Til that hit be so fer y-go
That hit at bothè brynkès be.
Al-thogh thou mowe hit not y-see
Above, hit goth yet alway under,
Although thou thenke hit a gret wonder.
And who-so seith of trouthe I varie,
Bid him provèn the contrarie.   300
And right thus every word, y-wys,
That loude or pryvee spoken is,
Moveth first an air aboute,
And of his movyng, out of doute,
Another air anoon is mevèd,
As I have of the water prevèd,
That every cercle causeth other.
Ryght so of air, my levè brother ;

237, 238. Cx. Th. invert these lines. Cx. Th.
Light thynges up; P *Light thynges upward;*
F B *upward* for *up.*
254. P Cx. Th. omit *this.*
260. P Cx. *an air.*
262. P Cx. Th. *is soun.*

284. P Cx. Th. insert *as* before *brood.*
285. P Cx. omit this and the next three lines ;
F B Th. insert *cercle* after *wheel,* to which it was
originally a gloss.
289. F B *Wyder than.*
292. F B *Caused.*
296. P Cx. Th. *see.*
297. F B omit *alway.*
303. P Cx. *in the air.*
304. F B *this* for *his.*

Everich air in other stereth
More and more, and speche up bereth   310
Or vois, or noise, or word, or soun,
Ay through multiplicacioun,
Til hit be atte House of Fame,—
Tak hit in ernest or in game.
    ' Now have I told, if thou have mynde,
How speche or soun, of puré kynde
Enclynéd is upward to meve ;
This, mayst thou felé, wel I preve.
And that same place, y-wys,
That every thyng enclyned to is,   320
Hath his kyndéliché stede :
That sheweth hit, withoutén drede,
That kyndély the mansioun
Of every speche, of every soun,
Be hit either foul or fair,
Hath his kyndé place in air.
And syn that every thyng that is
Out of his kyndé place, y-wys,
Moveth thider for to go,
If hit a-weyé be therfro,   330
As I before have prevéd thee,
Hit seweth, every soun, pardee,
Moveth kyndely to pace
Al up into his kyndely place.
And this place of which I telle,
Ther as Famé list to dwelle,
Is set amyddés of these three,
Heven, erthe, and eek the see,
As most conservatif the soun.
Than is this the conclusioun,   340
That every speche of every man,
As I thee tellé first began,
Moveth up on high to pace
Kyndély to Famés place.
    ' Tellé me this feithfully,
Have I not prevéd thus symply,
Withouten any subtilitee
Of speche, or gret prolixitee
Of termés of philosophýe,
Of figurés of poetrýe,   350
Or colours of rethorike ?
Pardee, hit oghté thee to lyke ;
For hard langage, and hard matére

Is encombrous for to here
Atonés ; wost thou not wel this ?'
And I answerde and seydé, ' Yis.'
    ' A ha !' quod he, ' lo, so I can,
Lewédly to a lewéd man
Speke, and shewe him swyché skiles,
That he may shake hem by the biles,   360
So palpable they shuldén be.
But tel me this now pray I thee,
How thinketh thee my conclusioun ?'
[Quod he,] ' A good persuasioun,'
Quod I, ' hit is ; and lyk to be
Right so as thou hast prevéd me.'
' By God,' quod he, ' and as I leve,
Thou shalt have yet, or hit be eve,
Of every word of this sentence
A prevé by experience ;   370
And with thyn erés herén wel
Top and tail, and everydel,
That every word that spokén is
Cometh into Famés House, y-wys,
As I have seyd ; what wilt thou more ?'
And with this word upper to sore
He gan, and seydé, ' By Seynt Jame !
Now wil we spekén al of game.
    ' How farest thou ?' quod he to me.
' Wel,' quod I.   ' Now see,' quod he,   380
' By thy trouthé, yond adoun,
Wher that thou knowest any toun,
Or hous, or any other thyng.
And whan thou hast of ought knowyng,
Loké that thou warné me,
And I anoon shal tellé thee
How fer thou art now therfro.'
    And I adoun gan lokén tho,
And beheld feldés,and playnes,
And now hilles, and now mountaynes,   390
Now valeys, and now forestes,
And now unethés greté bestes ;
Now ryvérés, now citees,
Now tounés, and now greté trees,
Now shippés seyllynge in the see.
    But thus sone in a while he
Was flowén fro the grounde so hÿe,
That al the world, as to myn ýe,
No more semedé than a prikke ;
Or elles was the air so thikke   400
That I ne myghté not discerne.

309. F B omit *in;* Willert reads *another* for *in other.*
319. F *And that sum place stide;* B *And that som styde;* Th. *And that some stede;* P Cx. omit ll. 827-864. *stede* is a gloss on *place,* which has crept into the text. *some* should be *same.*
364. All omit *Quod he;* Skeat inserts.
387. P omits *fer;* F B Th. insert *that* after *fer.*

With that he spak to me as yerne,
And seydè : 'Seestow any token,
Or ought that in the world is of spoken ?'
   I seydè, '⟨Nay.' 'No wonder nis,'
Quod he, 'for half so high as this
Nas Alexandre Macedo ;
Ne the kyng, dan Scipio,
That saw in dreme, at poynt devys,
Helle and erthe, and paradys ;   410
Ne eek the wrightè Dedalus,
Ne his child, nyce Icarus,
That fleigh so highè that the hete
His wyngès malt, and he fel wete
In-myd the see, and ther he dreynte,
For whom was maad a greet compleynte.
   'Now turn upward,' quod he, 'thy
         face,
And behold this largè place,
This eyr ; but lokè thou ne be
Adrad of hem that thou shalt see ;   420
For in this regioun, certeyn
Dwelleth many a citezeyn,
Of which that speketh dan Plato.
These ben the eyrysh bestès, lo !'
And tho saw I al that meynee,
Bothè goon and also flee.
'Now,' quod he tho, 'cast up thyn ẏe ;
See yonder, lo, the Galaxẏe,
The which men clepe the Milky Wey,
For hit is white : and somme, parfey   430
Callen hit Watlyngè strete,
That onès was brent wyth the hete,
Whan the sonnès sone, the rede,
That hightè Pheton, woldè lede
Algate his fader cart, and gye.
The cart-hors gonnè wel espye
That he [ne] coude no governaunce,
And gonnè for to lepe and daunce,
And berèn him now up, now doun,
Til that he saw the Scorpioun,   440
Which that in heven a sign is yit.
And he, for ferde, lost his wyt
Of that, and lat the reynès goon
Of his hors ; and they anoon

Gonne up to mounte, and doun descende,
Til bothe eyr and erthè brende ;
Til Jupiter, lo, atte laste
Him slow, and fro the cartè caste.
Lo, is it not a greet myschaunce,
To lete a fole han governaunce   450
Of thynges that he can not demeyne ?'
   And with this word, soth for to
         seyne,
He gan alwey upper to sore,
And gladded me ay more and more,
So feithfully to me spak he.
Tho gan I loken under me,
And behelde the eyrish bestes,
Cloudès, mystès, and tempestes,
Snowès, haylès, reynès, wyndes,
And thengendryng in hir kyndes,   460
Al the wey through which I cam ;
'O God,' quod I, 'that made Adam,
Moche is thy myght and thy noblesse.'
   And tho thoughte I upon Boëce,
That writ 'A thought may flee so hye,
With fetherès of Philosophye,
To passen everich element ;
And whan he hath so fer y-went,
Than may be seen, behynd his bak,
Cloud, and al that I of spak.'   470
Tho gan I wexen in a were,
And seyde, 'I woot wel I am here ;
But wher in body or in gost
I noot y-wys ; but God, thou wost !'
For morè clere entendèment
Nadde he me never yit y-sent.
And than thoughte I on Marcian,
And eek on Anteclaudian,
That sooth was hir descripcioun
Of al the hevenès regioun,   480
As fer as that I saw the preve ;
Therfor I can hem now beleve.
   With that this egle gan to crye :
'Lat be,' quod he, 'thy fantasye ;

449. F B *mochil.*
464. *Boece,* cp. Boethius, *De Consolatione
Philosophiæ,* bk. iv. met. i.
476. F B *Nas never ;* Th. *Nas me never.*
477. *Marcian,* Martianus Mineus Felix
Capella, the 8th book, l. 857, of whose *De
Nuptiis inter Mercurium et Philologiam* is
quoted by Copernicus in support of his system of
astronomy ; cp. also *March. Tale,* l. 1732 ff.
478. *Anteclaudian,* 'Anticlaudianus,' a Latin
poem by Alanus de Insulis ; cp. *P. of F.* l. 316.
480. P omits this line.

403, 404. F B omit. P reads, l. 404, *Or ought
thow knowest yonder down ;* Th. *this* for *the.*
408. *Scipio,* cp. *Parl. of Foules,* l. 31 note.
411. F B *wrecche Dedalus.*
416. F B *maked moch compleynte.*
427. P Cx. Th. *Lo, quod he, cast.*
437. All omit *ne.*

Wilt thou lere of sterrès aught?'
'Nay, certeynly,' quod I, 'right naught.'
'And why?' 'For I am now to old.'
'Ellès wolde I thee have told,'
Quod he, 'the sterrès namès, lo,
And al the hevenès signes ther to,   490
And which they been.' 'No fors,' quod
     I.
'Yis, pardee,' quod he, 'wostow why?
For whan thou redest poetrye,
How goddès gonnè stellifye
Brid, fish, beste, or him, or here,
As the Raven or eyther Bere,
Or Arionès harpè fyn,
Castor, Pollux, or Delphyn,
Or Atlantès doughtrès sevene,
How allè these are set in hevene;   500
For though thou have hem ofte on
     honde,
Yet nostow not wher that they stonde.'
'No fors,' quod I, 'hit is no nede,
As wel I leve, so God me spede,
Hem that write of this matere,
As though I knew hir places here;
An eke they shynen here so brighte
Hit shuldè shenden al my sighte,
To loke on hem.' 'That may wel be,'
Quod he. And so forth bar he me   510
A whil, and than he gan to crye,
That never herde I thyng so hye,
'Now up the heed; for al is wel;
Seynt Julyan, lo, bon hostel!
See here the Hous of Famè, lo!
Maistow not herèn that I do?'
'What?' quod I. 'The gretè soun,'
Quod he, 'that rumbleth up and doun
In Famès Hous, ful of tidynges,
Bothe of fair speche and chidynges,   520
And of fals and soth compouned.
Herkne wel; hit is not rouned.
Herestow not the gretè swogh?'
'Yis, pardee,' quod I, 'wel y-nogh.'
'And what soun is it lyk?' quod he.
'Peter! betyng of the see,'

Quod I, 'again the rochès holowe,
Whan tempest doth the shippès swalowe,
And lat a man stonde, out of doute,
A mylè thens, and here hit route.   530
Or ellès lyke the last humblynge
After the clappe of a thundrynge.
When Iovès hath the air y-bete;
But hit doth me for ferè swete.
'Nay, dred thee not therof,' quod he,
'Hit is nothyng wil beten thee,
Thou shalt non harm have trewèly.'
And with this word bothe he and I
As nygh the place arryvèd were
As men may casten with a spere.   540
I nystè how, but in a strete
He settè me faire on my fete,
And seydè, 'Walkè forth a pas,
And tak thyn aventure or cas,
That thou shalt fyndè in Famès place.'
'Now,' quod I, 'whil we han space
To speke, or that I go fro thee,
For the love of God, tel me,
In sooth, that wil I of thee lere,
If this noisè that I here   550
Be, as I have herd thee tellen,
Of folk that doun in erthè dwellen,
And cometh here in the samè wyse
As I thee herde or this devyse;
And that there lyvès body nys
In al that hous that yonder is,
That maketh al this loudè fare?'
'No,' quod he, 'by Seyntè Clare!
And, also wis God redè me,
But o thinge I wil warnè thee,   560
Of the which thou wolt have wonder.
Lo, to the House of Famè yonder,
Thou wost now how cometh every
     speche,
Hit nedeth noght eft thee to teche.
But understond now right wel this,
Whan any speche y-comen is
Up to the paleys, anon-right
Hit wexeth lyk the samè wyght,
Which that the word in erthè spak,
Be he clothèd reed or blak;   570

496. *eyther Bere*, Ursa Major and Ursa Minor.
497. *Arionès harpe*, cp. *Fasti*, ii. 82.
498. *Delphyn*, the dolphin.
499. *Atlantes doughtres*, the Pleiades.
514. *Seynt Julyan*, St. Julian, patron of hospitality; cp. *C.T.* Prol. l. 340.
520. P Cx. Th. *and of other thynges.*

536. Th. B *biten*; Cx. *greue.*
549. P Cx. Th. *I euil.*
552. P Cx. *forth* for *doun.*
558. *Seyntè Clare*, a disciple of St. Francis, whose day is Aug. 12th.

And hath so verray his lyknesse,　571
That spak the word, that thou wilt gesse
That it the same body be,
Man or woman, he or she.
And is not this a wonder thyng?'
'Yis,' quod I tho, 'by hevené kyng!'

576. P *hevenes*.

And with this worde, 'Farewel,' quod
　　he,
'And here I wol abyden thee,
And God of hevené sende thee grace,
Som good to lernén in this place.'　580
And I of him took leve anoon,
And gan forth to the paleys goon.

THIRD BOOK

(*The Invocation*)

O GOD of science and of light,
Apollo, through thy greté myght,
This lytel lasté book thou gye!
Nat that I wilné, for maistrýe
Here art poetical be shewed;
But, for the rym is light and lewed,
Yit make hit sumwhat agreable,
Thogh som vers faile in a sillable;
And that I do no diligence,
To shewé craft, but o sentence.　10
And if, divyné vertu, thou
Wilt helpé me to shewé now
That in myn hede y-markéd is,—
Lo, that is for to menén this,
The Hous of Fame for to descryve,—
Thou shalt see me go as blyve
Unto the nexté laure I see,
And kisse it, for hit is thy tree.
Now entreth in my breste anoon!

(*The Dream*)

Whan I was fro this egle goon,　20
I gan beholde upon this place.
And certein, or I ferther pace,
I wol yow al thys shap devyse
Of hous and site; and al the wyse
How I gan to this place aproche,
That stood upon so high a roche,
Hyer stant there noon in Spayne.
But up I clomb with allé payne,
And though to clymbe it grevedé me,
Yit I ententif was to see,　30
And for to pouren wonder lowe,
If I coude any weyés know

6. P Cx. *But the ryme that is so lewd*.
10. P Cx. omit *o*.

What maner stoon this roché was;
For hit was lyk alynéd glas,
But that hit shoon ful moré clere;
But of what congeléd matere
Hit was, I nysté redély.
　But at the laste espiéd I,
And found that hit was everydeel
A roche of yse, and not of steel.　40
Thoughte I, 'By Seynt Thomas of Kent!
This were a feble foundément,
To bilden on a placé hye;
He oughte him litel glorifýe
That her-on bilt, so God me save!'
　Tho saw I al the half y-grave
With famous folkés namés fele,
That hadde y-been in mochel wele,
And her famés wide y-blowe.
But wel unethés coude I knowe　50
Any lettrés for to rede
Hir namés by; for, out of drede,
They were almost of-thowéd so,
That of the lettrés oon or two
Were molte away of every name.
So unfamous was wexe hir fame;
But men seyn, 'What may ever laste?'
　Tho gan I in myn herté caste,
That they were molte awey with hete,
And not awey with stormés bete.　60
For on that other syde I sey
Of this hill, that northward lay,
How hit was written full of names
Of folk that haddén greté fames
Of oldé tyme, and yit they were

34. P *alymde*; Cx. Th. *a lymed*; F B *a thyng of*. I read *alyned* (=aligned, *i.e.* placed in lines).
35. P *shewen mor*; Cx. *shewed more*.
41. *Seynt Thomas*, Thomas à Becket.
53. P Cx. *ouerthowed*.
64. P *hedd after*; Cx. Th. *had afore*.

As fresshe as men had write hem here
The selvé day right, or that houre
That I upon hem gan to poure.
But wel I wisté what hit made;
Hit was conservéd with the shade,   70
Of a castel stood on hy,
Al the writynge that I sy;
And stood eek on so cold a place,
That heté myghte it not deface.
   Tho gan I up the hill to goon,
And fond upon the coppe a woon,
That alle the men that ben on lyve
Ne han the cunnyng to descryve
The beautee of that ilke place,
Ne coudé casten no compace   80
Swich another for to make,
That myghte of beautee be his make;
Ne so wonderliche y-wrought,
That hit astonyeth yit my thought,
And maketh al my wyt to swynke
On this castel for to thynke.
So that the greté craft, beautee,
The caste, the curiositee
Ne can I not to yow devyse,
My wyt ne may me not suffise.   90
   But nathéles al the substance
I have yit in my remembrance;
For-why me thoughté, by Seynt Geyle!
Al was of stone of beryle,
Bothe the castel and the tour,
And eek the halle, and every bour,
Wythouten pecés or ioynynges.
But many subtil compassynges,
Babéwynnés and pynacles,
Imageries and tabernacles,   100
I saw eek, and ful of wyndowes,
As flakés falle in greté snowes.
And eek in ech of the pynacles
Werén sondry habitacles,
In whiché stodén al withoute—
Ful the castel, al aboute—
Of allé maner of mynstrales,

And gestiours, that tellén tales
Bothe of weping and of game,
Of al that longeth unto Fame.   110
   Ther herde I pleyén on an harpe
That sownéd bothé wel and sharpe,
Orpheus ful craftély,
And on his sydé fasté by
Sat the harper Orion
And Eacidés Chiron,
And other harpers many oon.
And the Bret Glascurioun,
And smalé harpers with her gleés,
Seten under hem in seés,   120
And gonne on hem upward to gape,
And countrefet hem as an ape,
Or as craft countrefeteth kynde.
   Tho saw I stonden hem behynde,
A-fer fro hem, alle be hemselve,
Many thousand tymés twelve,
That madén loudé menstralcyes
In cornémusé, and shalmyes,
And many other maner pipe,
That craftély begunne to pipe,   130
Bothe in doucet and in rede,
That ben at festés with the brede,
And many floute and liltyng horne,
And pipés made of grené corne,
As han thise litel herde-gromes,
That kepén bestés in the bromes.
   Ther saw I than dan Cytherus,
And of Athenes dan Proserus,
And Marcia that lost hir skyn,
Bothe in face, bodý, and chyn,   140

112. P Cx. Th. omit *bothe*.
113. P inserts *And*, Cx. Th. insert *Hym* before *Orpheus*. Perhaps the original copy read *Dan Orpheus*, and the first word had become illegible.
115. *Orion*, Arion; cp. bk. ii. l. 497.
116. *Eacides Chiron*, i.e. Achilles' Chiron: Chiron, the centaur, was tutor to Achilles, son of Æacus; cp. Ovid, *Ars Am.* i. 17, *Æacidæ Chiron*.
118. *Bret Glascurioun*, the British Glasgerion; cp. Percy Folio MS. ed. Hales and Furnivall, i. 246.
128. *cornemuse*, a bagpipe. *shalmye*, a shawm, from Lat. 'calamus,' a reed.
137. F B invert this and the next line.
137. F B *Atiteris* for *dan Cytherus*, both perhaps corruptions for *dan Tityrus*.
138. F B *dan Pseustis*; P *dan presentus*. All three readings are corrupt.
139. *Marcia*, Dante's Marsia (*Parad.* i. 13-27), i.e. Marsyas the male flute-player; cp. *Metamorphoses*, vi. 382-400.

71. F B Th. invert the order of this and the next line. P Cx. Th. insert *that so* before *stood*; B inserts *that*.
87. F B omit *craft*; P Cx. Th. insert it wrongly in the next line.
99. F *Rabewyures*; B *Rabewynnes*; Cx. As *babewuryes*; Th. As *babeuries*; P *Babeweuries*. Skeat rightly reads *Babewinnes* (O. F. *babuin*, L. Lat. *babewynnus*, Mod. Engl. *baboon*); used of grotesque figures in architecture.

For that she wolde envýen lo !
To pipen bet than Apollö.

There saw I famous, olde and yonge,
Pipers of the Duchè tonge,
To lernè lovè-dauncès, sprynges,
Reyès, and these straungè thynges.

Tho saw I in another place,
Stondèn in a largè space
Of hem that makèn blody soun,
In trumpè, beme, and clarioun ; 150
For in fight and blod-shedynge
Is usèd gladly clarionynge.

Ther herde I trumpèn Messenus,
Of whom that speketh Virgilius.

Ther herde I Joab trumpe also,
Theodomas, and other mo ;
And al that usède clarion,
In Cataloigne and Aragon,
That in hir tymè famous were
To lernè, saw I trumpè there. 160

Ther saw I sit in other seès,
Pleyinge upon otherè gleès,
Whichè that I cannot nevene,
Mo than sterrès been in hevene,
Of whiche I nyl as now not ryme,
For ese of yow, and losse of tyme :
For tyme y-lost, this knowèn ye,
By no way may recoverèd be.

Ther saw I pleyèn jogelours,
Magiciens, and tregetours, 170
And phitonesses, charmeresses,
Oldè wycches, sorceresses,
That use exorsisaciouns,
And eek thise fumygaciouns ;
And clerkès eek, which connè wel
Al this magik naturel,

That craftèly don hir ententes,
To make, in certeyn ascendentes,
Imagès, lo, through swych magik,
To make a man ben hool or syk. 180
Ther saw I thee quene Medeá,
And Circès eek, and Calipsa ;
Ther saw I Hermes Ballenus,
Lymote, and eek Symon Magus.
Ther saw I, and knew hem by name,
That by such art don men han fame.
Ther saw I Colle tregetour
Upon a table of sicamour
Pleye an uncouth thyng to telle ;
I saw him carien a wynd-melle 190
Under a walsh-notè shale.

What shulde I makè lenger tale
Of al the peple that I say,
Fro hennès unto domèsday?

Whan I hadde al this folk beholde,
And fond me lous, and noght y-holde,
And eft y-musèd longè while
Upon these wallès of berile,
That shoon ful lighter than a glas,
And made wel morè than hit was, 200
To semèn, every thynge, y-wis,
As kyndè thyng of Famès is ;
I gan forth romen til I fond
The castel-yate on my right hond,
Which that so wel corvèn was,
That never swich another nas ;
And yit it was by aventure
Y-wrought, as often as by cure.

---

146. *Reyes*, round dances, from Dut. 'rey'; cp.
Ger. ' Reihentanz,' a circular dance.

150. *beme*, a horn, trumpet.

153. *Messenus*, Misenus, son of Æolus, trum-
peter first to Hector and then to Æneas ; cp. *Æn.*
iii. 239 and vi. 162 ff.

155. *Joab*, cp. 2 Sam. ii. 28 ; xviii. 16 ; xx. 22.

156. *Theodomas*, Thiodamas, augur in succes-
sion to Amphiaraus at the siege of Thebes ; cp.
Statius, *Thebaid* viii. 343, and *March. Tale*, l.
1720 ff.

162. F B *sondry* for *othere*; Th. *other sondry*.

169. *jogelours* played, sang, danced, and performed tricks by sleight of hand.

170. *tregetours* performed more elaborate tricks
requiring mechanical contrivances.

171. *phitonesses*, pythonesses; cp. *Freres Tale*,
l. 1510.

174. P omit this line.

178. *ascendentes*. The ascendent is that point
of the zodiac ascending above the horizon at a
given time. It was a factor of great importance
in calculating nativities.

181. *Medeá*, the wife of Jason.

182. *Circes*, Circe ; cp. *Odyssey* x. *Calipsa*,
Calypso ; cp. *Odyssey* i.

183. *Hermes Ballenus*. Belinous, the disciple
of Hermes. Belinous discovered beneath a statue
of Hermes a book explaining the secrets of the
universe. *Hermes* is here in the possessive case.

184. *Lymote*, Elymas the sorcerer (Acts xiii. 8),
according to Prof. Hale's. *Symon Magus;* cp.
Acts viii. 9.

187. *Colle tregetour*, Colle the juggler, a now
unknown celebrity.

194. Cx. Th. *I coud not telle tyl domesday*.

197. P *lengur a whyle*, perhaps rightly ; Cx. *a
lenger whyle*.

201. P omits this line ; Cx. Th. also omit but
insert the line *And thenne anon after this* after
l. 202.

208. Cx. Th. *Ywrought by grete and subtyl
cure*.

Hit nedeth noght yow for to tellen,
To makė yow to lenger duellen,   210
Of this yatės florisshynges,
Ne of compassės, ne of kervynges,
Ne how they hatte in masoneries,
As corbets, ful of ymageriės.
But, Lord! so fair it was to shewe
For hit was al of gold behewe.
But in I wente, and that anoon;
Ther mette I crying many oon,—
'A largės, largės! uphold wel!
God save the lady of this pel,   220
Our ownė gentil lady Fame,
And hem that wilne to have a name
Of us!'   Thus herde I criėn alle,
And fastė comėn out of halle,
And shokėn noblės and sterlynges.
And sommė crounėd were as kynges,
With crounės wroght ful of losenges;
And many riban, and many frenges
Were on hir clothes trewėly.

Tho attė laste aspyėd I   230
That pursėvauntės and heraudes,
That crien richė folkės laudes,
Hit weren alle; and every man
Of hem, as I yow tellėn can,
Hadde on him throwėn a vesture,
Which that men clepe a cote-armure,
Enbrowdėd wonderlichė riche,
Al-though they nerė nought y-liche.
But noght nyl I, so mote I thryve,
Been aboutė to dyscryve   240
Al this armės that ther weren,
That they thus on hir cotės beren,
For hit to me were impossible;
Men mȳghte make of hem a bible,
Twenty foot thikke, as I trowe.
For certeyn, who-so coude y-knowe
Myghte ther allė the armės seen,
Of famous folk that haddė been
In Auffrike, Europe, and Asýe,
Sith first began the chevalrýe.   250
Lo! how shulde I now telle al this?

Ne of the halle eek what nede is
To tellėn yow that every wal
Of hit, and floor, and roof wyth al,
Was plated half a fotė thikke
Of gold, and that nas no thyng wikke,
But, for to prove in allė wyse,
As fyn as ducat of Venyse,
Of whiche to litel in my pouche is?
And they were set as thikke of nouchis
Fulle of the fynest stonės faire,   261
That men rede in the Lapidaire,
As gresės growėn in a mede.
But hit were al to longe to rede
The namės; and therfore I pace.

But in this rychė lusty place,
That Famės hallė callėd was,
Ful mochė prees of folke ther nas,
Ne croudyng, for to mochė prees.
But al on hye, upon a dees,   270
Sitte in a see imperial,
That maad was of a rubee al,
Which that a carbuncle is y-called,
I saw perpetually y-stalled,
A femynynė crëature;
That never formėd by nature
Nas swich another thyng y-seye.
For altherfirst, soth for to seye,
Me thoughtė that she was so lyte,
That the lengthe of a cubite   280
Was lenger than she semedė be;
But thus sone in a whilė she
Hir-self tho wonderlichė streighte,
That with hir feet she therthė reighte,
And with hir heed she touchėde hevene,
Ther as shyne the sterrės sevene.
And therto eek, as to my wyt,
I saw as gret a wonder yit,
Upon hir eyėn to beholde,
But certeyn I hem never tolde.   290

259. P Th. *to lite al in;* Cx. *to lyte in;* F *to litel al.*
260. P Cx. *as owches.*
271. P Cx. *on* for *in.*
272. P omits *al;* Cx. Th. *Ryal (royal)* for *al.*
277. P Cx. omit *Nas;* Th. *Was.*
283. F B *This was gret marvaylle to me.*
284. F *Hir tho so wonderly streight;* B *Hir tho so wondirlich streyght;* P Cx. Th. *wonderly* for *wonderliche.* The original of F B probably read:—

    This was gret marvayile to me, she
    Hir tho so wonderliche streighte,

which is perhaps the right reading.

213. P Cx. Th. *how the hackynge in.*
214. P Cx. Th. *and* for *ful of.*
219. F B Th. *holde up;* P Cx. Th. repeat *a* before second *larges.*
227. P Cx. *full of lesynges.*
228. P *and moy thynges;* Cx. *and many thynges.*
250. P Cx. Th. *lo* for *begnn the.*

For as fele eyén haddé she,
As fetherés upon foulés be,
Or werén on the bestés foure,
That goddés troné gunne honoure,
As writ John in the Apocalips.
Hir heer that oundy was and crips,
As burnéd gold shoon for to see.
And sooth to tellén also, she
Had also fele up-stondyng eres
And tonges, as on a best ben heres ;   300
And on hir feet wexen saw I
Partrichés wingés redély.

    But, lord ! the perrie and the richesse
I saw sittyng on this godesse !
And, lord ! the hevenysh melodye,
Of songés ful of armonye,
I herde aboute her trone y-songe,
That al the paleys-wallés ronge !
So song the myghty Musé, she
That clepéd is Caliopee,   310
And hir eighté sustrén eek
That in her facé semén meke ;
And evermo, eternally
They synge of Fame as tho herde I :—
' Heriéd be thou and thy name,
Goddesse of renoun and of fame.'

    Tho was I war, lo, atté laste,
As I myn eyén gan up caste,
That this ilké noblé quene
On hir shuldrés gan sustene   320
Bothé tharmés, and the name
Of tho that haddé largé fame ;
Alexander, and Hercules
That with a sherté his lyf lees !
Thus fond I sittyng this goddesse,
In nobley honour and richesse ;
Of which I stynte a whilé now,
Other thyng to tellén yow.

    Tho saw I stonde on either syde,
Streight doun to the dorés wyde,   330
Fro the dees many a pileer
Of metal, that shoon not ful cleer,
But though they nere of no rychesse,
Yet they were maad for greet noblesse,

And in hem hy and greet sentence ;
And folk of digné reverence,
Of whiche I wol yow tellé fonde,
Upon the piler saw I stonde.

    Alderfirst, lo, ther I sigh,
Upon a piler stonde on high,   340
That was of lede and yren fyn,
Him of secté Saturnyn,
The Ebräyk Josephus the olde,
That of Jewés gestés tolde ;
And bar upon his shuldrés hye,
The fame up of the Iewérye.
And by him stoden other sevene,
Wyse and werthy for to nevene,
To helpen him bere up the charge,
Hit was so hevy and so large.   350
And for they writen of batailes,
As wel as of theré mervailes,
Therfor was, lo, this pileer,
Of which that I yow telle heer,
Of lede and yren bothe, y-wys.
For yren Martés metal is,
Which that god is of bataile ;
And the leed, withouten faile,
Is, lo, the metal of Saturne,
That hath ful largé wheel to turne.   360
Tho stoden forth on every rowe
Of hem which that I coudé knowe,
Thogh I hem noght be ordré telle,
To maké you to long to dwelle.

    These, of whiche I gynné rede,
There saw I stonden, out of drede :
Upon an yren piler strong,
That peyntéd was, al endélong,
With tigrés blode in every place,
The Tholosan that highté Stace,   370
That bar of Thebés up the name
Upon his shuldrés, and the fame

335. All omit *hy and*, which, however, Th. wrongly inserts in the next line ; P and Cx. alter *hy and* in l. 336 into *gret and* by contamination with the previous line.
342. P omits this line ; Cx. *Hym that wrote thactes dyuyne.*
347. P Cx. *ther stoden sevene.*
352. F B *as other olde mervayles.*
367. P omits this line ; Cx. *a pyler hye and stronge.*
369. *tigres blode ;* cp. *Thebaid,* bk. vii. The killing of two lions by the besiegers caused a renewal of the siege.
370. *The Tholosan . . . Stace.* According to Dante, Statius was a native of Toulouse. He was born at Naples A.D. 61.

297. P Cx. insert *as* before *for;* F B Th. *hit shoon to see.*
300. F B *as on bestes heres.*
321. F B P Cx. *Both (Bothe) armes.*
325. All read *And thus.*
329. P Cx. Th. *on thother.*

Also of cruel Achillés.
And by him stood, withoutén lees,
Ful wonder hye on a pileer
Of yren, he, the greete Omere ;
And with him Dares and Tytus
Before, and eek he, Lollius,
And Guydo eek de Columpnis,
And English Gaufride eek, y-wys.   380
And ech of these, as have I joye,
Was besy for to bere up Troye.
So hevy was therof the fame,
That for to bere hit was no game.
But yit I gan ful wel espie,
Betwix hem was a litel envye.
Oon seyde that Omere madé lyes,
Feynynge in his poetries,
And was to Grekés favorable ;
Therfor held he hit but fable.   390

Tho saw I stonde on a pileer,
That was of tynnéd yren cleer,
Thát Latyn poete Virgile,
That hath boren up longé while
The fame of Pius Eneas.

And next him on a piler was,
Of coper, Venus clerk, Ovyde,
That hath y-sowen wonder wyde
The greté god of Love his fame.
And ther he bar up wel his name,   400
Upon this piler, also hye,
As I hit myghte see with myn ye :
For-why this halle of whiche I rede
Was woxe on highte, lengthe and brede,
Wel moré, by a thousand dele,
Than hit was erst, that saw I wel.

Thoo saw I on a piler by,
Of yren wroght ful sternély,

The greté poete, dan Lucan,
And on his shuldrés bar up than,   410
As highe as that I myghté see,
The fame of Julius, and Pompee.
And by him stodén alle these clerkes,
That write of Romés myghty werkes,
That if I wolde her namés telle,
Alle to longé moste I dwelle.

And next him on a piler stood,
Of soulfre, lyk as he were wood,
Dan Claudian, soth for to telle,
That bar up al the fame of helle,   420
Of Pluto, and of Proserpyne,
That quene is of the derké pyne.

What shulde I moré telle of this ?
The hallé was al ful, y-wys,
Of hem that writen oldé gestes,
As ben on treés rokés nestes ;
But it is a ful confus matere
Were al the gestés for to here,
That they of write, and how they highte.
But whil that I beheld this sighte,   430
I herde a noise aprochén blyve,
That ferde as been don in an hyve,
Ayenst her tyme of out-comynge ;
Right swiche a maner murmurynge,
For al the world hit semedé me.

Tho gan I loke aboute and see,
That ther com entryng into the halle,
A right greet company withalle,
And that of sondry regiouns,
Of allé kynnes condiciouns,   440
That dwelle in erthe under the mone,
Pore and riche.   And also sone
As they were come into the halle,
They gonné doun on kneés falle,
Before this ilké noble quene,
And seydé, ' Graunte us, lady shene,
Eche of us, of thy grace, a bone ! '
And somme of hem she grauntéde sone,
And somme she wernedé wel and faire ;

377. *Dares and Tytus*, Dares Phrygius and Dictys Cretensis, the reputed authors of two late histories of the Trojan War.
378. *Lollius*, probably a misunderstanding on Chaucer's part of Horace, *Epist.* i. 2 :—
   ' Troiani belli scriptorem, maxime Lolli,
    Dum tu declamas Romæ, Prænestæ relegi.'
379. *Guydo . . . de Columpnis*, Guido delle Colonne, whose *Historia Troiana* (1287) is a translation of Benoît de Sainte-Maure's *Roman de Trois*. The M.E. *Geste Hystoriale* (E. E. T. S.) is a translation of the *Historia*.
380. *English Gaufride*, Geoffrey of Monmouth, author of the *Historia Britonum*.
387. So Th. ; F B omit *that* and read *was* for *made*; Cx. P read *Other* for *Oon*.
394. F B *bore hath up longe*; P Cx. Th. *hath bore up a longe*.

409. *Lucan*, author of the *Pharsalia*, which describes the war between Cæsar and Pompey.
419. *Claudian*; cp. *supra*, bk. i. l. 449 note.
427. P Cx. invert this and the next line.
433. F B *out-fleyinge*.
440. F *alle skynnes*; B *all skynys*; Cx. *alle kyns*; Th. *al kyns*.
444. P. *They gonne wy on knees doun falle*, which is probably a corruption of the true reading; perhaps *They gonne ny on knees doun falle*; Cx. Th. *They gonne (gan) on knees doun falle*.

And somme she grauntéde the contraire 450
Of her axyng utterly.
But this I seye yow trewély,
What hir causé was, I nyste.
For of this folk ful wel I wyste,
They haddé good fame ech deservéd,
Althogh they were diversly servéd.
Right as hir suster, dame Fortune,
Is wont to servén in comune.
  Now herkné how she gan to paye
That gonne hir of hir grácé praye ; 460
And yit lo, al this companye
Seyden sooth, and noght a lye.
  ' Madame,' seyden they, ' we be
Folk that heer besechen thee,
That thou graunte us now good fame,
And let our werkés han that name.
In ful recompensacioun
Of goodé werkes, yive us renoun.'
  ' I werne hit yow,' quod she, anoon,
' Ye gete of me good famé noon, 470
By god ! and therfor go your wey.'
  ' Allas,' quod they, ' and welaway !
Telle us what your cause may be.'
  ' For me list hit noght,' quod she,
' No wyght shal speke of yow, y-wys,
Good ne harm, ne that ne this.'
And with that word she gan to calle
Her messanger that was in halle,
And bad that he shulde fasté goon,
Upon peyne to be blynde anoon, 480
For Eolus, the god of wynde,
' In Tracé ther ye shul him finde,
And bid him bringe his clarioun,
That is ful dyvers of his soun,
And hit is clepéd Clere Laude,
With which he wonte is to heraude
Hem that me list y-preised be :
And also bid him how that he
Brynge his other clarioun,
That highté Sclaundre in every toun, 490

With which he wont is to diffame
Hem that me liste, and do hem shame.'
  This messanger gan fasté goon,
And found wher in a cave of stoon,
In a contree that highté Trace,
This Eolus, with hardé grace,
Held the wyndés in distresse,
And gan hem under him to presse,
That they gonne as berés rore,
He bond and pressédé hem so sore. 500
  This messanger gan fasté crie,
' Ris up,' quod he, ' and fasté hye,
Til thou at my lady be ;
And tak thy clarioun eek with thee,
And speed thee fast.' And he anon
Took to a man that hight Triton,
His clariouns to beré tho,
And leet a certeyn wynd to go,
And blew so hidously and hye,
That hit ne lefté not a skye 510
In al the welken longe and brood.
  This Eolus no-wher abood,
Til he was come at Famés feet,
And eek the man that Triton heet;
And ther he stood as still as stoon.
And her-withal ther com anoon
Another hugé companye
Of oldé folk and gunné crie,
' Lady, graunte us now good fame
And lat our werkés han that name, 520
Now in honour of gentilesse,
And also God your soulé blesse !
For we han wel deservéd hit,
Therfor is right that we ben quyt.'
  ' As thryve I,' quod she, ' ye shal failc,
Good werkés shal yow noght availe
To have of me good fame as now.
But wite ye what ? I graunté yow,
That ye shal have a shrewéd name,
And wikkéd loos and worsé fame, 530
Though ye good loos have wel deservéd.
Now go your wey, for ye be servéd ;
And thou, dan Eolus,' quod she,
' Tak forth thy trompe anon, let see,

451. P Cx. omit this and the next line.
453. P Cx. *What ther grace was ;* Th. *What her grace was.*
456. F B omit this line.
466. P Cx. Th. *good name.*
480. A line is left blank here in F B. The next two lines read :
    Upon the peyn to be blynde,
    For Eolus, the god of wynde.
842. P omits this line.

503. So all the authorities.
505. F B *forth* for *fast.*
506. *Triton ;* cp. Ovid, *Met.* i. 333.
518. F B Th. *gode* for *olde.*
534. F B
    Have doon, Eolus, let see,
    Take forth thy trumpe anon, quod she.

That is y-clepéd Sclaunder light,
And blow hir loos, that every wyght
Speke of hem harm and shrewédnesse,
In stede of good and worthynesse.
For thou shalt trumpe al the contraire
Of that they han don wel and faire.'　540
　'Alas,' thoughte I, 'what aventures
Han these sory creatures,
That they amongès al the pres,
Shulde thus be shaméd giltéles !
But what ! hit mosté nedès be.'
　What dide this Eolus, but he
Took out his blakké trompe of bras,
That fouler than the devil was,
And gan this trompé for to blowe,
As al the world shulde overthrowe.　550
Throughouten every regioun
Wente this foulé trumpès soun,
As swift as pelet out of gonne,
Whan fyr is in the poudré ronne.
And swiche a smoké gan out-wende,
Out of his foulé trumpès ende,
Blak, blo, grenysh, swartysh, reed,
As doth when that men melté leed,
Lo, al on hye fro the tuél !
And therto oo thing saw I wel,　560
That the ferther that hit ran,
The gretter wexèn hit began,
As doth the ryver from a welle,
And hit stank as the pit of helle.
Allas, thus was her shame y-ronge,
And giltélees, on every tonge.
　Tho com the thriddé companye,
And gunne up to the dëes, hye,
And doun on knees they fille anon,
And seydé, they ben everychon　570
Folk that han ful trewély
Deservéd famé rightfully,
And prayé that hit myghte be knowe,
Right as hit is, and forth y-blowe.
'I grauntè,' quod she, 'for me list
That now your godé werkes be wist ;
And yit ye shul han better loos,

Right in dispit of alle your foos,
Than worthy is ; and that anoon :
Lat now,' quod she, 'thy trumpé goon,
Thou Eolus, that is so blak ;　581
And out thyn other trompé tak
That highté Laude, and blow it so
That through the world her fame go,
Al esély and not to faste,
That hit be knowèn atté laste.'
　'Ful gladly, lady myn,' he seyde ;
And out his trompe of goldé he brayde
Anon, and sette hit to his mouthe,
And blew it est, and west, and southe,　590
And north, as loude as any thunder,
That every wyght hath of hit wonder,
So brode hit ran or that hit stente.
And, certès, al the breeth that wente
Out of his trumpès mouthé smelde
As men a pot of bawmé helde
Among a basket ful of roses ;
This favour dide he to her loses.
　And right with this I gan aspye,
Ther com the ferthé companye,——　600
But certeyn they were wonder fewe,——
And gonné stondèn in a rewe,
And seydèn, 'Certès, lady brighte,
We han don wel wyth al our myghte,
But we ne kepèn have no fame.
Hid our werkès and our name,
For goddès love ! for certès we
Han certeyn doon hit for bountee,
And for no maner other thyng.'
'I grauntè yow al your askyng,'　610
Quod she ; 'let alle your werkes be deed.
　With that aboute I clew myn heed,
And saw anoon the fifté route
That to this lady gonné loute,
And doun anoon on kneès falle ;
And hir tho besoughtèn alle,
To hide hir goodé werkès eek,
And seyde, they yevèn noght a leek
For famé, ne for swich renoun ;
For they for contemplacioun,　620

553. P Cx. Th. insert *a* before *pelet* and *gonne.*
554. P Cx. *fire is in to it ronne.*
558. P Cx. omit *that ;* F B Th. *wher that.*
568. Cx. *on hye ;* F B Th. *to hye.*
570. F B Th. *we* for *they.*
573. F B *praye yow it mot be ;* Cx. *prayd hyt myght ;* Th. *prayde you it might.*
575. P Cx. Th. insert *now* before *me.*
578. F B omit *Right.*
585. F B omit *Al.*
596. F B Th. *potte ful ;* P Cx. *pitte ful.* Koch and Skeat omit *of.*
602. P Cx. Th. insert *to* before *stonden.*
612. P Cx. Th. *turned* for *clew.*
619. F B Th. *For no fame.* F B omit *ne.* P Cx. Th. omit second *for.*

And goddès love, hadde y-wrought,
Ne of famè wolde they nought.
'What?' quod she, 'and be ye wood?
And wenè ye for to do good,
And for to have of that no fame?
Have ye dispit to have my name?
Nay, ye shul lyvèn everychoon!
Blow thy trompe and that anoon,'
Quod she, 'thou Eolus, I hote,
And ryng thise folkès werk by note, 630
That al the world may of hit here.'
And he gan blowe hir loos so clere,
In his golden clarioun,
That through the world wentè the soun,
And so kenely, and eek so softe,
That hir fame was blowen a-lofte.

Tho com the sextè companye,
And gan fastè to Famè crie.
Right verraily in this manere
They seydèn : 'Mercy, lady dere! 640
To tellè certeyn as hit is,
We han don neither that ne this,
But ydel al our lyf hath be.
But, nathéles, we preyè thee,
That we may have so good a fame,
And gret renoun and knowèn name,
As they that han don noblè gestes,
And achevèd alle hir lestes,
As wel of love as other thyng ;
Al was us never broche ne ryng, 650
Ne ellès nought from wymmen sent,
Ne onès in hir herte y-ment,
To make us only frendly chere,
But myghtè teme us upon bere,
Yit lat us to the peple seme
Swiche as the world may of us deme
That wymmen lovède us for wood.
Hit shal don us a mochè good,
And to our herte as moche availe
To countrepeise ese and travaile, 660

As we hadde wonne hit with labour ;
For that is derè boght honour,
At regard of our greet ese.
And yit thou most us morè plese ;
Let us be holden eek therto,
Worthy, wyse, and gode also,
And riche, and happy unto love.
For Goddès love that sit above,
Thogh we may not the body have
Of wymmen, yit, so God me save! 670
Let men glewe on us the name ;
Sufficeth that we han the fame.'
'I grauntè,' quod she, 'by my trouthe!
Now, Eolus, withoutèn slouthe,
Tak out thy trompe of gold,' quod she,
'And blow as they have axèd me,
That every man wene hem at ese,
Though they gon in ful bad lese.'
This Eolus gan hit so blowe,
That through the world hit was y-knowe.

Tho com the seventh route anoon, 681
And fel on kneès everychon,
And seydè, 'Lady, grauntè us sone
The samè thyng, the samè bone,
Thát thise nextè folke have doon.'
'Fy on yow,' quod she, 'everychoon!
Ye masty swyn, ye ydel wrecchès,
Ful of roten slowè tecchès!
What? falsè thevès! wher ye wolde
Be famous good, and nothing nolde 690
Deservè why, ne never thoughte
Men rather yow to-hangen oughte?
For ye be lyk the slepy cat,
That wolde have fish ; but wastow what?
He woldè no-thyng wete his clowes.
Yvel thrift come on your jowes,
And on myn if I hit graunte,
Or do yow favour yow to avaunte!
Thou Eolus, thou kyng of Trace!
Go, blow this folk a sory grace,' 700
Quod she, 'anoon ; and wostow how

621. P Cx. Th. *it wrought.*
623. P Cx. Th. omit *and.*
624. P Cx. Th. omit *for.*
630. All read *werkes*—the plural form caught from the preceding word—cp. *hit* in next line.
635. P Cx. Th. *kyndely* for *kenely ;* F B *Also* for *And so.*
636. P omits this line ; F B *But atte last (atlaste) it was on lofte ;* Cx. Th. *their* for *hir.*
645. F B *as good ;* Th. *as good a.*
648. P Cx. *eshued alle her bestes ;* Th. *acheued . . . questes.*

675. F B read *now let se* for *quod she.*
685. A loose construction. Cx. reads *That to thyse next folk hast done,* which is perhaps right.
689-691. F B read :

 What? false theves? or ye wolde
 Be famous good, and nothing nolde
 Deserve why, ne never ye roughte!
 Men rather yow to-hangen oughte!

693. F *swynt* for *slepy ;* B *sweynte,* rightly according to Skeat.
699. *Trace,* Thrace.

As I shal tellė thee right now.
Sey, "Thise ben they that wolde honour
Have, and do nòskynnės labour,
Ne do no good, and yit han laude ;
And that men wende that bele Isaude
Ne coud hem noght of lovė werne ;
And yit she that grynt at a querne
Is al to good to ese hir herte."'
　　This Eolus anon up sterte,　　　710
And with his blakkė clarioun
He gan to blasen out a soun,
As loude as belweth wynde in helle.
And eek thérwith, sooth to telle,
This soun was [al] so ful of japes,
As ever mowės were in apes.
And that wente al the world aboute,
That every wyght gan on hem shoute,
And for to laugh as they were wode ;
Such gamė fonde they in hir hode.　　720
　　Tho com another companye,
That had y-doon the trecherye,
The harme, the gretest wikkednesse,
That any hertė coudė gesse ;
And preyėde hir to han good fame,
And that she nolde doon hem no shame,
But yeve hem loos and good renoun,
And do hit blowe in clarioun.
'Nay, wis !' quod she, 'hit were a vyce ;
Al be ther in me no justice,　　　730
Me [ne] list not do hit now,
Ne this nyl I not grauntė yow.'
　　Tho com ther lepynge in a route,
And gan clappėn al aboute
Every man upon the croune,
That al the hallė gan to sowne,
And seydė, 'Lady, lefe and dere,
We ben swich folk as ye may here.
To tellėn al the tale aright,
We ben shrewės every wyght,　　　740
And han delyt in wikkednes,
As goodė folk have in goodnes ;
And joyė to be knowėn shrewes,
And ful of vyce and wikkėd thewes ;

Wherfor we preyen you, a-rowe,
That our fame be swich y-knowe,
In allė thyng right as hit is.'
'I grauntė hit yow,' quod she, 'y-wys.
But what art thou that seyst this tale,
That werest on thy hose a pale,　　　750
And on thy tipet swiche a belle ?'
'Madamė,' quod he, 'sooth to telle,
I am that ilkė shrewe, y-wys,
That brende the temple of Isidis
In Athenės, lo, that citee.'
'And wherfor didest thou so ?' quod she.
'By my troth,' quod he, 'madame,
I woldė fayn han had a fame,
As other folk hadde in the toune,
Al-thogh they were of greet renoun　　760
For hir vertu and hir thewes,
Thoughte I, as greet a fame han shrewes—
Though hit be noght—for shrewėdnesse
As godė folk han for goodnesse ;
And sith I may not have that oon,
That other nyl I noght forgoon.
And for to gette of Famės hire,
The temple sette I al a-fire.
Now do our loos be blowen swythe,
As wysly be thou ever blythe.'　　　770
'Gladly,' quod she.　'Thou Eolus,
Herestow not what they prayen us ?'
'Madamė, yis, ful wel,' quod he,
'And I wil trompen hit, parde !'
And tok his blakke trumpė faste,
And gan to puffen and to blaste,
Til hit was at the worldės ende.
　　With that I gan aboutė wende,
For oon that stood right at my bak,
Me thoughtė goodly to me spak,　　　780
And seydė, 'Frend, what is thy name ?
Artow come hider to han fame ?'
'Nay, for-sothė, frend !' quod I ;
'I cam noght hider, graunt mercy !
For no swich causė, by my heed !
Sufficeth me, as I were deed,
That no wyght have my name in honde.
I woot my-self best how I stonde,

705. P *hem* for *han*.
706. *Isaude*, Ysolt, the lover of Tristram ; cp.
P. *of F.* l. 290.
715. All omit *al*, which Skeat inserts. P reads
as, which is a contraction of *also*.
723. All read *grrt, grete* ; Willert reads *gretest*.
731. All omit *ne*. Cx. Th. read *to do*.
732. P *The nys* for *Ne this* ; Cx. *Ne I ne wyl* ;
Th. *I nyl grauntė it yow*.

753. P ends with this line.
754. *Isidis*, Isis.　Chaucer refers to Heros-
tratus, who set fire to the temple of Diana at
Ephesus on the night of Alexander the Great's
birth.
. 757. F B *thrift* for *troth*.
767. Cx. Th. *As for* . . . *a fame here*.

For what I drye or what I thynke,—
I wol my selven al hit drynke,   790
Certeyn for the moré part,
As ferforthe as I can myn art.'
What doost thou here than?' quod he.
Quod I, 'That wol I tellén the,
The causé why I stondé here.
Som newé tydyngs for to lere,
Som newé thyngés, I not what,
Tydyngés other this or that,
Of love, or swiché thingés glade.
For, certeynly, he that me made   800
To comen hider, seydé me
I shuldé bothé here and see,
In this placé, wonder thynges;
But these be no swiche tydynges
As I menté.' 'No?' quod he.
And I answerdé, 'No, pardé!
For wel I wysté ever yit,
Sith that first I haddé wit,
That som folk han desiréd fame
Dyversély, and loos and name;   810
But certeynly I nysté how,
Ne where that Famé dwellde, er now;
And eek of hir descripcioun,
Ne also hir condicioun,
Ne the ordre of hir dom,
Unto the tyme I hider com.'
'[Which] than, be lo, thise tidynges,
That [thee] now [thus] hider brynges,
That thou hast herd?' quod he to me;
'But now, no fors; for wel I see   820
What thou desirest for to here.
Com forth, and stond no lenger here,
And I wol the, withoutén drede,
In swich another placé lede,
Ther thou shalt heré many oon.'
Tho gan I forth with him to goon,

Out of the castel, soth to seye.
Tho saw I stonde in a valeye,
Under the castel, fasté by,
An hous, that *domus Dedali*,   830
That *Laboryntus* clepéd is,
Nas maad so wonderlich y-wys,
Ne half so queyntéliche y-wrought.
And evermo, so swyft as thought,
This queynté hous abouté wente,
That nevermo hit stillé stente.
And therout com so greet a noise,
That had hit stonden upon Oise,
Men myghte hit han herd esély
To Rome, I trowé sikerly   840
And the noise which that I herde,
For al the world right so hit ferde,
As doth the routyng of the stoon,
That from thengyn is leten goon.
And al this hous of whiche I rede
Was maad of twiggés, falwé, rede
And grene eek, and som werén white,
Swiche as men to these cagés thwyte,
Or makén of these panyers,
Or ellés hottés or dossers;   850
But for the swough and for the twygges,
This house was also ful of gigges,
And also ful eek of chirkynges,
And of many other werkynges;
And eek this hous hath of entrees
As fele of leves as ben on trees
In somer, whan they grené been,
And on the roof men may yit seen
A thousand holés, and wel moo,
To leten wel the soun out go.   860
And eek by day in every tyde
Been al the dorés openéd wide,
And by nyght echoon unshette;
Ne porter ther is non to lette
No maner tydyngs in to pace;

793. F omits *than* and inserts *But* before *What*.
797. All read *thing, thinge*; read with Skeat *thynges*.
805. F B *I mene of*; Th. *I ment of*.
807. All read *wote* for *wyste*.
816. Cx. Th. *Knewe I not tyl*.
817-819. All read:

     Why than be, lo, these tydynges
     That thou now hider bryngus
     That thou hast herd.

Skeat reads *Whiche* for *Why than* and inserts *thus* in l. 818; Koch reads:

     Which than be, lo I thise tydinges
     That bringe thee hider, and thlse thinges
     That thou wilt here.

830. *domus Dedali*, the labyrinth made by Dædalus for Minos; cp. Ovid, *Met.* viii. 159 ff.
838. *Oise*, a northern tributary of the Seine.
839. F B Th. *Men*; Cx. *I*; probably the right reading is *Me* (=one); Th. *myghte han herd hit*.
850. F B Cx. *hattes*; Th. *hutches*; Skeat reads *hottes*.
851. F B Th. *That* for *But*.
854. So Cx. Th., but certainly wrongly; B omits the line; F has only *As ful this lo*.
856. F B *yn* for *on*. B omits *as* before *ben* and inserts it before *of*; Cx. *As many as leues ben of trees*; Th. *As many as leues ben on trees*.

Ne never reste is in that place,
That hit nys fild ful of tydynges,
Other loude, or in whisprynges.
And over alle the housės angles,
Is ful of rounynges and of jangles,   870
Of werres, of pees, of mariages,
Of reste, of labour of viages,
Of aboode, of deeth, of lyfe,
Of love, of hate, acorde, of stryfe,
Of loos, of lore, and of wynnynges,
Of hele, of sekeness, of bildynges,
Of fairė wyndės, of tempestes,
Of qwalme of folk, and eek of bestes ;
Of dyvers transmutaciouns,
Of estats and eek of regions ;   880
Of trust, of drede, of jelousye,
Of wyt, of wynnynge, of folye ;
Of plentee, and of greet famyne,
Of chepe, of derth, and of ruyne ;
Of good or mysgovernément,
Of fire, of dyvers accident.
   And lo, this hous of whiche I write,
Siker be ye, hit nas not lyte ;
For hit was sixty myle of lengthe,
Al was the tymber of no strengthe ;   890
Yet hit was foundėd to endure
Whil that hit list to Aventure,—
That is the moder of tydynges,
As the see of welles and sprynges,—
And hit was shapėn lyk a cage.
   'Certės,' quod I, 'in al myn age,
Ne saw I swich a hous as this.'
And as I wondrėde me, y-wys,
Upon this hous, tho war was I
How that myn egle, fastė by,   900
Was perchėd hye upon a stoon ;
And I gan streightė to hym goon,
And seydė thus : 'I preyė thee
That thou a whil abidė me
For Goddės love, and let me seen
What wondrės in that placė been ;
For yit paraunter I may lere

Somme good therin, or sumwhat here
That leef me were, or that I wente.'
   'Peter ! that is myn entente,'   910
Quod he to me ; 'therfor I dwelle,
But certeyn, oon thyng I thee telle,
That, but I bringė thee therinne,
Ne shalt thou never cunnė gynne
To come into hit, out of doute,
So faste hit whirleth, lo, aboute.
But sith that Jovės, of his grace,
As I have seyd, wol thee solace
Fynally with thise thynges,
Unkouthe syghtės and tydynges,   920
To passė with thyn hevynesse,
Swiche routhe hath he of thy distresse,—
That thou suffrest debonairly,
And wost thy-selven utterly,
Desperat of all maner blis,
Sith that Fortune hath maad a-mys
The swote of al thyn hertės reste
Languisshe and eek in poynt to breste,—
That he through his myghty merite,
Wol do thee an ese, al be hit lyte,   930
And yaf expresse commaundėment,
To whiche I am obedient,
To furthrė thee with al my myght,
And wysse and techė thee aright,
Wher thou maist most tydyngės here ;
Thou shalt anoon heer many oon lere.'
   With this worde he right anoon
Hentė me up bytwene his toon,
And at a wyndowe in me broghte,
That in this hous was, as me thoghte,—   940
And therwithal me thoghte hit stente,
And no-thing hit aboutė wente,—
And me sette in the flore adoun.
But which a congregacioun
Of folk, as I saw rome aboute,

872. All *restes.*
876. Cx. Th. *lesynges* for *bildynges,* perhaps rightly.
877. Cx. Th. *wether and* for *wyndes.*
877. All *and eek of tempestes,* caught from line below.
886. All *and of.*
891. F B Th. *is* for *was.*
899. Cx. *Upon the hous that was ful hye.*
906. F B *this* for *that.*

908. F B *thereon.*
910. Cx. Th. insert *now* after *that.*
914. Cx. Th. *conne the gyn.*
919. So all authorities. The line is at least one syllable short.
925. F B *Disesperat of alle blis.*
927. F *frot* ; B *foot* ; Cx. Th. *swote* ; Koch *fruit.*
930. Cx. *the an* ; F *than* ; Th. B *the.* Cx. omits *Wol* and inserts *wyl* after *he* in line above.
931. All insert *in* after *yaf.*
936. F B *Shallow here anoon* ; Cx. Th. omit *anoon,* perhaps rightly ; Skeat *anoon heer.*
938. F B omit this line.
940. Cx. *Whyche on.*
944. Cx. *whyche a grete* ; Th. *suche a great.*

Some within and some withoute,
Nas never seen, ne shal ben eſt ;
That, certès, in the world nys left
So many forméd by Nature,
Ne deed so many a crëature ;   950
That wel unethe in that place
Hadde I oon foot brede of space ;
And every wyght that I saw there
Rounéde everych in otherès ere
A newè tydyng prevèly,
Or ellès tolde al openly
Right thus, and seydè, ' Nost not thou
That is betid, late or now ? '
' Nó,' quod he, ' tél me what.'
And than he tolde him this and that,   960
And swoor therto that hit was sooth,—
' Thus hath he sayd,' and 'Thus he dooth,'
' Thus shal hit be,' ' Thus herde I seye,'
' That shal be found,' ' That dare I leye.'
That al the folk that is a-lyve
Ne han the connyng to discryve
The thyngès that I herdè there,
What aloude, and what in ere.
But al the wonder-most was this :
Whan oon hadde herd a thyng y-wys,   970
He com forth to another wight,
And gan him tellén, anoon-right,
The samè that to him was told,
Or hit a forlong-way was old,
But gan somwhat for to eche
To this tidyng in his speche
More than ever hit spoken was.
And nat so sone departèd nas
Tho fro him, that he ne mette
With the thridde ; and, or he lette   980

Any stounde, he tolde him als ;
Were the tidyng sooth or fals,
Yit wolde he telle hit nathélees,
And evermo with more encrees
Than hit was erst.   Thus north and southe
Went every [thyng] fro mouth to mouthe,
And that encresyng evermo,
As fire is wont to quykke and go
From a sparkè spronge amys,
Til al a citee brent up is.   990
And whan that was ful up-spronge,
And woxèn more on every tonge
Than ever hit was, [hit] went anoon
Up to a wyndowe out to goon
Or, but hit myghte out ther pace,
Hit gan out crepe at som crevace,
And fleigh forth fastè for the nones.
And somtyme saw I ther, at ones
A lesyng and a sad soth-sawe,
That gonne of aventurè drawe   1000
Out to a wyndowe for to pace ;
And, when they mettèn in that place,
They were a-chekkéd bothè two,
And neither of hem myghte out go ;
For other so they gonnè croude,
Til eche of hem gan crièn loude,
' Lat me go first ! '   ' Nay, but lat me !
And here I wol ensuren thee
Wyth the nones that thou wolt do so,
That I shal never fro thee go,   1010
But be thyn ownè sworèn brother !
We wil medle us eche with other,
That no man, be they never so wrothe,
Shal han that oon [of] two, but bothe
At onès, al beside his leve,
Come we a-morwè or on eve,
Be we cried or stille y-rouned.'
Thus saw I false and sooth compouned.
Togeder flee for oo tidynge.
          Thus out at holès gonnè wrynge   1020

946. F B omit this line, which is probably corrupt. Koch *Many a thousand in a route.*
956. Cx. Th. insert *it* before *tolde.*
958. Cx. Th. *to right now.*
959. All *quod he ;* Willert *quod the other.*
963. All insert *and* before each *Thus ;* Cx. Th. *And thys (this) shall be.*
971. F B *come forth ryght to ;* Cx. *come forth unto ;* Th. *Came streyght to.* Probably *right* in the original of F B had the word *forth* written above it because of its recurrence in the next line, and it then crept into the text as well as *right.* This theory is supported by the reading of Th., which is an edited text.
973. P B Th. *that him was ;* Cx. *that was to him.*
976. F B Th. *this* for *his.*
977. F B *More than hit ever was.*
979. F B *That he fro . . . thoo,* etc.

986. F B *mouthe* for *thyng ;* Cx. Th. *tydyng ;* Skeat *word.*
991. F B *y-spronge.*
993. All read *and* for second *hit.*
999. Cx. *soth sayd sawe,* perhaps rightly.
1004. F B *most (must).*
1005. Cx. omits l. 1005 to the end, but prints twelve spurious lines as conclusion.
1006. Th. *For eche other they gonne so.*
1009. Th. omits *the.*
1012. Th. *in* for *with.*
1014. F *han on two ;* B omits *of two ;* Th. *hane one two.*

Every tidyng streight to Fame ;
And she gan yevèn-eche his name,
After hir disposicioun,
And yaf hem eek duracioun,
Some to wexe and wanè sone,
As dooth the fairè whitè mone,
And leet hem gon.   Ther myghte I seen
Wengèd wondrès fastè fleen,
Twenty thousand in a route,
As Eolus hem blew aboute.   1030
 And, lord ! this hous in allè tymes
Was ful of shipmen and pilgrymes,
With scrippès bret-ful of lesynges,
Entrèmedlèd with tidynges,
And eek alonè by hemselve.
O, many a thousand tymès twelve
Saw I eek of these pardoneres,
Currours, and eek messangeres,
With boistès crammèd ful of lyes,
As ever vessel was with lyes.   1040
And as I alther-fastest wente
Aboute, and dide al myn entente,
Me for to pleye and for to lere,
And eek a tydynge for to here,
That I hadde herd of som contree
That shal not now be told for me ;
For hit no nede is, redèly ;
Folk can synge hit bet than I.
For al mot out, other late or rathe,
Allè the shevès in the lathe.   1050
 I herde a gretè noise withalle
In a corner of the halle,
Ther men of lovè tydynges tolde,

And I gan thiderwarde beholde ;
For I saw rennynge every wyght,
As faste as that they haddèn myght ;
And everyche criede, 'What thing is that?'
And som sayde, ' I not never what.'
And whan they were alle on an hepe,
Tho behyndè gonne up lepe,   1060
And clamben up on other faste,
And up the nose and ÿen caste,
And troden faste on otherès heles,
And stampe, as men doon after eles.
 Attè laste I saw a man,
Which that I ne wot, ne kan,
But he semedè for to be
A man of greet auctoritè.
         (*Unfinished*)

Cx. Th. add the following spurious lines

[And therwithal I abraide
Out of my slepè, half afraide ;   1070
Remembring wel what I hadde seen,
And how hye and ferre I hadde been
In my goost ; and hadde gret wonder
Of that the god of thunder
Hadde let me knowe ; and began to write
Lyk as ye have herd me endite.
Wherefor to studye and rede alway,
I purpose to do day by day.
 Thus in dreaming and in game
Endeth this lytel book of Fame.]   1080

1062. Th. *the noyse on hyghen.*
1066. F B *nat ne kan;* Th. *naught ne can;*
Skeat *nevene naught ne can.*
1069-71. Cx.

    And wyth the noyse of them wo
    Sodeynly awoke anon tho,
    And remembryd, etc.

1036. Th. omits *a.*
1039. Th. *boxes,* B *bowgys.*
1049. Th. omits *other.*
1050. Th. *rathe* for *lathe.*

THE LEGENDE OF GOOD WOMEN

THE PROLOGUE

This prologue is extant in two different versions, an earlier and a later, between which there are many important variations (see Introduction). The portion in which most of these occur is here given in both forms, words and lines in the first version omitted or altered in the second being printed in italics.

THE PROLOGUE	THE PROLOGUE
FIRST VERSION	SECOND VERSION, B

A THOUSENT *sythis have* I herd men telle,
That there is joye in hevene and peyne in helle,
And I acordè wel that it *be* so ;
But, nathèles, *this* wit I wel also,
That there ne is non *that dwellyth* in this cuntre
That eythir hath in *helle or hevene* i-be,
Ne may of it non othere weyis wytyn
But as he hath herd seyd, or foundè it wrytyn ;
For by asay there may no man it preve.
But *goddis* forbodè but men schuldè leve   10
Wel morè thyng than men han seyn with eye !
Men schal nat wenyn everything a lye,
For that he say it nat of yore ago.
God wot *a* thyng is nevere the lessè *so,*
Thow every wyght ne may it nat i-se.
Bernard the monk ne say nat al pardee !
Thanne motyn we to bokys that we fynde,
Thourw whiche that oldè thyngis ben in mynde,
And to the doctryne of these oldè wyse,
Yevyn credence, in every skylful wyse ;   20
And trowyn on these olde aprovede storyis
Of holynesse, of regnys, of victoryis,
Of love, of hate, of othere sundery thyngis
Of which I may nat makè rèhersyngys.

A THOUSANDE tymès I have herd men telle,
That there is joy in hevene, and peyne in helle,
And I acordè wel that it is so ;
But, nathèles, yet wot I wel also,
That ther is noon dwellyng in this countree,
That eythir hath in hevene or in helle y-be,
Ne may of hit noon other weyès witen,
But as he hath herd seyde, or foundè it writen ;
For by assay ther may no man it preve.
But God forbedè but men shuldè leve   10
Wel morè thing than men han seen with eye !
Men shal not wenen everything a lye
But-if hymselfe it seeth, or ellès dooth ;
For, God wot, thing is never the lassè sooth,
Thogh every wight ne may it not y-see.
Bernarde, the monke, ne saugh nat al, parde !
Than motè we to bokès that we fynde,—
Thurgh which that oldè thingès ben in mynde,—
And to the doctrine of these oldè wyse,
Yevè credence, in every skylful wise,   20
That tellen of these olde apprevèd stories,
Of holynesse, of regnès, of victories,
Of love, of hate, of other sondry thynges,
Of whiche I may not maken rehersynges.

1. *men*, om. F³.
2. *That*, om. F².
16. *Bernard*, glossed in G F⁴. ‘Bernardus monachus (om. G) non vidit omnia.’

1-49. Cp. B 1-49.

FIRST VERSION	SECOND VERSION, B

FIRST VERSION

And if that oldė bokis weryn aweye,
I-loryn were of rémembrance the keye.
Wel oughte us thanne *on oldė bokys leve*,
There *as there is* non othyr *asay be* preve ;
And as for me, thow that *myn wit be* lite,
On bokys for to rede I me delyte, 30
And in myn herte have hem in reverence,
And to hem yeve *swich lust* and *swich*
  credence
That ther is *wel onethė* gamė non
That from myne bokys make[th]me to gon
But it be *other upon* the halyday,
Or ellis, in the jòly tyme of May,
Whan that I here the *smalė* foulys synge,
And that the flouris gynnė for to sprynge,—
Farwel myn *stodye, as lastynge that sesoun!*
  Now have I *therto* this condycyoun, 40
Thát of alle the flouris in the mede
Thanne love I most these flourys white
  and rede,
Swyche as men callė dayesyis in oure
  toun.
To hem have I so gret affecioun,
As I seyde erst, whan comyn is the may,
That in myn bed there dawith me no day
That I ne am up and walkynge in the mede,
To sen these flouris agen the sunne to-
  sprede,
Whan it upryseth be *the morwe schene*, 49
The longė day thus walkynge in the grene.

And whan the sunne *begynnys for to* weste,
Thanne closeth it, and drawith it to reste,
So sore it is a-ferid of the nyght,
Til on the morwe that it is dayis lyght.
This dayeseye, of allė flouris flour,
Fulfyld of vertu and *of alle* honour,
And evere i-likė fayr and frosh of hewe,
As wel in wyntyr as in somyr newe,
Fayn wolde I preysyn *if I coude* aright,
But, wo is me! it lyth nat in myn myght

51-59. Cp. B 60-67.

43. *our*, F *her*.
50-52, 57-60, 64-72. New lines.

SECOND VERSION, B

And if that oldė bokės were awey,
Y-lornė were of remembraunce the key.
Wel ought us, thanne, honóuren and beleve
These bokės, ther we han noon other
  preve.
And as for me, though that I konne
  but lyte,
On bokės for to rede I me delyte, 30
And to hem yive I feyth and ful credence,
And in myn herte have hem in reverence
So hertėly, that ther is gamė noon
That fro my bokės maketh me to goon,
But it be seldom on the holyday,
Save, certeynly, whan that the month
  of May
Is comen, and that I here the foulės synge,
And that the flourės gynnen for to
  sprynge,—
Farewel my boke, and my devocion !
  Now have I thanne suche a condicion,
Thát of alle the flourės in the mede, 41
Than love I most thise flourės white and
  rede,
Suche as men callen daysyes in our toun.
To hem have I so grete affeccioun,
As I seyde erst, whan comen is the May,
That in my bed ther daweth me no day,
That I nam up and walkyng in the mede,
To seen this floure agein the sonnė sprede,
Whan it uprysith erly by the morwe ;
That blisful sightė softneth al my sorwe, 50
So glad am I, whan that I have presence
Of it, to doon it allė reverence,
As she that is of allė flourės flour,
Fulfillėd of al vertue and honour,
And evere ilikė faire, and fresshe of hewe,
And I love it, and evere ylikė newe,
And ever shal, til that myn hertė dye ;
Al swere I nat, of this I wol nat lye ;
Ther lovėd no wight hotter in his lyve. 59
  And, whan that it is eve, I rennė blyve,
As sone as evere the sonnė gynneth weste,
To seen this flour, how it wol go to reste,
For fere of nyght, so hateth she derknesse !
Hir chere is pleynly sprad in the brightnesse
Of the sonnė, for ther it wol unclose.
Allas, that I ne had Englyssh, ryme or
  prose,
Súffisant this flour to preyse aryght !

FIRST VERSION

For wel I wot that *folk* han herebeforn 61
Of makynge ropyn and lad awey the corn,
[And] I come aftyr, glenynge here and
   ther,
And am ful glad if I may fynde an er
Of ony goodly word that *they* han laft.
And *if* it happé me rehersen eft
That *they* han in here froschè songis said,
I hope that they wele nat ben evele a-payed,
Sithe it is seyd in fortheryng and honour
Of hem that eythir servyn lef or flour ; 70
For trustyth wel I ne have nat undyrtake
As of the lef agayn the flour to make,
Ne of the flour *to* make ageyn the lef,
No more than of the corn agen the shef ;
For as to me is lefere non, ne lothere,
I *am* withholdè yit with never nothire ;
I not who servyth lef ne who the flour.
That nys nothyng the entent of myn
   labour ;
For this *werk* is al of anothyr tunne 79
Of oldè story, er swich *strif* was begunne.
But wherfore that I spak to yeve credence
To *bokys* olde and don hem reverence
Is for men *schulde autoriteis* beleve,
There as there lyth non othyr asay be preve.
For myn entent is, or I fro you fare,
The nakede tixt in Englis to declare
Of manye a story, or ellis of manye a geste,
As autourys seyn—leoyth hem if you leste.

61-70. Cp. B 73-82.
71-80. Cp. B 188-196.
81-84. Cp. B 97-100.

72. *With the Leef or with the Flour.* This
appears to be the earliest allusion to the dispute as
to the merits of the Flower and the Leaf on which
a follower of Chaucer afterwards wrote the Poem
with that title.
83-96. New lines.
96. *in* (2), B² only ; rest om.
100. *they,* Trin.² ; Arch. Seld. *man ;* F om. ;
rest *men.*
101-120. New lines.
102. *al,* om. F.

SECOND VERSION, B

But helpeth ye that han konnyng and
   myght,
Ye lovers, that kan make of sentèment ;
In this case oghté ye be diligent 70
To forthren me somwhat in my labour,
Whethir ye ben with the Leef or with
   the Flour ;
For wel I wot, that ye han her-biforne
Of makynge ropen, and lad awey the corne ;
And I come after, glenyng here and there,
And am ful glad if I may fynde an ere
Of any goodly word that ye han left.
And thogh it happen me rehercen eft
That ye han in your fresshè songès sayede,
Forbereth me, and beth not evele apayede,
Syn that ye see I do it in the honour 81
Of love, and eke in service of the flour
Whom that I serve as I have witte or myght.
She is the clerenesse and the verray lyght,
That in this derkè worlde me wynt and
   ledyth,
The herte in-with my sorwful brest yow
   dredith,
And loveth so sore, that ye ben verrayly
The maistresse of my witte, and nothing I.
My worde, my werk, is knyt so in youre
   bond
That as an harpe obeieth to the hond, 90
That maketh it soune after his fyngerynge,
Ryght so mowe ye oute of myn hertè bringe
Swich vois, ryght as yow lyst, to laughe
   or pleyne ;
Be ye my gide, and lady sovereyne.
As to my erthely god, to yowe I calle,
Bothe in this werke, and in my sorwès alle.
  But wherfore that I spake to yive
   credence
To oldè stories, and doon hem reverence,
And that men mosten morè thyng beleve
Then they may seen at eye or ellès preve,
That shal I seyn, whanne that I see my
   tyme— 101
I may nat al attonès speke in ryme.
My besy gost, that thursteth alwey newe,
To seen this flour so yong, so fresshe of
   hewe,
Constreynèd me with so gledy desire,
That in myn herte I feelè yet the fire,
That madè me to ryse er it wer day,

FIRST VERSION

Whan passed was *almost the monyth* of
     May
And I hadde roméd, al the somerys day, 90
The grené medewe, of which that I yow
     tolde,
Upon the frosché dayeseie to beholde,
And that the sonne out of the south gan
     weste
And *closede was* the flour and gon to reste
For derknesse of the nyht *of* which sche
     dradde,
Hom to myn hous, ful swiftly, I me spadde,
And in a lytyl erber that I have,
I-benchede *newe with* turvis, frosche i-
     grave,
I bad men schuldé me myn couché make ;
For deynté of the newé somerys sake, 100
I bad hem strowé flouris on my bed.
Whan I was layd and hadde myn eyen hid
I fel aslepe *withinne* an hour or two.
Me mette how *I was* in the medewe tho,
And that I romede in that samé gyse,
To sen *that* flour, *as ye han herd devyse.*
Fayr was this medewe, as thoughté me,
     overal ;
With flouris sote enbroudit *was it* al,
As for to speke of gomme, or erbe, or tre,
Comparisoun may non i-makede be ; 110
For it surmounte*de* pleynly alle odours.
Ánd of riché beuté allé flourys.
Forgetyn hadde the erthe his pore estat
Of wyntyr, that hym nakede made and
     mat,
And with his swerd of cold so sore *hadde*
     grevyd :
Now *hadde* the tempre sonne al that relevyd,
And clothede hym in grene al newe ageyn.
The smalé foulis, of the seson fayn,
That from the panter and the net ben
     skapid, 119
Upon the foulere, that hem made a-wapid

89-107. Cp. B 100, 180-182, 197-212.
108-137. Cp. B 119-151.

208. *this*, om. F.
111. *that*, om. F.
113. *the beste*, Taurus or the Bull.
114. *Agenores doghtre*, Europa.
124. *alle*, F. *of.*
143-144. New lines.

SECOND VERSION, B

And this was now the firsté morwe of May,
With dredful hert, and glad devocion
For to ben at the resurreccion 110
Óf this flour, whan that it shulde unclose
Agayne the sonne, that roos as rede as rose,
That in the brest was of the beste, that day,
That Agenorés doghtre ladde away.
And doun on knes anon-ryght I me sette,
And as I koude, this fresshé flour I grette,
Knelyng alwey, til it uncloséd was,
Upon the smalé, softé, swoté gras,
That was with flourés swote enbrouded al,
Of swich swetnesse, and swich odour
     over-al, 120
That for to speke of gomme, or herbe, or
     tree,
Comparisoun may noon y-makéd be ;
For it surmounteth pleynly alle odoures,
Ánd of riché beauté allé floures.
Forgeten had the erthe his pore estate
Of wyntir, that him naked made and mate,
And with his swerd of colde so soré greved ;
Now hath the atempré sonne al that releved
That naked was, and clad it new agayne.
The smalé foulés, of the sesoun fayne, 130
That of the panter and the nette ben scaped,
Upon the foweler, that hem made a-whaped
In wynter, and distroyéd hadde hire
     broode,
In his dispite hem thoghte it did hem goode
To synge of hym, and in hir songe dispise
The foulé cherle, that, for his coveytise,
Had hem betrayéd with his sophistrye.
     This was hir songe, 'The foweler we
     deffye,
And al his crafte.' And sommé songen clere
Layés of love, that joye it was to here, 140
In worshipynge and in preysing of hir
     make ;
And, for the newé blisful somers sake,
Upon the braunchés ful of blosmés softe,
In hire delyt, they turnéd hem ful ofte,
And songen, 'Bléssed be Seynt Valentyne !
For on his day I chees you to be myne,
Withouten répentyng myne herté swete !'
And therewithal hire bekés gonnen mecte,
Yeldyng honóur and humble obeysaunces
To love, and diden hire othere observaunces
That longeth onto love, and to nature ; 151

FIRST VERSION

In wyntyr, and distroyed hadde hire brood,
In his dispit hem thoughte it dede hem
    good
To synge of hym, and in here song despise
The foulè cherl that, for his coveytyse,
Hadde hem betrayed with his sophistrye.
This was here song 'The foulere we defye.'
Some songyn *on the* [   ] *braunchis* clere
[Layes] of love, that joye it was to here,
In *worschepe* and in preysyng of hire make,
And [for] the newè blysful somerys sake.
[And] sungyn 'Blyssede be seynt Valentyn,
[For] at his day I ches yow to be myn, 132
Withoutè répentynge, myn hertè swete !'
And therwithal here bekys gunnè mete,
[Yeldyng] honour and humble obey-
    saunces,
And after dedyn othere observauncys,
Ryht [longynge] onto love and to natures :
So eche of hem to cryaturys.
This song to herken I dede al myn entent,
Forwhy I mette I wistè what they ment.
Tyl at the laste a larkè song above,   141
' I se,' quod she, ' the myghty god of love.
Lo, yond he comyth. I se hise wyngis sprede.'
Tho gan I loken endèlong the mede
And saw hym come and in his honda quene
Clothed in ryal abyte, *al of* grene.

SECOND VERSION, B

Construeth that as yow lyst, I do no cure.
  And tho that haddè don unkyndè-
    nesse,—
As doth the tydif, for newfangelnesse,—
Besoghtè mercy of hir trespassynge,
And humblèly songen hir répentynge,
And sworen on the blosmès to be trewe,
So that hire makès wolde upon hem rewe,
And at the lastè maden hir acorde.   159
Al foundè they Daunger for a tyme a lord,
Yet Pitee, thurgh his strongè gentil myght,
Foryaf, and madè Mercy passen Ryght,
Thurgh Innocence, and rulèd Curtesye.
But I ne clepe it innocence folye,
Ne fals pitee, for vertue is the mene ;
As Ethike seith, in swich maner I mene.
And thus thise fowelès, voide of al malice,
Acordèden to love, and laften vice
Of hate, and songen alle of oon acorde,
'Welcome, Somer, oure governour and
    lorde.'   170
  And Zepherus and Flora gentilly
Yaf to the flourès, softe and tenderly,
Hir swootè breth, and made hem for to
    sprede,
As god and goddesse of the floury mede.
In whiche me thoght I myghtè, day by day,
Dwellen alwey, the joly month of May,
Withouten slepe, withouten mete or
    drynke.
Adoun ful softèly I gan to syhke,
And lenynge on myn elbowe and my syde,
The longè day I shoop me for to abide,   180
For nothing ellis, and I shal nat lye,
But for to loke upon the dayèsie,
That men by resoun wel it callè may
The dayèsie, or elles the ye of day,
The emperice, and fflourè of flourès alle.
I pray to God that fairè mote she falle,
And alle that loven flourès, for hire sake !
But, nathéles, ne wene nat that I make
In preysing of the Flour agayn the Leef,
No more than of the corne agayn the sheef ;
For as to me nys lever noon, ne lother,   191
I nam withholden yit with never nother.
Ne I not who serveth Leef, ne who the
    Flour.
Wel browken they hir service or labour !
For this thing is al of another tonne,

Lines 127-138 are very imperfect in the unique
MS., which omits several words and reads *and*
that for *that* in l. 128, *of* for *for* in l. 130, *That*
for *And* in l. 131, *The honour and the humble*
in l. 135. L. 138 seems hopeless.
144-166. Cp. B 211-234.

152-187. New lines.
164. *it,* Arch. Seld. *that;* F⁵ *it nat.*

FIRST VERSION

SECOND VERSION, B

Of oldė storye, er swiche thinge was
    begonne.
    Whan that the sonne out of the south gan
    weste,
And that this flour gan close, and goon to
    reste,
For derknesse of the nyght, the which she
    dredde,
Home to myn house full swiftly I me spedde
To goon to reste, and erly for to ryse,   201
To seen this flour to-sprede, as I devyse.
And in a litel herber that I have,
That benchėd was on turvės fressh y-grave,
I bad men sholdė me my couchė make ;
For deyntee of the newė someres sake,
I bad hem strawen flourės on my bed.
    Whan I was leydė, and haddė myn eyen
    hed,
I fel on slepe, in-with an houre or two.
Me mettė how I lay in the medewe tho,   210
To seen this flour that I love so and drede ;
And from a-fer come walkyng in the mede
The god of Love, and in his hand a quene,
And she was clad in real habite grene ;

A frette of goold sche haddė next hyre heer
And upon that a whit corone sche beer,
With *manye flourys*, and I schal nat lye ;
For al the world ryght as the dayseye   150
I-corounede is with whitė levys lite,
Swiche were the *flourys* of hire corone
    white.
For of o perle fyn *and* oriental
Hyre whitė coroun was i-makyd al.
For which the whitė coroun above the grene
Mádė hire lyk a dayseye for to sene,
Considerede ek *the* fret of gold above.
I-clothėd was this myhty god of love
Of silk, i-broudede ful of grenė grevys.
A garlond on his hed of rosė levys,   160
Stikid al with lylye flourys newe ;
But of his face I can not seyn the hewe,
For sekyrly his facė schon so bryhte
That *with the glem astonede was the syhte,*

A fret of gold she haddė next her heer,
And upon that a whitė crowne she beer,
With flourouns smalė, and I shal nat lye,
For al the worlde ryght as a daÿsye
Y-corouned is with whitė levės lyte,
So were the flourouns of hire coroune
    white ;   220
For of o perlė, fyne, óriental,
Hire whitė coroune was i-maked al,
For which the whitė coroune above the
    grene
Mádė hire lyke a daysie for to sene,
Considered eke hir fret of goldė above.
Y-clothėd was this mighty god of Love
In silke enbrouded, ful of grenė greves,
In-with a fret of redė rosė leves,
The fresshest syn the worlde was first by-
    gonne.
His giltė here was corowned with a sonne   230
In stede of golde, for hevynesse and wyghte ;
Therwith me thoght his facė shon so
    brighte
That wel unnethės myght I him beholde ;
And in his handė me thoght I saugh him
    holde

149. *manye*, text *mane*, with the *n* added as
a correction.

201. A new line.
211-212. F has these lines in reverse order,
perhaps rightly.
217. *And*, Arch. Seld. *and if*.
229-231. New lines.

FIRST VERSION

A furlongwey I myhte hym *not* beholde.
But at the laste in hande I saw hym holde
Two firy dartis, as the gleedys rede.
And aungellych hyse wengis *gan he* sprede.
And al-be that men seyn that blynd is he,
Algate me thoughte he myghte *wel i-see*,
For sternely on me he gan beholde,   171
So that his lokynge doth myn herte colde.
And be the hond he held *the* noble quene,
Corouned with whit and clothede al in
    grene,
So womanly, so benygne and so meke
That in this world, thow that men wolde
    seke,
Half hire beute schulde men not fynde
In cryature that formede is be Kynde.
Hire name was Alceste the *debonayre*.
I preye to God that evere falle *sche* fayre, 180
For ne hadde confort been of hire presence
I hadde be ded withoutyn ony defence,
For dred of Lovys wordys and his chere,
As, whan tyme is, hereaftyr ye schal here.
Byhynde this god of love, upon *this* grene,
I saw comynge of ladyis nynetene,
In ryal abyte, a ful esy pas,
And aftyr hem come of wemen swich a tras,
That syn that God Adam [hadde] made
    of erthe
The thredde part of *women*, ne the ferthe,
Ne wende I not by possibilite   191
Haddyn evere in this [wyde] world i-be.
And trewe of love these wemen were echon.
Now whether was that a wondyr thyng,
    or non,
That ryht anon as that they gunne espye
This flour whiche that I clepe the dayseye,
Ful sodeynly they styntyn alle atonys
And knelede adoun, as it were for the nonys.
And aftyr that they wentyn in cumpas,
Daunsynge about this flour an esy pas, 200
And songyn, as it were in carole-wyse,
This *balade, whiche that I schal yow devyse.*

Hyd, Absalon, thyne gilte tresses clere,
Ester, ley thow thy meknesse al adoun,

167-178. Cp. B 235-246.
167. For *two firy* the MS. reads *tho fery*, and
in l. 172 *both* for *doth.*
179-198. Cp. B 276-295.
203-224. Cp. B 259-270.

SECOND VERSION, B

Two firy dartes, as the gledes rede,
And aungelyke his wynges saugh I sprede.
And, al be that men seyn that blynd is he,
Algate me thoghte that he myghte se ;
For sternely on me he gan byholde,   239
So that his loking doth myn herte colde.
And by the hande he helde this noble quene,
Crowned with white, and clothed al in
    grene,
So womanly, so benigne, and so meke,
That in this world, thogh that men wolde
    seke,
Half hire beute shulde men nat fynde
In creature that formed is by Kynde.
And therfore may I seyn, as thynketh me,
This songe in preysyng of this lady fre.

Hyde, Absalon, thy gilte tresses clere ;
Ester, ley thou thy mekenesse al adoun ;   250
Hyde, Jonathas, al thy frendly manere ;
Penalopee, and Marcia Catoun,
Make of youre wifhode no comparysoun ;
Hyde ye youre beautes, Ysoude and
    Eleyne ;
My lady comith, that al this may disteyne.

Thy faire body lat it nat appere,
Lavyne ; and thou Lucresse of Rome toun,
And Polixene, that boghten love so dere,
And Cleopatre, with al thy passyoun,
Hyde ye your trouthe of love, and your
    renoun,   260
And thou, Tesbe, that hast of love suche
    peyne ;
My lady comith, that al this may disteyne.

Hero, Dido, Laudomia, alle yfere,
And Phillis, hangyng for thy Demophon,
And Canace, espied by thy chere,
Ysiphile, betraysed with Jason,

245. *Half,* Arch. Seld. *Half of.*
247-248. New lines.
252. *Marcia Catoun,* Cato's daughter Marcia,
who would not marry a second time.
257. *Lavyne,* Lavinia, wife of Aeneas.
258. *Polixene,* Polyxena, daughter of Priam,
betrothed to Achilles.
263. *Laudomia,* Laodamia.
264. *Phillis,* see ll. 2394-2560.
265. *Canace,* cp. *Cant. Tales,* B 78.
266. *Ysiphile,* Hypsipyle, see ll. 1368-1577.

FIRST VERSION

Hyde, Jonathas, al thy frendely manere ;
Penolope and Marcia Catoun,
Mak of youre wyfhod no comparisoun ;
Hyde ye youre beuteis, Ysoude and Elene :
Alceste is here that al *that* may destene.

Thyn fayrè body lat it nat apeere,   210
Laveyne, and thow, Lucresse of Romè
    town,
And Pollexene, that boughtè love so dere,
Ek Cleopatre with al thyn passioun,
Hide ye youre trouth *in* love and youre
    renoun ;
And thow Tysbe, that hast *for* love swich
    peyne ;
Alceste is here that al *that* may desteyne.

Herro, Dido, Laodomya, alle in fere,
Ek Phillis hangynge for thyn Demophoun,
And Canace espied be thyn chere,
Ysiphile bytrayed with Jasoun,   220
Mak of youre trouthe *in love* no bost, ne
    soun ;
Nor Ypermystre, or Adriane, *ne pleyne ;*
Alceste is here that al *that* may disteyne.

Whan that this balade al i-songyn was,
Upon the softe and sotè grenè gras
They settyn hem ful softèly adoun,
By ordere alle in cumpas, *alle* inveroun.
Fyrst sat the god of love and *thanne* this
    queene
With the whitè corone clad in grene,
And sithyn al the remenant by and by,   230
As they were of *degre,* ful curteysly ;
Ne nat a word was spokyn in that place
The mountenaunce of a furlongwey of
    space.
I *lenyngè fastè by, undyr a bente,*
Abod to knowè what this peple mente,
As stille as ony ston, til at the laste
The god of love on me his eyè caste
And seyde 'Who *restith* there ?' and I
    answerde
Unto his axsynge, whan that *I hym* herde,
And seyde ' *Sere,* it am I,' and cam hym
    nere   240

226-257. Cp. B 301-331.

SECOND VERSION, B

Maketh of your trouthè neythir boost ne
    soun,
Nor Ypermystre, or Adriane, ye tweyne :
My lady cometh, that al thys may dysteyne.

This balade may ful wel y-songen be,
As I have seyde erst, by my lady free ;   271
For certeynly al thise mowe nat suffise
To apperen wyth my lady in no wyse.
For as the sonnè wole the fire disteyne,
So passeth al my lady sovereyne,
That is so good, so faire, so debonayre,
I prey to God that ever falle hire faire.
For naddè comfort ben of hire presence,
I haddè ben dede, withouten any defence,
For drede of Lovès wordès, and his chere,
As, when tyme is, herafter ye shal here.

   Behynde this god of Love upon the
    grene   281
I saugh comyng of ladyès nynetene
In real habite, a ful esy paas ;
And after hem come of wymen swich a
    traas,
That syn that God Adam hadde made of
    erthe,
The thriddè part of mankynde, or the ferthe,
Ne wende I nat by possibilitee,
Had ever in this widè worlde y-bee ;
And trewe of love thise women were echon.

   Now wheither was that a wonder thing
    or non,   291
That ryght anon, as that they gonne espye
Thys flour, which that I clepe the dayèsie,
Ful sodeynly they stynten al attones,
And knelède doune, as it were for the nones,
And songen with o vois, ' Heel and honour
To trouthe of womanhede, and to this flour
That bereth our alder pris in figurynge !
Hire whitè corowne bèryth the witness-
    ynge ?'

   And with that word, a-compas enviroun,
They setten hem ful softèly adoun.   301
First sat the god of Love, and syth his
    quene

268. *Ypermystrè,* Hypermnestra, see ll. 2562-
2723.
268. *Adriane,* Ariadne, see ll. 1886-2225.
271. *by,* concerning.
271-275. New lines.
296-297. New lines.

FIRST VERSION

And salewede hym. Quod he, 'What
dost thow her
In myn presence, and that so boldèly?
For it were better worthi, trewèly,
A worm *to com in[to] myn syht* than thow.'
'And why, sere?' quod I, 'and it lykè yow?'
' For thow,' quod he, 'art therto nothyng
able,
Myne servauntis been alle wyse and hon-
ourable.
Thow *art* myn *mortal* fo and *me* warreyest,
And of myne oldè servauntis thow
mysseyest,
And hynderyst hem with thy translacyoun,
And lettist folk *to han* devocyoun   251
To servyn me, and haldist it folye
To *troste on me:* thow mayst it nat denye.
For in pleyn tixt, *it nedyth nat to* glose,
Thow hast translatid the Romauns of the
Rose
That is an eresye ageyns myn lawe,
And makyst wisè folk fro me withdrawe.
And thynkist in thyn wit, that is ful cole,
That he nys but a verray propre fole   259
That lovyth paramours to harde and hote.
Wel wot I therby thow begynnyst dote,
As oldè folis, whan here spiryt faylyth
Thanne blame they folk and wete nat what
hem ealyth.
Hast thow nat mad in Englys ek the bok
How that Crisseydè *Troylis forsok.*
In schewyng how that wemen han don mis.
But nathèles answere me now to this,
Why noldist thow as wel a seyd goodnes
Of wemen, as thow hast seyd wekedenes?
Was there no goodè matyr in thyn mynde,
Ne in alle thy bokys ne coudist thow nat
fynde   271
Sum story of wemen that were goode and
trewe;
Yis, God wot, sixty bokys, olde and newe,
Hast thow thyself, alle ful of storyès grete,
That bothe Romaynys and ek Grekis trete
Of sundery wemen, whiche lyf that they
ladde,
And evere an hunderede goode ageyn on
badde,—
This knowith God, and allè clerkis eke,

265-266. Cp. B 332-333.

SECOND VERSION, B

Wìth the whitè corowne, clad in grene;
And sithen al the remenaunt by and by,
As they were of estaat, ful curteysly,
Ne nat a worde was spoken in the place,
The mountaunce of a furlong wey of
space.
I, knelyng by this floure, in good entente
Abode, to knowen what this peple mente,
As stille as any ston; til at the laste 310
This god of Love on me his eighen caste,
And seyde, 'Who kneleth there?' And
I answerde
Unto his askynge, whan that I it herde,
And seydè, ' It am I,' and come him nere,
And salwed him. Quod he, 'What
dostow here,
So nygh myn ownè floure, so boldèly?
It werè better worthy trewèly
A worme to neghen ner my floure than
thow.'
'And why, sire,' quod I, 'and it lykè yow?'
' For thow,' quod he, ' art therto nothing
able.   320
It is my relyke, digne and delytable,
And thow my foo, and al my folke werreyest,
And of myn oldè servauntes thow mysseyest,
And hynderest hem, with thy translacioun,
And lettest folke from hire devocioun
To servè me, and holdest it folye
To servè Love. Thou maist it nat denye,
For in pleyne text, withouten nede of glose,
Thou hast translated the Romaunce of the
Rose,
That is an heresye ayeins my lawe,   330
And makest wisè folke fro me withdrawe;
And of Cresyde thou hast seydeas the lyste,
That maketh men to wommen lassè triste,
That ben as trewe as ever was any steel?
Of thyn answere avisè the ryght weel,
For thogh that thou reneyèd hast my lay,
As other wrecches han doon many a day,
By Seyntè Venus, that my moder ys,
If that thou lyve, thou shalt repenten this
So cruelly, that it shal wele be sene.' 340

321. A new line.
330. This line clearly points to Chaucer having
translated from the continuation of the *Roman*
de la Rose by Jean de Meung as well as from the
unfinished original by Guillaume Lorris.
335, 348-493. New lines.

2 Q   593

FIRST VERSION	SECOND VERSION, B

FIRST VERSION

That usyn sweche materis for to seke.
What seyth Valerye, Titus, or Claudyan,
What seyth Jerome agayns Jovynyan, 281
How clenè maydenys and how trewè wyvys,
How stedefaste wedewys durynge alle here
       lyvys,
Telleth Jerome, and that nat of a fewe
But, I dar seyn, an hunderede on a rewe,
That it is pitè for to rede, and routhe,
The wo that they endurè for here trouthe.
For to hyre lovè werè they so trewe,
That rathere than they wolè take a newe,
They chosè to be ded in sundery wyse, 290
And deiedyn, as the story wele devyse.
And some were brend and some were cut
       the hals,
And some dreynkt, for they woldyn not be
       fals ;
For allè kepid they here maydynhed,
Or ellis wedlok, or here wedewehed.
And this thyng was nat kept for holynesse,
But al for verray vertu and clennesse,
And for men schuldè set on hem no lak ;
And yit they werè hethene, al the pak,
That were so sore a-drad of allè schame. 300
These oldè wemen keptè so here name,
That in this world I trowe men shal nat
       fynde
A man that cowdè be so trewe and kynde
As was the lestè woman in that tyde !
What seyth also the epistelle of Ovyde
Of trewè wyvys and of here labour ?
What Vincent in his Estoryal Myrour ?
Ek al the world of autourys maystow here,
Cristene and hethene, trete of swich matere,
It nedyth nat al day thus for to endite. 310
But yit I seye what eylyth the to wryte
The draf of storyis and forgete the corn ?
Be Seynt Venus, *of whom that I was born,*
Althow [that] thow reney[ed] hast myn
       lay,
As othere *oldè folys* manye a day,
Thow shalt repente *it, that it schal be sene.*
Thanne spak *Alceste the worthyere queene,*
And seydè, 'God, ryght of youre curteysye

307. Vincent de Beauvais, in his *Miroir Historial.*
313-323. Cp. B 338-347.
316. *that,* MS. *so that.*

SECOND VERSION, B

Tho spake this lady, clothèd al in
       greene,   341
And seydè, 'God, ryght of youre curtesye,
Ye moten herken if he can replye
Agayns al this that ye have to him meved :
A god ne sholdè nat be thus agreved,

594

FIRST VERSION

Ye motyn herken, if he can replye
Ageyns *these poyntys* that ye han to hym
     mevid.   320
A god ne schuldė not thus been agrevyd,
But of his deitee he schal be stable,
And therto *ryghtful* and *ek* mercyable.
He schal nat ryghtfully his yrė wreke
Or he have herd the tothyr partye speke.
Al ne is nat gospel that is to you pleynyd ;
The god of love hereth many a tale i-feynyd.
For in youre court is many a losengeour,
And·manye a queynte totulour ácusour,
That tabouryn in youre eres manye a *thyng*,
For hate or for jelous ymagynyng,   331
And for to han *with you sum* dalyaunce.
Envye—*I preye to God yeve hire mys-*
     chaunce—
Is lavender in the *gretė* court alway ;
For sche ne partyth, neythir nyght ne day,
Out of the hous of Cesar—thus seyth
     Dante—
Whoso that goth, alwey sche *motė* wante.
This man to you may *wrongly* ben acused,
There as be ryght hym oughtė ben excusid.
Or ellis, sere, for *that* this man is nyce, 340
He *may translate a thyng in* no malyce
But for he usyth *bokis* for to make,
And takyth non hede of what matere he
     take,
Therfore he wrot the Rose and ek Crisseyde
Of innocence, and nystė what he seyde.
Or hym was bodyn makė thilkė tweye
Of sum persone, and durste it not withseye ;
For he hath wretė manye a bok er this.
He ne hath not don so grevously amys
To translatė that oldė clerkės wryte,   350
As thow that he of malyce wolde endyte
Despit of love, and haddė hymself·
     *i-*wrought.
This schulde a ryghtwys lord han in his
     thought
And not ben lyk tyrauntis of Lumbardye
That usyn *wilfulhed and* tyrannye.
For he that kyng or lord is naturel
Hym oughtė nat be tyraunt and crewel,
As is a fermour, to don the harm he can.

322. *deitee,* MS. *dede.*
328-343. Cp. B 352-361, 350-351, 362-365.
346 *sqq.* Cp. B 366 *sqq.*

SECOND VERSION, B

But of hys deitee he shal be stable,
And therto gracious and merciable.
And if ye nere a god that knowen alle,
Thanne myght it be as I yow tellen shalle ;
This man to yow may falsly ben accused,
That as by right him oughtė ben excused ;
For in youre courte ys many a losengeour,
And many a queinte totelere áccusour,
That tabourẹn in youre erės many a soun,
Ryght aftir hire ymagynacioun,
To have youre daliance, and for envie.
Thise ben the causes, and I shal nat lye,
Envie is lavendere of the court alway ;
For she ne parteth, neither nyght ne day,
Out of the house of Cesar,—thus seith
     Dante ;   360
Whoso that goth, algate she wol nat
     wante.
And eke, parauntere, for this man is nyce,
He myghtė doon it, gessyng no malice ;
But for he useth thyngės for to make,
Hym rekketh noght of what matere he
     take ;
Or him was boden maken thilkė tweye
Of somme persone, and durste it nat
     withseye
Or him repenteth outrély of this.
He ne hath nat doon so grevously amys,
To translaten that oldė clerkės writen,
As thogh that he of malice wolde enditen,
Despite of Love, and had himselfe it
     wroght.   372
This sholde a ryghtwis lord have in his
     thoght,
And nat be lyke tirauntes of Lumbardye,
That han no réward but at tyrannye.
For he that kynge or lorde is naturel,
Hym oghtė nat be tiraunt ne crewel,
As is a fermour, to doon the harme he kan ;

351. *That,* so *that* ; a better reading than the
Ther of the earlier version.
354. *soun,* F *swoun,* wrongly.
357. A new line.
359. In the *Inferno,* xvii. 64-65, Invidia is called
     La meretrice, che mal dall' ospizio Di
     Cesare non torse gli occhi putti.
361. *wants,* be missing.
364. *But,* F B om.
368. A new line.
371. *As,* F³ and Pepys *And,* wrongly.
374. *tirauntes of Lumbardye,* like the Visconti.

FIRST VERSION

He mustė thynke it is his ligė man.
And that hym owith o verry duėtee,　360
Schewyn his peple pleyn benygnete
And wel to heryn here excusacyouns,
And here compleyntys and petyciouns,
In duewė tymė, whan they schal it profre.
This is the sentens of the philosophre :
A kyng to kepe hise lygis in justice,
Withouten doutė that is his offise,
And therto is a kyng ful depe i-sworn
Ful manye an hunderede wyntyr here-
be-forn,
And for to kepe his lordys hir degre,　370
As it is ryght and skylful that they be
Enhaunsėde and honourėd [and] most dere
For they ben half goddys in this worldė
here.
This schal be don bothė to pore [and]
ryche, *etc.*

[For the rest of the Prologue and the
Legends the differences between this
MS. and the rest are slight enough
to be indicated in the notes.]

367. *Withouten,* MS. *which oughtyn.*

SECOND VERSION, B

He mostė thinke it is his leegė man,　379
And is his tresour, and his gold in cofre.
This is the sentence of the philosophre :
A kyng to kepe his leegės in justice,
Withouten doutė that is his office.
Al wol he kepe his lordės hire degree,
As it is ryght and skilful that they bee
Enhaunced and honourėd, and moste
dere,
For they ben half goddys in this worldė
here.—
Yit mote he doon bothe ryght, to poore and
ryche,
Al be that hire estaat be nat yliche,
And han of poorė folke compassyoun ;　390
For lo, the gentil kynde of the lyoun !
For whan a flye offendith him or biteth,
He with his tayle awey the flyė smyteth
Al esely ; for of his gentėrye
Hym deyneth nat to wreke hym on a flye,
As doth a curre, or elles another best.
' In noble corage oughtė ben arest,
And weyen every thing by equytee,
And ever have rėwarde to his owen
degree.
For, syr, it is no maistrye for a lorde　400
To dampne a man, without answere of
worde,
And for a lorde, that is ful foule to use.
And if so be he may hym nat excuse,
But asketh mercy with a dredeful herte,
And profereth him, ryght in his barė
sherte,
To ben ryght at your owen jugėment,
Than oght a god, by short avysėment,
Consydre his owne honour, and hys trespas :
For syth no cause of dethe lyeth in this
caas,
Yow oghte to ben the lyghter merciable.　410
Leteth youre ire, and beth sumwhat
tretable !
The man hath servėd yow of his kunnyng,
And furthrėd wel youre lawe in his makyng.

380. A new line.
384. *kepe, i.e.* keep for ; Trin. MS. reads : *At
well hys lordes to kepe theyr degre.*
400. *no maistrye,* no difficult matter.
403. *if,* F⁴ and Pepys *it.*
404. *dredeful,* Gg (390) *sorweful.*
405. It was thus that, as late as 1429, Alexander,
Lord of the Isles, presented himself to James I.

596

'Al be hit that he kan nat wel endite,
Yet hath he madè lewdè folke delyte
To servè you, in preysinge of your name.
He made the book that hight the Hous
  pf Fame,
And eke the Deeth of Blaunchè the
  Duchesse,
And the Parlèment of Foulès, as I gesse, 419
And al the Love of Palamoun and Arcíte
Of Thebès, thogh the storye ys knowen
  lyte ;
And many an ympné for your halydayes,
That highten balades, roundels, virelayes.
  'And for to speke of other holynesse,
He hath in prosè translated Boece,
And made the Lyfe also of Seynt Cecile.
He made also, gon ys a gretè while,
Origenes upon the Maudeleyne.
Hym oughtè now to have the lessè peyne,
He hath made many a lay, and many a
  thynge. 430
  'Now as ye be a god, and eke a kynge,
I youre Alcestè, whilom quene of Trace,
I askè yow this man, ryght of youre grace,
That ye him never hurte in al his lyve,
And he shal sweren to yow, and that as
  blyve,
He shal no more agilten in this wyse,
But he shal maken, as ye wol devyse,
Of wommen trewe in lovyng al hire lyf,
Wher so ye wol, of mayden or of wyf,
And forthren yow as muche as he mysseyde,
Or in the Rose, or ellès in Creseyde.' 441
  The god of Love answerede hire thus
    anoon,
'Madame,' quod he, 'it is so long agoon

That I yow knewe so charitable and trewe,
That never yit, syn that the worlde was
  newe,
To me ne founde I better noon than yee ;
If that I woldè savè my degree,
I may, ne wol, nat wernè your requeste ;
Al lyeth in yow,—dooth wyth hym what
  yow liste.
I al foryeve withouten lenger space ; 450
For who-so yeveth a gifte, or doth a grace,
Do it bytyme, his thank is wel the more ;
And demeth ye what he shal do therfore.
Go, thankè now my lady here,' quod he.
  I roos, and doun I sette me on my knee,
And seyde thus : 'Madame, the God above
Foryeldè yow that ye the god of Love
Han makèd me his wrathè to foryive,
And yeve me grace so longè for to lyve,
That I may knowè soothly what ye bee, 460
That han me holpe, and put me in this
  degree.
But trewély I wende, as in this cas,
Naught have a gilt, ne doon to Love trespas ;
For-why, a trewè man, withouten drede,
Hath nat to parten with a thevès dede ;
Ne a trewè lover oghtè me not blame,
Thogh that I spake a fals lovere som shame.
They oghtè rather with me for to holde,
For that I of Creseydè wroot or tolde,
Or of the Rose,—what-so myn auctour
    mente,— 470
Algatè, God woot, it was myn entente
To forthren trouthe in love, and it cheryce,
And to ben war fro falsnesse and fro vice,
By swiche ensample ; this was my men·
  ynge.'
  And she answerde, 'Lat be thyn
    arguynge,
For Love ne wol nat countrèpletèd be
In ryght ne wrong, and lernè that of me ;
Thow hast thy grace, and holde the ryght
  therto.
Now wol I seyn what penance thou shalt do
For thy trespas, and understonde it here :

414. *wel,* Gg *omits.* Gg (400-403) adds two lines
and presents the next couplet in a different form :
  Whil he was yong he keptè youre estat ;
  I not wher hè be now a renegat.
  But wel I wot with that he can endyte
  He hath makid lewede folk to delyte.
421. *thogh the storye ys knowen lyte,* cp.
Anelida, ll. 13, 14.
424. *other holynesse,* the religion of the church
as opposed to that of Cupid.
425. Gg (414, 415) adds the lines :
And of the Wrechede Engendrynge of Mankynde,
As man may in pope Innocent i-fynde.
426. *Lyfe of Seynt Cecile,* now the Second
Nun's Story in *Cant. Tales.*
428. *Origenes,* a homily, De Maria Magdalene,
wrongly attributed to Origen.

447. *I,* F *ye.*
450. *I,* Gg (440) *And.*
459. *yeve me,* om. F⁴.
461. *this,* Gg (451) *swich.*
466. *oghte me not,* MSS. *oght me not to.*
477. *that of,* Gg (467) *this at.*
478. *the,* i.e. *thee.*

Thou shalt while that thou lyvest, yere by
    yere   481
The mosté partye of thy tymé spende
In makyng of a glorious Legende
Of goodé wymmen, maydenés and wyves,
That weren trew in lovyng al hire lyves ;
And telle of falsé men that hem bytraien,
That al here lyf ne don nat but asayen
How many women they may doon a shame,
For in youre worlde that is now holde a
    game.
And thogh the lyké nat a lovere bee, 490
Speke wel of love ; this penance yive I the.
And to the god of Love I shal so preye,
That he shal charge his servantes, by any
    weye,
To forthren thee, and wel thy labour quyte :
Go now thy weye, thys penaunce is but lyte.
And whan this book is made, yive it the
    quene,
On my byhalfe, at Eltham, or at Sheene.'
    The god of Love gan smyle, and than
    he sayde,
' Wostow,' quod he, ' wher this be wyf or
    mayde,
Or queene, or countesse, or of what degre,
That hath so lytel penance yiven thee, 501
That hast deservéd sorere for to smerte ?
But pite renneth soone in gentil herte :
That maistow seen, she kytheth what
    she is.'
And I answerde, ' Nay, sire, so have I blys,
Na more, but that I see wel she is good.'
    ' That is a trewé talé, by myn hood ! '
Quod Love, ' and that thou knowest wel,
    pardee,
If it be so that thou avisé the.   509
Hastow nat in a book, lyth in thy cheste,
The greté goodnesse of the quene Alceste,
That turnéd was into a dayésye ?
She that for hire housbonde chees to dye,

And eke to goon to helle, rather than he,
And Ercules rescowéd hire, *pardé,*
And broght hir out of helle agayne to blys?'
    And I answerd ageyn, and saydé, ' Yis,
Now knowe I hire.   And is this good
    Alceste,
The daysie, and myn owene hertés reste ?
Now fele I weel the goodnesse of this wyf,
That both after hir deth, and in hire lyf, 521
Hir greté bounté doubleth hir renoun.
Wel hath she quyt me myn affeccioun,
That I have to hire flour the dayésye. ,
No wonder is thogh Jove hire stellyfye,
As telleth Agaton, for hire goodnesse,
Hire whité corowne berith of it witnesse ;
For also many vertues haddé shee,
As smalé florouns in hire corowne bee.
    ' In rémembraunce of hire and in honoure
Cibella made the daysye and the floure 531
Y-crowned al with white, as men may see,
And Mars yaf to hire corowne reede, pardee,
In stede of rubyes, sette among the white.'
    Therwith this queene wex reed for shame
    a lyte,
Whanne she was preyséd so in hire presence.
Thanne seydé Love, ' A ful grete neglygence
Was it to the, that ylké tyme thou made,
' Hyd, Absolon, thy tresses ' in balade,
That thou forgate hire in thy songe to sette,
Syn that thou art so gretly in hire dette, 541
And wost so wel that kalender ys she
To any woman that wol lover be :
For she taught al the crafte of fyne lovyng,
And namély of wyfhode the lyvyng,

521. *in*, Gg (509) *ek.*
526. *Agaton.* Prof Hales has shown that the
reference is to Plato's *Symposium* (in which the
poet Agathon is one of the speakers), where the
story of Alcestis is told.
528. *haddé*, so F⁴ Pepys, Arch. Seld.; Gg Trin ²
hath.
531. *Cibella*, Cybele.
539-541, 543. New lines.
537-542. The Gg text (ll. 525-534) reads :

Than seyde Love, ' A ful grete neglygence
Was it to the to write onstedefast-nesse
Of women, sithe thow knowist here goodnesse
By pref and ek by storyis hereby-forn.
Let be the chaf and writ wel of the corn.
Why noldist thow han writyn of Alceste
And latyn Criseide ben a-slepe and rest,
For of Alceste schulde thy wrytynge be,
Syn that thow wist that calandir is she
Of goodnesse, for sche taughte of fyn lovynge.

542. *so*, om. F⁴.

487. Omitted in Fairfax, Tanner, and Bodley.
490. *the lyke*, it pleases thee ; Gg (480) *the
lestyth.*
496, 497. New lines.
497. *Eltham.* Part of the royal house, built in
the thirteenth century, but enlarged by Edward
IV., still remains.
497. *Sheene,* now Richmond. It was at the
palace at Sheen that Anne of Bohemia died.
502. *sorere,* Bodl. and Tann. *sore.*
503. Cp. *Cant. Tales,* A 1761.
508. *that,* om. F⁴.

And al the boundès that she oghtè kepe ;
Thy litel witte was thilkè tyme aslepe.
But now I chargè the upon thy lyfe,   548
That in thy legende thou make of thys wyfe,
Whan thou hast other smale y-made before ;
And fare now wel, I chargè thee namore.
But er I go, thus muche I wol the telle,
Ne shal no trewè lover come in helle.
Thise other ladies sittynge here arowe
Ben in thy balade, if thou kanst hem knowe,
And in thy bookès alle thou shalt hem fynde ;
Have hem in thy Legende now alle in
    mynde,
I mene of hem that ben in thy knowyng.
For here ben twenty thousand moo sittyng
Thanne thou knowest, and ben good
    wommen alle,   560
And trewe of love for oght that may byfalle ;
Makè the metres of hem as the lest ;
I mot goon home, the sonnè draweth west,
To Paradys, with al thise companye ;
And serve alwey the fresshè dayèsye.
At Cleopatre I wole that thou begynne,
And so forthe, and my love so shalt thou
    wynne ;
For lat see now what man that lover be,
Wol doon so stronge a peyne for love as she.
I wot wel that thou maist nat al it ryme,
That swichè lovers dide in hirè tyme ;   571
It were to long to reden and to here ;
Sufficeth me thou make in this manere,
That thou reherce of al hir lyfe the grete,
After thise olde auctours lysten trete.
For who-so shal so many a storye telle,
Sey shortly, or he shal to longè dwelle.'
    And with that worde my bokès gan I
    take,
And ryght thus on my legende gan I make.

Incipit Legenda Cleopatrie, Martiris,
Egipti Regine.

After the deth of Tholome the kyng,   580
That al Egipte hadde in his governyng,

Regnèd hys queenè Cleopataras ;
Til on a tyme befel ther swich a cas,
That out of Rome was sent a senatour,
For to conquéren regnès and honour
Unto the toun of Rome, as was usaunce,
To have the worlde at hir obeÿsaunce,
And sooth to seye, Antonius was his name.
    So fil it, as Fortúne hym oght a shame,
Whanne he was fallen in prosperitee,   590
Rebel unto the toun of Rome is he.
And over al this, the suster of Cesar
He lafte hir falsly, er that she was war ;
And wold algatès han another wyf ;
For which he took with Rome and Cesar
    strif.
    Natheles, forsooth, this ylkè senatour
Was a full worthy gentil werreyour,
And of his deeth it was ful gret damage.
But Love had brought this man in swich
    a rage,
And him so narwè bounden in his laas,
Al for the love of Cleopataras,   601
That al the worlde he sette at no value ;
Him thoghte ther was nothing to him
    so due
As Cleopataras for to love and serve ;
Him roghtè nat in armès for to sterve
In the defence of hir and of hir ryght.
    This noble queene ek lovedè so this
    knyght,
Thurgh his desert and for his chivalrye ;
As certeynly, but-if that bookès lye,
He was of persone, and of gentilesse,   610
And of discrecion, and of hardynesse,
Worthy to any wight that lyven may ;
And she was faire as is the rose in May.
And, for to maken shortly is the beste,
She wax his wif, and hadde him as hir
    leste.
    The weddyng and the festè to devyse,
To me that have y-takè swich emprise,
Of so many a storye for to make,
It were to longe, lest that I sholdè slake
Of thing that beryth more effecte and
    charge ;   620
For men may overlade a shippe or barge.

552-565. New lines.
552-565, 568-577, not in the Gg text.
560. *and ben*, Trin.² *and*; Arch. Seld. *that ben*; F⁴ om.
575. *trete*, from Arch. Seld. ; F⁵ *for to trete*; Trin.² *to trete*.
578. *my bokes*, etc.; Gg *of slep I gan awake*.
580. *Tholome*, Ptolemy, probably the elder of the two sons of Ptolemy Auletes.

592. *the suster of Cesar*. Octavia, sister of Octavianus Cæsar, afterwards the Emperor Augustus.
611. *of* (2), om. Arch. Seld. and Trin.
614. *for*, om. F.

And forthy to effect than wol I skyppe,
And al the remenaunt I wol letè slyppe.
  Octavyan, that woode was of this dede,
Shoop him an ost on Antony to lede,
Al outerly for his destruccioun,
With stoutè Romaynes, crewel as lyoun ;
To shippe they wente, and thus I let
        hem sayle.   628
  Antonius, was war, and wol nat fayle
To meten with thise Romaynes, if he may,
Took eke his rede, and both upon a day,
His wyf and he, and al his ost, forthe wente
To shippe anon, no lenger they ne stente,
And in the see hit happèd hem to mete.
Up goth the trumpe, and for to shoute
        and shete,
And paynen hem to sette on with the sonne ;
With grisly soune out goth the gretè gonne,
And heterly they hurtelen al attones,
And for the top doun cometh the gretè
        stones.   639
In gooth the grapènel so ful of crokes,
Amonge the ropès, and the sheryng hokes ;
In with the polax preseth he and he ;
Byhynde the mastè begyneth he to fle,
And out agayn, and dryveth hem over
        borde ;
He stynteth hem upon his sperès orde ;
He rent the sayle with hokès lyke a sithe ;
He bryngeth the cuppe, and biddeth hem
        be blithe ;   647
He poureth pesen upon the hacches slidre ;
With pottès ful of lyme, they goon togidre ;
And thus the longè day in fight they spende,
Til at the last, as every thing hath ende,
Antony is shent, and put hym to the flyghte ;
And al his folke to-go, that best go myghte.
  Fleeth ek the queene with al hir
        purpre sayle,
For strokès which that wente as thik as
        hayle ;

No wonder was she myght it nat endure.
And whan that Antony saugh that àventure,
'Allas,' quod he, 'the day that I was borne !
My worshippe in this day thus have I lorne !'
And for dispeyre out of his wytte he sterte,
And roof hymself anon thurghout the herte,
Er that he ferther went out of the place.
His wyf, that koude of Cesar have no grace,
To Egipte is fled, for drede and for dis-
        tresse.
But herkeneth ye that speken of
        kyndenesse.
Ye men that falsly sweren many an othe,
That ye wol dye if that your love be wrothe,
Here may ye seen of women which a trouthe.
This woful Cleopatre hath made swich
        routhe,   669
That ther nys tongè noon that may it telle.
But on the morowe she wol no lenger dwelle,
But made hir subtil werkmen make a shryne
Of al the rubees and the stonès fyne
In al Egiptè that she koude espye ;
And puttè ful the shryne of spicerye,
And let the corps embawme ; and forth
        she fette
This dedè corps, and in the shryne it shette.
And next the shryne a pitte than doth
        she grave,
And alle the serpentes that she myghtè have,
She put hem in that grave, and thus she
        seyde :   680
' Now, love, to whom my sorweful herte
        obeyde
So ferforthely that fro that blysful houre
That I yow swor to ben al frely youre,—
I menè yow, Antonius, my knyght,—
That never wakyng in the day or nyght
Ye nere out of myn hertès rémembraunce,
For wele or woo, for carole, or for daunce ;
And in my self this covenaunt made I tho,
That ryght swich as ye felten wele or wo,
As ferforth as it in my powere lay,   690
Unréprováble unto my wifhood ay,
The samè wolde I felen, life or deethe :
And thilkè covenaunt, while me lasteth
        breethe,
I wol fulfille ; and that shal wel be seene,
Was never unto hir love a trewer queene.'

623. *lete*, Gg ; F⁵ *let it.*
638. *heterly*, F⁴ *hertely.*
642. *he* (2), Gg *sche*, as if the references were
personal to Antony and Cleopatra !
644. *hem*, Trin., Pepys, and Add. ; rest *hym.*
645. *stynteth hem*, Trin. and Add. ; rest *styngeth
hym.*
648. *pesen*, peas to make the decks slippery.
654. Chaucer here follows the 'regina cum
aurea puppe veloque purpureo se in altum dedit'
of Florus.

662. Actium was fought in Sept. of 31 B.C. ;
Antony killed himself the next year.

And wyth that worde, naked, with ful
    good herte,
Amonge the serpents in the pit she sterte;
And ther she chees to han hir buryinge.
Anon the neddres gonne hir for to stynge,
And she hir deeth receveth with good chere,
For love of Antony that was hir so dere.
And this is storial sooth, it is no fable. 702
    Now er I fynde a man thus trewe and
    stable,
And wolde for love his deeth so frely take,
I prey God lat oure hedes nevere ake!

Explicit Legenda Cleopatre, Martyris

Incipit Legende Tesba Babilon, Martiris

At Babiloyne whilom fil it thus,—
The whiche toun the queene Semyramus
Leet dichen al about, and walles make
Ful hye, of harde tiles wel y-bake: 709
There were dwellynge in this noble toune
Two lordes, which that were of grete
    renoune,
And woneden so neigh upon a grene,
That ther nas but a stoon wal hem betwene,
As ofte in grette tounes is the wone.
And sooth to seyn, that o man had a sone,
Of al that londe oon of the lustieste;
That other had a doghtre, the faireste
That esteward in the worlde was tho
    dwellynge. 718
The name of everyche gan to other sprynge,
By wommen that were neyghebores aboute;
For in that contre yit, withouten doute,
Maydens ben y-kept for jelousye
Ful streyte, leste they diden somme folye.
    This yonge man was cleped Piramus,
And Tesbe highte the maide,—Naso seith
    thus.
And thus by réporte was hir name y-shove,
That as they wex in age, wex hir love.
And certeyn, as by reson of hir age, 728
Ther myghte have ben betwex hem
    mariage,
But that hir fadres nold it not assente,
And both in love y-like soore they brente,
That noon of al hir frendes myghte it lette.

But prevely somtyme yit they mette
By sleight, and spoken somme of hir desire,
As wre the glede and hotter is the fire;
Forbeede a love, and it is ten so woode.
    This wal, which that bitwixe hem bothe
    stoode,
Was cloven a-two, right fro the toppe
    adoun,
Of olde tyme, of his foundacioun. 739
But yit this clyfte was so narwe and lite
It was nat seene, deere ynogh a myte;
But what is that that love kannat espye?
Ye lovers two, if that I shal nat lye,
Ye founden first this litel narwe clifte,
And with a soune as softe as any shryfte,
They leete hir wordes thurgh the clifte pace,
And tolden, while they stoden in the place,
Al hire compleynt of love, and al hire wo.
At every tyme whan they dorste so.
Upon the o syde of the walle stood he,
And on that other syde stood Tesbe, 751
The swoote soun of other to receyve.
    And thus here wardeyns wolde they
    disceyve,
And every day this walle they wolde threete,
And wisshe to God that it were doun y-bete,
Thus wolde they seyn: 'Allas, thou
    wikked walle!
Thurgh thyn envye thow us lettest alle!
Why nyltow cleve, or fallen al a-two?
Or at the leeste, but thow wouldest so,
Yit woldestow but ones let us meete, 760
Or ones that we myghte kyssen sweete,
Than were we covered of oure cares colde.
But natheles, yit be we to thee holde,
In as muche as thou suffrest for to goon
Our wordes thurgh thy lyme and eke thy
    stoon;
Yet oghte we with the ben wel apayede.'
    And whan these idel wordes weren sayde,
The colde walle they wolden kysse of stoon,
And take hir leve, and forth they wolden
    goon.
And this was gladly in the evetyde, 770
Or wonder erly, lest men it espyede.
And longe tyme they wroght in this manere,
Til on a day, whan Phebus gan to clere—

706-776. Missing in Pepys.
716. *of*, om. F³.
725. *And*, in Gg only.

741. *deere ynogh a myte*, ever so little.
747. *they*, Trin.²; rest *that they*.
770. *And*, F *Alle*.

Aurora with the stremés of hire hete
Had driéd uppe the dewe of herbés wete—
Unto this clyfte, as it was wont to be,
Come Piramus, and after come Tesbe.
And plighten trouthé fully in here faye,
That ilké samé nyght to steele awaye,
And to begile hire wardeyns everychone,
And forth out of the citee for to gone.   781
And, for the feeldés ben so broode and wide,
Fór to meete in o place at o tyde
They setté markes, hire metyng sholdé bee
Ther kyng Nynus was graven, under a
    tree,—
For oldé payens, that ydóles heriede,
Useden tho in feeldés to ben beriede,—
And fasté by his gravé was a welle.
And, shortly of this talé for to telle,   789
This covenaunt was afferméd wonder faste,
And longe hem thoghté that the sonné laste,
That it nere goon under the see adoun.

This Tesbe hath so greete affeccioun,
And so grete lykynge Piramus to see,
That whan she seigh hire tymé myghté bee,
At nyght she stale awey ful prevély,
With hire face y-wympled subtilly.
For al hire frendés, for to save hire trouthe,
She hath forsake ; allas, and that is routhe,
That ever woman woldé be so trewe   800
To trusten man, but she the bet hym knewe !

And to the tree she goth a ful goode paas,
For love made hir so hardy in this caas ;
And by the welle adoun she gan hir dresse.
Allas ! than comith a wildé leonesse
Out of the woode, withouten more arreste,
With blody mouth, of strangelynge of a
    beste,
To drynken of the welle ther as she sat.
And whan that Tesbe had espyéd that,
She ryst hir up, with a ful drery herte,   810
And in a cave with dredful foot she sterte,
For by the moone she saugh it wel withalle.
And as she ranne, hir wympel leet she falle,
And tooke noon hede, so sore she was
    awhaped,
And eke so gladé that she was escaped ;
And ther she sytte, and darketh wonder
    stille.

Whan that this lyonesse hath dronke hire
    fille,
Aboute the wellé gan she for to wynde,
And ryght anon the wympil gan she fynde,
And with hir blody mouth it al to-rente.
Whan this was don, no lenger she ne stente,
But to the woode hir wey than hath she
    nome.   822
    And at the laste this Piramus is come,
But al to longe, allas, at home was hee !
The mooné shone, men myghté wel y-see,
And in his wey, as that he come ful faste,
Hise eyen to the grounde adoun he caste ;
And in the sonde as he behelde adoun,
He seigh the steppés broode of a lyoun ;
And in his herte he sodeynly agroos,   830
And pale be wex, therwith his heer aroos,
And nere he come, and founde the wympel
    torne.
' Allas,' quod he, ' the day that I was borne !
This o nyght wol us lovers bothé slee !
How shulde I axen mercy of Tesbee,
Whan I am he that have yow slayne, allas?
My byddyng hath i-slayn yow in this caas !
Allas, to bidde a woman goon by nyghte
In placé ther as peril fallen myghte !
And I so slowe ! allas, I ne haddé be   840
Here in this place, a furlong wey or ye !
Now what lyon that be in this foreste,
My body mote he renten, or what beste
That wilde is, gnawen mote he now my
    herte ! '
And with that worde he to the wympel
    sterte,
And kiste it ofte, and wepte on it ful sore ;
And seydé, ' Wympel, allas ! ther nys no
    more,
But thou shalt feele as wel the blode of me,
As thou hast felt the bledynge of Tesbe.'
And with that worde he smot hym to the
    herte ;   850
The blood out of the wounde as brodé
    sterte
As water, whan the conduyte broken is.
    Now Tesbe, which that wysté nat of this,
But syttyng in hire drede, she thoghté thus :
' If it so fallé that my Piramus
Be comen hider, and may me nat y-fynde,

---

785. *Nynus*, the mythical founder of Nineveh,
for whom Semiramis built a tomb.
815. *glade*, Trin. *glad of*.

852. *whan the conduyte broken is*. The metaphor is transferred from Ovid, *Met.* iv. 122-124.

He may me holden fals, and eke unkynde.'
And oute she comith, and after hym gan
   espien
Bóthe with hire herte and with hire eyen ;
And thoghte, 'I wol him tellen of my
   drede, 860
Bothe of the lyonesse and al my dede.'
And at the laste hire love than hath she
   founde,
Bétynge with his helis on the grounde,
Al blody ; and therwithal abak she sterte,
And lyke the wawes quappé gan hir herte,
And pale as boxe she wax, and in a throwe
Avisèd hir, and gan him wel to knowe,
That it was Piramus, hire herté dere.
  Who koudé writé which a dedely chere
Hath Tesbe now ? and how hire heere she
   rente ? 870
And how she gan hir-selvé to turmente ?
And how she lyth and swowneth on the
   grounde ?
And how she wepe of terès ful his wounde?
How medleth she his blood with hir com-
   pleynte ?
How with his blood hir-selven gan she
   peynte ?
How clippeth she the dedé corps? allas !
How kysseth she his dedé corps? allas !
How kysseth she his frosty mouthe so
   colde?
' Who hath don this ? and who hath ben
   so bolde 879
To sleen my leefe ? O speké, Piramus !
I am thy Tesbe, that thee calleth thus ! '
And therwithal she lyfteth up his heed.
  This woful man, that was nat fully
   deed,
Whan that he herde the name of Tesbe
   crien,
On hire he caste his hevy dedely eyen,
And doun agayn, and yeldeth up the
   goste.
  Tesbe rist uppe, withouten noyse or
   boste,
And saugh hir wympel and his empty
   shethe,
And eke his swerde, that him hath don
   to dethe.

Than spake she thus : 'Thy woful hande,'
   quod she, 890
' Is strong ynogh in swiche a werke to me ;
For love shal me yive strengthe and
   hardynesse,
To make my woundé large ynogh, I gesse.
I wole the folowen ded, and I wol be
Felawe and cause eke of thy deeth,' quod
   she.
' And thogh that nothing save the deth only
Myghte the fro me departé trewély,
Thou shal no more departé now fro me
Than fro the deth, for I wol go with the.
  ' And now, ye wrecched jelouse fadrès
   oure, 900
Wé, that weren whilome children youre,
We prayen yow, withouten more envye,
That in o grave i-fere we moten lye,
Syn love hath broght us to this pitouse ende.
And ryghtwis God to every lover sende,
That loveth trewely, more prosperite
Than ever haddé Piramus and Tesbe.
And let no gentile woman hire assure,
To putten hire in swiche an áventure.
But God forbedé but a woman kan 910
Ben also trewe and lovynge as a man,
And for my parte I shal anon it kythe.'
And with that worde his swerde she took
   as swithe,
That warme was of hire lovès blood, and
   hote,
And to the herté she hire-selven smote.
  And thus are Tesbe and Piramus ago.
Of trewé men I fyndé but fewe mo
In al my bookés, save this Piramus,
And therfore have I spoken of hym thus
For it is deyntee to us men to fynde 920
A man that kan in love be trewe and
   kynde.
  Here may ye seen, what lover so he be,
A woman dar and kan as wel as he.

Explicit Legenda Tesbe

890. *Thy*, Gg corrects to *Myn* ; but perhaps a
couplet has fallen out. Chaucer is translating
Metamorphoses, iv. 147-149 :
    Tua te manus, inquit, amorque
  Perdidit, infelix. Est et nihl fortis in anum
  Hoc manus : est et amor, etc.
898. F³ *noo more now depart.*
903. *i-fere*, only in Trin. and Add.
904. F *hath us broght.*
911. *also*, Add. only ; Trin. *als* ; rest *as.*

866. *pale as boxe*, Ovid's ' oraque buxo Pallidi-
ora gerens,' *Met.* iv. 134, 135.

Incipit Legenda Didonis, Martiris,
Carthaginis Regine

Glorie and honour, Virgile Mantuan,
Be to thy name! and I shal, as I kan,
Folowe thy lanterne as thou goste byforn.
How Eneas to Dido was forsworne—
In thyne Eneyde and Naso wol I take   928
The tenour, and the grete effectès make.
  Whan Troyè broght was to destruccion
By Grekès sleight, and namely by Synon,
Feynyng the hors offred unto Minerve,
Thurgh which that many a Trojan mostè
      sterve,
And Ector had after his deeth appered,
And fire so woode it myghtè nat ben stered,
In al the noble tour of Ylion,
That of the citee was the cheef dungeon;
And al the contree was so lowe y-broght,
And Priamus, the kyng, fordoon and noght;
And Eneas was chargèd by Venus   940
To fleen away, he tooke Ascanius,
That was his sone, in his ryght hande
      and fledde,
And on his bakke he baar, and with him
      ledde,
His oldè fader, clepèd Anchises;
And by the wey his wyf Creusa he lees,
And mochel sorowe hadde he in his mynde,
Er that he koude his felawshippè fynde.
But at the lastè, whan he hadde hem
      founde,
He made him redy in a certeyn stounde,
And to the see ful faste he gan him hye,   950
And sayleth forth with al his companye
Towarde Ytayle, as wolde his destanee.
But of his àventurès in the see
Nys nat to purpos for to speke of here,
For it acordeth nat to my matere.
But as I seyde, of hym and of Dydo
Shal be my tale, til that I have do.
  So longe he sayllèd in the saltè see,
Til in Lybye unneth arryvèd he,
With schepis sevene and with no more
      navye,   960

And glad was he to londè for to hye,
So was he with the tempest al to-shake.
And whan that he the havene had y-take,
He had a knyghte was callèd Achates,
And him of al his felawshippe he ches
To goon with him, the contree for to spye.
He toke with him na morè companye,
But forth they goon, and lafte his shippès
      ride,
His fere and he, withouten any guyde.
  So longe he walketh in this wildernesse,
Til at the last he mette an hunteresse;   971
A bowe in hande, and arwès haddè shee;
Hire clothès cuttid were unto the knee.
But she was yit the fairest creature
That ever was y-formèd by nature;
And Eneas and Achates she grette,
And thus she to hem spak whan she hem
      mette,
'Sawe ye,' quod she, 'as ye han walked
      wide,
Any of my sustren walkè yow besyde,
With any wildè boor or other beste,   980
That they han hunted to in this foreste,
Y-tukkèd up, with arwès in hire cas?'
  'Nay soothly, lady!' quod this Eneas;
'But by thy beaute, as it thynketh me,
Thou myghtest never erthely woman be,
But Phebus suster artow, as I gesse.
And if so be that thou be a goddesse,
Have mercy on oure labour and oure wo.'
  'I nam no goddesse soothely,' quod
      she tho;
'For maydens walken in this contree
      here,   990
With arwès and with bowe, in this manere.
This is the regne of Libie ther ye been,
Of which that Dido lady is and queene.'
And shortly tolde al the occasioun
Why Dido come into that regioun,
Of which as now me lusteth nat to ryme:
It nedeth nat, it nere but los of tyme.
For this is al and somme; it was Venus,
His owene moder, that spake with him
      thus;

928. *Naso*, Ovid in his *Heroides*, Ep. vii.
931. *Synon*, cp. *Æneid*, ii. 57-198.
934. *Ector*. Hector's ghost warned Æneas to
flee from Troy, cp. *Æn.* ii. 270-277.
952. *his*, om. F⁵.
960, 961. Only in Gg and Pepys.

971 *sqq.* Cp. *Æn.* i. 314-417.
973. *cuttid*, F³ *knytte.* Virgil's 'nuda gens
nodoque sinus collecta fluentis' might suggest
either word.
982. *Y-tukked up*, etc., Virgil's 'succinctm
pharetra.'

And to Cartage she bad he sholde him
   dighte,   1000
And vanysshéd anoon out of his sighte.
I koudé folwe worde for worde Virgile,
But it wolde lasten al to longé while.
   This noble queene, that clepéd was
   Dido,
That whilom was the wife of Sitheo,
That fairer was than is the bryghté sonne,
This noble toun of Cartage hath begonne;
In which she regneth in so grete honoure,
That she was holde of allé quenés floure,
Of gentilesse, of fredome, of beautee,
That wel was him that myght hir onés see.
Of kyngés and of lordés so desired,   1012
That al the worlde hire beaute hadde
   y-fired,
She stoode so wel in every wyghtés grace.
   Whan Eneas was come unto that place,
Unto the maistre temple of al the toun,
Ther Dido was in hir devocioun,
Ful privély his wey than hath he nome.
Whan he was in the largé temple come,—
I kannat seye if that hit be possible,—
But Venus hadde him makéd invisible ;
Thus seith the booke, withouten any les.
   And whan this Eneas and Achates
Hadden in this temple ben over-alle,
Than foundé they depeynted on a walle
How Troy and al the londe distroyed
   was.
' Allas, that I was born ! ' quod Eneas.
' Thurghout the worlde oure shame is
   kid so wide,
Now it is peynted upon every side.
Wé, that weren in prosperitee,   1030
Be now disclaundréd, and in swiche degre,
No lenger for to lyven I ne kepe.'
And with that worde he braste out for to
   wepe
So tendirly that routhe it was to seene.
   This fresshé lady, of the citee queene,
Stoode in the temple, in hire estat royalle,
So richély, and eke so faire withalle,
So yonge, so lusty, with hire eyen glade,
That if that God, that hevene and erthé
   made,

Wolde han a love, for beaute and
   goodenesse,   1040
And womanhode, and trouthe, and
   semlynesse.
Whom sholde he loven but this lady swete ?
Ther nys no woman to him halfe so mete.
Fortune, that hath the worlde in
   governaunce,
Hath sodeynly broght in so newe a chaunce,
That never was ther yet so fremde a cas.
For al the companye of Eneas,
Which that he wende han loren in the see,
Aryved is, noght fer fro that citee.   1049
For which the grettest of his lordés, some,
By áventure ben to the citee come,
Unto that samé temple, for to seke
The queene, and of hire socour hir beseke ;
Swich rénowne was ther spronge of hir
   goodnesse.
   And whan they haddé tolde al hire
   distresse,
And al hir tempest and hire hardé cas,
Unto the queene apperéd Eneas,
And openly beknew that it was he.
Who haddé joyé thanne but his meynee,
That hadden founde hire lord, hire
   governour ?   1060
   The queené saugh they dide him swich
   honour,
And had herde ofte of Eneas er tho,
And in hir herté she hadde routhe and wo,
That ever swiche a noble man as hee
Shal ben disherited in swiche degree.
And saugh the man, that he was lyke a
   knyghte,
And suffisaunt of persone and of myghte,
And lyke to ben a verray gentilman.
And wel his wordés he besetté kan,   1069
And hadde a noble visage for the nones,
And forméd wel of brawnés and of bones;
For after Venus hadde he swich fairenesse,
That no man myghte be half so faire, I gesse,
And wel a lorde he semede for to be.
And for he was a straunger, somwhat she
Lýkéd him the bette, as, God do bote,
To somme folke often newé thinge is swote.

1005. *Sitheo*, Sichæus.
1006. *is*, om. all but Gg and Add.
1030. *weren*, Trin. and Add. *were whilom*.

1046. *never was ther yet*, so Trin. and Thynne ;
Arch. Seld. *never yet was sene*; Add. om. *yet*;
rest om. *ther*.
1074. *he*, so Gg Add. Pepys ; rest *him*.

Anon hire herte hath pitee of his wo,
And with that pitee, love come in also ;
And thus for pitee and for gentillesse,
Refresshéd mote he ben of his distresse.
　She seydé, certés, that she sory was
That he hath had swich peril and swiche
　　cas ;
And in hire frendely speche, in this manere
She to him spake, and seyde as ye may here.
　' Be ye nat Venus' sone and Anchises' ?
In good faythe, al the worshippe and encres
That I may goodly doon yow, ye shal have :
Youre shippés and youre meynee shal I
　　save.'
And many a gentil worde she spake him to,
And comaunded hire messagers to go
The samé day, withouten any faylle,   1092
His shippés for to seke and hem vitaylle.
Ful many a beeste she to the shippés sente,
And with the wyne she gan hem to presente,
And to hire royall paleys she hire spedde,
And Eneas alwey with hire she ledde.
What nedeth yow the festé to discryve ?
He never better at ese was in his lyve.
Ful was the feste of deyntees and richesse,
Of instruments, of songe, and of gladnesse,
And many an amorouse lokyng and devys.
　This Eneas is comen to Paradys
Out of the swolowe of helle ; and thus in joye
Remembreth him of his estaat in Troye.
To daunsyng chambres, ful of parements,
Of riché beddés, and of ornaments,
This Eneas is ladde after the meete.
And with the queené whan that he
　　hadde seete   1109
And spices parted, and the wyne agon,
Unto his chambrës was he lad anon
To take his ease, and for to have his reste
With al his folke, to doon what so hem leste.
　Thér nas coursere, wel y-bridléd, noon,
Ne stedé for the justyng wel to goon,
Ne largé palfrey, esy for the nones,
Ne juwel fretted ful of riché stones,
Ne sakkés ful of gold, of largé wyghte,
Ne rubee noon that shynédé by nyghte,

Ne gentil hawteyn faukone heroneer,
Ne hound for hert, or wildé boor or deer.
Ne coupe of golde, with floryns newe
　　y-bette,   1122
That in the londe of Lybye may ben gette.
That Dido ne hath hit Eneas i-sente ;
And al is payéd, what that he hath spente.
Thus gan this queene honoure hir gestes
　　talle,
As she that kan in fredome passen alle.
　Eneas soothly eke, withouten les,
Hath sent unto his shippe by Achates
After his sone, and after ryché thynges,
Both ceptre, clothés, brochés, and eke
　　rynges ;   1131
Somme for to were, and somme for to
　　presente
To hire, that alle thise noble thinges
　　him sente ;
And bad his sone how that he sholdé make
The presentynge, and to the queene it take.
　Repeyréd is this Achates agayne,
And Eneas ful blysful is and fayne,
To seen his yongé sone Ascanius.
But nathéles our autour tellith us   1139
That Cupido, that is the god of love,
At prayere of hys moder hye above,
Haddé the liknesse of the childe y-take,
This noble queen enamouréd to make
On Eneas.   But as of that scripture
Be as be may, I make of it no cure.
But sooth is this, the queene hath made
　　swich chere
Unto this childe that wonder is to here ;
And of the present that his fader sente,
She thankéd him ful ofte in goode intente.
　Thus is this queene in pleasaunce and
　　in joye,   1150
With al thise newé lusty folke of Troye.
And of the dedés hath she more enquered
Of Eneas, and al the storie lered

1126. MSS. read *Thus kan* (Add. *ganne*) *this
honourable queene hir gestes* (Pepys, *giftes*) *calle.*
where *calle* is plainly a misreading of the com-
plimentary epithet *talle.*   This would make the
verb *honoure* impossible, and so lead to the sub-
stitution of *honourable.*   Another possible restoration would be *Thus yaf this noble queene hir
giftes talle.*   The reading *talle* is due to Dr.
Heath.

1139. So Gg and Pepys ; F⁴ *For to him yt was
reported thus ;* other variants show that the line
was corrupted.

1099. Gg *He nevere at ese was betyr in al hese
lyve.*
1107. *ornaments,* so Gg Trin. Add. ; F⁹ *pave-
ments.*
1110. *shynede,* Gg Trin. Pepys ; Add. *shone ;*
F⁵ *shineth.*

Of Troye; and al the longé day they tweye
Entendeden to speken and to pleye.
Of which ther gan to breden swich a fire,
That sely Dido hath now swich desire
With Eneas, hir newé geste, to deele,
That she hath loste hire hewe and eke
 hire heele.
Now to theffecte, now to the fruyt of al,
Why I have tolde this storye, and tellen
 shal,   1161
Thus I bygynne : It fil upon a nyght,
Whan that the moone upreysėd had hire
 lyght,
This noble queene unto hire restė wente.
She siketh sore, and gan hire - selfe
 turmente ;
She waketh, walwithe, maketh many a
 brayde,
As doon thise lovers, as I have herde
 sayde;
And at the laste, unto hire suster Anne
She made hir mone, and ryght thus
 spake she thanne.   1169
' Now, derė suster myn, what may it be
That me agasteth in my dreme?' quod she.
' This ilkė Trojane is so in my thoghte,
For that me thinketh he is so wel y-wroghte,
And eke so likly for to ben a man,
And therwithal so mykel good he kan,
That al my love and lyf lyth in his cure.
Have ye nat herde hym telle his áventure ?
Now certes, Anne, gif that ye redė me,
I woldė fayne to him y-wedded be ; 1179
This is theffect ; what sholde I morė seyn?
In him lith alle, to doo me lyve or deyn.'
 Hir suster Anne, as she that kouth
 hire goode,
Seyde as hire thoght, and somdel it
 withstoode.
But herof was so longe a sermonynge,
It were to longe to makė rehersynge.
But, finally, it may nat be withstonde :
Lovė woll love, for no wyght wol it wonde.
 The dawėnyng upryst oute of the see ;
This amorouse queenė chargeth hire
 meynee

1155. So Gg; rest *For to speke and for to*
pleye.
1163. *hire,* Gg *his.*
1174. *for,* om. F⁵.
1178. *rede,* Gg *rede it.*

The nettės dresse, and sperės brood and
 kene ;   1190
An huntynge wol this lusty fresshėqueene,
So priketh hire this newė joly wo.
To hors is al hire lusty folke y-go ;
Unto the courte the houndės ben
 y-broughte,
And upon coursers, swyfte as any thoughte,
Hir yongė knyghtės hoven al aboute,
And of hir women eke an hugė route.
Upon a thikkė palfrey, paper white, 1198
With sadel rede, enbroudet with delyte,
Of golde the barrės up enbosėd heighe,
Sitte Dido, al in golde and perrey wreighe.
And she is faire as is the bryghtė morwe,
That heeleth sekė folkes of nyghtės sorwe.
 Upon a coursere, startlyng as the fire,—
Men myghtė turne him with a lytel wire,—
Sitte Eneas, like Phebus to devyse,
So was he fressh arrayėd in his wyse.
The fomy bridel, with the bitte of golde,
Governeth he, ryght as himselfe hathe
 wolde.   1209
And forth this noble queene, this lady, ride
On huntyng, with this Trojan by hire syde.
 The herde of hertės founden is anon,
With ' Hay ! ' ' Go bet ! ' ' Prik thou ! '
 ' Lat gon, lat gon ! '
' Why nyl the lyoun comen, or the bere,
That I myght hym onės meten with this
 spere ? '
Thus seyn thise yongė folke, and up they
 kylle
The wildė hertes, and han hem at here wille.
 Amongės al this, to romblen gan the
 hevene ;
The thonder rored with a grisly stevene ;
Doun come the rayne, with haile and
 sleet, so faste,   1220
With hevenes fire, that it so sore agaste
This noble quene, and also hire meynee,
That yche of hem was glad awey to flee ;
And shortly, fro the tempest hire to save,
She fled hire-selfe into a lytel cave,
And with hire wente this Eneas also.
I not with hem if ther went any mo ;
The auctour maketh of hit no mencioun.
And here beganne the depe affeccioun
Betwix hem two ; this was the firstė morwe

1195. *coursers,* F⁵ *coursers.*

Of hire gladnesse, and gynnynge of hir
    sorwe.   1231
For there hath Eneas y-kneléd so,
And tolde hir al his herte and al his wo,
And sworne so depé to hire to be trewe
For wele or wo, and chaungé for no newe,
And, as a fals lover, so wel kan pleyne,
That sely Dido rewéd on his peyne,
And toke hym for housbonde, and became
    his wife
For evermor, while that hem lasté lyfe.
And after this, whan that the tempest
    stente,   1240
With myrth, out as they comé, home they
    wente.

    The wikked fame up ros, and that anon,
How Eneas hath with the queene y-gon
Into the cave, and deméd as hem liste.
And whan the kynge that Yarbas hight
    hit wiste,
As he that had hire lovéd ever his lyfe,
And wowéd hire to have hire to hys wife,
Swiche sorowe as he hath makéd, and
    swiche chere,
It is a rewthe and pitee for to here.
But as in love alday it happeth so,   1250
That oon shal lawghen at anotherès wo ;
Now lawgheth Eneas, and is in joye,
And more richès than ever was in Troye.

    O sely woman, ful of innocence,
Ful of pitee, of trouthe, and conscience,
What makéd yow to men to trusten so ?
Have ye suche rewthe upon hir feynéd wo,
And han suche olde ensaumples yow
    beforne ?
Se ye nat allé how they ben forsworne ?
Where se ye oon that he ne hath lafte
    his leefe ?   1260
Or ben unkynde, or don hir some
    myscheefe ?
Or pilléd hir, or bosted of his dede ?
Ye may as wel hit seen as ye may rede.
Take hede now of this greté gentilman,
This Trojan, that so wel hire plesé kan,
That feyneth him so trewe and obeysinge,
So gentil, and so privy of his doynge ;
And kan so wel doon al his obeysaunces,

And waytyn hir, at festès and at daunces,
And whan she gooth to temple, and home
    ageyne,   1270
And fasten til he hath his lady seyne ;
And beren in his devyses for hire sake
Wot I not what ; and songès wolde he
    make,
Justen, and doon of armès many thynges,
Sénd hire letrès, tokens, brochès, rynges.
Now herkneth how he shal his lady serve.

    Ther as he was in peril for to sterve
For hunger and for myscheef in the see,
And desolate, and fledde fro his contree,
And al his folke with tempeste al to-driven,
She hath hir body and eke hir reamé yiven
Into his hande, theras she myghte have
    bene   1282
Of other lande than of Cartage a queene,
And lyved in joy ynogh ; what wolde ye
    more ?

    This Eneas, that hath thus depe y-swore,
Is wery of his crafte within a throwe ;
The hooté erneste is al overblowe.
And privély he doth his shippès dyghte,
And shapeth him to steele awey by nyghte.

    This Dido hath suspecion of this, 1290
And thoughté wel that hit was al amys ;
For in his bedde he lyth a nyght and siketh,
She asketh him anon what him mysliketh.

    ' My deré herté, which that I love moste,
Certès,' quod he, ' thys nyght my fadrès
    goste
Hath in my slepe so soré me turmentede,
And eke Mercure his message hath pre-
    sentede,
That nedès to the conqueste of Ytayle
My destany is sooné for to sayle,
For whiche me thynketh brosten is myn
    herte.'   1300
Therwith his falsé teerès oute they sterte,
And taketh hir within his armès two.

    ' Is that in ernest ? ' quod she ; ' wol ye
    so ?
Have ye nat sworne to wifé me to take ?
Allas, what woman wol ye of me make ?
I am a gentil woman, and a queene ;
Ye wol nat fro your wyfe thus foulé fleene !
That I was borne, allas !   What shal I do ? '

1235. *chaunge*, Gg and Pepys *chaunge hire.*
1242. *The wikked fame.* Virgil's ' Fama,
malum qua non aliud velocius ullum,' *Æn.* iv. 174.

1269. *And waytyn*, Gg only ; Trin.² *And
pleyn* ; rest *To.*

To telle in short, this noble queene Dido
She seketh halwès, and doth sacrifise ;
She kneleth, crieth, that routhe is to
    devyse ;   1311
Conjureth him, and profereth him to be
His thral, his servant, in the lest degree.
She falleth him to foote, and swowneth
    there,
Disshevely with hire bryghtè giltè here,
And seith, ' Have mercy l let me with
    yow ryde ;
These lordès, which that wonien me besyde,
Wol me destroien only for youre sake.
And so ye wole now me to wifè take,
As ye han sworn, than wol I yive yow leve
To sleen me with your swerd now soone
    at eve ;   1321
For than shal I yet dien as youre wife.
I am with childe, and yive my childe his
    lyfe !
Mércy, lorde, have pitee in youre thought !'
    But al this thing avayleth hire ryght
    nought,
For on a nyght sleping he let hir lye,
And staal awey upon his companye,
And as a traytour forthe he gan to sayle
Towarde the largè contree of Itayle.
And thus he lefte Dido in wo and pyne,
And weddid there a lady highte Lavyne.
A cloth he lefte, and eke his swerde
    stondynge,   1332
Whan he fro Dido staal in hire slepynge,
Righte at hir beddès hed : so gan he hye,
Whanne that he staal awey to his navye.
    Which cloth, whan sely Dido gan awake,
She hath it kyste ful oftè for hys sake ;
And seyde, ' O swetè cloth, while [Jove]
    hit leste,
Take now my soule, unbynde me of this
    unreste ;   1339

I have fulfilled of fortune al the cours.'
And thus, allas, withouten his socours,
Twénty tyme y-swownèd hath she thanne.
And whan that she unto hir suster Anne
Compleynèd had, of which I may not write,
So gretè routhe I have hit for to endite,
And bad hir noryce and hir sustren gon
To fechè fire, and other thinges anon,
And seydè that she woldè sacrifie,—
And whan she myght hir tymè wel espye,
Upon the fire of sacrifice she sterte, 1350
And with his swerde she roof hire to the
    herte.
But, as myn auctour seythe, yit thus she
    seyde,
Or she was hurte, beforne or she deide,
She wroot a letter anon, that thus biganne.
    ' Ryght so,' quod she, ' as that the whitè
    swanne
Ayenst his deeth begynneth for to synge,
Ryght so to yow I make my cómpleynynge,
Nat that I trowe to geten yow agayne,
For wel I woot that hit is al in vayne,
Syn that the goddys ben contrary to me.
But syn my name is loste thurgh yow,'
    quod she,   1361
' I may wel leese a worde on yow, or letter,
Albeit I shal be never the better.
For thilkè wynde that blew your shipaway,
The samè wynde hath blowe awey your fay.'
But who wol al this letter have in myndè,
Rede Ovyde, and in him he shal hit fynde.

Explicit Legenda Didonis, Martiris,
Cartagenis Regine

Incipit Legenda Ysiphilè et Medee,
Martiris

    Thou roote of falsè lovers, duke Jason !
Thou slye devourer, and confusyon
Of gentil women, gentil creàtures ! 1370
Thou madest thy reclaymynge and thy lures
To ladies of thy staately aparaunce,
And of thy wordès farsèd with plesaunce,

1319. *so*, om. F⁵.
1324. *have*, Gg *havyth.*
1330. *And thus he lefte*, Trin.³ ; Gg. *Thus he hath lefte*; F⁴ *And thus hath he lefte.*
1338. Trin.³ om. *swete*, but Chaucer is translating the ' Dulces exuviæ, dum fata deusque sinebant' of Æn. iv. 651, and, like ' dulces,' *swete* is emphatic. To mend the line I read *Jove* for *Jupiter* of MSS.
1339. *now*, om. F⁵.
1339. *unbynde me*, Virgil's 'accipite hanc animam meque his exsolvite curis'; Gg reads *and brynge it.*

1352. *myn auctour*, now Ovid (*Heroides*, vii.).
1360. *contrary*, F⁴ *contrariouse.*
1366. *who wol al*, so Pepys and Tan. ; Gg F² Th. *whoso wol al*; Trin.² *who that wyll*; Ar. Seld. *whoso wol.*
1367. Pepys MS. stops here.
1370. So F⁴ and P ; Gg for first and Trin.³ for second *gentil* read *tendre.*

2 R   609

And of thy feynéd trouthe, and thy manere,
With thyne obeÿsaunce and humble chere,
And with thy countrefeted peyn and wo !
Ther other falsen oon, thou falseste two !
O, ofté swore thou that thou woldest deye
For love, whan thou ne felteste maladeye,
Save foule delyte, which that thou callest
    love !   1380
If that I lyve, thy namé shal be shove
In Englyssh, that thy sleighté shal be
    knowe ;
Have at the, Jason ! now thyn horn is
    blowe !
But certés, it is bothé routhe and wo,
That love with falsé lovers werketh so ;
For they shalle have wel better and gretter
    chere
Than he that hath a-boughte his love ful
    dere,
Or had in armés many a blody box.
For ever as tender a capon eteth the fox,
Though he be fals, and hath the foule
    betrayed,   1390
As shal the good man that therfor hath
    payed ;
Al have he to the capon skille and ryghte,
The falsé fox wil have his part at nyghte.
On Jason this ensample is wel y-seene,
By Isiphile and Médea the queene.
    In Tessalye, as Guido telleth us,
Ther was a kyng that highté Pelléus,
That had a brother whiche that hight Eson ;
And whan for age he myghte unnethés gon,
He yaf to Pelléus the governynge   1400
Of al his regne, and made him lorde and
    kynge.
Of whiche Eson this Jason geten' was,
That in his tyme in al that lande ther nas
Nat suche a famouse knyghte of gentilesse,
Of fredome, and of strengthe, and lusty-
    nesse.
After his fader deeth he bar him so,
That there nas noon that lysté ben his fo,

1387. *a-boughte,* F³ *bought. his,* om. F⁴.
1391. *hath,* Gg only ; rest om.
1392. *Al have he,* F² *Alle thof he have.*
1395. *Isiphile,* Hypsiphile.
1396. *Guido, i.e.* Guido delle Colonne in his
Historia Trojana ; F⁴ *Ovyde.*
1397. *kyng,* F³ *knyght.*
1405. *and of strengthe,* etc., all but Gg read *of
strengthe and of lustynesse.*

But dide him al honóur and companye.
Of which this Pelléus hath grete envye,
Imagynynge that Jason myghté be   1410
Enhauncéd so, and put in suche degree,
With love of lordés of his regioun,
That from his regne he may be put adoun.
    And in his witte a-nyghte compasséd he
How Jason myghté beste destroyéd be,
Withouté sclaunder of his compassémente.
And at the laste he tooke avysémente,
To senden him into some fer contre,
There as this Jason may distroyéd be.
This was his witte, al made he to Jasoun
Grete chere of love and of affeccioun,   1421
For dredé lest his lordés hyt espyde.
    So felle hyt, so as famé renneth wide,
Ther was suche tidynge overal, and suche
    los,
That in an ile that calléd was Colcos,
Beyonde Troyé, estwarde in the see,
That ther a ram was that men myghté see,
That had a flees of gold, that shoon so
    bryghte,
That no-wher was ther suche another
    sighte,
But hit was kept alway with a dragoun,—
And many other mervels up and doun ;
And with two boles maked al of bras,
That spitten fire ; and muché thinge ther
    was.   1433
But this was eke the talé, nathélees,
That who-so woldé wynné thilké flees,
He mosté both—or he hyt wynné myghte—
With the bolés and the dragoun fyghte ;
And kyng Oëtes lorde was of that ile.
This Pelléus bethoughte upon this wile,
That he his nevewe Jason wolde enhorte
To saylen to that londe, him to disporte ;
And seydé, ' Nevewe, if hyt myghté be,
That suché worshippe myghté fallé the,
That thou this famous tresor myghté
    wynne,
And bryngyn hit my regyoun withinne,
It were to me grette plesaunce and honóure ;
Thanne were I holde to quyté thy laboure,
And al the cost I wol my-selfé make ;

1413. *may,* Gg and Arch. Seld. *mighte.*
1418. *To,* F⁵ *That to.*
1425. *Colcos,* Colchis.
1438. *Oëtes,* Æetes.

And chese what folke that thou wilte with
    the take. 1449
Let see nowe, darstow taken this viage?'
Jason was yonge, and lusty of corage,
And undertooke to doon this ilke emprise.
Anon Argus his shippės gan devyse.
With Jason wente the strongė Hercules,
And many another that he with him ches.
But who-so axeth who is with him gon,
Lėt him redė 'Argonauticon,'
For he wol telle a talė longe ynoughe.
Philotetes anon the sayle up droughe,
Whan that the wynde was good, and gan
    him hye 1460
Out of his contree callėd Tessalye.
So longe he saylėd in the saltė see,
Til in the ile of Lemnon arryvėd he.
Al be this not rehersėd of Guydo,
Yet seyth Ovyde in his Epistles so;
And of this ilė lady was, and queene,
The fairė yonge Ysiphilė, the shene,
That whilom Thoas doughter was, the
    kynge.
Ysiphylė was goon in hire pleynge,
And romynge on the clyvės by the see.
Under a brake anoon espiede she 1471
Where that the shippe of Jason gan arryve.
Of hire goodnesse adoun she sendeth blyve,
To weten, if that any straungė wyghte
With tempest thider were y-blow a-nyghte,
To doon hem socour, as was hir usaunce
To forthren every wyghte, and don
    plesaunce
Of very bountee, and of curteysie.
This messagere adoun him gan to hye,
And foundė Jason and Ercules also,
That in a cogge to londė were y-go, 1481
Hem to refresshen, and to take the eyr.
The morwènyng atempree was and fair,
And in his wey this messager hem mette;
Ful cunnyngely these lordės two he grette,
And did his message, askynge hem anon
If they were broken, or ought wo-begon,

Or haddė nede of lodesmen or vitayle;
For of socóure they shuldė no thinge fayle,
For it was outrėly the quenės wille. 1490
Jason answerdė mekėly and stille;
'My lady,' quod he, 'thanke I hertėly
Of hir goodnesse; us nedeth trewėly
Nothing as now, but that we wery be,
And comė for to pley out of the see,
Til that the wynde be better in oure weye.
This lady rometh by the clyffe to pleye
With hire meynee, endėlonge the stronde,
And fyndeth this Jason and thyse other
    stonde 1499
In spekynge of this thinge, as I yow tolde.
This Ercules and Jason gan beholde
How that the queene it was, and faire hir
    grette,
Anonryght as they with this lady mette.
And she tooke hede, and knew by hire
    manere,
By hire array, by wordės, and by chere,
That hit were gentil men of grete degree.
And to the castel with hir ledeth she
These straungė folke, and doth hem grete
    honour; 1508
And axeth hem of travaylle and labour
That they han suffrėd in the saltė see;
So that withynne a day, or two or three,
She knew by folke that in his shippės be,
That hyt was Jason, full of renomee,
And Ercules, that haddė the gretė los,
That soughten the áventurės of Colcos.
And did hem honour morė than before,
And with hem delėd ever lenger the more,
For they ben worthy folke, withouten les.
And, namely, she spake most with Ercules;
To him hir hertė bare, he shuldė be 1520
Sad, wise, and trewe, of wordės avysee,
Withouten any other affeccioun
Of love, or evyl ymaginacioun.
This Ercules hath so this Jason preysed,
That to the sonne he hath hym up areysed,
That halfe so trewe a man ther nas of love
Under the cope of hevene, that is above;
And he was wyse, hardy, secrė, and ryche;

1449. *that*, all but Gg and Arch. Seld. om.
1453. *Argus*, the builder of the Argo.
1457. *rede*, Trin.³ *go rede*.
1457. *Argonauticon, i.e.* the imitation of
Apollonius Rhodius by Valerius Flaccus.
1459. *Philotetes*, Philoctetes.
1460. *that*, all but Gg and Trin.² om.
1463. *Lemnon*, Lemnos.
1472. *that . . . of*, F⁴ *lay . . . that*.

1490. Fairfax, Tanner, and Bodley MSS. omit
this line.
1512. *folke*, so Gg and Arch. Seld.; F⁶ *the
folke* or *folkes*.
1523. *evyl*, all but Gg *any other*.
1525. *areysed*, all but Gg *reysed*.

Of these thre poyntés there nas noon hym
   liche.
Of fredome passéd he, and lustihede, 1530
Allé tho that lyven, or ben dede.
Therto so grete a gentil-man was he,
And of Tessalye likly kynge to be.
Ther nas no lakke, but that he was agaste
To love, and for to speké shaméfaste ;
He haddé lever himselfe to mordre and dye,
Than that men shulde a lover him espye.
' As wolde almychty God that I hadde yive
My bloode and flessh, so that I myghte lyve,
With the nonés that he hadde oughe-where
   a wife   1540
For his estaat ! for suche a lusty lyfe
She sholdé ledé with this lusty knyghte ! '
And all this was compasséd on the nyghte
Betwix him Jason, and this Ercules.
Of thesé two here was a shrewéde les,
To come to house upon an innocent !—
For, to bedote this queene was here assent.

   This Jason is as coy as is a mayde ;
He loketh pitously, but noght he sayde,
But freely yaf he to hir counselleres 1550
Yíftés grete, and to hire officeres,
As God wolde that I leyser had and tyme,
By processe al his wowyng for to ryme !
But in this house if any fals lover be,
Ryght as himselfe now doth, ryght so
   did he,
With feynynge, and with every sotil dede.
Ye gete no more of me, but ye wol rede
The original that telleth al the cas.

   The somme is this, that Jason weddid was
Unto this queene, and toke of hire sub-
   staunce   1560
What-so him lyste unto his purveyaunce ;
And upon hir begat he children two,
And drough his saylle, and saugh hir
   never mo.
A letter senté she to hym certeyn,
Which were to longe to written and to
   seyn ;

And him repreveth of his grete untrouthe,
And prayeth him on hir to have some
   routhe.
And of his children two, she sayede him
   this :
That they be lyke of allé thinge, y-wis,
To Jason, save they couthé nat begile. 1570
And prayede God, or hit were longé
   while,
That she that had his herte y-rafte hir fro
Most fynden him to hir untrewe also :
And that she mosté both hir children spille,
And allé tho that suffreth hym his wille.
And trewe to Jason was she al hir lyf,
And ever kept hir chaste, as for his wyf ;
Ne never hadde she joyé at hir herte,
But dyéd for his love of sorwés smerte.

   To Colcos comen is this duke Jasoun,
That is of love devourer and dragoun, 1581
As mater appetiteth forme alwey,
And from forme into forme it passen may ;
Or as a welle that weré botomles,
Rýght so kan fals Jason have no pes,
For to desiren, thurgh his appetite,
To doon with gentil wymmen his delyte ;
This is his luste, and his felicite.

   Jason is romed forth to the cite,
That whylom clepéd was Jaconitos, 1590
That was the maister toun of al Colcos,
And hath y-tolde the cause of his comynge
Unto Oetes, of that contree kynge ;
Prayinge him that he moste doon his assay
To gete the flese of golde, if that he may.
Of which the kynge assentith to his bone,
And doth him honour as hyt was to done,
So ferforth, that his doghtre and his eyre,
Medea, which that was so wise and feyre,
That feyrer saugh ther never man with ye,
He made hire doon to Jason companye
At mete, and sitté by him in the hall. 1602

   Now was Jason a semely man withalle,
And like a lorde, and had a grete renoun,
And of his loke as rial as a lyoun,
And goodly of his speche, and famulere,
And koude of love al crafte and arte
   plenere

1538. *almychty*, Arch. Seld. only ; probably
the scribe's insertion to mend the line.
   1540. *With the nones*, on condition.
   1547. *assent*, F⁴ and Ar. Seld. *intent*.
   1554. *in this house.* The phrase points to the
poem being read aloud, possibly at court.
   1558. *The original*, Ovid, *Her.* Ep. vi., from
which he translates closely in ll. 1564 *sq.*
   1559. *somme*, F⁴ *sothe ;* Ar. Seld. *text.*

1582. *mater*, F *nature.* Chaucer takes his
philosophy from Guido.
   1590. *Jaconitos* (F⁴ *Jasonicos*), Jaconites in
Colchis.
   1597. *was*, F⁴ *is.*

Withouté boke, with everyche observaunce.
And as fortune hir oughte a foule mes-
    chaunce.
She wex enamouréd upon this man. 1610
  'Jason,' quod she, 'for oght I se or kan,
As of this thinge the whiche ye ben aboute,
Ye, han your-selfe y-put in moché doute ;
For who-so wol this áventure acheve,
He may nat wele asterten, as I leve,
Withouten dethe, but I his helpé be.
But nathélesse, hit is my wille,' quod she,
'To furtheren yow, so that ye shal nat dye,
But turné sounde home to youre Tessalye.'
  'My ryghté lady,' quod thys Jason,
    'tho,   1620
That ye han of my dethe, or of my wo,
Any rewarde, and doon me this honour,
I wote wel that my myght, ne my labour,
May nat deserve hit in my lyvés day ;
God thanké yow, ther I ne kan nor may.
Youre man am I, and lowly yow beseche
To ben my helpe, withouté moré speche ;
But certés for my dethe shal I not spare.'
Tho. gan this Médea to him declare
The peril of this case, fro poynt to poynt
Of his bataylé, and in what disjoynt 1631
He moté stonde ; of whiche no creáture,
Save only she, ne myght his lyfe assure.
And shortely, to the poynt ryght for to go,
They been accorded ful betwex hem two,
That Jason shal hir wedde, as trewé knyght,
And terme y-sette to comé soone at nyght
Unto hir chambre, and make there his
    othe
Upon the goddys, that he for leve ne lothe
Ne shulde hire never falsen, nyght ne day,
To ben hir husbonde while he lyvé may,
As she that from his dethe hym savéd there.
  And here-upon at nyght they mete y-fere,
And doth his othe, and goth with hir to
    bedde,   1644
And on the morwé upwarde he him
    spedde,
For she hath taught him how he shal not
    faile
The flese to wynne, and stynten his batayle;
And savéd him his lyfe and his honour,

And gat a name ryght as a conquerour,
Ryght thurgh the sleyghte of hir en-
    chauntément.   1650
  Now hath Jason the fleese, and home
    is went
With Médea, and tresourés ful grete
    woon ;
But unwiste of hir fader she is goon
To Tessalye, with duke Jason hir leefe,
That afterwarde hath broght hir to
    myschefe.
For as a traytour he is from hire go,
And with hir lefté yongé children two,
And falsly hath betrayéd hir, allas !
And ever in love a chefe traytour he was ;
And wedded yet the thriddé wife anon,
That was the doghtre of the kynge Creon.
  This is the mede of lovynge and
    guerdoun,   1662
That Médea receyvéd of Jasoun
Ryght for hir trouthe, and for hir kyndé-
    nesse,
That loved hym beter thane hir-selfe, I
    gesse ;
And left hir fadir and hire heritage.
And of Jason this is the vassalage,
That in his dayes nas never noon y-founde
So fals a lover goynge on the grounde.
And therfore in her letter thus she sayde,
First of his falsnesse whan she hym up-
    brayde.   1671
'Why lykéde me thy yelow heere to see,
More than the boundés of myn honeste ?
Why lykéde me thy youthe and thy faire-
    nesse,
And of thy tonge the infinite gracious-
    nesse ?
O, haddest thou in thy conquest ded y-be,
Ful mykel untrouthé had ther dyed with
    the !'
  Wel kan Ovyde hir letter in verse endyte,
Which were as now to longe for me to
    write.

  Explicit Legenda Ysiphile et Medee,
        Martirum

1608. *with,* Gg *and.*
1640. Add.₃ begins here.
1643. Omitted in F³.

1659. *a chefe traytour,* Gg *a thef and traytour;* Trin. *a thyef traytour;* Add.₃ *traytour
and theffe.*
1670. *in her letter,* Ovid, *Her.* Ep. xii. 10. 11.

Incipit Legenda Lucrecie, Rome, Martiris

Now mote I sayne the exilynge of kynges
Of Romè, for here horrible doynges;   1681
Of the lastè kynge Tarquinius
As sayth Ovyde, and Titus Lyvius.
But for that causè telle I nat this story,
But for to preyse, and drawen to memory
The verray wife, the verray trewe Lucresse,
That for hir wifehode, and hir stedfast-
      nesse,
Nat only that these payens hir comende,
But he that y-clepèd is in oure legende 1689
The grete Austyne hath grete compassyoun
Of this Lucresse that starf at Romè toun.
And in what wise I wol but shortly trete,
And of this thynge I touchè but the grete.
  Whan Ardea besegèd was aboute
With Romaynes, that ful sternè were and
      stoute,
Ful longè lay the sege, and lytel wroghte,
So that they were halfe ydel, as hem
      thoghte.
And in his pley Tarquinius the yonge
Gan for to jape, for he was lyghte of tonge,
And saydè that hyt was an ydel lyfe,   1700
No man dide ther no morè than his wife.
'And lat us speke of wivès that is best;
Preise every man his ownè, as him lest,
And with oure spechè let us ease oure herte.'
  A knyght, that hightè Colatyne, up
      sterte,
And saydè thus : 'Nay, for hit is no nede
To trowen on the worde, but on the dede.
I have a wife,' quod he, 'that as I trowe
Is holden good of al that ever hir knowe.
Go we to Rome, to nyght, and we shul se.'
Tarquinius answerde, 'That lyketh me.'
  To Romè be they come, and faste
      hem dighte   1712
To Colatynès house, and doun they lyghte,
Tarquinius, and eke this Colatyne.
The housbonde knewe the estres wel
      and fyne,
And ful prevely into the house they goon,

For at the gatè porter was there noon :
And at the chambre dorè they abyde.
This noble wyfe sat by hir beddys syde
Disshevele, for no malice she ne thoghte,
And softè wolle saith our boke that
      she wroghte,   1721
To kepen hir fro slouthe and ydilnesse ;
And bad hir servauntes doon hir besynesse ;
And axeth hem, 'What tydynges heren ye?
How sayne men of the sege ? how
      shal it be ?
God wolde the wallès weren falle adoun !
Myn housbonde is to longe out of this toun,
For which the dredè doth me so to smerte ;
Ryght as a swerde hyt styngeth to myn
      herte,   1729
Whan I thenke on the sege, or of that place.
God save my lorde, I pray him for his grace !'
  And therwithal ful tendirly she wepe,
And of hir werke she toke no morè kepe,
But mekèly she let hire eyen falle,
And thilkè semblant sat hir wel withalle.
And eke the teerès ful of honeste
Embelysshèd hire wifely chastitee.
Hire countenance is to her hertè digne,
For they acordeden in dede and signe.
And with that worde hir husbonde
      Colatyne,   174c
Or she of him was ware, come stertyng ynne,
And saydè, 'Drede the noght, for
      I am here !'
And she anon up roos, with blysful chere,
And kyssed hym, as of wyvès is the wone.
  Tarquinius, this prowdè kyngès sone,
Conceyvèd hath hir beaute and hir chere,
Hire yelow heer, hir shap, and hire manere,
Hir hewe, hir wordès that she hath
      compleyned,
And by no craft hire beaute was not feyned ;
And kaughtè to this lady suche desire,
That in his hertè brent as any fire   1751
So wodely that his wittè was forgeten,
For wel thoghte he she shuldè nat be geten.
And ay the more that he was in dispaire,

1683. *Ovyde*, Ovid, *Fasti* ii. 685, 721-852.
1683. *Lyvius*, Livius, i. 57-58.
1684. *telle*, Gg *ne telle*.
1686. *trewe*, Gg only ; rest om.
1701. *no* (2), Gg only ; rest om.
1716. *ful*, Trin.² om.

1721. *our boke*, Thynne (wrongly) *L ivi* ; Gg om.
Perhaps Chaucer wrote *Ovyde* (cp. *Fasti* ii. 741-
742).
1730. *the sege*, Trin.⁴ ; F⁴ *these, this* ; Gg
corrupt.
1736. *honeste*, F⁹ *hevyte* ; Tan. and Th. *hery-
nesse.* Ovid has 'lacrimæ cecidere pudicæ.'
1753. Gg *For he wote wel she wolde.*

The more he covetyth, and thoght hir faire ;
His blyndė lust was al his covetynge.
  On morwė, whan the brid began to synge,
Unto the sege he cometh ful pryvely,
And by himselfe he walketh sobrely,
The ymage of hir recordyng alwey newe :
'Thus lay hir heer, and thus fressh
    was hir hewe ;   1761
Thus sate, thus spake, thus spanne,
    this was hir chere ;
Thus faire she was, and thys was hir
    manere.'
Al this conceyte his herte hath new y-take,
And as the see, with tempeste al to-shake,
That after, whan the storme is al ago,
Yet wol the watir quappe a day or two,
Ryght so, thogh that hir formė were absent,
The plesaunce of hir formė was present.
  But nathėles, nat plesaunce, but delyte,
Or an unryghtful talent with dispite, —
'For mawgree hir, she shal my lemman
    be :
Happe helpeth hardy man alway,' quod
    he,
'What endė that I make, hit shal be so !'
And gyrt hym with his swerde, and
    gan to go,
And forth he rit til he to Rome is come,
And al alone his way than hath he nome
Unto the hous of Colatyne ful ryght.
  Doun was the sonne, and day hath
    lost his lyght,   1779
And inne he come, unto a prevy halke,
And in the nyght ful thefely gan he stalke,
Whan every wyght was to his restė broght,
Ne no wyghte had of tresoun suche a thoght.
Whether by wyndow, or by other gynne,
With swerde y-drawe, shortly he cometh
    ynne
There as she lay, thys noble wyfe Lucresse,
And as she woke, hir bed she feltė presse.
'What best is that,' quod she, 'that
    weyeth thus ?'
'I am the kyngės sone, Tarquinius,'
Quod he, 'but and thow crye, or
    noysė make,   1790
Or if thou any creăture awake,
Be thilkė God that formede man on lyve,
This swerd thurghout thyn hertė shal
    I ryve.'

And therwithal unto hir throte he sterte,
And sette the swerde al sharpe unto
    hir herte.
  No worde she spake, she hath no
    myght therto ;
What shal she sayne ? hir wytte is al ago !
Ryght as a wolfe that fynt a lomb alone,
To whom shal she compleyne or
    makė mone ?
What ! shal she fyghtė with an hardy
    knyghte ?   1800
Wel wotė men a woman hath no myghte.
What ! shal she crye, or how shal she sterte
That hath hir by the throte, with swerde
    at herte ?
She axeth grace, and seyde al that she kan.
  'Ne wolt thou nat ?' quod tho this
    cruelle man,
'As wisly Jupiter my soulė save,
As I shal in the stable slee thy knave,
And lay him in thy bed, and lowdė crye,
That I the fynde in suche avowtrye ;
And thus thou shalt be ded, and also lese
Thy namė, for thou shalt non othir chese.'
  Thise Romaynes wyfės loveden so
    hir name   1812
At thilkė tyme, and dredden so the shame,
That, what for fere of sklaundre, and
    drede of dethe,
She lost attonės bothė wytte and brethe ;
And in a swowgh she lay, and woxe so ded,
Men myghten smyten of hir arme or hed,
She feleth nothinge, neither foule ne feyre.
  Tarquinius, thou art a kyngės eyre, 1819
And sholdest, as by lynage and by ryght,
Doon as a lorde and as a verray knyght ;
Why hastow doon dispite to chevalrye ?
Why hastow doon thys lady vylanye ?
Allas, of the thys was a vilenous dede !
  But now to the purpose ; in the
    story I rede
Whan he was goon and this myschaunce
    is falle.
Thys lady sent aftir hir frendės alle,
Fáder, moder, housbonde, alle y-fere,

1798. *fynt a lomb*, F⁴ (many of whose bad
readings are passed over) here have *fcyneth a
love !*
1805. *tho*, Trin. only ; Gg⁴ *ho*, rest om.
1815. *attones bothe* Gg only ; rest *both attones*.
1821. *verray*, Gg *worthi*.

And al dysshevelee with hir heeré clere,
In habyte suche as wymmen usede tho
Unto the buryinge of hir frendés go,   1831
She sytte in hallé with a sorowful syghte.
Hir frendés axen what hir aylen myghte,
And who was dede, and she sytte
        aye wepynge.
A worde for shame ne may she forthe
        out brynge,
Ne upon hem she dursté nat beholde,
But atté laste of Tarquyny she hem tolde
This rewful case, and al thys thing horrýble.
    The wo to telle hyt were an ímpossible
That she and al hir frendés made attones.
Al haddé folkés hertys ben of stones,   1841
Hyt myght have makéd hem upon hir rewe,
Hire herté was so wyfely and so trewe.
She sayde that for hir gylt, ne for hir blame,
Hir housbonde shulde nat have the
        foulé name,
That noldé she nat suffren by no wey.
And they answerdé alle upon hir fey,
That they foryaf hyt hyr, for hyt was ryght;
Hyt was no gilt ; hit lay not in hir myght,
And seyden hire ensamples many oon.
But al for noght, for thus she seyde anoon :
' Be as be may,' quod she, ' of foryifynge ;
I wol not have no foryift for nothinge.'
But pryvely she kaughté forth a knyfe,
And therwithal she rafte hir-selfe hir lyfe;
And as she felle adoun she kaste hire loke,
And of hir clothés yet she hedé toke ;
For in hir fallynge yet she haddé care,
Lest that hir fete or suché thynge lay bare,
So wel she lovéde clennesse, and eke
        trouthe !   1860
    Of hir had al the toun of Romé routhe,
And Brutus by hir chasté bloode hath swore,
That Tarquyn shulde y-banysshed be
        therfore,
And al his kynne ; and let the peple calle,
And openly the tale he tolde hem alle ;
And openly let cary her on a bere
Thurgh al the toun, that men may
        see and here   1867
The horrýblé dede of hir oppressyoun.
Ne never was ther kynge in Romé toun
Syn thilké day ; and she was holden there
A seynt, and ever hir day y-halwéd dere,

As in hire lawe.   And thus endeth Lucresse
The noble wyfe, as Titus beryth wittnesse.
    I telle hyt, for she was of love so trewe,
Ne in hir wille she chaungéde for no newe ;
And for the stable herté, sadde and kynde,
That in these wymmen men may al
        day fynde ;
Ther as they kaste hire herté, there
        it dwelleth.
For wel I wot that Criste himselfé telleth,
That in Israel, as wyde as is the londe,
Nat so grete feythe in al that londe
        he fonde,   1881
As in a woman ; and this is no lye.
And as for men, loketh which tirannye
They doon al day,—assay hem who-
        so lyste,
The trewest is ful brotil for to triste.

Explicit Legenda Lucrecie, Rome,
Martiris

Incipit Legenda Adriane de Athenes

Juge infernal Mynos, of Creté king,
Now cometh thy lotte, now comestow
        on the rynge !
Nat only for thy sake writen is this story,
But for to clepe ageyn unto memory 1889
Of Theseus, the grete untrewe of love,
For which the goddis of the heven above
Ben wrothe, and wreche han také for
        thy synne.
Be rede for shame ! now I thy lyfe begynne.
    Mynos, that was the myghty kynge
        of Crete,
That wan an hundred citees stronge
        and grete,
To scole hath sent his sone Androgeus
To Athenes, of the which hyt happeth thus,
That he was slayne, lernynge philosophie,
Ryght in that citee, nat but for envye.
    The greté Mynos, of the whiche I speke,
His sonés dethe is comé for to wreke,—
Alcathoë besegeth harde and longe ; 1902
But nathéles, the wallés be so stronge,

1872. *As in hire lawe,* in their religion.
1881. *Nat,* Trin.²; rest *that.*
1881. *he,* all but Add. *he ne.*
1902. *Alcathoë,* the name of the western
acropolis of Megara.

And Nysus, that was kynge of that citee,
So chyvalrous, that lytel dredeth he ;
Of Mynos or his oste toke he no cure.
Til, on a day, befel an áventure,
That Nisus doghtre stode upon the walle,
And of the segė sawe the maner alle. 1909
So happede hyt that at a skarmysshynge,
She caste hir hert upon Mynos the kynge,
For his beaute, and for his chevalerye,
So soré, that she wendė for to dye.

And, shortly of this processe for to pace,
She madė Mynos wynnen thilkė place,
So that the citee was al at his wille,
To saven whom hym lyst, or ellės spille.
But wikkidly he quytte her kyndénesse,
And let hir drenche in sorowe and distresse,
Nere that the goddys had of hir pite ; 1920
But that tale were to longe as now for me.
Athénés wanne this kynge Mynos also,
As Alcathoe and other tounės mo ;
And this theffect, that Mynos hath so dryven
Hem of Athénes, that they mote hym yiven
Fro yere to yere hir owene children dere
For to be slayne, as ye shal after here.

Thys Mynos hath a monstre, a wikked
    beste,
That was so cruelle that, withoute areste,
Whan that a man was broght in his
    presence, 1930
He wolde hym ete; ther helpeth no defence.
And every thriddė yere, withouten doute,
They casten lotte, and as hyt came aboute
On ryche, on pore, he most his soné take,
And of his childe he mostė present make
To Mynos, to save him or to spille,
Or lat his best devoure him at his wille.
And this hath Mynos doon right in dyspite ;
To wreke his sone was sette all his delyte,
And maken hem of Athenės his thralle
Fro yere to yere, while that he lyven shalle;
And home he saileth whan this toun is
    wonne 1942
This wikked custome is so longe y-ronne,
Til that of Athenės kynge Egėus
Moste senden his owne soné Thesėus,
Sith that the lotte is fallen hym upon,
To be devouréd, for grace is ther non.

And forth is lad thys woful yongė knyght
Unto the court of kynge Mynos full ryght,
And in a prison fetrėd faste is he, 1950
Til thilkė tyme he shulde y-freten be.

Wel maystow wepe, O woful Theseus,
That art a kyngės sone, and dampnėd thus !
Me thynketh this, that thow were depe
    y-holde
To whom that savėde the fro carės colde !
And now, if any woman helpė the,
Wel oughtestow hir servant for to be,
And ben hir trewė lover yere by yere !
But now to come agayn to my matere.
The tour, ther as this Theseus is throwe,
Doun in the bothome derke, and wonder
    lowe, 1961
Was joynynge in the walle to a foreyne,
And hyt was longynge to the doghtren
    tweyne
Of kyng Mynos, that in hire chambres grete
Dwelten above, toward the maystrė strete
Of Athenės, in joy and in solace.
Wot I not how, hyt happėdė parcase,
As Theseus compleynėd hym by nyghte,
The kyngės doghter Adriane that hyghte,
And eke hir suster Phedra, herden alle
His compleynt, as they stoden on the walle,
And lokėden upon the bryghtė mone ;
Hem listė nat to go to beddė sone. 1973
And of his wo they hadde compassyoun ;
A kyngės sone to be in swiche prisoun,
And be devouréd, thoughte hem grete
    pitee.

Than Adriane spake to hir suster free,
And seydė, ' Phedra, levė suster dere,
This woful lordės sone may ye not here,
How pitously compleyneth he his kynne,
And eke his pore estate that he is ynne,
And giltėles ? now certės hit is routhe !
And if ye wol assentė, by my trouthe,
He shal be holpen, how so that we do.'
Phedra answerde, ' Y-wys, me is as wo
For him, as ever I was for any man ;

1949. *court,* F⁴ *contree.*
1949. *ful ryght,* F⁴ *ful of myght.*
1964. *kyng,* Arch. Seld. only, probably an
emendation. Here again Gg has *Theseus* for
Mynos.
1966. *Athenes,* probably Chaucer's own slip;
T² *in mochell myrthe.*
1973. *sone,* F⁴ Trin.² *so sone.*
1986. Add. stops here.

1936. Trin.² botch this line by reading *unto* for
to (1), Arch. Seld. by *for to* instead of *to* (2), Gg
has *To Theseus* for *To Mynos.*

And to his helpe the besté rede I kan,
Is, that we doon the gayler prively
To come and speké with us hastely,
And doon this woful man with him to come;
For if he may the monstre overcome,   1991
Than were he quyte ; ther is noon other
    bote !
Lat us wel taste him at hys herte-rote,
That if so be that he a wepne have,
Wher that he dar, his lyfe to kepe or save,
Fighten with this fende and him defende.
For in the prison, ther he shal descende,
Ye wote wel that the best is in a place
That nys not derke, and hath roume and
    eke space
To welde an axe, or swerde, or staffe, or
    knyffe.   2000
So that, me thenketh, he shuldé save his
    lyffe ;
If that he be a man, he shal do so.
  ' And we shal make him ballés eke also
Of wexe and towe, that, whan he gapeth
    faste,
Into the bestés throte he shal hem caste,
To sleke his hunger, and encombre his teeth.
And ryght anon whan that Theséus seeth
The beste achokéd, he shal on hym lepe
To sleen hym or they comen more to-hepe.
This wepen shal the gayler, or that tyde,
Ful prively within the prisoun hyde :   2011
And for the house is crynkled to and fro,
And hath so queynté weyés for to go,
For it is shapen as the mase is wroght,
Therto have I a remedy in my thoght,
That by a clewe of twyne, as he hath gon,
The samé way he may returne anon,
Folwynge alway the threde, as he hath
    come.
And whan that he this beste hathe over-
    come,   2019
Thanne may he fleen away out of this drede,
And eke the gayler may he wyth him lede,
And him avaunce at home in his contree,
Syn that so grete a lordés sone is he.
Thys is my rede, if that ye dar hyt take ;
What shulde I lenger sermoun of hyt make ?'

1995. So Gg ; F *wher that hys lyfe he dar hope;*
rest vary.
1999. Gg *and hath bothe roum and space.*
2020. *drede,* F⁴ *stede.*
2024. *ye,* so Trin.² and Th. ; rest *he.*

  The gayler cometh, and with hym
    Theseus ;
Whan thesé thyngés ben acorded thus,
Adoun sytte Theseus upon his knee,   2028
' The ryghté lady of my lyfe,' quod he,
' I sorwful man, y-dampned to the deth,
Fro yow, whiles that me lasteth lyf or breth,
I wol not twynne aftir this áventure.
But in youre servise thus I wol endure ;
That as a wrecche unknowe I wol yow serve
For evermore, til that myn herté sterve.
Forsake I wol at home myn herytage,
And, as I sayde, ben of youre courte a page,
If that ye vouchésafe that in this place,
Ye graunté me to have so gret a grace,
That I may have not but my mete and
    drinke ;   2040
And for my sustenaunce yet wol I swynke,
Ryght as yow lyste ; that Mynos, ne no
    wyght,
Syn that he sawe me never with eyen syght,
Ne no man ellés shal me konne espye,
So slyly and so wel I shal me gye,
And me so wel disfigure, and so lowe,
That in this worlde ther shal no man me
    knowe,
To han my lyfe, and to have the presence
Of yow, that doon to me this excellence.
And to my fader shal I sendé here   2050
This worthy man that is now your gaylere,
And him to-guerdone that he shal wel bee
Oon of the gretest men of my contree.
And if I dursté sayne, my lady bryght,
I am a kyngés sone and eke a knyght,
As woldé God, if that hyt myghté bee,
Ye weren in my contree allé three,
And I with yow, to bere yow companye.
Than shulde ye seen if that I therof lye.
  ' And if I profre yow in lowe manere
To ben youre page and serven yow ryght
    here,   2061
But I yow serve as lowly in that place,
I prey to Mars to yevé me suche grace,
That shamés deth on me ther moté falle.
And dethe and poverte to my frendés alle.
And that my spirite be nyghté moté go
After my dethe, and walké to and fro,

2048. *to have the,* so Add.2; F⁴ *to have* ; Gg¹
for to have.
2051. *now,* only Gg.

Thát I mote of traytoure have a name,
For which my spirite goth to do meshame!
And if I ever clayme other degre, 2070
But of ye vouchésafe to yeve hyt me,
As I have seyde, of shamés deth I deye!
And mercy, lady! I kan nat ellès seye.'
  A semely knyght was Theseus to see,
And yongè, but of twenty yere and three.
But whoso hadde y-seen his contenaunce,
He wolde have wepte for routhe of his
      penaunce;
For which this Adriane in this manere
Answerde hym to his profre and to his chere.
' A kyngès sone, and eke a knyght,' quod
      she, 2080
' To ben my servant in so lowe degre,
God shelde hit, for the shame of wymmen
      alle,
And lene me never suche a case befalle!
But sende yow grace and sleyght of herte
      also
Yow to defende and knyghtly sleen your fo!
And lene hereaftir that I may yow fynde
To me and to my suster here so kynde,
That I repentè not to yeve yow lyfe!
  'Yet wer hyt better that I were your wife,
Syn that ye ben as gentil borne as I, 2090
And have a realmè nat but fastè by,
Then that I suffrede yow giltles to sterve,
Or that I lete you as a pagè serve;
Hyt is no profre, as unto youre kynrede.
But what is that man wol not do for drede?
And to my suster, syn that hyt is so,
That she mote goon with me, if that I goo,
Or ellés suffre deth as wel as I,
That ye unto your sone, as trewély, 2099
Doon hir be wedded at your home comynge.
This is the final ende of al this thynge;
Ye, swere hit here, upon al that may be
      sworne!'
  ' Yee, lady myn,' quod he, ' or ellès torne
Mote I be with the Minotawre to morowe!
And have here-of myn hertè-bloode to
      borowe,
If that ye wol! If I hadde knyfe or spere,
I wolde hit laten out, and theron swere,
For then at erst I wote ye wol me leve.

2092. *yow giltles*, F⁴ *your gentilesse.*
2094. *no profre*, etc., *i.e.* no proffer suitable to
your birth; F⁴ *not profet.*

By Mars, that is the chefe of my beleve,
So that I myghtè lyven, and nat fayle
To morowe for to achevè my batayle, 2111
I noldè never fro this placè flee,
Til that ye shulde the verray prefè see.
For now, if that the sothe I shal yow saye,
I have y-lovèd yow ful many a daye,
Thogh ye ne wiste it nat, in my contree,
And aldermoste desirèd yow to see
Of any erthely lyvynge creáture.
Upon my trouthe I swere, and yow assure,
These seven yere I have your servant bee.
Now have I yow, and also have ye mee,
My derè herte, of Athenès duchesse!'
  This lady smyleth at his stedfastnesse,
And at his hertely wordys, and his chere,
And to hir suster sayde in this manere:
  ' Al softèly now, suster myn,' quod she,
' Now be we duchesses, both I and ye,
And sykered to the regals of Athenes,
And both heraftir lykly to be queenes,
And savèd fro his deth a kyngès sone,   •
As ever of gentil wymen is the wone 2131
To save a gentilman, enforthe hir myght,
In honest cause, and namely in his ryght.
Me thinketh no wyght ought us here-of
      blame,
Ne beren us therfore an evel name.'
  And shortly of this matere for to make,
This Theseus of hir hath leve y-take,
And every poynt was performèd in dede,
As ye have in this covenant herde me rede;
His wepne, his clew, his thing that I
      have sayde, 2140
Was by the gayler in the house y-layde,
Ther as this Mynatour hath his dwellyng,
Ryght fastè by the dorre at his entrynge;
And Theseus is ladde unto his deth;
And forthe unto this Mynataure he geth,
And by the techynge of thys Adriane,
He overcome thys beste and was his bane,
And oute he cometh by the clewe agayne
Ful prively, when he thys beste hath
      slayne;
And by the gayler gotten hath a barge, 2150
And of his wivès tresure gan it charge,
And tok his wif, and eke hir suster free,
And eke the gayler, and wyth hem alle
      three
Is stole away out of the londe by nighte,

And to the contree of Ennopye hym dyghte,
There as he had a frende of his knowynge.
There festen they, there dauncen they
　　and synge,
And in his armès hath thys Adriane,
That of the beste hath kepte him from
　　his bane.　　　　　　　　　　2159
And gate him there a newè barge anoon,
And of his countre-folke a ful grete woon,
And taketh his leve, and homewarde
　　sayleth hee ;
And in an yle, amydde the wildè see,
There as ther dwelleth creâturè noon
Save wildè bestes, and that ful many oon,
He made his shippe a-londè for to sette,
And in that ile halfe a day he lette,
And sayde that on the londe he moste
　　him reste.
　　His maryners han don ryght as hym
　　leste ;
And, for to tellè shortly in thys cas, 2170
Whanne Adriane his wyfe aslepè was,
For that hir suster fairer was than she,
He taketh hir in his honde, and forth gooth
　　he
To shyppe, and as a traytour stale his way,
While that thys Adriane aslepè lay,
And to his contree-warde he sayleth
　　blyve,—
A twenty devel way the wynde him
　　dryve !—
And fonde his fader drenchèd in the see.
Me lyste no more to speke of hym, *pardee !*
These falsè lovers, poyson be her bane !
　　But I wol turne ageyne to Adryane,
That is with slepe for werynesse y-take ;
Ful sorwfully hir hertè may awake.　 2183
Allas, for the myn hertè hath pitee !
Ryght in the dawènynge awaketh she,
And gropeth in the bed, and fonde ryght
　　noght.
　　'Allas,' quod she, 'that ever I was
　　wroght :
I am betrayèd,' and hir heer to-rente,
And to the strondè barefote faste she wente,
And cryede, 'Theseus ! myn hertè swete !

Where be ye, that I may not wyth yov
　　mete ?　　　　　　　　　　2190
And myghtè thus with bestes ben y-slaync
　　The holowe roches answerde hir agayne.
No man she sawe, and yet shynède the
　　mone,
And hye upon a rokke she wentè sone,
And saw his bargè saylynge in the see.
Colde waxe hir herte, and ryght thus
　　saydè she :
'Meker than ye fynde I the bestès
　　wilde !'—
Hadde he not synnè that hir thus be-
　　gylde !—
She cried, 'O turne agayne for routhe
　　and synne,　　　　　　　　2200
Thy bargè hath not al his meyny ynne.'
Hir kerchefe on a pole up stykede she,
Ascauncè that he shulde hyt wel y-see,
And hym remembre that she was behynde,
And turne agayne, and on the stronde
　　hir fynde.
But al for noght ; his wey he is i-goon,
And doun she felle a-swowne upon a stoon :
And up she ryste, and kyssed in al hir care
The steppès of his fete, there he hath fare,
And to hir bedde ryght thus she speketh
　　tho :　　　　　　　　　　　2210
'Thow bedd,' quoth she, 'that hast
　　receyvèd two,
Thow shalt answere of two and not of oon.
Where is thy gretter parte away i-goon ?
Allas, where shal I wreched wyght become ?
For though so be that shyp or boot here
　　come,
Home to my contree dar I not for drede :
I kan my-selfè in this case not rede.'
　　What shulde I tellè more hir compleyn-
　　ynge ?
Hyt is so longe hyt were an hevy thynge.
In hyr Epistil Naso telleth alle ;　　2220
But shortly to the endè tel I shalle.
The goddys have hir holpen for pitee,
And in the sygne of Taurus men may see
The stonès of hir corowne shynè clere ;
I wol no morè speke of thys matere.

2155. *Ennopye,* 'Ænopia, another name for
Ægina' (Skeat); Gilman suggests Enope in
Messenia.
2184. *pitee,* Gg *now pitee ;* Trin.² *gret pitee.*
2188. *hir heer,* Gg *al hire her.*

2215. *ship or boot,* Trin.; Arch. Seld. and
Add.₂ *any tote ;* Gg *boot here ne ;* F⁴ *bote
noon here.* Ovid :
Finge, dari comitesque mihi, ventosque, ratemque.

But thus this falsė lover kan begyle
His trewe love, the devel quyte hym his while !

Explicit Legenda Adriane de Athenes

Incipit Legenda Philomene

Thow yiver of the formės, that hast wroght
The fairė worlde, and bare hit in thy thoght
Eternally or thow thy werke beganne, 2230
Why madest thow unto the sklaunder of manne,
Or—al be that hyt was not thy doynge,
As for that fyne to makė suche a thynge,—
Why suffrest thow that Terėus was bore,
That is in love so fals and so forswore,
That fro thys worlde up to the firstė hevene
Corrumpeth, whan that folke his namė nevene ?
And as to me, so grisly was his dede,
That whan that I this foulė story rede,
Myn eyen wexen foule and sore also ; 2240
Yet laste the venym of so longe ago,
That it infecteth hym that wolde beholde
The story of Terėus, of which I tolde.
 Of Trasė was he lorde, and kynne to Marte,
The cruelle god that stante with blody darte,
And wedded haddehe, with a blisful chere,
King Pandyónės fairė doghter dere,
That hyghtė Proygne, floure of hir contree ;
Thogh Juno lyst nat at the festė bee,
Ne Ymeneus, that god of weddyng is. 2250
But at the festė redy ben, y-wys,
The Furies thre, with al hire mortel bronde,
The owle al nyght about the balkės wonde,
That prophete is of wo and of myschaunce.
This revel, ful of songe, and ful of daunce,
Lasteth a fourtėnyght or lytel lasse.
But shortly of this story for to passe,—
For I am wery of hym for to telle,—
Fyve yere his wyfe and he togedir dwelle ;
Til on a day she gan so sorė longe 2260
To seen hir suster, that she saugh not longe,

That for desire she nystė what to seye,
But to hir husbonde gan she for to preye
For Goddys love, that she moste onės gon
Hir suster for to seen, and come anon.
Or ellės, but she mostė to hyr wende,
She preydė hym that he wolde aftir hir sende.
And thys was day be day al hir prayere,
With al humblesse of wyfehode, worde and chere. 2269
 This Terėus let make his shippės yare,
And into Grece hymselfe is forthe y-fare,
Unto his fader in lawe, and gan hym preye,
To vouchėsafe that for a moneth or tweye,
That Philomene, his wyfės suster, myghte
On Proigne his wyfe but onės have a syghte ;
' And she shal come to yow agayne anon,
Myselfe with hyr, I wil bothe come and gon,
And as myn hertės lyfe I wol hir kepe.'
 Thys oldė Pandėon, thys kynge, gan wepe
For tendernesse of hertė for to leve 2280
His doghtre gon, and for to yive hir leve ;
Of al thys worlde he lovede nothinge so ;
But at the lastė leve hath she to go.
For Philomene with saltė terės eke
Gan of hir fader gracė to beseke,
To seen hir sustre that she loveth so,
And hym embraceth with hir armės two.
And ther-with-alle so yonge and faire was she, 2288
That whan that Terėus saugh hir beaute,
And of array that ther nas noon hir lyche
(And yet of beaute was she two so ryche),
He caste his fiery hert upon hir so,
That he wol have hir, how-so that hyt go,
And with his wilės knelėd and so preyde,
Til at the lastė Pandėon thus seydė :
' Now, sone,' quod he, ' that arte to me so dere,
I the betake my yongė doghtre here,
That bereth the key of al myn hertės lyfe.
And gretė wel my doghter and thy wyfe,
And yeve hir leve sometymė for to pleye,
That she may seen me onės or I deye.'
And sothely he hath made him rychė feste,
And to his folke, the moste and eke the leste,

2228. *yiver of the formes,* ' Deus dator for-
marum,' Bodley gloss.
2256. *Lasteth,* Arch. Seld. *Lestith ;* rest *Laste.*

2286. *she loveth,* F⁴ *hir longeth.*
2291. *beaute,* F¹ *bounte.*

That with him come ; and yaf him yeftes grete,
And him conveyeth thurgh the maistir strete
Of Athenés, and to the see him broghte,
And turneth home ; no malyce he ne thoghte.
  The ores pulleth forthe the vessel faste,
And into Trace arryveth at the laste ;
And up into a forest he hir ledde,   2310
And to a cavé pryvely hym spedde,
And in this derké cavé, yif hir leste,
Or lesté noght, he bad hir for to reste ;
Of which hir hert agrose, and seyde thus :
' Where is my suster, brother Teréus ? '
And therewithal she wepté tendirly,
And quoke for feré, pale and pitously,
Ryghte as the lambe that of the wolfe is byten,
Or as the colver that of the egle is smyten,
And is out of his clawés forthe escaped,
Yét hyt is aferded and awhaped   2321
Lest hit be hent eftsonés : so sate she.
But utterly hyt may none other be,
By forcé hath this traytour done a dede,
That he hath refte hir of hir maydenhede
Maugree hir hede, by strengthe and by his myght.
  Lo, here a dede of men, and that aryght !
She crieth ' Suster ! ' with ful loudé stevene,
And ' Fader dere ! ' and ' Helpe me, God in hevene ! '
Al helpeth nat.   And yet this falsé thefe
Hath doon thys lady yet a more myschefe,
For ferdé lest she sholde his shamé crye,
And done hym openly a vilanye,   2333
And with his swerde hire tonge of kerveth he,
And in a castel made hir for to be
Ful privély in prison evermore,
And kept hir to his usage and to his store,
So that she myghte hym nevermore asterte.
  O sely Philomene, wo is in thyn herte !
God wreké the, and sendé the thy bone !
Now is hyt tyme I make an endé sone.
  This Teréus is to his wyfe y-come,
And in his armes hath his wyfe y-nome,

And pitously he wepe, and shoke his hede,
And swore hire that he fonde hir suster dede ;
For whiche the sely Proigne hath suche wo,
That nyghe hire sorwful herté brake a-two.
And thus in terés lat I Proigne dwelle,
And of hir suster forthe I wol yow telle.
  This woful lady y-lernéd had in yowthe,
So that she werken and enbrowden kowthe,   2351
And weven in hire stole the radevore,
As hyt of wymmen hath ben y-wovéd yore.
And, shortly for to seyn, she hath hir fille
Of mete and drynke, and clothyng at hire wille,
And kouthe eke rede and wel ynogh endyte,
But with a penné kouthe she nat write ;
But letteres kan she wevé to and fro.
So that by that the yere was al ago,   2360
She haddé woven in a stames large,
How she was broght from Athenes in a barge,
And in a cavé how that she was broght,
And al the thinge that Teréus hath wroght.
She wave hyt wel, and wrote the story above,
How she was servéd for hir suster love.
And to a knave a rynge she yaf anoon,
And prayéd hym by signés for to goon
Unto the quene, and beren hir that clothe ;
And by signés swor hym many an othe,
She shulde hym yevé what she geten myghte.   2370
  Thys knave anon unto the queene hym dyghte,
And toke hit hir, and al the maner tolde.
And whanne that Proigne hath this thing beholde,
No worde she spake, for sorwe and eke for rage,
But feynéd hyr to goon on pilgrymage
To Bachus temple.   And in a lytel stounde
Hire dombé suster syttyng hath she founde
Wépynge in the castel, hir-self allone.
Allas, the wo, the compleynt, and the mone

2329. and (2), om. F⁵.
2332. For ferde Gg² For fere.
2338. F³ om. and insert the spurious line Huge ben thy sorwes and wonder smerte after 2339.
2352. hire, F⁵ om.
2353. ben y-woved, so Arch. Seld. ; rest be woved, be woned.
2369. signes, F⁴ signe.
2369. hym, Gg only ; Trin. she ; rest om.

That Proigne upon hir dombë suster
    maketh !   2380
In armés everych of hem other taketh ;
And thus I lat hem in her sorwë dwelle.
  The remenant is no chargë for to telle,
For this is al and some,—thus was
    she served,
That never harm agyltë ne deservede
Unto thys cruelle man, that she of wyste.
Ye may be war of men, yif that yow lyste.
For al be that he wol not for his shame
Dóon as Tereus, to lese his name,   2389
Ne serve yow as a mordcrere or a knave,
Ful lytel whilë shul ye trewe hym have,—
That wol I seyne, al were he nowe
    my brother,—
But hit so be that he may have non other.

Explicit Legenda Philomene

Incipit Legenda Phillis

By preve, as wel as by auctorite,
That wikked frute cometh of a wikked tree,
That may ye fynde, if that hyt liketh yow.
  But for thys ende I spekë thys as now,
To tellë yow of falsë Demophon.
In love a falser herde I never non,
But if hit were hys fader Theseus ;   2400
God, for his gracë, fro suche oon kepe us !
Thus thesë wymen prayen that hit here ;
Now to theffect turne I of my matere.
  Distroyëd is of Troyë the citee ;
This Demophon come saylyng in the see
Towarde Athénës to his paleys large.
With hym come many a shippe and
    many a barge
Fúl of folke, of whiche ful many on
Is wounded sore, and seke, and wo begon,
And they han at a segë longe y-layne.
Byhynde him come a wynde and eke
    a rayne,   2411
That shofe so sore his saylle ne myghtë
    stonde,
Hym werë lever than al the worlde a-londe,
So hunteth hym the tempest to and fro !
So derke hyt was, he kouthë no-wher go,

And with a wawë brosten was his stere.
His shippe was rent so lowe, in suche
    manere,
That carpentere ne koude hit nat amende.
  The see by nyght as any torchë brende
For wode, and posseth hym now up now
    doun ;   2420
Til Neptune hath of hym compassyoun,
And Thetis, Chorus, Triton, and they alle,
And maden him upon a londe to falle,
Wherof that Phillis lady was and quene,
Lycurgus doghtre, fayrer on to sene
Than is the floure ageyn the bryghtésonne.
  Unneth is Demophoon to londe
    y-wonne,
Waykeand ekewery, and his folke forpyned
Of werynesse, and also enfamyned,   2429
And to the dethe he was almoste y-dreven.
His wisë folke to counseyle han hymyeven,
To seken helpe and socour of the quene,
And loken what his gracë myghtë bene,
And maken in that londe some chevis-
    saunce,
To kepen hym fro wo and fro myschaunce.
For seke he was, and almoste at the dethe ;
Unnethë myght he speke, or drawë brethe ;
And lyeth in Rhodopeya hym for to reste.
  Whan he may walke, hym thoght hit
    was the beste
Unto the court to seken for socoure.   2440
Men knewe hym welle and diden hym
    honoure ;
For at Athénës duke and lorde was he,
As Thesëus his fader hath y-be,
That in his tymë was of grete renoun,
No man so grete in al his regioun ;
And lyke his fader of face and of stature,
And fals of love ; hyt came hym of nature,
As doth the fox Renarde, the foxes sone ;
Of kynde he koude his oldë fadrës wone

2420. *now up now down*, F[4] *up and down.*
2422. *Chorus.* So Thynne (the MSS. read
Thorus), probably a misunderstanding of 'Et
senior Glauci chorus' in *Æn.* v. 823-825, where
Thetis, Triton 'and they all' ('exercitus omnis ')
are mentioned. See Skeat's note and Bech in
Anglia, vol. v.
2435. *To*, F[4] *And.*
2438. *Rhodopeya*, a mountain in Thrace.
2440. *court*, F[4] *contree.*
2441. *diden*, so Gg (*dedyn*); F[4] *dyd* ; Trin.[2] *did
him gret* ; Add.[2] *hym they dede.*
2442. *at*, Gg *of.*

2388. *his*, Gg only.
2400. *if*, F[5] om.
2408. *folke*, Gg *his folk.*

Withouté lore, as kan a drake swymme 2450
Whan hit is kaught and caried to the
  brymme.
  Thys honourable quené doth him chere,
Hir lyketh wel his porte and his manere.
But for I am agroteyd here beforne,
To write of hem that ben in love forsworne
And eke to hasté me in my Legende,
Which to performé, God me gracé sende ;
Therfore I passé shortly in thys wyse.
  Ye have wel herde of Theséus devise,
In the betraysyng of faire Adriane,   2460
That of hir pitee kepte hym fro his bane.
At shorté wordés, ryght so Demophon,
The samé way, the samé path hath gon,
That did his falsé fader Theséus.
For unto Phillis hath he sworen thus,
To wedden hir, and hir his trouthé plyghte,
And pikéd of hyr al the good he myghte,
Whan he was hole and sounde, and had
  his reste,
And doth with Phillis what-so that him
  leste,
As wel kouthe I, gif that me lesté so, 2470
Téllen al his doynges, to and fro.
  He sayde unto his contree moste he
  sayle,
For ther he wolde hire weddyng apparaylle
As fille to hir honour and his also,
And openly he tok his levé tho,
And to hir swore he woldé not sojourne,
But in a moneth ageyn he wolde retourne.
And in that londe let make his ordynaunce,
As verray lorde, and toke the obeisaunce
Wel and homely, and let his shippis dyghte,
And home he gooth the nexté wey he
  myghte.   2481
For unto Phillis yet ne come he noght,
And that hath she so harde and sore y-boght,
Allas, that as the storyes us recorde,
She was hir owné dethe ryght with a corde,
Whanne that she segh that Demophon
  her trayede.
But to hym firste she wrote, and faste hym
  prayede
He woldé come and hir delyver of peyne,

As I rehersè shal oo worde or tweyne.
Me lysté nat vouch-safe on him to swynke,
Ne spend on hym a penné ful of ynke, 2491
For fals in love was he, ryght as his syre ;
The devel set hire soulés both a-fire !
But of the letter of Phillis wol I wryte
A worde or tweyne, althogh hit be but lyte.
  'Thyn hostesse,' quod she, 'O thou
    Demophon,
Thy Phillis, which that is so wo begon,
Of Rhodopey, upon yow mot compleyne,
Over the termé sette betwix us tweyne,
That ye ne holden forwarde, as ye seyde.
Your anker, which ye in oure haven leyde,
Hyght us that ye wolde comen out of doute,
Or that the moné went onés aboute ;
But tymés foure the mone hath hid hir face
Syn thylké day ye wenté fro this place ;
And fouré tymés lyghte the worlde ageyn.
But for al that, yet I shal soothly seyn,
Yet hath the streme of Sithon nat i-broght
From Athenés the shippe ; yet cometh
  hit noght.
And if that ye the termé rekné wolde, 2510
As I or other trewé lovere sholde,
I pleyné nat, God wot ! beforne my day.'
But al hir letter writen I ne may
By ordre, for hit were to me a charge ;
Hir letter was ryght longe, and therto large.
But here and there in ryme I have hyt layde,
There as me thoghté that she hath wel
  sayde.
  She seyde, ' Thy sayllés cometh nat
    ageyn,
Ne to the worde there nys no fey certeyn ;
But I wote why ye comé nat,' quod she ;
' For I was of my love to yow so fre. 2521
And of the goddys that ye han forswore,
If hire vengeauncé fal on yow therfore,
Ye be nat suffisaunt to bere the peyne.
To muché trusted I, wel may I pleyne,
Upon youre lynage and youre fairé tonge,
And on youre terés falsély out-wronge.
How kouthe ye wepé so be crafte ?' quod
  she ;

2491. *Ne spend*, F⁴ *Dispenden*.
2496. *thou*, Trin. and Arch. Seld. only.
2508. *Sithon*, the name of the father of Phillis,
the King of Thrace.
2511. *lovere*, F⁴ *lovers*.
2523. *If*, F⁴ *That*.

2459. *devise*, F³ *the nyse*; Thynne *the gyse*.
2480. *homely*, Tan. *humble*; Thynne *humbly*.
2480. *let*, Gg only ; rest om.
2482. *For*, Trin. *But*.

'Máy there suché teres i-feynede be?
Now certes gif ye wolde have in memorye,
Hyt oughtè be to yow but lytel glorie, 2531
To have a sely maydè thus betrayed !
To God,' quod she, 'prey I, and ofte
    have prayed,
That hyt be nowe the gretest prise of alle,
And moste honour that ever yow shal
    befalle.
And when thyn olde auncetres peynted be,
In which men may her worthynessè se,
Then pray I God, thow peynted be also,
That folke may reden, for-by as they go, —
  " Lo, this is he, that with his flaterye
Betrayèd hath, and doon hir vilanye, 2541
That was his trewè love in thoghte and
    dede."
  But sothely of oo poynt yet may they
    rede,
That ye ben lyke youre fader, as in this ;
For he begilèd Adriane, y-wis,
With suche an arte, and suchè soteltee,
As thou thy-selven hast begiled me.
As in that poynt, althogh hit be nat feire,
Thou folwest hym certeyn, and art his
    eyre.
But syn thus synfully ye me begile, 2550
My body mote ye seen, within a while,
Ryght in the havene of Athenès fletynge,
Withouten sepulture and buryinge,
Though ye ben harder then is any stone.'
  And whan this letter was forthe sent
    anone,
And knew how brotel and how fals he was,
She for dispeyre fordide hir-self, allas !
Suche sorowe hath she, for she beset hire so !
Be war, ye wymmen, of youre sotile fo !
Syns yet this day men may ensample se,
And, as in love, trusteth no man but me.

    Explicit Legenda Phillis

    Incipit Legenda Ypermystre

  In Grecè whilom weren brethren two
Of which that oon was callèd Danao, 2563
That many a sone hath of his body wonne,
As suchè falsè lovers oftè konne.
  Among his sonès allè there was oon,
That aldermoste he loved of everychon.

And whan this childe was borne, this Danao
Shope hym a name, and callèd hym Lyno.
  That other brother callèd was Egiste,
That was in love as fals as ever hym lyste.
And many a doghtre gat he in his lyfe ;
Of which he gat upon his ryghtè wife 2573
A doughter dere, and did hir for to calle
Ypermystra, yongest of hem alle.
The whichè childe, of hir natyvite,
To allè goodè thewès borne was she,
As lykède to the goddes, or she was borne,
That of the shefe she shuldè be the corne.
  The Wirdes, that we clepen Destanye,
Hath shapen hir, that she moste nedès be
Pitousè, saddè, wise, and trewe as stele.
And to this woman hyt acordeth wele ;
For though that Venus yaf hir grete beaute,
With Jupiter compounèd so was she,
That consciencè, trouthe, and drede of
    shame,
And of hir wyfehode for to kepe hir name,
This thoghte hire was felicitè as here.
And redè Mars was that tyme of the yere
So feble, that his malice is him rafte ; 2590
Repressèd hath Venùs his cruelle crafte ;
And with Venùs, and other oppressyoun
Of houses, Mars his venym is adoun,
That Ypermystra dare not handel a knyfè
In malyce, thogh she shuldè lese hir lyfe.
  But nathéles, as heven gan tho turne,
To baddè aspectes hath she of Saturne,
That made hir for to dyen in prisoun,
As I shal after makè mencioun.
  To Danao and Egistes also, 2600
Al thogh so be that they were brethren
    two,
For thilkè tyme nas sparèd no lynage,
Hyt lyketh hem to maken mariage
Betwixè Ypermestre and hym Lyno,
And casten suche a day hyt shal be so,
And ful acorded was hit wittirly.
  The array is wroght, the tyme is fastè by,
And thus Lyno hath of his fadres brother
The doghter wedded, and eche of hem
    hath other.

2582. *and*, Trin.² only.
2592. *And with*, Gg⁴ *That* (Thynne *And*)
what with.
2598. *dyen*, MSS. *dy, dye.*
2599. *As*, F⁴ *And.*
2601. *Al*, F⁵ *And.*

2 S

The torches brennen, and the lampès
  bryghte,   2610
The sacrifices ben ful redy dyght,
Thencence out of the firè reketh sote,
The flour, the lefe, is rent up by the rote,
To maken garlandes and corounès hye ;
Ful is the place of sounde of mynstralcye,
Of songès amorouse of mariage,
As thilkè tymè was the pleyne usage.
And this was in the paleys of Egiste,
That in his house was lorde, ryght as hym
  lyste.
And thus that day they driven to an ende ;
The frendès taken leve, and home they
  wende ;   2621
The nyght is comen, the bride shal go to
  bedde.
Egistè to his chambre fast hym spedde,
And prively he let his doghter calle,
Whanne that the hous was voyded of hem
  alle.
He lokèd on his doghter with glad chere,
And to hir spak as ye shal after here.
  ' My ryghtè doghtèr, tresour of myn
  herte,
Syn firste that day that shapen was my
  sherte,   2629
Or by the fatale sustren hadde my dome,
So ny myn hertè never thinge me come
As thou, myn Ypermystra, doughter dere !
Take hedè what thy fader seyth the here,
And wirke after thy wiser ever mo.
For alderfirstè, doghter, I love the so
That al the worlde to me nys half so lefe,
Ne I noldè redè the to thy myschefe,
For al the good under the coldè moone ;
And what I meene, hyt shal be seyde
  ryght soone,   2639
With protestacioun, as seyn these wyse,
That, but thou do as I shal the devyse,
Thou shalt be ded,—by hym that al hath
  wrought !
At shortè wordès thou ne scapest nought
Out of my paleys or that thou be dede,
But thou consente and werke aftir my rede ;
Take this to the for ful conclusioun.'

This Ypermystra caste hir eyen doun,
And quoke as doth the lefe of aspè grene ;
Ded wex hir hewe, and lyke an ashe to sene :
And seydè, 'Lorde and fader, al youre wille,
After my myght, God wote I shal fulfille,
So hit to me be no confusioun.'   2652
  'I nyl,' quod he, 'have noon excepcioun ;
And out he kaughte a knyfe as rasour kene.
' Hyde this,' quod he, ' that hyt be not
  i-sene,
And whan thyn housbonde is to beddè go,
While that he slepeth kut his throte atwo :
For in my dremès hyt is warnèd me,
How that my nevew shal my banè be,
But which I not ; wherfore I wol be siker.
Gif thou say nay, we two shal have a byker,
As I have seyde, by him that I have sworne !'
  This Ypermystre hath nygh hire wytte
  forlorne,   2663
And, for to passen harmlesse of that place,
She grauntèd hym ; ther was noon other
  grace.
And therwithal a costrel taketh he
And seyde, ' Hereof a draught, or two, or
  thre,
Yif hym to drynkè, whan he gooth to reste,
And he shal slepe as longe as ever the leste ;
The narcotikes and opies ben so stronge.
And go thy way, lest that hym thynke to
  longe.'   2671
  Oute cometh the bride, and with ful
  sobre chere,
As is of maidenes oftè the manere,
To chambre is broght with revel and with
  songe.
And shortly, leste this talè be to longe,
This Lyno and she beth i-broght to bedde,
And every wight out at the dore hym
  spedde.
The nyght is wasted and he felle aslepe ;
Ful tenderly begynneth she to wepe ;
She riste hir up, and dredefully she quaketh,
As doth the braunchè that Zepherus
  shaketh,   2681

2632. *myn*, Gg only ; Trin.[2] have *my* before
doughter.
2633. *what*, Gg *what I.*
2637. *I noldè*, F[4] *noldè* ; Trin. *wold* ; Add.2
wolde I.

2649. *an*, F[4] *as.*
2666. *he*, F[4] add *tho*, omitting *or thre* in next
line.
2676. Trin. mends this line by reading *beth sent*
for *beth*, but Trin. and Arch. Seld. have *Danao*
for *Lino*, and this metre-saving slip may be
Chaucer's own.

And hussht were alle in Argone that citee.
As colde as eny froste now wexeth she,
For pite by the herte hir streyneth so,
And drede of dethe doth hir so moché wo,
That thriès doun she fil in swich a were,
She ryst hir up and stakereth here and there,
And on hir handès fastè loketh she.
'Allas, and shal myn handès blody be?
I am a mayde, and as by my nature, 2690
And by my semblant, and by my vesture,
Myn handès ben nat shapen for a knyfe,
As for to revè no man fro his lyfe!
What devel have I with the knyfe to do?
And shal I have my throtè korve a-two?
Than shal I blede, allas, and me be-shende!
And nedès-coste thys thing mot have an
    ende;
Or he or I mot nedès lese oure lyfe.
Now certès,' quod she, 'syn I am his wyfe,
And hathe my feythe, yet is hyt bet for me
For to be ded in wyfely honeste, 2701
Than be a traytour lyvyng in my shame.
Be as be may, for erneste or for game,
He shal awake and ryse and go his way
Out at this goter, or that hyt be day.'

And wepte ful tendirly upon his face,
And in hir armès gan hym to embrace,
And hym she roggeth and awaketh softe,
And at the wyndow lepe he fro the lofte,
Whan she hath warnèd hym and doon
    hym bote. 2710
This Lyno swyftè was and lyght of fote,
And from his wif he ranne a ful goode pas.
This sely womman ys so wayke, allas!
And helples, so that er that she fer wente
Her crewel fader did her for to hente,
Allas! Lyno, why art thou so unkynde?
Why ne haddist thou remembred in thy
    mynde
And taken hir and ledde hir forthe with
    the?
For when she sawe that goon away was he,
And that she mightè not so fastè go, 2720
Ne folowen hym she sat hir doun ryght tho,
Til she was caught and fetered in prysoun.
This tale is seyde for this conclusioun.

. . . . .

2712. *his wif he*, F⁴ *hir*.
2723. At this point Chaucer, after showing
many signs of tiredness, seems to have abandoned
the *Legend* altogether.

LATER MINOR POEMS

TO ROSEMOUNDE
A Balade

MADAME, ye ben of al beauté [the] shryne
As fer as cerclèd is the mappèmounde,
For as the cristal glorious ye shyne
And lykè ruby ben your chekès rounde.
Therwith ye ben so mery and so jocounde
That at a revel whan that I see you daunce,
It is an oynèment unto my wounde,
Though ye to me ne do no daliaunce.

For though I wepe of terès ful a tyne, 9
Yet may that wo myn hertè nat confounde;
Your seemly voys that ye so smal out-twyne
Maketh my thoght in joye and blis
    habounde.
So curteisly I go, with lovè bounde,
That to myself I sey, in my penaunce,

1. MS. Rawl. Poet. 163 omits *the*.
11. MS. reads *semy;* and *fynall* (i.e. *final*)
for *small*, according to Skeat.

Suffyseth me to love you Rosemounde,
Though ye to me ne do no daliaunce.

Nas never pyk walwèd in galauntyne
As I in love am walwèd and y-wounde,
For which ful ofte I of my-self dyvyne
That I am trewè Tristam the secounde, 20
My love may not refreyd be nor afounde;
I brenne ay in an amorous plesaunce.
Do what you lyst, I wyl your thral be
    founde
Though ye to me ne do no daliaunce.
TREGENTIL.   CHAUCER.

THE FORMER AGE
(ÆTAS PRIMA)

A BLISFUL lyf, a paisible and a swete,
Ledden the peplès in the former age;

They helde hem paied of fruités that they
    ete;
Whiche that the feldés yave hem by usage,
They ne weré nat for-pampred with out-
    rage.
Unknowén was the quern and eek the melle,
They eten mast, hawés, and swych pounage,
And dronken water of the coldé welle.

Yit nas the ground nat wounded with
    the plough,
But corn up-sprong, unsowe of mannés
    hond,   10
The which they gnodde and eete nat half
    y-nough;
No man yit knew the forwés of his lond;
No man the fyr out of the flynt yit fonde;
Unkorven and ungrobbéd lay the vyne;
No man yit in the morter spices grond
To clarré, ne to sause of galentyne.

No mader welde, or wood no litéstere
Ne knew; the flees was of his former hewe;
No flessh ne wyste offence of egge or spere;
No coyn ne knew man which was fals or
    trewe;   20
No ship yit karf the wawés grene and blewe;
No marchaunt yit ne fette outlandissh ware;
No trompés for the werrés folk ne knewe,
Ne towrés heye and wallés rounde or square.

What sholde it han avayléd to werreye?
Ther lay no profit, ther was no richesse;
But curséd was the tyme, I dar wel seye,
That men first dide hir swety besynesse
To grobbe up metal lurkyng in darknesse,
And in the ryverés fyrst gemmés soghte;
Allas! than sprong up al the cursédnesse
Of covetyse that fyrst our sorwé broughte!

Thise tyraunts putte hem gladly nat in
    pres
No wyldnesse ne no busshés for to wynne.
Ther póverte is, as seith Diogenes,
Ther as vitaile is eek so skars and thinne,
That noght but mast or apples is ther-inne;
But ther as baggés been and fat vitaile
Ther wol they gon and sparé for no synne
With al hir ost the cyte forto asayle.   40

Yit were no paleis chaumbrés, ne non
    halles;
In cavés and [in] wodés softe and swete,
Slepten this blisséd folk withowté walles,
On gras or leves in parfit joye and quiéte:
No down of fetherés, ne no blechéd shete
Was kid to hem, but in seurtee they slepte.
Hir hertés were al oon withouté galles,
Everich of hem his feith to other kepte.

Unforgéd was the hauberke and the
    plate;
The lambish peple, voydéd of alle vyce, 50
Haddén no fantasyé to debate,
But ech of hem wolde other wel cheryce;
No pridé, non envye, non avaryce,
No lord, no taylage by no tyranye,
Humblesse, and pes, good feith, the
    emperice,

.   .   .   .   .

Yit was nat Jupiter the likerous,
That first was fader of delicacye,
Come in this world, ne Nembrot desyrous
To reynen had nat maad his tourés hye. 60
Allas! allas! now may men wepe and
    crye!
For in our dayés nis but covetyse,
[And] dowblenesse, and tresoun, and
    envey,
Poysoun, manslaughtre, and mordre in
    sondry wyse.

FORTUNE

Balades de visage sans Peinture

I.—LE PLEINTIF COUNTRE FORTUNE

THIS wrecchéd worldés transmutacioun,
As wele or wo, now povre and now honour,
Withouten ordre or wys discrecioun
Governéd is by Fortunés errour;
But nathéles the lak of hir favour

---

3. Both MSS. read *the fruites.*
34. Ii reads *places wyldnesse;* Hh *place of
wyldnesse.*

42. Both omit *in* before *wodes.*
44. *quiete* is slurred so as to be practically
monosyllabic or dissyllabic if the final vowel is
pronounced. Cp. *B. of D.* l. 330 Medea.
56. This line is wanting in the MSS.
59. *Nembrot,* Nimrod.
63. Both omit first *And.*

Ne may not don me singen, though I dye.
' *Iay tout perdu mon temps et mon labour* ' :
For fynally, Fortune, I thee defye.

Yit is me left the light of my resoun
To knowen frend fro fo in thy mirour. 10
So muche hath yit thy whirlyng up and doun
Y-taught me for to knowen in an hour.
But trewély, no force of thy reddour
To him that over him-self hath the maystrye
My suffisaunce shal be my socour :
For fynally, Fortune, I thee defye.

O Socrates, thou stedfast champioun,
She never mighte be thy tormentour ;
Thou never dreddest hir oppressioun
Ne in hir cheré founde thou no savour. 20
Thou knewe wel the deceit of hir colour
And that hir mosté worshipe is to lye.
I know hir eek a fals dissimulour :
For fynally, Fortune, I thee defye !

II.—LA RESPOUNSE DE FORTUNE AU PLEINTIF

No man is wrecched, but him-self it wene
And he that hath him-self hath suffisaunce.
Why seystow than I am to thee so kene
That hast thy-self out of my governaunce?
Sey thus : 'Graunt mercy of thyn habound-
aunce
That thou hast lent or this.'   Why wol
thou strýve ?   30
What wostow yit how I thee wol avaunce ?
And eek thou hast thy besté frend alyve !

I have thee taught divisioun bi-twene
Frend of effect, and frend of countenaunce ;
Thee ñedeth nat the galle of noon hyéne,
That cureth ýen derke fro hir penaunce ;
Now seestow cleer, that were in ignoraunce.
Yit halt thyn ancre, ånd yit thou mayst
arryve
Ther bountee berth the keye of my sub-
staunce :   39
And eek thou hast thy besté frend alyve !

How many have I refuséd to sustene
Sin I thee fostred have in thy plesaunce !
Woltow than make a statute on thy quene
That I shal been ay at thyn ordinaunce ?
Thou born art in my regne of variaunce,
Aboute the wheel with other most thou
dryve.
My lore is bet than wikke is thy grevaunce :
And eek thou hast thy besté frend alyve !

III.—LA RESPOUNSE DU PLEINTIF COUNTRE FORTUNE

Thy lore I dampne, hit is adversitee.
My frend maystow nat reven, blynd
goddésse !   50
That I thy frendés knowe, I thanke it thee.
Tak hem agayn, lat hem go lye on presse !
The negardye in kepyng hir richesse
Prenostik is thou wolt hir tour assayle ;
Wikke appetyt comth ay before seknesse :
In general, this reulé may nat fayle.

IV.—LA RESPOUNSE DE FORTUNE COUNTRE LE PLEINTIF

Thou pinchest at my mutabilitee,
For I thee lente a drope of my richesse,
And now me lyketh to withdrawé me.
Why sholdestow my rëaltee oppresse ? 60
The see may ebbe and flowen more or lesse ;
The welkne hath might to shyné, reyne
or hayle ;
Right so mot I kythén my brotelnesse :
In general, this reulé may nat fayle.

Lo, thexecucion of the magestee
That al purveyeth of his rightwysnesse
That samé thyng 'Fortuné' clepen ye,
Ye blyndé bestés, ful of lewédnesse !
The hevene hath propretee of sikernesse ;
This world hath ever restéles travayle ; 70
Thy lasté day is ende of myn intresse :
In general, this reulé may nat fayle.

LENVOY DE FORTUNE

Princes, I prey you of your gentilesse
Lat nat this man on me thus crye and
pleyne,

11. All but Ii read *turnyng* for *whirlyng*.
30. All but Ii read *Thou shalt not stryve.*

51. Ii *to* for *it.*

And I shal quyté you your bisynesse 75
At my requeste, as three of you or tweyne ;
And but you list releve him of his peyne,
Preyeth his besté frend, of his noblesse
That to som bettre estat he may atteyne.

Made thee of noght, and in especiál
Draw unto him, and pray in general
For thee, and eek for other, hevenlich
   mede ;
And trouthé shall delivere, it is no drede.

Explicit le bon conseil de G. Chaucer.

TRUTH
BALADE DE BON CONSEYL

FLEE fro the prees, and dwelle with soth-
   fastnesse
Suffice unto thy thyng though hit be smal ;
For hord hath hate and clymbyng tikel-
   nesse,
Prees hath envye, and welé blent overal ;
Savour no more than thee bihové shal ;
Werk wel thy-self, that other folk canst
   rede,
And trouthé shal delivere, it is no drede.

Tempest thee noght al crokéd to redresse
In trust of hir that turneth as a bal :
Greet resté stant in litel besynesse ;   10
An eek be war to sporne ageyn an al ;
Stryve noght, as doth the crokke with the
   wal.
Daunté thy-self, that dauntest otherés dede,
And trouthé shall delivere, it is no drede.

That thee is sent, receyve in buxumnesse,
The wrastling for this worlde axeth a fal.
Her nis non hoom, her nis but wildernesse.
Forth, pilgrim, forth ! Forth, beste, out
   of thy stal,
Know thy contree, look up, thank God
   of al ;
Hold the hye wey, and lat thy gost thee
   lede,   20
And trouthé shall delivere, it is no drede.

ENVOY

Therfore, thou vache, leve thyn old
   wrecchednesse
Unto the world ; leve now to be thral ;
Crye him mercy, that of his hy goodnesse

76. Only in Ii. The meaning is doubtful.
20. *Hold the hye wey*, Harl. F₁ F₂ L Cx. T₁ T₂
Seld. *Weyve thy lust ;* Kk *Reull thi self.*
23. *world* is dissyllabic as in O.E.

GENTILESSE
MORAL BALADE OF CHAUCER

THE firsté stok and fader of gentilesse,—
   What man that claymeth gentil for to be
Moste folwe his trace and alle his wittés
   dresse
Vertu to sewe and vycés for to flee.
   For unto vertu longeth dignitee,
And nought the revers, saufly dar I deme,
Al were he mytre, croune, or diademe.

This firsté stok was ful of rightwysnesse,
   Trewe of his word, sobre, pitous and free,
Clene of his goste and lovéd besynesse,   10
   Ageynst the vyce of slouthe, in honestee ;
   And but his heir love vertu, as dide he,
He nis nought gentil though he richè seme,
Al were he mitre, croune, or diademe.

Vycé may wel be heyr to old richesse,
   But there may no man, as ye may wel
     see,
Bequethe his heyr his vertuous noblesse ;
   That is appropréd unto no degree,
   But to the firsté Fader in magestee,
That maketh his heyr him that wol him
     queme,   20
Al were he mytre, croune, or diademe.

LAK OF STEDFASTNESSE
BALADE

SOM tyme this world was so stedfast and
   stable
That mannés word was obligacioun,
And now hit is so fals and deceivable
That word and deed, as in conclusioun,

1. A *The first fader and founder ;* H *fader
and fynder ;* Harl. *fader fynder.*
2. T H C Ha. *desireth ;* Add. *coveyteth.*

630

Ben no-thyng oon, for turnėd up so doun
Is al this world through mede and wilful-
nesse
That al is lost for lak of stedfastnesse.

What maketh this world to be so variable
But lust that folk have in dissensioun?
For now adayes a man is holde unable 10
But if he can, by som collusioun,
Don his neighbour wrong or oppressioun.
What causeth this, but wilful wrecched-
nesse
That al is lost, for lak of stedfastnesse?

Trouthe is put doun, resoun is holden fable,
Vertu hath now no dominacioun,
Pitee exyled, no wyght is merciáble.
Through covetyse is blent discrecioun;
The world hath mad a permutacioun
Fro right to wrong, fro trouthe to fikel-
nesse,   20
That al is lost, for lak of stedfastnesse.

LENVOY TO KING RICHARD

O prince, desire for to be honourable,
Cherish thy folk and hate extorcioun!
Suffre no thyng, that may be reprevable
To thyn estat, don in thy regioun.
Shew forth thy swerd of castigacioun,
Dred God, do law, love trouthe and
worthynesse,
And dryve thy folk ageyn to stedfastnesse.

Explicit.

LENVOY DE CHAUCER A
SCOGAN

To-broken been the statutes hye in
hevene,
That crėat were eternally to dure,
Sith that I see the bryghtė goddės sevene

5. Ct. F Harl. 7578 *Is no thing lyke;* Add.
Ar nothing like.
10. Tr. Th. Ct. F Add. Harl. 7578 *For amonge
us;* Bann. *Among us now.*
17. Harl. 7578 Ct. F *man* for *wyght.*
28. Harl. 7578 Ct. F Tr. Th. *And wed.*

Mowe wepe and wayle, and passioun
endure,
As may in erthe a mortale crëature.
Allas! fro whennės may this thing pro-
cede?
Of whiche errour I deye almost for drede.

By worde eterne whilom was it y-shape,
That fro the fiftė cercle, in no manére,
Ne myghte a drope of terės doun eschape.
But now so wepeth Venus in hir spere, 11
That with hir terės she wol drenche us
here.
Allas, Scogan! this is for thyn offence!
Thou causest this deluge of pestilence.

Hast thou not seyd in blaspheme of this
goddės,
Through pride, or through thy gretė
rekelnesse,
Swich thing as in the lawe of love forbode
is?
That, for thy lady saw nat thy distresse,
Therfor thou yave hir up at Michelmesse?
Allas, Scogan! of oldė folk ne yonge, 20
Was never erst Scogan blamėd for his
tonge.

Thou drowe in scorn Cupide eek to
recorde
Of thilkė rebel word that thou hast spoken,
For which he wol no lenger be thy lord.
And, Scogan, thogh his bowė be nat
broken,
He wol nat with his arwės been y-wroken
On thee, ne me, ne noon of our figure;
We shul of him have neyther hurte ne cure.

Now certės, frend, I drede of thyn
unhappe,
Leste for thy gilte the wreche of love
procede   30
On alle hem that ben hore and rounde of
shape,
That ben so lykly folk in love to spede.
Than shul we for our labour han no mede;
But wel I wot, thou wilt answere and seye,
'Loo, tholdė Grisel list to ryme and pleye!'

4. *wepe and wayle.* Probably a reference to
the heavy rains and floods of 1393.

Nay, Scogan, say not so, for I mexcuse,
God helpe me so ! in no ryme doutèlees,
Ne thynke I never of sleep to wake my
     muse,   38
That rusteth in my shethè stille in pees ;
While I was yong I put hir forth in prees ;
But al shal passèn that men prose or ryme,
Take every man his turne as for his tyme.

ENVOY

Scogan, that knelest at the stremès hede
Of grace, of alle honour, and worthy-
 nesse !
In thende of which streme I am dul as
 dede,
Forgete in solitarie wildernesse ;
Yet, Scogan, thenke on Tullius kyndè-
 nesse ;
Mynnè thy frend ther it may fructifye,
Far-wel, and lok thou never eft love defye.

THE COMPLEYNT OF VENUS

I

THERE nys so hy comfort to my
  plesaunce,
Whan that I am in any hevynesse,
As for to have leyser of remembraunce
Upon the manhod and the worthynesse,
Upon the trouth and on the stedfastnesse
Of him whos I am al, whil I may dure.
Ther oghtè blamè me no crèature,
For every wyght preiseth his gentilesse.

In him is bountee, wysdom, govern-
  aunce,   9
Wel more then any mannès wyt can gesse ;
For grace hath wold so ferforth him
  avaunce,
That of knyghthode he is parfit richesse ;
Honour honoureth him for his noblesse ;
Therto so well hath formèd him Nature.
That I am his for ever, I him assure,
For every wyght preiseth his gentilesse.
 And not-withstandyng al his suffisaunce
His gentil herte is of so greet humblesse

47. *Tullius kyndenesse*, a reference to M.
Tullius Cicero's *De Amicitia*.

To me in word, in werk, in contenaunce,
And me to serve is al his besynesse, 20
That I am set in verrey sikirnesse.
Thus oghte I blessè wel myn aventure,
Sith that him list me serven and honoure,
For every wyght preiseth his gentilesse.

II

Now certès, Love, hit is right covènable,
That men ful derè bye the noble thyng,
As wake a-bedde, and fasten at the table,
Wepyng to laughe and singe in com-
  pleynyng,
And doun to castè visage and lokyng, 29
Often to chaungèn hewe and countenaunce,
Pleyne in slepyng, and dremèn at the
 daunce,
Al the revers of any glad felyng.

Ialousyè be hangèd by a cable !
She wolde al knowè through her espying.
Ther doth no wyght nothyng so resonable,
That al nys harm in her ymagynyng.
Thus dere abought is Love in his yevyng,
Which ofte he yiveth withoutèn ordyn-
  aunce,
As sorw ynogh, and litel of plesaunce,
Al the revers of any glad felyng.   40

A litel tyme his yift is agrèable,
But ful encombèrous is the usyng ;
For subtil jalosye, the deceyvable,
Ful often-tymè causeth destourbyng.
Thus be we ever in drede and sufferyng ;
In nouncerteyn we languisshe in penaunce,
And han ful often many an harde mys-
  chaunce,
Al the revers of any glad felyng.

III

But certès, Love, I sey not in such wyse,
That for tescape out of your lace I mente,
For I so longe have been in your servyse, 51
That for to lete of, wol I never assente.
No fors ! thogh jalousyè me tormente ;
Sufficeth me to see him when I may ;
And therfor certès to myn endyng-day,
To love him best, ne shal I never repente.

31. Granson *plaindre en dormant*; MSS
pleye.

And certés, Love, whan I me wel avyse
On any estat that man may represente,
Then have ye makéd me, through your
    franchise,   59
Chesé the beste that ever on erthé wente.
Now love wel, herte, and look thou never
    stente,
And let the jelouse put it in assay,
That for no peyné wol I not sey nay ;
To love him best, ne shal I never repente.

Herté, to thee hit oghte y-nogh suffyse
That Love so hy a gracé to thee sente
To chese the worthiest in allé wyse,
And most agrëable unto myn entente.
Seché no ferther, neyther way ne wente,
Sith I have suffisaunce unto my pay,— 70
Thus wol I endé this compleynt or lay,
To love him beste ne shal I never repente.

LENVOY

Princess ! receyveth this Compleynt in
    gree,
Unto your excellent benignitee,
    Direct after my litel suffisaunce.
For eld, that in my spirit dulleth me,
Hath of endyting al the subtilte
    Wel ny bereft out of my remembraunce ;
And eek to me hit is a greet penaunce,
Syth rym in English hath swich scarsitee,
    To folwé word by word the curiositee 81
    Of Graunson, flour of hem that make
    in Fraunce !

LENVOY DE CHAUCER A BUKTON

THE COUNSEIL OF CHAUCER TOUCH-ING MARIAGE, WHICH WAS SENT TO BUKTON

MY maister Bukton, whan of Criste
    our kyng
Was axéd, What is trouthe or sothfast-
    nesse ?

82. Sir Oto de Graunson, a knight of Savoy, received an annuity from Richard II. in 1393 for services to the king.

He nat a word answerde to that axyng,
As who saith, 'No man is al trewe,' I
    gesse.
And therfor, thogh I highté to expresse
The sorwe and wo that is in mariage,
I dar not wryte of hit no wikkednesse,
Lest I my-self falle eft in swich dotage.

I wol nat seyn how that hit is the
    cheyne
Of Sathanas, on which he gnaweth
    ever ;   10
But I dar seyn, were he out of his
    peyne,
As by his wille he wolde be boundé
    never.
But thilké dotéd fool that eft hath lever
Y-cheynéd be than out of prison crepe,
God lete him never fro his wo dissever,
Ne no man him bewaylé thogh he wepe !

But yit, lest thou do worsé, tak a wyf ;
Bet is to wedde than brenne in worsé
    wyse,
But thou shalt have sorwe on thy flessh,
    thy lyf,
And ben thy wyvés thral, as seyn these
    wyse,   20
And if that holy writ may nat suffyse,
Experience shal thee teché, so may happe,
That thee were lever to be take in Fryse
Than eft to falle of weddyng in the trappe.

ENVOY

This litel writ, proverbés, or figure
I sendé you, tak kepe of hit, I rede :
Unwys is he that can no wele endure.
If thou be siker, put thee nat in drede.
The Wyf of Bathe I pray yow that ye
    rede
Of this matéré that we have on honde. 30
God graunté you your lyf frely to lede
In fredom ; for ful hard is to be bonde.

Explicit.

23. *Fryse.* An expedition in which Englishmen took part was launched against Friesland in 1396. The Frieslanders refused to ransom their country-men when captured, so no exchange was possible, which gives force to Chaucer's line.

THE COMPLEYNT OF CHAUCER TO HIS PURSE

To you, my purse, and to noon other wyght
    Compleyne I, for ye be my lady dere !
I am so sory now that ye been light ;
    For, certès, but ye make me hevy chere,
    Me were as leef be leyd upon my bere,
For whiche unto your mercy thus I crye,—
Beth hevy ageyn, or ellès mot I dye !

Now voucheth sauf this day, or hit be
    nyght,   8
    That I of you the blisful soun may here,
Or see your colour lyk the sonnè bright,
    That of yelownesse haddè never pere.
Ye be my lyf ! ye be myn hertès stere !
Quene of comfort and of good companye !
Beth hevy ageyn, or ellès mot I dye.

Now, purse, that be to me my lyvès light
    And savèour, as doun in this worlde
    here,
Out of this toun help me throgh your
    myght,
    Syn that ye wole not been my tresorére ;
    For I am shave as nye as is a frere. 19

19. *as is a*, Harl. 7333 P Add. Harl. 2251 *als nyghe as any;* Ff *shave as ys any.*

But yet I pray unto your curtesye,
Beth hevy ageyn, or ellès mot I dye !

L'ENVOYE DE CHAUCER

O conquerour of Brutès Albioun,
Which that by lyne and free eleccioun
    Ben verray kyng, this song to you I
    sende,   -
    And ye that mowen al myn harm amende,
Have mynde upon my supplicacioun !

PROVERBE OF CHAUCER

I

WHAT shul these clothes thus many-
    folde,
    Lo, this hotè somers day ?
After greet heet cometh colde ;
    No man caste his pilche away.

II

Of al this worlde the large compas
    Hit wol not in myn armès tweyne ;
Whoso mochel wol embrace,
    Litel therof he shal distreyne.

DOUBTFUL MINOR POEMS

MERCILES BEAUTE

A TRIPLE ROUNDEL

I

YOUR ẏen two wol slee me sodenly ;
I may the beautee of hem not sustene,
So woundeth hit through-out my hertè kene.

And but your word wol helen hastily
My hertès woundè, while that hit is grene.

1. P reads *Youre two yen*, but cp. ll. 6 and 11.
3. *through-out, out* is in the margin.

Your ẏen two wol slee me sodenly ;
I may the beautee of hem not sustene.

Upon my trouthe I sey you feithfully
That ye ben of my lyf and deeth the
    quene ;
For with my deeth the trouthè shal be
    sene.   10
Your ẏen two wol slee me sodenly ;
I may the beautee of hem not sustene,
So woundeth it through-out my hertè
    kene.

II

So hath your beautee fro your herté chaced
Pitee, that me ne availeth not to pleyne ;
For Daunger halt your mercy in his cheyne.

Giltles my deeth thus han ye me purcháced ;
I sey you sooth, me nedeth not to feyne ;
  So hath your beautee fro your herté
    chaced   19
  Pitee, that me ne availeth not to pleyne.

Allas ! that nature hath in you compássed
So greet beautee, that no man may atteyne
To mercy, though he stervé for the peyne.
  So hath your beautee fro your herté
    chaced
  Pitee, that me ne availeth not to pleyne ;
  For Daunger halt your mercy in his
    cheyne.

III

Sin I fro Love escapèd am so fat
I never thenk to ben in his prison lene ;
Sin I am free, I counte him not a bene.

He may answere, and seyé this or that ; 30
I do no fors, I speke right as I mene.
  Sin I fro Love escapèd am so fat
  I never thenk to ben in his prison lene.

Love hath my name y-strike out of his sclat,
And he is strike out of my bokés clene
For evermo ; [ther] is non other mene.
  Sin I fro Love escapèd am so fat
  I never thenk to ben in his prison lene ;
  Sin I am free, I counte him not a bene.

Explicit.

BALADE

AGAINST WOMAN UNCONSTAN

MADAMÉ, for your newé-fangelnesse
Many a servaunt have ye put out of grace.
I take my leve of your unstedfastnesse,
For wel I wot, whyl ye have lyvés space,

36. P *this is ;* Skeat *ther is.*
2. F Ct. Stowe's ed. *of your.*
4. Ct. Stowe's ed. *to liue haue ;* Harl. *lyne
and space.*

Ye can not love ful half yeer in a place ;
To newé thyng your lust is ay so kene ;
In stede of blew, thus may ye were al
  grene.

Right as a mirour nothyng may enpresse
But, lightly as it cometh, so mot it pace,
So fareth your love, your werkés bereth
  witnesse.   10
Ther is no feith that may your herte
  embrace ;
But, as a wedercok, that turneth his face
With every wynd, ye fare, and that is sene ;
In stede of blew, thus may ye were al grene.

Ye might be shrynéd, for your brotelnesse,
Bet than Dalyda, Creseide, or Candáce ;
For ever in chaungyng stant your
  sikernesse,
That tache may no wyght fro your
  herte arace ;
If ye lese oon, ye can wel tweyn purchace ;
Al light for somer, ye woot wel what I
  mene,   .   20
In stede of blew, thus may ye were al grene.

Explicit.

COMPLEYNT DAMOURS

I, WHICH that am the sorwfullesté man
That in this world was ever yit lyvynge
And leest recoverer of him-selven can
Beginne thus my deedly compleynynge
On hir, that may to lif and deeth me
  brynge,
Which hath on me no mercy ne no
  rewthe
That love hir best, but sleeth me
  for my trewthe.

6. Ct. Harl. *ever so ;* Stowe's ed. (1561)
omits *so.*
8. Ct. Harl. Stowe *that nothyng.*
16. Ct. *bettir,* rest *better. Dalyda,* Delilah.
Creseide, the heroine of Chaucer's Troilus.
Candace, Queen Candace, who tricked Alexander.
17. *stant,* all *stondeth.*
4. F B insert *right* before *thus.*

Can I noght doon ne seye that may you
    lyke?
Ne, certes, now, allas! allas! the while!
Your plesaunce is to laughen whan I syke,
And thus ye me from all my blisse exile.
Ye han me cast in thilkė spitous ile   12
Ther never man on lyve ne mighte asterte;
This have I for I love you beste, swete
    herte!

Sooth is, that wel I woot, by lyklinesse,
If that it were a thing possible to do
For to acompte your beautee and good-
    nesse
I have no wonder thogh ye do me wo;
Sith I, thunworthiest that may ride or go
Durste ever thynken in so hy a place,   20
What wonder is, thogh ye do me no grace?

Allas! thus is my lif brought to an ende,
My deeth, I see, is my conclusioun;
I may wel singe 'in sory tyme I spende
My lif'; that song may have confusioun!
For mercy, pitee, and deep affeccioun,
I sey for me, for al my deedly chere,
Alle thise diden, in that, me love you dere.

And in this wyse and in dispaire I lyve
In lovė; nay, but in dispaire I dye!   30
Bút shal I thus you my deeth for-yive,
That causéles doth me this sorwė drye?
Ye, certės, I! For she of my folye
Hath nought to done, although she
    do me sterve;
Hit is not with hir wil that I hir serve!

Than sithėn I am of my sorwe the cause,
And sith that I have this, withoute hir
    reed,
Than may I seyn, right shortly in a clause,
It is no blame unto hir womanheed.
Though swich a wrecche as I be for hir
    deed;   40
Yít alwey two thingės doon me dye,
That is to seyn, hir beautee and myn ȳe.

So that algates she is the verray rote
Of my disese, and of my dethe also;
For with oon word she mightė be my bote,
If that she vouchėd sauf for to do so.
Bút than is hir gladnesse at my wo?
It is hir wone plesaunce for to take,
To seen hir servaunts dȳen for hir sake!

But certės, than is al my wonderyng— 50
Sithėn she is the fayrest crëature
As to my dom that ever was lyvyng,
The benignest and beste eek that nature
Hath wrought or shal, whyl that the
    world may dure,—
Why that she leftė pitee so behynde?
It was, y-wys, a greet defaut in kynde.

Yít is al this no lak to hir, pardee,
But God or nature hem sore woldė I blame;
For, though she shewe no pitee unto me,
Sithėn that she doth otherė men the same,
I ne oughtė to despise my lady's game;
It is hir pley to laugh when that men syketh,
And I assente, al that hir list and lyketh!

Yít wolde I, as I dar, with sorwful herte
Biseche un-to your mekė womanhede
That I now dorste my sharpė sorwės smerte
Shewė by worde that ye wolde onės rede

8. Harl. om. *doon*; F B *doon to seyn that yow*
may like.
9. So all MSS. *Ne* is the strong accented negative.
14. F B om. *beste.*
16. Harl. om. *that.*
20. F *neuer*; perhaps rightly.
22. F *myschefe*; B *myschef* for *my lif.*
24. F om. all after *tyme.*
25 ff. B reads:
    that song is my confusyoun!
  For mercy and pite and my saluacioun,
  I soy for me, I have noun felte,
  All thes diden me in dispeire to melte.
F om. all after *song* in l. 25.
26. F om. *and* before *pites* and all after second
and.
27. F om. all after *me.*
28. F om. all after *diden.*
31. F *thanne* for *thus.*

36. Harl. *sith* for *sithen.*
37. F B *sithen* for *sith* and om. *that.*
43. F B om. *the.*
44. B om. second *of.*
45. F B a for *oon.*
48. B ins. *to* before *plesaunce.*
49. B *scruaunte.*
51. B *Sith.*
55. F B *all* for *so.*
57. F B om. *al.*
58. F B om. *sore.*
62. Harl. om. *hir.* F B om. *that.*
64. Harl. *Yeo* for *Yit.*
66. F B om. *now.* Harl. *shoures* for *sorwes.*

The compleynt of me, which ful sore I drede
That I have seid here, through myn unconnynge,
In any worde to your displesynge.   70

Lothest of anything that ever was loth
Were me, as wysly God my soulė save !
To seyn a thyng through which ye mighte be wroth ;
And, to that day that I be leyd in grave,
A trewer servaunt shulle ye never have ;
And, though that I on you have pleynėd here,
Foryiveth it me, myn ownė hertė dere !

Ever have I been, and shal, how-so I wende
Outher to lyve or dye, your humble trewe ;
Ye been to me my gynnyng and myn ende,   80
Sonne of the sterre so bright and clere of hewe,
Alwey in oon to love you freshly newe,
By God and by my trouthe, is myn entente ;
To lyve or dye, I wol it never repente !

This compleynt on seynt Valentynės day,
Whan every foughel chesėn shal his make,
To hir whos I am hool, and shal alwey,
This woful song and this compleynt I make,
That never yit wolde me to mercy take ;
And yit wol I evermore hir serve   90
And love hir best, although she do me sterve.

Explicit.

68. Harl. *the which I fulle*, etc.
69. Harl. *unknowynge.* F B om. *here and myn.*
70. This line seems short unless *worde* is dissyllabic, which is improbable ; cp. ll. 31, 41, 47, 86, 90, which are short in all MSS.
71. F *Lothe* for *Lothest.*
77. Harl. *myne owne lady so dere.*
81. F B *ouer (ouyr) the sterre bright of hewe.*
82. Harl. *And I ay oon.*
83. F B ins. *this* before *is.*
86. If *foughel* (fowl) is not dissyllabic this is another nine-syllabled line. F *soule*, B *foule.*
87. F B om. *hool.*
91. F *though* for *although.*

BALADE OF COMPLEYNTE

COMPLEYNE ne coude, ne mighte myn hertė never
My peynės halve, ne what torment I have,
Though that I sholde in your presence ben ever,
My hertės lady, as wisly he me save
That bountee madė, beautee list to grave
In your persone, and bad hem bothe in-fere
Ever tawayte, and ay be wher ye were.

As wisly he gye alle my joyės here
As I am youres, and to you sad and trewe,
And ye, my lif and cause of my good chere
And deeth also, whan ye my peynės newe,
My worldės joye, whom I wol serve and sewe,   12
My heven hool, and al my suffisaunce,
Whom for to serve is set al my plesaunce.

Beseching yow in my most humble wyse
Taccepte in worth this litel povrė dyte
And for my trouthe my service nat despyte,
Myn observaunce eek have nat in despyse,
Ne yit to long to suffren in this plyte,
I you beseche, myn hertės lady dere,   20
Sith I you serve, and so will yeer by yere.

BALADE THAT CHAUCIER MADE

So hath myn hertė caught in remembraunce
Your beautee hool and stedfast governaunce,
Your vertues allė and your hie noblesse,
That you to serve is set al my plesaunce.
So wel me liketh your womanly contenaunce,
Your fresshė fetures and your comlynesse,
That whiles I lyve, myn herte to his maistresse

16. MS. *porr.*
20. *dere*, MS. *here* by mistake.
3. MS. *al* for *alle.*

You hath wel chose in trewe perséveraunce
Never to chaunge for no maner distresse.

And sith [that] I shal do this observaunce
Al my lif [long] withouten displesaunce,
You for to serve with al my besynesse,
And have me somwhat in your
     souvenaunce,   13
My woful herté suffreth greet duresse,
And [hoveth humblély] with al sym-
     plesse ;
My wyl I cónforme to your ordynaunce
As you best list, my peynes for to redresse ;

Considryng eek how I hange in balaunce,
In your servicé, swich lo ! is my chaunce,
Abidyng grace whan that your gentilnesse,
Of my grete wo listeth don alleggeaunce,

And wyth your pitee me som wyse avaunce,
In ful rebatyng of myn hevynesse,   23
And thynketh by resoun that womanly
     noblesse
Shulde nat desiré for til do the outrance
Ther as she fyndeth non unbuxomnesse.

LENVOYE

Auctour of norture ! Lady of plesaunce !
Soveraigne of beautee ! flour of woman-
     hede,
Take ye non hede unto my ignoraunce,
But this receyveth of your goodlihede,
Thenkyng that I have caught in
     remembraunce,
Your beautee hool, your stedfast
     governaunce.

8. MS. *trieve.*
10. MS. om. *that.*
11. MS. om. *long.*
15. MS. *And how humbly.*

24. Perhaps *And* should be *Me*, otherwise the construction of this stanza, like that of the preceding one, is very loose.
29. *Take ye* should probably be *Taketh ;* cp. *receyveth* in next line.

A TREATISE ON THE ASTROLABE

LYTE LOWYS my sone, I aperceyve wel by certeyne evydences thyn abilite to lerne sciences touching nombres and proporciouns ; and as wel considre I thy bisy praier in special to lerne the Tretys of the Astrelabie. Than for as mochel as a philosofre saith, 'he wrappith him in his frende, that condescendith to the rightfull praiers of his frende,' therefore have I yeven the a suffisant Astrolabie as for oure orizonte compowned after the latitude of Oxenforde ; upon which, by mediacioun of this litel tretys, I propose to teche the a certein nombre of conclusions perteynyng to the same instrument. I seie a certein of conclusions for thre causes.

The first cause is this : truste wel that alle the conclusions that han be founde, or ellys possibly might be founde in so noble an instrument as is an Astrelabie ben unknowe parfitly to eny mortal man in this regioun, as I suppose. Another cause is this, that sothly in any tretis of the Astrelabie that I have seyn there be somme conclusions that wol not in alle thinges parformen her bihestes; and somme of hem ben to harde to thy tendir age of x yere to conceyve. [5]

This tretis, divided in 5 parties, wol I shewe the under full light reules and naked wordes in Englisshe, for Latyn canst thou

B₁ M₁ B₂ have title *Brede and milke for children.*
2. R₁ A₁ add *the werkynge of* before *a suffisant.*

5. *and somme of hem*, etc., *i.e.* the third cause.
5. *to thy*, etc., R₁ *to understonde and to conceyve to the tender age of þe.*
5. *naked*, simple ; cp. Shak. *Two Gent.* II. iv. 142.

yit but small, my litel sone. But natheles suffise to the these trewe conclusions in Englisshe as wel as sufficith to these noble clerkes Grekes these same conclusions in Greke ; and to Arabiens in Arabike, and to Iewes in Ebrewe, and to the Latyn folk in Latyn ; whiche Latyn folke had hem first oute of othere dyverse langages, and writen hem in her owne tunge, that is to seyn in Latyn. And god woot that in alle these langages and in many moo han these conclusions ben suffisantly lerned and taught, and yit by diverse reules; right as diverse pathes leden diverse folke the right way to Rome. Now wol I preie mekely every discret persone that redith or herith this litel tretys to have my rude endityng for excused, and my superfluite of wordes, for two causes. The first cause is for that curiouse endityng and harde sentence is ful hevy at onys for such a childe to lerne. And the secunde cause is this, that sothly me semith better to writen un-to a childe twyes a gode sentence, than he forgete it onys. [11]

And Lowys, yf so be that I shewe the in my light Englisshe as trewe conclusions touching this mater, and not oonly as trewe but as many and as subtile conclusiouns, as ben shewid in Latyn in eny commune tretys of the Astrelabie, konne me the more thanke. And preie god save the king, that is lorde of this language, and alle that him feithe berith and obeieth, everiche in his degre, the more and the lasse. But considre wel that I ne usurpe not to have founden this werke of my labour or of myn engyn. I nam but a lewde compilator of the labour of olde astrologiens, and have it translatid in myn Englisshe oonly for thy doctrine. And with this swerde shal I sleen envie. [15]

Prima pars.—The firste partie of this tretys shal reherse the figures and the membres of thyn Astrelabie by cause that thou shalt have the gretter knowing of thyn owne instrument.

Secunda pars.—The secunde partie shal techen the worken the verrey practik of

the forseide conclusiouns as ferforth and as narwe as may be shewed in so small an instrument portatif aboute. For wel woot every astrologien that smallist fraccions ne wol not be shewid in so small an instrument as in subtile tables calculed for a cause.

Tertia pars.—The thirde partie shal contene diverse tables of longitudes and latitudes of sterres fixe for the Astrelabie, and tables of the declinacions of the sonne, and tables of longitudes of citees and townes ; and tables as well for the gover-naunce of a clokke, as forto synde the altitude meridian ; and many a-nothir notable conclusioun after the kalenders of the reverent clerkes, frere I. Somer and frere N. Lenne. [20]

Quarta pars.—The fourthe partie shal ben a Theorike to declare the moevyng of the celestiall bodies with the causes. The whiche fourthe partie in speciall shal shewen a table of the verrey moeving of the mone from houre to houre every day and in every signe after thyn almenak. Upon whiche table ther foleweth a canoun suffisant to teche as wel the manere of the worchynge of the same conclusioun as to knowe in oure orizonte with whiche degre of the zodiak that the mone ariseth in any latitude, and the arisyng of any planete after his latitude fro the ecliptik lyne.

Quinta pars.—The fifthe partie shal be an Introductorie, after the statutes of oure doctours, in whiche thou maist lerne a gret parte of the generall rewles of theorik in astrologie. In whiche fifthe partie shalt thou fynden tables of equaciouns of houses after the latitude of Oxenforde; and tables of dignitees of planetes, and othere notefull thinges, yf God wol vouche saaf and his Moder the Maide moo then I behete. [25]

PART I

Here begynneth the descripcioun of the Astralabie

1. *Annulus.*—Thyn Astrolabie hath a ringe to putten on the thombe of thi right

18. *smallist*, B₁ B₂ *the smale ;* A₂ R₂ *smale.*
25. Chaucer abandoned his task before he had finished Part II.

7. *sufficith.* We should expect *suffice*, cp. 13.

honde in taking the height of thinges. And take kepe, for from henes forthward I wol clepen the heighte of any thinge that is taken by the rewle 'the altitude' withoute moo wordes.

2. *Ansa.*—This rynge renneth in a maner toret fast to the moder of thyn Astrelabie in so rowme a space that it distourbith not the instrument to hangen after his right centre.

3. *Mater.*—The Moder of thin Astrelabye is thikkest plate perced with a large hool, that resceiveth in hir wombe the thynne plates compowned for diverse clymates and thy reet shapen in manere of a nett or of a webbe of a loppe.

4. This moder is divided on the bakhalf with a lyne that cometh descending fro the ringe doun to the netherist bordure. The whiche lyne, fro the forseide ringe unto the centre of the large hool amidde, is clepid the Southe Lyne, or ellis the Lyne Meridional. And the remenaunt of this lyne doun to the bordure is clepid the North Lyne, or ellis the Lyne of Midnyght. [32]

5. Overthwart this forseide longe lyne ther crossith him a-nother lyne of the same lengthe from est to west. Of the whiche lyne, from a litel cros (+) in the bordure unto the centre of the large hool, is clepid the Est Lyne, or ellis the Lyne Orientale. And the remenaunt of this lyne, fro the forseide centre unto the bordure, is clepid the West Lyne, or ellis the Lyne Occidentale. Now hast thou here the foure quarters of thin Astrolabie divided after the foure principales plages or quarters of the firmament.

6. The est syde of thyn Astrolabie is clepid the right syde, and the west syde is clepid the lefte syde. Forgete not thys, litel Lowys. Putte the rynge of thyn Astrolabie upon the thombe of thi right honde, and than wol his right side

be toward thi lifte side, and his lefte side wol be toward thy right side. Take this rewle generall, as wel on the bak as on the wombe syde. Upon the ende of this est lyne, as I first seide, is marked a litel cros (+) where as evere moo generaly is considerid the entring of the first degre in whiche the sonne arisith. [40]

7. Fro this litel cros (+) up to the ende of the Lyne Meridionall, under the rynge, shalt thou fynden the bordure divided wit 90 degrees; and by that same proporcioun is every quarter of thin Astrolabie divided. Over the whiche degrees there ben noumbres of Augrym that dividen thilke same degres fro 5 to 5, as shewith by longe strikes bitwene. Of whiche longe strikes the space bitwene contenith a myle wey, and every degre of the bordure conteneth 4 minutes, this to seien mynutes of an houre.

8. Under the compas of thilke degrees ben writen the names of the Twelve Signes: as Aries, Taurus, Gemini, Cancer, Leo, Virgo, Libra, Scorpio, Sagittarius, Capricornus, Aquarius, Pisces. And the nombre of the degrees of thoo signes be writen in augrym above, and with longe divisiouns fro 5 to 5, dyvidid fro tyme that the signe entrith unto the last ende. [45] But understonde wel that these degres of signes ben everiche of hem considred of 60 mynutes, and every mynute of 60 secundes, and so furthe into smale fraccions infinite, as saith Alkabucius. And therfore knowe wel that a degre of the bordure contenith 4 minutes, and a degre of a signe conteneth 60 minutes, and have this in mynde.

9. Next this folewith the Cercle of the Daies, that ben figured in manere of degres that contenen in nombre 365, dividid also with longe strikes fro 5 to 5, and the nombre in augrym writen under that cercle.

10. Next the cercle of the daies folewith the Cercle of the Names of the Monthes, that is to sayn Ianuarius, Februarius, Marcius, Aprilis, Maius, Iunius, Iulius, Augustus, September, October, November, December. The names of these monthes

---

30. In early editions and A₂ § 3 is preceded by a gloss on *mater*.

30. *thikkest plate* (late MSS. *the thikkest*, etc.), like *smallist fraccions*, 18, seems to be a Latinism, and to mean 'very thick plate.'

35. *centre* is reading of R₁ R₂; B₁ *hool*, A₁ B₂ Br. Edd. *oriental*, M₁ Dd₁ have +.

43. *myle way*, 20 minutes; cp. *Tales*, A 3637. for temporal use of *furlong*.

were clepid somme for her propirtees and somme by statutes of lordes Arabiens, somme by othre lordes of Rome. [50] Eke of these monthes as liked to Iulius Cesar and to Cesar Augustus somme were compouned of diverse nombres of daies, as Iulie and August. Than hath Ianuarie 31 daies, Februarie 28, Marche 31, Aprill 30, May 31, Iunius 30, Iulius 31, Augustus 31, September 30, October 31, November 30, December 31. Natheles all though that Iulius Cesar toke 2 daies oute of Feverer and putte hem in his monthe of Iuyll, and Augustus Cesar clepid the monthe of August after his name and ordeined it of 31 daies, yit truste wel that the sonne dwellith therfore nevere the more ne lasse in oon signe than in a-nother.

11. Than folewen the names of the Holy Daies in the Kalender, and next hem the lettres of the A B C on whiche thei fallen.

12. Next the forseide cercle of the A B C, under the crosse lyne, is marked the Skale in manere of 2 squyres, or ellis in manere of laddres, that serveth by his 12 pointes and his dyvisiouns of ful many a subtile conclusioun. Of this forseide skale fro the crosse lyne unto the verrey angle is clepid Umbra Recta, or ellis Umbra Extensa, and the nethir partie is clepid Umbra Versa.

13. *Regula.*—Than hast thou a brode Reule, that hath on either ende a square plate perced wit certein holes, somme more and somme lasse, to receyve the stremes of the sonne by day, and eke by mediacioun of thin eye to knowe the altitude of sterres by night. [57]

14. *Axis.*—Than is there a large Pyn in manere of an extre, that goth thorugh the hole that halt the tables of the clymates and the riet in the wombe of the moder.

Equus.—Thorugh whiche pyn ther goth a litel wegge, whiche that is clepid the Hors, that streynith all these parties to hepe. Thys forseide grete pyn in manere of an extre is ymagyned to be the Pool Artik in thyn Astralabie. [60]

15. *Secunda pars astrolabii: Venter.*— The wombe syde of thyn Astrelabie is also divided with a longe croys in 4 quarters from est to west, fro southe to northe, fro right syde to lefte side, as is the bak-side.

16. The bordure of whiche wombe side is divided fro the point of the est lyne unto the point of the southe lyne under the ringe in 90 degrees; and by that same propor-cioun is every quarter divided, as is the bak side. That amountith 360 degrees. And understonde wel that degres of this bordure ben aunswering and consentrike to the degrees of the Equinoxiall, that is dividid in the same nombre as every othir cercle is in the high hevene.

This same bordure is dividid also with 23 lettres capitals and a small crosse (+) above the south lyne, that shewith the 24 houres equals of the clokke. And, as I have seid, 5 of these degres maken a myle wey, and 3 mileweie maken an houre. And every degre of thys bordure contenith 4 minutes, and every minute 60 secundes. Now have I tolde the twyes. [65]

17. The plate under the riet is dis-crived with 3 cercles, of whiche the leest is clepid the Cercle of Cancre by cause that the heved of Cancre turnith evermo consentrik upon the same cercle. In this heved of Cancer is the grettist de-clinacioun northward of the sonne, and therfore is he clepid Solsticium of Somer; whiche declinacioun after Ptholome is 23 degrees and 50 minutes as wel in Cancer as in Capricorn. This signe of Cancer is clepid the Tropik of Somer of *Tropos*, that is to seien 'ageynward.' For than beginneth the sonne to passen from usward. [70]

50. *were clepid,* B₁ *were clepid thus;* A₁ R₂ *ben consideryd;* R₁ *were yeven;* Br. Edd. *taken ther names.*

50. *lordes Arabiens,* R₂ A₁ (var.) *clerkys;* B₂ A₂ *Arabiens;* R₁ Br. Edd. *Emperours.*

53. The scribe of B₁ inserts Latin note showing incorrectness of Chaucer's statement.

56. Chaucer or first copyist has made mistake here, the name of the lower part being the Umbra Recta, that of the upright one Umbra Versa.

67. *3 cercles,* B₁ *tropik cercles;* M₁ Dd₁ *3 tropical cercles;* R₁ *3 principal cercles.*

67. Chaucer begins here to expand Messahala's *Descriptio,* with extracts from John de Sacro-bosco's *Tractatus de Sphæra.*

The myddel cercle in wydnesse of these 3 is clepid the Cercle Equinoxiall, upon whiche turnith evermo the hevedes of Aries and Libra. And understonde wel that evermo thys Cercle Equinoxiall turnith iustly from verrey est to verrey west as I have shewed the in the speer solide. This same cercle is clepid also the Weyer of the day ; for whan the sonne is in the hevedes of Aries and Libra, than ben the dayes and the nightes ylike of lengthe in all the worlde. And therfore ben these 2 signes called the Equinoxiis. And alle that moeveth withinne the hevedes of these Aries and Libra, his moevyng is clepid Northward ; and alle that moevith withoute these hevedes, his moevyng is clepid Southward, as fro the equinoxiall. Take kepe of these latitudes North and South, and forgete it nat. [75] By this cercle equinoxiall ben considred the 24 houres of the clokke, for evermo the arisyng of 15 degrees of the equinoxiall makith an houre equal of the clokke. This equinoxiall is clepid the gurdel of the first moeving, or ellis of the first moevable. And note that the first moevyng is clepid moevyng of the first moevable of the 8 speer, whiche moeving is from est in-to west, and efte ageyn in-to est. Also it is clepid girdel of the first moeving for it departith the first moevable, that is to seyn the spere, in two ilike partyes evene distantes fro the poles of this world.

The widest of these 3 principal cercles is clepid the Cercle of Capricorne by cause that the heved of Capricorne turnith evermo consentrik upon the same cercle. In the heved of this forseide Capricorne is the grettist declinacioun southward of the sonne, and therfore it is clepid the Solsticium of Wynter. This signe of Capricorne is also clepid the Tropic of Wynter, for than begynneth the sonne to come ageyn to usward. [82]

18. Upon this forseide plate ben compassed certeyn cercles that highten Almycanteras, of whiche somme of hem semen parfit cercles and somme semen inparfit. The centre that stondith amyddes the narwest cercle is clepid the Cenyth. And the netherist cercle, or the first cercle, is clepid the Orizonte, that is to seyn the cercle that divideth the two emysperies, that is the partie of the hevene above the erthe and the partie by-nethe. These almykanteras ben compowned by 2 and 2, all be it so that on diverse Astrelabies somme almykanteras ben divided by oon, and some by two, and some by thre, after the quantite of the Astrelabie. This forseide Cenyth is ymagined to ben the verrey point over the crowne of thin heved. And also this Cenyth is the verray pool of the orizonte in every regioun. [88]

19. From this cenyth, as it semeth, there comen a maner croked strikes like to the clawes of a loppe, or elles like the werke of a wommans calle, in kervyng overtwart the almykanteras. And these same strikes or divisions ben clepid Azimutes, and thei dividen the orisounte of thin Astrelabie in 24 divisiouns. And these azymutes serven to knowe the costes of the firmament, and to othre conclusiouns, as forto knowe the cenyth of the sonne and of every sterre.

20. Next these azymutes under the cercle of Cancer ben there 12 divisiouns embelif, muche like to the shap of the azimutes, that shewen the spaces of the houres of planetes. [92]

21. *Aranea.*—The riet of thin Astrelabie with thy zodiak, shapen in manere of a net or of a lopwebbe after the olde descripcioun, whiche thou maist turnen up and doun as thiself liketh, contenith certein nombre of sterres fixes, with her longitudes and latitudes determinat, yf so be that the maker have not erred. The names of the sterres ben writen in the margyn of the riet there as thei sitte, of

73. *Weyer,* 'equator'; *euener?*
77. Cp. Sacrobosco : ' et dicitur cingulus primi motus unde sciendum quod primus motus dicitur motus primi mobilis, hoc est nonæ spheræ cœli ultimi,' etc. So ' 8 ' must be error for ' 9.' Likewise 9 seems to be omitted before *spere,* below ; cp. Sacrobosco : ' Dicitur ergo cingulus primi motus quia cingit sive dividit primum mobile, scilicet sphæram nonam,' etc.

whiche sterres the smale point is clepid the centre. And understonde also that alle the sterres sitting with-in the Zodiak of thin Astrelabie ben clepid Sterres of the North, for thei arise by northe the est lyne. And all the remenaunt fixed oute of the zodiak ben clepid Sterres of the South. But I seie not that thei arisen alle by southe the est lyne; witnesse on Aldeberan and Algomeyse. [97] Generaly understonde this rewle, that thilke sterres that ben clepid Sterres of the North arisen rather than the degre of her longitude, and alle the Sterres of the South arisen after the degre of her longitude—this is to seyn sterres fixed in thyn Astrelabie. The mesure of the longitude of sterres is taken in the Lyne Ecliptik of hevene, under whiche lyne whan that the sonne and the mone be lyne-right, or ellis in the superficie of this lyne, than is the eclipse of the sonne or of the mone, as I shal declare and eke the cause why. But sothely the ecliptik lyne of thy zodiak is the utterist bordure of thy zodiak there the degrees be marked. [100]

Thy Zodiak of thin Astrelabie is shapen as a compas whiche that contenith a large brede as after the quantite of thyn Astrelabie, in ensaumple that the zodiak in hevene is ymagyned to ben a superfice contenyng a latitude of 12 degrees, whereas alle the remenaunt of cercles in the hevene ben ymagyned verrey lynes withoute eny latitude. Amiddes this celestial zodiak is ymagined a lyne whiche that is clepid the Ecliptik Lyne, under whiche lyne is evermo the weye of the sonne. Thus ben there 6 degres of the zodiak on that oo syde of the lyne and 6 degrees on that othir. This zodiak is divided in 12 principale divisiouns that departen the 12 signes, and, for the streitnesse of thin Astrolabie, than is every smal divisioun in

a signe departed by two degrees and two, I mene degrees contenyng 60 mynutes. And this forseide hevenysshe zodiak is clepid the Cercle of the Signes, or the Cercle of the Bestes, for 'zodia' in language of Greke sowneth 'bestes' in Latyn tunge. And in the zodiak ben the 12 signes that han names of bestes, or ellis for whan the sonne entrith into eny of tho signes he takith the propirte of suche bestes, or ellis for that the sterres that ben ther fixed ben disposid in signes of bestes or shape like bestes, or elles whan the planetes ben under thilke signes thei causen us by her influence operaciouns and effectes like to the operaciouns of bestes. [108]

And understonde also that whan an hote planete cometh into an hote signe, than encresith his hete; and yf a planete be colde, than amenusith his coldenesse by cause of the hoot sygne. And by thys conclusioun maist thou take ensaumple in alle the signes, be thei moist or drie, or moeble or fixe, reknyng the qualite of the planete as I first seide. And everiche of these 12 signes hath respecte to a certeyn parcel of the body of a man, and hath it in governaunce, as Aries hath thin heved, and Taures thy nekke and thy throte, Gemini thin armeholes and thin armes, and so furthe as shal be shewid more pleyn in the 5 partie of this tretis.

This zodiak, whiche that is parte of the 8 speer, overkervith the equinoxial, and he overkervith him ageyn in evene parties; and that oo half declineth southward; and that othir northward, as pleinly declarith the Tretys of the Speer.

22. *Labellum.*—Than hast thou a Label that is shapen like a reule, save that it is streight and hath no plates on either ende with holes. But with the smale point of the forseide label shalt thou calcule thin

---

97. B₁ inserts *Menkar Algenze cor Leonis* after *Aldeberan* with marginal note saying that they are found on the Merton College Astrolabe.

100. Since only the north half of the Zodiacband is represented on the Astrolabe.

105. Chaucer omits to say that each sign contains 30°.

113. *8 speer*, again a mistake for '9 speer'; cp. 77. The nine spheres are those of the moon, of the six planets, of the fixed stars, and of the zodiac and primum mobile. Chaucer places the zodiac in the 9th in *Tales*, F 1283.

113. *i.e.* John de Sacrobosco's *Tractatus de Sphæra*, ii. 'de zodiaco circulo,' whence Chaucer derives the foregoing description.

equaciouns in the bordure of thin Astralabie, as by thin Almury. [115]

23. *Denticulus.* — Thin Almury is clepid the Denticle of Capricorne or ellis the Calculer. This same almury sitt fixe in the heved of Capricorne, and it serveth of many a necessarie conclusioun in equacions of thinges as shal be shewid.

Here endith the descripcioun of the Astrelabie and here begynne the conclusions of the Astrelabie.

PART II

1. *Conclusio. To fynde the degre in whiche the sonne is day by day, after his cours aboute*

Rekne and knowe whiche is the day of thy monthe, and ley thy rewle up that same day, and than wol the verrey poynt of thy rewle sitten in the bordure upon the degre of thy sonne.

Ensample as thus :—The yeer of oure lord 1391, the 12 day of Marche at midday, I wolde knowe the degre of the sonne. I soughte in the bakhalf of myn Astrelabie and fonde the Cercle of the Daies, the whiche I knowe by the names of the monthes writen under the same cercle. Tho leyde I my reule over this forseide day, and fonde the point of my reule in the bordure upon the firste degre of Aries, a litel with-in the degre. And thus knowe I this conclusioun. [121]

A-nothir day I wolde knowen the degre of my sonne, and this was at midday in the 13 day of December. I fonde the day of the monthe in manere as I seide ; tho leide I my rewle upon this forseide 13 day, and fonde the point of my rewle in the bordure upon the firste degre of Capricorne alite with-in the degre. And than had I of this conclusioun the ful experience.

2. *Conclusio. To knowe the altitude of the sonne or of othre celestial bodies*

Putte the rynge of thyn Astrelabie upon thy right thombe, and turne thi lifte syde ageyn the light of the sonne ; and remewe thy rewle up and doun til that the stremes of the sonne shine thorugh bothe holes of thi rewle. Loke than how many degrees thy rule is areised fro the litel crois upon thin est lyne, and take there the altitude of thi sonne. And in this same wise maist thow knowe by night the altitude of the mone or of brighte sterres. [127]

This chapitre is so generall evere in oon that there nedith no more declaracioun ; but forgete it not.

3. *Conclusio. To knowe every tyme of the day by light of the sonne ; and every tyme of the nyght by the sterres fixe ; and eke to knowe by nyght or by day the degre of eny signe that ascendith on the est orisonte, that is clepid comonly the ascendent, or ellis horoscopum*

Take the altitude of the sonne whan the list, as I have seide, and sette the degre of the sonne, in caas that it be beforne the myddel of the day, amonge thyn almykanteras on the est syde of thin Astrelabie ; and if it be after the myddel of the day, sette the degre of thy sonne upon the west syde. Take this manere of settyng for a general rule, ones for evere. And whan thou hast sette the degre of thy sonne upon as many almykanteras of height as was the altitude of the sonne taken by thy rule, ley over thi label upon the degre of the sonne ; and than wol the point of thi labelle sitte in the bordure upon the verrey tyde of the day. [132]

Ensample as thus :—The yere of oure lord 1391, the 12 day of Marche, I wolde knowe the tyde of the day. I toke the altitude of my sonne, and fonde that it was 25 degrees and 30 of minutes of height in

---

118. *up*, B₁ A₁ A₂ R₂ Br. Edd. *upon ;* B₂ *of.*
119. Probably the date at which Chaucer was writing.
120. *knowe*, A₂ B₂ Br. Edd. *knew.*
121. *knowe*, B₂ R₂ Br. Edd. *knew.*

123. In A₂ Add. 2302 Br. Edd. a spurious conclusio is inserted here.
134. *of minutes*, B₁ B₂ R₂ Br. Edd. omit *of :* perhaps an imitation of *triginta minutorum.*

the bordure on the bak side. Tho turned I myn Astrelabye, and by cause that it was beforne mydday, I turned my riet and sette the degre of the sonne, that is to seyn the first degre of Aries, on the right side of myn Astrelabye upon 25 degrees and 30 mynutes of height among myn almykanteras. Tho leide I my label upon the degre of my sonne, and fonde the point of my label in the bordure upon a capitale lettre that is clepid an X. Tho rekned I alle the capitale lettres fro the lyne of mydnight unto this forseide lettre X, and fonde that it was 9 of the clokke of the day. Tho loked I doun upon the est orizonte, and fonde there the 20 degre of Geminis ascendyng, whiche that I toke for myn ascendent. And in this wise had I the experience for evermo in whiche manere I shulde knowe the tyde of the day and eke myn ascendent. [139]

Tho wolde I wite the same nyght folewyng the houre of the nyght, and wroughte in this wise :—Among an heepe of sterres fixe it liked me for to take the altitude of the faire white sterre that is clepid Alhabor, and fonde hir sittyng on the west side of the lyne of midday, 12 degrees of heighte taken by my rewle on the bak side. Tho sette I the centre of this Alhabor upon 12 degrees amonge myn almykanteras upon the west syde, by cause that she was founde on the west side. Tho leyde I my label over the degre of the sonne, that was discendid under the west orisounte, and rekned all the lettres capitals fro the lyne of midday unto the point of my label in the bordure, and fonde that it was passed 9 of the clokke the space of 10 degrees. Tho lokid I doun upon myn est orisounte, and fonde ther 10 degrees of Scorpius

ascendyng, whom I toke for myn ascendent. And thus lerned I to knowe onys for evere in whiche manere I shuld come to the houre of the nyght, and to myn ascendent, as verrely as may be taken by so smal an instrument. [145]

But natheles this rule in generall wol I warne the for evere :—Ne make the nevere bolde to have take a just ascendent by thin Astrelabie, or elles to have sette justly a clokke, whan eny celestial body by whiche that thou wenyst governe thilke thinges be nigh the southe lyne. For truste wel whan the sonne is nygh the meridional lyne, the degre of the sonne renneth so longe consentrike upon the almykanteras that sothly thou shalt erre fro the just ascendent. The same conclusion sey I by the centre of eny sterre fixe by nyght. And, more over, by experience I wote wel that, in our orisounte, from xi of the clokke unto oon of the clokke in taking of a iust ascendent in a portatif Astrelabie it is harde to knowe —I mene from xi of the clokke before the houre of noon til oon of the clokke next folewyng. [150]

4. A special declaracioun of the Ascendent

The Ascendent sothly, as wel in alle Nativites as in questions and eleccions of tymes, is a thinge which that these Astrologiens gretly observen. Wherfore me semeth convenyent, syth that I speke of the Ascendent, to make of it speciall declaracioun.

The Ascendent, sothly to take it at the largest, is thilke degre that ascendith at eny of these forseide tymes upon the est orisounte. And therfore, yf that eny planete ascende at thatt same tyme in thilke forseide degre, than hath he no latitude fro the ecliptik lyne, but he is than in the degre of the ecliptik whiche that is the degre of his longitude. Men sayn that planete is *In Horoscopo.*

138. *doun upon,* A₁ A₂ B₂ R₂ *on.*
138. *Geminis,* so in MSS.
141. *12 degrees,* R₁ (whose numerals are not trustworthy) Dd₁ (corrected later) A₂ Edd. *18 degrees;* similarly in 142, except that *18* added later in R₁.
143. *9 of the clokke,* Dd₁ reads *8;* R₁ *5;* A₂ B₂ R₂ Edd. 7.
143. *10 degrees,* Dd₁ R₁ read *2;* A₂ B₂ R₂ Edd. *11.*
144. *10 degrees of Scorpius,* Dd₁ *23 degrees of*

Libra; R₁ R₂ Edd. *20 degrees of Libra;* R₂ *12 degrees of Libra;* M₁ *10 degrees of Taurus.*
154. *degre,* M₁ Dd₁ *latitude;* Dd₂ R₁ *same degre;* B₂ R₂ *orisounte;* corr. of R₁ (var.) A₂ *latitude oryzont.*
154. *degre . . . degre,* MSS. except B₁ omit.

But sothly the House of Ascendent, that is to seyn the first hous or the est angle, is a thinge more brode and large. For, after the statutes of Astrologiens, what celestial body that is 5 degrees above thilke degre that ascendith, or with inne that nombre, that is to seyn neer the degree that ascendith, yit rekne they thilke planete in the ascendent. [156] And what planete that is under thilke degre that ascendith the space of 15 degres, yit seyn thei that thilke planete is 'like to him that is the Hous of the Ascendent.' But sothly, if he passe the boundes of these forseide spaces, above or bynethe, thei seyn that the planete is 'fallyng fro the ascendent.' Yit saien these Astrologiens that the ascendent and eke the lorde of the ascendent may be shapen forto be fortunat or infortunat. As thus :—A 'fortunat ascendent' clepen they whan that no wicked planete, as Saturne or Mars or elles the Tayle of the Dragoun, is in the house of the ascendent, ne that no wicked planete have noon aspect of enemyte upon the ascendent. But thei wol caste that thei have a fortunat planete in hir ascendent, and yit in his felicite ; and than say thei that it is wel. [161]

Further over thei seyn that the infortunyng of an ascendent is the contrarie of these forseide thinges. The Lord of the Ascendent sey thei that he is fortunat whan he is in gode place fro the ascendent, as in an angle, or in a succident where as he is in hys dignite and comfortid with frendly aspectes of planetes and wel resceyved ; and eke that he may seen the ascendent ; and that he be not retrograd, ne combust, ne joyned with no shrewe in the same signe; ne that he be not in his discencioun, ne joyned with no planete in his descencioun, ne have upon him noon aspect infortunat ; and than sey thei that he is well. [165]

Natheles these ben observvaunces of judicial matere and rytes of payens in which my spirit hath no feith, ne knowing of her

horoscopum. For they seyn that every signe is departid in thre evene parties by 10 degrees, and thilke porcioun they clepe a face. And al though that a planete have a latitude fro the ecliptik, yit sey somme folke, so that the planete arise in that same signe with eny degre of the forseide face in which his longitude is rekned, that yit is the planete *in horoscopo*, be it in nativyte or in eleccion etc. [168]

5. *Conclusio.* *To knowe the verrey equacioun of the degre of the sonne yf so be that it falle bitwene thyn almykanteras*

For as muche as the almykanteras in thin Astrelabie ben compowned by two and two, where as somme almykanteras in sondry astrelabies be compowned by 1 and 1, or elles by 3 and 3, it is necessarie to thy lernyng to teche the first to knowe and worke with thin owne instrument. Wherfore whan that the degre of thi sonne fallith bytwixe 2 almykanteras, or ellis yf thin almykanteras ben graven with over gret a poynt of a compas (for bothe these thinges may causen errour as wel in knowing of the tide of the day, as of the verrey ascendent), thou must worken in this wise :—[170]

Sette the degre of thy sonne upon the hyer almykanteras of bothe, and wayte wel where as thin almury touchith the bordure and sette there a prikke of ynke. Sett doun agayn the degre of the sunne upon the nether almykanteras of bothe, and sett there another pricke. Remeve than thin almury in the bordure evene amiddes bothe prickes, and this wol lede justly the degre of thi sonne to sitte atwixe bothe almykanteras in his right place. Ley than thy label over the degre of thi sonne, and fynde in the bordure the verrey tyde of the day, or of the night. And as verraily shalt thou fynde upon thin est orisonte thin ascendent. [174]

---

157. *15* should be *25*. Probably Chaucer's mistake. Brae cites Ptolemy, iii. 10, 'viginti quinque.'

168. *eleccion, i.e.* election of times.
169. *by 3 and 3,* B₁ R₂ Dd₁ *by 2 and 2* ; R₁ *by 2 and ;* A₂ Br. *by 2.*
170. *of thi sonne,* B₁ B₂ Br. Th. *of the sonne. thy* and *the* are often thus confused.
173. *betwixe,* R₁ A₂ R₂ Br. *betwene* ; B₁ *atwixe.*

6. *To knowe the sprynge of the dawenyng and the ende of the evenyng the whiche ben called the two crepuscules*

Sette the nadir of thy sonne upon 18 degrees of height amonge thyn almykanteras on the west side; and ley thy label on the degre of thy sonne, and than shal the point of thy label shewen the sprynge of the day. Also set the nader of thy sonne upon 18 degrees of height among thin almykanteras on the est side, and ley over thy label upon the degre of the sonne, and with the point of thy label fynde in the bordure the ende of the evenyng, that is verrey nyght.

The nader of the sonne is thilke degre that is opposyt to the degre of the sonne in the 7 signe. As thus :—every degre of Aries by ordir is nadir to every degre of Libra by ordre, and Taurus to Scorpioun, Gemini to Sagittarie, Cancer to Capricorn, Leo to Aquarie, Virgo to Pisces. And yif eny degre in thy zodiak be derke, his nadir shal declare hym. [179]

7. *Conclusio. To knowe the Arch of the Day, that some folke callen the Day Artificial, fro sonne arisyng tyl it go to reste*

Sette the degre of thi sonne upon thin est orisonte, and ley thy label on the degre of the sonne and at the point of thy label in the bordure sette a pricke. Turne than thy riet aboute tyl the degre of the sonne sitte upon the west orisonte, and ley thy label upon the same degre of the sonne, and at the poynt of thy label sette there a nother pricke. Rekne than the quantite of tyme in the bordure bitwixe bothe prickes, and take there thyn arch of the day. The remenaunt of the bordure under the orisonte is the arch of the nyght. Thus maist thou rekne bothe arches or every porcioun of whether that the liketh. And by this manere of worching maist thou se how longe that eny sterre fixe dwelleth

180. Rubric. *go to reste*, A₂ Br. *goth doun.* The former is Chaucer's usual expression; cp. *Tales*, A 30, A 1779.

above the erthe, fro tyme that he risith til he go to rest. But the day natural, that is to seyn 24 houres, is the revolucioun of the equinoxial with as muche partie of the zodiak as the sonne of his propre moeving passith in the mene while. [185]

8. *Conclusio. To turne the houres inequales in houres equales*

Knowe the nombre of the degrees in the houres inequales, and depart hem by 15, and take there thin houres equales.

9. *Conclusio. To knowe the quantite of the day vulgar, that is to seyn fro sprynge of the day unto verrey nyght*

Knowe the quantite of thy crepuscules, as I have taught in the chapitre before, and adde hem to the arch of thy day artificial, and take there the space of alle the hool day vulgar unto verrey night. The same manere maist thou worche to knowe the quantite of the vulgar nyght. [188]

10. *Conclusio. To knowe the quantite of houres inequales by day*

Understonde wel that these houres inequales ben clepid houres of planetes. And understonde wel that som tyme ben thei lenger by day than by night, and som tyme the contrarie. But understonde wel that evermo generaly the houre inequal of the day with the houre inequal of the night contenen 30 degrees of the bordure, whiche bordure is evermo answeryng to the degrees of the equinoxial. Wherfore departe the arch of the day artificial in 12, and take there the quantite of the houre inequal by day. And if thou abate the quantite of the houre inequal by day out of 30, than shal the remenaunt that levith parforme the houre inequal by night. [193]

184. *fro tyme*, A₂ B₂ R₂ Br. *fro the tyme.*
188. *Knowe the*, R₁ A₂ *Knowe thou the.*
190. *And understonde*, B₁ *This understonde*; B₂ omits *And.*
191. *contenen*, A₂ R₂ Br. *contenyth.*
193. *30*, R₁ A₂ B₂ R₂ Br. Th. *360 degrees.*

11. Conclusio.   To knowe the quantite of houres equales

The quantite of houres equales, that is to seyn the houres of the clokke, ben departid by 15 degrees al redy in the bordure of thin Astrelaby as wel by night as by day, generaly for evere.   What nedith more declaracioun?

Wherfore whan the list to knowe how many houres of the clokke ben passed, or eny part of eny of these houres that ben passed, or ellis how many houres or parties of houres ben to come fro suche a tyme to suche a tyme by day or by night, knowe the degre of thy sonne, and ley thy label on it.   Turne thy ryet aboute joyntly with thy label, and with the poynt of it rekne in the bordure fro the sonne arise unto that same place there thou desirist, by day as by nyght.   This conclusioun wol I declare in the last chapitre of the 4 Partie of this tretys so openly that there shal lakke no worde that nedith to the declaracioun. [198]

12. Conclusio.   Special Declaracioun of the houres of planetes

Understonde wel that evermo, fro the arisyng of the sonne til it go to rest, the nadir of the sonne shal shewe the houre of the planete, and fro that tyme forward al the night til the sonne arise; than shal the verrey degre of the sonne shewe the houre of the planete.

Ensample as thus :—The xiij day of Marche fyl upon a Saturday, peraventure, and atte risyng of the sonne I fonde the secunde degre of Aries sittyng upon myn est orisonte, al be it that it was but litel. Than fonde I the 2 degre of Libra, nadir of my sonne, discending on my west orisonte, upon whiche west orisonte every day generaly atte sonne arist entrith the houre of every planete, after whiche planete the

day berith his name, and endith in the next strike of the planete under the forseide west orisonte.   And evere as the sonne clymbith upper and upper, so goth his nadir downer and downer, teching by suche strikes the houres of planetes by ordir as they sitten in the hevene.   The firste houre inequal of every Saturday is to Saturne, and the seconde to Iupiter, the thirde to Mars, the fourthe to the sonne, the fifte to Venus, the sixte to Mercurius, the seventhe to the mone.   And then ageyn the 8 is to Saturne, the 9 to Jupiter, the 10 to Mars, the 11 to the sonne, the 12 to Venus.   And now is my sonne gon to reste as for that Saturday. Than shewith the verrey degre of the sonne the houre of Mercurie entring under my west orisonte at eve ; and next him succedith the mone, and so furthe by ordir, planete after planete in houre after houre, all the nyght longe til the sonne arise.   Now risith the sonne that Sonday by the morwe, and the nadir of the sonne upon the west orisonte shewith me the entring of the houre of the forseide sonne.   And in this manere succedith planete under planete fro Saturne unto the mone, and fro the mone up ageyn to Saturne, houre after houre generaly. And thus knowe I this conclusyoun. [209]

13. Conclusio.   To knowe the altitude of the sonne in myddes of the day that is clepid the Altitude Meridian

Sette the degre of the sonne upon the lyne meridional, and rekne how many degrees of almykanteras ben bitwyxe thin est orisonte and the degre of thy sonne, and take there thin altitude meridian, this to seyn the highest of the sonne as for that day.   So maist thou knowe in the same lyne the heighst cours that eny sterre fixe

198. Cp. ' Quarta pars ' in Chaucer's Introd.
199. The ' Houres of Planetes ' is a matter of astrology, depending on the fact that each planet belonged to a particular day of the week.
200. The 13th of March fell on a Saturday in 1389 and in 1395.
200. *atte risyng*, M₁ Dd₁ B₂ R₂ Br. *atte the arisyng.*

205. *the 8*, B₁ B₂ *8 houre.*
205. And so with any other day, the series beginning with the planet whose name accord with the day ; e.g. Monday, to the moon ; Wednesday, to Mercury ; Friday, to Venus, etc.
207. *til the sonne*, B₂ R₂ *to the sonne.*
208. *that Sonday*, R₁ Br. *the Sonday* ; A₂ a: *Sonday* ; R₂ *on Sonday.*
210. Conclusions 13, 14, 15, 16, 17, 18 follow conclusion 21 in MSS. of group γ; cp. Introd.
210. *this to seyn*, A₂ R₂ Br. Th. *that ys to seyn.*

clymbeth by night. This is to seyn that whan eny sterre fixe is passid the lyne meridional, than begynneth it to descende; and so doth the sonne. [211]

14. *Conclusio. To knowe the degre of the sonne by thy ryet for a maner curiosite*

Seke besily with thy rule the highest of the sonne in mydde of the day. Turne than thin Astrelabie, and with a pricke of ynke marke the nombre of that same altitude in the lyne meridional; turne than thy ryet aboute tyl thou fynde a degre of thy zodiak according with the pricke, this is to seyn, sitting on the pricke. And in soth thou shalt finde but 2 degrees in al the zodiak of that condicioun; and yit thilke 2 degrees ben in diverse signes. Than maist thou lightly, by the sesoun of the yere, knowe the signe in whiche that is the sonne. [215]

15. *Conclusio. To knowe whiche day is like to whiche day as of lengthe*

Loke whiche degrees ben ylike fer fro the hevedes of Cancer and Capricorne, and loke when the sonne is in eny of thilke degrees; than ben the dayes ylike of lengthe. This is to seyn that as longe is that day in that monthe, as was suche a day in suche a monthe; there varieth but litel.

Also, yf thou take 2 dayes naturales in the yere ylike fer fro either pointes of the equinoxial in the opposyt parties, than as longe is the day artificiall of that oon day as is the night of that othir, and the contrarie. [218]

16. *Conclusio. This chapitre is a maner Declaracioun to Conclusiouns that folewen*

Understonde wel that thy zodiak is departed in two halfe circles, as fro the heved of Capricorne unto the heved of Cancer, and ageynward fro the heved of Cancer unto the heved of Capricorne. The heved of Capricorne is the lowest point whereas the sonne goth in wynter, and the heved of Cancer is

216. A₂ B₃ Edd. have slightly different rubric.

the heighist point in whiche the sonne goth in somer. And therfore understonde wel that eny two degrees that ben ylike fer fro eny of these two hevedes, truste wel that thilke two degrees ben of ilike declinacioun, be it southward or northward, and the daies of hem ben ilike of lengthe and the nyghtes also, and the shadewes ilyke, and the altitudes ylike atte midday for evere. [222]

17. *Conclusio. To knowe the verrey degre of eny maner sterre, straunge or un-straunge, after his longitude; though he be indetermynate in thin Astra-labye, sothly to the trouthe thus he shal be knowe*

Take the altitude of this sterre whan he is on the est syde of the lyne meridional, as neigh as thou mayst gesse; and take an ascendent anon right by som manere sterre fixe whiche that thou knowist; and forgete not the altitude of the firste sterre ne thyn ascendent. And whan that this is done, aspye diligently whan this same firste sterre passith eny thyng the southwestward; and cacche him anon right in the same nombre of altitude on the west syde of this lyne meridional, as he was kaught on the est syde; and take a newe ascendent anon ryght by som manere sterre fixe whiche that thou knowist, and forgete not this secunde ascendent. And whan that this is done, rekne than how many degrees ben bitwixe the first ascendent and the secunde ascendent; and rekne wel the myddel degre bitwene bothe ascendentes, and sette thilke myddel degre upon thyn est orizonte; and wayte than what degre that sitte upon the lyne meridional, and take there the verrey degre of the ecliptik in whiche the sterre stondith for the tyme. For in the ecliptik is the longitude of a celestial body rekned, evene fro the heved of Aries unto the ende of Pisces; and his latitude is rekned after

223. Rubric. *longitude*, A₂ Br. Th. *latitude*.
225. *passith eny thyng*, etc., *i.e.* passes west of the meridional line.
225. *cacche*, M₁ Dd₁ *hath*; A₂ Br. *take*; B₂ *sett*.
228. *wayte than*, A₂ R₂ Br. Th. *than loke*.

the quantite of his declynacioun north or south toward the polys of this world. [229]

As thus :—yif it be of the sonne or of eny fixe sterre, rekne hys latitude or his declinacioun fro the equinoxial cercle ; and if it be of a planete, rekne than the quantite of his latitude fro the ecliptik lyne, al be it so that fro the equinoxial may the declinacioun or the latitude of eny body celestial be rekned after the site north or south and after the quantite of his declinatioun. And right so may the latitude or the declinacioun of eny body celestial, save oonly of the sonne, after hys site north or south and after the quantite of his declinacioun, be rekned fro the ecliptik lyne, fro which lyne alle planetes som tyme declinen north or south save oonly the forseide sonne. [233]

18. *Conclusio. To knowe the degrees of longitudes of fixe sterres after that they be determynat in thin Astrelabye, yf so be that thei be trewey sette*

Sette the centre of the sterre upon the lyne meridional, and take kepe of thy zodiak and loke what degre of eny signe that sitte upon the same lyne meridional at that same tyme, and take there the degre in which the sterre stondith ; and with that same degre cometh that same sterre unto that same lyne fro the orisonte. [235]

19. *Conclusio. To knowe wit whiche degre of the zodiak eny sterre fixe in thin Astrelabie arisith upon the est orisonte al though his dwellyng be in a nother signe*

Sette the centre of the sterre upon the est orisonte, and loke what degre of eny signe that sitt upon the same orisonte at that same tyme. And understonde wel that

with that same degre arisith that same sterre. [236]

And thys merveylous arisyng with a straunge degre in a nother signe is by cause that the latitude of the sterre fixe is either north or south fro the equinoxial. But sothly the latitudes of planetes be commonly rekned fro the ecliptyk by cause that noon of hem declyneth but fewe degrees oute fro the brede of the zodiak. And take gode kepe of this chapitre of arisyng of celestial bodies ; for truste wel that neyther mone ne sterre, as in our embelif orisonte, arisith with that same degre of his longitude save in oo cas, and that is whan they have no latitude fro the ecliptik lyne. But natheles som tyme is everiche of these planetes under the same lyne. [240]

20. *Conclusio. To knowe the declinacioun of eny degre in the zodiak fro the equinoxial cercle*

Sette the degre of eny signe upon the lyne meridional, and rekne hys altitude in the almykanteras fro the est orisonte up to the same degre sette in the forseide lyne, and sette there a prik ; turne up than thy riet. and sette the heved of Aries or Libra in the same meridional lyne, and sette there a nother prik. And whan that this is done, considre the altitudes of hem bothe ; for sothely the difference of thilke altitudes is the declinacioun of thilke degre fro the equinoxial. And yf it so be that thilke degre be northward fro the equinoxial, than is his declinacyoun north ; yif it be southward, than is it south.

21. *Conclusio. To knowe fro what latitude in eny regioun the almykantera of eny table ben compowned*

Rekne how many degrees of almykanteras in the meridional lyne ben fro the cercle equinoxial unto the cenyth, or elles from the pool artyk unto the north orisonte : and for so gret a latitude, or for so smal a latitude, is the table compowned. [243]

231. *the site,* R₂ Br. Th. *the syght* ; B₁ *site* ; A₂ B₂ *that it sytteth.*
232. *site,* A₂ *syttyng* ; R₂ *syght.*
234. *centre, i.e.* the point of the tongue representing it in the Astrolabe.
235. *that same degre,* R₁ A₂ R₂ Br. Th. *the same degre* ; and frequently *the same* for *that same* in late MSS.
236. Rubric. *his dwellyng,* R₂ *his orisonte* ; Br. Th. *the orisonte.*
245. Rubric. *eny,* A₂ R₂ Th. *wey* ; Br. *thy.*

22. *Conclusio.   To know in special the latitude of oure countre, I mene after the latitude of Oxenford, and the height of oure pool*

Understonde wel that as fer is the heved of Aries or Libra in the equinoxial fro oure orisonte as is the cenyth fro the pool artik ; and as high is the pool artik fro the orisonte as the equinoxial is fer fro the cenyth. I prove it thus by the latitude of Oxenford : understonde wel that the height of oure pool artik fro oure north orisonte is 51 degrees and 50 mynutes ; than is the cenyth fro oure pool artik 38 degrees and 10 mynutes ; than is the equinoxial from oure cenyth 51 degrees and 50 mynutes ; than is oure south orisonte from oure equinoxial 38 degrees and 10 mynutes.   Understonde wel this rekenyng.   Also forgete not that the cenyth is 90 degrees of height from oure orisonte, and oure equinoxiall is 90 degres from oure pool artik.   Also this shorte rule is soth, that the latitude of eny place in a regioun is the distaunce fro the cenyth unto the equinoxial. [251]

23. *Conclusio.   To prove evidently the latitude of eny place in a regioun by the prove of the height of the pool artik in that same place*

In some wynters nyght whan the firmament is clere and thikke sterred, wayte a tyme til that eny sterre fixe sitte lyne right perpendiculer over the pool artik, and clepe that sterre A ; and wayte another sterre that sitte lyne right under A, and under the pool, and clepe that sterre F.   And understonde wel that F is not considrid but oonly to declare that A sitte evene over the pool.   Take than anoon right the altitude of A from the orisonte, and forgete it not ; lete A and F goo fare wel tyl ageynst the dawenyng a gret while, and come than ageyn, and abide til that A is evene under the pool, and under F ; for sothly than wol

F sitte over the pool, and A wol sitte under the pool.   Take than efte sonys the altitude of A from the orisonte, and note as wel his secunde altitude as hys first altitude. And whan that this is doon, rekene how many degrees that the first altitude of A excedith his secunde altitude, and take half thilke porcioun that is excedid and adde it to his secunde altitude, and take there the elevacioun of thy pool, and eke the latitude of thy regioun ; for these two ben of oo nombre, this is to seyn as many degres as thy pool is elevate, so muche is the latitude of the regioun. [258]

Ensample as thus :—peraventure the altitude of A in the evenyng is 56 degrees of height ; than wol his secunde altitude or the dawenyng be 48 degres, that is 8 degrees lasse than 56 that was his first altitude att even.   Take than the half of 8 and adde it to 48 that was is secunde altitude, and than hast thou 52.   Now hast thou the height of thy pool and the latitude of the regioun. But understonde wel that to prove this conclusioun and many a nother faire conclusioun, thou must have a plomet hangyng on a lyne, heygher than thin heved, on a perche ; and thilke lyne must hange evene perpendiculer bytwixe the pool and thin eye ; and than shalt thou seen yf A sitte evene over the pool, and over F atte evene ; and also yf F sitte evene over the pool and over A or day. [262]

24. *Conclusio.   Another conclusioun to prove the height of the pool artik fro the orisonte*

Take eny sterre fixe that never discendith under the orisonte in thilke regioun, and considre his heighist altitude and his lowist altitude fro the orisonte, and make a nombre of bothe these altitudes ; take than and abate half that nombre, and take

246. Rubric. *oure countre*, M₁ *the countre;* R₂ Br. Th. *oure centur;* MS. in St. John's Coll. Camb. (Skeat) *nostri centri.*

251. *place*, M₁ A₂ B₂ R₁ R₂ Edd. *planete.*

259. In this example MSS. of group β have a different set of observations, viz. 62 for the evening altitude, and 21 for that taken in the morning, giving as a result a latitude about that of Rome.

260. *52 degrees*, roughly the latitude of Oxford ; cp. 270.

263. *make a nombre, i.e.* add them together.

there the elevacioun of the pool artik in that same regioun.

25. *Conclusio. Another conclusioun to prove the latitude of the regioun*

Understonde wel that the latitude of eny place in a regioun is verrely the space bytwexe the cenyth of hem that dwellen there and the equinoxial cercle north or south, takyng the mesure in the meridional lyne, as shewith in the almykanteras of thin Astrelabye. And thilke space is as much as the pool artike is high in that same place fro the orisonte. And than is the depressioun of the pool antartik, that is to seyn than is the pool antartike, bynethe the orisonte the same quantite of space neither more ne lasse. [266]

Than ifthou desire to knowe this latitude of the regioun, take the altitude of the sonne in the myddel of the day, whan the sonne is in the hevedes of Aries or of Libra ; for than moeveth the sonne in the lyne equinoxial ; and abate the nombre of that same sonnes altitude oute of 90 degrees, and than is the remenaunt of the nombre that leveth the latitude of that regioun. As thus :—I suppose that the sonne is thilke day at noon 38 degrees of height ; abate than 38 oute of 90 ; so leveth there 52 ; than is 52 degrees the latitude. I say not this but for ensample ; for wel I wot the latitude of Oxenford is certeyn minutes lasse as thow might preve. [270]

Now yf so be that the semeth to longe atarieng to abide til that the sonne be in the hevedes of Aries or of Libra, than wayte whan the sonne is in eny othir degre of the zodiak and considre the degre of his declinacioun fro the equinoxial lyne ; and if it so be that the sonnes declinacioun be northward fro the equinoxial, abate than fro the sonnes altitude at none the nombre

of his declinacioun, and than hastow the height of the hevedes of Aries and Libra. [272]

As thus :—My sonne is peraventur in the first degre of Leoun, 58 degrees and 10 minutes of height at none, and his declinacioun is almost 20 degrees northward fro the equinoxial ; abate than thilke 20 degrees of declinacioun oute of the altitude at none ; than leveth there 38 degrees and odde minutes. Lo there the heved of Aries or Libra and thin equinoxial in that regioun. Also if so be that the sonnes declinacioun be southward fro the equinoxial, adde than thilke declinacioun to the altitude of the sonne at noon, and take there the hevedes of Aries and Libra and thin equinoxial ; abate than the height of the equinoxial oute of 90 degrees ; than leveth there the distance of the pool of that regioun fro the equinoxial. Or elles, if the list, take the highest altitude fro the equinoxial of eny sterre fixe that thou knowist, and take the netherest elongacioun (lengthing) fro the same equinoxial lyne, and worke in the manere forseid. [277]

26. *Conclusio. Declaracioun of the Ascensioun of signes*

The excellence of the Spere Solide, amonges othir noble conclusiouns, shewith manyfest the diverse ascenciouns of signes in diverse places, as wel in the right cercle as in the embelif cercle. These auctours writen that thilke signe is clepid of right ascensioun with whiche more parte of the cercle equinoxial and lasse part of the zodiak ascendith ; and thilke signe ascendith embelif with whiche lasse part of the equinoxiall and more part of the zodiak ascendith. Ferther-over, they seyn that

269. B$_1$ A$_2$ B$_2$ add *and 25 minutes* after *degrees*, and read *so leveth there 51 degrees and 50 minutes* (B$_2$ *15*, A$_2$ *51*), that is (A$_2$ B$_2$ omit) *the latitude*, an evident attempt to make the problem yield the latitude of Oxford exactly.
270. *as thow might preve*, A$_1$ A$_2$ R$_1$ R$_2$ Dd$_2$ Br. Th. omit ; M$_1$ B$_1$ omit *as ;* M$_1$ adds *the ;* B$_1$ adds *the same*.

273. There are two sets of readings for this problem, viz. that of the text found in B$_1$ (except that it reads *17* for *10*) M$_1$ Dd$_1$, and *10 degrees of Leo almost 56 of height at noon . . . declinacioun . . . 18 . . . ; abate . . . 18 than leveth ;* found in MSS. of group β (A$_2$ and B$_2$ showing contamination with B$_1$).
278. *Spere Solide, i.e.* the chapter 'De ascencionibus et descensionibus signorum rectis et obliquis' of John de Sacro Bosco's *De Sphæra* which Chaucer draws on for this conclusion.

in thilke cuntrey where as the senith of hem that dwellen there is in the equinoxial lyne, and her orisonte passyng by the two poles of this world, thilke folke han this right cercle and the right orisonte; and evermore the arch of the day and the arch of the night is there ilike longe ; and the sonne twies every yere passing thorugh the cenith of her heed, and two someres and two wynters in a yere han these forseide peple. And the almykanteras in her Astrelabyes ben streight as a lyne, so as it shewith in the figure. [284]

The utilite to knowe the ascensions of signes in the right cercle is this :—Truste wel that by mediacioun of thilke ascensions these astrologiens, by her tables and her instrumentes, knowen verreily the ascensioun of every degre and minute in all the zodiak in the embelif cercle as shal be shewed. And *nota* that this forseide right orisonte, that is clepid *Orison Rectum*, dividith the equinoxial in to right angles ; and the embelif orisonte, where as the pool is enhaunced up on the orisonte, overkervith the equinoxial in embilif angles as shewith in the figure. [286]

27. *Conclusio. This is the conclusioun to knowe the ascensions of signes in the right cercle, that is circulus directus*

Sette the heved of what signe the lyst to knowe his ascendyng in the right cercle upon the lyne meridional, and wayte where thyn almury touchith the bordure, and sette there a prikke ; turne than thy riet westward til that the ende of the forseide signe sitte upon the meridional lyne and efte sonys wayte where thin almury touchith the bordure, and sette there a nother pricke. Rekene than the nombre of degres in the bordure bitwixe both prikkes, and take the ascensioun of the signe in the right

286. *overkervith*, A₂ B₂ (var.) *overkeverеth*; Edd. *overcomith*.
287. *his ascendyng*, A₁ A₂ B₂ R₂ Br. *the ascendyng*.
287. *and sette ther a prikke*. Following this to end of conclusion B₁ has a different version, no traces of which are found in other MSS.

cercle. And thus maist thou werke with every porcioun of thy zodiak. [289]

28. *Conclusio. To knowe the ascensions of signes in the embelif cercle in every regioun, I mene, in circulo obliquo*

Sette the heved of the signe whiche as the list to knowe his ascensioun upon the est orisonte, and wayte where thin almury touchith the bordure, and there sette a prikke. Turne than thy riet upward til that the ende of the same signe sitte upon the est orisonte, and wayte efte sonys where as thin almury touchith the bordure, and sette there a nother prikke. Rekene than the nombre of degrees in the bordur bitwyxe bothe prikkes and take there the ascensioun of the signe in the embelif cercle. And understonde wel that alle the signes in thy zodiak, fro the heved of Aries unto the ende of Virgo, ben clepid Signes of the North fro the equinoxial. And these signes arisen bitwyxe the verrey est and the verrey northe in oure orisonte generaly for evere. [294] And alle the signes fro the heved of Libra unto the ende of Pisces ben clepid Signes of the South fro the equinoxial ; and these signes arisen ever- more bitwexe the verrey est and the verrey south in oure orisonte. Also every signe bitwixe the heved of Capricorne unto the ende of Geminis arisith on oure orisonte in lasse than 2 houres equales. And these same signes fro the heved of Capricorne unto the ende of Geminis ben cleped Tortuose Signes, or Croked Signes, for thei arise embelyf on oure orisonte. And these croked signes ben obedient to the signes that ben of right ascensioun. The signes of right ascencioun ben fro the heved of Cancer unto the [end] of Sagittarie; and these signes arisen more upright, and thei ben called eke Sovereyn Signes and everiche of hem arisith in more space than in 2 houres. Of whiche signes Gemini obeieth to Cancer, and Taurus to

299. *unto the end of Sagittarie.* B₂ is the only MSS. that has reading in text. Others *heued* for *end.*

Leo, Aries to Virgo, Pisces to Libra, Aquarius to Scorpioun, and Capricorne to Sagittarie. And thus evermore 2 signes that ben ilike fer fro the heved of Capricorne obeyen everiche of hem til othir. [301]

29. *Conclusio. To knowe iustly the 4 quarters of the worlde, as Est, West, North, and South*

Take the altitude of thy sonne whan the list, and note wel the quarter of the worlde in which the sonne is for the tyme by the azymutes. Turne than thin Astrelabie, and sette the degre of the sonne in the almykanteras of his altitude on thilke syde that the sonne stant, as is the manere in takyng of houres, and ley thy label on the degre of the sonne ; and rekene how many degrees of the bordure ben bitwexe the lyne meridional and the point of thy label, and note wel that nombre ; turne than ageyn thin Astrelabie, and sette the point of thy gret rule there thou takist thin altitudes upon as many degrees in his bordure fro his meridional as was the point of thy label fro the lyne meridional on the wombe side. Take than thin Astrelabie with bothe hondes sadly and slyly, and lat the sonne shyne thorugh bothe holes of thy rule, and slyly in thilke shynyng lat thin Astrelabie kouche adoun evene upon a smothe grounde, and than wol the verrey lyne meridional of thin Astrelabie lye evene south, and the est lyne wol lye est, and the west lyne west, and the northe lyne north, so that thou wirke softly and avysely in the kouching. And thus hast thou the 4 quarters of the firmament. [308]

30. *Conclusio. To knowe the altitude of planetes fro the weye of the sonne whethir so they be north or south fro the forseide weye*

Loke whan that a planete is in the lyne meridional, yf that hir altitude be of the same height that is the degre of the sonne for that day, and than is the planete in the verrey wey of the sonne and hath no latitude. And if the altitude of the planete be heigher than the degre of the sonne, than is the planete north fro the wey of the sonne suche a quantite of latitude as shewith by thin almykanteras. And if the altitude of the planete be lasse than the degre of the sonne, than is the planete south fro the wey of the sonne suche a quantite of latitude as shewith by thin almykanteras. This is to seyn fro the wey where as the sonne went thilke day, but not fro the wey of the sonne in every place of the zodiak. [312]

31. *Conclusio. To knowe the Cenyth of the arising of the sonne, this is to seyn the partie of the orisonte in whiche that the sonne arisith*

Thou must first considere that the sonne arisith not alwey verrey est, but somtyme by northe the est and somtyme by south the est. Sothly the sonne arisith nevere moo verrey est in oure orisonte, but he be in the heved of Aries or Libra. Now is thin orisonte departed in 24 parties by thin azimutes in significacioun of 24 parties of the world ; al be it so that shipmen rekene thilke parties in 32. Than is there no more but wayte in whiche azimutz that thy sonne entrith at his arisyng, and take there the cenith of the arisyng of the sonne. [316]

The manere of the divisioun of thin Astrelabie is this, I mene as in this cas :— First it is divided in 4 plages principalis with the lyne that goth from est to west : and than with a nother lyne that goth fro south to north ; than is it divided in smale parties of azymutz, as est, and est by south.

309. Chaucer in 312 explains *wey of the sonne* to mean the sun's apparent path on any given day
312. After *zodiak* group β adds *for on the morowe wyl the sonne be on another degre*.
313. Rubric. *Cenyth*, azimuth.
314. *nevere moo*, A₁ B₂ *evermore*.
315. As in the mariner's compass.

301. *til other*, B₁ A₂ B₂ R₂ Edd. *to other*.

where as is the first azymute above the est lyne ; and so furthe fro partie to partie til that thou come ageyn un to the est lyne.   Thus maist thou understonde also the cenyth of eny sterre in whiche partie he riseth. [319]

32. *Conclusio.   To knowe in whiche partie of the firmament is the conjunccyoun*

Considere the tyme of the conjunccyoun by the kalender, as thus :—Loke hou many houres thilke conjunccioun is fro the midday of the day precedent, as shewith by the canoun of thy kalender.   Rekene than thilke nombre of houres in the bordure of thin Astrelabie, as thou art wont to do in knowyng of the houres of the day or of the nyght, and ley thy label over the degre of the sonne, and than wol the point of thy label sitte upon the houre of the conjunccioun.   Loke than in whiche azymute the degre of thy sonne sittith, and in that partie of the firmament is the conjunccioun. [322]

33. *Conclusio.   To knowe the cenyth of the altitude of the sonne*

This is no more to seyn but eny tyme of the day take the altitude of the sonne, and by the azymut in whiche he stondith maist thou seen in whiche partie of the firmament he is.   And the same wise maist thou seen by night of eny sterre, whether the sterre sitte est or west, or north or southe, or eny partie bitwene, after the name of the azimute in whiche the sterre stondith. [324]

34. *Conclusio.   To knowe sothly the degre of the longitude of the mone, or of eny planete that hath no latitude for the tyme fro the ecliptik lyne*

Take the altitude of the mone, and rekne thy altitude up amonge thyn almykanteras on whiche syde that the mone

318. *above the est lyne.*   Because the points of the compass were reversed on the Astrolabe.
323. *eny tyme,* M₂ R₂ *on tyme.*
325. *altitude of the mone,* A₂ B₂ *latitude of the mone.*

stondith, and sette there a prikke.   Take than anon right upon the mones syde the altitude of any sterre fixe whiche that thou knowist, and sett his centre upon his altitude amonge thyn almykanteras there the sterre is founde.   Wayte than whiche degre of the zodiak touchith the prykke of the altitude of the mone, and take there the degre in whiche the mone stondith.   This conclusioun is verrey sothe, yf the sterres in thin Astrelabie stonden after the trouthe.   Comoun tretes of the Astrelabie ne maken non excepcioun whether the mone have latitude or noon, ne on wheyther syde of the mone the altitude of the sterre fixe be taken.

And *nota* that yf the mone shewe himself by light of day, than maist thou wyrke this same conclusioun by the sonne, as wel as by the fixe sterre. [330]

35. *Conclusio.   This is the wyrkynge of the conclusioun to knowe yf that eny planete be directe or retrograde*

Take the altitude of any sterre that is clepid a planete, and note it wel ; and take eke anon the altitude of any sterre fixe that thou knowist, and note it wel also.   Come than ageyn the thridde or the ferthe nyght next folewing, for than shalt thou perceyve wel the moeving of a planete, whether so he moeve forward or bakward.   Awayte wel than whan that thy sterre fixe is in the same altitude that she was whan thou toke hir firste altitude. And take than eft sones the altitude of the forseide planete and note it wel ; for truste wel yf so be that the planete be on the right syde of the meridional lyne, so that his secunde altitude be lasse than hys first altitude was, than is the planete directe ; and yf he be on the west syde in that condicioun, than is he retrograde.   And yf so be that this planete be upon the est side whan his altitude is taken, so that his secunde altitude be more than his first altitude, than is he retrograde.   And if he be on the west syde, than is he direct. But the contrarie of these parties is of the cours of the mone ; for certis the mone moeveth the contrarie from othre planetes as in hir epicicle, but in noon othir manere. [337]

36. *Conclusio. The conclusioun of equacioune of houses after the Astrelabie*

Sette the begynnyng of the degre that ascendith upon the ende of the 8 houre inequal, than wol the begynnyng of the 2 hous sitte upon the lyne of mydnight. Remove than the degre that ascendith, and sette him on the ende of the 10 houre inequal, and than wol the begynnyng of the 3 hous sitte up on the mydnight lyne. Bringe up ageyn the same degre that ascended first, and sette him upon the est orisonte, and than wol the begynnyng of the 4 hous sitte upon the lyne of mydnight. Take than the nader of the degre that first ascendid, and sette him in the ende of the 2 houre inequal ; and than wol the begynnyng of the 5 hous sitte upon the lyne of mydnight. Sette than the nader of the ascendent in the ende of the 4 houre inequal, and than wol the begynnyng of the 6 hous sitte on the mydnight lyne. The begynnyng of the 7 hous is nader of the ascendent, and the begynnyng of the 8 hous is nader of the 2 hous, and the begynnyng of the 9 hous is nader of the 3, and the begynnyng of the 10 hous is nader of the 4, and the begynnyng of the 11 hous is nader of the 5, and the begynnyng of the 12 hous is nader of the 6. [343]

37. *Conclusio. Another maner of equacioune of houses by the Astrelabie*

Take thin ascendent, and than hast thou thy 4 angles ; for wel thou wost that

the opposite of thin ascendent, that is to seyn, the begynnyng of the 7 hous, sitt upon the west orisonte, and the begynnyng of the 10 hous sitt upon the lyne meridional, and his opposyt upon the lyne of mydnight. Than ley thy label over the degre that ascendith, and rekne fro the point of thy label alle the degrees in the bordure tyl thou come to the meridional lyne ; and departe alle thilke degrees in 3 evene parties, and take there the evene equacions of 3 houses ; for ley thy label over everiche of these 3 parties, and than maist thou se by [ther] thy label lith in the zodiak, the begynnyng of everiche of these same houses fro the ascendent ; that is to seyn the begynnyng of the 12 hous next above thin ascendent, the begynnyng of the 11 hous, and than the 10 upon the meridional lyne, as I first seide. The same wise wirke thou fro the ascendent doun to the lyne of mydnyght, and thus hast thou othre 3 houses ; that is to seyn, the begynnyng of the 2, and the 3, and the 4 hous. Than is the nader of these 3 houses the begynnyng of the 3 houses that folewen. [350]

38. *Conclusio. To fynde the lyne meridional to dwelle fixe in eny certeyn place*

Take a rounde plate of metal, for werpyng the brodder the better ; and make there upon a just compas a lite with in the bordure. And ley this rounde plate upon an evene grounde, or on an evene ston, or on an evene stok fixe in the grounde ; and ley it evene by a level. And in the centre of the compas styke an evene pyn, or a wyre, upright, the smaller the better ; sette thy pyn by a plom-rule evene upright, and lete thy pyn be no lenger than a quarter of the dyametre of thy compas, fro the centre a-middes. And wayte bisely about 10 or 11 of the clokke, whan the sonne shineth, whan the shadewe of the pyn entrith any thynge with in the cercle

337. *certis*, R₁ *sothly* ; M₁ Dd₁ *he settes* ; A₂ omits.
338. After conclusion 36 the MSS. vary. The text represents MSS. B₁ M₁ Dd₁ R₁. R₂ ends with conclusion 35, B₂ with 36. Of the other MSS. some insert a number of spurious conclusions between 35 and 36; others place them after conclusion 40. The evidence that these are spurious is found in the fact that (*a*) they occur only in late MSS., and (*b*) are in a style quite different from Chaucer's.

348. *same*, M₂ *12* ; R₁ *3*.
351. *a just compas*, an exact circle.
353. *the centre a-middes*, R₁ *the pyn*.

of thy compas an heer mele ; and marke there a pricke with inke. Abide than stille waityng on the sonne til after 1 of the clokke, til that the shadwe of the wyre, or of the pyn, passe any thing oute of the cercle of the compas, be it nevere so lyte, and sette there another pricke of ynke. Take than a compas, and mesure evene the myddel bitwexe bothe prickes, and sette there a prikke. Take me than a rule and drawe a strike evene a-lyne, fro the pyn unto the middel prikke ; and take there thi lyne meridional for evermore as in that same place. And yif thou drawe a crosse lyne over-thwart the compas justly over the lyne meridional, than hast thou est and west and south, and par consequens, the opposite of the southe lyne is the northe. [358]

39. *Conclusio. The Description of the meridional lyne, of longitudes and latitudes of Citees and Townes, as wel as of Climates*

Thys lyne meridional is but a manere descripcioun, or lyne ymagined, that passith upon the poles of this world and by the cenyth of oure heved. And it is cleped the lyne meridional, for in what place that any man ys at any tyme of the yere, whan that the sonne, by mevynge of the firmament, cometh to his verrey meridian place, than is it verrey mydday, that we clepen oure none, as to thilke man. And therefore is it cleped the lyne of mydday.

And *nota* that evermore of any 2 cytes or 2 townes, of which that oo town approchith neer the est than doth that othir town, truste wel that thilke townes han diverse meridians. [362]

Nota also that the arch of the equinoxial that is contened or bownded bitwixe the 2 meridians is clepid the longitude of the

toun. And yf so be that two townes have ilike meridian or oon meridian, than is the distaunce of hem both ilike fer fro the est, and the contrarie ; and in this manere thei change not her meridian. But sothly thei chaungen her almykanteras, for the enhaunsyng of the pool and the distance of the sonne. [365]

The longitude of a climat is a lyne ymagined fro est to west ilike distant fro the equinoxiall. And the latitude of a climat may be cleped the space of the erthe fro the begynnyng of the first clymat unto the verrey ende of the same clymat evene direct ageyns the pool artyke. Thus sayn somme auctours ; and somme of hem sayn that yf men clepe the latitude of a cuntrey the arch meridian that is contened or intercept bitwixi the cenyth and the equinoxial, than say they that the distance fro the equinoxial unto the ende of a climat evene ageynst the pool artik is the latitude of a clymat forsoothe. [368]

40. *Conclusio. To knowe with whiche degre of the zodiak that any planete ascendith on the orisonte, whether so that his latitude be north or south*

Knowe by thin almenak the degre of the ecliptik of any signe in whiche that the planete is rckned forto be, and that is clepid the degre of his longitude. And knowe also the degre of his latitude fro the ecliptik north or southe. And by these ensamples folewynge in special maist thou wirke forsothe in every signe of the zodiak :— [371]

The degree of the longitude peraventure of Venus or of a nother planete was 6 of Capricorne, and the latitude of hir was northward 4 degrees fro the ecliptik lyne. Than toke I a subtile compas, and clepid that oo point of my compas A, and that other point F. Than toke I the point of

---

359. From this point B₁ is copied from a MS. like M₁ Dd₁. The readings of all three are very poor ; so that for the remaining conclusions the text is that of B₁ collated with R₁.
359. Conclusio 39 is taken largely from Sacrobosco.

366. *evene direct*, etc., 'versus polum articum.'
371. Dd₁ has different set of figures (in R₁ the figures have not been filled in), giving longitude 6 and latitude 2. In M₁ not all figures filled in.
372. *6 of Capricorne*, B₁ *1 degree of Capricorne* ; R₁ *of Capricorne* (in R₁ the figures have not been filled in) ; M₁ *planete*.

A and sette it in the ecliptik lyne in my zodiak in the degre of the longitude of Venus, that is to seyn, in the 1 degre of Capricorne ; and than sette I the point of F upward in the same signe by cause that latitude was north upon the latitude of Venus, that is to seyn, in the 4 degre fro the heved of Capricorne ; and thus have 4 degrees bitwixe my two prickes. Than leide I down softly my compas, and sette the degre of the longitude upon the orisonte ; tho toke I and waxed my label in manere of a peire tables to receyve distinctly the prickes of my compas. [376] Tho toke I thys forseide label, and leyde it fixe over the degre of my longitude ; tho toke I up my compas and sette the point of A in the waxe on my label, as evene as I koude gesse, over the ecliptik lyne in the ende of the longitude, and sette the point of F endelonge in my label upon the space of the latitude, inward and over the zodiak, that is to seyn northward fro the ecliptik. Than leide I doun my compas, and loked wel in the wey upon the prickes of A and of F ; tho turned I my ryet til that the pricke of F satt upon the orisonte ; than sawe I wel that the body of Venus in hir latitude of degrees septemtrionals ascendid in the ende of the 8 degre fro the heved of Capricorne.

And *nota* that in this manere maist thou wirke with any latitude septemtrional in alle signes. But sothly the latitude meridional of a planete in Capricorne ne may not be take by cause of the litel space bitwixe the ecliptyk and the bordure of the Astrelabie ; but sothely in all othre signes it may. [382]

375. *4 degrees*, Dd₁ *2 degrees*.
381. *8 degre fro*, Dd₁ *6 degre in*

2 pars hujus conclusio

Also the degre peraventure of Iupiter, or of a nother planete, was in the first degre of Piscis in longitude, and his latitude was 2 degrees meridional ; tho toke I the point of A and sette it in the first degre of Piscis on the ecliptike ; and than sette I the point of F dounward in the same signe by cause that the latitude was south 2 degrees, that is to seyn, fro the heved of Piscis ; and thus have 2 degrees bitwexe bothe prikkes. Than sette I the degre of the longitude upon the orisonte ; tho toke I my label, and leide it fixe upon the degre of the longitude ; tho sette I the point of A on my label evene over the ecliptik lyne in the ende of the degre of the longitude, and sette the point of F endlonge in my label the space of 2 degres of the latitude outward fro the zodiak (this is to seyn southward fro the ecliptik toward the bordure), and turned my riet til that the pricke of F saat upon the orisonte. Than say I wel that the body of Iupiter in his latitude of 2 degres meridional ascendid with 8 degres of Piscis *in horoscopo*. And in this manere maist thou wirke with any latitude meridional, as I first seide, save in Capricorne. And yf thou wilt pleye this crafte with the arisyng of the mone, loke thou rekne wel hir cours houre by houre, for she ne dwellith not in a degre of his longitude but litel while, as thow wel knowist. But natheles yf thow rekne hir verrey moevyng by thy tables houre after houre— [391]

(*Left unfinished.*)

383. *2 degrees*, Dd₁ *3 degrees*. Similarly :
384, 386, 388 (M₁ agrees with B₁).
388. *8 degres*, Dd₁ *14 degrees* ; M₁ *6 degre*.

THE ROMAUNT OF THE ROSE

MANY men sayn that in sweveninges
Ther nys but fables and lesynges ;
But men may some swevenes sene
Whiche hardély that false ne bene,
But afterwarde ben apparaunt.
This maye I drawé to warraunt
An authour that hight Macrobes,
That halte nat dremés false ne lees,
But undothe us the avysioun
That whilom metté kyng Cipioun.   10
And who-so saith, or weneth it be
A jape, or ellés nycete,
To wene that dremés after falle,
Lette who so lyste a fole me calle.
For this trowe I, and say for me,
That dremés signifiauncé be
Of good and harme to many wightes,
That dremen in her slepe a nyghtes
Ful many thyngés covertly,
That fallen after al openly.   20
   Within my twenty yere of age,
Whan that Love taketh his cariage
Of yongé folke, I wenté soone
To bedde, as I was wont to done,
And faste I slepte ; and in slepyng
Me metté suche a swevenyng
That lykéd me wonder wele.
But in that sweven is never a dele
That it nys afterwarde befalle,
Ryght as this dreme wol tel us alle.   30
   Nowe this dreme wol I ryme a-right
To make your hertés gaye and lyght,
For Love it prayeth and also
Commaundeth me that it be so.
And if there any aské me,
Whether that it be he or she,

Howe [wil I] this booke whiche is here
Shal hatté, that I rede you here ;
It is the Romance of the Rose,
In whiche al the Arte of Love I close.   40
   The mater fayre is of to make :
God graunt me in gree that she it take
For whom that it begonnen is !
And that is she that hath y-wis
So mochel pris, and therto she
So worthy is biloved to be
That she wel ought of pris and ryght
Be clepéd Rose of every wight.
   That it was May me thoughté tho—
It is .V. yere or more ago—   50
That it was May thus dreméd me,
In tyme of love and jolite,
That al thing gynneth waxen gay.
For ther is neither busk nor hay
In May that it nyl shrouded bene,
And it with newé levés wrene.
These wodés eek recoveren grene
That drie in wynter ben to sene.
And the erthé wexith proude withalle
For swoté dewes that on it falle,   60
And [al] the pore estat forgette
In which that wynter had it sette.
And than bycometh the ground so proude,
That it wole have a newé shroude,
And makith so queynt his robe and faire
That it hath hewes an hundred payre,
Of gras and flouris, ynde and pers,
And many hewés ful dyvers.
That is the robe I mene, y-wis,   69
Through whiche the ground to preisen is.
   The byrdés that han lefte her song
While thei suffridé cold so strong,
In wedres gryl and derk to sight,

1. For vv. 1-44 Thynne's edition is sole authority.
4. that false, ? to falseen ben, 'mensongier.'
7. Macrobes, cp. Dethe of Blaunche, l. 284, note.
12. Th. els.
22. cariage (Th. corage), i.e. toll, 'paage.'

37. wil I, supplied from Fr. 'ge voil.'
61. al, supplied by Skeat ; but perhaps povre.
66. hath, MSS. had.
71. MS., which is imperfect in vv. 69-72, . . . en.
72. Th. han suffred.

Ben in May, for the sonné bright,
So glade that they shewe in syngyng,
That in her hertis is sich lykyng,
That they mote syngen and be light.
Than doth the nyghtyngale hir myght
To maké noyse and syngen blythe ;
Thán is blisful many sithe   80
The chelaundre and [the] papyngay.
Than yongé folk entenden ay
Forto ben gay and amorous.
The tyme is than so saverous,
Hard is the hert that loveth nought
In May, whan al this mirth is wrought ;
Whan he may on these braunches here
The smalé briddés syngen clere
Her blesful sweté song pitous.
And in this sesoun delytous,   90
Whan love affraieth allé thing,
Me thoughte a-nyght, in my sleping
Right in my bed, ful redily
That it was by the morowe erly,
And up I roos, and gan me clothe.
Anoon I wisshe myn hondis bothe.
A sylvre nedle forth y droughe
Out of an aguler queynt ynoughe,
And gan this nedlé threde anon ;
For out of toun me list to gon   100
The song of briddés forto here,
That in thise buskés syngen clere.
And in the swete seson that lefe is,
With a threde bastyng my slevis,
Alone I wente in my plaiyng,
The smalé foulés song harknyng,
That peynéd hem ful many peyre
To synge on bowés blosméd feyre.
Iolyf and gay, ful of gladnesse,
Toward a ryver gan I me dresse,   110
That I herd renné fasté by,
For fairer plaiyng non saugh I
Than playen me by that ryvere.
For from an hill that stood ther nere,
Cam doun the streme ful stif and bold ;
Cleer was the water and as cold

As any welle is, soth to seyne.
And somdele lasse it was than Seyne,
But it was strayghter, wel away ;
And never saugh I, er that day,   170
The watir that so wel lykéd me,
And wondir glad was I to se
That lusty place and that ryvere.
And with that watir that ran so clere
My face I wysshe.   Tho saugh I well
The botmé pavéd everydell
With gravel ful of stonés shene.
The medewe softé, swote, and grene.
Béet right on the watir syde.
Ful clere was than the morowtyde,   13:
And ful attempre, out of drede.
Tho gan I walké thorough the mede,
Dóunward ay in my pleiyng
The ryver sydé costeiyng.
And whan I had a whilé goon,
I saugh a gardyn right anoon,
Ful long and brood, and euerydell
Enclôséd was, and wallèd well
With highé wallés enbatailled,
Portraied without and wel entailled   14:
With many riché portraitures.
And bothe the ymages and peyntures
Gan I biholdé bysyly ;
And I wole telle you redyly
Of thilk ymagés the semblaunce,
As fer as I have remembraunce.
   Amyddé saugh I HATÉ stonde,
That for hir wrathé, yre, and onde
Semede to ben a meveresse,
An angry wight, a chideresse ;   15:
And ful of gyle and felle corage
By semblaunt was that ilk ymage.
And she was no thyng wel arraied,
But lyk a wode womman afraied.
Y-frounced foule was hir visage
And grennyng for dispitous rage ;
Hir nosé snorted up for tene.
Ful hidous was she forto sene,
Ful foule and rusty was she this ;

76. Th. *herte.*
81. *chelaundre,* a kind of lark.
84. *saverous,* Fr. ' saverous,' G *faverous.*
91. *affraieth,* arouses ; cp. *B. of D.* 296.
103. As in Thynne ; MS. *And in* [erasure]
swete seson tha[t swete over erasure] *is.* The
Fr. is ' En icele saison novele,' which makes one
suspect that *And in that sesoun that newe is* was
the original form of the line.

119. *strayghter,* ' espandue.'
142. G *the peyntures.*
146. G *in remembraunce.*
149. *meveresse,* MSS. *mynoresse* ; Fr. ' c:: ⁻
resse,' fem. of *mouveur,* ' a troublesome f. ⁻
(Cotgr.).
159. A similar repetition of subject i: '
880.

Hir heed y-writhen was, y-wis,   160
Ful grymly with a greet towayle.
  An ymage of another entayle
A lyft half was hir fastè by ;
Hir name above hir heed saugh I,
And she was callèd FELONYE.
Another ymagè, that VILANYE
Y-clepid was, saugh I and fonde
Upon the wal on hir right honde.
Vilany was lyk somdel
That other ymage, and, trustith wel,   170
She semede a wikked creàture.
By countenaunce in portrayture
She semèd be ful dispitous,
And eek ful proude and outragious.
Wel coude he peynte, I undirtake,
That sich ymagè coudè make.
Ful foule and cherlysshe semèd she,
And eek vylayneus forto be,
And litel coude of norriture
To worshipe any creàture.   180
  And next was peynted COVEITISE,
That eggith folk in many gise
To take and yeve right nought ageyne,
And gret tresouris up to leyne.
And that is she that for usure
Leneth to many a creàture,
The lassè for the more wynnyng,
To coveteise is her brennyng.
And that is she for penyes fele,
That techith forto robbe and stele   190
These thevès and these smale harlotes ;
And that is routh, for by her throtes
Ful many oon hangith at the laste.
She makith folk compasse and caste
To taken other folkis thyng
Through robberie or myscounting.
And that is she that makith trechoures
And she makith falsè pleadoures,
That, with hir termès and hir domes,
Doon maydens, children, and eek gromes
Her heritagè to forgo.   201
Ful croked were hir hondis two,
For coveitise is evere wode
To gripen other folkis gode ;

Coveityse for hir wynnyng
Ful leef hath other mennès thing.
  Another ymage set saugh I
Next Coveitisè fastè by,
And she was clepid AVARICE.
Ful foule in peyntyng was that vice,   210
Ful fade and caytif was she eek,
And also grene as ony leek.
So yvel hewed was hir colour
Hir semed to have lyved in langour ;
She was lyk thyng for hungrè deed,
That ladde hir lyf oonly by breed
Kneden with eisel strong and egre ;
And therto she was lene and megre.
And she was clad ful porèly
Al in an old torn courtèpy,   220
As she were al with doggis torne ;
And both bihynde and eke biforne
Clóuted was she beggarly.
A mantyl henge hir fastè by,
Upon a perchè weike and small ;
A burnet cote henge therwith-all,
Furrèd with no menyvere
But with a furrè rough of here,
Of lambè skynnès hevy and blake ;
It was ful old I undirtake,   230
For Avarice to clothe hir well
Ne hastith hir neveradell.
For certeynly it were hir loth
To weren ofte that ilkè cloth ;
And if it were forwerèd she
Wolde have ful gret necessite
Of clothyng, er she bought hir newe,
Al were it bad of woll and hewe.
This Avarice hilde in hir hande
A purs that henge [doun] by a bande,   240
And that she hidde and bonde so
    strong,
Men must abydè wondir long,
Out of that purs er ther come ought ;
For that ne cometh not in hir thought.
It was not, certein, hir entent
That fro that purs a peny went.
  And by that ymage nygh ynough

---

166. *Another ymage*, etc. ; cp. 162, 170, 207.
179. MSS. *norture*.
185. G omits *she*.
188. *coveteise*, Th. *covetous*.
196. *myscounting*, 'mesconter.'   Kaluza's
emendation for *myscoueiting* of MSS.

208. MSS. *faste by*, also in 224, and frequently.
211. MSS. *sad*, but Fr. 'megre'; cp. 311, where
it translates *megre*.
212. *also*, just as.
220. Th. omits *old*; Fr. 'vies et desrumpue.'
240. Perhaps *hengde*.

Was peynted ENVYE, that never lough,
Nor never wel in hir herte ferde,
But if she outher saugh or herde   250
Som gret myschaunce, or gret disese.
Nó thyng may so moch hir plese
As myschef and mysaventure ;
Or whan she seeth discomfiture
Upon ony worthy man falle,
That likith hir wel with alle.
She is ful glade in hir corage,
If she se any grete lynage
Be brought to nought in shamful wise.
And if a man in honour rise,   260
Or by his witte or by his prowesse,
Of that hath she gret hevynesse.
For trustith wel she goth nygh wode,
Whan any chaunge happith gode.
Envie is of such crueltee
That feith ne trouth[é] holdith she
To freend ne felawe, bad or good.
Ne she hath kynne noon of hir blood,
That she nys ful her enemye ;
She nolde, I dar seyn hardelye,   270
Hir owne fadir ferde well.
And sore abieth she everydell
Hir malice and hir male talent,
For she is in so gret turment
And hath such [wo] whan folk doth good,
That nygh she meltith for pure wood ;
Hir herté kervyth and so brekith,
That god the puple wel a-wrekith.
Envie, i-wis, shal nevere lette
Som blame upon the folk to sette ;   280
I trowe that if Envie, i-wis,
Knewe the besté man that is
On this side, or biyonde the see,
Yit somwhat lakken hym wolde she ;
And if he were so hende and wis,
That she ne myght al abate his pris,
Yit wolde she blame his worthynesse,
Or by hir wordis make it lesse.
I saugh Envie in that peyntyng
Hádde a wondirful lokyng,   290
For she ne lokidé but awrie,

Or overthart all baggyngly.
And she hadde a foule usage,
She myght loke in no visage
Of man or womman forth-right pleyn,
But shette hir one eye for disdeyn ;
So for Envié brenned she,
Whan she myght any man y-se
That faire or worthi were, or wise,
Or elles stode in folkis pryse.   300
    SORWÉ was peynted next Envie
Upon that wall of masonrye,
But wel was seyn in hir colour
That she hadde lyvéd in langour ;
Hir seméde to havé the jaunyce.
Nought half so pale was Avarice,
Nor no thyng lyk [as] of lenesse ;
For sorowé, thought, and gret distresse,
That she hadde suffred day and nyght,
Made hir ful yolwe and no thyng bright.
Ful fadé, pale, and megre also.   311
Was never wight yit half so wo
As that hir seméde forto be,
Nor so fulfilled of ire as she.
I trowe that no wight myght hir please,
Nor do that thyng that myght hir ease ;
Nor she ne wolde hir sorowé slake
Nor comfort noon unto hir take,
So depé was hir wo bigonnen
And eek hir hert in angre ronnen.   320
A sorowful thyng wel seméd she,
Nor she hadde no thyng slowé be
Forto forcracchen al hir face,
And forto rent in many place
Hir clothis, and forto tere hir swire,
As she that was fulfilled of ire.
And al to-torn lay eek hir here
Aboute hir shuldris here and there,
As she that hadde it al to-rent
For angre, and for maltalent.   330
And eek I telle you certeynly
How that she wepe ful tendirly.
In worlde nys wyght so harde of herte
That had [he] sene her sorowes smerte,
That nolde have had of her pyte,

248. Kaluza reads *peynte* to avoid slurring *envye*, but *peynted* is the form in ll. 301, 349, 450, 807, 935.
256. MSS. *Than*, but Fr. ' Ice.' If anything is to be added to the verse, it should be *to se* after *wel ;* Fr. ' a veoir.'
266. *ne*, MSS. omit.
275. *wo*, supplied from Fr.

292. *baggyngly*, ' borgnoiant ' (Cotgr. ' tc loure '); cp. *B. of D.* v. 623.
296. *one eye*, MS. *eien ;* Fr. ' un œl.'
298. *y-se*, MSS. *se ;* cp. 1401.
305. Either omit *to*, or read *to have* as two syllables.
325. *swire*, throat ; nothing in Fr. corresponding.

So wo begone a thyng was she.
She al to-dassht her-selfe for woo,
And smote togyder her hondès two.
To sorowe was she ful ententyfe
That woful rechélesse caytyfe ; 340
Her roughté lytel of playing
Or of clypping, or [of] kissyng ;
For who so sorouful is in herte,
Him lusté not to play ne sterte,
Ne for to dauncen, ne to synge,
Ne may his herte in temper bringe,
To maké joye on even or morowe,
For joy is contrarie unto sorowe.
    ELDE was paynted after this,
That shorter was a foote, i-wys, 350
Than she was wonte in her yonghede.
Unneth her selfe she mighté fede ;
So feble and eke so olde was she
That faded was al her beaute.
Ful salowe was waxen her colour ;
Her heed for hore was whyte as flour,
I-wys great qualme ne were it none,
Ne synne, al though her lyfe were gone ;
Al woxen was her body unwelde,
And drie and dwynéd al for elde. 360
A foule forwelkéd thyng was she,
That whylom rounde and softe had be ;
Her eerès shoken faste withall,
As from her heed they woldé fall ;
Her facé frouncéd and forpyned,
And bothe her hondès lorne, fordwyned.
So olde she was that she ne went
A foote, but it were by potent.
The tyme that passeth nyght and daye,
And restélesse travayleth aye, 370
And steleth from us so privély,
That to us semeth so sykerly
That it in one poynt dwelleth ever ;
And certes it ne resteth never,
But gothe so faste, and passeth aye,
That there nys man that thynké may
What tymé that nowe present is ;
Ásketh at these clerkés this.
For [or] men thynke it redily
Thre tymés ben y-passed by. 380
The tymé that may not sojourne,

But goth and may never retourne,
As watir that doun renneth ay,
But never drope retourné may.
Ther may no thing as tyme endure,
Metall nor erthely creàture ;
For allé thing it frette and shall.
The tyme eke that chaungith all,
And all doth waxe and fostred be,
And allé thing distroieth he ; 390
The tyme that eldith our auncessours,
And eldith kynges and emperours,
And that us alle shal overcomen
Er that deth us shal have nomen ;
The tymé, that hath al in welde
To elden folk, had maad hir elde
So ynly, that to my witing,
She myght[é] helpe hir silf no thing,
But turned ageyn unto childhede.
She had no thing hir silf to lede, 400
Ne witte ne pithé in hir holde
More than a child of two yeer olde.
But nathéles I trowe that she
Was faire sumtyme, and fresh to se,
Whan she was in hir rightful age ;
But she was past al that passage,
And was a doted thing bicomen.
A furréd cope on had she nomen,
Wel had she clad hir silf and warme,
For colde myght ellès don hir harme. 410
These oldé folk have alwey colde,
Her kynde is sich whan they ben
    olde.
    Another thing was don there write,
That seméde lyk an ipocrite,
And it was clepid POOPE HOLY.
That ilk is she that pryvely
Ne spareth never a wikked dede
Whan men of hir taken noon hede.
And maketh hir outward precious
With palé visage and pitous, 420
And semeth a simple creáture.
But ther nys no mysaventure
That she ne thenkith in hir corage.
Ful lyk to hir was that ymage,
That makid was lyk hir semblaunce.
She was ful symple of countenaunce
And she was clothéd and eke shod
As she were, for the love of god,

348. Perhaps read *contraire ;* cp. 991.
368. *by potent,* with a crutch.
380. *i.e.* three moments are gone while one is thinking about it.

401. *in hir holde,* in her possession.
413. *don there write,* ' empres (apres ?) escrite.

663

Yolden to relygioun,
Sich seméde hir devocioun.   430
A sauter helde she faste in honde,
And bisily she gan to fonde
To maké many a feynt praiere
To god, and to his seyntis dere.
Ne she was gay, ne fresh, ne jolyf,
But semede to be ful ententyf
To gode werkis and to faire,
And therto she had on an haire ;
Ne certis she was fatt no thing,
But semed wery for fasting ;   440
Of colour pale and deed was she.
From hir the gate ay werned be
Of Paradys, that blisful place.
For sich folk maketh lene her face,
As Crist seith in his Evangile,
To geté prys in toun a while ;
And for a litel glorie veigne
They lesen god and ek his reigne.

    And alderlast of everychon
Was peynted POVERT al aloon,   450
That not a peny hadde in holde,
All though she hir clothis solde,
And though she shulde an hongéd be ;
For nakid as a worme was she,
And if the wedir stormy were,
For colde she shulde have dyéd there.
She nadde on but a streit olde sak,
And many a cloute on it ther stak ;
This was hir cote and hir mantell,
No more was there, never a dell,   460
To clothe hir with, I undirtake ;
Grete leyser haddé she to quake.
And she was putt, that I of talke,
Fer fro these other, up in an halke ;
There lurkéd and there couréd she.
For pover thing, where so it be,
Is shamefast and dispiséd ay ;
Acurséd may wel be that day
That povere man conceyvéd is,
For god wote al to selde, i-wys,   470
Is ony povere man wel fedde

Or wel araiéd or [wel] cledde,
Or welbilovéd in sich wise
In honour that he may arise.
Alle these thingis well avised,
As I have you er this devysed,
With gold and asure over all
Depeynted were upon the wall.
Square was the wall and high sumdell.
Enclosed and barred well,   480
In stede of hegge, was that gardyne ;
Come nevere shepherdé therynne.
Into that gardyn wel y-wrought
Who so that me coude have brought
By laddre, or ellés by degre,
It woldé wel have likéd me,
For sich solace, sich joie and play
I trowe that nevere man ne say,
As was in that place delytous.
The gardeyn was not daungerous   490
To herberwe briddés many oon,
So riche a yerde was nevere noon
Of briddés songe and braunches grene ;
Therynne were briddés mo I wene
Than ben in all the rewme of Fraunce.
Ful blisful was the accordaunce
Of swete and pitous songe thei made ;
For all this world it owghté glade.
And I my-silf so mery ferde,
Whan I her blisful songés herde,   500
That for an hundreth pounde nolde I,
If that the passage opunly
Háddé be unto me free,
That I nolde entren forto se
Thassemble—god kepe it fro care—
Of briddis whiche therynné ware.
That songen thorugh her mery throtes
Dauncis of love and mery notes.
Whan I thus herdé foulés synge,
I felle fast in a weymentyng,   510
By which art, or by what engyne,
I myght come into that gardyne.
But way I couthé fyndé noon
Into that gardyne for to goon.
Ne nought wist I if that ther were

437. *to faire*, ' bonnes ovres faire' ; ' faire'
carelessly misread ?
438. *haire*, O.F. ' haire,' a sleeveless shirt of
hair worn as a penance.
442. *gate*, perhaps plural.
444. *face*, ' vis' ; MSS. *grace*.
451. *holde*, G *wolde* ; but cp. 395.
454. *nakid as a worme*, ' nue comme vers ' ; cp.
Tales, E 880.

472. MSS. omit *wel*.
480. The verse has apparently but three accents.
492. MSS. *yerre*.
501. MSS. *wolde* ; i.e. I wouldn't take a
hundred pounds not to enter.
505. Prof. Skeat changes *god kepe it fro car.*
to *god it kepe and were* on account of the un-
Chaucerian rhyme.

Eýther hole or placé where,
Bý which I myght have entre.
Ne ther was noon to teché me,
For I was al aloone i-wys,
For-wo and angwishis of this.   520
Til atté last bithought I me,
That by no weye ne myght it be
That ther nas laddre, or wey to passe,
Or hole, into so faire a place.
Tho gan I go a full grete pas,
Envyronyng evene in compas
The closing of the squaré wall,
Tyl that I fonde a wiket small,
So shett that I ne myght in gon,
And other entre was ther noon.   530
Uppon this dore I gan to smyte
That was [so] fetys and so lite,
For other weye coude I not seke.
Ful long I shof, and knokkide eke,
And stood ful long and oft herknyng,
If that I herde ony wight comyng,
Til that dore of thilk entre
A mayden curteys openyde me.
Hir heer was as yelowe of hewe
As ony basyn scouréd newe,   540
Hir flesh [as] tendre as is a chike,
With benté browis smothe and slyke ;
And by mesure largé were
The openyng of hir yèn clere ;
Hir nose of good proporcioun,
Hir yèn grey as is a faucoun ;
With sweté breth and wel savoured,
Hir facé white and wel coloured,
With litel mouth and rounde to see ;
A clové chynne eke haddé she,   550
Hir nekké was of good fasoun,
In lengthe and gretnesse by resoun,
Withoute bleyné, scabbe, or royne ;
Fro Iersalem unto Burgoyne
Ther nys a fairer nekke, i-wys,
To fele how smothe and softe it is.
Hir throte also white of hewe
As snowe on braunché snowéd newe.
Of body ful wel wrought was she,
Men neded not in no cuntre   560

A fairer body forto seke.
And of fyn orfrays hadde she eke
A chapélet so semly oon
Ne werède never mayde upon.
And faire above that chapélet
A rosé gerland had she sett.
She hadde [in honde] a gay mirrour,
And with a riché gold tresour
Hir heed was tresséd, queyntély.
Hir slevés sewid fetously,   570
And forto kepe hir hondis faire
Of glovés white she had a paire.
And she hadde on a cote of grene
Of cloth of Gaunt, withouten wene.
Wel semyde by hir apparayle
She was not wont to gret travayle ;
For whan she kempte was fetisly,
And wel arayed and richély,
Thanne had she don al hir journe.
For merye and wel bigoon was she,   580
She ladde a lusty lyf in May ;
She hadde no thought by nyght ne day
Of no thyng, but it were oonly
To graythe hir wel and uncouthly.
Whan that this dore hadde opened me
This may[dé] semely forto see,
I thankéd hir as I best myght,
And axide hir how that she hight,
And what she was I axide eke.
And she to me was nought unmeke,   590
Ne of hir answer daungerous,
But faire answeride, and seidé thus :—
' Lo, sir, my name is YDELNESSE ;
So clepé men me, more and lesse ;
Ful myghty and ful riche am I,
And that of oon thyng namély,
For I entendé to no thyng,
But to my joye, and my pleyyng,
And forto kembe and tressé me.
Aqueynted am I and pryve   600
With Myrthé, lord of this gardyne,
That fro the lande Alexandryne
Madé the trees hidre be fette

516. Perhaps read *there* for *where*.
520. *For-wo*, very weary ; but perhaps mistake
or *ful wo*.
535. *and oft* (Th. *al*, G *and of*) *herknyng*, ' par
maintes fois escoutai.'
557. *also*, as. Perhaps read *was also*.

564. *upon*, adverb ; cp. 1085, *Tales*, D 568.
567. MSS. omit *in honde* ; ' en sa main.'
574. *Gaunt*, Ghent.
579. *journe*, day's work.
593. Cp. *Tales*, G 1-7, A 1940.
602. MSS. *of Alex.*
603. *be fette*, perhaps omit *be* ; cp. 607, 609,
where the infinitives are passive, Fr. ' fist . . .
faire,' ' fist portraire.'

That in this gardyne ben y-sette.
And whan the trees were woxen on hight,
This wall, that stant heere in thi sight,
Dide Myrthe enclosen al aboute.
And these ymages al withoute
He dide hem bothe entaile and peynte,
That neithir ben jolyf ne queynte,   610
But they ben ful of sorowe and woo,
As thou hast seen a while agoo.
And ofté tyme hym to solace
Sir Myrthé cometh into this place,
And eke with hym cometh his meynee,
That lyven in lust and jolite.
And now is Myrthe therynne to here
The briddis, how they syngen clere,
The mavys and the nyghtyngale,
And other joly briddis smale.   620
And thus he walketh to solace
Hym and his folk, for swetter place
To pleyen ynne he may not fynde,
Al though he sought oon in-tyl Ynde.
The alther-fairest folk to see
That in this world may founde be
Hath Mirthé with hym in his route,
That folowen hym always aboute.'
Whan Ydelnesse had tolde al this,
And I hadde herkned wel y-wys,   630
Thanne seide I to dame Ydelnesse :
' Now also wisly god me blesse,
Sith Myrthe that is so faire and fre
Is in this yerde with his meyne,
Fro thilk assemble, if I may,
Shal no man werné me to-day,
That I this nyght ne mote it see.
For wel wene I there with hym be
A faire and joly companye,
Fulfillèd of all curtesie.'   640
And forth, withouté wordis mo,
In at the wiket went I tho,
That Ydelnesse hadde opened me,
Into that gardyne faire to see.
And whan I was inne i-wys,
Myn herté was ful glad of this.
For wel wende I ful sikerly
Have ben in Paradys erthly ;
So faire it was that, trusteth wel,
It semede a place espirituel.   650
For certys, as at my devys,
Ther is no place in Paradys

645. Perhaps insert *ther* before *inne.*

So good inne forto dwelle or be,
As in that gardyne, thoughté me.
For there was many a bridde syngyng
Thorough-out the yerde al thringyng.
In many places were nyghtyngales,
Alpés, fynchés, and wodéwales,
That in her sweté song deliten.
In thilké places as they habiten,   660
There myght[e] men see many flokkes
Of turtles and [of] laverokkes.
Chalaundres felé sawe I there,
That wery, nygh forsongen were.
And thrustles, terins, and mavys,
That songen forto wynne hem prys,
And eke to sormounte in hir songe
That otheré briddés hem amonge.
By noté madé faire servyse
These briddés that I you devise ;   670
They songe her songe as faire and wele
As angels don espirituel.
And, trusteth wel, than I hem herde,
Ful lustily and wel I ferde,
For never yitt sich melodye
Was herd of man that myghté dye.
Sich sweté song was hem amonge,
That me thought it no briddis songe,
But it was wondir lyk to be
Song of mermaydens of the see,   680
That, for her syngyng is so clere,
Though we mermaydens clepe hem here
In English as is oure usaunce,
Men clepé hem sereyns in Fraunce.
Ententif weren forto synge
These briddis, that nought unkunnyng
Were of her craft and apprentys,
But of song sotil and wys.
And certis, whan I herde her songe,
And sawe the grené place amonge,   690
In herte I wexe so wondir gay,
That I was never erst er that day
So jolyf, nor so wel bigoo,
Ne merye in herte, as I was thoo.
And than wist I and sawe ful well,
That Ydelnesse me servèd well,
That me putte in sich jolite.

658. *Alpes*, bullfinches. *wodewales*, orioles (
668. *That othere* (MSS. *other*) can be used w—
plural nouns ; cp. 991.
673. *than* (Th. *whan*, G. *that*), whan.
680. Chaucer calls them *mermaids* in *B*—
32, where the French version has *seraines*.

Hir freend wel ought I forto be
Sith she the dore of that gardyne
Hadde openèd, and me leten inne.   700
From hennès forth how that I wroughte,
I shal you tellen as me thoughte.
First wherof Myrthè servèd there,
And eke what folk there with hym
    were,
Withoutè fable I wole discryve ;
And of that gardyne eke as blyve
I wole you tellen aftir this
The fairè fasoun all y-wys,
That wel y-wrought was for the nones.
I may not telle you all at ones,   710
But as I may and can, I shall
By ordre tellen you it all.
Ful faire servise, and eke ful swete,
These briddis maden, as they sete ;
Layès of love ful wel sownyng,
They songen in their jargonyng ;
Summe high and summe eke lowè songe
Upon the braunches grene y-spronge.
The swetnesse of her melodye
Made al myn herte in reverye.   720
And whan that I hadde herde, I trowe,
These briddis syngyng on a rowe,
Than myght I not withholdè me
That I ne wente inne forto see
Sir Myrthè ; for my desiryng
Was hym to seen, over allè thyng ;
His countenaunce and his manere,
That sightè was to me ful dere.
Tho wente I forth on my right honde
Doun by a lytel path I fonde,   730
Of mentès full and fenell grene.
And fastè by, withoutè wene,
Sir Myrthe I fonde, and right anoon
Unto sir Myrthè gan I goon,
There as he was, hym to solace.
And with hym in that lusty place
So faire folk and so fresh had he,
That whan I sawe I wondred me
Fro whennès sichè folk myght come,
So faire they weren all and some,   740
For they were lyk, as to my sighte,
To angels that ben fethered brighte.
    This folk, of which I telle you soo,
Upon a karole wenten thoo.

742. *fethered brighte*, with bright wings.
744. *karole*, a ring-dance to song.

A lady karolede hem, that hyght
GLADNESSE, [the] blisfull and the light.
Wel coude she synge and lustyly ;
Noon half so wel and semèly,
Couthe make in song sich refreynynge.
It sat hir wondir wel to synge ;   750
Hir voice ful clere was and ful swete,
She was nought rudè ne unmete,
But couthe ynow of sich doyng
As longeth unto karolyng.
For she was wont in every place
To syngen first, folk to solace,
For syngyng moost she gaf hir to,
No craft had she so leef to do.
Tho myghtist thou karoles sene,
And folk daunce and mery bene,   760
And makè many a faire tournyng
Upon the grenè gras springyng.
There myghtist thou see these flowtours,
Mynstrales, and eke jogèlours,
That wel to syngè dide her peyne ;
Somme songè songès of Loreyne,
For in Loreyn her notès bee
Full swetter than in this contre.
There was many a tymbester,
And saillouris that I dar wel swere,   770
Cóuthe her craft ful parfitly ;
The tymbres up ful sotilly,
They caste and hente full ofte,
Upon a fynger faire and softe,
That they [ne] failide never mo.
Ful fetys damysellès two,
Ryght yonge and full of semelyhede,
In kirtles and noon other wede
And fairè tressèd every tresse,
Hadde Myrthè doon, for his noblesse,   780
Amydde the karole forto daunce.
But herof lieth no remembraunce
How that they dauncèd queyntèly ;
That oon wolde come all pryvyly
Agayn that other, and whan they were
To-gidre almost, they threwe yfere
Her mouthis so that through her play
It semèd as they kiste alway.

749. MSS. *And couthe.*
768. *this contre*, Orleans.
770. *saillouris*, dancers.
771. *that* possibly belongs before *couthe* in next verse ; Fr. 'Qui moult savoient.'
773. *They casten and* [hem] *hente ful ofte* ; but perhaps a 3-beat line, cp. 480, 801.

To dauncen well koude they the gise,
What shulde I more to you devyse ;   790
Ne bode I never thennès go,
Whiles that I sawe hem dauncé so.

   Upon the karoll wonder faste
I gan biholde, til attè laste
A lady gan me forto espie ;
And she was clepèd CURTESIE
The worshipfull, the debonaire,
I pray to god evere falle hir faire.
Ful curteisly she calléde me,
' What do ye there, Beau ser ?' quod she,
' Come [here], and if it lykè yow   801
To dauncen, dauncith with us now.'
And I withoutè tariyng
Wénte into the karolyng.
I was abasshéd never a dell,
But it to me likèd right well
That Curtesie me clepèd so,
And bad me on the dauncè go.
For if I haddè durst, certeyn
I wolde have karolèd right fayn,   810
As man that was to dauncè blithe.
Thanne gan I loken oftè sithe
The shape, the bodies, and the cheres,
The countenaunce, and the maneres
Of all the folk that dauncèd there ;
And I shal tell [you] what they were.

   Ful faire was Myrthe, ful longe and high,
A fairer man I nevere sigh ;
As rounde as appille was his face,
Ful rody and white in every place.   820
Fetys he was and wel beseye,
With metely mouth and yèn greye,
His nose by mesure wrought ful right.
Crispe was his heer, and eek ful bright,
Hise shuldris of a largè brede,
And smalish in the girdilstede.
He semèd lyke a portreiture,
So noble he was of his stature,
So faire, so joly and so fetys,
With lymès wrought at poynt devys,   830
Delyver, smert, and of grete myght ;
Ne sawe thou nevere man so lyght.
Of berde unnethe hadde he no thyng,
For it was in the firstè spryng.

Ful yonge he was, and mery of thought ;
And in samette with briddis wrought,
And with gold beten ful fetysly,
His body was clad ful richèly.
Wrought was his robe in straungè gise
And al to-slytered for queyntise   842
In many a placè lowe and hie ;
And shode he was with grete maistrie,
With shoon decopèd and with laas.
By druèry and by solas,
His leef a rosyn chapèlet
Hadde made and on his heed it set.

   And witè ye who was his leef?
Dame Gladnesse there was hym so leef,
That syngith so wel with glad courage,
That from she was .XII. yeer of age,   851
She of hir lovè graunt hym made.
Sir Mirthe hir by the fynger hadde
Dàunsyng, and she_ hym also ;
Grete lovè was atwixe hem two.
Bothe were they faire and bright of hewe :
She semède lyke a rosè newe
Of colour, and hir flesh so tendre
That with a brerè smale and slendre
Men myght it cleve, I dar wel seyn ;
Hir forheed frouncèles, al pleyn ;   860
Bent were hir [brownè] browis two,
Hir yèn greye and glad also,
That laugheden ay in hir semblaunt
First or the mouth, by covenaunt.
I not what of hir nose descryve,
So faire hath no womman alyve.
Hir heer was yelowe, and clere shynyng.
I wot no lady so likyng.
Of orfrays fresh was hir gerland ;
I, which seyen have a thousand,   871
Saugh never y-wys no gerlond yitt,
So wel y-wrought of silk as it.
And in an overgilt samit
Cladde she was, by gretè delit,
Of which hir leef a robè werede ;
The myrier she in hir hertè ferede.

   And next hir wente, in hir other side.
The GOD OF LOVE, that can devyde
Love, and as hym likith it be,
But he can cherles daunten, he,   880

---

791. *bode*, mistake for *bede*, or *bad* ; cp. 808.
The same Fr. is differently rendered at 1854.
801. *here*, MSS. omit ; Fr. ' ça venez.'
806. Sk. *it me likede*.
811. MSS. *right blithe*.

861. *browne*, supplied from Fr.
865. MSS. insert *wot* before *not* and *I sha*
before *descryve*.
873. *samit*, robe of samite.

And maken folkis pridé fallen,
And he can wel these lordis thrallen,
And ladyes putt at lowe degre,
Whan he may hem to proudé see.
This God of Love of his fasoun
Was lyke no knavé, ne quystroun.
His beaute gretly was to preyse,
But of his robé to devise
I drede encombred forto be ;
For nought y-clad in silk was he,   890
But all in floures and in flourettes,
I-paynted all with amorettes,
And with losengés, and scochouns,
With briddés, lybardes, and lyouns,
And other beestis wrought ful well,
His garnément was everydell
Y-portreiéd, and wrought with floures,
By dyvers medlyng of coloures.
Floures there were of many gise,
Y-sett by compas in assise ;   900
Ther lakkide no flour to my dome,
Ne nought so mych as flour of brome,
Ne violete, ne eke pervynke,
Ne flour noon that man can on thynke ;
And many a rosé-leef ful longe,
Was entermelled ther amonge,
And also on his heed was sette
Of roses reed a chapélett.
But nyghtyngales, a full grete route
That flyen over his heed aboute,   910
The leeves felden as they flyen ;
And he was all with briddés wryen,
With popynjay, with nyghtyngale,
With chalaundre, and with wodéwale,
With fynche, with lark, and with arch-
     aungell.
He semede as he were an aungell,
That doun were comen fro hevene
     clere.
    Love hadde with hym a bachelere,
That he made alleweyes with hym be ;
SWETE LOKYNG clepéd was he.   920
This bachelere stode biholdyng
The daunce ; and in his honde holdyng

Turké bowés two had he.
That oon of hem was of a tree
That bereth a fruyt of savour wykke,
Ful crokid was that foulé stikke ;
And knotty here and there also,
And blak as bery, or ony slo.
That other bowe was of a plante
Withouten wem, I dar warante,   930
Ful evene, and by proporcioun
Treitys and long, of good fasoun ;
And it was peynted wel and thwyten,
And over al diapred and writen
With ladyes and with bacheleris,
Full lyghtsom and glad of cheris.
These bowés two helde Swete-lokyng,
That seméde lyk no gadélyng,
And ten brode arowis hilde he there,
Of which .V. in his righthond were ;   940
But they were shaven well and dight,
Nokkéd and fetheréd aright,
And all they were with gold bygoon,
And strongé poynted everychoon,
And sharpé forto kerven well.
But iren was ther noon, ne steell,
For al was golde, men myght it see,
Out-take the fetherés and the tree.
The swiftest of these arowis fyve
Out of a bowé forto dryve,   950
And besté fetheréd for to flee,
And fairest eke, was clepid Beaute ;
That other arowe that hurteth lesse
Was clepid, as I trowe, Symplesse ;
The thriddé clepéd was Fraunchise
That fethréd was in noble wise,
With valour and with curtesye ;
The fourthe was cleped Compaignye,
That hevy forto shoten ys ;
But who so shetith right y-wys,   960
May therwith doon grete harme and wo.
The fifte of these, and laste also,
Faire-Semblaunt men that arowe calle,
The leesté grevous of hem alle,
Yit can it make a ful grete wounde.
But he may hope his soris sounde,
That hurt is with that arowe y-wys ;
His wo the bette bistowéd is,

886. *quystroun* (O. F. coistron), scullion.
892. Found only in Th.
892. *with amorettes*, 'by amorous girls'; cp.
4755. 'With' in this sense is common in Middle
English ; cp. *Troilus*, iv. 80.
   915. *archaungell*; Fr. 'mesanges,' which
Cotgrave defines as titmouse.

923. *Turke bowes*, etc. MSS. add *full wel
devysed* (not in Fr.) after *two*. Cp. *Tales*, A 2895,
where 'Turkeis.'
   932. MSS. *ful good;* Fr. 'de bone façon.'

For he may sonner have gladnesse ;
His langour oughte be the lesse.   970
Five arowis were of other gise,
That ben ful foule to devyse,
For shaft and ende, soth forto telle,
Were also blak as fende in helle.
The first of hem is called Pride,
That other arowe next hym biside,
It was [y-]cleped Vylanye.
That arowe was al with felonye
Envenymed, and with spitous blame.
The thridde of hem was cleped Shame,
The fourthe Wanhope cleped is,   981
The fifte Newe-thought, y-wys.
These arowis that I speke of heere
Were alle fyve on oon maneere,
And alle were they resemblable.
To hem was wel sittyng and able,
The foule croked bowe hidous
That knotty was, and al roynous ;
That bowe semede wel to shete
These arowis fyve, that ben unmete   990
And contrarye to that other fyve.
But though I telle not as blyve
Of her power, ne of her myght,
Herafter shal I tellen right
The soothe, and eke signyfiaunce ;
As fer as I have remembraunce
All shal be seid, I undirtake,
Er of this book an ende I make.

   Now come I to my tale ageyn.
But aldirfirst I wole you seyn   1000
The fasoun and the countenaunces
Of all the folk that on the daunce is.
The God of Love, jolyf and lyght,
Ladde on his honde a lady bright,
Of high prys and of grete degre ;
This lady called was Beaute,
As an arowe of which I tolde,
Ful wel [y-]thewed was she holde ;
Ne she was derk, ne broun, but bright,
And clere as [is] the mone lyght,   1010
Ageyn whom all the sterres semen
But smale candels, as we demen.
Hir flesh was tendre as dewe of flour,
Hir chere was symple as byrde in bour,
As whyte as lylye or rose in rys ;

Hir face gentyl and tretys,
Fetys she was, and smale to se ;
No wyntred browis hadde she,
Ne popped hir, for it neded nought   1018
To wyndre hir, or to peynte hir ought.
Hir tresses yelowe, and longe straughten
Unto hir helys doun they raughten ;
Hir nose, hir mouth, and eyhe, and cheke
Wel wrought, and all the remenaunt eke
A ful grete savour and a swote
Me toucheth in myn herte rote,
As helpe me god, whan I remembre
Of the fasoun of every membre.
In world is noon so faire a wight ;
For yonge she was, and hewed bright,
Sore plesaunt, and fetys with all,   103:
Gente, and in hir myddill small.
Biside Beaute yede richesse,
An high lady of gret noblesse,
And gret of prys in every place ;
But who so durste to hir trespace,
Or til hir folk, in word or dede,
He were full hardy, out of drede.
For bothe she helpe and hyndre may ;
And that is nought of yisterday,   1c4
That riche folk have full gret myght
To helpe, and eke to greve a wyght.
The leste and grettest of valour
Diden Rychesse ful gret honour,
And besy weren hir to serve,
For that they wolde hir love deserve.
They cleped hir ' Lady,' grete and small :
This wide world hir dredith all,
This world is all in hir daungere.
Hir court hath many a losengere,   105:
And many a traytour envyous,
That ben ful besy and curyous
Forto dispreisen and to blame

---

978. MSS. read *as* for *al*, 'toute.'
991. Perhaps read *contraire;* cp. 348.
1014. *byrde*, bride.

1018. *wyntred*, 'guignie;' not elsewhere foun
in English unless in '*wintrede brumes*,' O.E
Homilies (Morris) ii. 213, where the meaning
seems to be 'ogling glances' as here. Si
changes to *wynered* as in 1020.
1019. *popped*, defined by Coles (1713) 'dres
fine.' v. Dyce's Skelton ii. 239, where *popte* f.v
is quoted.
1020. *wyndre*, to trim (the hair), Coles, cp.
1018.
1026. *toucheth*, Kaluza's emendation for *thought*
of the MSS.
1037. MSS. *werk*, 'par fais ou par dis.'
1043. MSS. *beste* for *leste*, 'li greignor et
menor.'

That best deserven love and name.
Bifore the folk, hem to bigilen,
These losengeris hem preyse, and smylen,
And thus the world with word anoynten;
And aftirward they prille, and poynten
The folk right to the baré boon,
Bihynde her bak whan they ben goon,
And foule abate the folkis prys.   1061
Ful many a worthy man, y-wys
An hundrid, havé do to dye
These losengers thorough flaterye ;
And maké folk ful straungé be
There hem oughté be pryve.
Wel yvel mote they thryve and thee,
And yvel arryvéd mote they be,
These losengers ful of envye ;
No good man loveth her companye.   1070
Richesse a robe of purpur on hadde,
Ne trowe not that I lye or madde,
For in this world is noon hir lyche,
Ne by a thousand deel so riche,
Ne noon so faire ; for it ful well
With orfrays leyd was everydeell
And portraied in the ribanynges
Of dukés storyes, and of kynges,
And with a bend of gold tasseled,
And knoppis fyne of gold ameled.   1080
Aboute hir nekke of gentyl entayle
Was shete the riché chevesaile,
In which ther was full gret plente
Of stones clere and bright to see.
Rychesse a girdell hadde upon,
The bokele of it was of a stoon,   ·
Of vertu gret and mochel of myght ;
For who so bare the stoon so bright,
Of venym durst hym no thing doute,
While he the stoon hadde hym aboute.
That stoon was gretly forto love,   1091
And, tyl a riché mannys byhove,
Worth all the gold in Rome and Frise.
The mourdaunt wrought in noble wise

Was of a stoon full precious,
That was so fyne and vertuous
That hole a man it koudé make
Of palasie, and [of] tothe ake.
And yit the stoon hadde such a grace
That he was siker in every place,   1100
All thilké day not blynde to bene,
That fastyng myght that stoon [have] seene.
The barres were of gold ful fyne
Upon a tyssu of satyne,
Full hevy, gret, and no thyng lyght,
In everiche was a besaunt-wight.
Upon the tresses of Richesse
Was sette a cercle, for noblesse,
Of brend gold that full lyghté shoon,
So faire trowe I was never noon.   1110
But she were kunnyng for the nonys,
That koude devysé alle the stonys,
That in that cercle shewen clere.
It is a wondir thing to here,
For no man koudé preyse or gesse
Of hem the valewe or richesse.
Rubyes there were, saphires, jagounces,
And emeraudes more than two ounces.
But all byfore ful sotilly
A fyn charboncle sette saugh I ;   1120
The stoon so clere was and so bright,
That also soone as it was nyght,
Men myght[é] seen to go for nede
A myle or two in lengthe and brede.
Sich lyght sprang oute of the stone,
That Richesse wondir brighté shone,
Bóthe hir heed and all hir face,
And eke aboute hir al the place.
    Dame Richesse on hir honde gan lede
A yong man full of semelyhede,   1130
That she best loved of ony thing.
His lust was mych in housholding,
In clothyng was he ful fetys,
And loved to have well hors of prys ;
He wende to have reproved be
Of theft or moordre, if that he
Hadde in his stable ony hakeney.
And therfore he desired ay

1058. *prille* (Th. *prill*, G. *prile*), Fr. 'poignent,'
may be right (cp. sb. *prill*, a top), and mean
'pirouette.' But probably the scribe's mistake for
thrill, pierce ; cp. 5556, where *depe* for *dothe.*
    1065. *And make*, Th. *And maketh* ; G *have
maad*, 'car il tout,' etc.
    1068. *arryved*, G *achyved.*
    1089. *durst*, need. The forms of *durren* and
thar were confused in Middle English ; cp. 1324,
1360.
    1094. *mourdaunt*, the pendant of the girdle.

1102. *have*, supplied from Fr., 'l'avoit veüe.'
    1106. *besaunt*, a gold coin worth about a half-
sovereign.
    1117. *jagounces*, cp. 'There is a stone whiche
called is jagounce. . . . Cytryne of colour, lyke
garnettes of entayle.' Lydgate's *Minor Poems,*
p. 188.

To be aqueynted with Richesse,
For all his purpos, as I gesse,   1140
Was forto makè gret dispense
Withoutè wernyng or diffense;
And Richesse myght it wel sustene
And hir dispencè well mayntene,
And hym alwey sich plentè sende
Of gold and silver forto spende
Withoutè lakking or daunger,
As it were poured in a garner.
    And after on the dauncè wente
LARGESSE, that sette al hir entente   1150
Forto be honourable and free.
Of Alexandres kyn was she;
Hir mostè joyè was y-wys
Whan that she yaf, and seide, ' Have
          this.'
Not Avarice, the foule caytyf,
Was half to gripe so ententyf,
As Largesse is to yeve and spende ;
And god ynough alwey hir sende,
So that the more she yaf awey
The more y-wys she hadde alwey.   1160
Gret loos hath Largesse and gret pris,
For bothè wyse folk and unwys
Were hooly to hir baundon brought,
So wel with yiftès hath she wrought.
And if she hadde an enemy,
I trowe that she coude tristèly
Make hym full soone hir freend to be,
So large of yift and free was she.
Therfore she stode in love and grace
Of riche and pover in every place.   1170
A full gret fool is he y-wys
That bothè riche and nygart is ;
A lord may have no maner vice
That greveth more than avarice.
For nygart never with strengthe of
          honde
May wynnè gret lordship or londe ;
For freendis all to fewe hath he
To doon his will perfourmèd be.
And who so wole have freendis heere,
He may not holde his tresour deere.   1180
For by ensample I tellè this,
Right as an adamaund y-wys
Can drawen to hym sotylly
The yren that is leid therby,

So drawith folkès hertis y-wis
Silver and gold that yeven is.
Largesse hadde on a robè fresh
Of richè purpur Sarsynesh.
Wel fourmèd was hir face and cleere,
And opened hadde she hir colere ;   1190
For she right there hadde in present
Unto a lady maad present
Of a gold brochè, ful wel wrought.
And certys it myssatte hir nought,
For thorough hir smokkè wrought with silk
The flesh was seen as white as mylk.
Largesse, that worthy was and wys,
Hilde by the honde a knyght of prys,
Was sibbe to Artour of Britaigne,
And that was he that bare the ensaigne
Of worship, and the gounfanoun.   1201
And yit he is of sich renoun
That men of hym seye fairè thynges
Byforè barouns, erles, and kynges.
This knyght was comen all newly
Fro [a] tourneiyng fastè by.
    Ther hadde he don gret chyvalrie
Through his vertu and his maistrie,
And for the love of his lemman
He caste doun many a doughty man.   1210
And next hym daunced dame FRAUNCHISE,
Arayèd in full noblè gyse.
She was not broune ne dunne of hewe,
But white as snowe y-fallen newe.
Hir nose was wrought at poynt devys,
For it was gentyl and tretys,
·With eyen gladde and browès bente,
Hir here doun to hir helis wente ;
And she was symple as dowve on tree.
Ful debonaire of herte was she ;   1220
SĦe durst neither seyn ne do
Bùt that that hir longèd to.
And if a man were in distresse,
And for hir love in hevynesse
Hir herte wolde have full gret pite,
She was so amiable and free.
For were a man for hir bistadde,
She woldè ben right sore adradde
That she dide over gret outrage ;
But she hym holpe his harme to aswage

1185. *hertis*, as in v. 76, is to be read as one
syllable.
1188. MSS. *Sarlynysh*.
1199. *i.e.* Who was sib, etc.
1206. MSS. omit *a*; Fr. ' d'un tornoiement.

1158. *sende*, sent.
1166. *tristely*, Th. *craftely*.

Hir thought it ell a vylanye. 1231
And she hadde on a sukkenye
That not of hempe ne heerdis was ;
So fair was noon in all Arras.
Lord, it was ridled fetysly !
Ther nas nat a poynt trewely
That it nas in his right assise.
Full wel y-clothed was Fraunchise,
For ther is no cloth sittith bet
On damysell than doth roket ; 1240
A womman wel more fetys is
In roket than in cote y-wis.
The whyte roket, rydled faire,
Bitokeneth that full debonaire
And swete was she that it bere.
 Bi hir daunced a bachelere ;
 I can not telle you what he hight,
But faire he was and of good hight,
All hadde he be, I sey no more,
The lordis sone of Wyndesore. 1250
 And next that daunced CURTESYE,
That preised was of lowe and hye,
For neither proude ne foole was she.
She forto daunce called me,
 I pray god yeve hir right good grace !
Whanne I come first into the place,
She was not nyce ne outrageous,
But wys and ware and vertuous ;
Of faire speche and of faire answere,
Was never wight mysseid of here, 1260
Ne she bar rancour to no wight.
Clere broune she was and therto bright
Of face, of body avenaunt ;
 I wot no lady so plesaunt.
She were worthy forto bene
An emperesse or crowned quene.
 And by hir wente a knyght dauncyng,
That worthy was and wel spekyng,
And ful wel koude he don honour.
The knyght was faire and styf in stour, 1271
And in armure a semely man,
And welbiloved of his lemman.
 Faire IDILNESSE thanne saugh I,
That alwey was me faste by ;
Of hir have I withoute fayle

Told yow the shap and apparayle.
For, as I seide, loo that was she
That dide to me so gret bounte,
That she the gate of the gardyn
Undide and lete me passen in. 1280
 And after daunced, as I gesse,
YOUTHE fulfilled of lustynesse,
That nas not yit XII yeer of age,
With herte wylde and thought volage.
Nyce she was, but she ne mente
Noon harme ne slight in hir entente,
But oonly lust and jolyte ;
For yonge folk wele witen ye
Have lytel thought but on her play.
Hir lemman was biside alway 1290
In sich a gise that he hir kyste
At alle tymes that hym lyste ;
That all the daunce myght it see,
They make no force of pryvete ;
For who spake of hem yvel or well,
They were ashamed neveradell,
But men myght seen hem kisse there,
As it two yonge dowves were.
For yong was thilke bachelere,
Of beaute wot I noon his pere, 1300
And he was right of sich an age
As Youthe his leef, and sich corage.
 The lusty folk that daunced there,
And also other that with hem were,
That weren all of her meyne,
Ful hende folk and wys and free
And folk of faire port trewely
They weren alle comunly.
Whanne I hadde seen the countenaunces
Of hem that ladden thus these daunces,
Thanne hadde I will to gon and see 1311
The gardyne that so lyked me,
And loken on these faire loreres,
On pyntrees, cedres, and olmeris.
The daunces thanne y-ended were,
For many of hem that daunced there
Were with her loves went awey,
Undir the trees to have her pley.
A lord, they lyved lustyly !
A gret fool were he sikirly 1320

1232. *sukkenye*, 'sorquanie,' a canvas jacket, frock, or gaberdine (Cotgr.).
1236. *a poynt*, one point.
1250. *i.e.* Edward I. the son of Henry III. of England.
1265. *were* (G omits) ; Kaluza reads *wel was*.

1282. *Youthe* (MSS. *And she*), proposed by Ten Brink.
1308. *They*, MSS. *There*.
1314. *olmeris* (G *oliueris* ?), elms. 'Moriers' was perhaps read as ormiers ; but *olyueris* in v. 1381 translates 'oliviers.'

That nolde his thankès such lyf lede.
For this dar I seyn oute of drede,
That who so myghtè so wel fare,
For better lyf durst hym not care ;
For ther nys so good paradys
As to have a love at his devys.
Oute of that placé wente I thoo,
And in that gardyn gan I goo,
Pleyyng alonge full meryly.
The God of Love full hastely   1330
Unto hym Swetè-Lokyng clepte.
No lenger wolde he that he kepte
His bowe of gold, that shoon so bright ;
He bad hym bend it anoon ryght.
And he full soonè sette an-ende,
And at a braid he gan it bende ;
And toke hym of his arowes fyve,
Full sharp and redy forto dryve.
    Now god that sittith in mageste,
Fro deedly woundes he kepè me,   1340
If so be that he hadde me shette !
For if I with his arowe mette,
It hadde me grevèd sore y-wys.
But I, that no thyng wist of this,
Wente up and doun full many awey,
And he me folwed faste alwey ;
But no where wolde I restè me,
Till I hadde in all the gardyn be.
    The gardyn was by mesuryng
Right evene and square ; in compassing
It was as long as it was large.   1351
Of fruyt hadde every tree his charge,
But it were any hidous tree,
Of which ther werè two or three.
There were, and that wote I full well,
Of pome garnettys a full gret dell,
That is a fruyt full well to lyke,
Namely to folk whanne they ben sike.
And trees there were of gret foisoun
That baren nottes in her sesoun   1360
Such as men notè myggès calle,
That swote of savour ben withalle ;
And almandèrès gret plente,

1321. his thankes, willingly.
1326. his is often indefinite in Middle English.
1336. at a braid, immediately.
1341. Skeat reads wol for hadde ; Fr. 'Se
il fait tant que a moi traie.' Perhaps join with
the next line by reading Or for For in 1342.
1363. almanderes, MSS. almandres, Fr.
'alemandiers.'

Fygès, and many a datè tree,
There wexen, if men haddè nede,
Thorough the gardyn in length and brede.
Ther was eke wexyng many a spice,
As clowe-gelofre, and lycorice,
Gyngevre, and greyn de Paradys,
Canell, and setèwale of prys,   1370
And many a spicè delitable
To eten whan men rise fro table.
And many homly trees ther were
That peches, coynes, and apples beere,
Mèdlers, plowmes, perys chesteynis,
Cherys, of which many oon fayne is,
Nótes, aleys, and bolas,
That forto seen it was solas ;
With many high lorer and pyn
Was renged clene all that gardyn,   1380
With cipres and with olyveris,
Of which that nygh no plente heere is.
There were elmès grete and stronge,
Maples, asshe, oke, aspè, planes longe,
Fyne ew, popler, and lyndes faire,
And othere trees full many a payre—
What shulde I tel you more of it ?
There were so many treès yit,
That I shulde al encombred be
Er I had rekened every tree.   1390
    These trees were sette, that I devyse,
One from another in assyse
Fyve fadome or sixe, I trowè so ;
But they were hye and great also,
And for to kepe out wel the sonne,
The croppès were so thicke y-ronne,
And every braunche in other knette,
And ful of grenè leves sette,
That sonnè myght there none discende.
Lest [it] the tender grasses shende.   1400
There myght men does and roes y-se,
And of squyrels ful great plente
From bowe to bowe alwaye lepynge :
Connès there were also plaiynge,
That comyn out of her clapers,
Of sondrie colours and maners,
And maden many a tourneiyng
Upon the fresshè grasse spryngyng.
    In places sawe I wellès there
In whichè there no froggès were,   1410
And fayre in shadowe was every welle
But I ne can the nombre telle

674

Of stremys smal, that by devyse
Myrthe had done come through condyse;
Of whiche the water in rennyng
Gan make a noysé ful lykyng.
 About the brinkés of these welles
And by the stremés over al elles
Sprange up the grasse, as thicke y-set
And softe as any veluet,   1420
On whiche men myght his lemman ley
As on a fetherbed to pley,
For the erthé was ful softe and swete.
Through moisture of the wellé wete
Spronge up the soté grené gras
As fayre, as thicke, as myster was.
But moche amended it the place
That therthé was of suche a grace
That it of flourés hath plente,
That bothe in somer and wynter be.   1430
There sprange the vyolet al newe,
And fresshe pervynké riche of hewe,
And floures yelowe, white, and rede,
Suche plente grewe there never in mede.
Ful gaye was al the grounde, and queynt
And poudred, as men had it peynt
With many a fresshe and sondrie floure,
That casten up ful good savour.
 I wol nat longe holde you in fable
Of al this garden delectable,   1440
I mote my tongé stynten nede ;
For I ne maye withouten drede
Naught tellen you the beaute al,
Ne halfe the bounte there with al.
 I went on right honde and on lefte
About the place ; it was nat lefte
Tyl I had al the garden [in] bene,
In the esters that men myghté sene.
And thus while I wente in my playe
The God of Love me folowed aye,   1450
Right as an hunter can abyde
The beest, tyl he seéth his tyde
To shoten at good messe to the dere,
Whan that hym nedeth go no nere.
 And so befyl I rested me
Besydes a wel under a tree,
Whiche tree in Fraunce men cal a pyne ;

1420. *veluet*, trisyllabic.
1426. *myster*, need ; cp. vv. 6519, 6581, 7324.
1429. *hath* ; cp. 1652 for a similar change of
tense.
1436. *poudred*, 'piolee.'
1447. Cp. v. 1348.

But sithe the tyme of kyng Pepyne,
Ne grewe there tree in mannés syght
So fayre, ne so wel woxe in hight,   1460
In al that yarde so high was none.
And springyng in a marble stone
Had nature set, the sothe to telle,
Under that pyné tree a welle ;
And on the border al withoute
Was written in the stone aboute
Letters smal, that sayden thus :
' Here starfe the fayré Narcisus.'
 Narcisus was a bachelere   1469
That Love had caught in his daungere,
And in his nette gan hym so strayne,
And dyd him so to wepe and playne,
That nede him must his lyfe forgo.
For a fayre lady that hight Echo
Him loved over any creáture,
And gan for hym suche payne endure,
That on a tymé she him tolde
Thát, if he her loven nolde,
That her behovéd nedés dye,
There laye none other remedye.   1480
 But nathélesse for his beaute
So feirs and daungerous was he
That he nolde grauntè hir askyng,
For wepyng ne for faire praiyng.
And whanne she herd hym werné soo,
She hadde in herté so gret woo,
And took it in so gret dispite,
That she withouté more respite
Was deed anoon.   But er she deied
Full pitously to god she preied,   1490
That proudé-hertid Narcisus,
That was in love so daungerous,
Myght on a day be hampred so
For love, and ben so hoot for woo,
That never he myght to joye atteyne,
Than he shulde feele in every veyne
What sorowe trewé lovers maken
That ben so velaynesly forsaken.
This prayer was but resonable,
Therfore god helde it ferme and stable.
For Narcisus, shortly to telle,   1501
By aventure come to that welle,
To resten hym in that shadowing
A day whanne he come fro huntyng.

1470. *daungere*, dominion.
1473. *nede*, adverbial.
1496. *Than*, when.

This Narcisus hadde suffred paynes
For rennyng alday in the playnes,
And was for thurst in grete distresse
Of heet, and of his werynesse
That hadde his breth almost bynomen.
Whanne he was to that welle y-comen,
That shadowid was with braunches grene,
He thoughte of thilkė water shene   1512
To drynke, and fresshe hym wel withalle;
And doun on knees he gan to falle,
And forth his heed and necke out-straught
To drynken of that welle a draught.
And in the water anoon was sene
His nose, his mouth, his yėn shene,
And he therof was all abasshed;
His ownė shadowe had hym bytrasshed,
For well wende he the formė see   1521
Óf a child of gret beaute.
Well kouthė Love hym wrekė thoo
Of daunger and of pride also,
That Narcisus somtyme hym beere.
He quytte hym well his guerdoun there;
For he musede so in the welle
That, shortly all the sothe to telle,
He lovede his ownė shadowe soo,
That attė laste he starf for woo.   1530
For whanne he saugh that he his wille
Myght in no maner way fulfille,
And that he was so fastė caught
That he hym kouthė comforte nought,
He loste his witte right in that place,
And deyde withynne a lytel space.
And thus his warisoun he took
Fro the lady that he forsook.
Ladyes I preye ensample takith,
Ye that ageyns youre love mistakith;   1540
For if her deth be yow to wite,
God kan ful well youre whilė quyte.
Whanne that this lettre of which I telle
Hadde taught me that it was the welle
Of Narcisus in his beaute,
I gan anoon withdrawė me,
Whanne it felle in my remembraunce
That hym bitiddė such myschaunce.

1537. *warisoun*, 'guerredon' (confused with
guerison ?), reward.
1538. *Fro*, MSS. *For*, 'de la meschine.'
1540. *love*, 'amis,' perhaps read *loves*; but cp.
v. 1965. *ageyns* here means 'in respect to.'
1541. *to wite*, gerundive, *i.e.* is to be imputed
to you.
1543. *lettre*, writing.

But at the lastė thanne thought I
That scathéles full sykerly   1550
I myght unto the wellė goo—
Wherof shulde I abaisshen soo?
Unto the welle than went I me,
And doun I loutede forto see
The clerė water in the stoon,
And eke the gravell which that shoon
Down in the botme as silver fyn.
For of the well this is the fyn,
In world is noon so clere of hewe.
The water is evere fresh and newe   1560
That welmeth up with wawis bright
The mountance of two fynger hight.
Abouten it is gras spryngyng
For moiste so thikke and wel likyng,
That it ne may in wynter dye
No more than may the see be drye.
  Downe at the botmė sette sawe I
Two cristall stonys craftély
In thilkė freshe and fairė welle.
But o thing sothly dar I telle   1570
That ye wole holde a gret mervayle
Whanne it is tolde, withouten fayle.
For whanne the sonnė clere in sight
Cast in that welle his bemys bright,
And that the heete descendid is,
Thanne taketh the cristall stoon y-wis
Agayn the sonne an hundrid hewis,
Blewe, yelowe, and rede that fresh and
          newe is.
Yitt hath the merveilous cristall
Such strengthė, that the place overall,   1580
Bothe flour, and tree, and leves grene,
And all the yerde in it is seene.
And forto don you to undirstonde,
To make ensample wole I fonde.
Ryght as a myrrour openly
Shewith allė thing that stont therby,
As well the colour as the figure,
Withouten ony coverture;
Right so the cristall stoon shynyng,
Withouten ony disseyvyng,   1590
The estrees of the yerde accusith,
To hym that in the water musith.
For evere in which half that ye be

1578. *rede that fresh and newe is*, 'vermeil.'
1581. *flour*, MSS. *foule*; Fr. 'flors.'
1586. *stont*, MSS. *stondith*; read *Shew'th a-
thing*, etc.
1591. *estrees* (MSS. *entrees*), 'l'estre.'

e may well half the gardyne se ;
nd if he turne, he may right well
ǝne the remenaunt everydell.
ɔr ther is noon so litil thyng
ɔ hidde ne closid with shittyng,
hat it ne is sene as though it were
ǝýntid in the cristall there.   1600
his is the mirrour perilous,
ı which the proudé Narcisus
ıwe all his facé faire and bright ;
hat made hym swithe to lie upright.
or who so loketh in that mirrour,
her may no thyng ben his socour,
hat he ne shall there sene some thyng
hat shal hym lede into lovyng.
ull many worthy man hath it
-blent, for folk of grettist wit   1610
en sooné caught heere and awayted ;
/ithouten respite ben they baited.
ʾeere comth to folk of newé rage,
ʾeere chaungith many wight corage ;
ʾeere lith no rede ne witte therto,
or Venus sone, daun Cupido,
ʾath sowen there of love the seed,
hat help ne lith there noon, ne rede,
ɔ cerclith it the welle aboute.
ʾis gynnés hath he sett withoute,   1620
yght forto cacche in his panters
hese damoysels and bachelers.
ove will noon other briddé cacche
hough he sette either nette or lacche.
nd for the seed that heere was sowen
his welle is clepid, as well is knowen,
he Welle of Love of verray right,
f which ther hath ful many a wight
póke in bookis dyversely.
ut they shull never so verily   1630
'escripcioun of the wellé heere,
e eke the sothe of this matere,
s ye shull, whanne I have undo
he craft that hir bilongith to.
   Allway me likéd forto dwelle
ɔ sene the cristall in the welle,

That shewide me full openly
A thousand thingés fasté by.
But I may say in sory houre
Stode I to loken or to poure,   1640
For sithen [have] I soré siked ;
That mirrour hath me now entriked.
But hadde I first knowen in my wit
The vertue and [the] strengthe of it,
I noldé not have mused there ;
Mé had bette bene ellis where,
For in the snare I fell anoon
That hath bitresshéd many oon.
In thilké mirrour sawe I tho,
Among a thousand thingés mo,   1650
A roser chargid full of rosis,
That with an hegge aboute enclos is.
Tho had I sich lust and envie,
That for Parys, ne for Pavie,
Nolde I have left to goon and see
There grettist hepe of roses be.
Whanne I was with this ragé hent,
That caught hath many a man and shent,
Toward the roser gan I go.
And whanne I was not fer therfro,   1660
The savour of the roses swote
Me smote right to the herté rote,
As I hadde all enhawméd be.
And if I ne hadde endouted me
To have ben hatid or assailed,
My thankis wolde I not have failed
To pulle a rose of all that route
To beren in myn honde aboute,
And smellen to it where I wente ;
But ever I dredde me to repente,   1670
And leste it grevede or forthought
The lord that thilké gardyn wrought.
Of roses ther were greté wone,
So fairé waxé never in rone.
Of knoppes clos some sawe I there,
And some wel beter woxen were ;
And some ther ben of other moysoun,
That drowé nygh to her sesoun,
And spedde hem fasté forto sprede.
I lové well sich roses rede,   1680

1595. he is the indefinite pronoun, i.e. 'one';
'. note to v. 1540.
1604. i.e. to lie dead ; cp. Tales, D 768.
1608. MSS. laughyng.
1610. Perhaps we should read Y - bleint,
ceived ; Fr. 'mis en rage.'
1613. of newe, anew.
1621. panters, cp. Leg. of G. W. 131.

1641. MSS. sighide, cp. Parl. of F. 404.
1666. My thankis (G Me thankis), for my
part.
1666. MSS. wole.
1673. wone, abundance, seems to be plural ;
cp. Zupitza's Guy of Warwick, 10329.
1674. rone seems to be a northern word meaning 'bush.' Fr. 'sous ciaus.'

For brodè roses and open also
Ben passèd in a day or two,
But knoppès wille [al] freshè be
Two dayès attè leest or thre.
The knoppès gretly liked me,
For fairer may ther no man se.
Whó-so myght have oon of all,
It ought hym ben full lief withall ;
Might I gerlond of hem geten,
For no richesse I wolde it leten.   1690
Among the knoppes I chese oon
So faire, that of the remenaunt noon
Ne preise I half so well as it,
Whanne I avise it in my wit.
For it so well was enlumýned
With colour reed, [and] as well fyned
As nature couthe it makè faire ;
And it hath levès wel foure paire,
That kynde hath sett thorough his knowyng
Aboute the redè roses spryngyng.   1700
The stalkè was as rishè right,
And theron stode the knoppe upright,
That it ne bowide upon no side.
The swotè smellè spronge so wide,
That it dide all the place aboute.
Whanne I haddè smelled the savour swote,
No will haddè I fro thens yit goo ;
Bot somdell neer it wente I thoo
To take it, but myn hond for drede
Ne dorste I to the rosè bede   1710
For thesteles sharpe of many maneeres,
Netles, thornes, and hokede breres ;
For mychè they distourbled me,
That sore I dradde to harmèd be.
    The God of Love with bowè bent,
That all day sette hadde his talent
To pursuen and to spien me,
Was stondyng by a figè tree.
And whanne he sawè how that I
Hadde chosen so ententifiy   1720
The bothoun more unto my paie

    1683. MSS. omit *al* ; Fr. 'tuit frois.'
    1705. *aboute*, Fr. 'replenist.' Skeat and Kaluza
think that the Chaucerian part of the translation ends here ; but it is possible that the absence
of rhyme is due to a later alteration of a rhyme
like *swete*, vb., with *swete*, adj. ; or *replete* with
swete (*replete*, vb., is given in Levin's rhyme-list).
    1713. *For*, Skeat reads *Ful*, Kaluza *Over*, but
no change is necessary.
    1714. *That* (MSS. *For*), Fr. 'Que.'
    1721. From this point 'botoun,' hitherto trans-
lated by *knoppe*, is rendered *bothoun* (= 'button')

Than ony other that I say,
He toke an arowe full sharply whette,
And in his bowe whanne it was sette,
He streight up to his erè drough
The strongè bowe, that was so tough,
And shette att me so wondir smerte,
That thorough myn ye unto myn herte
The takel smote, and depe it wente.
And therwith-all such colde mehente,   1730
That, under clothès warme and softe,
Sithen that day I have chevered ofte.
Whanne I was hurt thus, in [a] stounde
I felle doun platte unto the grounde ;
Myn hertè failed and feynted ay,
And longè tyme a-swoone I lay.
But whanne I come out of swounyng,
And haddè witt and my felyng,
I was all maate, and wende full well
Of bloode have loren a full gret dell.   1740
But certes the arowe that in me stode
Of me ne drewe no drope of blode,
For why I founde my wounde all dreye.
Thanne toke I with myn hondis tweie
The arowe, and ful fast out it plight,
And in the pullyng sore I sight ;
So at the last the shaft of tree
I drough out with the fethers thre
But yet the hokede heed y-wis,
The which that Beaute callid is,   1750
Gan so depe in myn hertè pace
That I it myghtè nought arace ;
But in myn hertè still it stode.
Al bledde I not a drope of blode.
I was bothe anguyssous and trouble
For the perill that I sawe double.
I nystè what to seye or do,
Ne gete a leche my woundis to ;
For neithir thorough gras ne rote
Ne hadde I helpe of hope ne bote.   1760
But to the bothoun evermo
Myn hertè drewe, for all my wo ;
My thought was in noon other thing,
For hadde it ben in my kepyng,
It wolde have brought my lyf agayn.

in the curious form *bothoum*. Kaluza see
this the evidence of a new translator. If so, the
new part probably begins at v. 1715. After this
the translation becomes more diffuse, the rhymes
have a northern colouring, and the verses more
frequently begin with an accented syllable.
    1733. *in a stounde*, 'tantost.'
    1750. *that*, MSS. *it*.

For certis evenly, I dar wel seyn,
The sight oonly and the savour
Aleggèd mych of my langour.
Thanne gan I forto drawè me
Toward the bothon faire to se.   1770
And Love hadde gete hym in this throwe
Another arowe into his bowe,
And forto shetè gan hym dresse ;
The arowis namè was Symplesse.
And whanne that Love gan nyghe me mere,
He drowe it up withouten were,
And shette at me with all his myght ;
So that this arowe anoon right
Thourghout [myn] eigh, as it was founde,
Into myn herte hath maad a wounde.   1780
Thanne I anoon dide al my crafte,
Fórto drawen out the shafte ;
And therwith-all I sighede efte,
But in myn herte the heed was lefte,
Which ay encreside my desire,
Unto the bothon drawè nere.
And evermo that me was woo,
The more desir hadde I to goo
Unto the roser, where that grewe
The freysshè bothun so bright of hewe.
Bétir me were to have laten be,   1791
But it bihovede nedè me
To done right as myn hertè badde,
For evere the body must be ladde
Aftir the herte, in wele and woo ;
Of force togidre they must goo.
But never this archer woldè feyne
To shete at me with all his peyne.
And forto make me to hym mete,
The thridde arowe he gan to shete,   1800
Whanne best his tyme he myght espie,
The which was named Curtesie.
Into myn herte it dide avale.
A-swoone I fell bothe deed and pale,
Long tyme I lay and stirèd nought,
Till I abraide out of my thought.
And faste thanne I avysede me

To drawè out the shafte of tree ;
But evere the heed was left bihynde, ·
For ought I couthè pulle or wynde.   1810
So sore it stikid whanne I was hit,
That by no craft I myght it flit.
But anguyssous and full of thought
I felt sich woo my wounde ay wrought,
That somonede me alway to goo
Toward the rose, that plesede me soo.
But I ne durste in no manere,
Bicause the archer was so nere ;
'For evermore gladly,' as I rede,
'Brent child of fier hath mychè drede.'
And certis yit, for al my peyne,   1821
Though that I sigh yit arwis reyne,
And groundè quarels sharpe of steele,
Ne for no payne that I myght feele,
Yit myght I not my-silf witholde
The fairè roser to biholde.
For Love me yaf sich hardèment
Forto fulfille his comaundement,
Upon my fete I rose up thanne,
Féble as a forwoundid man,   1830
And forth to gon [my] myght I sette,
And for the archer nolde I lette.
Toward the roser fast I drowe,
But thornès sharpe mo than ynowe
Ther were, and also thistèles thikke
And brerès brymmè forto prikke,
That I ne myghtè getè grace
The rowè thornès forto passe,
To sene the roses fresshe of hewe.
I must abide, though it me rewe,   1840
The hegge aboute so thikkè was,
That closide the roses in compas.
But o thing lykèd me right wele ;
I was so nygh I myghtè fele
Of the bothon the swote odour,
And also se the fresshe colour,
And that right gretly likèd me,
That I so neer myght it se.
Sich joie anoon therof hadde I,
That I forgate my maladie ;   1850
To sene I haddè siche delit,

1766. *evenly*, equally ; cp. v. 5280. There is no *certes* in Fr.
1776. *withouten were*, Fr. 'sans menacier,' ? without warning.
1791. *laten*, let.
1794-5-6. Seems to be a quotation ; not in Fr. ; cp. vv. 2084 ff.
1797, 1798. *feyne, peyne* (Thyn. *fyne, pyne*). Either an assonance or *fyne, pene* ; cp. vv. 1785, 1786, *desirè, nerè*.

1814. MSS. *lefte* ; Skeat proposed *felte*.
1842. *closide* is but one syllable.
1848. *neer*, either an adverbial form *nere*, from O.E. *neor* with adv. -*e*, or a scribe's mistake for *nerwe* ; Skeat reads *it myght*.
1851. Skeat's emendation, *it hadde I*, is perhaps right.

679

Of sorwe and angre I was al quyte,
And of my woundes that I hadde thore.
For no thing liken me myght more
Than dwellen by the roser ay,
And thennes never to passe away.
But whanne a while I hadde be thare,
The god of Love, which alto-share
Myn herte with his arwis kene,
Cast hym to yeve me woundis grene.
He shette at me full hastily   1861
An arwe named Company,
The whiche takell is full able
To make these ladies merciable.
Thanne I anoon gan chaungen hewe
For grevaunce of my wounde newe,
That I agayn fell in swounyng,
And sighede sore in compleynyng.
Soore I compleyned that my sore
On me gan greven more and more.   1870
I hadde noon hope of allegeaunce ;
So nygh I drowe to desperaunce,
I roughte [ne] of deth ne lyf.
Wheder that Love wolde me dryf,
Yf me a martir wolde he make,
I myght his power nought forsake.
And while for anger thus I woke,
The God of Love an arowe toke ;
Ful sharpe it was and [ful] pugnaunt.
And it was callid Faire Semblaunt,   1880
The which in no wise wole consente,
That ony lover hym repente
To serve his love with herte and all
For ony perill that may bifall.
But though this arwe was kene grounde,
As ony rasour that is founde
To kutte and kerve, at the poynt
The God of Love it hadde anoynt
With a precious oynement,
Somdell to yeve aleggement   1890
Upon the woundes that he hadde
Through the body in my herte made,
To helpe her sores and to cure,
And that they may the bette endure.
But yit this arwe, withoute more,
Made in myn herte a large sore,

That in full grete peyne I abode.
But ay the oynement wente abrode,
Thourgh-oute my woundes large and wide
It spredde aboute in every side.   1900
Through whos vertu and whos myght
Myn herte joyfull was and light ;
I hadde ben deed and alto-shent
But for the precious oynement.
The shaft I drowe out of the arwe,
Roukyng for wo right wondir narwe,
But the heed, which made me smerte,
Lefte bihynde in myn herte
With other foure, I dar wel say,
That never wole be take away.   1910
But the oynement halpe me wele ;
And yit sich sorwe dide I fele
That al day I chaunged hewe
Of my woundes fresshe and newe.
As men myght se in my visage,
The arwis were so full of rage,
So variaunt of diversitee,
That men in everiche myght se
Bothe gret anoy, and eke swetnesse
And joie meynt with bittirnesse.   1920
Now were they esy, now were they wode.
In hem I felte bothe harme and goode ;
Now sore without aleggement,
Now softyng with the oynement ;
It softed heere and prikked there,
Thus ese and anger to-gidre were.
The God of Love delyverly
Come lepande to me hastily,
And seide to me in gret rape,
'Yelde thee, for thou may not escape,   1930
May no defence availe thee heere ;
Therfore I rede make no daungere,
If thou wolt yelde thee hastely.
Thou shalt [the] rather have mercy.
He is a foole in sikernesse,
That with daunger or stoutenesse
Rebellith there that he shulde plese ;
In sich folye is litel ese.
Be meke where thou must nedis bowe.
To stryve ageyn is nought thi prowe :   1940
Come at oones and have y-doo,
For I wole that it be soo.
Thanne yelde thee heere debonairly.'

1853, 1854. *thore, more*, northern rhyme ;
perhaps *thare, mare;* cp. 1857.
1873. MSS. *rought of deth ne of lyf.*
1874. *Wheder,* whither.
1892. As in Thynne. G *That he hadde the
body hole made* written later over blank line.

1925. MSS. *softnede . . . prikkith.* Se[ʃ]
became less violent.
1940. *nought thi prowe,* not to thy advan[t];

And I answerid ful hombly :
'Gládly sir at youre biddyng
I wole me yelde in allé thyng ;
To youre servýse I wole me take,
For god defende that I shulde make
Ageyn youre biddyng résistence,
I wole not don so grete offence.   1950
For if I dide, it were no skile ;
Ye may do with me what ye wile,
Save or spille and also sloo.
Fro you in no wise may I goo,
My lyf, my deth is in youre honde,
I may not laste out of youre bonde ;
Pleyn at youre lyst I yeldé me,
Hopyng in herte that sumtyme ye
Comfort and esé shull me sende,
Or ellis shortly, this is the eende,   1960
Withouten helthe I mote ay dure,
But if ye take me to youre cure.
Comfort or helthe how shuld I have,
Sith ye me hurt, but ye me save ?
The helthe of lové mot be founde
Where as they token firste her wounde.
And if ye lyst of me to make
Youre prisoner, I wole it take
Of herte and willfully at gree ;
Hoolly and pleyn y yeldé me,   1970
Withouté feynyng or feyntise,
To be governed by youre emprise.
Of you I heré so mych pris,
I wole ben hool at youre devis
Forto fulfillé youre lykyng,
Aṅd repenté for no thyng,
Hopyng to have yit in some tide
The mercy of that I abide.'
And with that covenaunt yelde I me,
Anoon down knelyng upon my kne,   1980
Proferyng forto kisse his feete.
But for no thyng he wolde me lete,
And seide, 'I love thee bothe and preise,
Sens that thyn answer doth me ese,
For thou answerid so curteisly.
For now I wote wel uttirly

That thou art gentyll by thi speche ;
For, though a man fer woldé seche,
He shulde not fynden in certeyn
No sich answer of no vileyn,   1990
For sich a word ne myghté nought
Iſse out of a vilayns thought.
Thou shalt not lesen of thi speche,
For [to] thy helpyng wole I eche,
And eke encresen that I may.
But first I wole that thou obaye
Fúlly for thyn avauntage,
Anoon to do me heere homage ;
And sithé kisse thou shalt my mouthe,
Which to no vilayn was never couthe
Forto aproche it ne forto touche.   2001
For sauff of cherlis I ne vouche
That they shull never neigh it nere ;
For curteis and of faire manere,
Well taught and full of gentilnesse,
He musté ben that shal me kysse ;
And also of full high fraunchise,
That shal atteyne to that emprise.
And first of o thing warne I thee,
That peyne and gret adversite   2010
He mote endure, and eke travaile,
That shal me serve withouté faile.
But ther ageyns thee to comforte,
And with thi servise to desporte,
Thou mayst full glad and joyfull be
So good a maister to have as me,
Aṅd lord of so high renoun.
I bere of love the gonfenoun,
Of curtesié the banere.
For I am of the silf manere,   2020
Géntil, curteys, meke, and fre,
Thát who ever ententyf be
Mé to honouré, doute, and serve,
Néde is that he hym observe
Fro trespasse and fro vilanye,
And hym governe in curtesie
With will and with entencioun.
For whanne he first in my prisoun
Is caught, thanne must he uttirly
Fro thennes forth full bisily   2030

1960. *this is*, pronounce 'this.'
1965. Cp. note to 1540.
1976. Fr. 'Ge ne m'en puis de riens doloir.'
Perhaps *Me repente*.
1978. MSS. *Mercy;* but Fr. 'la merci que j'entens.'
1983. Fr. 'moult.' So probably *mocke* instead of *bothe*.

2016. Read *t' have.*
2024. *Nede is*, MSS. *And also.* 'Dedans lui ne puet demorer Vilonnie ne mesprison Ne nule mauvese aprison.' 'Aprison,' instruction, seems to have been confused with 'aprisonner,' 'to make prisoner,' hence vv. 2028-2032, to which there is nothing corresponding in Fr.

Cáste hym gentyll forto bee
If he desiré helpe of me.'
Anoon withouté more delay,
Withouten daunger or affray,
I bicome his man anoon,
And gave hym thankés many a oon,
And knelide doun with hondis joynt,
And made it in my port full quoint.
The joye wente to myn herté rote,   2039
Whanne I hadde kissed his mouth so swote;
I hadde sich myrthe and sich likyng
It curéd me of langwisshing.
He askide of me thanne hostages.
'I have,' he seide, 'taken fele homages
Of oon and other, where I have bene
Disceyved ofte withouten wene.
These felouns full of falsite
Have many sithes biguyléd me,
And through falshede her lust achieved,
Wherof I repente and am agreved.   2050
And I hem gete in my daungere,
Her falshede shull they bie full dere!
But for I love thee, I seie thee pleyn,
I wole of thee be more certeyn.
For thee so sore I wole now bynde,
That thou away ne shalt not wynde
Forto denyen the covenaunt
Or don that is not avenaunt.
That thou were fals it were gret reuthe,
Sith thou semest so full of treuthe.'   2060
'Sire, if thee lyst to undirstande,
I mérveile the askyng this demande.
For why or wherfore shuldé ye
Ostáges, or borwis aske of me,
Or ony other sikirnesse,
Sith ye wote in sothfastnesse
That ye have me suppriséd so,
And hole myn herté taken me fro,
That it wole do for me no thing
But if it be at youre biddyng;   2070
Myn herte is youres and myn right nought
As it bihoveth in dede and thought,
Rédy in all to worche youre will,
Whéther so turne to good or ill.
So sore it lustith you to plese,
No man therof may you desese.

Ye have theron sette sich justice,
That it is werreid in many wise.
And if ye doute it nolde obeye,
Ye may therof do make a keye,   2080
And holde it with you for ostage.'
'Now certis this is noon outrage,'
Quod Love, 'and fully I acorde;
For of the body he is full lord
That hath the herte in his tresour;
Outrage it were to asken more.'
Thanne of his awmener he drough
A litell keye, fetys ynowgh,
Which was of gold polisshéd clere;   2089
And seide to me, 'With this keye heere
Thyn herte to me now wole I shette:
For all my jowell, loke and knette,
I bynde undir this litel keye,
That no wight may carie aweye.
This keye is full of gret poste.'
With which anoon he touchide me
Under the side full softily,
That he myn herté sodeynly
Without anoyé haddé spered,   2009
That yit right nought it hath me dered.
Whanne he hadde don his will al oute,
And I hadde putte hym out of doute,
'Sire,' I seide, 'I have right gret wille
Youre lust and plesaunce to fulfille.
Loke ye my servise take atte gree
By thilké feith ye owe to me.
I seye nought for recreaundise,
For I nought doute of youre servise,
But the servaunt traveileth in vayne,
That forto serven doth his payne   2111
Unto that lord which in no wise
Kan hym no thank for his servyse.'
Lóvé seide, 'Dismaie thee nought,
Syn thou for sokour hast me sought:
In thank thi servise wole I take
And high of gre I wole thee make,
If wikkidnesse ne hyndre thee;
But as I hope it shal nought be,
To worshipe no wight by aventure
May come, but if he peyne endure: 2121
Abide and suffre thy distresse
That hurtith now; it shal be lesse.

2038. *it in*, (?) *in it*, *i.e.* in doing it.
2051. *And*, if.
2051. *in my daungere*; cp. v. 1470.
2074. *Whether*, monosyllable 'wher'; cp. 2128.

2077. *justice*, punishment.
2078. *werreid*, persecuted; cp. vv.
6264, 6926.
2084, 2085. Cp. vv. 1794 ff.
2116. MSS. *degre*.

I wote my silf what may thee save,
What medicyne thou woldist have ;
And if thi trouthe to me thou kepe,
I shal unto thyn helpyng eke,
To cure thy woundes and make hem clene,
Where so they be olde or grene ;
Thou shalt be holpen at wordis fewe.
For certeynly thou shalt well shewe 2130
Where that thou servest with good wille
Forto accomplysshen and fulfille
My comaundèmentis day and nyght
Whiche I to lovers yeve of right.'
' Ah Sire, for goddis love,' seide I,
' Er ye passe hens ententyfly,
Youre comaundèmentis to me ye say,
And I shall kepe hem if I may.
For hem to kepen is all my thought.
And if so be I wote hem nought, 2140
Thanne may I [erre] unwityngly.
Wherfore I pray you entierly,
With all myn hertè me to lere,
That I trespasse in no manere.'
The God of Love thanne chargide me,
Anoon as ye shall here and see,
Worde by worde by right emprise,
So as the Romance shall devise.
The maister lesith his tyme to lere
Whanne the disciple wole not here ; 2150
It is but veyn on hym to swynke
That on his lernyng wole not thynke.
Who so luste love, late hym entende,
For now the Romance bigynneth to
          amende ;
Now is good to here in fay
If ony be that can it say,
And poynte it as the resoun is.
Set forth [an] other gate ywys,
It shall nought well in allè thyng
Be brought to good undirstondyng. 2160
For a reder that poyntith ille
A good sentence may oftè spille.
The book is good at the eendyng
Màad of newe and lusty thyng.

For who so wole the eendyng here,
The crafte of love he shall mowe lere,
If that ye wole so long abide
Tyl I this Romance may unhide,
Añd undo the signifiance
Óf this dreme into Romance. 2170
The sothfastnesse that now is hidde
Without coverture shall be kidde,
Whanne I undon have this dremyng,
Wherynne no word is of lesyng.
  'Vylanye at the bigynnyng
I wole,' sayde Love, ' over alle thyng
Thou levè, if thou wolt nought be
Fáls and trespasse ageyns me.
I curse and blamè generaly
All hem that loven vilanye. 2180
For vilanye makith vilayn,
And by his dedis a cherle is seyn.
Thise vilayns arn withouten pitee,
Fréndshipe, love, and all bounte.
I nyl resseyve unto my servise
Hem that ben vilayns of emprise.
But undirstonde in thyn entent
That this is not myn entendement,
To clepe no wight in noo ages
Oonly gentill for his lynages. 2190
But who so [that] is vertuous,
And in his port nought outrageous,
Whanne sich oon thou seest thee biforn,
Thóugh he be not gentill born,
Thou maist well seyn this is in soth,
That he is gentil by cause he doth
As longeth to a gentilman,
Of hym noon other deme I can.
For certeynly withouten drede
A cherle is demèd by his dede 2200
Of hie or lowe, as ye may see,
Or of what kynrede that he bee.
Ne say nought, for noon yvel wille,
Thyng that is to holden stille ;
It is no worshipe to mysseye,
Thou maist ensample take of Keye,
That was somtyme, for mysseiyng,
Háted bothe of olde and ying.
As fer as Gaweyn the worthy
Was preisèd for his curtesie, 2210
Kay was hated, for he was fell,

2141. *erre* (MSS. omit), 'issir de la voie'
(Urry's emendation).
2149-2152. Should come after 2144 if we follow
Fr. original.
2154. *bigynneth to amende.* If the reading of
the text is retained it must be *gynnith t'amende.*
As Fr. is 'des or amende,' perhaps we should
read *wole amende.*

2185-2202. Not in Fr. It bears some resemblance to *Cant. Tales*, D 1109.
2188. *this is*, read *this.*

Of word dispitous and cruell.
Wherfore be wise and aqueyntable,
Goodly of word and resonable,
Bothe to lesse and eke to mare.
And whanne thou comest there men are,
Loke that thou have in custome ay
First to salue hym, if thou may ;
And if it fall that of hem somme
Salue thee first, be not domme,　　　2220
But quyte hym curteisly anoon,
Without abidyng, er they goon.
For no thyng eke thy tunge applye
To speke wordis of rebaudrye ;
To vilayne speche in no degre
Late never thi lippe unbounden be,
For I nought holde hym, in good feith,
Curteys that foule wordis seith.
And alle wymmen serve and preise,
And to thy power her honour reise ;　2230
And if that ony myssaiere
Dispise wymmen, that thou maist here,
Blame hym and bidde hym holde hym stille.
And set thy myght, and all thy wille,
Wymmen and ladies forto please,
And to do thyng that may hem ese,
That they ever speke good of thee ;
For so thou maist best preised be.
Loke fro pride thou kepe thee wele,
For thou maist bothe perceyve and fele,
That pride is bothe foly and synne.　2241
And he that pride hath hym withynne,
Ne may his herte in no wise
Meken ne souplen to servyse.
For pride is founde in every part
Contrarie unto loves art,
And he that loveth trew[e]ly
Shulde hym contene jolily
Withoute pride in sondry wise,
And hym disgysen in queyntise ;　　2250
For queynte array withoute drede
Is no thyng proude, who takith hede ;
For fresh array, as men may see,
Withoute pride may ofte be.
Mayntene thy silf aftir thi rent,
Of robe and eke of garnement ;
For many sithe faire clothyng
A man amendith in mych thyng.
And loke alwey that they be shape,
What garnement that thou shalt make,

2230. *to thy power*, according to thy power.

Of hym that kan [hem] beste do　　2261
With all that perteyneth therto.
Poyntis and sleves be well sittande,
Right and streght on the hande ;
Of shone and bootes newe and faire,
Loke at the leest thou have a paire,
And that they sitte so fetisly,
That these ruyde may uttirly
Merveyle, sith that they sitte so pleyn,
How they come on or off ageyn.　　2270
Were streite gloves with awmere
Of silk, and alwey with good chere
Thou yeve, if thou have [gret] richesse ;
And if thou have nought, spende the lesse.
Alwey be mery, if thou may,
But waste not thi good alway.
Have hatte of floures as fresh as May,
Chapelett of roses of Wissonday ;
For sich array ne costneth but lite.
Thyn hondis wasshe, thy teeth make white,
And lete no filthe upon thee bee ;　　2281
Thy nailes blak if thou maist see,
Voide it awey delyverly ;
And kembe thyn heed right jolily.
Farce not thi visage in no wise,
For that of love is not themprise,
For love doth haten, as I fynde,
A beaute that cometh not of kynde.
Alwey in herte, I rede thee,
Glad and mery forto be ;　　　　2290
And be as joyfull as thou can,
Love hath no joye of sorowful man.
That yvell is full of curtesie
That lowith in his maladie.
For ever of love the sikenesse
Is meynde with swete and bitternesse.
The sore of love is merveilous,
For now [is] the lover joyous,
Now can he pleyne, now can he grone,
Now can he syngen, now maken mone ;
To day he pleyneth for hevynesse,　2301
To morowe he pleyeth for jolynesse.
The lyf of love is full contrarie,
Which stounde-mele can ofte varie.

2271. *awmere*, same as *awmener*, v. 208 above.
2273. MSS. omit *gret* ; Fr. ' grant richesse.'
2285. *Farce*, paint ; variant form of *farde*.
2293. *That yvell*, that sick man.
2294. MSS. *knowith*, but Fr. ' L'en en nt (Kal.).
2302. *pleyeth*, MSS. *pleyneth*.

Bút if thou canst mirthis make,
That men in gre wole gladly take,
Do it goodly, I comaunde thee.
For men shulde, where so evere they be,
Do thing that [to] hem sittyng is ;
For therof cometh good loos and pris.
Where-of that thou be vertuous   2311
Ne be not straunge ne daungerous,
For if that thou good ridere be,
Prike gladly that men may [the] se.
In armès also, if thou konne,
Pursue tyl thou a name hast wonne.
And if thi voice be faire and clere
Thóu shalt make [no] gret daungere
Whánne to synge they goodly prey,
It is thi worship fortobeye.   2320
Also to you it longith ay
To harpe and gitterne, daunce and play ;
For if he can wel foote and daunce,
It may hym greetly do avaunce.
Among eke, for thy lady sake.
Songes and complayntes [se] that thou make,
For that wole meven in her herte,
Whanne they reden of thy smerte.
Loke that no man for scarce thee holde,
For that may greve thee many folde ;
Resoun wole that a lover be   2331
In his yiftes more large and fre
Than cherles that kan naught of lovyng.
For who therof can ony thyng,
He shall be leef ay forto yeve,
In lovès lore who so wolde leve.
For he that through a sodeyn sight,
Or for a kyssyng, anoon right
Yaff hoole his herte in will and thought,
And to hym silf kepith right nought,
Aftir swich gift is good resoun   2341
He yeve his good [al] in abandoun.
   Now wole I shortly heere reherce
Óf that I have seid in verce

Ál the sentence by and by,
In wordis fewe compendiously,
That thou the bet mayst on hem thynke,
Whether so it be thou wake or wynke.
Fór the wordis litel greve
A man to kepe, whanne it is breve.   2350
Who so with love wole goon or ride,
He mote be curteis and voide of pride,
Méry, and full of jolite,
And of largesse alosèd be.
Firste I joyne thee heere in penaunce
That evere, withoutè répentaunce,
Thou sette thy thought in thy lovyng
To laste withoutè répentyng,
And thenke upon thi myrthis swete,
That shall folowe aftir, whan ye mete.
And for thou trewe to love shalt be,   2361
Í wole, and comaundé thee
That in oo place thou sette all hoole
Thyn herte, withoutè halfen doole
Of trecherie and sikernesse ;
For I lovede nevere doublenesse.
To many his herte that wole departe,
Everiche shal have but litel parte ;
But of hym drede I me right nought
That in oo placè settith his thought.   2370
Tĥerfore in oo place it sette,
And lat it nevere thennys flette.
For if thou yevest it in lenyng,
I holde it but a wrecchid thyng.
Therfore yeve it hoole and quyte,
And thou shalt have the more merite ;
If it be lent, than aftir soone
The bounte and the thank is doone,
Bút in love fre yeven thing
Requyrith a gret guerdonyng.   2380
Yeve it in yift al quyte fully,
And make thi yifte debonairly,
For men that yifte holde morè dere
That yeven [is] with gladsome chere.
Tĥat yifte nought to preisen is
Thát man yeveth maugre his.
Whanne thou hast yeven thyn herte, as I
Have seid [to] thee heere openly,
Thanne áventurès shull thee fall

2311. *vertuous*, skilled.
2323. *he*, indefinite.
2323. *foote*. Kal. suggests *flout* because *foot* (saltare) is a later word.
2325. *Among*, i.e. from time to time.
2333. MSS. *ben not*. See next verse.
2336. MSS. *londes*.
2341. *swich gift*, Kal. for *this swifft it* of MSS. Perhaps *After so riche gift*, Fr. ' Apres si riche don.'
2342. MSS. omit *al*. Fr. ' tout a bandon.'

2349. *wordis*, perhaps read *word is*, 'la parole.'
2355. *joyne*, enjoin. MSS. *that heere*, but Fr. ' t'enjoing en penitence.'
2365. *Of trecherie*, etc. (MSS. *For trecherie*), i.e. half treacherous, half faithful.
2386. *maugre his*, in spite of himself.

Which harde and hevy ben with-all. 2390
For ofte, whan thou bithenkist thee
Of thy lovyng, where so thou be,
Fro folk thou must departe in hie,
That noon perceyve thi maladie.
But hyde thyne harme thou must alone,
And go forthe sole, and make thy mone.
Thou shalte no whyle be in o state,
But whylom colde and whilom hate,
Nowe reed as rose, now yelowe and fade.
Suche sorowe I trowe thou never hade ;
Cótidien, ne quarteyne,   2401
It is nat so ful of peyne.
For often tymès it shal fal
In love, among thy paynès al,
That thou thy selfè al holy
Foryeten shalte so utterly,
That many tymès thou shalte be
Stýl as an ymage of tree,
Domme as a stone, without steryng
Of fote or honde, without spekyng. 2410
Than, soone after al thy payne,
To memorye shalte thou come agayne,
A man abasshèd wonder sore,
And after syghen more and more.
For wytte thou wele, withouten wene,
In suche astate ful ofte have bene,
That have the yvel of love assayde,
Whérthrough thou arte so dismayde.
After a thought shal take the so,
That thy love is to ferre the fro ;   2420
Thou shalte saye "God ! What may this be
That I ne maye my lady se ?
Myne herte alone is to her go,
And I abyde al sole in wo,
Departed fro myne ownè thought,
And with myne eyen se right nought.
Alas ! myne eyen send I ne may
My careful hertè to convay !
Myne hertès gydè but they be,
I prayse nothyng what ever they se. 2430
Shul they abydè than ? nay,
But gone visyte without delay,
Thát myne herte desyreth so.
For certainly, but if they go,
A foole my selfe I maye wel holde,

2395-2442. Thynne is the only authority here,
the MS. lacking a leaf.
2416. Subject omitted as in 2367.
2427. Th. *sene* for *send*; Fr. 'envoier.'
2432. Th. *gone and visyten.*

Whan I ne se what myne hert wolde.
Wherfore I wol gone her to sene,
For eased shal I never bene,
Bút I have some tokenyng."
Than gost thou forthe without dwellyng.
But ofte thou faylest of thy desyre,   2441
Er thou mayst come her any nere,
And wastest in vayn thi passage.
Thanne fallest thou in a newè rage ;
For want of sight, thou gynnest morne.
And homewarde pensyf thou dost retorne.
In greet myscheef thanne shalt thou bee,
For thanne agayne shall come to thee
Síghes and pleyntes with newè woo,
Thát no yecchyng prikketh soo.   2450
Who wote it nought, he may go lere
Of hem that biën love so dere.
No thyng thyn herte appesen may
That ofte thou wole goon and assay,
If thou maist seen by aventure
Thi lyvès joy, thine hertis cure.
So that bi gracè if thou myght
Atteyne of hire to have a sight,
Thanne shalt thou done noon other dede.
But with that sight thyne eyen fede.   2460
That fairè fresh whanne thou maist see,
Thyne hertè shall so ravysshed be,
That nevere thou woldest, thi thankis, lete
Ne rémove forto see that swete.
The more thou seest, in sothfastnesse,
The more thou coveytest of that swetnesse :
The more thine hertè brenneth in fier,
The more thine herte is in desire.
For who considreth everydeell,
It may be likned wondir well   2470
The peyne of love unto a fere.
For evermore thou neighest nere,
Thou or whoo so that it bee,
For verray sothe I tell it thee,
The hatter evere shall thou brenne,
As experiencè shall thee kenne.
Where so comest in ony coost,
Who is next fuyre he brenneth moost.
And yitt forsothe for all thine hete,
Though thou for lovè swelte and swete.
Ne for no thyng thou felen may,   248.
Thou shalt not willen to passen away.

2463. *thi thankis,* willingly.
2477. Supply *thou.*
2478. *next,* nearest.

And though thou go, yitt must thee nede
Thenke allé day on hir fairhede,
Whom thou biheelde with so good wille,
And holde thi silf biguyléd ille
That thou ne haddest noon hardément
To shewe hir ought of thyne entent.
Thyn herte full sore thou wolt dispise,
And eke repreve of cowardise,   2490
That thou, so dulle in every thing,
Were domme for drede withoute spekyng.
Thou shalt eke thenke thou didest folye,
That thou were hir so fasté bye,
And durst not auntre thee to say
Sóm thyng er thou cam away.
Fór thou haddist nomore wonne,
To speke of hir whanne thou bigonne,
But yitt she woldé, for thy sake,
In armés goodly thee have take,   2500
It shulde have be more worth to thee
Thán of tresour gret plente.
Thus shalt thou morne and eke compleyne,
And gete enchesoun to goone ageyne
Unto the walke, or to the place
Where thou biheelde hir fleshly face.
And never, for fals suspeccioun,
Thou woldest fynde occasioun
Fórto gone unto hire hous.
Só art thou thanne desirous   2510
Á sight of hir forto have,
If thou thine honour myghtist save,
Or ony erande myghtist make,
Thíder for thi lovés sake
Full fayn thou woldist, but for drede
Thou gost not, lest that men take hede.
Wherfore I red [the] in thi goyng
And also in thyne ageyn comyng,
Thou be well ware that men ne wite ;
Feyne thee other cause than itte   2520
To go that weye or fasté bye ;
To helé wel is no folye.
And if so be it happé thee,
That thou thi lové there maist see,
In siker wise thou hir salewe,
Wherewith thi colour wole transmewe,
And eke thy blode shal alto quake,
Thyne hewe eke chaungen for hir sake ;

But word and witte with chere full pale
Shull wante [the] forto tell thy tale. 2530
And if thou maist so fer forth wynne,
That thou [thi] resoun dorst bigynne,
And woldist seyn thre thingis or mo,
Thou shalt full scarsly seyn the two.
Though thou bithenke thee never so well,
Thou shalt foryeté yit somdell,
But if thou dele with trecherie ;
For fals lovers mowe all folye
Seyn what hem lust withouten drede,
They be so double in her falshede ; 2540
For they in herte cunne thenke a thyng,
And seyn another in her spekyng.
And whanne thi speche is eendid all,
Ryght thus to thee it shall byfall,
If ony word thanne come to mynde
That thou to seye hast left bihynde.
Thanne thou shalt brenne in gret martire,
For thou shalt brenne as ony fiere,
This is the stryf and eke the affray,
And the batell that lastith ay ;   2550
This bargeyn eende may never take,
But if that she thi pees will make.
And whanne the nyght is comen anoon,
A thousande angres shall come uppon.
To bedde as fast thou wolt thee dight,
Where thou shalt have but smal delite ;
For whanne thou wenest forto slepe
So full of peyné shalt thou crepe,
Sterte in thi bedde aboute full wide,
And turne full ofte on every side,   2560
Now dounward groff and now upright,
And walowe in woo the longé nyght ;
Thine armys shalt thou sprede abrede
As man in werre were forwerede.
Thanne shall thee come a remembraunce
Óf hir shappe and hir semblaunce,
Whereto none other may be pere.
And wite thou wel withouté were,
That thee shal [seme] somtyme that nyght
That thou hast hir, that is so bright, 2570
Naked bitwene thyne armés there,
All sothfastnesse as though it were.
Thou shalt make castels thanne in Spayne
And dreme of joye, all but in vayne,
And thee deliten of right nought,

2497. The French suggests that we should
supply *though* before *thou* and read *that* for *yitt*
in v. 2499.
  2517. Cp. *I rede the* in v. 2856.
  2522. *hele*, conceal.

2530. Fr. 'Parole te faudra.'
2551. *bargeyn*, strife ; Kaluza changes to *batail*.
2564. Fr. 'Com fait homs qui a mal a dens.'

While thou so slomrest in that thought,
That is so swete and delitable ;
The which in soth[é] nys but sable,
For it ne shall no whilé laste.
Thanne shalt thou sighe and wepé faste
And say, "Dere god, what thing is
    this ?   2581
My dreme is turned all amys,
Which was full swete and apparent ;
But now I wake, it is al shent !
How yede this mery thought away !
Twenty tymes upon a day
I wolde this thought wolde come ageyne,
For it aleggith well my peyne ;
It makith me full of joyfull thought.
It sleth me that it lastith noght   2590
A lord, why nyl ye me socoure
Fro joye ? I trowe that I langoure ;
The deth I wolde me shuldé sloo
While I lye in hir armés twoo.
Myne harme is harde, withouten wene,
My gret unease full ofte I meene.
But woldé love do so I myght
Have fully joye of hir so bright,
My peyne were quytte me rychély.
Allas, to grete a thing aske I !   2600
Hit is but foly and wrong wenyng
To aske so outrageous a thyng ;
And who so askith folily,
He mote be warned hastily.
And I ne wote what I may say,
I am so fer out of the way.
For I wolde have full gret likyng
And full gret joye of lassé thing ;
For wolde she of hir gentylnesse
Withouté more me oonys kysse,   2610
It were to me a grete guerdoun,
Relees of all my passioun.
But it is harde to come therto,
All is but folye that I do ;
So high I have myne herté sette
Whére I may no comfort gette ;
I not where I seye well or nought,
But this I wote wel in my thought,
That it were better of hir alloone,
Fórto stynte my woo and moone,   2620

A loke on me I-caste goodly,
Than forto have al utterly
Of an other all hoole the pley.
A lord, where I shall byde the day
That evere she shall my lady be ?
He is full cured that may hir see.
A god, whanne shal the dawnyng springe ?
To lye thus is an angry thyng ;
I have no joye thus heere to lye
Whanne that my love is not me bye.   2630
A man to lye hath gret disese,
Which may not slepe ne reste in ese.
I wolde it dawed and were now day,
And that the nyght were went away ;
For were it day I wolde uprise.
A slowé sonne, shewe thine enprise !
Spede thee to sprede thy beemys bright,
And chace the derknesse of the nyght,
To putte away the stoundés stronge,
Whiche in me lasten all to longe !"   2640
The nyght shalt thou contené soo
Withouté rest, in peyne and woo.
If evere thou knewe of love distresse,
Thou shalt mowe lerne in that sicknesse,
And thus enduryng shalt thou lye,
And ryse on morwé up erly
Out of thy bedde, and harneyse thee,
Er evere dawnyng thou maist see.
All pryvyly thanne shall thou goon,
What weder it be, thi silf alloon,   2650
For reyne or hayle, for snowe, for slete,
Thider she dwellith that is so swete.
The which may fall a-slepé be,
And thenkith but lytel upon thee.
Thanne shalt thou goon ful foule a-feerd
Loke if the gaté be unspered,
And waite without in woo and peyne,
Full yvel acoolde, in wynde and reyne.
Thanne shal thou go the dore bifore,
If thou maist fyndé ony score,   2660
Or hoole, or reeft what evere it were.
Thanne shalt thou stoupe, and lay to ere.

2585. *How,* MSS. *Now.*
2592. *Fro joye,* MSS. *The joye,* which Skeat
retains, construing as object of *languor;* but
'langour' is not used in this sense.
2617. MSS. *wote not.*
2621. MSS. *on hir I-caste.* Skeat proposed the
reading in the text ; ? read *of hir.*
2624. *where,* whether ; introducing a direct
question.
2628. *lye,* MSS. *liggen,* but cp. rhymes in vv.
2629, 2630 ; 2645, 2646.
2631. *to lye, i.e.* in lying down.
2641. *contene,* continue ; but Fr. 'te contendras'
may have been rendered *contende.*
2650. *weder,* MSS. *whider,* Skeat's correction

f they withynne a-slepe be—
mene all save the lady free.
Whom wakyng if thou maist aspie,
Go putte thi-silf in jupartie,
To aske grace, and thee bimene,
That she may wite withoute wene
That thou [a-]nyght no rest hast hadde,
So sore for hir thou were bystadde ; 2670
Wommen wel ought pite to take
Of hem that sorwen for her sake.
And loke, for love of that relyke,
That thou thenke noon other lyke ;
For whanne thou hast so gret annoy,
Shall kysse thee er thou go away,
And holde that in full gret deynte.
And for that noman shal thee see
Bifore the hous, ne in the way,
Loke thou be goone ageyn er day.   2680
  Such comyng and such goyng,
Such hevynesse and such wakyng
Makith lovers, withouten wene,
Under her clothes pale and lene.
For love leveth colour ne cleernesse,
Who loveth trewe hath no fatnesse ;
Thou shalt wel by thy-silf [y-]see
That thou must nedis assaied be ;
For men that shape hem other weye
Falsly her ladyes to bitraye,   2690
It is no wonder though they be fatt,
With false othes her loves they gatt.
For oft I see suche losengours
Fatter than abbatis or priours.
It with o thing I thee charge,
That is to seye that thou be large
Unto the mayde that hir doith serve,
So best hir thanke thou shalt deserve.
Yéve hir yiftes, and gete hir grace,
For so thou may thank purchace,   2700
That she thee worthy holde and free,
Thi lady, and all that may thee see.
Also hir servauntes worshipe ay,
And please as mych as thou may ;
Grete good through hem may come to thee

Bi-cause with hir they ben pryve ;
They shal hir telle hoe they thee fande
Curteis, and wys, and well doande,
And she shall preise well the mare.
Loke oute of londe thou be not fare,   2710
And if such cause thou have that thee
Bihoveth to gone out of contree,
Leve hoole thin herte in hostage,
Till thou ageyn make thi passage.
Thenke longe to see the swete thyng,
That hath thine herte in hir kepyng.
Now have I tolde thee in what wise
A lovere shall do me servise ;
Do it thanne if thou wolt have
The meede that thou aftir crave.'   2720
Whanne Love all this hadde boden me,
I seide hym, ' Sire, how may it be
That lovers may in such manere
Endure the peyne ye have seid heere ?
I merveyle me wonder faste
How ony man may lyve or laste
In such peyne and [in] such brennyng ;
In sorwe and thought, and such sighing,
Aye unrelesed woo to make,
Whether so it be they slepe or wake,   2730
In such annoy contynuely,
As helpe me god, this merveile I
How man, but he were maad of stele,
Myght lyve a monthe such peynes to fele.'
  The God of Love thanne seide me,
' Freend, by the feith I owe to thee,
May no man have good but he it bye ;
A man loveth more tendirly
The thyng that he hath bought most
            dere.
For wite thou well, withouten were,   2740
In thanke that thyng is taken more
For which a man hath suffred sore.
Certis no wo ne may atteyne
Unto the sore of loves peyne ;
Noon yvel therto ne may amounte,
Nomore than a man [may] counte
The dropes that of the water be.
For drye as well the greete see
Thou myghtist, as the harmes telle
Of hem that with love dwelle   2750
In servyse ; for peyne hem sleeth,
And yet ech man wolde fle the deeth.

2669. a-nyght, MSS. nyght.
2673. ' Por l'amor du haut seintueire' ; cp.
the similar use of relyk in v. 2907.
2676. The Fr. directs the lover to kiss the door
before leaving ; so Kaluza reads wham for whan
in verse above, and suggests Thou kisse the dore
er thou go away for v. 2676.
2704. Read mychel, or insert ever before may.
2709. Perhaps insert thee before well.
2752. yet, ' toutes voies,' MSS. that.

And trowe thei shulde nevere escape,
Neré that hope couthe hem make
Glád, as man in prisoun sett,
And may not geten forto ete
But barly breed and watir pure,
And lyeth in vermyn and in ordure ;
Wíth all this yitt can he lyve,
Good hope such comfort hath hym yive,
Which maketh wene that he shall be   2761
Delyvered and come to liberte.
Iń fortune is [his] full trust,
Thóugh he lye in strawe or dust ;
In hoope is all his susteynyng.
And so for lovers in her wenyng,
Whiche Love hath shitte in his prisoun,
Good hope is her salvacioun.
Good hope how soré that they smerte
Yeveth hem bothé will and herte   2770
To profre her body to martire ;
For hope so sore doith hem desire
To suffre ech harme that meń devise
For joye that aftirward shall aryse.
Hope in desire hathe victorie,
In hope of love is all the glorie,
For hope is all that love may yive ;
Nere hope ther shulde no lover lyve.
Blessid be hope, which with desire
Avaunceth lovers in such manere !   2780
Good hope is curteis forto please,
To kepe lovers from all disese ;
Hope kepith his bonde, and wole abide
For ony perill that may betyde ;
For hope to lovers, as most cheef,
Doth hem enduré all myscheef ;
Hope is her helpe whanne myster is.
  And I shall yeve thee eke I-wys
Three other thingis, that gret solas
Doith to hem that be in my las.   2790
The firsté good that may be founde
To hem that in my lace be bounde
Is Sweté Thought, forto recorde
Tḱing wherwith thou canst accorde
Best in thyne herte, where she be.

Thenkyng in absence is good to thee.
Whanne ony lover doth compleyne,
And lyveth in distresse and in peyne,
Thanne Sweté-Thought shal come as blyve
Awey his angre forto dryve.   2800
It makith lovérs to have remembraunce,
Of comfort and of high plesaunce,
That hope hath hight hym forto wynne.
For Thought anoon thanne shall bygynne,
As ferre, god wote, as he can fynde,
To make a mirrour of his mynde ;
Forto biholde he wole not lette.
Hir persone he shall afore hym sette,
Hir laughing eyen, persaunt and clere,
Hir shappe, hir fourme, hir goodly chere :
Hir mouth, that is so gracious,   2811
So swete and eke so saverous ;
Of all hir fetures he shall take heede,
His eyen with all hir lymés fede.
Thus Sweté-Thenkyng shall aswage
The peyne of lovers and her rage.
Thi joye shall double withouté gesse
Whanne thou thenkist on hir semlynesse.
Or of hir laughing, or of hir chere
That to thee made thi lady dere.   2820
This comfort wole I that thou take ;
And if the next thou wolt forsake,
Which is not lessé saverous,
Thou shuldist ben to daungerous.
  The secounde shal be Sweté-Speche.
That hath to many oon be leche
To bringe hem out of woo and were,
And holpé many a bachilere,
And many a lady sent socoure,
Thát have lovéd paramour,   2830
Through spekyng whanne they myght heer
Of hir lovers, to hem so dere.
To hem it voidith all her smerte,
The which is closéd in her herte ;
In herte it makith hem glad and light.
Speche, whanne they mowe have [no] sight.
And therfore now it cometh to mynde
In oldé dawés, as I fynde,
That clerkis writen that hir knewe ;
Ther was a lady, fresh of hewe,   2840
Which of hir lové made a songe,

2753. *And trowe*, i.e. I trowe ; cp. vv. 2756, 2758.
2775. *hathe*, MSS. *cacche* ; 'Esperance par soffrir vaint.' Skeat amends *to cacche*, taking *hope* as imperative.
2783. *bonde*, MSS. *londe*,

      Iceste te garantira,
      Ne ja de toi ne partire.

2796. Kal. reads *Thought* for *Thenkyng* ; cp. v. 2815.
2808. *he shall* ; cp. note to v. 2945.
2809. *eyen*, one syllable ; cp. vv. 2913, 2814
2824. MSS. *shuldest not*, 'seroies.'

On hym forto remembre amonge,
In which she seyde : "Whanne that I here
Speken of hym that is so dere,
To me it voidith allé smerte.
I-wys, he sittith so nere myne herte
To speke of hym at eve or morwe
It cureth me of all my sorwe.
To me is noon so high plesaunce
As of his persone dalyaunce." 2850
She wist full well that Swete-Spekyng
Comfortith in full myché thyng.
Hir love she hadde full well assaid,
Of him she was full well apaid ;
To speke of hym hir joye was sett.
Therfore I rede thee that thou gett
A felowe that can well concele,
And kepe thi counsell, and well hele,
To whom go shewe hoolly thine herte,
Bothe well and woo, joye and smerte ;
To gete comfort to hym thou goo, 2861
And pryvyly bitwene yow twoo
Yee shall speke of that goodly thyng,
That hath thyne herte in hir kepyng.
Of hir beaute, and hir semblaunce,
And of hir goodly countenaunce ;
Of all thi state, thou shalt hym seye,
And aske hym counseill how thou may
Do ony thyng that may hir plese ;
For it to thee shall do gret ese, 2870
That he may wite thou trust hym soo,
Bothe of thi wele and of thi woo.
And if his herte to love be sett,
His companye is myche the bett,
For resoun wole he shewe to thee
All uttirly his pryvyte,
And what she is he loveth so.
To thee pleynly he shall undo,
Withouté drede of ony shame,
Bothe tell hir renoun and hir name. 2880
Thanne shall he forther, ferre and nere,
And namely to thi lady dere.
In syker wise yee every other
Shall helpen, as his owne brother,
In trouthe withouté doublenesse,
And kepen cloos in sikernesse ;
For it is noble thing in fay
To have a man thou darst say
Thy pryvé counsell every deell ; 2889

2881. Then shall he go further, etc.
2888. (T) Supply *that* before *thou.*

For that wole comforte thee right well,
And thou shalt holde thee well apayed,
Whanne such a freend thou hast assayed.
The thriddé good of gret comforte,
That yeveth to lovers moste disporte,
Comyth of sight and of biholdyng,
That clepid is SWETÉ-LOKYNG.
The which may [thee] noon esé do
Whanne thou art fer thy lady fro.
Wherfore thou prese alwey to be
In placé where thou maist hir see. 2900
For it is thyng most amerous,
Most delytable and saverous,
Forto a-swage a mannès sorowe,
To sene his lady by the morwe.
For it is a full noble thing,
Whánne thyne eyen have metyng
With that relike precious
Wherof they be so désirous.
But al day after, soth it is,
They have no drede to faren amysse ; 2910
They dreden neither wynde ne reyne,
Né noon other maner peyne.
For whanne thyne eyen were thus in blisse,
Yit of hir curtesie, y-wysse,
Alloone they can not have her joye,
But to the herte they [it] convoye ;
Parte of her blisse to hym they sende,
Of all this harme to make an ende.
The eye is a good messangere,
Which can to the herte in such manere
Tidyngis sendé, that hath sene 2921
To voide hym of his peynès clene.
Wherof the herte rejoiseth soo,
That a gret partye of his woo
Is voided, and putte awey to flight,
Right as the derknesse of the nyght
Is chased with clerenesse of the mone,
Right so is al his woo full soone
Devoided clene, whanne that the sight
Biholden may that freshé wight 2930
Thát the herte desireth soo,
That al his derknesse is agoo.
For thanne the herte is all at ese,
Whanne the eyen sene that may hem plese.

2902. MSS. *favorous*, 'savorous.'
2917. *they*, MSS. *thou.*
2920. The verse is made smoother by placing
can after the first word of the next line.
2925. *voided*, (T) *void.*
2934. *the eyen*, 'll oel,' MSS. *they.*

Now have I declared thee all oute
Of that thou were in drede and doute,
For I have tolde thee feithfully
What thee may curen utterly.
And allé lovers that wole be
Feithfull and full of stabilite,   2940
Good hope alwey kepe bi thi side,
And Sweté-Thought, make eke abide ;
Sweté-Lokyng and Sweté-Speche.
Of all thyne harmes thei shall be leche :
Of every thou shalt have gret plesaunce,
If thou canst bidé in suffraunce,
And servé wel withoute feyntise ;
Thou shalt be quyte of thyne emprise
With more guerdoun, if that thou lyve,
But at this tyme this I thee yive.'   2950
The God of Love, whanne al the day
Had taught me as ye have herd say,
And enfourmed compendiously,
He vanyshide awey all sodeynly ;
And I allooné lefte all soole,
So full of compleynt and of doole,
For I sawe no man there me by.
My woundes me grevéd wondirly ;
Me forto curen no thyng I knewe
Sáve the bothon bright of hewe,   2960
Wheron was sett hoolly my thought.
Of other comfort knewe I nought,
But it were thrugh the God of Love.
I knewe not elles to my bihove
That myght me ease or comfort gete,
But if he wolde hym entermete.
The roser was withouté doute
Clósed with an haye withoute,
As ye toforn have herd me seyne.
And fast I bisiede, and wolde fayne   2970
Have passed the hay, if [that] I myght
Have geten ynne by ony slight
Unto the bothon so faire to see.
But evere I draddé blamed to be,
If men wolde have suspeccioun
That I wolde of entencioun
Have stole the roses that there were ;

2945. Of every, i.e. from each of them. Kaluza
omits gret, but two unaccented syllables, one of
which is shall, are not uncommon in the poem ;
cp. vv. 2808, 2813.
2950. at, 'des ore,' MSS. all.
2953. enfourmed. Perhaps supply me before
enfourmed.
2954. awey does not seem to belong to the verse.
2968. haye, MSS. hegge ; but cp. v. 3007.

Therfore to entre I was in fere.
But at the last, as I bithought,
Whéther I shulde passe or nought,   2980
I sawe come with a glad chere
To me a lusty bachelere,
Of good stature and of good hight ;
And BIALACOIL forsothe he hight,
Sóne he was to Curtesie.
And he me grauntide full gladly
The passage of the outter hay,
And séidè 'Sir, how that yee may
Pásse, if [that] youre willé be
The freshé roser forto see,   2990
And yee the sweté savour fele,
Yóu warranté may [I] right wele.
So thou thee kepé fro folye,
Shall no man do thee vylanye ;
If I may helpé you in ought,
I shall not feyné, dredeth nought,
For I am bounde to youre servise,
Fully devoide of feyntise.'
Thanne unto Bialacoil saide I :
'I thanke you, sir, full hertély   3000
And youre biheesté take at gre,
That ye so goodly profer me.
To you it cometh of gret fraunchise
That ye me profer youre servise.'
Thanne aftir, full delyverly,
Thorough the breres anoon wente I,
Wherof encombred was the hay.
I was wel plesed, the soth to say,
To se the bothon faire and swote
So freshé spronge out of the rote.   3010
And Bialacoil me servéd well
Whanne I so nygh me myghté fele
Of the bothon the swete odour
Ánd so lusty hewed of colour.
But thanne a cherle (foule hym bityde ?)
Biside the roses gan hym hyde,
To kepe the roses of that roser
Of whom the namé was DAUNGER.
This cherle was hid there in the greves,
Kovered with gras and with leves,   3020
To spie and take whom that he fonde
Unto that Roser putte an honde.
He was not soole, for ther was moo ;

2988. how, (?) now ; cp. v. 2585.
2992. MSS. Youre warrante, and omit I ; 'Ge
vous i puis bien garantir.'
2998. Possibly devoided ; but cp. v. 3723.
3001. biheest, with inorganic -e as in Chaucer

For with hym weré other twoo
Of wikkid maners and yvel fame.
That oon was clepid by his name
WÝKKED-TONGE (god yeve hym sorwe !),
For neither at evé ne at morwe
He can of no man good [ne] speke ;
On many a just man doth he wreke. 3030
Ther was a womman eke that hight
SHÁME, that, who can reken right,
Tréspace was hir fadir name,
Hir moder Resoun ; and thus was Shame
Brought of these ilké twoo.
And yitt hadde Trespasse never adoo
With Resoun, ne never ley hir bye
He was so hidous and so ugly,
I mené this that Trespas hight ;
But resoun conceyved of a sight 3040
Shame, of that I spake aforne.
And whanne that Shame was thus [y-] borne,
It was ordeynéd that CHASTITE
Shulde of the Roser lady be,
Which of the bothons more and lasse
With sondre folk assailéd was,
That she ne wisté what to doo.
For Venus hir assailith soo,
That nyght and day from hir she stale
Bothons and roses over-all. 3050
To Resoun thanne praieth Chastite,
Whom Venus hath flemed over the see,
That she hir doughter wolde hir lene,
To kepe the Roser fresh and grene.
Anoon Resoun to Chastite
Is fully assented that it be,
And grauntide hir at hir request
That Shame, by cause she is honest,
Shall keper of the roser be.
And thus to kepe it ther were three, 3060
That noon shulde hardy be ne bolde,
Were he yong or were he olde,
Ageyn hir will awey to bere
Bothons ne roses that there were.
I hadde wel spedde, hadde I not bene
Awayted with these three and sene.
For Bialacoil, that was so faire,
So gracious and debonaire,
Quytt hym to me full curteislye,

And me to pleasé, bade that I 3070
Shulde drawe me to the bothon nere ;
Prese in to touché the rosere
Which bare the roses, he yaf me leve ;
This graunte ne myght but lytel greve.
And for he sawe it liked me,
Ryght nygh the bothon pullede he
A leef all grene and yaff me that ;
The whiche full nygh the bothon sat,
I made [me] of that leef full queynte.
And whanne I felte I was aqueynte 3080
With Bialacoil, and so pryve,
I wende all at my will hadde be.
Thanne waxe I hardy forto telle
To Bialacoil how me bifelle
Of love, that toke and wounded me ;
And seidé : 'Sir, so mote I thee,
I may no joye have in no wise
Uppon no sidé, but it rise.
For sithens, if I shall not feyne,
In herte I have hadde so gret peyne, 3090
So gret annoy and such affray,
That I ne wote what I shall say,
I drede youre wrathé to disserve.
Lever me were that knyvés kerve
My body shulde in pecys small,
Than any weyes it shuldé fall
That ye wratthéd shulde ben with me.'
'Sey boldély thi will,' quod he,
'I nyl be wroth, if that I may, 3099
For nought that thou shalt to me say.'
Thanne seide I, 'Ser, not you displease
To knowen of myn gret unnese,
In which oonly love hath me brought.
For peynés gret, disese, and thought,
Fro day to day he doth me drye—
Supposeth not, sir, that I lye.
In me fyve woundés dide he make,
The soore of whiche shall nevere slake ;
But ye the Bothon graunté me
Which is moost passaunt of beaute, 3110
My lyf, my deth, and my martire,
And tresour, that I moost desire.'
Thanne Bialacoil, affrayéd all,
Seydé, 'Sir, it may not fall—
That ye desire, it may not arise.
What ! Wolde ye shende me in this wise ?

3038. 'Si hidous et si ley'; it would seem, therefore, as if second *so* belonged in text, and should not be omitted as Kaluza suggests.

3096. *any weyes*, MSS. *in any wise* (Kaluza). 3115. *arise*, cp. 3088; perhaps originally *arive*, with assonance.

A mochel foolé thanne I were,
If I suffride you awey to bere
The fresh bothoun so faire of sight.
For it were neither skile ne right,   3120
Of the roser ye broke the rynde,
Or take the rose aforn his kynde ;
Ye are not curteys to aske it.
Late it still on the roser sitt,
And growe til it amended be
And parfytly come to beaute ;
I nolde not that it pulléd were
Fró the roser that it bere,
To me it is so leef and deere.'   3129
With that sterte oute anoon Daungere,
Out of the place were he was hidde ;
His malice in his chere was kidde.
Full grete he was and blak of hewe,
Stúrdy and hidous, who so hym knewe,
Like sharp urchouns his here was growe ;
His eyes reed as the fyré glowe,
His nosé frounced, full kirkéd stoode.
He come criande as he were woode,
And seide : 'Bialacoil, telle me why
Thou bryngest hider so booldely   3140
Hym that [is] so nygh the roser !
Thou worchist in a wrong manner ;
He thenkith to dishonoure thee.
Thou art wel worthy to have maugree,
To late hym of the roser wite ;
Who serveth feloun is yvel quitte.
Thou woldist have doon gret bounte,
And he with shame wolde quyté thee.
Fle hennés, Felowe ! I rede thee goo,
It wanteth litel I wole thee sloo ;   3150
For Bialacoil ne knewe thee nought,
Whanne thee to serve he sette his thought ;
For thou wolt shame hym, if thou myght,
Bóthe ageyns resoun and right.
I wole no more in thee affye,
That comest so slyghly for tespye ;
Fór it preveth wonder well
Thy sleight and tresoun every deell.'
I durst no more there make abode

3118. The verse would be smoother without *awey* ; cp. note to v. 2954.
3136. Only in Thynne, which reads *reed sparklingly* ; 's'ot les iex rouges comme feus.'
3137 *kirked*, 'froncie,' translated in v. 7259 'frouncen.' Morris suggested *kroked*, which Skeat thinks likely.
3150. *I*, Th. *he* ; Gl. *it* ; Fr. 'ge.

Fór the cherl, he was so wode ;   3160
So gan he threté and manace,
And thurgh the haye he dide me chace.
For feer of hym I tremblyde and quoke.
So cherlishly his heed it shoke ;
And seide, if eft he myght me take
I shulde not from his hondis scape.
Thanne Bialacoil is fledde and mate,
And I, all soole, disconsolate,
Was left aloone in peyne and thought.
For shame to deth I was nygh brought.
Thanne thought I on myn high foly,   3171
How that my body utterly
Was yeve to peyne and to martire ;
And therto hadde I so gret ire,
That I ne durst the hayé passe.
There was noon hope, there was no grace.
I trowe nevere man wiste of peyne,
But he were laced in lovés cheyne ;
Ne no man [not], and sooth it is,
But if he love, what anger is.   3180
Love holdith his heest to me right wele,
Whanne péyne he seide I shuldé fele.
Noon herte may thenke, ne tungé seyne
A quarter of my woo and peyne ;
I myght not with the anger laste.
Myn herte in poynt was forto brast,
Whanne I thought on the rose, that soo
Was thurgh Daunger cast me froo.
A longe while stode I in that state,   3189
Til that me saugh so madde and mate
The lady of the highe ward,
Which from hir tour lokide thiderward.
RESOUN men clepé that lady,
Which from hir tour delyverly,
Come doun to me withouté more.
But she was neither yong ne hoore,
Ne high ne lowe, ne fat ne lene,
But best as it were in a mene.
Hir eyen twoo were cleer and light
As ony candell that brenneth bright ;   3200
And in hir heed she hadde a crowne.
Hir semede wel an high persoune ;
For rounde enviroun hir crownet
Was full of riché stonys frett.
Hir goodly semblaunt by devys
I trowe were maad in Paradys ;
For nature hadde nevere such a grace
To forge a werk of such compace.

3175. MSS. *hayes*, 'la haie.'

or certeyn, but if the letter lye,
ód hym-silf, that is so high,   3210
áde hir aftir his ymage,
nd yaff hir sith sich avauntage,
hat she hath myght and seignorie
o kepé men from all folye.
Tho so wole trowe hir lore,
e may offenden nevermore.
   And while I stode thus derk and pale,
esoun bigan to me hir tale.
ıe seide : ' Al hayle, my swetė freende !
oly and childhoode wole thee sheende,
Thich the have putt in gret affray ;   3221
hou hast bought deere the tyme of May,
hat made thyn herte mery to be.
ı yvell tyme thou wentist to see
he gardyne, wherof Idilnesse
áre the keye and was maistresse,
Thánne thou yedest in the daunce
Tith hir, and haddest aqueyntaunce.
.ir aqueyntaunce is perilous,
irst softe and aftir noious ;   3230
ıe hath [thee] trasshed withoutė wene.
he God of Love hadde the not sene,
e hadde Idilnessé thee conveyed
ı the verger, where Myrthe hym pleyed.
˙ foly have supprisėd thee,
o so that it recovered be,
nd be wel ware to take nomore,
ounsel that greveth aftir sore.
.e is wise that wole hym-silf chastise ;
nd though a yong man in ony wise
respace amonge and do foly,   3241
ate hym not tarye, but hastily
ate hym amende what so be mys.
nd eke I counseile thee I-wys
he God of Love hoolly foryete,
hat hath thee in sich peynė sette,
nd thee in herte tourmented soo.
can not sene how thou maist goo
'ther weyės to garisoun ;
or Daunger that is so feloun   3250
elly purposith thee to werreye,
Thich is ful cruel, the soth to seye.
   And yitt of Daunger cometh no blame
ı réwarde of my doughter Shame,
Thich hath the roses in her warde,
.s she that may be no musarde.

3228. MSS. *hadde.*
3240. MSS. *in ony wise ;* cp. note to v. 3096.

And WIKKED-TUNGE is with these two,
That suffrith no man thider goo.
For er a thing be, do he shall,
Where that he cometh over-all,   3260
In fourty places, if it be sought,
Seye thyng that nevere was donne wrought ;
So moche tresoun is in his male,
Of falsnesse forto seyne a tale.
Thou delest with angry folk y-wis ;
Whérfore to thee bettir is
Fróm these folk awey to fare,
For they wole make thee lyve in care.
This is the yvell that love they calle,
Wherynne ther is but foly alle ;   3270
For love is foly everydell.
Who loveth in no wise may do well,
Ne sette his thought on no good werk.
His scole he lesith, if he be clerk ;
Of other craft eke if he be,
He shal not thryve therynne, for he
In love shal have more passioun
Than monkė, hermyte, or chanoun.
The peyne is hard out of mesure,
The joye may eke no while endure ;   3280
Añd in the possessioun,
Iś mych tribulacioun.
The joye it is so short lastyng,
And but in happe is the getyng.
For I see there many in travaill
That attė lastė foulė fayle.
I was no thyng thi counseler
Whanne thou were maad the omager
Of God of Love to hastily.
Ther was no wisdom, but foly ;   3290
Thyne herte was joly but not sage,
Whanne thou were brought in sich a rage,
To yeldė thee so redily.
   And to leve of his gret maistrie,
I rede thee Love awey to dryve,
That makith thee recche not of thi lyve.
The foly more fro day to day
Shal growe, but thou it putte away.
Take with thy teeth the bridel faste   3299
To daunte thyne herte, and eke thee caste,
If that thou maist gete thee defence,
Forto redresse thi first offence.
Who so his herte alwey wole leve
Shal fynde amonge that shal hym greve.'
   Whanne I hir herd thus me chastise,

3274. MSS. *a clerk;* Fr. 's'il est clers.'

I answerd in ful angry wise ;
I prayed hir ceessen of hir speche,
Outher to chastise me or teche,
To biddé me my thought refreyne,   3309
Which Love hath caught in his demeyne.
'What!   Wene ye Lové wole consente,
That me assailith with bowé bente,·
To drawe myne herte out of his honde,
Which is so qwikly in his bonde ?
That ye counseyle may nevere be ;
For whanne he firste arestide me,
He took myne herte so hoole hym tille,
That it is no thyng at my wille.
He taught it so hym forto obey,
That he it sparrede with a key.   3320
I pray yow late me be all stille,
For ye may well, if that ye wille,
Youre wordis waste in idilnesse.
For utterly, withouten gesse,
All that ye seyn is but in veyne.
Me were lever dye in the peyne,
Than Lové to-me-ward shulde arette
Falsheed, or tresoun on me sette.
I wole me geté prys or blame
And Lové trewe to save my name ;   3330
Who that me chastith I hym hate.'
With that word Resoun wente hir gate,
Whanne she saugh for no sermonynge
She myght me fro my foly brynge.
Thanne dismaiéd I, lefte all sool,
Forwery, forwandred, as a fool,
For I ne knewe no chevisaunce.
Thanne fell into my remembraunce
How Lové bade me to purveye
A felowe, to whom I myght seye   3340
My counsell and my pryvete,
For that shulde moche availé me.
With that bithought I me that I
Hádde a felowe fasté by
Tréwe and siker, curteys and hende ;
And he was called by name a FREENDE,
A trewer felowe was no wher noon.
In haste to hym I wente anoon,
And to hym all my woo I tolde,
Fro hym right nought I wold witholde.
I tolde him all withouté were,   3351
And made my compleynt on Daungere,
How forto see he was hidous,

3319. *taught*, MSS. *thought*.
3331. MSS. *chastiseth*.

And to-me-ward contrarious ;
The whiché, thurgh his cruelte
Was in poynt to have meygnéd me.
With Bialacoil whanne he me sey
Withynne the gardeyn walke and pley.
Fro me he made hym forto go ;
And I, bilefte aloone in woo,   3360
I durst no lenger with hym speke,
For Daunger seide he wolde be wreke.
Whanne that he sawé how I wente
The freshé bothon forto hente,
If I were hardy to come neer
Bitwene the hay and the Roser.
   This freend, whanne he wiste of my
     thought,
He discomforted me right nought,
But seidé, 'Felowe, be not so madde.
Ne so abaysshéd, nor bystadde ;   3370
My silf I knowe full well Daungere,
And how he is feers of his cheere
At primé temps love to manace.
Ful ofte I have ben in his caas ;
A feloun firste though that he be,
Aftir thou shalt hym souple se.
Of longé passed I knewe hym well ;
Ungoodly first though men hym feele,
He wole meke aftir in his beryng
Been, for service and obeyssyng.   3380
I shal thee telle what thou shalt doo :
Mekely I rede thou go hym to,
Of herté pray hym specialy
Of thy trespace to have mercy,
And hoté well, [hym] here to plese,
That thou shalt nevermore hym dis-
     plese.
Who can best serve of flaterie,
Shall please Daunger most uttirly.'
My freend hath seid to me so wel,
That he me esid hath somdell,   3390
And eke allegged of my torment.
For thurgh hym had I hardément
Agayn to Daunger forto go,
To preve if I myght meke hym soo.
To Daunger came I all ashamed,
The which aforn me hadde y-blamed,
Desiryng forto pese my woo.

3379. *meke*, MSS. *make*, 'amoloier.
3383. *Of herte*; cp. 3902.
3385. *well hym*, Skeat's emendation for *hyr well* of MSS. (?) *his ire to pese* (*pese* apothetic form of *appese*); cp. v. 3397.

But over hegge durst I not goo,
For he forbede me the passage.
I fonde hym cruel in his rage   3400
And in his honde a gret burdoun.
To hym I knelide lowe a-doun,
Ful meke of port and symple of chere,
And seide, 'Sir, I am comen heere
Donly to aske of you mercy ;
It greveth me full gretly
That evere my lyf I wratthèd you.
But forto amenden I am come now,
With all my myght, bothe loude and stille,
To doon right at youre ownè wille.   3410
For Lovè made me forto doo
That I have trespassed hidirto,
Fro whom I ne may withdrawe myne herte.
Yit shall never for joy ne smerte,
What so bifallè, good or ille,
Offendè more ageyn youre wille ;
Lever I have endure disese,
Than do that you shuldè displese.
I you require and pray that ye
Of me have mercy and pitee   3420
To stynte your ire that greveth soo.
That I wole swere for ever mo
To be redressid at youre likyng,
If I trespasse in ony thyng.
Save that I pray thee grauntè me
A thyng that may not warnèd be :
That I may lovè all oonly,
Noon other thyng of you aske I.
I shall doon ellès well I-wys,
If of youre grace ye graunte me this ;   3430
And ye may not letten me,
For wel wot ye that love is free,
And I shall loven sithen that I wille,
Who evere like it, well or ille.
And yit ne wold I for all Fraunce
Do thyng to do you displesaunce.'
     Thanne Daunger fille in his entent
Forto foryeve his male talent ;
But all his wratthe yit attè laste

3398. *hegge*, probably mistake for *haye*.
3406. *It greveth*, MSS. *That greveth*.
3407. *evere my lyf*, read (?) *ever in my lyf*.
3422. *That*, (?) *And*; Fr. 'et.'
3429. *elles*, Th. *all*. Bell: *I shal don al your*
vil iwys, which aptly gives sense of original.
3437. *fille in his entent*, (?) failed.

     Moult troval Dangier dur et lent.
     De pardonner son maltalent.

Skeat interprets 'condescended,' but has *fall*
such a meaning ?

He hath relesed, I preyde so faste.   3440
Shortly he seidè, 'Thy request
Is not to mochel dishonest,
Nè I wole not werne it thee ;
For yit no thyng engreveth me.
For though thou love thus evermore,
To me is neither softe ne soore.
Love where the list, what recchith me,
So [thou] fer fro my roses be ?
Trust not on me for noon assay,
If ony tyme thou passe the hay.'   3450
Thus hath he graunted my praiere.
Thanne wente I forth withouten were
Unto my freend, and tolde hym all,
Which was right joyfull of my tale.
He seide, 'Now goth wel thyn affaire,
He shall to thee be debonaire ;
Though he aforn was dispitous,
He shall heere aftir be gracious.
If he were touchid on somme good veyne,
He shuld yit rewen on thi peyne.   3460
Suffre I rede, and no boost make,
Till thou at good mes maist hym take.
By sufferaunce and wordis softe
A man may overcomè ofte
Hym that aforn he hadde in drede,
In bookis sothly as I rede.'
Thus hath my freend with gret comfort
Avaunced me with high disport,
Which wolde me good as mych as I.
And thanne anoon full sodeynly   3470
I toke my leve, and streight I wente
Unto the hay, for gret talent
I hadde to sene the fresh bothoun
Wherynne lay my salvacioun.
And Daunger toke kepe, if that I
Kepe hym covenaunt trewèly.
So sore I dradde his manasyng
I durst not brekè his biddyng,
For lest that I were of hym shent
I brake not his comaundèment,   3480
Fórto purchase his good wille.
It was [nat] forto come ther-tille,
His mercy was to ferre bihynde ;
I wepte for I ne myght it fynde.
I compleynèd and sighed sore,

3450. MSS. *I ony tyme to passe*, 'se tu james
passes la haie.'
3482. *nat*, MSS. omit. Morris, etc. supply
hard.

Añd langwisshéd evermore,
Fór I durst not over goo
· Unto the rose I loved soo.
Thurgh my demenyng outerly
[Thanne he had knowlege certanly,] 3490
That Love me ladde in sich a wise
That in me ther was no feyntise,
Fálsheed, ne no trecherie.
And yit he full of vylanye,
Of disdeyne, and cruelte,
Oñ me ne wolde have pite
His cruel will forto refreyne,
Though I wepe alwey and me compleyne.
And while I was in this torment,
Were come of gracé, by god sent, 3500
Ffaunchise and with hir Pite.
Fulfild the bothen of bounte,
They go to Daunger anoon-right,
To forther me with all her myght,
And helpé in worde and in dede;
For well they saugh that it was nede.
First of hir gracé dame Fraunchise
Hath taken [word] of this emprise;
She seide, 'Daunger, gret wrong ye do
To worche this man so myché woo, 3510
Or pynen hym so angerly;
It is to you gret villanye.
I can not see [ne] why ne how
That he hath trespassed ageyn you,
Save that he loveth; wherfore ye shulde
The more in cherete of hym holde.
The force of love makith hym do this;
Who wolde hym blame, he dide amys.
He leseth more than ye may do;
His peyne is harde, ye may see lo, 3520
And Love in no wise wolde consente
That he have power to repente.
For though that quyk ye wolde hym sloo,
Fro love his herté may not goo.
Now, sweté Sir, is it youre ese
Hym forto angre or disese?
Allas, what may it you avaunce

To done to hym so gret grevaunce?
What worship is it agayn hym take,
Or on youre man a werré make, 353?
Sith he so lowly every wise
Is redy, as ye lust devise?
If Love hath caught hym in his lace
You for tobeye in every caas,
And ben youre suget at youre will,
Shuld ye therfore willen hym ill?
Ye shulde hym sparé more all oute
Than hym that is bothe proude and stout,
Curtesie wole that ye socour
Hem that ben meke undir youre cure. 354?
His herte is hard that wole not meke,
Whanne men of mekenesse hym biseke.
'Thát is certeyn,' seide Pite,
'We se ofte that humilite
Bothe ire and also felonye
Venquyssheth, and also malencolye.
To stondé forth in such duresse,
This cruelte and wikkidnesse.
Wherfore I pray you, Sir Daungere,
Forto mayntene no lenger heere 355?
Such cruel werre agayn youre man,
As hoolly youres as ever he can;
Nor that ye worchen no more woo
On this caytif that langwisshith soo,
Which wole no more to you trespasse,
But putte hym hoolly in youre grace.
His offense ne was but lite;
The god of Love it was to wite,
That he youre thrall so gretly is;
And if ye harme hym, ye done amys. 356?
For he hath hadde full hard penaunce,
Sith that ye refte hym thaqueyntaunce
Of Bialacoil, his mosté joye,
Which alle hise peynés myght acoye.
He was biforn anoyed sore,
But thanne ye doubled hem well more.
For he of blis hath ben full bare,
Sith Bialacoil was fro hym fare.
Love hath to hym do gret distresse,
He hath no nede of more duresse; 357?
Voideth from hym youre ire, I rede,
Ye may not wynnen in this dede.
Makith Bialacoil repeire ageyn,

3489. MSS. *Thurgh out my demyng outerly That he had* . . . (Gl. omits) *Thanne love me ladde*, etc.; Fr. 'Tant fis qu'il a certainement Veü a mon contenement Qu'Amors,' etc.

3502. *the bothen, i.e.* both, full of kindness, visit Daunger immediately. MSS. *the bothom*, which Skeat refers to the rosebud; Fr. 'car l'une a l'autre me vodroit.'

3505. (?) Omit *in* before *dede*.

3522. *he*, MSS. *ye*, a common scribal error.

3546. *Venquyssheth*, two syllables; cp. 3554

3548. *This*, This is.

3554. *On*, MSS. *Upon*.

3566. *hem*, MSS. *hym*, 'ses anuis.'

And haveth pite upon his peyne ;
For Fraunchise wole and I, Pite,
That mercyful to hym ye be.
And sith that she and I accorde
Have upon hym misericorde,
For I you pray and eke moneste
Ought to refusen oure requeste.   3580
For he is hard and fell of thought,
That for us twoo wole do right nought.'
   Daunger ne myght no more endure,
He mekede hym unto mesure.
I wole in no wise,' seith Daungere,
Denye that ye have asked heere,
It were to gret uncurtesie ;
I wole he have the companye
Of Bialacoil, as ye devise ;
I wole hym lette in no wise.'   3590
To Bialacoil thanne wente in hye
Fraunchise, and seide full curteislye :
Ye have to longe be deignous
Unto this lover and daungerous,
Fro him to withdrawe your presence,
Whiche hath do to him great offence,
That ye not wolde upon him se ;
Wherfore a sorouful man is he.
Shape ye to paye him, and to please,
Of my love if ye wol have ease ;   3600
Fulfyl his wyl, sithe that ye knowe
Daunger is daunted and brought lowe
Through helpe of me and of Pyte ;
You dare no more aferde be.'
   ' I shal do right as ye wyl,'
Saith Bialacoil, ' for it is skyl,
Sithe Daunger wol that it so be.'
   Than Fraunchise hath him sent to me
Bialacoil at the begynnyng,
Salued me in his commyng ;   3610
No straungenesse was in him sene,
No more than he ne had wrathed bene.
As fayre semblaunt than shewed he me,
And goodly, as aforne dyd he.
And by the honde withoute doute,
Within the haye right al aboute
He ladde me with right good chere,
Al envyron the vergere
That Daunger hadde me chased fro.
Nowe have I leave over al to go,   3620

Nowe am I raysed at my devyse
Fro helle unto paradyse.
Thus Bialacoil of gentylnesse,
With al his payne and besynesse,
Hath shewed me onely of grace
The estres of the swote place.
   I sawe the Rose whan I was nygh
Was greatter woxen and more high,
Fresshe, roddy, and fayre of hewe,
Of coloure veer yliche newe.   3630
And whan I hadde it longe sene,
I sawe that through the leves grene
The Rose spredde to spaunysshinge,
To sene it was a goodly thynge.
But it ne was so sprede on brede
That men within myght knowe the sede ;
For it covert was and close
Bothe with the leves and with the rose.
The stalke was even and grene upright,
It was theron a goodly syght,   3640
And wel the better, withoute wene,
For the seed was nat [y-]sene.
Ful fayre it spradde (God it blesse),
For suche another, as I gesse,
Aforne ne was, ne more vermayle.
I was abawed for marveyle,
For ever the fayrer that it was,
The more I am bounde in Loves laas.
Longe I abode there, sothe to saye,
Tyl Bialacoil I ganne to praye,   3650
Whan that I sawe him, in no wyse
To me warnen his servyce,
That he me wolde graunt a thynge,
Whiche to remembre is wel syttynge.
This is to sayne, that of his grace
He wolde me yeve leysar and space,
To me that was so desyrous
To have a kyssynge precious
Of the goodly fresshe Rose,
That so swetely smelleth in my nose.   3660
' For if it you displeased nought
I wolde gladly, as I have sought,
Have a cosse therof freely
Of your yefte ; for certainly
I wol none have, but by your leve,
So lothe me were you for to greve.'
   He sayde, ' Frende, so god me spede,

3596 - 3690. From Thynne ; two leaves of Glasgow MS. missing.
3604. *dare*, cp. note to v. 1089.

3622. Th. *hell.*
3656. (?) Omit *me* and read *wolde.*
3667. Th. *said.*

Of Chastite I have suche drede,
Thou shuldest nat warnėd be for me ;
But I dare nat for Chastyte.   3670
Agayne her dare I nat mysdo,
For alwaye byddeth she me so
To yeve no lover leve to kysse.
For who therto maye wynne y-wisse,
He of the surplus of the praye
May lyve in hoope to gette some daye.
For who so kyssynge maye attayne
Of loves payne hath, soth to sayne,
The best and [the] most avenaunt,
And ernest of the remenaunt.'   3680
    Of his answere I sighed sore ;
I durst assaye him tho no more,
I hadde suche drede to greve him aye.
A man shulde nat to moche assaye
To chafe hys frende out of measure,
Nor putte his lyfe in aventure.
For no man at the firstė stroke
Ne maye nat fellė downe an oke,
Nor of the reysyns have the wyne,
Tyl grapes be rype, and wel afyne   3690
Be sore empressid, I you ensure,
And drawen out of the pressure.
But I forpeynėd wonder stronge,
Though that I aboode right longe
Aftir the kis in peyne and woo,
Sith I to kis desirėd soo ;
Till that, rewyng on my distresse,
Ther come Venus the goddesse,
Which ay werreyeth Chastite,
Came of hir grace to socoure me,   3700
Whos myght is knowė ferre and wide ;
For she is modir of Cupide,
The god of love, blynde as stoon,
That helpith lovers many oon.
This lady brought in hir right honde
Of brennyng fyre a blasyng bronde,
Wherof the flawme and hootė fire
Hath many a lady in desire
Of lovė brought, and sorė hette,
And in hir servise her hertes sette.   3710
This lady was of good entaile,
Right wondirfull of apparayle ;

3674. Th. *wynnen.*
3688. Th. *fel.*
3690. Skeat omits *be,* but unnecessarily.
3698. Skeat reads *to me* for *come.*
3700. *Came,* p. part. ? If so, *Come.*
3710. *hertes,* MSS. *herte is.*

Bi hir atyre so bright and shene
Men myght perceyvė well and sene
She was not of religioun.
Nor I nell makė mencioun
Nór of robe nor of tresour,
Of broche nor of hir riche attour,
Ne of hir girdill aboute hir side,
For that I nyll not longe abide.   3720
But knowith wel that certeynly
She was araiėd richėly ;
Devoyde of pruyde certeyn she was.
To Bialacoil she wente apas,
And to hym, shortly in a clause,
She seidė, ' Sir, what is the cause
Ye ben of port so daungerous
Unto this lover and deynous,
To graunte hym nothyng but a kisse.
To werne it hym ye done amysse,   3730
Sith well ye wotė how that he
Is loves servaunt, as ye may see,
And hath beåute, wher-through is
Worthy of love to have the blis.
How he is semely, biholde and see
How he is faire, how he is free,
How he is swoote and debonaire,
Of agė yonge, lusty and faire.
Ther is no lady so hawteyne,
Duchesse ne countesse, ne chasteleyne,   3740
That I nolde holde hir ungoodly
Forto refuse hym outterly.
His breth is also good and swete,
And eke his lippis rody, and mete
Oonly to pleyen and to kisse ;
Graunte hym a kis of gentilnysse.
His teth arn also white and clene.
Me thenkith [it] wrong, withouten wen,
If ye now werne hym, trustith me,
To grauntė that a kis have he.   3750
The lasse to helpe hym that ye haste,
The morė tymė shul ye waste.'
Whanne the flawme of the verry brond
That Venus brought in hir right honde,
Hadde Bialacoil with hetė smete,
Anoon he bade me withouten lette,
Grauntede to me the Rosė kisse.
Thanne of my peyne I gan to lysse,
And to the Rose anoon wente I,
And kisside it full feithfully.   3760

3718. *nor,* MSS. *neither.*
3751. *to helpe,* MSS. *ye helpe.*

Thar no man aske if I was blithe
Whanne the savour soft and lythe
Stroke to myn herte withouté more,
And me aleggéd of my sore,
So was I full of joye and blisse.
It is faire sich a flour to kisse ;
It was so swoote and saverous.
I myght not be so angwisshous,
That I [ne] mote glad and joly be,
Whanne that I remembre me.   3770
Yit ever among, sothly to seyne,
I suffre noye and moché peyne.
The see may never be so stille,
That with a litel wynde it nylle
Overwhelme and turne also,
As it were woode in wawis goo.
Aftir the calme, the trouble soone
Mote folowe, and chaunge as the moone.
Right so farith Love, that selde in oon
Holdith his anker : for right anoon,   3780
Whanne they in ese wene beste to lyve,
They ben with tempest all fordryve.
Who serveth love can telle of woo ;
The stoundemele joie mote overgoo ;
Now he hurteth and now he cureth,
For selde in oo poynt love endureth.
    Now is it right me to procede
How Shame gan medle, and také hede,
Thurgh whom fele angres I have hadde.
And how the strongé wall was maad,   3790
And the castell of brede and lengthe,
That God of Love wanne with his
        strengthe.
All this in Romance will I sette,
And for no thyng ne will I lette,
So that it lykyng to hir be
That is the flour of beaute.
For she may best my labour quyte,
That I for hir love shal endite.
    Wikkid-Tunge, that the covyne
Of every lover can devyne   3800
Worste, and addith more somdell
For wikkid tunge seith never well),
To-me-ward bare he right gret hate,
Espiyng me erly and late,

Till he hath sene the greté chere
Of Bialacoil and me I-feere.
He myghté not his tunge withstonde
Worse to reporté than he fonde,
He was so full of curséd rage ;
It satte hym well of his lynage,   3810
For hym an Irish womman bare.
His tunge was fyléd sharpe and square,
Póign[i]aunt, and right kervyng,
And wonder bitter in spekyng.
For whanne that he me gan espie,
He swoore, affermyng sikirlye,
Bitwené Bialacoil and me
Was yvel aquayntaunce and pryve.
He spake therof so folilye,
That he awakide Ielousye,   3820
Which all afrayed in his risyng,
Whanne that he herd [him] janglyng,
He ran anoon as he were woode
To Bialacoil there that he stode ;
Which hadde lever in this caas
Have ben at Reynes or Amyas.
For foot-hoot in his felonye,
To hym thus seidé Ielousie :
' Why hast thou ben so necligent
To kepen, whanne I was absent,   3830
This verger heere left in thi warde.
To me thou haddist no rewarde,
To truste, to thy confusioun,
Hym thus, to whom suspeccioun
I have right gret, for it is nede ;
It is well shewéd by the dede.
Grete faute in thee now have I founde ;
By God, anoon thou shalt be bounde,
And fasté loken in a tour,
Withouté refuyt or socour.   3840
For Shame to longe hath be thee froo ;
Over soone she was agoo.
Whanne thou hast lost bothe drede and
        feere,
It semede wel she was not heere.
Shé was bisy in no wyse
To kepé thee and [to] chastise,
And forto helpen Chastite
To kepe the roser, as thenkith me.
For thanne this boy knave so booldely
Ne shuldé not have be hardy,   3850

3773 ff. Cp. *Boece*, 253 ff.
3774. *nylle*, MSS. *wille*.
3775. *Overwhelme*, (?) *Overwhelve*.
3779. *selde*, MSS. *yelde* (through *selde*).
3786. *selde*, MSS. *elde*.
3796. *beaute*, three syllables, as in v. 3733.

3805. *grete chere*, kindly welcome.
3826. *Reynes*, Rennes in Brittany ; Fr. 'a
Estampes.' *Amyas* corresponds to Fr. 'a Miaus.'

Of Chastitė verger hadde such game,
Thou shul_y me turneth to gret shame.'
But I dar hyst what to sey ;
Agayne h'he wolde have fled awey,
For alwa; han hiddė, nere that he
To yeve _nly toke hym with me.
For whoinne I saugh he haddė soo,
He of thbusiė, take us twoo,
May ly_stoned, and knewe no rede,
For whidde awey for verrey drede.   3860
Of lov_e Shame cam forth full symplely.
The bende have trespaced full gretly,
And ene of hir port, and made it symple,
  Of l_g a vayle in stede of wymple,
I durs_nnys don in her abbey.
I hacuse hir herte was in affray,
A m_gan to speke withynne a throwe
To 'felousie right wonder lowe.
No_t of his gracė she bysoughte
For seidė, ' Sire, ne leveth noughte   3870
N_kkid-Tunge, that false espie,
N'hich is so glad to feyne and lye.
  _ hath you maad, thurgh flateryng,
Be Bialacoil a fals lesyng ;
A_s falsnesse is not now a-newe,
R is to long that he hym knewe ;
'This is not the firstė day,
'For Wikkid-Tunge hath custome ay
Yóngė folkis to bewreye,
And falsė lesynges on hem leye.   3880
Yit nevertheles I see amonge
Thát the loigne it is so longe
Of Bialacoil, hertis to lure
In Loves servyse forto endure,
Drawyng such folk hym too,
That he hath no thyng with to doo.
But in sothnesse I trowė nought
That Bialacoil haddė ever in thought
To do trespace or vylonye.
But for his modir Curtesie   3890
Háth taught hym ever to be
Good of aqueyntaunce and pryve.
For he loveth noon hevynesse,
But mirthe, and pley, and all gladnesse ;
He hateth all trechours,
Sóleyn folk and envyou[r]s ;

Fór ye witen how that he
Wole ever glad and joyfull be,
Hónestly with folk to pleye.
I have be negligent in good feye
To chastise hym ; therfore now I
Of herte I crye you heere mercy
That I have been so recheles
To tamen hym, withouten lees.
Of my foly I me repente.
Now wole I hoole sette myn entent
To kepė, bothė low[d]e and stille.
Biálacoil to do youre wille.'
' Sháme, shame,' seyde Ielousie,
' To be bytrasshed gret drede have I :
Léccherie hath clombe so hye,
That almoost blerėd is myn ye :
No wonder is if that drede have I ;
Over all regnyth Lecchery,
Whós myght growith nyght and day
Bóthe in cloistre and in abbey ;
Chástite is werried over all,
Therfore I wole with siker wall
Close bothė roses and roser.
I have to longe in this maner
Left hem unclosid wilfully ;
Wherfore I am right inwardly
Sorowfull, and repentė me.
But now they shall no lenger be
Unclosid, and yit I dredė sore
I shall repentė ferthermore ;
Fór the game goth all amys,
Coúnsell I must newe y-wys.
I have to longė tristed thee,
But now it shal no lenger be ;
For he may best in every cost
Disceyve that men tristen most.
I see wel that I am nygh shent,
But if I sette my full entent
Rémedyė to purveye.
Thérfore close I shall the weye,
Fro hem that wole the Rose espie,
And come to wayte me vilonye.
Fór in good feith and in trouthe,
I wole not lettė for no slouthe,
To lyve the more in sikirnesse,
To make anoon a fort[e]resse,
Tenclose the roses of good savour.

3861. MSS. *simply.*
3880. MSS. *lye.*
3885. This verse, like 3895, has but three accented syllables.

3942. *To*, MSS. *Do.*
3943. *Tenclose* (i.e. to enclose), MSS. *Tu
close*, ' qui . . . clorra entor.'

myddis shall I make a tour,
putte Bialacoil in prisoun;
r evere I drede me of tresoun.
rowe I shal hym kepè soo
ıat he shal have no myght to goo
ıoute, to makè companye
ı hem that thenke of vylanye;   3950
ı to no such as hath ben heere
orn, and founde in hym good chere;
hich han assailèd hym to shende,
ıd with her trowandyse to blynde.
foole is eythè to bigyle;
t, may I lyve a litel while,
ı shal forthenke his fair semblaunt.'
And with that word came DREDE avaunt,
hich was abasshed and in gret fere.
hanne he wiste Ielousie was there, 3960
ı was for drede in sich affray,
át not a word durst he say,
t quakyng stode full still aloone,
ı Ielousie his weye was gone,
ve Shamè, that him not forsoke.
the Drede and she ful sorè quoke,
an attè lastè Drede abreyde,
ıd to his cosyn Shamè seide:
hame,' he seide, 'in sothfastnesse,
me it is gret hevynesse   3970
át the noyse so ferre is go,
d the sclaundre of us twoo;
t sithe that it is byfall,
ı may it not ageyn call
hanne onys sprongen is a fame.
r many a yeer withouten blame
ı han ben, and many a day;
r many an Aprill and many a May
ı han passèd not [a-]shamed,
l Ielousiè hath us blamed   3980
mystrust and suspecioun,
useles, withoute enchesoun.
ı we to Daunger hastily,
d late us shewe hym openly
at he hath not aright [y-]wrought,
hanne that he settè nought his thought
kepè better the purprise.
his doyng he is not wise;
ı hath to us do gret wronge,
át hath suffred now so longe   3990
ïlacoil to have his wille,

3967. *Than*, MSS. *That*.
3974. Skeat supplies *do* before *call*.

Áll his lustès to fulfille.
He must amende it utterly,
Or ellys shall he vilaynesly
Exiled be out of this londe;
For he the werre may not withstonde
Of Ielousiè, nor the greef,
Sith Bialacoil is at myscheef.'
To Daunger, Shame and Drede anoon
The rightè weye ben goon.   4000
The cherle thei founden hem aforn
Liggyng undir an hawèthorn;
Undir his heed no pilowe was,
But in the stede a trusse of gras.
He slombred, and a nappe he toke,
Tyll Shamè pitously hym shoke,
And grete manace on hym gan make.
'Why slepist thou, whanne thou shulde
    wake?'
Quod Shame. 'Thou doist us vylanye;
Who tristith thee, he doth folye, 4010
To kepè roses or bothouns
Whanne thei ben faire in her sesouns.
Thóu art woxe to familiere,
Whére thou shulde be straunge of chere,
Stoute of thi porte, redy to greve.
Thou doist gret folye forto leve
Bialacoil here inne to calle
The yonder man, to shende us alle.
Though that thou slepè, we may here
Of Ielousie gret noysè heere. 4020
Art thou now late? Rise up an high,
And stoppe sone, and delyverly,
All the gappis of the hay;
Dó no favour, I thee pray.
It fallith no thyng to thy name
To make faire semblaunt, where thou
    maist blame.
Yf Bialacoil be sweete and free,
Doggèd and fell thou shuldist be,
Froward and outerageous y-wis.
A cherl chaungeth that curteis is. 4030
This have I herd ofte in seiyng,
"Thát man may, for no dauntyng,
Máke a sperhauke of a bosarde."
Alle men wole holde thee for musarde

3994. *vilaynesly*, stress on second syllable as in v. 178 (*ellys*, one syllable as usual).
3998. 'S'ele l'acueilloit en haine'; possibly misread as 'Se belacueil l'ait en haine.'
4021. 'Esties vous ore couchies?'
4026. *where*, as extra syllable after cæsura.

That debonair have founden thee.
It sittith thee nought curteis to be,
To do men plesaunce or servise ;
In thee it is recreaundise.
Léte thi werkis fer and nere
Be like thi name, which is Daungere.'
   Thanne, all abawid in shewing,   4041
Anoon spake Drede right thus seiyng,
And seide, ' Daungere, I dredé me
Thát thou ne wolt bisy be
To kepé that thou hast to kepe ;
Whanne thou shuldist wake thou art a slepe.
Thou shalt be grevéd certeynly,
If the aspié Ielousie,
Or if he fyndé thee to blame.
He hath to day assailéd Shame   4050
And chased awey, with gret manace,
Bialacoil oute of this place,
And swereth shortly that he shall
Enclose hym in a sturdy wall ;
And all is for thi wikkidnesse,
For that thee faileth straungénesse.
Thyne herte I trowe be failed all.
Thou shalt repente in speciall,
If Ielousié the sooth knewe ;
Thou shalt forthenke and soré rewe.' 4060
   With that the cherl his clubbe gan shake,
Frounyng his eyen gan to make,
And hidous chere ; as man in rage
For ire he brente in his visage.
Whanne that [he] herd hym blaméd soo,
He seide, ' Oute of my witte I goo ;
To be discomfyt I have gret wronge.
Certis I have now lyved to longe,
Sith I may not this rosér kepe.
All quykke I wolde be dolven deepe 4070
If ony man shal more repeire
Into this gardyne, for foule or faire.
Myne herte for ire goth a-fere
That I lete ony entre heere.
I have do folie, now I see ;
But now it shall amended bee.
Who settith foot heere ony more,
Truly he shall repente it sore,
For no man moo into this place
Of me to entre shal have grace.   4080
Lever I hadde with swerdis tweyne
Thurghoute myne herte in every veyne
Perced to be with many a wounde,

Thanne slouthé shulde in me be founde
From hennés forth, by nyght or day,
I shall defende it, if I may,
Withouten ony excepcioun
Of ech maner condicioun.
And if I it eny man graunte,
Holdeth me for recreaunte.'   40..
   Thanne Daunger on his feet gan stonde.
And hente a burdoun in his honde.
Wroth in his ire, ne lefte he nought
But thurgh the verger he hath sooght :
If he myght fyndé hole or trace,
Where-thurgh that me mote forth by pace.
Or ony gappe, he dide it close,
That no man myghté touche a rose.
Of the roser all aboute
He shitteth every man withoute.   41..
Thus day by day Daunger is wers,
More wondirfull, and more dyvers,
And feller eke than evere he was.
For hym full ofte I synge ' allas,'
For I ne may nought, thurgh his ire,
Recovere that I moost desire.
Myne herte, allas, wole brest a-twoo,
For Bialacoil I wrathéd soo ;
For certeynly in every membre
I quaké whanne I me remembre   41..
Of the bothon which I wolde
Full ofte a day sene and biholde.
And whanne I thenke upon the kisse,
And how mych joye and blisse
I haddé thurgh the savour swete,
For wante of it I grone and grete.
Me thenkith I fele yit in my nose
The sweté savour of the rose.
And now I woot that I mote goo
So fer the freshé flourés froo,   4..
To me full welcome were the deth.
Absens therof allas me sleeth.
For whilom with this Rose, allas,
I touched nosé, mouth, and face ;
But now the deth I must abide.
But love consente another tyde
That onys I touché may and kisse,
I trowe my peyne shall never lisse.
Theron is all my coveitise,
Which brent myn herte in many wise.
Now shal repaire agayn sighinge,   41..
Long wacche on nyghtis, and no sleping.

Thought in wisshing, torment and woo,
With many a turnyng to and froo.
That half my peyne I can not telle,
For I am fallen into helle
From paradys, and wel the more
My turment greveth more and more.
Anoieth now the bittirnesse,
That I to forn have felt swetnesse.   4140
And Wikkid-Tunge thurgh his falshede
Causeth all my woo and drede.
On me he leieth a pitous charge,
Bi-cause his tungė was to large.
  Now it is tyme shortly that I
Telle you som-thyng of Ielousie,
That was in gret suspecioun.
Aboute hym lefte he no masoun,
That stoon coude leyė, ne querrour ;
He hirede hem to make a tour.   4150
And first, the roses forto kepe,
Aboute hem made he a dichė deepe,
Right wondir large, and also broode.
Upon the whichė also stode
Of squarėd stoon a sturdy wall,
Which on a cragge was founded all.
And right grete thikkenesse eke it bare
Abouten it was founded square,
An hundred fademe on every side.
It was alichė longe and wide ;   4160
Lest ony tyme it were assayled,
Ful wel aboute it was batayled,
And rounde enviroun eke were sette
Ful many a riche and faire tourette.
At every corner of this wall
Was sette a tour full pryncipall,
And everich hadde, withoutė fable,
A portė-colys defensable
To kepe of enemyes, and to greve
That there her forcė woldė preve.   4170
And eke amyddė this purprise
Was maad a tour of gret maistrise ;
A fairer saugh no man with sight,
Large, and wide, and of gret myght.
They dreddė noon assaut
Of gynnė, gunnė, nor skaffaut.

4152. Possibly *he* is to be omitted. For *diche*
. 4205.
4160. *aliche*, MSS. *all liche*, (T) *all aliche*.
4166. *tour*, 'portaus'; (T) *port* or some such
word.
4172. *maistrise*, Fr. 'maistrise,' does not seem
be an English word.

The temprure of the mortere
Was maad of lycour wonder dere,
Of quykkė lyme, persant and egre,
The which was tempred with vynegre.
The stoon was hard of ademant,   4181
Wherof they made the foundėment.
The tour was rounde, maad in compas ;
In all this world no riccher was,
Ne better ordeigned therwith-all.
Aboute the tour was maad a wall,
So that bitwixt that and the tour
Rosers were sette of swete savour
With many roses that thei bere.
And eke withynne the castell were   4190
Spryngoldes, gunnes, bows and archers,
And eke aboven attė corners
Men seyn over the wallė stonde
Grete engynės, who were nygh honde.
And in the kernels heere and there
Of Arblasters grete plente were ;
Noon armure myght her stroke withstonde,
It were foly to prece to honde.
Withoute the diche were lystės maade
With wall bataylėd large and brade,   4200
For men and hors shulde not atteyne
To neighe the dyche over the pleyne.
Thus Ielousie hath enviroun
Sėtte aboute his garnysoun,
With wallės rounde and dichė depe,
Oonly the roser forto kepe.
And Daunger bere erly and late
The keyės of the utter gate,
The whichė openeth toward the eest.
And he hadde with hym attė leest   4210
Thritty servauntes, echon by name.
That other gatė keptė Shame,
Which openedė, as it was couth,
Toward the part[i]e of the south.
Sergeauntes assignėd were hir too
Ful many, hir willė forto doo.
Thanne Dredė hadde in hir baillie
The kepyng of the Conestablerye,
Toward the north I undirstonde,
That openyde upon the lyftė honde.   4220
The which for no thyng may be sure
Bůt if she do bisy cure,
Ėrly on morowe and also late,
Strongly to shette and barre the gate.
Of every thing that she may see
Drede is aferd, wher so she be ;

For with a puff of litell wynde
Drede is a-stonyed in hir mynde.
Therfore for stelyng of the Rose
I rede hir nought the yate unclose ;   4230
A foulis flight wole make hir flee,
And eke a shadowe if she it see.

Thanne Wikked-Tunge, full of envye,
With soudiours of Normandye,
As he that causeth all the bate,
Was keper of the fourthe gate.
And also to the tother three
He wente full ofte forto see.
Whanne his lotte was to wake anyght,
His instrumentis wolde he dight   4240
Forto blowe and make sowne
(Ofte thanne he hath enchesoun)
And walken oft upon the wall,
Corners and wikettis over all
Full narwe serchen and espie.
Though he nought fonde, yit wole he
    lye
Discordaunt ever fro armonye,
And distoned from melodie.
Controve he wolde, and foule fayle
With hornepipes of Cornewaile ;   4250
In floytes made he discordaunce.
And in his musyk with myschaunce,
He wolde seyn with notes newe
That he fonde no womman trewe,
Ne that he saugh never in his lyf
Unto hir husbonde a trewe wyf ;
Ne noon so ful of honeste,
That she nyl laughe and mery be
Whanne that she hereth, or may espie,
A man speken of leccherie.   4260
Everiche of hem hath somme vice ;
Oon is dishonest, another is nyce ;
If oon be full of vylanye,
Another hath a likerous ighe ;
If oon be full of wantonesse,
Another is a chideresse.

Thus Wikked Tunge (god yeve hem
    shame)

4249. *fayle*, make mistakes ; but it may be an
error for *fall* (rhyming with Cornewall), in which
case the meaning is to make mistakes in
counterpoint.
4250. *with hornepipes*, etc., 'as estives de
Cornaille.'
4254 ff. This seems to be the part of the Romaunce that Chaucer refers to in *L. of G. W.* 431.
4264. *ighe*, a form of *ye*.

Can putt hem everychone in blame
Withoute desert, and causeles.
He lieth, though they ben giltles.   4270
I have pite to sene the sorwe
That waketh bothe eve and morwe,
To Innocentis doith such grevaunce.
I pray god yeve hym evel chaunce,
That he ever so bisie is
Of ony womman to seyn amys.
Eke Ielousie God confounde,
That hath maad a tour so rounde,
And made aboute a garisoun
To sette Bealacoil in prisoun,   4280
The which is shette there in the tour
Ful longe to holde there sojour,
There forto lyven in penaunce.
And forto do hym more grevaunce
Ther hath ordeyned Ielousie
An olde vekke forto espye
The maner of his governaunce.
The whiche devel in hir enfaunce
Hadde lerned of loves arte,
And of his pleyes toke hir parte.   4290
She was expert in his servise,
She knewe eche wrenche and every
    gise
Of love, and every wile ;
It was [the] harder hir to gile.
Of Bealacoil she toke ay hede,
That evere he lyveth in woo and drede.
He kepte hym koy and eye pryve,
Lest in hym she hadde see
Ony foly countenaunce ;
For she knewe all the olde daunce.   4300
And aftir this, whanne Ielousie
Hadde Bealacoil in his baillie,
And shette hym up that was so fre ;
For seure of hym he wolde be.
He trusteth sore in his castell,
The stronge werk hym liketh well.
He dradde not that no glotouns
Shulde stele his roses or bothouns.
The roses weren assured all,
Defenced with the stronge wall.   4310
Now Ielousie full well may be
Of drede devoide in liberte,

4272. MSS. *walketh* ; cp. v. 2682 and note
thereto.
4285. *Ther*, MSS. *Which*.
4291. *expert*, MSS. *except*, which even :
sense of 'acceptable' is not very clear.

Whether that he slepe or wake,
For his roses may noon be take.
  But I allas now mornė shall
Bi-cause I was withoute the wall.
Full mochė doole and moone I made.
Who haddė wist what woo I hadde,
I trowe he wolde have had pite.
Lóve to deere hadde soolde to me   4320
The good, that of his love hadde I.
I wente a bought it all queyntly,
But now, thurgh doublyng of my peyne,
I see he wolde it selle ageyne,
And me a newė bargeyn leere,
The which all-oute the more is deere ;
For the solace that I have lorn,
Thanne I hadde it never aforn.
Certayn I am ful like in deede   4329
To hym that caste in erthe his seede,
And hath joie of the newė spryng,
Whanne it greneth in the gynnyng,
And is also faire and fresh of flour,
Lusty to seen, swoote of odour.
But er he it in shevės shere,
May falle a weder that shal it dere,
And makėn it to fade and falle,
The stalke, the greyne, and floures
    alle,
That to the tylyer is fordone
The hopė that he hadde to soone.   4340
I drede certeyn that so fare I ;
For hope and travaile sikerlye
Ben me byraft all with a storme ;
The floure nel seeden of my corne.
For Love hath so avauncėd me
Whanne I bigan my pryvite
To Bialacoil all forto telle,
Whom I ne fonde froward ne felle,
But toke a gree all hool my play.
But Love is of so hard assay,   4350
That all at oonys he revėd me,
Whanne I wente best aboven have be.
It is of love as of fortune,
That chaungeth ofte, and nyl contune ;

Which whilom wole on folkes smyle,
And glowmbe on hem another while ;
Now freend, now foo, shaltow hir feele.
For [in] a twynklyng, turne hir wheele,
Shé can writhe hir heed awey ;
This is the concours of hir pley.   4360
She canne arisė that doth morne,
And whirle adown, and over turne.
Who sittith hieghst, but as hir lust ?
A foole is he that wole hir trust.
For it is I that am come down
Thurgh change and revolucioun.
Sith Bealacoil mote fro me twynne,
Shette in the prisoun yonde withynne,
His absence at myn herte I fele.
For all my joye and all myne hele   4370
Wás in hym and in the rose,
That but yon walle, which hym doth close,
Ópene that I may hym see,
Love nyl not that I curėd be
Óf the peynes that I endure,
Nor of my cruel aventure.
A, Bialacoil, myn ownė deere,
Though thou be now a prisonere,
Kepe attė leste thyne herte to me,
And suffre not that it daunted be ;   4380
Ne late not Ielousie in his rage
Putten thine herte in no servage.
Al though he chastice thee withoute,
And make thy body unto hym loute,
Have herte as hard as dyamaunt,
Stédéfast, and nought pliaunt ;
In prisoun though thi body be,
At largė kepe thyne hertė free.
A trewė hertė wole not plie,
For no manace that it may drye.   4390
If Ielousiė doth thee payne,
Quyte hym his whilė thus agayne
To venge thee attė leest in thought,
If other way thou mai[e]st nought ;
And in this wisė sotilly
Wórche and wynnė the maistrie.
But yit I am in gret affray
Lést thou do not as I say ;
I drede thou canst me gret maugre
That thou enprisoned art for me.   4400
But that [is] not for my trespas,

4313. We get the best rhythm by reading *wher*
nd stressing *For* in the next line. *roses* is often
hus followed by an unaccented syllable ; cp.
g. 4314.
  4322. MSS. *I wente aboute.* The correction is
Kaluza's (except that he reads *wende* for *wente*,
p. v. 4352), and is justified by the Fr. original.
4339. MSS. *tilyers.*
4352. MSS. *abouen to.*

4355. MSS. *folk.*
4357. *shaltow,* MSS. *shalt.*
4372. *walle,* MSS. *wole.*

For thurgh me never discovred was
That thyng that oughté be secree.
Wel more anoyè is in me
Than is in thee of this myschaunce,
For I endure more harde penaunce
Than ony [man] can seyn or thynke ;
That for the sorwe almost I synke.
Whanne I remembre me of my woo,
Full nygh out of my witt I goo.   4410
Inward myn herte I feelé blede ;
For comfortles the deth I drede.
Owe I not wel to have distresse
Whanne falsé thurgh hir wikkednesse
And traitours, that arn envyous,
To noyen me be so curious ?
A, Bialacoil, full wel I see
That they hem shape to disceyve thee,
To make thee buxom to her lawe,
And with her cordé thee to drawe   4420
Where so hem lust, right at her wille ;
I drede they have thee brought thertille.
Withouté comfort thought me sleeth,
This game wole brynge me to my deeth ;
For if youre good[é] wille I leese,
I mote be deed, I may not chese ;
And if that thou foryeté me,
Myne herte shal nevere in likyng be,
Nor elles where fyndé solace,
If I be putt out of youre grace,   4430
As it shal never been, I hope.
Thanne shulde I fallen in wanhope.
Allas—in wanhope ? nay pardee,
For I wole never dispeired be.
If hope me failé, thanne am I
Ungracious and unworthy.
In hope I wole comforted be,
For Love, whanne he bitaught hir me,
Seidé that Hope, where so I goo,
Shulde ay be reles to my woo.   4440
But what and she my baalis beete,
And be to me curteis and sweete ?
Shé is in no thyng full certeyne.
Lovers she putt in full gret peyne,
And makith hem with woo to deele ;
Hir faire biheeste disceyveth feele.
For she wole byhote sikirly,
And failen aftir outrely.
A, that is a full noyous thyng !

4403. MSS. *Yit.*
4441. *what and*, what though.

For many a lover in lovyng   4450
Hangeth upon hir, and trusteth fast,
Whiche leese her travel at the last.
Of thyng to comen she woot right
     nought ;
Therfore if it be wysely sought,
Hir counseill foly is to take.
For many tymes whanne she wole make
A full good silogisme, I dreede
That aftirward ther shal in deede
Folwe an evell conclusioun.
This putte me in confusioun ;   4460
For many tymes I have it seen
That many have bigyled been
For trust that they have sette in hope,
Which felle hem aftirward a-slope.
But nevertheles yit gladly she wolde
That he, that wole hym with hir holde,
Hadde allé tymes his purpos clere,
Withoute deceyte or ony were ;
That she desireth sikirly.
Whanne I hir blamed, I dide foly.   4470
But what avayleth hir good wille ?
Whanne she ne may staunche my stounde
     ille,
That helpith litel that she may doo,
Outake biheest unto my woo.
And heesté certeyn, in no wise
Withouté yift is not to prise.
Whanne heest and deede a-sundry varie,
They doon a gret contrarie.
Thus am I posséd up and doun
With dool, thought, and confusioun ;   4480
Of my disese ther is no noumbre.
Daunger and Shamé me encumbre,
Drede also, and Ielousie,
And Wikked-Tunge full of envie,
Of whiche the sharpe and cruel ire
Full ofte me putte in gret martire.
They han my joyé fully lette,
Sith Bialacoil they have bishette
Fro me in prisoun wikkidly,
Whóm I love so entierly   4490
Thát it wole my bané bee
But I the sonner may hym see.
And yit more over, wurst of all,

4457. *silogisme*, read 'silogim.'
4467. *his*, MSS. *her.*
4472. *stounde*, perhaps read *woundѐ.*
4492. *The sonner may hym ser*, for syn::
cp. 4515.

Ther is sette to kepe (foule hir bifall !)
A rympled vekke, ferre ronne in age,
Frownyng and yelowe in hir visage,
Which in a-wayte lyth day and nyght,
That noon of hym may have a sight.
Now mote my sorwe enforcèd be ;
Full soth it is that Love yaf me   4500
Three wonder yiftès, of his grace,
Whiche I have lorn now in this place,
Sith they ne may, withoutè drede,
Helpen but lytel, who taketh heede.
For here availeth no Swetè-Thought,
And Sweetè-Spechè helpith right nought ;
The thridde was called Swetè-Lokyng,
That now is lorn without lesyng.
Yiftes were faire, but not forthy
They helpè me but symplèly   4510
But Bialacoil loosèd be,
To gon at large and to be free.
For hym my lyf lyth all in doute,
But if he come the rather oute.
Allas, I trowe it wole not bene !
For how shult I evermore hym sene ?
He may not oute, and that is wronge,
By cause the tour is so stronge.
How shulde he oute ? By whos prowesse,
Oute of so stronge a forteresse ?   4520
By me certeyn it nyl be doo ;
God woot I have no witte therto.
But wel I woot I was in rage,
Whonne I to Lovè dide homage.
Who was the cause, in sothfastnesse,
Bùt hir-silf Dame Idelnesse,
Which me conveièd, thurgh my praiere,
To entre into that faire verger ?
She was to blame me to leve,
The which now doth me soorè greve.
A foolis word is nought to trowe,   4531
Ne worth an appel forto love.
Men shulde hym snybbè bittirly
At prymè temps of his foly.

4494. Ther is, one syllable.
4498. hym, MSS. hem.
4511. But, unless. (?) Add all after Bialacoil.
4527. my, MSS. faire from line below ; 'ma
proiere.'
4532. love, MSS. lowe, but love, 'to value,' is
the regular word in this connection. Medial v
and w were sometimes rhymed together in northern
poems ; cp. note to v. 104. The scribe of Gl.
writes w sometimes as v ; cp. wode, v. 4709, where
MS. vode, Th. voyde.

I was a fool and she me leevede,
Thurgh whom I am right nought releeved ;
She accomplisshid all my wille,
That now me greveth wondir ille.
Resoun me seidè what shulde falle.
A fool my silf I may wel calle   4540
That love asyde I hadde not leyde,
And trowed that damè Resoun seide.
Resoun hadde bothè skile and ryght,
Whanne she me blamed with all hir
      myght
To medle of love that hath me shent ;
But certeyn now I wole repente.
    And shulde I repente ? Nay, parde,
A fals traitour thanne shulde I be.
The develes engynnes wolde me take,
If I my lorde woldè forsake,   4550
Or Bialacoil falsly bitraye.
Shulde I at myscheef hate hym ? Nay,
Sith he now for his curtesie
Is in prisoun of Ielousie.
Curtesie certeyn dide he me,
So mych that may not yolden be,
Whanne he the hay passen me lete
To kisse the Rosè faire and swete ;
Shulde I therfore cunne hym mawgre ?
Nay, certeynly, it shal not be ;   4560
For Love shall nevere, yif God wille,
Here of me, thurgh word or wille,
Offence or complaynt more or lesse,
Neither of Hope nor Idilnesse.
For certis it were wrong that I
Hated hem for her curtesie.
Ther is not ellys but suffre and thynke,
And waken whanne I shuldè wynke ;
Abide in hope til Love, thurgh chaunce,
Sende me socour or allegeaunce,   4570
Expectant ay till I may mete
To geten mercy of that swete.
    Whilom I thenke how love to me
Seide he woldè take att gree
My servise, if unpacience
Cáusèd me to done offence.
He seide, 'In thank I shal it take,
And high rhaister eke thee make,
If wikkednesse ne reve it thee ;   4579
But, sone, I trowe that shall not be.'
These were his wordis by and by ;
It semede he lovede me trewèly.
Now is ther not but serve hym wele,

If that I thenke his thanke to fele ;
My good, myne harme lyth hool in me.
In love may no defauté be,
For trewe Love ne failide never man ;
Sothly the faute mote nedys than,
As god forbede, be founde in me.
And how it cometh, I can not see ;   4590
Now late it goon as it may goo,
Whether Love wole socoure me or sloo ;
He may do hool on me his wille ;
I am so soré bounde hym tille,
From his servise I may not fleen ;
For lyf and deth, withouten wene,
Is in his hande, I may not chese,
He may me doo bothe wynne and leese.
And sith so sore he doth me greve,
Yit if my lust he wolde acheve   4600
To Bialacoil goodly to be,
I yeve no force what felle on me.
For though I dye as I mote nede,
I praye Love of his goodlyhede
To Bialacoil do gentylnesse,
For whom I lyve in such distresse,
That I mote deyen for penaunce.
But first withouté repentaunce,
I wole me confesse in good entent,
And make in haste my testament,   4610
As lovers doon that feelen smerte.
To Bialacoil leve I myne herte
All hool withouté departyng,
Or doublenesse of repentyng.

Thus as I madé my passage
In compleynt, and in cruel rage,
And I not where to fynde a leche
That couthe unto myne helpyng eche,
Sodeynly agayn comen doun
Out of hir tour I saugh Resoun,   4620
Discrete, and wis, and full plesaunt,
And of hir porte full avenaunt.
The righté weye she tooke to me,
Which stode in gret perplexite,
That was posshéd in every side,
That I nyst where I myght abide ;
Till she demurely sad of chere,
Seíde to me, as she come neré,
'Myne owné freend, art thou yit greved ?
How is this quarell yit acheved   4630
Of Lovés side?   Anoon me telle.
Hast thou not yit of Love thi fille ?

4592. *Whether*, read *Wher.*

Art thou not wery of thy servise
That the hath in siché wise ?
What joye hast thou in thy lovyng ?
Is it swete or bitter thyng ?
Canst thou yit chesé, late me see,
What best thi socour mygbt be ?
Thou servest a full noble lorde,
That maketh thee thrall for thi rewarde.
Which ay renewith thi turment,   4644
With foly so he hath thee blent.
Thou fell in mycheef thilké day
Whanne thou didist, the sothe to say,
Obeysaunce and eke homage.
Thou wroughtest no-thyng as the sage,
Whanne thou bicam his liegé man ;
Thou didist a gret foly than,
Thou wistest not what fell therto,
With what lord thou haddist to do ;   4652
If thou haddist hym wel knowe,
Thou haddist nought be brought so lowe.
For if thou wistest what it were,
Thou noldist serve hym half a yeer,
Not a weke nor half a day,
Ne yit an hour withoute delay,
Ne never ha lovede paramours.
His lordshipp is so full of shoures,
Knowest hym ought ?'
L'Amaunt.   'Ye, Dame, pardé.'
Raisoun. 'Nay, nay.'
L'Amaunt.   'Yis, I.'
Raisoun.   'Wherof? late se.
L'Amaunt. 'Of that he seidé I shulde be
Glád to have sich lord as he,   4668
And maister of sich seignorie.'
Raisoun. 'Knowist hym no more ?'
L'Amaunt.   'Nay, certis, I.
Save that he yaf me rewles there,
And wente his wey, I nysté where,
And I aboode bounde in balaunce.'
Raisoun. 'Lo, there a noble conisaunce'
But I wille that thou knowe hym now,
Gynnyng and eendé, sith that thou   4677
Art so anguisshous and mate,
Disfigured oute of a-state ;
Ther may no wrecche have more of woo.
Ne caytyfe noon enduren soo.
It were to every man sittyng
Of his lord have knowleching ;
For if thou knewe hym oute of doute,

4634. Insert some word like *harmed* after *hath*

710

Lightly thou shulde escapen oute
Of the prisoun that marreth thee.'
  L'Amaunt. 'Ye, Damė, sith my lord
    is he,   4680
And I his man maad with myn honde,
' woldė right fayne undirstonde
To knowen of what kynde he be,
If ony wolde enformė me.'
  Raisoun. 'I wolde,' seidė Resoun,
  ' thee lere
Sith thou to lerne hast sich desire,
And shewė thee withouten fable,
A thyng that is not demonstrable.
Thou shalt [wite] withouten science,
And knowe withouten experience,   4690
The thyng that may not knowen be,
Ne wist ne shewid in no degre.
Thou maist the sothe of it not witen,
Though in thee it werė writen.
Thou shalt not knowe therof more,
While thou art reuled by his lore.
But unto hym that love wole flee
The knottė may unclosed bee,
Which hath to thee, as it is founde,
So long be knette and not unbounde.
Now sette wel thyne entencioun,   4701
To here of love discripcioun.
  Love it is an hatefull pees,
A free acquitaunce withoute relees,
A truthe frette full of falsheede ;
A sikernesse all sette in drede,
In hertis a dispeiryng hope,
And full of hope it is wanhope ;
Wise woodnesse and wode resoun,
A swetė perell in to droune,   4710
An hevy birthen lyght to bere ;
A wikked wawe alwey to ware,
It is Karibdous perilous ;
Disagreable and gracious ;
It is discordaunce that can accorde,

And accordaunce to discorde ;
It is kunnyng withoute science,
Wisdome withoutė sapience,
Witte withoutė discrecioun,
Havoire withoute possessioun ;   4720
It is sike hele and hool sekenesse,
A thrust drownėd in dronknesse ;
An helthė full of maladie,
And charite full of envie ;
An hunger full of habundaunce,
And a gredy suffisaunce ;
Delite right ful of hevynesse,
And drerihed full of gladnesse ;
Bitter swetnesse and swete errour,
Right evell savoured good savour ;   4730
Syn[nė] that pardoun hath withynne,
And pardoun spotted oute with synne ;
A peyne also it is joious,
And felonyė right pitous ;
Also pley that selde is stable,
And stedefast [stat] right mevable.
A strengthe weykėd to stonde upright,
And feblenessė full of myght ;
Witte unavised, sage folie,
And joiė full of turmentrie ;   4740
A laughter it is, weping ay,
Reste that traveyleth nyght and day ;
Also a swetė helle it is,
And a soroufull paradys ;
A plesaunt gayl and esy prisoun,
And, full of froste, [a] somer sesoun,
Prýme temps full of frostės white,
And May devoide of al delite ;
With seer braunches blossoms ungrene,
And newe fruyt fillid with wynter tene.
It is a slowe may not forbere   4751
Ragges ribaned with gold to were ;
For also well wole love be sette
Under ragges as riche rochette,
And eke as wel by amourettes
In mournyng blak, as bright burnettes.

4687. withouten, perhaps dissyllabic.
4693, 4694. These obscure lines not in Fr. ; perhaps we should connect v. 4693 with v. 4692
reading now witen for not witen), and v. 4694
vith v. 4695.
  4705. MSS. And thurgh the. The correction
s Tyrwhitt's.
  4705. frette full ; cp. Leg. of G. W. 1117.
  4709. Cp. note to v. 4532.
  4712. 'A dangerous sea always to be avoided,
It is Charybdis perilous.' The MS. reading
wey to were (nothing in Fr. corresponding)
does not make good sense.

4722. MSS. A trust . . . and dronknesse.
4723. MSS. And helth.
4725. MSS. And anger.
4728. drerihed, MSS. dreried.
4732. oute with, MSS. withoute.
4751.   C'est taigne qui riens refuse
            Les porpres et les buriaus use.
The word taigne (moth) of the Fr. is probably a
mistake for caigne (cp. Hatzfeld-Darmesteter s. v.
cagne). At least that seems to be the word here
translated slowe, 'a vagabond.'

For noon is of so mochel pris,
Ne no man founden [is] so wys,
Ne noon so high is of parage,
Ne no man founde of witt so sage,   4760
No man so hardy, ne so wight,
Ne no man of so mychel myght,
Noon so fulfillèd of bounte,
That he with love [ne] may daunted be.
All the world holdith this wey,
Lóve makith all to goon myswey,
But it be they of yvel lyf
Whom Genius cursith man and wyf,
That wrongly werke ageyn nature.
Noon such I love, ne have no cure   4770
Of sich as lovès servauntes bene,
And wole not by my counsel flene.
For I ne preisè that lovyng,
Wherthurgh men at the laste eendyng
Shall calle hem wrecchis full of woo,
Love greveth hem and shendith soo.
But if thou wolt wel love eschewe
Forto escape out of his mewe,
And make al hool thi sorwe to slake,
No bettir counsel maist thou take   4780
Than thynke to fleen wel I-wis.
May nought helpe elles; for wite thou this:
It thou fie it, it shal flee thee;
Folowe it, and folowen shal it thee.'
    Whanne I hadde herde all Resoun
      seyne,
Which haddè spilt hir speche in veyne,
' Dáme,' seide I, ' I dar wel sey,
Of this avaunt me wel I may,
That from youre scole so devyaunt
I am, that never the more avaunt   4790
Right nought am I thurgh youre doctrine.
I dulle under youre discipline,
I wote no more than wist [I] ever ;
To me so contrarie and so fer
Is every thing that ye me lere,
And yit I can it all by *par cuer*,
Myne herte foryetith therof right nought,
It is so writen in my thought ;
And depè greven it is so tendir
That all by herte I can it rendre,   4800
And rede it over comunely ;
But to my-silf lewedist am I.
But sith ye love discreven so,
And lak and preise it bothè twoo,

4764. Cp. similar mistake in v. 3774.

Defyneth it into this letter
That I may thenke on it the better :
For I herde never diffyne it ere,
And wilfully I wolde it lere.'
    Raisoun. ' If love be serchèd wel an
      sought,
It is a sykenesse of the thought,   4811
Annexed and knet bitwixè tweyne
Which male and female with oo cheyne
So frely byndith that they nyll twynne,
Whether so therof they leese or wynne.
The rootè springith thurgh hootè brennyng
Into disordinat desiryng
Fórto kissen and enbrace,
And at her lust them to solace ;
Of other thyng love recchith nought
But setteth her herte and all her thought.
Móre for delectacioun   4821
Than ony procreacioun
Of other fruyt by engendrure ;
(Which love to god is not plesure),
For of her body fruyt to gete
They yeve no force, they are so sette
Upon delite to pley in-feere.
And somme have also this manere,
To feynen hem for lovè seke.
Sich love I preise not at a leke,   4831
For paramours they do but feyne,
To lovè truly they disdeyne ;
They falsen ladies traitoursly,
And swerne hem othes utterly,
With many a lesyng and many a fable,
And all they fynden deceyvable ;
And whanne they han her lust [y]geten.
The hootè ernes they al foryeten.
Wymmen the harme they bien full sore.
But men this thenken evermore ;   4841
That lasse harme is, so mote I the,
Deceyve them than deceyved be ;
And namèly where they ne may
Fynde none other menè wey.
For I wote wel, in sothfastnesse,
What wight doth now his bisynesse
With ony womman forto dele
For ony lust that he may fele,
But if it be for engendrure,
He doth trespasse, I you ensure.   4850

4807. MSS. *diffyned heerr*.
4814. *Whether* for *wher*.
4824. *plesure*, MSS. *plesyng*.

'or he shulde setten all his wille
To geten a likly thyng hym tille,
And to sustené, if he myght,
And kepé forth, by kyndés right,
His owné lyknesse and semblable.
'or because all is corumpable,
And failé shulde successioun,
Ve were ther generacioun
Dure sectis strené forto save,   4859
Vhanne fader or moder arn in grave,
Her children shulde, whanne they ben
    deede,
Full diligent ben in her steede
To use that werke on such a wise,
That oon may thurgh another rise.
Therfore sette Kynde therynne delite ;
'or men therynne shulde hem delite,
And of that deedé be not erke,
But ofté sithés haunt that werke.
'or noon wolde drawe therof a draught,
Ve were delite which hath hym kaught.
Thus hath sotilléd Dame Nature ;   4871
'or noon goth right, I thee ensure,
Ve hath entent hool ne parfit,
'or her desir is for delyte ;
The which for tené crece, and eke
The pley of love for-ofté seke,
And thrall hem silf they be so nyce
Jnto the prince of every vyce ;
'or of ech synne·it is the rote
Jnlefull lust, though it be sote,   4880
And of all yvell the racyne,
As Tulius can determyne
Which in his tymé was full sage,)
n a boke he made OF AGE,
Vhére that more he preyseth eelde,
Though he be croked and unweelde,
And more of commendácioun
Than youthe in his discripcioun,
'or youthé sette bothe man and wyf
n all perell of soule and lyf,   4890
And perell is, but men have grace,
The perell of yougth[é] forto pace
Vithoute ony deth or distresse,
t is so full of wyldénesse.

4871. *Thus hath sotilled* (MSS. *This had
)tilled*, etc.), 'soutiva,' *i.e.* thus hath Nature
subtly reasoned.
4875. *for tene crece* (MSS. *fortened crece*);
rese, i.e. increase.
4892. Skeat and Kaluza read *tyme* for *perell*.

So ofte it doth shame or damage
Tó hym, or to his lynage.
It ledith man now up, now doun,
In mochel dissolucioun,
And makith hym love yvell companye,
And lede his lyf disrewlilye,   4900
And halt hym payed with noon estate.
Withynne hym-silf is such debate,
He chaungith purpos and entente
And yalte [him] into somme covente,
To lyven aftir her emprise,
And lesith fredom and fraunchise,
That nature in hym haddé sette.
The which ageyne he may not gette,
If he there make his mansioun,
For to abide professioun.   4910
Though for a tyme his herte absente,
It may not fayle, he shal repente,
And eke abidé thilkè day
To leve his abite and gone his way ;
And lesith his worship and his name,
And dar not come ageyn for shame,
But al his lyf he doth so morne,
By cause he dar not hom retourne.
Fredom of kynde so lost hath he,
That never may recuréd be,   4920
But that if God hym graunté grace
That he may, er he hennés pace,
Conteyne undir obedience
Thurgh the vertu of pacience.
For youthe sett man in all folye,
In unthrift and [in] ribaudie,
In leccherie and in outrage,
So ofte it chaungith of corage.
Youthe gynneth ofté sich bargeyne
That may not eende withouten peyne.
In gret perell is sett youthede,   4931
Delite so doth his bridil leede.
Delite thus hangith, drede thee nought,
Bothe mannys body and his thought
Oonly thurgh youth, [his] chamberere,
That to done yvell is custommere,
And of nought elles taketh hede
But oonly folkés forto lede
Into disporte and wyldénesse,
So [she] is frowarde from sadnesse.   4940
But Eeldé drawith hem therfro,

4933. MSS. *this* for *thus*, 'ainsinc.'
4933. *drede thee nought, i.e.* you may be sure.
4940. Omitted subject.

Who wote it nought, he may wel goo
And moo of hem that now arn olde,
That whilom youthhed hadde in holde,
Which yit remembre of tendir age,
How it hem brought in many a rage,
And many a foly therynne wrought.
But now that Eelde hath hem thourgh
　　　sought,
They repente hem of her folye,
That youthe hem putte in jupardye,　4950
In perell, and in mychè woo,
And made hem ofte amys to do,
And suen yvell companye,
Ríot and avouterie.
　　But Eeldè can ageyn restreyne
From sich foly, and refreyne
And sette men by her ordinaunce
In good reule and in governaunce.
But yvell she spendith hir servise
For no man wole hir love ne preise,　4960
She is hated, this wote I welle,
Hir acqueyntaunce wolde noman fele
Ne han of Eeldè companye,
Men hate to be of hir alye ;
For noman wolde bicomen olde
Ne dye, whanne he is yong and bolde.
And Eelde merveilith right gretlye,
Whanne thei remembre hem inwardly,
Of many a perelous emprise,　4969
Whiche that they wrought in sondry wise,
How evere they myght, withoutè blame,
Escape awey withoutè shame.
In youthè withoutè damage
Or repreef of her lynage,
Losse of membre, shedyng of blode,
Perell of deth, or losse of good.
Woste thou nought where Youthe abit,
That men so preisen in her witt ?
With Delite she halt sojour,
For bothe they dwellen in oo tour.　4980
As longe as Youthe is in sesoun
They dwellen in oon mansioun.
Delite of Youthe wole have servise
To do what so he wole devise ;
And Youthe is redy evermore
Forto obey for smerte of sore

Unto Delite, and hym to yive
Hir servise while that she may lyve.
Where Elde abit I wole thee telle
Shórtly, and no whilè dwelle,　4??
For thidir byhoveth thee to goo.
If deth in youthe [hath] thee not sloo,
Of this journey thou maist not faile.
Wíth hir Labour and Travaile
Lógged ben, with Sorwe and Woo
That never out of hir court goo.
Peyne and Distresse, Syknesse and Ire
And Malencoly, that angry sire,
Ben of hir paleys senatours ;　4?
Gronyng and Grucchyng hir herbejours
The day and nyght hir to turment,
With cruell deth they hir present ;
And tellen hir, erliche and late,
That Deth stont armèd at hir gate.
Thanne brynge they to her remembrauncz
The foly dedis of hir infaunce,
Whiche causen hir to mourne in woo
That Youthe hath hir bigilèd so,
Which sodeynly awey is hasted.
She wepeth the tyme that she hath wasted
Compleynyng of the preterit　5.?
And the present, that not abit,
And of hir oldè vanite ;
That, but aforn hir she may see
Ín the future somme socour,
To leggen hir of hir dolour,
To graunte hir tyme of répentaunee,
Fór her synnes to do penaunce,
And at the laste so hir governe
To wynne the joy that is eterne,　?.?
Fro which go bakward Youthe her m??
In vanite to droune and wade,—
For present tyme abidith nought,
It is more swift than any thought,
So litel while it doth endure
That ther nys comptè ne mesure.
But how that evere the gamè go
Who list to have joie and mirth also
Of lovè, be it he or she

5004. MSS. *stondith*.
5022. The conclusion seems to have been fx::?
by the translator ; Fr.
　　　'Et qu'ele a sa vie perdue
　　　　Se du futur n'est secorue,' etc.
So supply after 5022 :
　　　　Al her lyf she hath forlorn.
5028. *have* (MSS. *love*), read *t'have*.

4943. *moo*, 'demant,' either verb meaning *to
ask* or mistake for some such word.　Cp. v. 5290
and note.
4944. *youthhed*, MSS. *youthe*.
4960. MSS. *neither* ; cp. v. 3718.

714

High or lowė, who it be,   5030
In fruyt they shuldė hem delyte ;
Her part they may not ellės quyte,
To save hem-silf in honeste.
And yit full many one I se
Of wymmen, sothly forto seyne,
Thát desire and woldė fayne
The pley of love, they be so wilde,
And not coveite to go with childe.
And if with child they be perchaunce,
They wole it holde a gret myschaunce ;
But what-som-ever woo they fele,   5041
They wole not pleynė but concele,
But if it be ony fool or nyce
In whom that Shame hath no justice.
For to delyte echone they drawe,
That haunte this werke bothe high and
        lawe,
Sáve sich that arn worth right nought
That for money wole be bought.
Such love I preisė in no wise,   5050
preise no womman though she be wood
That yeveth hir-silf for ony good.
For litel shulde a man telle,
Of hir that wole hir body selle,
Bė she maydė, be she wyf,
That quyk wole selle hir, bi hir lif.
How faire chere that evere she make
Se is a wrecche, I undirtake,
That loved such one, for swete or soure,
hough she hym calle hir paramoure,
nd laugheth on hym, and makith hym
        feeste ;   5061
Sr certeynly no such beeste
Só be loved is not worthy,
r bere the name of drueric.
Noon shulde hir please, but he were
        woode,
Thạt wole dispoile hym of his goode.
t nevertheles I wole not sey
Thạt she for solace and for pley
Se may a jewel or other thyng
Ake of her lovės fre yevyng ;   5070
t that she aske it in no wise,
r drede of shame of coveitise.
d she of hirs may hym certeyn
thoutė sclaundre yeven ageyn,

And joyne her hertes to-gidre so
In love, and take and yeve also.
Trówe not that I wolde hem twynne
Whanne in her love ther is no synne ;
I wole that they to-gedre go,
And don al that they han ado,   5080
As curteis shulde and debonaire,
And in her love beren hem faire,
Withoutė vice, bothe he and she,
So that alwey in honeste
Fro foly love they kepe hem clere,
That brenneth hertis with his fere,
And that her love in ony wise
Bė devoide of coveitise.
Góod love shulde engendrid be
Of trewė herte, just and secre,   5090
And not of such as sette her thought
To have her lust, and ellis nought.
So are they caught in lovės lace,
Truly for bodily solace.
Fleshly delite is so present
With thee, that sette all thyne entent,
Withoutė more (what shulde I glose ?)
Fórto gete and have the Rose,
Which makith [thee] so mate and woode,
That thou desirest noon other goode.   5100
But thou art not an inche the nerre,
But evere abidist in sorwe and werre,
As in thi facė it is sene ;
It makith thee bothe pale and lene ;
Thy myght, thi vertu goth away.
A sory geste, in goodė fay,
Thou herberest then in thyne inne,
The God of Love whanne thou let inne.
Wherfore I rede thou shette hym oute,
Or he shall greve thee, oute of doute ;
For to thi profit it wole turne,   5111
Iff he nomore with thee sojourne.
In gret myscheef and sorwe sonken
Ben hertis that of love arn dronken,
As thou peraunter knowen shall
Whanne thou hast lost thi tyme all,
And spent thy youth in ydilnesse
In waste and wofull lustynesse.
If thow maist lyve the tyme to se
Of love forto delyvered be,   5120

5085. *they*, MSS. *to*.
5107. *then*, MS. *hem;* Th. omits.
5116. *thi tyme*, 'ton tens,' MSS. *the tyme*.
5117. *thy youth*, 'ta jonesce,' MSS. *by thought*.

251. MSS. *though so be wood*; (?) read *to be*
7. ' Mes ja certes n'iert fame bone.'

Thy tyme thou shalt biwepe sore,
The whiche never thou maist restore,
For tyme lost, as men may see,
For no thyng may recured be.
And if thou scape yit atte laste
Fro Love that hath thee so faste
Knytt and bounden in his lace,
Certeyn I holde it but a grace.
For many oon, as it is seyne,
Have lost and spent also in veyne   5130
In his servise, withoute socour,
Body and soule, good and tresour,
Witte and strengthe and eke richesse,
Of which they hadde never redresse.'
    Thus taught and preched hath resoun,
But Love spilte hir sermoun,
That was so ymped in my thought,
That hir doctrine I sette at nought.
And yitt ne seide she never a dele
That I ne undirstode it wele,   5140
Word by word the mater all ;
But unto love I was so thrall,
Which callith over-all his pray,
He chasith so my thought al day,
And halt myne herte undir his sele,
As trust and trew as ony stele.
So that no devocioun
Ne hadde I in the sermoun
Of dame Resoun, ne of hir rede.
It toke no sojour in myne hede,   5150
For all yede oute at [that] oon ere,
That in that other she dide lere ;
Fully on me she lost hir lore.
Hir speche me greved wondir sore.
    Than unto hir for ire I seide,
For anger as I dide abraide :
' Dame, and is it youre wille algate
That I not love, but that I hate
Alle men, as ye me teche ?
For if I do aftir youre speche,   5160
Sith that ye seyne love is not good,
Thanne must I nedis say with mood,
If I it leve, in hatrede ay
To lyven, and voide love away
From me, [and be] a synfull wrecche,

Hated of all that [love that] tecche ;
I may not go noon other gate,
For other must I love or hate.
And if I hate men of newe
More than love, it wole me rewe,
As by youre preching semeth me,
For Love no thing ne preisith thee.
Ye yeve good counsel sikirly,
That prechith me al day that I
Shulde not loves lore alowe,
He were a foole wolde you not trowe
In speche also ye han me taught
Another love that knowen is naught,
Which I have herd you not repreve,
To love ech other.   By youre leve,
If ye wolde diffyne it me,
I wolde gladly here to se,
Atte the leest, if I may lere,
Of sondry loves the manere.'
    Raisoun. ' Certis freend a fool art thou
Whan that thou no thyng wolt allowe.
That I for thi profit say.
Yit wole I sey thee more in fay,
For I am redy at the leste
To accomplisshe thi requeste.
But I not where it wole avayle,
In veyn perauntre I shal travayle.
Love ther is in sondry wise,
As I shal thee heere devise.
For somme love leful is and good :
I mene not that which makith thee wo
And bringith thee in many a fitte
And ravysshith fro thee al thi witte,
It is so merveilouse and queynte ;
With such love be no more aqueynte.
    Love of freendship also ther is,
Which makith no man done amys,
Of wille knytt bitwixe two,
That wole not breke for wele ne wo
Which long is likly to contune
Whanne wille and goodis ben in comun
Grounded by goddis ordinaunce,
Hoole withoute discordaunce ;
With hem holdyng comunte
Of all her goode in charite ;
That ther be noon excepcioun
Thurgh chaungyng of entencioun :
That ech helpe other at her neede.

5144. *al day*, MSS. *ay* ; cp. v. 5174.
5145. *halt*, MSS. *holdith.*
5162. *say,* an aphetic form of *assay,* to attempt.
5164. MSS. omit *To.*
5165. The bracketed words (Skeat's readings)
seem necessary to the sense.

5172. *preisith thee,* ' Tout me vaille Am
denier.'

716

And wisely hele bothe word and dede;
Trewe of menyng, devoide of slouthe,
For witt is nought withoutė trouthe,
So that the ton dar all his thought,
Seyn to his freend and sparė nought
As to hym silf, withoute dredyng
To be discovered by wreying.   5220
For glad is that conjunccioun
Whanne ther is noon susspecioun,
Ne lak in hem] whom they wolde
     prove,
That trewe and parfit weren in love.
For no man may be amyable,
But if he be so ferme and stable
That fortune chaunge hym not, ne blynde;
But that his freend all-wey hym fynde,
Bothe pore and ríche, in oon estate.
For if his freend, thurgh ony gate,   5230
Wole compleyne of his poverte,
He shulde not bide so long til he
Of his helpyng hym requere;
For goode dedė done thurgh praiere
Is sold and bought to deere, I-wys,
To hert that of grete valour is.
For hert fulfilled of gentilnesse
Can yvel demenė his distresse,
And man, that worthy is of name,
To asken often hath gret shame.   5240
A good man brenneth in his thought
For shamė, whanne he axeth ought.
He hath gret thought, and dredeth ay
For his disese, whanne he shal pray
His freend, lest that he warnėd be,
Til that he preve his stabilte.
But whanne that he hath founden oon,
That trusty is and trewe as stone,
And [hath] assaied hym at alle,
And founde hym stedefast as a walle   5250
And of his freendship be certeyne,
He shal hym shewe bothe joye and
     peyne,
And all that [he] dar thynke or sey,
Withoutė shame, as he wel may.
For how shulde he a-shamėd be
Of sich one as I toldė thee?
For whanne he woot his secre thought,

The thridde shal knowe therof right
     nought;
For tweyne of noumbre is bet than thre
In every counsell and secre.   5260
Repreve he dredeth never a deele
Who that bisett his wordis wele.
For every wise man, out of drede,
Can kepe his tunge til he se nede;
And foolės can not holde her tunge —
"A foolės belle is soonė runge."
Yit shal a trewė freend do more,
To helpe his felowe of his sore,
And socoure hym, whanne he hath neede,
In all that he may done in deede;   5270
And gladder [be] that he hym plesith,
Thán his felowe, that he esith.
And if he do not his requeste,
He shal as mochel hym moleste
As his felow, for that he
May not fulfille his volunte
Fúlly, as he hath requered.
If bothe the hertis Love hath fered,
Jóy and woo they shull departe
And take evenly ech his parte;   5280
Half his anoy he shal have ay,
And comfort [him] what that he may;
And of his blissė parte shal he,
If lovė wel departed be.
   And whilom of this unyte
Spake Tulius in a ditee,
Man shuldė maken his requeste
Unto his freend that is honeste,
And he goodly shulde it fulfille,
But if the more were out of skile;   5290
And other wise not graunte therto,
Except oonly in causes twoo;
If men his freend to deth wolde drive,
Late hym be bisy to save his lyve;
Also if men wolen hym assayle
Of his wurship to make hym faile,
And hyndren hym of his renoun;

5223. Tiex mors (mœurs) avoir doivent et seulent
     Qui parfetement amer veulent.
The bracketed words were supplied by Professor
Kent.

5274. *He.* Perhaps read *That* or *It*, as a re-
flexive verb *molest* is unusual.
5282. *comfort him* (MSS. omit *him*), 'le
conforte.'
5284. *wel* (MSS. *wole*), 'a droit.'
5287. *Man* (MSS. *And*) *shuldė*, one should,
'devons.'
5290. MSS. *But if. more* is either a subst.
meaning *request*, or a similar mistake to that in
v. 4943.
5292. *causes* (MSS. *cause*), cases.

Late hym, with full entencioun,
His dever done in eche degre
Thát his freend ne shaméd be,   5300
In this two causes with his myght,
Taking no kepe to skile nor right
As ferre as love may hym excuse ;
Thís ought no man to refuse.
This love, that I have tolde to thee,
Is no thing contrarie to me ;
This wole I that thou folowe wele,
And leve the tother everydele ;
This love to vertu all entendith,
The tothir foolés blent and shendith. 5310
   Another love also there is,
That is contrarie unto this ;
Whích desire is so constreyned
Thát [it] is but willé feyned.
Awey fro trouthe it doth so varie,
That to good love it is contrarie,
Fór it maymeth in many wise
Síké hertis with coveitise.
All in wynnyng and in profit
Sich love settith his delite.   5320
This love so hangeth in balaunce,
That if it lese his hope perchaunce
Of lucre that he is sett upon,
Ít wole faile and quenche anoon.
For no man may be amerous,
Ne in his lyvyng vertuous,
Bút he lové more in moode
Men for him-silf than for her goode.
For love that profit doth abide
Is fals, and bit not in no tyde   5330
[This] lové cometh of Dame Fortune,
That litel whilé wole contune ;
For it shal chaungen wonder soone,
And take Eclips ; right as the moone
Whanne he is from us lett
Thurgh erthé, that bitwixe is sett
The sonne and hir, as it may falle,
Be it in partie or in all.
The shadowe maketh her bemys merke,
And hir hornes to shewe derke   5340
That part where she hath lost hir lyght
Of Phebus fully, and the sight ;
Til, whanne the shadowe is overpaste,

She is enlumyned ageyn as faste
Thurgh the brightnesse of the sonné bemes
That yeveth to hir ageyne hir lemes.
That love is right of sich nature,
Now is faire, and now obscure,
Now bright, now clipsi of manere,
And whilom dymme, and whilom clere.
As soone as poverte gynneth take,   5350
With mantel and [with] wedis blake
Hidith of love the light awey,
That into nyght it turneth day ;
It may not see richessé shyne,
Till the blaké shadowes fyne.
For whanne richessé shyneth bright
Love recovereth ageyn his light,
And whanne it failith, he wole flit ;
And as she groweth, so groweth it. 5360
Óf this love here what I sey :
The riché men are lovéd ay,
And namely tho that sparand bene,
That wole not wasshe her hertes clene
Óf the filthe, nor of the vice
Of gredy brennyng avarice.
The riche man full sonned is y-wys,
That weneth that he loved is ;
If that his herte it undirstode,
It is not he, it is his goode ;   5370
He may wel witen in his thought
His good is loved and he right nought
For if he be a nygard eke,
Men wole not sette by hym a leke,
But haten hym, this is the sothe.
Lo, what profit his catell doth ?
Of every man that may hym see,
It geteth hym nought but enmyte.
But he amende hym of that vice,
And knowe hym silf, he is not wys. 5380
Certys he shulde ay freendly be,
To gete him love also ben free,
Or ellis he is not wise ne sage,
Nomore than is a gote ramage.
   That he not loveth his dede proveth
Whan he his richesse so wel loveth
That he wole hide it ay and spare,
His poré freendis sene forfare
To kepen alway his purpose,

5301. MSS. *caas.*
5327. Perhaps inseit *if* after *But.*
5342. Such displacements as this of *and* were
common in 15th century verse.

5351. *take,* 'l'afuble.'
5353. *Hidith.* Skeat reads *It hit,* and per-
rightly.
5379. *hym,* MSS. *hymself.*
5389. *alway,* MSS. *ay ;* cp. v. 5144.

718

Til for drede his yen close,   5390
And til a wikked deth hym take.
Hym hadde lever a-sondre shake
And late hise lymes a-sondre ryve,
Than leve his richesse in his lyve ;
He thenkith parte it with no man.
Certayn no love is in hym than ;
How shuldé love withynne hym be,
Whanne in his herte is no pite ?
That he trespasseth wel I wat,
For ech man knowith his estate.   5400
For wel hym ought to be reproved
That loveth nought, ne is not loved.
But sen we arn to fortune comen,
And hath oure sermoun of hir nomen,
A wondir will y telle thee nowe ;
Thou herdist never sich oon I trowe.
note where thou me leven shall,
Though sothfastnesse it be at all.
As it is writen and is soth,
That unto men more profit doth   5410
The froward fortune and contraire,
Than the swote and debonaire ;
And if thee thynke it is doutable
It is thurgh argument provable ;
Fór the debonaire and softe
Fálsith and bigilith ofte.
For lyche a moder she can cherishe,
And mylken [hem] as doth a norys ;
And of hir goodé to hem deles,
And yeveth hem parte of her joweles,
With grete richesse and dignite ;   5421
And hem she hoteth stabilite
In a state that is not stable,
But chaungynge ay and variable ;
And sedith hym with glorie veyne,
In worldly blissé noncerteyne.
Whanne she hem settith on hir whele
Thanne wené they to be right wele,
And in so stable state withall
That never they wené forto falle.   5430
And whanne they sette so highé be,
They wene to have in certeynte

Of hertly freendis so grete noumbre
That no thyng mygbt her state encombre.
They trust hem so on every side,
Wenyng with hem they wolde abide
In every perell and myschaunce,
Withouté chaunge or variaunce
Bóthe of catell and of goode.
And also forto spende her bloode,   5440
And all her membris forto spille,
Oonly to fulfille her wille.
They maken it hole in many wise,
And hoten hem her full servise,
How soré that it do hem smerte,
Into her naked sherte.
Herte and all so hole they yive,
For the tyme that they may lyve.
Só that with her flaterie,
They maken foolis glorifie   5450
Of her wordis spekyng,
And han ther-of a rejoysyng,
And trowe hem as the Evangile :
And it is all falsheede and gile,
As they shal aftirwardé se
Whanne they arn falle in poverte,
And ben of good and catell bare ;
Thanne shulde they sene who freendis ware.
For of an hundred certeynly,
Nor of a thousande full scarsly,   5460
Ne shal they fynde unnethis oon
Whanne poverté is comen upon.
For this Fortune that I of telle
With men whanne hir lust to dwelle,
Makith hem to leese her conisaunce,
And norishith hem in ignoraunce.
    But froward Fortune and perverse,
Whanne high estatis she doth reverse,
And maketh hem to tumble doune
Óf hir whele, with sodeyn tourne,   5470
And from her richesse doth hem fle,
And plongeth hem in poverte,
As a stepmoder envyous
And leieth a plastre dolorous
Unto her hertis wounded egre,
Which is not tempred with vynegre

5393. MSS. late all.
5399. MSS. wel I wot.
5401. For, (?) read Full, 'moult.'
5405. Cp. Boece, 583 ff.
5408. at all (MSS. it all), altogether.
5419. deles, (?) dele infinitive construed with
in and rhyming with jowele; cp. v. 2092. If so,
ad yeve in v. 5420.
5426. In, MSS. And, Fr. 'en.'

5433. so, MSS. to, Fr. 'tant.'
5452. ther-of, MSS. cheer of, (Kaluza).
5463. this, MSS. thus, 'ceste.'
5470. Of, off.
5473. The And of next verse seems to belong
before As, else v. 5474 precedes v. 5473.
    Et lor assiet comme marastre
    Au cuer un dolereus emplastre.

But with poverte and indigence—
Forto shewe by experience
That she is Fortune verelye,
In whom no man shulde affye,   5480
Nor in hir yeftis have fiaunce,
She is so full of variaunce.
Thus kan she maken high and lowe,
Whanne they from richesse arn [y-]throwe,
Fully to knowen without were
Freend of affect and freend of chere ;
And which in love were trewe and stable,
And whiche also were variable,
After Fortune her goddesse,
In poverte outher in richesse.   5490
For all she yeveth here, out of drede,
Unhappe bereveth it in dede ;
For in-fortune late not oon
Of freendis, whanne Fortune is gone—
I mene tho freendis that wole fle
Anoon, as entreth poverte ;
And yit they wole not leve hem so,
But in ech placé where they go,
They calle hem " wrecché," scorne, and
        blame,
And of her myshappe hem diffame.   5500
And namely siche as in richesse
Pretendid moost of stablenesse,
Whanne that they sawe hym sette on lofte,
And were of hym socouréd ofte,
And most yholpe in all her neede ;
But now they take no maner heede,
But seyn in voice of flaterie,
That now apperith her folye
Over-all where so they fare,
And syngé " Go fare-wel, feldefare." 5510
All suché freendis I beshrewe,
For of trewe ther be to fewe.
But sothfast freendis, what so bitide,
In every fortune wolen abide ;
Thei han her hertis in suche noblesse
That they nyl love for no richesse,
Nor for that fortune may hem sende

Thei wolen hem socoure and defende,
And chaunge for softe ne for sore ;
For who is freend loveth evermore.   5520
Though men drawe swerde his freend to s..
He may not hewe her love a-two,
But in case that I shall sey ;
For pride and ire lese it he may,
And for reprove by nycete,
And discovering of privite ;
With tongé woundyng as feloun,
Thurgh venemous detraccioun.
Frende in this case wole gone his way,
For no thyng greve hym more ne may.
And for nought ellis wole he fle,   5531
If that he love in stabilite.
And certeyn he is wel bigone,
Among a thousand that fyndith oon :
For ther may be no richesse
Ageyns frendshipp of worthynesse ;
For it ne may so high atteigne
As may the valoure, soth to seyne,
Of hym that loveth trew and well.
Frendshipp is more than is catell,   5540
For freend in court ay better is,
Than peny in purs certis.
And Fortune myshappyng,
Whanne upon men she is fallyng
Thúrgh mysturnyng of hir chaunce,
And casteth hem oute of balaunce,
She makith thurgh hir adversite
Mén full clerly forto se
Hym that is freend in existence,
From hym that is by apparence.   5550
For yn-fortune makith anoon,
To knowe thy freendis fro thy foon,
By experience right as it is.
The which is more to preise y-wis,
Than is myche richesse and tresour.
For more dothe profit and valour
Poverte and such adversite
Bi fer than doth prosperite ;
For the toon yeveth conysaunce,
And the tother ignoraunce.   5560
    And thus in poverte is in dede
Tróuthe declaréd fro falsheed,
For feynté frendis it wole declare,
And trewe also what wey they fare.

5486. *affect*, see *New English Dictionary*, s.v.
5486. Cp. Chaucer's *Fortune*, v. 34, and *Boece*,
590 ff.
5491. *she*, MSS. *that* ; ' Car ceus que beneurte
donne.'
5493. *late*, (?) *leveth*, 'remaint.'
5493. *oon* is subject of *late*, 'remains.'
5502. MSS. *pretendith*.
5510. *Go fare-wel*, etc., v. *New English Dict.*
under Farewell.

5519. *And*. *Ne* with semicolon after ...
would make better sense.
5544. *fallyng*, MS. *fablyng*, 'cheans.'

For whanne he was in his richesse,
These freendis ful of doublenesse
Offrid hym in many wise
Hért, and body, and servise ;
What wolde he thanne ha yove to ha bought
To knowen openly her thought,   5570
That he now hath so clerly seen ?
The lasse bigiled he shulde have bene,
And he hadde thanne perceyved it ;
But richesse nold not late hym witte.
Wel more avauntage doth hym thanne,
Sith that it makith hym a wise man,
The gret myscheef that he receyveth,
Than doth richesse that hym deceyveth.
Richesse richè ne makith nought
Hym that on tresour sette his thought,
For richesse stonte in suffisaunce   5581
And no-thyng in habundaunce ;
For suffisaunce all oonly
Makith men to lyvè richély.
Fór he that at mycches tweyne,
Ne valued [is] in his demeine,
Lyveth more at ese, and more is riche,
Than doth he that is chiche,
And in his berne hath, soth to seyn,·
An hundred mowis of whete greyne, 5590
Though he be chapman or marchaunte,
And have of golde many [a] besaunte.
For in the getyng he hath such woo,
And in the kepyng drede also,
And sette evermore his bisynesse
Forto encrese, and not to lesse,
Forto aument and multiplie.
And though on hepis that lye hym bye
Yit never shal makè his richesse
Asseth unto his gredynesse.   5600
But the povere that recchith nought,
Save of his lyflode, in his thought,
Which that he getith with his travaile,

He dredith nought that it shall faile,
Though he have lytel worldis goode,
Mete, and drynke, and esy foode,
Upon his travel and lyvyng,
And also suffisaunt clothyng.
Or if in syknesse that he fall,
And lothè mete and drynke withall,   5610
Though he have not his mete to bye
He shal bithynke hym hastily
To putte hym oute of all daunger,
That he of mete hath no myster ;
Or that he may with lytel eke
Be founden, while that he is seke ;
Or that men shull hym berne in haste,
To lyvè til his syknesse be paste,
Tó somme maysondewe biside ;   5619
Or he caste nought what shal hym bitide—
He thenkith nought that evère he shall
Into ony sykènessè fall.
And though it falle, as it may be,
That all be-tymè spare shall he
As mochel, as shal to hym suffice
While he is sike in ony wise,
He doth [that] for that he wole be
Cóntente with his poverte,
Withoutè nede of ony man.
So myche in litel have he can,   5630
He is apaied with his fortune ;
And for he nyl be importune
Unto no wight, ne honerous,
Nor of her goodès coveitous,
Therfore he spareth, it may wel bene,
His pore estate forto sustene.
Or if hym lust not forto spare,
But suffrith forth as not ne ware,
Atte last it hapneth as it may
Right unto his lastè day,   5640
And taketh the world as it wolde be ;
For evere in hertè thenkith he,
The sonner that [the] deth hym slo,
To paradys the sonner go
He shal, there forto lyve in blisse,

5569. yove, MSS. yow, p. pt. of yive. Read
to ha as one word. The thought is borrowed
from Boethius ; see Chaucer's Boece, 590.
5573. And, if.
5577. receyveth, MSS. perceyveth, 'recoit.'
5585. at, MSS. hath. 'Car tex n'a pas voillant
deus miches.'
5586. Ne valued is, MSS. Ne value; cp. v.
above.
5590. mowis, MSS. mavis, 'mius.'
5598. that, i.e. the gold ; (?) read they, referring
to the besauntes.
5599. He shall never make his riches satisfy
(asseth) his greed.

5617. berne for beren ; cp. myxnes, v. 6496.
5620. Or supplied from Fr. 'ou.'
5638, 5639. Fr.

> Ainsi viengnent li froit et li chaut
> En la fin qui morir le face ;

so perhaps read :

> But suffrith frost as hot ne ware,
> He lat it hapne as it may.

5641. MSS. take.

Where that he shal noo good misse ;
Thider he hopith God shal hym sende,
Aftir his wrecchid lyves ende.
Pictagoras hym silf reherses
In a book, that the Golden Verses   5650
Is clepid for the nobilite
Of the honourable ditee,
That whanne thou goste thy body fro,
Fre in the eir thou shalt up go,
And leven al humanite,
And purely lyve in deïte.
He is a foole withouten were
That trowith have his Countre heere ;
In erthè is not oure Countre—   5659
That may these clerkis seyn, and see
In Boice of Consolacioun,
Where it is makèd mencioun
Of oure countre pleyn at the yë
By teching of Philosophie ;
Where lewid men myght lerè witte,
Who so that wolde translaten it.
If he be sich that can wel lyve
Aftir his rentè may hym yive,
And not desireth more to have,
Than may fro poverte hym save.   5670
A wise man seide, as we may seen,
Is no man wrecche but he it wene,
Be he kyng, knyght, or ribaude ;
And many a ribaude is mery and baude
That swynkith and berith bothe day and
    nyght
Many a burthen of gret myght,
The whichè doth hym lasse offense
Fór he suffrith in pacience.
They laugh and dauncè, trippe and synge,
And ley not up for her lyvyng,   5680
But in the taverne all dispendith
The wynnyng that God hem sendith.
Thanne goth he fardeles forto bere,
With as good chere as he dide ere ;
To swynke and traveile he not feynith,
For for to robben he disdeynith ;
But right anoon aftir his swynke

He goth to taverne forto drynke.
All these ar riche in abundaunce,
That can thus havè suffisaunce   5691
Wel more than can an usurere,
As God wel knowith, withoute were.
For an usurer, so God me se,
Shal nevere for richesse richè be,
But evermore pore and indigent,
Scarce and gredy in his entent.
For soth it is, whom it displese,
Ther may no marchaunt lyve at ese.
His herte in sich a werre is sett,
That it quyk brenneth more to gete,   5700
Ne never shal enough have geten,
Though he have gold in gerners yeten.
Forto be nedy he dredith sore,
Wherfore to geten more and more
He sette his herte and his desire.
So hote he brennyth in the fire,
Of coveitise, that makith hym woode
To purchace other mennès goode.
He undirfongith a gret peyne
That undirtakith to drynke up Seyne ;
For the more he drynkith ay   5711
The more he leveth, the soth to say.
Thús is thurst of fals getyng,
Thát laste ever in coveityng,
Ánd the angwisshe and distresse,
Wíth the fire of gredynesse.
She fightith with hym ay and stryveth,
That his herte a-sondre ryveth ;
Such gredynessè hym assaylith,
That whanne he most hath, most he failith.
Phisiciens and advocates   5721
Góne right by the samè yates ;
They selle her science for wynnyng,
And haunte her crafte for gret getyng.
Her wynnyng is of such swetnesse,
That if a man falle in sikenesse,
They are full glad for ther encrese ;
For by her wille, withoutè lees,
Everichè man shuldè be seke,   5729
And though they die, they sette not a lekc.
After, whanne they the gold have takc.
Full litel care for hem they make ;
They wolde that fourty were seke atonys—

5650. (?) Omit *the* ; there is no article in the Fr.
The book referred to is the *Aurea Carmina*, extant in the Middle Ages as a work of Pythagoras.
5653. *That*, MSS. *Thanne*.
5661. *of Consolacioun*, 'de Consolatione.'
Jehan de Meung refers to I, pr. v.
5663. MSS. *eye*.
5672. MSS. *wrecched* ; cp. *Boece*, 394.

5701. *enough have*, MSS. *though he ha:t*
(Kaluza).
5706. Cp. *Boece*, 325.
5713. Kaluza reads *This* for *Thus*.

Ye ii hundred in flesh and bonys,
And yit ii thousand, as I gesse,
Forto encrecen her richesse.
They wole not worchen in no wise,
But for lucre and coveitise.
For Fysic gynneth first by 'Fy'
(The Phisicien also sothely);   5740
And sithen it goth fro "Fy" to "Sy,"
To truste on hem [it] is foly,
For they nyl, in no maner gre,
Do right nought for charite.
　Eke in the same secte ar sette
All tho that prechen forto gete
Worshipes, honour, and richesse.
Her hertis arn in grete distresse,
That folk [ne] lyve not holily.
But aboven all specialy   5750
Sich as prechen [in] veynglorie,
And toward god have no memorie,
But forth as ypocrites trace,
And to her soules deth purchace
An outward shewing holynesse,
Though they be full of cursidnesse,
Not liche to the apostles twelve.
They deceyve other and hem selve ;
Bigiled is the giler thanne,
For prechyng of a cursed man   5760
Though [it] to other may profite,
Hymsilf it vaileth not a myte.
For ofte goode predicacioun
Cometh of evel entencioun.
To hym not vailith his preching,
All helpe he other with his teching.
For where they good ensaumple take,
There is he with veynglorie shake.
But late us leven these prechoures,
And speke of hem that in her toures   5770
Hepe up her gold, and faste shette,
And sore theron her herte sette.
They neither love God ne drede,
They kepe more than it is nede,
And in her bagges sore it bynde ;

Out of the soune, and of the wynde,
They putte up more than nede ware.
Whanne they seen pore folk forfare,
For hunger die, and for cold quake,
God can wel vengeaunce therof take.   5780
Thre gret myscheves hem assailith,
And thus in gadring ay travaylith :
With mychel peyne they wynne richesse,
And drede hem holdith in distresse
To kepe that they gadre faste,
With sorwe they leve it at the laste ;
With sorwe they bothe dye and lyve
That unto richesse her hertis yive.
And in defaute of love it is,
As it shewith ful wel I-wys ;   5790
For if this gredy, the sothe to seyn,
Loveden and were loved ageyn,
And goode Love regned over-all,
Such wikkidnesse ne shulde fall.
But he shulde yeve, that most good hadde,
To hem that weren in nede bistadde ;
And lyve withoute false usure,
For charite, full clene and pure.
If they hem yeve to goodnesse,
Defendyng hem from ydelnesse,   5800
In all this world thanne pover noon
We shulde fynde, I trowe not oon.
But chaunged is this world unstable,
For love is over-all vendable ;
We se that no man loveth nowe,
But for wynnyng and for prowe.
And love is thralled in servage,
Whanne it is sold for avauntage ;
Yit wommen wole her bodyes selle—
Suche soules goth to the devel of helle.

　.　　.　　.　　.　　.

Whanne Love hadde told hem his entent,

5801. *pover*, MSS. *pore*; cp. v. 6489.
5811. The translation is here interrupted, ll. 5137-10694 of the French (*Michel*, i. p. 171, l. 5876—p. 355, l. 11443; *Marteau*, ii. p. 70, l. 5397—iii. p. 48, l. 11060) not having been translated. The following is a synopsis (abridged from Bell's Chaucer) of the missing portion :—Reason shows the vanity of natural love and the caprice of Fortune, and exhorts l'Amant to fix his heart on Charity. L'Amant maintains his loyalty to the God of Love, and Reason leaves him. He then consults l'Ami, who advises him to approach Bel-Acueil's prison by a road called Trop-Donner, constructed by Largesse. L'Ami then gives l'Amant directions as to how he is to conduct himself towards his mistress and his wife, and leaves him to pursue his adventure. L'Amant

5739-5742. The key of the pun is found in v. 5742 : 'Physyc' goes from 'fying'=trusting, to 'sying'=sighing and groaning. The joke was probably an old one in our author's time, for it depends for its fullest point on the earlier form of 'sien,' viz. 'sicen,' still used by Chaucer, and by the translator of the 'A' part of the Romaunt (cp. v. 1641).
5755. *An*, MSS. *And*.
5762. MSS. *availeth* ; cp. v. 5765.

The baronage to councel went ;   5812
In many sentences they fille,
And dyversly they seide hir wille.
But aftir discorde they accorded,
And her accord to Love recorded :
'Sir,' seiden they, 'we ben atone
Bi evene accorde of everichone,
Outaké Richesse al oonly,
That sworne hath ful hauteynly,   5820
That she the castell nyl not assaile,
Ne smyte a stroke in this bataile
With darte ne macé, spere ne knyf,
For man that spekith or berith the lyf,
And blameth youre emprise, I-wys,
And from oure hoost departed is,
Atte lest wey as in this plyte,
So hath she this man in dispite.
For, she seith, he ne loved hir never,
And therfore she wole hate hym evere.
For he wole gadre no tresoure,   5831
He hath hir wrath for evermore ;
He agylte hir never in other caas,
Lo, heere all hoolly his trespas.
She seith wel that this other day
He axide hir leve to gone the way
That is clepid "To-moche-yevyng,"
And spak full faire in his praiyng.
But whanne he praide hir, pore was he,
Therfore she warned hym the entre ;   5840
Ne yit is he not thryven so
That he hath geten a peny or two,
That quytly is his owne, in holde.
Thus hath Richesse us all[é] tolde ;
And whanne Richesse us this recorded,
Withouten hir we ben accorded.
And we fynde in oure accordaunce
That False-Semblant and Abstinaunce,
With all the folk of her bataille,
Shull at the hyndre gate assaile,   5850
That Wikkid-Tunge hath in kepyng
With his Normans full of janglyng ;
And with hem Curtesie and Largesse,
Thát shull shewe her hardynesse
To the oldé wyf, that kepte so harde
Fair-Welcomyng withynne her warde ;

Thanne shal Delite and Wel-Heelynge
Fóndé Shame adowne to brynge,
With all her oost early and late
They shull assailen that ilké gate ;   5860
Agaynes Drede shall Hardynesse
Assayle, and also Sikernesse
With all the folk of her ledyng,
That never wist what was fleyng ;
Fraunchise shall fight and eke Pite
With Daunger, full of Cruelte ;
Thus is youre hoost ordeyned wele.
Doune shall the castell every-dele,
If everiché do his entent,
Só that Venus be present,   5870
Youre modir full of vesselage
That can ynough of such usage.
Withouten hir may no wight spede
This werk, neithir for word ne deede ;
Therfore is good ye for hir sende,
For thurgh hir may this werk amende.'
    ' Lordynges, my modir, the goddesse,
That is my lady and my maistresse,
Nis not [at] all at my willyng,
Ne doth not all my desiryng ;   5880
Yit can she some tyme done labour,
Whanne that hir lust, in my socour,
As my nede is forto a-cheve.
But now I thenke hir not to geve ;
My modir is she, and of childehede,
I bothé worshipe hir and drede.
For who that dredith sire ne dame,
Shal it abye in body or name.
And netheles yit kunné we
Sende aftir hir if nedé be ;   5890
And were she nygh she comen wolde,
I trowe that no thyng myght hir holde.
Mi modir is of gret prowesse,
She hath tan many a forteresse,
That cost hath many a pounde, er this,
There I nas not present y-wis ;
And yit men seide it was my dede.
But I come never in that stede,
Ne me ne likith, so mote I the,   5899
That suche toures ben take withoute me.
For why me thenkith that in no wise
It may bene clepid but marchandise.

approaches the castle, but Richesse bars his entrance.   The God of Love comes to his assist-ance, first convoking a council of his barons. Here the English begins again.
    5856. Fair-Welcomyng, hitherto called Bial-acoil.

5883. As my nede is. Kaluza reads Al my nedis, and perhaps rightly ; ' mes besoignes,' 'affairs,' read as ' mes besoinges ('needs '). Cp. similar translation in Boece, 147.
    5886. MSS. eke drede.

Go bye a courser, blak or white,
And pay therfore, than art thou quyte ;
The marchaunt owith thee right nought,
Né thou hym, whanne thou it bought.
I wole not sellyng clepé " yevyng,"
For sellyng axeth no guerdonyng,
Here lith no thank ne no merite ;
That oon goth from that other al quyte.
But this sellyng is not sémblable ;   5911
For whanne his hors is in the stable,
He may it selle ageyn, parde,
And wynnen on it, such happe may be ;
All may the man not leese I·wys,
For at the leest the skynne is his.
Or ellis if it so bitide
That he wole kepe his hors to ride,
Yit is he lord ay of his hors.
But thilké chaffare is wel wors,   5920
There Venus entremetith ought.
For who-so such chaffare hath bought,
He shal not worchen so wisely,
That he ne shal leese al outerly
Bóthe his money and his chaffare.
But the seller of the ware
The prys and profit havé shall,
Certeyn the biér shal leese all.
For he ne can so dere it bye
To have lordship and full maistrie,   5930
Ne have power to maké lettyng
Neithir for yift ne for prechyng,
That of his chaffare, maugré his,
Another shal have asmoche, I-wis,
If he wole yeve as myche as he,
Of what contrey so that he be ;
Or for right nought, so happé may,
If he can flater hir to hir pay.
Bén thanne siché marchauntz wise ?
Nó but fooles in every wise,   5940
Whanne they bye sich thyng wilfully
There as they leese her good fully.
But nathéles this dar I say,
My modir is not wont to pay,
For she is neither so fool ne nyce
To entremete hir of sich vyce.
But trusteth wel he shal pay all,
That répent of his bargeyn shall,

Whanne poverte putte hym in distresse,
All were he scoler to Richesse,   5950
That is for me in gret yernyng
Whanne she assentith to my willyng.
But [by] my modir seint Venus,
And by hir fader Saturnus,
That hir engendride by his lyf
(But not upon his weddid wyf)—
Yit wole I more unto you swere
To make this thyng the sikerere :—
Now by that feith and that leaute
That I owe to all my britheren fre,   5960
Of which ther nys wight undir heven
That kan her fadris names neven,
So dyverse and so many ther be,
That with my modir have be prive ;
Yit wolde I swere for sikirnesse,
The pole of helle to my witnesse,
Now drynke I not this yeere claire,
If that I lye or forsworne be !
(For of the goddes the usage is,
That who so hym forswereth amys   5970
Shal that yeer drynké no clarre.)
Now have I sworne ynough pardee,
If I forswere me, thanne am I lorne—
But I wole never be forsworne.
Syth Richesse hath me failed heere,
She shal abye that trespas dere,
Átté leest wey but hir arme
With swerd, or sparth or [with] gysarme.
For certis sith she loveth not me
Fro thilké tyme that she may se   5980
The castell and the tour to-shake,
In sory tyme she shal awake.
If I may grype a riché man,
I shal so pulle hym, if I can,
That he shal in a fewé stoundes
Lese all his markis and his poundis ;
I shal hym make his pens outslynge,
Bút they in his gerner sprynge.
Oure maydens shal eke pluk hym so,
That hym shal neden fetheres mo,   5990
And make hym selle his londe to spende,
But he the bet kunne hym defende.
Pore men han maad her lord of me ;

5915. *All* is object of *leese*.
5931. *make leityng*, *i.e.* put hindrance in his way.
5942. *fully*, MSS. *folyly*, ' ou tant perdent.'
5947. MSS. *trust*.

5958. *sikererе*, MSS. *sеuererr*, (Kaluza's emendation) based on vv. 6147, 7308.
5959. *leaute*, MSS. *beaute*. The same error occurs in v. 6006.
5976. *dere*, MSS. *ful dere*, ' chiers.'
5988. ' S'il ne li sourdent en greniers.'

Al though they not so myghty be
That they may fede me in delite,
I wole not have hem in despite ;
No good man hateth hem as I gesse.
For chynche and feloun is richesse ;
That so can chase hym and dispise,
And hem defoule in sondry wise.   6000
They loven full bet, so God me
     spede,
Than doth the richė chynchy gnede ;
And ben in goode feith morė stable,
And trewer and more serviable.
And therfore it suffisith me
Her goodė herte and her leaute.
They han on me sette all her thought,
And therfore I forgete hem nought ;
I wolde hem bringe in grete noblesse,
If that I were god of richesse,   6010
As I am god of love sothely,
Sich routhe upon her pleynt have I.
Therfore I must his socour be
That peyneth hym to serven me,
For if he deide for love of this,
Thanne semeth in me no love ther is.'
   'Sir,' seide they, 'soth is every deel
That ye reherce, and we wote wel
Thilke oth to holde is resonable.
For it is good and covenable   6020
That ye on richė men han sworne ;
For, Sir, this wote we wel biforne :
If Richė men done you homage,
That is, as foolės done, outrage.
But ye shull not forsworen be,
Ne lette, therfore, to drynke clarre
Or pyment makid fresh and newe.
Ladies shull hem such pepir brewe,
If that they fall into her laas,   6029
That they for woo mowe seyn, "Allas ! "
Ladyes shullen evere so curteis be,
That they shal quyte youre oth all
     free.
Ne sekith never othir vicaire,
For they shal speke with hem so faire,
That ye shal holde you paied full wele,
Though ye you medle never a dele.
Late ladies worchė with her thyngis
They shal hem telle so fele tidynges,
And moeve hem eke so many requestis,
Bi flateri, that not honest is ;   6040

6002. MSS. *grede* for *gnede*.

And therto yeve hym such thankynges,
What with kissyng, and with talkynges,
That certis, if they trowėd be,
Shal never leve hem londe ne fee,
That it nyl as the moeble fare
Of which they first delyverid are.
Now may ye telle us all youre wille,
And we youre heestės shal fulfille.
   But Fals-Semblaunt dar not for drede
Of you, Sir, medle hym of this dede ;
For he seith that ye ben his foo,   6051
He note if ye wole worche hym woo.
Wherfore we pray you alle, Beausire,
That ye forgyve hym now your Ire,
And that he may dwelle as your man
With Abstinence, his dere lemman.
This oure accord and oure wille nowe.'
   'Parfay,' scide Love, 'I graunte it yowe :
I wole wel holde hym for my man,   6059
Now late hym come.' And he forth ran.
   'Fals-Semblant,' quod Love, ' in this wise
I take thee heere to my servise,
That thou oure freendis helpe away,
And hyndreth hem neithir nyght ne day,
But do thy myght hem to releve ;
And eke oure enemyes that thou greve ;
Thyne be this myght, I graunte it thee,
My Kyng of Harlotes shalt thou be,
We wole that thou have such honour.
Certeyne thou art a fals traitour,   6070
And eke a theef ; sith thou were borne,
A thousand tyme thou art forsworne ;
But nethėles in oure heryng,
To putte oure folk out of doutyng
I bidde thee teche hem, wostowe howe,
Bi somme general signė nowe,
In what place thou shalt founden be,
If that men had myster of thee,
And how men shal thee best espye ;
For thee to knowe is gret maistrie.   6081
Télle in what place is thyn hauntyng.'
   'Sir, I have felė dyverse wonyng,
That I kepe not rehersed be ;
So that ye wolde respiten me.

6041, 6042. *thankynges*, 'colees'; Kaluza suggests *thwakkynges*. Similarly *talkynges* does n :
seem happy for 'acolees'; (?) read *wakynges*, c?
vv. 2682, 4272.
6057. *This*, this is.
6068. *Kyng of Harlotes*, 'rois des ribauds.' i ?
provost-marshal.

For if that I tellé you the sothe,
I may have harme and shamé bothe ;
If that my felowes wisten it,
My talis shulden me be quytt,
For certeyne they wolde haté me
If ever I knewe her cruelte. 6090
For they wolde overall holde hem stille
Of trouthe that is ageyne her wille ;
Suche tales kepen they not here.
I myght eftsoone bye it full deere,
If I seide of hem ony thing
That ought displesith to her heryng.
For what word that hem prikketh or biteth,
In that word noon of hem deliteth,
Al were it gospel the Evangile,
That wolde reprove hem of her gile. 6100
For they are cruel and hauteyne,
And this thyng wote I well certeyne ;
If I speke ought to peire her loos,
Your court shal not so well be cloos
That they ne shall wite it atté last.
Of good men am I nought agast,
For they wole taken on hem no thyng,
Whanne that they knowe al my menyng.
But he that wole it on hym take,
He wole hym-silf suspecious make 6110
That he his lyf let covertly,
In gile and in Ipocrisie
That me engendred and yaf fostryng.'
' They made a full good engendryng,'
Quod Love, ' for who so sothly telle,
They engendred the Devel of Helle.
But nedely, how so evere it be,'
Quod Love, ' I wole and chargé thee
To telle anoon thy wonyng places, 6119
Heryng ech wight that in this place is,
And what lyf that thou lyvest also ;
Hide it no lenger now—Wherto ?
Thou most discovere all thi wurchyng,
How thou servest, and of what thyng,
Though that thou shuldist for this othe-sawe
Ben alto beten and to-drawe.
And yit art thou not wont pardee.
But natheles though thou beten be,
Thou shalt not be the first that so
Háth for sothsawe suffred woo.' 6130
' Sir, sith that it may liken you,
Though that I shulde be slayne right now,
I shal done youre comaundément,

6111. *let*, leads.

For therto have I gret· talent.'
Withouten wordis mo right thanne
Fals-Semblant his sermon biganne,
And seide hem thus in audience :
' Barouns, take heede of my sentence :
That wight that list to have knowing
Of Fals-Semblant, full of flatering, 6140
He must in worldly folk hym seke,
And certes in the cloistres eke,
I wone no where but in hem twey ;
But not lyk even, soth to sey.
Shortly, I wole herberwe me
There I hope best to holstred be ;
And certeynly sikerest hidyng,
Is undirnethé humblest clothing.
Religiouse folk ben full covert,
Seculer folk ben more appert. 6150
But nathéles I wole not blame
Religious folk, ne hem diffame ;
In what habit that ever they go,
Religioun umble and trewe also,
Wole I not blamé, ne dispise,
But I nyl love it in no wise—
I mene of false religious,
That stouté ben and malicious,
That wolen in an abit goo,
And setten not her herte therto. 6160
Religious folk ben al pitous,
Thou shalt not seen oon dispitous ;
They loven no pridé, ne no strif,
But humbely they wole lede her lyf.
With which folk wole I never be,
And if I dwelle, I feyne me.
I may wel in her abit go,
But me were lever my nekke a-two
Than lete a purpose that I take,
What covenaunt that ever I make, 6170
I dwelle with hem that proudé be,
And full of wiles and subtilte,
That worship of this world coveiten,
And grete nedes kunnen espleiten,
And gone and gadren gret pitaunces,
And purchace hem the acqueyntaunces
Of men that myghty lyf may leden,
And feyne hem pore, and hem silf feden
With godé morcels delicious,

6146. MSS. *hulstred*.
6172. MSS. *subtilite*.
6174. MSS. *grete nede*, ' les grans besoignes ';
cp. note to 5883.

And drinken good wyne precious,   6180
And preche us povert and distresse,
And fisshen hem silf gret richesse
With wily nettis that they cast ;
It wole come foule out at the last.
They ben fro clene religioun went,
They make the world an argument,
That [hath] a foule conclusioun :
"I have a robe of religioun,
Thanne am I all religious."
This argument is all roignous,   6190
It is not worth a croked brere ;
Abit ne makith neithir monk ne frere,
But clene lyf and devocioun
Makith godé men of religioun.
Nétheles ther kan noon answere,
How high that evere his heed he shere
With rasour whetted never so kene,
That Gile in braunches kut thrittene ;
Ther can no wight distincte it so,
That he dare sey a word therto.   6200
   But what herberwe that ever I take
Or what Semblant that evere I make,
I mene but gile, and folowe that.
For right no mo than Gibbe oure cat,
That awaiteth myce and rattes to kyllen,
Ne entende I but to bigilen.
Ne no wight may by my clothing
Wite with what folk is my dwellyng,
Ne by my wordis yit, parde,
So softe and so plesaunt they be.   6210
Biholde the dedis that I do,
But thou be blynde thou oughtest so.
For varie her wordis fro her deede,
They thenke on gile withouté dreede,
What maner clothing that they were
Or what estate that evere they bere
Lered or lewdé, lord or lady,
Knyght, squyér, burgeis, or bayly.'
   Right thus while Fals - Semblant
     sermoneth
Eftsones Love hym aresoneth,   6220
And brake his tale in his spekyng,
As though he had hym tolde lesyng,

6197. MSS. *resoun* for *rasour*.
6198. *That* has *noon* for its antecedent, and
the allusion is to the twelve monks and prior
who made up a convent.
6204. *Gibbe, i.e.* 'Gib,' a common English
name for a cat.
6205. Only in Th., but found in Fr.
6206. G *bigilyng*.

And seide, ' What Devel is that I here
What folk hast thou us nempned heere?
Máy men fyndé religioun
In worldly habitacioun ?'
' Ye, Sir, it folowith not that they
Shulde lede a wikked lyf, parfey,
Ne not therfore her soulés leese,
That hem to worldly clothés chese ; 6230
For certis it were gret pitee.
Men may in seculer clothés see
Florishen hooly religioun.
Full many a seynt in feeld and toune,
With many a virgine glorious,
Devoute and full religious
Han deied, that comyn cloth ay beerer.
Yit seyntés nevere the lesse they weren.
I cowdé reken you many a ten,   6240
Ye wel nygh [al] these hooly wymmen,
That men in chirchis herie and seke,
Bothe maydens and these wyves eke,
That baren full many a faire child heere.
Wered alwey clothis seculere,
And in the samé dieden they,
That seyntes weren, and ben alwey.
The xi. thousand maydens deere,
That beren in heven her ciergis clere,
Of whiche men rede in chirche and synge.
Were take in seculer clothing,   6250
Whanne they resseyvéd martirdome,
And wonnen hevene unto her home.
Good herté makith the goodé thought,
The clothing yeveth ne reveth nought :
The goodé thought and the worching
That makith the religioun flowryng—
Ther lyth the goode religioun,
Aftir the right entencioun.
   Whoso took a wether's skynne,
And wrapped a gredy wolf therynne 6260
For he shulde go with lambis whyte,
Wenest thou not he wolde hem bite ?
Yis, neverthelasse, as he were woode,
He wolde hem wery and drinke th..
     bloode,
And wel the rather hem disceyve ;
For sith they cowdé not perceyve
His treget and his cruelte,
They wolde hym folowe al wolde he fle.
If ther be wolves of sich hewe

6243. Perhaps omit *full*.
6264. MSS. *the bloode*, 'lor sanc.'

Amongės these apostlis newe,   6270
Thou, Hooly Chirche, thou maist be
  wailed,
Sith that thy Citee is assayled
Thourgh knyghtis of thyn ownė table.
God wote thi lordship is doutable,
If thei enforce [hem] it to wynne,
That shulde defende it fro withynne.
Who myght defense ayens hem make?
Withoutė stroke it mote be take
Of trepeget, or mangonel,
Without displaiyng of pensel.   6280
And if God nyl done it socour,
But lat [it] renne in this colour,
Thou most thyn heestis laten be;
Thanne is ther nought but yeldė thee,
Or yeve hem tribute doutėlees,
And holde it of hem to have pees.
But gretter harme bitideth thee
That they al maister of it be.
Wel konne they scornė thee withal;
By dayė stuffen they the wall,   6290
And al the nyght they mynen there.
Nay, thou planten most elles where
Thyn ympės, if thou wolt fruyt have;
Abide not there thi-silf to save.

  But now pees! Heere I turne ageyne,
I wole nomore of this thing seyne,
If I may passen me herby.
I myghtė maken you wery;
But I wole heten you al-way
To helpe youre freendis, what I may,   6300
Sō they wollen my company;
For they be shent al outerly,
But if so fallė that I be
Ófte with hem and they with me.
And eke my lemman mote they serve,
Or they shull not my love deserve.
Forsothe I am a fals traitour,
God jugged me for a theef trichour;
Forsworne I am, but wel nygh none
Wote of my gile til it be done.   6310
Thurgh me hath many oon deth
  resseyved,
That my treget nevere aperceyved;
And yit resseyveth, and shal resseyve,

That my falsnesse shal nevere aperceyve.
But who so doth, if he wise be,
Hym is right good be war of me.
But so sligh is the deceyvyng
That to hard is the aperceyvyng.
For Protheus, that cowde hym chaunge,
In every shap homely and straunge,   6320
Cowde nevere sich gilė ne tresoune
As I. For I come never in toune,
Thére as I myght knowen be;
Though men me bothe myght here and see,
Full wel I can my clothis chaunge,
Take oon and make another straunge.
Now am I knyght, now chastėleyne,
Now prelat, and now chapėleyne,
Now prest, now clerk, and now forstere;
Now am I maister, now scolere,   6330
Now monke, now chanoun, now baily;
What ever myster man am I,
Now am I prince, now am I page,
And kan by herte every langage;
Somme tyme am I hore and olde,
Now am I yonge, [and] stoute, and bolde;
Now am I Robert, now Robyn,
Now Frere Menour, now Iacobyn.
And with me folwith my loteby,
To done me solas and company,   6340
That hight Dame Abstinencė-Streyned.
In many a queynte array feyned,
Ryght as it cometh to hir lykyng,
I fulfille al hir desiryng;
Sómtyme a wommans cloth take I,
Now am I maydė, now lady;
Somtyme I am religious,
Now lyk an anker in an hous;
Somtyme am I Prioresse,
And now a nonne, and now Abbesse;   6350
And go thurgh allė regiouns,

6314. *shal* often thus makes an extra unaccented syllable.
6317, 6318. Supplied by Kaluza from Fr.
MSS. have *aperceyvyng* for *deceyvyng* in 6317,
and G leaves blank space for 6318, which appears
in Th. as *That al to late cometh knowyng.*
6337. *Robert,* i.e. gentleman.
6337. *Robyn,* i.e. clown.
6338. *Frere Menour,* i.e. Franciscan.
6338. *Iacobyn,* i.e. Dominican.
6341. MSS. *and reyned* for *streyned.*
6344. *To fulfille,* with comma after *streyned*
and full stop after *desiryng,* would better translate Fr.
6346. MSS. *a maydė.*

6281. 'Et se d'eus (misread as *deus*) ne la vues
rescorre.'
6290. MSS. *day.* Skeat supplies *wel* before
stuffen.

729

Sekyng all religiouns.
But to what ordre that I am sworne,
I take the strawe, and lete the corne
To joly folk I enhabite ;
I axe nomore but her abite.
What wole ye more ? In every wise,
Right as me lyst, I me disgise ;
Wel can I wre me undir wede,
Unlyk is my word to my dede.   6360
[I] make into my trappis falle,
Thurgh my pryveleges, alle
That ben in Cristendome alyve,
I may assoile and I may shryve
(That no prelat may lettè me) .
All folk where evere thei foundè be ;
I note no prelate may done so,
But it the pope be, and no mo,
That madè thilk establisshing.
Now is not this a propre thing ?   6370
But where my sleight is aperceyved,
Of hem I am nomore resceyved,
As I was wont ; and wostow why ?
For I dide hem a tregetrie.
But therof yeve I lytel tale ;
I have the silver and the male.
So have I prechid, and eke shriven,
So have I take, so have me yiven
Thurgh her foly husbonde and wyf,
That I lede right a joly lyf,   6380
Thurgh symplesse of the prelacye ;
They knowe not al my tregettrie.
But for asmoche as man and wyf
Shulde shewe her paroch-prest her lyf
Onys a yeer, as seith the book,

Er ony wight his housel took,
Thanne have I pryvylegis large
That may of mychè thing discharge.
For he may seie right thus, parde :—
" Sir Preest, in shrift I telle it thee,
That he to whom that I am shryven
Hath me assoilèd, and me yiven
For penaunce sothly for my synne
Which that I fonde me gilty ynne :
Ne I ne have nevere entencioun,
To makè double confessioun,
Ne reherce efte my shrift to thee ;
O shrift is right ynough to me.
This oughtè thee sufficè wele,
Ne be not rebel never a dele,
For certis, though thou haddist it swor
I wote no prest ne prelat borne
That may to shrift efte me constreyne
And if they done, I wole me pleyne,
For I wote where to pleynè wele.
Thou shalt not streynè me a dele
Ne enforcè me, ne not me trouble
To makè my confessioun double.
Ne I have none affeccioun,
To have double absolucioun.
The firste is right ynough to me,
This latter assoilyng quyte I thee.
I am unbounde—What ! Maist thou
More of my synnes me to unbynde !
For he that myght hath in his honde
Of all my synnès me unbonde,
And if thou wolt me thus constreyne
That me mote nedis on thee pleyne,
There shall no jugge imperial
Ne bisshop, ne official,
Done jugèment on me ; for I
Shal gone and pleyne me openly
Unto my shriftefadir newe,
That hightè not Frere Wolf untrewe '
And he shal chevys hym for me,
For I trowe he can hampre thee.
But lord ! he wolde be wrooth withall,
If men hym woldè Frere Wolf call ;
For he wolde have no pacience,
But done al cruel vengeaunce ;
He wolde his myght done at the lees
No thing spare, for goddis heest.
And god so wys be my socour,
But thou yeve me my Savyour
At Ester, whanne it likith me,

6354. *lete*, MSS. *bete* ; cp. 5544, 5959, 6006.
6355. The Fr. texts vary here. The verse should run : *To blynde folk ther I enhabit*, and be taken with v. 6356. *Joly* is perhaps a mistake for *sely*, translating 'por gens avugler' misread as 'por gens avugles.'
6359. *wre*, MSS. *were* ; Skeat and Kaluza here ; 'Moult sont en moi mûé li vers.'
6365. *That*, 'ce.'
6371. *where*, MSS. *were*.
6371. *sleight is*, MSS. *sleightis*. Other editions retain reading of MSS. See next note.
6372. Missing from MSS. ; here supplied from Fr. :
    Mes mes trais ont aperceûs
    Si n'en sui mes si receûs.
Bell :
    I shulde no lenger ben received.
Morris :
    Ne shulde I more ben receyved.
But the statement in Fr. is not conditional.
6375. MSS. *a litel tale* ; cp. v. 6346.

'ithouté presyng more on thee,
wole forth and to hym gone,
nd he shal housel me anoon,
ɔr I am out of thi grucching ;
kepe not dele with thee no thing." 6440
hus may he shryve hym that forsaketh
is paroch prest, and to me takith ;
nd if the prest wole hym refuse,
am full redy hym to accuse,
nd hym punysshe and hampre so
hat he his chirché shal forgo.
ɪt who so hath in his felyng
ɪe consequence of such shryvyng,
ɪal sene that prest may never have myght
ɔ knowe the conscience a-right 6450
f hym that is undir his cure.
nd this ageyns Holy Scripture,
ɪat biddith every heerde honeste
ave verry knowing of his beeste.
ɪt poré folk that gone by strete,
ɪat have no gold, ne sommés grete,
em wolde I lete to her prelates ;
r lete her prestis knowe her states.
ɔrto me right nought yevé they.'
' And why?'
　　　　' It is for they ne may.
ɪey ben so bare I take no kepe, 6461
ɪt I wole have the fatté sheepe ;
ɪt parish prestis have the lene,
yeve not of her harme a bene,
nd if that prelates grucché it,
ɪat oughten wroth be in her witt
ɔ leese her fatté beestes so,
ɪhal yeve hem a stroke or two
ɪat they shal leesen with [her] force
ɛ bothe her mytre and her croce. 6470
ɪus jape I hem, and have do longe,
y pryveleges ben so stronge.'
Fals - Semblaunt wolde have stynted
　　　　heere,
ɪt Love ne made hym no such cheere
ɪat he was wery of his sawe,
ɪt forto make hym glad and fawe

He seide : ' Telle on more specialy,
How that thou servest untrewly ;
Telle forth, and shame thee never a dele,
For as thyn abit shewith wele 6480
Thou semest an hooly heremyte.'
' Sothe is, but I am an ypocrite.'
' Thou goste and prechest poverte.'
' Ye sir but richesse hath pouste.'
' Thou prechest abstinence also.'
' Sir, I wole fillen, so mote I go,
My paunche of good mete and [good]
　　　　wyne,
As shulde a maister of dyvyne ;
For how that I me pover feyne,
Yit all[é] pore folk I disdeyne. 6490
I Lové bettir thacqueyntaunce
Ten tymé of the Kyng of Fraunce,
Than of a pore man of mylde mode,
Though that his soule be also gode.
For whanne I see beggers quakyng
Naked on myxnes al stynkyng
For hungre crie, and eke for care,
I entremete not of her fare.
They ben so pore and ful of pyne, 6499
They myght not oonys yeve me a dyne,
For they have no thing but her lyf ;
What shulde he yeve that likketh his
　　　　knyf?
It is but foly to entremete,
To seke in houndés nest fat mete.
Lete bere hem to the spitel anoon,
But for me comfort gete they noon.
　Bút a riché sike usurere
Wolde I visite and drawé nere ;
Hym wole I comforte and rehete,
For I hope of his gold to gete. 6510
And if that wikkid deth hym have,
I wole go with hym to his grave ;
And if ther ony reprove me
Why that I lete the pore be,
Wóstow how I mot a-scape ?

5436. *presyng*, pressing.
5440. *i.e.* I don't care to deal with you in
y way.
5452. *this*, this is.
5466. MSS. *woth*.
5469. *her*, Skeat *the*, Kaluza suggests *by seint*
:e, referring to *Tales*, D 483. Fr. :
　　Que lever ferai tex boces
　　Qu'il en perdront mitres et croces.

6481. *semest*, MSS. *seruest*.
6482. *an*, MSS. *but an*.
6492. *Ten tyme*, Fr. ' cent mil tans.'
6493. Skeat omits *a*. Kaluza *mylde*, which
seems better ; cp. Fr. ' Que d'un povre par nostre
Dame ' ; *pover*, too, is more frequent than *pore*
in the poem.
6500. Kaluza and Skeat omit *a*.
6507. *usurere* seems to be dissyllabic here, like
seculer in v. 6263.
6515. *mot*, MSS. *not*.

731

I sey and swerè hym ful rape
That richè men han morè tecches,
Of synnè than han porè wrecches,
And han of counsel more mister,
And therfore I wole drawe hem ner.
But as grete hurt, it may so be,   6521
Hath soule in right grete poverte
As soule in grete richesse, forsothe,
Al be it that they hurten bothe ;
For richesse and mendicitees
Ben clepid ii. extremytees ;
The mene is clepèd suffisaunce,
Ther lyth of vertu the aboundaunce.
For Salamon, full wel I wote,
In his Parablis us wrote,   6530
As it is knowe to many a wight,
In his thrittene chapitre right :
" God thou me kepe, for thi pouste,
Fro richesse and mendicite ;
For if a richè man hym dresse,
To thenke to myche on [his] richesse,
His herte on that so fer is sett,
That he his creàtour foryett ;
And hym that begging wole ay greve,
How shulde I bi his word hym leve ?
Unnethe [is] that he nys a mycher   6541
Forsworne or ellis God is lyer."
Thus seith Salamones sawes.
Ne we fynde writen in no lawis
And namely in oure Cristen lay
(Whoso seith, " Ye," I dar sey, " Nay,")
That Crist ne his apostlis dere,
While that they walkide in erthè heere,
Were never seen her bred beggyng ;
For they nolde beggen for no thing. 6550
And right thus was men wont to teche,
And in this wisè wolde it preche
The maistres of divinite
Somtyme in Parys the citee.
And if men wolde ther-geyn appose
The nakid text and lete the glose,
It myghtè soone assoiled be.

For men may wel the sothè see,
That, parde, they myght aske a thir;
Pléynly forth without begging ;
For they were Goddis herdis deere,
And cure of soulès hadden heere.
They noldè no thing begge her fode :
For aftir Crist was done on rode
With ther propre hondis they wro?
And with travel, and ellis nought,
They wonnen all her sustenaunce,
And lyveden forth in her penaunce.
And the remenaunt yaf awey
To other porè folkis alwey.
They neither bilden tour ne halle,
But ley in houses smale with-alle.
A myghty man that can and may,
Shulde with his honde and body alv.
Wynne hym his fode in laboring,
If he ne have rent or sich a thing,
Al though he be religious,
And god to serven curious.
Thus mote he done, or do trespas,
But if it be in certeyn cas,
That I can reherce if myster be
Right wel, whanne the tyme I se.
Seke the book of seynt Austyne,
Be it in papir or perchemyne,
There as he writ of these worchyng?
Thou shalt seen that noon excusyng?
A parfit man ne shuldè seke
Bi wordis, ne bi dedis eke,
Al though he be religious
And god to serven curious,
That he ne shal, so mote I go,
With propre hondis and body also,
Géte his fode in laboryng,
If he ne have proprete of thing.
Yit shulde he selle all his substaunce
And with his swynk have sustenau?
If he be parfit in bounte ;
Thus han tho bookès toldè me.
For he that wole gone ydilly
And usith it ay besily
To haunten other mennès table,
He is a trechour ful of fable,

6522. MSS. *a soule.*
6532. *thrittene,* it should be thirtieth (Prov. xxx. 8, 9), 'trentiesne.'
6536. *his richesse,* 'sa richesse.'
6539. *begging,* MSS. *beggith* (corrected by Kaluza).
6539. *wole greve,* 'mendicité guerroie.'
6542. *God is,* MSS. *goddis.* Cp. 6541.
6543. *Salamones,* MSS. *Salamon* (Kaluza).
6551. *men,* one.

6568. *penaunce,* 'en pacience, so perha? Kaluza suggests, read *pacience.*
6581. Perhaps omit *That.*
6592. Kaluza reads *honde,* citing v. ??? cp. v. 6565.
6600. *besily,* MSS. *desily.*

: he ne may by gode resoun
:cuse hym by his orisoun ;
r men bihoveth in somme gise
ynne somtyme in Goddis servise
, gone and purchasen her nede.
:n mote eten, that is no drede,
,d slepe, and eke do other thing ;
  longe may they leve praiyng ;   6610
  may they eke her praier blynne,
hile that they werke her mete to wynne.
ynt Austyn wole therto accorde
 thilke book that I recorde.
stinian eke, that made lawes,
,th thus forboden, by old dawes.
, man up peyne to be dede,
ghty of body, to begge his brede,
he may swynke it forto gete ;
:n shulde hym rather mayme or bete,
  done of hym aperte justice,   6621
,an suffren hym in such malice.
,ey done not wel, so mote I go,
,at taken such almesse so,
t if they have somme pryvelege,
,at of the peyne hem wole allege.
t how that is, can I not see,
t if the prince disseyved be.
: I ne wene not sikerly
,at they may have it rightfully.   6630
t I wole not determine
pryncee power, ne defyne,
: by my word comprende, I-wys,
it so ferre may strecche in this ;
vole not entremete a dele.
t I trowe that the book seith wele,
ho that takith almessis that be
:we to folk, that men may se
me, feble, wery and bare,
re or in such maner care,   6640
,at konne wynne hem never mo,
r they have no power therto,
: etith his owne dampnyng,
t if he lye that made al thing.
,d if ye such a truaunt fynde,
,astise hym wel, if ye be kynde.
t they wolde hate you percas,
,d if ye fillen in her laas,

They wolde eftsoonys do you scathe,
If that they myghte, late or rathe.   6650
For they be not full pacient,
That han the world thus foule blent.
And witeth wel, that [though] God bad
The good-man selle al that he had,
And folowe hym, and to pore it yive,
He wolde not therfore that he lyve
To serven hym in mendience,
For it was nevere his sentence.
But he bad wirken whanne that neede is,
And folwe hym in goode dedis.   6660
Seynt Poule, that loved al Hooly Chirche,
He bade thappostles forto wirche,
And wynnen her lyflode in that wise,
And hem defended truaundise ;
And seide, "Wirketh with youre honden" ;
Thus shulde the thing be undirstonden.
He nolde, I-wys, have bidde hem begging,
Ne sellen gospel ne prechyng,
Lest they berafte, with her askyng,
Folk of her catel or of her thing.   6670
For in this world is many a man
That yeveth his good for he ne can
Werne it for shame, or ellis he
Wolde of the asker delyvered be ;
And for he hym encombrith so,
He yeveth hym good to late hym go.
But it can hem no thyng profit
They lese the yift and the meryte.
The goode folk that Poule to preched
Profred hym ofte, whan he hem teched,
Somme of her good in charite.   6681
But therfore right no thing toke he,
But of his hondwerk wolde he gete
Clothes to wryne hym, and his mete.'
'Telle me thanne how a man may lyven,
That al his good to pore hath yiven,
And wole but oonly bidde his bedis,
And nevere with hondes labour his nede is.
May he do so ?'
         'Ye sir.'
             'And how ?'

6653. *though*, supplied by Kaluza ; but *ther*
(=where) would come closer to Fr. 'la au Diex
comande.'
6654. *The good-man*, Fr. 'prodons.'
6677. *hem*, MSS. *hym*, Fr. 'lor prouffite.'
6688. Found only in Thynne, but according
nearly enough with Fr. *nede is*, Th. *nedis ;*
labour in sense of 'to labour for' is not otherwise
known in M.E.

606. *Blynne*, MSS. *Ben.* Skeat and Kaluza
d *somtyme leven.*
615. *Justinian*, cod. Justin. xi. 25. *De*
ndicantibus validis (Bell).

Sir, I wole gladly tellė yow.   6690
Seynt Austyn seith a man may be
In houses that han proprete,
As Templers, and Hospitelers,
And as these Chanouns Regulers,
Or Whitė monkės or these Blake—
I wole no mo ensamplis make—
And take therof his sustenyng,   ,
For therynne lyth no begging ;
But other wey[ė]s not, y-wys,
Yif Austyn gabbith not of this.   6700
And yit full many a monke laboreth,
That God in hooly chirche honoureth ;
For whanne her swynkyng is agone,
They rede and synge in chirche anone.
And for ther hath ben gret discorde,
As many a wight may bere recorde,
Upon the estate of mendience,
I wole shortly, in youre presence,
Telle how a man may begge at nede,
That hath not wherwith hym to fede.
Maugre this felones jangelyngis,   6711
For sothfastnesse wole none hidyngis ;
And yit percas I may abey,
That I to yow sothly thus sey.
   Lo heere the caas especial :
If a man be so bestial,
That he of no craft hath science,
And nought desireth ignorence,
Thanne may he go a-begging yerne,
Til he somme maner craftė kan lerne ;
Thurgh which withoutė truaundyng   6721
He may in trouthė have his lyvyng.
Or if he may done no labour
For elde, or sykenesse, or langour,
Or for his tendre age also,
Thanne may he yit a-begging go.
Or if he have peraventure,
Thurgh usage of his norriture,
Lyved over deliciously,
Thanne oughten good folk comunly   6730
Han of his myscheef somme pitee,
And suffren hym also that he
May gone aboute and begge his breed,
That he be not for hungur deed.
Or if he have of craft kunnyng,

And strengthe also, and desiryng
Tó wirken as he had what
But he fynde neithir this ne that,
Thanne may he beggė, til that he
Have geten his necessite.
Or if his wynnyng be so lite
That his labour wole not acquyte
Sufficiantly al his lyvyng,
Yit may he go his breed begging ;
Fro dore to dore he may go trace.
Til he the remenaunt may purchace
Or if a man wolde undirtake
Ony emprisė forto make
In the rescous of oure lay,
And it defenden as he may,
Be it with armės or lettrure
Or other covenable cure,
If it be so he pore be,
Thanne may he beggė til that he
May fynde in trouthė forto swynke.
And gete hym clothė, mete and dry:
Swynke he with hondis corporell
And not with hondis espirituell.
In al this caas and in semblables,
If that ther ben mo resonables,
He may begge as I telle you heere.
And ellis nought in no manere ;
As William Seynt Amour wolde pre
And oftė wolde dispute and teche,
Of this mater all openly.
At Parys full solempnely.
And, also god my soulė blesse,
As he had in this stedfastnesse
The accorde of the universite
And of the puple, as semeth me,
No good man oughte it to refuse,
Ne ought hym therof to excuse.
Be wrothe or blithė who-so be,
For I wole speke and telle it thee,
Al shulde I dye, and be putt doun
As was seynt Poule in derke prison
Or be exiled in this caas
With wrong, as maister William wa
That my moder, Ypocrysie,
Bányssbėd for hir gret envye.

6700. I'*if*, MSS. I'*it*, 'Se.'
6707. MSS. *mendicence.*
6711. MSS. *his felones*, Fr. ' Maugre les felon-
esses jangles,' *i.e.* these felonous janglings.

6749. *i.e.* in the defence of our religio
6759. *this*, plural.
6763. William Seynt Amour, a doctor
Sorbonne who wrote a book against t..
the 13th century.
6769. *Th'accord of th'universite.*

My modir flemed hym, Seynt Amour :
The noble didé such labour
To susteyne evere the loyalte,
That he to moche agilté me ;
He made a book, and lete it write
Wheryn hys lyfe he dyd al write,
And wolde ich reneyéd begging,
And lyvéd by my traveylyng,
If I ne had rent ne other goode.
What! Wenéd he that I were woode ? 6790
For labour myght me never plese,
I have more wille to bene at ese,
And have wel lever, soth to sey,
Bifore the puple patre and prey ;
And wrie me in my foxerie
Under a cope of papelardie.'
Quod Love, 'What devel is this that I heere?
What wordis tellest thou me heere ?'
　　'What, Sir ?'
　　　　　　'Falsnesse that apert is ;
Thanne dredist thou not god?'
　　　　　　　　'No certis ;
For selde in grete thing shal he spede
In this worldé, that god wole drede. 6802
For folk that hem to vertu yyven,
And truly on her owné lyven,
And hem in goodnesse ay contene,
On hem is lytel thrift y-sene.
Súch folk drinken gret mysese ;
Thát lyf may me never plese.
But se what gold han usurers
And silver eke in [her] garners, 6810
Taylagiers and these monyours,
Bailifs, bedels, provost countours
These lyven wel nygh by ravyne.
The smalé puple hem mote enclyne,
And they as wolvés wole hem eten.
Upon the poré folk they geten
Full moche of that they spende or kepe.
Nis none of hem that he nyl strepe,
And wrine hem silf wel atté fulle ;
Withouté scaldyng they hem pulle. 6820
The stronge the feble overgoth,
But I, that were my symple cloth,

Robbe bothé robbéd and robbours,
And gilé giléd and gilours.
By my treget, I gadre and threste
The gret tresour into my cheste,
That lyth with me so fasté bounde.
Myn highé paleys do I founde,
And my delités I fulfille
With wyne at feestés at my wille 6830
And tables full of entremees.
I wole no lyf but ese and pees,
And wynné gold to spende also.
For whanne the greté bagge is go,
It cometh right with my japes.
Make I not wel tümble myn apes ?
To wynnen is alwey myn entent,
My purchace is bettir than my rent ;
For though I shuldé beten be,
Over-al I entremeté me ; 6840
Withouté me may no wight dure.
I walké soulés forto cure,
Of al the worldé cure have I
In brede and lengthé. Bold[é]ly
I wole bothe preche and eke counceilen ;
With hondis wille I not traveilen,
For of the Pope I have the bull,
I ne holde not my wittés dull.
I wole not stynten in my lyve
These emperouris forto shryve, 6850
Or kyngis, dukis, lordis grete ;
But poré folk al quyte I lete,
I love no such shryvyng, parde ;
But it for other causé be,
I rekké not of poré men—
Her astate is not worth an hen ;
Where fyndest thou a swynker of labour
Have me unto his confessour ?
But emperesses and duchesses,
Thise queenes, and eke countesses, 6860
Thise abbessis, and eke bygyns,
These greté ladyes palasyns,
These joly knyghtis and baillyves,
Thise nonnes, and thise burgeis wyves
That riché ben and eke plesyng,
And thisé maidens welfaryng,
Wher so they clad or naked be,
Uncounceiled goth ther noon fro me.

6786. As in Th. and Fr. ; G in late hand,
Of thyngis that he beste myghte.
6802. MSS. *world*, but as in v. 6843 the metre
requires two syllables.
6810. MSS. omit *her*, 'lor greniers.'
6819. *wrine*, (?) *wrcen*. The scribe frequently
confuses *i* and *e*.

6823, 6824. MSS. *robbyng, giling.*
6838. Cp. *Tales*, D 145.
6850. MSS. *emperours.*
6862. *ladyes palasyns, i.e.* court ladies.

And for her soulés savete
At lord and lady and her meyne   6870
I axe, whanne thei hem to me shryve,
The proprete of al her lyve,
And make hem trowe, bothe meest and
    leest,
Hir paroch prest nys but a beest
Ayens me and my companye,
That shrewis ben as gret as I.
Fro whiche I wole not hide in holde
No pryvete that me is tolde,
That I, by word or signe y-wis,
[Nyl] make hem knowe what it is.   6880
And they wolen also tellen me,
They hele fro me no pryvyte,
And forto make yow hem perceyven,
That usen folk thus to disceyven,
I wole you seyn withouten drede
What men may in the gospel rede
Of seynt Mathew, the gospelere,
That seith as I shal you sey heere :
    " Uppon the chaire of Moyses
(Thus is it gloséd doutéles :   6890
That is the Oldé Testament,
For ther-by is the chairé ment)
Sitte Scribes and Pharisen
(That is to seyn, the cursid men
Whiche that we ypocritis calle).
Doth that they preche, I rede you alle,
But doth not as they don a dele ;
That ben not wery to seye wele,
But to do wel no will have they.
And they wolde bynde on folk al-wey, 6900
Thát ben to be giléd able,
Búrdons that ben importable.
On folkés shuldris thinges they couchen,
That they nyl with her fyngris touchen."
    ' And why wole they not touche it ?'
    ' Why,
For hem ne lyst not sikirly,
For saddé burdons that men taken,
Make folkes shuldris aken.
And if they do ought that good be,
That is for folk it shuldé se.   6910
Her bordurs larger maken they,
And make her hemmes wide alwey,
And loven setés at the table,

6880. *Nyl*, MSS. *Wole.*
6887. Matt. xxiii. 1-8.
6911. MSS. *burdons*, 'philateres.'

The firste and mosté honourable,
And forto han the firste chaieris
In synagogis to hem full deere is,
And willen that folk hem loute and gr.
Whanne that they passen thurgh the str.
And wolen be cleped " Maister " also.
But they ne shulde not willen so,   f.
The gospel is ther-ageyns, I gesse,
That shewith wel her wikkidnesse.
    Another custome usé we
Of hem that wole ayens us be ;
We hate hym deedly everichone,
And we wole werrey hym as oon ;
Hym that oon hatith hate we alle,
And congecte how to done hym falle.
And if we seen hym wynne honour,
Richesse, or preis, thurgh his valour, x:
Provendé, rent, or dignyte,
Full fast y-wys compassen we
Bi what ladder he is clomben so ;
And forto maken hym doun to go
With traisoun we wole hym defame,
And done hym leese his goodé name.
Thus from his ladder we hym take,
And thus his freendis foes we make.
But word ne wité shal he noon,
Till all hise freendis ben his foon.   &.
For if we dide it openly
We myght have blamé redily :
For hadde he wist of oure malice,
He hadde hym kept, but he were nyc.
    Another is this, that if so falle
That ther be oon amonge us alle
That doth a good turne out of drede.
We seyn it is oure alder deede.
Ye sikerly though he it feyned,
Or that hym list, or that hym deyned
A man thurgh hym avauncéd be,
Therof all parseners be we,
And tellen folk where so we go,
That man thurgh us is sprongen so.
And forto have of men preysyng,
We purchace thurgh oure flateryng
Of riché men of gret pouste
Lettres to witnesse oure bounte,
So that man weneth that may us see
That allé vertu in us be.
And al-wey poré we us feyne ;

6926. *as oon*, 'par accort,' ? *al oon.*
6950. *hym deyned*, be vouchsafed.

But how so that we begge or pleyne,
We ben the folk without lesyng
That all thing have without havyng.
Thus be we dred of the puple y-wis.
And gladly my purpos is this :
I delé with no wight but he
Have gold and tresour gret plente ;
Her acqueyntaunce wel love I,
This is moche my desire shortly.   6970
I entremete me of brokages,
I maké pees and mariages,
I am gladly executour,
And many tymés procuratour ;
I am somtymé messager
(That fallith not to my myster),
And many tymes I make enquestes—
For me that office not honest is.
To dele with other mennes thing,
That is to me a gret lykyng.   6980
And if that ye have ought to do
In place that I repeiré to,
I shal it speden thurgh my witt,
As soone as ye have told me it.
So that yé servé me to pay,
My servyse shal be youre alway ;
But who-so wole chastisé me,
Anoon my lové lost hath he.
For I love no man in no gise
That wole me repreve or chastise ;   6990
But I wolde al folk undirtake,
And of no wight no teching take ;
For I that other folk chastie,
Wole not be taught fro my folie.
I love noon hermitagé more ;
All desertés, and holtés hore,
And greté wodés everichon,
I lete hem to the Baptist Iohn.
I quethe hym quyte, and hym relese
Of Egipt all the wildirnesse.   7000
To ferre were alle my mansiouns
Fro al citees and goodé tounes ;
My paleis and myn hous make I
There men may renne ynne openly ;
And sey that I the world forsake,
But al amydde I bilde and mak

My hous, and swimme and pley therynne,
Bet than a fish doth with his fynne.
Of Antecristes men am I,
Of whiche that Crist seith openly,   7010
They have abit of hoolynesse,
And lyven in such wikkednesse.
Oútward lambren semen we,
Full of goodnesse and of pitee,
And inward we withouten fable
Ben gredy wolvés ravysable.
We enviroune bothe londe and se,
With all the worldé werrien we ;
We wole ordeyne of allé thing,
Of folkis good and her lyvyng.   7020
If ther be castel or citee
Wherynne that ony bourgerons be,
Al though that they of Milayne were
(For therof ben they blaméd there) ;
Or if a wight out of mesure
Wolde lene his gold and take usure,
For that he is so coveitous ;
Or if he be to leccherous,
Or these that haunté symonye,
Or provost full of trecherie,   7030
Or prelat lyvyng jolily,
Or prest that halt his quene hym by,
Or oldé horis hostilers,
Or other bawdes or bordillers,
Or ellés blamed of ony vice
Of whiche men shulden done justice :
Bi all the seyntés that me pray,
But they defende them with lamprey,
With luce, with elys, with samons,
With tendre gees, and with capons,   7040
With tartés, or with chesis fat,
With deynté flawns brode and flat,
With caleweis, or with pullaylle,
With conynges, or with fyne vitaille,
That we undir our clothés wide
Maken thourgh oure golet glide,
Or but he wole do come in haste
Roo-venysoun bake in paste,
Whether so that he loure or groyne,

7007. *swimme*, G *swimme* ; cp. *Tales*, D 1926.
7021 ff. The conclusion to these conditions
is found in v. 7049 ff.
7022. *bourgerons* (G *begger*), 'bogre,' sodomites.
7029. Skeat reads *thefe or* for *these that*,
following 'lerres ou' ; but this may have been
misread (?) 'lesses au,' etc.
7041. MSS. *chefis*.

6970. 'Ce sont auques tuit mi desir.'
6974. MSS. *a procuratour*. We have seen
that the scribe frequently inserts *a* in such
cases.
6998. *i.e.* the reputed founder of asceticism.
7002. G omits *al*.

He shal have of a corde a loigne   7050
With whiche men shal hym bynde and
    lede
To brenne hym for his synful deede,
That men shull here hym crie and rore,
A mylė-wey aboute and more ;
Or ellis he shal in prisoun dye,
But if he wole his frendship bye,
Or smerten that that he hath do
More than his gilt amounteth to.
But and he couthė thurgh his sleight
Do maken up a tour of height,—   7060
Nought rought I whethir of stone, or tree,
Or erthe or turvės though it be,
Though it were of no voundė stone
Wrought with squyre and scantilone,
So that the tour were stuffėd well
With allė richesse temporell—
And thanne that he wolde updresse
Engyns bothė more and lesse,
To cast at us by every side
To bere his goodė namė wide,   7070
Such flightės [as] I shal yow nevene,
Barelles of wyne by sixe or sevene
Or gold in sakkis gret plente,
He shuldė soone delyvered be.
And if he have noon sich pitaunces,
Late hym study in equipolences,
And latė lyes and fallaces,
If that he wolde deserve oure graces ;
Or we shal bere hym such witnesse
Of synne and of his wrecchidnesse,   7080
And done his loos so widė renne,
That al quyk we shulden hym brenne,
Or ellis yeve hym suche penaunce
That is wel wors than the pitaunce.
For thou shalt never for no thing
Kon knowen a-right by her clothing
The traitours full of trecherie,
But thou her werkis can a-spie.
And ne hadde the good kepyng be
Whilom of the universite   7090
That kepith the key of Cristendome
We had bene turmented, al and some.

Suche ben the stynkyng prophetis ;
Nys none of hem that good prophete is,
For they thurgh wikked entencioun,
The yeer of the Incarnacioun
A thousand and two hundred yeer,
Fyve and fifty, ferther ne ner,
Broughten a book with sory grace
To yeven ensample in comune place,   7100
That seidė thus though it were fable :
"This is the Gospel Perdurable,
That fro the Holy Goost is sent."—
Wel were it worthi to bene brent !
Entitled was in such manere
This book, of which I tellė heere
Ther nas no wight in all Parys
Biforne Oure Lady at parvys
That he ne mightė bye the book
To copy, if hym talent toke.   7110
There myght he se by gret tresoun
Full many fals comparisoun :—
"As moche as thurgh his gretė myght,
Be it of hetė or of lyght,
The sonnė sourmounteth the mone,
That troublė is and chaungith soone,
And the notė kernell the shell—
(I scornė not, that I yow tell)—
Right so, withouten ony gile,
Sourmounteth this noble Evangile   7120
The word of ony evangelist."
And to her title they token Crist.
And many such comparisoun
Of which I make no mencioun,
Mightė men in that book fynde
Who so coude of hem have mynde.
    The Universite, that tho was a-slepe,
Gan forto braide and taken kepe,
And at the noys the heed upcast,
Ne never sithen slept it fast ;   7131
But up it stert, and armės toke

7098. *ferther ne ner* (G *ferther neuer*). 'c's hons vivans qui m'en demente,' *i.e.* neither earlier nor later.
7099. *a book*, the *Evangelium Eternas* Skeat refers to Southey's *Book of the Chur* ch. xi.
7104. MSS. *worth*.
7109. G omits ; Th. *That they me mighte ̄ ̄ booke by.*
7110. Th. inserts before 7110 *The sente pleased hem well trewly*, and adds after *Of the Evangelistes book.* Fr. contains ̄ ̄ G's single line.
7115. G (*same* for *sonne*).
7116. MSS. *troublere*, 'troble.'

7056. *his frendship bye, i.e.* pay for his relief ; Skeat changes *his* to *our.*
7057. *that that*, (?) *for that.*
7063. *vounde*, Skeat reads *founde*; Fr. 'de quel pierre.' Cole's *Dictionary* glosses *vound stone,* 'free-stone,' with query 'found or foundation.'
7092. As in Th. ; G *Of al that here axe juste their dome*, in late hand over blank space.

Ayens this false horrible boke,
Al redy bateil for to make,
And to the juge the book to take.
But they that broughten the boke there
Hent it anoon awey for fere ;
They noldė shewė more a dele
But thenne it kept, and kepen will,
Til such a tyme that they may see
That they so strongė woxen be,   7140
That no wyght may hem wel withstonde.
For by that book they durst not stonde.
Awey they gonne it forto bere,
For they ne durstė not answere
By exposicioun ne glose
To that that clerkis wole appose
Ayens the cursednesse y-wys
That in that bookė writen is.
Now wote I not, ne I can not see
What maner eende that there shal be 7150
Of al this [bokes] that they hyde ;
But yit algate they shal abide
Til that they may it bet defende,
This trowe I best wole be her ende.
Thus Antecrist abiden we,
For we ben alle of his meyne ;
And what man that wole not be so,
Right soone he shal his lyf forgo.
We wole a puple upon hym areyse,
And thurgh oure gilė done hym seise,
And hym on sharpė speris ryve,   7161
Or other weyes brynge hym fro lyve,
But if that he wole folowe y-wis
That in oure booke writen is.
Thus mych wole oure book signifie,
That whilė Petre hath maistrie,
May never Iohn shewe well his myght.
Now have I you declarėd right
The menyng of the bark and rynde,
That makith the entenciouns blynde ; 7170
But now at erst I wole bigynne,
To expownė you the pith withynne :—

.   .   .   .   .

And the seculers comprehende,
That Cristes lawė wole defende,
And shulde it kepen and mayntenen
Ayenės hem that all sustenen,

And falsly to the puple techen.
That Iohn bitokeneth hem that prechen
That ther nys lawė covenable
But thilkė Gospel Perdurable,   7180
That fro the Holygost was sent
To turnė folk that ben myswent.
The strengthe of Iohn, they undirstonde
The grace in whiche they seie they stonde,
That doth the synfull folk converte
And hem to Iesus Crist reverte.
Full many another orriblite
May men in that booke se,
That ben comaunded doutėles
Ayens the lawe of Rome expres ;   7190
And all with Antecrist they holden,
As men may in the book biholden.
And thanne comaunden they to sleen
Alle tho that with Petre been ;
But they shal nevere have that myght,
And God to-forne for strif to fight,
That they ne shal enowė fynde,
That Petres lawė shal have in mynde,
And evere holde, and so mayntene ;
That at the last it shal be sene   7200
That they shal allė come therto
For ought that they can speke or do.
And thilkė lawė shal not stonde
That they by Iohn have undirstonde,
But, maugre hem, it shal adowne,
And bene brought to confusioun.
   But I wole stynt of this matere,
For it is wonder longe to here.
But hadde that ilkė book endured,
Of better estate I were ensured ;   7210
And freendis have I yit pardee
That han me sett in gret degre.
Of all this world is Emperour
Gylė my fadir, the trechour,
And Emperis my moder is,
Maugre the Holygost y-wis.
Oure myghty lynage and oure rowte
Regneth in every regne aboute.
And well is worthy we [maystres] be ;
For all this world governė we,   7220
And can the folk so wel disceyve,
That noon oure gilė can perceyve ;
And though they done, they dar not sey,

7151. MSS. omit *bokes*, 'cis livres.'
7172. One or two verses have been lost corresponding to 'Par Pierre voil le Pape entendre.'
7173. *the seculers*, (?) read *clerkes seculers*,
'clercs seculiers.'

7178. *that*, MSS. *to.*
7197. *enowe*, MSS. *ynough.*
7219. *maistres*, MSS. *mynstres.*

The sothé dar no wight bywray.
But he in Cristis wrath hym ledith
That more than Crist my britheren dredith.
He nys no full good champioun
That dredith such similacioun,
Nor that for peyné wole refusen
Us to correcté and accusen.   7230
He wole not entremete by right,
Ne have God in his eyé-sight;
And therfore God shal hym punyce.
But me ne rekketh of no vice,
Sithen men us loven comunably,
And holden us for so worthy,
That we may folk repreve echoon,
And we nyl have repref of noon.
Whom shulden folk worshipen so
But us, that stynten never mo   7240
To patren while that folk may us see,
Though it not so bihynde hem be.
And where is moré wode folye
Than to enhauncé chyvalrie,
And lové noble men and gay,
That joly clothis weren alway?
If they be sich folk as they semen,
So clene as men her clothis demen,
And that her wordis folowe her dede,
It is gret pité, out of drede,   7250
For they wole be noon ypocritis!
Of hem me thynketh [it] gret spite is;
I can not love hem on no side.
But beggers with these hodés wide,
With sleigh and palé faces lene,
And greyé clothis not full clene,
But fretted full of tatarwagges,
And highé shoés knopped with dagges,
That frouncen lyke a quailé-pipe,
Or botis revelyng as a gype;   7260
To such folk as I you dyvyse
Shulde princes and these lordis wise
Take all her londis and her thingis,
Bothe werre and pees in governyngis;
To such folk shulde a prince hym yive,
That wolde his lyf in honour lyve.
And if they be not as they seme,
That serven thus the world to queme,
There wolde I dwellé to disceyve
The folk, for they shal not perceyve.   7270
But I ne speke in no such wise

7268. *serven*, (T) *semen*; but 'emblent.'
7270. G *To* for *The.*

That men shulde humble abit dispise,
So that no pride ther-undir be.
No man shulde hate, as thynkith me,
The poré man in sich clothyng.
But God ne preisith hym no thing
That seith he hath the world forsake,
And hath to worldly glorie hym take,
And wole of siche delices use.
Who may that begger wel excuse,
That papelard that hym yeldith so,
And wole to worldly esé go,
And seith that he the world hath left,
And gredily it grypeth efte?
He is the hounde, shame is to seyn,
That to his castyng goth ageyn.
But unto you dar I not lye;
But myght I felen or aspie
That ye perceyvéd it no thyng,
Ye shuldé have a stark lesyng
Right in youre honde thus, to bigynne.
I nolde it letté for no synne.'
    The god lough at the wondir tho,
And every wight gan laugh also,
And seide:—'Lo heere a man, a right
Forto be trusty to every wight!'
    'Falssemblant,' quod Love, 'sey
       me,
Sith I thus have advauncéd thee
That in my court is thi dwellyng,
And of ribawdis shalt be my kyng,
Wolt thou wel holden my forwardis?'
'Yhe, sir, from hennes forewardis;
Hadde never youre fadir heere bifore,
Servaunt so trewe, sith he was borne.
    'That is ageynés all nature.'
    'Sir, putte you in that aventure;
For though ye borowes take of me,
The sikerer shal ye never be
For ostages, ne sikirnsese,
Or chartres, forto bere witnesse
I take youre silf to recorde heere,
That men ne may, in no manere,
Teren the wolf out of his hide,
Til he be flayen bak and side,
Though men hym bete and al defile.
What! Wene ye that I wole bigile?
For I am clothéd mekély,
Ther-undir is all my trechery;
Myn herté chaungith never the mo

7314. *flayen*, MSS. *slayn*, 'escorchiés.

For noon abit in which I go.   7320
Though I have chere of symplenesse,
I am not wery of shrewidnesse.
Myn lemman Streyneth-Abstinence,
Hath myster of my purveaunce ;
She hadde ful longe ago be deede,
Nere my councel and my rede ;
Lete hir allone and you and me.'
    And Love answerde : ' I trusté thee
Withouté borowe for I wole noon.'
    And Falssemblant, the theef, anoon
Ryght in that ilké samé place,   7331
That hadde of tresoun al his face
Ryght black withynne and white withoute,
Thankyth hym, gan on his knees loute.
    Thanne was ther nought but ' Every man
Now to assaut that sailen can,'
Quod Love, ' and that full hardyly ! '
Thanne armed they hem communly
Of sich armour as to hem felle.   7339
Whanne the were armed fers and felle,
They wente hem forth all in a route,
And set the castel al aboute.
They will nought away for no drede,
Till it so be that they ben dede,
Or till they have the castel take.
And fouré batels they gan make,
And parted hem in foure anoon,
And toke her way and forth they gone,
The fouré gatés forto assaile,
Of whiche the kepers wole not faile.   7350
For they ben neithir sike ne dede,
But hardy folk and stronge in dede.
    Now wole I seyn the countynaunce
Of Falssemblant and Abstynaunce,
That ben to Wikkid-Tongé went.
But first they heelde her parlement
Whether it to doné were
To maken hem be knowen there,
Or elles walken forth disgised.
But at the lasté they devysed   7360
That they wolde gone in tapinage,
As it were in a pilgrimage,
Lyke good and hooly folk unfeyned.
And Damé Abstinencé-Streyned
Toke on a robe of kamelyne,
And gan hir graithe as a Bygynne.
A largé coverechief of threde
She wrappéd all aboute hir heede ;
But she forgate not hir sawter ;

A peire of bedis eke she bere   7370
Upon a lace all of white threde,
On which that she hir bedés bede.
But she ne bought hem never a dele,
For they were geven her I wote wele,
God wote, of a full hooly frere,
That seide he was hir fadir dere
To whom she haddé ofter went
Than ony frere of his covent.
And he visited hir also,
And many a sermoun seide hir to ;   7380
He noldé lette for man on lyve
That he ne wolde hir osté shryve,
And with so great devocion
They madé her confession,
That they had osté, for the nones,
Two heedes in one hoode at ones.
    Of fayre shappe I devyse her the,
But pale of face somtyme was she ;
That falsé traytouresse untrewe,
Was lyke that salowe horse of hewe,   7390
That in the Apocalips is shewed,
That signifyeth tho folke beshrewed,
That ben al ful of trecherye
And palé through hypocrisye.
For on that horse no colour is,
But onely deed and pale y-wis,
Of suche a colour enlangoured
Was Abstynence i-wys coloured ;
Of her estate she her repented,
As her visagé represented.   7400
    She had a burdowne al of Thefte,
That Gyle had yeve her of his yefte ;
And a skryppe of Faynte Distresse,
That ful was of elengénesse.
And forthe she walkéd sobrely ;
And False Semblant saynt *je vous dîe*,
Had, as it were for suche mistere,
Done on the copé of a frere.
With cheré symple and ful pytous,
Hys lokyng was not disdeynous   7410
Ne proude, but meke and ful pesyble.
    About his neck he bare a byble,
And squierly forthé gan he gon ;

7385-7576 are lost from G.
7387. Th. *devysed.*
7392. Th. *to ;* cp. note to 7270.
7406. *saynt* is generally taken for *ceint,*
' girdled ' ; but no such Eng. adj. is known. Fr.
is ' qui bien se ratorne.' ? read *faynt, i.e.* pale.
7407. MSS. *And* for *Had.*

And, for to rest his lymmes upon,
He had of Treson a potent;
As he were feble his way he went.
But in his sleve he gan to thring
A rasour sharpe, and wel bytyng,
Thát was forgéd in a forge,   7419
Whiche that men clepen Coupé-gorge.
So longé forthe her waye they nomen,
Tyl they to Wicked-Tongé comen.
That at his gaté was syttyng,
And sawe folke in the way passyng.
The pilgrymes sawe he fasté by,
That beren hem ful mekely,
And humbly they with him mette,
Dame Abstynence first him grette,
And sythe him False-Semblant salued,
And he hem; but he not remeued   7430
For he ne dredde hem not a dele.
For whan he sawe her faces wele,
Alway in herté hem thought so,
He shuldé knowe hem bothé two;
For wel he knewe Dame Abstynaunce,
But he ne knewe not Constreynaunce.
He knewe nat that she was constrayned,
Ne of her thevés lyfe [y-]fayned,
But wende she come of wyl al free;
But she come in another degree;   7440
And if of good wyl she beganne
That wyl was fayléd her [as] thanne.
And False-Semblant had he sayne alse,
But he knewe nat that he was false.
Yet false was he, but his falsnesse
Ne coude he nat espye nor gesse;
For Semblant was so slyé wrought,
That Falsenesse he ne espyed nought.
    But haddest thou knowen hym beforne
Thou woldest on a boke have sworne, 7450
Whan thou him saugh in thylke araye,
That he that whilome was so gaye,
And of the dauncé joly Robyn,
Was tho become a Iacobyn.
But sothely what so menne hym calle,
Freres Prechours bene good menne alle,
Her order wickedly they beren,
Suche myn[é]strelles if they weren.
    So bene Augustyns and Cordyleres
And Carmés, and eke Sackéd freeres 7460
And allé frerés, shodde and bare,

(Though some of hem ben gret and squ...
Ful hooly men, as I hem deme.
Everyche of hem wolde good man se...
But shalte thou never of apparence
Séne conclude good consequence
In none argument y-wis
If existens al fayled is.
For menne maye fynde alwaye sophr...
The consequence to envenyme,   :·
Who so that hath hadde the subtek·
The double sentence for to se.
    Whan the pylgrymes commen we·
To Wicked-Tonge that dwelled ther·.
Her harneys nygh hem was algate;
By Wicked-Tonge adowne they sate,
That badde hem nere him for to com·
And of tidyngés telle him some,
And sayd hem: 'What case maketh r·
To come in-to this placé nowe?'   ·.
    'Sir,' sayd Straynéd-Abstynaunce,
'We, for to dryé our penaunce
With hertés pytous and devoute
Are commen, as pylgrimes gon abo·t·
Wel nygh on fote alway we go;
Ful dousty ben our heeles two.
And thus bothé we ben sent
Throughout this worlde that is misw·
To yeve ensample, and preche also.
To fysshen synful menne we go,   ·'
For other fysshynge, ne fysshé we.
And, sir, for that charyte,
As we be wonte, herborowe we crav·
Your lyfe to amendé, Christ it save,
And so it shulde you nat displese,
We wolden, if it were your ese,
A shorte sermon unto you sayne.'
And Wicked-Tonge answered agayn·
    'The house,' quod he, 'such as ye·
Shal nat be warnéd you for me,   ·
Say what you lyst, and I wol here.'
    'Graunt mercy, sweté sir, dere,'
Quod alderfirst Dame Abstynence,
And thus began she her sentence:
'Sir, the firste vertue certayne,
The greatest, and moste soverayne
That may be founde in any man
For havynge or for wytte he can,
That is his tongé to refrayne.
Therto ought every wight him payn·.

7442. MSS. omit *as.*
7459. *Augustyns,* read *Austins.*

7486. Th. *doughty.*

742

For it is better styllé be   7511
Than for to speken harme, parde ;
And he that herkeneth it gladly,
He is no good man sykerly.
    And, sir, aboven al other synne,
In that arte thou moste gylty inne.
Thou spake a jape not long a-go
(And, sir, that was ryght yvel do)
Of a yonge man, that here repayred
And never yet this place apayred.   7520
Thou saydest he awayted nothyng
But to disceyve Fayre-Welcomyng.
Ye saydé nothyng sothe of that ;
But, sir, ye lye, I tel you plat ;
He ne cometh no more, ne gothe, parde !
I trowe ye shal him never se.
Fayre-Welcomyng in prison is,
That ofte hath played with you er this
The fayrest gamés that he coude,
Withouté fylthé, styl or loude ;   7530
Nowe dare he nat him selfe solace.
Ye han also the manne do chace,
That he dare neyther come ne go ;
What meveth you to hate him so,
But properly your wicked thought,
That many a false lesyng hath thought,
That meveth your foole eloquence,
That jangleth ever in audyence,
And on the folke areyseth blame,
And doth hem dishonour and shame,   7540
For thynge that maye have no prevyng
But lykelynesse, and contryvyng ?
    For I dare sayne that reason demeth,
It is nat al sothe thynge that semeth ;
And it is synné to controve
Thynge that is to reprove ;
This wote ye wele ; and, sir, therfore
Ye arne to blamé [wel] the more.
And nathelesse he recketh lyte
He yeveth nat nowe therof a myte,   7550
For if he thoughté harme, parfaye,
He woldé come and gone al daye ;
He coudé himselfe nat abstene.
Nowe cometh he nat, and that is sene,
For he ne taketh of it no cure,
But if it be through aventure,
And lasse than other folke, algate.
And thou her watchest at the gate,
With speare in thyne arest alwaye ;

7531. Th. *she nat her selfe.*

There musé, musarde, al the daye.   7560
Thou wakest night and day for thought ;
I-wis thy traveyle is for nought.
And Ielousye, withouten fayle,
Shal never quyte the thy traveyle.
And skathe is that Fayre-Welcomyng
Withoutén any trespassyng,
Shal wrongfully in prison be,
There wepeth and languyssheth he.
And though thou never yet, y-wis,
Agyltest manne no more but this,—   7570
Take nat a grefe,—it were worthy
To putte the out of this bayly,
And afterwards in prison lye,
And fettre the, tyl that thou dye.
For thou shalt for this synné dwelle
Right in the devels ers of helle,
But if that thou repenté thee.'
'Mafay, thou liest falsly !' quod he.
'What? welcome with myschauncé nowe !
Have I therfore herberd yowe   7580
To seye me shame, and eke reprove
With sory happe, to youre bihove ?
Am I to day youre herbegere ?
Go herber yow elles-where than heere,
That han a lyer calléd me !
Two tregetours art thou and he,
That in myn hous do me this shame,
And for my sothe-saugh ye me blame.
Is this the sermoun that ye make ?
To all the develles I me take,   7590
Or elles, God, thou me confounde !
But er men diden this castel founde,
It passith not ten daies or twelve
But it was tolde right to my selve,
And as they seide, right so tolde I :
He kyst the Rosé pryvyly !
Thus seide I now and have seid yore ;
I not where he dide ony more.
Why shulde men sey me such a thyng
If it haddé bene gabbyng ?   7600
Ryght so seide I and wol seye yit ;
I trowe I liéd not of it.
And with my bemés I wole blowe
To allé neighboris a-rowe,
How he hath bothé comen and gone.'
Tho spake Falssemblant right anone :
' All is not gospel, oute of doute,
That men seyn in the towne aboute ;

7603. *bemes,* 'besuines,' trumpets.

Ley no deef ere to my spekyng :
I swere yow, sir, it is gabbyng ;   7610
I trowe ye wote wel certeynly,
That no man loveth hym tenderly
That seith hym harme, if he wote it,
All be he never so pore of wit.
And soth is also sikerly
(This knowe ye, sir, as wel as I)
That lovers gladly wole visiten
The places there her loves habiten.
This man yow loveth and eke honoureth,
This man to servé you laboureth,   7620
And clepith you "his freend so deere,"
And this man makith you good chere,
And every-where that [he] you meteth
He yow saloweth and he you greteth.
He preseth not so ofte that ye
Ought of his come encombred be ;
Ther presen other folk on yow
Fúll ofter than he doth now.
And if his herte hym streynéd so,
Unto the Rosé forto go,   7630
Ye shulde hym sene so ofté nede,
That ye shulde take hym with the dede.
He cowde his comyng not forbere
Though he hym thrilléd with a spere ;
It nere not thanne as it is now.
But trustith wel, I swere it yow,
That it is clene out of his thought ;
Sir, certis he ne thenkith it nought,
No more ne doth Faire-Welcomyng,
That sore abieth al this thing.   7640
And if they were of oon assent,
Full sooné were the Rosé hent,
The maugre youres woldé be.
And, sir, of o thing herkeneth me :
Sith ye this man that loveth yow
Han seid such harme and shamé now,
Witeth wel if he gesséd it,
Ye may wel demen in youre wit
He nolde no thyng love you so,
Ne callen you his freende also ;   7650
But nyght and day he wolde wake
The castell to destroie and take,
If it were soth as ye devise ;
Or some man in some maner wise,
Might it warne hym everydele,

       7612. *hym*, etc., indefinite pronouns.

Or by hymsilf perceyven wele.
For sith he myght not come and gone
As he was whilom wont to done,
He myght it soné wite and see.
But now all other wise doth he.   76...
Thanne have, [ye] sir, al outerly
Deserved helle, and Iolyly
The deth of hellé doutéles,
That thrallen folk so giltéles.'
      Fals Semblant proveth so this thing.
That he can noon answeryng,
And seth alwey such apparaunce,
That nygh he fel in repentaunce
And seidé hym :—'Sir, it may wel be.
Semblant, a good man semen ye ;   7...
And, Abstinence, full wise ye seme :
Of o talent you bothe I deme.
What counceil wole ye to me yeven ?'
'Ryght heereanoon thou shalt be shryven,
And sey thy synne withouté more ;
Of this shalt thou repenté sore.
For I am prest, and have pousté
To shryve folk of most dignyte
That ben, as wide as world may dure,
Of all this world I have the cure,   76...
And that hadde never yit persoun,
Ne vicarie of no maner toun.
And, God wote, I have of thee
A thousand tymé more pitee
Than hath thi' preest parochial,
Though he thy freend be special.
I have avauntage in o wise
That youre prelatis ben not so wise,
Ne half so lettred as am I.
Í am licenced boldély   76...
To redé in Divinite
And to confesséñ, out of drede.
If ye wol you now confesse,
And leve your sinnés more and lesse
Withoute abood, knele down anon,
And you shal have absolucion.'

       7660. MSS. *wote* for *doth*.
       7662. *Iolyly* is generally interpreted to be a strengthening adverb equivalent to 'bien' of Fr. but that is translated by *douteles*. Such a se of 'jollyly' is difficult to explain. ? *fully*.
       7691. G ends here with
             To reden in Divinite
             And longe have red.
The French original goes on 9488 verses furthe...

GLOSSARY

Words still in use, with substantially the same meaning, are not included in this Glossary, which is intended for working purposes and not as a concordance. In most cases, to help identification, one reference is given to each word, for each of its obsolete meanings; but in a few words of common occurrence, transferred to this Glossary from that in the Eversley Edition of the *Canterbury Tales*, these references are omitted. In the references the letters A-I denote the various sections of the *Canterbury Tales*, An. *Anelida and Arcite*, As. the *Treatise on the Astrolabe*, Bl. the *Dethe of Blaunche*, Bo. the *Boece*, HF the *Hous of Fame*, L the *Legende of Good Women*, PF the *Parlement of Foules*, R the *Romaunt of the Rose*, T *Troilus and Criseyde*. In the case of the *Hous of Fame* and *Troilus*, the index figures give the number of the book in which the line quoted occurs, thus T² 357 denotes *Troilus*, Bk. ii. l. 357. The letters *i* and *y* being often used interchangeably in manuscripts, most *y*-forms are arranged in the order of *i*.

A, *card. num.* one. T⁴ 1407
A, *interj.* ah. A 1078, R 2627
A, *prep.* on, in. A 3516, A 854
A, *v.* have. R 4322
Abaysed, Abayssched, Abayst, *p.p.* abashed. T³ 1233, Bo. 36, E 317
Abaved, Abawed, *p.p.* abashed, confounded. Bl. 613, R 3646
Abegge, *v.* atone for. A 3938
Abet, *sb.* instigation. T² 357
Abit, abideth. G 1175
Abite, *sb.* habit, dress. R⁻4914
Able, *adj.* fit, apt. A 167
Ablynge, *p. pres.* giving power to. Bo. 220
Abluciona, *sb.* washings. G 856
Abood, *sb.* abiding, delay. A 965; **Abodes**, *pl.* T³ 854
Aboughte, *pret.* of **Abye**. A 2303
Aboven, *adv.* uppermost in luck. R 4352
Abrayde. *See* **Abreyde**.
Abregge, *v.* abridge. A 2999
Abreyde, *v.* awake, start. T² 1113, A 2999 (*p.p.*)
Abroche, *v.* broach. D 177
Abusioun, *sb.* an abuse, scandal. T⁴ 990, 1060
Abye, *v.* pay for. C 765, Bo. 1350
Accesse, *sb.* fever-fit. T² 1543
Accident, *sb.* occurrence, T² 918; changing attribute, E 607
Accidie, *sb.* moral sloth. I 677
Accordaunt, *adj.* agreeable to. A 37
Accorden. *See* **Acorde**.
Accusement, *sb.* accusation. T⁴ 556
Achaat, *sb.* buying. A 571
Achatours, *sb.* buyers. A 568
Achekked, *p.p.* checked. HF² 1003
Achoken, *v.* suffocate, Bo. 443; **Achoked**, *p.p.* choked, L 2008
Acloieth, *pres.* lames, hinders. PF 517
Acontynge, *sb.* reckoning. Bo. 41
Acorde, *pres.* agree. L 3

Acorded, *pret.* suited. A 243
Acorse, *v.* accurse. T³ 1072
Acoye, *v.* caress, appease. T⁵ 782, R 3564
Adamant, Adamaund, *sb.* ironstone, A 1990; magnet, R 1182
Adawe, *v.* awake, T³ 1120; **Adawed**, *p.p.* E 2400
Adrad, *p.p.* afraid. A 605
Advertence, *sb.* attention. G 467
Advocacyes, *sb. pl.* pleas. T² 1469
Aferd, *p.p.* afraid. A 628
Affeccioun, *sb.* desire. A 1158, L 1522
Affectes, *sb. pl.* desires. T³ 1391
Affye, *v.* trust. R 3155
Afile, *v.* polish. A 712
Affraye, *v.* affright. E 455
Afyne, *adv.* finally. R 3690
Aforne, *adv.* before. R 3614
Afor-yein, *prep.* opposite. T² 1188
Afounde, *v.* perish. *Rosemounde* 21
After-tales, *adv.* afterwards. T³ 224
Agayn, Agayns, *prep.* toward, against, in the presence of. B 391, A 1509, C 743
Agaynward, *adv.* back. B 441
A-game, *adv.* in sport. T² 568
Agaste, *v.* terrify. T³ 901
Aggregeden, *p.p.* aggravated. B 2205
Aggreggeth, *v. pres.* aggravates. B 2475
Agilten, *v.* offend. L 435
Ago, Agon, *p.p.* departed, E 1764; past, C 246
Agree, *v.* please. T¹ 409
Agrief, *adv.* sorrowfully. B 4083
Agryse, *v.* be horrified, shudder at. B 614, D 1649
Agroos, Agrose, *pret.* of **Agryse**. L 830, 2314
Agroteyd, *p.p.* surfeited. L 2454
Aguler, *sb.* needle-case. R 98
Aiel, *sb.* grandfather. A 2477
Ajourne, *v.* adjourn. *ABC* 158
Aketoun, *sb.* quilted tunic. B 2050

745

Aknowe, v. acknowledge. Bo. 140

Al, adj. all, A 2959; Al and som, the whole, everybody, A 2761, 3136

Al, adv. wholly, A 2968; Al, conj. although, L 1392

Al, sb. awl. Truth 11

Alambio, sb. alembic. T⁴ 520

Alaunts, sb. boarhounds. A 2148

Alayes, sb. alloys. E 1167

Al-day, adv. continually. B 1702

Alder-, prefix, of all; Oure alder, of us all, R 6948

Alenge, adj. wretched. B 1412

Alestake, sb. pole bearing alehouse sign. A 667

Aleye, sb. alley. B 1758

Aleys, sb. pl. fruit of the wild service tree. R 1377

Algate, adv. always, A 571; any way, A 3962

Algates, adv. any way. T³ 24

Aliene, v. alienate. Bo. 237

Alyned, p.p. placed in lines. HF³ 34 (emend.)

Alkamystre, sb. alchemist. G 1204

Alle, dat. sing. (Bl. 1284) and nom. plur. (Bl 1051) of Al

Allegge, v. (1) allege, E 1658; quote (pres.) HF¹ 314; (2) alleviate (aleggith), R 2588

Aller, gen. plur. of Al. A 823

All-oute, adv. entirely. R 4326

Allowe, v. pres. approve. F 676

Almanderes, sb. pl. almond-trees. R 1363

Almesse, sb. alms. B 168

Almycanteras, sb. pl. circles or parallels of altitude. As. i. § 18

Almury, sb. the pointer of an astrolabe. As. i. § 22

Along on, prep. owing to. T³ 1001

Alose, v. praise, T⁴ 1473; Alosed, p.p. R 2354

Alpes, sb. pl. bullfinches. R 658

Als, adv. as. A 170

Alswa, adv. also. A 4085

Alther-, prefix, of all

Altitude, sb. the elevation of a star, etc., above the horizon. As. i. §§ 1, 13

Al to-, intensive prefix, e.g. Alto-share, pret. cut in pieces. R 1858

Alweys, adv. at all events. T⁵ 298

Amadriades, sb. pl. hamadryads. A 2928

Amalgamyng, sb. the compounding of quicksilver with some other metal. G 771

Amanuced, p.p. diminished. Bo. 118

Amayed, p.p. dismayed. T⁴ 641

Ambages, sb. pl. duplicities. T⁵ 897

Ambes as, both aces, double ace. B 124

Amblere, sb. easy-paced horse. A 469

Ameled, p.p. enamelled. R 1080

Amenuse, v. diminish, I 358; depreciate, I 496

Amenusynge, sb. diminution. Bo. 428

Amerciments, sb. pl. fines. I 752

Ameved, pret. changed; Amoeved, p.p. disturbed. Bo. 25

Amyddes, prep. in the midst of. A 2009

Amynistreth, pres. administers. Bo. 1467

Amoeved. See Ameved

Amonesten, v. warn, admonish. I 76

Amorettes, sb. pl. amorous girls. R 892, 4755

Amphibologyes, sb. pl. equivocations. T⁴ 1406

An, prep. in, on. Bo. 1668

Ancille, sb. handmaid. ABC 109

Anclee, sb. ankle. A 1660

Ancre, sb. anchor. Fortune 38

And, conj. if. L 1790

Angerly, adv. grievously. R 3511

Angres, sb. pl. griefs. R 2554

Angry, adj. grievous. R 2628

Anguyssohous, Angwyssous, adj. anxious. Bo. 482, 603

Anientissed, p.p. annihilated. B 2435

Anker, sb. (1) anchor, R 3780; (2) anchoress, R 6348

Anlaas, sb. dagger. A 357

Annueleer, sb. priest singing anniversary masses. G 1012

Anon-right, adv. forthwith. L 115

Anoyouse, adj. pl. troublesome. I 728

Antiphoner, sb. book of anthems. B 1709

Anvelt, sb. anvil. Bl. 1164

Aornement, sb. adornment. I 432

Apayed, p.p. pleased, contented. L 766, T¹ 649

Apaisen, pres. pl. appease. T³ 22

Apalled. See Appalled

Aparaunce, sb. appearance. L 1372

Apassed, p.p. passed away. Bo. 429

Apeyren, v. impair, depreciate. I 1078, A 3147

Apert, adj. open, frank. D 1114

Apertenant, adj. belonging to. Pite 70

Apertenen, v. belong to. I 410

Apertly, adv. openly, clearly. I 294

Apiked, p.p. trimmed. A 365

A-poynt, adv. exactly. T⁵ 1620

Apointe, reflex v. make up one's mind. T³ 691

Appalled, p.p. made pale or feeble. F 365, B 1292

Apparaille, sb. apparel. ABC 153

Apparaillements, sb. pl. garments. Bo. 465

Apparaillen, v. prepare. B 2530

Appetite, sb. desire, lust. A 1680, L 1586

Appetiteth, pres. s. seeks. L 1582

Apposed, pret. examined. G 363

Appreved, p.p. approved, confirmed. E 1349, L 21

Appropred, p.p. appropriated, peculiar to. Gentilesse 18

Approwours, sb. pl. informers. D 1343

Aqueyntaunce, sb. acquaintance. A 245

Aqueynte, v. acquaint. Bl. 531

Arace, v. tear away, F 1393; Araced, torn, Bo. 80

Arbitre, sb. choice. Bo. 1674

Arblasters, sb. pl. crossbowmen. R 4196

Archaungell, sb. titmouse. R 915

Ardaunt, adj. ardent, burning. Bo. 1394

Arede, v. interpret. Bl. 289

Aresoneth, pres. controverts. R 6220

Arest, sb. See Arrest

Arette, v. account, attribute, A 726, R 337; Aretted, A 2729

Arewe, adv. in a row. D 1254

Argoille, sb. crude tartar made from crust of wine. G 813

Arguments, sb. pl. angles on which tabulated quantities depend in astronomy. F 1277

Aryght, adv. exactly. A 267

Arist, pres. ariseth. B 265

Arist, sb. arising. As. ii. § 12 [200]

Aryve, sb. disembarkation. A 60 (var.)

Aryved, p.p. sent to land. Bo. 1312

Armee, sb. expedition. A 60 (Ellesmere)

Armypotente, adj. mighty in arms. A 2441

Armonyak, adj. Armenian; ammoniac. G 77

Armonye, sb. harmony. PF 63

Arn, pres. pl. are. T⁴ 972

A-roume, *adv.* at large. HF² 33
A-rowe, *adv.* in a row. L 554
Arrest, *sb.* socket of a spear. A 2602
Arreste, *sb.* restraint, delay. L 397, 896
Arryvage, *sb.* disembarking. HF¹ 223
Arsmetrik, *sb.* arithmetic. A 1898
Arten, *v.* constrain. T¹ 388
Artyk, *adj.* arctic. As. i. § 14
Artow, art thou. A 1141
Arwes, *sb. pl.* arrows. A 107
Ascapen, *pres. pl.* escape. Bo. 1361
Ascaunce, *adv.* as though, forsooth. G 838
Ascendent, *sb.* planetary influence. A 417 ; *see* As. ii. § 4 [151-165]
Ascry, *sb.* shout. T² 611
Ashen, *sb. pl.* ashes. A 1364
Aslake, *v.* abate, A 3553 ; **Aslaked,** A 1760
Aslope, *adv.* aside, crossly. R 4464
Aspe, *sb.* aspen tree. A 2921, PF 180
Aspectes, *sb. pl.* planetary relations. T² 682
Aspyen, *v.* espy. T² 649
Aspre, *adj.* rough, bitter. An. 23, Bo. 590
Asprenesse, *sb.* bitterness. Bo. 1370
Assautes, *sb. pl.* assaults. I 729
Assay, *sb.* experiment. L 9
Assaye, *v.* assay, try. Bl. 346
Asseged, *p.p.* besieged. A 881
Assent, *sb.* agreement, plot. C 758, L 1547
Assente, *v.* agree to. A 374
Asseth, *adv.* enough ; **Make asseth,** satisfy, R 5600
Asshy, *adj.* sprinkled with ashes. A 2883
Assise, *sb.* assize. A 314
Assoilen, *v.* absolve, C 939 ; discharge, Bo. 1621 ; resolve, Bo. 1677
Assoilyng, *sb.* absolution. A 661
Assure, *sb.* assurance. An. 331
Astate, *sb.* estate. R 6856
Asterte, *v.* start away, escape, A 1595 ; **A-stert, Asterted,** *p.p.* A 1592, B 437
Astonyed, *p.p.* astonished. HF² 41, A 2361
Astonynge, *sb.* astonishment. Bo. 55
A-stored, *p.p.* stored, provided. A 609
Astromye, *sb.* astronomy. A 3451
Asure, *sb.* blue. An. 330
A-swevad, *p.p.* dazed. HF² 41
At-after, *prep.* after. E 1921, F 302
Atake, *v.* overtake. G 556
Atanes, *adv.* at once. A 4074
Atazir, *sb.* adverse planetary influence. B 305
Ateyne, *v.* attain, *Mars* 161 ; **Ateynt,** *p.p.* attained, comprehended, Bo. 275
Atempraunce, *sb.* temperament. Bo. 1496
Atempre, *adj.* temperate. L 128, 1483, B 2177
Athinken, *v.* vex. T⁵ 878
Atyr, *sb.* attire. I 430, T¹ 181
Aton, *adv.* together. E 437
Atones, Attones, *adv.* at once. L 102
At-rede, *v.* outwit, surpass in advice. A 2449
At-renne, *v.* outrun. A 2449
Attamed, *p.p.* broached. B 4008
Atte, at the. A 125, R 4192
Attempre. *See* **Atempre**
Atthamaunt, *sb.* adamant. A 1305
Attour, *sb.* attire. R 3718
Attricioun, *sb.* contrition. T¹ 557
Attry, *adj.* venomous. I 583
Atwixe, Atwixen, *adv.* between. As. ii. § 5 [173], T² 886
Atwynne, *adv.* apart. A 3589

Auctoritee, *sb.* authority, especially of an esteemed writer. R 2394
Auctour, *sb.* author. L 470
Augrym, *sb.* arithmetical notation, As. i. § 8 ; **Augrym stones,** arithmetical counters, A 3210
Aument, *v.* augment. R 5597
Aungelyke, *adv.* angel-like. L 236
Auntred, *pret.* adventured. A 4205
Auntrous, *adj.* adventurous. A 2099
Autentyke, *adj.* authentic. Bl. 1085
Auter, *sb.* altar. A 1905
Avale, *v.* fall, T² 626 ; doff, A 3122 ; descend, Bo. 1558
Avaunce, *v.* profit. A 246
Avaunt, *adv.* forward. R 4790
Avaunt, *sb.* boast, bold statement. T² 289, A 227
Avauntour, *sb.* boaster. B 4107
Avenaunt, *adj.* comely, suitable. R 1263, 3679
Aventaille, *sb.* helmet's front. E 1204
Aventourous, *adj.* accidental. Bo. 248
Aventure, *sb.* adventure, chance. A 1160, 844
Avys, *sb.* deliberation. A 786, T³ 453
Avyse, *pres.* observe, look to. E 1988
Avysement, *sb.* deliberation. T⁴ 936
Avisioun, *sb.* vision. Bl. 285
Avowtrie, *sb.* adultery. B 2220
Await, *sb.* watch, H 149 ; delay, T² 580 ; **Awaytes,** ambushes, strategies, Bo. 778
Awaytour, *sb.* one who lies in wait. Bo. 1306
Awen, *adj.* own. A 4239
Awmenere, Awmere, *sb.* alms-bag. R 2087, 2271
Awreke, *v.* avenge, *Pite* 11 ; **Awroken,** *p.p.* A 3752
Axe, *pres.* ask. A 1739
Axyng, *sb.* asking, question. A 1826, Bl. 33
Ay, *adv.* always. A 63
Ayeins, *prep.* against. L 330
Ayeynward, *adv.* on the other hand. T⁴ 1097
Azimutes, *sb. pl.* divisions of an astrolabe. As. i. § 19

Ba, *imperat.* kiss. A 3709
Baar, *pret.* bare. A 1180
Babewynnes, *sb. pl.* (baboons) grotesques. HF³ 99
Bachelrye, *sb.* the bachelors. E 270
Baggeth, *pres.* squints. Bl. 622
Baggyngly, *adv.* squintingly. R. 292
Baillie, *sb.* jurisdiction. R. 4217 ; **Baily,** bailiff, R 6331
Baiten, *v.* feed. B 466, T¹ 193
Bak, *sb.* backcloth. G 881 (*var.*)
Balaunce, *sb. ;* **In balaunce,** at hazard, in uncertainty. G 611, R 4667
Bale, *sb.* harm. Bl. 534
Balkes, *sb. pl.* beams. A 3626
Balled, *adj.* bald. A 198
Banes, *sb. pl.* bones. A 4073
Bar, *pret.* bare ; **Bar on honde,** accused, T² 1154, An. 158
Barbe, *sb.* a kind of veil. T² 110
Barbour, *sb.* barber-surgeon. A 2025
Barbre, *adj.* barbarous. A 281
Bareyne, *adj.* barren. A 1244
Barel, *sb.* barrel. B 3083
Bargeyn, *sb.* strife. R 2551
Barm, *sb.* bosom. F 631
Barm-clooth, *sb.* apron. A 3236

Barres, sb. pl. cross-stripes. A 329, R 1103
Barrynge, sb. cross-striping. I 417
Basiliook, sb. basilisk. I 853
Batailled, p.p. battlemented, indented. B 4050
Batailles, sb. pl. battle. A 61
Bate, sb. strife. R 4235
Bathe, adj. both. A 4087
Baudarie, sb. gaiety. A 1926
Baudy, adj. dirty. G 635
Baundon, sb. control. R 1163
Bawdryk, sb. baldrick, belt. A 116
Bawme, sb. balm. T² 53, HF³ 596
Bayard, sb. proverbial name for a horse. G 1413
Be-. See also Bi
Be, prep. by. Bl. 1330
Beautee, sb. beauty. A 1926
Bechen, adj. made of beech. G 1160
Bede, Beede, v. offer. T⁶ 185, G 1065
Bedes, sb. pl. beads. A 159
Bedrede, adj. bedridden. E 1292
Beele, adj. good, fine. B 1599
Been, v. to be. A 140; pres. pl. B 122
Been, sb. pl. bees. F 205
Beere, sb. bier. B 1815
Beet, pret. touched. R 129
Beete, v. kindle. A 2253
Beete, v. mend. A 3927
Beggestere, s. (beggar woman) beggar. A 242
Behoteth, pres. promises. Bl. 620
Bekked, pret. nodded. T² 1260
Beknew, pret. confessed. L 1058
Bele, adj. fair. T² 288
Belweth, pres. bellows. HF³ 703
Bely, sb. bellows. I 353
Bely-naked, adj. stark naked. E 1326
Beme, sb. trumpet. B 4588
Bend, sb. strap. R 1079
Bendynge, sb. slant-striping. I 417
Benedicite, Benediste, bless ye. B 1170, T¹ 780
Bente, sb. dat. grassy slope. A 1981
Be-nymen, v. take away. Bo. 1282
Berd, sb. beard, A 332; Make a berd, outwit, A 4096; so Berdes, deceits, HF³ 181
Bere, sb. (1) bear, A 1640; (2) bier, Pite 105; (3) pillow-case, Bl. 254; pillow, T² 1638
Bere, v. bear, carry. B 3564
Bere on hond, accuse falsely, D 393; cheat into believing, D 232
Bere thurgh, pierce. A 2256
Berynge, sb. behaviour. B 2022
Berme, sb. yeast. G 813
Berne, sb. dat. barn. A 3258
Besaunt-wight, weighing a bezant. R 1106
Beseye, p.p. beseen. Bl. 828
Best, sb. beast. A 1976
Bet, adj. comp. better, B 311; adv. A 242; Go bet, go quickly, L 1213
Bete. See Beete
Beth, pres. be, are. A 178
Betten, p.p. kindled. G 518
Beye, v. buy. G 637
Bibbed, p.p. drunk. A 4162
Bi-bledde, p.p. bloodied. A 2002
Bioched, p.p. cursed. C 656
Bi-clappe, v. clap down, trap. G 9
Bidaffed, p.p. fooled. E 1191
Biddynge, sb. praying. G 140
Bien, pres. pl. buy. R 2452
Bier, sb. buyer. R 5928

Bygyns, sb. pl. béguines. R 6861
Bygoon, p.p. begone, clothed. R 943
Biheste, sb. promise. B 41
Bihete, Bihote, v. promise. A 1854
Bihight, p.p. promised
Byhove, sb. profit. R 1092
Bihovely, adj. advantageous. T² 261
Bijaped, p.p. tricked. A 1585
Biknowe, v. confess. A 1556
Bildere, sb. for adj. builder. PF 176
Biles, sb. pl. beaks. HF³ 360
Bileve, sb. belief, creed. A 3456
Bille, sb. petition. C 166
Bimene, v. bemoan. R 2667
Bynymeth, pres. takes away from. I 335
Biseken, pres. pl. beseech. A 918
Bisemare, sb. abusiveness. A 3965
Bisette, pret. employed. A 279
Biseye, p.p. beseen ; Yvele (richely) biseye, of an ill (rich) appearance. E 965, 984
Bi-shet, p.p. shut up. T³ 602
Bismotered, p.p. soiled. A 76
Bistad, p.p. bestead. B 649
Bit, biddeth. A 187
Bitake, pret. commend to. A 3750
Biteche, pres. commit to. B 2114
Bitymes, adv. betimes, speedily. G 1006
Bitit, betideth. T² 48
Bitore, sb. bittern. D 972
Bitraysed, Bitresshed, p.p. betrayed. B 3570, R 1648
Bitrent, pres. clasps, encircles. T⁴ 1231, T⁴ 870
Biwreye, v. betray. A 2229
Blakeberyed, goon a, go blackberrying, go where they will. C 406
Blaked, p.p. blackened. B 3321
Bianche, adj. white. T¹ 916
Blankmanger, sb. blanc-mange. A 387
Blasen, v. blare. HF³ 712
Bleyne, sb. blain. R 553
Bleynte, pret. blenched. A 1078
Blemesached, p.p. injured. Bo. 170
Blendith, pres. blinds. Bo. 1381
Blere, v. blind. A 4049
Bleve, v. remain. T³ 623
Blynne, v. cease. G 1171, R 6611
Blyve, adv. quickly. A 2697
Blo, adj. blue. HF³ 557
Bloames, sb. pl. blossoms. L 143
Blowynge, p. pres. panting. Bo. 1267
Bobaunce, sb. boast. D 569
Boch, sb. swelling. Bo. 693
Bocher, sb. butcher. A 2025
Bode, sb. delay. An. 119
Boden, p.p. bidden. L 366
Boes, pres. it behoves. A 4027
Boydekin, sb. bodkin, dagger. B 3892
Boyste, sb. box. C 307
Boystous, adj. rough. H 211
Bokeler, sb. buckler. A 112, 3266
Boket, sb. bucket. A 1533
Bolas, sb. bullace. R 1387
Boles, sb. pl. bulls. A 2139
Bon, adj. good. HF³ 514
Bone, sb. prayer. Bl. 834
Boole, sb. astringent earth. G 790
Boon, sb. bone. A 1177
Boor, sb. boar. A 3070
Boos, sb. boss. A 3266
Boost, Boste, sb. talk, outcry. A 4001, L 857

GLOSSARY

Boot, *pret.* bit. B 3791
Boot, *sb.* boat. E 1424
Boots, *sb.* remedy. A 424
Boras, *sb.* borax. A 630
Bord, *sb.* (1) a table, A 52 ; (2) ship's side, A 3585
Bordels, *sb. pl.* brothels. I 885
Bordillers, *sb. pl.* keepers of brothels. R 7034
Borel, Burel, *adj.* coarse, common. B 3145, D 1872, F 716
Borken, *pret.* barked. Bo. 196
Borneth, *pres.* burnishes. T¹ 327
Borwe, *sb.* pledge, surety. A 1622, B 2995
Bosarde, *sb.* buzzard. R 4033
Boste. *See* Boost
Bote, (1) remedy ; (2) boat. *See* Boot
Botel, *sb.* bottle. H 141
Boteler, *sb.* butler. HF² 84
Bother, *gen.* of both. T⁴ 168
Bothon, *sb.* bud. R 2960
Botme, *sb.* bottom. G 1321
Botoun, *sb.* bud. R 1721
Bouk, *sb.* body. A 2746
Boun. *See* Bown
Bountee, *sb.* goodness. B 1656
Bourde, *pres.* jest, C 778 ; Bourded, *p.p.* jested, PF 589
Bourde, *sb. dat.* jest. H 81
Boures, *sb. gen.* bedchamber. A 3677
Bourgerons, *sb. pl.* sodomites. R 7022
Bowes, *sb. pl.* boughs. A 1642
Bown, *adj.* ready. F 1503
Bracer, *sb.* arm-guard. A 111
Brade, *adj.* broad. R 4200
Bragot, *sb.* ale and mead. A 3261
Brayd, *p.p.* started. An. 124
Brayde, *sb.* restless turn, L 1166 ; At a braid, immediately, R 1366
Brak, *pret.* broke
Brast, *pret.* burst
Brat, *sb.* cloak. G 811
Bratful, *adj.* *See* Bretful
Brawn, *sb.* muscle, A 546 ; *pl.* A 2135
Brede, *sb.* roast meat. HF² 132
Brede, *sb.* breadth. A 3811
Breyde, *v.* start, awake. A 4283
Breke, *v.* break. A 551
Brekke, *sb.* flaw. Bl. 939
Breme, *adj.* fierce, T⁴ 184 ; *adv.* A 1699
Bren, *sb.* bran. A 4053
Brennen, *v.* burn, B 111 ; *p.p.* brent, brend, R 1109
Brennynge, *sb.* burning. A 996
Breres, *sb. pl.* briars. R 3006
Bresten, *v.* burst. A 1980
Bretful, Bratful, *adj.* full to the brim. A 687, 2164
Breve, *adj.* brief. R 2350
Brybe, *v.* steal, cheat. A 4417, D 1378
Briberyes, *sb. pl.* rascalities. A 1367
Bryd, *sb.* bird. A 3805
Bryge, *sb.* quarrel. B 2870
Brihte, *adj.* bright. ABC 181
Brike, *sb.* trap. B 3580
Brocage, *sb.* brokery, jobbery. A 3375
Broche, *sb.* brooch. Mars 245
Brode, *adj.* broad. A 739
Broyded, *p.p.* braided. A 1049
Brokkynge, *p. pres.* warbling. A 3377
Bromes, *sb. pl.* broom bushes. HF² 136

Brondes, *sb. pl.* brands, torches. A 2338
Brood, *adj.* broad. A 549
Brotel, Brutel, *adj.* brittle, unstable. L 1885, 2556, Bo. 421
Brouke, *v.* enjoy, use. B 4490, L 194
Browdynge, *sb.* embroidery. A 2498
Browken. *See* Brouke
Brustles, *sb. pl.* bristles. A 556
Brutel. *See* Brotel
Bukke, *sb.* buck ; Blow the bukkes horn, have trouble for nothing. A 3387
Bulte, *v.* sift. B 4430
Bulte, *pret.* built. A 1548
Burdons, *sb. pl.* burdens. R 6908
Burdoun, *sb.* (1) bass, A 673 ; (2) cudgel, R 3401
Burel. *See* Borel
Burned, *p.p.* burnished. A 1983
Burnet, *adj.* of brown material, R 226 ; Burnettes, *pl.* dresses of brown, R 4756
Busk, *sb.* bush. A 2013, R 54
But-if, *conj.* unless. A 351
Buxom, *adj.* obedient. B 1432
By, *prep.* concerning. L 271
By and by, *adv.* side by side, in order. A 1011, L 304
Byle, *sb.* beak. B 4051
Bynt, bindeth. Mars 47
Bytrasshed, *p.p.* betrayed. R 3910

Caas. *See* Cas
Caytyves, *sb. pl.* wretches. A 924
Calcening, *sb.* calcination. G 771
Calculinge, *sb.* reckoning. T¹ 71
Caleweis, *sb. pl.* pears. R 7043
Calkuler, *sb.* the pointer of an astrolabe
Calle, *sb.* head-dress. D 1018, T³ 775 ; cp. Howve
Cam, *pret.* came. A 547
Camaille, *sb.* camel. E 1196
Camuse, *adj.* flat. A 3934
Canel-boon, *sb.* collar-bone. Bl. 942
Canell, *sb.* cinnamon. R 1370
Canevas, *sb.* canvas
Canker-dort, *sb.* state of suffering. T³ 1752
Cantel, *sb.* portion. A 3008
Cape, *pres. pl.* gape. T⁵ 1133
Capitayn, *sb.* captain. B 3741
Capul, *sb.* palfrey. A 4088
Cardynacle, *sb.* heart-disease. C 313
Careyne, *sb.* carcase, B 3814 ; corpse, A 2013
Carf, *pret.* carved. A 100
Cariage, *sb.* toll, tax. R 21, I 752, Bo. 118
Carl, *sb.* churl. A 545
Carmes, *sb. pl.* Carmelites. R 7460
Carpe, *v.* chatter. A 194
Carryk, *sb.* ship of burden. D 1688
Cas, *sb.* case, quiver. A 2080
Cas, *sb.* case, fortune, A 1411 ; chance, A 844 ; Caas, *pl.* law-cases, A 323
Caste, *pret.* devised, B 406 ; reckoned, A 2172
Castes, *sb. pl.* contrivances. A 2468
Catel, *sb.* chattels. A 373
Celebrable, *adj.* famous. Bo. 820
Celle, *sb.* (1) cellar, A 3822 ; (2) religious house, A 172 ; (3) brain, B 3162
Cenyth, *sb.* zenith. As. i. § 18
Ceptre, *sb.* sceptre. B 3563
Cered, *p.p.* sealed. G 808
Cerial ook, *sb.* holm oak. A 2290

749

Certeyn, (1) *adv.* certainly; (2) *sb.* a certain quantity, G 776; (3) In certeyn, certainly, T⁴ 908
Ceruce, *sb.* white lead. A 630
Cetewale, *sb.* valerian. A 3207
Ceynt, *sb.* girdle. A 3235
Chaar, *sb.* car. A 2138
Chaffare, *sb.* merchandise, B 1475; business, E 2438
Chalaundre, Chelaundre, *sb.* sort of lark. R 914, 81
Chalons, *sb.* coverlets from Chalons. A 4140
Chamberere, *sb.* maid-servant. E 819
Champartie, *sb.* partnership. A 1949
Chanoun, *sb.* canon. G 720
Chaped, *p.p.* capped. A 366
Chapeleyne, *sb.* nun who said minor offices. A 164
Chapmanhode, *sb.* business. B 143
Chapmen, *sb. pl.* merchants. B 136
Charboole, *sb.* carbuncle. B 2061
Charge, *sb.* harm, A 2287; load, An. 32
Chargeant, *adj.* burdensome. B 2430
Chartres, *sb. pl.* agreements. T³ 340
Chasted, *p.p.* chastised. F 491
Chasteleyne, *sb.* chatelaine. R 3740
Chasteyne, *sb.* chestnut. A 1921
Chaunterie, *sb.* endowment for singing masses for the dead. A 510
Cheere, *sb.* manner, A 139; countenance, A 913
Cheese, *imperat.* choose. A 1595
Cheeste, *sb.* strife. I 556
Cheeve, *v.* succeed. G 1225
Chek, *interj.* check. Bl. 658
Chekkere, *sb.* chess-board. Bl. 659
Chelaundre. *See* Chalaundre
Chepe, *sb.* purchase, bargain, cheapness. HF³ 884
Cherete, *sb.* dearness. R 3516
Cheste, *sb.* coffin. E 29
Chevered, *p.p.* shivered. R 1732
Chevesaile, *sb.* collar. R 1082
Chevise, *v.* procure. *Mars* 290, R 6425
Chevyssaunce, *sb.* borrowing. B 1519, A 281
Chiche, *adj.* parsimonious. R 5588
Chideresse, Chidestere, *sb.* scold. R 4266, E 1535
Chiertee, *sb.* affection, F 881; dearness, B 1526
Chike, *sb.* chick. R 541
Chiknes, *sb. pl.* chickens. A 380
Chilyndre, *sb.* pocket sundial. B 1396
Chymbe, *v.* chime. A 3896
Chyngerie, *sb.* parsimony. B 2790
Chinynge, *p. pres.* splitting. Bo. 231
Chirche, *sb.* church. A 460
Chirche-hawes, *sb. pl.* churchyards. I 801
Chirketh, *pres.* twitters. D 1804
Chirkyng, *sb.* murmuring. A 2004
Chit, chideth. G 921
Chiteren, *pres.* chatter. G 1397
Chivachie, *sb.* expedition. A 86
Choys, *sb.* choice. B 2273
Ciergis, *sb. pl.* tapers. R 6248
Ciser, *sb.* cider. B 3245
Citole, *sb.* stringed instrument of music. A 1959
Citrinacioun, *sb.* turning citron colour. G 816
Clapers, *sb. pl.* burrows. R 1405
Clappe, *pres.* babble. G 965
Clappen, *v.* (1) beat, HF³ 734; (2) clatter, babble, G 965, E 1200

Clappyng, *sb.* chatter. E 999
Claree, *sb.* spiced wine. A 1471
Clawe, *v.* rub, scratch. A 4326, D 940
Cleped, *p.p.* called. A 121
Clergeoun, *sb.* chorister. B 1693
Clergial, *adj.* clerkly. G 752
Clerk, *sb.* scholar. A 285
Clew, *pret.* clawed, rubbed. HF³ 612
Clifte, *sb.* cranny. Bo. 1406
Clyket, *sb.* latch-key. E 2046
Clippeth, *pres.* hugs. E 2413
Clipsi, *adj.* eclipsed, obscure. R 5349
Clyven, *pres. pl.* cleaves. Bo. 376
Clyves, *sb. pl.* cliffs. L 1470
Clyvyng, *p. pres.* cleaving. Bo. 1460
Cloysterer, *sb.* monk. A 259
Clom, *int.* hush. A 3638
Clos, Cloos, *adj.* secret. T² 1534, R 6104
Clos, *sb.* a pen, enclosure. A 4550, Bo. 203
Closer, *sb.* enclosure. R 4069
Cloteleef, *sb.* burdock-leaf. G 571
Clothered, *p.p.* clotted. A 2745
Clowes, *sb. pl.* claws. HF³ 696
Cod, *sb.* bag. C 534
Cofedred, *p.p.* confederated. *Pite* 52
Cogge, *sb.* small boat. L 1481
Coillons, *sb. pl.* testicles. C 952
Cokenay, *sb.* milksop. A 4208
Cokewold, *sb.* cuckold. A 3152
Cokkow, *sb.* cuckoo. A 1930
Col-blak, *adj.* coal-black. A 2142
Colde, *v.* grow cold. B 879, L 240
Colered, *p.p.* collared. A 2152
Col-fox, *sb.* brant-fox. B 4405
Collacioun, *sb.* conference, E 325; comparison. Bo. 1862
Collect, *sb.* table of planetary motions. F 1275
Colours, *sb. pl.* ornaments of style. F 39
Colpons, *sb. pl.* shreds. A 679
Columbyn, *adj.* dove-like. E 2141
Colver, *sb.* dove. L 2319
Combre-world, *sb.* useless creature. T⁴ 279
Combust, *p.p.* burnt up. T³ 717, As. ii. § 4 [164
Come, *sb.* coming. B 4517
Commoeveden, *pret. pl.* influenced. T³ 17
Commune, *sb.* the commons. E 70
Compassement, *sb.* contrivance. L 1416
Composicioun, *sb.* agreement. A 2651
Compotent, *adj.* almighty. Bo. 1871
Compowned, *p.p.* composed. As. ii. § 5
Comprehended, *p.p.* summed up. An. 83
Comunte, *sb.* community. R 5209
Comyn, *sb.* cummin. B 2045
Concours, *sb.* course. R 4360
Condicioun, *sb.* temperament. L 40
Conestablerye, *sb.* constable's jurisdiction. R 4218
Confedred, *p.p.* confederated. *Pite* 42
Confus, *adj.* confused. A 2230
Congeyen, *v.* dismiss. T⁵ 479
Conyes, *sb. pl.* rabbits. PF 193
Coninges, *sb. pl.* conies. R 7044
Conisaunce, *sb.* acquaintance, R 4668; knowledge, R 5465, 5559
Conjecte, Congecte, *v.* conjecture. Bo. 221, R 6928
Conne, *v.* can be able, know
Connes, *sb. pl.* conies, rabbits. R 1404
Conporte, *v.* bear. T⁵ 1397
Consistorie, *sb.* judgment-seat. C 162

Contek, sb. strife, A 2003; Contekes, pl. dissensions, B 4122

Controve, v. contrive. R 7545

Contubernyal, sb. fellow-soldier. I 760

Contune, v. continue. R 5205

Convenably, adv. suitably. B 2420

Convoyen, v. convey. E 55

Cope, sb. dat. top. A 554

Cope, sb. cape. A 260

Coppe, sb. dat. cup. A 134

Corageous, adj. ardent. I 585

Corages, sb. pl. hearts. A 11

Corbets, sb. pl. architectural ornaments. HF³ 214

Cornemuse, sb. bagpipe. HF³ 128

Corniculer, sb. adjutant. G 369

Corrumpable, adj. corruptible. A 3010

Corrumpen, v. rot, Bo. 987; Corrumped, p.p. corrupted, I 819

Cors, sb. body, corpse. B 2098, A 3429

Corseint, sb. holy body, relic. HF¹ 117

Cosynage, sb. kinship. B 1226

Cosse, sb. kiss. R 3663

Cost, s. coast, place. R 3931

Costage, sb. expense. B 1235

Costeiyng, p. pres. coasting, skirting. R 134

Costrel, sb. bottle. L 2666

Cote, sb. dat. dungeon. A 2457

Couched, p.p. laid, A 2933; inlaid, A 2161

Couchen, v. lay. G 1152, R 6903

Coude, pret. knew. A 327

Counter-taille, sb. counter-tally. E 1190

Countour, sb. auditor. A 359

Countrepeise, v. balance. HF³ 660

Countre-pleted, p.p. controverted. L 476

Countrewayte, v. watch against. B 2505, I 100

Coupable, adj. guilty. Bo. 70

Coured, pret. cowered. R 465

Courtepy, sb. cape. A 290

Couth, p.p. plain, evident. R 4213

Couthe, adv. patently. HF² 249

Covenable, adj. suitable. I 80

Covent, sb. convent of monks. B 1827

Coverchiefs, sb. pl. kerchiefs. A 453

Covercle, sb. lid of a cup. HF² 284

Covered, p.p. recovered. L 762

Covyne, sb. craft, intriguing. R 3799, A 604

Coye, v. quiet. T² 801

Coynes, sb. pl. quinces. R 1374

Cracchynge, sb. scratching. A 2834

Craketh, pres. sings hoarsely. E 1850

Crampisseth, pres. cramps. An. 171

Creaunce, sb. belief, B 340; debt, ABC 61

Creaunce, v. get credit, B 1479; creanced, p.p. raised on credit, B 1556

Crece, sb. increase. R 4875

Crekes, sb. pl. devices. A 4051

Crepil, sb. cripple. T⁴ 1458

Cryke, sb. creek. A 409

Crips, adj. crisp, curly. HF³ 296

Cristophere, sb. image of St. Christopher worn as an amulet. A 115

Croce, sb. cross, crozier. R 6470

Crois, sb. cross. ABC 60, A 699

Crop, sb. top, summit. T⁶ 25, A 1533

Cropen, p.p. crept. A 4259

Crosselet, sb. crucible, G 1117; Croslets, pl. G 793

Crouche, pres. sign with the cross. A 3479

Crowke, sb. crock. A 4158

Crownet, sb. coronet. R 3203

Crulle, adj. pl. curly. A 81

Cucurbites, sb. pl. flasks for distilling. G 794

Culpe, sb. guilt. I 336

Cure, sb. care, keeping. Bo. 227

Curiositee, sb. fastidiousness. I 829

Currours, sb. pl. runners. HF³ 1038

Custommere, adj. accustomed. R 4936

Cut, sb. lot. A 835

Daf, sb. fool. A 4208

Daggynge, sb. slitting. I 418

Dagoun, sb. fragment. D 1751

Dayerye, sb. dairy. A 597

Dayesie, sb. daisy. L 182

Daliaunce, sb. pleasantry. A 211

Dampned, p.p. condemned. A 1175

Dan, sb. See Daun

Dare, v. daze. D 1294

Darketh, pres. hides. L 816

Darreyne, v. contest. A 1609

Daswed, p.p. dazed. HF³ 151

Daun, sb. lord, sir. A 1379, B 3982

Daunce, sb. dance, game. A 476

Daunger, sb. influence, dominion. A 663, R 1470

Daungerous, adj. difficult, hard to please. A 517, B 2129

Daunten, v. subdue. Bo. 743

Dawes, sb. pl. days. F 1180, R 2838

Daweth, pres. dawns. A 1676

Dawing, sb. dawn. T³ 1466

Debate, v. do battle, oppose. B 2058, T⁴ 166

Debonairte, sb. meekness. Bl. 985

Debonerly, adv. gently. T² 1259

Decooped, p.p. slit. R 843

Ded, p.p. dead. A 942

Deduyt, sb. delight. A 2177

Deed, p.p. dead. See Ded

Deef, adj. deaf. A 446

Deel, sb. part, whit. A 415

Deemen, v. judge. B 3045

Deer, sb. wild animals

Deere, adv. dearly. A 3100

Deerelyng, sb. darling. A 3793

Deerne, adj. secret. A 3200

Dees, sb. pl. dice. T³ 1347

Defaute, sb. default, defect. Bl. 5, I 182

Defende, v. (1) imper. defend, ABC 95; (2) Deffendeth, forbids, B 2945; p.p. forbidden, B 475

Defet, p.p. enfeebled. T⁶ 618

Deffeted, p.p. defeated. Bo. 261

Defusioun, sb. diffuseness. T³ 296

Degise, adj. fashionable. I 417

Degree, sb. rank, A 1168; pl. steps, A 1890

Deydest, pret. didst die. T³ 263

Deye, sb. dairy-woman. B 4036

Deyned, pret. deigned

Deynous, adj. bumptious. A 3941

Deys, sb. dais. A 370

Del, sb. part, whit

Delyces, sb. pl. delights. C 547

Delit, sb. pleasure. A 335

Delyvere, adj. active. A 84

Delyverly, adv. adroitly. B 4606

Delivernesse, sb. agility. I 452

Deme, v. judge, B 2219; Demeth, imper. A 1353

Demeyne, (1) sb. dominion, B 3855; (2) v. govern, HF² 451

Demene, *v.* endure. R 5278

Departe, *v.* distinguish, T³ 404; *pres. subj.* separate, A 1134; **Departed,** *p.p.* A 1621

Depeynted, *p.p.* depicted. A 2031

Depper, *adv. comp.* more deeply. B 630

Dere, *v.* harm. F 240, A 1822

Dereworth, Derworth, *adj.* precious. Bo. 281, 491

Derke, *sb. dat.* darkness. Bl. 608

Derre, *adv. comp.* more dearly. A 1448

Descensories, *sb. pl.* vessels for extracting oil. G 792

Desolaundre, *v.* slander. G 993

Descryve, *v.* describe. *See* **Discryve**

Desese, *v.* dispossess. R 2076

Desespaired, *p.p.* despaired. *Comp. to his Lady* 7

Deslavee, *adj.* unbridled. I 629

Desordeynee, *adj.* inordinate. I 818

Desordinat, *adj.* disorderly. I 415

Despense, *sb.* expenditure. A 1928

Despitous, *adj.* scornful. A 516

Desray, *sb.* disarray, confusion. I 927

Destynal, *adj.* fated. Bo. 1465

Destreyne, Distreyne, *v.* vex, constrain, grasp. F 820, A 1455, 1816, Bo. 513, PF 337

Determine, *v.* come to an end. T³ 379

Devyaunt, *adj.* divergent. R 4789

Devoided, *p.p.* banished. R 2929

Devoir, *sb.* duty. I 764

Dextrer, *sb.* steed. B 2103

Dyapred, *p.p.* diapered. A 2158

Dych, *sb.* ditch. I 718

Diffense, *sb.* prohibition. R 1142

Dight, *p.p.* dressed. A 1041

Digne, *adj.* worthy, A 141; haughty, repellent, A 517, 3964; | **Dignelich,** *adv.* haughtily, T³ 1024

Dilatacioun, *sb.* enlargement. B 232

Disavaunce, *v.* hinder. T³ 511

Disaventure, *sb.* mischance. T⁴ 741

Dischevelee, *adj.* with hair loose. A 683

Disclaundred, *p.p.* slandered. L 1031

Discorden, *pres. pl.* disagree. Bo. 1495

Discreven, Discryven, Diskryve, *v.* describe. R 4803, I 533, Bl. 915

Discure, *v.* reveal, abide. Bl. 548

Disfigurat, *adj.* deformed. PF 222

Disjoynt, *sb.* dilemma, disadvantage, danger. B 1601, A 2962, L 1631

Dismal, *sb.* evil day. Bl. 1205

Dispence, *sb.* expenditure. R 1144

Dispitouse, *adj.* despiteful. Bl. 623

Dispone, *imper.* dispose. T³ 300

Disponyth, *pres.* disposes. Bo. 1457

Disrewlily, *adv.* irregularly. R 4900

Dissert, *sb.* deserving. Bo. 1302

Disserved, *p.p.* deserved. A 1716

Disteyne, *v.* stain, obscure. L 255

Distincte, *v.* distinguish. R 6199

Distyngwed, *p.p.* distinguished. Bo. 439

Distoned, *p.p.* put out of tune. R 4248

Distreyne. *See* **Destreyne**

Disturne, *v.* turn aside. T³ 718

Dite, *sb.* song, poem, story. Bo. 1453, 602, 315

Divinistre, *sb.* diviner. A 2811

Divynailes, *sb. pl.* divinations. I 605

Divisioun, *sb.* difference. A 1780

Doande, *p. pres.* doing. R 2708

Doke, *sb.* duck, A 3576; *pl.* H 4580

Doked, *p.p.* cropped. A 590

Dolven, *p.p.* buried. Bl. 222

Dom, *sb.* judgment. PF 480

Domme, *adj.* dumb. R 2220

Donne, *adj.* dun. T³ 908, PF 334

Doole, *sb.* portion. R 2364

Doole, *sb.* dolefulness. R 2956

Doom, *sb.* judgment. C 257

Dormaunt, *adj.* (of a table) fixed. A 353

Doucet, *sb.* a kind of flute. HF³ 132

Douteles, *adv.* doubtless

Doutas, *adj. pl.* dubious. Bo. 591

Doutous, *adj.* deceitful. Bo. 275

Dowe, *pres. s.* bestow. T³ 230

Dradde, *pret.* feared

Draf, *sb.* dregs, refuse. I 35, A 4207

Drasty, *adj.* worthless. B 2113

Drat, dreadeth. T³ 328

Draughte, *sb.* move at chess. Bl. 681

Drawe, *v.* move at chess. Bl. 682

Drecched, *p.p.* harassed. B 4077

Drecchynge, *sb.* delaying. I 1000, T³ 853

Dredeles, *adv.* undoubtedly. Bl. 763

Dredful, Dredeful, *adj.* (1) timorous, PF 195, A 1479; (2) terrible, B 3558

Dreinte, *pret.* drowned, Bl. 72; was drowned. B 923

Dreynt, *p.p.* drowned. A 3520

Drenchen, *v.* drown. B 455

Drenchyng, *sb.* drowning. A 2456

Drerihed, *sb.* dreariness. R 4728

Dresse, *v.* make ready. B 1100

Drye, *v.* endure, suffer. *Mars* 251, T³ 42, R 3105

Dryve, *p.p.* driven. F 1230

Drogges, *sb. pl.* drugs. A 426

Dronkelewe, *adj.* tipsy. C 495

Droppynge, *p. pres.* dripping. I 633

Drough, *pret.* drew. B 1710, F 965, T³ 978

Drovy, *adj.* turbid. I 816

Drusry, *sb.* love, affection. R 844, 5063

Drugge, *v.* drudge. A 1416

Duo, *sb.* duke. A 860

Dulcarnon, *sb.* perplexity. *See* note, T³ 931

Dulle, *pres.* grow dull. R 4792

Dulve, *pret.* dug. Bo. 1639

Dure, *v.* endure, abide, live. E 166, A 1276, *Comp. to his Lady* 31

Durre-don, dare do. T³ 840

Durring-don, *sb.* daring. T³ 837

Duweliche, *adv.* duly. Bo. 190

Dwale, *sb.* sleeping draught. A 4161

Dwyned, *p.p.* dwindled. R 360

Ech, *adj.* each. A 39

Eche, *v.* eke, increase. T¹ 705, T³ 110

Eched, Echid, *p.p.* increased. T³ 1329, Bo. 71

Echynnys, *sb. pl.* sea-urchins. Bo. 798

Echon, each one

Eek, *adv.* also. A 41

Eem, Em, *sb.* uncle. T¹ 1022, T³ 162

Eft, *adv.* again. A 1669

Eft-sones, *adv.* soon again. T³ 1468

Egal, *adj.* equal. T³ 137, Bo. 575

Egalitee, Egalyte, *sb.* equality, equanimity. I 949, Bo. 395

Egaly, *adv.* equably. Bo. 398

Egge, *sb.* edge. T⁴ 927, *Former Age* 19

Eggement, *sb.* incitement. B 842

Egre, *adj.* sharp, bitter. Bo. 215, I 117, R 5475

gremoyne, *sb.* agrimony. G 800
gren, *v.* excite. Bo. 1530
rleth, *pres. s.* ails. A 1081
r, *sb.* air. A 1246
rre, *sb.* heir. L 2549
rryah, *adj.* aerial. HF² 424
sel, *sb.* vinegar. R 217
rthe, *adj.* easy. R 3955
t, *adv.* also. T⁵ 1510
defather, *sb.* grandfather. Bo. 372
den, *v.* grow old. Bo. 528
engenesse, *sb.* wretchedness. R 7494
l, *adv.* else. R 1231, 2964
lebor, *sb.* hellebore. B 4154
les, *adv.* else. C 315
vysahe, *adj.* elf-like, abstracted. G 842
n, *sb.* uncle. T² 162
nbawme, *v.* embalm. L 676
nbelif, *adj.* oblique. As. i. § 20
nbelysed, *p.p.* embellished. Bo. 439
nbosed, *p.p.* sheltered in the woods. Bl. 353
nbrouded, *p.p.* embroidered. A 89
neraude, *sb.* emerald. PF 175
nforth, *prep.* to the extent of, according to. T² 243, 997, A 2235
nysperies, *sb. pl.* hemispheres. As. i. § 18
npeyre, *pres.* impair. E 2198
npeireden, *pret. pl.* made worse. B 2205
nplastre, *pres. pl.* plaster over, 'whitewash.' E 2297
nplieth, *pres. pl.* unfold. Bo. 1648
nprise, *sb.* enterprise. G 605, Bl. 1092
npte, *adj.* empty. G 741
ncens, *sb.* incense. A 2938
nchesoun, *sb.* occasion. B 2780
ncombrous, *adj.* burdensome. HF² 354
ncrees, *sb.* increase. A 2184
ncreascoeden, *pret.* enlarged on. B 2466
ncreassen, *pres. pl.* increase. A 1338
ndelong, *adv.* lengthways. A 1991
ndentynge, *sb.* scalloping. I 417
ndyte, *v.* write, compose. A 95, L 2356
nforcest thee, *pres.* endeavourest. Bo. 775
ngyn, *sb.* (1) wit, contrivance, G 339, T³ 274; (2) military machine, R 4194
ngyned, *p.p.* racked. B 4250
ngreggen, *pres. pl.* weigh upon. I 978
ngreveth, *pres.* grieves. R 3444
nhabite, *pres.* dwell. R 6355
nhaunced, *p.p.* elevated. As. ii. § 26 -
nlaceth, *pres.* entangles, Bo. 97; Enlaced, *p.p.* Bo. 774
nlumyned, *p.p.* illuminated. *ABC* 73
nlutyng, *sb.* plastering with clay. G 766
noynt, *p.p.* anointed. A 199
nseled, *p.p.* sealed up, confirmed. T⁵ 151, T⁴ 559
ntaile, *v.* carve, R 619, 3711; Entailled, *p.p.* R 140
ntayle, *sb.* shape, R 162; cutting, jagging, R 1081
ntame, *v.* begin. *ABC* 79
nteoched, *p.p.* endued with (good) qualities, T⁵ 832; infected, Bo. 1292
ntende, *pres. s.* perceive. T⁴ 1649
ntermete, *v.* interpose. R 2966
ntre, *sb.* entry. Bo. 266, 316
ntrechaungynges, *sb. pl.* interchanges. Bo. 357
ntrecomunen, *v.* communicate. T⁴ 1354

Entredited, *p.p.* under an interdict. I 905
Entremedled, *p.p.* intermingled. Bo. 512
Entremees, *sb.* entremet, a between-course. PF 665
Entremete, *v.* interpose, interfere. D 834, B 2730, Bo. 1094, R 2966
Entriketh, *pres.* entangles. PF 403
Entunes, *sb. pl.* intonings. Bl. 309
Envenyme, *v.* poison. Bl. 640
Environ, *adv.* round about. R 4203
Envyned, *p.p.* supplied with wine. A 342
Envoluped, *p.p.* enveloped. C 942
Equipolences, *sb. pl.* equivalents. R 7076
Er, *adv. conj. prep.* before
Ercedeken, *sb.* archdeacon. A 655
Ere, *sb.* ear; Erys, *pl.* A 556
Ere, *v.* plough, A 886; Ered, *p.p.* HF¹ 485
Erke, *adj.* irked, weary. R 4867
Erme, *v.* grieve. Bl. 80, C 312
Ernes, *sb.* earnestness. R 4838
Ernestful, *adj.* serious. E 1175
Erraunt, *adj.* wandering. Bl. 660
Ers, *sb.* arse. A 3734
Eschaufede, *pret.* chafed. Bo. 211
Eschaufeth, *pres.* grows warm. Bo. 216
Eschaunges, *sb. pl.* exchanges. HF² 189
Eschew, Eschu, *adj.* unwilling. I 971, E 1812
Esed, *p.p.* entertained. A 29
Esoyne, *sb.* excuse for absence. I 164
Espleiten, *v.* perform. R 6174
Estat, *sb.* state. A 926
Estatlich, *adj.* stately. A 140
Estatutes, *sb. pl.* statutes. Bo. 269
Estres, *sb. pl.* inner parts of a house. A 1971, 4295, L 1715
Ethe, *adj.* easy. T⁵ 850
Evene, *adj.* average. A 82
Everich, *pron.* each. A 371
Everychon, each one. A 31
Everydel, every whit. A 368
Ew, *sb.* yew-tree. A 2923, PF 180
Exces, *sb.* excess, extravagance. T¹ 626
Expans, *adj.* separate. F 1275
Extre, *sb.* axle. As. i. § 14
Ey, *sb.* egg. B 4035

Facound, *sb.* eloquence. C 50, Bl. 925
Facound, *adj.* eloquent. PF 520
Fader, *sb.* (*gen.*) father's. R 781
Fadme, *sb.* fathom. A 2916, Bl. 422
Fayle, *v.* make mistakes. R 4249
Fair, *adj.*; A fair, a good one, A 165, T³ 850
Faire, *adv.* fairly. A 94
Fairye, *sb.* fairyland. E 95
Faldyng, *sb.* coarse cloth. A 391
Fallaces, *sb. pl.* fallacies. R 7077
Falle, *v.* happen
Falsen, *v.* falsify. A 3175
Falwe, *adj.* brown, yellow. HF² 846
Falwes, *sb. pl.* fallows. D 656
Famulier, *adj.* familiar. A 215
Fan, *sb.* quintain. H 42
Fantastik, *adj.* imaginative. A 1376
Fantome, *sb.* fantasy. B 1037
Faros, *imperat.* paint. R 2285
Pardeles, *sb. pl.* burdens. R 5683
Fare, *sb.* fuss, disturbance. A 3999, T³ 860
Fare, *v.* go, speed, behave
Fare, *p.p.* gone. F 1546
Fare-carte, *sb.* cart. T⁵ 1162

3 C

Farsed, *p.p.* stuffed. A 233
Fasoun, *sb.* fashion. R 708
Fancon, *sb.* falcon. F 411
Fasooners, *sb. pl.* falconers. F 1196
Fawe, *adj.* fain, R 6477; *adv.* T⁴ 887
Fay, *sb.* faith. L 778, R 2887
Fecches, *sb. pl.* vetches. T² 936
Feeld, *sb.* field. A 1522
Feendly, *adj.* fiendish. Bl. 593
Feffe, *v.* fee, present. T² 901
Feffed in, *p.p.* invested with. E 1698
Feirs, *adj.* fierce. R 1482
Feyne, *v.* feign. A 735
Feyntise, *sb.* feigning. R 2947, 2998
Fel, *adj.* fierce. B 2019
Fel, *sb.* skin. T¹ 91
Felawe, *sb.* fellow. A 1525
Feldefare, *sb.* field-fare. PF 364, T² 861
Fele, *adj.* many. E 917, Bo. 262, R 189
Felle, *adj. pl.* cruel. T¹ 470
Felliche, Felly, *adv.* cruelly. Bo. 355, R 3251
Felnesse, *sb.* fierceness. Bo. 217
Femenye, *sb.* womankind. A 866
Femininitee, *sb.* womanhood, feminine appearance. B 360
Fend, *sb.* fiend. I 584
Fenix, *sb.* phœnix. Bl. 981
Fer, *adj.* and *adv.* far
Ferde, *sb. dat.* fear. Bl. 981, T¹ 557, L 2332
Ferde, *pret.* fared, behaved. A 1372, 3600
Fere, *sb.* fellow, companion, L 969; In fere, I-fere, together
Perforth, *adv.* far forward; So forforth, So ferforthly, to such an extent. B 372, A 960
Ferfulleste, *adj. sup.* most timorous. T² 450
Ferly, *adj.* wonderful. A 4173
Fermacies, *sb. pl.* pharmacies, medicines. A 2713
Fermerer, *sb.* keeper of the infirmary. D 1859
Fermour, *sb.* farmer, contractor. L 378
Fern, *adv.* of long time. F 255
Ferne, *adj. pl.* ancient, A 14; Ferne yere, past years, T⁵ 1176
Ferre, *adv. comp.* farther. A 47
Ferreste, *adj. super.* farthest. A 494
Fers, *sb.* piece at chess. Bl. 653
Ferthe, *card. num.* fourth. H 823
Ferther, *adv.* further. A 36
Ferthyng, *sb.* morsel. A 134
Fesaunt, *sb.* pheasant. PF 357
Fest, *sb.* fist. C 802
Feste, *sb.* feast, festival. A 906
Festeiynge, *p. pres.* feasting. F 345
Festyvally, *adv.* joyously. Bo. 560
Festne, *v.* fasten. A 195
Fet, *pret.* fetched. A 810
Fetys, *adj.* neat, graceful. A 157, C 478
Fetisly, *adv.* neatly, skilfully. A 273, A 124
Fiaunce, *sb.* confidence. R 5481
Fycchen, *v.* fix. Bo. 419
Fil, *pret.* fell. A 1034, Bl. 275
Fille, *v.* fell, cut down. A 1702
Fyn, *sb.* end. B 424, Mars 218
Finaliche, *adv.* finally. T² 556
Fine, *v.* finish, cease, stop. T⁴ 26, T⁵ 776, T² 1460.
Fynt, findeth
Fir, *sb.* fire. A 1502, 1246
Fizycien, *sb.* physician. Bo. 66
Fit, *sb.* stave, canto. B 2078

Fithele, *sb.* fiddle. A 296
Flayne, *p.p.* flayed. I 425
Flammes, *sb. pl.* flames. ABC 89
Fleemeth, *pres.* chases away. H 182
Fleen, *sb. pl.* fleas. H 17
Fleen, *v.* flee. ABC 148
Fleete, *pres. s.* float. A 2397
Fleigh, *pret.* flew. T² 104
Flemed, *pret.* exiled, R 3052; *p.p.* exiled fugitive, G 58
Flemen, *v.* put to flight. T² 852
Flemere, *sb.* banisher. B 460
Fleteth, *pres. s.* floateth. B 901
Fletynge, *p. pres.* floating. A 1956
Flex, *sb.* flax. A 676
Flo, *sb.* dart. H 264
Flokmeele, *adv.* in a crowd. E 86
Floteren, *pres. pl.* flutter, are tossed about. Bo 1037
Flotery, *adj.* dishevelled. A 2883
Flourouns, *sb. pl.* flower-ornaments. L 217
Floute, *sb.* flute. HF² 133
Floytynge, *p. pres.* fluting. A 91
Fneseth, *pres. s.* snorts. H 62
Foynen, *pres. pl.* thrust. A 1654
Foysoun, *sb.* increase. A 3167
Foleyen, *v.* act foolishly. Bo. 644
Foly, *adv.* foolishly. Bl. 873
Folye, *adj.* foolish. L 164
Folily, *adv.* foolishly. Mars 158, R 2603
Fonde, *v.* try, prove. B 347, T² 1155
Fonge, *v.* take. B 377
Fonne, *sb.* fool. A 4089
Fonned, *p.p.* fooled. R 5367
Foore, *sb.* course. D 1935
Foot-hoot, *adv.* in haste. B 438
For-, *as an intensive prefix.* For-blak, A 2144. For-dronk, For-dry, For-old, A 2142; For-pampered, *Former Age* 5, etc.; very black, very drunk, very dry, very old, very pampered, etc.
For, *conj.* because. T¹ 802
For, *prep.* in fear of, T¹ 748, T² 194, 868; against. T¹ 928
For al, notwithstanding. T⁴ 55 note
Forbede, Forbode, *pres. subj.* forbid. L 10
Forbise, *v.* exemplify. T² 1390
For-brak, *pret.* interrupted. Bo. 1143
Forby, *adv.* by, past. A 175
For-craccheth, *v.* scratch. R 323
For-do, *v.* destroy. T¹ 238
For-do, For-done, *p.p.* destroyed, ruined. T¹ 7. R 4339
For-drede, *sb.* fear. B 2383
For-dryve, *p.p.* driven astray. A 3782
For-dwyned, *p.p.* wasted. R 366
Foreyn, *sb.* outer room. L 1962
Forseyne, *adj.* foreign, external, public. E. 680, 755
For-fare, *v.* fare ill. R 5778
Forheed, Forheved, *sb.* forehead. G 580, Bo. 1.
Forlete, *v.* resign, forgo, forsake, B 184, C 864, I 720; Forleten, *p.p.* forsaken, HF² 3.
Forloyn, *sb.* note on horn recalling hounds when at fault. Bl. 386
Forlyved, *p.p.* decrepit. Bo. 763
Forlyven, *v.* degenerate. Bo. 758
Forme, *adj.* first. B 2290
Formel, *sb.* any hen-bird of prey. PF 371
Formest, *adj.* foremost. Bl. 889

Forncast, *p.p.* planned. I 448
Forneys, *sb.* furnace. A 559
For-pyned, *p.p.* tormented. A 205
Fors, *sb.* force ; **No fors,** no matter. B 285
For-shapen, *p.p.* misshapen. T² 66
For-shright, *p.p.* tired with shrieking. T⁴ 1147
For-sleweth, *pres.* is over-slothful. I 685
Forslewthen, *v.* over-tarry. B 4286
For-sluggeth, *pres.* is over-sluggish. I 685
For-songen, *p.p.* exhausted with singing. R 664
Forster, *sb.* forester. A 120
For-straught, *p.p.* exhausted. B 1295
For-thenke, For-thinke, *v.* repent. R 3957, T²
 1414
For-thy, *adv.* therefore. Bo. 375
Forthren, *v.* further, help. A 1137
Forth-right, *adv.* directly. E 1503
Fortunen, *v.* presage. A 417
Fortunous, *adj.* fortuitous. Bo. 224
For-waked, *p.p.* tired with watching. B 596,
 Bl. 126
Forwandred, *p.p.* tired with wandering. R 3336
Forward, *sb.* agreement. A 33
Forwelked, *p.p.* withered. R 361
For-weped, *p.p.* exhausted with weeping. Bl.
 126
For-wered, *p.p.* worn out. R 235
Forwes, *sb. pl.* furrows. *Former Age* 12
For-why, *conj.* because. T² 12
Forwityng, *sb.* foreknowledge. B 4433
Forwot, *pret.* foreknew. HF¹ 45
Foryaf, *pret.* forgave, respited. T² 1577
Foryede, *pret.* forwent, desisted from. T² 1330
Foryelde, *v.* repay. E 831
Foryete, *v.* forget. Bl. 1124
Foryive, *pres.* forgive. B 1615
Fother, *sb.* cartload. A 530
Foudre, *sb.* lightning. HF¹ 335
Foules, *sb. pl.* fowls, birds. PF 203
Founde. *See* **Fonde.**
Foundred, *pret.* fell. A 2687
Founes, *sb. pl.* fawns. Bl. 429
Frayneth, *pres. s.* asks. B 1790
Frakenes, *sb. pl.* freckles. A 2169
Frape, *sb.* company. T³ 410
Freel, *adj.* frail. Bo. 889
Freeten, *pres. pl.* eat. A 2068
Freyned, *pret.* prayed. B 3020
Freletee, *sb.* frailty. I 449
Fremde, *adj.* foreign. F 429
Fret, *sb.* ornament. L 215
Frete, *v.* eat, B 3294 ; *p.p.* eaten, B 475
Freteth, *pres. s.* rubs. A 3747
Frounce, *sb.* wrinkle. Bo. 61
Frounced, *p.p.* wrinkled. R 365, 3137
Frounceles, *adj.* unwrinkled. R 850
Frutesteres, *sb. pl.* fruit-women. C 478
Fumetere, *sb.* the herb fumitory. B 4153
Fumosltee, *sb.* headiness, vapouriness. C 567,
 F 358
Furial, *adj.* raging. F 448
Furlong-wey, short space. L 841
Further-over, *adv.* furthermore. T⁴ 1027

Gabbe, *v.* talk idly, gossip. A 3510, Bl. 1074,
 T³ 301
Gadelyng, *sb.* vagabond. R 938
Gadrede, *pret.* gathered. A 824
Gayl, *sb.* gaol. R 4745
Gayler, *sb.* gaoler. A 1064

Gaillard, Gaylard, *adj.* gay, merry. A 4367,
 3336
Gayneth, *pres. s.* availeth. A 1787
Gaitrys beryis, *sb. !pl.* berries of the dog-wood
 tree. B 4155
Galauntyne, Galentyne, *sb.* a kind of sauce.
 Rosam. 17, *Former Age* 16
Galaxye, *sb.* the Milky Way. PF 56
Gale, *v.* cry out. D 832
Galyngale, *sb.* sweet cypress root. A 381
Galoche, *sb.* patten, high shoe. F 555
Galpyng, *adj.* gaping. F 350
Galwes, *sb. pl.* gallows. B 3941
Gan, *pret.* began, did, used to. A 301
Ganeth, *pres. s.* yawns. A 4037
Gargat, *sb.* throat. B 4525
Garisoun, *v.* cure. R 3249
Garnisoun, *sb.* garrison. B 2215
Gas, goes. A 4037
Gastnes, *sb.* terror. Bo. 728
Gat-tothed, *adj.* goat-toothed, lascivious. A
 468
Gauded, *p.p.* dyed. A 159
Gauren, *v.* gaze. A 3827
Gaureth, *pres. s.* stares. B 3559
Gawdes, *sb. pl.* toys, fineries. I 651
Geaunt, *sb.* giant. B 1997
Geere, Gere, *sb.* (1) clothing, accoutrement, A
 365, 1016 ; (2) behaviour, manners, A 1372,
 1531
Geery, *adj.* changeable. A 1536
Geestes, *sb. pl.* stories. F 211
Geyn, *sb.* gain. An. 206
Geldehalle, *sb.* guild-hall. A 370
Gent, *adj.* gentle, courteous. B 1905, PF 558
Gentrie, *sb.* gentle birth, nobility. I 452
Geomancie, *sb.* divination by figures made on
 the earth. I 605
Gerdon, Gerdoun, *sb.* reward ; **For alle ger-**
 dons, at all costs. B 2240
Gerdoned, *p.p.* rewarded. B 2460
Gere, *sb. See* **Geere**
Gere, *sb.* changeableness. Bl. 1256
Gereful, Gerful, *adj.* changeable. A 1538, T⁴
 286
Gesse, *pres. s.* guess. A 82
Geste, *sb.* guest, stranger. L 1158
Geste, *sb.* romance, story. B 2123, T³ 450
Gestiours, *sb. pl.* reciters. HF³ 108
Get, *sb.* contrivance. G 1277
Gye, *v.* guide. A 1950, E 75, An. 6
Gif, *conj.* if. Bl. 224
Gigges, *sb. pl.* fiddles. HF³ 852
Giggynge, *p. pres.* strapping. A 2504
Giltelees, *adj.* guiltless. B 1062
Gyn, Gynne, *sb.* engine, contrivance. F 128, R
 4176
Gynne, *v.* begin
Gypon, *sb.* short vest. A 75
Gipser, *sb.* pouch. A 357
Girden, *v.* strike. B 3736
Girles, *sb. pl.* youths. A 664
Gysarme, *sb.* halberd. R 5978
Gise, *sb.* fashion. A 663
Gyser, *sb.* gizzard. Bo. 1132
Gyte, *sb.* some part of a woman's dress, A 3954 ;
 pl. D 559
Gladere, *sb.* one who makes glad. A 2223
Glareth, *pres. s.* shines. HF¹ 272
Glase, *v.* glaze. T⁵ 469. *See* **Howve**

Gledy, *adj.* fiery. L 105
Gleyre, *sb.* white of egg. G 806
Glente, *pret.* glanced. T⁴ 1223
Glewe, *v.* glue, fasten. HF³ 671
Glymsyng, *sb.* glimmering. E 2383
Glood, *pret.* glided. F 393
Glose, *sb.* gloss, comment. L 328, Bl. 333
Glose, *v.* flatter, B 3330 ; expound, B 1180
Glowmbe, *v.* frown. R 4356
Gnodde, *pret.* rubbed, crushed. *Former Age* 11
Gnof, *sb.* churl. A 3188
Gobet, *sb.* shred. A 696
Godsibbes, *sb. pl.* godparents. I 908
Goldlees, *adj.* without gold. B 1480 .
Golee, *sb.* mouthful. PF 556
Goliardeys, *sb.* ribald. A 560
Gonfanoun, Gounfanoun, *sb.* pennon, banner. R 2018, 1201
Gonge, *sb.* privy. I 885
Gonne, *pret.* began, A 1658 ; Gonnen, *pl.* L 148
Good, *sb.* goods, property. A 581
Gooldes, *sb. pl.* marigolds. A 1929
Goore, *sb.* gusset, A 3237 ; Under my goore, at my side, B 1979
Goosissh, *adj.* foolish. T³ 584
Goost, Gost, *sb.* spirit. A 2768, T⁴ 187
Goter, *sb.* gutter. Bo. 689, T³ 787, L 2705
Governeresse, *sb. fem.* governess. *Pite* 80
Grayn, *sb.* dye. B 1917
Grame, *sb.* harm, anger. G 1403, An. 276, T³ 1028
Grange, *sb.* farm, granary, A 3668 ; Graunges, *pl.* B 1256, HF² 190
Graspe, *v.* grope. T⁵ 223
Graunt, *sb.* decree. A 1306
Graven, *p.p.* buried. L 785
Gre, Gree, (1) pleasure, favour, E 1151 ; (2) superiority, pre-eminence, A 2733
Grehoundes, *sb. pl.* greyhounds. A 191
Greithen, *v.* prepare, make ready, A 4309 ; *pres. pl.* B 3784
Greythed, *p.p.* prepared. Bo. 161
Grenehede, *sb.* immaturity. B 163
Gres, *sb.* grass, T² 515 ; Gresses, *pl.* grasses, HF³ 263
Grete, *sb.* ; The grete, the sum, Bl. 1241
Grete See, *sb.* the Mediterranean. A 59, R 2748
Greve, *sb.* grove, B 4013 ; *pl.* A 1495
Greven, *p.p.* graven, engraved. R 4799
Griffhon, *sb.* griffin. A 2133
Gryl, *adj.* rough. R 73
Grynt, grindeth. HF³ 708
Grynte, *pret.* gnashed. D 2161
Grys, *adj.* grey. G 559
Grys, *sb.* grey fur. A 194
Grislich, *adj.* grisly. T² 1700
Groff, *adv.* prone, face downwards. R 2561
Groynynge, *sb.* groaning. A 2460
Gromes, *sb. pl.* men. R 200
Grope, *v.* probe, try. A 644, D 1817
Gruochen, *pres. pl.* grumble. A 3058
Gruf, *adv.* prone, face downwards. A 949, B 1865
Gunne, *pret. pl.* began. PF 257

Ha, *v.* have. R 4657
Haaf, *pret.* heaved. A 3470
Habergeon, *sb.* coat of mail. A 76
Habitacle, *sb.* habitation. Bo. 540
Hacches, *sb. pl.* hatches. L 648
Haf, Haaf, *pret.* heaved. A 2428, 3470

Hay, *sb.* hedge, R 2987 ; Hayis, *pl.* T³ 351
Haynselyns, *sb. pl.* smocks. I 422
Haire, *sb.* hair-shirt. G 133, R 438
Haleth, *pres. s.* draws. *ABC* 68
Halfe, *sb.* ; On my halfe, on my part, Bl. 139
Halke, *sb.* corner. L 1780
Hals, *sb.* neck. B 73
Halse, *pres. s.* conjure. B 1835
Halt, *pres. s.* (1) holdeth, performs, B 721, Bl. 620 ; (2) halteth, limps, Bl. 621
Halten, *v.* limp. T⁴ 1457
Halvendel, *adv.* half. T³ 707
Halwed, *p.p.* accounted holy. T² 268
Halwes, *sb. pl.* saints, shrines. Bl. 830, A 14. D 657
Halydayes, *sb. pl.* holidays, festivals. L 422
Hameled, *p.p.* mutilated, cut off. T² 964
Hande-brede, *sb.* hand-breadth. A 3811
Hard, *adj.* ; Of hard, with difficulty, T² 1236
Hardement, *sb.* hardihood. R 3392
Hardily, *adv.* surely. A 156
Harlot, *sb.* rascal. A 647, D 1754
Harneys, *sb.* armour. A 1006
Harneised, *p.p.* equipped. A 114
Harre, *sb.* hinge. A 550
Harwed, *p.p.* harrowed, devastated. A 3512, D 2107
Hasardrye, *sb.* gambling. C 590
Hasel - wodes, *sb. pl.* hazel-woods (haselwodes shaken), ‘Queen Anne is dead.’ T³ 890, T³ 1174
Hatte, *v.* be called. R 38, T³ 798
Hatter, *adv.* more hotly. R 2475
Haubergeon, *sb.* hauberk. A 2119
Haunt, *sb.* practice. A 447
Haunten, *pres. pl.* practise. I 780
Hauteyn, *adj.* haughty. C 330
Havoire, *v.* to have. R 4720
Hawe, *sb.* hedge. C 855
Hawebake, *sb.* baked haws, *i.e.* poor stuff. B 95
Hawteyn, *adj.* haughty, high-flying. R 3739, L 1120
Hed, *p.p.* hidden. L 208
Hede, *v.* put a head on. T² 1042
Heele, *sb.* health. B 1540
Heeng, *pret.* hung. A 676
Heer, *sb.* hair. A 589
Heerde, *sb.* herdsman. R 6453
Heer-mele, *sb.* hair's-breadth. As. ii. § 38
Heete, *pres. subj.* promise. A 2398
Heete, *pret.* was named. Bl. 200
Hey, *sb.* hedge. H 14
Heye, *v.* rise. Bo. 875
Heyly, *adv.* highly, urgently. T² 1733
Heyne, *sb.* villain. G 1319
Heyre, *sb.* heir. Bl. 168
Heyres, *sb. pl.* hair-shirts. I 105
Heysugge, *sb.* hedge-sparrow. PF 612
Heythen, *adv.* hence. A 4033
Hele, *sb.* *See* Heele
Hele, *v.* hide, conceal. B 2275, D 950
Heled, *p.p.* hidden. B 4245
Heleles, *adj.* without health. T⁵ 1593
Helply, *adj.* helpful. T⁵ 128
Hende, *adj.* prompt, polite, gracious. D 1258, 628, A 3199
Heng, *pret.* hung. Bl. 122
Henne, *adv.* hence. A 2356
Hennesfurth, *adv.* henceforth. T³ 167

Hente, *pret.* seized. B 4525
Henteres, *sb. pl.* seizers. Bo. 91
Hepe, *sb.* hip. B 1937
Heraudes, *sb. pl.* heralds. A 2672
Herbejours, *sb. pl.* receivers of guests. R 5000
Herber, *sb.* arbour. L 203
Herbergage, *sb.* lodging. A 4329, B 147
Herbergeours, *sb. pl.* harbingers. B 997
Her-biforn, *adv.* herebefore. L 73
Herd, *p.p.* haired. A 2518
Herde, *sb.* herdsman. T³ 1235
Herde-gromes, *sb. pl.* herdsmen. HF³ 136
Herdesse, *sb. fem.* herdswoman. T¹ 653
Herdis, *sb.* refuse of flax. R 1233
Here and houne, one and all (?). T⁴ 210
Herieth, *pres. s.* praises, B 1808; Heryest, praisest, B 3419; Heryed, *p.p.* praised, B 872; Heriynge, *p. pres.* praising, B 1649
Herys, *sb. pl.* hairs. A 555
Herne, *sb.* corner. F 1121
Heroner, *sb.* heron-killer. T⁴ 413, L 1120
Heronsewes, *sb. pl.* young herons. F 68
Hert, *sb.* hart. A 1689
Herte, *pret.* hurt. Bl. 882
Herte, *sb.* heart. A 954
Hertely, *adj.* heartfelt. Bl. 85
Herte-spon, *sb.* breast-bone. A 2606
Hete, *pret.* was called. Bl. 947
Heterly, *adv.* fiercely. L 638
Hethyng, *sb.* mockery. A 4110
Heve, *v.* heave. A 550
Hevedes, *sb. pl.* heads. B 2032
Hevenysh, *adj.* heavenly. *Mars* 30
Hevenyshly, *adv.* celestially. A 1055
Hewe, *sb.* colour. An. 147
Hewe, *sb.* domestic servant. E 1785
Hye, *v.* hasten, F 291; Hy, *imperat.* Bl. 152
Hyene, *sb.* hyena. *Fortune* 35
Hierde, *sb.* herdsman, A 603; Hierdes, *pl.* T³ 619
Hight, *p.p.* promised. A 2472
Highte, *sb.*; On highte, aloud. A 1784
Highteth, *pres. s.* adorns. Bo. 45
Hyne, *sb.* servant. A 603, C 688
Hir, (1) her, *pers. pron.* B 624; (2) her, *poss. pron.* B 625; (3) their, *poss. pron.* A 365; (4) of them, *gen. pers. pron.* A 586
Hit, *pron.* it. Bl. 18
Hit, hideth. F 512
Hoker, *sb.* mockery. A 3965
Hokerly, *adv.* scornfully. I 584
Holour, *sb.* lecher. D 524
Holsom, *adj.* wholesome. PF 206
Honerous, *adj.* onerous, burdensome. R 5633
Honestee, *sb.* purity. G 89
Hoodles, *adj.* without hood. Bl. 1027
Hool, *adj.* whole. G 111, Bl. 552
Hoold, *sb.* a stronghold. B 507
Hooly, *adv.* wholly. A 599, Bl. 15
Hoors, *adj.* hoarse. T⁴ 1147
Hoot, *adj.* hot. A 420
Hoppesteres, *sb. pl.* dancers. A 2017
Hord, *sb.* hoard, plenty. *Truth* 3
Hors, Hoors, *adj.* hoarse. Bl. 347, T⁴ 1147
Horwe, *adj.* filthy. *Mars* 206
Hostiler, *sb.* innkeeper. A 241
Hote, *v.* promise, R 3385; Hoten, be called, D 144
Hottes, *sb. pl.* baskets. HF³ 850
Houndfyssch, *sb.* shark. E 1825

Houres, *sb. pl.* (astrological) hours. A 416
Housel, *sb.* the Eucharist. R 6386
Housled, *p.p.* having received the Eucharist. I 1027
Hoved, *pret.* waited, T⁶ 33; Hoveth, *pres. Balade that C. made* 15 (*emend.*)
How, *adv.* however. R 6489
Howve, *sb.* cap, 'sette his howve,' A 3911; 'make him an howve above a calle,' T³ 775; 'glase his howve,' T⁶ 469, all phrases for 'to befool.' *See also* Cappe
Hulstred, *p.p.* concealed. R 6146
Humblesse, *sb.* humility. B 1660
Hunte, *sb.* hunter, A 1678; Huntes, *pl.* Bl. 540
Hurtlen, *v.* attack. Bo. 266
Hust, *p.p.* hushed. A 2981, T³ 1094
Hwed, *p.p.* hued, coloured. R 3014

I-, y-, *prefix of past participles*
Ich, *pron.* I. T³ 282
Iche, *adj.* each. Bo. 1812
I-fyochid, *p.p.* fixed. Bo. 1473
Ik, *pron.* I. A 3867
Il-hayl, ill-luck to you. A 4089
Ilke, *adj.* same
Imperie, *sb.* imperium, official dignity. Bo. 487
Impetren, *pres. pl.* obtain. Bo. 1725
Importable, Inportable, *adj.* unbearable. B 3792, E 1144
In, *sb.* inn. B 1632
Infaunce, *sb.* infancy. R 5006
Infect, *p.p.* invalidated. A 320
Infortunat, *adj.* unfortunate. B 302
In-hielde, *pres. pl.* infuse. T³ 44
Injure, *sb.* injury. T³ 1018
In-knette, *pret.* confined. T³ 1088
Inned, *p.p.* housed. A 2192
In-set, *p.p.* implanted. Bo. 330
In-thringe, *v.* press in. T⁴ 66
Intresse, *sb.* interest. *Truth* 71
In-with, *prep.* within
Irous, *adj.* passionate. D 2086
I-shad, *p.p.* shed. Bo. 481
Isse, *v.* issue. R 1992
I-thrungen, *p.p.* pressed. Bo. 538

Jagounces, *sb. pl.* jacinths. R 1117
Jakke of Dover. *See note*, A 4347
Jambeux, *sb. pl.* leggings. B 2065
Jane, *sb.* small Genoese coin. B 1925, E 999
Jangiere, *sb.* prater. A 560
Janglynge, *sb.* chattering, talking idly. I 649
Jape, *sb.* trick, jest. B 1639
Japeres, *sb. pl.* jesters. I 651
Jape-worthi, *adj.* burlesque. Bo. 1707
Jaunyce, *sb.* jaundice. R 305
Jet, *sb.* fashion. A 682
Jeupardyes, *sb. pl.* problems. Bl. 665
Jewerye, *sb.* Jews' quarter. B 1679
Jo, *v.* come about. T³ 33
Jogelours, *sb. pl.* jugglers. HF³ 169
Joynant, *adj.* adjoining. A 1060
Joyne, *v.* enjoin. R 2355
Jolitee, *sb.* jolliness. A 680
Jompre, *imp. s.* jumble. T² 1037
Jouken, *v.* repose. T⁶ 409 (*note*)
Journe, *sb.* day's work. R 579
Jowes, *sb. pl.* jaws. HF³ 696
Jubbe, *sb.* jug. A 3628
Juge, *sb.* judge. A 1712

Jupartie, *sb.* jeopardy. F 1495, R 2666
Jurdones, *sb. pl.* chamber-pots. C 305
Justice, *sb.* punishment. R 2077
Juwise, Juyse, *sb.* judgment. A 1739, B 795

Kaynard, *sb.* coward. D 235
Kalenderes, *sb. pl.* calendars in illuminated prayer-books. *ABC* 70
Kalendes, *sb. pl.* calends, the first or beginning. T⁵ 1634
Kamelyne, *sb.* camel's hair. R 7365
Kamuse, *adj.* flat-nosed. A 3974
Kan, *v.* know, be able. A 371
Karole, *sb.* singing dance. R 744
Keoche, *v.* catch. T² 1375
Kechyl, *sb.* cake. D 1747
Keen, *sb.* kine. B 4021
Keepe, *sb.* heed. A 503
Kempe, *adj.* shaggy. A 2134
Kenned, *p.p.* known. Bl. 786
Kepe, *v.* care, reck. A 2238, 1593
Kepte, *pret.* observed. A 415
Kernels, *sb. pl.* R 4197
Kers, *sb.* curse. A 3756
Kesse, *v.* kiss. E 1057
Kevere, *v.* recover. T1 917
Kevered, *p.p.* covered. PF 271, HF¹ 275
Kid, *p.p.* known. L 1028, E 1943
Kidde, *pret.* showed. T1 208
Kiked, *pret.* peeped. A 3445
Kymelyn, *sb.* brewing-tub. A 3518
Kynde, *sb.* nature. A 2451
Kirked, *p.p.* See note, R 3167
Kithe, *v.* show, B 636 ; Kytheth, *pres.* L 504
Kitte, *pret.* cut. B 600
Knarre, *sb.* knot. A 549
Knarry, *adj.* gnarled. A 1977
Knave, *sb.* boy, servant. A 3431
Knopped, *p.p.* knobbed. R 7258
Knoppes, *sb. pl.* buds. R 1675
Knotteles, *adj.* like an unknotted string. T⁵ 769
Knowe, *sb.* knee, T² 1202 ; Knowes, *pl.* B 1719
Konnyng, *sb.* ability. B 1099
Koude, *pret.* knew. A 110
Kowthe, *p.p.* renowned. A 14

Laas, *sb.* cord, snare. A 392, 1817
Labbe, *sb.* tell-tale, blabber. A 3509, T³ 300
Label, *sb.* a kind of ruler. As. i. § 22
Laoche, *sb.* snare. R 1624
Laos, *sb.* net. R 2792
Lacerte, *sb.* muscle. A 2753
Lache, *adj.* lazy. Bo. 1309
Lachesse, *sb.* negligence. I 720
Lad, *p.p.* led. A 2620
Ladde, *pret.* took. B 1524
Lafte, *pret.* left, ceased. A 492
Laghyng, *p. prs.* laughing. Bl. 632
Lay, *sb.* creed. F 18
Layneres, *sb. pl.* straps. A 2504
Lake, *sb.* linen cloth. B 2048
Lakken, *v.* depreciate. T1 189
Lambish, *adj.* lamblike. *Former Age* 50
Lambren, *sb. pl.* lambs. R 7013
Lampe, *sb.* a thin plate. G 764
Lapidaire, *sb.* treatise on precious stones. HF³ 262
Lappe, *sb.* lap, border. G 12

Large, *adj.* liberal, extravagant. B 3489, 1621
Las, *adv. comp.* less. Bl. 674
Las, Laas, *sb.* snare. A 1951, 1817
Last, *pres.* lasteth, reaches. E 266
Last, *sb.* load. B 1628
Late, *adv.* lately. A 690
Laten, *v.* let. L 3007
Laterede, *adj.* slow. I 718
Lathe, *sb.* stable, barn. A 4088, HF² 1050
Latis, *sb.* lattice. T² 615
Latoun, *sb.* brass. A 699, B 2067
Laudes, *sb. pl.* (1) the service said between midnight and 6 A.M. ; (2) praises. HF² 232
Launcegay, *sb.* kind of lance. B 1942
Launde, *sb.* clearing in the wood. A 1691, PF 302
Laurer, *sb.* laurel. A 1027
Laus, *adj.* loose, A 4064 ; Lause, *pl.* Bo. 417
Laven, *v.* exhaust. Bo. 1446
Lavendere, *sb.* washerwoman. L 358
Lavyd, *p.p.* poured out, drawn. Bo. 1127
Lawe, *adj.* low. R 5046
Lazar, *sb.* leper. A 242
Leche, *sb.* physician. R 2944
Leden, *sb.* language. F 435
Leed, *sb.* leaden vessel. A 202
Leef, *adj.* dear. Bl. 8
Leef, *sb.* leaf. E 1211
Leefful, *adj.* lawful. I 41
Leefsel, *sb.* bower. I 411
Leepe, *pret.* leapt. A 2687
Leere, Lere, *v.* learn, teach. B 181, 630
Leere, *sb.* skin. B 2047
Lees, *sb.* net, leash. G 19, I 387
Lees, *pret.* lost. L 945
Lees, *adj.* false. R 8
Leet, *pret.* (1) let, A 175 ; (2) caused, B 1810 ; (3) left, A 508
Leeve, *pres. s.* believe. G 213
Leeve, *adj.* dear. G 257
Lef, *imper.* leave. T⁴ 896
Lefte, *pret.* delayed. R 4093
Legge, *v.* (1) lay, A 3937 ; (2) relieve, R 5016
Leye, *v.* wager, assert. T² 1658
Leygheth, *pres.* laughs. Bo. 294
Leigh, *pret.* lied. T² 1077
Leyser, *sb.* leisure. Bl. 172
Leyt, *sb.* flame, lightning. I 839, Bo. 94
Leke, *sb.* leek. R 4830
Lemaille, *sb.* filing, thin plate. G 1162
Lemes, *sb. pl.* (1) gleams, flashes, B 4120, R 5346 ; (2) limbs, A 3886
Lemman, *sb.* sweetheart. A 3278
Lendes, *sb. pl.* loins. A 3237
Lene, *v.* lend. A 611
Lenger, *adv. ccmp.* longer
Leoun, *sb.* lion. B 3106
Lepande, *p. pres.* leaping. R 1928
Lere, Leere, *v.* teach, learn. B 630, 181
Les, *sb.* lie. L 1022
Lese, *v.* lose ; Leseth, B 19
Lesyng, *sb.* lie. G 479
Lest, *sb.* pleasure. A 132, Bl. 907
Leste, *pret.* it pleased. A 750
Lette, *sb.* hindrance, delay. T² 235
Letten, *v.* (1) hinder, A 889, B 2116 ; (2) for—. A 1317, B 4274
Lette-game, *sb.* spoil-sport. T³ 527
Letterure, Lettrure, *sb.* literature. G 846, B 3486

Letuarie, *sb.* electuary, remedy, C 307, T⁶ 741;
  Letuaries, *pl.* A 426
Leve, *sb.* permission. T³ 622
Leveful, *adj.* lawful. A 3912
Leven, *v.* believe. B 1181
Levere, *adj. comp.* pleasanter to. A 293
Levesel, *sb.* leafy bower. A 4061
Lewed, *adj.* ignorant. A 502
Lewednesse, *sb.* stupidity. A 502
Lyard, *adj.* grey. D 1563
Lybardes, *sb. pl.* leopards. R 874
Libel, *sb.* bill of complaint. D 1595
Lyche-wake, *sb.* corpse-watch. A 2958
Lief, *sb.* darling. B 3084
Liflode, *sb.* livelihood. I 685, R 5602
Lifly, *adv.* lively, life-like. A 2087
Liggen, *pres. pl.* lie. A 2205
Lyghter, *adv.* more lightly. L 410
Ligne-aloes, *sb.* aloes-wood. T⁴ 1137
Liken, *v.* please. T¹ 431
Likerous, *adj.* lustful. C 540
Liltyng, *p. pres.* playing a lilt. HF³ 133
Lymaille, *sb.* filings. G 853
Lymeres, *sb. pl.* hounds in leash. Bl. 362
Lymerod, *sb.* lime-twig. B 3754
Lymytour, *sb.* licensed beggar. A 209
Lynde, *sb.* lime-tree. A 2922, E 1211
Lipsed, *pret.* lisped. A 264
Lisse, *sb.* relief, comfort. Bl. 1039, F 1238
Lisse, *v.* relieve, Bl. 210; Lissed, *p.p.* F 1170
Lyst, *sb.* edge. D 634
Listow, liest thou. H 276
Lytarge, *sb.* white lead. A 629, G 775
Litargye, *sb.* lethargy. Bo. 57, T¹ 730
Lyte, *adj.* little, B 2153; A lite, a little, B 713
Litestere, *sb.* dyer. *Former Age* 17
Lith, *pres.* lies. A 1795
Lith, *sb.* limb. B 4065, Bl. 952
Lythe, *adj.* smooth, easy. HF¹ 118, R 3762
Lithe, *v.* soften. T⁴ 740
Litherly, *adv.* badly. A 3299
Lyves, *adj.* living. A 2395
Lixt, liest. D 1618
Lodemenage, *sb.* pilotage. A 403
Lodesmen, *sb. pl.* pilots. L 1488
Loigne, *sb.* tether. R 3882
Longes, *sb. pl.* lungs. A 2752
Longeth, *pres.* belongs to. G 716
Loodesterre, *sb.* loadstar. A 2059
Loone, *sb.* loan. D 1861
Loos, *sb.* report, fame, praise. HF³ 530, B 3035
Looth, *adj.* hateful to. A 486
Loppe, *sb.* spider. As. i. § 19
Lopwebbe, *sb.* spider's web. As. i. § 21
Lore, *p.p.* lost. Bl. 1134
Lorel, *sb.* rascal. D 273, Bo. 178
Los, *sb.* praise, fame. L 1424, 1514
Losengeour, *sb.* flatterer. B 4516, L 352
Losengerie, *sb.* flattery, false praise. I 613
Losenges, *sb. pl.* lozenges. HF³ 227
Loteby, *sb.* paramour. R 6339
Lotynge, *p. pres.* lurking. G 186
Lough, *adj.* low. A 817
Lovedayes, *sb. pl.* days for settling disputes. A 258
Love-drury, *sb.* courtship. B 2085
Lous, *adj.* at large. HF³ 196
Loute, *v.* bow, T³ 683; Loutede, *pret.* R 1554
Lowke, *sb.* fellow-rascal. A 4415

Lowteth, *pres. s.* bows. B 2375
Lufsom, *adj.* lovable. T³ 465
Lunarie, *sb.* moonwort. G 800
Lust, *sb.* pleasure. A 192, T¹ 326

M', before a verb beginning with a vowel, *pers. pron.* me.
Maad, *p.p.* made. A 394
Maat, *adj.* dejected, discomfited. A 955, B 933
Madde, *v.* go mad. *Mars* 253
May, *sb.* maiden. B 851
Maydenhede, *sb.* virginity. B 30
Mayme, *sb.* maiming. I 625
Maysondewe, *sb.* hospital. R 5619
Maystow, mayst thou. A 1918
Maistre, *sb.* master; *adj.* chief. L 1016
Maystre-, chief; Maystre-strete, Maister-toun. L 1965, 1591
Maistrye, *sb.* mastery. L 400
Make, *sb.* husband, mate, match. D 85, B 1982, A 2556
Maked, *pret.* made. A 1907
Makeles, *adj.* matchless. T¹ 172
Makynge, *sb.* poetry. L 74
Malapert, *adj.* impudent. T³ 87
Male, *sb.* wallet. C 920
Malefice, *sb.* evil-doing. Bo. 169
Malgre, *prep.* in spite of. *Mars* 220
Malt, *pret.* melted. HF³ 414
Mal-talent, *sb.* ill-will. R 330
Manace, *sb.* menace. A 2003
Manasynge, *p. pres.* menacing. Bo. 416
Maner, *sb.* manor. Bl. 1003
Maner, Manere, *sb.* manner. *Pite* 24, L 251
Manye, *sb.* mania. A 1374
Mansuete, *adj.* gentle. T³ 194
Mappemounde, *sb. mappa mundi,* map of the world. *Rosemounde* 2
Marc, *sb.* thirteen shillings and fourpence. G 1026
Marcial, *adj.* martial. T⁴ 1669
Mare, *adv. comp.* more. R 2709
Mareys, *sb.* marsh. D 970, Bo. 536
Mary, *sb.* marrow. C 542, Bo. 1008
Marybones, *sb. pl.* marrow-bones. A 380
Market-beters, *sb.* bully at fairs. A 3936
Markys, *sb.* marquis. E 786
Markysesse, *sb.* marchioness. E 283
Martire, *sb.* torment. T⁴ 818
Mased, *p.p.* dazed. Bl. 12
Mast, *sb.* acorns. *Former Age* 6
Masty, *adj.* acorn-eating. HF³ 687
Mate, *adj.* depressed, discomfited. L 126, R 3167
Matere, *sb.* matter, subject. Bl. 43
Maugree, *prep.* despite. A 1169
Maugree, *sb.* ill-will, R 3144; Can maugree, owe a grudge, R 4399, 4559
Maumettrie, *sb.* Mohammedism, idolatry. B 236
Maunciple, *sb.* purveyor. A 510
Mawmet, *sb.* idol. I 749
Mazelyn, *sb.* maple-bowl. B 2042
Mede, Meede, (1) reward, bribe, A 3380; (2) mead, a drink, B 2042; (3) meadow, A 89
Medlee, *adj.* of mixed stuff. A 328
Medleth, *pres.* mingles, mixes. L 874, Bo. 1313
Medlynge, *sb.* mixture. Bo. 1356
Meede, *sb. See* Mede
Meene, *pres.* bemoan. R 2596
Meeth, *sb.* mead, a drink. A 2279

Msignes, *sb.* household. I 894
Meygned, *p.p.* maimed. R 3356
Meynee, *sb.* retinue, household. A 1258
Meynt, *p.p.* mingled. R 1920
Meyntenaunce, *sb.* demeanour. BL 833
Mekede, *pret.* meekened. R 3584
Mel-tid, *sb.* meal-time. T² 1556
Melle, *sb.* mill. A 3923
Memoire, Memorie, *sb.* memory, commemoration. BL 944, A 1906
Mencioun, *sb.* mention. B 54
Mendience, *sb.* mendicancy. R 6657
Mendynantz, *sb. pl.* begging friars. D 1906
Mene, *pres.* mean, intend. A 2063, 2216
Mene, *adj.* middle, of middle size. T⁵ 806
Meneliche, *adj.* moderate. Bo. 251
Mentes, *sb. pl.* mint. R 731
Merciable, *adj.* merciful. L 348
Mere, *sb.* mare. A 541
Merke, *adj.* dark. R 5339
Merlion, *sb.* merlin-hawk. PF 339
Marvaille, *sb.* marvel. E 1186
Mes, Messe, *sb.; At good mes,* at advantage, R 3462, 1453
Meschief, *sb.* mischief; *At meschief,* in danger, A 2551
Mesel, *sb.* leper. I 624
Message, *sb.* messenger. B 144
Messagere, *sb.* messenger. BL 133
Messe, *sb.* mass. B 1413
Meste, *adj. pl.* most; *The meste,* the most important, T⁵ 440
Mester, *sb.* occupation. A 1340
Mesurable, *adj.* moderate. F 362
Mesure, *sb.* moderation. E 622
Met, *pres.* dreams. PF 104
Met, *sb.* measure. I 799
Mete, *pres. sub.* dream. BL 1233
Mette, *pret.* dreamt. B 4084, L 210
Meve, *v.* move
Meveresse, *sb. fem.* agitator. R 149
Mewe, *sb.* cage, coop. F 643, T³ 602
Myoohes, *sb. pl.* small loaves. R 5585
Mych, *adj.* much. R 2704
Mycher, *sb.* thief. R 6541
Mihti, *adj.* mighty. ABC 6
Mile-wey, Milewey, *sb.* 5 degrees of angular measurement, the third part of an hour. As. i. § 16
Milne-stones, *sb. pl.* mill-stones. T² 1384
Mynour, *sb.* miner. A 2465
Myntynge, *p. pres.* meaning. Bo. 38
Mirre, *sb.* myrrh. A 2938
Mys, *sb. pl.* mice. Bo. 492
Misaccounted, *p.p.* misreckoned. T⁵ 1185
Misbileved, *p.p.* as *sb.* unbelievers. ABC 146
Mysboden, *p.p.* abused, harmed. A 909
Mysdeparteth, *pres. s.* divides unfairly. B 107
Misericorde, *sb.* mercy. ABC 35
Mysese, *sb.* discomfort. I 177
Mis-foryaf, *pret.* sorely misgave. T⁴ 1426
Myslay, *pret.* lay awry. A 3647
Mislived, *p.p.* ill-behaved. T⁴ 330
Mismetre, *pres. sub.* scan wrongly. T⁵ 1796
Missatte, *pret.* suited ill. R 1194
Mysseyest, *pres. s.* speakest ill of. L 323
Myster, *sb.* (1) craft, A 613 ; (2) need, R 1426, 6078 ; *What mysters men,* what manner of men, A 1710
Mystihede, *sb.* mystery. *Mars* 224

Mystorned, *p.p.* turned aside. Bo. 1236
Miswey, *adv.* astray. R 4766
Mysweyes, *sb. pl.* by-paths, wrong roads. Bo. 1623
Miswent, *pret.* erred. T¹ 633
Myxnes, *sb. pl.* middens, dungheaps. R 6496
Mo, Moo, *adj.* more, others. A 1715, E 1039
Moche, Mochel. *See* Muche, Muchel
Moder, *sb.* mother, ABC 49 ; the large plate in an astrolabe, As. i. § 2
Moeble, *adj.* moveable. As. i. § 21
Moeble, *sb.* furniture, T⁴ 1380 ; **Moebles,** *sb. pl.* moveables, chattels, E 1314
Moysoun, *sb.* crop. R 1677
Mokeren, *pres. pl.* heap up. Bo. 425
Mokererea, *sb. pl.* heapers up, hoarders. Bo. 425
Mokre, *v.* heap up. T³ 1375
Molte, *pret.* melted. T⁵ 10
Mone, *sb.* moon
Moneste, *pres. s.* admonish. R 3579
Montaunce, *sb.* value, amount. A 1570, C 863
Monyours, *sb. pl.* money-changers. R 6811
Mood, *sb.* anger. R 5162
Moote, *pres.* must, may. A 735
Mordre, *sb.* murder. B 4211
More, *sb.* root. T⁵ 25
Mormal, *sb.* gangrene. A 386
Morter, *sb.* night-light. T⁴ 1245
Mortifye, *v.* transmute. G 1126
Mortrer, *sb.* murderer. PF 353
Mortreux, *sb.* a kind of stew. A 384
Morwe, *sb.* morrow, morning. A 334
Morwenynge, *sb.* morning. A 1062
Mosel, *sb.* muzzle. A 2151
Moste, *pres.* must
Mote, *pres.* must, may
Mote, *sb.* speck. T³ 1603
Motteleye, *sb.* motley. A 271
Mountaunce, *sb.* amount. R 1562
Mourdaunt, *sb.* pendant of a girdle. R 1094
Moustre, *sb.* show-piece. BL 911
Mowes, *sb. pl.* grimaces. R 5590, HF³ 716
Mowynge, *sb.* ability. Bo. 1372
Mowled, *p.p.* grown mouldy. A 3870
Mowlen, *v.* moulder. B 32
Muable, *adj.* fleeting. T³ 822, Bo. 1455
Muche and lite, great and small. A 494
Muchel, *adj.* much. A 132
Mullok, *sb.* refuse. A 3873
Murierly, *adv. comp.* more merrily. A 714
Musarde, *sb.* dreamer. R 3256, 4034, 7560
Muttre, *v.* mutter. T² 541
Muwe, *sb.* mew, cage. A 349, T³ 1784
Muwe, *v.* change. T³ 1258
Muwet, *adj.* mute. T⁵ 194

N', before a vowel, = Ne, not
Na, *adj.* no. A 4026
Nadde, Ne hadde, had not. L 278
Naddre, *sb.* adder. E 1786
Nadir, *sb.* the point of the heavens diametrically opposite to the zenith. As. ii. § 5
Nadstow, hadst thou not. A 4088
Na fors, no matter. A 4176
Nayles, *sb. pl.* nails. A 2141
Nayte, *v.* say no to, deny. I 1013
Nake, *pres. pl.* bare. Bo. 1616
Nakers, *sb. pl.* drums. A 2511
Nale, Atte nale, at the ale-house. D 1349

Nam, Ne am, am not. A 1122
Nam, *pret.* took. G 1297
Namely, *adv.* especially. B 1233
Na mo, no more. A 1589
Nart, Ne art, art not. *ABC* 26, G 497
Narwe, *adj.* narrow, close. E 1988
Nas, Ne was, was not. A 1649, 2105
Nat, *adv.* not. A 1145, 4087
Nath, Ne hath, hath not
Natheles, *adv.* nevertheless. E 377
Natureel, Naturel, *adj.* natural, by birth A 415, L 375
Ne, *adv.* not, nor. A 923, 1649
Neddres, *sb. pl.* adders. L 699
Nede, *sb.* need. B 4643
Nedeles, *adv.* needlessly. E 621
Nedely, *adv.* of necessity. B 4435
Nedescost, *adv.* of necessity. A 1477
Neen, *adj.* none, no. A 4185
Neet, *sb.* cattle. A 597
Negardye, *sb.* niggardy. *Truth* 53
Neghen, *v.* draw near. L 318
Neigh, *adv.* nigh, near. Bl. 104
Nel, Ne wil, will not. R 4344
Nempnen, name, B 507; Nempned, *pret.* E 609
Ner, *adj.* nearer. Bl. 887
Nere, Ne were, were not. B 547
Nevene, *v.* name. G 821
Neveradeel, not a whit. C 670
Newe, *adv.* newly. A 4239
Newed, *pret.* renewed itself. Bl. 905
Nexte, *adj. sup.* nearest. B 807
Nyce, *adj.* foolish. B 1088
Nyfles, *sb. pl.* trifles. D 1760
Nyghtertale, *sb.* night-time. A 97
Nigromanciens, *sb. pl.* magicians. I 603
Nil, Ne will, will not. T¹ 1020
Nillynge, *sb.* refusing. Bo. 1656
Nyn, Ne in, nor in. E 2088
Nys, Ne is, is not. A 1677
Nyste, Ne wiste, knew not. B 384
Noble, *sb.* coin worth 6s. 8d. A 3256
Nobleye, *sb.* nobility. E 828
No fors, no matter. B 285
Noye, *v.* harm. R 3772
Noious, *adj.* harmful. R 3231
Nolde, Ne wolde, would not. A 1024
Nome, *p.p.* taken. L 822
Non, *adj.* none
Nones, For the nones, for the occasion. A 545
Nonne, *sb.* nun. A 118
Noon, *adj.* none. A 773
Noot, *pres.* Ne woot, know not. A 1340, Bl. 29
Noote, *sb.* note, music. B 1711
Norice, *sb.* nurse. E 561
Nortelrie, *sb.* good manners. A 3967
Nory, *sb.* foster-child. Bo. 850
Nosethirles, *sb. pl.* nostrils. A 557
Noskinnes, *adj.* no kind of. HF³ 704
Nost, Ne wost, knowest not
Note, *sb.* need, business. A 4068
Noteful, *adj.* useful. Bo. 33
Notemygges, *sb. pl.* nutmegs. R 1362
Not-heed, *sb.* close-cropped head. A 109
Nother, Ne other, nor other
Nouncerteyn, *sb.* uncertainty. *Venus* 46
Noun-power, *sb.* impotence. Bo. 726
Nouther, *adj.* neither. Bl. 530
Novelrie, *sb.* novelty. F 619
Nowches, *sb. pl.* jewels. E 382

Nowthe, *adv.* now. A 462

O, *num.* one. A 2725, G 335, R 6398
Obeissaunce, *sb.* obedience. A 2974
Observaunce, *sb.* respect, ceremony. A 1045
Observe, *v.* respect, countenance. B 1821
Octogamye, marrying eight times. D 33
Of, *adv.* off. A 782
Of-caste, *imper.* cast off. PF 132
Offended, *p.p.* hurt. A 909
Offensioun, *sb.* opposition. A 2416
Offici, *sb.* secular employment. A 292
Of-thowed, *p.p.* thawed. HF³ 53
Oynement, *sb.* ointment. A 631
Oynons, *sb. pl.* onions. A 634
Oystre, *sb.* oyster. A 182
Olifauntes, *sb. pl.* elephants. Bo. 782
Olmeris, *sb. pl.* elms. R 1314
O-loft, *adv.* aloft. T¹ 950
Omager, *sb.* one who does homage, vassal. R 3288
On, *prep.* on, in, at
Onde, *sb.* malice. R 148
Ones, *adv.* once. A 1836
Onloft, *adv.* aloft. E 229
Oo, *num.* one
Ook, *sb.* oak. A 1702, 2921
Oon, *num.* one. A 2969
Ooned, *p.p.* united. Bo. 1463
Oones, *adv.* once
Ooning, *sb.* unifying. Bo. 1464
Oonly, *adv.* only. H 143
Oore, *sb.* compassion. A 3726
Oost, *sb.* host, army. L 626, Bo. 88
Openers, *sb. pl.* medlars. A 3871
Open-heveded, *p.p.* bareheaded. D 645
Opie, *sb.* opium. A 1472
O-point, at point, ready. T⁴ 1638
Ordal, *sb.* ordeal. T³ 1046
Orde, *sb. dat.* point. L 645
Ordeyne, *adj.* ordered. T¹ 892
Ordeynly, *adv.* in order. Bo. 1524
Ordred, *p.p.* ordained. I 782
Orfrays, *sb.* gold embroidery. R 1076
Orisonte, *sb.* horizon. T⁵ 276
Orloge, *sb.* sundial, clock. PF 530, B 4044
Orphelyn, *sb.* orphan. Bo. 334
Ost, *sb.* host, army. *Former Age* 40
Ostelements, *sb. pl.* utensils, furniture. Bo. 455
Other, *conj.* either, or
Ouche, *sb.* jewel. D 743
Oules, *sb. pl.* awls. D 1730
Oultrage, *sb.* excess. Bo. 455
Ounces, *sb. pl.* small pieces. A 677
Ounded, *adj.* wavy. T⁴ 743
Outen, *v.* publish, display. E 2438, G 834
Out-hees, *sb.* hue and cry. A 2012
Outher, *conj.* either, or. A 1485, 1593
Outlandissh, *adj.* foreign. *Former Age* 22
Outrage, *sb.* excess. *Former Age* 5
Outreye, *v.* pass beyond control. E 643
Outrely, *adv.* utterly. C 849
Out-taken, *prep.* except. B 277
Over-al, *prep.* above, besides
Over-al, *adv.* everywhere, generally. A 547, 1664
Overeste, *adj. sup.* uppermost. A 270
Overkervith, *pres.* intersects. As. i. § 21
Overlad, *p.p.* overborne. B 3101
Overslope, *sb.* upper garment. G 633

761

Oversprat, *pres.* overspreadeth. T³ 767
Overte, *adj.* open. HF² 210
Overthrowynge, *adj.* hasty, biassed. Bo. 1530
Overthwart, *adv.* across. A 1991, T² 685
Overwhelveth, *pres.* agitates. Bo. 356
Owen, *v.* ought
Owgh, *interj.* alas. Bo. 228
O-wher, *adv.* anywhere. A 653
Owndynge, *sb.* waving. I 417
Owtrayen, Outreye, *v.* act outrageously, pass beyond control. Bo. 758, E 643

Paas, *sb.* pace, especially walking-pace. A 2897, G 575
Pace, *v.* pass. A 175
Paye, *v.* content. R 3599
Payde, *p.p.* pleased
Payen, *adj.* pagan. A 2370
Payens, *sb. pl.* pagans. L 786
Pallet, *sb.* pallet. T² 229
Palasie, *sb.* palsy. R 1098
Paleys, *sb.* palace. A 2199
Palestral, *adj.* athletic. T⁵ 304
Palynge, *sb.* the making a perpendicular stripe. I 417
Palys, *sb. pl.* pales, palisade. Bo. 231
Pan, *sb.* brain-pan, skull. A 1165
Panade, *sb.* knife. A 3929
Pandemayne, *sb.* fine bread. B 1915
Panyers, *sb. pl.* panniers. HF³ 849
Panter, *sb.* snare. L 131
Papeer, *sb.* pepper. G 762
Papejay, *sb.* parrot, popinjay. B 1957, B 1559
Papelard, *sb.* deceiver. R 7281
Papelardie, *sb.* deceit. R 6796
Paper, *sb.* indenture. A 4404
Parage, *sb.* dignity, high-priest. D 250, 1120, R 4759
Paramentz, Parementz, *sb. pl.* rich array. A 2501, F 269
Paramour, *sb.* sweet-heart. D 454
Paramours, *adv.* passionately. T⁵ 158
Paraventure, Paraunter, *adv.* peradventure. B 190, L 362
Parcel, *sb.* part. *Pite* 106
Pardee, *par Dieu*, B 1977
Paregal, *adj.* equal. T⁵ 840
Parements. *See* Paramentz
Parentele, *sb.* relationship. I 908
Parfay, *par foi.* B 110
Parfit, *adj.* perfect. A 72
Parfourned, *p.p.* consummated. B 1646
Parfournest, *pres.* accomplishest. B 1797
Parisshens, *sb. pl.* parishioners. A 482
Paritory, *sb.* pellitory. G 581
Parlement, *sb.* parliament, deliberation. A 1306
Parooh prest, *sb.* parish priest. R 6384
Parodie, *sb.* period. T² 1548
Parsoners, *sb. pl.* partners. R 6952
Parten, *v.* take part, share. L 465
Partie, *sb.* partisan. A 2657
Partyng-felawes, *sb. pl.* partners. I 637
Parvys, *sb.* church-porch. A 310
Pas, *sb.* *See* Paas
Passant, *adj.* surpassing. A 2107
Passen, *v.* surpass. L 162
Patre, Patren, *v.* patter, chatter. R 6794, 7241
Paumes, *sb. pl.* palms. T³ 1114

Pax, *sb.* a painted tablet kissed during the celebration of mass. I 407
Pecunyal, *adj.* pecuniary. D 1314
Pees, *sb.* peace. A 1671
Peyned, *pret.* pained, troubled. A 139
Peytrel, *sb.* breast-piece. G 564
Pel, *sb.* castle. HF³ 220
Pelet, *sb.* shot. HF³ 553
Penant, *sb.* penitent. B 3124
Pencel, Pensel, *sb.* small banner. T² 1043, R 6282
Penyble, *adj.* painstaking. B 3490
Penner, *sb.* pen-case. E 1879
Penoun, *sb.* pennant, banner. A 978
Pens, *sb. pl.* pence. C 402
Peple, *sb.* people. A 995
Peroas, *adv.* perchance. R 6647
Percely, *sb.* parsley. A 4350
Perchemyne, *sb.* parchment. R 6584
Perdurable, *adj.* lasting. I 75
Perdurablete, *sb.* immortality. Bo. 552
Peregryn, *adj.* pilgrim. F 428
Peredonette, *sb.* pear-tree. A 3248
Perfit, *adj.* perfect. A 1271
Perissed, *p.p.* destroyed. I 579
Perree, *sb.* precious stones, jewellery. A 2936, B 3495, D 344
Pers, *adj.* blue. A 439
Persaunt, *adj.* piercing. R 2809
Persone, Persoun, (1) person, A 2725; (2) parson, A 478
Perturben, *pres. pl.* disturb. A 906
Pervynke, *sb.* periwinkle. R 903
Pese, *v.* appease. R 3397
Pesene, *sb. pl.* peas. L 648
Pesible, *adj.* peaceful. Bo. 169
Philosophre, *sb.* philosopher, esp. an alchemist. A 297
Phitonesses, *sb. pl.* diviners, witches. HF³ 171
Pye, *sb.* magpie, chatterer. T³ 527
Piggesnye, *sb.* pig's eye, a term of endearment. A 3268
Pike, *v.* (1) peep, T² 60; (2) pick; Pyketh, *pres.* picks over, smartens, E 2011; (3) Pike on, prick against, T² 1274
Piked, *pret.* stole. L 2467
Pykepurs, *sb.* pick-pocket. A 1998
Pykerel, *sb.* young pike. E 1419
Piloche, *sb.* fur coat. *Proverbs* 4
Piled, *adj.* plucked, scanty, bald. A 67, 3935, 4306
Pilere, *sb.* pillow. Bl. 738
Pilled, *p.p.* plundered. L 1262
Pilours, *sb. pl.* plunderers. A 1007
Pilwe, *sb.* pillow. Bl. 884
Pilwe-beer, *sb.* pillow-case. A 694
Pyment, *sb.* spiced wine. A 3378, Bo. 476, R 6027
Pynchen, *v.* cavil at, A 326; Pynchest, *Fortune* 57
Pyne, *sb.* pain, torture. T³ 676, A 1746
Pyn-trees, *sb. pl.* pine-trees. Bo. 477
Piper, *adj.* used for pipes or horns. PF 178
Pyrie, *sb.* pear-tree. E 2217
Pissemyre, *sb.* ant. D 1825
Pistel, *sb.* epistle, story. D 1021
Pitaunce, *sb.* portion of food. A 224
Place, *sb.* chief house. B 1910
Plages, *sb. pl.* coasts, quarters. B 543, As. i. § 5
Playes, *sb. pl.* devices. Bl. 569

Plat, *adj.* flat. B 3947
Platly, *adv.* flatly. T³ 786
Pleye, *v.* play, jest. A 1127
Pleyn, *adj.* (1) full, A 315; (2) plain, frank, L 328, An. 278
Pleyn, Playn, *adv.* (1) fully, A 327; (2) plainly, B 219
Pleyne, *v.* complain. D 1313
Pleyng, *p. pres.* arguing. PF 495
Pleynlioh, *adv.* plainly. T² 272
Plesaunce, *sb.* pleasure. L 1446
Plete, Pleten, *v.* plead. T² 1468, Bo. 296
Plye, *v.* bend. E 1169, R 4389
Plyght, *p.p.* plucked, D 790; Plighte, *pret.* pulled, B 15
Plit, *sb.* plight. T² 712
Plite, *v.* fold. T³ 1204
Plowngy, *adj.* moist, Bo. 64, 616
Poepliszh, *adj.* vulgar. T⁴ 1677
Poileys, *adj.* Apulian. F 195
Poynaunt, *adj.* pungent. A 352
Poynt, *sb.*; In good poynt, in good condition, A 200; At poynt devys, carefully, A 3689
Poyntel, *sb.* pencil, stylus. D 1742, Bo. 1810
Poke, *sb.* pocket, bag. A 3780
Pokettes, *sb. pl.* bags. G 608
Polyve, *sb.* pulley. F 184
Pome-garnettys, *sb. pl.* pomegranates. R 1356
Pomel, *sb.* crown, top. A 2689
Pomely, *adj.* dappled. A 616
Pool, *sb.* pole. Bo. 1435, As. i. § 14
Popelote, *sb.* puppet. A 3254
Popet, *sb.* poppet, doll. B 1891
Popped, *pret.* bedizened. R 1019
Poppere, *sb.* dagger. A 3931
Poraille, *sb.* poor folk. A 247
Porismes, *sb. pl.* corollaries. Bo. 924
Portatif, *adj.* portable. As. [17]
Portecolys, *sb.* portcullis. R 4168
Porthors, *sb.* breviary. B 1321
Portreitour, *sb.* artist. A 1899
Pose, *sb.* a cold. A 4152
Pose, *pres. s.* put the case, suppose. A 1162, T³ 310
Possessioners, *sb. pl.* members of endowed orders. D 1772
Posseth, *pres. s.* pushes, L 2420; Possed, Posshed, *p.p.* pushed, driven, T¹ 415, R 4625
Postum, *sb.* abscess. Bo. 694
Potente, *sb.* staff. D 1776, T⁶ 1222, R 368
Potestat, *sb.* potentate. D 2007
Poudremarchant, *sb.* flavouring powder. A 381
Pounage, *sb.* food for pigs. *Former Age* 7
Poune, *sb.* pawn in chess. Bl. 660
Pouped, *pret.* blown. H 90
Pourely, *adv.* poorly. A 1412
Pous, *sb.* pulse. T³ 1114
Pouste, *sb.* power. Bo. 1423, R 6484
Pownsonynge, *sb.* puncturing. I 418
Prece, *v.* press. R 4198
Predicacioun, *sb.* preaching. B 1176
Prees, *sb.* press, crowd. B 393, 865
Preest, *sb.* priest. B 4010
Preeve, *v.* stand testing. G 645
Preferre, *pres. subj.* surpass. D 96
Preye, *pres. s.* pray. B 3995
Preyneth, *pres. s.* preens. E 2011
Preyse, *v.* praise. L 67
Prenostik, *adj.* prophetic. *Fortune* 54
Prenten, *v.* imprint. T³ 900

Prea, *sb.* crowd. T² 1718
Prese, Presen, *v.* press, R 2899, *Pite* 19; Presyng, *p. pres.* R 6437
Prest, *adj.* ready. T² 785, T³ 485
Pretende, *v.* intend. T⁴ 922
Preterit, *adj.* past. R 5011
Preve, *sb.* proof. T¹ 470, 690
Preve, *v.* prove. L 9
Prydeles, *adj.* without pride. *Compleynte to his Lady* 25
Prighte, *pret.* pricked. F 418
Prihte, *pret.* pierced. *ABC* 163
Prikasour, *sb.* hard rider. A 189
Priketh, *pres. s.* spurs. A 1043
Prikyng, *sb.* spurring. A 191
Prikke, *sb.* point, centre. Bo. 1030
Prille. *See note*, R 1058
Prime, *sb.* the time between 6 and 9 A.M. B 1278, 4387
Prime, At prime face, *primâ facie*, at first glance
Prymerole, *sb.* primrose. A 3268
Prys, *sb.* value, estimation. A 67, B 2285
Pryvee, *adj.* secret. D 1136
Pryvely, *adv.* secretly. A 1443
Prolacions, *sb. pl.* preludes. Bo. 270
Prolle, *pres. pl.* prowl. G 1412
Propre, *adj.* proper, own. T² 1487
Proprete, *sb.* property. T⁴ 392
Prow, *sb.* profit. B 1598, T² 1664
Pruesse, *sb.* prowess. Bo. 1291
Pulle, *v.* pluck, A 652; Pulled, *p.p.* A 177
Purchace, *v.* obtain. T⁴ 557
Purchas, *sb.* earnings. A 256
Purchasyng, *sb.* prosecuting. A 320
Purchasour, *sb.* prosecutor. A 319
Pure, *adj.* mere, very. A 1279
Pured, *p.p.* refined. F 1560
Purpre, *adj.* purple. L 654
Pursewing, *adj.* following, in accordance with. Bl. 958
Purtreye, *v.* draw. A 96
Purveiable, *adj.* providential. Bo. 655
Purveiaunce, *sb.* providence. A 1252
Purveye, *v.* provide. E 191
Put, *pres.* putteth. L 652
Put, *sb.* pit. I 170
Putours, *sb. pl.* whoremongers. I 886

Quaad, *adj.* evil. A 4357
Quakke, *sb.* hoarseness. A 4152
Qualm, *sb.* disease, A 2014; death-note, T⁵ 382
Quappe, *v.* flutter. T³ 57
Queerne, *sb.* mill. B 3264
Queynte, *pl. adj.* quaint. A 1531
Queynte, *sb.* pudendum muliebre. A 3276
Queynte, *pret.* was quenched. A 2334
Queyntise, *sb.* elegance, I 932; contrivance, I 733
Quelle, *v.* kill. B 4580
Quemen, *v.* please. T⁶ 695; *pres. pl.* T² 803
Querne, *sb.* mill. HF² 708
Querrour, *sb.* quarryman. R 4149
Questemongers, *sb. pl.* holders of inquests. I 797
Quethe, *pres. s.* say, cry. R 6999
Quyke, *adj. pl.* alive. A 1015
Quyked, *pret.* revived. A 2335
Quyknesse, *sb.* liveliness. Bl. 26
Quynyble, *sb.* a part sung a fifth above the air. A 3332

763

Quyrboilly, *sb.* leather boiled and hardened. B 2065

Quisshin, *sb.* cushion. T² 1229

Quystron, *sb.* scullion. R 886

Quite, *v.* pay, redeem, satisfy. A 770, 1032, B 354

Quitly, *adv.* freely. A 1792

Quod, *pret.* said. B 1644

Quoint, *adj.* quaint. R 2038

Quook, *pret.* quaked. A 1576

Raa, *sb.* roe. A 4086

Racyne, *sb.* root. R 4881

Rad, *p.p.* read, A 2595 ; **Radde**, *pret.* PF 21

Radevore, *sb.* tapestry (?). L 2352

Rafte, *pret.* reft. L 1855

Rayed, *p.p.* striped. Bl. 252

Rakel, *adj.* hasty. T³ 429, H 278

Rakelnesse, Rekelnesse, *sb.* hastiness. H 283, *Scogan* 16

Rake-stele, *sb.* rake-handle. D 949

Rakle, *v.* be rash. T³ 1642

Ramage, *adj.* wild. R 5384

Rammyssh, *adj.* ram-like. G 887

Rape, *sb.* haste, *Adam* 7 ; *adv.* hastily, R 6516

Rape and renne, rob and plunder. G 1422

Rather, *adv. comp.* earlier, sooner. Bo. 260, B 2265

Raughte, *pret.* reached. A 136

Ravyne, *sb.* rapine, Bo. 323; **Ravynes**, *pl.* I 793

Ravyners, *sb. pl.* plunderers, Bo. 91; **Ravynour**, Bo. 1304

Ravysable, *adj.* ravenous. R 7006

Real, *adj.* royal. B 4366

Realtee, *sb.* royalty. *Fortune* 60

Reawme, *sb.* realm. B 797

Rebekke, *sb.* abusive term for an old woman. D 1573

Recche, *pres. subj.* expound. B 4086

Reccheles, *adj.* careless. A 179

Rechased, *p.p.* chased back. Bl. 379

Reche, *v.* reach. Bl. 47

Recorde, *pres. s.* confirm. A 1745

Recourses, *sb. pl.* retrogressions. Bo. 41

Recreaundise, *sb.* cowardice. B 4038

Recured, *p.p.* recovered. R 4920

Reddour, *sb.* violence. *Fortune* 13

Rede, *sb.* reed-pipe. HF³ 131

Rede, Reed, *sb.* counsel. Bl. 203

Redeless, *adj.* deviceless. *Pite* 27

Redoutynge, *sb.* glorifying. A 2050

Redowte, *v.* respect. Bo. 73

Reed, *adj.* red. B 1301

Reed, Rede, *sb.* counsel. A 1216

Reenden, *pres. pl.* rend, destroy. Bo. 1092

Rees, *sb.* race ; **in a rees**, hastily. T⁴ 350

Refect, *p.p.* refreshed. Bo. 1550

Refreyden, *v.* cool, T⁵ 507 ; **Refreyded, Refreyd**, *p.p.* frozen, cool, I 341, *Rosemounde* 21

Refut, *sb.* refuge. B 852, *ABC* 14

Regalye, *sb.* majesty. *Pite* 65

Regals, *sb. pl.* royal privileges. L 2128

Regne, *sb.* kingdom. A 1638

Reyes, *sb. pl.* round dances. HF³ 146

Reighte, *pret.* reached. HF³ 284

Reysed, *p.p.* (1) raised, Bl 1277 ; (2) raided, A 54

Rekelnesse, *sb.* hastiness. *Scogan* 16

Reken, Rekne, *v.* reckon, recount. B 110, A 1933

Relees, *sb.* release, *ABC* 3 ; **Out of relees**, ceaselessly, G 46

Relente, *v.* melt. G 1278

Remes, *sb. pl.* realms. B 4326, Bo. 723

Remewed, *p.p.* removed. F 181

Remorde, *pres. subj.* cause remorse, T⁴ 1491 ; **Remordith**, vexes, Bo. 1519

Remounted, *p.p.* caused to rise again. Bo. 603

Remuable, *adj.* changeable. T⁴ 1682

Ren, *sb.* run. A 4079

Renably, *adv.* eloquently. D 1509

Reneyen, *v.* deny, B 3751 ; **Reneyed**, *p.p.* B 340

Renges, *sb. pl.* ranks. A 2594

Renomee, *sb.* renown. D 1159, L 1513

Renovelaunces, *sb. pl.* renewals. HF² 185

Renovellen, *pres. pl.* renew. I 1027

Rent, rendeth. L 646

Rente, *sb.* income. B 4017

Replicacioun, *sb.* reply. A 1846, PF 536

Reprende, *v.* reprehend, blame. T¹ 510

Requerable, *adj.* desirable, Bo. 491

Resalgar, *sb.* rat's-bane. G 814

Rescous, Rescus, *sb.* rescue. T¹ 478, A 2643

Rescowe, *v.* rescue. T³ 857

Rese, *v.* shake. A 1986

Resons, *sb. pl.* opinions. A 274

Resport, *v.* regard. T⁴ 850

Restelees, *adj.* restless. C 728

Rethor, *sb.* rhetorician. B 4397

Rethorien, *sb.* rhetorician. Bo. 341

Retorninge, *part. pres.* turning over. T⁵ 1023

Retracciouns, *sb. pl.* recantations. I 1085

Revelous, *adj.* sportive. B 1194

Revers, *sb.* reverse. B 416

Revesten, *pres. pl.* clothe anew. T³ 353

Revoken, *v.* call back, restore. T² 1118

Reward, *sb.* regard. B 2445

Rewe, *sb.* row. A 2866

Rewel boon, *sb.* smooth bone, ivory (?). B 2068

Rewliche, *adj.* pitiable. Bo. 312

Rewme, *sb.* realm. R 495

Rial, *adj.* royal. *Pite* 59

Ribibe, *sb.* old woman. D 1377

Ribible, Rubible, *sb.* fiddle. A 4396, 3331

Richesse, *sb.* riches. B 107

Ridyng, *sb.* a jousting or procession. A 4377

Ridled, *p.p.* pleated. R 1235

Riet, *sb.* the net or perforated plate revolving within the 'mother' of an Astrolabe. As. i. § 14

Righte, *adj.* direct. B 556

Rightful, *adj.* righteous. *ABC* 31

Rihte, *adj.* right. *ABC* 75

Rympled, *p.p.* wrinkled. R 4494

Rys, *sb.* twig. A 3324

Rishe, Risshe, *sb.* rush. R 1701, T³ 1161

Rist, riseth. B 864, L 810

Rit, rideth. A 974

Roche, *sb.* rock. HF² 40

Rochette, *sb.* rochet, linen vest. R 4754

Rode, *sb.* ruddiness. B 1917

Rode, *sb.* rood, cross. HF¹ 57

Roggeth, *pres. s.* shakes. L 2708

Roghte, *pret.* recked. E 685

Roignous, *adj.* rotten. R 6190

Royleth, *pres. s.* rolls. Bo. 256

Royne, *sb.* itch. R 553

Roynous, *adj.* scabby, rough. R 988

Roket, *sb.* rochet, linen vest. R 1242

Rombel. *See* **Rumbel**.

Rommer, *adj. comp.* roomier. A 4145

Ron, *pret.* rained. T³ 640

Rone. *See* note, R 1673

Ronne, *pres. pl.* ran. B 4578

Rood, *pret.* rode. A 966

Roof, *pret.* clave. HF¹ 373

Rootes, *sb. pl.* astrological roots. F 1276

Ropen, *p.p.* reaped. L 74

Rore, *sb.* uproar. T⁵ 45

Rosene, *adj.* rosy. Bo. 353

Roser, *sb.* rose-tree. R 1651, 3059

Rosyn, *adj.* made of roses. R 845

Rote, *sb.* a small harp. A 236

Roughte, *pret.* recked. T¹ 496

Rouken, *v.* cower, huddle, T⁵ 409; **Rouketh,** *pres. s.* A 1308

Rouncy, *sb.* hack. A 390

Roundel, *sb.* circlet. HF² 283

Rounynges, *sb. pl.* whisperings. HF³ 870

Route, *sb.* assembly. B 776

Route, *v.* assemble together. B 540

Routeth, *pres. s.* snores. A 3647

Routhe, *sb.* pity. A 914

Routyng, *sb.* rumbling. HF³ 843

Rove, *sb.* roof. A 3837

Rowe, *adj. pl.* rough. R 1838

Rowe, *adv.* roughly. G 861, T¹ 206

Rowe, *sb.* row, line, HF¹ 448; **Rowes,** *pl.* rays, beams, *Mars* 2

Rowne, *pres. pl.* whisper. D 241

Rowtyng, *sb.* snoring. A 4166

Rubible, *sb.* kind of fiddle. A 3331

Ruddok, *sb.* robin. PF 349

Ruggy, *adj.* unkempt. A 2883

Rumbel, *sb.* moaning wind, A 1979; rumour, E 997

Sachelis, *sb. pl.* satchels, bags. Bo. 90

Sad, *adj.* steadfast. E 220

Sadly, *adv.* firmly, seriously, steadfastly. A 2602, B 1266, 743

Say, *pret.* saw. B 809, Bl. 1088

Say, *v.* assay. R 5162

Saillouris, *sb. pl.* dancers. R 770

Sale, *sb.* soul. A 4187

Salue, *v.* salute, B 1723; **Salued,** *pret.* R 3610; **Salewed,** *p.p.* F 1310

Salwes, *sb. pl.* willows. D 655

Samyt, *sb.* samite. T¹ 109

Sangwyn, *adj.* red. A 439

Sarge, *sb.* serge. A 2568

Sarpleris, *sb. pl.* sacks. Bo. 90

Sarsynish, *adj.* made of Saracen cloth, soft silk. R 1188

Sat, *pret.* fitted, suited, L 1735; **Sate,** *subj.* would befit, T² 117

Sauf, *adj.* safe. G 950

Sauter, *sb.* psalter. R 431

Sautrie, *sb.* psaltery, small harp. A 296

Savacioun, *sb.* salvation. E 1677

Save, *adj.* safe. An. 267

Save, *sb.* sage. A 2713

Save-garde, *sb.* safe-conduct. T⁴ 139

Saverous, *adj.* pleasant, toothsome. R 84, 2812

Savete, *sb.* safety. R 6869

Sawcefleem, *adj.* pimpled. A 625

Sawe, *sb.* saying. G 691

Scaled, *adj.* scabby. A 627

Scalle, *sb.* scab. *Adam* 3

Scantilone, *sb.* mason's rule. R 7064

Scarmuch, *sb.* skirmish. T² 611

Scathe, *sb.* harm, misfortune. A 446

Schad, *p.p.* scattered. Bo. 1478

Schrewes, *sb. pl.* rascals. Bo. 1365

Solat, *sb.* slate. *Merciles Beaute* 34

Solaundre, *sb.* slander, scandal. E 722

Slendre, *adj.* slender. A 587

Soochouns, *sb. pl.* escutcheons. R 893

Soole, *sb.* school. B 1685

Sooleye, *v.* attend school. A 302

Soomes, *sb. pl.* foamings. Bo. 1612

Soorklith, *pres. s.* scorches. Bo. 525

Scripture, *sb.* inscription. T² 1369

Sorit, *sb.* writing. T² 1130

Scrivenisshly, *adv.* like a scribe. T² 1026

Seche, *v.* seek. A 784

Secree, *adj.* secret. B 4105

See, *sb.* sea. Bl. 67

See, *sb.* seat. T⁴ 1023

Seeke, *adj.* sick. A 18

Seel, *sb.* happiness. A 4239

Seeld, *adv.* seldom. B 2340, Bo. 1442

Seele, *sb.* seal. B 882

Sege, *sb.* seat. Bo. 102

Seigh, Sey, *pret.* saw. A 192, T² 277

Seyl, *sb.* sail. A 696

Seyn, *p.p.* seen. B 624

Seyn, *pres. pl.* say. B 622

Seynd, *p.p.* singed. B 4035

Seintuarie, Seyntwarie, *sb.* sanctuary. I 781, Bo. 131

Seistow, sayest thou. D 292

Selde, *adv.* seldom. A 1539, T⁴ 423

Sely, *adj.* innocent, simple, good, A 3404, B 682, 1702; strange, HF² 5

Selyly, *adv.* happily. Bo. 386

Selinesse, *sb.* happiness. T⁵ 825

Selve, *adj.* self-same. A 2584

Semblable, *adj.* like. I 408

Semblant, *sb.* appearance. L 1736, R 3205

Semelyhede, *sb.* goodliness. R 1130

Semycope, *sb.* short cloak. A 262

Semysoun, *sb.* low noise. A 3697

Sencer, *sb.* censer. A 3340

Sendal, *sb.* fine silk. A 440

Senith, *sb.* zenith. As. ii. § 26

Sent, *pres.* sendeth. T² 1123

Sentence, *sb.* meaning, purport. A 306, C 157

Septemtrioun, *sb.* the north. B 3657

Serenous, *adj.* serene. *Pite* 92 (*emend.*)

Sereyns, *sb. pl.* sirens. R 684

Servage, *sb.* servitude. A 1946

Servaunt, *sb.* lover. A 1814

Sesons, *sb. pl.* seasons. A 347

Sete, *v.* were seated. T² 81

Setewale, *sb.* valerian. R 1370

Sette ... cappe, befool. A 586

Seur, *adv.* surely. T³ 1633

Seurte, *sb.* surety. A 1604

Sewed, pursued. B 4527

Sewes, *sb. pl.* dishes. F 67

Shal, *pres. s.* owe. T³ 791

Shale, *sb.* shell. HF³ 191

Shalmyes, *sb. pl.* shawms. HF³ 128

Shaltow, shalt thou

Shapen, *pres. pl.* prepare. A 772

Shaply, *adv.* likely. T⁴ 1452

Shawe, *sb.* grove. A 4367, T³ 720

Sheeldes, *sb. pl.* French crowns. A 278

Sheene, *adj.* beautiful. A 166

Sheete, *v.* shoot. A 3928

Shende, harm, A 4410; **Shendeth,** confounds, B 28

765

Shendshipe, *sb.* ignominy. I 273
Shent, *p.p.* scolded, discomfited, spoilt. B 1731, A 2754, L 652, R 2584
Shepne, *sb. pl.* sheep-folds. A 2020
Sherte, *sb.* shirt. A 1566
Shet, *p.p.* shut. A 2597
Sheter, *sb.* as *adj.* shooter. PF 180
Shette, *pret.* shut. T³ 1086
Shilde, *subj. pres. s.*; God shilde, God forbid, A 3427, B 1356
Shynes, *sb. pl.* shins. A 1279
Shipnes, *sb. pl.* stables. D 871
Shiten, *p.p.* befouled. A 504
Shode, *sb.* parting of the hair. A 2007
Shof, *pret.* shoved. T³ 487, R 533
Sholde, *sb.* shouldest. D 348
Shonde, *sb.* harm. B 2098
Shoof, *pret.* shoved. PF 154
Shoop, *pret.* shaped, determined. *Pite* 20, B 1244
Shotwyndowe, *sb.* window with a bolt. A 3358
Shour, *sb.* onslaught, T⁴ 47; Shoures, *pl.* T³ 1064
Shrewednesse, *sb.* rascality. B 2721
Shrewes, *sb. pl.* rascals. C 835
Shryfte, *sb.* confession. L 745
Shrighte, *pret.* shrieked. A 2817
Shuldres, *sb. pl.* shoulders. A 6787
Sy, *pret.* saw, HF³ 72; Sye, *pret. pl.* E 1804
Syb, *adj.* related, akin. B 2565, R 1199
Sikerly, *adv.* certainly. A 137
Sye, *v.* sink. T⁵ 182
Syen, Sye, *pret. pl.* saw. G 110, E 1804
Siggen, *pres. pl.* say. T⁴ 194
Sighte, *pret.* sighed. B 1035
Sik, *sb.* sigh. T⁴ 1527
Sike, *v.* sigh. A 1540
Sike, *adj.* sick. A 245
Sikernesse, *sb.* security, surety. B 425, R 7309
Siklich, *adj.* sickly. T³ 1528
Syn, *conj.* since. A 601
Synguler, *adj.* particular. I 300
Synwes, *sb. pl.* sinews. I 685
Sys-aas, six and ace. B 3851
Sisoures, *sb. pl.* scissors. HF² 182
Sit, *pres. s.* sitteth, sits, A 1599, Bl. 1107; fits, B 1353
Sith, Sithen, *conj.* and *adv.* since. A 930, 1521
Sithe, *sb.* scythe. L 646
Sithe, *sb. pl.* times. B 733
Sittande, *pres. part.* fitting. R 2263
Sittyngest, *adj. sup.* most fitting. PF 551
Skaffaut, *sb.* scaffold. R 4176
Skale, *sb.* scale, circle under cross-line of Astrolabe. As. i. § 12
Skye, *sb.* cloud. HF³ 510
Skylatoun, *sb.* fine cloth. B 1924
Skiles, *sb. pl.* reasons. F 205
Skilful, *adj.* reasonable. Bl. 533
Skilfully, *adv.* reasonably. G 320
Skryppe, *sb.* scrip. R 7493
Slawe, Slawen, *p.p.* slain. A 943, An. 59
Sle, *imper.* slay thou. A 1740
Sledys, *sb. pl.* sledges, carriages. Bo. 1165
Slee, *v.* slay. A 661
Sleep, *pret.* slept. A 98, Bl. 169
Sleere, *sb.* slayer. A 2005
Sleighe, *adj.* sly, clever. T⁴ 972
Slider, *adj.* slippery. A 1264

Slye, *adj. pl.* clever. Bl. 569
Slyk, *adj.* sleek. D 351
Slyk, *adj.* such. A 4130
Slyly, *adv.* cleverly. A 1444
Slit, *pres. s.* slideth. G 682, PF 3
Slivere, *sb.* sliver, part. T³ 1013
Slomrest, *pres. s.* slumberest. R 2576
Slow, Slough, *pret.* slew. B 984, Bl. 738, A 980. An. 56
Slowe, *sb.* moth. R 4751
Smerte, *adv.* smartly. A 149
Smote, *p.p.* smitten. R 3735
Smyt, *pres. s.* smiteth. E 122
Smoterlich, *adj.* smutty. A 3963
Snewed, *pret.* snowed, abounded. A 345
Snybben, *v.* reprove, A 523; Snybbed, *p.p.* A 4401
Socoour, *sb.* succour. A 918
Sodeynliche, *adv.* suddenly. A 1575
Sojour, *sb.* sojourn. R 5151
Sokene, *sb.* tolls. A 3987
Sokyngly, *adv.* suckingly, gently. B 2765
Solaas, *sb.* solace. A 798
Soleyn, *adj.* solitary. PF 607, R 3896
Solempne, *adj.* solemn, famous. A 209
Somdel, *adv.* somewhat. A 174
Some, *num. pron.* one; Tenthe some, ten in all, T³ 1249; Al and som, one and all
Somer, *sb.* summer. A 394
Somne, *v.* summon. D 1377
Somonour, *sb.* summoner of offenders to the church courts. A 623
Sond, Soond, *sb.* sand. PF 243, B 4457
Sonde, *sb.* sending, message, messenger. B 1400, 760, 388
Sone, *adv.* soon
Sone, *sb.* son. A 2261
Sonne, *sb.* sun. A 7
Sonnish, *adj.* sunny. T⁴ 743
Soole, *adj.* solitary, alone. R 2955, 3023
Soond, *sb.* sand. B 4457
Soote, *adj. pl.* sweet. A 1
Sope, *sb.* sop. A 334
Soper, *sb.* supper. A 799
Sophyme, *sb.* problem, E 5; Sophymes. *p.* sophistries, F 554
Sort, *sb.* lot, fate, oracle. A 844, T¹ 76
Sorwe, *sb.* sorrow. ABC 3
Sorwful, *adj.* sorrowful. *Pite* 25
Sory, *adj.* sad, luckless. A 2004
Sothsawe, Sothesaugh, *sb.* true tale. HF 999, R 6130, 7588
Sotil, *adj.* subtle. L 1556
Soudiours, *sb. pl.* soldiers. R 4234
Soughe, *sb.* sow. I 156
Soulfre, *sb.* sulphur. HF³ 418
Soun, *sb.* sound. Bl. 1165
Sourden, *pres. pl.* rise from. I 448
Soures, *sb. pl.* bucks. Bl. 429
Sours, *sb.* rising, ascent. D 1938, HF² 36
Soutere, *sb.* cobbler. A 3904
Soutil, *adj.* thin, subtle. A 2030, 2049
Sowdan, *sb.* Sultan. B 177
Sowdanesse, *sb.* Sultaness. B 358
Sowded, *p.p.* attached, devoted. B 1769
Sowe, *v.* sew, fasten. T³ 1201
Sowke, *v.* suck. A 4157
Sowne, *v.* sound, play. A 565
Sowned, *pret.* tended to, B 3348; Sownynge *pres. part.* A 275

Space, *sb.* spare time, opportunity. A 35, T³ 505
Spak, *pret.* spoke. A 304
Span-newe, *adj.* newly spun, fresh. T³ 1665
Sparand, *part. pres.* sparing. R 5363
Sparrede, *pret.* locked. R 3320
Sparth, *sb.* halberd. A 2520, R 5978
Spauysshinge, *sb.* blooming. R 3633
Spece, *sb.* species, kind, class. Bo. 1791, I 407
Speculacioun, *sb.* contemplation. Bo. 1660
Speere, *sb.* sphere. F 1280
Spelle, *sb. dat.* recital. B 2083
Spence, *sb.* buttery. D 1931
Spered, *p.p.* shut. R 2008
Speres, *sb. pl.* spheres. PF 59
Sperhauk, *sb.* sparrow-hawk. T³ 1192, R 4033
Spete, *v.* spit. T³ 1617
Spille, *v.* die, perish, destroy, B 285, A 3278, *Pite* 46 ; **Spilt**, *p.p.* killed, B 857
Spitously, *adv.* angrily. A 3476
Spores, *sb. pl.* spurs. A 473
Sporneth, *pres. s.* tramples, T² 797 ; **Sporned**, *pret.* stumbled, A 4280
Spousaille, *sb.* marriage. E 115
Sprad, *p.p.* spread, scattered. Bl. 873
Spraynd, Spreynd, *p.p.* mingled. Bo. 397, B 422
Spryngoldes, *sb. pl.* stone-hurlers. R 4191
Squames, *sb. pl.* scales. G 759
Squaymous, *adj.* squeamish. A 3337
Squyre, *sb.* measuring-square, R 7064 ; **Squyres**, *pl.* As. i. § 12
Stadye, *sb.* race-course. Bo. 1275
Stak, *pret.* stuck. T³ 1372
Stal, *pret.* stole. Bl. 652, 1250
Stamyn, Stames, *sb.* linsey-woolsey, coarse cloth. I 1052, L 2360
Stank, *sb.* pool. I 841
Stant, *pres. s.* standeth. B 1704
Stape, Stapen, *p.p.* advanced. B 4011, E 1514
Stare, *sb.* starling. PF 348
Starf, *pret.* died. A 933
Starke, *adj. pl.* strong, stiff. B 3560
Steere, *sb.* steersman. B 448
Steereless, *adj.* without rudder. B 439
Steyen, *v.* ascend. B 877
Steyre, *sb.* stair. *Mars* 129, T³ 1705
Stel, Stele, *sb.* steel. T² 593, HF² 175
Stele, *sb.* handle. A 3785
Stellifye, *v.* turn into a star. L 525
Stemed, *pret.* shone. A 202
Stenten, *v.* cease, A 903 ; **Stente**, *pret.* Bl. 154
Stepe, *adj.* bright. A 201
Steppes, *sb. pl.* tracks. Bo. 80
Stere, *sb.* steersman, guide, HF¹ 437, T³ 1291 : rudder, T³ 641
Stere, *v.* steer, guide. T³ 910
Stere, *v.* stir, HF² 59; discuss, T⁴ 1451 ; **Steryng**, *pres. part.* moving, HF² 59
Stered, *p.p.* controlled, L 935
Sterlynges, *sb. pl.* sterling pennies, C 907, HF³ 225
Sterres, *sb. pl.* stars. A 268
Sterte, *pret.* started, L 1301 ; alighted, A 952
Sterve, *pres. sub.* die. A 1144
Stevene, *sb.* voice, A 2562 ; appointment, *Mars* 47, A 1524
Stewe, *sb.* closet. T³ 601
Stiborne, *adj.* stubborn. D 456
Stye, *v.* climb. Bo. 1550

Styere, *sb.* rudder. Bo. 1078
Stiked, *pret.* pierced. B 3897
Stillatorie, *sb.* vessel for distilling. G 580
Stynt, *pres. s.* stinteth, ceases. A 2421
Stirte, *pret.* started. A 1579
Styth, *sb.* anvil. A 2026
Styves, *sb. pl.* stews, brothels. D 1332
Styward, *sb.* steward. B 914
Stoke, *v.* stab. A 2546
Stokked, *p.p.* set in the stocks. T³ 380
Stonde, *v.* stand. A 745
Stoon, *sb.* stone. A 774
Stoor, *sb.* farm-stock. A 598
Stoore, *adj.* stubborn. E 2367
Storial, *adj.* historical. L 702
Stot, *sb.* cob. A 615
Stounde, *sb.* while, time, B 1021 ; **Stoundes**, *pl.* Bo. 220
Stoundemele, *adv.* momently. T⁵ 674, R 2304
Stour, *sb.* conflict. R 1270
Strake, *v.* run. Bl. 1311
Straughte, *pret.* stretched. A 2916
Strecche, *v.* stretch. An. 341, T¹ 888
Stree, *sb.* straw. A 2918, Bl. 670
Streen, Strene, *sb.* race, lineage. E 157, R 4859
Streit, *adj.* narrow. A 174
Stremes, *sb. pl.* beams. Bl. 338
Strene, *sb.* lineage. R 4859
Strenges, *sb. pl.* strings. PF 98, T¹ 732
Strike, *sb.* hank, A 676 ; **Strikes**, *pl.* strokes, As. i. § 19
Stroof, *pret.* strove. A 1038
Strouted, *pret.* spread. A 3315
Stubbes, *sb. pl.* stumps. A 1978
Studies, *sb. pl.* desires, purposes. Bo. 659, 1309
Stuwe, *sb.* stew, fish-pond. A 350
Submitted to, *p.p.* subsumed under. Bo. 1628
Succident, *sb.* subordinate house in astrology. As. ii. § 3
Sucred, *p.p.* sugared. T² 384
Suffisaunce, *sb.* sufficiency. Bl. 1037
Suffraunt, *adj.* patient. Bl. 1009
Suget, *sb.* subject. R 3535
Sukkenye, *sb.* gaberdine. R 1232
Surement, *sb.* surety, pledge. F 1534
Surquidrie, *sb.* arrogance, over-confidence. I 405, 1067
Sursanure, *sb.* surface-healed wound. F 1113
Sustren, *sb. pl.* sisters. A 1019
Suwe, *v.* follow. T¹ 379
Swa, *adv.* so. A 4040
Swal, *pret.* swelled. B 1750
Swalwe, *sb.* swallow. T² 64
Swappe, Swape, *v.* strike. E 586, G 366
Swappe, *sb.* stroke. HF² 35
Sweigh, *sb.* sway, movement. B 296
Swelte, *pret.* fainted. E 1776, T³ 347
Swelwe, *pres. sub.* swallow, E 1188 ; **Swelweth**, *pres. ind. s.* swallows, B 2805
Swerd, *sb.* sword. A 2546
Swete, *v.* sweat. G 579
Swevene, *sb.* dream. B 4086
Swich, *adj.* such. D 281
Swynk, *sb.* toil. A 188
Swynke, *v.* toil. A 186
Swynkere, *sb.* labourer. A 531
Swire, *sb.* throat. R 325
Swythe, *adv.* quickly. C 796, An. 226

Swyve, *v.* have sexual intercourse with. A 4178
Swogh, *sb.* swoon, *Pite* 16 ; groan, A 3619
Swolowe, *sb.* gullet, gulf. L 1104
Swoot, *sb.* sweat. G 578
Swough, *sb.* soughing wind. A 1979

T', before a verb beginning with a vowel, to ; a
few instances given below
Taa, *v.* take. A 4129
Taas, *sb.* heap. A 1005
Tabard, *sb.* short coat for a herald, A 20 ; for
a labourer, A 541
Tabyde, to abide. B 797
Tables, *sb. pl.* backgammon. F 900
Tabouren, *pres. pl.* drum. L 354
Tache, *sb.* quality. *Balade* 20
Taffata, *sb.* fine silk. A 440
Taffraye, to affray, frighten. E 455
Taylagiers, *sb. pl.* tax-gatherers. R 6811
Taillages, *sb. pl.* taxes. I 567
Taille, *sb.* a tally, credit. A 570
Takel, *sb.* tackle. A 106
Tale, *sb.* speech. Bl. 535
Tale, Talen, *v.* talk, tell stories. T³ 231, A
772
Talent, *sb.* desire. B 1137, Bo. 260
Talyghte, to alight
Talynge, *sb.* story-telling. B 1624
Talle, *adj.* compliant, seemly, manly. *Mars* 38,
L 1127 (emend. for 'calle')
Tallege, to allege
Tamen, *v.* make trial of. R 3904
Tamende, to amend
Tan, *p.p.* taken. R 5894
Tapes, *sb. pl.* ribands. A 3241
Tapinage, *sb.* hiding ; In tapinage, incognito.
R 7361
Tapycer, *sb.* tapestry maker. A 362
Tapite, *sb.* carpet. Bl. 260
Tappestere, *sb.* barmaid, tapster. A 241
Targe, *sb.* shield. *ABC* 176
Tarraye, to array. E 961
Tassaye, to assay. E 454
Tassaile, to assail
Tatarwagges, *sb. pl.* tatters. R 7257
Tavyse, to advise. B 1426
Teoches, *sb. pl.* ill qualities. T³ 935, HF³ 688,
R 6517
Teche, *v.* teach. A 308
Teene, *sb.* sorrow. *ABC* 3
Teyne, *sb.* thin plate of metal. G 1225
Tembrace, to embrace. B 1891
Teme, *v.* bring forth. HF³ 654
Temple, *sb.* inn of court. A 567
Temprure, *sb.* tempering. R 4177
Tempus, *sb.* tense. G 875
Ten, Ten so woode, ten times as mad. L 733
Tendyte, to endite
Tendure, to endure. E 756
Tene, *sb.* sorrow. T¹ 814
Tenqueren, to enquire
Tentifly, *adv.* attentively. E 334
Tercel, *adj.* male (of birds of prey). PF 393
Tercelet, *sb.* male falcon. F 504
Tery, *adj.* tearful. T⁴ 821
Terins, *sb.* tarins. R 665
Terme, *sb.* ; In terme, In termes, precisely,
C 311, A 323
Termyne, *v.* determine. PF 530
Terved, *p.p.* stripped. G 1171

Tespye, to espy
Testeres, *sb. pl.* headpieces. A 2499
Testes, *sb. pl.* vessels for testing metals. G 818
Testif, *adj.* headstrong. A 4004
Texpounden, to expound
Textuel, *adj.* verbally accurate. I 57
Th', before substantives beginning with a vowel,
the ; a few instances are given below
Thakked, *p.p.* stroked. A 3304
Thankes, *sb. pl.* ; Hir thankes, His thankes,
willingly, A 1626, 2107
Thanne, *conj.* and *adv.* then
Thar, *pres. s.* it behoves. A 4320
That, *conj.* when. T² 910
That, introducing an optative clause. T⁵ 944
Thavys, the advice. A 3076
The, *pron. acc.* thee
Thedam, *sb.* prosperity ; Yvel thedam, ill-luck,
B 1595
Thee, Theen, *v.* thrive. B 4622, C 309
Theech, Theek, *subj. pres.* thrive I. C 947,
A 3864
Theffect, the effect
Thaigh, *conj.* though. T⁴ 175
Their, the air. D 1939
Thenche, *v.* think. A 3253
Thencrees, the increase. A 275
Thennes, *adv.* thence
Theorik, *sb.* theory. As. ii. pref.
Ther, *adv.* there, where. A 2809, T² 618
Ther, introducing an optative clause. T³ 947,
1015, 1437
Ther-geyn, there against. R 6555
Therthe, the earth
Thestat, the estate, rank
Thewed, *p.p.* endowed with virtues. *Mars* 180
Thewes, *sb. pl.* good qualities. E 1542
Thider, *adv.* thither
Thilke, that same. A 182
Thyng, *sb.* ; Make a thyng, draw up a docu-
ment ; Thynges, *pl.* prayers, acts of devotion,
business, A 2293, B 1281, 4280
Thinke, *v.* seem. T¹ 405
Thirled, *p.p.* pierced. A 2710
This, These, *dem. pl.* thiese. Bl. 166
This, this is. T² 363
Tho, *adv.* then. Bl. 1053
Tho, 'these
Tholed, *p.p.* suffered. D 1546
Thoo, *adv.* then. L 787
Thought, *sb.* anxiety. R 308
Thraste, *pret.* thrust. T³ 1155
Threpe, *pres. pl.* call. G 826
Threste, *v.* thrust, A 2612 ; Thresten, *pres. pl.*
Bo. 460
Thretynge, *sb.* threatening. G 698
Thridde, *num.* third
Thrye, *num. adv.* thrice. T² 89
Thringe, *v.* thrust. T⁴ 66
Thritten, *card. num.* thirteen. D 2259
Throf, *pret.* thrived. Bo. 717
Thrope, *sb.* hamlet. I 12
Throte-bolle, *sb.* wind-pipe. A 4273
Throwe, *sb.* short space of time. B 953, E 452,
Pite 86
Throwes, *sb. pl.* throes. T⁵ 206, 1201
Thrust, *sb.* thirst. R 4722
Thurfte, *pret.* needed. T³ 572
Thurgh-girt, *p.p.* pierced. A 1010
Thurrok, *sb.* hold of a ship, sink. I 363, 715

Thwyte, *pres.* whittle, HF³ 848 ; Thwyten, *p.p.* R 933

Thwitel, *sb.* short knife. A 3933

Tyden, *v.* betide. B 337

Tydif, *sb.* small bird ; Tidyves, *pl.* F 648

Tikel, *adj.* frail. A 3428

Tikelnesse, *sb.* instability. *Truth* 3

Til, *prep.* to. A 180

Tylyers, *sb. pl.* tillers. R 4339

Tylyinge, *sb.* tilling. Bo. 1637

Tymbres, *sb. pl.* timbrels. R 772

Typet, *sb.* hood. A 233

Tire, *v.* feed on, Bo. 1132 ; Tiren, *pres. pl.* T¹ 787

Tit, *pres. s.* betides. T¹ 333

Titerynge, *sb.* hesitating. T² 1744

Title, *sb.* pretext. T¹ 488

Titled, *p.p.* devoted. I 894

To, The to, that one. Bo. 1587

To-, *intensive prefix;* a few instances are given below

To-breste, *pres. pl.* break in pieces. A 2611

Tode, *sb.* toad. I 636

To-forn, *prep.* before. T³ 335

Toft, *sb.* tuft. A 555

Toght, *adj.* taut. D 2267

To-hepe, *adv.* together, at close quarters. Bo. 1461, L 2008

To-yere, *adv.* this year. T² 241

Tolde, *pret.* accounted. B 3676

Toles, *sb. pl.* tools. T¹ 632

Tollen, *v.* take toll. A 562

Tollen, *v.* allure. Bo. 531

Tolletanes, *adj. pl.* of Toledo. F 1273

Tombesteres, *sb. pl.* female tumblers. C 477

To-medes, as reward. T² 1201

Ton, The ton, that one. Bo. 1066, R 5217

Tonge, *sb.* tongue. B 1666

Tonne, *sb.* tun, cask. E 215

Too, *sb.* toe, A 2726 ; Toon, *pl.* B 4052

Toord, *sb.* excrement. C 955

Tope, *sb.* crown of head. A 590

To-point, *adv.* point by point, exactly. T² 497, T³ 1620

To-race, *subj. pr.* tear in pieces. E 572

To-rente, *pret.* rent in pieces. C 709

Torney, *sb.* tournament. T⁴ 1669

To-slytered, *p.p.* slashed. R 840

To-tar, *pret.* lacerated. B 3801

Totelere, *sb.* tattler. L 353

Toty, *adj.* dizzy. A 4253

To-tore, *p.p.* torn. G 635

Touret, *sb.* turret. A 1909

Tourettes, *sb. pl.* round holes. A 2152

Toute, *sb.* backside. A 3812

Toverbyde, to outlive. D 1260

Towayle, *sb.* towel. R 161

To-wonde, *pret.* went to pieces. *Mars* 102

Traas, *sb.* train. L 285

Trace, *sb.* track. *Gentilesse* 3

Trad, *pret.* trod, *sens. ob.* B 4368

Trayed, *pret.* betrayed. HF¹ 390

Trays, *sb. pl.* traces. A 2139, T¹ 222

Traitorye, *sb.* treachery. An. 156

Transmuwen, *v.* transmute. T⁴ 467

Trappures, *sb. pl.* trappings. A 2499

Trattor, *sb.* go-between, pimp. T³ 273

Traunce, *v.* tramp. T³ 690

Trave, *sb.* frame for unruly horses. A 3282

Travers, *sb.* curtain, screen. E 1817, T³ 674

Trechour, *sb.* traitor. R 6602

Tredefowel, *sb.* treader of fowls, *sens. ob.* B 3135

Treget, *sb.* deceit. R 6267

Tregetour, *sb.* juggler, HF³ 167 ; Tregetoures, *pl.* F 1141

Trenden, *v.* roll. Bo. 1043

Trental, *sb.* series of masses for the dead. D 1717

Trepeget, *sb.* engine for casting stones. R 6279

Tresoun, *sb.* treason. L 1783

Tresour, *sb.* head-dress. R 568

Tretable, *adj.* tractable, communicative. L 411, Bl. 532

Tretee, *sb.* treaty. A 1288

Tretys, *adj.* well-made. A 152

Tretis, *sb.* treatise, document. T² 1697

Trewe, *adj.* true. A 531

Trewe, *sb.* truce. T³ 1779

Trewe-love, *sb.* condiment to sweeten breath. A 3692

Triacle, *sb.* balm, panacea. B 479, C 314

Trice, *v.* pull. B 3715

Trichour, *sb.* traitor. R 6308

Trille, *v.* turn, twist. F 316

Trype, *sb.* morsel. D 1747

Trist, *sb.* trust. T³ 403, I 473

Triste, *sb.* tryst. T² 1534

Tristed, *p.p.* trusted. R 3929

Trone, *sb.* throne. A 2529

Trouble, *adj.* troubled. *Comp. to his Lady* 128

Trowandyse, Truandise, *sb.* vagrancy. R 3954, 6604

Trowblable, *adj.* troublesome. Bo. 1268

Truaundyng, *sb.* vagrancy. R 6721

Trubly, *adj.* troublous. Bo. 1443

Trufles, *sb. pl.* trifles. I 715

Trye, *adj.* choice. B 2046

Tuel, *sb.* pipe, tube. HF³ 559

Tulle, *v.* lure. A 4134

Turmentrie, *sb.* torture. R 4740

Tweyfold, *adj.* folded in two. G 566

Twight, *p.p.* twitched, pulled, D 1563 ; Twighte, *pret.* T⁴ 1185

Twynne, *v.* sunder, B 517 ; *pres. subj.* depart, A 835

Twiste, *sb.* branch. E 2349

Umble, *adj.* humble. R 6155

Unaraced, *p.p.* untorn. Bo. 1156

Unconning, *adj.* stupid. T⁵ 1139

Uncouthe, *adj.* strange, rare. HF³ 189

Uncovenable, *adj.* unsuitable. I 431

Undergrowe, *p.p.* undergrown. A 156

Undermeles, *sb. pl.* morning meal-time. D 875

Undernome, *p.p.* blamed, I 401 ; Undernoom, *pret.* perceived, G 243

Underpighte, *pret.* stuffed. B 789

Underspore, *v.* lever up. A 3465

Undertake, *pres. s.* assert. A 289

Undigne, *adj.* unworthy. E 359

Undirfongeth, *pres. s.* undertakes. R 5709

Undo, *v.* unravel. Bl. 898

Undren, *sb.* morning, the time between 9 A.M. and noon. B 4412, E 260

Uneschuable, *adj.* inevitable. Bo. 1643

Unespyed, *p.p.* undiscovered. T⁴ 1457

Unfestlich, *adj.* unfestive, worn. F 366

Ungiltif, *adj.* innocent. T³ 1018

Ungrobbed, *p.p.* undigged. *Former Age* 14

3 D

Unhappes, *sb. pl.* mishaps. T² 456
Unheele, *sb.* misfortune. C 116
Unkynde, *adj.* unnatural. B 88
Unkyndely, *adv.* unnaturally. C 485
Unkonnynge, *sb.* ignorance. I 1082
Unkorven, *p.p.* unpruned. *Former Age* 14
Unkouth, *adj.* rare. A 2497
Unlefull, *adj.* unlawful. Bo. 274, R 4880
Unneste, *imper.* quit thy nest. T⁴ 305
Unnethe, Unnethes, *adv.* hardly. B 1050, 1675
Unparygal, *adj.* unequal. Bo. 603
Unplitable, *adj.* perilous. Bo. 122
Unplyten, *v.* unfold. Bo. 583
Unresty, *adj.* restless. T⁵ 1355
Unsad, *adj.* inconstant. E 995 ·
Unsely, *adj.* unhappy. A 4210, Bo. 361
Unset, *adj.* unappointed. A 1524
Unsittinge, *adj.* unbefitting. T² 307
Unspered, *p.p.* unlocked. R 2656
Unthank, *sb.* ingratitude, little thank. T⁵ 699
Unwar, *adj.* unawares. F 1356
Unweelde, *adj.* impotent. A 3886
Unwemmed, *adj.* undefiled, pure. B 924, *ABC* 91
Unwist, *adj.* ignorant. T¹ 93
Unwit, *sb.* folly. *Mars* 271
Unwrye, *v.* uncover. T¹ 858
Unyolden, *adj.* without yielding. A 2642
Up, *prep.* upon. Bl. 921
Up-bounde, *p.p.* bound up. T² 517
Up-frete, *v.* eat up. T⁵ 1470
Uprighte, *adv.* full length, whether standing or lying. A 4194
Upriste, *sb.* rising. A 1051
Up-so-doun, *adv.* topsy-turvy. Bo. 1695
Up-swal, *pret.* swelled up. B 1750
Urchouns, *sb. pl.* hedgehogs. R 3135
Utter, *adj.* outer. R 4208

Vache, *sb.* cow. *Truth* 22
Vailith, Valeth, *pres.* avails. R 5765, 5762
Valance, *sb.* failure. *Mars* 145 (*see* note)
Vane, *sb.* weather-vane. E 996
Vanytee, *sb.* folly. A 3835
Vassalage, Vassellage, *sb.* prowess, good service. L 1667, A 3054
Vavasour, *sb.* landholder. A 360
Vekke, *sb.* old woman. R 4286
Vendable, *adj.* saleable. R 5804
Venerie, *sb.* hunting. A 166, 2308
Veniaunce, *sb.* vengeance. Bo. 1375
Venym, *sb.* poison. A 2751
Venymous, *adj.* poisonous. *ABC* 149
Ventusinge, *sb.* cupping. A 2747
Ver, *sb.* spring. T¹ 157
Verdit, *sb.* verdict. A 787
Verger, *sb.* orchard. B 3234, 3618
Verye, *imper.* guard (?). A 3485
Verytrot, *sb.* quick-trot. A 3770
Vermayle, *adj.* red. R 3645
Vernage, *sb.* white wine. B 1261
Vernycle, *sb.* St. Veronica cloth. A 685
Vernysshed, *pret.* varnished. A 4149
Verray, Verreie, *adj.* genuine, true. I 1012, Bo. 1729
Verrayment, *adv.* truly. B 1903
Verre, *sb.* glass. T³ 867
Vertuous, *adj.* skilled. R 2311
Vesselage, *sb.* prowess. R 5871

Vese, *sb.* rush of wind. A 1985
Viage, *sb.* voyage, journey. A 723
Vigilies, *sb. pl.* wakes. A 377
Vileynye, *sb.* anything unbecoming a gentleman. A 70
Virytrate, *sb.* hag. D 1582
Vitaille, *sb.* victuals. A 248
Vitremyte, *sb.* woman's cap. B 3562
Voidé, *sb.* sleeping cup. T³ 674
Voyde, *adj.* empty, penniless. Bo. 471
Volage, *adj.* giddy. H 239
Voltor, *sb.* vulture. Bo. 1132
Volunte, *sb.* will. R 5276
Voluper, *sb.* cap. A 3241
Vounde, *adj.* *See* note. R 7063

Waget, *sb.* blue cloth. A 3321
Wayfereres, *sb. pl.* confectioners. C 479
Wayke, *adj.* weak. A 887, B 1671
Waymentynge, *sb.* lamentation. A 902, 1921
Wayted, *pret.* watched. A 571
Walsh-note, *sb.* walnut. HF³ 191
Walwe, *v.* wallow. T¹ 699
Walwynge, *pres. part.* wallowing. A 3616
Wan, *pret.* won. A 442
Wanges, *sb. pl.* cheek-teeth, A 4030 ; Wang-tooth, B 3234
Wanhope, *sb.* despair. A 1249
Wanye, *v.* wane. A 2078
Wanten, *pres. pl.* are lacking. *Pite* 76
Wantrust, *adj.* distrustful. H 281
War, *adj.* wary, aware. A 309, 896
Warde, *sb.* guardianship. BL 248
Wardecors, *sb.* bodyguard. D 359
Warderere, look out behind ! A 4101
Wardright, *sb.* guardianship. Bo. 492
Wardrobe, *sb.* privy. B 1762
Ware, *imp.* beware that. B 4146
Waryangles, *sb. pl.* butcher birds. D 1408
Warice, *v.* heal. C 906
Warien, Warye, *v.* curse. T² 1619, B 372
Warisoun, *sb.* reward. R 1537
Warisshe, *v.* recover, B 2170 ; Warisshed, *p.p.* cured, F 1138, Bl. 1103
Warisshyng, *sb.* healing. B 2205
Warly, *adv.* warily. T⁵ 454
Warne, *v.* repulse. *ABC* 11
Warnestoore, *sb.* garrison. B 2485
Wast, *sb.* waste. B 1609
Wastel-breed, *sb.* cake of fine flour. A 147
Wawes, *sb. pl.* waves. A 1958
Webbe, *sb.* weaver. A 362
Wedde, *sb. dat.* pledge. A 1218
Wede, *sb.* clothing. A 1006
Weder, *sb.* weather, D 2253 ; Wedres, *pl.* R 73
Weeply, *adj.* tearful. Bo. 1120
Weerdes, *sb. pl.* fates. Bo. 92
Weex, *pret.* waxed. B 563
Wegge, *sb.* wedge. As. i. § 14
Weyeth, *pres. s.* weighs. A 1781
Weyked, *p.p.* weakened. R 4737
Weylawey, *interj.* alas. Bl. 718
Weymentyng, *sb.* lamentation. R 510
Weyven, *v.* depart from, E 1483 ; Weyve. *imper.* abandon, Bo. 957
Welde, *sb.* a plant. *Former Age* 17
Welde, *v.* rule. D 271
Weldy, *adj.* powerful. T² 636
Wele, *sb.* well-being. A 895
Welk, *pret.* walked. T⁵ 1235

Welken, *v.* wither. Bo. 1590
Welkne, *sb.* welkin. *Fortune* 62
Welmeth, *pres. s.* wells. R 1561
Welte, *pret.* ruled. B 3200
Wel-willy, *adj.* benevolent. T³ 1257
Wem, *sb.* spot, harm. F 121
Wemmelees, *adj.* spotless. G 47
Wende, *pret. subj.* thought. T⁴ 1650
Wene, *sb.* doubt. R 574
Wente, *sb.* turn, passage. T² 815, T³ 787
Wepene, Wepne, *sb.* weapon. A 1591, 1601
Werble, *sb.* song. T² 1033
Were, *sb.* doubt, L 2686, Bl. 1294 ; danger, R 2827
Were, *v.* guard. A 2550
Were, *sb.* weir, pool. T³ 35, PF 138
Werne, *v.* turn away, refuse. L 448, T⁴ 111, HF³ 469
Werre, *adv.* worse. Bl. 615
Werre, *sb.* war. A 1671
Werre, *v.* make war on. *ABC* 116
Werreye, *v.* make war on, persecute, A 1484, R 6926 ; **Werreieth**, *pres. s.* battles against, I 401 ; **Werreid**, *p.p.* persecuted, R 2078
Wert, *sb.* wart. A 555
Wessh, *pret.* washed
Weste, *v.* turn westward. L 61
Weten, *v.* know. L 1474
Wetheres, *sb. pl.* weathers. A 3542
Wex, *sb.* wax. G 1268
Wex, *pret.* waxed, increased, A 1362 ; **Wexynge**, *pres. part.* A 2077
What, *inter.* why. A 184
Whelkes, *sb. pl.* pimples. A 632
Wher, (1) where, A 1351 ; (2) whether, A 1101
Wheston, *sb.* whetstone. T¹ 631
Whiche, *pron.* of what kind. A 40, 2675
Whiel, *sb.* wheel. T¹ 839
Whielen, *v.* wheel. T¹ 139
Whyle, *sb.* time. A 3329
Whippeltre, the cornel-tree. A 2923
Wyde-where, *adv.* widely. B 136, T³ 404
Wierdes, Wirdes, *sb. pl.* fates. T³ 617, L 2580
Wight, *adj.* strong, swift, brave. A 4086, B 3457
Wighte, *sb.* weight, A 2145, T² 1385 ; **A lite wight**, a little while, A 4283
Wyke, *sb.* week. B 1461
Wikke, *adj. pl.* evil. B 118
Wilne, *v.* will, desire, I 517 ; **Wilned**, *pret.* willed, Bl. 1261
Wiltow, wilt thou
Wylugh, *sb.* willow. A 2922
Wympul, *sb.* wimple. A 151
Wyn ape. H 44. *See* note
Wyndas, *sb.* windlass. F 184
Wyndre, *v.* trim. R 1020
Wynsynge, *adj.* lively. A 3263
Wynt, *pres. s.* windeth, turns. L 85
Wirdes, *sb. pl.* Fates. L 2580
Wys, *adv.* certainly, surely. A 2786, T² 887
Wise, *sb.* fashion. A 2370
Wisly, *adv.* surely. B 1061
Wisse, *v.* guide, D 1415, T¹ 622 ; *imp. ABC* 155
Wisshe, *pret.* washed. R 96
Wyst, *p.p.* known. HF¹ 351
Wyte, *imper.* blame, A 3140 ; **Wite at**, impute, G 621
Witen, *pres. pl.* know. A 1794
Withholden, *v.* restrain, B 1512 ; **Withholdeth**,

pres. retains, Bo. 1245 ; **Withholde**, retained, B 2200
Withouton, *prep.* besides. A 461
Withseye, *pres. subj.* contradict, abjure, G 447 ; **Withseyn**, A 1140
Wityng, *s.* knowledge. A 1611
Wivere, *sb.* viper. T² 1010
Wlatsom, *adj.* loathsome. B 4243
Wodewales, *sb. pl.* orioles. R 658
Wol, *pres. s.* will. A 723
Wolde, *pret.* would. A 954
Wolle, *sb.* wool. C 910
Woltow, wilt thou. A 1544
Wombe, *sb.* belly. I 769
Won, *sb.* hope. T⁴ 1181
Wonde, *v.* turn aside, change. L 1187
Wonde, *pret.* dwelt. L 2253
Wonder, *adj.* wondrous. B 1045
Wondermost, *adj. sup.* most wonderful. HF³ 969
Wone, *sb.* custom, wont. A 335, B 1694
Wone, *sb.* plenty. R 1673
Woned, *p.p.* accustomed. Bl. 150
Wonger, *sb.* pillow. B 2102
Wonynge, *sb.* living, dwelling. A 388, 606
Wonned, *pret.* dwelt. B 4406
Wood, *adj.* mad. A 184
Wood, *sb.* blue dye. *Former Age* 17
Woodeth, *pres. s.* is distraught, rages. G 467, Bo. 1328
Woodly, *adv.* madly. A 1301
Woodnesse, *sb.* madness. C 496
Woon, *sb.* place, dwelling. B 1991, HF³ 76
Woot, *pres. s.* know, A 1813 ; *pret.* knew, A 1525
Wopen, *p.p.* wept. T¹ 941
Word, *sb.* for **Ord**, beginning. T³ 702
Wortes, *sb. pl.* vegetables. B 4411
Worthen, *v.* fare ; **Lete him worthen**, let him alone, T⁵ 320 ; **Worth**, *imperat.* Bo. 310
Worthy, *adj.* brave. B 2107
Wost, knowest
Wowe, *v.* woo. T⁵ 791
Wowke, *sb.* week. A 1539
Wraw, *adj.* indignant. H 46
Wrawful, *adj.* perverse. I 677
Wre, Wren, Wrene, *v.* cover. I 735, R 6359, T² 539, R 56
Wreche, *sb.* vengeance, punishment. B 3403, T² 784
Wreighe, *p.p.* covered, L 1201 ; *pret.* T³ 1056
Wreye, *sub. pres.* betray. A 3507
Wreying, *sb.* betrayal. R 5220
Wrekere, *sb.* avenger. Bo. 1385
Wrenche, *sb.* deceit, R 4292 ; **Wrenches**, *pl.* G 1081
Wreththe, *sb.* wrath. T³ 110
Wrye, *p.p.* hidden. T³ 620
Wrye, Wryen, *v.* turn, twist, T² 906, H 262, Bl. 626 ; **Wryed**, *p.p.* twisted, A 3283
Wryne, *v.* cover. R 6683, 6819
Wryth, *pres. s.* winds. T³ 1231
Writhen, *v.* turn. Bo. 1676
Wroken, *p.p.* avenged. T¹ 88
Wroteth, *pres.* digs with the snout. I 157

Y-, *prefix to past participles* ; a few instances are given below
Yaf, *pret.* gave. A 227
Yalte, *pret.* yielded ; **Yalte him**, betook himself, R 4904

Yare, *adj.* ready. L 2270
Y-bet, *p.p.* beaten. D 1285
Y-bete, stamped, illuminated. A 979
Y-blent, *p.p.* blended. A 3808
Y-bleynt, *p.p.* blenched, started aside. A 3753
Y-brent, *p.p.* burnt. A 946
Y-clenched, *p.p.* clamped. A 1991
Y-corve, *p.p.* cut. A 2013
Y-crased, *p.p.* broken. Bl. 324
Ydel, *adj.* idle ; **In ydel**, in vain
Ydolastre, *sb.* idolater. I 749
Ye, *adv.* yea, yes. B 1841
Yeechynge, *sb.* itching. R 2450
Yed, *p.p.* eyed. T⁴ 1459
Yeddynges, *sb. pl.* proverbial sayings. A 257
Yede, *pret.* went, G 1141 ; **Yeden**, *pl.* T² 936
Yelpe, *v.* boast. A 2238
Yelw, *adj.* yellow. Bl. 856
Yerde, *sb.* rod, stick. T² 154, A 149, T² 1427, A 1387
Yerne, *adv.* readily, eagerly, quickly. C 398, D 993, PF 21, T² 376
Yerne, *adj.* brisk. A 3257
Yeten, *v.* get. Bo. 253
Yexeth, *pres. s.* hiccups. A 4151
Y-feere, *adv.* together. B 394
Y-frounced, *p.p.* wrinkled. R 155
Y-go, *p.p.* gone. A 286
Y-grave, *p.p.* dug. L 204
Y-hede, *p.p.* hid. Bl. 175
Y-hent, *p.p.* seized. C 868
Y-herd, *p.p.* haired. A 3737
Yif, *conj.* if. T² 1063
Y-korven, *p.p.* cut. B 1801
Y-lad, *p.p.* lead, carted. A 530

Y-lik, *adv.* alike. A 592
Ymages, *sb. pl.* astrological figures
Y-meynd, *p.p.* mingled. A 2170
Ymel, *prep.* among. A 4172
Ymped, *p.p.* grafted. R 5137
Ympes, *sb. pl.* grafts, shoots, saplings. R 6293, B 3146
Ympne, *sb.* hymn. L 422
Ynde, *sb.* indigo. R 67
Ynly, *adv.* inwardly. Bl. 276
Y-nome, *p.p.* taken. T¹ 242, L 2343
Yolden, *p.p.* yielded. A 3052, Bo. 211
Yolleden, *pret. pl.* yelled. B 4579
Youlyng, *sb.* yelling. A 1278
Yow, you. B 4610
Y-piked, *p.p.* picked out. G 941
Y-plited, *p.p.* pleated. Bo. 61
Y-preved, *p.p.* proved. A 483
Y-purfiled, *p.p.* trimmed. A 193
Y-reke, *p.p.* spread about. A 3882
Ys, *sb.* ice. HF² 40
Y-shete, *p.p.* shut. B 560
Y-shore, *p.p.* shorn, shaven. T⁴ 996
Y-spreynd, *p.p.* sprinkled. A 2169
Y-stalled, *p.p.* throned. HF² 274
Y-stikked, *p.p.* stabbed. F 1476
Y-strawed, *p.p.* strewed. Bl. 628
Yvele, *adv.* ill. B 1897
Yvy leef, *sb.* ; **Pipen in an yvy leef**, ‘ go whistle.’ A 1838
Yvoire, *sb.* ivory. Bl. 945
Y-wis, *adv.* certainly. A 3277
Y-worth, *p.p.* become. Bl. 578
Y-wrien, **Y-wrye**, *p.p.* veiled, hid. Bl. 627, A 2904, T⁴ 1654
Y-writhen, *p.p.* wrapped. R 160

THE END

Printed by R. & R. CLARK, LIMITED, *Edinburgh.*

NEW UNIFORM AND COMPLETE EDITIONS OF THE POETS.

Large Crown 8vo, cloth gilt, $1.75. Bound in morocco, extra, $4.00.

ALFRED, LORD TENNYSON, POET LAUREATE, COMPLETE WORKS. *With a New Portrait.*

"This latest edition of his works, which as a book is every way what a complete, compact edition should be, and contains the only portrait we have ever seen which does his genius justice." — *N. Y. Mail and Express.*

ROBERT BROWNING'S POETICAL WORKS.

Edited by AUGUSTINE BIRRELL. In two volumes.

"An edition which in every point of excellence will satisfy the most fastidious taste." — *Scotsman.*

COLERIDGE'S COMPLETE POETICAL WORKS.

Edited, with Introduction, by J. DYKES CAMPBELL.

MATTHEW ARNOLD'S POETICAL WORKS.

"Contains some of the wisest and most melodious verse that this age has produced." — *Athenæum.*

PERCY BYSSHE SHELLEY'S POETICAL WORKS.

Edited by PROFESSOR DOWDEN. With Portrait.

WILLIAM WORDSWORTH'S COMPLETE POETICAL WORKS.

With an Introduction by JOHN MORLEY, and Portrait.

"Mr. Morley has seldom written anything fresher or more vigorous than the essay on Wordsworth which he has prefixed to Macmillan's new and admirable one-volume edition of the poet — the only complete edition." — *Spectator.*

"The finest of all tributes to the memory of Wordsworth is a complete edition of his poetical works, printed in one volume, and sold at a few shillings. It runs to near a thousand pages, and is all that it need be in type and clearness of arrangement. It stands midway oetween the *éditions de luxe* and the cheap typographical renderings of other classics of the English school. In a good binding it would do perfectly well for the library of a millionaire; in serviceable cloth it would make almost a library in itself for the student of humble means. It has a good bibliography of all the poet's writings, a catalogue of biographies, an index of first lines and a complete list of the poems in the order of their production year by year. Above all, it has an introduction from the pen of Mr. John Morley." — *Daily News.*

SHAKESPEARE'S COMPLETE WORKS.

Edited by W. G. CLARK, M.A., and W. ALDIS WRIGHT, M.A. With Glossary. New Edition.

MORTE D'ARTHUR.

SIR THOMAS MALORY'S Book of King Arthur, and of his Noble Knights of the Round Table. The Edition of Caxton, revised for modern use. With an Introduction, Notes, and Glossary, by SIR EDWARD STRACHEY. New Edition.

ROBERT BURNS' COMPLETE WORKS.

The POEMS, SONGS, and LETTERS. Edited, with Glossarial Index, and Biographical Memoir, by ALEXANDER SMITH. New Edition.

SIR WALTER SCOTT'S POETICAL WORKS.

With Biographical and Critical Essay by FRANCIS TURNER PALGRAVE. New Edition.

OLIVER GOLDSMITH'S MISCELLANEOUS WORKS.

With Biographical Introduction by PROFESSOR MASSON. New Edition.

EDMUND SPENSER'S COMPLETE WORKS.

Edited with Glossary by R. MORRIS, and Memoir by J. W. HALES. New Edition.

ALEXANDER POPE'S POETICAL WORKS.

Edited, with Notes and Introductory Memoir, by PROFESSOR WARD. New Edition.

JOHN DRYDEN'S POETICAL WORKS.

Edited, with a Revised Text and Notes, by W. D. CHRISTIE, M.A., Trinity College, Cambridge. New Edition.

COWPER'S POETICAL WORKS.

Edited, with Notes and Biographical Introduction, by Rev. W. BENHAM, B.D. New Edition.

MILTON'S POETICAL WORKS.

With Introductions by PROFESSOR MASSON.

THE MACMILLAN COMPANY,

66 FIFTH AVENUE, NEW YORK.

www.ingramcontent.com/pod-product-compliance
Lightning Source LLC
LaVergne TN
LVHW012209040326
832903LV00003B/215